Child Maltreatment Law

Child Maltreatment Law

Foundations in Science, Practice and Policy

SECOND EDITION

Roger J.R. Levesque
PROFESSOR OF CRIMINOLOGY AND CRIMINAL JUSTICE
INDIANA UNIVERSITY BLOOMINGTON

CAROLINA ACADEMIC PRESS
Durham, North Carolina

ISBN 978-1-5310-2904-3
eISBN 978-1-5310-2905-0
LCCN 2024936414

Carolina Academic Press
700 Kent Street
Durham, NC 27701
(919) 489-7486
www.cap-press.com

Printed in the United States of America

Contents

Preface

This book examines how society, researchers, and the law conceptualize and respond to child maltreatment. It provides a wide variety of cases and situations to help us understand how the legal system views children and responds to their environments. The approach suits readers with a broad variety of interests, needs, and backgrounds. The materials have been used to teach law school students as well as graduate and undergraduate students in psychology and criminology. Courses using these materials have attracted students from other fields of inquiry, especially human development, family studies, political science, social work, education, and journalism. Undoubtedly, many disciplines now seek to understand and address child maltreatment by examining legal issues. That interest mirrors those of practitioners who study and operate in the legal system and voice a need to learn from other fields of study.

Interest in these materials by individuals from diverse fields of inquiry reflects more than a broadening concern for child maltreatment and the emergence of a new specialty, "Child Maltreatment Law." The broad reach is deliberate. How diverse fields of inquiry and practice can talk to each other remains one of the most challenging issues confronting efforts to address the maltreatment of children. The position taken in the pages that follow is that we learn about issues foreign to us by examining others' real-life situations. To do so, we examine cases and research to see how the law works, how it often fails, and how we can envision alternative approaches. Most of the materials are quite unpleasant and depressing. Child maltreatment is a multisystemic problem with no easy solutions, and efforts to understand it must adapt to that reality. Understanding what we know about maltreatment is no easy task. It means acquiring a very broad understanding of cultural diversity, human development, and interdisciplinary research. It also means understanding basic principles guiding many areas of law that regulate human relationships, ranging from child welfare law, criminal law, juvenile justice, civil/tort law, family law, labor law, education law, poverty law, constitutional law, laws of evidence, and civil rights law, to human rights law. Equally importantly, it means understanding the limits of our knowledge and determining how to proceed in directions fraught with uncertainties.

This book rests on the claim that understanding how to respond to maltreatment means moving beyond the boundaries of the child welfare system and examining, for example, the welfare system and how the legal system privileges some family dynamics and structures over others. If there is only one point that emerges from this text, it hopefully is that we only will be situated to respond more effectively to child maltreatment when we understand the many ways the legal system addresses and can address the ways we treat children, those with whom they interact, and one another. If there is any other point that emerges, it hopefully is the realization that legal systems remain profoundly limited and that addressing intractable social problems like child maltreatment requires broad social reform guided, but not straightjacketed, by law.

Given the multiple areas of law and the remarkable complexity of maltreatment, it is important to note that the categories of maltreatment and the legal topics should be viewed as analytical tools rather than self-contained categories. For example, sexual maltreatment often involves psychological maltreatment and neglect; and many legal systems regulate responses to sexual maltreatment. Likewise, all cases are loaded with information, insights, and points that need further elaboration. As a result, a case often foreshadows discussions developed in other chapters. For example, the termination of parental rights often plays a pivotal role in many forms of state responses to maltreatment. That requires introducing the rules of termination when examining the various forms of maltreatment and then returning to those rules when examining how the law terminates relationships in a manner that protects the rights of parents, children, and broader society. The rules are again revisited when considering broad policy objectives that balance the extent to which families can be preserved or children must be removed from them. Taking a more categorical approach likely would prove unsatisfactory given that it would not allow for really knowing what transpires in the cases selected as illustrative of complex issues and how broad principles guide different responses to maltreatment. The short of it is that understanding what is happening at a particular point in legal responses to child maltreatment requires thinking of that point from a broad, systemic lens.

It may be helpful to provide a brief overview of the manner I have organized the chapters. The beginning chapters explore how the legal system defines what constitutes the major forms of maltreatment and risks of harm deemed worthy of state intervention. It then details the nature of families deemed problematic and how the state directly intervenes in families to address allegations of maltreatment. Chapters then focus on the complexities of how court proceedings and broad legal mandates seek to protect children's rights and safety as well as protect the rights of those entrusted with their care. The last chapters address the challenges of legal reform efforts seeking to stop and prevent child maltreatment, including laws that both directly and indirectly shape the extent to which families protect children. These chapters also complement legal analyses with what empirical research reveals about the law's efforts. The appendices assist those unfamiliar with legal cases, legal terminology, the legal system, and the place of social sciences in law. Together, the materials provide a firm foundation for understanding key social science findings, policy directions, and practices in child maltreatment law.

ROGER J. R. LEVESQUE
Bloomington, Indiana, January 2024

Notes on Case Editing

Many citations and footnotes, as well as sizeable portions of texts, have been omitted to keep materials at a manageable size and to facilitate reading. Ellipses, or brackets containing summaries of omitted material, indicate where other text has been deleted. Notes often appear at the end of the cases; those notes are not from the cases unless specifically noted. Many citations and footnotes considered nonessential for understanding the cases or child maltreatment law have been omitted without indication.

Child Maltreatment Law

Chapter 1

The Scope and Nature of Child Maltreatment

Many challenges and criticisms face research that examines the occurrence and distribution of intractable social problems like child maltreatment. Yet our understanding of child maltreatment has advanced dramatically through a wide variety of increasingly sophisticated and comprehensive epidemiological studies. The most extensive investigations tend to use incidence studies that analyze data from cases reported during specific time periods. Such studies typically provide information about the number of children who have been victimized annually, the number of investigations conducted, and the general characteristics of victims, their families, and perpetrators. Prevalence studies also have attempted to provide estimates of child maltreatment; and these studies examine rates in a population at any one point in time and tend to interview adults about what happened during their childhoods. Less frequently, some studies indirectly have asked children about the occurrence of maltreatment while other studies have inferred maltreatment by identifying relevant risk factors in children's environments. Although impressive, important limitations associate with each form of epidemiological study. We will return to the advantages and limitations of these studies throughout our investigation, since different maltreating actions and conditions bring their own challenges to research endeavors. For now, we examine incidence studies given that they most readily highlight the significance of the legal system in defining, understanding, and responding to child maltreatment.

Fourth National Incidence Study of Child Abuse and Neglect (NIS–4): Executive Summary

Sedlak, A. J., Mettenburg, J., Basena, M., Petta, I., McPherson, K., Greene, A., and Li, S. (2010). Washington, DC: U.S. Department of Health and Human Services, Administration for Children and Families.

The National Incidence Study (NIS) is a congressionally mandated, periodic effort of the United States Department of Health and Human Services.... The principal objectives of the NIS–4 were to provide updated estimates of the incidence of child abuse and neglect in the United States and measure changes in incidence from the earlier studies.

...

In the NIS classifications, maltreatment encompasses both abuse and neglect. Abuse includes physical abuse, sexual abuse, and emotional abuse. Neglect includes physical neglect, emotional neglect, and educational neglect. Each of these categories comprises more specific forms of abuse or neglect....

The NIS applies two definitional standards in parallel: the Harm Standard and the Endangerment Standard. The Harm Standard ... is relatively stringent in that it generally requires that an act or omission result in demonstrable harm in order to be classified as abuse or neglect. It permits exceptions in only a few specific maltreatment categories, where the nature of the maltreatment itself is so egregious that one can infer that the child was harmed. The chief advantage of the Harm Standard is its strong objectivity. Its principal disadvantage is that it is so stringent that it provides a perspective that is too narrow for many purposes, excluding even many children whom CPS substantiates or indicates as abused or neglected.

The Endangerment Standard ... includes all children who meet the Harm Standard but adds others as well. The central feature of the Endangerment Standard is that it counts children who were not yet harmed by abuse or neglect if a sentinel [sentinels are community professionals who work in categories of agencies that have duties relating to child maltreatment] thought that the maltreatment endangered the children or if a CPS investigation substantiated or indicated their maltreatment. In addition, the Endangerment Standard is slightly more lenient than the Harm Standard in allowing a broader array of perpetrators, including adult caretakers other than parents in certain maltreatment categories and teenage caretakers as perpetrators of sexual abuse.

Incidence of Harm Standard maltreatment. Using the stringent Harm Standard definition, more than 1.25 million children (an estimated 1,256,600 children) experienced maltreatment during the NIS–4 study year (2005–2006). This corresponds to one child in every 58 in the United States. A large percentage (44%, or an estimated total of 553,300) were abused, while most (61%, or an estimated total of 771,700) were neglected. The NIS classifies children in every category that applies, so the components (here and throughout the NIS findings) sum to more than 100%. Most of the abused children experienced physical abuse (58% of the abused children, an estimated total of 323,000). Slightly less than one-fourth were sexually abused (24%, an estimated 135,300), while slightly more than one-fourth were emotionally abused (27%, an estimated 148,500). Almost one-half of the neglected children experienced educational neglect (47% of neglected children, an estimated 360,500 children), more than one-third were physically neglected (38%, an estimated 295,300 children), and one-fourth were emotionally neglected (25%, an estimated 193,400 children).

. . .

Incidence of Endangerment Standard maltreatment. Defining maltreatment according to the more inclusive Endangerment Standard provides a very different picture of the incidence and distribution of child abuse and neglect. Nearly 3 million children (an estimated 2,905,800) experienced Endangerment Standard maltreatment during the NIS–4 2005–2006 study year. This corresponds to one child in every 25 in the United States. While 29% (an estimated 835,000 children) were abused, more than three-fourths (77%, an estimated 2,251,600 children) were neglected. Most abused children (57%, or 476,600 children) were physically abused, more than one-third (36%, or 302,600 children) were emotionally abused, and less than one-fourth (22%, or 180,500 children) were sexually abused. Under the Endangerment Standard definitions, more than one-half of the neglected children were physically neglected (53%, or 1,192,200 children) and a similar percentage were emotionally neglected (52%, or 1,173,800), whereas 16% (an estimated 360,500) were educationally neglected.

Distribution of Child Abuse and Neglect by the Child's Characteristics

The child's sex, age, race, disability status, and school enrollment were all related to rates of maltreatment.

Child's sex. Girls were sexually abused much more often than boys, under both the Harm Standard and the Endangerment Standard. This finding is consistent with earlier NIS results, so females' disproportionately greater risk of sexual abuse has been stable over time. This sex difference in incidence rates of sexual abuse leads to higher rates of abuse in general among girls. Also, because the definitional guidelines permit the inference that injury or harm occurred in connection with the more extreme forms of sexual abuse, girls' greater risk of sexual abuse also accounts for their higher incidence rates for inferred injury.

Boys' rates of Harm Standard physical neglect and of serious harm under both standards decreased more since the NIS–3 than the corresponding rates for girls. The incidence of boys who experienced Endangerment Standard emotional neglect increased less since the NIS–3 than that of girls. Moreover, trends in the incidence of inferred harm from Endangerment Standard maltreatment moved in opposite directions for girls and boys — the incidence of girls with inferred harm declined slightly since the NIS–3, while the incidence of boys with inferred harm rose.

Child's age. A consistent feature of the age differences in NIS–4 incidence rates is the lower incidence of maltreatment among the youngest children in the Harm

Standard abuse and neglect rates and in the rates of Endangerment Standard abuse. In most cases, the 0- to 2-year-olds had significantly lower maltreatment rates than older children. It is possible that the lower rates at these younger ages reflect some undercoverage of these age groups. That is, prior to attaining school age, children are less observable to community professionals.

In contrast, the age differences in Endangerment Standard neglect (overall, as well as in the specific categories of physical neglect and emotional neglect) revealed a distinctly different pattern. In these categories, the oldest children (15- to 17-year-olds) have the lowest rates and 6- to 8-year-olds have the highest rates. This curvilinear age pattern may reflect the combination of opposing age distributions for different maltreatment outcomes — rates of children with serious and moderate harm from maltreatment generally increase with increasing age, whereas rates of children who were endangered, but not demonstrably harmed, by their maltreatment experiences sharply decrease across the age continuum. Because the endangered children are more prevalent among those who experienced Endangerment Standard physical and emotional neglect, this opposing age trend primarily affected the age distribution in these categories, shaping the curvilinear pattern.

. . .

Race/ethnicity. Unlike previous NIS cycles, the NIS–4 found strong and pervasive race differences in the incidence of maltreatment. In nearly all cases, the rates of maltreatment for Black children were significantly higher than those for White and Hispanic children. These differences occurred under both definitional standards in rates of overall maltreatment, overall abuse, overall neglect, and physical abuse and for children with serious or moderate harm from their maltreatment. They also occurred in the incidence of Harm Standard sexual abuse, in the incidence of children who were inferred to be harmed by Harm Standard maltreatment, and in Endangerment Standard rates for physical neglect, emotional maltreatment, and children who were endangered but not demonstrably harmed by their maltreatment.

Disability. The NIS–4 is the first NIS cycle to examine the relationship between the incidence of maltreatment and children's disability status. Under the Harm Standard, children with confirmed disabilities had significantly lower rates of physical abuse and of moderate harm from maltreatment, but they had significantly higher rates of emotional neglect and of serious injury or harm. Using the Endangerment Standard to define maltreatment revealed more extensive differences, some similar to the Harm Standard findings, but also some quite different results. Children with disabilities had a significantly lower rate of Endangerment Standard abuse overall, consistent with their lower rate of physical abuse under both standards. Children with disabilities also had significantly lower rates of Endangerment Standard sexual abuse, neglect, physical neglect, and emotional neglect; and they were significantly less likely to be moderately harmed or endangered but not demonstrably harmed by the maltreatment. Similar to the Harm Standard finding, the children with disabilities were significantly more likely to be seriously injured or harmed when they experienced maltreatment.

The findings on the incidence of emotional neglect are exactly opposite under the two standards. This indicates that, although children with confirmed disabilities were less likely to be emotionally neglected, they more often suffered harm from that maltreatment (in fact, serious harm) and so were more often countable under the Harm Standard in this category.

School enrollment. For the first time in the NIS, the NIS–4 gathered information about children's enrollment in school. Across both definitional standards, school-aged children who were not enrolled in school were sexually abused more often than enrolled children and more often qualified for inferred harm, an outcome frequently associated with sexual abuse. Enrolled children had significantly higher rates of moderate harm as a result of maltreatment and they were at marginally higher risk of educational neglect. This latter finding warrants explanation. On the one hand, simply knowing that a school-age child is not enrolled in school is not sufficient to classify the child as educationally neglected in NIS. Data on most nonenrolled children lacked details that would exclude legitimate reasons for their circumstance, such as the child being seriously ill, suspended, expelled, or recently moved and not yet enrolled at a new location. On the other hand, since schools regularly track absences of enrolled children, NIS sentinels are likely to describe these to the study. Enrolled children had higher rates of Harm Standard physical abuse and of overall Harm Standard maltreatment. In contrast, nonenrolled school-age children had higher rates of Endangerment Standard maltreatment, overall and in the categories of neglect, physical neglect, and emotional neglect. The nonenrolled children were also more likely to be classified as endangered, but not demonstrably harmed, by their Endangerment Standard maltreatment.

Distribution of Child Abuse and Neglect by Family Characteristics

. . .

Parents' employment. Unemployed parents were those described as unemployed or laid off but looking for work either currently (at the time of maltreatment) or at any time during the past year. Employed parents were those who had steady full-or part-time work, with no reported unemployment currently or in the previous year. Parents who were not in the labor force were not employed or actively looking for work. These included parents who were retired, disabled, homemakers, receiving Temporary Assistance for Needy Families (TANF), on maternity leave, in the hospital, or in jail. Under both definitional standards, the incidence of maltreatment and of all severities of injury or harm was higher for children with no parent in the labor force and those with an unemployed parent and lowest for those with employed parents. Compared to children with employed parents, those with no parent in the labor force had 2 to 3 times the rate of maltreatment overall, about 2 times the rate of abuse, and 3 or more times the rate of neglect. Children with unemployed parents had 2 to 3 times higher rates of neglect than those with employed parents.

Socioeconomic status. To contend with missing data on individual items, the NIS–4 analyses combined three indicators into a general measure of socioeconomic status: household income, household participation in any poverty program, and parents' education. Low socioeconomic status households were those in the bottom tier on any indicator: household income below $15,000 a year, parents' highest education level less than high school, or any member of the household a participant in a poverty program, such as TANF, food stamps, public housing, energy assistance, or subsidized school meals. Children in low socioeconomic status households had significantly higher rates of maltreatment in all categories and across both definitional standards. They experienced some type of maltreatment at more than 5 times the rate of other children; they were more than 3 times as likely to be abused and about 7 times as likely to be neglected.

Family structure and living arrangement. Family structure reflects the number of parents in the household and their relationship to the child; living arrangement reflects their marital or cohabitation status. Considering both factors, the NIS–4 classified children into six categories: living with two married biological parents, living with other married parents (e.g., step-parent, adoptive parent), living with two unmarried parents, living with one parent who had an unmarried partner in the household, living with one parent who had no partner in the household, and living with no parent. The groups differed in rates of every maltreatment category and across both definitional standards. Children living with their married biological parents universally had the lowest rate, whereas those living with a single parent who had a cohabiting partner in the household had the highest rate in all maltreatment categories. Compared to children living with married biological parents, those whose single parent had a live-in partner had more than 8 times the rate of maltreatment overall, over 10 times the rate of abuse, and nearly 8 times the rate of neglect.

...

Grandparents as caregivers. The NIS–4 could identify a grandparent as a child's caregiver under three conditions: when the grandparent was the child's primary caregiver, when the primary caregiver did not have a spouse or partner and the grandparent was the secondary caregiver, and when the grandparent was a caregiver and maltreated the child. Children whose grandparent cared for them had lower rates of physical abuse compared to those with no identified grandparent caregiver: they had two thirds the rate of Harm Standard physical abuse and less than four-fifths the rate of Endangerment Standard physical abuse.

Family size. The incidence of maltreatment was related to the number of dependent children in the family, in Harm Standard categories of overall maltreatment and all neglect and in Endangerment Standard maltreatment, abuse, neglect, and in physical and emotional maltreatment, both abuse and neglect. The general pattern was nonlinear: the incidence rates were highest for children in the largest families (those with 4 or more children), intermediate for "only" children and those in households with 3 children, and lowest for children in families with two children. The largest differences occurred in the Endangerment Standard maltreatment rates, especially for the neglect categories, where the incidence rates for children in the largest households were more than twice the rates for children in households with 2 children.

County metropolitan status. Except for educational neglect, the incidence of all categories of Endangerment Standard maltreatment was higher in rural counties than in urban counties and similar patterns also emerged in rates of most categories of Harm Standard maltreatment. Rural children had a nearly 2 times higher rate of overall Harm Standard maltreatment and nearly 2 times higher rate of overall Endangerment Standard maltreatment. Whether this reflects better coverage of maltreated children in the rural counties or higher rates of actual maltreatment in rural communities is not clear. Nor is it clear how differential distribution of other factors, such as socioeconomic status and family size differences, may contribute to these metropolitan status differences.

Distribution of Child Abuse and Neglect by Perpetrator Characteristics

. . .

Perpetrator's relationship to the child. The majority of all children countable under the Harm Standard (81%) were maltreated by their biological parents. This held true both for the abused children (64% were abused by biological parents) and for those neglected (92% were neglected by biological parents). Biological parents were the most closely related perpetrators for 71% of physically abused children and for 73% of emotionally abused children. The pattern was distinctly different for sexual abuse. More than two-fifths (42%) of the sexually abused children were sexually abused by someone other than a parent (whether biological or nonbiological) or a parent's partner, whereas just over one-third (36%) were sexually abused by a biological parent. In addition, severity of harm from physical abuse varied by the perpetrator's relationship to the child. A physically abused child was more likely to sustain a serious injury when the abuser was not a parent.

Perpetrator's sex. Children were somewhat more likely to be maltreated by female perpetrators than by males: 68% of the maltreated children were maltreated by a female, whereas 48% were maltreated by a male. (Some children were maltreated by both.) Of children maltreated by biological parents, mothers maltreated the majority (75%) whereas fathers maltreated a sizable minority (43%). In contrast, male perpetrators were more common for children maltreated by nonbiological parents or parents' partners (64%) or by other persons (75%).

The predominant sex of perpetrators of abuse was different from that of neglect. Female perpetrators were more often responsible for neglect (86% of children neglected by females versus 38% by males). This finding is congruent with the fact that mothers (biological or other) tend to be the primary caretakers and are the primary persons held accountable for any omissions and/or failings in caretaking. In contrast, males more often were abusers (62% of children were abused by males versus 41% by females). The prevalence of male perpetrators was strongest in the category of sexual abuse, where 87% of children were abused by a male compared to only 11% by a female.

Among all abused children, those abused by their biological parents were about equally likely to have been abused by mothers as by fathers (51% and 54%, respectively), but those abused by nonbiological parents or parents' partners, or by other, perpetrators were much more likely to be abused by males (74% or more by males versus 26% or less by females).

Perpetrator's age. Among all maltreated children, only a small percentage (11%) was maltreated by a perpetrator in the youngest age bracket (under 26 years of age). However, younger perpetrators were much more predominant among children who were maltreated by someone who was not a parent (34%).

Child's race and relationship to the perpetrator. The NIS–4 explored whether the children's race was systematically related to the perpetrator's relationship to them, either overall or in specific maltreatment categories. Overall, and across most maltreatment categories, the racial distribution of maltreated children did not vary with their perpetrator's relationship. The exceptions were in overall neglect and in the specific category of physical neglect, which displayed the same pattern. The majority of children physically neglected by a biological parent were White (58%), whereas children neglected by a nonbiological parent or parent's partner were predominantly Black (53%).

Perpetrator's alcohol use, drug use, and mental illness. CPS investigators and NIS–4 sentinels indicated whether they considered these issues to be factors in the child's maltreatment. Perpetrator's alcohol use and drug use were approximately equivalent factors in Harm Standard maltreatment, each applying to 11% of the countable children, while mental illness was a factor in the maltreatment of 7% of the children. Perpetrator's alcohol use was slightly more often implicated in abuse situations than drug use (13% versus 10%), largely because alcohol was more frequently involved in physical abuse and emotional abuse. Alcohol use was most involved in emotional abuse (22% of the children), while drug use was most involved in emotional neglect (21% of the children). The perpetrator's mental illness was most often cited as a factor in emotional abuse (17% of the children). All three factors were more often involved in maltreatment when the perpetrator was a biological parent.

Sources of Recognition for Maltreated Children

School staff predominated as a source of recognition for maltreated children. School sentinels recognized 52% of the children who suffered Harm Standard maltreatment and 39% of the Endangerment Standard total. Other important sources of abused and neglected children were hospitals (11% and 13%), police and sheriff departments (12% and 19%), and the general public (6% and 10%). For maltreatment defined under the Endangerment Standard, day care centers and mental health agencies also joined the group of agency categories that recognized more than an estimated 100,000 abused and neglected children nationwide.

. . .

Child Protective Services (CPS) Investigation of Maltreated Children

Throughout its history, the NIS has consistently found that child protective services agencies (CPS) investigate maltreatment of only a minority of the children the NIS identifies. The NIS–4 again verified that result, finding that CPS investigated the maltreatment of only 32% of children who experienced Harm Standard maltreatment and of 43% of those whose maltreatment fit the Endangerment Standard. Moreover, this was not an artifact of the relatively short (3-month) NIS reference period. The NIS–4 examined an additional full month of CPS data to increase the opportunity for more maltreated children to enter CPS investigations. This additional time made essentially no difference to the percentages of children investigated.

Overall, the percentages of maltreated children who received CPS investigation represented more than one-half of the children in only a few maltreatment categories except fatalities. Under both definitional standards, the highest investigation rates (50% or higher) occurred for physically abused (52% or more) and sexually abused children (55% or more), and for those with maltreatment so severe that their harm could be inferred (53% or more). Also, among children with Endangerment Standard maltreatment, those who were deemed to be endangered, but not demonstrably harmed, also had a high rate of CPS investigation (60%). Considering the sentinel sources that recognized the children as maltreated, investigation rates were above 50% only among children with Harm Standard maltreatment recognized in police or sheriff departments (53%) or at public housing agencies (68%) and among children with Endangerment Standard maltreatment recognized at juvenile probation departments (63%), police or sheriff departments (64%), mental health agencies (53%), social services agencies (94%), and public housing agencies (67%). The lowest rates of investigation occurred for children recognized at schools (20% or less across the definitional standards), day care (12% or less), or shelters (19% or less).

. . .

Child Maltreatment 1999: Reports from the States to the National Child Abuse and Neglect Data System

U.S. Department of Health and Human Services.
Washington, DC: U.S. Printing Office, 2001.

. . .

Fatalities

Child fatality estimates are based on data recorded by CPS agencies and/or other agencies. An estimated 1,100 children died of abuse and neglect, a rate of approximately 1.62 deaths per 100,000 children in the general population. Slightly more than 2 percent (2.1%) of all fatalities occurred while the victim was in foster care. Children younger than 1-year-old accounted for 42.6 percent of the fatalities, and 86.1 percent were younger than 6 years of age. Maltreatment deaths were more often associated with neglect (38.2%) than with any other type of abuse. Slightly more than one-tenth (12.5%) of the families of child fatalities had received family preservation services in the 5 years prior to the deaths, while only 2.7 percent of the child fatality victims had been returned to the care of their families prior to their deaths.

Services Provided

CPS agencies provide services to prevent future instances of child abuse and neglect and to remedy harm that has occurred as a result of child maltreatment. Preventive services are provided to parents whose children are at risk of abuse or neglect. Remedial or post-investigative services are offered to families that have experienced a child maltreatment episode. Nationwide, an estimated 1,563,000 children (22.3 out of every 1,000 children in the population) received preventive services. The average time from the start of investigation to provision of service was 47.4 days. Nationally, 55.8 percent of child victims (an estimated 461,000) received post-investigative services, and an additional 14.2 percent of children with unsubstantiated reports (an estimated 217,000) also received services. Nationally, an estimated 171,000 child victims were placed in foster care. An estimated additional 49,000 children who were not victims (i.e., children with unsubstantiated reports) were placed in foster care. About one-fifth (21.2%) of victims had received family preservation services within the previous 5 years, while more than 5 percent (5.1% of victims) had been reunited with their families in the previous five years. Court actions were initiated for an estimated 26.1 percent of maltreatment victims. Four-fifths of these victims (79.3%) were provided with court-appointed representatives.

Notes and Queries

1. How is maltreatment indexed? Do you agree that we should count children *at risk* for maltreatment as victims of maltreatment? Why would it be reasonable to include children at risk in incidence studies of maltreatment?

2. Incidence studies help counter many problems that arise from prevalence reports: biases in sample selection, response rates, methods of data collection, definitions of maltreatment, definitions of childhood, the accuracy of adults' memories, and the relative skills of interviewers. However, many of the same issues remain: different criteria for counting what constitutes maltreatment, counting abuse by family or by individual child victims, and multiple reports per victim.

3. Reality makes it unlikely that we can ever obtain true epidemiological figures. Many barriers exist: controversial topics may not get funding for research, the rights of individuals may prohibit researchers from asking certain questions to certain groups (e.g., children), and the challenge of countering problems resulting from underreporting and stigma. Given these issues, how close do you think existing reports are to revealing the actual incidence of maltreatment?

4. CPS receives nearly three million yearly reports of alleged maltreatment and finds nearly three-quarters of the allegations unsubstantiated. What do you make of this finding? Are we to conclude that the system misallocates resources to investigation and that it should devote itself more to remediation? How can we get around this problem? Is it clear that before remediation begins, we must find those who need it?

5. Nearly 60 percent of abused children suffer from neglect. What does that tell you about the needed legal response to child maltreatment?

6. A quick look at family characteristics reveals that child maltreatment links to poverty. Correct? Why do you suppose that is?

7. Who tends to be maltreated?

8. Do fatally maltreated children generally receive services prior to their death? What does that tell you about prevention?

9. How can nonmaltreated children be placed in foster care?

10. Why do so few victims receive family preservation services?

11. What significance do you attach to race/ethnic differences in reports of maltreatment?

Research Comments

1. What accounts for massive race/ethnic differences in victimization rates? Evidence suggests that factors other than race and ethnicity account for differences in children being served and that there actually are no differences in victimization rates by race. See Sheila Ards, Chanjin Chung & Samuel L. Myers, Jr. (1998). The effects of sample selection bias on racial differences in child abuse reporting. *Child Abuse & Neglect*, 22, 103–115. Why do you suppose that reporting rates by race and by maltreatment type may differ? Reporting bias may be a concern, but it seems that reports of child deaths would reveal considerably less bias; instead they too show important differences. Children of color are over represented in child maltreatment fatalities compared to the proportion of children in the general population. While children of color make up 34 percent of the population of children in the United States, they make up 48 percent of the children who die as a result of child maltreatment. African American children make up 40 percent of the proportion of children who die as a result of maltreatment, while comprising only 15 percent of the U.S. population of children. See Michael R. Petit & Patrick A. Curtis (1997). *Child Abuse and Neglect: A Look at the States.* Washington, DC: Child Welfare League of America. What do those findings tell you? What do they tell you about the persistent finding that African American children are overrepresented throughout the progression from substantiated abuse to adoption? See Stephen A. Kapp, Thomas P. McDonald & Kandi L. Diamond (2001). The path to adoption for children of color. *Child Abuse & Neglect*, 25, 215–229.
2. Child maltreatment is commonly regarded as a child welfare problem. However, law enforcement may also be involved when children are assaulted. Regrettably, the law enforcement perspective on child maltreatment remains greatly neglected. The first multistate study to examine incidents coming to the attention of police officers reported important findings: Incidents of child maltreatment committed by parents and other caretakers make up about one-fifth (19 percent) of violent crimes against children aged 0 to 17. The majority of these crimes are physical assaults (73 percent) and sexual assaults (23 percent). Child maltreatment constitutes more than half of the crimes against children age 2 or younger reported to police. Male offenders are responsible for 92 percent of sexual assaults and 68 percent of physical assaults; they also are responsible for three-quarters of all child maltreatment incidents reported to police. The research confirms several findings from the child welfare system: Parents and caretakers are the most common abusers; male caretakers are responsible for the majority of severe maltreating incidents; and there is substantially more physical than sexual maltreatment, with ratios of nearly three to one. David Finkelhor & Richard Ormrod (2001). Child abuse reported to police. *Bulletin.* Washington, DC: Department of Justice, Office of Justice Programs, Office of Juvenile Justice and Delinquency Prevention.

Recurring Themes and Considerations

Several concerns arise when considering the appropriateness of defining certain circumstances or events as maltreating.

1. How widely or narrowly should we draw definitions of maltreatment? Addressing this concern immediately raises the issue of the definition's ultimate purpose. The answer may well differ depending on whether the definition is meant for criminal law enforcement, civil child welfare practice, research, reporting, or fostering public awareness. More specificity tends to help (1) clarify the seriousness of the form of maltreatment and its importance in relation to other forms of abuse; (2) promote specific research; (3) implement policy, especially in terms of the proper allocation of resources and determinations of program effectiveness; (4) provide those who implement laws (social workers) guidance and reduce the risk of destructive intervention in families; and (5) more clearly specify who is at risk and thereby protect children from the potentially damaging effects of "cures" like removing children from their homes. On the other hand, broader approaches (1) allow for reaching more children, (2) can help devise broader intervention programs that could be more preventative, (3) allow for greater intervention in families that may be deemed at risk, and (4) provide professionals with much-needed discretion in attempts to address necessarily ambiguous circumstances.

2. What subcategories of circumstances or events can be deemed maltreating? Most typically, maltreatment includes physical abuse, neglect, sexual abuse, and emotional abuse. Less frequently used subcategories include moral issues, educational neglect, and witnessing family violence. The *Child Abuse Prevention and Treatment Act* (CAPTA), Pub. L. No. 93-247, 88 Stat. 4 (1974), codified as amended at 42 U.S.C. 5101–5120 (West Supp. 2001), defines child abuse and neglect as: "at a minimum, any recent act or failure to act on the part of a parent or caretaker, which results in death, serious physical or emotional harm, sexual abuse or exploitation, or an act or failure to act which presents an imminent risk of serious harm" (42 U.S.C.A. § 5106g(2) (West Supp. 2001)). Under CAPTA, there exists only four forms of child maltreatment: sexual abuse, neglect, physical abuse, and emotional abuse. Using this minimum standard as a foundation, each state provides its own definitions for child abuse and neglect. Three places in state statutes generally define abuse and neglect: (1) reporting laws for child maltreatment, (2) criminal codes, and (3) juvenile or family court statutes.

3. To what extent should perpetrator (or parental) intention factor in definitions? An indefinite number of conditions create and perpetuate the occurrence of child maltreatment. For example, ecological approaches place equal emphasis on the environmental and familial contributions to the occurrence of child maltreatment. Given that understanding and depending on the type of abuse, it may seem less appropriate to focus on parents' intentions.

4. How do definitions of maltreatment shift with children's developmental ages and developmental levels? For CAPTA, the term *child* is someone who has not reached the age of 18; or (except in the case of sexual abuse) the age specified by the child protection law of the state in which the child resides. *Child Abuse Prevention and Treatment Act*, 42 U.S.C.A. § 5106g(1)(B) (West Supp. 2001). The consequences of maltreatment manifest themselves differently according to the child's developmental level and needs. Child maltreatment undermines issues salient to developmental stages (e.g., attachment in infancy, self- and language development in toddlerhood, and peer relations in middle childhood represent the central emotional tasks children confront during their early development).

5. Should we focus mostly on the actual harm to the child? Ultimately, maltreatment involves identifying that a child is harmed (or about to be harmed). In that determination, concern arises as to whether a normative or a more ideographic focus would best assist victims. This dilemma raises many issues in that we may want to focus on the particular needs of vulnerable children or attempt to devise what would be harmful for "normal" children. Such a focus, in turn, raises issues regarding what we are to do with resilient children or children who may have a delayed response to maltreatment. Further complicating factors is the reality that not all child maltreatment immediately or easily presents harm that can be documented.

6. What concerns are we to weigh in designing effective policies responding to child maltreatment? The following are among some of the most critical factors to consider: (1) severity, whether we should focus on the most serious or less serious circumstances of maltreatment; (2) occurrence, whether we should focus on risk of occurrence and future harm or actual occurrences that already have happened; (3) type of maltreatment, whether we should devote resources unevenly to physical, sexual, neglect, etc., or should focus more on some types of abuse, such as criminal child abuse; (4) type of offender, whether we should treat family members or strangers differently; (5) determinative burden of proof, whether we should seek objective truth or follow the subjective impressions of investigators; (6) intervention focus, whether we should focus on preserving families or on child protection through removing children from their families; and (7) targeting intervention, whether intervention should focus on broad, universal benefits and services or categorical and narrowly-tailored services.

For further analyses, see:

Peter J. Pecora, James K. Whittaker, Anthony N. Malcusio, Richard P. Barth & Robert D. Plotnick (2000). *The Child Welfare Challenge: Policy, Practice, and Research.* New York: Aldine deGruyter.

Jeanne Giovannoni (1989). Definitional issues in child maltreatment. In Dante Cicchetti & Vicki Carlson (Eds.). *Child Maltreatment: Theory and Research on the Causes and Consequences of Child Abuse and Neglect* (pp. 3–37). New York: Cambridge University Press.

Taina Laajasalo, Laura Elizabeth Cowley, Gabriel Otterman, Diogo Lamela, Leonor Bettencourt Rodrigues, Andreas Jud, Alison Kemp et al. (2023). Current issues and challenges in the definition and operationalization of child maltreatment: A scoping review. *Child Abuse & Neglect*, 140, 106187.

Roger J. R. Levesque (2008). *Child Maltreatment and the law: Returning to First Principles.* New York: Springer.

Chapter 2

Controlling Child Development

Numerous factors influence children's developmental outcomes. Among the most frequently identified and researched determinants are children's inherited temperamental qualities, parental practices and personalities, peer relationships, neighborhood qualities, cultural institutions, and the characteristics of the particular historical era. No one doubts that the power and effectiveness of these factors vary, particularly as a function of children's changing developmental needs. Few agree, however, on the manner specific factors operate and their relative influences. Despite a wide variety of views and assumptions, discussions of the socializing influences on children frequently favor one of three positions.

Different Orienting Models of Child Development

Before understanding how the law addresses the rights of children, it is important to consider the three general approaches to understanding the influences of children's outcomes. Among other reasons is the reality that the legal system tends to embrace only one approach. The law's limited perspective, which is entrenched for important reasons, sets up this entire area of law as fundamentally at odds with much of what researchers have long learned and, in many ways, now view as incredibly limited. Understanding how researchers approach children's outcomes, then, provides an opportunity to evaluate legal perspectives, understand the limitations of particular perspectives, appreciate why some gain prominence and remain so powerful, and consider how they may be improved.

Taking a long view of research focusing on how children develop reveals strong adherence to the notion of parental influence. From this view, parents typically impact their children through four different mechanisms. First, parents influence their children through direct interactions. For example, much research examines the nature of parenting styles and generally links authoritative ("democratic") parenting to more healthy outcomes. Second, children may identify with parents. For example, children may unconsciously adopt some of their parents' attributes. Children also can identify with the class, ethnic, or religious group to which their family belongs and often feel an imperative to honor the identification. Third, parents direct their children's social environment. For example, parents highly influence with whom their children play, the schools they attend, the media they watch, and the health services they receive. Lastly, parents greatly influence their children by contributing genetic and physical predispositions. A child's physical attributes, such as their attractiveness and pubertal timing, profoundly influence developmental outcomes.

Much research supports the claim that parents highly determine their children's outcomes. For example, attachment theory proposes that the relationships established between an infant and its caretakers during the first two years of life permanently shape the child's future. The extent to which parents' actions do influence their children probably finds its most important support in the area of pathology. When children are severely maltreated, for example, no one doubts the potentially long-term effects of parental actions. Attachment theories explain these long-term influences as arising from "internal working models." Internal working models simply are mental representations that children form through their interactions with primary caregivers. As children develop, these representations guide what to expect from their relationships with others and even their general environments. For example, children who have not been maltreated tend to have "working models" to the extent that they evince the hallmarks of secure relationships because they reevaluate each relationship on its own terms. Maltreated children tend to operate on a closed working model, or ones known as not properly functioning as they tend to generalize their negative relationships to others. See Patricia M. Crittenden & Mary D. S. Ainsworth (1989). Child maltreatment and attachment theory. In Dante Cicchetti & Vicki Carlson (Eds.). *Child Maltreatment: Theory and Research on the Causes and Consequences of Child Abuse and Neglect* (pp. 432–463). New York: Cambridge University Press. For a broader and authoritative analysis of internal working models, see Inge Bretherton & Kristine A. Munholland (2008). Internal working models in attachment relationships: Elaborating a central construct in attachment theory. In J. Cassidy & P. R. Shaver (Eds.). *Handbook of Attachment: Theory, Research, and Clinical Applications* (pp. 102–127). New York: Guilford Press.

The second approach to understanding child development proposes that parents have little or no permanent influence on their child's future personality. Researchers adopting this position typically argue that parents tend to impact their children only to the extent that they biologically impact their children, and that the remaining influences derive from their environment. This line of research suggests that parental *behavior* has little effect on the intellectual or personality development of their children as well as their overall outcomes. One of the leading voices in this group champions the claim, for example, that children would develop essentially the same way if one simply left them in their neighborhoods and switched the parents from one family to another. That suggestion highlights the powerful effects of neighborhoods and peers on child development. Although many may be quick to discount this approach, much research supports the view. The general contention is that children only need an "average expectable environment" to be healthy. These environments include the wide range in the environment that supports adaptive functioning. Stated differently, most homes provide similar developmental opportunities and, as long as the environments are not abusive, it does not matter much which homes raise children. See Judith R. Harris (2011). *The Nurture Assumption*. New York: The Free Press.

As much as the image of lack of parental influence on their children's development may seem off, this approach underscores the need to take a developmental perspective when thinking of child development. This is particularly important to consider as children begin to move outside their homes, such as when they attend school and become influenced by peers as well as "super peers" in the form of social media. A long history of developmental research focuses on the influence of peers on children's development and socializing experiences. Kenneth H. Rubin, William M. Bukowski & Brett Laursen (Eds.) (2011). *Handbook of Peer Interactions, Relationships, and Groups*. New York: Guilford Press.

The view that peers socialize each other may make intuitive sense, but this area of research can become quite contentious as it focuses more on how individuals engage their social environments. Among the most heated contentions is the claim that people select their own social class, a position mainly based on the argument that genetic variation accounts for differences in social class outcomes. Typically, the proposal is that genetic variation arises from differences in the "Big 5" personality dimensions that are highly influenced by genetics: extroversion, agreeableness, conscientiousness, emotional stability, and intellectual openness. The argument also posits that children make their own environments in three major ways: Children *evoke* different reactions from parents; children *interpret* other people's behaviors in idiosyncratic ways; and people who influence children (parents, teachers, and coaches) are *selected* by children who choose to be influenced in a certain manner. See Sandra Scarr (1996). How people make their own environments: Implications for parents and policy makers. *Psychology, Public Policy, & Law*, 2, 204–228.

Although the above example may be contentious, it does highlight well how individuals are the ones in charge of their own development, regardless of whether they are aware of it. The focus on the individual reflects much of developmental science that frequently adopts a middle position reflected in research examining how parents affect their child's psychological growth. That research typically reveals that the contribution of parental practices to children's personalities cannot be viewed in isolation of numerous social, psychological, and biological factors. Each parental behavior or parental personality trait is part of a complex system unique to each parent–child relationship. Although empirical data affirm that parental behaviors and personality traits influence their children's personalities and social behavior, their influence is part of a larger web of conditions that includes inherited temperamental biases, ordinal position, social class, ethnicity, quality of peer friendships, and even the historical era. For example, some find it is unreasonable to expect that one parenting style will have the same effect on children given that children possess different temperaments; they also argue that different parenting strategies may be necessary to achieve similar outcomes in different children. See W. Andrew Collins, Eleanor E. Maccoby, Laurence Steinberg, E. Mavis Hetherington & Marc H. Bornstein (2000). Contemporary research on parenting: The case for nature and nurture. *American Psychologist*, 55, 218–232.

As researchers seek to take a middle ground in terms of parents or children's influence on child development, a third approach has appeared and now arguably receives the most attention from researchers interested in understanding child maltreatment and its effects. For example, many view development in terms of transactional/ecological systems. Among other important characteristics, this third approach emphasizes the need to focus on several domains (biological, social, psychological, etc.), understands the domains as in transaction or in recursive relationships (rather than simply interacting) with each other, and views healthy development as arising from a balance of risk and protective factors (e.g., poverty, marital instability, poor education, poor parenting skills, unemployment, domestic violence, or their opposite). See Dante Cicchetti, Sheree L. Toth & Angeline Maughan (2000). An ecological-transactional model of child maltreatment. In Arnold J. Sameroff, Michael Lewis & Suzanne M. Miller (Eds.). *Handbook of Developmental Psychopathology* (2nd ed.) (pp. 689–722). New York: Kluwer Academic/Plenum Publishers.

Transactional models that focus on multiple factors influencing child development have gained increasing interest along with the development of longitudinal research and statistical modeling. It should not be surprising that people change as they age and respond to their environments. New models allow for considering how individuals at different times are differently influenced and differently influence their surroundings. In a real sense, there is no real "individual" as that individual changes. It may be that core characteristics develop and remain influential. But this approach helps highlight that we do not really "interact" with our environments. Instead, we "transact" as we both influence and are influenced by people, places, and things.

Transactional models may make for cutting-edge research and theory, but it is important to underscore that most of the research being produced does not really engage them as much as what would be expected. Longitudinal research that is sufficiently longitudinal and appropriately useful remains rare. As a result, even comprehensive reviews of research focusing on risk and protective factors for child maltreatment continue to focus on different levels of analysis, such as the individual, interpersonal, community, and broader societal levels. They do not focus much on how each level actually influences how others change and develop. In fact, they typically focus on identifying specific risk factors within specific levels without even considering how other levels might influence them, let alone influence them in a transactional way. See, e.g., Anna E. Austin, Alexandria M. Lesak & Meghan E. Shanahan (2020). Risk and protective factors for child maltreatment: A review. *Current Epidemiology Reports*, 7, 334–342. Joel S. Milner, Julie L. Crouch, Randy J. McCarthy, Joe Ammar, Rodrigo Dominguez-Martinez, Courtney L. Thomas & Audra P. Jensen (2022). Child physical abuse risk factors: A systematic review and a meta-analysis. *Aggression and Violent Behavior*, 101778.

Why Different Orienting Models Matter

In considering the models, it is appropriate to evaluate each on their own merit and in light of their own limitations. The usefulness of each approach, however, depends on the nature of the issues it is called upon to address.

The broad, integrative model, for example, may help us realize that intervention in families is highly problematic in that intervention may affect many systems. The approach emphasizes the need to intervene on many levels and that interventions actually will intervene in many ways even though they may be viewed as narrowly tailored to specific concerns. The approach emphasizes the need to focus on support systems outside of families. It also underscores that those support systems need not be positive or negative; they simply shape and are being shaped by multiple factors.

In seeking to understand child development through research, however, it seems much easier to adopt either of the first two approaches. It is easier given that they assume the existence of entities influencing one another, rather than constantly changing entities in a sea of influences. This approach makes managing information more possible. In addition, despite the reality that many factors influence child development, some factors do have greater influence at particular times. As an example, the influence of social class runs through parents particularly when children are young; as children age, the influence of class influences them more directly.

In terms of therapeutic interventions, different models have different strengths. For example, a model that focuses on individual children offers much. Even if the intervention includes families and the need to enhance family interactions, the notion of internal working models helps recognize the importance of understanding children's perceptions of issues. Relatedly, in terms of broad interventions, the ecological approach gains considerable relevance given its focus on attempting to understand the impact of broad social forces on individual development and the need to also focus outside of families. One of the most important findings relating to the success of therapeutic interventions is that they often fail; and failure comes when efforts mismatch the intervention to actual needs. As much as that may seem obvious, the reality is that much mismatch continues. It continues not necessarily because it is not known what intervention would work best but more because of the lack of resources to engage in interventions that would be needed.

Different orientations matter much more than for understanding children's development. They matter because they can shape researchers and practitioners' responses to children. They also matter because those responses are constrained by societal responses to children. They point to the types of rights and frameworks that would need to be developed in efforts to address child maltreatment.

As you read the cases that follow, consider which approach the legal system seems to adopt in the manner it regulates children and their family life. On what developmental assumptions do the cases rest their rulings? Do the assumptions really matter? If they do matter, would you expect different outcomes if cases adopted alternative assumptions? As you seek to understand the dominant approach to understanding how the legal system envisions child protection through children's rights, consider dissenting voices. Dissenting voices highlight alternative ways and the challenges of moving toward them in light of what the cases stand for in this area of law.

Notes and Queries

1. Which approach seems to have the firmest hold on understanding the influences on children's development?

2. Diana Baumrind pioneered research on three commonly identified parenting styles: (a) authoritative (parents explain rules with children, place less emphasis on strict obedience, and are more likely to encourage autonomy), (b) authoritarian (parents emphasize obedience and tend to favor more punitive measures of discipline management), and (c) permissive (parents use little apparent control over their children's behavior, rarely use punishment, and allow children to make their own decisions). Why do you think she proposes that authoritative parenting offers the most optimal environment? Would those who espouse a transactional/ecological model agree? Do you think the model should gain greater relevance depending on the child's age? Would you expect cultural differences in parenting styles' relative effectiveness? What significance would you attach to this model as a way to understand and address child maltreatment? See Diana Baumrind (1995). *Child Maltreatment and Optimal Caregiving in Social Contexts*. New York: Garland.

3. Ecological models help identify children at risk and the extensive challenges facing intervention efforts. Illustrative is the manner disabled children are at higher risk of maltreatment. Recent research emphasizes the need to examine disability in cultural contexts, with some cultural beliefs positing that disability results from someone's evilness or from supernatural causes. These views will lead different groups to use folk remedies, natural healers, prayer, spiritualists, or nothing. See Susan H. Kapitanoff, John R. Lutzker & Kathryn M. Bigelow (2000). Cultural issues in the relation between child disabilities and child abuse. *Aggression and Violent Behavior*, 5, 227–244. That research highlights well how efforts to intervene must consider parents' views of disability and the extent to which those views are culturally determined. Equally importantly, the findings reveal how intervention requires examining cultural issues (e.g., role of families) and how intervention necessarily changes cultural values. It is difficult to imagine more ethically challenging issues than intervening in and deliberately seeking to change families and entire cultures.

4. How would legal systems differ if they championed the regulation of the influences on child development according to a particular view of child development? Which model do you suppose our legal system adopts?

Meyer v. Nebraska

262 U.S. 390; 43 S. Ct. 625 (1923)

Mr. Justice McReynolds delivered the opinion of the Court.

Plaintiff in error was tried and convicted in the District Court for Hamilton County, Nebraska, under an information which charged that on May 25, 1920, while an instructor in Zion Parochial School, he unlawfully taught the subject of reading in the German language to Raymond Parpart, a child of ten years, who had not attained and successfully passed the eighth grade. The information is based upon "An act relating to the teaching of foreign languages in the State of Nebraska". . . .

> Section 1. No person, individually or as a teacher, shall, in any private, denominational, parochial or public school, teach any subject to any person in any language other than the English language.
>
> Sec. 2. Languages, other than the English language, may be taught as languages only after a pupil shall have attained and successfully passed the eighth grade as evidenced by a certificate of graduation issued by the county superintendent of the county in which the child resides.
>
> Sec. 3. Any person who violates any of the provisions of this act shall be deemed guilty of a misdemeanor and upon conviction, shall be subject to a fine of not less than twenty-five dollars ($25), nor more than one hundred dollars ($100) or be confined in the county jail for any period not exceeding thirty days for each offense.

. . .

The Supreme Court of the State affirmed the judgment of conviction. It declared the offense charged and established was "the direct and intentional teaching of the German language as a distinct subject to a child who had not passed the eighth grade," in the parochial school maintained by Zion Evangelical Lutheran Congregation, a collection of Biblical stories being used therefor. And it held that the statute forbidding this did not conflict with the Fourteenth Amendment, but was a valid exercise of the police power. The following excerpts from the opinion sufficiently indicate the reasons advanced to support the conclusion.

The salutary purpose of the statute is clear. The legislature had seen the baneful effects of permitting foreigners, who had taken residence in this country, to rear and educate their children in the language of their native land. The result of that condition was found to be inimical to our own safety. To allow the children of foreigners, who had emigrated here, to be taught from early childhood the language of the country of their parents was to rear them with that language as their mother tongue. It was to educate them so that they must always think in that language, and, as a consequence, naturally inculcate in them the ideas and sentiments foreign to the best interests of this country. The statute, therefore, was intended not only to require that the education of all children be conducted in the English language, but that, until they had grown into that language and until it had become a part of them, they should not in the schools be taught any other language. The obvious purpose of this statute was that the English language should be and become the mother tongue of all children reared in this state. The enactment of such a statute comes reasonably within the police power of the state.

It is suggested that the law is an unwarranted restriction, in that it applies to all citizens of the state and arbitrarily interferes with the rights of citizens who are not of foreign ancestry, and prevents them, without reason, from having their children taught foreign languages in school. That argument is not well taken, for it assumes that every citizen finds himself restrained by the statute. The hours which a child is able to devote to study in the confinement of school are limited. It must have ample time for exercise or play. Its daily capacity for learning is comparatively small. A selection of subjects for its education, therefore, from among the many that might be taught, is obviously necessary. The legislature no doubt had in mind the practical operation of the law. The law affects few citizens, except those of foreign lineage. Other citizens, in their selection of studies, except perhaps in rare instances, have never deemed it of importance to teach their children foreign languages before such children have reached the eighth grade. In the legislative mind, the salutary effect of the statute no doubt outweighed the restriction upon the citizens generally, which, it appears, was a restriction of no real consequence.

The problem for our determination is whether the statute as construed and applied unreasonably infringes the liberty guaranteed to the plaintiff in error by the Fourteenth Amendment. "No State shall . . . deprive any person of life, liberty, or property, without due process of law."

While this Court has not attempted to define with exactness the liberty thus guaranteed, the term has received much consideration and some of the included things have been definitely stated. Without doubt, it denotes not merely freedom from bodily restraint but also the right of the individual to contract, to engage in any of the common occupations of life, to acquire useful knowledge, to marry, establish a home and bring up children, to worship God according to the dictates of his own conscience, and generally to enjoy those privileges long recognized at common law as essential to the orderly pursuit of happiness by free men. The established doctrine is that this liberty may not be interfered with, under the guise of protecting the public interest, by legislative action which is arbitrary or without reasonable relation to some purpose within the competency of the State to effect. Determination by the legislature of what constitutes proper exercise of police power is not final or conclusive but is subject to supervision by the courts. The American people have always regarded education and acquisition of knowledge as matters of supreme importance which should be diligently promoted. The Ordinance of 1787 declares, "Religion, morality, and knowledge being necessary to good government and the happiness of mankind, schools and the means of education shall forever be encouraged." Corresponding to the right of control, it is the natural duty of the parent to give his children education suitable to their station in life; and nearly all the States, including Nebraska, enforce this obligation by compulsory laws.

Practically, education of the young is only possible in schools conducted by especially qualified persons who devote themselves thereto. The calling always has been regarded as useful and honorable, essential, indeed, to the public welfare. Mere knowledge of the German language cannot reasonably be regarded as harmful. Heretofore it has been commonly looked upon as helpful and desirable. Plaintiff in error taught this language in school as part of his occupation. His right thus to teach and the right of parents to engage him so to instruct their children, we think, are within the liberty of the Amendment.

. . .

Evidently the legislature has attempted materially to interfere with the calling of modern language teachers, with the opportunities of pupils to acquire knowledge, and with the power of parents to control the education of their own.

It is said the purpose of the legislation was to promote civic development by inhibiting training and education of the immature in foreign tongues and ideals before they could learn English and acquire American ideals; and "that the English language should be and become the mother tongue of all children reared in this State." It is also affirmed that the foreign born population is very large, that certain communities commonly use foreign words, follow foreign leaders, move in a foreign atmosphere, and that the children are thereby hindered from becoming citizens of the most useful type and the public safety is imperiled.

That the State may do much, go very far, indeed, in order to improve the quality of its citizens, physically, mentally and morally, is clear; but the individual has certain fundamental rights which must be respected. The protection of the Constitution extends to all, to those who speak other languages as well as to those born with English on the tongue. Perhaps it would be highly advantageous if all had ready understanding of our ordinary speech, but this cannot be coerced by methods which conflict with the Constitution — a desirable end cannot be promoted by prohibited means.

For the welfare of his Ideal Commonwealth, Plato suggested a law which should provide: "That the wives of our guardians are to be common, and their children are to be common, and no parent is to know his own child, nor any child his parent. . . . The proper officers will take the offspring of the goods parents to the pen or fold, and there they will deposit them with certain nurses who dwell in a separate quarter; but the offspring of the inferior, or of the better when they chance to be deformed, will be put away in some mysterious, unknown place, as they should be." In order to submerge the individual and develop ideal citizens, Sparta assembled the males at seven into barracks and intrusted their subsequent education and training to official guardians. Although such measures have been deliberately approved by men of great genius, their ideas touching the relation between individual and State were wholly different from those upon which our institutions rest; and it hardly will be affirmed that any legislature could impose such restrictions upon the people of a State without doing violence to both letter and spirit of the Constitution.

The desire of the legislature to foster a homogeneous people with American ideals prepared readily to understand current discussions of civic matters is easy to appreciate. Unfortunate experiences during the late war and aversion toward every characteristic of truculent adversaries were certainly enough to quicken that aspiration. But the means adopted, we think, exceed the limitations upon the power of the State and conflict with rights assured to plaintiff in error. The interference is plain enough and no adequate reason therefor in time of peace and domestic tranquility has been shown.

The power of the State to compel attendance at some school and to make reasonable regulations for all schools, including a requirement that they shall give instructions in English, is not questioned. Nor has challenge been made of the State's power to prescribe a curriculum for institutions which it supports. Those matters are not within the present controversy. Our concern is with the prohibition approved by the Supreme Court . . . mere abuse incident to an occupation ordinarily useful is not enough to justify its abolition, although regulation may be entirely proper. No emergency has arisen which renders knowledge by a child of some language other than English so clearly harmful as to justify its inhibition with the consequent infringement of rights long freely enjoyed. We are constrained to conclude that the statute as applied is arbitrary and without reasonable relation to any end within the competency of the State.

As the statute undertakes to interfere only with teaching which involves a modern language, leaving complete freedom as to other matters, there seems no adequate foundation for the suggestion that the purpose was to protect the child's health by limiting his mental activities. It is well known that proficiency in a foreign language seldom comes to one not instructed at an early age, and experience shows that this is not injurious to the health, morals or understanding of the ordinary child.

The judgment of the court below must be reversed and the cause remanded for further proceedings not inconsistent with this opinion.

Reversed.

Justice Holmes, concurring and joined by Justice Sutherland. [omitted]

Notes and Queries

1. *Myer* is one of the leading "parental rights" cases. What are the foundations of parental rights?

2. What does *Myer* reveal about children's rights?

3. What developmental assumptions of childhood does the Court make? What assumptions does the Court make about a child's relationship to his community?

4. Given that parents retain an interest in directing their children's learning, what would be the outcome of a case involving parents teaching their children only German?

5. One of the most important parts of the *Myer* decision is the Court's take on Plato's view of what an effective child welfare law would provide. The Court rejects the view. Still, the image is of significance as it helps to understand this entire area of law, including the challenges met by efforts to reform.

Pierce v. Society of Sisters

268 U.S. 510; 45 S. Ct. 571 (1925)

Mr. Justice McReynolds delivered the opinion of the Court.

These appeals are from decrees, based upon undenied allegations, which granted preliminary orders restraining appellants from threatening or attempting to enforce the Compulsory Education Act adopted November 7, 1922, under the initiative provision of her Constitution by the voters of Oregon. They present the same points of law; there are no controverted questions of fact. Rights said to be guaranteed by the federal Constitution were specially set up, and appropriate prayers asked for their protection.

The challenged Act, effective September 1, 1926, requires every parent, guardian or other person having control or charge or custody of a child between eight and sixteen years to send him "to a public school for the period of time a public school shall be held during the current year" in the district where the child resides; and failure so to do is declared a misdemeanor. There are exemptions—not specially important here—for children who are not normal, or who have completed the eighth grade, or who reside at considerable distances from any public school, or whose parents or guardians hold special permits from the County Superintendent. The manifest purpose is to compel general attendance at public schools by normal children, between eight and sixteen, who have not completed the eighth grade. And without doubt enforcement of the statute would seriously impair, perhaps destroy, the profitable features of appellees' business and greatly diminish the value of their property.

Appellee, the Society of Sisters, is an Oregon corporation, organized in 1880, with power to care for orphans, educate and instruct the youth, establish and maintain academies or schools, and acquire necessary real and personal property....

After setting out the above facts the Society's bill alleges that the enactment conflicts with the right of parents to choose schools where their children will receive appropriate mental and religious training, the right of the child to influence the parents' choice of a school, the right of schools and teachers therein to engage in a useful business or profession, and is accordingly repugnant to the Constitution and void.

And, further, that unless enforcement of the measure is enjoined the corporation's business and property will suffer irreparable injury.

...

No answer was interposed in either cause, and after proper notices they were heard by three judges on motions for preliminary injunctions upon the specifically alleged facts. The court ruled that the Fourteenth Amendment guaranteed appellees against the deprivation of their property without due process of law consequent upon the unlawful interference by appellants with the free choice of patrons, present and prospective. It declared the right to conduct schools was property and that parents and guardians, as a part of their liberty, might direct the education of children by selecting reputable reachers and places. Also, that these schools were not unfit or harmful to the public, and that enforcement of the challenged statute would unlawfully deprive them of patronage and thereby destroy their owners' business and property. Finally, that the threats to enforce the Act would continue to cause irreparable injury; and the suits were not premature.

No question is raised concerning the power of the State reasonably to regulate all schools, to inspect, supervise and examine them, their teachers and pupils; to require that all children of proper age attend some school, that teachers shall be of good moral character and patriotic disposition, that certain studies plainly essential to good citizenship must be taught, and that nothing be taught which is manifestly inimical to the public welfare.

The inevitable practical result of enforcing the Act under consideration would be destruction of appellees' primary schools, and perhaps all other private primary schools for normal children within the State of Oregon. These parties are engaged in a kind of undertaking not inherently harmful, but long regarded as useful and meritorious. Certainly there is nothing in the present records to indicate that they have failed to discharge their obligations to patrons, students or the State. And there are no peculiar circumstances or present emergencies which demand extraordinary measures relative to primary education.

Under the doctrine of *Meyer v. Nebraska* we think it entirely plain that the Act of 1922 unreasonably interferes with the liberty of parents and guardians to direct the upbringing and education of children under their control. As often heretofore pointed out, rights guaranteed by the Constitution may not be abridged by legislation which has no reasonable relation to some purpose within the competency of the State. The fundamental theory of liberty upon which all governments in this Union repose excludes any general power of the State to standardize its children by forcing them to accept instruction from public teachers only. The child is not the mere creature of the State; those who nurture him and direct his destiny have the right, coupled with the high duty, to recognize and prepare him for additional obligations.

...

The decrees below are Affirmed.

Notes and Queries

1. What does *Pierce* add to *Meyer v. Nebraska*? Is it significant for the manner it confirms the liberty of parents? How does it envision that liberty in relation to the state: What would legitimize state intervention in parent–child relationships?

2. Under *Pierce*, what is the role of schools in fostering child development?

3. The Court notes, in what has become a highly cited sentence, that "[t]he child is not the mere creature of the State; those who nurture him and direct his destiny have the right, coupled with the high duty, to recognize and prepare him for additional obligations." What do you suppose the Court meant by those "additional obligations"? The answer can be found in the case *Wisconsin v. Yoder*, found later in this chapter.

Prince v. Massachusetts

321 U.S. 158; 64 S. Ct. 438 (1944)

Mr. Justice Newmark delivered the opinion of the Court.

The case brings for review another episode in the conflict between Jehovah's Witnesses and state authority. This time Sarah Prince appeals from convictions for violating Massachusetts' child labor laws, by acts said to be a rightful exercise of her religious convictions.

When the offenses were committed she was the aunt and custodian of Betty M. Simmons, a girl nine years of age. Originally there were three separate complaints. They were, shortly, for (1) refusal to disclose Betty's identity and age to a public officer whose duty was to enforce the statutes; (2) furnishing her with magazines, knowing she was to sell them unlawfully, that is, on the street; and (3) as Betty's custodian, permitting her to work contrary to law. The Supreme Judicial Court reversed the conviction under the first complaint on state grounds; but sustained the judgments founded on the other two. They present the only questions for our decision. These are whether [the statute], as applied, contravene the Fourteenth Amendment by denying or abridging appellant's freedom of religion and by denying to her the equal protection of the laws.

. . .

The story told by the evidence has become familiar. It hardly needs repeating, except to give setting to the variations introduced through the part played by a child of tender years. Mrs. Prince, living in Brockton, is the mother of two young sons. She also has legal custody of Betty Simmons, who lives with them. The children too are Jehovah's Witnesses and both Mrs. Prince and Betty testified they were ordained ministers. The former was accustomed to go each week on the streets of Brockton to distribute "Watchtower" and "Consolation," according to the usual plan. She had permitted the children to engage in this activity previously, and had been warned against doing so by the school attendance officer, Mr. Perkins. But, until December 18, 1941, she generally did not take them with her at night.

That evening, as Mrs. Prince was preparing to leave her home, the children asked to go. She at first refused. Childlike, they resorted to tears; and, motherlike, she yielded. Arriving downtown, Mrs. Prince permitted the children "to engage in the preaching work with her upon the sidewalks." That is, with specific reference to Betty, she and Mrs. Prince took positions about twenty feet apart near a street intersection. Betty held up in her hand, for passers-by to see, copies of "Watch Tower" and "Consolation." From her shoulder hung the usual canvas magazine bag, on which was printed: "Watchtower and Consolation 5 cents per copy." No one accepted a copy from Betty that evening and she received no money. Nor did her aunt. But on other occasions, Betty had received funds and given out copies.

Mrs. Prince and Betty remained until 8:45 p.m. A few minutes before this, Mr. Perkins approached Mrs. Prince. A discussion ensued. He inquired and she refused to give Betty's name. However, she stated the child attended the Shaw School. Mr. Perkins referred to his previous warnings and said he would allow five minutes for them to get off the street. Mrs. Prince admitted she supplied Betty with the magazines and said, "Neither you nor anybody else can stop me.... This child is exercising her God-given right and her constitutional right to preach the gospel, and no creature has a right to interfere with God's commands." However, Mrs. Prince and Betty departed. She remarked as she went, "I'm not going through this any more. We've been through it time and time again. I'm going home and put the little girl to bed." It may be added that testimony, by Betty, her aunt and others, was offered at the trials, and was excluded, to show that Betty believed it was her religious duty to perform this work and failure would bring condemnation "to everlasting destruction at Armageddon."

As the case reaches us, the questions are no longer open whether what the child did was a "sale" or an "offer to sell" ... or was "work"....

The only question remaining therefore is whether, as construed and applied, the statute is valid. Upon this the court said: "We think that freedom of the press and of religion is subject to incidental regulation to the slight degree involved in the prohibition of the selling of religious literature in streets and public places by boys under twelve and girls under eighteen, and in the further statutory provisions herein considered, which have been adopted as means of enforcing that prohibition."

Appellant does not stand on freedom of the press. Regarding it as secular, she concedes it may be restricted as Massachusetts has done. Hence, she rests squarely on freedom of religion under the First Amendment, applied by the Fourteenth to the states. She buttresses this foundation, however, with a claim of parental right as secured by the due process clause of the latter Amendment. These guaranties, she thinks, guard alike herself and the child in what they have done. Thus, two claimed liberties are at stake. One is the parent's, to bring up the child in the way he should go, which for appellant means to teach him the tenets and the practices of their faith. The other freedom is the child's, to observe these; and among them is "to preach the gospel . . . by public distribution" of "Watchtower" and "Consolation," in conformity with the scripture: "A little child shall lead them."

If by this position appellant seeks for freedom of conscience a broader protection than for freedom of the mind, it may be doubted that any of the great liberties insured by the First Article can be given higher place than the others. All have preferred position in our basic scheme. All are interwoven there together. Differences there are, in them and in the modes appropriate for their exercise. But they have unity in the charter's prime place because they have unity in their human sources and functionings. Heart and mind are not identical. Intuitive faith and reasoned judgment are not the same. Spirit is not always thought. But in the everyday business of living, secular or otherwise, these variant aspects of personality find inseparable expression in a thousand ways. They cannot be altogether parted in law more than in life.

To make accommodation between these freedoms and an exercise of state authority always is delicate. It hardly could be more so than in such a clash as this case presents. On one side is the obviously earnest claim for freedom of conscience and religious practice. With it is allied the parent's claim to authority in her own household and in the rearing of her children. The parent's conflict with the state over control of the child and his training is serious enough when only secular matters are concerned. It becomes the more so when an element of religious conviction enters. Against these sacred private interests, basic in a democracy, stand the interests of society to protect the welfare of children, and the state's assertion of authority to that end, made here in a manner conceded valid if only secular things were involved. The last is no mere corporate concern of official authority. It is the interest of youth itself, and of the whole community, that children be both safeguarded from abuses and given opportunities for growth into free and independent well-developed men and citizens. Between contrary pulls of such weight, the safest and most objective recourse is to the lines already marked out, not precisely but for guides, in narrowing the no man's land where this battle has gone on.

The rights of children to exercise their religion, and of parents to give them religious training and to encourage them in the practice of religious belief, as against preponderant sentiment and assertion of state power voicing it, have had recognition here. . . . Previously in *Pierce v. Society of Sisters* this Court had sustained the parent's authority to provide religious with secular schooling, and the child's right to receive it, as against the state's requirement of attendance at public schools. And in *Meyer v. Nebraska*, children's rights to receive teaching in languages other than the nation's common tongue were guarded against the state's encroachment. It is cardinal with us that the custody, care and nurture of the child reside first in the parents, whose primary function and freedom include preparation for obligations the state can neither supply nor hinder. And it is in recognition of this that these decisions have respected the private realm of family life which the state cannot enter.

But the family itself is not beyond regulation in the public interest, as against a claim of religious liberty. And neither rights of religion nor rights of parenthood are beyond limitation. Acting to guard the general interest in youth's well being, the state as parens patriae may restrict the parent's control by requiring school attendance, regulating or prohibiting the child's labor and in many other ways. Its authority is not nullified merely because the parent grounds his claim to control the child's course of conduct on religion or conscience. Thus, he cannot claim freedom from compulsory vaccination for the child more than for himself on religious grounds. The right to practice religion freely does not include liberty to expose the community or the child to communicable disease or the latter to ill health or death. The catalogue need not be lengthened. It is sufficient to show what indeed appellant hardly disputes, that the state has a wide range of power for limiting parental freedom and authority in things affecting the child's welfare; and that this includes, to some extent, matters of conscience and religious conviction.

But it is said the state cannot do so here. This, first, because when state action impinges upon a claimed religious freedom, it must fall unless shown to be necessary for or conducive to the child's protection against some clear and present danger and, it is added, there was no such showing here. The child's presence on the street, with her guardian, distributing or offering to distribute the magazines, it is urged, was in no way harmful to her, nor in any event more so than the presence of many other children at the same time and place, engaged in shopping and other activities not prohibited. Accordingly, in view of the preferred position the freedoms of the First Article occupy, the statute in its present application must fall. It cannot be sustained by any presumption of validity. And, finally, it is said, the statute is, as to children, an absolute prohibition, not merely a reasonable regulation, of the denounced activity.

Concededly a statute or ordinance identical in terms with except that it is applicable to adults or all persons generally, would be invalid. But the mere fact a state could not wholly prohibit this form of adult activity, whether characterized locally as a "sale" or otherwise, does not mean it cannot do so for children. Such a conclusion granted would mean that a state could impose no greater limitation upon child labor than upon adult labor. Or, if an adult were free to enter dance halls, saloons, and disreputable places generally, in order to discharge his conceived religious duty to admonish or dissuade persons from frequenting such places, so would be a child with similar convictions and objectives, if not alone then in the parent's company, against the state's command.

The state's authority over children's activities is broader than over like actions of adults. This is peculiarly true of public activities and in matters of employment. A democratic society rests, for its continuance, upon the healthy, well-rounded growth of young people into full maturity as citizens, with all that implies. It may secure this against impeding restraints and dangers within a broad range of selection. Among evils most appropriate for such action are the crippling effects of child employment, more especially in public places, and the possible harms arising from other activities subject to all the diverse influences of the street. It is too late now to doubt that legislation appropriately designed to reach such evils is within the state's police power, whether against the parent's claim to control of the child or one that religious scruples dictate contrary action.

It is true children have rights, in common with older people, in the primary use of highways. But even in such use streets afford dangers for them not affecting adults. And in other uses, whether in work or in other things, this difference may be magnified. This is so not only when children are unaccompanied but certainly to some extent when they are with their parents. What may be wholly permissible for adults therefore may not be so for children, either with or without their parents' presence.

Street preaching, whether oral or by handing out literature, is not the primary use of the highway, even for adults. While for them it cannot be wholly prohibited, it can be regulated within reasonable limits in accommodation to the primary and other incidental uses. But, for obvious reasons, notwithstanding appellant's contrary view, the validity of such a prohibition applied to children not accompanied by an older person hardly would seem open to question. The case reduces itself therefore to the question whether the presence of the child's guardian puts a limit to the state's power. That fact may lessen the likelihood that some evils the legislation seeks to avert will occur. But it cannot forestall all of them. The zealous though lawful exercise of the right to engage in propagandizing the community, whether in religious, political or other matters, may and at times does create situations difficult enough for adults to cope with and wholly inappropriate for children, especially of tender years, to face. Other harmful possibilities could be stated, of emotional excitement and psychological or physical injury. Parents may be free to become martyrs themselves. But it does not follow they are free, in identical circumstances, to make martyrs of their children before they have reached the age of full and legal discretion when they can make that choice for themselves. Massachusetts has determined that an absolute prohibition, though one limited to streets and public places and to the incidental uses proscribed, is necessary to accomplish its legitimate objectives. Its power to attain them is broad enough to reach these peripheral instances in which the parent's supervision may reduce but cannot eliminate entirely the ill effects of the prohibited conduct. We think that with reference to the public proclaiming of religion, upon the streets and in other similar public places, the power of the state to control the conduct of children reaches beyond the scope of its authority over adults, as is true in the case of other freedoms, and the rightful boundary of its power has not been crossed in this case.

In so ruling we dispose also of appellant's argument founded upon denial of equal protection. It falls with that based on denial of religious freedom, since in this instance the one is but another phrasing of the other. Shortly, the contention is that the street, for Jehovah's Witnesses and their children, is their church, since their conviction makes it so; and to deny them access to it for religious purposes as was done here has the same effect as excluding altar boys, youthful choristers, and other children from the edifices in which they practice their religious beliefs and worship. The argument hardly needs more than statement, after what has been said, to refute it. However Jehovah's Witnesses may conceive them, the public highways have not become their religious property merely by their assertion. And there is no denial of equal protection in excluding their children from doing there what no other children may do.

Our ruling does not extend beyond the facts the case presents. We neither lay the foundation "for any [that is, every] state intervention in the indoctrination and participation of children in religion" which may be done "in the name of their health and welfare" nor give warrant for "every limitation on their religious training and activities." The religious training and indoctrination of children may be accomplished in many ways, some of which, as we have noted, have received constitutional protection through decisions of this Court. These and all others except the public proclaiming of religion on the streets, if this may be taken as either training or indoctrination of the proclaimer, remain unaffected by the decision.

The judgment is

Affirmed.

Mr. Justice Jackson, joined by Mr. Justice Roberts and Mr. Justice Frankfurter, concurring.

The novel feature of this decision is this: the Court holds that a state may apply child labor laws to restrict or prohibit an activity of which, as recently as last term, it held: "This form of religious activity occupies the same high estate under the First Amendment as do worship in the churches and preaching from the pulpits. It has the same claim to protection as the more orthodox and conventional exercises of religion." . . .

It is difficult for me to believe that going upon the streets to accost the public is the same thing for application of public law as withdrawing to a private structure for religious worship. But if worship in the churches and the activity of Jehovah's Witnesses on the streets "occupy the same high estate" and have the "same claim to protection" it would seem that child labor laws may be applied to both if to either. . . . [A] foundation is laid for any state intervention in the indoctrination and participation of children in religion, provided it is done in the name of their health or welfare. . . .

My own view may be shortly put: I think the limits begin to operate whenever activities begin to affect or collide with liberties of others or of the public. Religious activities which concern only members of the faith are and ought to be free — as nearly absolutely free as anything can be. But beyond these, many religious denominations or sects engage in collateral and secular activities intended to obtain means from unbelievers to sustain the worshippers and their leaders. They raise money, not merely by passing the plate to those who voluntarily attend services or by contributions by their own people, but by solicitations and drives addressed to the public by holding public dinners and entertainments, by various kinds of sales and Bingo games and lotteries. All such money-raising activities on a public scale are, I think, Caesar's affairs and may be regulated by the state so long as it does not discriminate against one because he is doing them for a religious purpose, and the regulation is not arbitrary and capricious, in violation of other provisions of the Constitution.

The Court . . . now draws a line based on age that cuts across both true exercise of religion and auxiliary secular activities. I think this is not a correct principle for defining the activities immune from regulation on grounds of religion. . . . I have no alternative but to dissent from the grounds of affirmance of a judgment which I think was rightly decided, and upon right grounds, by the Supreme Judicial Court of Massachusetts.

Mr. Justice Murphy dissenting.

This attempt by the state of Massachusetts to prohibit a child from exercising her constitutional right to practice her religion on the public streets cannot, in my opinion, be sustained.

The record makes clear the basic fact that Betty Simmons, the nine-year-old child in question, was engaged in a genuine religious, rather than commercial, activity. She was a member of Jehovah's Witnesses and had been taught the tenets of that sect by her guardian, the appellant. Such tenets included the duty of publicly distributing religious tracts on the street and from door to door. Pursuant to this religious duty and in the company of the appellant, Betty Simmons on the night of December 18, 1941, was standing on a public street corner and offering to distribute Jehovah's Witness literature to passersby. There was no expectation of pecuniary profit to herself or to appellant. It is undisputed, furthermore, that she did this of her own desire and with appellant's consent. She testified that she was motivated by her love of the Lord and that He commanded her to distribute this literature; this was, she declared, her way of worshipping God. She was occupied, in other words, in "an age-old form of missionary evangelism" with a purpose "as evangelical as the revival meeting."

Religious training and activity, whether performed by adult or child, are protected by the Fourteenth Amendment against interference by state action, except insofar as they violate reasonable regulations adopted for the protection of the public health, morals and welfare. Our problem here is whether a state, under the guise of enforcing its child labor laws, can lawfully prohibit girls under the age of eighteen and boys under the age of twelve from practicing their religious faith insofar as it involves the distribution or sale of religious tracts on the public streets. No question of freedom of speech or freedom of press is present and we are not called upon to determine the permissible restraints on those rights. Nor are any truancy or curfew restrictions in issue. The statutes in question prohibit all children within the specified age limits from selling or offering to sell "any newspapers, magazines, periodicals or any other articles of merchandise of any description . . . in any street or public place." Criminal sanctions are imposed on the parents and guardians who compel or permit minors in their control to engage in the prohibited transactions. The state court has construed these statutes to cover the activities here involved, thereby imposing an indirect restraint through the parents and guardians on the free exercise by minors of their religious beliefs. This indirect restraint is no less effective than a direct one. A square conflict between the constitutional guarantee of religious freedom and the state's legitimate interest in protecting the welfare of its children is thus presented.

As the opinion of the Court demonstrates, the power of the state lawfully to control the religious and other activities of children is greater than its power over similar activities of adults. But that fact is no more decisive of the issue posed by this case than is the obvious fact that the family itself is subject to reasonable regulation in the public interest. We are concerned solely with the reasonableness of this particular prohibition of religious activity by children.

In dealing with the validity of statutes which directly or indirectly infringe religious freedom and the right of parents to encourage their children in the practice of a religious belief, we are not aided by any strong presumption of the constitutionality of such legislation. On the contrary, the human freedoms enumerated in the First Amendment and carried over into the Fourteenth Amendment are to be presumed to be invulnerable and any attempt to sweep away those freedoms is prima facie invalid. It follows that any restriction or prohibition must be justified by those who deny that the freedoms have been unlawfully invaded. The burden was therefore on the state of Massachusetts to prove the reasonableness and necessity of prohibiting children from engaging in religious activity of the type involved in this case.

The burden in this instance, however, is not met by vague references to the reasonableness underlying child labor legislation in general. The great interest of the state in shielding minors from the evil vicissitudes of early life does not warrant every limitation on their religious training and activities. The reasonableness that justifies the prohibition of the ordinary distribution of literature in the public streets by children is not necessarily the reasonableness that justifies such a drastic restriction when the distribution is part of their religious faith. If the right of a child to practice its religion in that manner is to be forbidden by constitutional means, there must be convincing proof that such a practice constitutes a grave and immediate danger to the state or to the health, morals or welfare of the child. The vital freedom of religion, which is "of the very essence of a scheme of ordered liberty," cannot be erased by slender references to the state's power to restrict the more secular activities of children.

The state, in my opinion, has completely failed to sustain its burden of proving the existence of any grave or immediate danger to any interest which it may lawfully protect. There is no proof that Betty Simmons' mode of worship constituted a serious menace to the public. It was carried on in an orderly, lawful manner at a public street corner. And "one who is rightfully on a street which the state has left open to the public carries with him there as elsewhere the constitutional right to express his views in an orderly fashion. This right extends to the communication of ideas by handbills and literature as well as by the spoken word." The sidewalk, no less than the cathedral or the evangelist's tent, is a proper place, under the Constitution, for the orderly worship of God. Such use of the streets is as necessary to the Jehovah's Witnesses, the Salvation Army and others who practice religion without benefit of conventional shelters as is the use of the streets for purposes of passage.

It is claimed, however, that such activity was likely to affect adversely the health, morals and welfare of the child. Reference is made in the majority opinion to "the crippling effects of child employment, more especially in public places, and the possible harms arising from other activities subject to all the diverse influences of the street." To the extent that they flow from participation in ordinary commercial activities, these harms are irrelevant to this case. And the bare possibility that such harms might emanate from distribution of religious literature is not, standing alone, sufficient justification for restricting freedom of conscience and religion. Nor can parents or guardians be subjected to criminal liability because of vague possibilities that their religious teachings might cause injury to the child. The evils must be grave, immediate, substantial. Yet there is not the slightest indication in this record, or in sources subject to judicial notice, that children engaged in distributing literature pursuant to their religious beliefs have been or are likely to be subject to any of the harmful "diverse influences of the street." Indeed, if probabilities are to be indulged in, the likelihood is that children engaged in serious religious endeavor are immune from such influences. Gambling, truancy, irregular eating and sleeping habits, and the more serious vices are not consistent with the high moral character ordinarily displayed by children fulfilling religious obligations. Moreover, Jehovah's Witness children invariably make their distributions in groups subject at all times to adult or parental control, as was done in this case. The dangers are thus exceedingly remote, to say the least. And the fact that the zealous exercise of the right to propagandize the community may result in violent or disorderly situations difficult for children to face is no excuse for prohibiting the exercise of that right.

No chapter in human history has been so largely written in terms of persecution and intolerance as the one dealing with religious freedom. From ancient times to the present day, the ingenuity of man has known no limits in its ability to forge weapons of oppression for use against those who dare to express or practice unorthodox religious beliefs. And the Jehovah's Witnesses are living proof of the fact that even in this nation, conceived as it was in the ideals of freedom, the right to practice religion in unconventional ways is still far from secure. Theirs is a militant and unpopular faith, pursued with a fanatical zeal. They have suffered brutal beatings; their property has been destroyed; they have been harassed at every turn by the resurrection and enforcement of little used ordinances and statutes. To them, along with other present-day religious minorities, befalls the burden of testing our devotion to the ideals and constitutional guarantees of religious freedom. We should therefore hesitate before approving the application of a statute that might be used as another instrument of oppression. Religious freedom is too sacred a right to be restricted or prohibited in any degree without convincing proof that a legitimate interest of the state is in grave danger.

Notes and Queries

1. Which opinion evinces greater respect for children's rights? Nine-year-old Simmons is an ordained minister, as are all members of her congregation. Should she receive direct First Amendment protection? What does the manner in which the Court frames her rights tell us about the rights of children? Does the Court grant children rights in disputes with their parents? The Court no longer doubts that children have rights. The major concern now involves the extent to which children's own individual interests may prevail over parental opposition and the extent to which children should control their rights (or have a parent or other adult control them). What do *Prince*'s lessons tell us about how to address these issues?

2. Are you persuaded that the activities of Mrs. Prince were the type contemplated as problematic by child labor and solicitation laws? Assuming the state has an interest in enacting child labor laws, how are those affected by the facts presented in *Prince*? If the goal is to protect children, was the child not protected enough by Mrs. Prince? The Court evinces concern about child labor in public places; is that concern legitimate? Is it legitimate in this case? Should we be more concerned about child labor in families or places more hidden from public view?

3. Justice Newmark quotes from a prior case to note that:

   > It is cardinal with us that the custody, care and nurture of the child reside first in the parents, whose primary function and freedom include preparation for obligations the state can neither supply nor hinder. And it is in recognition of this that these decisions have respected the private realm of family life which the state cannot enter.

   What is it that the state cannot supply? Does he refer to moral standards? If so, then what is the role of law and why is the state interfering?

4. Justice Murphy's dissent would find that the real issue is not the reasonableness of the statute but the need to have "convincing proof that such a practice constitutes a grave and immediate danger to the state or to the health, morals or welfare of the child." Whose rights do you suppose such a rule would really protect?

5. The Court again projects an image of childhood. Has it changed from prior cases?

Wisconsin v. Yoder

406 U.S. 205; 92 S. Ct. 1526 (1972)

Mr. Chief Justice Burger delivered the opinion of the Court.

On petition of the State of Wisconsin, we granted the writ of certiorari in this case to review a decision of the Wisconsin Supreme Court holding that respondents' convictions of violating the State's compulsory school-attendance law were invalid under the Free Exercise Clause of the First Amendment to the United States Constitution made applicable to the States by the Fourteenth Amendment. For the reasons hereafter stated we affirm the judgment of the Supreme Court of Wisconsin.

Respondents Jonas Yoder and Wallace Miller are members of the Old Order Amish religion, and respondent Adin Yutzy is a member of the Conservative Amish Mennonite Church. They and their families are residents of Green County, Wisconsin. Wisconsin's compulsory school-attendance law required them to cause their children to attend public or private school until reaching age 16 but the respondents declined to send their children, ages 14 and 15, to public school after they completed the eighth grade. The children were not enrolled in any private school, or within any recognized exception to the compulsory-attendance law, and they are conceded to be subject to the Wisconsin statute.

On complaint of the school district administrator for the public schools, respondents were charged, tried, and convicted of violating the compulsory-attendance law in Green County Court and were fined the sum of $5 each. Respondents defended on the ground that the application of the compulsory-attendance law violated their rights under the First and Fourteenth Amendments. The trial testimony showed that respondents believed, in accordance with the tenets of Old Order Amish communities generally, that their children's attendance at high school, public or private, was contrary to the Amish religion and way of life. They believed that by sending their children to high school, they would not only expose themselves to the danger of the censure of the church community, but, as found by the county court, also endanger their own salvation and that of their children. The State stipulated that respondents' religious beliefs were sincere.

In support of their position, respondents presented as expert witnesses scholars on religion and education whose testimony is uncontradicted. They expressed their opinions on the relationship of the Amish belief concerning school attendance to the more general tenets of their religion, and described the impact that compulsory high school attendance could have on the continued survival of Amish communities as they exist in the United States today. ...

Formal high school education beyond the eighth grade is contrary to Amish beliefs, not only because it places Amish children in an environment hostile to Amish beliefs with increasing emphasis on competition in class work and sports and with pressure to conform to the styles, manners, and ways of the peer group, but also because it takes them away from their community, physically and emotionally, during the crucial and formative adolescent period of life. During this period, the children must acquire Amish attitudes favoring manual work and self-reliance and the specific skills needed to perform the adult role of an Amish farmer or housewife. They must learn to enjoy physical labor. Once a child has learned basic reading, writing, and elementary mathematics, these traits, skills, and attitudes admittedly fall within the category of those best learned through example and "doing" rather than in a classroom. And, at this time in life, the Amish child must also grow in his faith and his relationship to the Amish community if he is to be prepared to accept the heavy obligations imposed by adult baptism. In short, high school attendance with teachers who are not of the Amish faith — and may even be hostile to it — interposes a serious barrier to the integration of the Amish child into the Amish religious community. Dr. John Hostetler, one of the experts on Amish society, testified that the modern high school is not equipped, in curriculum or social environment, to impart the values promoted by Amish society.

The Amish do not object to elementary education through the first eight grades as a general proposition because they agree that their children must have basic skills in the "three R's" in order to read the Bible, to be good farmers and citizens, and to be able to deal with non-Amish people when necessary in the course of daily affairs. They view such a basic education as acceptable because it does not significantly expose their children to worldly values or interfere with their development in the Amish community during the crucial adolescent period. While Amish accept compulsory elementary education generally, wherever possible they have established their own elementary schools in many respects like the small local schools of the past. In the Amish belief higher learning tends to develop values they reject as influences that alienate man from God.

On the basis of such considerations, Dr. Hostetler testified that compulsory high school attendance could not only result in great psychological harm to Amish children, because of the conflicts it would produce, but would also, in his opinion, ultimately result in the destruction of the Old Order Amish church community as it exists in the United States today. The testimony of Dr. Donald A. Erickson, an expert witness on education, also showed that the Amish succeed in preparing their high school age children to be productive members of the Amish community. He described their system of learning through doing the skills directly relevant to their adult roles in the Amish community as "ideal" and perhaps superior to ordinary high school education. The evidence also showed that the Amish have an excellent record as law-abiding and generally self-sufficient members of society.

Although the trial court in its careful findings determined that the Wisconsin compulsory school-attendance law "does interfere with the freedom of the Defendants to act in accordance with their sincere religious belief" it also concluded that the requirement of high school attendance until age 16 was a "reasonable and constitutional" exercise of governmental power, and therefore denied the motion to dismiss the charges. The Wisconsin Circuit Court affirmed the convictions. The Wisconsin Supreme Court, however, sustained respondents' claim under the Free Exercise Clause of the First Amendment and reversed the convictions. A majority of the court was of the opinion that the State had failed to make an adequate showing that its interest in "establishing and maintaining an educational system overrides the defendants' right to the free exercise of their religion."

I

There is no doubt as to the power of a State, having a high responsibility for education of its citizens, to impose reasonable regulations for the control and duration of basic education. Providing public schools ranks at the very apex of the function of a State. Yet even this paramount responsibility was, in *Pierce*, made to yield to the right of parents to provide an equivalent education in a privately operated system. There the Court held that Oregon's statute compelling attendance in a public school from age eight to age 16 unreasonably interfered with the interest of parents in directing the rearing of their offspring, including their education in church-operated schools. As that case suggests, the values of parental direction of the religious upbringing and education of their children in their early and formative years have a high place in our society. Thus, a State's interest in universal education, however highly we rank it, is not totally free from a balancing process when it impinges on fundamental rights and interests, such as those specifically protected by the Free Exercise Clause of the First Amendment, and the traditional interest of parents with respect to the religious upbringing of their children so long as they, in the words of *Pierce*, "prepare [them] for additional obligations."

It follows that in order for Wisconsin to compel school attendance beyond the eighth grade against a claim that such attendance interferes with the practice of a legitimate religious belief, it must appear either that the State does not deny the free exercise of religious belief by its requirement, or that there is a state interest of sufficient magnitude to override the interest claiming protection under the Free Exercise Clause. Long before there was general acknowledgment of the need for universal formal education, the Religion Clauses had specifically and firmly fixed the right to free exercise of religious beliefs, and buttressing this fundamental right was an equally firm, even if less explicit, prohibition against the establishment of any religion by government. The values underlying these two provisions relating to religion have been zealously protected, sometimes even at the expense of other interests of admittedly high social importance. The invalidation of financial aid to parochial schools by government grants for a salary subsidy for teachers is but one example of the extent to which courts have gone in this regard, notwithstanding that such aid programs were legislatively determined to be in the public interest and the service of sound educational policy by States and by Congress.

The essence of all that has been said and written on the subject is that only those interests of the highest order and those not otherwise served can overbalance legitimate claims to the free exercise of religion. We can accept it as settled, therefore, that, however strong the State's interest in universal compulsory education, it is by no means absolute to the exclusion or subordination of all other interests.

II

We come then to the quality of the claims of the respondents concerning the alleged encroachment of Wisconsin's compulsory school-attendance statute on their rights and the rights of their children to the free exercise of the religious beliefs they and their forebears have adhered to for almost three centuries. In evaluating those claims we must be careful to determine whether the Amish religious faith and their mode of life are, as they claim, inseparable and interdependent. A way of life, however virtuous and admirable, may not be interposed as a barrier to reasonable state regulation of education if it is based on purely secular considerations; to have the protection of the Religion Clauses, the claims must be rooted in religious belief. Although a determination of what is a "religious" belief or practice entitled to constitutional protection may present a most delicate question, the very concept of ordered liberty precludes allowing every person to make his own standards on matters of conduct in which society as a whole has important interests. Thus, if the Amish asserted their claims because of their subjective evaluation and rejection of the contemporary secular values accepted by the majority, much as Thoreau rejected the social values of his time and isolated himself at Walden Pond, their claims would not rest on a religious basis. Thoreau's choice was philosophical and personal rather than religious, and such belief does not rise to the demands of the Religion Clauses.

... [T]he record in this case abundantly supports the claim that the traditional way of life of the Amish is not merely a matter of personal preference, but one of deep religious conviction, shared by an organized group, and intimately related to daily living.

... The respondents freely concede, and indeed assert as an article of faith, that their religious beliefs and what we would today call "life style" have not altered in fundamentals for centuries. Their way of life in a church-oriented community, separated from the outside world and "worldly" influences, their attachment to nature and the soil, is a way inherently simple and uncomplicated, albeit difficult to preserve against the pressure to conform. Their rejection of telephones, automobiles, radios, and television, their mode of dress, of speech, their habits of manual work do indeed set them apart from much of contemporary society; these customs are both symbolic and practical.

...

The impact of the compulsory-attendance law on respondents' practice of the Amish religion is not only severe, but inescapable, for the Wisconsin law affirmatively compels them, under threat of criminal sanction, to perform acts undeniably at odds with fundamental tenets of their religious beliefs. Nor is the impact of the compulsory-attendance law confined to grave interference with important Amish religious tenets from a subjective point of view. It carries with it precisely the kind of objective danger to the free exercise of religion that the First Amendment was designed to prevent. As the record shows, compulsory school attendance to age 16 for Amish children carries with it a very real threat of undermining the Amish community and religious practice as they exist today; they must either abandon belief and be assimilated into society at large, or be forced to migrate to some other and more tolerant region.

. . .

III

Neither the findings of the trial court nor the Amish claims as to the nature of their faith are challenged in this Court by the State of Wisconsin. Its position is that the State's interest in universal compulsory formal secondary education to age 16 is so great that it is paramount to the undisputed claims of respondents that their mode of preparing their youth for Amish life, after the traditional elementary education, is an essential part of their religious belief and practice. Nor does the State undertake to meet the claim that the Amish mode of life and education is inseparable from and a part of the basic tenets of their religion—indeed, as much a part of their religious belief and practices as baptism, the confessional, or a Sabbath may be for others.

. . .

We turn, then, to the State's broader contention that its interest in its system of compulsory education is so compelling that even the established religious practices of the Amish must give way. Where fundamental claims of religious freedom are at stake, however, we cannot accept such a sweeping claim; despite its admitted validity in the generality of cases, we must searchingly examine the interests that the State seeks to promote by its requirement for compulsory education to age 16, and the impediment to those objectives that would flow from recognizing the claimed Amish exemption.

The State advances two primary arguments in support of its system of compulsory education. It notes, as Thomas Jefferson pointed out early in our history, that some degree of education is necessary to prepare citizens to participate effectively and intelligently in our open political system if we are to preserve freedom and independence. Further, education prepares individuals to be self-reliant and self-sufficient participants in society. We accept these propositions.

However, the evidence adduced by the Amish in this case is persuasively to the effect that an additional one or two years of formal high school for Amish children in place of their long-established program of informal vocational education would do little to serve those interests. Respondents' experts testified at trial, without challenge, that the value of all education must be assessed in terms of its capacity to prepare the child for life. It is one thing to say that compulsory education for a year or two beyond the eighth grade may be necessary when its goal is the preparation of the child for life in modern society as the majority live, but it is quite another if the goal of education be viewed as the preparation of the child for life in the separated agrarian community that is the keystone of the Amish faith.

The State attacks respondents' position as one fostering "ignorance" from which the child must be protected by the State. No one can question the State's duty to protect children from ignorance but this argument does not square with the facts disclosed in the record. Whatever their idiosyncrasies as seen by the majority, this record strongly shows that the Amish community has been a highly successful social unit within our society, even if apart from the conventional "mainstream." Its members are productive and very law-abiding members of society; they reject public welfare in any of its usual modern forms. The Congress itself recognized their self-sufficiency by authorizing exemption of such groups as the Amish from the obligation to pay social security taxes.

It is neither fair nor correct to suggest that the Amish are opposed to education beyond the eighth grade level. What this record shows is that they are opposed to conventional formal education of the type provided by a certified high school because it comes at the child's crucial adolescent period of religious development. Dr. Donald Erickson, for example, testified that their system of learning-by-doing was an "ideal system" of education in terms of preparing Amish children for life as adults in the Amish community. . . .

We must not forget that in the Middle Ages important values of the civilization of the Western World were preserved by members of religious orders who isolated themselves from all worldly influences against great obstacles. There can be no assumption that today's majority is "right" and the Amish and others like them are "wrong." A way of life that is odd or even erratic but interferes with no rights or interests of others is not to be condemned because it is different.

The State, however, supports its interest in providing an additional one or two years of compulsory high school education to Amish children because of the possibility that some such children will choose to leave the Amish community, and that if this occurs they will be ill-equipped for life. The State argues that if Amish children leave their church they should not be in the position of making their way in the world without the education available in the one or two additional years the State requires. However, on this record, that argument is highly speculative. There is no specific evidence of the loss of Amish adherents by attrition, nor is there any showing that upon leaving the Amish community Amish children, with their practical agricultural training and habits of industry and self-reliance, would become burdens on society because of educational short-comings. Indeed, this argument of the State appears to rest primarily on the State's mistaken assumption, already noted, that the Amish do not provide any education for their children beyond the eighth grade, but allow them to grow in "ignorance." To the contrary, not only do the Amish accept the necessity for formal schooling through the eighth grade level, but continue to provide what has been characterized by the undisputed testimony of expert educators as an "ideal" vocational education for their children in the adolescent years.

There is nothing in this record to suggest that the Amish qualities of reliability, self-reliance, and dedication to work would fail to find ready markets in today's society. Absent some contrary evidence supporting the State's position, we are unwilling to assume that persons possessing such valuable vocational skills and habits are doomed to become burdens on society should they determine to leave the Amish faith, nor is there any basis in the record to warrant a finding that an additional one or two years of formal school education beyond the eighth grade would serve to eliminate any such problem that might exist.

Insofar as the State's claim rests on the view that a brief additional period of formal education is imperative to enable the Amish to participate effectively and intelligently in our democratic process, it must fall. The Amish alternative to formal secondary school education has enabled them to function effectively in their day-to-day life under self-imposed limitations on relations with the world, and to survive and prosper in contemporary society as a separate, sharply identifiable and highly self-sufficient community for more than 200 years in this country. In itself this is strong evidence that they are capable of fulfilling the social and political responsibilities of citizenship without compelled attendance beyond the eighth grade at the price of jeopardizing their free exercise of religious belief. When Thomas Jefferson emphasized the need for education as a bulwark of a free people against tyranny, there is nothing to indicate he had in mind compulsory education through any fixed age beyond a basic education. Indeed, the Amish communities singularly parallel and reflect many of the virtues of Jefferson's ideal of the "sturdy yeoman" who would form the basis of what he considered as the ideal of a democratic society. Even their idiosyncratic separateness exemplifies the diversity we profess to admire and encourage.

The requirement for compulsory education beyond the eighth grade is a relatively recent development in our history. Less than 60 years ago, the educational requirements of almost all of the States were satisfied by completion of the elementary grades, at least where the child was regularly and lawfully employed. The independence and successful social functioning of the Amish community for a period approaching almost three centuries and more than 200 years in this country are strong evidence that there is at best a speculative gain, in terms of meeting the duties of citizenship, from an additional one or two years of compulsory formal education. Against this background it would require a more particularized showing from the State on this point to justify the severe interference with religious freedom such additional compulsory attendance would entail.

We should also note that compulsory education and child labor laws find their historical origin in common humanitarian instincts, and that the age limits of both laws have been coordinated to achieve their related objectives. In the context of this case, such considerations, if anything, support rather than detract from respondents' position. The origins of the requirement for school attendance to age 16, an age falling after the completion of elementary school but before completion of high school, are not entirely clear. But to some extent such laws reflected the movement to prohibit most child labor under age 16 that culminated in the provisions of the Federal Fair Labor Standards Act of 1938. It is true, then, that the 16-year child labor age limit may to some degree derive from a contemporary impression that children should be in school until that age. But at the same time, it cannot be denied that, conversely, the 16-year education limit reflects, in substantial measure, the concern that children under that age not be employed under conditions hazardous to their health, or in work that should be performed by adults.

The requirement of compulsory schooling to age 16 must therefore be viewed as aimed not merely at providing educational opportunities for children, but as an alternative to the equally undesirable consequence of unhealthful child labor displacing adult workers, or, on the other hand, forced idleness. The two kinds of statutes — compulsory school attendance and child labor laws — tend to keep children of certain ages off the labor market and in school; this regimen in turn provides opportunity to prepare for a livelihood of a higher order than that which children could pursue without education and protects their health in adolescence.

In these terms, Wisconsin's interest in compelling the school attendance of Amish children to age 16 emerges as somewhat less substantial than requiring such attendance for children generally. For, while agricultural employment is not totally outside the legitimate concerns of the child labor laws, employment of children under parental guidance and on the family farm from age 14 to age 16 is an ancient tradition that lies at the periphery of the objectives of such laws. There is no intimation that the Amish employment of their children on family farms is in any way deleterious to their health or that Amish parents exploit children at tender years. Any such inference would be contrary to the record before us. Moreover, employment of Amish children on the family farm does not present the undesirable economic aspects of eliminating jobs that might otherwise be held by adults.

IV

Finally, the State, on authority of *Prince v. Massachusetts*, argues that a decision exempting Amish children from the State's requirement fails to recognize the substantive right of the Amish child to a secondary education, and fails to give due regard to the power of the State as parens patriae to extend the benefit of secondary education to children regardless of the wishes of their parents. Taken at its broadest sweep, the Court's language in *Prince*, might be read to give support to the State's position. However, the Court was not confronted in *Prince* with a situation comparable to that of the Amish as revealed in this record; this is shown by the Court's severe characterization of the evils that it thought the legislature could legitimately associate with child labor, even when performed in the company of an adult. The Court later took great care to confine *Prince* to a narrow scope in *Sherbert v. Verner*, when it stated:

> On the other hand, the Court has rejected challenges under the Free Exercise Clause to governmental regulation of certain overt acts prompted by religious beliefs or principles, for 'even when the action is in accord with one's religious convictions, [it] is not totally free from legislative restrictions.' The conduct or actions so regulated have invariably posed some substantial threat to public safety, peace or order.

This case, of course, is not one in which any harm to the physical or mental health of the child or to the public safety, peace, order, or welfare has been demonstrated or may be properly inferred. The record is to the contrary, and any reliance on that theory would find no support in the evidence.

Contrary to the suggestion of the dissenting opinion of Mr. Justice Douglas, our holding today in no degree depends on the assertion of the religious interest of the child as contrasted with that of the parents. It is the parents who are subject to prosecution here for failing to cause their children to attend school, and it is their right of free exercise, not that of their children, that must determine Wisconsin's power to impose criminal penalties on the parent. The dissent argues that a child who expresses a desire to attend public high school in conflict with the wishes of his parents should not be prevented from doing so. There is no reason for the Court to consider that point since it is not an issue in the case. The children are not parties to this litigation. The State has at no point tried this case on the theory that respondents were preventing their children from attending school against their expressed desires, and indeed the record is to the contrary. The State's position from the outset has been that it is empowered to apply its compulsory-attendance law to Amish parents in the same manner as to other parents—that is, without regard to the wishes of the child. That is the claim we reject today.

Our holding in no way determines the proper resolution of possible competing interests of parents, children, and the State in an appropriate state court proceeding in which the power of the State is asserted on the theory that Amish parents are preventing their minor children from attending high school despite their expressed desires to the contrary. Recognition of the claim of the State in such a proceeding would, of course, call into question traditional concepts of parental control over the religious upbringing and education of their minor children recognized in this Court's past decisions. It is clear that such an intrusion by a State into family decisions in the area of religious training would give rise to grave questions of religious freedom comparable to those raised here and those presented in *Pierce v. Society of Sisters*. On this record we neither reach nor decide those issues.

The State's argument proceeds without reliance on any actual conflict between the wishes of parents and children. It appears to rest on the potential that exemption of Amish parents from the requirements of the compulsory-education law might allow some parents to act contrary to the best interests of their children by foreclosing their opportunity to make an intelligent choice between the Amish way of life and that of the outside world. The same argument could, of course, be made with respect to all church schools short of college. There is nothing in the record or in the ordinary course of human experience to suggest that non-Amish parents generally consult with children of ages 14–16 if they are placed in a church school of the parents' faith.

Indeed it seems clear that if the State is empowered, as parens patriae, to "save" a child from himself or his Amish parents by requiring an additional two years of compulsory formal high school education, the State will in large measure influence, if not determine, the religious future of the child. Even more markedly than in *Prince*, therefore, this case involves the fundamental interest of parents, as contrasted with that of the State, to guide the religious future and education of their children. The history and culture of Western civilization reflect a strong tradition of parental concern for the nurture and upbringing of their children. This primary role of the parents in the upbringing of their children is now established beyond debate as an enduring American tradition. If not the first, perhaps the most significant statements of the Court in this area are found in *Pierce v. Society of Sisters*, in which the Court observed:

> ... The fundamental theory of liberty upon which all governments in this Union repose excludes any general power of the State to standardize its children by forcing them to accept instruction from public teachers only. The child is not the mere creature of the State; those who nurture him and direct his destiny have the right, coupled with the high duty, to recognize and prepare him for additional obligations.

The duty to prepare the child for "additional obligations," referred to by the Court, must be read to include the inculcation of moral standards, religious beliefs, and elements of good citizenship. Pierce, of course, recognized that where nothing more than the general interest of the parent in the nurture and education of his children is involved, it is beyond dispute that the State acts "reasonably" and constitutionally in requiring education to age 16 in some public or private school meeting the standards prescribed by the State.

However read, the Court's holding in *Pierce* stands as a charter of the rights of parents to direct the religious upbringing of their children. And, when the interests of parenthood are combined with a free exercise claim of the nature revealed by this record, more than merely a "reasonable relation to some purpose within the competency of the State" is required to sustain the validity of the State's requirement under the First Amendment. To be sure, the power of the parent, even when linked to a free exercise claim, may be subject to limitation under *Prince* if it appears that parental decisions will jeopardize the health or safety of the child, or have a potential for significant social burdens. But in this case, the Amish have introduced persuasive evidence undermining the arguments the State has advanced to support its claims in terms of the welfare of the child and society as a whole. The record strongly indicates that accommodating the religious objections of the Amish by forgoing one, or at most two, additional years of compulsory education will not impair the physical or mental health of the child, or result in an inability to be self-supporting or to discharge the duties and responsibilities of citizenship, or in any other way materially detract from the welfare of society.

In the face of our consistent emphasis on the central values underlying the Religion Clauses in our constitutional scheme of government, we cannot accept a parens patriae claim of such all-encompassing scope and with such sweeping potential for broad and unforeseeable application as that urged by the State.

V

For the reasons stated we hold, with the Supreme Court of Wisconsin, that the First and Fourteenth Amendments prevent the State from compelling respondents to cause their children to attend formal high school to age 16. Our disposition of this case, however, in no way alters our recognition of the obvious fact that courts are not school boards or legislatures, and are ill-equipped to determine the "necessity" of discrete aspects of a State's program of compulsory education. This should suggest that courts must move with great circumspection in performing the sensitive and delicate task of weighing a State's legitimate social concern when faced with religious claims for exemption from generally applicable educational requirements. It cannot be overemphasized that we are not dealing with a way of life and mode of education by a group claiming to have recently discovered some "progressive" or more enlightened process for rearing children for modern life.

Aided by a history of three centuries as an identifiable religious sect and a long history as a successful and self-sufficient segment of American society, the Amish in this case have convincingly demonstrated the sincerity of their religious beliefs, the interrelationship of belief with their mode of life, the vital role that belief and daily conduct play in the continued survival of Old Order Amish communities and their religious organization, and the hazards presented by the State's enforcement of a statute generally valid as to others. Beyond this, they have carried the even more difficult burden of demonstrating the adequacy of their alternative mode of continuing informal vocational education in terms of precisely those overall interests that the State advances in support of its program of compulsory high school education. In light of this convincing showing, one that probably few other religious groups or sects could make, and weighing the minimal difference between what the State would require and what the Amish already accept, it was incumbent on the State to show with more particularity how its admittedly strong interest in compulsory education would be adversely affected by granting an exemption to the Amish.

Nothing we hold is intended to undermine the general applicability of the State's compulsory school-attendance statutes or to limit the power of the State to promulgate reasonable standards that, while not impairing the free exercise of religion, provide for continuing agricultural vocational education under parental and church guidance by the Old Order Amish or others similarly situated. The States have had a long history of amicable and effective relationships with church-sponsored schools, and there is no basis for assuming that, in this related context, reasonable standards cannot be established concerning the content of the continuing vocational education of Amish children under parental guidance, provided always that state regulations are not inconsistent with what we have said in this opinion.

Affirmed.

Mr. Justice Stewart, with whom Mr. Justice Brennan joins, concurring.

This case involves the constitutionality of imposing criminal punishment upon Amish parents for their religiously based refusal to compel their children to attend public high schools. Wisconsin has sought to brand these parents as criminals for following their religious beliefs, and the Court today rightly holds that Wisconsin cannot constitutionally do so.

This case in no way involves any questions regarding the right of the children of Amish parents to attend public high schools, or any other institutions of learning, if they wish to do so. As the Court points out, there is no suggestion whatever in the record that the religious beliefs of the children here concerned differ in any way from those of their parents. Only one of the children testified. The last two questions and answers on her cross-examination accurately sum up her testimony:

> Q. So I take it then, Frieda, the only reason you are not going to school, and did not go to school since last September, is because of your religion?
>
> A. Yes.
>
> Q. That is the only reason?
>
> A. Yes.

It is clear to me, therefore, that this record simply does not present the interesting and important issue discussed in Part II of the dissenting opinion of Mr. Justice Douglas. With this observation, I join the opinion and the judgment of the Court.

Mr. Justice White, with whom Mr. Justice Brennan and Mr. Justice Stewart join, concurring.

Cases such as this one inevitably call for a delicate balancing of important but conflicting interests. I join the opinion and judgment of the Court because I cannot say that the State's interest in requiring two more years of compulsory education in the ninth and tenth grades outweighs the importance of the concededly sincere Amish religious practice to the survival of that sect.

This would be a very different case for me if respondents' claim were that their religion forbade their children from attending any school at any time and from complying in any way with the educational standards set by the State. Since the Amish children are permitted to acquire the basic tools of literacy to survive in modern society by attending grades one through eight and since the deviation from the State's compulsory-education law is relatively slight, I conclude that respondents' claim must prevail, largely because "religious freedom—the freedom to believe and to practice strange and, it may be, foreign creeds—has classically been one of the highest values of our society."

The importance of the state interest asserted here cannot be denigrated, however....

In the present case, the State is not concerned with the maintenance of an educational system as an end in itself, it is rather attempting to nurture and develop the human potential of its children, whether Amish or non-Amish: to expand their knowledge, broaden their sensibilities, kindle their imagination, foster a spirit of free inquiry, and increase their human understanding and tolerance. It is possible that most Amish children will wish to continue living the rural life of their parents, in which case their training at home will adequately equip them for their future role. Others, however, may wish to become nuclear physicists, ballet dancers, computer programmers, or historians, and for these occupations, formal training will be necessary. There is evidence in the record that many children desert the Amish faith when they come of age. A State has a legitimate interest not only in seeking to develop the latent talents of its children but also in seeking to prepare them for the life style that they may later choose, or at least to provide them with an option other than the life they have led in the past. In the circumstances of this case, although the question is close, I am unable to say that the State has demonstrated that Amish children who leave school in the eighth grade will be intellectually stultified or unable to acquire new academic skills later. The statutory minimum school attendance age set by the State is, after all, only 16.

Decision in cases such as this and the administration of an exemption for Old Order Amish from the State's compulsory school-attendance laws will inevitably involve the kind of close and perhaps repeated scrutiny of religious practices, as is exemplified in today's opinion, which the Court has heretofore been anxious to avoid. But such entanglement does not create a forbidden establishment of religion where it is essential to implement free exercise values threatened by an otherwise neutral program instituted to foster some permissible, nonreligious state objective. I join the Court because the sincerity of the Amish religious policy here is uncontested, because the potentially adverse impact of the state requirement is great, and because the State's valid interest in education has already been largely satisfied by the eight years the children have already spent in school.

Mr. Justice Douglas, dissenting in part.

I

I agree with the Court that the religious scruples of the Amish are opposed to the education of their children beyond the grade schools, yet I disagree with the Court's conclusion that the matter is within the dispensation of parents alone. The Court's analysis assumes that the only interests at stake in the case are those of the Amish parents on the one hand, and those of the State on the other. The difficulty with this approach is that, despite the Court's claim, the parents are seeking to vindicate not only their own free exercise claims, but also those of their high-school-age children. It is argued that the right of the Amish children to religious freedom is not presented by the facts of the case, as the issue before the Court involves only the Amish parents' religious freedom to defy a state criminal statute imposing upon them an affirmative duty to cause their children to attend high school.

First, respondents' motion to dismiss in the trial court expressly asserts, not only the religious liberty of the adults, but also that of the children, as a defense to the prosecutions. It is, of course, beyond question that the parents have standing as defendants in a criminal prosecution to assert the religious interests of their children as a defense. Although the lower courts and a majority of this Court assume an identity of interest between parent and child, it is clear that they have treated the religious interest of the child as a factor in the analysis.

Second, it is essential to reach the question to decide the case, not only because the question was squarely raised in the motion to dismiss, but also because no analysis of religious-liberty claims can take place in a vacuum. If the parents in this case are allowed a religious exemption, the inevitable effect is to impose the parents' notions of religious duty upon their children. Where the child is mature enough to express potentially conflicting desires, it would be an invasion of the child's rights to permit such an imposition without canvassing his views. As in *Prince v. Massachusetts*, it is an imposition resulting from this very litigation. As the child has no other effective forum, it is in this litigation that his rights should be considered. And, if an Amish child desires to attend high school, and is mature enough to have that desire respected, the State may well be able to override the parents' religiously motivated objections.

Religion is an individual experience. It is not necessary, nor even appropriate, for every Amish child to express his views on the subject in a prosecution of a single adult. Crucial, however, are the views of the child whose parent is the subject of the suit. Frieda Yoder has in fact testified that her own religious views are opposed to high-school education. I therefore join the judgment of the Court as to respondent Jonas Yoder. But Frieda Yoder's views may not be those of Vernon Yutzy or Barbara Miller. I must dissent, therefore, as to respondents Adin Yutzy and Wallace Miller as their motion to dismiss also raised the question of their children's religious liberty.

II

This issue has never been squarely presented before today. Our opinions are full of talk about the power of the parents over the child's education. And we have in the past analyzed similar conflicts between parent and State with little regard for the views of the child. Recent cases, however, have clearly held that the children themselves have constitutionally protectible interests.

These children are "persons" within the meaning of the Bill of Rights. We have so held over and over again....

On this important and vital matter of education, I think the children should be entitled to be heard. While the parents, absent dissent, normally speak for the entire family, the education of the child is a matter on which the child will often have decided views. He may want to be a pianist or an astronaut or an oceanographer. To do so he will have to break from the Amish tradition.

It is the future of the student, not the future of the parents, that is imperiled by today's decision. If a parent keeps his child out of school beyond the grade school, then the child will be forever barred from entry into the new and amazing world of diversity that we have today. The child may decide that that is the preferred course, or he may rebel. It is the student's judgment, not his parents', that is essential if we are to give full meaning to what we have said about the Bill of Rights and of the right of students to be masters of their own destiny. If he is harnessed to the Amish way of life by those in authority over him and if his education is truncated, his entire life may be stunted and deformed. The child, therefore, should be given an opportunity to be heard before the State gives the exemption which we honor today.

The views of the two children in question were not canvassed by the Wisconsin courts. The matter should be explicitly reserved so that new hearings can be held on remand of the case.

III

I think the emphasis of the Court on the "law and order" record of this Amish group of people is quite irrelevant. A religion is a religion irrespective of what the misdemeanor or felony records of its members might be. I am not at all sure how the Catholics, Episcopalians, the Baptists, Jehovah's Witnesses, the Unitarians, and my own Presbyterians would make out if subjected to such a test. It is, of course, true that if a group or society was organized to perpetuate crime and if that is its motive, we would have rather startling problems akin to those that were raised when some years back a particular sect was challenged here as operating on a fraudulent basis. But no such factors are present here, and the Amish, whether with a high or low criminal record, certainly qualify by all historic standards as a religion within the meaning of the First Amendment.

Notes and Queries

1. Is the parental interested asserted in *Yoder* more compelling than the one in *Prince*?
2. What parental, child, and state interests does education serve?
3. Does *Yoder* compromise the state's interest in an educated citizenry capable of democratic participation?
4. How do you distinguish *Yoder* from situations in which a parent could be deemed neglectful if they exploited their child's labor and earning power rather than sending them to school?
5. Suppose Justice Douglas prevailed. What should be the outcome of a case where significant differences of opinion existed between parent and child? Did the Court allow parents to preempt their children's worldviews?
6. Do Justices Stewart and Brennan really address the dissent's claim?
7. How would you distinguish *Yoder* from *Prince* in terms of the impact of parental religious freedom on children?

Review Problems

1. The United States has a long history of hostility to bilingual education programs, as revealed in "English Only" laws that, in many ways, simply confirm dominant practices. How could *Myer* help challenge these popular initiatives?

2. Following *Yoder*, what would be the outcome of a law that allowed a Hispanic community to have their children, age 16 and above, taught only in Spanish?

3. It is important to not ignore how several states have sought to protect bilingualism. Dual-language programs have emerged in many school districts and states and take a variety of forms. See Kathryn J. Lindholm-Leary (2001). *Dual Language Education* (Vol. 28). Tonawanda, NY: Multilingual Matters.

4. Despite the rise of dual and bilingual education, one of the most dominant themes coming from this area of research suggests two key findings. First, a broad social consensus on the benefits of linguistic diversity has resulted in a "New Bilingualism." Second, despite that pivot toward respecting bilingualism, its benefits are not reaching multilingual communities that have long demanded support for bilingual programing. Instead, the support comes from (and goes to) places of privilege, namely English-dominant, middle- and upper-class communities. See Chris K. Chang-Bacon (2021). Monolingual language ideologies and the idealized speaker: The "new bilingualism" meets the "old" educational inequities. *Teachers College Record*, 123(1), 1–28. This line of research reveals, for example, how teaching of Spanish as a resource now dissociates it from the large population that uses it, Mexican Americans. This unmarking of language from those who speak it has been viewed as "converse racialization" to understand how bilingual education can have profound social, economic, and racializing consequences that rearticulates the deficiency perspective that perpetuated structural inequalities and supported "English Only" laws. Mike Mena and Ofelia García (2021). "Converse racialization" and "un/marking" language: The making of a bilingual university in a neoliberal world. *Language in Society*, 50(3), 343–364. This area of research gains significance for the understanding of child development, parenting, family life, and social integration. As such, it has important implications for understanding and responding to what could be deemed child well-being and child maltreatment.

Troxel v. Granville

530 U.S. 57 (2000)

Justice O'Connor announced the judgment of the Court and delivered an opinion, in which The Chief Justice, Justice Ginsburg, and Justice Breyer join.

Section 26.10.160(3) of the Revised Code of Washington permits "any person" to petition a superior court for visitation rights "at any time," and authorizes that court to grant such visitation rights whenever "visitation may serve the best interest of the child." Petitioners Jenifer and Gary Troxel petitioned a Washington Superior Court for the right to visit their grandchildren, Isabelle and Natalie Troxel. Respondent Tommie Granville, the mother of Isabelle and Natalie, opposed the petition. The case ultimately reached the Washington Supreme Court, which held that § 26.10.160(3) unconstitutionally interferes with the fundamental right of parents to rear their children.

I

Tommie Granville and Brad Troxel shared a relationship that ended in June 1991. The two never married, but they had two daughters, Isabelle and Natalie. Jenifer and Gary Troxel are Brad's parents, and thus the paternal grandparents of Isabelle and Natalie. After Tommie and Brad separated in 1991, Brad lived with his parents and regularly brought his daughters to his parents' home for weekend visitation. Brad committed suicide in May 1993. Although the Troxels at first continued to see Isabelle and Natalie on a regular basis after their son's death, Tommie Granville informed the Troxels in October 1993 that she wished to limit their visitation with her daughters to one short visit per month.

In December 1993, the Troxels commenced the present action by filing, in the Washington Superior Court for Skagit County, a petition to obtain visitation rights with Isabelle and Natalie. The Troxels filed their petition under two Washington statutes. Only the latter statute is at issue in this case. Section 26.10.160(3) provides: "Any person may petition the court for visitation rights at any time including, but not limited to, custody proceedings. The court may order visitation rights for any person when visitation may serve the best interest of the child whether or not there has been any change of circumstances." At trial, the Troxels requested two weekends of overnight visitation per month and two weeks of visitation each summer. Granville did not oppose visitation altogether, but instead asked the court to order one day of visitation per month with no overnight stay. In 1995, the Superior Court issued an oral ruling and entered a visitation decree ordering visitation one weekend per month, one week during the summer, and four hours on both of the petitioning grandparents' birthdays.

Granville appealed, during which time she married Kelly Wynn. Before addressing the merits of Granville's appeal, the Washington Court of Appeals remanded the case to the Superior Court for entry of written findings of fact and conclusions of law. On remand, the Superior Court found that visitation was in Isabelle and Natalie's best interests:

> The Petitioners [the Troxels] are part of a large, central, loving family, all located in this area, and the Petitioners can provide opportunities for the children in the areas of cousins and music.
>
> ... The court took into consideration all factors regarding the best interest of the children and considered all the testimony before it. The children would be benefitted from spending quality time with the Petitioners, provided that that time is balanced with time with the childrens' [sic] nuclear family. The court finds that the childrens' [sic] best interests are served by spending time with their mother and stepfather's other six children.

Approximately nine months after the Superior Court entered its order on remand, Granville's husband formally adopted Isabelle and Natalie.

The Washington Court of Appeals reversed the lower court's visitation order and dismissed the Troxels' petition for visitation, holding that nonparents lack standing to seek visitation under § 26.10.160(3) unless a custody action is pending. In the Court of Appeals' view, that limitation on nonparental visitation actions was "consistent with the constitutional restrictions on state interference with parents' fundamental liberty interest in the care, custody, and management of their children." Having resolved the case on statutory grounds, however, the Court of Appeals did not expressly pass on Granville's constitutional challenge to the visitation statute.

The Washington Supreme Court granted the Troxels' petition for review and ... affirmed.... The Washington Supreme Court nevertheless agreed with the Court of Appeals' ultimate conclusion that the Troxels could not obtain visitation of Isabelle and Natalie pursuant to § 26.10.160(3). The court rested its decision on the Federal Constitution, holding that § 26.10.160(3) unconstitutionally infringes on the fundamental right of parents to rear their children. In the court's view, there were at least two problems with the nonparental visitation statute. First, according to the Washington Supreme Court, the Constitution permits a State to interfere with the right of parents to rear their children only to prevent harm or potential harm to a child. Section 26.10.160(3) fails that standard because it requires no threshold showing of harm. Second, by allowing "'any person' to petition for forced visitation of a child at 'any time' with the only requirement being that the visitation serve the best interest of the child," the Washington visitation statute sweeps too broadly. "It is not within the province of the state to make significant decisions concerning the custody of children merely because it could make a 'better' decision." The Washington Supreme Court held that "parents have a right to limit visitation of their children with third persons," and that between parents and judges, "the parents should be the ones to choose whether to expose their children to certain people or ideas." ...

We granted certiorari and now affirm the judgment.

II

The demographic changes of the past century make it difficult to speak of an average American family. The composition of families varies greatly from household to household. While many children may have two married parents and grandparents who visit regularly, many other children are raised in single-parent households....

The nationwide enactment of nonparental visitation statutes is assuredly due, in some part, to the States' recognition of these changing realities of the American family. Because grandparents and other relatives undertake duties of a parental nature in many households, States have sought to ensure the welfare of the children therein by protecting the relationships those children form with such third parties. The States' nonparental visitation statutes are further supported by a recognition, which varies from State to State, that children should have the opportunity to benefit from relationships with statutorily specified persons — for example, their grandparents. The extension of statutory rights in this area to persons other than a child's parents, however, comes with an obvious cost. For example, the State's recognition of an independent third-party interest in a child can place a substantial burden on the traditional parent–child relationship....

The Fourteenth Amendment provides that no State shall "deprive any person of life, liberty, or property, without due process of law." We have long recognized that the Amendment's Due Process Clause, like its Fifth Amendment counterpart, "guarantees more than fair process." The Clause also includes a substantive component that "provides heightened protection against government interference with certain fundamental rights and liberty interests."

The liberty interest at issue — in this case the interest of parents in the care, custody, and control of their children — is perhaps the oldest of the fundamental liberty interests recognized by this Court....

...

Section 26.10.160(3), as applied to Granville and her family in this case, unconstitutionally infringes on that fundamental parental right. The Washington nonparental visitation statute is breathtakingly broad. According to the statute's text, "any person may petition the court for visitation rights at any time," and the court may grant such visitation rights whenever "visitation may serve the best interest of the child." That language effectively permits any third party seeking visitation to subject any decision by a parent concerning visitation of the parent's children to state-court review. Once the visitation petition has been filed in court and the matter is placed before a judge, a parent's decision that visitation would not be in the child's best interest is accorded no deference. Section 26.10.160(3) contains no requirement that a court accord the parent's decision any presumption of validity or any weight whatsoever. Instead, the Washington statute places the best-interest determination solely in the hands of the judge. Should the judge disagree with the parent's estimation of the child's best interests, the judge's view necessarily prevails. Thus, in practical effect, in the State of

Washington a court can disregard and overturn any decision by a fit custodial parent concerning visitation whenever a third party affected by the decision files a visitation petition, based solely on the judge's determination of the child's best interests. The Washington Supreme Court had the opportunity to give § 26.10.160(3) a narrower reading, but it declined to do so.

Turning to the facts of this case, the record reveals that the Superior Court's order was based on precisely the type of mere disagreement we have just described and nothing more. The Superior Court's order was not founded on any special factors that might justify the State's interference with Granville's fundamental right to make decisions concerning the rearing of her two daughters. To be sure, this case involves a visitation petition filed by grandparents soon after the death of their son — the father of Isabelle and Natalie but the combination of several factors here compels our conclusion that § 26.10.160(3), as applied, exceeded the bounds of the Due Process Clause.

First, the Troxels did not allege, and no court has found, that Granville was an unfit parent. That aspect of the case is important, for there is a presumption that fit parents act in the best interests of their children. . . .

. . .

The problem here is not that the Washington Superior Court intervened, but that when it did so, it gave no special weight at all to Granville's determination of her daughters' best interests. More importantly, it appears that the Superior Court applied exactly the opposite presumption. . . .

The judge's comments suggest that he presumed the grandparents' request should be granted unless the children would be "impacted adversely." In effect, the judge placed on Granville, the fit custodial parent, the burden of disproving that visitation would be in the best interest of her daughters. The judge reiterated moments later: "I think [visitation with the Troxels] would be in the best interest of the children and I haven't been shown it is not in [the] best interest of the children." . . .

Finally, we note that there is no allegation that Granville ever sought to cut off visitation entirely. Rather, the present dispute originated when Granville informed the Troxels that she would prefer to restrict their visitation with Isabelle and Natalie to one short visit per month and special holidays. In the Superior Court proceedings Granville did not oppose visitation but instead asked that the duration of any visitation order be shorter than that requested by the Troxels. While the Troxels requested two weekends per month and two full weeks in the summer, Granville asked the Superior Court to order only one day of visitation per month (with no overnight stay) and participation in the Granville family's holiday celebrations. . . . The court instead rejected Granville's proposal and settled on a middle ground, ordering one weekend of visitation per month, one week in the summer, and time on both of the petitioning grandparents' birthdays.

Considered together with the Superior Court's reasons for awarding visitation to the Troxels, the combination of these factors demonstrates that the visitation order in this case was an unconstitutional infringement on Granville's fundamental right to make decisions concerning the care, custody, and control of her two daughters....

...

Accordingly, the judgment of the Washington Supreme Court is affirmed.

It is so ordered.

Justice Souter, concurring in the judgment. [omitted]

Justice Thomas, concurring in the judgment.

...

Consequently, I agree with the plurality that this Court's recognition of a fundamental right of parents to direct the upbringing of their children resolves this case.... [P]arents have a fundamental constitutional right to rear their children, including the right to determine who shall educate and socialize them. The opinions of the plurality, Justice Kennedy, and Justice Souter recognize such a right, but curiously none of them articulates the appropriate standard of review. I would apply strict scrutiny to infringements of fundamental rights. Here, the State of Washington lacks even a legitimate governmental interest—to say nothing of a compelling one—in second-guessing a fit parent's decision regarding visitation with third parties. On this basis, I would affirm the judgment below.

Justice Stevens, dissenting. [omitted]

Justice Scalia, dissenting.

In my view, a right of parents to direct the upbringing of their children is among the "unalienable Rights" with which the Declaration of Independence proclaims "all Men ... are endowed by their Creator." And in my view that right is also among the "other [rights] retained by the people" which the Ninth Amendment says the Constitution's enumeration of rights "shall not be construed to deny or disparage." The Declaration of Independence, however, is not a legal prescription conferring powers upon the courts; and the Constitution's refusal to "deny or disparage" other rights is far removed from affirming any one of them, and even farther removed from authorizing judges to identify what they might be, and to enforce the judges' list against laws duly enacted by the people. Consequently, while I would think it entirely compatible with the commitment to representative democracy set forth in the founding documents to argue, in legislative chambers or in electoral campaigns, that the state has no power to interfere with parents' authority over the rearing of their children, I do not believe that the power which the Constitution confers upon me as a judge entitles me to deny legal effect to laws that (in my view) infringe upon what is (in my view) that unenumerated right.

...

... I think it obvious—whether we affirm or reverse the judgment here, or remand ... that we will be ushering in a new regime of judicially prescribed, and federally prescribed, family law. I have no reason to believe that federal judges will be better at this than state legislatures; and state legislatures have the great advantages of doing harm in a more circumscribed area, of being able to correct their mistakes in a flash, and of being removable by the people.

For these reasons, I would reverse the judgment below.

Justice Kennedy, dissenting.

. . .

While it might be argued as an abstract matter that in some sense the child is always harmed if his or her best interests are not considered, the law of domestic relations, as it has evolved to this point, treats as distinct the two standards, one harm to the child and the other the best interests of the child. The judgment of the Supreme Court of Washington rests on that assumption, and I, too, shall assume that there are real and consequential differences between the two standards.

. . .

To say that third parties have had no historical right to petition for visitation does not necessarily imply, as the Supreme Court of Washington concluded, that a parent has a constitutional right to prevent visitation in all cases not involving harm. True, this Court has acknowledged that States have the authority to intervene to prevent harm to children, but that is not the same as saying that a heightened harm to the child standard must be satisfied in every case in which a third party seeks a visitation order. It is also true that the law's traditional presumption has been "that natural bonds of affection lead parents to act in the best interests of their children" and "simply because the decision of a parent is not agreeable to a child or because it involves risks does not automatically transfer the power to make that decision from the parents to some agency or officer of the state." The State Supreme Court's conclusion that the Constitution forbids the application of the best interests of the child standard in any visitation proceeding, however, appears to rest upon assumptions the Constitution does not require.

My principal concern is that the holding seems to proceed from the assumption that the parent or parents who resist visitation have always been the child's primary caregivers and that the third parties who seek visitation have no legitimate and established relationship with the child. That idea, in turn, appears influenced by the concept that the conventional nuclear family ought to establish the visitation standard for every domestic relations case. As we all know, this is simply not the structure or prevailing condition in many households. . . .

. . . Some pre-existing relationships, then, serve to identify persons who have a strong attachment to the child with the concomitant motivation to act in a responsible way to ensure the child's welfare. . . .

. . .

In light of the inconclusive historical record and case law, as well as the almost universal adoption of the best interests standard for visitation disputes, I would be hard pressed to conclude the right to be free of such review in all cases is itself "'implicit in the concept of ordered liberty.'" In my view, it would be more appropriate to conclude that the constitutionality of the application of the best interests standard depends on more specific factors. In short, a fit parent's right vis-a-vis a complete stranger is one thing; her right vis-a-vis another parent or a de facto parent may be another....

...

It should suffice in this case to reverse the holding of the State Supreme Court that the application of the best interests of the child standard is always unconstitutional in third-party visitation cases. Whether, under the circumstances of this case, the order requiring visitation over the objection of this fit parent violated the Constitution ought to be reserved for further proceedings. Because of its sweeping ruling requiring the harm to the child standard, the Supreme Court of Washington did not have the occasion to address the specific visitation order the Troxels obtained. More specific guidance should await a case in which a State's highest court has considered all of the facts in the course of elaborating the protection afforded to parents by the laws of the State and by the Constitution itself. Furthermore, in my view, we need not address whether, under the correct constitutional standards, the Washington statute can be invalidated on its face. This question, too, ought to be addressed by the state court in the first instance.

In my view the judgment under review should be vacated and the case remanded for further proceedings.

Notes and Queries

1. Justice Kennedy makes important distinctions between the harm and best interests standards. Would you conclude that the best interests standard would be appropriate if the person seeking visitation already had an established relationship?
2. The Court rested its decision on the "sweeping breadth" of the statute, which it found impermissible. Therefore, it did not consider whether the Due Process Clause requires all nonparental visitation statutes to include a showing of harm or potential harm to the child as a condition precedent to granting visitation. How should legislatures respond to this mandate?
3. This case seems of considerable significance in that it actually is the first time the Court recognized specifically that parents have a fundamental liberty interest in controlling the associational rights of their children. Despite the long list of parental rights cases, the Court apparently had never before addressed this issue squarely. Now, at least five justices—Justices O'Connor, Rehnquist, Ginsburg, Breyer, and Thomas—seem prepared to recognize that determination of a child's associations is a fundamental liberty interest held by parents. Do you find this a sound policy development? Would a statutory presumption in favor of parents best serve the parents, the child, and the legal system that seeks to protect them all?

4. It would seem that an approach that requires deference to parents must be safeguarded by high standards, and a harm standard offers a particularly strong and coherent means of screening out encroachment on parental freedoms. Yet the Court rejected the harm-based approach, which may reveal its lack of commitment to such a strongly deferential approach. For those interested in devising a workable standard, does the case leave you unsatisfied by the way the Court did not offer guidance to legislatures that need to articulate a standard allowing them to favor parents? What directions and assumptions should a legislature take from this case?

Chapter 3
Psychological Maltreatment

The emotional development that occurs in infancy and later childhood lays the foundations for good mental health. As attachment theorists convincingly demonstrate and theorize, the groundwork for healthy development depends on the quality and frequency of response to an infant or child from a parent or primary caregiver. The parental response to the infant's emotions or expressive behaviors usually results in the formation of an attachment bond between them. This bond develops in the early months and years of life, and closely links to the behavioral response of the parent and the ongoing cycle of parent–child interaction. Obvious hypotheses arise from this developmental perspective. Where a child experiences a warm, intimate and continuous relationship with a primary caregiver, that child would thrive. Conversely, an unresponsive caregiver, or one who responds inappropriately to a child's needs, would increase the likelihood of the child becoming anxious and insecure in its attachment and, at extremes, evince signs of pathology.

Considerable evidence suggests that inappropriate parenting practices may be viewed as psychological maltreatment. At extremes, it results in three general forms of destructive outcomes: (1) interpersonal maladjustment, such as insecure attachment to caregiver, difficulties with peers, and low social competence; (2) intellectual deficits, such as academic problems, lack of creativity, and deficits in problem solving and in cognitive abilities; and (3) emotional and behavioral problems, such as aggression, hostility, anger, depression, and self-destructive behavior. Yet this form of maltreatment remains one of the least studied of all the forms of child maltreatment. See National Research Council (1993). *Understanding Child Abuse and Neglect*. Washington, DC: National Academy Press. The status of research relates to the challenges associated with this form of maltreatment. The very nature of adult–child relationships and cultural influences involves inflicting emotional maltreatment on children. As a result, while behavior may be emotionally damaging to a child, it may not necessarily be considered emotionally abusive by child protection or child welfare staff. The converse is also true.

Neither the federal government nor individual states provide clear direction to child protective service agencies. The most frequently referenced definition is the one provided by the American Professional Society on the Abuse of Children, which provides a broad definition of psychological maltreatment as *a repeated pattern of caregiver behavior or extreme incidents that convey to children that they are worthless, flawed, unloved, unwanted, endangered, or only of value in meeting another's needs.* American Professional Society on the Abuse of Children (APSAC) (1995). Psychosocial evaluation of suspected psychological maltreatment in children and adolescents. *Practice Guidelines.* Chicago, IL: APSAC. The most recent survey of state laws revealed that 30 states have specific statutes defining emotional/psychological abuse, often along with "mental injury." That survey also revealed that most state statutes focus on harm to the child rather than on parental actions. In doing so the states use similar language that define it as "injury to the psychological capacity or emotional stability of the child as evidenced by an observable or substantial change in behavior, emotional response, or cognition." Injury itself is deemed to exist when it is evidenced by "anxiety, depression, withdrawal, or aggressive behavior." U.S. Department of Health and Human Services (2022). *Child Abuse and Neglect State Statutes Elements: Reporting Laws, Number 1, Definitions of Child Abuse and Neglect.* Washington, DC: U.S. Department of Health and Human Services.

Social science research addressing psychological maltreatment frequently involves disputes regarding whether we should use a broad or narrow definition. Researchers who adopt broad definitions typically define psychological maltreatment as psychological acts, or non-acts, committed by a caretaker that results in emotional, cognitive, or educational neglect. These researchers emphasize the consequences for the child rather than specific, inadequate parental behaviors. Researchers who adopt narrower approaches restrict psychological maltreatment to certain parent–child communications that may be psychologically damaging to children, such as ignoring, isolating, swearing, or terrorizing.

The intangible nature of emotional trauma makes medical and legal interventions troublesome, especially when similar provoking actions may be classified as "bad parenting" by some and "abuse" by others. To understand psychological maltreatment, consider the writings of a leading commentator, James Garbarino. He and his colleagues have proposed, as now have many others, the following categories: (1) Rejecting, which occurs when the adult fails to acknowledge the child's worth and the legitimacy of the child's needs, such as when adults refuse to show affection to the child; (2) isolating, which involves a pattern by which the adult deprives the child of normal social experiences, prevents the child from forming friendships, and makes the child believe that he or she is alone in the world; examples include not allowing the child normal contact with peers, not allowing the child to participate in the normal family routine, and locking the child in a room, basement, or attic; (3) terrorizing, which involves relationships where the adult verbally assaults the child, creates a climate of fear, bullies and frightens the child, and makes the child believe that the world is capricious and hostile; examples include threatening and frightening the child with guns, knives, whips, or other weapons; (4) ignoring, which occurs when the adult deprives the child of essential responsiveness; examples include failing to stimulate the child in an appropriate manner and not calling the child by name; and (5) corrupting, which occurs when the adult stimulates engagement in destructive antisocial behavior, reinforces deviance, and makes the child unfit for normal social experience;

examples include encouraging and instructing the child in antisocial activity, teaching the child sexually exploitative behavior, and teaching the child that "bad is good and good is bad." James Garbarino, Edna Guttmann & Janis Wilson Seeley (1986). *The Psychologically Battered Child.* San Francisco: Jossey-Bass. These types of psychological maltreatment enhanced the recognition of this form of maltreatment and contributed to much important research that has expanded the list of abusive practices. Garbarino and his colleagues also have offered another approach that highlights four principles of psychological maltreatment. The first principle states that punishing positive, normal behaviors such as smiling, mobility, exploration, vocalization, and manipulation of objects is psychological maltreatment; it stifles the child's development of competence. The second principle finds that discouraging caregiver–infant attachment is psychological maltreatment. The third principle holds that punishing self-esteem is psychological maltreatment because it damages one's positive identity. Lastly, the fourth principle states that punishing the interpersonal skills necessary for adequate performance in nonfamilial contexts, such as schools and peer groups, is psychological maltreatment. See James Garbarino & John Eckenrode (1997). *Understanding Abusive Families: An Ecological Approach to Theory and Practice.* San Francisco: Jossey-Bass.

Notes and Queries

1. Which of Garbarino's approaches seems more effective? In determining effectiveness, consider the goals of defining psychological maltreatment: Is it for research, broad policies, aggressive intervention in schools and families, etc.? Also consider how definitions in one domain may transfer to another, which runs the risk of inappropriately using definitions and concepts.

2. Several alternative choices exist for those who would wish to engage in policy development. They could focus on the severity of the maltreatment (on the most serious or include the less serious), on risk vs. actual occurrence (risk of future harm or past harm), on the type of offender (parent, sibling stranger, teacher, or peer), or on determinations of the burden of proof (objective truth or the subjective impression of investigators), or adopt a normative vs. idiographic focus (focus on the vulnerable child or include resilient children who appear unharmed because their situations should be harmful for the normal child).

Research Comments

1. One of the most popular proposals for dealing with problems that arise from definitional ambiguities would have states focus only on the most severe cases and provide intensive intervention for those cases. The approach would rely on voluntary community services for the rest of maltreating conditions. What issues

would you expect to arise with relying on a voluntary system? See Jane Waldfogel (1998). *The Future of Child Protection: How to Break the Cycle of Abuse and Neglect*. Cambridge, MA: Harvard University Press. The centerpiece of her proposal is a differential response paradigm for child protection. The new system would include the following central features: (1) a customized response to families, built on the availability of skilled social workers who are capable of functioning autonomously; (2) a community-based system of child protection in which frontline workers have access to services that cross agency lines and public and private sector boundaries; and (3) a larger role for informal and natural helpers, based on assessment of the family's needs and available resources. What are your thoughts about her proposal?

2. New paradigms calling for the reform do not necessarily result in avoiding old issues. Revamping of CPS through the development of a community-based alternative response to some reports of child maltreatment presents many concerns. One of the leading studies to examine diversion revealed that risk assessments and conclusions remain problematic. By examining outcomes for 1,263 "low" risk CPS referrals diverted to a community-based alternative response system, they found that the risk level and severity of some of the referrals were inappropriately high. The reason for this finding may be that increasing pressure on social services to reduce their capacity seems to result in a tendency to raise referral criteria. Importantly, they also found the opposite: Very serious allegations were classified as low risk. Approximately one-third of the families were re-referred for services, and these were mostly families with chronic histories of substance abuse, domestic violence, and other problems. One of the key findings was that the majority of families did not come back into the system in either the group who agreed to voluntary services or those who did not. These findings and areas of research gain increasing significance as efforts seek to rely on voluntary systems. Diana J. English, Tom Wingard, David Marshall, Matt Orme & Anna Orme (2000). Alternative responses to child protective services: Emerging issues and concerns. *Child Abuse & Neglect*, 24, 375–388.

Review Problems

1. Taking Garbarino's principles seriously may have important implications. Consider this situation. Roger and his wife both work full time. Instead of placing their three children in childcare, they alternate the times they work. The arrangement means that they often run a tight schedule. One day, Marc, who is five and the oldest, has an appointment with his dentist to replace a filling that has fallen off. Understanding that not all of the children can be in the small room while Marc is with the dentist, Roger and his wife take the unusual step of ensuring that both do not work at the same time so that one of them can stay at home with the other

children. Roger accompanies Marc to the dentist. Both patiently wait for the dentist to arrive. Once she arrives, she asks Roger to leave the room. Concerned that Marc may be hesitant to stay in the room alone with the dentist, Roger asks Marc if he would prefer to have him stay. Marc agrees. The dentist, however, refuses to see Marc unless his father leaves. She explains that it is her policy to work with children alone, that parents need to stay in the main office, that it is her right to do her work as she deems fit, and that the American Dental Association's dentist–patient guidelines support her. She also says that, if they do not like it, they can reschedule with another dentist (who is overbooked at the moment) or simply take their business elsewhere. Roger counters that it should be the child's right to decide whether his parent should stay, that their insurance severely limits their pool of potential dentists, that they cannot wait weeks before a next visit, and that he and his wife cannot easily change their schedules, which they had a difficult time accommodating for this visit. If Roger allows the dentist to do as she wishes, is he maltreating Marc who does not want him to leave?

2. Garbarino's principles also point us in other directions in that it encourages a look at all adult actions. Is the dentist psychologically abusive? Should she be more accommodating to children's wishes? Should the American Dental Association (ADA) change the discretion it gives to dentists? Is the argument that dentists are mandated reporters enough to prevail over the argument that we should respect a fearful child's wish to be with his parent? Suppose Roger respects Marc's wishes but the tooth quickly develops an infection; who should be held responsible?

3. Are the ADA's policies the type of policies that symbolize adults' maltreatment of children that goes unnoticed? Are these policies something that should concern child advocates? If you do find the policies problematic, could you envision an alternative? If you were a dentist, would you prefer to keep policies discretionary? Would you prefer to have the parent there to, for example, protect yourself from false claims of maltreating children? Suppose a dentist not only adopts the policy that the parent must be absent but also adopts the policy that each child under five must be shackled so they cannot resist, a shackling that includes a contraption that forces and keeps their mouths open. Abusive? Would you prefer a policy that at least requires the dentist to try to do without the shackles and frightening head gear? How hard would you require a dentist to try avoiding such instruments? Would you attach liability to the failure to take appropriate steps to avoid their use? Suppose a dentist, the only one within a hundre-mile radius, uses these instruments for all patients under ten years of age? What if the same dentist found it so effective that he decided to use them for all his patients? What arguments would justify differential treatment based on age?

In the Matter of Catherine W.

116 Misc. 2d 377; 455 N.Y.S.2d 519 (NY Fam. Ct., 1982)

Judge Willen delivered the opinion of the court.

The fundamental issue in this case is the determination of a father's obligation to provide child support when his adolescent children refuse to see him.

There is no doubt that such obligation may be suspended when a former wife-custodian actively deprives the father of his visitation rights. Under section 241 of the Domestic Relations Law which does not apply in the instant matter because of the former wife's remarriage, alimony may also be terminated. Other remedies exist as well, which will be discussed below.

Where the father's conduct towards the children clearly is such that his acts render it inimical to their physical or emotional well-being, then the children's refusal to see him does not excuse his obligation to support them.

There is a grey zone, however, where the children perceive their father with anger and resentment, do not wish to see him, and conflicting allegations are made as to the basis. When this occurs, typically either a petition for contempt or to enforce or vacate support or visitation or to make support and visitation mutually dependent, follows, and a hearing held to determine the adequacy of the children's reaction. If, for example, their refusal to have visitation is fueled by their mother's hurts, old or new, and she is overtly or covertly undermining visitation, and the alleged conduct of the father is blown up to undeserved proportions, then the misalliance between mother and children rather than the father's conduct is the root cause for nonvisitation and the courts will afford him relief.

Stated another way, if the acts of the father with the children are of such magnitude as to reasonably excuse their refusal to see him, then his obligation to support them will be enforced. Where on the other hand, resentment, the anticipated fallout of a defunct marriage, results in noncompliance with the duty of the custodial parent to foster and encourage a positive relationship between the children and noncustodial parent, our law quite properly provides a range of remedies, including change of custody, contempt, suspending child support or alimony where applicable, and making child support dependent upon visitation.

The courts must take especial care not to provide children as allies to either side when former spouses elect to continue litigation warfare.

This petition by the father seeks a finding of willful contempt against the mother and an order making support dependent upon visitation. The parties were married in 1960 and divorced in 1979. There are two children, Cathleen, 17, and Robert (Robbie), 16. A nonmerged separation agreement provided custody to the mother, alimony, support for the children, specified visitation (one full weekend and all remaining Sundays of the month), prompt disclosure of serious illness of the children, and mutual access to their medical and school records. Additionally the parties agreed to: "exert every reasonable effort to maintain free access and unhampered contact between the children and each of the parties and to foster a feeling of affection between the children and the other party. Neither party shall do anything which may estrange the children from the other party or injure the children's opinion as to their mother or father or which may hamper the free and natural development of the children's love and respect for the other party."

In previous litigation, following the recommendation of the Consultation Services Center, Cathleen was excused from compliance with visitation with her father while Robbie was compelled to continue. The father is currently paying child support of $120 per week ($60 per week per child), as a result of an order of this court on December 10, 1980.

At this time the father has not had visitation with either of the children for over two years, based he says, on the mother having turned his daughter against him, and as to his son, based on the mother's wrongful removal of the boy to a Pennsylvania boarding school without the father's consent nor even consultation with him. No serious refutation was made by the mother that her placing the son in the Pennsylvania school was clandestine and effectively deprived the father of agreed upon as well as court-ordered visitation.

The testimony adduced showed continuous efforts by the father to obtain visitation. There were a huge number of telephone calls which resulted in either the phone being hung up, or his being told the children were not home when they actually were there, or his being told to call back at a later time at which time no one was home and eventually total frustration when the mother obtained an unlisted telephone number. He attempted on a large number of occasions to go to the mother's house and was denied visitation in each instance. In at least one instance he was told his son was not home while he was seen at an upstairs window. Additionally the police were called frequently by the mother upon very little pretext. The father sent many letters as well as birthday and Christmas cards to the children and these were returned to him, unopened, and on one occasion, the boy, Robbie, responded with a vitriolic hate letter.

The main thrust of the mother's defense was that the decision to forego visitation was made by the children solely, despite her advice to the contrary. The testimony of the mother persuades the court that she is ambivalent about fostering an appropriate father–child relationship, paying lip service to its virtue but covertly approving any negative reaction by the children to their father. On cross-examination the mother's present husband indicated that the mother was partially responsible for the children's refusal of visitation by her overreaction to her former husband, and the court so finds.

The incidents which the children allege sustain their decision not to see their father consist of Cathleen's claim that her father demeaned her in front of her friends, that he was a phony, that he badgered her about her mother, that he asked her to live with him, that she resented his present wife and her teenage daughter. She claimed her father called her a "whore", "bitch", "stupid" and that she looked like a prostitute.

She was criticized by him at age 14 for wearing too much make-up, for low grades in school and for going out with boys.

The father denied all of the name calling except that he admitted telling his daughter, "If that's the way you feel, you can go to hell." He stated that his former wife's reaction to the children's refusal to see him was illustrated by her statement to him in a telephone conversation, "I am glad you are getting it stuffed up your ass." Notwithstanding all of Cathleen's negativism she admitted that during a period of regular visitation with her father they went rollerskating, to the movies and even picnics. The father's present wife also indicated that at one time there was discussion of Cathleen living with them and sharing a bedroom with her 16-year-old daughter. After hearing all the versions of what was said and done, the court is satisfied that the father was truthful, sincere and is not looking to avoid his support obligations. He emphatically denies calling Cathleen the names she attributes to him and the court believes him. He testified that if he is required to support the children but is unable to see them, that they would continue to regard him as "just money". His present wife described him as a gentle person, who when angry says "Go to hell, or to hell with you", but nothing worse, and that he is a caring father as well as stepfather to her daughter. He impressed the court substantially that way.

Robbie's version of his father's wrongdoing consisted of his father allegedly hitting him with a strap, being called a "faggot" and being struck by his father. These incidents were sharply controverted, with the father, however, admitting the following. Once Robbie climbed up on the roof after being told not to and he was punished by being hit lightly with a strap. Clearly Robbie should not have climbed on the roof and clearly the father's use of a strap was not the most sensible way of disciplining him. However no claim was made that the boy was hurt, or genuinely beaten. The incident of Robbie being struck was described by the father as Robbie having placed too much wood in a lighted wood stove. When the fire got too large, he pushed him away from the stove. This, the court finds, was appropriate. As to Robbie being called a "faggot" the father admitted that on two occasions he told Robbie that "you act like a queer" when Robbie told him he did not fight back when he was hit by another boy. Undoubtedly these remarks should never have been made, particularly to a boy of Robbie's sensitivity. Robbie and Cathleen are adopted children and both of them know this. Robbie has asthma and many emotional problems for which he is receiving therapy. He has been a poor student in the past as well as a behavioral problem and he was asked not to return to a parochial school he had been attending. Lately he has been doing better with the assistance of psychotherapy. Some time after the litigants were divorced Robbie left his mother to live with his father but after one week elected to return to his mother. Since then he has refused visitation with his father, written vitriolic letters to him, returned his birthday and Christmas cards, and told his mother to tell his father he was not home when he called or came to see him. He testified that he did not speak to his father on the telephone while in school in Pennsylvania and persisted in his story even when confronted with irrefutable documentary evidence to the contrary. The proof showed Robbie to be inconsistent, manipulative and troubled. Small wonder in view of his history of adoption, perceived perhaps as a rejection of him by his biological parents, plus a severe trauma in boyhood while at school that need not be discussed herein, and the divorce by his parents, which he may again feel to be a rejection of him. Notwithstanding all of the foregoing Robbie and his father had a good relationship for a long time which his father wishes devoutly to continue. Giving Robbie the unilateral power to cut it off for all time strikes the court as beyond his best interests. Robbie is not always the clearest of persons in knowing what is best for him and the court feels that the father's motive in this lawsuit is a most natural one, to establish and have as normal a parent–child relationship as is possible under all the troubled circumstances everyone has endured.

The children's mother clearly is struggling with the sure knowledge that it would be good for the children to relate to their father and her own disdain for him. She is unable to get out of her own way, vacillating between encouraging such relations and approving the children's rebellion. This, as much as anything else, the court finds, is the reason for the litigiousness of this couple.

The mother has not obeyed her obligations under the separation agreement to disclose serious illnesses of the children to the father, nor has she permitted the father to have access to the children's school records. The removal of Robbie to an out-of-State school without consultation with the father was in total disregard of his rights of visitation.

Under the law established by a host of decisions in our State, "The father's right to see his children is tied into his covenant to [pay] *** for their support."

The record is entirely silent as to any "pressing concern" or "exceptional circumstances" to warrant the removal of Robbie to an out-of-State school under the doctrine established in *Abraham v. Abraham*. . . .

While the court recognizes that Robbie's needs were somewhat special, the court questions the necessity of such a distant placement by his mother. Nevertheless, the court justifiably surmises that Mr. F. would have encountered the same visitation obstacles even if Robbie were attending a local New York school. Indeed, while the distance between the father and son may well have been substantial in terms of miles, there is even a greater distance with respect to attitudes and perceptions. The court finds no fault on the part of Mr. F. in this regard. The father's conduct is well short of any forfeiture by him of his previous right of visitation.

The court is obliged to encourage the visceral feeling of a parent to see his or her children. Accordingly, the decision of the court is that Mr. F.'s support obligation shall be dependent upon his being afforded actual visitation with both of his children. A finding of contempt at this time would likely exacerbate the hostility of the litigants for each other and perhaps ill serves the goal of promoting a reconciliation between the father and children and the court declines, therefore, to make such finding.

Settle order specifying realistic visitation, telephone access and related matters in conformance with this decision.

Notes and Queries

1. The court notes that the father would be obliged to support the child if the father's actions are detrimental to the child's physical or emotional well-being. Is this such a case?

2. Even though the father may have impressed the court as a "gentle person," if the children do not want to see their father, should they be forced to see him? Should he still be required to support them if he does not see them?

3. The court does not focus much on Robbie's particular sensitivities. The court also seems to blame the mother for vacillating between encouraging and discouraging the children's relationship with their father. Should those issues matter to the court?

4. How does this case potentially involve psychological maltreatment?

Research Comments

1. This case raises issues that have been the subject of considerable controversy. Although research may reveal that allegations of abuse are not as high as expected, some leading commentators suggest that allegations of abuse are much higher. Most notably, Dr. Richard Gardner, a psychiatrist at Columbia University, coined the term *Parental Alienation Syndrome* (PAS) for the psychological manipulations he viewed in custody disputes. PAS is characterized by a cluster of symptoms that may include: (1) a campaign of denigration; (2) weak, absurd, or frivolous rationalizations for the deprecation; (3) lack of ambivalence; (4) absence of guilt over cruelty to and/or exploitation of the alienated parent; (5) the presence of borrowed scenarios; and (6) spread of the animosity to the friends and/or extended family of the alienated parent. The primary manifestation of PAS is the child's campaign of denigration against a parent, a campaign that has no justification. In the extreme cases, these behaviors include an allegation of sexual abuse. PAS often is understood as resulting from the combination of a programming (brainwashing) parent's indoctrinations and the child's own contributions to the vilification of the target parent. Although it typically involves denigration of a parent by the other, the child provides his own contributions to the alienating parent's own campaign of denigration against the alienated parent. According to Dr. Gardner, PAS has emerged because of changes in approaches to custody proceedings. He asserts that the replacement of the tender years presumption with the best interests principle and the increased popularity of the concept of joint custody have increased the amount and intensity of child custody litigation. See Richard A. Gardner (1998). *The Parental Alienation Syndrome* (2nd ed.). Cresskill, NJ: Creative Therapeutics, Inc.

2. PAS has been highly criticized. The most frequent accusations are that: (1) Dr. Gardner's books are self-published; (2) he inappropriately testifies in custody cases; (3) PAS cannot be reliably diagnosed (different mental health professionals may not obtain the same diagnosis from the same circumstances); (4) the syndrome is based on his earlier and now discredited attempt to create a test to determine whether children were fabricating allegations of sexual abuse, the Sex Abuse Legitimacy Scale; (5) children may become alienated from a parent for a variety of different reasons; and (6) he has not provided research findings to substantiate his assertions. See Kathleen Coulborn Faller (1998). The parental alienation syndrome: What is it and what data support it? *Child Maltreatment*, 3, 100–116.

3. The outcomes of cases that use parental alienation claims to discredit a mother's allegation of a father's abusive and unsafe parenting have been an ongoing area of concern. Studies from U.S. cases reveal that mothers' claims of abuse, especially child physical or sexual abuse, increase their risk of losing custody. They also reveal that fathers' cross-claims of alienation virtually double that risk. Importantly, fathers making allegations against mothers do not result in that risk when mothers cross-claim alienation. The gender-specific impact is not found in nonabuse cases. Joan S. Meier (2020). U.S. child custody outcomes in cases involving parental alienation and abuse allegations: what do the data show? *Journal of Social Welfare and Family Law*, 42(1), 92–105. As might be expected, those findings have been challenged. Jennifer J. Harman & Demosthenes Lorandos (2021). Allegations of family violence in court: How parental alienation affects judicial outcomes. *Psychology, Public Policy, and Law*, 27(2), 184–208.

4. The case also involves the extent to which children may suffer in families that no longer are intact. One of the most highly cited studies examining these issues is a meta-analysis, of ninety-two studies and thirteen thousand children, that compared children from divorced and from intact families to assess the differences in well-being between these two groups and the potential outcomes that may be significant. The researchers found that children from divorced families had poorer psychological and behavioral adjustment, more social difficulties, and poorer self-concepts than did children from intact two-parent families. Importantly, they also found that family conflict in both intact and divorced families associates with poorer children's functioning. Paul R. Amato & Bruce Keith (1991). Parental divorce and the well-being of children: A meta-analysis. *Psychological Bulletin*, 110, 26–46.

5. Is parental divorce itself maltreating? Current research often focuses on those divorce-related factors that place children at risk for poor emotional functioning following divorce. Researchers estimate that approximately 30 percent of divorcing couples with children engage in serious interparental conflict for three to five years following divorce. Not surprisingly, children may be adversely affected by their involvement in an acrimonious divorce with conflict over custody and visitation issues. As a result, parental divorce has been cited in the literature as leading

to poorer outcomes for children in school, in emotional functioning, in behavioral functioning, and in self-esteem. Catherine C. Ayoub, Robin M. Deutsch & Andronicki Maraganore (1999). Emotional distress in children of high-conflict divorce: The impact of marital conflict and violence. *Family & Conciliation Courts Review*, 37, 297–314. A number of factors have been considered and found to place children at greater risk for poorer psychological adjustment following divorce. For example, the age of the child, the gender of the child, the level of interparental conflict, custody or visitation disputes, and the parent–child relationship all associate with psychological maladjustment in children from divorced populations. Again, there is consistent evidence indicating that interparental conflict is more strongly associated with problems in children than is the divorce itself. See Abigail J. Stewart, Anne P. Copeland, Nia L. Chester, Janet E. Malley & Nicole B. Barenbaum (1997). *Separating Together: How Divorce Transforms Families*. New York: Guilford. In support of this finding, research has shown that children in intact families with high levels of interparental conflict fair no better than children in divorced families. See Paul R. Amato (1993). Children's adjustment to divorce: Theories, hypotheses, and empirical support. *Journal of Marriage and the Family*, 55, 23–38. The severity of fighting has been documented in many studies to have a central role. High-intensity fighting is associated with more insecure attachments and anxiety in infants and toddlers. In older children and adolescents, severity of conflict has the largest and most consistent impact on children's adjustment, with intense conflict leading to more externalizing (disobedience, aggression, delinquency) and internalizing (depression, anxiety, poor self-esteem) symptoms in both boys and girls, compared with children experiencing low-intensity conflict. Joan B. Kelly (2000). Children's adjustment in conflicted marriage and divorce: A decade review of research. *Journal of the American Academy of Child and Adolescent Psychiatry*, 39, 963–73. Research has identified buffers that help protect children in high-conflict marriages, including a good relationship with at least one parent or caregiver, parental warmth, the support of siblings, and for adolescents, having good self-esteem and peer support. Interestingly, parental warmth diminishes the effects of high marital conflict in girls, but does not serve the same buffering function for boys. Instead, parental warmth directly associates with boys' positive outcomes, independent of marital conflict levels. Preadolescents in high-conflict homes with close sibling relationships seem to be as well-adjusted as comparable children in low-conflict homes. Furthermore, positive sibling support in high-conflict families in childhood associates with more positive adjustment in late adolescence, particularly in self-esteem and social relationships, compared with those with low sibling support or only children. Michelle L. Caya & Joan H. Liem (1998). The role of sibling support in high-conflict families. *American Journal of Orthopsychiatry*, 68, 327–333; Robert Emery (1999). *Marriage, Divorce, and Children's Adjustment* (2nd ed.). Thousand Oaks, CA: Sage.

6. Determining whether parental divorce itself may be maltreating may require an understanding of broad social influences. Consider the results of a meta-analysis

that supplemented findings of the leading study cited in note 4. The study in note 4 had found that the negative implications of divorce for children's well-being (including measures of academic achievement, conduct, psychological adjustment, self-concept, social relations, and quality of relationships with parents) were much more pronounced in studies of the 1950s and 1960s than they were in studies of the 1970s and 1980s. Good reasons could be hypothesized for the significant trend: (1) people's attitudes toward divorce became more accepting; (2) parenting courses for divorcing parents became available; (3) states started to encourage and even mandate mediation for divorcing parents involved in contested cases; and (4) organizations and institutions, such as schools, started to offer numerous therapeutic interventions. All of these interventions and perceptions could reasonably lead one to conclude that the negative effects of divorce would be expected to stabilize or even decline over time. Yet the follow-up analysis using literature published in the 1990s actually found the opposite. The gap between negative outcomes of children with divorced parents and of children with married parents significantly increased during the 1990s. See Paul R. Amato (2001). Children of divorce in the 1990s: An update of the Amato and Keith (1991) meta-analysis. *Journal of Family Psychology*, 15, 355–370. The author of the new study attributed the unexpected finding to a decline in the threshold of marital unhappiness needed to trigger divorce. The author argued that divorce marked by low discord may represent a greater proportion of all marital dissolutions and that low-discord divorces appear to be especially distressing to children because children from these families are more likely to view the separation as an unexpected and inexplicable event that launches a series of stressful challenges, such as a decline in household income, a move to new schools and neighborhoods, or a loss of contact with one parent. What are we to make of these findings? Note that the author attributed the decline in the thresholds to trigger divorce to policies allowing for no-fault divorces, softening public attitudes toward divorce, and resulting in a dramatic growth of divorcing couples. Assuming the findings are correct, would they justify efforts to secure a policy or attitudinal shift? Further note that the findings do not support the argument that legal and attitudinal changes have not benefitted children; rather, the findings indicate that these social forces have operated even more strongly to disadvantage children from divorced families. How would that impact your attempts to develop policies to address the needs of children in disrupted families? What do you make of this new research in light of what we know from note 5 above relating to high-conflict families? Recent research further complicates efforts to design policies to address the manner marital disruption impacts children's mental health. Longitudinal studies now find that, even before disruption, children in families that will end up divorced already exhibit the academic, psychological, and behavioral problems that will distinguish them from their peers from families that will remain intact. Likewise, families on the verge of disruption compared to those who are not are characterized by many of the problems thought to arise after disruption: less intimate parental and parent–child relationships, less commitment to children's educations, and fewer economic and human resources. See Yongmin Sun (2001). Family environments and adolescents' well-being before and after parents' marital disruption: A longitudinal analysis. *Journal of Marriage and the Family*, 63, 697–713. What do these findings contribute to efforts to address the needs of children in disrupted families?

7. Children often experience a substantial decline in their standard of living in the custodial home after divorce, leading to greater economic instability and reduced access to resources that never-divorced children are more likely to have, including better schools and neighborhoods. The general belief is that inadequate child support and weak enforcement policies are largely responsible for the decline, although some of these families were poor before divorce. In 1992, 14 percent of white and nearly one-half of African American households were below the poverty level after divorce, which was found to be more a consequence rather than cause of the divorce. It is estimated that the economic problems of divorced households account for as much as half of the adjustment problems seen in divorced children. Sarah S. McLanahan (1999). Father absence and the welfare of children. In E. Mavis Hetherington (Ed.), *Coping With Divorce, Single Parenting, and Remarriage: A Risk and Resiliency Perspective* (pp. 117–145). Mahwah, NJ: Lawrence Erlbaum.

8. Another controversy worth considering in families with separating parents involves sexual abuse allegations. More accusations of sexual abuse may be made in the context of family breakups than in other situations. Among the many reasons this may in fact be so are the possibilities that (1) the mother finds out about the sexual abuse and decides to divorce her husband, (2) sexual abuse is only revealed during the marital breakup, or (3) sexual abuse has been precipitated by the marriage dissolution. It seems, however, that allegations are made much less frequently than suggested by popular beliefs and many commentaries. The leading study in this area examined nine thousand cases from domestic relations courts involving custody or visitation disputes. These cases came from twelve jurisdictions in the United States. Of these nine thousand cases, 1.9 percent (169 cases) involved allegations of sexual abuse. Nancy Thoennes & Patricia G. Tjaden (1990). The extent, nature, and validity of sexual abuse allegations in custody/visitation disputes. *Child Abuse & Neglect*, 14, 151–163. Whether allegations of sexual abuse in contested divorce are false is difficult to determine. One of the few studies to address this issue examined 215 allegations of sexual abuse assessed at a university-based multidisciplinary clinic. To determine the likelihood that the allegations were likely, the study used a team of experts. A higher percentage was deemed likely, 72.6 percent, with 20 percent considered unlikely and 7.4 percent uncertain. Kathleen Coulborn Faller & Ellen R. DeVoe (1995). Allegations of sexual abuse in divorce. *Journal of Child Sexual Abuse*, 4, 1–25.

In the Matter of Shane T.

115 Misc. 2d 161; 453 N.Y.S.2d 590 (NY Fam. Ct., 1982)

Judge Leddy, Jr. delivered the opinion of the court.

Today, this court finds that 14-year-old Shane T. is an abused child in that he has been repeatedly called a "fag", "faggot", and "queer" by his natural father, a respondent herein. His father also taunted him continually by saying that he should have been a girl. In holding that Shane is an abused child, the court concludes that the phrase "physical injury" as contemplated by section 1012 (subd [e], par [I]) of the Family Court Act need not be inflicted by physical force and that it encompasses the stomach pain experienced by Shane when his father challenged the boy's sexual identity.

The instant proceeding arose from petitions filed by the Commissioner of Social Services on February 8, 1982 against the natural parents seeking an adjudication that Shane and his two sisters are abused children. After carefully considering all of the testimony adduced and evaluating the demeanor of the respective witnesses, the court finds that the following facts have been established beyond a reasonable doubt.

Shane is the natural child of the respondents and presently resides with his mother and two sisters. His father is a construction worker who has been separated from his wife for some time, although they continue to see each other.

Over the course of the last several years, Shane has been subjected to an unrelenting torrent of verbal abuse by his father directed at his sexual identity. Specifically, he has been regularly called a "fag", "faggot", and "queer". In desperation, the boy pleaded with his mother to intervene on his behalf and prevail upon his father to cease making these accusations. However, the mother's efforts were abortive, resulting only in a repetition of the taunts by the father with the added assertion that they were true.

Nor were these accusations limited to the home. On one particular occasion, the respondent father humiliated the boy by calling him a "fag" while they were shopping in a store.

Section 1012 of the Family Court Act defines an "abused child" as one "[Less] than eighteen years of age whose parent or other person legally responsible for his care *** inflicts or allows to be inflicted upon such child physical injury by other than accidental means which causes or creates a substantial risk of death, or serious or protracted disfigurement, or protracted impairment of physical or emotional health or protracted loss or impairment of the function of any bodily organ". . . .

As defined in the Penal Law, "'[physical] injury' means impairment of physical condition or substantial pain."

Whether "substantial pain" has been established is ordinarily a question for the trier of fact. In reaching a determination, the subjective reaction of the injured party is a proper factor to be considered although there is an objective level below which the question is one of law. Thus, such things as "petty slaps, shoves, kicks and the like delivered out of hostility, meanness and similar motives", are not within the contemplation of assault as defined in the Penal Law.

In deciding whether Shane has experienced "substantial pain", the court initially considers the observation of Chief Judge Cooke: "Pain is, by definition, a subjective concept and cannot be quantified or expressed with precision. Knowledge of the circumstances and the description of the sensation accompanying the use of force, however, provide a ready basis for measuring, within one's own experience, the degree of pain felt by another." It must be immediately observed that there is no specific requirement of the use of force in the definition of an abused child. Thus, Chief Judge Cooke's statement relating to "the use of force" is specifically referenced to the assault statute. . . . In fact, while . . . the Family Court Act is derived from . . . the Penal Law, there are substantial differences between the statutes. Thus, it is sufficient for a finding of abuse that there be protracted impairment of emotional health or a substantial risk thereof. It is clear, therefore, that it is the actual or potential impact on the child, as opposed to the per se seriousness of the injury, that forms the predicate for abuse. In this regard, the Family Court Act provision differs markedly from the Penal Law definition of "serious physical injury". Furthermore, while . . . the Family Court Act makes specific reference to "emotional health" . . . the Penal Law refers merely to "health".

The foregoing is consistent with the fact that . . . the Family Court Act is a civil proceeding "designed to establish procedures to help protect children from injury or mistreatment and to help safeguard their physical, mental, and emotional well-being." Therefore, this court concludes that the "physical injury" referred to in . . . the Family Court Act need not be inflicted by physical force. Rather, to constitute abuse, mere words are sufficient provided that their effect on the child falls within the language of the statute. To hold otherwise would constitute an unjustifiably narrow interpretation of the statute that would frustrate the Legislature's intent.

As he testified, Shane repeatedly tried to forestall tears, but they besieged his eyes, nonetheless. He told the court how he would cry and his stomach would twist when his father called him a "fag". At one point, he was asked whether he was beginning to believe that he was a homosexual. He clenched his hands, sat forward, and cried out "No!" His demeanor strongly suggested, however, that he would like someone, anyone to reassure him.

It should be noted that, in addition to the verbal indignities to which he was subjected, Shane was frequently forced to remove his father's shoes and massage his feet. The boy complied without protest since he was constantly in fear of his father. This fear was well founded since the father has a history of assaultive behavior in the home. Against this background, it is hardly surprising that Shane is now in therapy. This sensitive, handsome little boy has been trapped in an emotional roller coaster that seemingly plunges only downward, at a terrifying speed, toward an end that seems never to come.

To fail to acknowledge this boy's plight would be an affront to the clear legislative intent of . . . the Family Court Act; to fail to label the father's actions as child abuse would strip the phrase of all meaning; to fail to warn other parents against this insidious type of abuse would perpetuate the suffering of countless other defenseless children.

The respondent father seeks to justify his verbal abuse of Shane as a form of legitimate parental discipline designed to cure the child of certain unspecified "girlie" behavior. He stated that it would be embarrassing to him if Shane were "queer". It is very sad and even shocking that, at this late date in our constitutional development, many parents continue to view their home as a kingdom where they reign as king and queen and their children are relegated to the role of indentured servants.

While a parent's right to raise his or her child remains fundamental, it is equally fundamental that children have constitutional rights which must be respected by all, including their parents.... Time and again, courts have reiterated the validity of State interference in the parental–child relationship when necessary to protect the child's health and welfare. Cases such as these and the principles that underline them form the constitutional predicate for child protective statutes such as ... the Family Court Act. Accordingly, the father's defense is not only legally insufficient but, rather, it is singularly ludicrous.

The behavior of this respondent father is as serious a form of abuse as if he had plunged a knife into the stomach of this child. In fact, it's probably worse since the agony and heartache suffered by Shane has already assailed him for several years and constitutes a grave and imminent threat to his future psychological development.

The respondent mother testified that she tried to keep peace in the marital home. And the court does find that she attempted to dissuade her husband from continuing his verbal abuse of Shane. Despite this, the fact remains that she failed to protect her son from an ongoing, serious abuse.

She hardly discharged her parental duty to Shane by, in effect, keeping peace at his expense. When her husband persisted in his abuse of the child, she had an obligation to act meaningfully to protect the boy. And, in this regard, no action is meaningful unless and until it results in a cessation of the abuse and protection of the child. To uphold any lesser standard would seriously undercut legislative efforts to halt the senseless abuse and neglect of children.

It is also significant that the respondent mother continues to speak of a reconciliation with her husband despite the absence of any indication that he recognizes the seriousness of his actions toward Shane or the need to involve himself in therapy.

Accordingly, the court finds that the respondent mother allowed physical injury to be inflicted upon Shane which created a substantial risk of protracted impairment of his emotional health.

Therefore, on the entire record it is ordered that Shane T. be, and he hereby is, declared to be an abused child by both respondents, and it is further ordered that he be, and he so is, remanded to the Commissioner of Social Services....

Notes and Queries

1. The court focuses on the plight of the "handsome little boy" (who is 14) who suffers from verbal abuse. In light of the previous cases you have read, do the father's actions constitute maltreatment?

2. How would you defend the father?

3. The mother also has been found abusive. The court found that she physically abused Shane by letting the father emotionally abuse him. Is this a fair finding? What is the practical significance of finding the mother abusive?

In the Interests of M. A.

781 S.W.2d 94 (Mo. App. Ct. 1989)

Judge Gaertner delivered the opinion of the court.

This is an appeal from a decision of the Juvenile Court of St. Louis County adopting the findings and recommendations of Commissioner Walton Lemay that the Juvenile, M. A., was in need of care and treatment under RSMo section 211.031.1(1) (1986).

M. A. was born January 23, 1975, and is the youngest of four children. In November of 1987 he was attending religion classes on Wednesday nights at Crestview Junior High. Due to his misbehavior in class, the class teacher expelled M. A. To discipline M. A., his father took M. A. into the basement of their home and ordered him to get into a 3' × 4' dog cage used to transport the family's German Shepherd dog. The cage was then pushed between a metal beam of the house and some shelves to prevent M. A. from escaping. The duration of the confinement is in dispute but at a minimum M. A. was to remain in the cage for the same two hour period he would usually be in the religion class. This practice continued every Wednesday until January of 1988 when M. A. was taken into protective custody. The testimony also contains evidence of the cage being used on at least one Saturday. While so confined M. A. was not permitted use of the restroom.

M. A. ultimately told his teacher and school principal about the cage and the police investigated. A search warrant was obtained and the cage was seized from the minor's home. In addition, M. A. was taken into protective custody.

A hearing was held on this matter on May 8, 1988. A commissioner found that M. A. was without proper care by reason of confinement in the cage and ordered M. A. returned to his home "subject to the supervision by the juvenile officer." The circuit court adopted these findings.

Juvenile proceedings and the appellate review of them are civil proceedings and the scope of review is as in court-tried cases. Thus, the court must affirm the decision of the trial court unless there is no substantial evidence to support it.

Appellants first claim that, as they housed, fed and clothed the minor, there was no violation of section 211.031.1(1). That section provides in part:

> 211.031. Juvenile court to have exclusive jurisdiction when—exceptions—1. Except as otherwise provided herein, the juvenile court shall have exclusive original jurisdiction in proceedings:
>
> (1) Involving any child who may be a resident of or found within the county and who is alleged to be in need of care and treatment because:
>
> > (a) The parents or other persons legally responsible for the care and support of the child neglect or refuse to provide proper support, education which is required by law, medical, surgical or other care necessary for his well-being; except that reliance by a parent, guardian or custodian upon remedial treatment other than medical or surgical treatment for a child shall not be construed as neglect when the treatment is recognized or permitted under the laws of this state; or
> >
> > (b) The child is otherwise without proper care, custody or support.

Appellants claim that the juvenile court based its decision on subsection (1)(a) of section 211.031 and that their method of discipline does not fall within its provisions. Respondent argues, however, that the juvenile court relied on subsection (1)(b).

The findings and recommendations of the commissioner cite section 211.031.1(1)(a). This court also has stated in the past that where a question of parental neglect or neglect by another person who has received custody of a child by court order is raised, subsection (1)(a) should be applied.

This does not aid the appellants, however. The appellants claim that putting their child into a cage is not "neglect" under the statute. To support this proposition the appellants cite several cases in which section 211.031.1(1)(a) was applied and claim that these cases show that the statute only applies where the parents "fail to provide the necessities of life to children." This court refuses to give the statute such a narrow construction.

Neglect is to be determined in light of societal norms. To limit its meaning to matters of physical deprivation would be to "require a completely amoral approach to juvenile matters and restrict the juvenile court to an examination of the physical health and environment of children. No such restriction is stated or implied in the Juvenile Code and its purpose. No doubt some factual situations might present a determination by the court of the fine line between proper parental discretion in the care and training of children and societal needs in general, but the instant case requires no such determination."

The issue here is not a termination of parental rights case. The juvenile court took jurisdiction and the order of the court places the child under supervision in his own home with his parents. Under the circumstances, the order is not unreasonable. This leads us to the question of whether or not the disciplining of a child by placing him into a dog cage is consistent with societal norms. This determination is necessarily a judicial function. The juvenile court, after hearing all of the evidence, determined the caging of M. A. to constitute neglect. We find that there was substantial evidence to support this finding.

The appellants argue that the juvenile court erred in forbidding them from testifying as to the care and support they provided M. A. This evidence, while relevant in a hearing to terminate parental rights, is immaterial where the sole issue was to determine if the caging, in itself, constituted neglect.

The decision of the juvenile court is affirmed.

Judge Crist, dissenting.

I dissent. Confining a twelve-year-old child in a dog cage may or may not be neglect. The State has admitted, and the majority opinion reflects, the only question presented is whether the caging was neglect per se. The caging was unusual punishment, but under the facts of this case it was not neglect per se because the child was not harmed, physically or mentally.

. . .

In the case at bar, parents had a mischievous boy. They had tried numerous forms of punishment, but with little success. They provided him with two years of professional counseling. They were actively involved in his training. They gave him proper care and support. They were caring and loving parents, and tried to do the right thing. The caging was done for disciplinary reasons, but was tempered with parental love.

There were no more than eight confinements, and on each of those confinements, the child had the run of his parents' well-lighted basement, and was in and out of the cage as he pleased. There was no evidence the confinements caused any deleterious effect on his physical or mental well being.

Contrary to the majority opinion, evidence of care and support provided to this child was relevant to determine if the caging was neglect. From the evidence, it appears parents did everything right except for the caging.

There was insufficient evidence for supervision by the State. The mere confinement in a 4' by 3' dog cage, for short periods of time, without harm to the child, was not neglect per se. I believe the parents are better able to discipline this boy without hindrance from the State.

Notes and Queries

1. Sometime during the first night M. A. learned that the door to the cage swung in, thus allowing him to escape. The actual time of confinement, therefore, was usually only a few minutes. Both parents discovered M. A.'s ability to escape the confinement but felt that M. A.'s belief that he would be put into the cage was sufficient

punishment. Are the parents still abusive? The acts seem to have been part of a consistent form of discipline, why does the court ignore the rights of parents to discipline and control their children as they see fit?

2. How is a cage different from a crib since both prohibit the child from roaming freely?

3. Did the child actually have adequate care, as the dissent states?

Research Comments

1. Important research investigates behavior that appears quite normative but still problematic. Research indicates that yelling has an independent, negative effect on child well-being; it links to: (1) higher rates of antisocial behavior, (2) lower levels of self-esteem, and (3) child psychopathology. These findings have led to interesting debates, such as whether parents should yell or use corporal punishment. Some religious groups allow corporal punishment as a better alternative to yelling. They argue that yelling (1) is harmful to the child's self-esteem, (2) links to physical abuse, (3) violates children's inherent sense of human dignity, and (4) indicates parental loss of control, which is dangerous. Preliminary findings suggest, however, that increased corporal punishment is associated with increased rates of yelling regardless of religious tradition. Thus, parents who use corporal punishment are not less likely to yell; and religious parents who use corporal punishment are as likely to yell as are nonreligious parents. See John P. Bartkowski & W. Bradford Wilcox (2000). The Conservative Protestant child discipline: The case of parental yelling. *Social Forces*, 79, 265–290.

2. Nonorganic failure to thrive is one of the few forms of psychological maltreatment that generates observable physical symptomology for the child. It also stands out as one of the earliest recognized forms of psychological maltreatment that has produced a specific body of literature. Generally, "failure to thrive" describes infants and children whose growth and development is significantly below age-related norms. Typically, cases can be classified into two categories. The first category, organic failure to thrive, is diagnosed when a disease has caused the problem and medical treatment is prescribed. The second category, nonorganic failure to thrive, is diagnosed when psychosocial factors are responsible and the treatment involves adequate feeding in combination with efforts to meet the child's emotional needs. It remains unclear whether emotional deprivation alone can lead to growth failure. Early evidence from studies investigating the causes of failure to thrive was conflictual. Some studies found insufficient diet the sole cause of nonorganic failure to thrive. Yet others concluded that the probable cause involved a combination of emotional abuse and inadequate diet. More recent investigations of nonorganic failure to thrive cases have indicated that there are often multiple family problems occurring, including poverty, housing problems, unemployment,

and marital discord. Likewise, the parents may have unconventional beliefs or perceptions about what constitutes a normal diet for an infant; the primary caregiver may be emotionally unresponsive to the child. Caregivers in these cases have been found to have poor parenting skills, to be immature or depressed, or to have a knowledge of parenting but to have failed to use it because of the overwhelming nature of other family problems. Some caretakers of failure to thrive children have wholly negative perceptions of their infants, accusing them of deliberately trying to annoy them. The infants in such cases have been described as being lethargic, anxious, fussier, more demanding, more unsociable, more inconsolable, and less happy than other babies. Importantly, it is unknown whether these factors merely increase the likelihood of failure to thrive or result from it. See Kim Oates (1996). *The Spectrum of Child Abuse: Assessment, Treatment, and Prevention*. New York: Brunner/Mazel Inc.; Dorota Iwaniec, Martin Herbert & Alice Sluckin (1988). Helping emotionally abused children who fail to thrive. In Kevin Browne, Cliff Davies & Peter Stratton (Eds.). *Early Prediction and Prevention of Child Abuse* (pp. 229–244). New York: Wiley.

3. In the early 1950s, a British physician wrote about patients who feigned illness very much the same way the famous Von Munchausen told stories, so he found them as suffering from Munchausen Syndrome. Like Von Munchausen, persons affected by the Munchausen Syndrome have always traveled widely and their stories are both dramatic and untruthful. Unlike Von Munchausen, however, they feign illness. Twenty-five years later, another British physician recognized the syndrome's existence by proxy, which has now led many to view it as a form of child maltreatment. Although not widely known, this form of maltreatment carries substantial morbidity and mortality, with mortality rates ranging from 10 percent to 30 percent. Key features of the syndrome include: (1) repetitive illness in the victim; (2) comorbidity in siblings of the index child; (3) victim passivity; (4) high risk of serious physical and psychological harm and death; (5) false allegations of sexual and physical abuse of victims; (6) mothers with high incidence of various personality disorders, including depression; and (7) disturbed marital and family relationships. The most commonly reported cases of the syndrome include a wide range of abuses: (1) apnea, sudden infant death, seizure, and cerebral palsy due to imposed upper airway obstruction; (2) coma, unsteadiness, and epilepsy; (3) developmental disability due to repetitive anoxia; (4) anticonvulsant, opiate, laxative, diuretics, barbiturate, codeine, imipramine, phenothiazine, chlorpromazine, theophylline, and arsenic poisonings; (5) salt poisoning and adding salt to breast milk; (6) feeding problems, vomiting, diarrhea, and failure to thrive; (7) false allegations of sexual and physical abuse; (8) tampering with medical specimens, hospital records, and legal documents; (9) altering urine specimens and temperature charts and heating a thermometer in a cup of tea; (10) insertion of factitious stones in the lower urinary tract or inducing urinary tract infections; (11) causing false diagnosis of diabetes mellitis, hypoglycemia, hyperglycemia, cystic fibrosis, gastroduodenal motility disorder, Crohn's disease, gastrointestinal

bleeding, and hemoptysis; (12) inducing asthma, migraine, recurrent pneumonia, gastrointestinal bleeding, esophageal perforation, intussusception, tooth loss, and preterm delivery; (13) inducing fevers and nephritis from injections of immunizing agents; (14) drawing large quantities of blood; (15) fabricating hearing impairment; and (16) coating skin with povidone-iodine (Betadine) to fake jaundice. See John B. Murray (1997). Munchausen Syndrome/Munchausen Syndrome by proxy. *Journal of Psychology*, 131, 343–354; Abdul-Kader Souid, David V. Keith & Allan S. Cunningham (1998). Munchausen Syndrome by proxy. *Clinical Pediatrics*, 37, 497–504.

4. There is growing recognition that children who witness domestic violence, but who are not actually physically assaulted, may suffer significant social and mental health problems as a result. These problems seem quite significant. In order to determine the prevalence of children exposed to substantiated cases of domestic violence, one highly cited study undertook a secondary analysis of a U.S. domestic violence database from the Spousal Assault Replication Program. The database contains cases of adult female assaults in five major American cities collected by police and researchers in response to calls for police assistance. Results indicated that, relative to the general population in these cities, the families experiencing domestic violence were significantly more likely to have children living in the household and had a significantly higher proportion of children aged five years or less. On average, children under five years were present as witnesses in 48 percent of domestic violence cases and in 21 percent of cases involving multiple incidents. John Fantuzzo, Robert Boruch, Beriama Abdullahi & Marc Atkins (1997). Domestic violence and children: Prevalence and risk in five major U.S. cities. *Journal of the American Academy of Child and Adolescent Psychiatry*, 36, 116–122. Note, however, that there may be an overlap between adult violence in the family and child maltreatment, but the link creates many challenges and leads many to urge caution before assuming that children are in fact maltreated because they are in families marked by adult violence. See Jeffrey L. Edleson (1999). The overlap between child maltreatment and woman battering. *Violence Against Women*, 5, 134–154; Lois A. Weithorn (2001). Protecting children from exposure to domestic violence: The use and abuse of child maltreatment. *Hastings Law Journal*, 53, 1–156.

5. As we already have seen, Garbarino's broad approach urges us to look outside of families. A particular form of abuse that is not frequently mentioned in the literature is psychological maltreatment within educational settings. A number of studies indicate that a proportion of teachers commonly use emotional maltreatment in conjunction with other punitive disciplining practices as a means of exerting control. While physical punishment has been banned or guided by important procedural protections in most educational settings, psychological maltreatment often passes without comment. Many studies find that teachers maltreat children by overly restricting access to toilets for very young children, threatening to tell parents of a child's misbehavior or unsatisfactory work, rejecting the child or

their work, verbally abusing children, harassing, allowing other children to harass others, labeling children as "dumb" or "stupid," screaming at children until they cried, and providing a continuous experience of failure by setting tasks inappropriate for their stages of development. Finally, some highlight as psychologically maltreating the failure of teachers to deal with allegations or suspicions of child maltreatment, along with the experience of bullying by peers. See Marla R. Brassard, Robert Germain & Stuart N. Hart (Eds.) (1987). *Psychological Maltreatment of Children and Youth*. New York: Pergamon Press.

Review Problems

1. Consider the following scenarios. Bob, a single parent, does not believe in corporal punishment. Instead of spanking his three-year-old daughter, Marla, he tells her that, "Unless you start behaving better, I will go to sleep and let the night ants eat your feet." Abusive? Suppose Bob does not say such things. To get Marla to nap, though, he lets her five-year-old brother, Sam, tell her the same thing. Sam is highly effective in getting his sister to nap, much more effective than Bob who often ends up in a screaming match with Marla. Is Sam maltreating Marla? Is Bob abusive for knowingly letting and encouraging Sam to say such things?

2. Jeff and Sally work nights. While they work, Sally's mother watches Billy, age 2. After they finish work, they get Billy from his grandmother's house and bring him home, put him in his room, tie the door shut, and try to sleep for 6 to 8 hours. In order to ensure that he is safe, they turn on their "baby monitor," which alerts them to any worrisome noises from his room. Psychologically maltreating?

3. Mrs. Falvo is alarmed by the way her three children are treated in school. She has learned that a number of her children's teachers sometimes have their students grade one another's work assignments and then have the students call out their own grades to the teacher. She complained about this grading practice to school counselors and to the School District superintendent, claiming it severely embarrassed her children by allowing other students to learn their grades. The District refused to disallow the practice. Teachers like to use this type of "peer grading" as a way to help students learn the correct answers. Is this an instance of pervasive psychological maltreatment? Suppose Mrs. Falvo was told her children always had the option of confidentially reporting their grades to the teacher. Does that solve the problem? The issue eventually found itself on the Supreme Court docket as a case involving expectations of privacy in schoolwork. In *Owasso Independent School District v. Falvo*, No. 00-1073 (Feb. 19, 2002), Mrs. Falvo contended the right to privacy under the Fourteenth Amendment prohibits public disclosure of students' grades. The lower court had found that while the Fourteenth Amendment right may prevent disclosure of certain types of personal information, the school work and test grades of presecondary school students do not rise to the level of this

constitutionally protected category of information. In assessing whether a specific category of information is constitutionally protected, the Court used the following test: (1) if the party asserting the right has a legitimate expectation of privacy [in that information], (2) if disclosure serves a compelling state interest, and (3) if disclosure can be made in the least intrusive manner. In this case, however, the court ruled that it did not even reach the second and third prong of the test. Given that Mrs. Falvo and her children do not have a legitimate expectation of privacy in the children's school work and test grades, they have no Fourteenth Amendment privacy right protecting those grades from disclosure. Falvo contended that she and her children have a legitimate expectation of privacy in these grades given to them through a federal statute, the *Family Educational Rights and Privacy Act* (FERPA), 20 U.S.C. § 1232g, commonly known as the "Buckley Amendment." FERPA provides in pertinent part that an educational agency or institution "which has a policy or practice of permitting the release of educational records ... of students without the written consent of their parents" is in violation of FERPA. 20 U.S.C. § 1232g(b)(1). FERPA defines "educational records" as "those records, files, documents, and other materials which (i) contain information directly related to a student; and (ii) are maintained by an educational agency or institution or by a person acting for such agency or institution." 20 U.S.C. § 1232g(a)(4)(A). The Supreme Court, however, ruled that the statute did not apply to peer grading, that the papers were not educational records protected by the statute in that the peers did not maintain the papers they graded and were not acting on behalf of the school district. Lest you think that the matter is trivial, the United States Court of Appeals had concluded that the Fourteenth Amendment did not preclude the grading practice, but that the FERPA did. *Falvo v. Owasso Independent School District*, 229 F.3d 956 (10th Cir. Ct. App., 2000). Should the practice be stopped?

Chapter 4
Physical Maltreatment

Physical maltreatment is the most visible form of maltreatment as it typically involves 15 to 20 percent of all substantiated cases of child maltreatment. Physical maltreatment is the second highest percentage of maltreatment types responded to by child welfare systems in the United States. U.S. Department of Health and Human Services (2021). *Child Maltreatment 2021*. Washington, DC: U.S. Government Printing Office. Generally, physical maltreatment refers to a situation in which a child suffers, or is likely to suffer, significant harm from an injury inflicted by the child's parent or caregiver. Others take a broader approach and define it as any act that results in a nonaccidental trauma or physical injury. The injury may be inflicted intentionally or may be the inadvertent result of physical punishment or physically aggressive treatment of a child. Behavior by a parent or caregiver that may cause significant physical harm to a child generally takes the following forms: hitting, biting, shaking, punching, burning, administering poison, suffocating, and drowning.

One of the striking aspects of this form of maltreatment is that its most severe forms seem to disproportionately affect young children. Sixty percent of the major physical injuries inflicted by caregivers occur in children under age four. Every year, nearly 1,400 cases of fatal child abuse are reported. Recent information from investigators of child fatality records suggests that the actual number of children killed by their caregivers may be much larger. Head injuries are the leading cause of traumatic death and the leading cause of child abuse fatalities. Homicide is the leading cause of injury-related deaths in infants younger than four years. The "Shaken Baby Syndrome" is viewed as a leading cause of death to children under four. See U.S. Advisory Board on Child Abuse & Neglect (1995). *A Nation's Shame: Fatal Child Abuse and Neglect in the United States*. Washington, DC: Department of Health and Human Services.

Many difficulties challenge efforts to define physical maltreatment. One of the most difficult issues includes whether we approach this form of maltreatment as actual injuries sustained or as violent acts that could cause injuries. Relatedly, controversies surround efforts to identify what would be legitimate physical violence, such as corporal punishment and reasons for its use. Inflicted physical injury most often represents unreasonable, severe corporal punishment or unjustifiable punishment. These issues are highlighted by the manner states approach physical maltreatment.

Most states view physical child maltreatment as physical injury caused by other than accidental means that result in a substantial risk of physical harm. The injuries can be due to striking, kicking, burning, or biting the child, or any action that results in a physical impairment. Most statutes emphasize the overt consequences of abuse, such as bruises or broken bones. States allow parents to use "reasonable" corporal punishment with children. The major concern involves determining what is reasonable in the way children are treated, which frequently raises the controversial issue of corporal punishment. See U.S. Department of Health and Human Services (2022). *Child Abuse and Neglect State Statutes Elements: Reporting Laws, Number 1, Definitions of Child Abuse and Neglect.* Washington, DC: U.S. Department of Health and Human Services.

By far, one of the most critical challenges in addressing the gray area between appropriate physical chastisement and inappropriate maltreatment involves the need to respect cultural values and cultural diversity. The leading study in this area found that the use of physical punishment varies by ethnic group but, across a wide array of cultures examined, most agree that physical punishment is more appropriate if the child is 3 than if the child is 9 or 15. This finding serves to emphasize that individuals believe physical means of discipline are most appropriate for those with less of an understanding of verbal reprimands; but some would argue that it also ends up emphasizing that all cultures disrespect and harm the most vulnerable. See Helen Noh Ahn (1994). Cultural diversity and the definition of child abuse. In Richard Barth, Jill Duer Berrick & NeilGilbert (Eds.). *Child Welfare Research Review* (pp. 28–55). New York: Columbia University Press.

In addition to issues of cultural diversity, other challenges involve how to address the manner by which some children appear at greater risk of physical punishment that turns into maltreatment. Children with mental health needs provide the clearest example of a group at higher risk. Comparing clinical and community groups, children between ages two and seven are not differently subjected to corporal punishment; yet adolescents (13–17) are treated differently. Parents are twice as likely to use corporal punishment with adolescents who need mental health treatment. Indexes of physical aggression reveal similar trends: Children in need of mental health services are two to three times more likely to suffer physical aggression from parents, *and* the aggression continues with age in clinical groups although it declines in the general population. These findings suggest a bidirectionality between parent and child actions, which supports the contention that coercive interactions escalate. See Annette Mahoney, William O. Donnelly, Terri Lewis & Carri Maynard (2000). Mother and father self-reports of corporal punishment and severe physical aggression toward clinic-referred youth. *Journal of Clinical Child Psychology,* 29, 266–281.

Research Comments

1. Research examining physical aggression viewed as punishment presents one of the most intriguing set of findings. Child protection workers pervasively believe that corporal punishment should be limited in that it links to negative outcomes. Yet over 90 percent of parents use it and all states allow it as long as it is "reasonable and justifiable." These two findings have important implications. Most notably, it has been suggested that they lead professionals to intervene more aggressively in some cultural groups than others, which becomes potentially problematic given that children of color receive more coercive intervention in their families *but* receive fewer and less adequate services. See Roger J. R. Levesque (2000). Cultural evidence, child maltreatment, and the law. *Child Maltreatment*, 5, 146–160. The reality is, though, that research remains highly inconclusive, at least in terms of dynamics of relationships involved in corporal punishment. Reviews of research reveal the following: (1) Relationships between ethnic group and corporal punishment are inconclusive, some studies find white parents to be more likely to use corporal punishment while others find Black parents use it more; (2) few relationships exist between income and frequency of corporal punishment, but there may be class differences in reasons for using it; (3) younger mothers use it more frequently; (4) mothers use it more often than fathers, but fathers are more deadly; and (5) it is used more often with boys and with children under age six. See Tracy L. Dietz (2000). Disciplining children: Characteristics associated with the use of corporal punishment. *Child Abuse & Neglect*, 24, 1529–1524. In addition to these findings, it seems that whether corporal punishment in fact is harmful remains debatable. Some find it essential to (1) help children learn to obey and respect authority, (2) impose discipline, (3) prevent bad behavior, and (4) effect immediate compliance. Yet some propose that it has long-term negative effects, that it (1) leads to depression and suicide, (2) contributes to a culture of violence, (3) increases the likelihood that children will assault siblings and future partners (corporal punishment links to depression, which is linked to domestic violence in the form of both child physical abuse and partner abuse), (4) lowers IQ scores, (5) increases suicidal ideation, (6) increases alcohol abuse, (7) increases the probability of engaging in masochistic sex, and (8) decreases income. See Murray A. Straus (2001). *Beating the Devil Out of Them: Corporal Punishment in American Families and Its Effects on Children*. New Brunswick, NJ: Transaction Publishers. As with other effects of parents' treatment of their children, it seems that the nature of the parent–child relationship may influence the effects of corporal punishment. One study, for example, examined adolescents and parents' reports of parents hitting, pushing, grabbing, or shoving them *during adolescence* (7th–10th grades), its relationship to quality of parenting (warmth/affection, monitoring, inductive reasoning to explain rules and expectations, and consistency), and its impact of adolescent aggressiveness, delinquency, and psychological well-being. The study

found that quality of parenting, not harsh corporal punishment, relates to adolescent adjustment. Ronald L. Simons, Christine Johnson & Rand D. Conger (1994). Harsh corporal punishment versus quality of parental involvement as an explanation of adolescent maladjustment. *Journal of Marriage & the Family*, 56, 591–607.

2. Why does corporal punishment continue? Several myths about corporal punishment have been examined: (1) it is legal, (2) it is effective, (3) it is believed to be used only as a last resort, (4) it is thought to be harmless and actually good for children, (5) its infrequent use is not harmful, (6) parents need extensive parenting skills to adopt alternative disciplinary approaches, (7) if it is not used, children will engage in problem behavior, (8) parents spank only rarely or only for very serious reasons, (9) parents stop using it as children grow older, and (10) not using it is unrealistic. All except the first point are questionable, and their opposite seems to be supported by existing research. See Murray A. Straus (2001). *Beating the Devil Out of Them: Corporal Punishment in American Families and Its Effects on Children*. New Brunswick, NJ: Transaction Publishers.

3. Given the challenges we encounter in addressing an issue plagued by controversy and difficulties, some have argued that the legal system could address the issue through more symbolic laws. These proposals draw from laws passed in other countries. Over the past two decades, European courts and governments increasingly have moved toward banning physical punishment. In 1979, Sweden became the first nation to legally abolish all forms of corporal punishment by all caretakers. The Swedish law states that "Children are to be treated with respect for their person and individuality, and may not be subjected to physical punishment or other injurious or humiliating treatment." The law, however, is precatory; it does not attach civil or criminal penalties to the failure of those who would not follow the mandate. Since the Swedish law was passed, seven other countries have implemented similar bans: Finland in 1984, Denmark in 1986 (made more explicit in 1997), Norway in 1987, Austria in 1989, Cyprus in 1994, Latvia in 1998, and Croatia in 1999. In addition, in 1996, the highest court in Italy ruled that physical punishment of children is no longer permitted by law, declaring it anachronistic and legally unsustainable. Other European nations are moving in a similar direction. Although examining the impact of these laws remains complex, those who have attempted to examine the impact of these trends suggest that legislative reform has started to alter parental attitudes and behavior. For example, the majority of Swedish youth report never having been physically punished by their mothers; a majority of the remainder report having been struck only once or twice in their entire childhood. See Joan E. Durrant (2000). Trends in youth crime and well-being since the abolition of corporal punishment in Sweden. *Youth and Society*, 31, 437–456. Research also reveals that public support for corporal punishment has declined, identification of children at risk has increased, child abuse mortality is rare, prosecution rates have remained steady, and social service intervention has become increasingly supportive and preventive. Joan E. Durrant (1999).

Evaluating the success of Sweden's corporal punishment ban. *Child Abuse & Neglect*, 23, 435–448. Importantly, because it may have helped alter beliefs, effects of the ban are difficult to evaluate. For example, by making the problem more recognized, it is likely to lead to increased reports of maltreatment, which seems to have become the case. Robert E. Larzelere & Byron Johnson (1999). Evaluations of the effects of Sweden's spanking ban on physical child abuse rates: A literature review. *Psychological Reports*, 85, 381–392. Likewise, support for physical punishment began declining before the reform was passed, which makes it difficult to evaluate the extent to which reforms impacted public attitudes and leads some to conclude that the reforms have had no impact. Julian V. Roberts (2000). Changing public attitudes toward corporal punishment: The effects of statutory reform in Sweden. *Child Abuse & Neglect*, 24, 1027–1035. After reviewing the cases that follow, consider revisiting this approach to dealing with corporal punishment and consider its potential contribution to efforts in the United States.

Notes and Queries

1. As may be expected, the manner, frequency, and severity of corporal punishment seems to influence effects. Assuming that conclusion is accurate, how should the legal system respond? Assuming Straus's conclusions are accurate, how should the legal system respond to his suggestion that all forms of corporal punishment should be banned?

In re S. K. and V. L.

564 A.2d 1382 (D.C. Ct. App., 1989)

Judge Rogers, per curiam.

This is an appeal by a mother and her eight-year-old child from a finding by the trial judge that the mother had abused and neglected her child under D.C. Code. The judge based his finding of neglect on the fact that the mother had beaten the child with a belt notwithstanding her knowledge of the child's severe psychological problems when the child had denied setting fire to her bed. Appellants contend that the key findings of fact are unsupported by the record, and that the judge failed to consider the mother's mitigating actions and shifted the burden of proof by relying on a statutory inference of neglect under D.C. Code. The government must prove by a preponderance of the evidence that a child is abused. All parties agree, as do we, that the judge must apply an objective standard in determining whether the parental action constitutes abuse. On that basis, the judge found that S. K. was an abused child because a reasonable person, knowing of S. K.'s severe mental problems, would have restrained his or her reaction in responding to an admittedly potentially life-threatening circumstance. We concur in all except Part IV and footnote 10 of Judge Schwelb's opinion, concluding that the evidence on which the trial judge relied supports his findings.

Dr. Vernberg testified about S. K.'s mental condition and opined that the reaction of the mother and the stepfather in beating S. K. for starting the fire was inappropriate. The mother admitted that she was aware of S. K.'s severe mental problems and still had beaten her with a belt when S. K. denied her culpability and stared blankly into space. When S. K. was admitted to the psychiatric ward of Children's Hospital several welts were visible on her body, and one was still visible a week and one-half later. Under these circumstances we hold that there was sufficient evidence for the judge to find that the corporal punishment of S. K. by the mother was excessive, and consequently, that S. K. was a neglected child as a result of abuse.

That the record also contains evidence that is, arguably, supportive of the mother's viewpoint of what happened is not dispositive. The trial judge was in the best position to evaluate the mother's and S. K.'s credibility. In finding abuse, the judge could properly emphasize the mother's knowledge of S. K.'s severe mental problems in view of the assessment by hospital officials that the mother, although able to present herself well, lacked appropriate appreciation of the effect of her treatment of S. K. and was unwilling to acknowledge its consequence.

In addition, we disagree with appellants' contention that the trial judge made four critical findings of fact that require reversal. First, they claim there was no evidence that the mother acted in a rage. Regardless of whether we agree with appellants that this was a critical finding, there was evidence from which the judge could make such a reasonable inference. Although the mother realized S. K. was acting inappropriately, she repeatedly beat her with a belt and admitted to Dr. Vernberg that she was afraid that she would not have been able to control herself if she had not stopped to seek assistance.

Appellants' second contention, that there was no evidence the beatings resulted in abrasions, is meritless in view of evidence of welts on S. K.'s body, at least one of which was still visible when the police investigated on July 25, more than a week after the beatings. Their third contention, that there was no evidence to support the judge's finding the mother, knowing of S. K.'s emotional problems, should have acted differently, also is meritless. Again, there was Dr. Vernberg's testimony on which the judge was entitled to rely in applying an objective standard. Finally, appellants' contention that there was no evidence that such physical discipline was likely to exacerbate S. K.'s condition ignores the expert testimony about the nature of S. K.'s mental condition, its causes, the inappropriateness of such behavior, and the effect of the beatings. Therefore, the evidence was sufficient to support the trial judge's finding that beatings were likely to exacerbate S. K.'s fear of her mother and cause her to withdraw and to experience hallucinations and death wishes.

Accordingly, declining to exercise our jurisdiction to decide the vagueness challenge, we affirm the judgment.

Judge Schwelb, concurring in part and dissenting in part.

I agree with my colleagues that there was evidence before the trial judge from which he could have found facts which would constitute child abuse within the meaning of D.C. Code. I do not believe, however, that the facts actually found by the judge were sufficient to sustain the government's burden of persuasion. Accordingly, although my colleagues and I are in agreement as to substantially all of the legal principles which govern this case, I cannot join in the affirmance of the judgment. Rather, I would vacate the finding of abuse and remand for further proceedings.

I

On July 13, 1986, S. K., who was then eight years old, set her bed on fire. Her mother and stepfather, who were asleep at the time, awoke to the smell of smoke. S. K. initially denied knowing anything about the fire and pretended to help her parents look for its origin. She eventually admitted that she was responsible.

After the mother and stepfather had put out the fire, the mother struck S. K. approximately twice with a belt. S. K. acted strangely, staring into space, and the mother ran out to telephone for help. While the mother was doing so, the stepfather administered another whipping. S. K. had several welts on her body, apparently as a result of these beatings. Concerned about S. K.'s behavior and emotional condition, the mother took her to Children's Hospital. S. K.'s welts did not require medical treatment, but she was admitted to the psychiatric ward.

Children's Hospital authorities immediately referred the case to the Child Abuse unit of the Metropolitan Police Department's Youth Division. After a somewhat perfunctory inquiry, a police detective concluded that there was no need for police inervention. Children's Hospital then requested a "hold" to prevent S. K.'s removal from the hospital, but the police again found insufficient evidence of abuse. Finally, a hold was placed on the child at the hospital's request; the mother learned about it when she was not permitted to take S. K. to the cafeteria.

On July 28, 1986, more than two weeks after the beating, the Hospital's Associate Director of Inpatient Psychiatric Services and the psychiatric social worker assigned to the case directed a letter to the Chief of Intake of Child and Family Services which began as follows:

> We are writing to strongly request that [S. K.] be immediately removed from her parents' care and placed in the custody of the Department of Human Services. We believe this child is in imminent danger of continued physical and emotional abuse and that this should be regarded as an emergency situation.
>
> [S. K.] has sustained documented physical and sexual abuse at the hands of family members since 1978 when she was an infant. She is now eight years old. Two other children in the home died in unusual circumstances. We feel that the system has largely closed its eyes to this child's pleas for help and has taken no effective action to stop this abuse despite a lengthy history of

> violence in the home and repeated reports of abuse by medical personnel and others.

After describing both the incident that precipitated S. K.'s hospitalization and her prior history of mistreatment, which ranged from the melancholy to the unspeakable, [note—describing the death of her two brothers by her father and her hallucinations regarding speaking to her dead brothers—omitted] the letter concluded as follows:

> In summary, we implore you to act swiftly to remove this child from her family. How much more abuse can her frail body withstand? How much more pain can her frail psyche endure?

...

On the same day, a hearing was held before Judge Steffen Graae. Judge Graae found probable cause to believe that S. K. was a neglected child and ordered that she be placed in shelter care pending trial, with supervised visitation rights for the mother and stepfather. Pursuant to Judge Graae's order, S. K. was placed at St. Ann's Infant Home, where she remained for more than a year.

While the case was awaiting trial, the government struck from its petition the allusion to the deaths of S. K.'s siblings. In fact, the government apparently agreed to go further and to eliminate the allegations of the family's past history as well. Judge Truman Morrison "indicated displeasure" with this plan, however, and the "history of child abuse" allegation remained in the petition, albeit almost ornamentally.

Following several continuances, the case was brought to trial before Judge Ricardo Urbina on April 27, 1987. After hearing the evidence, the judge found S. K. to be a neglected child and ordered that she be continued in shelter care pending disposition. On August 24, 1987, the judge ordered that S. K. be returned to the care of her mother and placed for one year under the protective supervision of the court. S. K. and V. L. both appeal, contending principally that the District's neglect statute is unconstitutionally vague, that the evidence was insufficient to show neglect, that the trial judge improperly shifted the burden of proof, and that several specific factual findings were erroneous. Finding appellants' other arguments unpersuasive, I address in detail only their contention that the mother's conduct of July 13, 1986 did not constitute child abuse.

II

At the beginning of the trial, Judge Urbina announced, restating a prior ruling, that the scope of the relevant evidence would be limited so that "the events immediately leading up to the July 1986 alleged incident would be the focus of the government's case." He subsequently held that evidence of earlier incidents would be admitted only if they shed some light on the state of mind that is compatible with [what] you allege led into the events of July '86. If not, they're excluded.

This meant, in effect, that the mother and stepfather were basically to be tried for beating S. K. with a belt on July 13, 1986, and that other incidents of abuse were to be considered only if they qualified under the kind of analysis under which evidence of "other crimes" is admitted in criminal cases, e.g. to show intent, motive, or lack of accident. This conception of the issue before the court, which was not opposed by the government, shaped the evidence which the judge heard and formed the basis for his decision.

At trial, Dr. Douglas Tebor, who conducted an emergency psychiatric evaluation of S. K. at Children's Hospital, was qualified as an expert in psychiatry. He testified that when she was brought to the hospital, S. K. was quiet, sad and withdrawn. He noticed some redness on her body, three or four welts on the upper thigh of the left leg, and several red welts on her upper left arm. The welts were approximately three to four inches in length. S. K. initially denied setting the fire and said she was not going to say anything because she was afraid she would be whipped. She later told Dr. Tebor that she had auditory hallucinations, disturbed sleep, and violent thoughts about hurting her peers. Dr. Tebor also interviewed the mother, whom he found to be upset and overwhelmed. He testified that the mother told him that she was afraid that if she had not taken S. K. to the hospital, she might not have been able to stop hitting her. In Dr. Tebor's opinion, whipping a child for setting a fire was inappropriate.

Eric Vernberg, a clinical psychology intern, was S. K.'s case manager at Children's Hospital and her outpatient therapist after her discharge. He testified that S. K. told him that she had set her bed on fire because she wished she was dead and because she thought that the fire would kill her. She told him, almost cheerfully, that she would consider using a knife to kill herself. She reported "seeing" her dead brother frequently. She claimed that her mother beat her about three times a week, but had promised not to beat her any more. Vernberg also testified that the mother had stated that the hospital's proposed behavior management program would not work with S. K. and that the only thing you could do with the child was to beat her.

Lorraine Lougee, a psychiatric social worker from Children's Hospital, who was one of the persons who had signed the letter of July 28, 1986, testified that the mother had said she thought S. K. "needs the belt daily," and had ridiculed alternative ways to discipline S. K. Although, in Ms. Lougee's view, the mother genuinely wanted to help S. K., she tended to minimize how often she beat S. K. and was not open to exploring alternatives to whipping. Ms. Lougee was not asked any questions about S. K.'s prior history of abuse.

Testifying in her own behalf, the mother confirmed that S. K. had serious psychological problems. She related that she had observed S. K.'s behavior deteriorate over the past year. Specifically, S. K. did not do her school work. She was disobedient at home. She frequently lied. Although she generally had a poor appetite, S. K. sometimes stuffed herself to the point of vomiting. She complained of headaches and told of hearing imaginary voices. The mother testified that in the spring of 1986 she had called Children's Hospital's Psychiatric Ward for an appointment for S. K., but was told that no appointment was available until July.

The mother admitted having beaten S. K. with a belt on July 13. She also acknowledged that on past occasions she had struck her with a belt and on the hand with a ruler, but denied making the damaging statements which the government witnesses had attributed to her. She explained that on July 13, she had taken S. K. to the hospital because she was upset and afraid, not about S. K.'s bruises, but because S. K. had set the fire. In response to questioning by the trial judge, the mother testified that she did not know at the time whether or not she should discipline S. K. for setting the fire. She said she knew it was not normal for children to set fires, and that it was for this reason that she had secured medical help for S. K. She testified that she visited S. K. in the hospital daily and that "I let [her] know I love her." She stated that S. K. was easily led, and that this might explain her statements to hospital personnel to the effect that she was often beaten and afraid of further beatings.

In announcing his oral decision at the conclusion of the trial, and again in written findings dated September 3, 1987, the judge focused entirely on the July 13 incident. Although the judge made a number of comments about credibility, some of them favorable to the mother, he never made a finding, explicit or implicit, as to whether the mother had made the more damaging comments and admissions attributed to her by the government witnesses. Rather, he eschewed any determination as to whether the mother's (or stepfather's) habitual conduct towards S. K. was abusive, and elected to decide the case on the basis of the single incident that precipitated it. The judge concluded that, while it was not abuse per se to whip a youngster who had started a dangerous fire, the mother should have exercised greater restraint in light of her knowledge of her daughter's emotional condition, and that her failure to do so constituted neglect. The judge expressly found that the mother acted reasonably after the beating in taking the child to the hospital but, in the light of his analysis, this evidently made no difference.

Judge Urbina also held that

> the stepfather's conduct was equally insensitive, but not enough evidence was generated during the trial regarding his awareness of the child's background to permit the court to reach the conclusion that he too is guilty of what the statute contemplates as neglect.

Essentially, the judge, focusing on the culpability of the parents' behavior on a single occasion, rather than on the effect of their overall conduct on the child, "convicted" the mother and "acquitted" the stepfather of child abuse.

III

When a child is battered by a parent, the state can address the problem in two different ways. The parent may be criminally prosecuted for cruelty to children. Alternatively, or in addition, the appropriate governmental authority may institute a civil action alleging neglect or abuse under remedial legislation designed to protect the welfare of the child. These two types of proceedings may be triggered by the same kind of conduct, but they are profoundly different in purpose and character. If the distinction between the two is blurred, the results can be unfortunate.

In a criminal proceeding, the focus is, as it must be, on the alleged wrongdoer. The child is, at most, a witness or a victim. The accused enjoys all of the rights accorded by our Constitution and laws to a criminal defendant. Proof of guilt must be beyond a reasonable doubt. The statute under which the alleged abuser is charged must sufficiently apprise him or her of what conduct is prohibited. If that statute is ambiguous, it is strictly construed, for the rule of lenity applies. The case centers on the specific acts of cruelty alleged, and evidence of other bad acts is excluded unless it bears on a legitimate disputed issue such as intent, motive, or lack of accident; even then, such evidence is admitted only if it is found to be more probative than prejudicial.

A civil proceeding predicated on child neglect or abuse, on the other hand, is remedial in character. Its focus is, or should be, on the child. The purpose of the state's intervention as parens patriae is to promote the child's best interest, which is paramount. Civil neglect statutes are designed to enable the state to identify and protect children who are in need of assistance; they are remedial and should be liberally construed. The "void for vagueness" doctrine has substantially less application, for the Supreme Court has expressed "a greater tolerance of enactments with civil rather than criminal penalties because the consequences of imprecision are qualitatively less severe."

Since a civil proceeding is designed to protect the child rather than to punish the offender, it is essential that the court avoid an unduly narrow focus. One cannot determine whether a child's welfare requires the intervention of the state, with all of the disruption which such intervention often entails, by simply examining the most recent episode. Rather, the judge must be apprized of the entire mosaic.

Frequently, as in this case, the incident that precipitated the institution of the proceeding was not an isolated one, but rather a part of an alleged pattern of mistreatment. Where this is so, I do not believe that the government can adequately carry out its obligations as parens patriae, or that the judge can make an informed determination as to the best interests of the child, if the inquiry is restricted to the single whipping or other similar event which brought the parties to the attention of the court. To do the right thing by the child, the judge must know as much as reasonably possible about his or her situation. To resort to an imperfect but revealing analogy, the investigation must go beyond the straw that broke the camel's back, and the judge should assess the entire burden which the child has had to bear.

The present case was presented and tried more like a quasi-criminal proceeding, focusing on the guilt or innocence of the mother and stepfather in connection with the events of a particular day, than like a remedial action designed to determine if state intervention was warranted to protect the safety and welfare of the child. As a result, what might well have been a very powerful case if the trial judge had utilized a broader approach and considered the poignant history of S. K.'s troubles became, at best, a marginal one in terms of the limited evidence presented to the court, and the trial judge's findings were based on only a part of the evidence presented.

IV

In the present case, there would be ample evidence to sustain a finding of abuse if any significant portion of the events predating July 13, 1986, which are described in the Children's Hospital submission had been found by the judge to have occurred. Besides that submission, there was evidence that the mother had in fact regularly and inappropriately beaten the child, and that she had made the statements attributed to her by the government witnesses (but denied by her) to the effect that regular beatings were the only way to deal with her daughter. The apparent deterioration of S. K.'s psychological condition, including her matter-of-fact discussion of suicide, her violent thoughts about hurting peers, her burning of the mattress, and other events described by Dr. Tebor and Dr. Vernberg, could also provide evidence of abuse to supplement the July 13 whipping, if the judge had found in the record the requisite nexus between these developments and the mother's behavior. The problem, for me, is that the judge made no findings on these important matters, restricting himself exclusively to the events of July 13 and the mother's knowledge of S. K.'s psychological condition.

Given the restricted scope of the findings, I cannot agree with my colleagues or with the trial judge that the conduct of the mother on July 13, standing alone, constituted child abuse, or that it could justify the drastic interference with the life of this family which a finding of abuse may precipitate. The question whether the state should interpose itself into the relationship between a parent and child is a sensitive one. The primary role of the parents in the upbringing of their children is now established beyond debate as an enduring American tradition. Although I view the welfare of the child as paramount, the child's best interest is presumptively served by being with a parent, provided that the parent is not abusive or otherwise unfit.

State intervention in the lives of families does not come without cost to the child. . . .

I do not doubt that a single act, if sufficiently drastic, could constitute abuse within the meaning of our statute. Most cases of physical chastisement in which abuse or neglect has been found, however, involve the kind of continuous pattern of mistreatment alleged here by Children's Hospital, rather than the single whipping, severe enough to leave welts for several days, but administered under extenuating circumstances, which formed the basis of the judge's decision. In the present case, the judge correctly concluded that the two or so blows with a belt would not, under ordinary circumstances, be sufficient to constitute child abuse within the meaning of the statute. He found against the mother because, in his words,

> the likelihood of making the child's already disturbed mental state worse should have been evident to any reasonable person and restraint should have been exercised.

I am unable to discern in the record, however, any basis for concluding that the mother knew or should have known that corporal punishment which would otherwise have been a permissible exercise of parental discipline was converted into child abuse as a result of S. K.'s psychological condition. Although Dr. Tebor testified that whipping the child for setting a fire was inappropriate, this does not establish that the mother should have known this, or that a single overreaction under great pressure (which was all that the judge explicitly considered) was sufficient to make her a child abuser or to lay a predicate for major intervention in the life of this family for several years to come. Accordingly, I would vacate the judge's finding of abuse and his order placing the child under protective supervision, and remand for any further proceedings which might still be appropriate so long after the events complained of.

Notes and Queries

1. How does the dissent envision differences between criminal and civil proceedings? Do you agree with the contention that the case was indeed quasi-criminal?
2. The court places considerable emphasis on the child's mental condition. Without such findings, would the mother's behavior have been accepted as permissible disciplinary responses to problem behavior?
3. Why was the parents' disciplinary behavior inappropriate?

Keser v. State

706 P.2d 263 (Sup. Ct. Wyo., 1985)

Judge Cardine delivered the opinion of the court.

This appeal is from a criminal conviction for child abuse. Appellant was sentenced to a term of not less than one nor more than two years in the Wyoming State Penitentiary; the sentence was suspended and appellant ordered to serve six months in the Natrona County jail with a subsequent supervised probation of one year. We affirm.

...

Appellant, Randy Keser, is the stepfather of fourteen-year-old Kevin Padilla. During December 1983, Kevin's mother was visiting relatives in Honduras. Appellant had made arrangements for Kevin to stay with neighbors while he was out of town on business. When appellant returned, he discovered that Kevin had taken the bus to school but had not arrived and that he had been absent from his classes. Appellant called the neighbors around 10:30 p.m. to see if Kevin had been found and discovered that they had picked him up around 8:30 p.m. When appellant sought to take Kevin home, he refused to leave. Appellant called the sheriff's office, then called Kevin, and advised him that the sheriff's office required that he return home with him. Appellant drove to the neighbors; Kevin entered the car, and they started traveling to appellant's house.

Kevin testified that while they were in the car his stepfather hit him three or four times with a metal spatula used to scrape ice off the window, backhanded him on the mouth, called him names, and threatened to kill him. After they arrived home, he was hit on his bare bottom and thighs with a leather belt fourteen or fifteen times as hard as appellant could hit, four or five times on the face, and at least once on the arm.

Appellant conceded that Kevin was disciplined. He testified, however, that Kevin was hit with the window scraper only twice and that it was not metal but a flat piece of plastic; that Kevin preferred the belt to having his privileges withdrawn, and that he only hit Kevin with the belt four to six times; that he was afraid Kevin would run away; that he suspected an involvement with drugs and sex; and that he was worried about Kevin's school work.

The morning after Kevin was "disciplined," he saw the school nurse who reported the incident to the Department of Public Assistance and Social Services. Kevin was examined by an emergency room physician who later testified to the existence of bruises on Kevin's face and posterior. Subsequently charges were brought against appellant for child abuse. At the beginning of the trial, appellant's attorney moved for a dismissal of the case contending that the child abuse statute with which he was charged was unconstitutional. At the end of the Stat's case, the court ruled the statute constitutional.

The statute in question, § 6-2-503, W.S.1977, reads as follows:

> Except under circumstances constituting a violation of W.S. 6-2-502, any adult who intentionally or in reckless disregard of the consequences causes physical injury or mental trauma to a child under the age of sixteen (16) years **** is guilty of child abuse ****.
>
> . . .
>
> The applicable constitutional standards are not disputed by the parties.
>
> The constitutional requirement of definiteness is violated by a criminal statute that fails to give a person of ordinary intelligence fair notice that his contemplated conduct is forbidden by the statute. The underlying principle is that no man shall be held criminally responsible for conduct which he could not reasonably understand to be proscribed.
>
> On the other hand, if the general class of offenses to which the statute is directed is plainly within its terms, the statute will not be struck down as vague even though marginal cases could be put where doubts might arise. And if this general class of offenses can be made constitutionally definite by a reasonable construction of the statute, this Court is under a duty to give the statute that construction.

An ordinance or statute is void for vagueness if it fails to give a person of ordinary sensibility fair notice that the contemplated conduct is forbidden. Part of the rationale for this rule is that vagueness encourages arbitrary and erratic arrests and convictions. Wyoming has followed the constitutional guideline that a criminal statute violates an essential principle of due process if "men must necessarily guess at its meaning and differ as to its application."

> We have previously defined the principles of due process.
>
> In approaching a problem involving a decision which is concerned with whether a statute is constitutional or not, we do so with certain well-established rules in mind. The law in this regard was summarized in State v. Stern, when we said that in determining the constitutionality of a statute, '**** the plain, ordinary, and usual meaning of words used in a statute controls in the absence of clear statutory provisions to the contrary; that where there is plain, unambiguous language used in a statute there is no room for construction, and a court may not properly look for and impose another meaning; that where legislative intent is discernible a court should give effect to that intent; that every law must be presumed to be constitutional, with all reasonable doubt resolved in its favor; and that while generally speaking penal statutes are to be strictly construed, they need not be given overnarrow meaning in disregard of the obvious purpose of the legislative body.'
>
> Since no other states have statutory provisions similar to ours, we must determine the constitutionality of this section on the basis of the general requirements of due process.

Appellant contends that the phrases "physical injury" and "mental trauma" contained in the child abuse statute are vague and not defined in the statute. We have not hesitated to declare child protection statutes unconstitutional because the language was vague and indefinite. A statute, however, is not considered vague to the extent of being unconstitutional merely because a reviewing court believes the statute could have been drafted with greater precision. [Note 1 provides the relevant statutory language: 'Abuse' means inflicting or causing physical or mental injury, harm or imminent danger to the physical or mental health or welfare of a child other than by accidental means, including abandonment, excessive or unreasonable corporal punishment, malnutrition or substantial risk thereof by reason of intentional or unintentional neglect, and the commission or allowing the commission of a sexual offense against a child as defined by law: (A) 'Mental injury' means an injury to the psychological capacity or emotional stability of a child as evidenced by an observable or substantial impairment in his ability to function within a normal range of performance and behavior with due regard to his culture; (B) 'Physical injury' means death or any harm to a child including but not limited to disfigurement, impairment of any bodily organ, skin bruising, bleeding, burns, fracture of any bone, subdural hematoma or substantial malnutrition.]

. . .

The statute is concerned with abuse. It is not fatal to the statute that child abuse is defined in general terms. Abuse is something other than normal parental action.

Criminal statutes should be as explicit as is possible and still accomplish their intended goals.

> The relationship between parents or guardians and children is a delicate and complex one, and standards designed to regulate this relationship must necessarily provide some flexibility while at the same time effectuating the state policy of protecting children from abuse.

. . .

These statutes are basically protective in nature. Consequently, they are designed to cover a broad spectrum of conduct. There is an infinite variety of conduct which may be involved in order to safeguard the welfare of the children. The statutes must be broadly drawn and reasonably definite in the area of legislation involved so that an ordinary person would know the conduct proscribed.

In this case, the statute, provides that child abuse is the causing of physical injury or mental trauma intentionally or in reckless disregard of the consequences. "Physical injury" has been defined by Black's Law Dictionary as "bodily harm or hurt ****"; "mental" has been defined as "relating to or existing in the mind; intellectual, emotional, or psychic, as distinguished from bodily or physical," and "trauma" is defined as a "**** psychologically damaging emotional experience." We do not find these phrases to have such esoteric meanings as to be unintelligible.

Physical injury is harm to the body. It is a term of common usage generally understood by the average person. It includes the bruises and welts and trauma of the kind suffered by the victim in this case. "Mental trauma" is harm to the mind or spirit. It is also a commonly understood term. The statute is violated upon the occurrence of physical injury and mental trauma—what society would consider child abuse. Appellant here should have known that his conduct was violative of the statute; and, if the definition of child abuse is not as precise as he would like it, that, in itself, does not render the statute unconstitutional. The right to have children does not include a corresponding right to abuse them by omission or commission. Children need protection. This statute accomplishes that purpose and is sufficiently definite to satisfy constitutional requirements.

Parental Discipline

Appellant contends that this statute fails to separate discipline from child abuse and, since it does not make a provision for recognizing and honoring fundamental rights of a parent to discipline his child, it is unconstitutional. Appellant contends that the judge's instruction referring to reasonable parental discipline being an affirmative defense did not cure the unconstitutionality of the statute, stating that requiring a parent to prove that "**** the force used was reasonable and appropriate increases the risk of an erroneous deprivation of a fundamental right and violates due process."

The State concedes that parents have a right to raise and reasonably discipline their children as they see fit, arguing however that no adult has a protected right to severely beat or abuse a child. The child abuse statute, together with the common-law defenses available to one charged, are complete and fairly apprize one of prohibited acts and conduct. We do not easily impute "to the legislature an intention to include innocent acts as criminal felonies."

> . . .
>
> Wyoming has previously addressed the question of parental authority, stating:

Courts are agreed that since parents, or those standing in their place, are charged with the duty of educating their children and bringing them up in accordance with certain standards, they have the right to exercise such control and restraint and to adopt such disciplinary measures as will enable them to discharge their parental duty; that accordingly it is not an assault and battery for a parent, or one standing in such place, to strike a child in punishment for disobedience or other misconduct, but is in the exercise of a legal right in doing so. Courts are not agreed as to the extent of punishment. In 2 R.C.L. 542, the rule is stated as follows:

> The decided preponderance of authority, however, is that a parent in punishing his children must act in good faith with parental affection, must not exceed the bounds of moderation, and must not be cruel or merciless, and that any act of punishment in excess of such limits is unlawful. **** Whether in any case punishment exceeded the bounds referred to is a question of fact for the jury, and they may determine it from the injuries inflicted.

It is well established that the legislature enacts existing statutes with knowledge of pre-existing statutes and common law. Common-law defenses do not necessarily have to be set forth within the applicable statutes. . . .

Instructions

Appellant contends, however, that the parental discipline instruction to the jury augmented the statute in an unconstitutional manner; that this judicial amendment was within the province of the legislature and not the courts. The court instructed the jury upon the affirmative defense of reasonable and appropriate discipline as follows: "You are instructed that the use of reasonable and appropriate physical force is an affirmative defense to the crime of child abuse when it is employed by one entrusted with care of the child for the purpose of maintaining discipline."

The prosecuting attorney read that instruction to the jury in closing argument and then stated:

> Again I don't see how any of us can disagree with that. That is our parental right to do that. We have to discipline children sometimes, and I would focus your attention primarily on the use of reasonable and appropriate physical force. Is it reasonable to be scarred for life? To be hit in the face? Is that appropriate to be bruised and bleeding, to not be able to sleep that

> night from the pain, to hide from your own stepfather a week afterward? Not at all, not at all.

The defense attorney reiterated this concept in his closing argument stating:

> As I told you at the beginning of this whole thing, it all boils down to reasonableness and justified actions. You have been instructed by the Judge [in] Instruction Number 6. The prosecution must show beyond a reasonable doubt that the discipline which Randy gave his son was not reasonable, was not justifiable. We again submit to you that this has not been shown.

All parties recognized the applicability of reasonable parental discipline; the defense was based upon the theory that although Kevin had been hit with an ice scraper and a belt, appellant's actions constituted justifiable discipline rather than abuse. The jury was advised that reasonable parental discipline was a defense. Appellant took the stand and testified that he beat Kevin and that he had also been beaten as a child. He testified to his concerns about Kevin's behavior, attitude and school work. The jury did not accept this action as reasonable. The defense asserted that the conduct charged was appropriate parental discipline. The trial court properly instructed the jury upon this defense, and the instruction given was a correct statement of the law.

Looking at the statute on child abuse and being mindful of the constitutional requirements and the applicable rules of statutory construction, we cannot find this statute unconstitutional. The statutory prohibition of child abuse encompasses a very difficult and nebulous area; it is not an easy task to clearly distinguish child abuse from parental punishment. This statute, in conjunction with the common-law defense of justifiable parental discipline, is adequate to apprise one of the unlawfulness of abusing children; and of the acts to be avoided. The legislature has coped with this problem in a reasonable way.

The judgment from which this appeal is taken is, therefore, affirmed.

Notes and Queries

1. The court notes that child welfare statutes are "protective in nature" to cover an "infinite variety of conduct." Why does that not in itself prove that the statute is too vague and therefore fails to provide sufficient notice to individuals?

2. Why did the defense complain about the instruction to the jury regarding the parental discipline defense? Does the instruction seem fair? The "reasonableness" instruction saves the statute from being impermissibly vague. Do you agree that the instruction has that effect?

3. What makes the stepfather's actions abusive?

4. The court describes the limits of the parental right to reasonable discipline: (1) it must not be cruel or merciless, (2) the parent must act in good faith, and (3) the parent must not exceed the bounds of moderation. Appropriate standard?

People v. Whitehurst

9 Cal. App. 4th 1045; 12 Cal. Rptr. 2d 33 (Ca. App. Ct., 1992)

Acting Judge Hollenhorst delivered the opinion of the court.

Defendant was charged with two counts of inflicting corporal punishment on a child resulting in a traumatic condition, the first count involving Natalie P. and the second count Stephen W. After a jury trial, he was convicted of misdemeanor battery on count I and was acquitted on count II. Imposition of sentence was suspended and defendant was placed on three years' probation.

On appeal he raises three instructional errors: (1) the court erred in failing to instruct sua sponte on a parent's right to discipline a child; (2) the court erred in failing to instruct on the lesser included offense of misdemeanor child beating; and (3) the court erred in instructing on prior bad acts. We find merit to the first contention and therefore reverse.

Facts

On the morning of September 26, 1990, defendant and his wife, Donna Whitehurst, were sitting at the table in their home in Murrietta discussing custody arrangements regarding defendant's natural son, Stephen. Donna was planning on taking Stephen as well as Donna's five children from a prior marriage and leaving defendant.

While they were discussing custody of Stephen, Natalie, defendant's stepdaughter, age nine, came running into the house and approached the table to interrupt Donna and defendant for the fifth time. As Natalie approached, defendant backhanded her, hitting her in the rib cage on her left side. Natalie fell and cried.

Before Donna left her house with the children, she called her cousin, Dorothy McGill in Sacramento, and asked her if she could stay with her for a few days. Donna told Mrs. McGill that defendant had hit Natalie and had kicked Stephen. When Mrs. McGill agreed to Donna's visit, Donna took the children and drove to Sacramento.

Donna and the children arrived in Sacramento that evening. Mrs. McGill noticed that Natalie was guarding her ribs with her arms but Natalie refused to let Mrs. McGill look at her ribs. Mrs. McGill further noticed a bruise on Natalie's left arm between her shoulder and her elbow. Mrs. McGill also noticed that Stephen had a bruise on his stomach.

On September 27, 1990, Mrs. McGill called child protective services in Sacramento and reported the incident. On October 1, 1990, Donna returned to defendant with the children. Before leaving, Natalie told Mrs. McGill that she did not want to go back to Southern California because she was afraid defendant might hit her again.

Mrs. McGill also testified that defendant had called her twice in January of 1991 before the preliminary hearing, threatening to "come and get her" if she did not drop the charges.

On November 19, 1990, Detective Williams of the Riverside Sheriff's Department interviewed Donna in follow-up to the report of child abuse. Donna told him that defendant abused the children physically, verbally and emotionally. She told him that on September 26, defendant struck Natalie in the chest, knocking her out of a chair. Donna further told the detective that Natalie's ribs were sore after the blow.

On November 20, 1990, Donna again told the detective that defendant slapped, hit and kicked the children but this time claimed that it was their own fault.

At trial, Donna said that defendant hit Natalie because she was interrupting them. She denied that defendant knocked Natalie out of a chair. She said she had lied previously because she was mad at defendant. Donna also testified that she was standing next to defendant when he called Mrs. McGill in November and did not hear defendant threaten Mrs. McGill.

Defendant admitted backhanding Natalie but claimed that he did not hit her very hard. He said he hit her because she continued interrupting Donna and defendant although she had been told to stay outside. He denied kicking Stephen.

Riverside child protective services worker, Ranee McNeill, saw no bruises on any of the children on November 20, 1990.

Parent's Right to Discipline

Defendant contends the trial court had a sua sponte duty to instruct the jury regarding a parent's right to discipline his child. We agree.

...

Thus as these cases make clear, whether the corporal punishment falls within the parameters of a parent's right to discipline involves consideration of not only the necessity for the punishment but also whether the amount of punishment was reasonable or excessive. Reasonableness and necessity therefore are not two separate defenses but rather two aspects of the single issue of parental right to discipline by physical punishment. Thus we reject respondent's claim that the trial court was excused from instructing on the right to discipline because it was not defendant's "primary" defense.

Nor can we accept respondent's contention that instruction on this issue was not necessary to the jury's understanding of the case. As we see the issue it was of critical importance to the jury's understanding of the case. Here there was no dispute that defendant hit Natalie, and the only real issue in this case was whether the punishment was necessary and, if so, whether it was reasonable. Yet the jury received no guidance on this issue.

For the same reason we cannot accept respondent's conclusion that the right was self-evident. Instructions are given on the relevant law simply because we do not presume a jury composed of lay persons is knowledgeable in the law. Here the jury admittedly may have known that some parents do use corporal punishment to discipline a child without incurring either civil or criminal liability while others are subject to liability. But we cannot presume the jury knew when corporal punishment is lawful (and therefore a complete defense), or when it becomes a misdemeanor battery or when it forms the basis of a felony offense. Nor can we presume the jury knew that a parent's subjective belief that the punishment was necessary and reasonable and, therefore, justifiable does not preclude the jury from objectively determining that the punishment was either unnecessary or excessive.

We therefore conclude the court erred in not instructing on the scope of a parent's right to discipline by corporal punishment and the jury's duty to objectively evaluate defendant's conduct to determine whether the punishment was justified. We cannot conclude the error was harmless.

Because of the failure to instruct on parental discipline and particularly in light of the other instructions given, there is a reasonable probability the jury convicted defendant solely because he struck Natalie and without ever considering whether the punishment was unjustified.... Thus, rather than being informed that necessary and reasonable corporal punishment is permissible and will not subject defendant to criminal liability, the jury was advised that "the slightest unlawful touching" is sufficient to constitute a battery. With this instruction and without any instructions on the right to use corporal punishment as discipline, including the issues of necessity and reasonableness, a guilty verdict was virtually compelled in light of defendant's admission that he hit Natalie. The failure to instruct on the right to discipline was prejudicial.

Disposition

Judgment reversed.

Notes and Queries

1. Should a jury be instructed about the parental discipline defense? Is it really necessary for a "reasonable jury" to hear the instruction?

2. How could the hitting be deemed reasonable? According to the court, it would be reasonable if it (1) is controlled rather than done in anger and (2) involves a single incident. Appropriate standard? Do you find the standard more appropriate than the one *Keser v. State* announced?

Chapter 5

Neglect and Passive Maltreatment

Child neglect is the most frequently substantiated form of maltreatment. Estimates reveal that neglect accounts for over half of all reported cases of child maltreatment. For example, analyses of the 2021 national reports revealed 76 percent of all child maltreatment victims were found to have been neglected. U.S. Department of Health and Human Services (2021). *Child Maltreatment 2021.* Washington, DC: U.S. Government Printing Office. According to the 1988 NIS-2 study, almost 43 percent of the identified neglect was physical neglect, which included children living in unsafe housing, not being fed nutritionally adequate meals, being consistently without adequate clothing, and receiving grossly inadequate care for personal hygiene. The second largest category of neglect was inadequate supervision of children (36.6 percent) and failure or delay in providing health care (20.8 percent). U.S. Department of Health and Human Services (NIS) (1988). *Study of National Incidence and Prevalence of Child Abuse and Neglect.* Washington, DC: U.S. Government Printing Office.

The federal *Child Abuse Prevention and Treatment Act* (CAPTA) provides minimum standards for definitions. CAPTA states that "the term 'child abuse and neglect' means, at a minimum, any recent act or failure to act on the part of a parent or caretaker, which results in death, serious physical or emotional harm, sexual abuse or exploitation, or an act or failure to act which presents an imminent risk of serious harm." 42 U.S.C.A. § 5106g(2) (West Supp. 2001). Using this minimum standard as a foundation, each state provides its own definition for child neglect. A review of state reporting laws reveals that neglect frequently is defined as deprivation of adequate food, clothing, shelter, or medical care. However, states vary considerably in the manner by which they operationalize their definitions. For example, approximately one-fifth of the states do not define neglect separately from abuse. Of those that do define neglect separately, some also define particular types of neglect, such as abandonment or medical neglect. In addition, many states address related issues in their statutes, such as parental incapacity (i.e., parent is hospitalized or incarcerated) or injurious environments (i.e., child is exposed to criminal activity in the home). Most states also specify exemptions or issues to be taken into consideration, including religious exemptions for medical neglect and financial considerations for physical neglect. See

U.S. Department of Health and Human Services (2000). *Child Abuse and Neglect State Statutes Elements: Reporting Laws, Number 1, Definitions of Child Abuse and Neglect.* Washington, DC: U.S. Department of Health and Human Services.

The NIS research sought to overcome the problem of nonuniform definitions of child neglect by adopting a standard definition. The NIS definitions are categorized as follows: physical neglect, refusal of health care, delay in health care, abandonment, and expulsion. The definition also provides an "other" category that includes: conspicuous inattention to avoidable hazards in the home; inadequate nutrition, clothing, or hygiene; and other forms of reckless disregard of the child's safety and welfare (such as driving with the child while intoxicated, leaving a young child unattended in a motor vehicle, and so forth); inadequate supervision; emotional neglect (inadequate nurturance/affection, chronic/extreme abuse or domestic violence, permitted drug/alcohol abuse, refusal or delay of psychological care, permitting maladaptive behavior); and educational neglect (permitting chronic truancy, failure to enroll, and inattention to special education needs). U.S. Department of Health and Human Services (NIS) (1988). *Study of National Incidence and Prevalence of Child Abuse and Neglect.* Washington, DC: U.S. Government Printing Office.

Although experts may be making progress in defining neglect, there continues to be a lack of consensus among parents and even among child development researchers on what is essential for child development. Standards continue to change as we learn more about child development and factors that impede or enhance children's physical, cognitive, emotional, and social development. Defining neglect is complicated by the necessity of considering the following: What are the indispensable, minimally adequate types of care that children require? What actions or failures to act on the part of the caretakers constitute neglectful behavior? Are the caretaker's action or inaction intentional? What are the effects of the actions or inactions on the child's health, safety, and development? Do the family's circumstances result from poverty or parental neglect?

Definitions of what is minimally adequate care for children must also take into account cultural variations in standards. Significant differences seem to exist in ratings of the severity of specific indicators of abuse and neglect among social workers, police, attorneys, and judges and among African American, Hispanic, and white subjects. One study found, for example, that African American subjects rate indicators of physical neglect as significantly more severe instances of inadequate care than do white or Hispanic subjects. Other studies conclude that when presented with critical incidents descriptive of child neglect, substantial agreement emerges among white, Hispanic, and African American subjects on basic standards of care for children. This has led one review to conclude that, while there may be differences in definitional emphases, such as African American parents including behaviors of neglect and European American parents including behaviors of physical abuse, all groups tend to concur on the catalogue of behaviors that parents would define as child abuse and neglect. See Jill E. Korbin, Claudia J. Coulton, Heather Lindstrom-Ufuti & James Spilsbury (2000). Neighborhood views on the definition and etiology of child maltreatment. *Child Abuse & Neglect*, 24, 1509–1527; see also Roger J. R. Levesque (2001). *Culture and Family Violence: Fostering Change through Human Rights Law*. Washington, DC: American Psychological Association.

Poverty also remains a significant confounding factor in defining child neglect. Although most impoverished families manage to provide strong and nurturing care for their children, child neglect links to poverty. These realities complicate holding parents accountable for providing minimally adequate necessities for their children, such as after-school supervision and medical care, in the face of inadequate income and the absence of accessible, affordable medical and supportive social services. We will pay close attention to these issues and consider their significance.

Notes and Queries

1. Conceptual definitions of neglect vary, in part, depending on the definition's intended purpose. Legal advocates may prefer clear evidence of serious harm to a child before court intervention to remove a child from parents. On the other hand, for caseworkers intervening with a family to prevent placement and to protect the child from further harm, the definition of neglect should perhaps include parental omissions in care that are likely to increase the risk of harm to the child. For researchers interested in studying the long- and short-term consequences of neglect for the child, definitions of neglect would need to consider parental behaviors that result in harm to the child.

Research Comments

1. More children suffer from neglect in the United States than from physical and sexual abuse combined. In spite of this, neglect has received significantly less attention than physical and sexual abuse by practitioners, researchers, and the media. Compared to physical and sexual abuse, why does child neglect remain so ignored by researchers? Some (inaccurately) believe that neglect does not result in serious consequences, that it is inappropriate to judge parents involved in poverty-related neglect, that its problems are too insurmountable, other forms of maltreatment seem more compelling, and what constitutes neglect involves too much ambiguity and vagueness. Howard Dubowitz (1994). Neglecting the neglect of neglect. *Journal of Interpersonal Violence*, 9, 556–560.

2. Sudden Infant Death Syndrome (SIDS), also called crib or cot death, is the sudden death of an infant under one year of age that remains unexplained after thorough

case investigation, including performance of a complete autopsy, examination of the death scene, and a review of the clinical history. SIDS is the most common cause of death between one and six months of age. The incidence of SIDS peaks between two and four months of age. Approximately 90 percent of SIDS deaths occur before the age of six months. The SIDS rates are two to three times higher among African American and some American Indian populations. Research links SIDS to prone sleep position, sleeping on a soft surface, maternal smoking during or after pregnancy, overheating, late or no prenatal care, young maternal age, prematurity, low birth weight, and male gender. See American Academy of Pediatrics (2001). Distinguishing Sudden Infant Death Syndrome from child abuse fatalities. *Pediatrics*, 107, 437–441. Given the known links to SIDS, what arguments could be made for approaching SIDS as child neglect?

Review Problems

1. The legal requirement that children be restrained in car seats clearly defines a new standard for "minimally adequate care" of children while traveling in cars. Why do you suppose that many have little problem holding parents responsible for failing to secure their children's safety belts while hesitating to hold parents responsible for corporal punishment? Some argue that failure to use safety belts is clearly illegal while corporal punishment is not. Do you find that a satisfying distinction?

2. Operational definitions of neglect are highly dependent upon the standards of the local community and of the caseworker who investigates reports of neglect. Good idea?

3. Child neglect typically involves a focus on caretaker failures and involves acts of omission. These inabilities typically include four considerations: (1) inability to plan, such as low frustration levels and an inability to reach goals; (2) lack of knowledge or skills, such as a basic failure to understand the types of foods young children cannot eat; (3) lack of judgment, such as leaving young children unsupervised for extended periods of time; and (4) lack of motivation, such as no desire to learn about childcare. Are these considerations appropriate? Do they place too much emphasis on parental responsibility and parental blame? Another approach to defining adequacy simply lists major forms of neglect: medical, hygiene, educational, and fatal neglect. Also among situations deemed neglectful are abandonment and fostering delinquency. Is this approach more effective?

In the Matter of Billy Jean II.

226 A.D.2d 767; 640 N.Y.S.2d 326 (NY App. Ct., 1996)

Judge Peters delivered the opinion of the court.

Respondents are the parents of Billy Jean II., born in 1989. As a result of four reports made to the State Central Registry of Child Abuse and Maltreatment (hereinafter State Central Registry) between November 1990 and July 1993, all alleging inadequate guardianship either due to domestic violence, poor hygiene, or unsanitary and unsafe living conditions, a neglect petition was filed on July 29, 1993 by petitioner. Hearings were held on March 10, 1994 and June 29, 1994, at the conclusion of which findings were made that Billy Jean was neglected by respondent Ray II. (hereinafter respondent). A dispositional order was entered on September 7, 1994 which, inter alia, placed the child in the custody of petitioner [the state, which has placed the child in foster care] and provided for visitation with respondent. Respondent now appeals, alleging that there was insufficient proof to sustain the finding of neglect.

We are satisfied, upon the evidence here presented, that there was sufficient proof to sustain the finding of Family Court. Testimony at the fact-finding hearing primarily addressed an incident occurring on July 10, 1993 when respondent allegedly became intoxicated and violent, physically attacking respondent Colleen II. in the presence of the child. State Troopers James La Plant and Thomas Ward interviewed Colleen from her hospital bed. She claimed that respondent had beat her with his fists and had choked her almost to the point of her becoming unconscious. Both officers observed her face to be swollen with bruising about the face and neck. The emergency room report, dated July 10, 1993, was admitted in evidence. Notations therein corroborate the Troopers' testimony as to Colleen's description of the incident. When La Plant and Ward arrived at respondent's trailer in the early morning hours of July 11, 1993, they testified that respondent appeared highly intoxicated. They testified that when they entered one of the bedrooms to get Billy Jean to bring her to Colleen at the hospital, due to their belief that the two other individuals in the trailer were not capable of properly caring for the child, they noticed clothing strewn about the floor and dirty dishes with encrusted food all over the kitchen, and thus described the living area as "disgusting".

Various preliminary and follow-up investigative reports made by petitioner, as well as reports made to the State Central Registry, were offered and admitted into evidence. Such reports document a history of domestic violence between respondent and Colleen in the presence of the child, describe respondent as "violent" with a "total disregard of others", and detail that due to respondent's alcohol and physical abuse, the child is "at risk". The reports describe Billy Jean as "dirty", inadequately dressed and unsafe due to the living conditions in the trailer. Included in such proffer was a report detailing the July 10, 1993 incident which corroborated the testimony given by the State Troopers. A follow-up report detailed Colleen's admission that the child was present at the time of the beating.

Respondent testified that although he is an alcoholic, he ceased drinking in 1985. While admitting that he consumed alcohol on July 10, 1993, he contended that during such time, Billy Jean was being cared for by Edward Dominic and that he was unaware of how Colleen received her injuries. He did admit that in April 1993, he was visited by Joyce Di Donna of petitioner who, after assessing the unsanitary condition of the trailer, gave him three days to clean it up. At such time, the trailer housed his truck engine and other automobile parts in the living room.

Dominic, a 72-year-old hearing-impaired friend of respondent, testified that he had never seen respondent drink alcohol or argue, hit, choke or be aggressive in any manner with Colleen. He stated, instead, that both he and respondent had raised Billy Jean and that he frequently babysat for her. Respondent also proffered the testimony of Colleen, who recanted all of her prior statements to the hospital, police and social workers. She testified that prior to her diagnosis and placement on medication approximately six months before, she consistently lied about respondent beating her. She now testified that he has never hit, kicked, punched or choked her. With respect to the incident which warranted her hospitalization on July 10, 1993, she claimed that an unknown individual attempted to rape her.

Mindful of the deference to which the findings of Family Court are entitled regarding issues of credibility, we find that the evidence amply supports a finding of neglect against respondent. Not only do we agree that the testimony of respondent, Dominic and Colleen were incredible, we find, as did Family Court, that the child at issue is a neglected child within the meaning of Family Court Act § 1012 "whose physical, mental or emotional condition has been impaired or is in imminent danger of becoming impaired" due to respondent's failure to provide her with proper clothing and shelter. We find proper Family Court's finding that the neglect determination is also based upon respondent's failure to provide the child with "proper supervision or guardianship . . . by misusing alcoholic beverage to the extent that he loses self-control of his actions" and by the history of domestic violence occurring in the home, "acts of a similarly serious nature requiring the aid of the court". The lack of actual injury to the child does not preclude such finding.

Ordered that the order is affirmed, without costs.

Notes and Queries

1. Do the facts of the case warrant removal of a child from either parent?
2. How has the child been "injured"? What standard does the court use to find neglect?

Research Comment

1. Cultural and community values largely determine the point at which childcare moves from adequate to inadequate. Regrettably, one of the most important findings emerging from a review of the literature is the lack of research and lack of important findings on ethnicity's impact on parenting. See Vonnie C. McLoyd, Ana Mari Cauce, David Takeuchi & Leon Wilson (2000). Marital processes and parental socialization in families of color: A decade review of research. *Journal of Marriage & the Family*, 62, 1070–1093. Despite the lack of research, the review reveals some important conclusions. First, social location, rather than cultural differences, appears to be the key source of ethnic and racial variation in family life in the United States. Second, family conflict appears to have less of a negative impact on children of color. Different groups appear to evince different forms of socialization to account for racial and ethnic differences; groups appear to be preparing children for different social environments. What implications arise from these findings?

In the Interest of S. H. A.

728 S.W.2d 73 (Tex App. Ct., 1987)

Justice Scales delivered the opinion of the court.

Appellants, A. A. and A. S. ("the parents") appeal from the trial court's judgment terminating their parental rights to their son ("the child"). The suit was brought by appellee Dallas County Child Welfare Unit of the Texas Department of Human Resources ("Child Welfare"). Based on the jury's answers to special issues, the trial court entered judgment that: (1) each parent had engaged in conduct, or knowingly placed the child with persons who engaged in conduct, which endangered the physical or emotional well-being of the child, and (2) that termination of parental rights would be in the child's best interest. In six points of error, the parents attack the jury's findings, contending that the evidence is legally and factually insufficient. We overrule the parents' points of error and affirm the judgment of the trial court.

The record reflects that the parents are illegal aliens who came to the United States in 1981. The child, the parents' fourth, was born in the United States on February 12, 1982. The father has been employed, from time to time, working as a construction worker and as a dishwasher at a restaurant. The family's economic situation was characterized by several witnesses as "low-income." At the time of trial in March 1985, the parents had another child. The parents do not speak English, and they testified at trial through an interpreter.

The child's situation was first brought to the attention of Child Welfare in 1983, when the child was approximately sixteen months old. The child had been hospitalized in

May 1983 for an ear infection and anemia. The treating physician notified the public health department about the child's condition. Consequently, Barbara Brown, a public health nurse, visited the child's home on May 25, just after the child was released from the hospital. Brown testified that the child was filthy; that he was crying; and that he was eating cookies off of the dirty floor. Brown discussed the child's medication and the need to improve the child's hygiene with the mother. Brown stated that the mother "seemed disinterested in anything I had to say."

After the mother missed a doctor's appointment for the child, Brown made a second visit to the home on June 15. At that time, Brown testified, the child had "pus, very thick, white pus" coming out of his right ear, and he had a burn on his arm that was "pussy and oozing." Brown stated that the child's condition, if left untreated, could be dangerous to the child's health because of the risk of infection. Brown observed that the child appeared to be "very poorly cared for" and that the mother did not pick up the child when he was crying.

After the mother did not keep another appointment for the child at the public health clinic, Brown rescheduled the child's appointment for June 22. Brown performed nutritional, medical, and developmental tests on the child. The child was 28 inches in height and weighed sixteen pounds, eight ounces. This height and weight is below the thirtieth percentile for an average sixteen-month-old infant, and Brown testified that "that is a medical definition for failure to thrive." The statistics indicated that "the child was not growing as a normal child should." The mother told Brown that she fed the child about one-half gallon of milk each day; tortillas; soup once a week; eggs about four times a week; chicken once a week; occasionally fruits and cheese; and soup and beans. Brown stated that this was not a proper diet for an infant. Brown advised the mother that the child should be hospitalized immediately. Brown referred the family to a federally funded program that offers food to infants, and also made a referral to Child Welfare.

As a consequence of Brown's referral, Melba Martinez, an "in-take" worker for Child Welfare, visited the parents' home on June 23. Martinez testified that the child appeared very thin, very weak, and sluggish; his rib cage showed; he had a "protruding stomach or abdomen"; and his face "looked very sad." The older children appeared to be relatively healthy. The mother told Martinez that she fed the child twice a day, and that she fed him "sopas," a mixture of rice and pasta. Martinez expressed concern about the child's health to the mother, but the mother felt that the child was "just naturally thin, as one of her other children had been." Martinez testified that the mother "did not appear to understand that she needed to be concerned." As a result of the home visit, Martinez arranged for food to be provided to the family and to take the child to see a doctor. The next day, June 24, Martinez transported the mother and the child to Children's Medical Center.

The child was hospitalized on June 24 at Parkland Hospital for six days for treatment of the burn on his arm and an ear infection. Part of the diagnosis was that the child was a "failure to thrive" child, and Dr. Paul Prescott was called in as a consultant on the child's case. Dr. Prescott testified that failure to thrive "means a child is not living up to his own growth potential." He said that the "failure to thrive" syndrome is best explained as a "symptom," like a headache or backache; there are "five-hundred and some-odd causes of failure to thrive," including organic, nutritional, and "psychosocial" causes, such as where a mother has failed to nurture the child in some way.

Dr. Prescott stated that once failure to thrive is diagnosed, medical causes are ruled out first. Here, the child's failure to thrive was not due to medical reasons. Dr. Prescott testified that the cause of this child's failure to thrive was malnutrition. Dr. Prescott could not, however, positively exclude the possibility of emotional causes of the child's failure to thrive. The failure to thrive syndrome, in a child of this age, can have long-term effects, such as decreased intelligence, learning disabilities, permanently stunted growth, and increased risk of infection. Prescott testified that it is common for one child in a family of several children to suffer from failure to thrive. He stated that "if there is no medical reason, and it's malnutrition, that's actually more worrisome, because we then start calling it the maternal deprivation syndrome. Then you get into emotional deprivation. And for some reason, this one child is being scapegoated." Dr. Prescott testified that the maternal deprivation syndrome may be based on purely nutritional problems, but that only one child "is neglected, for who knows what reason."

Dr. Prescott stated that his diagnosis of malnutrition as the cause of this child's failure to thrive was in part based on the child's comparative weight gain over three time periods. During the child's May hospitalization, he gained about 1 1/2 to 1 3/4 ounces in weight each day. During the child's June hospital stay, he gained almost 3 ounces in weight each day. During the thirty-day period between hospital stays, the child gained an average of 1/4 ounce in weight per day while he was at home. An average child of this age gains about 1/2 ounce per day.

For this reason, Dr. Prescott recommended that the child be placed in foster care when he was discharged from the hospital on June 30. Dr. Prescott testified that he then believed the child's health was in danger.

The child was placed in a foster home upon discharge from the hospital. The foster parent, Molly Green, testified that when the child arrived at her home, he had existing bruises, "bite marks," and sores that looked like cigarette burns on his arm. Green stated that the child needed constant attention; that he became "hysterical" if the Greens were out of his sight; that he did not cry, but screamed, "piercing screams," until he was picked up by Green; and that he was a "tremendously emotional child." The child would not eat voluntarily, and Green testified that this was very unusual for a child of this age. Green stated that she had problems in getting the child to go to sleep, and that this, too, was unusual for a child of this age.

The child was removed from Green's home, after he sustained injuries to his head and face. Green stated that she discovered bruises on the child's chin and neck, and determined that the child was injuring himself in the baby bed by jumping up and down, hitting his head on the railing. Green later learned that the child had never before been in a baby bed. Martinez, the first Child Welfare caseworker, testified that the child was removed from Green's home because he needed constant attention in order to protect him from self-inflicted injuries. The child was placed in a home where he was the only child.

The child was placed in the Richmire home on July 9. Marlene Richmire testified that, in July 1983, the child was lethargic and depressed; he did not respond to pain; and he "didn't have the will to live" — "he was just like an inanimate object." The child would wake from sleep at night every thirty minutes, screaming. Richmire stated that it seemed "that he had repressed anger of something." The child did not want to eat; he was a "very picky" eater; and he occasionally hoarded food, putting it in a napkin and taking it to bed with him. Richmire testified that the child "progressed quickly" while in her care; he became more active, gained weight, and seemed "happy and more secure."

Richmire stated that, when the child was returned to her home after a visit with his parents, he was "really unmanageable." The child woke from sleep at night with "terrible anger." During those visits at which Richmire was present, there was nothing "done to the child" by the mother to cause sleepless nights, "unless it would be very little interaction, ignoring him."

Richmire stated that the child has inordinate fears of loud noises, such as sirens; bugs; and Mexican-American men. "Different times, when we've been out in public, . . . a Mexican-American man has approached him, just being nice and kind and trying to talk with him, and he screams." The child does not react in this manner to other men.

Mario Zuniga was assigned to this case in July 1983 as the permanent caseworker for Child Welfare. He testified at trial that his role was to help the family create a safe environment for the child, so that the child could be returned to the family. Zuniga first visited the parents' home after the child had been placed in foster care. Zuniga stated that the house was unsanitary and that he located a better apartment for the family near a day-care center. He arranged for and transported the mother and the other children to doctors' appointments. Zuniga obtained soap for the family; gave them a heater; provided diapers and formula for the baby, and some clothing and toys for the older children. Zuniga stated that the mother, with four small children at home excluding the child in issue, was "very overloaded" and "very, very depressed." Child Welfare arranged for the three older children to be placed in a nearby day-care center operated by Child Care Dallas. Zuniga testified that the older children in the family were being cared for, as far as Child Welfare was concerned, because they were receiving meals at day care.

From June 30 to December 4, 1983, the child remained in foster care. During this time, various workers from Child Welfare and Child Care Dallas worked with the family and offered support services to the family. The agencies arranged for the parents to attend parenting skills classes; the mother went to four out of the five classes, and the father attended one class.

On December 4, 1983, Child Welfare, in accordance with its goal of keeping the child with his natural parents if possible, returned the child to the parents' home. However, the child was removed and placed in foster care again on December 29. Zuniga testified that during this period he visited the parents' home and found the child outside, barefoot, and in dirty diapers, when it was "very cold" weather. Zuniga testified that the child was removed from the parents' home on December 29 after Zuniga found the child injured and the parents absent from the home.

Zuniga testified that he went to the parents' home on December 29 to take the mother and the new baby to a doctor's appointment, as had been pre-arranged with the mother. When he arrived, he found the family car was gone from the driveway, the parents were not there, and the child, with a "real deep gash over his eye," was lying on a bed. The child was "glassy-eyed" and did not respond to Zuniga when he walked into the room. The child had on a dirty diaper. A "young girl," apparently a baby-sitter, was at the home; Zuniga stated that she "appeared to be mentally retarded." The girl told Zuniga: "They want you to take [the child] to the hospital." Zuniga took the new baby to her doctor's appointment and then took the child to Parkland Hospital.

Zuniga's case notes state that the treating physician at Parkland told Zuniga that the injury had occurred at least one day earlier; that the parents should have immediately sought medical treatment; and that it was too late to put stitches in the cut. Zuniga had to hold the child down while the wound was cleaned because the child "became hysterical due to the pain." After medical treatment, Zuniga took the child to the foster parents' home.

The following day, Zuniga met with the mother and father at the Child Welfare Office. Zuniga testified that the father was "very angry" because "it was not that bad of an accident, [and] that we had no business going in there and taking the child out, and that these things happen all the time." Zuniga's report states: "The parents stated that they had not taken [the child] to the hospital since they were out looking for money to borrow to pay for the rent and that [the child] had sustained that injury jumping off a bed." The mother testified at trial that she and the father had gone to look for "money and transportation" to take the child to a doctor.

Also on December 30, the foster parent, Marlene Richmire, took the child to a general practice physician, Dr. Robert Fong. Fong's affidavit states that the child had a one-inch-long cut above his eye that had caused excessive swelling; multiple cuts, bruises, and contusions on his body; and a first-degree burn on his left hand. Fong testified that, in his opinion, the injury was due to "physical, you know, from some blow." Fong also stated, however, that he did not know with one-hundred-percent certainty exactly how the injury was caused. A photograph of the child's face shows the cut and the child's eye swollen shut. In his affidavit, Fong stated: "It is my opinion that [the child's] life could be in danger if he continues to live with his natural parents." Fong testified that he advised Richmire to treat the cut by applying ointments and ice.

Marlene Richmire, the foster parent, testified that after the child's three-week stay with his natural parents, "he had just regressed terribly." At first, the child was "lethargic." "He appeared to us to have lost the will to live again. He just sat and stared. He didn't respond." Once the child got past that, he became a discipline problem. Richmire stated: "He was self-destructive before, but he wasn't the discipline problem that he was when he came back." Richmire testified that the child was aggressive; that he would hit another child's head against the wall; and that he would spill food or rub it in his own hair. In December 1983, the child was approximately twenty-two months old.

Roxanne Purse, a supervisor for Child Welfare, testified that she was "very alarmed by the regression" of the child after his stay with his natural parents; "when he returned home he regressed so dramatically."

Georgette Speers, a Child Welfare caseworker, has been assigned to this case since June 1984, and she was on the case in March 1985, the time of trial. Speers arranged visits between the child and the natural parents and services to the parents and the other children. She testified that the visits where only the mother is present are "relatively quiet"; when the older siblings are present, however, the visit is "very stressful" for the child. During one visit, the child's older sisters were picking him up, and "they actually started to throw him across the room and throw things at him." Speers had to "extract" the child from the situation; the child was "terrified," and the mother could not control her daughters. Speers testified that she believes "very strongly" that the parental rights should be terminated, because if the child were returned home, he would "suffer profound regression." Speers recommended termination "because of the severely limited capacity of the parents to parent this child."

On January 3, 1984, Child Welfare filed its petition for temporary managing conservatorship over the child. The trial court ordered psychological evaluations of the parents and the child, and Dr. Nadine Palau performed the tests in May.

Dr. Palau testified that the intellectual assessment of the mother and the father indicated they are both in the mentally retarded range (I.Q. tested approximately 65), but this was probably an underestimate due to cultural differences, even though all tests were given in Spanish. Dr. Palau testified that the father's personality tests showed mental confusion; sensitivity to criticism; low frustration tolerance; and a possibility that he may "be given to episodes of explosive behavior," where he reacts "angrily and aggressively." Dr. Palau stated that her impression of the father during her clinical interview with him was that "he was trying hard to say the right things."

During her interview with the mother, Dr. Palau learned that the mother had been a "parental child" in her own family, assuming parenting duties for her siblings, because her mother had a "nervous condition." The mother told Dr. Palau that her mother had committed suicide by setting herself on fire, in front of the mother, about three years previously. The personality tests confirmed that the mother might have a "resistance to wanting to parent as an adult," a product of the parental child experience, and that the mother had difficulty in dealing with the trauma of her mother's death. The tests indicated a very intense anxiety that is internally repressed; a great deal of depression leading to difficulty carrying out every-day activities; and difficulty in being "emotionally available to her children." Dr. Palau testified that the mother had difficulty understanding the seriousness of the child's problems; she thought that the child was only thin.

Based on her observations of the child and his behavioral history, Dr. Palau concluded that the child conformed with battered child syndrome and failure to thrive syndrome. Dr. Palau stated that this child displayed emotional consequences of failure to thrive, such as "not wanting to live and self-destructing." Dr. Palau's written report stated that the child had "special needs for structure," and she explained that in an "unstructured environment, an environment in which he was neglected," the child "could become a very self-destructive child." Dr. Palau testified that "in families such as these, it could be that this one child is what is called the 'identified patient,' or the 'symptom bearer,'" and that this child is being scapegoated; "whether that is happening to other siblings or not does not necessarily mean that that child is safe in that relationship."

Dr. Palau stated that, as of the time she saw the parents and the child, she would not recommend returning the child to the natural parents. In regard to the family's limited financial resources, Dr. Palau stated that this was a factor in the family's problems in that "financial stress can affect family functioning." Dr. Palau testified that, while the parents may have the intellectual capacity to learn parenting skills, she was "not sure" that they would be able to "follow through" and put into practice what they learned.

Roxanne Purse, the Child Welfare supervisor on this case, was responsible for deciding whether Child Welfare should seek to terminate the parents' parental rights to the child. Purse testified that she decided, after the psychological tests were reported, that the parental rights should be terminated in this case. Child Welfare had been on the case for about nine months at that time. Purse testified that she was concerned "that in spite of all the efforts that had been expended, we seemed to be still at square one, in terms of [the parents'] ability to care for" the child. Purse stated that she strongly believes that the parents do not have the capacity to care for the child, and that the child "cannot survive in that family environment"—if the child were returned, he would "wither emotionally." Zuniga, the Child Welfare caseworker, testified that when he left the case in May 1984, the family still needed "24-hour family services." He stated that, with the various agencies' help, the mother's only responsibilities were to keep the new baby's doctor appointments and to keep the children clean, and that the mother "was not able to do so." He recommended termination of parental rights.

Mary Byrne, a volunteer for a court-appointed agency "Focus," gathered information on the case and also recommended termination. She testified that, in her opinion, if the child were returned, "I don't think he would make it."

At the time of trial in March 1985, the child was approximately three years old, and he was still in foster care at the Richmire home. Richmire testified that, at the time of trial, the child was affectionate, and he hugs and kisses her. She testified that she did not recommend that the child be returned to his natural parents, even if the testimony during the trial indicated that the parents have "the ability to parent" the child, because the child "has such emotional problems." She stated that the child is "emotionally handicapped." On cross-examination, Richmire stated: "No, sir, I have no degrees, but I have experience."

Dr. Carol Owen testified that she examined the child for his complaints about leg cramps on February 20, 1985, about two weeks before trial. She stated that the child was small for his age, three years, but that he was well-nourished, cheerful and affectionate. Dr. Owen did not find any problem with the child's legs, but she did find that one ear was infected. She stated that ear infections are common for small children and that there was not any pus draining out of the infected ear.

Several Child Care Dallas workers testified on behalf of the parents. They testified that the parents had made significant improvement in their "parenting skills" and that the child should be returned to the natural parents. Nancy Morales, a social worker for Child Care Dallas and manager of the day-care center, testified that the family's problems were largely economic; that the parents were capable of addressing the child's needs; and that "with the proper help, I think the family will do well and can do well." Morales stated that the family's problems were due, in part, to cultural differences. She explained that in Mexico, the "extended family is very important, and the care of the children, if the parents don't do one-hundred percent, there is always a grandmother or godmother or a neighbor, even, who can care for the child." When this family moved to the United States, "they were really isolated," and the responsibility of caring for the children fell totally on the mother.

Morales testified that Zuniga, the Child Welfare caseworker, had told her that Child Welfare would not return the child to the parents after the three-week period in December because the parents "did not make any attempt to seek medical care" for the child after he was hurt. Morales also testified that she had asked the mother why she didn't take the child to a doctor after he was injured in December 1983; the mother told Morales that she wanted to, but that the father told her no, because "the case worker was coming tomorrow, and he would take care of it."

Morales explained that failure to thrive is caused by malnutrition and that "another factor is dysfunctional relationship between the mother and infant."

Diane Banda, a social worker for Child Care Dallas, had been on this case since April of 1984. She testified that, with proper support services to the family, the child could be returned to his natural parents. She stated that Child Care Dallas could take care of the child during the day and offer services to the family. Banda did not recommend termination of parental rights.

Joan Weiser, the director of social work for Child Care Dallas, testified that there was not enough preparation for the child's return to the parents' home in December 1983. She also stated, however, that the parents had "progressed enough" for the child to return home at that time. Weiser said that Child Care Dallas had been providing support services to the family for about three-and-a-half months prior to December 1983.

Weiser did not recommend termination of parental rights. She testified that the child could enter the day home program offered by Child Care Dallas. Weiser commented that Child Care Dallas has "raised the children of many families" in Dallas and that they "raise other people's children that can't handle them."

Both of the parents testified at trial through an interpreter. The father stated that he would like the child returned "because before I was mean to him, not mean, but I did not have contact with him." He said that his relationship with the child "wasn't normal, because I did badly with him. My facts weren't right with the children." He stated: "Today I am different." The father testified that, while at his home, the child had never put food in his own hair or appeared fearful of Mexican men.

The mother testified that, at the time of trial, she was 25 years old, and she had six children. She stated that the only reason the child was removed from her care was because he had an ear infection and a burn on his arm. The mother said that they did not seek medical attention for the child when he hurt himself in December 1983 because it was at night and "we didn't have transportation."

The mother testified that if the child were returned to her, she would "feed him better food"; "take care of him"; feed him "three time a day"; "feed him on the hour"; and "take him outside to enjoy himself." She stated that she could care for the child "because now we have improved a lot." She said that she learned how to feed and care for the children at the parenting classes which she attended in November 1983, just before the child was returned to her home in December.

. . .

. . . [W]e believe the evidence in this case supports the jury's findings that the parents engaged in conduct which endangered the child's physical and emotional well-being.

The evidence in this case which supports the jury's findings reflects parental conduct which endangered the child's physical and emotional well-being. First, the parents did not give the child enough food or did not properly feed the child. There is little direct evidence as to what foods were fed to the child on a daily basis. The mother told one worker that she fed the child "sopas" twice a day; she told another worker that she regularly fed the child milk, tortillas, soup, and beans, and occasionally fed him soup, eggs, chicken, fruit, and cheese. There is, however, ample circumstantial evidence which shows that the parents did not provide the child with enough food or nutritionally adequate food, and circumstantial evidence may be sufficient to prove the grounds for termination under section.

Melba Martinez testified that, in June 1983, the child appeared very thin, weak, and sluggish and that his abdomen protruded and his rib cage showed. Dr. Prescott testified that the child gained significantly in body weight while in the hospital in May and June 1983, and that the child's weight gain between hospital visits, while in his parents' custody, averaged about one-half of that which the typical child of that age gains in weight per day. The child's failure to thrive syndrome was diagnosed after the child had been within the care and control of the parents. This is circumstantial evidence of the parents' conduct, namely failure to properly feed the child.

The record reflects that this conduct endangered both the physical and emotional well-being of the child. Dr. Prescott stated that the cause of this child's failure to thrive was malnutrition. The testimony at trial, we think, fully developed the seriousness of the failure to thrive syndrome and its physical and emotional ramifications.

In June 1983, the child was very thin, lethargic, and not of normal physical development for a sixteen-month-old child. The physical dangers of failure to thrive include increased susceptibility to infections as well as such long-term effects as learning disabilities, stunted growth, and decreased intelligence.

The parents' conduct which resulted in the child's failure to thrive also endangered the emotional well-being of the child. The testimony reflects that the failure to thrive disorder may have severe, permanent emotional consequences, and Dr. Palau, the psychologist, testified that this child displayed emotional problems consistent with failure to thrive syndrome. There is ample evidence in the record that this child has emotional problems, manifested in self-destructive tendencies, unusual aggressiveness towards other children, and behavioral problems. Marlene Richmire's testimony that the child occasionally hides food from the dinner table in his napkin and takes it to bed with him is strong evidence of an emotional problem which can be inferentially linked to the parents' conduct. Further, the testimony indicates that the child's physical and emotional health improved while he was in the custody of the foster parents in the late summer and fall of 1983; after his three-week stay with his parents in December, however, the child had "regressed dramatically."

Second, the parents engaged in conduct which endangered the physical well-being of the child in that they did not seek appropriate medical treatment for the child. The record is replete with testimony that the mother missed doctors' appointments for the child on several occasions. The public health nurse testified that when she visited the family on June 15, 1983, the child had "very thick, white pus" draining from one ear, and a burn on one arm that the nurse feared would become infected if left untreated. The burn on the child's arm had indeed become infected by June 24, when the child was hospitalized. There is evidence which reflects that early ear infections, if left untreated, could be dangerous to the child's health.

Moreover, after the child was injured in December 1983, the parents did not take the child to the doctor immediately after the injury or the next day. There is testimony from which the jury may have inferred that, instead of learning to take the child to the doctor when he was ill or injured, the parents had come to rely on the social workers to take care of the child's injuries.

Thus, we hold that there is some evidence to support the jury's findings . . . that the parents engaged in conduct which endangered the child's physical and emotional well-being. The record reflects that the parents did not properly feed the child and did not seek appropriate medical treatment for the child. This is conduct which, the evidence shows, endangered the child's physical and emotional well-being.

We next consider the evidence to the contrary, and whether the evidence as a whole is factually sufficient to support the jury's findings. . . .

First, the parents argue that the child's failure to thrive cannot be causally linked to any "conduct" on the part of the parents. They point to testimony by both foster parents that the child was a "picky eater" and would not eat voluntarily. In their brief, the parents argue that this evidence shows that "the problem was the child's eating habits" and that "it was inherent on the part of the child not to eat." Ms. Martinez, a Child Welfare worker, testified that the parents were not intentionally neglecting the child nor purposefully denying the child food. She stated that there was no "overt act or conduct" by the parents which caused the child to develop failure to thrive syndrome. Although this evidence conflicts with the jury's findings it was the jury's prerogative to weigh the conflicting evidence and to judge the credibility of the witnesses.

In addition, as we have stated, it is not necessary that the parent "knowingly or intentionally" engage in conduct in order to support a jury finding. . . . Moreover, there is circumstantial evidence, outlined above, which shows that the child developed failure to thrive symptoms while in the parents' care. The jurors, relying on their experience and common knowledge, were free to infer that a sixteen-month-old child could not feed himself and that the child's malnourished condition, therefore, was a result of the parents' conduct.

The parents also point to evidence that the child's various physical problems, other than the failure to thrive symptoms, were not attributable to the parents' conduct. Dr. Owen stated that ear infections are common for small children, and the child had an ear infection on February 20, 1985, at a time when he had been in foster care for over one-and-a-half years. There was testimony that the child's arm was burned when the mother, while holding the child, had a cooking accident, and that the injury to the child's face and eye, sustained during his three-week stay with his natural parents in December 1983, was accidental; the child hurt himself when he was playing and fell off the bed.

Molly Green, the first foster parent, testified that, while in her care, the child hurt himself by jumping up and down in the baby bed and by jumping out of the high chair. Zuniga, a Child Welfare caseworker, stated that the child was "energetic" and "accident-prone."

We agree that the overwhelming weight of the evidence reflects that the child's ear infections, burns, bruises, scrapes, and cuts were not inflicted upon the child by the parents and were not the result of mistreatment. Other than Dr. Fong, all the witnesses agreed that these problems were not the result of mistreatment. Georgette Speers, a Child Welfare caseworker, testified: "There is no evidence of active abuse" of the child. The evidence tending to show that the parents did not cause these problems is not, however, evidence tending to show that the parents appropriately cared for the child's injuries or sought professional medical treatment for the child when necessary.

The jury could distinguish between the injuries and common ailments of childhood on the one hand, and the parents' failure to appropriately care for the child's injuries after they occurred on the other; several witnesses also pointed out this distinction at trial. We conclude that the evidence showing that the parents did not cause these problems does not meet, and therefore does not rebut, the evidence reflecting that the parents endangered the physical well-being of the child by not seeking appropriate medical treatment for the child.

In summary, we hold that the evidence is sufficient to support the jury's findings that the parents engaged in conduct which endangered the child's physical and emotional well-being. The parents' first and fourth points of error are overruled.

...

... [T]he parents attack the jury's answers to special issues numbers three and six which find that it would be in the child's best interest to terminate the parental rights of each parent. The parents first contend that the trial court erred, as a matter of law, in entering judgment based on these findings because "any lack of ability [on the part of the parents] to provide a desirable degree of care [for the child] was due to [the parents'] lack of education, training, and misfortune." The parents also contend that there was insufficient evidence to support these findings. We disagree.

...

At the outset, we note that, although the parents' brief appears to treat it as such, "lack of education, training, or misfortune" is not an affirmative defense which, if properly pled and proved, would negate all evidence tending to show that termination is in the best interest of the child. Rather, the parents' lack of education, training, and misfortune is only one of several factors to be considered by the trier of fact in determining whether termination is in the child's best interest....

... [W]e consider only the evidence and inferences tending to support the jury's findings and disregard all evidence and inferences to the contrary.

The record reflects that Child Welfare and Child Care Dallas offered extensive services and training to the parents over a period of months which did not have a significant impact on the parents' ability to care for the child. The Child Welfare supervisor testified that in spite of all the efforts to assist the parents, "we seemed to be still at square one, in terms of [the parents'] ability" to care for the child. The Child Welfare caseworker testified that the family still needed "24-hour family services" in May 1984. A Child Care Dallas social worker testified that the parents did not seek medical treatment for the child after he was injured in December 1983 because they believed that the Child Welfare worker "would take care of it." Several witnesses testified that they believed the emotional needs of the child exceeded the parents' ability to care for and nurture the child; the foster parent stated that the child needs constant attention and a great deal of attention.

Dr. Palau stated that, as of the time she saw the parents and the child, she would not recommend returning the child to the natural parents. Dr. Palau further testified that, while the parents may have the intellectual capacity to learn parenting skills, she was "not sure" that they would be able to "follow through" and put into practice what they learned.

Roxanne Purse, the Child Welfare supervisor on the case, testified that the parental rights should be terminated in this case. Purse stated that she strongly believes that the parents do not have the capacity to care for the child, and that the child "cannot survive in that family environment" — if the child were returned, he would "wither emotionally."

Mary Byrne, a volunteer for a court-appointed agency, "Focus," gathered information on the case and also recommended termination. She testified that, in her opinion, if the child were returned, "I don't think he would make it."

Richmire, the foster parent, testified that she did not recommend that the child be returned to his natural parents because the child "has such emotional problems." She stated that the child is "emotionally handicapped." Child Welfare witnesses testified that the child would be put up for adoption if the parental rights were terminated and that the child would be "adoptable."

Dr. Prescott testified that there was a possibility of "maternal deprivation syndrome" in this family, where one of several children is being emotionally deprived and "scapegoated." The psychologist, Dr. Palau, echoed that the child may be the "symptom bearer" who is being used as a scapegoat. This testimony reflects the possibility of an emotional cause, other than lack of education, training, and misfortune, of the parents' conduct and the resulting failure to thrive symptoms displayed by the child.

Several Child Welfare caseworkers testified that they believed termination of parental rights would be in the child's best interest. Two physicians who examined the child testified that the child should not be returned to the parents because his health would be seriously jeopardized.

We conclude that the foregoing evidence is some evidence to support the jury's findings that termination as to each parent is in the best interest of the child....

...

The parents point to testimony in the record that tended to show that the parents' inability to care for the child was due to their ignorance and lack of training and education. It is undisputed that the parents are a "low-income" family; that the parents have low mental abilities; and that they are struggling to overcome the many cultural differences which confront them in the United States. The parents and several Child Care Dallas workers testified that the parents had improved their parenting skills and that the parents were capable of taking care of the child in the future. The parents testified that they had learned what kinds of food to feed the child and how to care for and nurture the child.

There was also testimony, however, which indicates that, even with the extensive support services offered to the family by Child Welfare and Child Care Dallas, the parents did not improve the quality of care for the child. The record shows that the child was returned to the parents in December 1983, after Child Welfare had been involved for three to four months. During December, the Child Welfare caseworker found the child in diapers outside the house in cold weather; the child was removed when he was found injured and the parents had not taken appropriate action in treating his injuries nor taken him to the doctor. This testimony indicates that the social programs to assist the parents in caring for the child were made available to the parents and that these programs were not capable of significantly affecting the parents' ability to care for the child.

In weighing the evidence, the jury was not required to find that the parent is "unfit" in order to find that termination is in the best interest of the child. Nor was the jury required to accept the truth or accuracy of the parents' explanations for past actions and statements as to future intentions. Here, there was ample evidence that Child Welfare offered extensive services designed to preserve the family unit and to avoid a termination suit. And, although the record reflects that the parents' inability to adequately care for the child was due in part to the parents' lack of education, training, and misfortune, there is sufficient evidence from which the jury could conclude that the child's problems were not due solely to these factors and could conclude that this was not an appropriate situation in which to leave the child with his parents, and that termination would be in the child's best interest.

We hold that the evidence was sufficient to support the jury findings that termination of parental rights would be in the best interest of the child....

Finally, we fully recognize that because fundamental constitutional rights are involved, severance of the parent–child relationship will survive constitutional scrutiny only if: the asserted governmental interest is compelling; a particularized showing is made that the state interest is promoted by terminating the relationship; it is impossible to achieve the goal through any less restrictive means; and procedural due process protections are met. Each of these requirements, however, has been satisfied in the present case.

First, the parents were represented by an attorney both at trial and on appeal and that a guardian ad litem was appointed to represent the child's interest. The parents were afforded a jury trial and they do not contend that they were in any way denied procedural due process. Accordingly, the question is whether the three remaining factors have been met.

The governmental interest at stake here is the protection of the physical and emotional safety and well-being of the child and the provision of a stable, permanent home for him. Clearly, protecting the lives, and promoting the stability of the lives, of its citizens are legitimate concerns of the government and are compelling interests.

Next, several witnesses testified that unless the child was removed from his parents' home, the child "wouldn't make it." Testimony of this nature satisfied the requirement that a particularized showing be made that protecting the life and well-being of the child would be promoted by termination.

Finally, it would be impossible to promote the goals of providing for the physical and emotional safety of the child and providing for a stable, permanent home for the child through a means less drastic than termination of the parents' rights. A permanent home for the child can be obtained only through adoption and the child cannot be adopted unless the parents' rights are terminated. The less drastic alternatives available to the state, such as day care or foster homes, cannot achieve the state's goal of providing a safe, stable, and permanent home for the child. To hold otherwise puts the state to a cruel choice: abolish all programs designed to temporarily assist families such as that in the present case so that no less drastic alternative is ever available, or, keep the temporary programs, thus ensuring that a less drastic alternative to termination is available but, in doing so, also ensuring that children such as the one in the present case will never obtain a safe, permanent home. We hold that the constitutional safeguards have been met.

The judgment of the trial court is affirmed.

Justice McClung, dissenting

...

The jury found that the parents had not knowingly placed or knowingly allowed the child to remain in conditions or surroundings which endangered the physical or emotional well being of the child. However, the jury found that the parents had engaged in conduct or knowingly placed the child with persons who engaged in conduct which endangered the physical or emotional well being of the child, and also found that termination was in the best interest of the child.

I conclude that the evidence is insufficient to support either of the affirmative findings....

Involuntary Termination

The evidence before the jury to support the State's contention that the parents engaged in conduct which endangered the physical or emotional well-being of the child was the following (1) the child was undernourished and (2) the parents did not immediately take the child to the hospital for treatment of a gash over his eye.

These parents have five children. The older three were examined and found not to be malnourished. These children are all in school and in day care provided by Child Welfare. Indeed, as pointed out by the majority, a social worker for Child Welfare testified that the other children were being adequately cared for because they were receiving meals at day care. Child Care Dallas, a United Way agency, offered to enroll this child in their special programs with his brothers and sisters but Child Welfare refused, opting instead to pursue termination of the parents' rights. The youngest child, born after the time that this child was removed from the home, is also adequately nourished. This is due to the parents' improved financial condition and parenting skills.

While in the parents' home, this child was fed a diet consisting primarily of dairy and cheese products as well as a dish called "sopas," described as "like rice, pastas, baked with spices." This diet was said to be nutritionally inadequate for the child both for the inadequacy of the portions and the lack of meat and vegetable items. The parents were getting free milk, dairy and cereal products from the "WIC" program. Consequently, the child's diet consisted heavily of milk and dairy products. The only form of assistance the family was receiving in the way of food was free milk, cheese and cereal. It naturally follows that the child's diet was heavy on milk and dairy products. As the parents were not receiving free meat and vegetable products, likewise, the child was not being fed a diet replete with meat and vegetables. The parents were not American citizens so the family was unable to get government assistance in the form of welfare benefits, food stamps and medical care paid for by the federal government.

The inadequacy of the meal portions was caused by the family's poverty. The lack of nutritionally balanced meals was also caused by poverty as well as the ignorance of the parents in the proper proportion of food groups to be fed to an infant of that age. The pediatrician that examined, tested, and followed the child's progress in the hospital stated conclusively that any failure of the child to meet his optimum growth potential was solely the result of malnutrition. Further, he excluded physical or emotional abuse by the parents and the home environment along some 500 other possible causes, stating, "In that particular child, it was 100-percent nutrition." In this regard, the record reflects that the other children were as thin as this child at his age. It is also interesting to note the child's nutritional state did not originally so concern Child Welfare that they thought termination was needed. Child Welfare originally returned the child to the home even after he was found to be undernourished. This child's nutritional woes were exacerbated by his eating habits. One foster parent testified that the child refused to eat during his stay with her family and that she, therefore, had to forcefeed him. This behavior was consistent with the parents' testimony of their difficulty in getting the child to eat.

As stated earlier, the child was malnourished because of the poverty and ignorance of the parents. Termination is not justified where the evidence shows that a parent's failure to provide a desirable degree of care and support of the child is due to lack of intelligence, training, or misfortune. The parents fall into this category by having the misfortune of possessing insufficient funds to purchase adequate food for their children. The majority's response is to summarily dismiss the statement in these cases as mere dicta. However, as even the majority concedes, the natural right existing between parent and child is of constitutional dimension. This natural parental right has been characterized by the United States Supreme Court as "essential," "a basic civil right" and "far more precious than property rights." This right is protected from infringement by the State in the due process and equal protection clauses of the Fourteenth Amendment as well as the Ninth Amendment. Therefore, the majority's holding that parental rights may be terminated because of a situation resulting from a parent's impoverished condition contravenes established constitutional law. This is so because it has been constantly held that it is impermissible to infringe upon fundamental constitutional rights on the basis of individual wealth. . . .

An examination of the only remaining basis on which termination was sought finds it to be lacking as well. The child was again removed from the home and termination proceedings brought when the child was discovered by a social worker to be suffering from a gash over his eye. The babysitter in the home at that time told the social worker that the parents wanted the social worker to take the child to the hospital. The parents testified that they did not take the child to the hospital because they were out looking for money to buy food and they knew that the social worker was coming by the next day and he could take the child to the doctor. The social worker further testified that the injury was an accident resulting from the active nature of the child, and that the parents had tried to reach him about the accident when it happened at 8:30 p.m. the evening before his scheduled visit but that he was unavailable. There was no evidence that this wound was life-threatening, or that the one-day delay was an impediment to treatment. Indeed, there was no evidence that this delay had any ill effects at all on the child.

It must be remembered that these parents are undocumented aliens from Mexico, unable to speak English. There was evidence that test scores show them to be mentally retarded. The parents are uneducated, ill-trained, and scared of deportation. The record shows that the social workers assigned to this family performed many tasks for them. The workers found them a place to live, brought food and appliances they needed, and generally tended to their needs. It would seem quite natural for these parents to grow dependent upon this individual. When this child needed medical attention the parents quite naturally looked to their "guardian and provider" for help. While these workers' substantial efforts to assist the family in whatever way possible are to be applauded and encouraged, it is cruel and unfair to allow these parents to become dependent on the Child Welfare Department and then have the department use acts of the parents caused by this dependency as a basis for terminating their parental rights.

. . . That is, the majority is holding that unknowing neglect of the child caused by ignorance and poverty is sufficient to support termination. This is . . . inconsistent with the accepted definitions of neglect used in the overwhelming majority of cases dealing with the parent–child relationship.

"Neglect" has been defined as a disregard of duty resulting from indifference or wilfulness. It has also been defined as "the intentional, deliberate and unjustifiable failure to perform a duty with which the parent is charged by law according to acceptable community standards."

"Neglected child" has been defined as a child who is abandoned or who lacks proper parental care by reason of the fault or habits of the parent.

"Child Neglect" has been defined as wilfully failing to provide proper and sufficient food, clothing, maintenance or a failure to do or permit any act necessary for a child's well being.

The common thread running through all of these definitions is the requirement of affirmative and deliberate action on the part of the parent. In other words, a culpable mental state is required before neglect can justify termination....

In our case the verdict establishes that the only neglect alleged or shown was committed unknowingly and the evidence shows that no aggressive conduct by the parents occurred. Therefore, we do not even need to reach the question of whether "aggressive conduct" must be directed at the child. I believe the majority is without legal foundation to support its holding that unknowing neglect can constitute the culpable neglect required to support termination....

... I would hold the evidence legally insufficient to support the affirmative finding regarding the conduct of the parents.

Best Interest

...

When making a determination of whether termination is in the best interest of the child, the fact finder may consider a number of factors, including, but not limited to: (A) the desires of the child; (B) the emotional and physical needs of the child now and in the future; (C) the emotional and physical danger to the child now and in the future; (D) the parental abilities of the individuals seeking custody; (E) the programs available to the individuals seeking custody; (F) the programs available to assist in promoting the best interest of the child; (G) the plans for the child by the individuals or agencies seeking custody; (H) the stability of the home or proposed placement; (I) the acts or omissions of the parent which may indicate that the existing parent–child relationship is not a proper one; and (J) any excuse for the acts or omissions of the parent.... [Applying these factors], it is apparent that it has not been shown by clear and convincing evidence that termination is in the best interest of the child. The child is too young to express his desires. The emotional and physical needs of the child now and in the future would best be served by staying with his natural parents, if possible. The evidence shows that the parents have worked hard to improve their parenting skills and can now more adequately care for the child. The emotional and physical danger to the child now and in the future is slight. There is no evidence that either parent ever physically abused the child. There is also no evidence that the parents knowingly emotionally abused the child. There is no evidence that the parents use drugs or intoxicants of any kind. There is no evidence that either parent uses profane, obscene, or objectionable language at home or in the presence of their children. Furthermore, the parents now have a greater realization that this child is a "special needs" child and are prepared to give him more attention. As to the cluster of factors dealing with the persons seeking custody, it is noteworthy that Child Welfare said that this child is "adoptable" and they are planning to place him with an American family. While it is true that this child was "Born in the U.S.A." his heritage and culture are Hispanic. To tear asunder the parent–child bond would also entail separating him from his brothers, sisters, grand-parents, etc. This would destroy the extended family bond that is especially important. It cannot be said that it is in this child's best interest to be torn apart from not only his parents but his other relatives that love him, and be placed with strangers.

There were and are programs available to assist in promoting the best interest of this child that did not encompass termination. A representative of Child Care Dallas testified that they could and would assist these parents in caring for this child and in seeing that he is fed and educated. Child Welfare had workers who were helping this family with the care of this child. Improvement was being made. There was no evidence improvement could not have continued to be made and the child protected without having to terminate these parents' rights.

Certainly it is true that the Family Code does not require the State to seek less drastic alternatives before filing suit for termination of parental rights. It is no doubt true that Child Welfare has a right to file suit for termination without seeking less drastic alternatives as indeed anyone can file suit against anyone else for whatever reason he or she chooses. I vehemently disagree, however, that a parent's rights can be terminated without a showing that less drastic means are unavailable....

There was testimony that Child Care Dallas was willing and able to assist this family in supplying the needed care for the child. Additional evidence was also introduced showing alternatives other than termination to protect this child....

...

Conclusion

It is undisputed that these parents are not "ideal." They are poverty-stricken, ignorant, uneducated, ill-trained in child-rearing and are of limited intelligence.

It is also apparent that the child has emotional problems and requires special attention. But surely the majority would not and is not advocating that the parental rights of all parents who have autistic children, hyperactive children, or children with any other handicap that requires special attention be terminated because the parents may be ill-equipped to handle these problems. These parents love their child very much, so much so that they willingly increased their risk of deportation in order to regain their son. The testimony at trial was sharply divided with one-half of the social workers who testified stating that they would not recommend termination. It is significant to note that the guardian ad litem appointed to protect the best interest of the child also refused to recommend termination. The social workers who did recommend termination did so because "The parents had limited parental ability," "the child needs special attention," "the parents are overwhelmed with too many other kids," and other reasons of equally questionable validity. These parents had made improvement and there were agencies willing to assist them so that additional improvement could be made. It is apparent that there was a period of crisis that occurred within this family at the period this child was removed from the home. The parents were in severe financial difficulty and were unprepared to parent a "special needs" child. Since that time they have worked hard to improve and have improved their parenting skills. Their financial condition has also improved. Consequently, their youngest child is not "failing to thrive" and their other children are doing well. There is no indication that this child would not also do well if he were returned to the home. Any rational examination of the facts could only lead to the conclusion that the State has not met their onerous burden of showing by clear and convincing evidence that ... termination is in the best interest of the child.

It is not the purpose of the Family Code of this state to prescribe just how often a child should be scrubbed, or exactly what diet should be slavishly adhered to and it by no means follows that a child's welfare is always necessarily promoted by removing him from a home of poverty and hard work, and transplanting him in another home of luxury and ease. Within the writer's knowledge, a generation of vigorous men and women have grown up under conditions that would not likely meet the approval of this majority.

...

For the multitude of reasons stated above, I dissent.

Justice Devay, dissenting. [omitted]

Notes and Queries

1. In considering an attack on the legal sufficiency of the evidence, the court only considers evidence and inferences that support the trial court's findings and will "disregard all evidence and inferences to the contrary." Appropriate standard? In considering an attack on the factual sufficiency of the evidence, the court considers all of the evidence to ascertain if the evidence is so weak that it could not produce a firm belief or conviction in the mind of the trier of facts that the challenged finding is true. Appropriate?

2. Are the parents to blame? Does it matter if they are? The court agrees that the overwhelming weight of the evidence reflects that the child's ear infections, burns, bruises, scrapes, and cuts were not inflicted upon the child by the parents and were not the result of mistreatment. So why remove the child from these parents?

3. Is this a case of cultural differences that deserve respect? In addition to cultural differences, the court notes that this is a low-income family with parents who have low mental abilities. Should that matter to findings of neglect?

4. Are you convinced that the child "wouldn't make it" if it were not removed from its parents?

5. Did the legal system properly follow the presumption that children are better off with their parents?

6. If the major concern is the child's nourishment and a local agency offers to provide services that have proven adequate for the other children, how would you justify removing the child from his home?
7. Did the majority opinion properly distinguish neglect from poverty?

Research Comments

1. Although most poor families may not neglect their children, numerous studies have linked poverty to an increased risk of child neglect. A number of stressing factors may explain the association: (1) unemployment, (2) single parenthood, (3) housing instability or frequent moves, (4) depleted or high-risk communities, (5) household crowding, (6) limited access to health care, and (7) exposure to environmental hazards such as lead paint or dangerous neighborhoods. See Howard Dubowitz (1999). The families of neglected children. In Michael E. Lamb (Ed.). *Parenting and Child Development in "Nontraditional" Families* (pp. 327–345). Mahwah, NJ: Lawrence Erlbaum. Importantly, the effects of poverty interact with community values. For example, for African Americans, poverty is much *less* linked to child maltreatment than for European American families. That is, poverty impacts African American rates of maltreatment less. Qualitative analyses reveal that neighborhood quality matters, especially factors relating to social connectedness and neighborhood support of children. One of the most interesting findings to emerge from this research is that the absence of middle-class neighbors has a negative effect on child health. Thus, having poor neighbors is not necessarily problematic so long as there are middle-class neighbors as well. Jill E. Korbin, Claudia J. Coulton, Sarah Chard, Candis Platt-Houston & Marilyn Su (1998). Impoverishment and child maltreatment in African American and European American neighborhoods. *Development and Psychopathology*, 10, 215–235.
2. Approximately one-third of the states provide room in their definitions of neglect for consideration of a family's financial means. U.S. Department of Health and Human Services (2000). *Child Abuse and Neglect State Statutes Elements: Reporting Laws, Number 1, Definitions of Child Abuse and Neglect.* Washington, DC: U.S. Department of Health and Human Services. These caveats usually address the family's access and response to available services that may help alleviate the neglectful conditions. For example, if a family living in poverty was not providing adequate food for their children, it may only be considered neglect if the parents were made aware of food assistance programs but did not use them. Does focusing on parents' use of available options seem appropriate? What about circumstances where there are few options? Is the child still neglected?
3. One of the major concerns about including poverty as a factor in defining neglect is that poverty tends to not involve absolutes. Most notably, poor families differ in terms of their resources, and there are many subgroups, such as the extreme poor

and the near poor. Likewise, the experience of poverty varies, from persistent to transitory poverty. The most problematic group is the persistently poor. Research generally concludes that poverty increases children's health risk. Most notably, less early intervention or access to health care leads to increased risk for accidents and illnesses, such as higher risk of ear infections, hearing loss, and asthma. Likewise, poverty relates to low birth weight, which increases health risks in childhood and contributes to higher levels of infant mortality. In addition, poverty contributes to strained parent–child relations, which increases the risk of maltreatment. Lawrence J. Aber, Neil G. Bennett, Dalton G. Conley & Jiali Li (1997). The effects of poverty on child health and development. *Annual Review of Public Health,* 18, 463–83.

4. In considering child maltreatment and poverty, several commentators now note that the legal system increasingly punishes poor parents, especially poor minority parents. Dorothy Roberts, most notably, argues that the criminal justice system is increasingly used to fight child maltreatment. She notes at least three ways the criminal justice system focuses on poor parents. First, it does so by not considering poverty as a mitigator for criminal offenses. She argues that although poor parents may be responsible, they may be less morally culpable if we understand their conditions. Doing so would allow the legal system, for example, to consider poverty-induced stress in determining sentencing. Second, crimes are detected differently because of parental poverty. She proposes that there is a bias in the reporting system, which makes poor parents already subject to heightened scrutiny. She proposes that the legal system would benefit from granting poor parents greater respect for their parental autonomy, that there should be less surveillance of poor people. Third, she proposes that some crimes are defined by parental poverty. Poor families are deemed problematic and held to a higher standard even though poverty is an exception to neglect. She provides important examples by noting that poverty increases risks for children and that parental responsibility laws to address delinquency differentially impact poor parents. Dorothy Roberts (2000). The ethics of punishing indigent parents. In William C. Heffernan & John Kleinig (Eds.). *From Social Justice to Criminal Justice: Poverty and the Administration of Criminal Law* (pp. 161–188). New York: Oxford University Press.

5. One critical issue in defining child neglect involves consideration of "incidents" of neglect versus a pattern of behavior that indicates neglect. By focusing on incidents, intervention would focus on incidents that are severe enough to warrant state intervention. Some recommend that some behaviors should present a "chronic pattern" to be considered neglectful. Examples include lack of supervision, inadequate hygiene, and failure to meet a child's educational needs. This suggests that rather than focusing on individual incidents that may or may not be classified as "neglectful," one should look at an accumulation of incidents that may together constitute neglect. In most CPS systems, however, the criteria for identifying neglect focuses on recent, discrete, and verifiable incidents. If CPS

focuses only on the immediate allegation before them and not the pattern reflected in multiple referrals, then many neglected children will continue to be inappropriately excluded from the CPS system. For example, a family exhibiting a pattern of behavior that may constitute neglect might include frequent reports of not having enough food in the home or keeping older children home from school to watch younger children. See Susan J. Zuravin (1991). Research definitions of child physical abuse and neglect: Current problems. In Raymond H. Starr & David A. Wolfe (Eds.). *The Effects of Child Abuse and Neglect* (pp. 100–128). New York: Guilford. Deborah English (1999). Evaluation and risk assessment of child neglect in public child protection services. In Howard Dubowitz (Ed.). *Neglected Children: Research, Practice and Policy* (pp. 191–210). Thousand Oaks, CA: Sage. It appears that families deemed chronically neglectful are similar yet different from those that would be deemed recently neglectful or their neglect is unconfirmed. All three family types are poor, and all three groups are poorer than their neighbors. But it appears that those deemed chronically neglectful support more people and that this group has more less educated parents and experience multiple problems as opposed to one major crisis. See Kristine E. Nelson, Edward J. Saunders & Miriam J. Landsman (1993). Chronic child neglect in perspective. *Social Work*, 38, 661–671.

6. The principal case discusses the concept of scapegoating, a process worth thinking about in the context of child maltreatment. Although the extent to which scapegoating occurs remains unknown, family systems therapists have explored and described how the process works. The scapegoating serves as a method of maintaining family coherence. The scapegoated individual in a family channels family tensions, which provide a basis of solidarity for the family. Most commonly assumed sources of tension tend to be those between adults, such as tensions due to different cultural or value orientations or due to different levels of self-esteem. In addition, it is believed that skewed families, where the couple relationship is characterized by one strong partner and one weak partner, and schismatic families, where the couple relationship is characterized by chronic hostility and mutual withdrawal, contain unresolved tensions that could lead to scapegoating. In addition, commentators have described the factors that determine who is selected as the scapegoat. Children typically are scapegoats because of their dependence and relative powerlessness in relation to their parents. The scapegoated child is chosen because of some characteristic that distinguishes him/her as being different from the family. These characteristics are significant as they relate to the real source of tension in the family. Other factors, such as the ordinal position of the child in the family or the sex of the child, also influence the choice of the scapegoat. Once a child is selected as the scapegoat, he/she is assigned the role of "problem child." The scapegoat becomes very sensitive to family tensions and acts out to reduce the tension and maintain homeostasis. Vimala Pillari (1991). *Scapegoating in Families: Intergenerational Patterns of Physical and Emotional Abuse*. New York: Brunner/Mazel.

Walker v. Superior Court

47 Cal. 3d 112; 763 P.2d 852 (Cal. Sup. Ct., 1988)

Judge Mosk delivered the opinion of the court.

We consider in this case whether a prosecution for involuntary manslaughter and felony child endangerment can be maintained against the mother of a child who died of meningitis after receiving treatment by prayer in lieu of medical attention. We conclude that the prosecution is permitted by statute as well as the free exercise and due process clauses of the state and federal Constitutions.

Defendant Laurie Grouard Walker is a member of the Church of Christ, Scientist (hereafter the Church). Her four-year-old daughter, Shauntay, fell ill with flu-like symptoms on February 21, 1984, and four days later developed a stiff neck. Consistent with the tenets of her religion, defendant chose to treat the child's illness with prayer rather than medical care. Defendant contacted an accredited Christian Science prayer practitioner who thereafter prayed for Shauntay and visited the child on two occasions. Defendant also engaged a Christian Science nurse who attended Shauntay on February 27 and again on March 6 and 8. Shauntay nevertheless lost weight, grew disoriented and irritable during the last week of her illness, and died on March 9 of acute purulent meningitis after a period of heavy and irregular breathing. During the 17 days she lay ill, the child received no medical treatment.

The People charged defendant with involuntary manslaughter and felony child endangerment based on allegations that her criminal negligence proximately caused Shauntay's death. Defendant moved to dismiss the prosecution on the grounds that (1) her conduct was specifically protected by law, and (2) the statutes under which she had been charged failed to provide fair notice that her conduct was criminal. The court denied her motion.

. . .

Defendant and amici curiae offer a variety of statutory and constitutional arguments in support of their claim that the prosecution of defendant under Penal Code section 192, subdivision (b) (hereafter section 192(b)), and section 273a, subdivision (1) (hereafter section 273a(1)), is barred as a matter of law. For the reasons set forth below, we reject their contentions and conclude that defendant can be prosecuted as charged.

I. Statutory Contentions

A. Section 270 as a complete defense to prosecution

Defendant first contends that the provisions of Penal Code section 270 (hereafter section 270) provide a complete defense to any prosecution based on her treatment of Shauntay's illness with prayer rather than medical care. Section 270 enumerates certain necessities that parents must furnish their children and imposes misdemeanor liability for the failure to do so. As enacted in 1872, the statute provided that "Every parent of any child who willfully omits, without lawful excuse, to perform any duty imposed upon him by law, to furnish necessary food, clothing, shelter, or medical attendance for such child, is guilty of a misdemeanor." The Legislature amended the provision in 1925 by inserting the phrase "or other remedial care" after "medical attendance." The statute was again amended in 1976 to specify that "treatment by spiritual means through prayer alone" constitutes "other remedial care."

1.

As a threshold consideration we must ascertain whether prayer treatment constitutes an acceptable substitute for medical care under the terms of section 270, as defendant contends. If it does not, then a fortiori the statute provides no defense to prosecutions under separate manslaughter and child endangerment provisions for the use of prayer in lieu of medicine. This determination hinges on whether "other remedial care," defined in section 270 to include prayer, represents an alternative to "medical attendance" or rather identifies a distinct and additional necessity that parents must provide their children.

. . .

Well-settled principles guide our review of the statutory analysis set forth in Arnold and embraced by the decision below. 'The fundamental rule of statutory construction is that the court should ascertain the intent of the Legislature so as to effectuate the purpose of the law.' In determining such intent, the court turns first to the words of the statute. '[Where] . . . the language is clear, there can be no room for interpretation.'

. . .

. . . It thus is apparent that the Legislature intended "other remedial care" to represent an alternative to medical attendance under the terms of section 270.

Any doubt regarding this interpretation cannot survive examination of the legislative history of the 1976 amendment defining "other remedial care" to include prayer. . . . We accordingly conclude that section 270 exempts parents who utilize prayer treatment from the statutory requirement to furnish medical care. . . .

2.

We next consider whether section 270 bars the prosecution of defendant under the manslaughter and child endangerment statutes. Again we turn to its plain language for initial guidance. Citing the statutory provision that "treatment by spiritual means through prayer alone . . . shall constitute 'other remedial care', as used in this section", the Court of Appeal concluded that section 270 expressly precludes any extension of its religious exemption to other statutes. This analysis confuses the statutory limitation on the definition of "other remedial care" with a limitation on possible defenses implied by that definition.

. . .

Defendant conversely asserts that the plain language of section 270 requires the extension of its religious exemption to her prosecution. She focuses on the reference in the statute to the provision of "necessary clothing, food, shelter or medical attendance, or other remedial care. . . ." Observing that "necessary" is defined, inter alia, as "absolutely required: essential, indispensable," she contends that there can be no circumstance involving the illness of a child in which the use of prayer in lieu of medicine is unlawful.

It is true that the statute recognizes "other remedial care" as an acceptable substitute for "medical attendance" when care is "necessary'; however, this conclusion does not address the question whether compliance with the terms of section 270 absolves defendant of liability under all other provisions of the Penal Code. "When used in a statute words must be construe in context, keeping in mind the nature and obvious purpose of the statute where they appear. . . ." Conduct that is legal in one statutory context thus may be actionable under separate statutes created for different legislative purposes. It follows that the legality of defendant's conduct under the terms of section 270 cannot be read to create a parallel exemption from prosecution under sections 192(b) and 273a(1) unless the statutes reflect some shared legislative objective.

"Rather than punishment of the neglectful parents, the principal statutory objectives [of section 270] are to secure support of the child and to protect the public from the burden of supporting a child who has a parent able to support him." The provision is 'designed to supplement civil statutes for effective enforcement of child support obligations." A parent thus may comply with the requirements of the statute simply by providing financial assistance to another individual with physical custody of the child. A parent who is financially incapable of furnishing support, without fault, is likewise excused from compliance. Indeed, the dispositional section of the statutory scheme explicitly contemplates protection of the fisc by stipulating that "If the children are receiving public assistance, all fines, penalties or forfeitures imposed and all funds collected from the defendant [for violations of section 270 or section 270a] shall be paid to the county department. Money so paid shall be applied first to support . . . and any balance remaining shall be applied to future needs, or be treated as reimbursement for past support furnished from public assistance funds."

. . .

We thus reaffirm our determination . . . that section 270 requires able parents to furnish certain routine necessities for their children so that the public need not unnecessarily assume that obligation. While certainly reflecting concern for the general welfare of children, the fiscal objectives of this support provision are so manifestly distinguishable from the specific purposes of the involuntary manslaughter and felony child-endangerment statutes — designed to protect citizens from immediate and grievous bodily harm — that section 270 cannot be read to create express exemptions from prosecution under those separate provisions as a matter of parallel construction. The Legislature has determined that the provision of prayer is sufficient to avert misdemeanor liability for neglecting one's financial responsibility to furnish routine child support. This hardly compels the conclusion that in so doing the Legislature intended to create an unqualified defense to felony manslaughter and child endangerment charges for those parents who continue to furnish prayer alone in the rare instance when a gravely ill child lies dying for want of medical attention.

In the absence of support from the plain language and purpose of section 270, defendant points to the legislative history of certain amendments to the statute as evidence of an intent to exempt prayer treatment from the reach of sections 192(b) and 273a(1). . . .

Defendant next contends that the 1976 amendment identifying prayer treatment as a form of "other remedial care" was similarly intended to shield Christian Scientists from manslaughter prosecutions. She observes that the amendment was sponsored by the Church in response to our dictum in Arnold, a case involving a misdemeanor-manslaughter prosecution. While legislative materials demonstrate that the amendment was indeed sponsored by the Church in response to Arnold, there is no evidence that the Legislature intended the modification to affect manslaughter, as opposed to misdemeanor, liability. . . .

The ineluctable conclusion we must draw from these materials is that the members of the Legislature were fully conscious of the potential liability remaining under sections 192(b) and 273a(1) for conduct they had legalized with respect to section 270, but simply chose to leave the matter unaddressed. Needless to say, considered silence is an insufficient basis to infer that the Legislature, by amending a misdemeanor support provision, actually exempted from felony liability all parents who offer prayer alone to a dying child. "The failure of the Legislature to change the law in a particular respect when the subject is generally before it and changes in other respects are made is indicative of an intent to leave the law as it stands in the aspects not amended." The plain language, purpose, and legislative history of section 270 thus fail to establish a discernible legislative intent to exempt prayer treatment, as a matter of law, from the reach of the manslaughter and felony child-endangerment statutes.

B. Expressions of legislative intent in related statutes

Defendant next contends that an intent to exempt prayer treatment from conduct within the reach of sections 192(b) 273a(1) is implied by a number of other civil and criminal measures relating to the provision of prayer in lieu of medical care to children. She first cites a plethora of statutes exempting prayer practitioners and their facilities from medical licensure requirements or variously accommodating individuals who choose to rely on such treatment for their own care. These accommodative provisions, however, evince no legislative sanction of prayer for the treatment of children in life-threatening circumstances.

More useful are statutes dealing with the definition of neglected or abused children for purposes of the state's child welfare services program, the activities of the Office of Child Abuse Prevention, and a criminal provision requiring certain individuals to report instances of suspected child abuse. Utilizing substantially similar language, each of these three statutes provides that children receiving treatment by prayer shall not "for that reason alone" be considered abused or neglected for its purposes.

Defendant cites these provisions as evidence that the Legislature does not consider prayer treatment to be a threat to the health of children, and thus that the imposition of criminal liability for the results of its use is inconsistent with legislative intent.

The Attorney General urges a different construction of the statutory language. He contends that the phrase "for that reason alone" denotes that a child receiving prayer treatment can still fall within the reach of the statutory definitions if the provision of such treatment, coupled with a grave medical condition, combine to pose a serious threat to the physical well-being of the child. While defendant contends the phrase merely indicates that a child receiving prayer treatment can come within the purview of the statutes for other reasons, her construction renders the use of the word, "alone" surplusage and thus must be rejected under the rule that "'[every] word, phrase and provision employed in a statute is intended to have meaning and to perform a useful function. . . .'"

. . .

Thus in any circumstance involving the threat of "serious physical harm or illness," the Legislature has empowered the juvenile court to intercede and assume custody for the express purpose of assuring medical care for a child whose parent is furnishing spiritual treatment by prayer alone. The expression of legislative intent is clear: when a child's health is seriously jeopardized, the right of a parent to rely exclusively on prayer must yield. This intent is implicit in the enumeration of necessities a parent must furnish to avert a dependency proceeding under W&I section 300; conspicuously absent from the list is any substitute for adequate medical treatment. It follows that the only tenable construction of the related provisions defining the relationship of prayer treatment to child neglect or abuse is the analysis offered by the Attorney General.

While dependency proceedings are civil rather than criminal, their relevance to our inquiry is plain. Parents possess a profound interest in the custody of their children. . . . Consistent with the gravity of the prerogative at stake, parents involved in W&I section 300 proceedings are assured notice and a due process hearing while those who are indigent receive appointed counsel. The Legislature's willingness to intrude on a parental interest of such magnitude to assure that children receiving prayer treatment are spared serious physical harm certainly evinces no contrary intent with respect to the application of the penal laws, which in significant respects constitute a less intrusive method of advancing the state's paramount interest in the protection of its children.

Defendant's argument by analogy to civil neglect and dependency provisions therefore corroborates rather than refutes our previous determination that the Legislature has created no exemption under sections 192(b) and 273a(1) for parents who are charged with having killed or endangered the lives of their seriously ill children by providing prayer alone in lieu of medical care. The legislative design appears consistent: prayer treatment will be accommodated as an acceptable means of attending to the needs of a child only insofar as serious physical harm or illness is not at risk.

When a child's life is placed in danger, we discern no intent to shield parents from the chastening prospect of felony liability.

C. Defendant's conduct and the standard for criminal culpability

Taking a wholly different tack, defendant next contends that she cannot be convicted under either the manslaughter or felony child-endangerment statutes regardless of the availability of a religious exemption. She rests this contention on a claim that the People will be unable to prove the degree of culpability necessary to convict her under either provision, both of which require criminal negligence in the commission of an offending act. We have defined criminal negligence as "'aggravated, culpable, gross, or reckless, that is, the conduct of the accused must be such a departure from what would be the conduct of an ordinarily prudent or careful man under the same circumstances as to be incompatible with a proper regard for human life, or, in other words, a disregard of human life or an indifference to consequences.... [Such negligence] is ordinarily to be determined pursuant to the general principles of negligence, the fundamental of which is knowledge, actual or imputed, that the act of the slayer tended to endanger life.'"

...

... [W]e must reject defendant's assertion that no reasonable jury could characterize her conduct as criminally negligent for purposes of sections 192(b) and 273a(1)....

...

In sum, we reject the proposition that the provision of prayer alone to a seriously ill child cannot constitute criminal negligence as a matter of law. Whether this defendant's particular conduct was sufficiently culpable to justify conviction of involuntary manslaughter and felony child endangerment remains a question in the exclusive province of the jury.

II. Constitutional Defenses

A. Free exercise under the First Amendment

In the absence of a statutory basis to bar defendant's prosecution, we necessarily reach her constitutional claims. Defendant and the Church first contend that her conduct is absolutely protected from criminal liability by the First Amendment to the United States Constitution and article I, section 4, of the California Constitution. We do not agree.

The First Amendment bars government from "prohibiting the free exercise" of religion. Although the clause absolutely protects religious belief, religiously motivated conduct "remains subject to regulation for the protection of society." To determine whether governmental regulation of religious conduct is violative of the First Amendment, the gravity of the state's interest must be balanced against the severity of the religious imposition. If the regulation is justified in view of the balanced interests at stake, the free exercise clause requires that the policy additionally represent the least restrictive alternative available to adequately advance the state's objectives.

Defendant does not dispute the gravity of the governmental interest involved in this case, as well she should not. Imposition of felony liability for endangering or killing an ill child by failing to provide medical care furthers an interest of unparalleled significance: the protection of the very lives of California's children, upon whose "healthy, well-rounded growth . . . into full maturity as citizens" our "democratic society rests, for its continuance. . . ." Balanced against this interest is a religious infringement of significant dimensions. Defendant unquestionably relied on prayer treatment as an article of genuine faith, the restriction of which would seriously impinge on the practice of her religion. We note, however, that resort to medicine does not constitute "sin" for a Christian Scientist, does not subject a church member to stigmatization, does not result in divine retribution, and, according to the Church's amicus curiae brief, is not a matter of church compulsion.

Regardless of the severity of the religious imposition, the governmental interest is plainly adequate to justify its restrictive effect. . . .

. . . As the court in Prince recognized, parents have no right to free exercise of religion at the price of a child's life, regardless of the prohibitive or compulsive nature of the governmental infringement. Furthermore, the United States Supreme Court has specifically sustained the compulsion of religiously prohibited conduct for interests no more compelling than here implicated. . . .

The imposition of felony liability for failure to seek medical care for a seriously ill child is thus justified by a compelling state interest. To survive a First Amendment challenge, however, the policy must also represent the least restrictive alternative available to the state. Defendant and the Church argue that civil dependency proceedings advance the governmental interest in a far less intrusive manner. This is not evident. First, we have already observed the profoundly intrusive nature of such proceedings; it is not clear that parents would prefer to lose custody of their children pursuant to a disruptive and invasive judicial inquiry than to face privately the prospect of criminal liability. Second, child dependency proceedings advance the governmental interest only when the state learns of a child's illness in time to take protective measures, which quite likely will be the exception rather than the rule: "Under ordinary circumstances, . . . the case of a true believer in faith healing will not even come to the attention of the authorities, unless and until someone dies." Finally, the imposition of criminal liability is reserved for the actual loss or endangerment of a child's life and thus is narrowly tailored to those instances when governmental intrusion is absolutely compelled.

We conclude that an adequately effective and less restrictive alternative is not available to further the state's compelling interest in assuring the provision of medical care to gravely ill children whose parents refuse such treatment on religious grounds. . . .

B. Due process right to fair notice of illegal conduct

Article I, section 7, of the California Constitution and the Fourteenth Amendment to the United States Constitution both assure that no person shall be deprived of "life, liberty, or property without due process of law." Among the implications of this constitutional command is that the state must give its citizenry fair notice of potentially criminal conduct. This requirement has two components: "due process requires a statute to be definite enough to provide (1) a standard of conduct for those whose activities are proscribed and (2) a standard for police enforcement and for ascertainment of guilt." Defendant contends that sections 192(b) and 273a(1), when read together with section 270, violate this constitutional dictate.

We initially observe that these statutes do not invite standardless law enforcement....

With respect to the remaining component of the due process analysis, defendant makes two arguments why the statutory scheme fails to provide fair notice. She first contends that sections 192(b) and 273a(1) provide no notice of the point at which lawful prayer treatment becomes unlawful, thus requiring her "at peril of life, liberty or property to speculate as to the meaning of penal statutes." ... The "matter of degree" that persons relying on prayer treatment must estimate rightly is the point at which their course of conduct becomes criminally negligent. In terms of notice, due process requires no more.

Defendant contends in conclusion that the statutory scheme violates her right to fair notice by allowing punishment under sections 192(b) and 273a(1) for the same conduct that is assertedly accommodated under section 270. She argues in essence that the statutes issue "inexplicably contradictory commands" and thus violate due process by precluding "an ordinary person [from] intelligently [choosing], in advance, what course it is lawful for him to pursue."

In considering whether a legislative proscription is sufficiently clear to satisfy the requirements of fair notice, "we look first to the language of the statute, then to its legislative history, and finally to California decisions construing the statutory language."

...

As we have discussed at length above, the purposes of the statutes here at issue are evidently distinguishable: sections 192(b) and 273a(1) protect against grievous and immediate physical harm while section 270 assures the routine provision of child support at parental expense. In light of these distinguishable objectives, it cannot be said that the legality of defendant's conduct under section 270 constitutes an "inexplicably contradictory command" with respect to the separate requirements of sections 192(b) and 273a(1). Indeed, the legislative history of section 270 specifically demonstrates the Legislature's unwillingness to extend the statute's religious exemption to the felony provisions. Sections 270, 192(b), and 273a(1) thus provided constitutionally sufficient notice to defendant that the provision of prayer alone to her daughter would be accommodated only insofar as the child was not threatened with serious physical harm or illness.

III. Disposition

We conclude that the prosecution of defendant for involuntary manslaughter and felony child endangerment violates neither statutory law nor the California or federal Constitution. The judgment of the Court of Appeal is affirmed.

Justice Broussard, concurring and dissenting. [omitted]

Notes and Queries

1. The court follows a *pari materia* analysis. This analysis reflects the rule that different statutes should be construed together only if they stand in *pari materia*. In theory, statutes are deemed to be in *pari materia* when they relate to the same person or thing, to the same class of person or things, or have the same purpose or object. Characterization of the object or purpose is more important than characterization of subject matter in determining whether different statutes are closely related enough to justify interpreting one in light of the other. The court notes that it has been held that where the same subject is treated in several acts having different objects the statutes are not in *pari materia*. "The adventitious occurrence of . . . similar subject matter, in laws enacted for wholly different ends will normally not justify applying the rule." Even if statutes stand in *pari materia*, "each retains its independence and a violation of one is not necessarily a violation of the other." Similarly, a defense to one is not necessarily a defense to the other. Is the application of this concept fair in this context?

2. The court notes that resorts to medicine do not constitute "sin" for Christian Scientists, do not subject church members to stigmatization, do not result in divine retribution, and are not a matter of church compulsion. Then how could the parent make her First Amendment claim?

3. Do spiritual exemption statutes misconstrue the doctrine of parental autonomy? Commentators find that spiritual treatment exemptions fail to protect children's interests and deprive them of equal protection of laws.

4. The religious exemption laws serve two main purposes. They help further ensure the free exercise of religion and guard against arbitrary intrusion upon the family by agents of the state. In addition, many other points support the need to respect parents' religious rights through religious exemptions: (1) the religious exemptions do not completely remove liability from parents who refuse necessary medical treatment based on their religious beliefs; (2) even with these religious exemptions, courts still have found parents criminally liable, and therefore, both the children and the parents are protected; (3) traditional medical treatment may be harmful and, in cases where the child still dies, the child (and the parent) is denied a spiritual life hereafter and will suffer eternal damnation; (4) exceptions respect spiritual life and do not place it above physical life; and (5) they respect

the parents' otherwise presumed ability to act in their child's best interests. See Jennifer Stanfield (2000). Faith healing and religious treatment exemptions to child-endangerment laws: Should parents be allowed to refuse necessary medical treatment for their children based on their religious beliefs? *Hamline Journal of Public Law and Policy*, 22, 45–86.

5. The major arguments against exemption laws proceed on constitutional grounds. Two arguments are illustrative. First, some argue that exemptions give preference to some religious groups while they hold others accountable, which violates the First Amendment's bar to the extent that it discriminates among religions by preferring recognized religions over those not recognized and because they necessarily engage the courts in an evaluation of the nature of the basic tenets of religious sects. See Ann MacLean Massie (1994). The religion clauses and parental health care decisionmaking for children: Suggestions for a new approach. *Hastings Constitutional Law Quarterly*, 21, 725–775. Second, some commentators present the creative argument that spiritual healing exemptions violate the Equal Protection Clause of the Fourteenth Amendment to the United States Constitution. By exempting parents who rely on spiritual healing from child welfare laws or criminal proscriptions, it is argued, state statutes inappropriately treat households that practice spiritual healing differently from other households. James G. Dwyer (1996). The children we abandon: Religious exemptions to child welfare and education laws as denials of equal protection to children of religious objectors. *North Carolina Law Review*, 74, 1321–1478.

Review Problem

1. Heather Verzi's labor suddenly seemed to stop. That abrupt change, which came as Spencer Verzi's legs and abdomen dangled from his mother's birth canal, was the first sign there might be a problem with the newborn's foot-first birth. When the child's foot first appeared about 3:46 p.m., Cryns, the midwife, said, she took no action because midwives believe births should proceed at a natural pace. She said she didn't detail for the Verzis what complications could occur or ask if they wanted to go to a hospital. "They made it clear they wanted to stay at home during a breech, unless there was a good reason not to," Cryns said. The midwife said the labor continued until Spencer's other leg appeared about 4:20 p.m., then his belly and umbilical cord appeared. But then the labor suddenly seemed to stall, she said. Heather wasn't able to quickly push the baby out as expected. Unable to locate the infant's heartbeat, the midwife then tried to extract the baby's upper body and head. When he was delivered about 4:31 p.m., she immediately began trying to resuscitate him. When she couldn't revive him after about twelve minutes she asked someone to call 911. Cryns testified she wasn't dissuaded from seeking help by a state order barring her from presiding over any births. "I kept thinking this baby was coming. I had this sensation the baby was going to be born," she said, adding that the

state order "didn't come into play at all." The midwife, who has presided over about 300 births, is accredited by a national midwives organization but is not licensed in Illinois. The state, which licenses only doctors and nurse-midwives to deliver babies, had ordered Cryns in April 2000 not to attend any more births. An autopsy concluded that Spencer, an 8-pound, 12-ounce, full-term baby, suffocated during the foot-first delivery. Two expert witnesses called earlier by prosecutors criticized Cryns's handling of the birth, including testifying that foot-first deliveries are high-risk procedures best done in hospitals. Prosecutors argued that the midwife failed to deliver the infant quickly enough after his feet appeared. They also charged that she waited too long to summon medical help after he was born. The midwife was charged with involuntary manslaughter. Should the parents be charged as well?

In re E. G.

133 Ill. 2d 98; 549 N.E.2d 322 (Ill. Sup. Ct., 1989).

Justice Ryan delivered the opinion of the court.

Appellee, E. G., a 17-year-old woman, contracted leukemia and needed blood transfusions in the treatment of the disease. E. G. and her mother, Rosie Denton, refused to consent to the transfusions, contending that acceptance of blood would violate personal religious convictions rooted in their membership in the Jehovah's Witness faith. Appellant, the State of Illinois, filed a neglect petition in juvenile court in the circuit court of Cook County. The trial court entered an order finding E. G. to be neglected, and appointed a guardian to consent to the transfusions on E. G.'s behalf.

The appellate court reversed the trial court in part. The court held that E. G. was a "mature minor," and therefore could refuse the blood transfusions through the exercise of her first amendment right to freely exercise her religion. Nevertheless, the court affirmed the finding of neglect against Denton.

We . . . now affirm the appellate court's decision in part, but on other grounds. We also remand this case to the trial court for the purpose of expunging the finding of neglect.

In February of 1987, E. G. was diagnosed as having acute nonlymphatic leukemia, a malignant disease of the white blood cells. When E. G. and her mother, Rosie Denton, were informed that treatment of the disease would involve blood transfusions, they refused to consent to this medical procedure on the basis of their religious beliefs. As Jehovah's Witnesses, both E. G. and her mother desired to observe their religion's prohibition against the "eating" of blood. Mrs. Denton did authorize any other treatment and signed a waiver absolving the medical providers of liability for failure to administer transfusions.

As a result of Denton's and E. G.'s refusal to assent to blood transfusions, the State filed a neglect petition in juvenile court. At the initial hearing on February 25, 1987, Dr. Stanley Yachnin testified that E. G. had approximately one-fifth to one-sixth the normal oxygen-carrying capacity of her blood and consequently was excessively fatigued and incoherent. He stated that without blood transfusions, E. G. would likely die within a month. Dr. Yachnin testified that the transfusions, along with chemotherapy, achieve remission of the disease in about 80% of all patients so afflicted. Continued treatment, according to Dr. Yachnin, would involve the utilization of drugs and more transfusions. The long-term prognosis is not optimistic, as the survival rate for patients such as E. G. is 20 to 25%.

Dr. Yachnin stated that he discussed the proposed course of treatment with E. G. He testified that E. G. was competent to understand the consequences of accepting or rejecting treatment, and he was impressed with her maturity and the sincerity of her beliefs. Dr. Yachnin's observations regarding E. G.'s competency were corroborated by the testimony of Jane McAtee, the associate general counsel for the University of Chicago Hospital. At the conclusion of this hearing, the trial judge entered an order appointing McAtee temporary guardian, and authorizing her to consent to transfusions on E. G.'s behalf.

On April 8, 1987, further hearings were held on this matter. E. G., having received several blood transfusions, was strong enough to take the stand. She testified that the decision to refuse blood transfusions was her own and that she fully understood the nature of her disease and the consequences of her decision. She indicated that her decision was not based on any wish to die, but instead was grounded in her religious convictions. E. G. further stated that when informed that she would undergo transfusions, she asked to be sedated prior to the administration of the blood. She testified that the court's decision upset her, and said: "[I]t seems as if everything that I wanted or believe in was just being disregarded."

Several other witnesses gave their opinions extolling E. G.'s maturity and the sincerity of her religious beliefs. One witness was Dr. Littner, a psychiatrist who has special expertise in evaluating the maturity and competency of minors. Based on interviews with E. G. and her family, Dr. Littner expressed his opinion that E. G. had the maturity level of an 18 to 21 year old. He further concluded that E. G. had the competency to make an informed decision to refuse the blood transfusions, even if this choice was fatal.

On May 18, 1987, the trial court ruled that E. G. was medically neglected, and appointed a guardian to consent to medical treatment. The court felt this was in E. G.'s best interests. The court did state, however, that E. G. was "a mature 17-year-old individual," that E. G. reached her decision on an independent basis, and that she was "fully aware that death [was] assured absent treatment." The court noted that it considered E. G.'s maturity and the religion of her and her parents, and that it gave great weight to the wishes of E. G. Nevertheless, the court felt that the State's interest in this case was greater than the interest E. G. and her mother had in refusing to consent to treatment. . . .

The paramount issue raised by this appeal is whether a minor like E. G. has a right to refuse medical treatment. In Illinois, an adult has a common law right to refuse medical treatment, even if it is of a life-sustaining nature. This court has also held that an adult may refuse life-saving blood transfusions on first amendment free exercise of religion grounds. An infant child, however, can be compelled to accept life-saving medical treatment over the objections of her parents. In the matter before us, E. G. was a minor, but one who was just months shy of her eighteenth birthday, and an individual that the record indicates was mature for her age. Although the age of majority in Illinois is 18, that age is not an impenetrable barrier that magically precludes a minor from possessing and exercising certain rights normally associated with adulthood. Numerous exceptions are found in this jurisdiction and others which treat minors as adults under specific circumstances.

In Illinois, our legislature enacted "An Act in relation to the performance of medical, dental or surgical procedures on and counseling for minors" which grants minors the legal capacity to consent to medical treatment in certain situations. For example, a minor 12 years or older may seek medical attention on her own if she believes she has venereal disease or is an alcoholic or drug addict. Similarly, an individual under 18 who is married or pregnant may validly consent to treatment. Thus, if E. G. would have been married she could have consented to or, presumably, refused treatment. Also, a minor 16 or older may be declared emancipated under the Emancipation of Mature Minors Act and thereby control his or her own health care decisions. These two acts, when read together in a complementary fashion, indicate that the legislature did not intend that there be an absolute 18-year-old age barrier prohibiting minors from consenting to medical treatment.

In an analogous area of law, no "bright line" age restriction of 18 exists either. Under the Juvenile Court Act, individuals much younger than 18 may be prosecuted under the Criminal Code, if circumstances dictate.... When a minor is mature enough to have the capacity to formulate criminal intent, both the common law and our Juvenile Court Act treat the minor as an adult.

Another area of the law where minors are treated as adults is constitutional law, including the constitutional right of abortion. The United States Supreme Court has adopted a mature minor doctrine, which allows women under the age of majority to undergo abortions without parental consent.... Moreover, children enjoy the protection of other constitutional rights, including the right of privacy, freedom of expression, freedom from unreasonable searches and seizures, and procedural due process. Nevertheless, the Supreme Court has not held that a constitutionally based right to refuse medical treatment exists, either for adults or minors. While we find the language from the cases cited above instructive, we do not feel, as the appellate court did, that an extension of the constitutional mature minor doctrine to the case at bar is "inevitable." These cases do show, however, that no "bright line" age restriction of 18 is tenable in restricting the rights of mature minors, whether the rights be based on constitutional or other grounds. Accordingly, we hold that in addition to these constitutionally based rights expressly delineated by the Supreme Court, mature minors may possess and exercise rights regarding medical care that are rooted in this State's common law.

The common law right to control one's health care was also the basis for the right of an incompetent patient to refuse life-sustaining treatment through a surrogate.... We see no reason why this right of dominion over one's own person should not extend to mature minors....

...

The trial judge must determine whether a minor is mature enough to make health care choices on her own. An exception to this, of course, is if the legislature has provided otherwise, as in the Consent by Minors to Medical Operations Act. We feel the intervention of a judge is appropriate for two reasons.

First, Illinois public policy values the sanctity of life. When a minor's health and life are at stake, this policy becomes a critical consideration. A minor may have a long and fruitful life ahead that an immature, foolish decision could jeopardize. Consequently, when the trial judge weighs the evidence in making a determination of whether a minor is mature enough to handle a health care decision, he must find proof of this maturity by clear and convincing evidence.

Second, the State has a parens patriae power to protect those incompetent to protect themselves. "[I]t is well-settled that the State as parens patriae has a special duty to protect minors and, if necessary, make vital decisions as to whether to submit a minor to necessary treatment where the condition is life threatening, as wrenching and distasteful as such actions may be." The State's parens patriae power pertaining to minors is strongest when the minor is immature and thus incompetent (lacking in capacity) to make these decisions on her own. The parens patriae authority fades, however, as the minor gets older and disappears upon her reaching adulthood. The State interest in protecting a mature minor in these situations will vary depending upon the nature of the medical treatment involved. Where the health care issues are potentially life threatening, the State's parens patriae interest is greater than if the health care matter is less consequential.

Therefore, the trial judge must weigh these two principles against the evidence he receives of a minor's maturity. If the evidence is clear and convincing that the minor is mature enough to appreciate the consequences of her actions, and that the minor is mature enough to exercise the judgment of an adult, then the mature minor doctrine affords her the common law right to consent to or refuse medical treatment. The right must be balanced against four State interests: (1) the preservation of life; (2) protecting the interests of third parties; (3) prevention of suicide; and (4) maintaining the ethical integrity of the medical profession. Of these four concerns, protecting the interests of third parties is clearly the most significant here. The principal third parties in these cases would be parents, guardians, adult siblings, and other relatives. If a parent or guardian opposes an unemancipated mature minor's refusal to consent to treatment for a life-threatening health problem, this opposition would weigh heavily against the minor's right to refuse. In this case, for example, had E. G. refused the transfusions against the wishes of her mother, then the court would have given serious consideration to her mother's desires.

Nevertheless, in this case both E. G. and her mother agreed that E. G. should turn down the blood transfusions. They based this refusal primarily on religious grounds, contending that the first amendment free exercise clause entitles a mature minor to decline medical care when it contravenes sincerely held religious beliefs. Because we find that a mature minor may exercise a common law right to consent to or refuse medical care, we decline to address the constitutional issue.

The final issue we must address is whether the finding of neglect entered against Rosie Denton, E. G.'s mother, should stand. If the trial judge had ruled that E. G. was a mature minor, then no finding of neglect would be proper. Although the trial judge was impressed with E. G.'s maturity and sincerity, the judge did not explicitly hold that E. G. was a mature minor. The trial judge, guided only by the law as it existed prior to this opinion, rightly felt that he must protect the minor's health and well-being. This case is one of first impression with this court. Therefore, the trial judge had no precedent upon which to base a mature minor finding. Because E. G. is no longer a minor, nothing would be gained by remanding this case back to the trial court for an explicit determination of E. G.'s maturity. Nevertheless, since the trial judge did not have any clear guidance on the mature minor doctrine, we believe that the finding of neglect should not stand. Accordingly, we affirm the appellate court in part and reverse in part, and remand this case to the circuit court of Cook County for the sole purpose of expunging the finding of neglect against Denton.

Appellate court affirmed in part and reversed in part; circuit court reversed; case remanded with directions.

Justice Ward, dissenting.

I must respectfully dissent. I consider the majority has made an unfortunate choice of situations to announce, in what it calls a case of first impression, that a minor may with judicial approval reject medical treatment, even if the minor's death will be a medically certain consequence. The majority cites decisions where a minor was permitted to exercise what was called a common law right to consent to medical treatment. The safeguarding of health and the preservation of life are obviously different conditions from one in which a minor will be held to have a common law right, as the majority puts it, to refuse medical treatment and sometimes in effect take his own life. That violates the ancient responsibility of the State as parens patriae to protect minors and to decide for them, as the majority describes, vital questions, including whether to consent to or refuse necessary medical treatment....

Unless the legislature for specific purposes provides for a different age, a minor is one who has not attained legal age. It is not disputed that E. G. has not attained legal age. It is a fundamental that where language is clear there is no need to seek to interpret or depart from the plain language and meaning and read into what is clear exceptions or limitations. The majority nevertheless would in effect define a minor in these grave situations to be one who has not attained legal age unless it is a "mature" minor who is involved. If so this protection that the law gives minors has been lost and the child may make his own decision even at the cost of his life. The majority acknowledges that this is a case of first impression. It may now be critically described by some as a holding without precedent. I point out again that this is not a holding where consent to treatment is the question but rather a unique one where a minor's injury or very self-destruction may be involved.

I am sure that in a host of matters of far lesser importance it would not be held that a minor however mature could satisfy a requirement of being of legal age. It would not be held that a minor was eligible to vote, to obtain a driver's or a pilot's license, or to enlist in one of the armed services before attaining enlistment age.

...

Justice Clark, also dissenting

...

Because I do not believe that any of the exceptions to the mootness doctrine are applicable here, I would dismiss this appeal as moot without addressing the merits of the parties' claims. I therefore respectfully dissent.

Notes and Queries

1. Under the court's holding, have mature and competent minors gained the right to reject life-sustaining treatment regardless of its effectiveness?
2. What factors would you consider appropriate, if any, in determining the competency of minors to reject life-saving treatment? Would the extent to which they and their parents agree matter? Would you prefer to put a minimal age limit, such as 15?

Review Problem

1. At 16, Chad and his mother discuss a case involving Joseph Gardner, 21, who was the stepgrandson of a close friend of Chad's grandmother. In Gardner's case, the court had held that "when an individual has clearly and convincingly in advance of treatment expressed his decision not to be maintained by life-sustaining procedures in a persistent vegetative state, health care professionals must respect that decision." Chad told his mother that he would not want to be left in a vegetative state. In late January 1989, Chad, with his older brother Scott, visited Joey Rollins, one of Scott's friends who was comatose in a hospital after a car accident. After briefly seeing Joey, Chad said, "I don't ever want to get like that.... I would want somebody to let me leave—to go in peace." Both of Chad's expressions were made in the context of serious discussions with family members about people Chad knew, whose plight he understood. Eight days after seeing Joey, on January 20, 1989, Chad, a normally mature high school senior then 17 1/3 years of age,

suffered "severe facial injuries and a permanent and totally disabling head injury" in an auto accident. He was taken to Central Maine Medical Center (CMMC) in Lewiston and hospitalized in intensive care. "Chad has never regained consciousness or any voluntary bodily function since the accident. He is totally incapable of feeding himself or ingesting food and drink by normal means. He is unable to chew or swallow voluntarily, making it necessary for him to be tube fed." "Although Chad is not brain dead he is in a persistent vegetative state with virtually no hope of improvement or of regaining any form of cognitive function. Any physical movement or eye tracking is non-purposeful and he has no appropriate reaction to specific stimuli." His parents and older brother decide to withdraw treatment. When Chad's body rejected the feeding tube, however, the hospital, in a departure from its neutral position, sought to maintain treatment. The hospital sought judicial relief. How should the court rule? See *In re Swan*, 569 A.2d 1202 (Me. 1990). The court found that the fact that Chad made these declarations as to medical treatment before he reached the age of 18 is at most a factor to be considered by the factfinder in assessing the seriousness and deliberativeness with which his declarations were made. The court reasoned that, in light of *Gardner* and after careful analysis of the specific facts of the case at bar, the Superior Court committed no error in refusing to order the reinsertion of a feeding tube in these circumstances in which the patient, a normally mature high school senior, had expressed well-formed desires as to medical treatment to his family, which now urges that those desires be respected.

Research Comments

1. A very careful review of cases involving children's right to refuse treatment for life-threatening conditions reported interesting findings. The cases were bimodal in distribution. Subjects were either under 2 years of age of above 13 years of age. Among the adolescents, many were in persistent vegetative states. The review found that the courts did consider children's wishes (as stated prior to the onset of their conditions and reported by family members). However, rulings were still made on the basis of the parents' wishes and children's wishes had not conflicted with those of their parents. Jennifer L. Evans (1995). Are children competent to make decisions about their own deaths? *Behavioral Sciences & the Law*, 13, 27–41.

2. Research addressing adolescents' decisional competence may be of assistance. Many researchers have concluded that the cognitive decision-making process of 14-year-olds is comparable to that of adults. The general contention is that the cognitive ability to compare information improves between the ages of 10 and 13. Much of this research has been done in the context of adolescents' rights to make medical decisions involving abortions. See Roger J. R. Levesque (2000). *Adolescents, Sex, and the Law: Preparing Adolescents for Responsible Citizenship.* Washington, DC: American Psychological Association.

3. Some argue that there is more to competent decision making than cognitive competence. Critics charge that a purely cognitive approach fails to include: (1) peer influence, (2) tendency to focus on immediate rather than long-term consequences, and (3) an inclination to make risky choices when evaluating adolescents' decision-making capabilities. See Elizabeth S. Scott, N. Dickon Reppucci & Jennifer L. Woolard (1995). Evaluating adolescent decision making in legal contexts. *Law & Human Behavior*, 19, 221–244. Researchers have expanded on this criticism and argued that, in addition to cognitive abilities, it would be appropriate to consider at least three psychosocial aspects of maturity of judgment: responsibility, temperance, and perspective. For several psychosocial dimensions of maturity that are likely to affect judgment, the existing evidence indicates that we are more likely to find differences between adults and adolescents and perhaps find more adolescents less mature/competent. See Laurence Steinberg & Elizabeth Cauffman (1996). Maturity of judgment in adolescence: Psychosocial factors in adolescent decision making. *Law & Human Behavior*, 20, 249–272.

4. Which approach makes most sense: one that focuses on minimal cognitive understanding or one that seeks to ensure that adolescents are making a decision in a "mature" manner? Are we asking more of adolescents than we are of adults? To complicate matters, the vast majority of research in this area does not study adolescents suffering from chronic illness and generally does not address the attendant psychosocial effects of severe illness. Compared to those who are healthy, chronic or seriously ill adolescents may feel more uncertainty about their future, have more doubts that they will ever be happy, and experience more psychosocial problems. These factors would seem to affect decision-making competencies given that they also would impact adolescents' normative developmental tasks. Most notably, such stresses could lower self-esteem and compromise their sense of personal identity. Does this mean that we should hold adolescents to higher standards?

Bowen v. American Hospital

476 U.S. 610; 106 S. Ct. 2101 (1986)

Justice Stevens announced the judgment of the Court and delivered an opinion, in which Justice Marshall, Justice Blackmun, and Justice Powell join.

This case presents the question whether certain regulations governing the provision of health care to handicapped infants are authorized by § 504 of the Rehabilitation Act of 1973. That section provides, in part:

> No otherwise qualified handicapped individual . . . shall, solely by reason of his handicap, be excluded from the participation in, be denied the benefits of, or be subjected to discrimination under any program or activity receiving Federal financial assistance.

[Note 1 defines "Handicapped individual" as "any person who (i) has a physical or mental impairment which substantially limits one or more of such person's major life activities, (ii) has a record of such an impairment, or (iii) is regarded as having such an impairment."]

I

The American Medical Association, the American Hospital Association, and several other respondents challenge the validity of Final Rules promulgated on January 12, 1984, by the Secretary of the Department of Health and Human Services. These Rules establish "Procedures relating to health care for handicapped infants," and in particular require the posting of informational notices, authorize expedited access to records and expedited compliance actions, and command state child protective services agencies to "prevent instances of unlawful medical neglect of handicapped infants."

Although the Final Rules comprise six parts, only the four mandatory components are challenged here. Subsection (b) is entitled "Posting of informational notice" and requires every "recipient health care provider that provides health care services to infants in programs or activities receiving Federal financial assistance"—a group to which we refer generically as "hospitals"—to post an informational notice in one of two approved forms. Both forms include a statement that § 504 prohibits discrimination on the basis of handicap, and indicate that because of this prohibition "nourishment and medically beneficial treatment (as determined with respect for reasonable medical judgments) should not be withheld from handicapped infants solely on the basis of their present or anticipated mental or physical impairments." The notice's statement of the legal requirement does not distinguish between medical care for which parental consent has been obtained and that for which it has not. The notice must identify the telephone number of the appropriate child protective services agency and, in addition, a toll-free number for the Department that is available 24 hours a day. Finally, the notice must state that the "identity of callers will be kept confidential" and that federal law prohibits retaliation "against any person who provides information about possible violations."

Subsection (c), which contains the second mandatory requirement, sets forth "Responsibilities of recipient state child protective services agencies." Subsection (c) does not mention § 504 (or any other federal statute) and does not even use the word "discriminate." It requires every designated agency to establish and maintain procedures to ensure that "the agency utilizes its full authority pursuant to state law to prevent instances of unlawful medical neglect of handicapped infants." Mandated procedures must include (1) "[a] requirement that health care providers report on a timely basis ... known or suspected instances of unlawful medical neglect of handicapped infants;" (2) a method by which the state agency can receive timely reports of such cases; (3) "immediate" review of those reports, including "on-site investigation," where appropriate; (4) protection of "medically neglected handicapped infants" including, where appropriate, legal action to secure "timely court [orders] to compel the provision of necessary nourishment and medical treatment;" and (5) "[timely] notification" to HHS of every report of "suspected unlawful medical neglect" of handicapped infants. The preamble to the Final Rules makes clear that this subsection applies "where a refusal to provide medically beneficial treatment is a result, not of decisions by a health care provider, but of decisions by parents."

The two remaining mandatory regulations authorize "[expedited] access to records" and "[expedited] action to effect compliance." Subsection (d) provides broadly for immediate access to patient records on a 24-hour basis, with or without parental consent, "when, in the judgment of the responsible Department official, immediate access is necessary to protect the life or health of a handicapped individual." Subsection (e) likewise dispenses with otherwise applicable requirements of notice to the hospital "when, in the judgment of the responsible Department official, immediate action to effect compliance is necessary to protect the life or health of a handicapped individual." The expedited compliance provision is intended to allow "the government [to] [seek] a temporary restraining order to sustain the life of a handicapped infant in imminent danger of death." Like the provision affording expedited access to records, it applies without regard to whether parental consent to treatment has been withheld or whether the matter has already been referred to a state child protective services agency.

II

The Final Rules represent the Secretary's ultimate response to an April 9, 1982, incident in which the parents of a Bloomington, Indiana, infant with Down's syndrome and other handicaps refused consent to surgery to remove an esophageal obstruction that prevented oral feeding. On April 10, the hospital initiated judicial proceedings to override the parents' decision, but an Indiana trial court, after holding a hearing the same evening, denied the requested relief. On April 12 the court asked the local Child Protection Committee to review its decision. After conducting its own hearing, the Committee found no reason to disagree with the court's ruling. The infant died six days after its birth.

Citing "heightened public concern" in the aftermath of the Bloomington Baby Doe incident, on May 18, 1982, the director of the Department's Office of Civil Rights, in response to a directive from the President, "[reminded]" health care providers receiving federal financial assistance that newborn infants with handicaps such as Down's syndrome were protected by § 504.

. . .

On April 6, 1983, respondents American Hospital Association et al. filed a complaint in the Federal District Court for the Southern District of New York seeking a declaration that the Interim Final Rule was invalid and an injunction against its enforcement. Little more than a week later, on April 14, in a similar challenge brought by the American Academy of Pediatrics and other medical institutions, the Federal District Court for the District of Columbia declared the Interim Final Rule "arbitrary and capricious and promulgated in violation of the Administrative Procedure Act." The District Judge in that case "[concluded] that haste and inexperience [had] resulted in agency action based on inadequate consideration" of several relevant concerns and, in the alternative, found that the Secretary had improperly failed to solicit public comment before issuing the Rule.

On July 5, 1983, the Department issued new "Proposed Rules" on which it invited comment. Like the Interim Final Rule, the Proposed Rules required hospitals to post informational notices in conspicuous places and authorized expedited access to records to be followed, if necessary, by expedited compliance action. In a departure from the Interim Final Rule, however, the Proposed Rules required federally assisted state child protective services agencies to utilize their "full authority pursuant to State law to prevent instances of medical neglect of handicapped infants." Mandated procedures mirrored those contained in the Final Rules described above. The preamble and appendix to the Proposed Rules did not acknowledge that hospitals and physicians lack authority to perform treatment to which parents have not given their consent.

After the period for notice and comment had passed, HHS, on December 30, 1983, promulgated the Final Rules and announced that they would take effect on February 13, 1984. On March 12 of that year respondents American Hospital Association et al. amended their complaint and respondents American Medical Association et al. filed suit to declare the new regulations invalid and to enjoin their enforcement. The actions were consolidated in the Federal District Court for the Southern District of New York, which awarded the requested relief on the authority of the decision of the United States Court of Appeals for the Second Circuit in *United States v. University Hospital.* On appeal, the parties agreed that the reasoning of the Court of Appeals in *University Hospital,* if valid, required a judgment against the Government in this case. In accordance with its earlier decision, the Court of Appeals summarily affirmed the District Court. Since the judgment here thus rests entirely on the reasoning of *University Hospital,* it is appropriate to examine that case now.

III

On October 11, 1983, after the Department's Interim Final Rule had been declared invalid but before it had promulgated the Final Rules challenged here, a child with multiple congenital defects known as "Baby Jane Doe" was born in Long Island, New York, and was promptly transferred to University Hospital for corrective surgery. After consulting with physicians and other advisers, the parents decided to forgo corrective surgery that was likely to prolong the child's life, but would not improve many of her handicapping conditions.

On October 16, 1983, an unrelated attorney named Washburn filed suit in the New York Supreme Court, seeking the appointment of a guardian ad litem for the infant who would direct the hospital to perform the corrective surgery. The trial court granted that relief on October 20, but was reversed the following day by the Appellate Division which found that the "concededly concerned and loving parents" had "chosen one course of appropriate medical treatment over another" and made an informed decision that was "in the best interest of the infant." On October 28, the New York Court of Appeals affirmed, but on the ground that the trial court should not have entertained a petition to initiate child neglect proceedings by a stranger who had not requested the aid of the responsible state agency.

While the state proceedings were in progress, on October 19, HHS received a complaint from a "private citizen" that Baby Jane Doe was being discriminatorily denied medically indicated treatment. HHS promptly referred this complaint to the New York State Child Protective Service. (The agency investigated the charge of medical neglect and soon thereafter concluded that there was no cause for state intervention.) In the meantime, before the State Child Protective Service could act, HHS on October 22, 1983, made repeated requests of the hospital to make its records available for inspection in order to determine whether the hospital was in compliance with § 504. The hospital refused the requests and advised HHS that the parents had not consented to a release of the records.

Subsequently, on November 2, 1983, the Government filed suit in Federal District Court invoking its general authority to enforce § 504.... The District Court allowed the parents to intervene as defendants, expedited the proceeding, and ruled against the Government.... Since the uncontradicted evidence established that the hospital "[had] at all times been willing to perform the surgical procedures in question, if only the parents ... would consent," the hospital "failed to perform the surgical procedures in question, not because Baby Jane Doe [was] handicapped, but because her parents [had] refused to consent."

The Court of Appeals affirmed.... It ... held that although Baby Jane Doe was a "handicapped individual," she was not "otherwise qualified" within the meaning of § 504 because "where medical treatment is at issue, it is typically the handicap itself that gives rise to, or at least contributes to the need for services"; as a result "the 'otherwise qualified' criterion of section 504 cannot be meaningfully applied to a medical treatment decision." ...

...

We granted certiorari, and we now affirm.

...

... Our recognition of Congress' need to vest administrative agencies with ample power to assist in the difficult task of governing a vast and complex industrial Nation carries with it the correlative responsibility of the agency to explain the rationale and factual basis for its decision, even though we show respect for the agency's judgment in both.

Before examining the Secretary's reasons for issuing the Final Rules, it is essential to understand the pre-existing state-law framework governing the provision of medical care to handicapped infants. In broad outline, state law vests decisional responsibility in the parents, in the first instance, subject to review in exceptional cases by the State acting as parens patriae. Prior to the regulatory activity culminating in the

Final Rules, the Federal Government was not a participant in the process of making treatment decisions for newborn infants. We presume that this general framework was familiar to Congress when it enacted § 504. It therefore provides an appropriate background for evaluating the Secretary's action in this case.

The Secretary has identified two possible categories of violations of § 504 as justifications for federal oversight of handicapped infant care. First, he contends that a hospital's refusal to furnish a handicapped infant with medically beneficial treatment "solely by reason of his handicap" constitutes unlawful discrimination. Second, he maintains that a hospital's failure to report cases of suspected medical neglect to a state child protective services agency may also violate the statute. We separately consider these two possible bases for the Final Rules.

VI

In the immediate aftermath of the Bloomington Baby Doe incident, the Secretary apparently proceeded on the assumption that a hospital's statutory duty to provide treatment to handicapped infants was unaffected by the absence of parental consent. He has since abandoned that view. Thus, the preamble to the Final Rules correctly states that when "a non-treatment decision, no matter how discriminatory, is made by parents, rather than by the hospital, section 504 does not mandate that the hospital unilaterally overrule the parental decision and provide treatment notwithstanding the lack of consent." A hospital's withholding of treatment when no parental consent has been given cannot violate § 504, for without the consent of the parents or a surrogate decisionmaker the infant is neither "otherwise qualified" for treatment nor has he been denied care "solely by reason of his handicap." Indeed, it would almost certainly be a tort as a matter of state law to operate on an infant without parental consent. This analysis makes clear that the Government's heavy reliance on the analogy to race-based refusals which violate § 601 of the Civil Rights Act is misplaced. If, pursuant to its normal practice, a hospital refused to operate on a black child whose parents had withheld their consent to treatment, the hospital's refusal would not be based on the race of the child even if it were assumed that the parents based their decision entirely on a mistaken assumption that the race of the child made the operation inappropriate.

Now that the Secretary has acknowledged that a hospital has no statutory treatment obligation in the absence of parental consent, it has become clear that the Final Rules are not needed to prevent hospitals from denying treatment to handicapped infants. The Solicitor General concedes that the administrative record contains no evidence that hospitals have ever refused treatment authorized either by the infant's parents or by a court order....

The Secretary's belated recognition of the effect of parental nonconsent is important, because the supposed need for federal monitoring of hospitals' treatment decisions rests entirely on instances in which parents have refused their consent. Thus, in the Bloomington, Indiana, case that precipitated the Secretary's enforcement efforts in this area, as well as in the University Hospital case that provided the basis for the summary affirmance in the case now before us, the hospital's failure to perform the treatment at issue rested on the lack of parental consent. The Secretary's own summaries of these cases establish beyond doubt that the respective hospitals did not withhold medical care on the basis of handicap and therefore did not violate § 504 [note 16 clarifies that they did not perform surgery because the parents refused to consent]; as a result, they provide no support for his claim that federal regulation is needed in order to forestall comparable cases in the future.

. . .

As a backstop to his manifestly incorrect perception that withholding of treatment in accordance with parental instructions necessitates federal regulation, the Secretary contends that a hospital's failure to report parents' refusals to consent to treatment violates § 504, and that past breaches of this kind justify federal oversight. By itself, § 504 imposes no duty to report instances of medical neglect — that undertaking derives from state-law reporting obligations or a hospital's own voluntary practice. Although a hospital's selective refusal to report medical neglect of handicapped infants might violate § 504, the Secretary has failed to point to any specific evidence that this has occurred. . . .

The particular reporting mechanism chosen by the Secretary — indeed the entire regulatory framework imposed on state child protective services agencies — departs from the nondiscrimination mandate of § 504 in a more fundamental way. The mandatory provisions of the Final Rules omit any direct requirement that hospitals make reports when parents refuse consent to recommended procedures. Instead, the Final Rules command state agencies to require such reports, regardless of the state agencies' own reporting requirements (or lack thereof). Far from merely preventing state agencies from remaining calculatedly indifferent to handicapped infants while they tend to the needs of the similarly situated nonhandicapped, the Final Rules command state agencies to utilize their "full authority" to "prevent instances of unlawful medical neglect of handicapped infants." The Rules effectively make medical neglect of handicapped newborns a state investigative priority, possibly forcing state agencies to shift scarce resources away from other enforcement activities — perhaps even from programs designed to protect handicapped children outside hospitals. The Rules also order state agencies to "[immediately]" review reports from hospitals, to conduct "on-site [investigations]," ibid., and to take legal action "to compel the provision of necessary nourishment and medical treatment," — all without any regard to the procedures followed by state agencies in handling complaints filed on behalf of nonhandicapped infants. . . .

. . . Section 504 is essentially concerned only with discrimination in the relative treatment of handicapped and nonhandicapped persons and does not confer any absolute right to receive particular services or benefits under federally assisted programs.

The Final Rules, however, impose just the sort of absolute obligation on state agencies that the Secretary had previously disavowed. The services state agencies are required to make available to handicapped infants are in no way tied to the level of services provided to similarly situated nonhandicapped infants. Instead, they constitute an "absolute right to receive particular services or benefits" under a federally assisted program. Even if a state agency were scrupulously impartial as between the protection it offered handicapped and nonhandicapped infants, it could still be denied federal funding for failing to carry out the Secretary's mission with sufficient zeal.

. . .

Section 504 authorizes any head of an Executive Branch agency—regardless of his agency's mission or expertise—to promulgate regulations prohibiting discrimination against the handicapped. As a result of this rulemaking authority, the Secretary of HHS has "substantial leeway to explore areas in which discrimination against the handicapped [poses] particularly significant problems and to devise regulations to prohibit such discrimination."

Even according the greatest respect to the Secretary's action, however, deference cannot fill the lack of an evidentiary foundation on which the Final Rules must rest. The Secretary's basis for federal intervention is perceived discrimination against handicapped infants in violation of § 504, and yet the Secretary has pointed to no evidence that such discrimination occurs. Neither the fact that regulators generally may rely on generic information in a particular field or comparable experience gained in other fields, nor the fact that regulations may be imposed for preventative or prophylactic reasons, can substitute for evidence supporting the Secretary's own chosen rationale. For the principle of agency accountability recited earlier means that "an agency's action must be upheld, if at all, on the basis articulated by the agency itself."

The need for a proper evidentiary basis for agency action is especially acute in this case because Congress has failed to indicate, either in the statute or in the legislative history, that it envisioned federal superintendence of treatment decisions traditionally entrusted to state governance.... The administrative record does not contain the reasoning and evidence that is necessary to sustain federal intervention into a historically state-administered decisional process that appears—for lack of any evidence to the contrary—to be functioning in full compliance with § 504.

The history of these regulations exposes the inappropriateness of the extraordinary deference—virtually a carte blanche—requested by the Government. The Secretary's present reading of § 504 has evolved only after previous, patently erroneous interpretations had been found wanting....

. . .

The administrative record demonstrates that the Secretary has asserted the authority to conduct on-site investigations, to inspect hospital records, and to participate in the decisional process in emergency cases in which there was no colorable basis for believing that a violation of § 504 had occurred or was about to occur. The District Court and the Court of Appeals correctly held that these investigative actions were not authorized by the statute and that the regulations which purport to authorize a continuation of them are invalid.

The judgment of the Court of Appeals is affirmed.

It is so ordered.

Chief Justice Burger concurs in the judgment.

Justice Rehnquist took no part in the consideration or decision of this case.

Justice White, with whom Justice Brennan joins and with whom Justice O'Connor joins as to Parts I, II, IV, and V, dissenting.

...

II

Section 504 of the Act, which was construed in *University Hospital*, provides:

> No otherwise qualified handicapped individual in the United States, as defined in section 706(7) of this title, shall, solely by reason of his handicap, be excluded from the participation in, be denied the benefits of, or be subjected to discrimination under any program or activity receiving Federal financial assistance.

...

Although infants with birth defects are clearly handicapped individuals covered by § 504, there is one manner in which they may differ from most other handicapped individuals for § 504 purposes. Specifically, they may have a combination of conditions—some of which are medically correctable and some of which are not. In older handicapped individuals, medically correctable conditions may have been corrected so that only irreparable handicapping conditions remain. In a newborn infant, however, both correctable and incorrectable conditions may exist. Thus, since both of these may interfere with major life activities, both types of conditions may be considered to be handicaps. In this context, however, it might make more sense to consider as handicaps only those conditions that cannot be medically treated to the point that they will not impair major life activities. For such correctable conditions would not be likely to cause the infant to be regarded as handicapped. In any case, I believe that defining an infant's handicap may well be a delicate problem and one that deserves some consideration.

It would appear that for an infant to be qualified for treatment his or her parents must have consented to such treatment. For the purposes of this discussion of whether the Court of Appeals was correct that medical treatment decisions may never be regulated by § 504, I assume that parental consent has been given and that the arguably discriminatory treatment decision is being made by the hospital or doctor. The Court of Appeals in *University Hospital* concentrated on the nature of these decisions in concluding that § 504 may not properly be applied, and I concentrate on that as well. That a situation in which treatment is refused where parental consent has been given may not have been shown to have arisen does not undermine this assumption here. The critical question is whether the operative provisions of § 504 may ever apply here given the nature of the decision.

...

Even under the Court of Appeals' interpretation of "otherwise qualified," however, it does not follow that § 504 may never apply to medical treatment decisions for the newborn. An esophageal obstruction, for example, would not be part and parcel of the handicap of a baby suffering from Down's syndrome, and the infant would benefit from and is thus otherwise qualified for having the obstruction removed in spite of the handicap. In this case, the treatment is completely unrelated to the baby's handicapping condition. If an otherwise normal child would be given the identical treatment, so should the handicapped child if discrimination on the basis of the handicap is to be avoided.

It would not be difficult to multiply examples like this. And even if it is true that in the great majority of cases the handicap itself will constitute the need for treatment, I doubt that this consideration or any other mentioned by the Court of Appeals justifies the wholesale conclusion that § 504 never applies to newborn infants with handicaps. That some or most failures to treat may not fall within § 504, that discerning which failures to treat are discriminatory may be difficult, and that applying § 504 in this area may intrude into the traditional functions of the State do not support the categorical conclusion that the section may never be applied to medical decisions about handicapped infants. And surely the absence in the legislative history of any consideration of handicapped newborns does not itself narrow the reach of the statutory language. Furthermore, the broad remedial purpose of the section would be undermined by excluding handicapped infants from its coverage; and if, as the plurality indicates, the Secretary has substantial leeway to explore areas in which discrimination against the handicapped poses serious problems and to devise regulations to prohibit the discrimination, it is appropriate to take note of the Secretary's present view that § 504 properly extends to the subject matter at issue here. Thus, I believe that the Court of Appeals in *University Hospital* incorrectly concluded that § 504 may never apply to medical treatment decisions concerning handicapped newborn infants. Where a decision regarding medical treatment for a handicapped newborn properly falls within the statutory provision, it should be subject to the constraints set forth in § 504. Consequently, I would reverse the judgment below.

III

Having determined that the stated basis for the Court of Appeals' holding in *University Hospital* was incorrect and that the decision below cannot be supported by *University Hospital*'s blanket prohibition, I would remand the case to the Court of Appeals....

...

First, the Secretary's proof that treatment is in fact being withheld from handicapped infants is unquestioned by the plurality. It is therefore obvious that whoever is making them, decisions to withhold treatment from such infants are in fact being made. This basic understanding is critical to the Secretary's further reasoning, and the discussion accompanying the proposed regulations clearly indicates that this was the

Secretary's starting point. Proceeding with this factual understanding, the next question is whether such withholding of treatment constitutes prohibited discrimination under § 504 in some or all situations. It is at this point that the plurality errs. . . .

The studies cited by the Secretary in support of the regulations and other literature concerning medical treatment in this area generally portray a decisionmaking process in which the parents and the doctors and often other concerned persons as well are involved — although the parental decision to consent or not is obviously the critical one. Thus, the parental consent decision does not occur in a vacuum. In fact, the doctors (directly) and the hospital (indirectly) in most cases participate in the formulation of the final parental decision and in many cases substantially influence that decision. Consequently, discrimination against a handicapped infant may assume guises other than the outright refusal to treat once parental consent has been given. Discrimination may occur when a doctor encourages or fails to discourage a parental decision to refuse consent to treatment for a handicapped child when the doctor would discourage or actually oppose a parental decision to refuse consent to the same treatment for a nonhandicapped child. Or discrimination may occur when a doctor makes a discriminatory treatment recommendation that the parents simply follow. Alternatively, discrimination may result from a hospital's explicit laissez-faire attitude about this type of discrimination on the part of doctors.

Contrary to the plurality's constrained view of the Secretary's justification for the regulations, the stated basis for those regulations reveals that the Secretary was cognizant of this more elusive discrimination. For example, the evidence cited most extensively by the Secretary in his initial proposal of these regulations was a study of attitudes of practicing and teaching pediatricians and pediatric surgeons This study indicated that a substantial number of these doctors (76.8% of pediatric surgeons and 49.5% of pediatricians) would "acquiesce in parents' decision to refuse consent for surgery in a newborn with intestinal atresia if the infant also had . . . Down's syndrome." It also indicated that a substantial minority (23.6% of pediatric surgeons and 13.2% of pediatricians) would in fact encourage parents to refuse consent to surgery in this situation and that only a small minority (3.4% of pediatric surgeons and 15.8% of pediatricians) would attempt to get a court order mandating surgery if the parents refused consent. In comparison, only a small minority (7.9% of pediatric surgeons and 2.6% of pediatricians) would acquiesce in parental refusal to treat intestinal atresia in an infant with no other anomaly. And a large majority (78.3% of pediatric surgeons and 88.4% of pediatricians) would try to get a court order directing surgery if parental consent were withheld for treatment of a treatable malignant tumor. The Secretary thus recognized that there was evidence that doctors would act differently in terms of attempts to affect or override parental decisions depending on whether the infant was handicapped.

Based on this evidence, the Secretary conceded that "[the] full extent of discriminatory and life-threatening practices toward handicapped infants is not yet known" but concluded "that for even a single infant to die due to lack of an adequate notice and complaint procedure is unacceptable." Thus, the Secretary promulgated the regulations at issue here....

I therefore perceive a rational connection between the facts found by the Secretary and the regulatory choice made....

...

Justice O'Connor, dissenting. [omitted]

Notes and Queries

1. Footnote 13 explained the basic pattern of medical decision making for children:

> The paucity of directly relevant cases makes characterization of the law in this area somewhat problematic, but certain points stand out. First, there is a presumption, strong but rebuttable, that parents are the appropriate decisionmakers for their infants. Traditional law concerning the family, buttressed by the emerging constitutional right of privacy, protects a substantial range of discretion for parents. Second, as persons unable to protect themselves, infants fall under the parens patriae power of the state. In the exercise of this authority, the state not only punishes parents whose conduct has amounted to abuse or neglect of their children but may also supervene parental decisions before they become operative to ensure that the choices made are not so detrimental to a child's interests as to amount to neglect and abuse.
>
> ... [As] long as parents choose from professionally accepted treatment options the choice is rarely reviewed in court and even less frequently supervened. The courts have exercised their authority to appoint a guardian for a child when the parents are not capable of participating in the decisionmaking or when they have made decisions that evidence substantial lack of concern for the child's interests. Although societal involvement usually occurs under the auspices of governmental instrumentalities—such as child welfare agencies and courts—the American legal system ordinarily relies upon the private initiative of individuals, rather than continuing governmental supervision, to bring the matter to the attention of legal authorities.

2. The Secretary of the Department of Human Health and Services undoubtedly faced an incredibly challenging task. Discrimination appeared at several levels: (1) by parents who opted not to proceed with medical intervention; (2) by CPS, which did not intervene in reported cases or did not actively enforce reporting statutes; (3) by state statutes and courts that allowed parents to withhold consent to treatment; and (4) by medical professionals who did not challenge parents, who

did not provide parents with appropriate information, and who failed to report. The Secretary focused on the last level. How could you use antidiscrimination laws to address the other levels?

3. Cases involving disabled infants continue to emerge as civil rights law address the rights of individuals with disabilities. *In re Baby "K,"* 16 F.3d 590 (4th Cir. 1994), aff'g and modifying *In re Baby "K,"* 832 F. Supp. 1022 (E.D. Va. 1993) addressed the question of whether the mother of an anencephalic child could insist on medical treatment that a hospital's physicians believed to be futile, and therefore inappropriate. After Baby "K" was born, she was diagnosed as anencephalic (lacking major portions of her brain, skull, and scalp, and as a result, permanently unconscious). Believing that she would soon die, hospital physicians recommended that Baby "K" be provided only comfort care (nutrition, hydration, and warmth), but urged that she not be placed on a respirator if she began to experience difficulty in breathing, which was a normal outgrowth of her anencephalic condition. Baby "K"'s mother rejected the physicians' proposal, and refused to agree to a "Do Not Resuscitate Order." Instead, she insisted that Baby "K" receive mechanical respiratory support when necessary. As the hospital sought, and was unable, to find another hospital with a pediatric intensive care unit, Baby "K" progressed to the point that she no longer needed acute hospital care and was moved to a nursing home. Thereafter, she occasionally suffered severe respiratory distress and would be brought to the original hospital's emergency room, where her mother would request respiratory support to stabilize her breathing, which was provided under protest. The hospital brought suit seeking a declaratory judgment that it was not obligated to provide treatment that it believed to be futile and therefore ethically inappropriate. The district court ruled in favor of the mother and the Fourth Circuit Court of Appeals affirmed by relying on the Emergency Medical Treatment and Active Labor Act (EMTALA). The court found that EMTALA preempted all state law to the contrary, including medical malpractice and professional ethics laws. Under this view, the extent to which parents can demand, and get, treatment may well depend on the extent to which infants receive treatment in the emergency room. Note too that parents' rights may also be overruled to the extent that the law mandates treatment to all who present themselves at hospital emergency rooms. What do you make of these developments?

Research Comments

1. Over the past decades, the medical and legal systems have witnessed a remarkable evolution in attitudes and practice toward the treatment of children with disabilities. Infants born with severe physical and mental anomalies are no longer routinely allowed to die. Many receive aggressive life-saving medical treatment as well as continuing medical and habilitative care. Even though the approaches to treatment of disabled children have changed significantly during the last quarter

century, the fundamental legal, ethical, and resource allocation issues remain constant. Issues essentially arise in two contexts: Acute care and habilitative care. In the acute care context, which includes urgent and emergent care, the paradigmatic cases involve severely disabled newborns. In these cases, analyses necessarily focus on parents' capacity and power to make appropriate health care decisions for their children, when their authority to do so has been challenged by physicians, hospitals, or the government. Similar issues arise when children become candidates for aggressive medical care, and their parents do not want to pursue it. The habilitative care context involves access to continuing medical and supportive services. These cases involve gaining access to medical and other services in order to maximize a child's opportunities for effective functioning. Disputes in this area usually raise two types of concerns: (1) whether services are related to a medical condition and thus are medically necessary, and (2) whether a child's disabilities are sufficiently severe to meet government criteria for financial assistance. The acute care context involves the most relevant issues to child maltreatment as it illustrates the allocation of the responsibility and authority among the medical profession, the state, and parents involved in medical care decision making.

2. In its own response to the "Baby Doe" cases, Congress sought to provide the authority for federal involvement in medical decision making for seriously ill newborns, which was alleged to be lacking in § 504 of the Rehabilitation Act. Under the most resent amendments to the *Child Abuse Prevention and Treatment Act* (CAPTA), Pub. L. No. 93-247, 88 Stat. 4 (1974), codified as amended at 42 U.S.C. 5101–5120 (West Supp. 2001), medical neglect is approached as "withholding of medically indicated treatment" to mean "the failure to respond to the infant's life-threatening conditions by providing treatment (including appropriate nutrition, hydration, and medication) which, in the treating physician's or physicians' reasonable medical judgment, will be most likely to be effective in ameliorating or correcting all such conditions, except that the term does not include failure to provide treatment (other than appropriate nutrition, hydration, or medication) to an infant when, in the treating physician's or physicians' reasonable medical judgment—

    (A) the infant is chronically and irreversibly comatose;

    (B) the provision of such services would—

    (i) merely prolong dying;

    (ii) not be effective in ameliorating or correcting all of the infant's life threatening conditions; or

    (iii) otherwise be futile in the survival of the infant; or

    (C) the provision of such treatment would be virtually futile in terms of the survival of the infant and the treatment itself under such circumstances would be inhumane. Id. § 5106g(6).

Ambiguity still remains, such as in the inherent ambiguity and subjectivity in such terms as "merely prolong dying," "futile," and "inhumane." Yet the new rules have had a significant impact on the practice of medicine in hospital delivery rooms and neonatal intensive care units. Studies have indicated that the new legislation has made physicians and other health care professionals much more aggressive in their treatment of extremely premature, low birth weight infants, or other infants born with severe and multiple anomalies. See Loretta M. Kopelman, Thomas G. Irons & Arthur E. Kopelman (1988). Neonatologists judge the "Baby Doe" regulations. *New England Journal of Medicine*, 318, 677–683; Jeffrey J. Pomerance, Teresita C. Yu & Sharyn J. Brown (1988). Changing attitudes of neonatologists toward ventilator support. *Journal of Perinatology*, 8, 232–241. How do you think it has done so? Has the new legislation limited physician autonomy and authority to make medical treatment decisions for seriously ill newborns, and indirectly constrain parental autonomy and authority as well, by limiting the options that physicians can provide to parents in discussing their child's condition and prognosis?

3. The Supreme Court reviewed the history of the "Baby Doe" regulations and found no evidence that hospitals were discriminating against disabled newborns by withholding treatment, because whenever treatment was not provided, it was because the parents had not consented. The Court concluded that there was no basis for the Secretary of Health and Human Services' decision to invoke § 504's prohibition against federally funded facilities discriminating on the basis of handicap. Instead, the Court found that state child abuse agencies were providing ample protection against the medical neglect of disabled newborns and had intervened to seek judicial authorization of medical treatment when necessary. Given the Court's rationale and ultimate holding, does *Bowen* vindicate the authority and autonomy of physicians or of parents? The Court did affirm the ability of parents to decide what was appropriate medical care for their children, so long as the parents had consulted with medical professionals, and had gained some medical support for their decision. As such, *Bowen*'s invalidation of the "Baby Doe" regulations in their entirety can be seen as affirming parental autonomy and authority. The decision also upholds the authority of physicians and other health care providers to guide parents through difficult health care decisions, free from outside interference. The government was permitted to intervene only in extreme cases of medical neglect and child abuse (where, presumably, physicians disagreed with parents about the appropriate treatment approach), and then it was the state, not federal government, that was deemed to have authority to second guess the parents' decision. At another level, however, the apparent recognition of parental autonomy and authority may be illusory. In reality, parents' choices are affirmed only when the doctors agree with the parents. Where the physicians believed that treatment should be given, the parents' authority can be overruled, ignored, or reported to state child abuse authorities, as noted in *Bowen*. This lends support to the view that *Bowen* vindicated physician, not parental, autonomy and authority.

Review Problems

1. Jack, the 60-year-old grandfather of 2-month-old Susan, has been awarded her custody. On the way home from court, they are involved in a car accident. Little Susan, who was not secured in a car seat, dies from massive trauma. Is this a case of criminal child neglect?

2. Alex, a 6-month-old boy, is found dead. The medical examiner finds no anatomical cause of death and determines that Alex died of Sudden Infant Death Syndrome. After the report is filed, a neighbor reports that he was there when the mother discovered the dead boy. He also reports that he saw the mother remove roaches from the child's mouth and trying to flush them down the toilet. It was obvious, according to the reporter, that the plumbing was not working. He also reports that he saw the mother turn on the heat in the apartment, which had been turned off for days because she had arranged with the landlord to have a rent discount if she did not incur heating expenses. Jennifer, a social worker, investigates the report and finds that the mother has two other children who are 2 and 4 years old. Should the mother be deemed neglectful of Alex? Is she neglecting his living brothers?

3. Bob, a 33-year-old single-father of three, fears walking home from his night shift. Because he does not want to get killed and have his children raised by strangers, he carries a loaded gun. One day, exhausted after a double shift, he forgets to not leave his coat on the sofa and inadvertently leaves the gun in his coat pocket. At 6:00 a.m. he is awaken by a gunshot. His 6-year-old had found the gun and killed his 4-year-old brother. Neglect? Assume that he is in a state that has not passed "gun access" laws making Bob's actions a criminal offense because his gun was not properly secured out of children's reach.

4. Judy has been smoking since she was a teenager. She has tried, but failed, repeatedly to quit. She has been told repeatedly, by her 3-year-old daughter's physician, that she must quit because it worsens her daughter's asthma. The girl dies from a severe asthma attack. Neglect?

5. Assume that all the above situations did not involve harm to the children. Are the caretakers' actions still neglectful?

Chapter 6
Sexual Maltreatment

Child sexual maltreatment provides some of the most controversial topics in the study of child maltreatment. Much of the controversy arises from what some view as the "secret ecology" of this form of maltreatment. This secrecy results from the manner in which the nature of sexual maltreatment reduces the likelihood of victim disclosure and leads to a wide variety of outcomes. Not surprisingly, these factors make recognizing and responding to victimization highly problematic. As with other forms of maltreatment, the behaviors and situations that constitute sexual maltreatment range from those that might be considered abusive in some situations to those that are always considered abusive. A guiding concern and controversy involves how and whether the encounter traumatically impacts children and the extent to which the legal system addresses the actual harm, possibility of harm, or assumed harm. Although these controversies ensure that available statistics estimating the prevalence and incidence of sexual maltreatment do not completely reflect the extent of the problem, estimates do provide useful starting points. Estimates come from three main sources: (1) research asking adults to recount their experiences of sexual victimization as children, (2) annual summaries of the accumulated reports of sexual maltreatment filed with child protection agencies, and (3) the National Incidence Studies.

Prevalence studies, those that examine the extent to which adults experienced sexual victimization during their childhoods, reveal a wide range of estimates. Rates of victimization for females range from 6 to 62 percent, with many professionals estimating that between one in three and one in four women are sexually maltreated in some manner during their childhoods. The rates for men are quite lower, ranging from 3 to 24 percent, with many professionals believing that one in ten men and perhaps as many as one in six are sexually maltreated as children. See Roger J. R. Levesque (1999). *Child Sexual Abuse: A Human Rights Perspective*. Bloomington, IN: Indiana University Press. Several reasons help explain the vast inconsistencies in findings. First, data are gathered using a variety of methodologies, such as telephone interviews, face-to-face interviews, and written questionnaires. Second, a study may focus entirely on sexual maltreatment, or a study may address sexual maltreatment as one of several issues. Third, some studies survey the general population, while the vast majority survey special populations, such as psychiatric patients, incarcerated sex offenders, or college students. Fourth, the definition of sexual maltreatment varies from study to study. Dimensions on which definitions may differ are maximum age for a victim, the age difference required between victim and offender, whether or not noncontact acts are included, and whether the act is unwanted. Finally, cultural values impact responses. For example, many believe that male victimization is more underreported than female victimization, in part because of societal failure to identify the behavior as problematic and boys' own definitions of sexual victimization. Although the potentially vast differences in prevalence estimates often lead to accusations that researchers and advocates inflate victimization rates, the variations and reasons for them are important to keep in mind. All estimates must be taken on their own terms and their sources carefully evaluated. If anything, they help us realize how sexual maltreatment actually does vary across populations.

Other estimates of child sexual maltreatment come from incidence studies. These studies define incidence as the number of reports during a given time frame, yearly in the case of sexual maltreatment. Research has examined data available on the number of sexual maltreatment cases reported per year to child protection agencies, as part of data collection on all types of maltreatment. In 1986, for example, the number of reported cases of sexual maltreatment was 132,000, a rate of 20.89 per 10,000 children. These reports comprised 15 percent of all reports. American Association for Protecting Children (AAPC) (1988). *Highlights of Official Child Neglect and Abuse Reporting, 1986.* Denver, CO: American Humane Association. Although these are important findings, they too are not without limitations. First, current data are not available. Second, cases included in this data set are limited to those that would warrant a CPS referral, which generally are cases in which the abuser is a caretaker or the caretaker fails to protect a child from sexual maltreatment. Thus, cases do not necessarily include those involving an extrafamilial abuser or a protective parent. Third, the data only index reported cases. As a result, the data sets do not include incidents unknown to professionals and those known but not reported. Moreover, the estimates are reports, not substantiations, of sexual maltreatment.

The National Incidence Studies (NIS-1, NIS-2, and NIS-3) provide additional data on the rates of child sexual maltreatment. Information from these studies provides estimates of annual incidence rates, as the child protection data do. In addition, these studies project a national rate of child maltreatment based on information from a sample of counties, rather than based on reports from all states. Importantly, though, the NIS studies gather information on unreported as well as reported cases. An estimated 133,600 cases were identified by professionals in 1986. These figures represent a rate of 21 cases per 10,000. Somewhat surprisingly, these are very similar to the rates reported by the most recent surveys: 135,300 cases were reported, constituting 23 percent of cases in 2010. See U.S. Department of Health and Human Services (1988). *Study Findings: Study of National Incidence and Prevalence of Child Abuse and Neglect: 1988.* Washington, DC: U.S. Government Printing Office; also see the 2010 report.

As we have seen, both the child protection (civil) and criminal justice systems define sexual maltreatment. The *Child Abuse Prevention and Treatment Act*, 42

U.S.C.A. § 5106g(4) (West Supp. 2001), views sexual maltreatment as sexual abuse and exploitation, which it delineates as a subcategory of child abuse and neglect. The statute defines this form of maltreatment to include: "(A) the employment, use, persuasion, inducement, enticement, or coercion of any child to engage in, or assist any other person to engage in, any sexually explicit conduct or simulation of such conduct for the purpose of producing a visual depiction of such conduct; or (B) the rape, molestation, prostitution, or other form of sexual exploitation of children, or incest with children. . . ." Importantly, the statute does not apply the maximum age of 18 it does for other types of maltreatment, but rather indicates that the age limit in the state law shall apply. Id. § 5106g(1)(B). The federal statute also has a limited reach. With the exception of situations involving Native American children, crimes committed on federal property, interstate transport of minors for sexual purposes, and the shipment or possession of child pornography, state criminal statutes regulate child sexual maltreatment. State criminal statutes generally provide very detailed definitions of sexual maltreatment. Statutes classify types of sexual maltreatment in terms of their degree of severity, first degree being the most serious and fourth degree the least; or classify sexual maltreatment in terms of class, with a class A felony being more serious than a class B or C felony. The penalties also vary considerably and mostly differ depending on: the age of the child, with crimes against younger children being regarded as worse; the level of force, with force making the crime more severe; the relationship between victim and offender, with an act against a relative or household member being considered more serious; or the type of sexual act, with penetration receiving more severe penalties.

As the criminal justice approach suggests, it seems important not to assume that all sexual encounters experienced by children are abusive in the same manner. Not surprisingly, then, social scientists examine how we may distinguish maltreating from nonmaltreating encounters and seek to understand the traumatic effects of encounters. Researchers and clinicians deem three interrelated factors useful in differentiating abusive from nonabusive acts. Although interrelated, the presence of any one of these factors raises concern that the sexual encounter was abusive. The first factor concerns power differentials, which implies that one party (the offender) controls the other (the victim) and that the sexual encounter is not mutually conceived and undertaken. Importantly, power differentials may derive from the role relationship between offender and victim, which allows for including the possibility, for example, that a young child can sexually maltreat another. The second factor involves knowledge differentials, which considers encounters abusive when one party (the offender) has a more sophisticated understanding of the significance and implications of the sexual encounter. This factor tends to include situations in which the offender is either older, more developmentally advanced, or more intelligent than the victim. Lastly, gratification differentials often indicate maltreatment. In most sexual maltreatment cases, perpetrators seek to obtain gratification and may delude themselves into believing that they sexually satisfy their victims. These three approaches are important as they highlight how determinations of what constitutes maltreatment involves the nature of the relationship and the meaning of the act(s) to the child, with some acts that even the law may not view as "traumatic" but in effect may still leave the child with cognitive distortions or problematic beliefs. See Roger J. R. Levesque (1999). *Child Sexual Abuse: A Human Rights Perspective*. Bloomington, IN: Indiana University Press.

A number of attempts have been made to conceptualize the effects of sexual maltreatment. Social scientists have found that the most important factors that contribute to variations in traumatic outcomes include the age of the victim (both at the time of the maltreatment and the time of the assessment), the sex of the victim, the sex of the offender, the extent of the sexual maltreatment, the relationship between offender and victim, the reaction of others to knowledge of the sexual maltreatment, other life experiences, and the length of time between the maltreatment and information gathering. Recent efforts to understand the impact of sexual maltreatment have specifically controlled research in which sexually maltreated children are compared to a normal or nonsexually maltreated clinical population. However, even despite more sophisticated studies and analytic techniques, our understanding of the impact of sexual maltreatment still remains frustrated by the wide variety of possible effects. Research still often does not focus on similar effects, and studies frequently use different methodologies and instruments. Consequently, a particular symptom, such as substance abuse, may not be studied or may be examined by using different measures. Furthermore, although most studies find significant differences between sexually maltreated children from study to study, there is no symptom universally found in every victim. In addition, often lower proportions of sexually maltreated children exhibit a particular symptom than do nonmaltreated clinical comparison groups. Finally, although some victims suffer pervasive and debilitating effects, others are found to be asymptomatic. See Kathleen A. Kendall-Tackett, Linda Meyer Williams & David Finkelhor (1993). Impact of sexual abuse on children: A review and synthesis of recent empirical studies. *Psychological Bulletin*, 113, 164–180.

The clinical approach to understanding trauma associated with sexual maltreatment should not be read as condoning some forms of sexual relationships with children. Much controversy surrounds definitions of what should constitute sexual maltreatment. Controversies should not be surprising given the wide range of possible forms of interactions individuals have with children, the necessary sexual development of individuals as they move from childhood to adulthood, the need to allow some form of contact between individuals and children, and the manner we live in a "sexualized" society (how sexuality infuses our popular culture and how great tension exists between controlling and liberating sexual activities and attitudes). These concerns are complicated further by the increasing use of the criminal justice system in responding to sexual maltreatment, which complicates matters given the higher standard of proof needed to convict offenders, the utility of having children participate in prosecutorial processes, and the tensions that may emerge between the criminal justice and child welfare systems. We already have seen how other forms of maltreatment may also implicate the criminal justice system (e.g., fatal physical maltreatment), but this category of maltreatment seems to receive the most attention from both systems.

Notes and Queries

1. It often is difficult to understand that children's sexual encounters may not be abusive in an experiential sense and also in a legal sense. Keep in mind that the legal category of childhood ranges widely, and often reaches the age of 18. Yet the vast majority of individuals have engaged in sexual activity (but not necessarily sexual intercourse) before the age of 18, which raises the issue of whether we should view most of these experiences as abusive. The legal system attempts to address these issues, and does so in very complicated ways, most notably through statutory rape laws. See Roger J. R. Levesque (2000). *Adolescents, Sex, and the Law: Preparing Adolescents for Responsible Citizenship.* Washington, DC: American Psychological Association.

2. Research examining the impact of sexual maltreatment on children often reports lack of affirmative findings. A leading meta-analytic study found that from 20 to nearly 50 percent of subjects reported no negative symptoms and did not significantly differ from control groups who, presumably, had not been sexual maltreated. Kathleen A. Kendall-Tackett, Linda Meyer Williams & David Finkelhor (1993). Impact of sexual abuse on children: A review and synthesis of recent empirical studies. *Psychological Bulletin*, 113, 164–180.

3. The results of the studies by Kendall-Tackett, Williams, and Finkelhor were similar to those reported in a more recent article that focused on the effects sexual maltreatment may have on college students. The authors questioned the dominant belief, held by many lay persons and professionals, that child sexual maltreatment causes intense harm, regardless of gender. Their meta-analyses revealed that students who had been sexually maltreated were, on average, slightly less well adjusted than controls. However, they also found that this poorer adjustment could not be attributed to child sexual maltreatment because family environment was consistently confounded with maltreatment. Family environment explained considerably more adjustment variance than maltreatment, and maltreatment–adjustment relations generally became nonsignificant when studies controlled for family environment. The authors concluded that self-reported reactions to and effects from maltreatment indicated that negative effects were neither pervasive nor typically intense, and that men reacted much less negatively than women. Bruce Rind, Philip Tromovitch & Robert Bauserman (1998). A meta-analytic examination of assumed properties of child sexual abuse using college samples. *Psychological Bulletin*, 124, 22–53. Unlike the previous meta-analysis, this one resulted in considerable political controversy, which eventually prompted Congress to pass a formal resolution condemning the article. H. Con. Res. 107, July 12, 1999.

4. The above findings have important implications when we think of intervening to help children who have been sexually maltreated. They do not mean, though,

that children are not harmed even though no negative findings are found. What could explain such a pervasive lack of findings? The children may be resilient or may have had appropriate support when the maltreatment occurred, the victims probably had appropriate therapeutic responses, the nature of maltreatment differs greatly, researchers simply may not have researched well, the control groups probably were maltreated in other ways, the harm was repressed and will reveal itself in later developmental stages, college students probably adapted better than those who did not go to college, or the victims experienced "normative confusion" (they think what they experienced is normal, a real possibility given how children become involved in sexually abusive relationships). What implications do these possibilities hold for the law's effort to conceive of sexual maltreatment? What does it tell you about harm?

5. Research examining the extent of juvenile sex offending reports startling statistics. Juvenile sex offenders (those 18 and below) commit sex crimes against younger children at rates apparently similar to those committed by adult offenders. Estimates reveal that adolescents commit more than 50 percent of sex offenses perpetrated against children under 12 years of age. These rates may appear incredibly high, but they actually seem to be underestimates of the magnitude of sex offending against children. Research examining the incidence of adolescents' sex offenses against children relies mainly on official reports of child sexual maltreatment, which often classify sexual offenses as assaults or neglect noncontact offenses, and, as with other offenses, involve underreporting to authorities. In addition, offenses by young offenders may be more underreported than those committed by adults. See, e.g., Gail Ryan, Thomas J. Miyoshi, Jeffrey L. Metzner, Richard D. Krugman & George Fryer (1996). Trends in a national sample of sexually abusive youths. *Journal of the American Academy of Child and Adolescent Psychiatry*, 35, 17–25; Glen E. Davis & Harrold Leitenberg (1987). Adolescent sex offenders. *Psychological Bulletin*, 101, 417–427; Michael L. Bourke & Brad Donohue (1996). Assessment and treatment of juvenile sex offenders: An empirical review. *Journal of Child Sexual Abuse*, 5, 47–70. Official reports of arrest rates also show a similar trend that urges us to take juvenile sex offending seriously. As an age group, juveniles appear to commit sex crimes at rates at least comparable to older age groups. Crime reports indicate that juvenile offenders account for 16 percent of all arrests for forcible rape and approximately one-fifth of all arrests for every remaining sex offense other than prostitution. Although it often is believed that juvenile offenders tend to be nearing the age of majority, evidence indicates otherwise. Thirteen- and fourteen-year-olds account for the largest number of arrests for forcible rape and all other reported sex crimes (except prostitution). Offenders 14 and younger account for 34 percent of forcible rapes and half of all other sex offenses committed by minors. United States Department of Justice (1993). *Uniform Crime Reports*. Washington, DC: Author. Lastly, the above studies also show that the modal age of juvenile sex offenders is 14 and the modal age of their victims is 7.

6. Although juveniles now constitute an important and increasing category of sex offenders, how we are to address children's relationships creates many controversies. Although it may be less difficult to find relationships with wide age gaps abusive, considerable difficulties arise when the children are close in age. Developmental psychologists seeking to understand the sexual maltreatment of children by children suggest that, for any age groups, we should deem abusive sexual acts between children that involve coercion, aggression, bribery, secrecy, a significant age or peer difference, or developmentally inappropriate behaviors. Sharon Araji (1997). *Sexually Aggressive Children: Coming to Understand Them.* Thousand Oaks, CA: Sage. These issues become significant and take different turns depending on the response to children's sexual behaviors, which can range from simply ignoring the situation, encouraging parents to teach their children differently, and requiring family therapy, to transferring the juvenile to adult court for adult penalties. Note that, theoretically, responses to juvenile offenses incorporate the need to assess offender needs and provide appropriate services to them. Yet numerous challenges arise that increase the risk of inappropriate responses. Most notably, assessments of juvenile sexual offenders that are intended to aid in dispositional decisions occur at a multitude of decision points within the juvenile justice system. Despite the ubiquity of decisions that include considerations of risk, relatively little empirical work has been done on the development and validation of any risk assessment procedure for those deemed young offenders. Robert Prentky, Bert Harris, Kate Frizell & Sue Righthand (2000). An actuarial procedure for assessing risk with juvenile sex offenders. *Sexual Abuse: Journal of Research & Treatment*, 12, 71–93. As a result, the reality is that mental health placements are rarely used, which is also true of other juvenile offenses; see Denise C. Herz (2001). Understanding the use of mental health placements by the juvenile justice system. *Journal of Emotional & Behavioral Disorders*, 9, 172–181.

Review Problem

1. Existing research from nonclinical samples in the United States indicates that more than 50 percent of 8- to 10-year-old daughters were reported as touching their mother's genitals and breasts, and more than 30 percent to be touching their father's genitals, while more than 40 percent of 8- to10-year-old sons were reported as touching their mother's genitals and about 20 percent their father's genitals. Alvin Rosenfeld, Robert Bailey, Bryna Siegel & Gwyn Bailey (1986). Determining incestuous contact between parent and child: Frequency of children touching parents' genitals in a nonclinical population. *Journal of the American Academy of Child Psychiatry*, 25, 481–484. What issues do these findings raise about the use of social science, our values when we try to understand sexual activity, and the legal system's response?

Commonwealth v. Rhodes

510 Pa. 537; 510 A.2d 1217 (Pa. Sup. Ct., 1986)

Judge Larsen delivered the opinion of the court.

...

At approximately 4:20 p.m. on February 18, 1982, the victim, a third grader at the Hunter School in Philadelphia, left her home to go to a cooking class at the nearby Waterloo Playground. The victim had celebrated her eighth birthday the prior month (January 9th). After playing tag for awhile with a playmate at the playground, she went inside a building there and watched two men playing chess. One of the men was twenty year old Nicholas Rhodes, the appellee in this case. Nicholas Rhodes lived across the street from the victim and her family and knew her for about three years. The victim knew the appellee as "Nicky."

When he was done playing chess, appellee asked the victim if she wanted to go somewhere, whereupon he led her to an abandoned building near the playground and took her upstairs to a dirty, unfurnished room on the second floor. Appellee instructed her to lay down on the dirty floor and to pull her legs up. He then laid on top of her and touched her "butt" with "something" in his pubic area. The victim felt pain when appellee "touched her" this way, and she "told him to stop." In a short while, appellee left the building with the victim who then walked to her home in the dark.

When the victim arrived at her home at about 7:30 p.m.–8:00 p.m., her mother observed her crying, frightened and smelling of dog feces which was on her clothing and in her hair. The victim's mother immediately examined her and found her underwear bloody and turned inside out, her rectum torn and bleeding, and her vagina red. The victim's mother called the police and the child was taken to a hospital where a medical examination tested positively for sperm in both the "vulvular sample" and the "rectal sample", and revealed a "recto-vaginal fissure" (a tear). Lab results confirmed the presence of blood and "seminal stains" on the victim's underwear.

Appellee was arrested at his home later that evening, and charged with rape, statutory rape, involuntary deviate sexual intercourse, indecent assault, indecent exposure, corruption of minors and unlawful restraint.

...

Judge DiBona adjudicated appellee guilty of rape, statutory rape, involuntary deviate sexual intercourse, indecent assault, indecent exposure and corruption of minors. Post trial motions were denied and appellee was sentenced to a term of imprisonment of six to twenty years on the conviction for rape (a felony of the first degree) and to a concurrent term of imprisonment of six to twenty years on the conviction for involuntary deviate sexual intercourse (a felony of the first degree). Additionally, appellee received a sentence of five years probation on the conviction for corruption of minors (a misdemeanor of the first degree) and a suspended sentence on the conviction for statutory rape (a felony of the second degree). No sentences were imposed on the remaining convictions.

Appellee's appeal to the Superior Court challenged the sufficiency of the evidence to sustain his convictions, challenged the sentences as "too harsh and severe for a sexual assault upon a young girl without violence or injury" .... A panel of the Superior Court found the evidence sufficient to sustain the convictions for involuntary deviate sexual intercourse, statutory rape, and corruption of minors, but insufficient to sustain the conviction for rape under 18 Pa.C.S.A. § 3121. The Superior Court further held that since "we cannot be certain that the trial court's sentences for [involuntary deviate sexual intercourse and corruption of minors] would have been the same if it had known that the conviction for forcible rape would be set aside ... we will vacate all judgments of sentence and remand for resentencing." ...

We granted the Commonwealth's petition for allowance of appeal from the Superior Court's order, and we now reverse.

Section 3121 of the Crimes Code establishes the crime of rape and its elements as follows:

> A person commits a felony of the first degree when he engages in sexual intercourse with another person not his spouse:
>
> (1) by forcible compulsion;
>
> (2) by threat of forcible compulsion that would prevent resistance by a person of reasonable resolution;
>
> (3) who is unconscious; or
>
> (4) who is so mentally deranged or deficient that such person is incapable of consent.

Labeling this section as "forcible rape," the Superior Court held:

> It is ... apparent ... that the Commonwealth failed to prove a forcible rape. There is not one iota of evidence that sexual intercourse was accomplished by forcible compulsion or by threat of forcible compulsion. Similarly, there was no evidence that the child was unconscious or mentally deficient. Although we do not minimize the heinous nature of appellant's act, it seems clear that the act of vaginal intercourse was criminal because of the provisions of 18 Pa.C.S. § 3122 defining statutory rape and not because it was a forcible rape as defined in 18 Pa.C.S. § 3121.

While we agree with the Superior Court that there was no evidence that the child victim in this case was unconscious, we find the evidence sufficient to establish beyond a reasonable doubt the crime of rape by forcible compulsion, threat of forcible compulsion and with a victim who was so mentally deficient by virtue of her young age as to be legally incapable of consent....

Thus, the Crimes Code provides:

> The provisions of this title shall be construed according to the fair import of their terms but when the language is susceptible of differing constructions it shall be interpreted to further the general purposes stated in this title and the special purposes of the particular provision involved. The discretionary powers conferred by this title shall be exercised in accordance with the criteria stated in this title and, in so far as such criteria are not decisive, to further the general purposes stated in this title.

The preceding section of the Crimes Code sets forth its purposes:

> Purposes
>
> The general purposes of this title are:
>
> (1) To forbid and prevent conduct that unjustifiably inflicts or threatens substantial harm to individual or public interest.
>
> (2) To safeguard conduct that is without fault from condemnation as criminal.
>
> (3) To safeguard offenders against excessive, disproportionate or arbitrary punishment.
>
> (4) To give fair warning of the nature of the conduct declared to constitute an offense, and of the sentences that may be imposed on conviction of an offense.
>
> (5) To differentiate on reasonable grounds between serious and minor offenses, and to differentiate among offenders with a view to a just individualization in their treatment.

The Crimes Code's provisions on Sexual Offenses are an amalgam of prior criminal law (judicial and statutory) . . . defined the crime of rape, as did most jurisdictions. . . . Since the focus of the element of force was on its use to overbear a victim's will and demonstrate lack of consent, the cases held that the "requisite force need not have been actually applied, but may have been constructive or implied", as where the victim was unconscious, insane, drugged, or so young as to have been legally incapable of consenting to the act of sexual intercourse.

. . .

With this background in mind, we now turn to construction of section 3121 of the Crimes Code. . . .

. . .

In common usage, therefore, the phrase "forcible compulsion" clearly connotes more than the exercise of sheer physical force or violence as the Superior Court has so limited section 3121(1) in this case and others. The phrase also connotes the act of using superior force — physical, moral psychological, or intellectual — to compel a person to do a thing against that person's volition and/or will.

. . .

... [W]e hold that "forcible compulsion" as used in section 3121(1) includes not only physical force or violence but also moral, psychological or intellectual force used to compel a person to engage in sexual intercourse against that person's will.

Closely related to section 3121(1) is section 3121(2) which applies to the situation where "forcible compulsion" is not actually used but is threatened. That section uses the phrase "by threat of forcible compulsion that would prevent resistance by a person of reasonable resolution."

...

The determination of whether there is sufficient evidence to demonstrate beyond a reasonable doubt that an accused engaged in sexual intercourse by forcible compulsion (which we have defined to include "not only physical force or violence, but also moral, psychological or intellectual force used to compel a person to engage in sexual intercourse against that person's will," or by the threat of such forcible compulsion that would prevent resistance by a person of reasonable resolution) is, of course, a determination that will be made in each case based upon the totality of the circumstances that have been presented to the fact finder. Significant factors to be weighed in that determination would include the respective ages of the victim and the accused, the respective mental and physical conditions of the victim and the accused, the atmosphere and physical setting in which the incident was alleged to have taken place, the extent to which the accused may have been in a position of authority, domination or custodial control over the victim, and whether the victim was under duress. This list of possible factors is by no means exclusive.

It is neither desirable nor appropriate to attempt to delineate all of the possible circumstances that might tend to demonstrate that sexual intercourse was engaged in by forcible compulsion or by the threat of forcible compulsion within the meaning of section 3121(1) and (2). That delineation will evolve in the best tradition of the common law....

...

Reviewing the evidence in the instant case, we find it sufficient to demonstrate beyond a reasonable doubt that appellee engaged in sexual intercourse with his eight year old victim by forcible compulsion and by the threat of forcible compulsion. Appellee, a twenty year old man who knew the child victim and her family for three years and who the victim knew as Nicky, lured the victim into an abandoned, filthy building and instructed her to lay down and pull her legs up, whereupon he forced his will upon her and engaged in acts of sexual and deviate sexual intercourse to the extent that she was bleeding and torn.

There is an element of forcible compulsion, or the threat of forcible compulsion that would prevent resistance by a person of reasonable resolution, inherent in the situation in which an adult who is with a child who is younger, smaller, less psychologically and emotionally mature, and less sophisticated than the adult, instructs the child to submit to the performance of sexual acts. This is especially so where the child knows and trusts the adult. In such cases, forcible compulsion or the threat of forcible compulsion derives from the respective capacities of the child and the adult sufficient to induce the child to submit to the wishes of the adult ("prevent resistance"), without the use of physical force or violence or the explicit threat of physical force or violence.... Accordingly, the evidence was sufficient to sustain his conviction for rape under 18 Pa.C.S.A. § 3121(1) and (2).

Additionally, section 3121(4) creates the category of rape where the actor engages in sexual intercourse with a person "who is so mentally deranged or deficient that such person is incapable of consent." ...

We do not address all of the possible conditions that would demonstrate that a person "is so mentally deranged or deficient that such person is incapable of consent." Suffice it to say that the eight year old child in this case was "so mentally deficient," as a matter of law, that she was incapable of consenting to an act whose nature she could not appreciate or comprehend; this is the "fair import" of § 3121(4).

...

We hold, therefore, that the evidence was sufficient to demonstrate beyond a reasonable doubt that appellee engaged in sexual intercourse with a person (an eight year old child) who was "so mentally ... deficient that such person [was] incapable of consent."

The Superior Court also stated in the instant case that "it seems clear that the act of vaginal intercourse was criminal because of the provisions of § 18 Pa.C.S. § 3122 defining statutory rape and not because it was a forcible rape as defined in 18 Pa.C.S. § 3121." We reject the implication of this passage that an act of sexual intercourse with a victim who is under the age of fourteen years cannot constitute rape as well as statutory rape where the elements of each distinct offense have been proven beyond a reasonable doubt. As we have held, the elements of the crime of rape have been proven beyond a reasonable doubt as appellee engaged in sexual intercourse with a person not his spouse by forcible compulsion, the threat of forcible compulsion and with a victim so mentally deficient because of her youth as to be legally incapable of consenting to the act of sexual intercourse. Additionally, there is no doubt that appellee was guilty of statutory rape under section 3122 which provides that: "A person who is 18 years of age or older commits statutory rape ... when he engages in sexual intercourse with another person not his spouse who is less than 14 years of age." The absence, existence or effectiveness of the victim's consent is immaterial to the crime of statutory rape. Appellee's guilt of this crime was established by the proven elements that he was older than eighteen (he was twenty) years and that he engaged in sexual intercourse with a victim who was younger than fourteen (the child victim was eight) years.

...

Nor do double jeopardy principles or the doctrine of merger of lesser included offenses prohibit the conviction and sentence for both rape and statutory rape arising from a single act of sexual intercourse. . . . [T]he Commonwealth has suffered two injuries from appellee's single act in that he not only engaged in sexual intercourse by forcible compulsion, the threat of forcible compulsion, and with a victim so mentally deficient as to be incapable of consent, he has also engaged in such acts with a victim under the statutory age of fourteen while he was older than eighteen. The separate injuries are proscribed by separate offenses with distinct elements.

. . .

For the foregoing reasons, we hold that the Superior Court erred in finding the evidence insufficient to establish the crime of rape under 18 Pa.C.S.A. § 3121, and we reinstate appellee's conviction and judgment of sentence for rape.

. . .

Accordingly, the order of the Superior Court is reversed, the conviction for rape is reinstated, and all judgments of sentence are reinstated.

Chief Justice Nix, concurring. [omitted]

Justice Hutchinson, concurring. [omitted]

Justice Zappala, concurring. [omitted]

Notes and Queries

1. The court adopts a "totality of the circumstances" standard to determine the presence of "forcible compulsion" to qualify the acts as sufficient to charge rape. Do you find this approach more effective than simply applying a minimum age, such as 10, to serve as a proxy for force?
2. Using the "totality of circumstances" test to determine the presence of force in child sexual abuse cases might involve the following considerations: age differences between participants, relationship between participants, the perpetrator's deviancy, the victim's sexual and cognitive maturity, and particularities of the events themselves. Are these appropriate considerations?
3. Efforts to devise a minimum age standard seek to use age as a proxy for numerous characteristics involving minors, especially their ability to exercise sexual agency and to exhibit cognitive and emotional competency. In addition, the age standard relates to chid-bearing capacity and beliefs regarding the appropriateness of children as sexual objects. What age best serves as proxy for forcible rape? If age seems inadequate, what factors should be considered to determine the presence of forcible compulsion?
4. The case addresses recurring concerns about double jeopardy. Do you agree with the court's decision allowing for a finding of guilt for both the criminal offense of rape and statutory rape for the same sexual acts? In sex crimes cases, as with some

other crimes, it is not unusual to have defendants charged with a slew of crimes. Does that seem appropriate given that they derive from the same acts? What rationale would you use to charge defendants in this manner?

5. The majority finds that forcible compulsion may be established by a showing of the respective capacities of the defendant and victim. Would you agree that their view eradicates the distinction between the criminal offenses of rape and statutory rape?

6. It seems reasonable to concur with the majority's holding that the victim's testimony and the physical evidence of trauma was sufficient to establish the element of forcible compulsion. Do you find it more difficult to accept the majority's conclusion that forcible compulsion has been established in the absence of that evidence?

7. The court defines forcible compulsion as "not only physical force or violence, but also moral, psychological or intellectual force used to compel a person to engage in sexual intercourse against that person's will, or by the threat of such forcible compulsion that would prevent resistance by a person of reasonable resolution." Would you define force that broadly? Note that, under this statute, forcible compulsion would apply to all ages. Does that make the definition too broad?

State v. Etheridge

319 N.C. 34; 352 S.E.2d 673 (N.C. Sup. Ct., 1987)

Justice Martin delivered the opinion of the court.

...

Briefly summarized, the state's evidence tended to show that defendant began engaging in sexual activity with his daughter and son when they were six and eight years old, respectively. The most recent incidents, from which the criminal charges at issue arose, consisted of the following acts: On 10 April 1985 defendant drove his daughter, then aged twelve, to an isolated area in Perquimans County known as Bear Swamp. Defendant stopped his truck about halfway into the swamp and told the child to open the door of the truck, remove her clothes, and lie down on the seat. She complied with these demands. Defendant then unzipped his pants and had vaginal intercourse with her. Afterward defendant warned her not to tell anyone admonishing that "we'll both get in trouble." Other episodes of intercourse, perpetrated in an essentially identical manner, occurred in Bear Swamp on 21 December 1984 and 5 January 1985 and in the child's room at home on 15 February 1985.

The state's evidence further tended to show that on 28 April 1985 defendant was at home alone with his son, then aged thirteen. Defendant told the boy to go upstairs and, having followed him to his room, directed him to remove his clothes. At first the child refused. However, when told to "[d]o it anyway," he obeyed defendant's order. Defendant then took off his own pants and had anal intercourse with his son. He threatened to hurt the boy if anyone found out what had transpired between them.

A friend to whom the boy later confided details of the incident informed the Department of Social Services (DSS), and defendant's children were removed from the home. This friend and Debbie Spence of the DSS testified as to what the children had told them about defendant's abuse. These statements were consistent with the children's testimony at trial. Public health nurse Louise Ervin provided additional corroboration, testifying that she had interviewed defendant at Perquimans Health Department on 21 May 1985 because he was concerned about symptoms of a sexually transmittable disease. Defendant stated to Ms. Ervin that he had had sexual contact with his son and daughter.

Defendant did not testify on his own behalf but presented evidence tending to show that his daughter vaguely remembered telling her mother when she was six years old that defendant had touched her breasts. Otherwise she had never complained of sexual abuse to friends or family members until DSS workers began asking questions about her father in May of 1985. Defendant's son learned about sexual abuse from a film at school and knew defendant would get into trouble if accused of molesting his children. He admitted that defendant had previously threatened to send him to training school because of disciplinary problems at home.... Medical examinations of the children on 4 May 1985 revealed no bruising or tearing of the tissues or other physical evidence of sexual abuse.

Defendant presents four assignments of error for our consideration.

...

Defendant next contends that the trial court erroneously denied his motion to dismiss the charge of sexual offense in the second degree. He argues that the state failed to present the evidence of force necessary to sustain his conviction of the offense under N.C.G.S. § 14-27.5. In overruling this assignment of error, we take this opportunity to elaborate upon our recent limitation of the holding in *State v. Alston* and to disavow its misbegotten offspring.

For the act of anal intercourse with his son, defendant was convicted under section 14-27.5, which provides in pertinent part:

> (a) A person is guilty of a sexual offense in the second degree if the person engages in a sexual act with another person:
>
> (1) By force and against the will of the other person;

...

The phrase "by force and against the will of the other person" means the same as it did at common law when it was used to describe an element of rape. The requisite force may be established either by actual, physical force or by constructive force in the form of fear, fright, or coercion. Constructive force is demonstrated by proof of threats or other actions by the defendant which compel the victim's submission to sexual acts. Threats need not be explicit so long as the totality of circumstances allows a reasonable inference that such compulsion was the unspoken purpose of the threat.

Defendant argues that both actual and constructive force were conspicuously absent from the incident of anal intercourse as described by his son. He bases this contention on the reasoning in *State v. Alston* and *State v. Lester*. We hold that *Lester* carried *Alston* far beyond its intended scope and that defendant's reliance on the two decisions is inappropriate under the facts of this case.

The facts giving rise to *Alston* were unusual ones. The prosecutrix, one Ms. Brown, had engaged in a consensual, though somewhat turbulent, sexual relationship with the defendant for six months prior to the alleged rape. The relationship involved some violence by the defendant, who struck Ms. Brown when she refused him money, and some passivity by Ms. Brown, who on several occasions remained entirely motionless while the defendant undressed her and had intercourse with her. On the day of the alleged rape, the defendant waited outside the school which Ms. Brown attended. He grabbed her arm and told her she was going with him. As they walked away, he threatened to "fix" her face. The two then walked around the neighborhood and discussed their relationship, eventually arriving at the home of the defendant's friend. The defendant began to undress Ms. Brown and told her to lie down on the bed. She complied, whereupon he pushed her legs apart and had intercourse with her. She cried but attempted no physical resistance.

This Court, recognizing that Ms. Brown's prior consensual relationship with the defendant rendered any inquiry on the issue of force more difficult, determined that the acts complained of were committed against Ms. Brown's will but were not committed forcibly. We noted that the defendant's grabbing of Ms. Brown and his threat to "fix" her face, "although they may have induced fear, appeared to have been unrelated to the act of sexual intercourse between Brown and the defendant." We thereupon concluded that "absent evidence that the defendant used force or threats to overcome the will of the victim to resist the sexual intercourse alleged to have been rape, such general fear was not sufficient to show that the defendant used the force required to support a conviction of rape."

In *Lester*, the Court of Appeals applied the *Alston* "general fear" rationale to an intrafamilial sexual assault. The defendant in that case was convicted of two counts of raping his fifteen-year-old daughter. He had engaged in sexual intercourse with the child since she was eleven years old and had threatened to kill her if anyone learned of his actions. The defendant had also beaten the child's mother in her presence and had pointed a gun at his children. Before each of the two incidents charged, the defendant told his daughter to remove her clothes. Both times she initially refused but capitulated upon the second demand because her father seemed to be getting angry. The defendant then had intercourse with her. He neither used physical force nor threatened its use expressly, and the child made no attempt to resist. The Court of Appeals held that, in light of *Alston*, "the victim's fear of defendant, however justified by his previous conduct" was insufficiently related to the intercourse to show that it had been forcible. This Court summarily affirmed.

We now disavow *Lester*'s misapplication of the *Alston* "general fear" rationale to a case of intrafamilial sexual abuse. As we noted in . . . the "general fear" theory should be applied only to those situations which are factually similar to *Alston*. Sexual activity between a parent and a minor child is not comparable to sexual activity between two adults with a history of consensual intercourse. The youth and vulnerability of children, coupled with the power inherent in a parent's position of authority, creates a unique situation of dominance and control in which explicit threats and displays of force are not necessary to effect the abuser's purpose. We therefore expressly overrule *State v. Lester*.

Having overruled *Lester* and limited *Alston* to its peculiar facts, we return to our consideration of whether the evidence of force presented in the instant case was sufficient to withstand defendant's motion to dismiss. . . .

We hold that constructive force could be reasonably inferred from the circumstances surrounding the parent–child relationship in this case. Defendant began abusing his son when the boy was only eight years old. Like his sister, the child was conditioned to succumb to defendant's illicit advances at an age when he could not yet fully comprehend the implications of defendant's conduct. Not until he saw a film at school did the boy realize that defendant's behavior was considered improper and abusive. The incidents of abuse all occurred while the boy lived as an unemancipated minor in defendant's household, subject to defendant's parental authority and threats of disciplinary action.

In the incident charged, defendant said no more than "[d]o it anyway" when his son initially refused to disrobe. It is nonetheless reasonable to conclude that these words carried a great deal more menace than is apparent on the surface, for a father's threat to impose punishment upon a child who refuses to obey his commands need not be stated in so many words. The child's knowledge of his father's power may alone induce fear sufficient to overcome his will to resist, and the child may acquiesce rather than risk his father's wrath. As one commentator observes, force can be understood in some contexts as the power one need not use.

In such cases the parent wields authority as another assailant might wield a weapon. The authority itself intimidates; the implicit threat to exercise it coerces. Coercion, as stated above, is a form of constructive force. For this reason, we hold that the state presented sufficient evidence from which the jury could reasonably infer that defendant used his position of power to force his son's participation in sexual acts.

. . .

No error.

Justice Webb, dissenting. [omitted]

Notes and Queries

1. Do you agree that parents are inherently coercive in cases of intrafamily sexual abuse? For purposes of intrafamily abuse, which approach protects children more effectively: the new rule held in this case or the *Alston* "general fear" rule this case rejects?

2. If you were to review this case as an appellate court, would you find that the court had abused its power in its decision to interpret force?

3. What would you make of a state statute that provides child victims with the ability to veto criminal prosecution of their parents in favor of using the child welfare system and its rehabilitative approach? Good idea to try to keep the family together? Although this approach may seem to unfairly place a very heavy burden on child victims who, for example and in effect, can determine whether to send a parent to prison, some states statutes allow for the possibility; see Roger J. R. Levesque (1999). *Child Sexual Abuse: A Human Rights Perspective.* Bloomington, IN: Indiana University Press.

Research Comment

1. How does family sexual maltreatment differ from abuse by strangers? One study reported findings that generally are replicated in other studies using case files: (1) earlier onset, longer duration, higher level of intrusion, and greater physical and emotional injury for intrafamilial victims, and (2) less use of physical/verbal force, or enticements, and greater use of instructions "not to tell" by intrafamilial offenders. Although statistically significant, there is little difference in level of intrusion perpetrated by intrafamilial and extrafamilial offenders; both are highly intrusive. Both intrafamilial and extrafamilial offenders use physical/verbal force with older victims; extrafamilial offenders more often choose older victims, and therefore more often use force. Intrafamilial victims suffer greater physical and emotional injury, resulting from greater intrusion not duration of abuse. Donald G. Fischer & Wendy L. McDonald (1998). Characteristics of intrafamilial and extrafamilial child sexual abuse. *Child Abuse & Neglect*, 22, 915–929.

Rider v. State

544 So. 2d 994 (Ala. Crim. App. Ct., 1989)

Justice Bowen delivered the opinion of the court.

Robin Rider was convicted of sexual abuse in the first degree and sodomy in the first degree. He was given consecutive sentences of four years' and twenty years' imprisonment.

The defendant argues that his convictions are not supported by the evidence because there was no evidence of "forcible compulsion" as alleged in each indictment.

We must agree.

Forcible compulsion is an element of the offenses of both sexual abuse in the first degree and sodomy in the first degree. Forcible compulsion is "physical force that overcomes earnest resistance or a threat, express or implied, that places a person in fear of immediate death or serious physical injury to himself or another person."

The defendant is the 27-year-old stepfather of the victim. The victim testified that, when she and the defendant were sitting on the sofa alone, the defendant would put a movie on the VCR showing "people have sex." She testified that as they watched the movie, the defendant "would force [her] hand on one of his private spots . . . between his legs." After the movie, the defendant "took [her by the hand] back to the bedroom and touched [her] private part[s] . . . between [her] legs and on [her] chest." When this touching occurred, both the defendant and the victim were undressed. The victim testified that the defendant touched her private part with his mouth and that the defendant "asked" or "made" her touch his private part with her mouth.

This touching began after the victim's ninth birthday and continued until around her twelfth birthday. The defendant told her not to tell anyone "because he would probably go to jail." The victim testified that, after each incident, he usually told her he was sorry and promised that it would not happen again.

When the prosecutor asked the victim if she "voluntarily" performed oral acts on the defendant, the victim did not answer. The victim testified that she tried to "mind" her stepfather because she "liked the way he treated [her], like [she] was his only child," and she considered him her father. The victim testified that she did not have a father when she was born and when she was "a little baby." The victim's mother married the defendant when the victim was seven. On direct examination, the victim explained her passive conduct:

> Q. Okay. The things that Robin did to you, why did you let him do those things to you? Why didn't you scream and yell and scratch him and claw him and all of that? Why did you, you know, just why did you let him do those things to you?
>
> A. Because I thought if I would stop, that he wouldn't treat me the way he did.

On cross-examination, the victim testified that she knew "it was wrong." She was "afraid" to tell her mother and did not know how her mother would "react." She did not tell her grandmother because she "thought it would break her heart." She did not tell anyone because she did not want the defendant to go to jail. She stated that the defendant had never done anything to make her afraid of him and that she was not afraid of him.

...

Here, there was never any evidence that the victim made any protest or complaint to the defendant....

Here, the totality of the circumstances simply does not support a finding of the existence of the element of forcible compulsion which overcame the victim's earnest resistance. The victim, who was between 9 and 12 years old when the repeated acts of sexual abuse occurred, testified that the defendant "forced" her hand on his "private part." The defendant was the victim's stepfather, who treated her like his "only child." The victim was afraid that if she protested the defendant would not treat her like his daughter anymore. She did not tell anyone about the abuse because she was afraid the defendant would go to jail.

There are two kinds of forcible compulsion. First, forcible compulsion may be that physical force which overcomes earnest resistance. Second, forcible compulsion may be a threat, either express or implied, that places a person in fear of immediate death or serious physical injury to himself or another person. Here, it is clear that there is absolutely no evidence to support this second type. The problem is whether there is any evidence to support the first type.

There is evidence that some physical force was involved because the victim testified that the defendant "forced" her hand on his "private spot." With regard to this first type of forcible compulsion, there must also be some evidence of earnest resistance, which, ... requires some "genuine physical effort ... [by the victim] to discourage and prevent her assailant from accomplishing his intended purpose." We fail to find any earnest resistance....

...

... A conviction not supported by proof of the offenses as charged in the indictment cannot stand. This Court cannot embrace a nebulous and ever-expanding construction of a crime in order to supply the proof of facts which the prosecution has failed to provide.

The judgment of the circuit court is reversed and a judgment is rendered for the defendant.

Reversed and judgment rendered.

Justice McMillan, concurring. [omitted]

Notes and Queries

1. How do you distinguish this case from *State v. Etheridge*? Is it the number of victims, the nature of the relationship, simply a different court, or something else?

2. This case defines forcible rape as "physical force that overcomes earnest resistance or a threat, express or implied, that places a person in fear of immediate death or serious physical injury to himself or another person." Compare this approach to that of *Commonwealth v. Rhodes*. Which makes most sense if we are to protect children from harm *and* protect their autonomous development? Is this even a fair question to the extent that it asks us to consider protecting sexual autonomy?

In re M. D.

38 Ohio St. 3d 149; 527 N.E.2d 286 (Oh. Sup. Ct., 1988)

On July 25, 1985, appellant, M. D. (a female, then age twelve), was charged with one count of complicity to rape, in violation of R.C. 2907.02 and 2923.03(A)(4). The complaint alleged that on July 8, 1985, M. D. unlawfully caused an innocent and irresponsible person, David (then age five), to commit the rape of one Cassie (then age five). A denial was entered on October 4, 1985, and defense counsel later moved to dismiss the charge, arguing that the prosecution of a twelve year old for a felony sex crime involving an incident of "playing doctor" was unconstitutional and contrary to R.C. Chapter 2151. This motion was overruled.

A trial to the court began on April 14, 1986. Both of the children involved in the alleged rape were deemed competent to testify, as was M. D.'s nine-year-old sister. The three children testified that they, with M. D., were "playing doctor," and that at the direction of M. D., David dropped his pants and placed his penis in Cassie's mouth, ostensibly because M. D. had instructed them to take temperature that way. M. D., who had originally denied being present when these events took place, testified at trial that she was present and observed the conduct between David and Cassie. The trial court found each element of the offense charged had been established beyond a reasonable doubt and adjudicated M. D. a delinquent child, pursuant to Juv. R. 29(F). She was placed on probation under the supervision of her parents.

The court of appeals affirmed, holding that appellant had raised for the first time on appeal the issue of the constitutionality of applying the rape statute to children under the age of thirteen, and had thus waived such challenge. A motion for reconsideration was denied.

...

Disposition: Judgment reversed.

Justice Holmes delivered the opinion of the court.

This case presents an issue involving the prosecution of juveniles under the age of thirteen as delinquents for conduct, characterized as "playing doctor," allegedly constituting felony sex crimes. We hold that to bring such charges in juvenile court, under the instant circumstances, is contrary to R.C. Chapter 2151 and Juv. R. 9(A), violates the intake policy of the Cuyahoga County Juvenile Court, and public policy in general, and thus constitutes a denial of due process of law. We must, therefore, reverse the judgment of the court of appeals and vacate the adjudication of delinquency in this case.

. . .

In considering appellant's constitutional challenge herein, we are somewhat hampered, as was the court of appeals, by appellant's failure to provide a transcript of the proceedings below. We must, therefore, presume the validity of the proceedings in juvenile court. We are not, however, required to affirm on this basis alone, as appellant challenges only the discretion initially exercised by the prosecutor in bringing the instant charges. Such a challenge may be decided on the documents and exhibits found in the record certified to this court, in addition to the findings of the juvenile court below. Our review leads to the inescapable conclusion that the conduct of appellant and the other children involved herein did not constitute a sexual assault or complicity thereto, as proscribed by R.C. 2907.02 and 2923.03, but rather could more accurately be characterized as childhood curiosity and exploration.

The events giving rise to the instant charges did not meet each element of the offense of complicity to rape. R.C. 2923.03 provides, in pertinent part:

> (A) No person, acting with the kind of culpability required for the commission of an offense, shall do any of the following:
>
> ***
>
> (4) Cause an innocent or irresponsible person to commit the offense.
>
> ***
>
> (C) No person shall be convicted of complicity under this section unless an offense is actually committed, but a person may be convicted of complicity in an attempt to commit an offense in violation of section 2923.02 of the Revised Code.

It is axiomatic, as reflected in subsection (c) of this statute, that an offense must actually be committed before a person may be convicted as an accomplice. Here, the underlying offense of rape did not occur. We emphasize, first, that all sections of the Revised Code defining offenses must be liberally construed in favor of the accused. The offense of rape is generally defined in R.C. 2907.02 as follows: . . .

> Sections of the Revised Code defining offenses or penalties shall be strictly construed against the state, and liberally construed in favor of the accused.
>
> (A)(1) No person shall engage in sexual conduct with another who is not the spouse of the offender or who is the spouse of the offender but is

> living separate and apart from the offender, when either of the following apply:
>
> ***
>
> (b) The other person is less than thirteen years of age, whether or not the offender knows the age of such person.

The key term in this section is "sexual conduct," which is specifically defined in R.C. 2907.01(A):

> (A) 'Sexual conduct' means vaginal intercourse between a male and female, and anal intercourse, fellatio, and cunnilingus between persons regardless of sex. Penetration, however slight, is sufficient to complete vaginal or anal intercourse.

Fellatio is the only proscribed act which resembles what occurred herein. Although fellatio is not defined in the Revised Code, our construction of that term according to common usage is guided by its dictionary definition, i.e., "the practice of obtaining sexual satisfaction by oral stimulation of the penis." In addition, other jurisdictions that have considered the term have defined fellatio to encompass elements of either stimulation or sexual satisfaction, or both. Finally, we note that mere penetration of the oral cavity is not sufficient to complete the offense, unlike vaginal or anal intercourse. Here, the record demonstrates neither an element of sexual satisfaction nor of oral stimulation. We seriously doubt whether either element is physiologically or emotionally possible in a child of the tender age of five, and the record presented to us does not suggest otherwise. Furthermore, it is a well-established presumption that an infant under the age of fourteen is incapable of committing the crime of rape, rebuttable only upon proof that such child has reached the age of puberty. Fellatio did not occur here, thus no rape was committed to which appellant could be an accessory.

Adjudicating a child as "delinquent" under circumstances where, as here, the child has neither committed a crime nor violated a lawful order of the juvenile court is obviously contrary to R.C. Chapter 2151. Even assuming, however, given the paucity of the record before us, that the conduct here technically involved a "rape" as that term is statutorily defined, we hold that prosecution of M. D. under these circumstances violates the underlying public policy of this state as expressed in R.C. Chapter 2151 and the Rules of Juvenile Procedure. R.C. 2151.01 provides, in pertinent part:

> The sections in Chapter 2151. of the Revised Code, with the exception of those sections providing for the criminal prosecution of adults, shall be liberally interpreted and construed so as to effectuate the following purposes:
>
> (A) To provide for the care, protection, and mental and physical development of children subject to Chapter 2151. of the Revised Code;
>
> (B) To protect the public interest in removing the consequences of criminal behavior and the taint of criminality from children committing delinquent

> acts and to substitute therefor a program of supervision, care, and rehabilitation; ***.

The best interests of the child and the welfare and protection of the community are paramount considerations in every juvenile proceeding in this state. This is further emphasized in the Rules of Juvenile Procedure. These goals are effectuated at every step in the juvenile court system, but are most effectively met at the initial intake of the juvenile by the juvenile court. The overriding rule upon intake of a child is that formal court action should be a last resort to resolving juvenile problems.

. . .

That rule is reflected in the intake policy of the Cuyahoga County Juvenile Court as it relates to allegations of statutory rape, R.C. 2907.02, between children who are under thirteen years of age:

> Rape—Complaint shall be taken and set before a JUDGE unless subject is under age 13 years, in which case matter may be diverted.

A memorandum from the legal department of the Cuyahoga County Juvenile Court attached to the record in this case further emphasizes this policy:

> In situations where there is an allegation of sexual conduct involving no force and both the alleged offender and the victim are under 13 years of age, charges are not to be taken under the above statute. As an alternative, the intake mediator may consider unruly charges on one or both children.

The prosecution of M. D. under the facts as found by the trial court below constitutes a significant variance from this specific, local intake policy, and fails to conform to the general policies of R.C. Chapter 2151. Nothing in the record or in the arguments of the prosecutor persuades us that the "best interest of the child and the public" were served by the filing of the instant complaint. Quite to the contrary, legal counsel for the family of the alleged five-year-old "rapist" petitioned the juvenile court judge prior to trial to dismiss this action, as "the trauma which the impending trial is causing and could cause the family is far more serious than the alleged acts, which *** [the family] truly believe[s] [were] just kids playing doctor."

Nor was the "care, protection, and mental and physical development of children" provided for herein. The report of a mental health counselor who was assigned to M. D.'s case after her being adjudicated delinquent below indicates a normal pre-teen who enjoys being with her friends, listening to music, roller skating and swimming. The battery of tests and evaluations performed on her "gave no compelling evidence to suggest or support *** [her] involvement in the crime for which she has been found guilty. Her profile deviates markedly when compared with the profiles of other sex offenders. *** Negative community relationships as identified by *** [her] and her parents and supported by the testing are of particular concern. *** [She] (and her family) ha[ve] had to endure incredible and persistent harassment as a result of this incident."

Appellant has been saddled with the "taint of criminality" by this adjudication for a felony sex offense under circumstances where "sex" played but a minute role.

It was inappropriate that this case was filed in juvenile court. The case having been filed, it reasonably devolved on the juvenile judge to dismiss it pursuant to the mandates of R.C. Chapter 2151. The failure to dismiss resulted in a denial of M. D.'s constitutional rights to due process under the law which should have been vindicated by the court of appeals. We proceed to rectify that court's failure to do so, and accordingly reverse the judgment of the court of appeals, and hereby vacate appellant's adjudication as a delinquent child.

Notes and Queries

1. This case challenges prosecutorial discretion and reverses the case without a trial transcript. Did the court abuse its own discretion? Recall that the weight and credibility of evidence generally are issues left to the trier of fact. In addition, recall, as stated in previous cases, that the court must view the evidence in the light most favorable to the state, giving the state the benefit of every reasonable inference that might be drawn therefrom. The trial judge must decide if there is substantial evidence of each element of the offense charged. Substantial evidence means such relevant evidence as a reasonable mind might accept as adequate to support a conclusion.

2. Have the prosecutors in this case acted reasonably? Should they not have the discretion to proceed forward with charges and prosecution in cases like M. D.'s?

3. The Supreme Court of Ohio essentially does not view the incident as constituting a sex crime. Does the harassment of M. D. and her family suggest otherwise? Should there be cause for concern? Would you feel differently if M. D. had been a 12-year-old boy?

4. Developmental psychologists report that it is normal for children within ages 6 and 10 to engage in games that show interest in others' bodies. Does that affect your opinion? See Sharon Araji (1997). *Sexually Aggressive Children: Coming to Understand Them*. Thousand Oaks, CA: Sage.

Research Comments

1. Should we be concerned about sex play and sexual touching in childhood? Recent research examined results from the National Health and Social Life Survey to study sexual touching and social origin variables in childhood and incarceration variables during teen years. The sample was a stratified, random sample of 3,362 adults (18 to 59 years of age) throughout the United States. After having been asked if they had

"been touched sexually before puberty," subjects were asked if it involved one of the following: kissing, touching/fondling of genitals, oral sex, vaginal intercourse, and anal intercourse. Results indicated that respondents reporting touching *before* puberty were significantly more likely to experience incarceration. These subjects were also more likely to engage in behaviors as teenagers that were associated with an increased probability of jailing, such as sexual promiscuity and early departure from the parental family. Importantly, the authors included touching by peers as well as by adults, since they found no differences in estimates of the impact by different kinds of agent, a difference suggesting that peer experiences including "sexual abuse" have emotional and behavioral consequences comparable to adult sexual contact. Note, however, that incarceration rates were statistically significant and much higher for respondents who were touched, 19 percent versus 12 percent, but 80 percent of those touched did not report later incarceration. Russell L. Curtis Jr., Patrick Leung, Elroy Sullivan, Karl Eschbach & Margie Stinson (2001). Outcomes of child sexual contacts: Patterns of incarcerations from a national sample. *Child Abuse & Neglect*, 25, 719–736.

2. The authors of the prepubertal sexual touching study were highly criticized for not distinguishing between voluntary and involuntary sexual touching, for inappropriately denying normal child sexuality, and for linking child sexuality to maladaptive adult behavior. In response, they explained that: (1) The touching may be traumatizing, which may increase the probability that the individual will engage in illegal activity; (2) the association reflects the effects of dysfunctional peer and family groups, which increase the probability of engaging in illegal activities; and (3) the association reflects personality traits that correlate with later decisions to engage in illegal activity. They also explained why there may be no significant relationship between the age of the person who does the touching and later incarceration: Individuals who report touching tend to report touching by more than one age category. Karl Eschbach, Russell L. Curtis Jr. & Patrick Leung (2002). Letter to the editor. *Child Abuse & Neglect*, 26, 5–10.

3. The National Task Force on Juvenile Sexual Offending defines sexually abusive behavior as sexual acts perpetrated on another without consent, without equality, or as a result of coercion. Under this framework, consent includes all of the following: (1) understanding what is proposed, (2) knowledge of societal standards for what is proposed, (3) awareness of potential consequences and alternatives, (4) assumption that agreement or disagreement will be respected equally, (5) voluntary decision, and (6) mental competence. Coercion is defined as exploitation of authority, use of bribes, threats of force, or intimidation to gain compliance or cooperation. Equality is defined as two participants operating with the same level of power in a relationship, neither controlled nor coerced by the other. The National Task Force on Juvenile Sexual Offending (1993). National Adolescent Perpetrator Network Revised Report. *Juvenile & Family Court Journal*, 44 (Supp. 4), 3–108. Based on this standard, should M. D. be considered a juvenile sex offender?

In re Washington

75 Ohio St. 3d 390; 662 N.E.2d 346 (Oh. Sup. Ct., 1996)

Appellee, Rhodell Washington, was adjudicated delinquent on two separate counts of rape, and was placed on intensive probation. On September 4, 1992, the date of the rape, Rhodell Washington was eight years old, as were the victims, Camille Pearman and Ashley Anderson. The codefendant, William Little, age twelve, was separately tried.

On December 15, 1992, the Juvenile Division of the court of common pleas conducted an inquiry hearing at which appellee reluctantly admitted to an intake mediator that he had anal intercourse with Camille and Ashley. Despite appellee's young age, the Juvenile Division determined to make the complaint an official filing since appellee showed no remorse for the rapes. The Cleveland Police Department filed a two-count formal complaint against appellee, Rhodell Washington, which alleged he raped Camille Pearman and Ashley Anderson, purposely compelling them to submit to such sexual conduct by force or threat of force, in violation of R.C. 2907.02(A)(1), rape, an aggravated felony of the first degree.

The following evidence was adduced at trial. Camille Pearman testified that in September 1992, appellee hurt her and Ashley. Camille was given anatomically correct dolls and asked to show the court how she was hurt. Camille stated that Dell (the appellee) put his penis into her anus and that this caused her pain. She stated that Little, but not appellee, had threatened her that day, yet she was afraid of both boys at the time that the sexual conduct occurred. Camille also stated that appellee did nothing to help her while Little was threatening the girls.

Camille's mother, Victoria Pearman, testified that she learned of the incident from a neighbor and then questioned her daughter. Camille related to her mother the same set of facts which Camille testified to at trial.

Ashley Anderson testified that on September 4, 1992, appellee was playing with Little. Ashley was also given anatomically correct dolls to aid in her testimony. She stated that appellee touched her private part without asking her permission. She stated that it hurt when appellee touched her. Ashley also stated that she was afraid of appellee on that day. When her mother found out what happened, she was beaten.

Ashley's mother testified that appellee's father contacted her about the incident and stated that his son had something to tell her. Appellee told Ashley's mother "that he had done it too." Upon returning home, she questioned her daughter. Ashley did not want to tell her, so she hit her several times until Ashley related the incident.

The state then presented Alan Maragliano, a social worker at University Hospitals. Maragliano testified that he conversed with both girls, Ashley and Camille, when they were brought into the hospital. He testified that the girls were reluctant to describe the sexual conduct, but did state the two boys took off their shirts and dropped their pants.

Cleveland Police Officer Pamela Berg from the Sex Crimes and Child Abuse Unit testified that she interviewed appellee who, after being advised of his legal rights, admitted in the presence of one of his parents that he inserted his penis into the rectums of both girls. The state then rested. Defense counsel moved for acquittal which was denied by the trial court, and the defense rested.

The trial court thereafter found the allegations of rape proved beyond a reasonable doubt and adjudged appellee delinquent. Appellee was placed on intensive probation, he and his parents were ordered into the pre-adolescent sex offender's program, and his father was ordered into drug rehabilitation.

The court of appeals reversed the trial court's finding that appellee was delinquent. The court of appeals held (1) that the evidence was insufficient to support the trial court's finding, and (2) that a rebuttable presumption existed that appellee was incapable of committing rape because he was under age fourteen, and that the state failed to rebut this presumption.

This matter is now before this court upon an allowance of a discretionary appeal.

Disposition: Judgment reversed.

Justice Sweeney delivered the opinion of the court.

The issues before this court are whether a rebuttable presumption exists that a child under the age of fourteen is incapable of committing the crime of rape and whether sufficient evidence existed to support the trial court's finding that appellee was delinquent. For the following reasons, we find that (1) no such presumption exists in Ohio, and (2) in the present case the evidence was sufficient to support the trial court's finding that appellee was delinquent. Accordingly, we reverse the court of appeals' judgment.

In determining the legal sufficiency of the state's evidence, "the relevant question is whether, after viewing the evidence in the light most favorable to the prosecution, any rational trier of fact could have found the essential elements of the crime beyond a reasonable doubt." The weight and credibility of the evidence are best left to the trier of fact.

R.C. 2907.02(A) states in relevant part as follows:

> (2) No person shall engage in sexual conduct with another when the offender purposely compels the other person to submit by force or threat of force.

R.C. 2907.01(A) defines "sexual conduct" in relevant part as follows:

> 'Sexual conduct' means vaginal intercourse between a male and female, and anal intercourse, fellatio, and cunnilingus, between persons regardless of sex. Penetration, however slight, is sufficient to complete vaginal or anal intercourse.

In the present case, appellee was indicted as follows:

"[Rhodell Washington did] unlawfully engage in sexual conduct with another *** a person who was not his spouse at the time, the said Rhodell Washington purposely compelled [the others] *** to submit to such sexual conduct by force or threat of force ***." At trial, Camille Pearman testified that appellee inserted his penis into her rectum causing her pain. Pamela Berg testified appellee admitted inserting his penis into the rectums of both girls. Both Ashley and Camille testified they were afraid of appellee at the time the sexual incidents occurred. Camille testified that appellee had not threatened her, but he did nothing to help when Little made the threats to them.

Upon viewing the foregoing evidence and the reasonable inferences drawn therefrom in the light most favorable to the state, we conclude that any rational trier of fact could have found beyond a reasonable doubt that appellee penetrated, however slightly, the rectums of both girls with his penis which, pursuant to R.C. 2907.01(A), constituted anal intercourse. Applying the same sufficiency analysis, we likewise conclude that any rational trier of fact could have found beyond a reasonable doubt that appellee, acting in concert with Little, used threats and force to compel Ashley and Camille to submit to anal intercourse. Accordingly, sufficient evidence exists to support the trial court's finding that appellee committed rape.

...

Accordingly, we conclude that a child under the age of fourteen is capable of committing rape and that, in the present case, sufficient evidence existed to support the trial court's finding that appellee committed rape.

The judgment of the court of appeals is reversed.

Judgment reversed.

Justice Wright, dissenting.

Ignore the defendant's age in this case and most of the problems with the majority's decision disappear. Pretend that the defendant was not eight years old when these "serial rapes" were committed and the outcome—probation—appears so mild as to invite outrage. But, focus on the defendant's age and the issue becomes, "did the defendant have criminal intent?" An ancillary question might be, "could the defendant have had criminal intent?"

This case was originally filed because the "appellee showed no remorse for the rapes." To have remorse, a person must understand the nature and consequences of the wrong. I cannot seriously believe that an eight-year-old child intended to commit a rape and then callously ignored the consequences.

It appears from the facts that the parents attempted to resolve this problem. Somehow, in a manner that defies explanation, the problem turned into a court case and is now before this state's highest court. Perhaps I am missing, something, but this strikes me as a scenario out of a Franz Kafka novel.

The majority's reasoning hinges on a reading of R.C. 2907.01(A) that overrules earlier case law which raised a rebuttable presumption that a child under the age of puberty was not capable of committing a rape. The majority apparently finds that when the legislature revised the statute, it intended to broaden the class of potential rape defendants to include young children.

I am satisfied that the focus in this case should be the requisite intent of a defendant. R.C. 2907.02(A)(2) defines rape, in part, as "sexual conduct with another where the offender purposely compels the other person to submit by force or threat of force." There is no showing that the defendant "intended" to have "sexual conduct" with his eight-year-old victims. The child admitted what he did, but nowhere in the facts in there any suggestion that he knew that what he was doing amounted to "sexual conduct." Absent some showing that the defendant had an appreciation of the sexual nature of his conduct, how is it possible to find him guilty of this charge?

Furthermore, the statute requires that the act be committed by "force or threat of force." There is not evidence in the record that the defendant used either. While there is evidence that the girls where "afraid" of the defendant and his twelve-year-old accomplice, and that the twelve-year-old threatened the girls after the "rapes," there is not evidence that force or the threat of force was employed before the "rapes" occurred. Similarly, there is not evidence that the appellee employed any force or threat before or after the "rapes." The majority notes that the appellee did not help the girls when they were threatened. I am at a loss about what the majority would have the eight-year-old do to the threatening twelve-year-old.

. . .

. . . This is an issue better suited to legislative examination than judicial fiat. Respectfully, I dissent.

Justice Pfeifer concurs in the foregoing dissenting opinion.

Notes and Queries

1. Are you convinced that there was force, coercion, or even constructive force in this case?

2. What facts would be needed to demonstrate that an 8-year-old had the requisite intent to rape?

3. The court orders the parents into a sex offender program and requires drug rehabilitation for the father. Does this seem appropriate to you? What should happen to the offender if his parents refuse or drop from treatment?

4. Recall *In re M. D.*, when, "playing doctor," a 12-year-old girl directed two 5-year-olds to perform a sexual act. Are those facts clearly distinguishable from the present forced sexual conduct? Do you agree with the dissent's contention that the defendant lacked appreciation of the sexual nature of his conduct?

In the Matter of Juvenile Action No. JV-121430

172 Ariz. 604; 838 P.2d 1365 (Az. App. Ct., 1992)

Justice Jacobson delivered the opinion of the court.

The sole issue in this appeal is whether an adjudication of delinquency based upon child molestation must be accompanied by a motivation to act with "an unnatural or abnormal sexual interest with respect to children."

The male juvenile was thirteen years old at the time of the incident that gave rise to the charge of delinquency. The act of child molestation consisted of the juvenile placing his finger or fingers into the vagina of a three-year-old girl who was a visitor in his home. The medical evidence showed that as a result, the three-year-old's vagina was severely bruised, bleeding, and the hymen was torn.

At the adjudication hearing, the defense centered upon whether the juvenile's acts were motivated by an unnatural or abnormal sexual interest in children. In support of this defense, Dr. Phillip Esplin, a psychologist, testified:

> Q. Could we say that the act was clinically abnormal?
>
> A. No.
>
> Q. Why not?
>
> A. Because of the base rate frequency with which 13-year-olds, 14-year-olds would engage in behavior of that nature. It's not to say it is [appropriate]. That is a different issue. The issue is, whether you would classify it as an indication of a sexual deviance, and that would be inappropriate to classify it as sexual deviance before the adolescent['s] sexuality solidified.
>
> Q. If a person committed, if an adolescent, age 13 year [old] male, committed the act of inserting his finger into the vagina of a three-year-old girl, is it your opinion that would not be a sexual deviation?
>
> A. Well, you couldn't classify it as a sexual deviation.
>
> Q. Let me stop you, what is the reason for that?
>
> A. Because it is not outside the scope of exploratory sexual behavior of youngsters in that age classification.

The juvenile judge found the juvenile delinquent based upon an act of child molestation. This appeal followed.

The sole issue raised on appeal is whether the evidence presented proved beyond a reasonable doubt that an act of child molestation occurred. The juvenile's contention is that an act of child molestation can only be committed if the act is motivated by an unnatural or abnormal sexual interest in children. His argument continues that, because the sole expert testimony in this case shows that such motivation is not present in a thirteen-year-old male, the evidence fails to support the requisite intent to commit child molestation.

The state responds that the juvenile judge was free to reject the opinion of the expert, that the juvenile judge was free to make his own assessment whether an act of molestation occurred and that, therefore, given the undisputed acts of the juvenile, a delinquency finding is supportable.

The juvenile's argument is premised upon the supposition that a necessary element of the crime of molestation under A.R.S. § 13-1410 is that the actor must be motivated by "an unnatural sexual interest with respect to children." Although the state does not specifically reject this contention, it argues that Dr. Esplin's testimony was immaterial . . . that the "unnatural and abnormal" mental state is merely articulated to distinguish criminal conduct from innocent conduct, and that motivational factors are to be judged by normal societal standards. The narrow issue before us, then, is the nature of the mental state required to adjudicate an adolescent juvenile delinquent for the crime of child molestation.

We begin our analysis of the requisite mental state to commit child molestation by noting that the "unnatural or abnormal sexual interest" language is not contained in the statute. . . .

. . .

. . . Particularly important is the legislative determination as to the defense to molestation:

It is a defense to prosecution pursuant to § 13-1410 that the defendant was not motivated by a sexual interest.

Thus, the logical correlation to this defense is that the intent necessary to commit the crime of molestation is not an "abnormal or unnatural sexual interest," but only that the actor be motivated by a "sexual interest." In our opinion, therefore, the case law that previously used the "abnormal or unnatural" language to distinguish innocent conduct from prohibited conduct has in reality been superseded by the less stringent statutory defense of lack of "sexual interest."

. . .

We thus turn to the issue whether, in the absence of expert testimony, the juvenile's "sexual interest" was established, thus enabling the juvenile judge to find that a child molestation occurred. The juvenile does not dispute that the touching occurred, nor does he claim it was privileged by a parent–child or doctor–patient relationship or that it was authorized by the victim's parents as part of her nonsexual daily care. Under such circumstances, the juvenile's acts, "by their very nature manifest that he was motivated by" a sexual interest, an interest that even Dr. Esplin characterized as "inappropriate" and "clearly unacceptable behavior."

We therefore hold that the evidence supports the juvenile court's conclusion that the acts of this thirteen-year-old juvenile involving a three-year-old victim constituted the offense of child molestation.

Judgment affirmed.

Notes and Queries

1. Since the juvenile's acts seem to be deemed normal, why has he been deemed delinquent? Does the age disparity mean that the acts were coercive?
2. Would you agree with the expert witness that it would be inappropriate to classify acts as sexual deviance before an adolescent's sexuality becomes solidified? What problems do you envision with the expert's approach? Is he nevertheless correct?

Review Problem

1. Thirteen-year-old Junior appeals an adjudication for the acts of indecent assault and involuntary deviate sexual intercourse. The 4-year-old female victim, A. B., testifies that she was left at her aunt's home by her mother and played in the woods with her cousins, Daniel Powell, age 8, Jeff Powell, age 4, and Junior. While in the woods, A. B. testified that Junior took off her shorts, lifted her up, and licked her vaginal area with his tongue five times. Do the actions constitute a sex crime, or is it normative, permissible child play? See *In the Interest of J. R.*, 436 Pa. Super. 416 (1994).

In the Interests of C. P. & R. D.

212 N.J. Super. 222; 514 A.2d 850 (NJ Sup. Ct., 1986)

Judge Ferrante delivered the opinion of the court.

This matter is before the court on juvenile co-defendants' motions seeking dismissal of complaints and presently pending against them. The complaints allege that the two juvenile co-defendants C. P. and R. D. physically restrained the victim, pinning her to the ground, while they inserted their fingers into her vagina. The juveniles were charged with aggravated sexual assault, under N.J.S.A. 2C:14-2(a)(1) and -2(a)(5). These motions seek to dismiss those charges; the arguments proffered by counsel in the matter revolve around the young ages of the juvenile co-defendants. At the outset, the court finds that at the time of the alleged assault, the victim, E. Z., was six years old, juvenile co-defendant C. P. was six years old and juvenile co-defendant R. D. was nine years old. The ages of these young people, while not determinative of the court's decision, are viewed by the court as a tragic circumstance; nonetheless, and without minimizing the tragic consequences this incident has had on the lives of the juveniles involved, and particularly on that of the victim, the court grants the motions to dismiss the charges against both juvenile co-defendants C. P. and R. D.

The issue presented in this matter is one of first impression to the courts of this State. The question is whether juvenile defendants six and nine years of age can be held to trial in juvenile court on the serious charge of aggravated sexual assault.

The statute N.J.S.A. 2C:14-2(a)(1) and -2(a)(5) reads as follows:

> a. An actor is guilty of aggravated sexual assault if he commits an act of sexual penetration with another person under any one of the following circumstances:
>
> (1) The victim is less than 13 years old . . .
>
> (5) The actor is aided or abetted by one or more other persons and either of the following circumstances exists:
>
> (a) The actor uses physical force or coercion, or
>
> (b) The victim is one whom the actor knew or should have known was physically helpless, mentally defective or mentally incapacitated.

Thus, for our purposes, the actus reus of this crime is the act of sexual penetration (as defined, inter alia, in N.J.S.A. 2C:14-1(c) as "insertion of the . . . finger . . . into the . . . vagina . . . by the actor") upon another, either where the victim is under 13 years of age, or else where the act of penetration is accomplished by force and is aided by another person. The mens rea requirement is read into the crime from N.J.S.A. 2C:2-2(c)(3), and the result is, of course, that the actus reus must be accompanied by the mental state described in N.J.S.A. 2C:2-2(b)(2) as 'knowingly,' in which the actor is aware of the nature of his conduct. Juvenile defendants C. P. and R. D. can be convicted of this crime if they are aware of the significance of the events going on around them to the extent that they can engage in their own defense, and also if they are shown to be capable of each element of the crime: the sexual penetration, the involvement of a victim less than 13 years of age, the use of force, and the aid of another actor. Further, it must be shown that these acts were all perpetrated with a 'knowing' awareness of the nature of the acts.

The old common law rule of juvenile responsibility . . . has been statutorily superseded by a single linear test, dependent only on the degree of intellectual and emotional maturity displayed by the defendant. . . .

The written reports on juvenile defendant R. D. are revealing. R. D. is described by Martinez as dysphoric to one degree or another, and subject to anxiety stemming both from family stressors as well as an inadequate sense of self-esteem. It was difficult for Martinez to speculate on the source of the family stress insofar as the adult authorities in the home had indicated their parenting styles had changed since the incident under consideration here. In addition, R. D.'s father is incarcerated and therefore absent from the home. Despite these findings, Martinez indicates that R. D. has, overall, a positive sense of family and interpersonal relations.

More importantly, R. D.'s examination revealed that, in Martinez' words, "he (R. D.) is very naive, and ignorant of most sexual facts . . . he lacks the cognitive development to fully comprehend the impact of what he has done to the victim." Martinez describes R. D.'s risk of recidivism as "low to moderate," based chiefly on his essential lack of understanding of the nature of the acts alleged. Martinez also states that the mother's denial behavior, meant to be protective, has more to do with R. D.'s "moderate" rating than the boy's own clinical status. Summarizing his profile of R. D., Martinez states that R. D. is developmentally delayed, thereby lacking the awareness and knowledge necessary to understand the full meaning and nature of the behavior under consideration, which he also notes occurred spontaneously and in the context of unsupervised play. Martinez concludes by suggesting family and group therapy, as well as counselling for R. D. at an appropriate age level.

Klaatsch's psychiatric evaluation of R. D. is very similar to that of Martinez. He found R. D. to be emotionally immature, and "quite uninformed" on sexual matters; R. D. reportedly knew he was involved in something wrong because of his required court appearances, but could not elaborate. His intellectual functioning was described by Klaatsch as below average, and was emotionally similar to youths several years younger. Klaatsch also recommends only counselling. Both experts reiterated the findings of their reports when called to the witness stand. Both experts denied that R. D. had the ability to understand the acts required in the commission of an aggravated sexual assault, though the experts were never directly questioned as to their own knowledge of the acts requisite to the commission of an aggravated sexual assault.

The situation is similar with regard to juvenile co-defendant C. P.; it is not necessary to reiterate the details, which are in essence identical with the details of the testimony on behalf of R. D. These, then, are the facts on which this court must base its decision. Considering this evidence, can it be that the juvenile co-defendants here are capable of knowingly perpetrating the actus reus indicated by the statute? The court finds, based on the evidence presented by the expert witnesses, and the lack of controverting evidence presented by the prosecution, that the answer must be no. I am satisfied by a preponderance of the evidence that these juveniles could not possibly have formed the mental intent necessary, the "knowing awareness," required by the statute. It is important to point out that the specific actus reus of sexual penetration is, because of the knowledge requirement, more than a mechanical operation or simply a "penetration." This is not a strict liability crime; it requires specifically a knowing sexual penetration, which would entail an awareness of intangible elements, of symbolic knowledge, which the court is convinced by the evidence presented these juvenile co-defendants could not possibly have had.

. . .

Notes and Queries

1. The court focuses on the co-defendant's responsibility. To do so, the court highlights what would constitute "knowingly" for this case. In addition, the court highlights the singular test of responsibility. Are those two tests the same? Should the tests focus on sexual knowledge or other factors?

Michael M. v. Superior Court

450 U.S. 464; 101 S. Ct. 1200 (1981)

Justice Rehnquist announced the judgment of the Court and delivered an opinion, in which The Chief Justice, Justice Stewart, and Justice Powell joined.

The question presented in this case is whether California's "statutory rape" law, § 261.5 of the Cal. Penal Code Ann., violates the Equal Protection Clause of the Fourteenth Amendment. Section 261.5 defines unlawful sexual intercourse as "an act of sexual intercourse accomplished with a female not the wife of the perpetrator, where the female is under the age of 18 years." The statute thus makes men alone criminally liable for the act of sexual intercourse.

In July 1978, a complaint was filed in the Municipal Court of Sonoma County, Cal., alleging that petitioner, then a 17 1/2-year-old male, had had unlawful sexual intercourse with a female under the age of 18, in violation of § 261.5. The evidence adduced at a preliminary hearing showed that at approximately midnight on June 3, 1978, petitioner and two friends approached Sharon, a 16 1/2-year-old female, and her sister as they waited at a bus stop. Petitioner and Sharon, who had already been drinking, moved away from the others and began to kiss. After being struck in the face for rebuffing petitioner's initial advances, Sharon submitted to sexual intercourse with petitioner. Prior to trial, petitioner sought to set aside the information on both state and federal constitutional grounds, asserting that § 261.5 unlawfully discriminated on the basis of gender. The trial court and the California Court of Appeal denied petitioner's request for relief and petitioner sought review in the Supreme Court of California.

The [California] Supreme Court held that "section 261.5 discriminates on the basis of sex because only females may be victims, and only males may violate the section." The court then subjected the classification to "strict scrutiny," stating that it must be justified by a compelling state interest. It found that the classification was "supported not by mere social convention but by the immutable physiological fact that it is the female exclusively who can become pregnant." Canvassing "the tragic human costs of illegitimate teenage pregnancies," including the large number of teenage abortions, the increased medical risk associated with teenage pregnancies, and the social consequences of teenage childbearing, the court concluded that the State has a compelling interest in preventing such pregnancies. Because males alone can "physiologically cause the result which the law properly seeks to avoid," the court further held that the gender classification was readily justified as a means of identifying offender and victim. For the reasons stated below, we affirm the judgment of the California Supreme Court.

... Our cases have held, however, that the traditional minimum rationality test takes on a somewhat "sharper focus" when gender-based classifications are challenged....

Underlying these decisions is the principle that a legislature may not "make overbroad generalizations based on sex which are entirely unrelated to any differences between men and women or which demean the ability or social status of the affected class." But ... this Court has consistently upheld statutes where the gender classification is not invidious, but rather realistically reflects the fact that the sexes are not similarly situated in certain circumstances....

Applying those principles to this case, the fact that the California Legislature criminalized the act of illicit sexual intercourse with a minor female is a sure indication of its intent or purpose to discourage that conduct....

The justification for the statute offered by the State, and accepted by the Supreme Court of California, is that the legislature sought to prevent illegitimate teenage pregnancies. That finding, of course, is entitled to great deference. And although our cases establish that the State's asserted reason for the enactment of a statute may be rejected, if it "could not have been a goal of the legislation," this is not such a case.

We are satisfied not only that the prevention of illegitimate pregnancy is at least one of the "purposes" of the statute, but also that the State has a strong interest in preventing such pregnancy. At the risk of stating the obvious, teenage pregnancies, which have increased dramatically over the last two decades, have significant social, medical, and economic consequences for both the mother and her child, and the State. Of particular concern to the State is that approximately half of all teenage pregnancies end in abortion. And of those children who are born, their illegitimacy makes them likely candidates to become wards of the State.

We need not be medical doctors to discern that young men and young women are not similarly situated with respect to the problems and the risks of sexual intercourse. Only women may become pregnant, and they suffer disproportionately the profound physical, emotional, and psychological consequences of sexual activity. The statute at issue here protects women from sexual intercourse at an age when those consequences are particularly severe.

The question thus boils down to whether a State may attack the problem of sexual intercourse and teenage pregnancy directly by prohibiting a male from having sexual intercourse with a minor female. We hold that such a statute is sufficiently related to the State's objectives to pass constitutional muster.

Because virtually all of the significant harmful and inescapably identifiable consequences of teenage pregnancy fall on the young female, a legislature acts well within its authority when it elects to punish only the participant who, by nature, suffers few of the consequences of his conduct. It is hardly unreasonable for a legislature acting to protect minor females to exclude them from punishment. Moreover, the risk of pregnancy itself constitutes a substantial deterrence to young females. No similar natural sanctions deter males. A criminal sanction imposed solely on males thus serves to roughly "equalize" the deterrents on the sexes.

. . .

Accordingly the judgment of the California Supreme Court is

Affirmed.

Justice Stewart, concurring.

. . .

At the outset, it should be noted that the statutory discrimination, when viewed as part of the wider scheme of California law, is not as clearcut as might at first appear. Females are not freed from criminal liability in California for engaging in sexual activity that may be harmful. It is unlawful, for example, for any person, of either sex, to molest, annoy, or contribute to the delinquency of anyone under 18 years of age. All persons are prohibited from committing "any lewd or lascivious act," including consensual intercourse, with a child under 14. And members of both sexes may be convicted for engaging in deviant sexual acts with anyone under 18. Finally, females may be brought within the proscription of § 261.5 itself, since a female may be charged with aiding and abetting its violation.

Section 261.5 is thus but one part of a broad statutory scheme that protects all minors from the problems and risks attendant upon adolescent sexual activity. To be sure, § 261.5 creates an additional measure of punishment for males who engage in sexual intercourse with females between the ages of 14 and 17. The question then is whether the Constitution prohibits a state legislature from imposing this additional sanction on a gender-specific basis.

. . .

Young women and men are not similarly situated with respect to the problems and risks associated with intercourse and pregnancy, and the statute is realistically related to the legitimate state purpose of reducing those problems and risks.

C

As the California Supreme Court's catalog shows, the pregnant unmarried female confronts problems more numerous and more severe than any faced by her male partner. She alone endures the medical risks of pregnancy or abortion. She suffers disproportionately the social, educational, and emotional consequences of pregnancy. Recognizing this disproportion, California has attempted to protect teenage females by prohibiting males from participating in the act necessary for conception.

. . .

Justice Blackmun, concurring in the judgment.

. . .

I, however, cannot vote to strike down the California statutory rape law, for I think it is a sufficiently reasoned and constitutional effort to control the problem at its inception. . . .

. . .

I think, too, that it is only fair, with respect to this particular petitioner, to point out that his partner, Sharon, appears not to have been an unwilling participant in at least the initial stages of the intimacies that took place the night of June 3, 1978. Petitioner's and Sharon's nonacquaintance with each other before the incident: their drinking; their withdrawal from the others of the group; their foreplay, in which she willingly participated and seems to have encouraged; and the closeness of their ages (a difference of only one year and 18 days) are factors that should make this case an unattractive one to prosecute at all, and especially to prosecute as a felony, rather than as a misdemeanor chargeable under § 261.5. But the State has chosen to prosecute in that manner, and the facts, I reluctantly conclude, may fit the crime.

Justice Brennan, with whom Justices White and Marshall join, dissenting.

. . .

Until very recently, no California court or commentator had suggested that the purpose of California's statutory rape law was to protect young women from the risk of pregnancy. Indeed, the historical development of § 261.5 demonstrates that the law was initially enacted on the premise that young women, in contrast to young men, were to be deemed legally incapable of consenting to an act of sexual intercourse. Because their chastity was considered particularly precious, those young women were felt to be uniquely in need of the State's protection. In contrast, young men were assumed to be capable of making such decisions for themselves; the law therefore did not offer them any special protection.

It is perhaps because the gender classification in California's statutory rape law was initially designed to further these outmoded sexual stereotypes, rather than to reduce the incidence of teenage pregnancies, that the State has been unable to demonstrate a substantial relationship between the classification and its newly asserted goal. . . . It has therefore not met its burden of proving that the statutory classification is substantially related to the achievement of its asserted goal. . . .

Justice Stevens, dissenting.

Local custom and belief—rather than statutory laws of venerable but doubtful ancestry—will determine the volume of sexual activity among unmarried teenagers. The empirical evidence cited by the plurality demonstrates the futility of the notion that a statutory prohibition will significantly affect the volume of that activity or provide a meaningful solution to the problems created by it. Nevertheless, as a matter of constitutional power, unlike my Brother Brennan, I would have no doubt about the validity of a state law prohibiting all unmarried teenagers from engaging in sexual intercourse. The societal interests in reducing the incidence of venereal disease and teenage pregnancy are sufficient, in my judgment, to justify a prohibition of conduct that increases the risk of those harms.

My conclusion that a nondiscriminatory prohibition would be constitutional does not help me answer the question whether a prohibition applicable to only half of the joint participants in the risk-creating conduct is also valid. It cannot be true that the validity of a total ban is an adequate justification for a selective prohibition; otherwise, the constitutional objection to discriminatory rules would be meaningless. The question in this case is whether the difference between males and females justifies this statutory discrimination based entirely on sex.

...

In this case, the fact that a female confronts a greater risk of harm than a male is a reason for applying the prohibition to her — not a reason for granting her a license to use her own judgment on whether or not to assume the risk. Surely, if we examine the problem from the point of view of society's interest in preventing the risk-creating conduct from occurring at all, it is irrational to exempt 50% of the potential violators. And, if we view the government's interest as that of a parens patriae seeking to protect its subjects from harming themselves, the discrimination is actually perverse. Would a rational parent making rules for the conduct of twin children of opposite sex simultaneously forbid the son and authorize the daughter to engage in conduct that is especially harmful to the daughter? That is the effect of this statutory classification.

... But from the standpoint of fashioning a general preventive rule — or, indeed, in determining appropriate punishment when neither party in fact has suffered any special harm — I regard a total exemption for the members of the more endangered class as utterly irrational.

...

Finally, even if my logic is faulty and there actually is some speculative basis for treating equally guilty males and females differently, I still believe that any such speculative justification would be outweighed by the paramount interest in evenhanded enforcement of the law. A rule that authorizes punishment of only one of two equally guilty wrongdoers violates the essence of the constitutional requirement that the sovereign must govern impartially.

I respectfully dissent.

Notes and Queries

1. Many agree with the dissent's charge that the plurality perpetuates stereotypes. What would be the outcome of a more gender-neutral law? A major rationale for statutory rape laws is that prosecutors could charge rapists in cases where there may be a doubt regarding the victim's nonconsent. Good idea? Why not just rely on laws that would require proving lack of consent? Would that be fairer to minors?

2. Are you persuaded by the overall theme that boys and girls are differently situated enough that they should be treated differently?

3. Consider Sharon's testimony at the preliminary hearing. Is the law applied fairly? Should that matter? Would you view the facts as sufficient to uphold forcible rape charges? Relatedly, Justice Blackmun observes that, based on the testimony, the sexual acts were consensual. Does the transcript Justice Blackmun relies on support his view?

> Q. [by the Deputy District Attorney]. On June the 4th, at approximately midnight—midnight of June the 3rd, were you in Rohnert Park? . . .
>
> Q. Did anything unusual happen to you that night in Rohnert Park?
>
> A. Yes.
>
> Q. Would you briefly describe what happened that night? Did you see the defendant that night in Rohnert Park?
>
> A. Yes.
>
> Q. Where did you first meet him?
>
> A. At a bus stop.
>
> Q. Was anyone with you?
>
> A. My sister.
>
> Q. Was anyone with the defendant?
>
> A. Yes.
>
> Q. How many people were with the defendant?
>
> A. Two.
>
> Q. Now, after you met the defendant, what happened?
>
> A. We walked down to the railroad tracks.
>
> Q. What happened at the railroad tracks?
>
> A. We were drinking at the railroad tracks and we walked over to this bush and he started kissing me and stuff, and I was kissing him back, too, at first. Then, I was telling him to stop—
>
> Q. Yes.
>
> A. —and I was telling him to slow down and stop. He said, 'Okay, okay.' But then he just kept doing it. He just kept doing it and then my sister and two other guys came over to where we were and my sister said—told me to get up and come home. And then I didn't—
>
> Q. Yes.
>
> A. —and then my sister and—
>
> Q. All right.

A. —David, one of the boys that were there, started walking home and we stayed there and then later—

Q. All right.

A. —Bruce left Michael, you know.

The Court: Michael being the defendant?

The Witness: Yeah. We was laying there and we were kissing each other, and then he asked me if I wanted to walk him over to the park; so we walked over to the park and we sat down on a bench and then he started kissing me again and we were laying on the bench. And he told me to take my pants off. I said, 'No,' and I was trying to get up and he hit me back down on the bench and then I just said to myself, 'Forget it,' and I let him do what he wanted to do and he took my pants off and he was telling me to put my legs around him and stuff."

...

Q. Did you have sexual intercourse with the defendant?

A. Yeah.

Q. He did put his penis into your vagina?

A. Yes.

Q. You said that he hit you?

A. Yeah.

Q. How did he hit you?

A. He slugged me in the face.

Q. With what did he slug you?

A. His fist.

Q. Where abouts in the face?

A. On my chin.

Q. As a result of that, did you have any bruises or any kind of an injury?

A. Yeah.

Q. What happened?

A. I had bruises.

The Court: Did he hit you one time or did he hit you more than once?

The Witness: He hit me about two or three times.

...

Q. Now, during the course of that evening, did the defendant ask you your age?

A. Yeah.

Q. And what did you tell him?

A. Sixteen.

Q. Did you tell him you were sixteen?

A. Yes.

Q. Now, you said you had been drinking, is that correct?

A. Yes.

Q. Would you describe your condition as a result of the drinking?

A. I was a little drunk.

Cross-Examination

. . .

Q. Now, you and Mr. M., as I understand it, went off into the bushes, is that correct?

A. Yes.

Q. Okay. And what did you do when you and Mr. M. were there in the bushes?

A. We were kissing and hugging.

Q. Were you sitting up?

A. We were laying down.

Q. You were lying down. This was in the bushes?

A. Yes.

Q. How far away from the rest of them were you?

A. They were just bushes right next to the railroad tracks. We just walked off into the bushes; not very far.

. . .

Q. So your sister and the other two boys came over to where you were, you and Michael were, is that right?

A. Yeah.

Q. What did they say to you, if you remember?

A. My sister didn't say anything. She said, 'Come on, Sharon, let's go home.'

Q. She asked you to go home with her?

A. (Affirmative nod.)

Q. Did you go home with her?

A. No.

Q. You wanted to stay with Mr. M.?

A. I don't know.

Q. Was this before or after he hit you?

A. Before.

. . .

Q. What happened in the five minutes that Bruce stayed there with you and Michael?

A. I don't remember.

Q. You don't remember at all?

A. (Negative head shake.)

Q. Did you have occasion at that time to kiss Bruce?

A. Yeah.

Q. You did? You were kissing Bruce at that time?

A. (Affirmative nod.)

Q. Was Bruce kissing you?

A. Yes.

Q. And were you standing up at this time?

A. No, we were sitting down.

. . .

Q. Okay. So at this point in time you had left Mr. M. and you were hugging and kissing with Bruce, is that right?

A. Yeah.

Q. And you were sitting up.

. . .

Q. Whose idea was it for you and Bruce to kiss? Did you initiate that?

A. Yes.

Q. What happened after Bruce left?

A. Michael asked me if I wanted to go walk to the park.

Q. And what did you say?

A. I said, 'Yes.'

Q. And then what happened?

A. We walked to the park.

. . .

4. Statutory rape laws attempt to protect teenagers from themselves, as well as from those who would prey upon their vulnerabilities. These laws complement

conventional rape law largely on the rationale that it offers little protection to the teenager who is not competent enough to "consent" to unwanted sex. Although it may be difficult to draw "bright lines" marking the ability to consent to sexual activity, it seems true that numerous factors make teenage girls susceptible to coercion and abuse in sexual encounters. The vulnerability inherent in adolescence, including severely diminished self-esteem, ambivalence about one's changing body, and a marked reluctance to assert one's self, leads teenagers to consent to undesired sexual contact. The peculiarities of adolescence complicate matters; it may well be that sexual desire and love plays a role, while it also may be that teenagers engage in sexual activity out of fear, confusion, coercion, peer pressure, and a desire for attention. See Roger J. R. Levesque (2000). *Adolescents, Sex, and the Law: Preparing Adolescents for Responsible Citizenship.* Washington, DC: American Psychological Association.

Review Problem

1. In 1993, a group of California teenage boys called the Spur Posse gained considerable notoriety for having developed a "game" in which members of the group sought to score points by having sexual encounters with as many females as possible. Members scored points for each time a girl gave them an orgasm. The boys were from the popular crowd and used their popularity to "encourage" girls to engage in "consensual" sex with them. Estimates are that each had sexual relations with anywhere from twenty to seventy-three different girls. Should peer pressure count as a reason to find coercion? Should the boys be held for statutory rape? Other states have recently had cases involving similar games, which, like the Spur Posse case, resulted in few prosecutions and minimal penalties. See Michelle Oberman (2000). Regulating consensual sex with minors: Defining a role for statutory rape. *Buffalo Law Review*, 48, 703–784.

State v. Yanez

716 A.2d 759 (Sup. Ct. R. I. 1998)

Justice Goldberg delivered the opinion of the court.

The principal issue presented by this case is whether a reasonable mistake of fact concerning a complainant's age may be asserted as a defense to a charge of statutory-rape. For the reasons articulated in this opinion, we hold that with respect to the age requirement first-degree child-molestation sexual assault is a strict-liability offense. Consequently a defendant charged with this offense may not introduce evidence that he or she was mistaken regarding the child's age, nor is a defendant entitled to a jury instruction regarding the same. A recitation of the facts is in order.

Facts

The defendant, Alejandro Yanez (Yanez), was eighteen-years-old when he engaged in consensual sexual intercourse with Allison (a fictitious name), the victim in this case, who was thirteen-years-old at the time. The two were first introduced to each other, albeit ever so briefly, in August 1992, nearly a year before this incident. Allison testified that she was attending a Portuguese festival with a girlfriend when she saw her aunt's boyfriend, Victor Yanez (Victor), defendant's brother. According to Allison, who at that time was only twelve-years-old, Victor introduced her to Yanez. For the next eleven months Allison and Yanez had virtually no contact with each other except for the obligatory "Hello" in passing. Then one day in mid-July 1993, while Allison was walking to the local park to meet friends, she saw Yanez cruise by in his white Trans Am convertible with the top down. She testified that she waved to Yanez, who proceeded to turn the Trans Am around and offer her a ride. Since the park was only across the street, Allison declined Yanez's invitation, but when he persisted, Allison acceded. The two briefly talked during the quarter-mile trip. Yanez gave Allison his name and telephone number, and the two conversed again briefly that night on the telephone.

The next day Allison received a telephone message from either her mother or her sister that Yanez had called her and asked that she call him back. Allison returned Yanez's telephone call, and the two made arrangements to meet in the parking lot behind St. Joseph's Church in West Warwick. From the church the two left in Yanez's car and went for a ride. According to Allison, they proceeded to the home of a friend of Yanez's where they engaged in consensual sexual intercourse on the floor in a back bedroom.

Following the conclusion of their first "date" Allison returned home quite late. After entering the house, Allison proceeded directly to the bathroom to shower whereupon she was subsequently confronted by her mother. While in the bathroom, Allison's mother noticed her underwear on the floor and asked if she had engaged in sexual intercourse. Allison initially denied having had sexual intercourse that evening but later admitted the truth. Subsequently Allison's mother contacted the police, whereupon Allison admitted that she had engaged in sexual intercourse but named as her partner a person called Derek. Allison later explained that she had lied about Yanez's identity because she did not want her mother to know that she had engaged in sexual intercourse with Yanez. A subsequent police investigation revealed that Yanez admitted having had sexual intercourse with Allison but insisted that Allison had told him that she was sixteen-years-old. Allison denied having told Yanez that she was sixteen years of age and, in fact, testified that on the two or three occasions when Yanez had inquired about her age, she had responded that she was only thirteen.

Yanez was indicted on one count of first-degree child-molestation sexual assault in violation of G.L. 1956 §§ 11-37-8.1 and 11-37-8.2, although the trial testimony would later reveal that this was not an isolated incident and that there were two more equally sordid, uncharged encounters. At trial defense counsel made numerous attempts to introduce evidence not only demonstrating Yanez's mistaken belief concerning Allison's age but also evidence concerning Allison's apparent maturity in light of her appearance, physical development, and demeanor. The trial justice rejected this evidence and determined that in cases in which conduct is made criminal because the victim is a minor, the defense of ignorance or mistaken belief with respect to the victim's age is not available. The trial justice further indicated that he intended to charge the jury with respect to the unavailability of this defense and consequently declined to charge in accordance with Yanez's requested mistake of fact instructions.

...

Following deliberations a Superior Court jury convicted Yanez of first-degree child-molestation sexual assault....

We note that even though we do not agree with the account of the facts set forth by the dissent—and reiterate that we saw no evidence that Allison and Yanez were actually dating—we are satisfied that even if this version was true, the General Assembly never intended that a charge of statutory-rape should be sorted out by a jury. With this assertion in mind we begin our analysis.

I

Mistake of Fact Defense

...

... Yanez argues that ... we are constrained to imply a mens rea requirement with respect to the age requirement (the second element of § 11-37-8.1) in a charge of first-degree child-molestation sexual assault. We disagree.

A. Statutory Interpretation

"It is well established that the Legislature may, pursuant to its police powers, define criminal offenses without requiring proof of a specific criminal intent and so provide that the perpetrator proceed at his own peril regardless of his defense of ignorance or an honest mistake of fact." ... Against this backdrop we examine our first-degree child-molestation sexual assault statute.

Section 11-37-8.1 provides that:

> [a] person is guilty of first degree child molestation sexual assault if he or she engages in sexual penetration with a person fourteen (14) years of age or under.

The term "sexual penetration" is defined in § 11-37-1(8) as follows:

> 'Sexual penetration'—sexual intercourse, cunnilingus, fellatio, and anal intercourse, or any other intrusion, however slight, by any part of a person's body or by any object into the genital or anal openings of another person's body, but emission of semen is not required.

Clearly the plain words and meaning of § 11-37-8.1 prohibit the sexual penetration of an underaged person and make no reference to the actor's state of mind, knowledge, or belief. In our opinion this lack of a mens rea results not from negligent omission but from legislative design.

Yanez correctly asserts that this Court has previously declared the existence of an implied mens rea element with respect to the term "sexual contact" in cases of second-degree sexual assault and to some but not all acts of "sexual penetration" in cases of first-degree child-molestation sexual assault. These opinions represent our determination that conduct that the Legislature has included within the definitions of "sexual contact" or "sexual penetration," other than sexual intercourse, anal intercourse, cunnilingus, or fellatio, may in the absence of a mens rea element embrace conduct that is intended for an innocent purpose and not for purposes of sexual arousal or gratification.

For instance, in *Bryant* with respect to the count of the indictment charging the defendant with first-degree child-molestation sexual assault for engaging in the digital penetration of the victim, we declared that necessity required "an instruction concerning sexual arousal or gratification in order to preclude the possibility that a defendant could be convicted because of an innocent touching." However, with respect to the count charging penile penetration, we held that this mens rea instruction was not necessary because purposeful penile penetration precludes a finding of innocent touching.... Thus in most but not all cases of statutory-sexual assault, and except in the most limited instances of child-molestation sexual assault, the "legislative focus is not dependent upon the question of whether the perpetrator at the time of the penetration was sufficiently aroused and gratified."

However, this debate concerning penetration but not gratification should in no way suggest our willingness to imply an element of mens rea with respect to the child's age. We decline to permit a defendant charged with the sexual penetration of a child fourteen years of age or younger to escape responsibility on the basis of the purported consent of the victim or a defendant's mistaken, albeit reasonable, belief that the child was over the age of consent. Our position has both historical and legislative support.

. . .

It can be inferred from this statutory classification that the child-molestation sexual assault statutes silence with regard to a mens rea "is designed to subserve the state interest of protecting female children from the severe physical and psychological consequences of engaging in coitus before attaining the age of consent in the statute." . . .

B. Due-Process Argument

Despite the Legislature's design Yanez nonetheless continues to argue that § 11-37-8.1 contains an implicit element that the accused must have knowledge that the victim is fourteen years of age or younger. Yanez suggests that § 11-37-8.1 violates his due-process rights because he had neither the opportunity to learn Allison's true age nor the opportunity to present a meaningful defense concerning his reasonable mistake. . . .

Indeed Yanez correctly states that "the existence of a mens rea is the rule of, rather than the exception to, the principles of Anglo-American criminal jurisprudence." . . .

Despite this well-recognized judicial principle, in order for Yanez to prove that the Legislature's exercise of its power runs afoul of the protections guaranteed by the due-process clause, Yanez must demonstrate that this practice "offends some principle of justice so rooted in the traditions and conscience of our people as to be ranked as fundamental." Yanez cannot satisfy this test.

. . .

We note that at the sentencing hearing the trial justice was fully cognizant of Yanez's favorable presentence report, his work history, his expressed remorse, and his supportive family. However, there is no escaping the fact that on their very first "date" following a brief encounter lasting only two or three minutes the previous day, this eighteen-year-old defendant engaged in sexual intercourse on the bedroom floor of his friend's house with this thirteen-year-old girl. The trial justice appropriately observed that there was some measure of planning involved in Yanez's encounters with Allison, which were aimed at avoiding detection by her mother. The trial justice further noted that the fact that Allison may have been "experienced" for someone her age or that her unfortunate past might have been somewhat unstable or troubled is not a defense. Indeed, the trial justice appropriately concluded that Allison is exactly the type of victim whose vulnerability the Legislature had intended to protect and that an offense perpetrated upon one in her circumstances "is more harmful than one committed upon someone who has a stable environment." Thus, although observing that "it is the public policy of this state *** that those who engage in sexual intercourse with a person under 14, should be treated harshly," the trial justice nonetheless fashioned a compassionate sentence designed to promote not only rehabilitation but also deterrence. In the words of the trial justice, this sentence is "not only to deter this young man from committing similar crimes, but to discourage or deter others in the community; to let them know that if they're going to succumb to passion with someone under 14 years of age, there's a very high price to pay." We agree with the trial justice and find no error in his decision.

We recognize that the dissent firmly believes that the General Assembly intended for jurors "to sort out true cases of child molestation from those involving consensual premarital sex between teenagers based upon a mistaken but reasonably held belief that both were old enough to do so legally." We observe, however, the social and policy considerations such a defense would engender in future prosecutions for child-molestation.

First, it would open the door to the introduction of evidence concerning a victim's past sexual conduct, evidence that the General Assembly has already sought to restrict through the enactment of the rape-shield statute. . . . Therefore if a victim, in this case Allison, is to be subject to cross-examination, as the dissent suggests, concerning her "evident sexual experience," as well as her "developed physical appearance, her poise, [and] her association with older teenagers," in order for a defendant to establish his or her reasonable belief that the victim was at least sixteen-years-old, we conclude that such action should come from the Legislature and not from this Court. This is a door best left closed until it is opened, if at all, by those who are better able to debate all the consequences.

Second, we are mindful that were we to adopt a mistake of age defense in cases of child-molestation sexual assault, this defense would be available to all persons charged with engaging in sexual contact with children under the age of fourteen and not only this eighteen-year-old defendant. The availability of this defense would, of course, inevitably lead to the presentation of evidence concerning the issue of consent. In order to avail oneself of the mistake of age defense, the accused, like Yanez in this case, would be required to allege not only that he or she reasonably believed the victim to have been at least sixteen years of age but also that the victim consented to the act. This defense would result in the prosecution having the burden of proving beyond a reasonable doubt the fact that the victim did not consent to a crime in which the Legislature has decreed that consent is irrelevant.

. . .

Conclusion

For the reasons articulated, we deny the defendant's appeal and affirm the judgment of conviction. . . .

Justice Flanders, dissenting.

I respectfully dissent. I cannot believe that the Legislature intended that (Rhode Island's statutory-rape law) — carrying a mandatory-minimum sentence of twenty years in jail — should be construed by the Judiciary to bar an accused teenager's reasonable mistake-of-age defense to charges based upon his engaging in consensual sexual acts with his teenaged girlfriend. The unavoidable result of such a draconian interpretation of this law is the imposition on this defendant, Alejandro Yanez (Alex) — a young man who was barely eighteen years old at the time of this incident — of an uncommonly brutal, harsh, and undeserved punishment that is so out of whack with reality that it is virtually without parallel in any jurisdiction of the United States.

[The dissent also notes, in note 1, the following: Although Alex received the minimum twenty-year sentence after the trial justice refused to consider his mistake-of-age defense, the trial justice ordered him to serve the first two years of his sentence in prison and suspended the remaining eighteen years while placing Alex on probation for this period. Thus, even after Alex finishes serving his prison sentence, he will be subject to re-imprisonment for up to eighteen years if he fails to keep the peace or engages in any other conduct that causes a hearing justice to be reasonably satisfied that he has violated the terms of his probation. Moreover, he will be required to register as a convicted sex offender and will be forever stigmatized as a convicted felon and child molester. Accordingly, in the circumstances of this case I disagree with the majority's conclusion that this outcome represents "a compassionate sentence."]

If any legislative intent is apparent in the language used in § 11-37-8.1 to criminalize sex with children, it is the intent manifest in its title to outlaw sexual abuse of children by adults and to punish severely those who commit such "child molestation." But there is a world of difference between a crime involving intentional child molestation and a situation like this one in which two teenage lovers engage in a fully consensual act (or acts) of sexual intercourse in the mistaken belief on the part of one of them that they are both of a legal age to do so. Although their exuberant sexual behavior may be sniffed at by a tongue-clucking majority as "sordid," it is certainly not "child molestation" within the meaning of Rhode Island's statutory-rape law. Any criminal statute that carries a mandatory twenty-year jail sentence and imposes a lifelong stigma as a sexual predator on any violator should be rationally interpreted to draw a distinction between these two very different scenarios — especially when, as here, the sexual conduct in question would have been unquestionably legal if Alex's sexual partner had been sixteen years old, as she allegedly said she was.

In this case, two versions of what happened vie for acceptance. According to the defense, Alex, an eighteen-year-old (who was only six months too old for participation in our juvenile court system), had been dating a mature-looking young woman whom he had met several times previously and who phoned him and asked him to go out on that fateful evening. Alex claims that the young woman told him she was sixteen when (unbeknownst to him) she was really a month and a half shy of her fourteenth birthday. Her deceit was made more credible, Alex contends, by her mature and developed physical appearance, her poise, her association with older teenagers, and her evident sexual experience. The defense was prepared to produce witnesses to corroborate the reasonableness of Alex's being taken in by these misrepresentations but the trial justice barred him from doing so. In any event, there is no dispute that Alex and his date engaged in fully consensual sexual relations with each other. The prosecution, on the other hand, paints Alex as a fully accountable eighteen-year-old adult who, after having been warned that the young woman was not old enough to be seeing him, nonetheless proceeded to take advantage of her, knowing full well that the allure of his relative sophistication — together with his ownership of a car and access to a friend's apartment — would work its magic on an impressionable thirteen-year-old. But because the trial justice prevented Alex from introducing any evidence concerning the reasonableness of his mistaken belief that his teenage girlfriend was of legal age to engage in consensual sex, the jury never got to hear any of this testimony.

I would hold that in this type of situation the General Assembly intended that a jury—not judges or prosecutors—is the appropriate body to sort out true cases of child molestation from those involving consensual premarital sex between teenagers based upon a mistaken but reasonably held belief that both were old enough to do so legally. To this end, a criminal defendant indicted under § 11-37-8.1 should be afforded the opportunity to defend against such charges by showing a reasonable and good-faith mistake concerning the age of his or her consenting sexual partner.

. . .

Notes and Queries

1. Some would probably consider the defendant's awareness of the age of the victim in a statutory rape case to be crucial to the moral quality of the defendant's act, but this case highlights that the traditional and still very common rule is to impose strict liability on that element of the offense. Do you find compelling the argument that strict liability is necessary to fulfill the protective functions of the statutory rape statutes?
2. Do you concur with the court's social policy considerations?
3. Are you convinced that the court must exclude challenges to the victim's credibility because the mistake of fact defense is not available to defendants? Do you think this simply goes too far?

State v. Tevay

707 A.2d 700 (Sup. Ct. R.I., 1998)

Per Curiam.

. . . The defendant, Nolan R. Tevay (Tevay), appeals his conviction on one count of second-degree child molestation in violation of G.L. 1956 § 11-37-8.3. . . .

The victim in this case, Jody (a fictitious name), was twelve years old when she testified to an incident involving Tevay, her stepfather, which had occurred some months prior to August 1994. Jody testified that one afternoon at her mother's request she entered the bedroom where Tevay had been sleeping to wake him for work. After entering the room, Jody stated, she told Tevay to wake up and then proceeded to shake him with her hands. At this point Tevay grabbed Jody, pulled her into his bed, touched her buttock, and forced Jody to touch his penis. Jody testified that during the two-minute incident Tevay's eyes were halfway open and that he warned her later not to tell anyone or he would beat her.

After freeing herself from Tevay's grasp, Jody testified, she ran down the stairs where she encountered her mother, who stated: "Are you okay? You look like you saw a ghost." Jody responded, "Mommy, I think Nolan thought I was you." Jody refused to explain, however, and suggested that they just "forget about it." Thereafter, for reasons apparently unrelated to this incident, Tevay moved out of the home. This separation was only temporary.

On February 14, 1995, Jody's mother informed Jody that Tevay would be returning home. On that same day Jody confided in a cousin, and later told her mother, about the earlier bedroom incident with Tevay. Subsequently, Jody gave a police statement in which she stated that Tevay had forced her to touch his penis and that Tevay had also touched her vagina. Tevay was later charged with two counts of second-degree child molestation. Count 1 charged that Tevay had touched Jody's vagina with his hand, and count 2 charged that Tevay had forced Jody's hand to touch his penis. Both counts related to the same incident.

. . .

Tevay first argues that the trial justice did not adequately inform the jury of the mens rea requirement needed to find him guilty of second-degree child molestation in light of his defense that if he did commit the charged act, he did so while semiconscious and under the mistaken belief that Jody was his wife. The trial justice initially instructed the jurors that they must find beyond a reasonable doubt that Tevay's conduct was intentional and had as its purpose sexual arousal or gratification. Following defense counsel's objection to the failure to instruct on the defense of accident or mistake-of-fact, the trial justice expanded upon his instruction by reiterating that the state must prove Tevay's conduct intentional beyond a reasonable doubt and "that [Tevay] may not be found guilty of conduct which you feel from the evidence, causes you to conclude that the conduct was accidental." After this instruction defense counsel again objected and repeated his request for a mistake-of-fact instruction. This request was denied.

. . .

The trial justice instructed the jurors that they must find Tevay's conduct intentional beyond a reasonable doubt and not as a result of an accident. Although the trial justice denied Tevay's request to instruct on mistake-of-fact, we are of the opinion that both accident and mistake-of-fact in the context of this case relate to the same defense theory. In other words the accident was the mistaken belief that Jody was Tevay's wife. Therefore, we conclude the jurors were adequately informed that if they had found Tevay's conduct toward Jody was unintentional, for any reason, they were to return a verdict of not guilty.

. . .

For the foregoing reasons we deny and dismiss the defendant's appeal. . . .

Notes and Queries

1. The *Tevay* court reaffirmed the requirement that the prosecution must prove intentional wrongdoing for the defendant to be guilty of child molestation and specifically endorsed a mistake-of-fact defense by approving a jury instruction that would excuse a defendant's conduct if it was based on a mistake of identity or "was unintentional, for any reason." Moreover, *Tevay* emphasized that if an accused's sexual conduct with a minor was indeed based on a reasonable mistake of fact, the jury was required to return a not-guilty verdict—notwithstanding the undeniable fact that the defendant's sexual contact with a 12-year-old girl was admittedly for the purpose of his sexual arousal or gratification. Is this a more just rule than the one announced in *State v. Yanez*?

2. Can you imagine a scenario in which a court should uphold a mistaken identity claim?

Review Problem

1. On trial for rape of a child and indecent assault and battery on a child under the age of 14, the defendant testifies that there was only one sexual episode between himself and the victim. One night in September 1989, after he had taken his girlfriend to work and returned home, he went to bed for a nap, which was his usual custom. He was awakened by someone massaging him, and then felt a hand go between his legs. He assumed his girlfriend was in bed with him. He responded by engaging in oral intercourse. After a few minutes, he realized that the person was not his girlfriend. He jumped up and turned on the light and saw the babysitter, who was naked. He knew she was 13 years old. He told her to get out of the bed. The victim testifies that they had had sexual relations for several months. The defendant is found guilty. On appeal, should the court rule for the defendant if the trial court did not instruct the jury that the defendant should not be held liable if he made a reasonable mistake as to the identity of the victim? See *Commonwealth v. Knap*, 412 Mass. 712; 592 N.E.2d 747 (1992), which rejected the defendant's argument, finding that statutory rape and indecent assault and battery on a child are strict liability crimes.

New York v. Ferber

458 U.S. 747; 102 S. Ct. 3348 (1982)

Justice White delivered the opinion of the Court.

At issue in this case is the constitutionality of a New York criminal statute which prohibits persons from knowingly promoting sexual performances by children under the age of 16 by distributing material which depicts such performances.

. . .

At issue in this case is § 263.15, defining a class D felony:

> A person is guilty of promoting a sexual performance by a child when, knowing the character and content thereof, he produces, directs or promotes any performance which includes sexual conduct by a child less than sixteen years of age."

To "promote" is also defined:

> 'Promote' means to procure, manufacture, issue, sell, give, provide, lend, mail, deliver, transfer, transmute, publish, distribute, circulate, disseminate, present, exhibit or advertise, or to offer or agree to do the same.

A companion provision bans only the knowing dissemination of obscene material.

This case arose when Paul Ferber, the proprietor of a Manhattan bookstore specializing in sexually oriented products, sold two films to an undercover police officer. The films are devoted almost exclusively to depicting young boys masturbating. Ferber was indicted on two counts of violating § 263.10 and two counts of violating § 263.15, the two New York laws controlling dissemination of child pornography. After a jury trial, Ferber was acquitted of the two counts of promoting an obscene sexual performance, but found guilty of the two counts under § 263.15, which did not require proof that the films were obscene. Ferber's convictions were affirmed without opinion by the Appellate Division of the New York State Supreme Court.

The New York Court of Appeals reversed, holding that § 263.15 violated the First Amendment. . . .

II

. . . This case, however, constitutes our first examination of a statute directed at and limited to depictions of sexual activity involving children. We believe our inquiry should begin with the question of whether a State has somewhat more freedom in proscribing works which portray sexual acts or lewd exhibitions of genitalia by children.

A

In *Chaplinsky v. New Hampshire*, the Court laid the foundation for the excision of obscenity from the realm of constitutionally protected expression:

> There are certain well-defined and narrowly limited classes of speech, the prevention and punishment of which have never been thought to raise any Constitutional problem. These include the lewd and obscene. . . . It has been well observed that such utterances are no essential part of any exposition of ideas, and are of such slight social value as a step to truth that any benefit that may be derived from them is clearly outweighed by the social interest in order and morality.

. . .

. . . In *Miller v. California*, a majority of the Court agreed that a "state offense must also be limited to works which, taken as a whole, appeal to the prurient interest in sex, which portray sexual conduct in a patently offensive way, and which, taken as a whole, do not have serious literary, artistic, political, or scientific value." Over the past decade, we have adhered to the guidelines expressed in *Miller*, which subsequently has been followed in the regulatory schemes of most States.

B

The *Miller* standard, like its predecessors, was an accommodation between the State's interests in protecting the "sensibilities of unwilling recipients" from exposure to pornographic material and the dangers of censorship inherent in unabashedly content-based laws. Like obscenity statutes, laws directed at the dissemination of child pornography run the risk of suppressing protected expression by allowing the hand of the censor to become unduly heavy. For the following reasons, however, we are persuaded that the States are entitled to greater leeway in the regulation of pornographic depictions of children.

First. It is evident beyond the need for elaboration that a State's interest in "safeguarding the physical and psychological well-being of a minor" is "compelling." "A democratic society rests, for its continuance, upon the healthy, well-rounded growth of young people into full maturity as citizens." Accordingly, we have sustained legislation aimed at protecting the physical and emotional well-being of youth even when the laws have operated in the sensitive area of constitutionally protected rights. In *Prince v. Massachusetts*, the Court held that a statute prohibiting use of a child to distribute literature on the street was valid notwithstanding the statute's effect on a First Amendment activity. In *Ginsberg v. New York*, we sustained a New York law protecting children from exposure to nonobscene literature. Most recently, we held that the Government's interest in the "well-being of its youth" justified special treatment of indecent broadcasting received by adults as well as children.

The prevention of sexual exploitation and abuse of children constitutes a government objective of surpassing importance. The legislative findings accompanying passage of the New York laws reflect this concern:

> [There] has been a proliferation of exploitation of children as subjects in sexual performances. The care of children is a sacred trust and should not be abused by those who seek to profit through a commercial network based

> upon the exploitation of children. The public policy of the state demands the protection of children from exploitation through sexual performances.

We shall not second-guess this legislative judgment.... The legislative judgment, as well as the judgment found in the relevant literature, is that the use of children as subjects of pornographic materials is harmful to the physiological, emotional, and mental health of the child. That judgment, we think, easily passes muster under the First Amendment.

Second. The distribution of photographs and films depicting sexual activity by juveniles is intrinsically related to the sexual abuse of children in at least two ways. First, the materials produced are a permanent record of the children's participation and the harm to the child is exacerbated by their circulation. Second, the distribution network for child pornography must be closed if the production of material which requires the sexual exploitation of children is to be effectively controlled. Indeed, there is no serious contention that the legislature was unjustified in believing that it is difficult, if not impossible, to halt the exploitation of children by pursuing only those who produce the photographs and movies. While the production of pornographic materials is a low-profile, clandestine industry, the need to market the resulting products requires a visible apparatus of distribution. The most expeditious if not the only practical method of law enforcement may be to dry up the market for this material by imposing severe criminal penalties on persons selling, advertising, or otherwise promoting the product....

...

Third. The advertising and selling of child pornography provide an economic motive for and are thus an integral part of the production of such materials, an activity illegal throughout the Nation. "It rarely has been suggested that the constitutional freedom for speech and press extends its immunity to speech or writing used as an integral part of conduct in violation of a valid criminal statute." We note that were the statutes outlawing the employment of children in these films and photographs fully effective, and the constitutionality of these laws has not been questioned, the First Amendment implications would be no greater than that presented by laws against distribution: enforceable production laws would leave no child pornography to be marketed.

Fourth. The value of permitting live performances and photographic reproductions of children engaged in lewd sexual conduct is exceedingly modest, if not de minimis. We consider it unlikely that visual depictions of children performing sexual acts or lewdly exhibiting their genitals would often constitute an important and necessary part of a literary performance or scientific or educational work. As a state judge in this case observed, if it were necessary for literary or artistic value, a person over the statutory age who perhaps looked younger could be utilized. Simulation outside of the prohibition of the statute could provide another alternative. Nor is there any question here of censoring a particular literary theme or portrayal of sexual activity. The First Amendment interest is limited to that of rendering the portrayal somewhat more "realistic" by utilizing or photographing children.

Fifth. Recognizing and classifying child pornography as a category of material outside the protection of the First Amendment is not incompatible with our earlier decisions. . . . Thus, it is not rare that a content-based classification of speech has been accepted because it may be appropriately generalized that within the confines of the given classification, the evil to be restricted so overwhelmingly outweighs the expressive interests, if any, at stake, that no process of case-by-case adjudication is required. When a definable class of material, such as that covered by § 263.15, bears so heavily and pervasively on the welfare of children engaged in its production, we think the balance of competing interests is clearly struck and that it is permissible to consider these materials as without the protection of the First Amendment.

C

There are, of course, limits on the category of child pornography which, like obscenity, is unprotected by the First Amendment. As with all legislation in this sensitive area, the conduct to be prohibited must be adequately defined by the applicable state law, as written or authoritatively construed. Here the nature of the harm to be combated requires that the state offense be limited to works that visually depict sexual conduct by children below a specified age. The category of "sexual conduct" proscribed must also be suitably limited and described.

. . .

D

Section 263.15's prohibition incorporates a definition of sexual conduct that comports with the above-stated principles. The forbidden acts to be depicted are listed with sufficient precision and represent the kind of conduct that, if it were the theme of a work, could render it legally obscene: "actual or simulated sexual intercourse, deviate sexual intercourse, sexual bestiality, masturbation, sado-masochistic abuse, or lewd exhibition of the genitals." The term "lewd exhibition of the genitals" is not unknown in this area and, indeed, was given in *Miller* as an example of a permissible regulation. A performance is defined only to include live or visual depictions: "any play, motion picture, photograph or dance . . . [or] other visual representation exhibited before an audience." Section 263.15 expressly includes a scienter requirement.

We hold that § 263.15 sufficiently describes a category of material the production and distribution of which is not entitled to First Amendment protection. It is therefore clear that there is nothing unconstitutionally "underinclusive" about a statute that singles out this category of material for proscription. It also follows that the State is not barred by the First Amendment from prohibiting the distribution of unprotected materials produced outside the State.

III

It remains to address the claim that the New York statute is unconstitutionally overbroad because it would forbid the distribution of material with serious literary, scientific, or educational value or material which does not threaten the harms sought to be combated by the State. Respondent prevailed on that ground below, and it is to that issue that we now turn.

...

The scope of the First Amendment overbreadth doctrine, like most exceptions to established principles, must be carefully tied to the circumstances in which facial invalidation of a statute is truly warranted. Because of the wide-reaching effects of striking down a statute on its face at the request of one whose own conduct may be punished despite the First Amendment, we have recognized that the overbreadth doctrine is "strong medicine" and have employed it with hesitation, and then "only as a last resort." We have, in consequence, insisted that the overbreadth involved be "substantial" before the statute involved will be invalidated on its face.

We accordingly held that "particularly where conduct and not merely speech is involved, we believe that the overbreadth of a statute must not only be real, but substantial as well, judged in relation to the statute's plainly legitimate sweep."

... This case, which poses the question squarely, convinces us that the rationale ... is sound and should be applied in the present context involving the harmful employment of children to make sexually explicit materials for distribution.

The premise that a law should not be invalidated for overbreadth unless it reaches a substantial number of impermissible applications is hardly novel. ...

B

... we hold that § 263.15 is not substantially overbroad. We consider this the paradigmatic case of a state statute whose legitimate reach dwarfs its arguably impermissible applications. New York, as we have held, may constitutionally prohibit dissemination of material specified in § 263.15. While the reach of the statute is directed at the hard core of child pornography, the Court of Appeals was understandably concerned that some protected expression, ranging from medical textbooks to pictorials in the *National Geographic* would fall prey to the statute. How often, if ever, it may be necessary to employ children to engage in conduct clearly within the reach of § 263.15 in order to produce educational, medical, or artistic works cannot be known with certainty. Yet we seriously doubt, and it has not been suggested, that these arguably impermissible applications of the statute amount to more than a tiny fraction of the materials within the statute's reach. Nor will we assume that the New York courts will widen the possibly invalid reach of the statute by giving an expansive construction to the proscription on "lewd [exhibitions] of the genitals." Under these circumstances, § 263.15 is "not substantially overbroad and ... whatever overbreadth may exist should be cured through case-by-case analysis of the fact situations to which its sanctions, assertedly, may not be applied."

...

Justice Blackmun concurs in the result. [omitted]

Justice O'Connor, concurring.

Although I join the Court's opinion, I write separately to stress that the Court does not hold that New York must except "material with serious literary, scientific, or educational value," from its statute. The Court merely holds that, even if the First Amendment shelters such material, New York's current statute is not sufficiently overbroad to support respondent's facial attack. The compelling interests identified in today's opinion, suggest that the Constitution might in fact permit New York to ban knowing distribution of works depicting minors engaged in explicit sexual conduct, regardless of the social value of the depictions. For example, a 12-year-old child photographed while masturbating surely suffers the same psychological harm whether the community labels the photograph "edifying" or "tasteless." The audience's appreciation of the depiction is simply irrelevant to New York's asserted interest in protecting children from psychological, emotional, and mental harm.

. . .

Justice Brennan, with whom Justice Marshall joins, concurring in the judgment.

I agree with much of what is said in the Court's opinion. . . . [T]he State has a special interest in protecting the well-being of its youth. This special and compelling interest, and the particular vulnerability of children, afford the State the leeway to regulate pornographic material, the promotion of which is harmful to children, even though the State does not have such leeway when it seeks only to protect consenting adults from exposure to such material. I also agree with the Court that the "tiny fraction" of material of serious artistic, scientific, or educational value that could conceivably fall within the reach of the statute is insufficient to justify striking the statute on the grounds of overbreadth.

But in my view application of § 263.15 or any similar statute to depictions of children that in themselves do have serious literary, artistic, scientific, or medical value, would violate the First Amendment. As the Court recognizes, the limited classes of speech, the suppression of which does not raise serious First Amendment concerns, have two attributes. They are of exceedingly "slight social value," and the State has a compelling interest in their regulation. The First Amendment value of depictions of children that are in themselves serious contributions to art, literature, or science, is, by definition, simply not "de minimis." At the same time, the State's interest in suppression of such materials is likely to be far less compelling. For the Court's assumption of harm to the child resulting from the "permanent record" and "circulation" of the child's "participation" lacks much of its force where the depiction is a serious contribution to art or science. The production of materials of serious value is not the "low-profile, clandestine industry" that according to the Court produces purely pornographic materials. In short, it is inconceivable how a depiction of a child that is itself a serious contribution to the world of art or literature or science can be deemed "material outside the protection of the First Amendment."

Justice Stevens, concurring in the judgment. [omitted].

Notes and Queries

1. Suppose New York desired to move the prohibited age group to include those 18, up from the current 16 years of age. Would *Ferber* permit such a move?

2. According to *Ferber*, what effects does child pornography have on the community?

3. According to *Ferber*, should a university be held liable for allowing students to buy materials that describe the facts of *Ferber*? What about a junior high school?

4. *United States v. Dost,* 636 F. Supp. 828 (1986), provided a list of factors to help determine whether depictions of nude children are punishable. The court noted that, "[b]ecause of the sexual innocence of children, that which constitutes a 'lascivious exhibition' of a child's genitals will be different from that of a 'lascivious or lewd exhibition' of an adult's genitals." Does the list protect parents from taking pictures of their own children who are nude or partially nude, without sexual activity?

    > . . . in determining whether a visual depiction of a minor constitutes a "lascivious exhibition of the genitals or pubic area" under § 2255(2)(E), the trier of fact should look to the following factors, among any others that may be relevant in the particular case:
    >
    > 1) whether the focal point of the visual depiction is on the child's genitalia or pubic area;
    >
    > 2) whether the setting of the visual depiction is sexually suggestive, i.e., in a place or pose generally associated with sexual activity;
    >
    > 3) whether the child is depicted in an unnatural pose, or in inappropriate attire, considering the age of the child;
    >
    > 4) whether the child is fully or partially clothed, or nude;
    >
    > 5) whether the visual depiction suggests sexual coyness or a willingness to engage in sexual activity; and
    >
    > 6) whether the visual depiction is intended or designed to elicit a sexual response in the viewer.
    >
    > Of course, a visual depiction need not involve all of these factors to be a "lascivious exhibition of the genitals or pubic area." The determination will have to be made based on the overall content of the visual depiction, taking into account the age of the minor.

5. The Court finds that some materials that depict children will inappropriately fall within the statute's prohibitions. Despite that possibility, the Court still finds that the statute is not impermissibly overbroad. How does the statute protect the rights of defendants who would be "inappropriate" targets?

Massachusetts v. Oakes

491 U.S. 576; 109 S. Ct. 2633 (1989)

Justice O'Connor delivered the opinion of the Court.

This case involves an overbreadth challenge to a Massachusetts criminal statute generally prohibiting adults from posing or exhibiting nude minors for purposes of visual representation or reproduction in any book, magazine, pamphlet, motion picture, photograph, or picture.

I

The statute at issue in this case, Mass. Gen. Laws § 272:29A (1986), was enacted in 1982. It provides as follows:

> Whoever with knowledge that a person is a child under eighteen years of age, or whoever while in possession of such facts that he should have reason to know that such person is a child under eighteen years of age, hires, coerces, solicits or entices, employs, procures, uses, causes, encourages, or knowingly permits such child to pose or be exhibited in a state of nudity or to participate or engage in any live performance or in any act that depicts, describes or represents sexual conduct for purpose of visual representation or reproduction in any book, magazine, pamphlet, motion picture film, photograph, or picture shall be punished by imprisonment in the state prison for a term of not less than ten nor more than twenty years, or by a fine of not less than ten thousand dollars nor more than fifty thousand dollars, or by both such a fine and imprisonment.
>
> It shall be a defense in any prosecution pursuant to this section that such visual representation or reproduction of any posture or exhibition in a state of nudity was produced, processed, published, printed or manufactured for a bona fide scientific or medical purpose, or for an educational or cultural purpose for a bona fide school, museum or library.
>
> As used in this section, the term 'performance' shall mean any play, dance or exhibit shown or presented to an audience of one or more persons.

Another statute, Mass. Gen. Laws § 272:31 (1986), defines "nudity" as

> uncovered or less than opaquely covered post-pubertal human genitals, pubic areas, the post-pubertal human female breast below a point immediately above the top of the areola, or the covered male genitals in a discernibly turgid state. For purposes of this definition, a female breast is considered uncovered if the nipple or the nipple or areola only are covered. In the case of pre-pubertal persons nudity shall mean uncovered or less than opaquely covered pre-pubertal human genitals or pubic area.

In 1984, respondent Douglas Oakes took approximately 10 color photographs of his partially nude and physically mature 14-year-old stepdaughter, L. S., who at the time was attending modeling school. The photographs depict L. S. sitting, lying, and reclining on top of a bar, clad only in a red and white striped bikini panty and a red scarf. The scarf does not cover L. S.'s breasts, which are fully exposed in all the photographs. The dissent below described the photographs as "sexually provocative photographs of the type frequently found in magazines displayed by storekeepers in sealed cellophane wrappers."

Oakes was indicted and tried for violating § 29A. The jury returned a general verdict of guilty, and Oakes was sentenced to 10 years' imprisonment. Because the jury was not instructed on the "sexual conduct" portion of § 29A, its verdict rested on a finding that Oakes "hire[d], coerce[d], solicit[ed] or entice[d], employ[ed], procure[d], use[d], cause[d], encourage[d], or knowingly permit[ted]" L. S. to "pose or be exhibited in a state of nudity." The acts proscribed by § 29A are listed disjunctively, so it is impossible to ascertain which of those acts the jury concluded Oakes had committed. The jury was instructed on the exemptions set forth in § 29A, but its guilty verdict indicates that the exemptions were found to be inapplicable.

. . .

We granted certiorari to review the decision of the Massachusetts Supreme Judicial Court and now vacate and remand.

II

. . .

. . . After we granted certiorari, § 29A was amended. The current version of § 29A, which is set forth in the margin, adds a "lascivious intent" requirement to the "nudity" portion, but not the "sexual conduct" portion, of the former version of § 29A. In addition, the current version of § 29A contains no exemptions. Because it has been repealed, the former version of § 29A cannot chill protected expression in the future. Thus, . . . the overbreadth question in this case has become moot as a practical matter, and we do not address it.

. . .

Vacated and remanded.

Justice Scalia, concurring (In Part). [omitted]

Justice Scalia, dissenting (In Part). [omitted]

Justice Brennan, dissenting. [omitted]

Notes and Queries

1. Does the statutory change adding "lascivious intent" really cure the statute from its broad reach?

2. Should the intent of the photographer matter if we are interested in child protection?

Free Speech Coalition v. Reno

198 F.3d 1083 (9th Cir. App., 1999)

Circuit Judge Molloy delivered the opinion of the court.

I.

The question presented in this case is whether Congress may constitutionally proscribe as child pornography computer images that do not involve the use of real children in their production or dissemination. We hold that the First Amendment prohibits Congress from enacting a statute that makes criminal the generation of images of fictitious children engaged in imaginary but explicit sexual conduct.

II.

In this case, the district court found that the Child Pornography Prevention Act of 1996 ("CPPA" or the "Act") was content-neutral, was not unconstitutionally vague or overbroad, and did not constitute an improper prior restraint of speech. The district court also found that the Child Pornography Prevention Act's affirmative defense did not impermissibly shift the burden of proof to a defendant by virtue of an unconstitutional presumption.

While we agree that the plaintiffs have standing to bring this case and that the Act is not an improper prior restraint of speech, the balance of the district court's analysis does not comport with what we believe is required by the Constitution. We find that the phrases "appears to be" a minor, and "conveys the impression" that the depiction portrays a minor, are vague and overbroad and thus do not meet the requirements of the First Amendment. Consequently we hold that while these two provisions of the Act do not pass constitutional muster, the balance of the Child Pornography Prevention Act is constitutional when the two phrases are stricken. Whether the statutory affirmative defense is constitutional is a question that we leave for resolution in a different case.

A.

The appellants consist of a group that refers to itself as "The Free Speech Coalition." The Free Speech Coalition is a trade association of businesses involved in the production and distribution of "adult-oriented materials." Bold Type, Inc. is a publisher of a book "dedicated to the education and expression of the ideals and philosophy associated with nudism;" Jim Gingerich is a New York artist whose paintings include large-scale nudes; and Ron Raffaelli is a professional photographer whose works include nude and erotic photographs.

The Free Speech Coalition sought declaratory and injunctive relief by a pre-enforcement challenge to certain provisions of the Child Pornography Prevention Act of 1996. The complaint was filed in the Northern District of California. Both parties moved for summary judgment. The district court determined the CPPA was constitutional and granted the government's motion for summary judgment. At the same time it denied Free Speech's cross motion for summary judgment. After the district court's adverse ruling, Free Speech appealed.

In this appeal, Free Speech argues the district court was mistaken in its determination that the legislation is content neutral. They also argue that the district court was wrong to hold that the Act is not unconstitutionally vague. The argument is that where the statute fails to define "appears to be" and "conveys the impression," it is so vague a person of ordinary intelligence cannot understand what is prohibited. Free Speech also questions the district court's holding that the affirmative defense provided in the Act is constitutional. Finally, Free Speech appeals the lower court's determination that the Act does not impose a prior restraint on protected speech and that it does not create a permanent chill on protected expression.

B.

. . .

Throughout the legislative history, Congress has defined the problem of child pornography in terms of real children. Up until 1996 the actual participation and abuse of children in the production or dissemination or pornography involving minors was the sine qua non of the regulating scheme. . . . The 1996 law, the law at issue here, changed course. The regulation direction shifted from defining child pornography in terms of the harm inflicted upon real children to a determination that child pornography was evil in and of itself, whether it involved real children or not. This shift forms the basis of the constitutional challenge Free Speech makes here.

6.

The Child Pornography Prevention Act of 1996 expanded the law to combat the use of computer technology to produce pornography containing images that look like children. The new law sought to stifle the use of technology for evil purposes. This of course was a marked change in the criminal regulatory scheme. Congress had always acted to prevent harm to real children. In the new law, Congress shifted the paradigm from the illegality of child pornography that involved the use of real children in its creation to forbid a "visual depiction" that "is, or appears to be, of a minor engaging in sexually explicit conduct."

The premise behind the Child Pornography Prevention Act is the asserted impact of such images on the children who may view them. The law is also based on the notion that child pornography, real as well as virtual, increases the activities of child molesters and pedophiles.

7.

18 U.S.C. § 2256(8)defines child pornography as "any visual depiction, including any photograph, film, video, picture, or computer or computer-generated image or picture, whether made or produced by electronic, mechanical, or other means, of sexually explicit conduct[.]" At issue in this appeal are the definitions contained in subsections (B) and (D) of § 2256(8). Section 2256(8)(B) bans sexually explicit depictions that appear to be minors. Section 2256(8)(D) bans visual depictions that are "advertised, promoted, presented, described or distributed in such a manner that conveys the impression" that they contain sexually explicit depictions of minors.

...

IV.

A.

...

1.

The district court held that the contested provisions of the Child Pornography Prevention Act are content-neutral regulations. The district judge reasoned that the law was passed to prevent the secondary effects of the child pornography industry, specifically the exploitation and degradation of children. The court also found that the Act addressed the need to control child pornography because virtual pornography led to the encouragement of pedophilia and the molestation of children. This reasoning was based on a finding that the CPPA is intended "to counteract the effect that [real or virtual child pornography] has on its viewers, on children, and to society as a whole." The lower court expressly found the legislation was not intended to regulate or outlaw the ideas themselves.

We do not agree....

The CPPA prohibits any sexually explicit depiction that "appears to be" of a minor or that is distributed or advertised in such a manner as to "convey the impression" that the depiction portrays a minor. Thus, the CPPA distinguishes favored from disfavored speech on the basis of the content of that speech.

...

2.

Under the circumstances, if the CPPA is to survive the constitutional inquiry the government must establish a compelling interest that is served by the statute, and it must show that the CPPA is narrowly tailored to fulfill that interest.

The district court found that even if no children are involved in the production of such materials the devastating secondary effect that sexually explicit materials involving the images of children have on society, and on the well being of children, merits the regulation of such images. This legislative finding supported the lower court's finding of a compelling state interest. We believe this legal determination is wrong.

There are three compelling interests put forward when instituting efforts to curb child pornography using images of actual children. The first interest is that child pornography requires the participation of actual children in sexually explicit situations to create the images. The second interest stems from the belief that dissemination of such pornographic images may encourage more sexual abuse of children because it whets the appetite of pedophiles. The third interest is that such images are morally and aesthetically repugnant.

The Supreme Court has required state statutes criminalizing child pornography to limit the offense to "works that visually depict explicit sexual conduct by children below a specified age." The *Ferber* Court specifically focused on the harm to children. It also found that distribution of pornographic images is "intrinsically related" to the harm suffered by child victims because the images produced are a permanent record of the child's participation, exacerbated by its dissemination. The Court reasoned that the distribution network for such images needs to be terminated if it is to be effectively controlled. The *Ferber* Court acknowledged that "if it were necessary for literary or artistic value, a person over the statutory age who perhaps looked younger could be utilized."

The language of the statute questioned here can criminalize the use of fictional images that involve no human being, whether that fictional person is over the statutory age and looks younger, or indeed, a fictional person under the prohibited age. Images that are, or can be, entirely the product of the mind are criminalized. The CPPA's definition of child pornography extends to drawings or images that "appear" to be minors or visual depictions that "convey" the impression that a minor is engaging in sexually explicit conduct, whether an actual minor is involved or not. The constitutionality of this definition is not supported by existing case law.

The rationale articulated in *Ferber* and the constitutional permissibility of regulating the category of child pornography as a separate class is not justified by consideration of the effects such images have on others, even if those effects exist. Instead the focus of analysis is on the harm to the children actually used in the production of the materials. Nothing in *Ferber* can be said to justify the regulation of such materials other than the protection of the actual children used in the production of child pornography. The language of the statute criminalizes even those materials that do not involve a recognizable minor. This shift is a significant departure from *Ferber*. While the government is given greater leeway in regulating child pornography, materials or depictions of sexual conduct "which do not involve live performance or photographic or other visual reproduction of live performances, retains First Amendment protection."

Ferber considered the possibility of simulations of sexually explicit acts involving non-recognizable minors and implicitly found them to be constitutionally protected. The Court also implicitly rejected the regulation of pornography that does not involve minors. Thus, the case law demonstrates that Congress has no compelling interest in regulating sexually explicit materials that do not contain visual images of actual children....

...

The critical ingredient of our analysis is the relationship between the dissemination of fabricated images of child pornography and additional acts of sexual abuse. Factual studies that establish the link between computer-generated child pornography and the subsequent sexual abuse of children apparently do not yet exist. The legislative justification for the proposition was based upon the Final Report of the Attorney General's Commission on Pornography, a report that predates the existing technology. The Final Report emphasized the victimization of real children by adult distribution of the pornographic material. The report shows that the use of sexually explicit photos or films of actual children to lure other children played a small part in the overall problem involving harm to children. Thus, while such images are unquestionably morally repugnant, they do not involve real children nor is there a demonstrated basis to link computer-generated images with harm to real children. Absent this nexus, the law does not withstand constitutional scrutiny.

. . .

In short, we find the articulated compelling state interest cannot justify the criminal proscription when no actual children are involved in the illicit images either by production or depiction. Because we find that Congress has not provided a compelling interest, we do not address the "narrow tailoring" requirement.

3.

. . . The judgment of the district court is REVERSED on the questions of the constitutionality of the statutory language "appears to be a minor" and "conveys the impression."

. . .

Affirmed in Part, Reversed and Remanded in Part.

Circuit Judge Ferguson, dissenting:

The majority holds that Congress cannot regulate virtual child pornography because it does not require the use of actual children in its production. Without the use of actual children, the majority believes that Congress is simply attempting to regulate "evil ideas." I disagree. Congress has provided compelling evidence that virtual child pornography causes real harm to real children. As a result, virtual child pornography should join the ranks of real child pornography as a class of speech outside the protection of the First Amendment. In addition, I do not believe that the statutory terms "appears to be" or "conveys the impression" are substantially overbroad or void for vagueness. Accordingly, I would find the Child Pornography Prevention Act of 1996 ("CPPA") constitutional.

I.

. . .

First. The majority improperly suggests that preventing harm to depicted children is the only legitimate justification for banning child pornography. Although this was the Supreme Court's focus in *New York v. Ferber*, the Court has subsequently indicated a willingness to consider additional factors. In *Osborne*, the Supreme Court addressed the issue of whether Ohio could ban the possession of child pornography. In finding it could, the Court relied not only on the harm caused to the children who were used in its production (i.e., *Ferber*), but also on the harm that children suffer when child pornography is used to seduce or coerce them into sexual activity. Thus, in *Osborne*, the Court indicated that protecting children who are not actually pictured in the pornographic image is a legitimate and compelling state interest. . . .

Second. The majority ignores the fact that many of the justifications Congress relied on when it passed the CPPA have already been endorsed by the Supreme Court. For example, the Court in *Osborne* recognized that states have a legitimate interest in preventing pedophiles from "using child pornography to seduce other children into sexual activity." Virtually parroting this justification, Congress enacted the CPPA after finding that "child pornography is often used as part of a method of seducing other children into sexual activity; a child who is reluctant to engage in sexual activity with an adult, or to pose for sexually explicit photographs, can sometimes be convinced by viewing depictions of other children 'having fun' participating in such activity." In addition, Congress found that when child pornography is "used as a means of seducing or breaking down a child's inhibitions," the images are equally as effective regardless of whether they are real photographs or computer-generated pictures that are "virtually indistinguishable."

The Supreme Court has also recognized that states have a legitimate interest in destroying the child pornography market. . . .

. . .

Third. Even though Congress presented some new justifications that the Supreme Court has not specifically endorsed, the majority still had an obligation to consider them as long as they advance the general goal of protecting children. In both *Ferber* and *Osborne*, the Court stated that "it is evident beyond the need for elaboration that a State's interest in 'safeguarding the physical and psychological well-being of a minor' is 'compelling.'" "A democratic society rests, for its continuance, upon the healthy, well-rounded growth of young people into full maturity as citizens." Thus, the Court will generally "sustain[ ] legislation aimed at protecting the physical and emotional well-being of children even when the laws . . . operate[ ] in sensitive areas."

The lesson from *Ferber* and *Osborne* is that legislators should be given "greater leeway" when acting to protect the well-being of children. . . .

Fourth. The majority ignores the fact that child pornography, real or virtual, has little or no social value. . . .

Why should virtual child pornography be treated differently than real child pornography? Is it more valued speech? I do not think so. Both real and virtual child pornography contain visual depictions of children engaging in sexually explicit activity. The only difference is that real child pornography uses actual children in its production, whereas virtual child pornography does not. While this distinction is noteworthy, it does not somehow transform virtual child pornography into meaningful speech. Virtual child pornography, like its counterpart real child pornography, is of "slight social value" and constitutes "no essential part of the exposition of ideas." Therefore, the majority is wrong to accord virtual child pornography the full protection of the First Amendment.

Fifth. The majority improperly analyzes the CPPA under a strict scrutiny approach. In so doing, the majority misreads the Supreme Court's previous child pornography decisions. These decisions indicate that the proper mode of analysis is to weigh the state's interest in regulating child pornography against the material's limited social value. The Supreme Court used this test in *Ferber* and found that "the balance of competing interests [was] clearly struck and that it [was] permissible to consider these materials as without the protection of the First Amendment."

Virtual child pornography should be evaluated in a similar fashion....

II.

The analysis does not end with a finding that virtual child pornography is without First Amendment protection. Statutes can be found unconstitutional if they are worded so broadly that they "criminalize an intolerable range of constitutionally protected conduct." This case focuses on the CPPA's new definition of child pornography which prohibits visual depictions that "appear[ ] to be," or are promoted or distributed "in such a manner that conveys the impression," that they are "of a minor engaging in sexually explicit conduct." The majority holds that this language is overbroad because it bans "material that has been accorded First Amendment protection." Slip Op. at 14664. I disagree.

...

Appellants suggest that the "appears to be" language is so broad that everyday artistic expressions like paintings, drawings, and sculptures that depict youthful looking subjects in a sexual manner will be criminalized under the CPPA. However, even a glancing look at the legislative history belies this assertion. Congress enacted the CPPA to address the problem of "computer-generated" child pornography....

...

There has also been concern that the CPPA prohibits constitutionally protected photographic images of adults in sexually explicit poses. This contention, however, is also without merit. The CPPA explicitly states that "it shall be an affirmative defense" to a charge of distributing, reproducing or selling child pornography that the pornography (1) "was produced using an actual person or persons," (2) each of whom "was an adult at the time the material was produced," and (3) "the defendant did not advertise, promote, present, describe, or distribute the material in such a manner as to convey the impression that it is or contains visual depictions of a minor engaging in sexually explicit conduct." The CPPA thus shields from prosecution sexually explicit visual depictions so long as they are produced using actual adults and "the material has not been pandered as child pornography." Persons—like the appellants in this case—who produce and distribute works depicting the sexual conduct of actual adults, and do not market the depictions as if they contain sexual images of children, are thus explicitly protected from culpability under the CPPA.

...

IV.

In sum, the CPPA is not, as the majority claims, an attempt to regulate "evil ideas." Instead, the CPPA is an important tool in the fight against child sexual abuse. The CPPA's definition of child pornography provides adequate notice of the type of images that are prohibited and does not substantially encroach on protected expression. Accordingly, I would find the CPPA constitutional.

Notes and Queries

1. The case fundamentally involves the extent to which Congress should be given a wide berth when legislating to protect children. The majority focuses on the state's interest in banning child pornography as based on the need to protect actual children. One of this case's central concerns involves child pornography's potential use as a tool to seduce other children into sexual acts. Do you find that interest compelling enough to override concerns against barring child pornography?
2. The majority indicates that a proper demonstration of a nexus between computer-generated child pornography and harm to real children could effectively recast the issue. What do you think about relying on such evidence? While there may be no empirical proof immune from criticism, Congressional hearings on the Act had produced testimony from a number of scholars and practitioners supporting the goals of the Act; many authorities had testified that pedophiles use child pornography to seduce children into engaging in sexual acts with them. Should that suffice?
3. What do you make of the argument that the Congressional findings track the Supreme Court's decision in *Osborne v. Ohio*? Should the Supreme Court's findings of fact in that case impact this case?
4. Which of the two opinions in this case remains most faithful to *Ferber*?

Ginsberg v. New York

390 U.S. 629; 88 S. Ct. 1274 (1968)

Mr. Justice Brennan delivered the opinion of the Court.

This case presents the question of the constitutionality on its face of a New York criminal obscenity statute which prohibits the sale to minors under 17 years of age of material defined to be obscene on the basis of its appeal to them whether or not it would be obscene to adults.

Appellant and his wife operate "Sam's Stationery and Luncheonette" in Bellmore, Long Island. They have a lunch counter, and, among other things, also sell magazines including some so-called "girlie" magazines. Appellant was prosecuted under two informations, each in two counts, which charged that he personally sold a 16-year-old boy two "girlie" magazines on each of two dates in October 1965, in violation of § 484-h of the New York Penal Law. He was tried before a judge without a jury in Nassau County District Court and was found guilty on both counts. The judge found (1) that the magazines contained pictures which depicted female "nudity" in a manner defined in subsection 1 (b), that is "the showing of . . . female . . . buttocks with less than a full opaque covering, or the showing of the female breast with less than a fully opaque covering of any portion thereof below the top of the nipple . . . ," and (2) that the pictures were "harmful to minors" in that they had, within the meaning of subsection 1 (f) "that quality of . . . representation . . . of nudity . . . [which] . . . (I) predominantly appeals to the prurient, shameful or morbid interest of minors, and (ii) is patently offensive to prevailing standards in the adult community as a whole with respect to what is suitable material for minors, and (iii) is utterly without redeeming social importance for minors." He held that both sales to the 16-year-old boy therefore constituted the violation under § 484-h of "knowingly to sell . . . to a minor" under 17 of "(a) any picture . . . which depicts nudity . . . and which is harmful to minors," and "(b) any . . . magazine . . . which contains . . . [such pictures] . . . and which, taken as a whole, is harmful to minors." The conviction was affirmed without opinion by the Appellate Term, Second Department, of the Supreme Court. Appellant was denied leave to appeal to the New York Court of Appeals and then appealed to this Court. . . . We affirm.

I.

The "girlie" picture magazines involved in the sales here are not obscene for adults. But § 484-h does not bar the appellant from stocking the magazines and selling them to persons 17 years of age or older, and therefore the conviction is not invalid under our decision in *Butler v. Michigan*.

Obscenity is not within the area of protected speech or press. The three-pronged test of subsection 1 (f) for judging the obscenity of material sold to minors under 17 is a variable from the formulation for determining obscenity under *Roth* stated in the plurality opinion in *Memoirs v. Massachusetts*. Appellant's primary attack upon § 484-h is leveled at the power of the State to adapt this *Memoirs* formulation to define the material's obscenity on the basis of its appeal to minors, and thus exclude material so defined from the area of protected expression. He makes no argument that the magazines are not "harmful to minors" within the definition in subsection 1 (f). Thus "no issue is presented . . . concerning the obscenity of the material involved."

The New York Court of Appeals "upheld the Legislature's power to employ variable concepts of obscenity" in a case in which the same challenge to state power to enact such a law was also addressed to § 484-h. In sustaining state power to enact the law, the Court of Appeals said:

> Material which is protected for distribution to adults is not necessarily constitutionally protected from restriction upon its dissemination to children. In other words, the concept of obscenity or of unprotected matter may vary according to the group to whom the questionable material is directed or from whom it is quarantined. Because of the State's exigent interest in preventing distribution to children of objectionable material, it can exercise its power to protect the health, safety, welfare and morals of its community by barring the distribution to children of books recognized to be suitable for adults.

Appellant's attack is not that New York was without power to draw the line at age 17. Rather, his contention is the broad proposition that the scope of the constitutional freedom of expression secured to a citizen to read or see material concerned with sex cannot be made to depend upon whether the citizen is an adult or a minor. He accordingly insists that the denial to minors under 17 of access to material condemned by § 484-h, insofar as that material is not obscene for persons 17 years of age or older, constitutes an unconstitutional deprivation of protected liberty.

We have no occasion in this case to consider the impact of the guarantees of freedom of expression upon the totality of the relationship of the minor and the State. It is enough for the purposes of this case that we inquire whether it was constitutionally impermissible for New York, insofar as § 484-h does so, to accord minors under 17 a more restricted right than that assured to adults to judge and determine for themselves what sex material they may read or see. We conclude that we cannot say that the statute invades the area of freedom of expression constitutionally secured to minors.

. . . We do not regard New York's regulation in defining obscenity on the basis of its appeal to minors under 17 as involving an invasion of such minors' constitutionally protected freedoms. Rather § 484-h simply adjusts the definition of obscenity "to social realities by permitting the appeal of this type of material to be assessed in terms of the sexual interests . . ." of such minors. That the State has power to make that adjustment seems clear, for we have recognized that even where there is an invasion of protected freedoms "the power of the state to control the conduct of children reaches beyond the scope of its authority over adults. . . ."

The well-being of its children is of course a subject within the State's constitutional power to regulate, and, in our view, two interests justify the limitations in § 484-h upon the availability of sex material to minors under 17, at least if it was rational for the legislature to find that the minors' exposure to such material might be harmful.

First of all, constitutional interpretation has consistently recognized that the parents' claim to authority in their own household to direct the rearing of their children is basic in the structure of our society. "It is cardinal with us that the custody, care and nurture of the child reside first in the parents, whose primary function and freedom include preparation for obligations the state can neither supply nor hinder." The legislature could properly conclude that parents and others, teachers for example, who have this primary responsibility for children's well-being are entitled to the support of laws designed to aid discharge of that responsibility. Indeed, subsection 1 (f)(ii) of § 484-h expressly recognizes the parental role in assessing sex-related material harmful to minors according "to prevailing standards in the adult community as a whole with respect to what is suitable material for minors." Moreover, the prohibition against sales to minors does not bar parents who so desire from purchasing the magazines for their children.

The State also has an independent interest in the well-being of its youth. . . .

> While the supervision of children's reading may best be left to their parents, the knowledge that parental control or guidance cannot always be provided and society's transcendent interest in protecting the welfare of children justify reasonable regulation of the sale of material to them. It is, therefore, altogether fitting and proper for a state to include in a statute designed to regulate the sale of pornography to children special standards, broader than those embodied in legislation aimed at controlling dissemination of such material to adults.

. . . [T]his Court, too, recognized that the State has an interest "to protect the welfare of children" and to see that they are "safeguarded from abuses" which might prevent their "growth into free and independent well-developed men and citizens." The only question remaining, therefore, is whether the New York Legislature might rationally conclude, as it has, that exposure to the materials proscribed by § 484-h constitutes such an "abuse."

Section 484-e of the law states a legislative finding that the material condemned by § 484-h is "a basic factor in impairing the ethical and moral development of our youth and a clear and present danger to the people of the state." It is very doubtful that this finding expresses an accepted scientific fact. But obscenity is not protected expression and may be suppressed without a showing of the circumstances which lie behind the phrase "clear and present danger" in its application to protected speech. To sustain state power to exclude material defined as obscenity by § 484-h requires only that we be able to say that it was not irrational for the legislature to find that exposure to material condemned by the statute is harmful to minors. . . . To be sure, there is no lack of "studies" which purport to demonstrate that obscenity is or is not "a basic factor in impairing the ethical and moral development of . . . youth and a clear and present danger to the people of the state." But the growing consensus of commentators is that "while these studies all agree that a causal link has not been demonstrated, they are equally agreed that a causal link has not been disproved either." We do not demand of legislatures "scientifically certain criteria of legislation." We therefore cannot say that § 484-h, in defining the obscenity of material on the basis of its appeal to minors under 17, has no rational relation to the objective of safeguarding such minors from harm.

...

Affirmed.

Mr. Justice Stewart, concurring in the result.

A doctrinaire, knee-jerk application of the First Amendment would, of course, dictate the nullification of this New York statute. But that result is not required, I think, if we bear in mind what it is that the First Amendment protects.

The First Amendment guarantees liberty of human expression in order to preserve in our Nation what Mr. Justice Holmes called a "free trade in ideas." To that end, the Constitution protects more than just a man's freedom to say or write or publish what he wants. It secures as well the liberty of each man to decide for himself what he will read and to what he will listen. The Constitution guarantees, in short, a society of free choice. Such a society presupposes the capacity of its members to choose.

When expression occurs in a setting where the capacity to make a choice is absent, government regulation of that expression may co-exist with and even implement First Amendment guarantees....

I think a State may permissibly determine that, at least in some precisely delineated areas, a child—like someone in a captive audience—is not possessed of that full capacity for individual choice which is the presupposition of First Amendment guarantees. It is only upon such a premise, I should suppose, that a State may deprive children of other rights—the right to marry, for example, or the right to vote—deprivations that would be constitutionally intolerable for adults.

I cannot hold that this state law, on its face, violates the First and Fourteenth Amendments.

Mr. Justice Doouglas, with whom Mr. Justice Black concurs, dissenting. [omitted]

Mr. Justice Fortas, dissenting.

This is a criminal prosecution. Sam Ginsberg and his wife operate a luncheonette at which magazines are offered for sale. A 16-year-old boy was enlisted by his mother to go to the luncheonette and buy some "girlie" magazines so that Ginsberg could be prosecuted. He went there, picked two magazines from a display case, paid for them, and walked out. Ginsberg's offense was duly reported to the authorities. The power of the State of New York was invoked. Ginsberg was prosecuted and convicted. The court imposed only a suspended sentence. But as the majority here points out, under New York law this conviction may mean that Ginsberg will lose the license necessary to operate his luncheonette.

The two magazines that the 16-year-old boy selected are vulgar "girlie" periodicals. However tasteless and tawdry they may be, we have ruled (as the Court acknowledges) that magazines indistinguishable from them in content and offensiveness are not "obscene" within the constitutional standards heretofore applied. These rulings have been in cases involving adults.

The Court avoids facing the problem whether the magazines in the present case are "obscene" when viewed by a 16-year-old boy, although not "obscene" when viewed by someone 17 years of age or older. It says that Ginsberg's lawyer did not choose to challenge the conviction on the ground that the magazines are not "obscene." He chose only to attack the statute on its face. Therefore, the Court reasons, we need not look at the magazines may be excluded from the ambit of the First Amendment as "obscene" for purposes of this case. But this Court has made strong and comprehensive statements about its duty in First Amendment cases — statements with which I agree.

In my judgment, the Court cannot properly avoid its fundamental duty to define "obscenity" for purposes of censorship of material sold to youths, merely because of counsel's position. By so doing the Court avoids the essence of the problem; for if the State's power to censor freed from the prohibitions of the First Amendment depends upon obscenity, and if obscenity turns on the specific content of the publication, how can we sustain the conviction here without deciding whether the particular magazines in question are obscene?

The Court certainly cannot mean that the States and cities and counties and villages have unlimited power to withhold anything and everything that is written or pictorial from younger people. But it here justifies the conviction of Sam Ginsberg because the impact of the Constitution, it says, is variable, and what is not obscene for an adult may be obscene for a child. This it calls "variable obscenity." I do not disagree with this, but I insist that to assess the principle — certainly to apply it — the Court must define it. We must know the extent to which literature or pictures may be less offensive than *Roth* requires in order to be "obscene" for purposes of a statute confined to youth.

I agree that the State in the exercise of its police power — even in the First Amendment domain — may make proper and careful differentiation between adults and children. But I do not agree that this power may be used on an arbitrary, free-wheeling basis. This is not a case where, on any standard enunciated by the Court, the magazines are obscene, nor one where the seller is at fault. Petitioner is being prosecuted for the sale of magazines which he had a right under the decisions of this Court to offer for sale, and he is being prosecuted without proof of "fault" — without even a claim that he deliberately, calculatedly sought to induce children to buy "obscene" material. Bookselling should not be a hazardous profession.

The conviction of Ginsberg on the present facts is a serious invasion of freedom. To sustain the conviction without inquiry as to whether the material is "obscene" and without any evidence of pushing or pandering, in face of this Court's asserted solicitude for First Amendment values, is to give the State a role in the rearing of children which is contrary to our traditions and to our conception of family responsibility. It begs the question to present this undefined, unlimited censorship as an aid to parents in the rearing of their children. This decision does not merely protect children from activities which all sensible parents would condemn. Rather, its undefined and unlimited approval of state censorship in this area denies to children free access to books and works of art to which many parents may wish their children to have uninhibited access. For denial of access to these magazines, without any standard or definition of their allegedly distinguishing characteristics, is also denial of access to great works of art and literature.

If this statute were confined to the punishment of pushers or panderers of vulgar literature I would not be so concerned by the Court's failure to circumscribe state power by defining its limits in terms of the meaning of "obscenity" in this field. The State's police power may, within very broad limits, protect the parents and their children from public aggression of panderers and pushers. This is defensible on the theory that they cannot protect themselves from such assaults. But it does not follow that the State may convict a passive luncheonette operator of a crime because a 16-year-old boy maliciously and designedly picks up and pays for two girlie magazines which are presumably not obscene.

I would therefore reverse the conviction....

Notes and Queries

1. The Court has defined obscene as the following: "Obscene material is material which deals with sex in a manner appealing to prurient interest." The Court has also accepted the following standard to determine obscenity: "whether to the average person, applying contemporary community standards, the dominant theme of the material taken as a whole appeals to prurient interest." See *Roth v. United States*, 354 U.S. 476 (1957). Does *Ginsberg* stand for the proposition that, when involving adolescents and children, a court must use a variable definition of obscenity and judge it from the vulnerable groups' perspective? Would that standard be workable?

2. The Court recognizes that no research supports the state's claim of harm to minors. It also finds that, even despite any evidence, the state acted rationally. What implications arise from this approach to protecting minors from harm?

3. Research indicates that by age 6 children seek information like pictures that explain body functions, and by age 10 that interest may include looking at photos and published materials that reveal others' bodies. See Sharon Araji (1997). *Sexually Aggressive Children: Coming to Understand Them*. Thousand Oaks, CA: Sage. In addition, by adolescence, "pornography" and other sexualized materials seem to become a major source of sexual information that contributes to adolescents'

sexual socialization. Roger J. R. Levesque (2000). *Adolescents, Sex, and the Law: Preparing Adolescents for Responsible Citizenship.* Washington, DC: American Psychological Association. What implications arise from that research?

4. The Court places emphasis on parental rights and finds them protected by the statute, at least to the extent that it could be assumed that parents would not want their children exposed to materials obscene as to minors. Why does the state permit parents to provide "obscene" materials to their minor children if the state's major rationale for the statute is to protect the moral and healthy development of minors?

5. Justice Stewart proposes that restrictions on minors' First Amendment rights are permissible given their limited capacity for individual choice in a free market of ideas? What capacity seems needed in this context? Following this logic, if minors can be deemed mature and capable, should they not have a right to "obscene' materials? What arguments can be made to support the contention that adolescents should have a right to obscene materials?

Chapter 7

Considering Child Welfare in Different Families

Much evidence supports the conclusion that traditional families (two married, heterosexual parents with their own biological children) are in many ways a minority. Yet the myth of the traditional family carries much weight in law and often serves as the standard on which to evaluate the relative normalcy of other families and the extent to which parents in those families may be fit to have or raise children. The legal system generally reflects and often supports society's attitude toward parenthood, and why it is that some people are judged fit to be parents while others are deemed inadequate. As a result, some parents and families may be assumed harmful to children or too burdensome on society, which justifies intervening in family relationships and breaking familial bonds even without proof of actual harm to the children removed from their families. Given the significance of the law's power to determine who is fit, how the legal system conceives of families and what would constitute normal family structures and relationships necessarily must serve as the starting point to understand the goals of child welfare law and efforts to regulate family life.

A look at family patterns and relationships that the legal system views as inadequate helps us envision what the legal system views, and assumes, as parenting adequate enough to escape direct state intervention. Presumably, well-functioning parents routinely provide children with safety and material well-being, but also with the interpersonal skills, personal values, and emotional development required to flourish as adults. Presumably, family structure would not matter and what would really matter is the quality of family life or parent–child relationship where the parent assumes the role of emotional, physical, social, and intellectual caretaker. Yet parent–child relationships do not take place within a social vacuum. The social circumstances of the family, the neighborhood in which the family lives, and the relationship between parents all impact a parent's effectiveness. It is precisely because parent–child relationships are socially located that we must consider what constitutes appropriate, competent parenting.

Considering factors outside of a particular relationship that is at stake when the law intervenes creates many challenges. Fundamentally, it raises the likelihood of intervening when there is no demonstrable harm to a particular child because of the parents' actions toward the child. It also increases the chances of intervening to preserve social values and perceptions of what parents owe children and broader society.

The legal system evinces considerable tension as it seeks to balance the rights of families and their children. On the one hand, it seeks to uphold the normative image of the traditional family as the basis to shape social and legal doctrines about the bases for parental status and for determining who stands in an appropriate relationship to a particular child. On the other hand, efforts are made to take into account the variety of ways in which adults may stand in valuable parental relationships to children and resist succumbing unreflectively to the normative pressure of picturing parenthood molded on the heterosexual, patriarchal, self-sustaining, nuclear family. The tension strikes our moral sensibilities and underscores the extent to which our moral sensibilities may resist decisions consistent with social science findings regarding adequate parent–child relationships.

This chapter seeks to help us understand the key concerns and rationales used to determine the fitness of parents and families. The cases and social science materials examine the right to marry (issues involving polygamy, interracial, same sex, and poverty), the right to plan families, the rights of parents making biological claims (unwed parents, biological v. adoptive parents, and parents through surrogacy and artificial insemination), the rights of parents sometimes deemed *per se* inadequate (mentally incompetent, criminal, immoral, and incestuous parents), and the rights of parents who reject extended family members (e.g., grandparents and communal groups). To understand these rights, we examine them in light of their potential impact on children, the place of children in society, and the law's approach to child maltreatment.

Review Problem

1. Before exploring how the state regulates parenting, it is useful to consider the extent to which you think the state could be more aggressive in regulating parents. For example, consider this possibility. To help prevent child abuse, a number of proposals include calls to license parents. Different versions of licensing usually include a credentialing process by the government to ensure that parents are capable and willing to act as parents, that they are at least 18 years of age in order to prevent children from raising children, that they sign a pledge not to neglect or abuse their children, and that they complete a certified course in parenting before being allowed to function as parents. Seem reasonable? To what extent do we already "license" parents or regulate how they will have children and how they will raise them?

Research Comments

1. Several rationales have been offered to support parental licensing proposals: (1) Children have a human right to be free from child maltreatment; (2) the government can regulate activities that are potentially harmful to others and to society; (3) most of our societal ills can be blamed on incompetent parents; (4) a licensing process for parents would demonstrate that our society values competent parenting; (5) responsibility would fall on parents to demonstrate their competence before a child is damaged rather than on the state to prove unfitness after a child has been damaged; and (6) we have the technology to determine who should not have children given that we would not attempt to distinguish between "good" and "less good" parenting or to prescribe parenting styles but rather exclude only those who are obviously unqualified. See Jack C. Westman (1994). *Licensing Parents: Can We Prevent Child Abuse and Neglect*? New York: Insight Books/Plenum Press. Do you find these rationales convincing?

2. Most may find it challenging to take seriously the various proposals offered in support of licensing parents; many simply may view the proposals as too offensive. One of the obvious controversies involves the extent to which scientific approaches support such proposals and the extent to which we wish to rely on science to further policy making in a way that plays down prevailing moral values. Consider the lively discussion that ensued when a senior psychologist wrote a provocative piece, in a leading psychology journal, proposing licensing *married* parents as the cure for addressing crime and other antisocial acts. His conclusion stemmed from his review of the literature that found the causes of crime and violence due to single and inept parents who neglect and abuse their children. We could stem crime, he argued, if we ensured joint parental responsibility. David T. Lykken (2000). The causes and costs of crime and a controversial cure. *Journal of Personality*, 68, 559–605. One critic responded that the vast majority of crimes and antisocial acts are committed by youth, that the majority who commit crimes during their adolescence tend not to do so in adulthood, and that changes in criminality over time are less due to factors in the family of origin and more due to the normative transitions of the life course. Robert J. Sampson (2000). Crime, criminals, and cures: Medical model revisited. *Journal of Personality*, 68, 607–613. Another critic argued that the absence of a father is a correlate of criminal behavior in offspring, but not its cause. Other correlations that are usually interpreted as the effects of good or bad child-rearing practices are similarly ambiguous and subject to other explanations. Judith Rich Harris (2000). The outcome of parenting: What do we really know? *Journal of Personality*, 68, 625–637. Yet another commentator argued that the evidence may be right but that proposing mandated marriage and parental licensure is wrong and unacceptable in our civilized society. She argued that, given reproductive rights, it would make more sense to foster voluntary parenthood through making effective contraception and abortion services available to all

women. Sandra Scarr (2000). Toward voluntary parenthood. *Journal of Personality*, 68, 615–623. What do these criticisms and proposals tell you about the role of social sciences in furthering social policy? In this instance, taking directions from social science findings does seem to require a considerable leap of faith. It requires concluding that an individual who is not yet a parent would be incompetent because that individual has characteristics similar to a group of individuals deemed suspect. Does that affront your sense of a need for individualized justice? To what extent does the legal system already embrace this approach?

3. More recent discussions focusing on parental licensing adopt harm reduction lenses. These approaches accept that problematic practices exist and will continue. Rather than harshly responding to those practices, harm reduction approaches suggest a need to focus on mitigating undesirable consequences. When it comes to licensing parents to prevent harm to children, commentators suggest the need for caution. That need stems from a long history of state abuse of power and, for example, its discriminatory effects. Liam Shields (2020). Parental licensing as harm reduction. *Health Care Analysis*, 28(4), 424–433.

Reynolds v. United States

98 U.S. 145; 25 L. Ed. 244 (1878)

Mr. Chief Justice Waite delivered the opinion of the court.

. . .

As to the defense of religious belief or duty.

. . . the accused proved that at the time of his alleged second marriage he was, and for many years before had been, a member of the Church of Jesus Christ of Latter-Day Saints, commonly called the Mormon Church, and a believer in its doctrines; that it was an accepted doctrine of that church "that it was the duty of male members of said church, circumstances permitting, to practice polygamy; . . . that this duty was enjoined by different books which the members of said church believed to be to divine origin, and among others the Holy Bible, and also that the members of the church believed that the practice of polygamy was directly enjoined upon the male members thereof by the Almighty God, in a revelation to Joseph Smith, the founder and prophet of said church; that the failing or refusing to practice polygamy by such male members of said church, when circumstances would admit, would be punished, and that the penalty for such failure and refusal would be damnation in the life to come." He also proved "that he had received permission from the recognized authorities in said church to enter into polygamous marriage . . . that Daniel H. Wells, one having authority in said church to perform the marriage ceremony, married the said defendant on or about the time the crime is alleged to have been committed, to some woman by the name of Schofield, and that such marriage ceremony was performed under and pursuant to the doctrines of said church."

Upon this proof he asked the court to instruct the jury that if they found from the evidence that he "was married as charged — if he was married — in pursuance of and in conformity with what he believed at the time to be a religious duty, that the verdict must be 'not guilty.'" This request was refused, and the court did charge "that there must have been a criminal intent, but that if the defendant, under the influence of a religious belief that it was right, — under an inspiration, if you please, that it was right — deliberately married a second time, having a first wife living, the want of consciousness of evil intent — the want of understanding on his part that he was committing a crime — did not excuse him; but the law inexorably in such case implies the criminal intent."

Upon this charge and refusal to charge the question is raised, whether religious belief can be accepted as a justification of an overt act made criminal by the law of the land. The inquiry is not as to the power of Congress to prescribe criminal laws for the Territories, but as to the guilt of one who knowingly violates a law which has been properly enacted, if he entertains a religious belief that the law is wrong.

Congress cannot pass a law for the government of the Territories which shall prohibit the free exercise of religion. The first amendment to the Constitution expressly forbids such legislation. Religious freedom is guaranteed everywhere throughout the United States, so far as congressional interference is concerned. The question to be determined is, whether the law now under consideration comes within this prohibition.

The word "religion" is not defined in the Constitution. We must go elsewhere, therefore, to ascertain its meaning, and nowhere more appropriately, we think, than to the history of the times in the midst of which the provision was adopted. The precise point of the inquiry is, what is the religious freedom which has been guaranteed.

. . .

Polygamy has always been odious among the northern and western nations of Europe, and, until the establishment of the Mormon Church, was almost exclusively a feature of the life of Asiatic and of African people. At common law, the second marriage was always void and from the earliest history of England polygamy has been treated as an offence against society. After the establishment of the ecclesiastical courts, and until the time of James I., it was punished through the instrumentality of those tribunals, not merely because ecclesiastical rights had been violated, but because upon the separation of the ecclesiastical courts from the civil the ecclesiastical were supposed to be the most appropriate for the trial of matrimonial causes and offences against the rights of marriage, just as they were for testamentary causes and the settlement of the estate of Deceased persons.

By the statute of 1 James I., the offence, if committed in England or Wales, was made punishable in the civil courts, and the penalty was death. As this statute was limited in its operation to England and Wales, it was at a very early period re-enacted, generally with some modifications, in all the colonies. In connection with the case we are now considering, it is a significant fact that on the 8th of December, 1788, after the passage of the act establishing religious freedom, and after the convention of Virginia had recommended as an amendment to the Constitution of the United States the declaration in a bill of rights that "all men have an equal, natural, and unalienable right to the free exercise of religion, according to the dictates of conscience," the legislature of that State substantially enacted the statute of James I., death penalty included, because, as recited in the preamble, "it hath been doubted whether bigamy or poligamy be punishable by the laws of this Commonwealth." From that day to this we think it may safely be said there never has been a time in any State of the Union when polygamy has not been an offence against society, cognizable by the civil courts and punishable with more or less severity. In the face of all this evidence, it is impossible to believe that the constitutional guaranty of religious freedom was intended to prohibit legislation in respect to this most important feature of social life. Marriage, while from its very nature a sacred obligation, is nevertheless, in most civilized nations, a civil contract, and usually regulated by law. Upon it society may be said to be built, and out of its fruits spring social relations and social obligations and duties, with which government is necessarily required to deal. In fact, according as monogamous or polygamous marriages are allowed, do we find the principles on which the government of the people, to a greater or less extent, rests. Professor Lieber says, polygamy leads to the patriarchal principle, and which, when applied to large communities, fetters the people in stationary despotism, while that principle cannot long exist in connection with monogamy. Chancellor Kent observes that this remark is equally striking and profound. An exceptional colony of polygamists under an exceptional leadership may sometimes exist for a time without appearing to disturb the social condition of the people who surround it; but there cannot be a doubt that, unless restricted by some form of constitution, it is within the legitimate scope of the power of every civil government to determine whether polygamy or monogamy shall be the law of social life under its dominion.

In our opinion, the statute immediately under consideration is within the legislative power of Congress. It is constitutional and valid as prescribing a rule of action for all those residing in the Territories, and in places over which the United States have exclusive control. This being so, the only question which remains is, whether those who make polygamy a part of their religion are excepted from the operation of the statute. If they are, then those who do not make polygamy a part of their religious belief may be found guilty and punished, while those who do, must be acquitted and go free. This would be introducing a new element into criminal law. Laws are made for the government of actions, and while they cannot interfere with mere religious belief and opinions, they may with practices. Suppose one believed that human sacrifices were a necessary part of religious worship, would it be seriously contended that the civil government under which he lived could not interfere to prevent a sacrifice? Or if a wife religiously believed it was her duty to burn herself upon the funeral pile of her dead husband, would it be beyond the power of the civil government to prevent her carrying her belief into practice?

So here, as a law of the organization of society under the exclusive dominion of the United States, it is provided that plural marriages shall not be allowed. Can a man excuse his practices to the contrary because of his religious belief? The permit this would be to make the professed doctrines of religious belief superior to the law of the land, and in effect to permit every citizen to become a law unto himself. Government could exist only in name under such circumstances.

A criminal intent is generally an element of crime, but every man is presumed to intend the necessary and legitimate consequences of what he knowingly does. Here the accused knew he had been once married, and that his first wife was living. He also knew that his second marriage was forbidden by law. When, therefore, he married the second time, he is presumed to have intended to break the law. And the breaking of the law is the crime. Every act necessary to constitute the crime was knowingly done, and the crime was therefore knowingly committed. Ignorance of a fact may sometimes be taken as evidence of a want of criminal intent, but not ignorance of the law. The only defense of the accused in this case is his belief that the law ought not to have been enacted. It matters not that his belief was a part of his professed religion: it was still belief, and belief only.

...

Upon a careful consideration of the whole case, we are satisfied that no error was committed by the court below.

Judgment affirmed.

...

Mr. Justice Field, concurring. [omitted]

Notes and Queries

1. Why is polygamy deemed criminal? Do you find the historical arguments persuasive? If not, then why is the practice still criminal?
2. The law can limit the practice of religious convictions, an approach which grants considerable power to governments. How would you distinguish withholding medical treatment from withholding food from a child? How can one be permissible on religious grounds while the other is not?
3. What limit does the court place on religion's impact on family life? Can you discern a standard? Is it that the practice is simply "odious"? Is it that the practice is simply socially harmful? If these are the standards, many other actions could come under the reach of the state. Any thought as to what should be included in the limit the law should place on the state's regulation of marriage?
4. Arguably, *Reynolds* involves motives more than consequences. How would you address the claim that polygamy is no different from families with numerous children due to "serial monogamy"? What evidence can you locate in *Reynolds* to support or deny any useful difference between these two positions?

Loving v. Virginia

388 U.S. 1; 87 S. Ct. 1817 (1967)

Mr. Justice Warren delivered the opinion of the Court.

In June 1958, two residents of Virginia, Mildred Jeter, a Negro woman, and Richard Loving, a white man, were married in the District of Columbia pursuant to its laws. Shortly after their marriage, the Lovings returned to Virginia and established their marital abode in Caroline County. At the October Term, 1958, of the Circuit Court of Caroline County, a grand jury issued an indictment charging the Lovings with violating Virginia's ban on interracial marriages. On January 6, 1959, the Lovings pleaded guilty to the charge and were sentenced to one year in jail; however, the trial judge suspended the sentence for a period of 25 years on the condition that the Lovings leave the State and not return to Virginia together for 25 years. He stated in an opinion that:

> Almighty God created the races white, black, yellow, malay and red, and he placed them on separate continents. And but for the interference with his arrangement there would be no cause for such marriages. The fact that he separated the races shows that he did not intend for the races to mix.

After their convictions, the Lovings took up residence in the District of Columbia. On November 6, 1963, they filed a motion in the state trial court to vacate the judgment and set aside the sentence on the ground that the statutes which they had violated were repugnant to the Fourteenth Amendment. The motion not having been decided by October 28, 1964, the Lovings instituted a class action in the United States District Court for the Eastern District of Virginia requesting that a three-judge court be convened to declare the Virginia antimiscegenation statutes unconstitutional and to enjoin state officials from enforcing their convictions. On January 22, 1965, the state trial judge denied the motion to vacate the sentences, and the Lovings perfected an appeal to the Supreme Court of Appeals of Virginia. On February 11, 1965, the three-judge District Court continued the case to allow the Lovings to present their constitutional claims to the highest state court.

The Supreme Court of Appeals upheld the constitutionality of the antimiscegenation statutes and, after modifying the sentence, affirmed the convictions. The Lovings appealed this decision, and we noted probable jurisdiction on December 12, 1966.

. . .

Virginia is now one of 16 States which prohibit and punish marriages on the basis of racial classifications. Penalties for miscegenation arose as an incident to slavery and have been common in Virginia since the colonial period. The present statutory scheme dates from the adoption of the Racial Integrity Act of 1924, passed during the period of extreme nativism which followed the end of the First World War. The central features of this Act, and current Virginia law, are the absolute prohibition of a "white person" marrying other than another "white person," a prohibition against issuing marriage licenses until the issuing official is satisfied that the applicants' statements as to their race are correct, certificates of "racial composition" to be kept by both local and state registrars, and the carrying forward of earlier prohibitions against racial intermarriage.

. . .

While the state court is no doubt correct in asserting that marriage is a social relation subject to the State's police power, the State does not contend in its argument before this Court that its powers to regulate marriage are unlimited notwithstanding the commands of the Fourteenth Amendment. . . . Instead, the State argues that the meaning of the Equal Protection Clause, as illuminated by the statements of the Framers, is only that state penal laws containing an interracial element as part of the definition of the offense must apply equally to whites and Negroes in the sense that members of each race are punished to the same degree. Thus, the State contends that, because its miscegenation statutes punish equally both the white and the Negro participants in an interracial marriage, these statutes, despite their reliance on racial classifications, do not constitute an invidious discrimination based upon race. The second argument advanced by the State assumes the validity of its equal application theory. The argument is that, if the Equal Protection Clause does not outlaw miscegenation statutes because of their reliance on racial classifications, the question of constitutionality would thus become whether there was any rational basis for a State to treat interracial marriages differently from other marriages. On this question, the State argues, the scientific evidence is substantially in doubt and, consequently, this Court should defer to the wisdom of the state legislature in adopting its policy of discouraging interracial marriages.

Because we reject the notion that the mere "equal application" of a statute containing racial classifications is enough to remove the classifications from the Fourteenth Amendment's proscription of all invidious racial discriminations, we do not accept the State's contention that these statutes should be upheld if there is any possible basis for concluding that they serve a rational purpose. . . .

. . .

There can be no question but that Virginia's miscegenation statutes rest solely upon distinctions drawn according to race. The statutes proscribe generally accepted conduct if engaged in by members of different races. Over the years, this Court has consistently repudiated "distinctions between citizens solely because of their ancestry" as being "odious to a free people whose institutions are founded upon the doctrine of equality." At the very least, the Equal Protection Clause demands that racial classifications, especially suspect in criminal statutes, be subjected to the "most rigid scrutiny," and, if they are ever to be upheld, they must be shown to be necessary to the accomplishment of some permissible state objective, independent of the racial discrimination which it was the object of the Fourteenth Amendment to eliminate. . . .

There is patently no legitimate overriding purpose independent of invidious racial discrimination which justifies this classification. The fact that Virginia prohibits only interracial marriages involving white persons demonstrates that the racial classifications must stand on their own justification, as measures designed to maintain White Supremacy. We have consistently denied the constitutionality of measures which restrict the rights of citizens on account of race. There can be no doubt that restricting the freedom to marry solely because of racial classifications violates the central meaning of the Equal Protection Clause.

. . .

These statutes also deprive the Lovings of liberty without due process of law in violation of the Due Process Clause of the Fourteenth Amendment. The freedom to marry has long been recognized as one of the vital personal rights essential to the orderly pursuit of happiness by free men.

Marriage is one of the "basic civil rights of man," fundamental to our very existence and survival. To deny this fundamental freedom on so unsupportable a basis as the racial classifications embodied in these statutes, classifications so directly subversive of the principle of equality at the heart of the Fourteenth Amendment, is surely to deprive all the State's citizens of liberty without due process of law. The Fourteenth Amendment requires that the freedom of choice to marry not be restricted by invidious racial discriminations. Under our Constitution, the freedom to marry, or not marry, a person of another race resides with the individual and cannot be infringed by the State.

These convictions must be reversed.

Mr. Justice Stewart, concurring. [omitted]

Notes and Queries

1. The Court grants marriage a very high status as it finds that it is one of the "basic civil rights of man," fundamental to our very existence and survival. Why is it so fundamental? Is it because of its link to procreation and child-rearing?

2. Do you understand the Court to mean that marriage is a fundamental right? If so, what compelling interest would be needed to infringe on that right?

3. Although the Court refers to marriage as a basic civil right, it may in fact not be fundamental in the jurisprudential sense of the term. The core holding of the case hinged on an equal protection, rather than a fundamental rights, analysis. The Court held that the ban on interracial marriages constituted racial discrimination and therefore violated the Equal Protection Clause of the Fourteenth Amendment. Do you agree?

Zablocki v. Redhail

434 U.S. 374; 98 S. Ct. 673 (1978)

Mr. Justice Marshall delivered the opinion of the court.

At issue in this case is the constitutionality of a Wisconsin statute, which provides that members of a certain class of Wisconsin residents may not marry, within the State or elsewhere, without first obtaining a court order granting permission to marry. The class is defined by the statute to include any "Wisconsin resident having minor issue not in his custody and which he is under obligation to support by any court order or judgment." The statute specifies that court permission cannot be granted unless the marriage applicant submits proof of compliance with the support obligation and, in addition, demonstrates that the children covered by the support order "are not then and are not likely thereafter to become public charges." No marriage license may lawfully be issued in Wisconsin to a person covered by the statute, except upon court order; any marriage entered into without compliance with § 245.10 is declared void; and persons acquiring marriage licenses in violation of the section are subject to criminal penalties.

...

Appellee Redhail is a Wisconsin resident who, under the terms of § 245.10, is unable to enter into a lawful marriage in Wisconsin or elsewhere so long as he maintains his Wisconsin residency. The facts, according to the stipulation filed by the parties in the District Court, are as follows. In January 1972, when appellee was a minor and a high school student, a paternity action was instituted against him in Milwaukee County Court, alleging that he was the father of a baby girl born out of wedlock on July 5, 1971. After he appeared and admitted that he was the child's father, the court entered an order on May 12, 1972, adjudging appellee the father and ordering him to pay $109 per month as support for the child until she reached 18 years of age. From May 1972 until August 1974, appellee was unemployed and indigent, and consequently was unable to make any support payments.

On September 27, 1974, appellee filed an application for a marriage license with appellant Zablocki, the County Clerk of Milwaukee County, and a few days later the application was denied on the sole ground that appellee had not obtained a court order granting him permission to marry, as required by § 245.10.

Although appellee did not petition a state court thereafter, it is stipulated that he would not have been able to satisfy either of the statutory prerequisites for an order granting permission to marry. First, he had not satisfied his support obligations to his illegitimate child, and as of December 1974 there was an arrearage in excess of $3,700. Second, the child had been a public charge since her birth, receiving benefits under the Aid to Families with Dependent Children program. It is stipulated that the child's benefit payments were such that she would have been a public charge even if appellee had been current in his support payments.

...

The leading decision of this Court on the right to marry is *Loving v. Virginia*. In that case, an interracial couple who had been convicted of violating Virginia's miscegenation laws challenged the statutory scheme on both equal protection and due process grounds. The Court's opinion could have rested solely on the ground that the statutes discriminated on the basis of race in violation of the Equal Protection Clause. But the Court went on to hold that the laws arbitrarily deprived the couple of a fundamental liberty protected by the Due Process Clause, the freedom to marry....

...

More recent decisions have established that the right to marry is part of the fundamental "right of privacy" implicit in the Fourteenth Amendment's Due Process Clause....

...

It is not surprising that the decision to marry has been placed on the same level of importance as decisions relating to procreation, childbirth, child rearing, and family relationships. As the facts of this case illustrate, it would make little sense to recognize a right of privacy with respect to other matters of family life and not with respect to the decision to enter the relationship that is the foundation of the family in our society....

...

By reaffirming the fundamental character of the right to marry, we do not mean to suggest that every state regulation which relates in any way to the incidents of or prerequisites for marriage must be subjected to rigorous scrutiny. To the contrary, reasonable regulations that do not significantly interfere with decisions to enter into the marital relationship may legitimately be imposed....

...

When a statutory classification significantly interferes with the exercise of a fundamental right, it cannot be upheld unless it is supported by sufficiently important state interests and is closely tailored to effectuate only those interests. Appellant asserts that two interests are served by the challenged statute: the permission-to-marry proceeding furnishes an opportunity to counsel the applicant as to the necessity of fulfilling his prior support obligations; and the welfare of the out-of-custody children is protected. We may accept for present purposes that these are legitimate and substantial interests, but, since the means selected by the State for achieving these interests unnecessarily impinge on the right to marry, the statute cannot be sustained.

...

With regard to safeguarding the welfare of the out-of-custody children, appellant's brief does not make clear the connection between the State's interest and the statute's requirements. At argument, appellant's counsel suggested that, since permission to marry cannot be granted unless the applicant shows that he has satisfied his court-determined support obligations to the prior children and that those children will not become public charges, the statute provides incentive for the applicant to make support payments to his children. This "collection device" rationale cannot justify the statute's broad infringement on the right to marry.

First, with respect to individuals who are unable to meet the statutory requirements, the statute merely prevents the applicant from getting married, without delivering any money at all into the hands of the applicant's prior children. More importantly, regardless of the applicant's ability or willingness to meet the statutory requirements, the State already has numerous other means for exacting compliance with support obligations, means that are at least as effective as the instant statute's and yet do not impinge upon the right to marry. Under Wisconsin law, whether the children are from a prior marriage or were born out of wedlock, court-determined support obligations may be enforced directly via wage assignments, civil contempt proceedings, and criminal penalties. And, if the State believes that parents of children out of their custody should be responsible for ensuring that those children do not become public charges, this interest can be achieved by adjusting the criteria used for determining the amounts to be paid under their support orders.

There is also some suggestion that § 245.10 protects the ability of marriage applicants to meet support obligations to prior children by preventing the applicants from incurring new support obligations. But the challenged provisions of § 245.10 are grossly underinclusive with respect to this purpose, since they do not limit in any way new financial commitments by the applicant other than those arising out of the contemplated marriage. The statutory classification is substantially overinclusive as well:

> Given the possibility that the new spouse will actually better the applicant's financial situation, by contributing income from a job or otherwise, the statute in many cases may prevent affected individuals from improving their ability to satisfy their prior support obligations. And, although it is true that the applicant will incur support obligations to any children born during the contemplated marriage, preventing the marriage may only result in the children being born out of wedlock, as in fact occurred in appellee's case. Since the support obligation is the same whether the child is born in or out of wedlock, the net result of preventing the marriage is simply more illegitimate children.

The statutory classification . . . thus cannot be justified by the interests advanced in support of it. The judgment of the District Court is, accordingly,

Affirmed.

Mr. Chief Justice Burger, concurring. [omitted]

Mr. Justice Stewart, concurring. [omitted]

Mr. Justice Powell, concurring. [omitted]

Mr. Justice Stevens, concurring. [omitted]

Mr. Justice Rehnquist, dissenting.

I substantially agree with my Brother Powell's reasons for rejecting the Court's conclusion that marriage is the sort of "fundamental right" which must invariably trigger the strictest judicial scrutiny. . . . I would view this legislative judgment in the light of the traditional presumption of validity. I think that under the Equal Protection Clause the statute need pass only the "rational basis test," and that under the Due Process Clause it need only be shown that it bears a rational relation to a constitutionally permissible objective. The statute so viewed is a permissible exercise of the State's power to regulate family life and to assure the support of minor children, despite its possible imprecision in the extreme cases envisioned in the concurring opinions.

. . .

Notes and Queries

1. *Zablocki v. Redhail* arguably established marriage as a fundamental right, although the holding in this case also was based ultimately upon equal protection. Recall that the statute at issue forbade marriage for residents who were under court order to support minor children unless they proved they were complying in all respects with the order. The Court held that the statute violated equal protection. Justice Marshall asserted that "by reaffirming the fundamental character of the right to marry, we do not mean to suggest that every state regulation which regulates in any way to the incidents of or prerequisites for marriage must be subjected to rigorous scrutiny. To the contrary, reasonable regulations that do not significantly interfere with decisions to enter into the marital relationship may legitimately be imposed." Again, the Court concedes that there is in fact a "fundamental character" to the right to marry, but the fundamental character of the right is within legitimate regulatory control of state laws so long as the regulations meet the demands of equal protection.

Review Problems

1. *Zablocki v. Redhail* and *Loving v. Virginia* conclude that the decision to marry is a fundamental right at least at some level. What circumstances could allow for prohibiting the exercise of that right? In *Turner v. Safley*, 482 U.S. 78 (1987), the Supreme Court addressed what rule should be applied in a prison forum. In that context, prisoners arguably have lost many of their basic rights and the state has legitimate security and rehabilitation concerns that may provide compelling reasons. Justice O'Connor delivered the opinion of the Court and reasoned as follows:

   > We disagree with petitioners that *Zablocki* does not apply to prison inmates. It is settled that a prison inmate "retains those [constitutional] rights that are not inconsistent with his status as a prisoner or with the

> legitimate penological objectives of the corrections system." The right to marry, like many other rights, is subject to substantial restrictions as a result of incarceration. Many important attributes of marriage remain, however, after taking into account the limitations imposed by prison life. First, inmate marriages, like others, are expressions of emotional support and public commitment. These elements are an important and significant aspect of the marital relationship. In addition, many religions recognize marriage as having spiritual significance; for some inmates and their spouses, therefore, the commitment of marriage may be an exercise of religious faith as well as an expression of personal dedication. Third, most inmates eventually will be released by parole or commutation, and therefore most inmate marriages are formed in the expectation that they ultimately will be fully consummated. Finally, marital status often is a pre-condition to the receipt of government benefits (e. g., Social Security benefits), property rights (e. g., tenancy by the entirety, inheritance rights), and other, less tangible benefits (e. g., legitimation of children born out of wedlock). These incidents of marriage, like the religious and personal aspects of the marriage commitment, are unaffected by the fact of confinement or the pursuit of legitimate corrections goals....
>
> The Missouri marriage regulation prohibits inmates from marrying unless the prison superintendent has approved the marriage after finding that there are compelling reasons for doing so. As noted previously, generally only pregnancy or birth of a child is considered a "compelling reason" to approve a marriage....
>
> Petitioners have identified both security and rehabilitation concerns in support of the marriage prohibition. The security concern emphasized by petitioners is that "love triangles" might lead to violent confrontations between inmates. With respect to rehabilitation, prison officials testified that female prisoners often were subject to abuse at home or were overly dependent on male figures, and that this dependence or abuse was connected to the crimes they had committed. The superintendent at Renz, petitioner William Turner, testified that in his view, these women prisoners needed to concentrate on developing skills of self-reliance and that the prohibition on marriage furthered this rehabilitative goal....
>
> We conclude that on this record ... [t]he Missouri regulation, however, represents an exaggerated response to such security objectives.... Nor, on this record, is the marriage restriction reasonably related to the articulated rehabilitation goal.

2. Justice O'Connor's analysis is quite significant not only for its holding but also for its reasoning. Most notably, it finds many reasons, beyond procreation as emphasized in earlier cases, to find marriage so central to our lives and thus worthy of considerable protection. Do you find her list persuasive?

Obergefell v. Hodges

576 U.S. 644 (2015)

Justice Kennedy delivered the opinion of the Court.

The Constitution promises liberty to all within its reach, a liberty that includes certain specific rights that allow persons, within a lawful realm, to define and express their identity. The petitioners in these cases seek to find that liberty by marrying someone of the same sex and having their marriages deemed lawful on the same terms and conditions as marriages between persons of the opposite sex.

These cases come from Michigan, Kentucky, Ohio, and Tennessee, States that define marriage as a union between one man and one woman. The petitioners are 14 same-sex couples and two men whose same-sex partners are deceased. The respondents are state officials responsible for enforcing the laws in question. The petitioners claim the respondents violate the Fourteenth Amendment by denying them the right to marry or to have their marriages, lawfully performed in another State, given full recognition. Petitioners filed these suits in United States District Courts in their home States. Each District Court ruled in their favor. Citations to those cases are in Appendix A, infra. The respondents appealed the decisions against them to the United States Court of Appeals for the Sixth Circuit. It consolidated the cases and reversed the judgments of the District Courts. The Court of Appeals held that a State has no constitutional obligation to license same-sex marriages or to recognize same-sex marriages performed out of State. The petitioners sought certiorari. This Court granted review, limited to two questions. The first, presented by the cases from Michigan and Kentucky, is whether the Fourteenth Amendment requires a State to license a marriage between two people of the same sex. The second, presented by the cases from Ohio, Tennessee, and, again, Kentucky, is whether the Fourteenth Amendment requires a State to recognize a same-sex marriage licensed and performed in a State which does grant that right.

. . .

After years of litigation, legislation, referenda, and the discussions that attended these public acts, the States are now divided on the issue of same-sex marriage.

III

Under the Due Process Clause of the Fourteenth Amendment, no State shall "deprive any person of life, liberty, or property, without due process of law." The fundamental liberties protected by this Clause include most of the rights enumerated in the Bill of Rights. In addition these liberties extend to certain personal choices central to individual dignity and autonomy, including intimate choices that define personal identity and beliefs. The identification and protection of fundamental rights is an enduring part of the judicial duty to interpret the Constitution. That responsibility, however, "has not been reduced to any formula." Rather, it requires courts to exercise reasoned judgment in identifying interests of the person so fundamental that the State must accord them its respect. That process is guided by many of the same considerations relevant to analysis of other constitutional provisions that set forth broad principles rather than specific requirements. History and tradition guide and discipline this inquiry but do not set its outer boundaries. That method respects our history and learns from it without allowing the past alone to rule the present.

The nature of injustice is that we may not always see it in our own times. The generations that wrote and ratified the Bill of Rights and the Fourteenth Amendment did not presume to know the extent of freedom in all of its dimensions, and so they entrusted to future generations a charter protecting the right of all persons to enjoy liberty as we learn its meaning. When new insight reveals discord between the Constitution's central protections and a received legal stricture, a claim to liberty must be addressed.

Applying these established tenets, the Court has long held the right to marry is protected by the Constitution. In *Loving v. Virginia*, which invalidated bans on interracial unions, a unanimous Court held marriage is "one of the vital personal rights essential to the orderly pursuit of happiness by free men." The Court reaffirmed that holding in *Zablocki v. Redhail*, which held the right to marry was burdened by a law prohibiting fathers who were behind on child support from marrying. The Court again applied this principle in *Turner v. Safley*, which held the right to marry was abridged by regulations limiting the privilege of prison inmates to marry. Over time and in other contexts, the Court has reiterated that the right to marry is fundamental under the Due Process Clause. It cannot be denied that this Court's cases describing the right to marry presumed a relationship involving opposite-sex partners. The Court, like many institutions, has made assumptions defined by the world and time of which it is a part. This was evident in *Baker v. Nelson*, a one-line summary decision issued in 1972, holding the exclusion of same-sex couples from marriage did not present a substantial federal question.

Still, there are other, more instructive precedents. This Court's cases have expressed constitutional principles of broader reach. In defining the right to marry these cases have identified essential attributes of that right based in history, tradition, and other constitutional liberties inherent in this intimate bond. And in assessing whether the force and rationale of its cases apply to same-sex couples, the Court must respect the basic reasons why the right to marry has been long protected.

This analysis compels the conclusion that same-sex couples may exercise the right to marry. The four principles and traditions to be discussed demonstrate that the reasons marriage is fundamental under the Constitution apply with equal force to same-sex couples.

A first premise of the Court's relevant precedents is that the right to personal choice regarding marriage is inherent in the concept of individual autonomy. This abiding connection between marriage and liberty is why *Loving* invalidated interracial marriage bans under the Due Process Clause. Like choices concerning contraception, family relationships, procreation, and child rearing, all of which are protected by the Constitution, decisions concerning marriage are among the most intimate that an individual can make. Indeed, the Court has noted it would be contradictory "to recognize a right of privacy with respect to other matters of family life and not with respect to the decision to enter the relationship that is the foundation of the family in our society."

Choices about marriage shape an individual's destiny. As the Supreme Judicial Court of Massachusetts has explained, because "it fulfils yearnings for security, safe haven, and connection that express our common humanity, civil marriage is an esteemed institution, and the decision whether and whom to marry is among life's momentous acts of self-definition."

The nature of marriage is that, through its enduring bond, two persons together can find other freedoms, such as expression, intimacy, and spirituality. This is true for all persons, whatever their sexual orientation. There is dignity in the bond between two men or two women who seek to marry and in their autonomy to make such profound choices.

A second principle in this Court's jurisprudence is that the right to marry is fundamental because it supports a two-person union unlike any other in its importance to the committed individuals. This point was central to *Griswold v. Connecticut*, which held the Constitution protects the right of married couples to use contraception. Suggesting that marriage is a right "older than the Bill of Rights," *Griswold* described marriage this way:

> Marriage is a coming together for better or for worse, hopefully enduring, and intimate to the degree of being sacred. It is an association that promotes a way of life, not causes; a harmony in living, not political faiths; a bilateral loyalty, not commercial or social projects. Yet it is an association for as noble a purpose as any involved in our prior decisions.

And in *Turner*, the Court again acknowledged the intimate association protected by this right, holding prisoners could not be denied the right to marry because their committed relationships satisfied the basic reasons why marriage is a fundamental right. The right to marry thus dignifies couples who "wish to define themselves by their commitment to each other." Marriage responds to the universal fear that a lonely person might call out only to find no one there. It offers the hope of companionship and understanding and assurance that while both still live there will be someone to care for the other.

As this Court held in *Lawrence*, same-sex couples have the same right as opposite-sex couples to enjoy intimate association. *Lawrence* invalidated laws that made same-sex intimacy a criminal act. And it acknowledged that "[w]hen sexuality finds overt expression in intimate conduct with another person, the conduct can be but one element in a personal bond that is more enduring." But while *Lawrence* confirmed a dimension of freedom that allows individuals to engage in intimate association without criminal liability, it does not follow that freedom stops there. Outlaw to outcast may be a step forward, but it does not achieve the full promise of liberty.

A third basis for protecting the right to marry is that it safeguards children and families and thus draws meaning from related rights of child rearing, procreation, and education. The Court has recognized these connections by describing the varied rights as a unified whole: "[T]he right to 'marry, establish a home and bring up children' is a central part of the liberty protected by the Due Process Clause." Under the laws of the several States, some of marriage's protections for children and families are material. But marriage also confers more profound benefits. By giving recognition and legal structure to their parents' relationship, marriage allows children "to understand the integrity and closeness of their own family and its concord with other families in their community and in their daily lives." Marriage also affords the permanency and stability important to children's best interests.

As all parties agree, many same-sex couples provide loving and nurturing homes to their children, whether biological or adopted. And hundreds of thousands of children are presently being raised by such couples. Most States have allowed gays and lesbians to adopt, either as individuals or as couples, and many adopted and foster children have same-sex parents. This provides powerful confirmation from the law itself that gays and lesbians can create loving, supportive families.

Excluding same-sex couples from marriage thus conflicts with a central premise of the right to marry. Without the recognition, stability, and predictability marriage offers, their children suffer the stigma of knowing their families are somehow lesser. They also suffer the significant material costs of being raised by unmarried parents, relegated through no fault of their own to a more difficult and uncertain family life. The marriage laws at issue here thus harm and humiliate the children of same-sex couples. That is not to say the right to marry is less meaningful for those who do not or cannot have children. An ability, desire, or promise to procreate is not and has not been a prerequisite for a valid marriage in any State. In light of precedent protecting the right of a married couple not to procreate, it cannot be said the Court or the States have conditioned the right to marry on the capacity or commitment to procreate. The constitutional marriage right has many aspects, of which childbearing is only one.

Fourth and finally, this Court's cases and the Nation's traditions make clear that marriage is a keystone of our social order. Alexis de Tocqueville recognized this truth on his travels through the United States almost two centuries ago:

> There is certainly no country in the world where the tie of marriage is so much respected as in America . . . [W]hen the American retires from the turmoil of public life to the bosom of his family, he finds in it the image of order and of peace. . . . [H]e afterwards carries [that image] with him into public affairs.

In *Maynard v. Hill*, the Court echoed de Tocqueville, explaining that marriage is "the foundation of the family and of society, without which there would be neither civilization nor progress." Marriage, the *Maynard* Court said, has long been "'a great public institution, giving character to our whole civil polity.'" This idea has been reiterated even as the institution has evolved in substantial ways over time, superseding rules related to parental consent, gender, and race once thought by many to be essential. Marriage remains a building block of our national community.

For that reason, just as a couple vows to support each other, so does society pledge to support the couple, offering symbolic recognition and material benefits to protect and nourish the union. Indeed, while the States are in general free to vary the benefits they confer on all married couples, they have throughout our history made marriage the basis for an expanding list of governmental rights, benefits, and responsibilities. These aspects of marital status include: taxation; inheritance and property rights; rules of intestate succession; spousal privilege in the law of evidence; hospital access; medical decision making authority; adoption rights; the rights and benefits of survivors; birth and death certificates; professional ethics rules; campaign finance restrictions; workers' compensation benefits; health insurance; and child custody, support, and visitation rules. Valid marriage under state law is also a significant status for over a thousand provisions of federal law. The States have contributed to the fundamental character of the marriage right by placing that institution at the center of so many facets of the legal and social order.

There is no difference between same- and opposite-sex couples with respect to this principle. Yet by virtue of their exclusion from that institution, same-sex couples are denied the constellation of benefits that the States have linked to marriage. This harm results in more than just material burdens. Same-sex couples are consigned to an instability many opposite-sex couples would deem intolerable in their own lives. As the State itself makes marriage all the more precious by the significance it attaches to it, exclusion from that status has the effect of teaching that gays and lesbians are unequal in important respects. It demeans gays and lesbians for the State to lock them out of a central institution of the Nation's society. Same-sex couples, too, may aspire to the transcendent purposes of marriage and seek fulfillment in its highest meaning.

The limitation of marriage to opposite-sex couples may long have seemed natural and just, but its inconsistency with the central meaning of the fundamental right to marry is now manifest. With that knowledge must come the recognition that laws excluding same-sex couples from the marriage right impose stigma and injury of the kind prohibited by our basic charter.

Objecting that this does not reflect an appropriate framing of the issue, the respondents refer to *Washington v. Glucksberg*, which called for a "'careful description'" of fundamental rights. They assert the petitioners do not seek to exercise the right to marry but rather a new and nonexistent "right to same-sex marriage." *Glucksberg* did insist that liberty under the Due Process Clause must be defined in a most circumscribed manner, with central reference to specific historical practices. Yet while that approach may have been appropriate for the asserted right there involved (physician-assisted suicide), it is inconsistent with the approach this Court has used in discussing other fundamental rights, including marriage and intimacy. *Loving* did not ask about a "right to interracial marriage"; *Turner* did not ask about a "right of inmates to marry"; and *Zablocki* did not ask about a "right of fathers with unpaid child support duties to marry." Rather, each case inquired about the right to marry in its comprehensive sense, asking if there was a sufficient justification for excluding the relevant class from the right.

That principle applies here. If rights were defined by who exercised them in the past, then received practices could serve as their own continued justification and new groups could not invoke rights once denied. This Court has rejected that approach, both with respect to the right to marry and the rights of gays and lesbians.

The right to marry is fundamental as a matter of history and tradition, but rights come not from ancient sources alone. They rise, too, from a better informed understanding of how constitutional imperatives define a liberty that remains urgent in our own era. Many who deem same-sex marriage to be wrong reach that conclusion based on decent and honorable religious or philosophical premises, and neither they nor their beliefs are disparaged here. But when that sincere, personal opposition becomes enacted law and public policy, the necessary consequence is to put the imprimatur of the State itself on an exclusion that soon demeans or stigmatizes those whose own liberty is then denied. Under the Constitution, same-sex couples seek in marriage the same legal treatment as opposite-sex couples, and it would disparage their choices and diminish their personhood to deny them this right.

The right of same-sex couples to marry that is part of the liberty promised by the Fourteenth Amendment is derived, too, from that Amendment's guarantee of the equal protection of the laws. The Due Process Clause and the Equal Protection Clause are connected in a profound way, though they set forth independent principles. Rights implicit in liberty and rights secured by equal protection may rest on different precepts and are not always coextensive, yet in some instances each may be instructive as to the meaning and reach of the other. In any particular case one Clause may be thought to capture the essence of the right in a more accurate and comprehensive way, even as the two Clauses may converge in the identification and definition of the right. This interrelation of the two principles furthers our understanding of what freedom is and must become.

The Court's cases touching upon the right to marry reflect this dynamic. In *Loving* the Court invalidated a prohibition on interracial marriage under both the Equal Protection Clause and the Due Process Clause. The Court first declared the prohibition invalid because of its unequal treatment of interracial couples. It stated: "There can be no doubt that restricting the freedom to marry solely because of racial classifications violates the central meaning of the Equal Protection Clause." With this link to equal protection the Court proceeded to hold the prohibition offended central precepts of liberty: "To deny this fundamental freedom on so unsupportable a basis as the racial classifications embodied in these statutes, classifications so directly subversive of the principle of equality at the heart of the Fourteenth Amendment, is surely to deprive all the State's citizens of liberty without due process of law." The reasons why marriage is a fundamental right became more clear and compelling from a full awareness and understanding of the hurt that resulted from laws barring interracial unions.

The synergy between the two protections is illustrated further in *Zablocki*. There the Court invoked the Equal Protection Clause as its basis for invalidating the challenged law, which, as already noted, barred fathers who were behind on child-support payments from marrying without judicial approval. The equal protection analysis depended in central part on the Court's holding that the law burdened a right "of fundamental importance."

It was the essential nature of the marriage right, discussed at length in *Zablocki* that made apparent the law's incompatibility with requirements of equality. Each concept—liberty and equal protection—leads to a stronger understanding of the other.

Indeed, in interpreting the Equal Protection Clause, the Court has recognized that new insights and societal understandings can reveal unjustified inequality within our most fundamental institutions that once passed unnoticed and unchallenged. To take but one period, this occurred with respect to marriage in the 1970's and 1980's. Notwithstanding the gradual erosion of the doctrine of coverture, invidious sex-based classifications in marriage remained common through the mid-20th century. These classifications denied the equal dignity of men and women. One State's law, for example, provided in 1971 that "the husband is the head of the family and the wife is subject to him; her legal civil existence is merged in the husband, except so far as the law recognizes her separately, either for her own protection, or for her benefit." Responding to a new awareness, the Court invoked equal protection principles to invalidate laws imposing sex-based inequality on marriage. Like *Loving* and *Zablocki*, these precedents show the Equal Protection Clause can help to identify and correct inequalities in the institution of marriage, vindicating precepts of liberty and equality under the Constitution.

Other cases confirm this relation between liberty and equality. In *M. L. B. v. S. L. J.*, the Court invalidated under due process and equal protection principles a statute requiring indigent mothers to pay a fee in order to appeal the termination of their parental rights. In *Eisenstadt v. Baird*, the Court invoked both principles to invalidate a prohibition on the distribution of contraceptives to unmarried persons but not married persons. And in *Skinner v. Oklahoma ex rel. Williamson*, the Court invalidated under both principles a law that allowed sterilization of habitual criminals.

In *Lawrence* the Court acknowledged the interlocking nature of these constitutional safeguards in the context of the legal treatment of gays and lesbians. Although *Lawrence* elaborated its holding under the Due Process Clause, it acknowledged, and sought to remedy, the continuing inequality that resulted from laws making intimacy in the lives of gays and lesbians a crime against the State. *Lawrence* therefore drew upon principles of liberty and equality to define and protect the rights of gays and lesbians, holding the State "cannot demean their existence or control their destiny by making their private sexual conduct a crime."

This dynamic also applies to same-sex marriage. It is now clear that the challenged laws burden the liberty of same-sex couples, and it must be further acknowledged that they abridge central precepts of equality. Here the marriage laws enforced by the respondents are in essence unequal: same-sex couples are denied all the benefits afforded to opposite-sex couples and are barred from exercising a fundamental right. Especially against a long history of disapproval of their relationships, this denial to same-sex couples of the right to marry works a grave and continuing harm. The imposition of this disability on gays and lesbians serves to disrespect and subordinate them. And the Equal Protection Clause, like the Due Process Clause, prohibits this unjustified infringement of the fundamental right to marry.

These considerations lead to the conclusion that the right to marry is a fundamental right inherent in the liberty of the person, and under the Due Process and Equal Protection Clauses of the Fourteenth Amendment couples of the same-sex may not be deprived of that right and that liberty. The Court now holds that same-sex couples may exercise the fundamental right to marry. No longer may this liberty be denied to them. *Baker v. Nelson* must be and now is overruled, and the State laws challenged by Petitioners in these cases are now held invalid to the extent they exclude same-sex couples from civil marriage on the same terms and conditions as opposite-sex couples.

IV

There may be an initial inclination in these cases to proceed with caution—to await further legislation, litigation, and debate. The respondents warn there has been insufficient democratic discourse before deciding an issue so basic as the definition of marriage. In its ruling on the cases now before this Court, the majority opinion for the Court of Appeals made a cogent argument that it would be appropriate for the respondents' States to await further public discussion and political measures before licensing same-sex marriages.

...

No union is more profound than marriage, for it embodies the highest ideals of love, fidelity, devotion, sacrifice, and family. In forming a marital union, two people become something greater than once they were. As some of the petitioners in these cases demonstrate, marriage embodies a love that may endure even past death. It would misunderstand these men and women to say they disrespect the idea of marriage. Their plea is that they do respect it, respect it so deeply that they seek to find its fulfillment for themselves. Their hope is not to be condemned to live in loneliness, excluded from one of civilization's oldest institutions. They ask for equal dignity in the eyes of the law. The Constitution grants them that right. The judgment of the Court of Appeals for the Sixth Circuit is reversed.

It is so ordered.

Chief Justice Roberts, with whom Justice Scalia and Justice Thomas join, dissenting.

Petitioners make strong arguments rooted in social policy and considerations of fairness. They contend that same-sex couples should be allowed to affirm their love and commitment through marriage, just like opposite-sex couples. That position has undeniable appeal; over the past six years, voters and legislators in eleven States and the District of Columbia have revised their laws to allow marriage between two people of the same sex.

But this Court is not a legislature. Whether same-sex marriage is a good idea should be of no concern to us. Under the Constitution, judges have power to say what the law is, not what it should be. The people who ratified the Constitution authorized courts to exercise "neither force nor will but merely judgment."

Although the policy arguments for extending marriage to same-sex couples may be compelling, the legal arguments for requiring such an extension are not. The fundamental right to marry does not include a right to make a State change its definition of marriage. And a State's decision to maintain the meaning of marriage that has persisted in every culture throughout human history can hardly be called irrational. In short, our Constitution does not enact any one theory of marriage. The people of a State are free to expand marriage to include same-sex couples, or to retain the historic definition.

Today, however, the Court takes the extraordinary step of ordering every State to license and recognize same-sex marriage. Many people will rejoice at this decision, and I begrudge none their celebration. But for those who believe in a government of laws, not of men, the majority's approach is deeply disheartening. Supporters of same-sex marriage have achieved considerable success persuading their fellow citizens — through the democratic process — to adopt their view. That ends today. Five lawyers have closed the debate and enacted their own vision of marriage as a matter of constitutional law. Stealing this issue from the people will for many cast a cloud over same-sex marriage, making a dramatic social change that much more difficult to accept.

I

Petitioners and their amici base their arguments on the "right to marry" and the imperative of "marriage equality." There is no serious dispute that, under our precedents, the Constitution protects a right to marry and requires States to apply their marriage laws equally. The real question in these cases is what constitutes "marriage," or — more precisely — who decides what constitutes "marriage"?

...

The Constitution itself says nothing about marriage, and the Framers thereby entrusted the States with "[t]he whole subject of the domestic relations of husband and wife."

...

The majority purports to identify four "principles and traditions" in this Court's due process precedents that support a fundamental right for same-sex couples to marry. In reality, however, the majority's approach has no basis in principle or tradition, except for the unprincipled tradition of judicial policymaking that characterized discredited decisions such as *Lochner v. New York*. Stripped of its shiny rhetorical gloss, the majority's argument is that the Due Process Clause gives same-sex couples a fundamental right to marry because it will be good for them and for society. If I were a legislator, I would certainly consider that view as a matter of social policy. But as a judge, I find the majority's position indefensible as a matter of constitutional law.

. . .

Neither *Lawrence* nor any other precedent in the privacy line of cases supports the right that petitioners assert here. Unlike criminal laws banning contraceptives and sodomy, the marriage laws at issue here involve no government intrusion. They create no crime and impose no punishment. Same-sex couples remain free to live together, to engage in intimate conduct, and to raise their families as they see fit. No one is "condemned to live in loneliness" by the laws challenged in these cases—no one. At the same time, the laws in no way interfere with the "right to be let alone."

In sum, the privacy cases provide no support for the majority's position, because petitioners do not seek privacy. Quite the opposite, they seek public recognition of their relationships, along with corresponding government benefits. Our cases have consistently refused to allow litigants to convert the shield provided by constitutional liberties into a sword to demand positive entitlements from the State. Thus, although the right to privacy recognized by our precedents certainly plays a role in protecting the intimate conduct of same-sex couples, it provides no affirmative right to redefine marriage and no basis for striking down the laws at issue here.

. . .

III

In addition to their due process argument, petitioners contend that the Equal Protection Clause requires their States to license and recognize same-sex marriages. The majority does not seriously engage with this claim. Its discussion is, quite frankly, difficult to follow. The central point seems to be that there is a "synergy between" the Equal Protection Clause and the Due Process Clause, and that some precedents relying on one Clause have also relied on the other. Absent from this portion of the opinion, however, is anything resembling our usual framework for deciding equal protection cases. It is casebook doctrine that the "modern Supreme Court's treatment of equal protection claims has used a means-ends methodology in which judges ask whether the classification the government is using is sufficiently related to the goals it is pursuing." The majority's approach today is different:

> Rights implicit in liberty and rights secured by equal protection may rest on different precepts and are not always co-extensive, yet in some instances each maybe instructive as to the meaning and reach of the other. In any particular case one Clause may be thought to capture the essence of the right in a more accurate and comprehensive way, even as the two Clauses may converge in the identification and definition of the right.

The majority goes on to assert in conclusory fashion that the Equal Protection Clause provides an alternative basis for its holding. Yet the majority fails to provide even a single sentence explaining how the Equal Protection Clause supplies independent weight for its position, nor does it attempt to justify its gratuitous violation of the canon against unnecessarily resolving constitutional questions. In any event, the marriage laws at issue here do not violate the Equal Protection Clause, because distinguishing between opposite-sex and same-sex couples is rationally related to the States' "legitimate state interest" in "preserving the traditional institution of marriage."

Justice Scalia, with whom Justice Thomas joins, dissenting. [opinion omitted]

Justice Thomas, with whom Justice Scalia joins, dissenting.

The Court's decision today is at odds not only with the Constitution, but with the principles upon which our Nation was built. Since well before 1787, liberty has been understood as freedom from government action, not entitlement to government benefits. The Framers created our Constitution to preserve that understanding of liberty. Yet the majority invokes our Constitution in the name of a "liberty" that the Framers would not have recognized, to the detriment of the liberty they sought to protect. Along the way, it rejects the idea—captured in our Declaration of Independence—that human dignity is innate and suggests instead that it comes from the Government. This distortion of our Constitution not only ignores the text, it inverts the relationship between the individual and the state in our Republic. I cannot agree with it.

. . .

Justice Alito, with whom Justice Scalia and Justice Thomas join, dissenting.

Until the federal courts intervened, the American people were engaged in a debate about whether their States should recognize same-sex marriage. The question in these cases, however, is not what States should do about same-sex marriage but whether the Constitution answers that question for them. It does not. The Constitution leaves that question to be decided by the people of each State.

. . .

For today's majority, it does not matter that the right to same-sex marriage lacks deep roots or even that it is contrary to long-established tradition. The Justices in the majority claim the authority to confer constitutional protection upon that right simply because they believe that it is fundamental.

. . .

Today's decision usurps the constitutional right of the people to decide whether to keep or alter the traditional understanding of marriage. The decision will also have other important consequences. It will be used to vilify Americans who are unwilling to assent to the new orthodoxy. In the course of its opinion, the majority compares traditional marriage laws to laws that denied equal treatment for African-Americans and women. The implications of this analogy will be exploited by those who are determined to stamp out every vestige of dissent.

Perhaps recognizing how its reasoning may be used, the majority attempts, toward the end of its opinion, to reassure those who oppose same-sex marriage that their rights of conscience will be protected. We will soon see whether this proves to be true. I assume that those who cling to old beliefs will be able to whisper their thoughts in the recesses of their homes, but if they repeat those views in public, they will risk being labeled as bigots and treated as such by governments, employers, and schools.

Notes and Queries

1. It is important to note that, in *Dobbs v. Jackson Women's Health Organization* (2022), the Supreme Court overruled *Roe v. Wade* (1973). In doing so, it held that the right to privacy does not extend to that of abortion on the criteria from *Washington v. Glucksberg* (1997) that a right must be "deeply rooted in the Nation's history," and abortion was considered a crime, a view that some historians argued is incomplete. What do you make of that reasoning for the rights recognized in *Obergefell*?

2. Justice Samuel Alito, writing for the majority in *Dobbs*, indicated that the ruling would not affect other substantive due process cases. Yet Justice Thomas, who dissented in *Obergefell*, concurred in *Dobbs* by urging the Court to revisit this case. How much doubt does *Dobbs*'s overruling the fundamental right to privacy as unenumerated right implied in *Roe* cast doubt over substantive due process protecting rights in *Obergefell*?

3. What do you make of the distinction between the right to marriage and the right to define marriage?

4. *Obergefell* inserts a focus on children's right to be raised by their parents without being marginalized or demeaned by the state. It explicitly includes the right to raise children and to safeguard them from inappropriate governmental intrusion as a rationale to recognize the right to same-sex marriage. What do you make of the ramifications of centering on marriage to protect children? For an analysis of the case's reflection on nonmarital families, see Gregg Strauss (2018). What's wrong with *Obergefell*? *Cardozo Law Review*, 40, 631. For an analysis of potential impact on single parenting and custody law, see Melanie Kalmanson (2017). "[R]elegated through no fault of their own to a more difficult system": Applying the *Obergefell* opinion to custody principles. *The Modern American*, 10, 1.

Rust v. Sullivan

500 U.S. 173; 111 S. Ct. 1759 (1991)

Chief Justice Rehnquist delivered the opinion of the Court.

These cases concern a facial challenge to Department of Health and Human Services (HHS) regulations which limit the ability of Title X fund recipients to engage in abortion-related activities. The United States Court of Appeals for the Second Circuit upheld the regulations, finding them to be a permissible construction of the statute as well as consistent with the First and Fifth Amendments to the Constitution. We granted certiorari to resolve a split among the Courts of Appeals. We affirm.

I

A

In 1970, Congress enacted Title X of the Public Health Service Act (Act), which provides federal funding for family-planning services. The Act authorizes the Secretary to "make grants to and enter into contracts with public or nonprofit private entities to assist in the establishment and operation of voluntary family planning projects which shall offer a broad range of acceptable and effective family planning methods and services." Grants and contracts under Title X must "be made in accordance with such regulations as the Secretary may promulgate." Section 1008 of the Act, however, provides that "none of the funds appropriated under this subchapter shall be used in programs where abortion is a method of family planning." That restriction was intended to ensure that Title X funds would "be used only to support preventive family planning services, population research, infertility services, and other related medical, informational, and educational activities."

In 1988, the Secretary promulgated new regulations designed to provide "'clear and operational guidance' to. . . ." The regulations "focus the emphasis of the Title X program on its traditional mission: The provision of preventive family planning services specifically designed to enable individuals to determine the number and spacing of their children, while clarifying that pregnant women must be referred to appropriate prenatal care services."

The regulations attach three principal conditions on the grant of federal funds for Title X projects. First, the regulations specify that a "Title X project may not provide counseling concerning the use of abortion as a method of family planning or provide referral for abortion as a method of family planning." Because Title X is limited to preconceptional services, the program does not furnish services related to childbirth. Only in the context of a referral out of the Title X program is a pregnant woman given transitional information. Title X projects must refer every pregnant client "for appropriate prenatal and/or social services by furnishing a list of available providers that promote the welfare of mother and unborn child." The list may not be used indirectly to encourage or promote abortion, "such as by weighing the list of referrals in favor of health care providers which perform abortions, by including on the list of referral providers health care providers whose principal business is the provision of abortions, by excluding available providers who do not provide abortions, or by 'steering' clients to providers who offer abortion as a method of family planning." The Title X project is expressly prohibited from referring a pregnant woman to an abortion provider, even upon specific request. One permissible response to such an inquiry is that "the project does not consider abortion an appropriate method of family planning and therefore does not counsel or refer for abortion."

Second, the regulations broadly prohibit a Title X project from engaging in activities that "encourage, promote or advocate abortion as a method of family planning." Forbidden activities include lobbying for legislation that would increase the availability of abortion as a method of family planning, developing or disseminating materials advocating abortion as a method of family planning, providing speakers to promote abortion as a method of family planning, using legal action to make abortion available in any way as a method of family planning, and paying dues to any group that advocates abortion as a method of family planning as a substantial part of its activities.

Third, the regulations require that Title X projects be organized so that they are "physically and financially separate" from prohibited abortion activities. To be deemed physically and financially separate, "a Title X project must have an objective integrity and independence from prohibited activities. Mere bookkeeping separation of Title X funds from other monies is not sufficient." The regulations provide a list of nonexclusive factors for the Secretary to consider in conducting a case-by-case determination of objective integrity and independence, such as the existence of separate accounting records and separate personnel, and the degree of physical separation of the project from facilities for prohibited activities.

. . .

II

We begin by pointing out the posture of the cases before us. Petitioners are challenging the facial validity of the regulations. Thus, we are concerned only with the question whether, on their face, the regulations are both authorized by the Act and can be construed in such a manner that they can be applied to a set of individuals without infringing upon constitutionally protected rights. Petitioners face a heavy burden in seeking to have the regulations invalidated as facially unconstitutional. "A facial challenge to a legislative Act is, of course, the most difficult challenge to mount successfully, since the challenger must establish that no set of circumstances exists under which the Act would be valid. The fact that [the regulations] might operate unconstitutionally under some conceivable set of circumstances is insufficient to render [them] wholly invalid."

. . .

A

The broad language of Title X plainly allows the Secretary's construction of the statute. By its own terms, § 1008 prohibits the use of Title X funds "in programs where abortion is a method of family planning." . . .

The District Courts and Courts of Appeals that have examined the legislative history have all found, at least with regard to the Act's counseling, referral, and advocacy provisions, that the legislative history is ambiguous with respect to Congress' intent in enacting Title X and the prohibition of § 1008. . . .

. . .

When we find, as we do here, that the legislative history is ambiguous and unenlightening on the matters with respect to which the regulations deal, we customarily defer to the expertise of the agency. Petitioners argue, however, that the regulations are entitled to little or no deference because they "reverse a longstanding agency policy that permitted nondirective counseling and referral for abortion," and thus represent a sharp break from the Secretary's prior construction of the statute. . . .

We find that the Secretary amply justified his change of interpretation with a "reasoned analysis." . . . We believe that these justifications are sufficient to support the Secretary's revised approach. Having concluded that the plain language and legislative history are ambiguous as to Congress' intent in enacting Title X, we must defer to the Secretary's permissible construction of the statute.

. . .

III

Petitioners contend that the regulations violate the First Amendment by impermissibly discriminating based on viewpoint because they prohibit "all discussion about abortion as a lawful option — including counseling, referral, and the provision of neutral and accurate information about ending a pregnancy — while compelling the clinic or counselor to provide information that promotes continuing a pregnancy to term." They assert that the regulations violate the "free speech rights of private health care organizations that receive Title X funds, of their staff, and of their patients" by impermissibly imposing "viewpoint-discriminatory conditions on government subsidies" and thus penalize speech funded with non-Title X monies. Because "Title X continues to fund speech ancillary to pregnancy testing in a manner that is not evenhanded with respect to views and information about abortion, it invidiously discriminates on the basis of viewpoint." . . . petitioners also assert that while the Government may place certain conditions on the receipt of federal subsidies, it may not "discriminate invidiously in its subsidies in such a way as to 'aim at the suppression of dangerous ideas.'"

There is no question but that the statutory prohibition contained in § 1008 is constitutional.

In *Maher v. Roe*, we upheld a state welfare regulation under which Medicaid recipients received payments for services related to childbirth, but not for nontherapeutic abortions. The Court rejected the claim that this unequal subsidization worked a violation of the Constitution. We held that the government may "make a value judgment favoring childbirth over abortion, and . . . implement that judgment by the allocation of public funds." Here the Government is exercising the authority it possesses . . . to subsidize family planning services which will lead to conception and childbirth, and declining to "promote or encourage abortion." The Government can, without violating the Constitution, selectively fund a program to encourage certain activities it believes to be in the public interest, without at the same time funding an alternative program which seeks to deal with the problem in another way. In so doing, the Government has not discriminated on the basis of viewpoint; it has merely chosen to fund one activity to the exclusion of the other....

...

To hold that the Government unconstitutionally discriminates on the basis of viewpoint when it chooses to fund a program dedicated to advance certain permissible goals, because the program in advancing those goals necessarily discourages alternative goals, would render numerous Government programs constitutionally suspect....

...

... [T]he Government is not denying a benefit to anyone, but is instead simply insisting that public funds be spent for the purposes for which they were authorized....

...

... Congress has merely refused to fund such [abortion-related] activities out of the public fisc, and the Secretary has simply required a certain degree of separation from the Title X project in order to ensure the integrity of the federally funded program.

...

IV

We turn now to petitioners' argument that the regulations violate a woman's Fifth Amendment right to choose whether to terminate her pregnancy....

That the regulations do not impermissibly burden a woman's Fifth Amendment rights is evident from the line of cases beginning with *Maher* and *McRae* and culminating in our most recent decision in *Webster*. Just as Congress' refusal to fund abortions in *McRae* left "an indigent woman with at least the same range of choice in deciding whether to obtain a medically necessary abortion as she would have had if Congress had chosen to subsidize no health care costs at all," and "Missouri's refusal to allow public employees to perform abortions in public hospitals leaves a pregnant woman with the same choices as if the State had chosen not to operate any public hospitals," Congress' refusal to fund abortion counseling and advocacy leaves a pregnant woman with the same choices as if the Government had chosen not to fund family-planning services at all. The difficulty that a woman encounters when a Title X project does not provide abortion counseling or referral leaves her in no different position than she would have been if the Government had not enacted Title X.

Petitioners also argue that by impermissibly infringing on the doctor–patient relationship and depriving a Title X client of information concerning abortion as a method of family planning, the regulations violate a woman's Fifth Amendment right to medical self-determination and to make informed medical decisions free of government-imposed harm. . . . Under the Secretary's regulations, however, a doctor's ability to provide, and a woman's right to receive, information concerning abortion and abortion-related services outside the context of the Title X project remains unfettered. It would undoubtedly be easier for a woman seeking an abortion if she could receive information about abortion from a Title X project, but the Constitution does not require that the Government distort the scope of its mandated program in order to provide that information.

Petitioners contend, however, that most Title X clients are effectively precluded by indigency and poverty from seeing a health-care provider who will provide abortion-related services. But once again, even these Title X clients are in no worse position than if Congress had never enacted Title X. "The financial constraints that restrict an indigent woman's ability to enjoy the full range of constitutionally protected freedom of choice are the product not of governmental restrictions on access to abortion, but rather of her indigency."

The Secretary's regulations are a permissible construction of Title X and do not violate either the First or Fifth Amendments to the Constitution. Accordingly, the judgment of the Court of Appeals is

Affirmed.

Justice Blackmun, with whom Justice Marshall joins, with whom Justice Stevens joins as to Parts II and III, and with whom Justice O'Connor joins as to Part I, dissenting.

Casting aside established principles of statutory construction and administrative jurisprudence, the majority in these cases today unnecessarily passes upon important questions of constitutional law. In so doing, the Court, for the first time, upholds viewpoint-based suppression of speech solely because it is imposed on those dependent upon the Government for economic support. Under essentially the same rationale, the majority upholds direct regulation of dialogue between a pregnant woman and her physician when that regulation has both the purpose and the effect of manipulating her decision as to the continuance of her pregnancy. I conclude that the Secretary's regulation of referral, advocacy, and counseling activities exceeds his statutory authority, and, also, that the regulations violate the First and Fifth Amendments of our Constitution. Accordingly, I dissent and would reverse the divided-vote judgment of the Court of Appeals.

. . .

Finally, it is of no small significance that the speech the Secretary would suppress is truthful information regarding constitutionally protected conduct of vital importance to the listener. One can imagine no legitimate governmental interest that might be served by suppressing such information. Concededly, the abortion debate is among the most divisive and contentious issues that our Nation has faced in recent years. "But freedom to differ is not limited to things that do not matter much. That would be a mere shadow of freedom. The test of its substance is the right to differ as to things that touch the heart of the existing order."

III

By far the most disturbing aspect of today's ruling is the effect it will have on the Fifth Amendment rights of the women who, supposedly, are beneficiaries of Title X programs. The majority rejects petitioners' Fifth Amendment claims summarily. . . .

. . .

Contrary to the majority's characterization, this is not a situation in which individuals seek Government aid in exercising their fundamental rights. The Fifth Amendment right asserted by petitioners is the right of a pregnant woman to be free from affirmative governmental interference in her decision. . . . Those cases serve to vindicate the idea that "liberty," if it means anything, must entail freedom from governmental domination in making the most intimate and personal of decisions. By suppressing medically pertinent information and injecting a restrictive ideological message unrelated to considerations of maternal health, the Government places formidable obstacles in the path of Title X clients' freedom of choice and thereby violates their Fifth Amendment rights.

. . .

The undeniable message conveyed by this forced speech, and the one that the Title X client will draw from it, is that abortion nearly always is an improper medical option. Although her physician's words, in fact, are strictly controlled by the Government and wholly unrelated to her particular medical situation, the Title X client will reasonably construe them as professional advice to forgo her right to obtain an abortion. As would most rational patients, many of these women will follow that perceived advice and carry their pregnancy to term, despite their needs to the contrary and despite the safety of the abortion procedure for the vast majority of them. Others, delayed by the regulations' mandatory prenatal referral, will be prevented from acquiring abortions during the period in which the process is medically sound and constitutionally protected.

. . . Both the purpose and result of the challenged regulations are to deny women the ability voluntarily to decide their procreative destiny. For these women, the Government will have obliterated the freedom to choose as surely as if it had banned abortions outright. The denial of this freedom is not a consequence of poverty but of the Government's ill-intentioned distortion of information it has chosen to provide.

. . .

Justice Stevens, dissenting. [omitted]

Justice O'Connor, dissenting. [omitted]

Notes and Queries

1. Constitutionally, this case stands for a powerful defense of governmental free speech restrictions. It does so by giving the government the power to limit its own speech. Essentially, the government can choose the speech that it wishes to promote. That approach may make sense, as the government is the one supporting the speech and it is not limiting the speech of others who can afford to access other services. Yet this may be problematic in that it gives the government the power to ignore alternative views on a variety of grounds. It particularly may be problematic in instances, such as health care, where individuals would expect professionals to act in a particular manner, including in their patients' best interest and to provide them with materials to make informed decisions supportive of their self-determination. In this instance, that expectation is complicated by how the speech that the government limits ends up differentially impacting women based on their socioeconomic status. The rule involves Title X patients who rely on the government for their reproductive health and autonomy, which means that they do not get the care affluent women could receive when they access their service providers who are not limited by the government's views. The rule has important consequences for the government's role in addressing more than health services; it can apply to a variety of services and programs that the government supports. It remains unclear how expansive the effect may be, but the major lesson from the case is that the government's message can be controlled by the government even in instances when they can go against the interests of the recipients of services.

2. For readers who find the *Rust v. Sullivan* rule legally problematic in the context of reproductive rights, consider the leading case involving the Hyde Amendment. *Harris v. McRae*, 448 U.S. 297 (1980), upheld the amendment, which is a federal law that proscribed federal funding for abortions except when necessary to preserve life or as a result of rape or incest. It also is important to consider that *Dobbs v. Jackson Women's Health Organization*, 597 U.S. 215 (2022), overruled both *Roe v. Wade* (1973) and *Planned Parenthood v. Casey* (1992), returning to individual states the power to regulate any aspect of abortion not protected by federal law. Some states use their own funds to pay for all or most medically necessary abortions, but how these rules eventually develop remains to be seen.

3. Suppose a 15-year-old girl believes she is pregnant. She does not want anyone to know, even her boyfriend. She sees a sign stating "Pregnant? Need some guidance? See us NOW." When seeking the services from the organization, does she have a right to know that she may have a right to an abortion (if she is in a state that would grant her the right)?

4. What does *Rust v. Sullivan* tell you about the power the state may wield as it offers services?

5. Any thoughts on how the state's power may be harnessed to address child maltreatment? Could social service departments encourage parents to place children up for adoption and not tell parents the rights they have to alternative services? Should the state be allowed to encourage severing parent–child bonds in alleged maltreatment cases? Could what case workers tell their clients be circumscribed to further the government's position on how parents are to raise their children? Keep in mind that the majority of families in the child welfare system live in poverty. Also keep in mind that the major federal antipoverty programs, such as TANF, exclude some poor families from receiving assistance; in 2020, for example, less than a quarter of families in poverty received TANF benefits; see Center for Budget and Policy Priorities (2022). *Policy Basics: Temporary Assistance for Needy Families*. Washington, DC: Author. Essentially, then, the likelihood seems quite high that a family involved in a child welfare system would require some type of state-supported service; and keep in mind that those services could be mandated if parents seek their children's return. The reality, of course, is that case workers already promote the government's view of what constitutes appropriate childrearing. When thinking of what case workers could do, the image that comes to mind is that they could not infringe on the fundamental rights of parents to raise their children as they deem fit. The wrench that the *Rust v. Sullivan* rule throws into this situation is the apparent reduced concern for the rights of recipients when they receive services. While there likely would be limits to what the government can do, the case makes that limit unclear.

In re Clausen

442 Mich. 648; 502 N.W.2d 649 (Sup. Ct. Mich., 1993)

Per Curiam.

. . .

. . . Briefly, on February 8, 1991, Cara Clausen gave birth to a baby girl in Iowa. Proceedings in Iowa have established that defendant Daniel Schmidt is the child's father. [Note 6 reports that Clausen and Daniel Schmidt married in April 1992.] On February 10, 1991, Clausen signed a release of custody form, relinquishing her parental rights to the child. Clausen, who was unmarried at the time of the birth, had named Scott Seefeldt as the father. On February 14, 1991, he executed a release of custody form.

On February 25, 1991, petitioners Roberta and Jan DeBoer, who are Michigan residents, filed a petition for adoption of the child in juvenile court in Iowa. A hearing was held the same day, at which the parental rights of Cara Clausen and Seefeldt were terminated, and petitioners were granted custody of the child during the pendency of the proceeding. The DeBoers returned to Michigan with the child, and she has lived with them in Michigan continuously since then.

However, the prospective adoption never took place. On March 6, 1991, nine days after the filing of the adoption petition, Cara Clausen filed a motion in the Iowa Juvenile Court to revoke her release of custody. In an affidavit accompanying the request, Clausen stated that she had lied when she named Seefeldt as the father of the child, and that the child's father actually was Daniel Schmidt. Schmidt filed an affidavit of paternity on March 12, 1991, and on March 27, 1991, he filed a petition in the Iowa district court, seeking to intervene in the adoption proceeding initiated by the DeBoers.

On November 4, 1991, the district court in Iowa conducted a bench trial on the issues of paternity, termination of parental rights, and adoption. On December 27, 1991, the district court found that Schmidt established by a preponderance of the evidence that he was the biological father of the child; that the DeBoers failed to establish by clear and convincing evidence that Schmidt had abandoned the child or that his parental rights should be terminated; and that a best interests of the child analysis did not become appropriate unless abandonment was established. On the basis of these findings, the court concluded that the termination proceeding was void with respect to Schmidt, and that the DeBoers' petition to adopt the child must be denied. Those decisions have been affirmed by the Iowa appellate courts.

On remand from the Iowa Supreme Court, the district court ordered the DeBoers to appear on December 3, 1992, with the child. The DeBoers did not appear at the hearing; instead, their Iowa attorney informed the court that the DeBoers had received actual notice of the hearing but had decided not to appear. In an order entered on December 3, 1992, the district court terminated the DeBoers' rights as temporary guardians and custodians of the child. The court found that

> Mr. and Mrs. De[B]oer have no legal right or claim to the physical custody of this child. They are acting outside any legal claim to physical control and possession of this child.

On the same day their rights were terminated in Iowa, the DeBoers filed a petition in Washtenaw Circuit Court, asking the court to assume jurisdiction under the UCCJA. The petition requested that the court enjoin enforcement of the Iowa custody order and find that it was not enforceable, or, in the alternative, to modify it to give custody to the DeBoers. On December 3, 1992, the Washtenaw Circuit Court entered an ex parte temporary restraining order, which directed that the child remain in the custody of the DeBoers, and ordered Schmidt not to remove the child from Washtenaw County.

On December 11, 1992, Schmidt filed a motion for summary judgment to dissolve the preliminary injunction and to recognize and enforce the Iowa judgment. The Washtenaw Circuit Court held a hearing on Schmidt's motion on January 5, 1993. It found that it had jurisdiction to determine the best interests of the child. It denied Schmidt's motion for summary judgment, and directed that the child remain with the DeBoers until further order of the court. [Note 9 reports that after the Washtenaw

Circuit Court's denial of the natural father's motion for summary judgment, proceedings have continued in Iowa. On January 27, 1993, the Iowa district court held the DeBoers in contempt of court, and issued bench warrants for their arrest. The Iowa juvenile court entered an order on February 17, 1993, restoring Cara (Clausen) Schmidt's parental rights. A best interests of the child determination hearing began in Washtenaw Circuit Court on January 29, 1993, and continued for eight days. In a decision rendered from the bench on February 12, 1993, the Washtenaw Circuit Court found that it was in the best interests of the child for her to remain with the DeBoers. That decision is not at issue in the instant appeal.]

On March 29, 1993, the Court of Appeals reversed the Washtenaw Circuit Court's denial of Schmidt's motion for summary judgment, concluding that court lacked jurisdiction under the UCCJA, and that under our decision in Bowie v Arder, supra, the DeBoers lacked standing to bring the action.

Following the Court of Appeals decision, on April 14, 1993, a complaint for "child custody, declaratory relief, and injunctive relief" was filed in Washtenaw Circuit Court. The plaintiff was described as "Jessica DeBoer (a/k/a Baby Girl Clausen), by her next friend, Peter Darrow." Mr. Darrow, a Washtenaw County attorney, had been appointed as one of the co-guardians ad litem for the child in the earlier custody case. On that date, the Washtenaw Circuit Court entered an order appointing Darrow as next friend in the new action, and an order to show cause directing the DeBoers and Schmidts to appear on April 22. The latter included language that pending that hearing, "the minor child's residence status quo shall be maintained." At the hearing on April 22, after hearing argument by counsel for the Schmidts and the DeBoers, the circuit court entered an "order continuing status quo." It provided, in part:

> 1. The status quo as to the residence of the Plaintiff, Jessica DeBoer, with Defendants, Roberta and Jan DeBoer shall be maintained during the pendency of this action or until further order of this Court, or any appellate court.
>
> 2. Counsel for the parties, and all other interested persons, if they obtain permission from the Court, may file briefs on the legal and constitutional issues raised by this action within 21 days from the date of this Order.

...

[After reviewing the history of the Uniform Child Custody Jurisdiction Act (UCCJA) and the federal Parental Kidnapping Prevention Act (PKPA), the court explained:]

Where the custody determination is made consistently with the provisions of the PKPA, the jurisdiction of the court that made the decision is exclusive and continuing as long as that state "remains the residence of the child or of any contestant," and it still has jurisdiction under its own laws. Unquestionably, Daniel Schmidt continues to reside in Iowa. Furthermore, Iowa law provides for continuing jurisdiction in custody matters, and the Iowa courts regarded themselves as continuing to have jurisdiction of the custody proceeding because they continued to issue orders in the case: the order of December 3, 1992, terminating the DeBoers' right to custody and appointing Daniel Schmidt as custodian, and the order of January 27, 1993, holding the DeBoers in contempt. Because the Iowa custody determination was made consistently with the terms of the PKPA, and because Iowa's jurisdiction continues, the Iowa court's order must be enforced.

. . .

The courts of this state may only modify Iowa's order if Iowa has declined to exercise its jurisdiction to modify it. Iowa has not declined to exercise its jurisdiction to modify its custody order; it has simply declined to order the relief sought by the DeBoers. Modification is not permitted on these facts: Iowa continues to have jurisdiction, it has not declined to exercise that jurisdiction, its jurisdiction is, therefore, exclusive, and Iowa's exclusive continuing jurisdiction precludes the courts of this state from exercising jurisdiction to modify the Iowa order.

. . .

The DeBoers argue that the Iowa judgment should not be enforced because the Iowa courts did not conduct a hearing into the best interests of the child in making the custody decision. They maintain that this undercuts the Iowa decision in two respects. First, they say this means that the Iowa decision was not in conformity with the UCCJA and therefore not entitled to enforcement under that statute. Second, they believe that the Iowa proceeding was repugnant to Michigan public policy.

We reject the contention that the decision of the Iowa courts not to conduct a best interests of the child hearing in the circumstances of this case justifies the refusal to enforce the Iowa judgments.

The UCCJA and the PKPA are procedural statutes. To be sure, they express the purpose of assuring that the state that is in the best position to make a proper determination regarding custody of the child be the one in which the action is brought, and that other states will follow the decision made there. That purpose has been achieved in this case. There can be no doubt that at the time the Iowa proceedings commenced in February 1991, that state was the appropriate one to take jurisdiction; it was in the best position to resolve the issues presented. As was conceded by counsel for the DeBoers during oral argument, the statutes do not provide that a best interests of the child standard is the substantive test by which all custody decisions are to be made. Each state, through legislation and the interpretative decisions of its courts, is free to fashion its own substantive law of family relationships within constitutional limitations.

. . .

After passage of the PKPA, we are not free to refuse to enforce the Iowa judgment as being contrary to public policy. That statute says:

> The appropriate authorities of every State shall enforce according to its terms, and shall not modify except as provided in subsection (f) of this

section, any child custody determination made consistently with the provisions of this section by a court of another State.

. . .

Justice Levin, dissenting.

. . .

Since the majority has decided that a best interests hearing is not required by the Child Custody Act or the PKPA, the Court should consider and decide whether the child"s interests in protecting her family relationship with the DeBoers is as constitutionally protected as a liberty interest as Daniel Schmidt's asserted constitutionally protected liberty interest in having an opportunity to establish a family relationship with the child. The Court should also consider and decide how those interests can be reconciled, either by a hearing concerning the best interests of the child, or by another standard or other means.

If the danger confronting this child were physical injury, no one would question her right to invoke judicial process to protect herself against such injury. There is little difference, when viewed from the child's frame of reference, between a physical assault and a psychological assault.

The law provides compensation for mental distress in countless situations, and has recognized that persons who suffer psychological injury are entitled to the protection of the law. It is only because this child cannot speak for herself that adults can avert their eyes from the pain that she will suffer.

Notes and Queries

1. This case highlights the significance of the parental rights model. Under this approach, the natural parents' right to custody is not to be disturbed absent a showing of parental unfitness.

2. Do you agree that a child could have no right to a hearing on her best interests when her custody is at issue? Note that Jessica was not claiming the right to bring an action to dictate the outcome of a custody dispute between her biological and psychological parents. Instead, she claimed a right to have the court decide what would be in her best interests. Do you think that the court, which simply is following statutory mandates, fosters the belief that children are property or "subpersons"? If not, then why not grant children the right to access the courts for a best interests determination? How would such a determination appropriately recognize their sense of personhood? If it would not, how could the law better respect children as persons in their own right? Does your conclusion return you to the standard this court adopted?

Stanley v. Illinois

405 U.S. 645; 92 S. Ct. 1208 (1972)

Mr. Justice White delivered the opinion of the Court.

Joan Stanley lived with Peter Stanley intermittently for 18 years, during which time they had three children. When Joan Stanley died, Peter Stanley lost not only her but also his children. Under Illinois law, the children of unwed fathers become wards of the State upon the death of the mother. Accordingly, upon Joan Stanley's death, in a dependency proceeding instituted by the State of Illinois, Stanley's children were declared wards of the State and placed with court-appointed guardians. Stanley appealed, claiming that he had never been shown to be an unfit parent and that since married fathers and unwed mothers could not be deprived of their children without such a showing, he had been deprived of the equal protection of the laws guaranteed him by the Fourteenth Amendment....

Stanley presses his equal protection claim here. The State continues to respond that unwed fathers are presumed unfit to raise their children and that it is unnecessary to hold individualized hearings to determine whether particular fathers are in fact unfit parents before they are separated from their children. We granted certiorari to determine whether this method of procedure by presumption could be allowed to stand in light of the fact that Illinois allows married fathers — whether divorced, widowed, or separated — and mothers — even if unwed — the benefit of the presumption that they are fit to raise their children.

I

At the outset we reject any suggestion that we need not consider the propriety of the dependency proceeding that separated the Stanleys because Stanley might be able to regain custody of his children as a guardian or through adoption proceedings. The suggestion is that if Stanley has been treated differently from other parents, the difference is immaterial and not legally cognizable for the purposes of the Fourteenth Amendment. This Court has not, however, embraced the general proposition that a wrong may be done if it can be undone. Surely, in the case before us, if there is delay between the doing and the undoing petitioner suffers from the deprivation of his children, and the children suffer from uncertainty and dislocation.

It is clear, moreover, that Stanley does not have the means at hand promptly to erase the adverse consequences of the proceeding in the course of which his children were declared wards of the State. It is first urged that Stanley could act to adopt his children. But under Illinois law, Stanley is treated not as a parent but as a stranger to his children, and the dependency proceeding has gone forward on the presumption that he is unfit to exercise parental rights. Insofar as we are informed, Illinois law affords him no priority in adoption proceedings. It would be his burden to establish not only that he would be a suitable parent but also that he would be the most suitable of all who might want custody of the children. Neither can we ignore that in the proceedings from which this action developed, the "probation officer," the assistant state's attorney, and the judge charged with the case made it apparent that Stanley, unmarried and impecunious as he is, could not now expect to profit from adoption proceedings. The Illinois Supreme Court apparently recognized some or all of these considerations, because it did not suggest that Stanley's case was undercut by his failure to petition for adoption.

Before us, the State focuses on Stanley's failure to petition for "custody and control"—the second route by which, it is urged, he might regain authority for his children. Passing the obvious issue whether it would be futile or burdensome for an unmarried father—without funds and already once presumed unfit—to petition for custody, this suggestion overlooks the fact that legal custody is not parenthood or adoption. A person appointed guardian in an action for custody and control is subject to removal at any time without such cause as must be shown in a neglect proceeding against a parent. He may not take the children out of the jurisdiction without the court's approval. He may be required to report to the court as to his disposition of the children's affairs. Obviously then, even if Stanley were a mere step away from "custody and control," to give an unwed father only "custody and control" would still be to leave him seriously prejudiced by reason of his status.

We must therefore examine the question that Illinois would have us avoid: Is a presumption that distinguishes and burdens all unwed fathers constitutionally repugnant? We conclude that, as a matter of due process of law, Stanley was entitled to a hearing on his fitness as a parent before his children were taken from him and that, by denying him a hearing and extending it to all other parents whose custody of their children is challenged, the State denied Stanley the equal protection of the laws guaranteed by the Fourteenth Amendment.

II

Illinois has two principal methods of removing nondelinquent children from the homes of their parents. In a dependency proceeding it may demonstrate that the children are wards of the State because they have no surviving parent or guardian. In a neglect proceeding it may show that children should be wards of the State because the present parent(s) or guardian does not provide suitable care.

The State's right—indeed, duty—to protect minor children through a judicial determination of their interests in a neglect proceeding is not challenged here. Rather, we are faced with a dependency statute that empowers state officials to circumvent neglect proceedings on the theory that an unwed father is not a "parent" whose existing relationship with his children must be considered. "Parents," says the State, "means the father and mother of a legitimate child, or the survivor of them, or the natural mother of an illegitimate child, and includes any adoptive parent," but the term does not include unwed fathers.

Under Illinois law, therefore, while the children of all parents can be taken from them in neglect proceedings, that is only after notice, hearing, and proof of such unfitness as a parent as amounts to neglect, an unwed father is uniquely subject to the more simplistic dependency proceeding. By use of this proceeding, the State, on showing that the father was not married to the mother, need not prove unfitness in fact, because it is presumed at law. Thus, the unwed father's claim of parental qualification is avoided as "irrelevant."

. . .

For its part, the State has made its interest quite plain: Illinois has declared that the aim of the Juvenile Court Act is to protect "the moral, emotional, mental, and physical welfare of the minor and the best interests of the community" and to "strengthen the minor's family ties whenever possible, removing him from the custody of his parents only when his welfare or safety or the protection of the public cannot be adequately safeguarded without removal. . . ." These are legitimate interests, well within the power of the State to implement. We do not question the assertion that neglectful parents may be separated from their children.

But we are here not asked to evaluate the legitimacy of the state ends, rather, to determine whether the means used to achieve these ends are constitutionally defensible. What is the state interest in separating children from fathers without a hearing designed to determine whether the father is unfit in a particular disputed case? We observe that the State registers no gain towards its declared goals when it separates children from the custody of fit parents. Indeed, if Stanley is a fit father, the State spites its own articulated goals when it needlessly separates him from his family.

. . .

It may be, as the State insists, that most unmarried fathers are unsuitable and neglectful parents. It may also be that Stanley is such a parent and that his children should be placed in other hands. But all unmarried fathers are not in this category; some are wholly suited to have custody of their children. This much the State readily concedes, and nothing in this record indicates that Stanley is or has been a neglectful father who has not cared for his children. Given the opportunity to make his case, Stanley may have been seen to be deserving of custody of his offspring. Had this been so, the State's statutory policy would have been furthered by leaving custody in him.

. . .

Procedure by presumption is always cheaper and easier than individualized determination. But when, as here, the procedure forecloses the determinative issues of competence and care, when it explicitly disdains present realities in deference to past formalities, it needlessly risks running roughshod over the important interests of both parent and child. It therefore cannot stand.

. . .

We think the Due Process Clause mandates a similar result here. The State's interest in caring for Stanley's children is de minimis if Stanley is shown to be a fit father. It insists on presuming rather than proving Stanley's unfitness solely because it is more convenient to presume than to prove. Under the Due Process Clause that advantage

child, Victoria D., who was born on May 11, 1981. Gerald was listed as father on the birth certificate and has always held Victoria out to the world as his daughter. Soon after delivery of the child, however, Carole informed Michael that she believed he might be the father.

In the first three years of her life, Victoria remained always with Carole, but found herself within a variety of quasifamily units. In October 1981, Gerald moved to New York City to pursue his business interests, but Carole chose to remain in California. At the end of that month, Carole and Michael had blood tests of themselves and Victoria, which showed a 98.07% probability that Michael was Victoria's father. In January 1982, Carole visited Michael in St. Thomas, where his primary business interests were based. There Michael held Victoria out as his child. In March, however, Carole left Michael and returned to California, where she took up residence with yet another man, Scott K. Later that spring, and again in the summer, Carole and Victoria spent time with Gerald in New York City, as well as on vacation in Europe. In the fall, they returned to Scott in California.

In November 1982, rebuffed in his attempts to visit Victoria, Michael filed a filiation action in California Superior Court to establish his paternity and right to visitation. In March 1983, the court appointed an attorney and guardian ad litem to represent Victoria's interests. Victoria then filed a cross-complaint asserting that if she had more than one psychological or de facto father, she was entitled to maintain her filial relationship, with all of the attendant rights, duties, and obligations, with both. In May 1983, Carole filed a motion for summary judgment. During this period, from March through July 1983, Carole was again living with Gerald in New York. In August, however, she returned to California, became involved once again with Michael, and instructed her attorneys to remove the summary judgment motion from the calendar.

For the ensuing eight months, when Michael was not in St. Thomas he lived with Carole and Victoria in Carole's apartment in Los Angeles and held Victoria out as his daughter. In April 1984, Carole and Michael signed a stipulation that Michael was Victoria's natural father. Carole left Michael the next month, however, and instructed her attorneys not to file the stipulation. In June 1984, Carole reconciled with Gerald and joined him in New York, where they now live with Victoria and two other children since born into the marriage.

In May 1984, Michael and Victoria, through her guardian ad litem, sought visitation rights for Michael pendente lite. To assist in determining whether visitation would be in Victoria's best interests, the Superior Court appointed a psychologist to evaluate Victoria, Gerald, Michael, and Carole. The psychologist recommended that Carole retain sole custody, but that Michael be allowed continued contact with Victoria pursuant to a restricted visitation schedule. The court concurred and ordered that Michael be provided with limited visitation privileges pendente lite.

On October 19, 1984, Gerald, who had intervened in the action, moved for summary judgment on the ground that under Cal. Evid. Code § 621 there were no triable issues of fact as to Victoria's paternity. This law provides that "the issue of a wife cohabiting with her husband, who is not impotent or sterile, is conclusively presumed to be a child of the marriage." The presumption may be rebutted by blood tests, but only if a motion for such tests is made, within two years from the date of the child's birth, either by the husband or, if the natural father has filed an affidavit acknowledging paternity, by the wife.

On January 28, 1985, having found that affidavits submitted by Carole and Gerald sufficed to demonstrate that the two were cohabiting at conception and birth and that Gerald was neither sterile nor impotent, the Superior Court granted Gerald"s motion for summary judgment, rejecting Michael's and Victoria's challenges to the constitutionality of § 621. The court also denied their motions for continued visitation pending the appeal under Cal. Civ. Code § 4601, which provides that a court may, in its discretion, grant "reasonable visitation rights . . . to any . . . person having an interest in the welfare of the child." It found that allowing such visitation would "violat[e] the intention of the Legislature by impugning the integrity of the family unit."

On appeal, Michael asserted, inter alia, that the Superior Court's application of § 621 had violated his procedural and substantive due process rights. Victoria also raised a due process challenge to the statute, seeking to preserve her de facto relationship with Michael as well as with Gerald. She contended, in addition, that as § 621 allows the husband and, at least to a limited extent, the mother, but not the child, to rebut the presumption of legitimacy, it violates the child's right to equal protection. Finally, she asserted a right to continued visitation with Michael under § 4601. After submission of briefs and a hearing, the California Court of Appeal affirmed the judgment of the Superior Court and upheld the constitutionality of the statute. It interpreted that judgment, moreover, as having denied permanent visitation rights under § 4601, regarding that as the implication of the Superior Court's reliance upon § 621 and upon an earlier California case which had held that once an assertion of biological paternity is "determined to be legally impossible" under § 621, visitation against the wishes of the mother should be denied under § 4601.

The Court of Appeal denied Michael's and Victoria's petitions for rehearing, and, on July 30, 1987, the California Supreme Court denied discretionary review. . . . Before us, Michael and Victoria both raise equal protection and due process challenges. We do not reach Michael's equal protection claim, however, as it was neither raised nor passed upon below.

II

The California statute that is the subject of this litigation is . . . as follows:

> § 621. Child of the marriage; notice of motion for blood tests
>
> > (a) Except as provided in subdivision (b), the issue of a wife cohabiting with her husband, who is not impotent or sterile, is conclusively presumed to be a child of the marriage.

> (b) Notwithstanding the provisions of subdivision (a), if the court finds that the conclusions of all the experts, as disclosed by the evidence based upon blood tests performed pursuant to Chapter 2 (commencing with Section 890) of Division 7 are that the husband is not the father of the child, the question of paternity of the husband shall be resolved accordingly.
>
> (c) The notice of motion for blood tests under subdivision (b) may be raised by the husband not later than two years from the child's date of birth.
>
> (d) The notice of motion for blood tests under subdivision (b) may be raised by the mother of the child not later than two years from the child's date of birth if the child's biological father has filed an affidavit with the court acknowledging paternity of the child.
>
> (e) The provisions of subdivision (b) shall not apply to any case coming within the provisions of Section 7005 of the Civil Code [dealing with artificial insemination] or to any case in which the wife, with the consent of the husband, conceived by means of a surgical procedure.

III

We address first the claims of Michael. At the outset, it is necessary to clarify what he sought and what he was denied. California law, like nature itself, makes no provision for dual fatherhood. Michael was seeking to be declared the father of Victoria. The immediate benefit he evidently sought to obtain from that status was visitation rights. But if Michael were successful in being declared the father, other rights would follow—most importantly, the right to be considered as the parent who should have custody a status which "embrace[s] the sum of parental rights with respect to the rearing of a child, including the child's care; the right to the child's services and earnings; the right to direct the child's activities; the right to make decisions regarding the control, education, and health of the child; and the right, as well as the duty, to prepare the child for additional obligations, which includes the teaching of moral standards, religious beliefs, and elements of good citizenship." All parental rights, including visitation, were automatically denied by denying Michael status as the father. While Cal. Civ. Code . . . places it within the discretionary power of a court to award visitation rights to a nonparent, the Superior Court here, affirmed by the Court of Appeal, held that California law denies visitation, against the wishes of the mother, to a putative father who has been prevented by § 621 from establishing his paternity.

Michael raises two related challenges to the constitutionality of § 621. First, he asserts that requirements of procedural due process prevent the State from terminating his liberty interest in his relationship with his child without affording him an opportunity to demonstrate his paternity in an evidentiary hearing. We believe this claim derives from a fundamental misconception of the nature of the California statute. While § 621 is phrased in terms of a presumption, that rule of evidence is the implementation of a substantive rule of law. California declares it to be, except in limited circumstances, irrelevant for paternity purposes whether a child conceived during, and born into, an existing marriage was begotten by someone other than the husband and had a prior relationship with him.... Of course the conclusive presumption not only expresses the State's substantive policy but also furthers it, excluding inquiries into the child's paternity that would be destructive of family integrity and privacy.

This Court has struck down as illegitimate certain "irrebuttable presumptions." Those holdings did not, however, rest upon procedural due process. A conclusive presumption does, of course, foreclose the person against whom it is invoked from demonstrating, in a particularized proceeding, that applying the presumption to him will in fact not further the lawful governmental policy the presumption is designed to effectuate. But the same can be said of any legal rule that establishes general classifications, whether framed in terms of a presumption or not. In this respect there is no difference between a rule which says that the marital husband shall be irrebuttably presumed to be the father, and a rule which says that the adulterous natural father shall not be recognized as the legal father. Both rules deny someone in Michael's situation a hearing on whether, in the particular circumstances of his case, California's policies would best be served by giving him parental rights. Thus, as many commentators have observed, our "irrebuttable presumption" cases must ultimately be analyzed as calling into question not the adequacy of procedures but—like our cases involving classifications framed in other terms—the adequacy of the "fit" between the classification and the policy that the classification serves. We therefore reject Michael's procedural due process challenge and proceed to his substantive claim.

Michael contends as a matter of substantive due process that, because he has established a parental relationship with Victoria, protection of Gerald's and Carole's marital union is an insufficient state interest to support termination of that relationship. This argument is, of course, predicated on the assertion that Michael has a constitutionally protected liberty interest in his relationship with Victoria.

It is an established part of our constitutional jurisprudence that the term "liberty" in the Due Process Clause extends beyond freedom from physical restraint....

In an attempt to limit and guide interpretation of the Clause, we have insisted not merely that the interest denominated as a "liberty" be "fundamental" (a concept that, in isolation, is hard to objectify), but also that it be an interest traditionally protected by our society. As we have put it, the Due Process Clause affords only those protections "so rooted in the traditions and conscience of our people as to be ranked as fundamental." Our cases reflect "continual insistence upon respect for the teachings of history [and] solid recognition of the basic values that underlie our society...."

This insistence that the asserted liberty interest be rooted in history and tradition is evident, as elsewhere, in our cases according constitutional protection to certain parental rights. Michael reads the landmark case[s] ... as establishing that a liberty interest is created by biological fatherhood plus an established parental relationship — factors that exist in the present case as well. We think that distorts the rationale of those cases. As we view them, they rest not upon such isolated factors but upon the historic respect — indeed, sanctity would not be too strong a term — traditionally accorded to the relationships that develop within the unitary family. . . .

Thus, the legal issue in the present case reduces to whether the relationship between persons in the situation of Michael and Victoria has been treated as a protected family unit under the historic practices of our society, or whether on any other basis it has been accorded special protection. We think it impossible to find that it has. In fact, quite to the contrary, our traditions have protected the marital family (Gerald, Carole, and the child they acknowledge to be theirs) against the sort of claim Michael asserts.

The presumption of legitimacy was a fundamental principle of the common law. Traditionally, that presumption could be rebutted only by proof that a husband was incapable of procreation or had had no access to his wife during the relevant period. . . .

We have found nothing in the older sources, nor in the older cases, addressing specifically the power of the natural father to assert parental rights over a child born into a woman's existing marriage with another man. Since it is Michael's burden to establish that such a power (at least where the natural father has established a relationship with the child) is so deeply embedded within our traditions as to be a fundamental right, the lack of evidence alone might defeat his case. But the evidence shows that even in modern times — when, as we have noted, the rigid protection of the marital family has in other respects been relaxed — the ability of a person in Michael's position to claim paternity has not been generally acknowledged.

. . .

Moreover, even if it were clear that one in Michael's position generally possesses, and has generally always possessed, standing to challenge the marital child's legitimacy, that would still not establish Michael's case. As noted earlier, what is at issue here is not entitlement to a state pronouncement that Victoria was begotten by Michael. It is no conceivable denial of constitutional right for a State to decline to declare facts unless some legal consequence hinges upon the requested declaration. What Michael asserts here is a right to have himself declared the natural father and thereby to obtain parental prerogatives. What he must establish, therefore, is not that our society has traditionally allowed a natural father in his circumstances to establish paternity, but that it has traditionally accorded such a father parental rights, or at least has not traditionally denied them. Even if the law in all States had always been that the entire world could challenge the marital presumption and obtain a declaration as to who was the natural father, that would not advance Michael's claim. Thus, it is ultimately irrelevant, even for purposes of determining current social attitudes towards the alleged substantive right Michael asserts, that the present law in a number of States appears to allow the natural father — including the natural father who has not established a relationship with the child — the theoretical power to rebut the marital presumption. What counts is whether the States in fact award substantive parental rights to the natural father of a child conceived within, and born into, an extant marital union that wishes to embrace the child. We are not aware of a single case, old or new, that has done so. This is not the stuff of which fundamental rights qualifying as liberty interests are made.

In *Lehr v. Robertson*, a case involving a natural father's attempt to block his child's adoption by the unwed mother's new husband, we observed that "[t]he significance of the biological connection is that it offers the natural father an opportunity that no other male possesses to develop a relationship with his offspring," and we assumed that the Constitution might require some protection of that opportunity. Where, however, the child is born into an extant marital family, the natural father's unique opportunity conflicts with the similarly unique opportunity of the husband of the marriage; and it is not unconstitutional for the State to give categorical preference to the latter. In *Lehr* we quoted approvingly from Justice Stewart's dissent . . . to the effect that although "'[i]n some circumstances the actual relationship between father and child may suffice to create in the unwed father parental interests comparable to those of the married father,'" "'the absence of a legal tie with the mother may in such circumstances appropriately place a limit on whatever substantive constitutional claims might otherwise exist.'" In accord with our traditions, a limit is also imposed by the circumstance that the mother is, at the time of the child's conception and birth, married to, and cohabitating with, another man, both of whom wish to raise the child as the offspring of their union. It is a question of legislative policy and not constitutional law whether California will allow the presumed parenthood of a couple desiring to retain a child conceived within and born into their marriage to be rebutted.

We do not accept Justice Brennan's criticism that this result "squashes" the liberty that consists of "the freedom not to conform." It seems to us that reflects the erroneous view that there is only one side to this controversy — that one disposition can expand a "liberty" of sorts without contracting an equivalent "liberty" on the other side. Such a happy choice is rarely available. Here, to provide protection to an adulterous natural father is to deny protection to a marital father, and vice versa. If Michael has a "freedom not to conform" (whatever that means), Gerald must equivalently have a "freedom to conform." One of them will pay a price for asserting that "freedom" — Michael by being unable to act as father of the child he has adulterously begotten, or Gerald by being unable to preserve the integrity of the traditional family unit he and Victoria have established. Our disposition does not choose between these two "freedoms," but leaves that to the people of California. Justice Brennan's approach chooses one of them as the constitutional imperative, on no apparent basis except that the unconventional is to be preferred.

IV

We have never had occasion to decide whether a child has a liberty interest, symmetrical with that of her parent, in maintaining her filial relationship. We need not do so here because, even assuming that such a right exists, Victoria's claim must fail. Victoria's due process challenge is, if anything, weaker than Michael's. Her basic claim is not that California has erred in preventing her from establishing that Michael, not Gerald, should stand as her legal father. Rather, she claims a due process right to maintain filial relationships with both Michael and Gerald. This assertion merits little discussion, for, whatever the merits of the guardian ad litem's belief that such an arrangement can be of great psychological benefit to a child, the claim that a State must recognize multiple fatherhood has no support in the history or traditions of this country. Moreover, even if we were to construe Victoria's argument as forwarding the lesser proposition that, whatever her status vis-a-vis Gerald, she has a liberty interest in maintaining a filial relationship with her natural father, Michael, we find that, at best, her claim is the obverse of Michael's and fails for the same reasons.

Victoria claims in addition that her equal protection rights have been violated because, unlike her mother and presumed father, she had no opportunity to rebut the presumption of her legitimacy. We find this argument wholly without merit. We reject, at the outset, Victoria's suggestion that her equal protection challenge must be assessed under a standard of strict scrutiny because, in denying her the right to maintain a filial relationship with Michael, the State is discriminating against her on the basis of her illegitimacy. Illegitimacy is a legal construct, not a natural trait. Under California law, Victoria is not illegitimate, and she is treated in the same manner as all other legitimate children: she is entitled to maintain a filial relationship with her legal parents.

We apply, therefore, the ordinary "rational relationship" test to Victoria's equal protection challenge. The primary rationale underlying § 621's limitation on those who may rebut the presumption of legitimacy is a concern that allowing persons other than the husband or wife to do so may undermine the integrity of the marital union. When the husband or wife contests the legitimacy of their child, the stability of the marriage has already been shaken. In contrast, allowing a claim of illegitimacy to be pressed by the child — or, more accurately, by a court-appointed guardian ad litem — may well disrupt an otherwise peaceful union. Since it pursues a legitimate end by rational means, California's decision to treat Victoria differently from her parents is not a denial of equal protection.

The judgment of the California Court of Appeal is

Affirmed.

Justice O'Connor, with whom Justice Kennedy joins, concurring in part. [omitted].

Justice Stevens, concurring in the judgment.

. . .

On the first issue I agree with Justice Scalia that the Federal Constitution imposes no obligation upon a State to "declare facts unless some legal consequence hinges upon the requested declaration." "The actions of judges neither create nor sever genetic bonds."

On the second issue I do not agree with Justice Scalia's analysis. He seems to reject the possibility that a natural father might ever have a constitutionally protected interest in his relationship with a child whose mother was married to, and cohabiting with, another man at the time of the child's conception and birth. I think cases like *Stanley v. Illinois* and *Caban v. Mohammed* demonstrate that enduring "family" relationships may develop in unconventional settings. I therefore would not foreclose the possibility that a constitutionally protected relationship between a natural father and his child might exist in a case like this. Indeed, I am willing to assume for the purpose of deciding this case that Michael's relationship with Victoria is strong enough to give him a constitutional right to try to convince a trial judge that Victoria's best interest would be served by granting him visitation rights. I am satisfied, however, that the California statute, as applied in this case, gave him that opportunity.

...

Justice Brennan, with whom Justice Marshall and Justice Blackmun join, dissenting.

...

Today's plurality, however, does not ask whether parenthood is an interest that historically has received our attention and protection; the answer to that question is too clear for dispute. Instead, the plurality asks whether the specific variety of parenthood under consideration — a natural father's relationship with a child whose mother is married to another man — has enjoyed such protection.

If we had looked to tradition with such specificity in past cases, many a decision would have reached a different result. . . .

...

. . . This is not a case in which we face a "new" kind of interest, one that requires us to consider for the first time whether the Constitution protects it. On the contrary, we confront an interest — that of a parent and child in their relationship with each other — that was among the first that this Court acknowledged in its cases defining the "liberty" protected by the Constitution and I think I am safe in saying that no one doubts the wisdom or validity of those decisions. Where the interest under consideration is a parent–child relationship, we need not ask, over and over again, whether that interest is one that society traditionally protects.

. . . The better approach — indeed, the one commanded by our prior cases and by common sense — is to ask whether the specific parent–child relationship under consideration is close enough to the interests that we already have protected to be deemed an aspect of "liberty" as well. On the facts before us, therefore, the question is not what "level of generality" should be used to describe the relationship between Michael and Victoria, but whether the relationship under consideration is sufficiently substantial to qualify as a liberty interest under our prior cases.

...

The evidence is undisputed that Michael, Victoria, and Carole did live together as a family; that is, they shared the same household, Victoria called Michael "Daddy," Michael contributed to Victoria's support, and he is eager to continue his relationship with her. Yet they are not, in the plurality's view, a "unitary family," whereas

Gerald, Carole, and Victoria do compose such a family. The only difference between these two sets of relationships, however, is the fact of marriage. The plurality, indeed, expressly recognizes that marriage is the critical fact in denying Michael a constitutionally protected stake in his relationship with Victoria: no fewer than six times, the plurality refers to Michael as the "*adulterous* natural father" (emphasis added) or the like. However, the very premise of Stanley and the cases following it is that marriage is not decisive in answering the question whether the Constitution protects the parental relationship under consideration. . . .

. . .

The atmosphere surrounding today's decision is one of make-believe. Beginning with the suggestion that the situation confronting us here does not repeat itself every day in every corner of the country moving on to the claim that it is tradition alone that supplies the details of the liberty that the Constitution protects, and passing finally to the notion that the Court always has recognized a cramped vision of "the family," today's decision lets stand California's pronouncement that Michael—whom blood tests show to a 98 percent probability to be Victoria's father—is not Victoria's father. When and if the Court awakes to reality, it will find a world very different from the one it expects.

Justice White, with whom Justice Brennan joins, dissenting.

California law, as the plurality describes it, tells us that, except in limited circumstances, California declares it to be "*irrelevant* for paternity purposes whether a child conceived during, and born into, an existing marriage was begotten by someone other than the husband" (emphasis in original). This I do not accept, for the fact that Michael H. is the biological father of Victoria is to me highly relevant to whether he has rights, as a father or otherwise, with respect to the child. Because I believe that Michael H. has a liberty interest that cannot be denied without due process of the law, I must dissent.

. . .

The interest in protecting a child from the social stigma of illegitimacy lacks any real connection to the facts of a case where a father is seeking to establish, rather than repudiate, paternity. The "stigma of illegitimacy" argument harks back to ancient common law when there were no blood tests to ascertain that the husband could not "by the laws of nature" be the child's father. Judicial process refused to declare that a child born in wedlock was illegitimate unless the proof was positive. The only such proof was physical absence or impotency. But we have now clearly recognized the use of blood tests as an authoritative means of evaluating allegations of paternity. I see no reason to debate the plurality's multilingual explorations into "spousal nonaccess" and ancient policy concerns behind bastardy laws. It may be true that a child conceived in an extramarital relationship would be considered a "bastard" in the literal sense of the word, but whatever stigma remains in today's society is far less compelling in the context of a child of a married mother, especially when there is a father asserting paternity and seeking a relationship with his child. It is hardly rare in this world of divorce and remarriage for a child to live with the "father" to whom her mother is married, and still have a relationship with her biological father.

The State's professed interest in the preservation of the existing marital unit is a more significant concern. To be sure, the intrusion of an outsider asserting that he is the father of a child whom the husband believes to be his own would be disruptive to say the least. On the facts of this case, however, Gerald was well aware of the liaison between Carole and Michael. . . .

. . .

Notes and Queries

1. Under California law, husbands may challenge the presumption of paternity. How does this shape the argument that the challenged law is permissible because it protects children from the stigma of illegitimacy?
2. The Court reasons that Victoria has no legal claim. Given that, how does the case protect children's interests?
3. What does this case tell you about the nature of family life deemed worth protecting?
4. As we have seen, *Obergefell* revisited the notion of marriage, does that analysis impact the assumptions of marriage in this case?

Review Problem

1. Linda and Michael were friends before they started dating. When Michael's feelings became more than platonic, he told her that he was a transsexual who had successfully completed a sex change 10 years earlier. Their relationship continued and survived many challenges, including her getting pregnant by a boyfriend who had recently left her. Michael was present in the delivery room when Linda gave birth to her son. The couple married in a civil ceremony the following month, and Michael adopted the baby that year. Wanting to expand their family, Linda was artificially inseminated with sperm donated by Michael's brother. She gave birth to a daughter, and Michael also adopted her. Ten years later, Michael left Linda after he had begun a relationship with his current girlfriend. Linda tells her husband's secret to their now 12-year-old son and 10-year-old daughter. After having provided over $65,000 in child support, Michael seeks to maintain a relationship with his children. Linda refuses, stating that "The kids don't want to see Michael, they don't need Michael, Michael's not their father, period." Should Michael have a right to see his children? Suppose the state in which they were married does not

permit same-sex marriage; are they in fact married? Does that matter? Should the court render its ruling based on the child's best interests? Is there a need to show that he is unfit as a parent?

In re Thomas S.

209 A.D.2d 298; 618 N.Y.S.2d 356 (NY Sup. Ct. App., 1994)

Judges Rosenberger, Ellerin, Rubin, Nardelli, Williams, rendering a memorandum decision.

The child, Ry R.-Y., now 12 years old, lives with her mother, respondent Robin Y., the mother's lifetime companion, Sandra R., and Sandra's child, Cade, now 14, who was also conceived through artificial insemination by a donor known to her mother. Petitioner, who is also gay, was sought out by Robin Y. as a known donor and, after several attempts in both New York and California, Robin Y. successfully inseminated herself with petitioner's semen in February 1981 at the home of a mutual friend.

Ry was born on November 16, 1981 in San Francisco, where the household temporarily relocated in connection with Sandra R.'s employment. Like Cade, Ry was given the last names of R. and Y. Petitioner is not listed on Ry's birth certificate, and R. and Y. paid all expenses associated with the pregnancy and delivery. Petitioner was, however, informed of the birth and brought congratulatory flowers to R. and Y.'s home. Later that year, the household moved back to New York where they currently occupy an apartment located in a building owned by Sandra R.

For the first three years of her life, petitioner saw Ry only once or twice while in New York on business. In accordance with an oral agreement with R. and Y., he did not call, support or give presents to her during this period. When Cade, at the age of approximately five years, started asking questions about her father, R. and Y., as they had agreed between themselves, made arrangements for Ry and Cade to meet their biological fathers.

Petitioner testified that there were approximately 26 visits with the R. and Y. family over the following six-year period, ranging in duration from a few days to two weeks. Robin Y. estimates that appellant spent a total of sixty days with the R.-Y. family over the course of those six years, and petitioner estimates 148 days. Whatever the figure, it appears that all parties concerned developed a comfortable relationship with one another. Photographs included in the exhibits depict a warm and amicable relationship between petitioner and Ry, and there are numerous cards and letters from Ry to petitioner in which she express her love for him.

In July 1990, petitioner asked Robin Y. for permission to take Ry and Cade to see his parents and stay at a beach house with some of his siblings and their children. It seems that petitioner felt awkward about introducing R. and Y. to his parents. R. and Y., however, were not willing to allow petitioner to take the girls unless the mothers accompanied them.

It was apparently during the course of these negotiations that petitioner revealed his desire to establish a paternal relationship with Ry. Y. and R. regarded this as a breach of their oral agreement, insisting that visitation continue on the same terms as over the past six years, viz., with their supervision. They also rejected petitioner's suggestion to consult a family counselor or mediator. Unable to resolve his differences with R. and Y. and unable to see his daughter for a period of several months, petitioner moved, by order to show cause, for an order of filiation and for visitation.

During the course of the proceedings, Family Court ordered blood tests and a psychiatric evaluation of Ry. Petitioner, Robin Y. and Ry all submitted to blood genetic marker tests pursuant to Family Court Act § 532. The tests indicated a 99.9% probability of petitioner's paternity. Psychiatric evaluation revealed a belief on Ry's part that any relationship with petitioner would necessarily disrupt her relationship with Robin Y. and Sandra R. and might therefore undermine the legitimacy of her perception of the family unit. It also revealed that, since these proceedings were instituted, Ry has expressed a desire to end all contact with petitioner.

Family Court found by clear and convincing evidence, based upon the blood tests, that petitioner is the biological father of Ry. Nevertheless, citing the doctrine of equitable estoppel, the court refused to enter an order of filiation and dismissed the proceeding. The court characterized petitioner as an "outsider attacking her [Ry's] family and refusing to give it respect", concluding that "a declaration of paternity would be a statement that her family is other than what she knows it to be and needs it to be" and, therefore, "would not be in her best interests." The court added, "Even were there an adjudication of paternity, I would deny [petitioner's] application for visitation."

It is appropriate to begin with the observation that the effect of Family Court's order is to cut off the parental rights of a man who is conceded by all concerned — the child, her mother and the court — to be the biological father. The legal question that confronts us is not, as Family Court framed it, whether an established family unit is to be broken up. Custody of the child is not now, and is unlikely ever to be, an issue between the parties. Rather the question is whether the rights of a biological parent are to be terminated. Absent strict adherence to statutory provisions, termination of those rights is in violation of well established standards of due process and cannot stand.

The asserted sanctity of the family unit is an uncompelling ground for the drastic step of depriving petitioner of procedural due process. Whatever concerns and misgivings Family Court and the dissenters may entertain about visitation, custody and the child's best interests, it is clear that they are appropriately reserved for a later stage of the proceedings. . . .

The reasoning advanced by the dissent to obviate further proceedings involves the predetermination of the very issues that would normally be resolved by hearings on visitation and, if warranted, termination of parental rights. Without the order of filiation to which the law entitles him, petitioner lacks standing to seek visitation or challenge respondent's (and the dissent's) concept of what may or may not be in the child's best interests. Apparently convinced that petitioner could not possibly contribute anything beneficial to the court's consideration of this issue, the dissent would deny petitioner the right to his day in court. . . .

Even more disturbing is the suggestion that the judicial process will pose "severe traumatic consequences" to the child whose interests it is designed to protect. Petitioner is portrayed by the dissent as the villain of this case for having the temerity to request that Ry and her sister accompany him on an unsupervised visit to meet his parents, causing a "rift" and precipitating this litigation. The record, however, indicates that it was Robin Y. and Sandra S. who opposed this visit and does not reflect any initial resistance on the part of Ry. It was only some period of time after Robin Y. and Sandra S. refused petitioner any further visitation with his daughter that Ry developed overt animosity towards the man she had called "Dad" and regarded with great affection. As the Court of Appeals has noted, "The desires of young children, capable of distortive manipulation by a bitter, or perhaps even well-meaning, parent, do not always reflect the long-term best interest of the children".

The apparent manipulation of an innocent child's affections and the obvious damage wreaked upon the once harmonious relationship with her father do not deter the dissent from the view that the child's "haunting fear" of being taken away from "the woman whom she has consistently thought of as her second parent" must have been instilled by petitioner. Whether Ry will come to regret the poisoning of her formerly amicable relationship with her father is beyond the meager ken of a court of law and must be consigned to the conscience of whoever must abide the consequences. It remains to be seen whether petitioner's is the only parent–child relationship to be damaged by this dispute.

The emphasis placed on custody both by respondent and the dissent, is out of all proportion to its relevance to this proceeding. . . .

. . .

It is clear that the dissent does not construe the issues presented by this case in the limited context of a filiation proceeding or even the more expansive proceeding for an order of visitation, which is the matter ultimately to be determined. Without apparent regard for the interests of the parties to this litigation, the dissent proceeds to analyze the issues from the context of an adoption, particularly the necessity for petitioner's consent. . . .

The first observation is the obvious one, that Sandra R. has not filed an adoption petition and that the issues presented by such a proceeding, including the necessity for petitioner's consent are simply not before us. . . .

The other observation is that it is in no one's best interest to require a father, in the position of petitioner, to choose between asserting full parental rights, encompassing support and custody of the child in order to achieve the limited relief sought — an order of filiation and, ultimately, visitation. This Court would perform a disservice to the litigants by expanding the proceeding to place custody in issue. As a matter of sound appellate jurisprudence, the Court should limit its consideration to questions embraced by the relief actually sought and not attempt to address issues which may or may not arise in the course of future proceedings. The gratuitous interjection of custody, in particular, raises the very threat to the relationship between Ry and her mothers that respondent and the dissent posits in support of the termination of petitioner's parental rights. Clearly, the resolution of this matter should not be predicated on avoiding judicial consideration of petitioner's right to relief that he has not thus far sought and which he might well never seek.

Family Court's disposition is no more compelled by the equities of this matter than by the law. The notion that a lesbian mother should enjoy a parental relationship with her daughter but a gay father should not is so innately discriminatory as to be unworthy of comment. Merely because petitioner does not have custody of his daughter does not compel the conclusion, embraced by the dissent, that he may not assert any right to maintain a parental relationship with her. While much is made by Family Court of the alleged oral understanding between the parties that petitioner would not assume a parental role towards Ry, any such agreement is unenforceable for failure to comply with explicit statutory requirements for surrender of parental rights, as the dissent concedes.

...

We reject the dissent's view that the alleged agreement between the parties constitutes evidence of a lack of committment to his child on the part of petitioner. As the dissenters concede, legal impediments and public policy considerations bar enforcement of the oral agreement, and it can therefore be accorded no force or effect. It is the longstanding rule of equity, now extended to law, that the facts be viewed in their fullest. The Court cannot simply ignore the significant events that have transpired since Ry's third birthday. In any event, we regard the determination of this matter in any manner that departs from the express procedures delineated in article 5 of the Family Court Act as a violation of petitioner's statutory and Constitutional rights.

Having initiated and encouraged, over a substantial period of time, the relationship between petitioner and his daughter, respondent is estopped to deny his right to legal recognition of that relationship. . . . Having found that petitioner is the father of Ry R.-Y., Family Court was commanded by statutory direction to enter an order of filiation.

All concur except Rosenberger, J.P., and Ellerin, J., who dissent in a memorandum by Ellerin, J.

Justice Ellerin, dissenting.

. . . Since, however, I believe that the overriding factor which must guide us is the best interests of this child, I dissent. . . .

...

Notwithstanding the agreement [that the father has no parental rights or obligations], it is the manner in which the parties acted during the period from the child's birth up to the time of the commencement of this proceeding that is of critical significance....

...

The record clearly establishes that for Ry's first 9 and half years of life the appellant at no time sought to establish a true parental relationship with her either by way of seeking to legally establish his paternity and assuming the responsibilities and obligations which that status entailed or by any involvement in her upbringing or schooling or by attempting to provide any support for her....

The net of petitioner's relationship with Ry during the 6 years that he occasionally saw her until she was almost 10 years old was that of a close family friend or fond surrogate uncle who, while acknowledging that he was her biological sperm donor, fully recognized that her family unit consisted of her two mothers and her sister Cade and that he was not a family member of that unit....

The trial court, sensitive to the issues involved, appointed a law guardian for the child and obtained the agreement of all parties to submit the child to a psychiatric evaluation.... Both the law guardian and the court appointed psychiatrist make clear that the best interests of Ry, now 12 years old, will be served by an affirmance of the denial of filiation, which will also eliminate Ry's custody concerns....

...

The threshold issue that must first be determined is what rights, if any, arise from the fact that petitioner was the sperm donor and paternal biological progenitor of the child Ry. The Court of Appeals has made clear that absent "a full commitment to the responsibilities of parenthood" the mere existence of a biological link does not merit constitutional protection. Thus, an unwed biological father does not automatically have parental rights which must be recognized by the state independent of the child's best interests, since such rights come into existence only if the father has sufficiently grasped the opportunity to "promptly manifested his willingness to take on parental responsibilities" and it is only when "the opportunity, of limited duration, to manifest a willingness to be a parent" is grasped that an interest arises worthy of protection as a Matter of due process.

...

If the child's best interests are to be the touchstone of the analysis, the attempts by both parties to argue the equities of their own respective personal positions are not germane. It is neither petitioner's nor respondent's feelings of aggrievement that are the determinative consideration, although one may sympathize and understand those feelings. Rather, it is the impact which petitioner's past assurances and representations to Ry during her first 9 1/2 years of life—as to who her family were, how it functioned and his non-family status have had upon her stability and security and the consequences which would stem from permitting a dramatic abrogation of those representations by giving petitioner family status with all that it entails.... To now grant him the standing to claim the very considerable authority and power held by a parent, against her wishes, would change her life in drastic ways. For this reason, I believe that the elements of misrepresentation, reliance and detriment have clearly been established and that the evidence demonstrates that an order of filiation is not in this child's best interests. Under these circumstances, the doctrine should be applied.

. . .

For all these reasons, I believe that the evidence overwhelmingly supports the Family Court's decision that the entry of an order of filiation would not be in this child's best interests and that there should, therefore, be an affirmance.

Notes and Queries

1. What policy arguments would you offer to support the conclusion that the father should honor his original agreement? A rule to that effect would lead to more predictable outcomes, but would it lead to more just outcomes?
2. The court rejects the claim that the judicial process will pose "severe traumatic consequences" to the child whose interests it is designed to protect. Do you agree?

Review Problem

1. Alison and Virginia had lived as partners in a loving relationship. After three years together they decided to have a child. Together they planned the conception, obtained a semen donor, and prepared for the birth. After Virginia gave birth to the baby boy, the women shared the parenting tasks, and both developed strong emotional bonds to their son. Two years later, Alison and Virginia had a daughter through donor insemination, this time with Alison as the biological mother. Six months later, when the son was 2 and 1/2 years old, the women separated. For the next three and a half years, Alison was allowed to visit the son. When the boy was 6 years old, however, Virginia barred Alison from visiting the child. Alison sought visitation rights under the New York State statute that gives a "parent" standing to request visitation rights of her child. Importantly, the statute did not define "parent" Equally importantly, the court did not have to decide whether to grant Alison visitation rights but only the narrow issue of whether she had standing to show that visitation would be in the best interest of Alison and Virginia's child. How should a court rule? The court that addressed these issues foreshadowed its holding in the opening sentence of the decision: "At issue in this case is whether petitioner, a biological stranger to a child who is properly in the custody of his biological mother, has standing to seek visitation with the child. . . ." The court rejected Alison's claim that she had "acted as a 'de facto' parent or that she should be viewed as a parent 'by estoppel.'" *Alison D. v. Virginia M.*, 572 N.E.2d 27, 28–29 (N.Y. 1991).

Buck v. Bell

274 U.S. 200; 47 S. Ct. 584 (1927)

Mr. Justice Holmes delivered the opinion of the Court.

This is a writ of error to review a judgment of the Supreme Court of Appeals of the State of Virginia, affirming a judgment of the Circuit Court of Amherst County, by which the defendant in error, the superintendent of the State Colony for Epileptics and Feeble Minded, was ordered to perform the operation of salpingectomy upon Carrie Buck, the plaintiff in error, for the purpose of making her sterile. The case comes here upon the contention that the statute authorizing the judgment is void under the Fourteenth Amendment as denying to the plaintiff in error due process of law and the equal protection of the laws.

Carrie Buck is a feeble minded white woman who was committed to the State Colony above mentioned in due form. She is the daughter of a feeble minded mother in the same institution, and the mother of an illegitimate feeble minded child. She was eighteen years old at the time of the trial of her case in the Circuit Court, in the latter part of 1924. An Act of Virginia, approved March 20, 1924, recites that the health of the patient and the welfare of society may be promoted in certain cases by the sterilization of mental defectives, under careful safeguard, etc.; that the sterilization may be effected in males by vasectomy and in females by salpingectomy, without serious pain or substantial danger to life; that the Commonwealth is supporting in various institutions many defective persons who if now discharged would become a menace but if incapable of procreating might be discharged with safety and become self-supporting with benefit to themselves and to society; and that experience has shown that heredity plays an important part in the transmission of insanity, imbecility, etc. The statute then enacts that whenever the superintendent of certain institutions including the above named State Colony shall be of opinion that it is for the best interests of the patients and of society that an inmate under his care should be sexually sterilized, he may have the operation performed upon any patient afflicted with hereditary forms of insanity, imbecility, etc., on complying with the very careful provisions by which the act protects the patients from possible abuse.

...

The attack is not upon the procedure but upon the substantive law. It seems to be contended that in no circumstances could such an order be justified. It certainly is contended that the order cannot be justified upon the existing grounds. The judgment finds the facts that have been recited and that Carrie Buck "is the probable potential parent of socially inadequate offspring, likewise afflicted, that she may be sexually sterilized without detriment to her general health and that her welfare and that of society will be promoted by her sterilization," and thereupon makes the order. In view of the general declarations of the legislature and the specific findings of the Court, obviously we cannot say as matter of law that the grounds do not exist, and if they exist they justify the result. We have seen more than once that the public welfare may call upon the best citizens for their lives. It would be strange if it could not call upon those who already sap the strength of the State for these lesser sacrifices, often not felt to be such by those concerned, in order to prevent our being swamped with incompetence. It is better for all the world, if instead of waiting to execute degenerate offspring for crime, or to let them starve for their imbecility, society can prevent those who are manifestly unfit from continuing their kind. The principle that sustains compulsory vaccination is broad enough to cover cutting the Fallopian tubes. Three generations of imbeciles are enough.

But, it is said, however it might be if this reasoning were applied generally, it fails when it is confined to the small number who are in the institutions named and is not applied to the multitudes outside. It is the usual last resort of constitutional arguments to point out shortcomings of this sort. But the answer is that the law does all that is needed when it does all that it can, indicates a policy, applies it to all within the lines, and seeks to bring within the lines all similarly situated so far and so fast as its means allow. Of course so far as the operations enable those who otherwise must be kept confined to be returned to the world, and thus open the asylum to others, the equality aimed at will be more nearly reached.

Judgment affirmed.

Mr. Justice Butler dissents. [omitted]

Notes and Queries

1. What is the state's compelling interest that justifies sterilization of individuals deemed incompetent?
2. If there is no link between a parent's mental retardation and the intelligence of their offspring, should the law still stand? What arguments would you make to support sterilization?
3. The Court notes that public welfare often asks for sacrifices, and that this is just one of them. What do you think of this reasoning?

Review Problems

1. A private group wishes to address problems associated with drug-abusing women who have babies. It pays $200 as an incentive to drug addicts to be medically sterilized or to use long-term birth control. Is this a legitimate way to coerce a vulnerable group into limiting their reproductive rights? Even though private cash-for-contraception agreements have been deemed permissible, do they violate basic rights? Are these contracts unconscionable? Could the state adopt a similar program? See Jennifer Mott Johnson (2001). Reproductive ability for sale, Do I hear

$200?: Private cash-for contraception agreements as an alternative to maternal substance abuse. *Arizona Law Review*, 43, 205–243.

2. Efforts to address poverty frequently involve efforts to condition welfare benefits on permanent or long-lasting birth control. Measures have been proposed that provide for increased welfare benefits contingent on welfare mothers' agreement not to have more children. Other proposed measures provide for the payment of state-funded benefits to welfare women who submit to sterilization procedures, usually in the form of tubal ligations and Norplant. These proposals have been quite popular, even though they have raised many issues regarding coercion and discrimination based on race and poverty. Following *Buck*, should these efforts survive? See Meredith Blake (1995). Welfare and coerced contraception: Morality implications of state sponsored reproductive control. *University of Louisville Journal of Family Law*, 34, 311–344. Note that several states already impose a "Family Cap," which provides that when children are born into families already on welfare, the family will not receive increased benefits despite the increase in family size. Why would that be deemed less problematic? See Wendy Chavkin, Tammy A. Draut, Diana Romero & Paul H. Wise (2000). Sex, reproduction, and welfare reform. *Georgetown Journal on Poverty Law & Policy*, 7, 379–393.

Research Comments

1. Although many view sterilization of the mentally incompetent as obsolete, the practice continues. See Roger J. R. Levesque (1996). Regulating the private relations of adults with mental disabilities: Old laws, new policies, hollow hopes. *Behavioral Sciences & the Law*, 14, 83–106; Deborah W. Denno (1997). Sexuality, rape, and mental retardation. *University of Illinois Law Review*, 1997, 315–434.

2. Parenting by learning disabled persons is a highly emotive issue that elicits strong arguments from both extremes. Many of the arguments against such parenting have their basis in eugenic theory, whereas those in favor often cite human rights declarations and philosophies such as normalization. Both sides may have considerable merit. However, it does seem clear that, whereas parents with learning difficulties may be more predisposed to having problems, they can perform as adequate parents, given appropriate training and support. The reality, however, is that, depending on their level of disability, they face important challenges. Young or expectant parents with intellectual disabilities, often with less formal education and with uncertain incomes below the community poverty level, often live in chaotic circumstances having few supports and limited resources. As a result, they often encounter substantial obstacles acquiring childcare knowledge and services. They also have a limited base of self- and child health care, safety, and well-being knowledge from which to draw and upon which to build; have difficulty understanding information in complex English (or in their primary language); and have

fewer information acquisition and application skills. At the same time, however, there is substantial clinical empirical evidence demonstrating that when services match parental learning needs, health and safety risk status of both children and parents can be reduced and well-being can be promoted. See Alexander J. Tymchuk (1999). Moving towards integration of services for parents with intellectual disabilities. *Journal of Intellectual & Developmental Disability*, 24, 59–74.

3. Sterilization efforts clearly address child maltreatment, such as through the obvious fact that children may not be born to be maltreated and the manner that sterilization may impact maltreatment rates through its links to poverty. But these are contentious matters. Not being born may be the ultimate form of maltreatment and not everyone in poverty maltreats his children. Recent efforts, though, even more directly address child maltreatment. In response to sex crimes, some states mandate chemical castration. For example, a Florida castration law requires judges to sentence sexual offenders to chemical alteration of their bodies after committing their second offense, while leaving it within judges' discretion to impose the same sentence for the first offense. What do you make of these responses to sex crimes? See Bryan Keene (1997). Chemical castration: An analysis of Florida's new "cutting-edge" policy towards sex criminals. *Florida Law Review*, 49, 803–829.

Pena v. Mattox

84 F.3d 894 (7th Cir. Ct. App., 1996)

Chief Judge Posner delivered the opinion of the court.

This appeal from the dismissal of a complaint for failure to state a claim, and from the denial of a motion for reconsideration and for leave to file an amended complaint, presents two questions. The first is whether a man who becomes a father as a result of his criminal intercourse with a minor has an interest in the child that is protected by the due process clause of the Fourteenth Amendment as a form of liberty. The second (which we shall not have to decide, however) is whether interference by state officials with the filing of a suit under state law violates the federal Constitution.

The only source of facts is the allegations of the complaint, and we therefore take those allegations as true for purposes of this appeal. The plaintiff, Ruben Pena, began dating Amanda Mattox in 1991. Ruben was 19 and Amanda 15. Both were living in Illinois, Amanda with her parents. Amanda became pregnant by Ruben the following year. When Amanda's parents discovered her pregnancy they forbade her to continue seeing Ruben, but she disobeyed their order.

He visited her on the evening of December 8, 1992. Her pregnancy was far advanced. She complained to him that she felt sick. He urged her to tell her parents about the feeling. Sometime after he left he called to find out how she was doing. He could not reach her, and no one at her home would give him any information about her. He visited several hospitals looking for her, but without success.

The next night, Amanda's father, defendant Mattox, called Ruben and asked him to meet him at a restaurant. When Ruben arrived he was arrested on the basis of a felony criminal complaint signed by Mattox. The complaint charged Ruben with the felony of sexual intercourse with a person who is at least 13 but no older than 16 and at least five years younger than the defendant. Mattox knew that Amanda was not five years younger than Ruben. The complaint had been drafted or authorized by, and the warrant for Ruben's arrest procured by, a state prosecutor named Charles Bretz, who is also a defendant, and who also knew that the charges were false. Bail was set at $30,000.

When Ruben's sister learned of his arrest she called the Mattox home. Patricia Schneider, who was at the time an Illinois state judge and who is Amanda's aunt and another defendant, answered the phone, identified herself as a judge, told the sister not to call the Mattox residence again, and added that Ruben's bail would be increased the next day. Increased it was, to $45,000. Although the complaint does not charge Schneider with any role other than to field the phone call from Ruben's sister, the fact that she told the sister that Ruben's bail would be raised the next day, and that it was raised, suggests that she may have spoken to the judge who handled Ruben's case.

Ruben could not make bail and remained in jail. Two days later, however, the charges against him were reduced to criminal sexual abuse, a misdemeanor that differs from the felony with which he had been charged originally in not requiring the defendant to be at least five years older than his sexual partner. Had he been charged with a misdemeanor in the first place, his bail could not have exceeded $1,000. Ruben pleaded guilty to this offense the same day, received a sentence of 24 months supervision, and was released. One condition of his release was that he have no contact with Amanda or any member of her immediate family until April 19, 1994. Ruben left Illinois, fearful that the defendants would "continue to exert improper influence" over the law enforcement authorities of Illinois, as his complaint puts it.

The scheme to arrest and prosecute Ruben had been activated when Amanda, seven and a half months pregnant, went into labor on December 8, 1992 (that was the "sickness" which, unbeknownst to him, she was complaining of). Her parents spirited her off to Indiana, where she gave birth. The child was immediately placed for adoption. Ruben was not informed of the adoption or even that the child had been born and Amanda removed to Indiana, a state that has an unusual law, dispensing with the requirement that the father consent to adoption, if, as in this case, the mother was under 16 when the child was conceived.

This suit was brought in June of 1994, some 18 months after the birth and arrest. The principal claim is that the defendants conspired to deprive the plaintiff of his parental rights. Since Bretz certainly and Schneider arguably were acting under color of state law, the conspiracy is actionable under 42 U.S.C. § 1983 even though the third defendant, Amanda's father, was not. The plaintiff seeks damages, not rights in the child which in any event these defendants have no power to give him.

Bretz claims immunity as a prosecutor (Schneider makes no claim of immunity), and rightly so with regard to everything that he did, such as the drafting or authorization of the original criminal complaint against the plaintiff, the procuring of the warrant, the request to increase Pena's bail, and the request that Pena be forbidden, as a condition of his punishment, to see Amanda. But the complaint alleges that he was a member of a conspiracy that went beyond the criminal prosecution of the plaintiff. A prosecutor has no immunity for the acts that he does outside his role as a prosecutor; and the law of conspiracy would impute to him, as a coconspirator, the acts of the other, nonprosecutor members of the conspiracy. The acts directly connected with the criminal prosecution were not the most significant acts committed in furtherance of the conspiracy. What really defeated Ruben's effort to establish a parental right (besides Indiana law) was the fact that Amanda was taken out of the state, and the child put up for adoption, without his knowledge, and the further fact that he found himself, a stripling of 19, up against Illinois officialdom in the persons of a judge and a prosecutor.

. . .

The claim here is that the defendants deprived Pena of a species of liberty that the Constitution protects from more than merely procedural infringements—denied him, that is, what is called "substantive due process" He claims that a father has a right to his child, a right shared with the mother but a genuine right nonetheless. . . .

. . .

But the suit must fail nevertheless. The reason is that the plaintiff has no constitutionally protected interest in the offspring of his relationship with Amanda Mattox. We do not reach this conclusion because the Constitution is silent on the rights of parents or because the due process clause speaks of process rather than of substance. We regard these bridges as having been crossed, and we therefore assume that the Constitution forbids a state to deprive parents—fathers as well as mothers, including natural fathers—of their children without good reasons for doing so. But in the word "their" is concealed an important qualification. It is not the brute biological fact of parentage, but the existence of an actual or potential relationship that society recognizes as worthy of respect and protection, that activates the constitutional claim. . . .

. . .

But no court has gone so far as to hold that the mere fact of fatherhood, consequent upon a criminal act that our society does take seriously and that is not cemented (whoever's fault that is) by association with the child, creates an interest that the Constitution protects in the name of liberty. The plaintiff's counsel conceded in response to a question at argument that had Amanda's child been conceived as the result of a violent rape, the rapist would have acquired no constitutional right to interfere with the adoption of the child or otherwise to assert a parent's rights. . . . The criminal should not be rewarded for having committed the aggravated form of the offense by receiving parental rights which he may be able to swap for the agreement of the victim's family not to press criminal charges.

... The sexual act was consensual, Ruben was 19 rather than 40, and Amanda was 15 rather than 12. The offense was a misdemeanor rather than a felony. But statutory rape, even in its misdemeanor form, that is, even if not aggravated by an extreme disparity in ages or the extreme youth of one of the sexual partners, is not one of those crimes like adultery or fornication that remain on the statute books, archaic and unenforced, as a residue of legislative inertia. It is not merely some quirk of Hoosier morality or religious conservatism. AIDS, abortion, and welfare have heightened public concern with teenage sex and pregnancy. In most states of the United States sex with a 15-year-old is a crime and is likely (somewhat, not highly, likely) to be prosecuted if a complaint is filed. A Congressman from Illinois was sent to prison recently for having sex with a 16-year-old. The conduct in which Ruben engaged with Amanda, and the sequel, her pregnancy, are conduct and consequence of which most societies, even today, strongly disapprove and for excellent reasons. A pregnancy is a serious misfortune for a 15-year-old. The Constitution does not forbid the states to penalize the father's illicit and harmful conduct by refusing to grant him parental rights that he can use to block an adoption or simply enjoy as the fruit of his crime.

The maxim that a wrongdoer shall not profit from his wrong is deeply inscribed in the Anglo-American legal tradition. . . .

In denying him the benefit of this argument we are not rewarding the defendants for having prevented Pena from obtaining parental rights in the first place by spiriting Amanda out of the state and putting the child up for adoption as soon as it was born. The cases that we have cited in which parental rights were granted to statutory rapists are not cases in which the rapist was trying to block an adoption. A statutory rapist who has managed somehow to establish a relationship with his child or who in default of adoption is being dunned for child support may have a claim to parental rights. But he does not have a right to create such a relationship by blocking the adoption of the child. To recognize a blocking right would be to allow the wrongdoer to benefit from his wrongdoing. . . .

. . .

When we asked the plaintiff's counsel what his strongest argument (apart from arguments based on the cases, which do not support his claim) was, he told us that the father deserves the child and the child the father. We have adequately discussed the first half of this proposition. As for the second, we think a state has discretion to decide whether it is better to encourage the kind of conduct in which the plaintiff engaged by giving him parental rights or discourage it by refusing to bestow legal protection on the relationship between father and child. The interest asserted by the plaintiff is not so compelling as to warrant our overriding the state's choice in the name of the Constitution.

. . .

Affirmed.

Notes and Queries

1. Would you agree that the court seems more interested in a parent's moral turpitude (contrary to good morals) than in a parent's interest in caring for his or her child?

2. The court denies that the father has cognizable rights as it reasons that "[i]t is not the brute biological fact of parentage, but the existence of an actual or potential relationship that society recognizes as worthy of respect and protection, that activates the constitutional claim." Given that, does the father's reasons for not having a relationship matter?

Bartasavich v. Mitchell

324 Pa. Super. 270; 471 A.2d 833 (Penn. Sup. Ct., 1984)

Judge Brosky delivered the opinion of the court.

These consolidated appeals are from three orders of the same date which: (1) terminated appellant Michael Bartasavich's parental rights; (2) denied Mr. Bartasavich's petition for visitation; and (3) granted custody of Michelle Bartasavich to Clearfield County Children's Services for purposes of placing her for adoption. For the reasons that follow we reverse and remand for further proceedings.

Appellant is the father of Michelle who was born on December 22, 1971 to Mr. Bartasavich and his wife, Mary. On October 14, 1974, during a domestic dispute, appellant stabbed and killed his wife. He immediately took his then two year old daughter to the home of a neighbor, returned home and stabbed himself with a fork. Mr. Bartasavich was arrested and charged with his wife's homicide while in the hospital recuperating from his self-inflicted wounds.

On October, 1974 while an inmate at the Clearfield County Jail, appellant signed a petition which led to the placement of Michelle in the custody of Clearfield County Child Welfare Services.

The Child Welfare service permitted Michelle's maternal grandparents, with whom she had been staying since her mother's tragic death, to retain custody of her. Michael Bartasavich entered a guilty plea to a charge of voluntary manslaughter, and in February 1975, was sentenced to a term of imprisonment of 5 to 10 years.

From October, 1974 to June, 1976 Michelle was taken by her grandparents to visit with her father who was incarcerated from October, 1974 to October, 1979.

In June, 1976, Clearfield County Child Welfare Services permitted the Gepperts to stop taking Michelle to visit her father, because she had apparently displayed a negative reaction to the visits. The Gepperts reported that Michelle suffered stomach ailments and other manifestations of anxiety during the periods surrounding the visits.

The Gepperts claim that Michelle feared her father. A psychologist retained by appellant when the visits ceased concluded that Michelle had "ambivalent" feelings about her father, and did seem to fear him. Prior to the cessation of the visits, Michelle began to refer to her father as "Mike" although she had formerly called him "Dad."

In May, 1978, while still incarcerated, appellant filed a Petition for Writ of Habeas Corpus, seeking a resumption of visitation.

On June 15, 1978, Clearfield County Children's Services filed a petition seeking the termination of appellant's parental rights.

...

The lower court terminated appellant's parental rights on the basis of Section 311(2) of the Adoption Act. That section required that three things be shown before a natural parent's right in a child will be terminated: (1) repeated and continued incapacity, abuse, neglect or refusal must be shown; (2) such incapacity, abuse, neglect or refusal must be shown to have caused the child to be without essential parental care, control or subsistence; and (3) it must be shown that the causes of the incapacity, abuse, neglect or refusal cannot or will not be terminated.

...

While the trial court opinion in this case suggests that it found the evidence "compelling" ... it is clear to us from a thorough reading of the opinion that the lower court did not place upon the petitioners the burden to prove their case by clear and convincing evidence.

The trial court opinion indicates that aside from the question of which burden of proof should be utilized, the Court assessed the burden against appellant, rather than appellee. The Court suggested that the appellant had failed to show his mental capacity or financial ability to care for his daughter. We note most emphatically that it is not appellant's burden to show his capability, but rather, it is the burden of the petitioner who seeks the termination of his parental rights to show his incapacity.

As the trial court opinion notes, the evidence adduced at the hearing in this case shows that appellant has made efforts to see his daughter many times since the cessation of visitation. He has corresponded to this end with Clearfield County Child Welfare Services and has employed a psychologist to evaluate his daughter. Mr. Bartasavich has attempted to write to his daughter many times, but his letters have been returned to him. He has paid his daughter's elementary school tuition. Appellant attempted, while incarcerated, to provide some financial support to Michelle, but the Gepperts returned his checks to him. Mr. Bartasavich has written to his daughter's school seeking information about her and has asked for pictures of her.

Additionally, officers in charge of appellant during his incarceration verified his testimony that he was virtually unsupervised at the prison and that he would be recommended for parole.

Having noted the above recited findings, the trial court nonetheless terminated appellant's parental rights saying that appellant lacks the ability to satisfy Michelle's psychological and physical needs. Specifically the court found that appellant had been rendered incapable of parenting Michelle because he had killed her mother. The court also noted the lack of evidence of appellant's financial and occupational situation, implying incorrectly that appellant had the burden of proof.

Appellant's killing of his wife was certainly a tragic event, which has surely caused harm to Michelle. We are not prepared to conclude that it alone, however, meets the statutory requirements for termination of parental rights which were relied upon by the petitioner, Children's Services.

. . . the incapacity must be repeated and continuous. Appellant's action was not repeated, although it could be argued that it is continuous in its effect.

The incapacity must have caused the child to be without essential parental care. Appellant's action certainly did cause Michelle to be without essential parental care.

The incapacity cannot be terminated. We cannot say based on the evidence before us that appellant's incapacity cannot be terminated. It is, of course true that because of appellant's action, Michelle will be permanently deprived of her mother's care. Her loss in this regard is complete and irretrievable. However, she may not be without essential parental care insofar as she may have available to her the care of her father. We do not agree with the trial court's conclusion that the permanence of the loss of her mother necessarily rendered appellant permanently incapable of parenting her.

. . .

We note that our review is of a record made in the spring of 1979. Three and one-half years have passed since then. Appellant has been paroled. Michelle has grown. We are unwilling to make any final determination on the basis of such an out of date record and we therefore remand for a new evidentiary hearing to be conducted in light of *Santosky* and its progeny.

. . .

Order terminating parental rights reversed.

Order denying visitation reversed.

Order granting permanent custody to Clearfield County Children's Services reversed.

. . .

Judge McEwen, concurring and dissenting. [omitted]

Notes and Queries

1. Returning again to *Pena*, which urged a focus on morality and a focus on the fact that the actions were indeed criminal, do you think this court was unnecessarily harsh on a statutory rapist-parent when other courts allow parents who commit a multitude of crimes, including murder, to retain rights to their children? At least this court examined the circumstances of the actual crime to determine if the parent is unfit. Do you find the crime in *Pena* that immoral given that Ruben and Amanda were both young and theirs was an ongoing consensual relationship?

Review Problems

1. Jack was convicted of the January 1992 murder of his wife, P. J. N. (Patty), a class AA felony, and he was sentenced to life imprisonment with no possibility of parole for at least 25 years. Jack violated a protection order restraining him from Patty's home and bribed his children to gain entrance to the home. When Patty returned from work, Jack shot her several times with a handgun in the presence of Joan, Jeff, and Justin, who were then ages 11, 8, and 4, respectively. Jack fled the scene, leaving the children with their dying mother. Patty was dead when police arrived and Jack was arrested shortly thereafter. Joan and Jeff testified against Jack at his murder trial. Shortly after the murder, the children were placed in the physical custody of Patty's sister, Sandy, who successfully petitioned the court for guardianship of the children. In December 1993, Sandy and her husband, Mark, petitioned the court to adopt the children and terminate Jack's parental rights. The trial court terminated Jack's parental rights and granted the adoption. He appealed. Would your decision render a *per se* rule that revokes parental rights in situations like these? Such a rule may be significant in that, without it, there may be a hearing or trial to determine the parents' fitness. Such adjudications may be problematic to the extent that they may involve the children in proceedings where they do not want to be with the offender and may prolong efforts to adopt the children. In this case, the court agreed that his incarceration alone is insufficient to warrant termination of his parental rights, that incarceration for the crime of murder may be insufficient in itself to warrant termination of parental rights, and that one parent's killing the other parent may not in itself warrant termination. The court nevertheless ruled against him as it found that the circumstances of Jack's crime present a paradigm of parental unfitness and resulting continuing deprivation of the children. *In the Matter of the Adoption of J. S. P. L.*, 532 N.W.2d 653 (Sup. Ct. N. D., 1995).

2. The *Bartasavich* and *Adoption of J. S. P. L.* analyses are contrary to that of *Pena* at least to the extent that they consider one crime alone inadequate for parental termination. How would you distinguish these two cases from *Pena*? Are they

distinguishable from *Pena* because the parent had already formed a relationship with the child beyond the mere biological relationship in *Pena*? Does it seem reasonable to make that distinction given that the *Pena* court made the crime, not the lack of a relationship, the deciding factor?

3. Would sexual abuse of a child render a father unfit to parent his other children? Consider the following case. Following an investigation conducted in connection with a child abuse report, in May 1991, an abuse and neglect petition was filed against respondent relative to two children: Amanda, the nine-year-old daughter of respondent's girlfriend, Veronica, and David, the three-year-old biological son of Veronica and respondent. The foundation for the charges relative to both children and the subject of the child abuse report was respondent's alleged sexual abuse of Amanda on several occasions between December 1990 and April 1991. Respondent challenged the derivative finding of abuse as to David. The reviewing court responded that evidence of the sexual abuse of one child, standing alone, does not, *ipso facto*, establish a prima facie case of derivative abuse or neglect against others. Nonetheless, in appropriate circumstances it can support a finding of derivative abuse or neglect as to other children, even those of the opposite sex. Appropriate circumstances include the nature of the direct abuse, notably its duration, the circumstances surrounding its commission and whether, on the whole, it can be said to evidence fundamental flaws in the respondent's understanding of the duties of parenthood. In terms of the present case, the court noted that the continuing nature of the abuse, the fact that it was accomplished, at times, by physical violence and was perpetrated while David was in the same room, revealed that the respondent's acts demonstrated a total lack of understanding of the parental role and placed David in imminent danger of harm. Accordingly, by affirmatively creating a substantial risk of physical injury that would likely cause protracted impairment of David's physical and/or emotional health, the actions could reasonably be viewed as making David derivatively abused. *In the Matter of Amanda L. L.*, 195 A.D.2d 708 (N.Y. 1993).

Research Comment

1. As we will explore in more detail later, prior to termination of parental rights, states typically must make reasonable efforts to preserve the family. This requirement has now changed dramatically with the enactment of the federal *Adoption and Safe Families Act of 1997* (ASFA), Pub. L. No. 105-89, 111 Stat. 2115 (codified in scattered sections of 42 U.S.C.). ASFA has sought to transform child welfare by moving from a philosophy of family preservation to child safety. This is reflected in ASFA's clarification of the reasonable efforts requirement, which mandates that the child's health and safety be the primary concern when making reasonable efforts determinations. ASFA provides that states are not required to make reasonable efforts to preserve or reunify families if a court has determined, among

other things, that the parent has committed murder or voluntary manslaughter of another child of the parent or aided or abetted, conspired or solicited to commit such a crime. It also removes reasonable efforts requirements if the parent has committed felony assault resulting in serious bodily injury to the child or another child of the parent.

Whitner v. State

328 S.C. 1; 492 S.E.2d 777 (S.C. Sup. Ct., 1997)

Justice Toal delivered the opinion of the court.

This case concerns the scope of the child abuse and endangerment statute in the South Carolina Children's Code. We hold the word "child" as used in that statute includes viable fetuses.

Facts

On April 20, 1992, Cornelia Whitner (Whitner) pled guilty to criminal child neglect for causing her baby to be born with cocaine metabolites in its system by reason of Whitner's ingestion of crack cocaine during the third trimester of her pregnancy. The circuit court judge sentenced Whitner to eight years in prison. Whitner did not appeal her conviction.

Thereafter, Whitner filed a petition for Post Conviction Relief (PCR), pleading the circuit court's lack of subject matter jurisdiction to accept her guilty plea as well as ineffective assistance of counsel. Her claim of ineffective assistance of counsel was based upon her lawyer's failure to advise her the statute under which she was being prosecuted might not apply to prenatal drug use. The petition was granted on both grounds. The State appeals.

Law/Analysis

A. Subject Matter Jurisdiction

The State first argues the PCR court erred in finding the sentencing circuit court lacked subject matter jurisdiction to accept Whitner's guilty plea. We agree.

Under South Carolina law, a circuit court lacks subject matter jurisdiction to accept a guilty plea to a nonexistent offense. For the sentencing court to have had subject matter jurisdiction to accept Whitner's plea, criminal child neglect would have to include an expectant mother's use of crack cocaine after the fetus is viable. All other issues are ancillary to this jurisdictional issue.

S.C. Code provides:

> Any person having the legal custody of any *child* or helpless person, who shall, without lawful excuse, refuse or neglect to provide, as defined in § 20-7-490, the proper care and attention for such *child* or helpless person, so that the life, health or comfort of such *child* or helpless person is endangered

> or is likely to be endangered, shall be guilty of a misdemeanor and shall be punished within the discretion of the circuit court (emphasis added).

The State contends this section encompasses maternal acts endangering or likely to endanger the life, comfort, or health of a viable fetus.

Under the Children's Code, "child" means a "person under the age of eighteen." The question for this Court, therefore, is whether a viable fetus is a "person" for purposes of the Children's Code.

In interpreting a statute, this Court's primary function is to ascertain the intent of the legislature. Of course, where a statute is complete, plain, and unambiguous, legislative intent must be determined from the language of the statute itself. We should consider, however, not merely the language of the particular clause being construed, but the word and its meaning in conjunction with the purpose of the whole statute and the policy of the law. Finally, there is a basic presumption that the legislature has knowledge of previous legislation as well as of judicial decisions construing that legislation when later statutes are enacted concerning related subjects.

South Carolina law has long recognized that viable fetuses are persons holding certain legal rights and privileges. In 1960, this Court decided *Hall v. Murphy*. . . . That case concerned the application of South Carolina's wrongful death statute to an infant who died four hours after her birth as a result of injuries sustained prenatally during viability. The Appellants argued that a viable fetus was not a person within the purview of the wrongful death statute, because, inter alia, a fetus is thought to have no separate being apart from the mother.

We found such a reason for exclusion from recovery "unsound, illogical and unjust," and concluded there was "no medical or other basis" for the "assumed identity" of mother and viable unborn child. In light of that conclusion, this Court unanimously held: "We have no difficulty in concluding that a fetus having reached that period of prenatal maturity where it is capable of independent life apart from its mother is a person."

Four years later, in *Fowler v. Woodward*, we interpreted *Hall* as supporting a finding that a viable fetus injured while still in the womb need not be born alive for another to maintain an action for the wrongful death of the fetus.

. . .

Fowler makes particularly clear that *Hall* rested on the concept of the viable fetus as a person vested with legal rights.

More recently, we held the word "person" as used in a criminal statute includes viable fetuses. *State v. Horne*, concerned South Carolina's murder statute. The defendant in that case stabbed his wife, who was nine months' pregnant, in the neck, arms, and abdomen. Although doctors performed an emergency caesarean section to deliver the child, the child died while still in the womb. The defendant was convicted of voluntary manslaughter and appealed his conviction on the ground South Carolina did not recognize the crime of feticide.

This Court disagreed. In a unanimous decision, we held it would be "grossly inconsistent . . . to construe a viable fetus as a 'person' for the purposes of imposing civil liability while refusing to give it a similar classification in the criminal context." Accordingly, the Court recognized the crime of feticide with respect to viable fetuses.

Similarly, we do not see any rational basis for finding a viable fetus is not a "person" in the present context. Indeed, It would be absurd to recognize the viable fetus as a person for purposes of homicide laws and wrongful death statutes but not for purposes of statutes proscribing child abuse. Our holding in *Hall* that a viable fetus is a person rested primarily on the plain meaning of the word "person" in light of existing medical knowledge concerning fetal development. We do not believe that the plain and ordinary meaning of the word "person" has changed in any way that would now deny viable fetuses status as persons.

The policies enunciated in the Children's Code also support our plain meaning reading of "person." . . . South Carolina's policy concerning children, expressly states: "It shall be the policy of this State to concentrate on the prevention of children's problems as the most important strategy which can be planned and implemented on behalf of children and their families." The abuse or neglect of a child at any time during childhood can exact a profound toll on the child herself as well as on society as a whole. However, the consequences of abuse or neglect which takes place after birth often pale in comparison to those resulting from abuse suffered by the viable fetus before birth. This policy of prevention supports a reading of the word "person" to include viable fetuses. Furthermore, the scope of the Children's Code is quite broad. It applies "to all children who have need of services." When coupled with the comprehensive remedial purposes of the Code, this language supports the inference that the legislature intended to include viable fetuses within the scope of the Code's protection.

Whitner advances several arguments against an interpretation of "person" as used in the Children's Code to include viable fetuses. We shall address each of Whitner's major arguments in turn.

Whitner's first argument concerns the number of bills introduced in the South Carolina General Assembly in the past five years addressing substance abuse by pregnant women. Some of these bills would have criminalized substance abuse by pregnant women; others would have addressed the issue through mandatory reporting, treatment, or intervention by social service agencies. Whitner suggests that the introduction of several bills touching the specific issue at hand evinces a belief by legislators that prior legislation had not addressed the issue. Whitner argues the introduction of the bills proves that [the child abuse law] section 20-7-50 was not intended to encompass abuse or neglect of a viable fetus.

We disagree with Whitner's conclusion about the significance of the proposed legislation. Generally, the legislature's subsequent acts "cast no light on the intent of the legislature which enacted the statute being construed." Rather, this Court will look first to the language of the statute to discern legislative intent, because the language itself is the best guide to legislative intent. Here, we see no reason to look beyond the statutory language. Additionally, our existing case law strongly supports our conclusion about the meaning of the statute's language.

Whitner also argues an interpretation of the statute that includes viable fetuses would lead to absurd results obviously not intended by the legislature. Specifically, she claims if we interpret "child" to include viable fetuses, every action by a pregnant woman that endangers or is likely to endanger a fetus, whether otherwise legal or illegal, would constitute unlawful neglect under the statute. For example, a woman might be prosecuted under section 20-7-50 for smoking or drinking during pregnancy. Whitner asserts these "absurd" results could not have been intended by the legislature and, therefore, the statute should not be construed to include viable fetuses.

We disagree for a number of reasons. First, the same arguments against the statute can be made whether or not the child has been born. After the birth of a child, a parent can be prosecuted under section 20-7-50 for an action that is likely to endanger the child without regard to whether the action is illegal in itself. For example, a parent who drinks excessively could, under certain circumstances, be guilty of child neglect or endangerment even though the underlying act — consuming alcoholic beverages — is itself legal. Obviously, the legislature did not think it "absurd" to allow prosecution of parents for such otherwise legal acts when the acts actually or potentially endanger the "life, health or comfort" of the parents born children. We see no reason such a result should be rendered absurd by the mere fact the child at issue is a viable fetus.

Moreover, we need not address this potential parade of horribles advanced by Whitner. In this case, which is the only case we are called upon to decide here, certain facts are clear. Whitner admits to having ingested crack cocaine during the third trimester of her pregnancy, which caused her child to be born with cocaine in its system. Although the precise effects of maternal crack use during pregnancy are somewhat unclear, it is well documented and within the realm of public knowledge that such use can cause serious harm to the viable unborn child. There can be no question here Whitner endangered the life, health, and comfort of her child. We need not decide any cases other than the one before us.

We are well aware of the many decisions from other states' courts throughout the country holding maternal conduct before the birth of the child does not give rise to criminal prosecution under state child abuse/endangerment or drug distribution statutes. Many of these cases were prosecuted under statutes forbidding delivery or distribution of illicit substances and depended on statutory construction of the terms "delivery" and "distribution." Obviously, such cases are inapplicable to the present situation. The cases concerning child endangerment statutes or construing the terms "child" and "person" are also distinguishable, because the states in which these cases were decided have entirely different bodies of case law from South Carolina. For example, in *Commonwealth v. Welch*, the Kentucky Supreme Court specifically noted Kentucky law has not construed the word "person" in the criminal homicide statute to include a fetus (viable or not). In *Reyes v. Superior Court*, the California Court of Appeals noted California law did not recognize a fetus as a "human being" within the purview of the state murder and manslaughter statutes, and that it was thus improper to find the fetus was a "child" for purposes of the felonious child endangerment statute.

Massachusetts, however, has a body of case law substantially similar to South Carolina's, yet a Massachusetts trial court has held that a mother pregnant with a viable fetus is not criminally liable for transmission of cocaine to the fetus. Specifically, Massachusetts law allows wrongful death actions on behalf of viable fetuses injured in utero who are not subsequently born alive. Similarly, Massachusetts law permits homicide prosecutions of third parties who kill viable fetuses. Because of the similarity of the case law in Massachusetts to ours, the *Pellegrini* decision merits examination.

In *Pellegrini*, the Massachusetts Superior Court found that state's distribution statute does not apply to the distribution of an illegal substance to a viable fetus. The statute at issue forbade distribution of cocaine to persons under the age of eighteen. Rather than construing the word "distribution," however, the superior court found that a viable fetus is not a "person under the age of eighteen" within the meaning of the statute. In so finding, the court had to distinguish *Lawrence* and *Cass*, supra, both of which held viable fetuses are "persons" for purposes of criminal laws in Massachusetts.

The Massachusetts trial court found *Lawrence* and *Cass* "accord legal rights to the unborn only where the mother's or parents' interest in the potentiality of life, not the state's interest, are sought to be vindicated." In other words, a viable fetus should only be accorded the rights of a person for the sake of its mother or both its parents. Under this rationale, the viable fetus lacks rights of its own that deserve vindication. Whitner suggests we should interpret our decisions in *Hall*, *Fowler*, and *Horne* to accord rights to the viable fetus only when doing so protects the special parent–child relationship rather than any individual rights of the fetus or any State interest in potential life. We do not think *Hall*, *Fowler*, and *Horne* can be interpreted so narrowly.

If the *Pellegrini* decision accurately characterizes the rationale underlying *Mone*, *Lawrence*, and *Cass*, then the reasoning of those cases differs substantially from our reasoning in *Hall*, *Fowler*, and *Home*, First, *Hall*, *Fowler*, and *Horne* were decided primarily on the basis of the meaning of "person" as understood in the light of existing medical knowledge, rather than based on any policy of protecting the relationship between mother and child. As a homicide case, *Horne* also rested on the State's — not the mother's — interest in vindicating the life of the viable fetus. Moreover, the United States Supreme Court has repeatedly held that the states have a compelling interest in the life of a viable fetus. If, as Whitner suggests we should, we read *Horne* only as a vindication of the mother's interest in the life of her unborn child, there would be no basis for prosecuting a mother who kills her viable fetus by stabbing it, by shooting it, or by other such means, yet a third party could be prosecuted for the very same acts. We decline to read *Horne* in a way that insulates the mother from all culpability for harm to her viable child. Because the rationale underlying our body of law — protection of the viable fetus — is radically different from that underlying the law of Massachusetts, we decline to follow the decision of the Massachusetts Superior Court in *Pellegrini*.

. . .

C. Constitutional issues

1. Fair Notice/Vagueness

Whitner argues that section 20-7-50 does not give her fair notice that her behavior is proscribed. We disagree.

The statute forbids any person having legal custody of a child from refusing or neglecting to provide proper care and attention to the child so that the life, health, or comfort of the child is endangered or is likely to be endangered. As we have found above, the plain meaning of "child" as used in this statute includes a viable fetus. Furthermore, it is common knowledge that use of cocaine during pregnancy can harm the viable unborn child. Given these facts, we do not see how Whitner can claim she lacked fair notice that her behavior constituted child endangerment as proscribed in section 20-7-50. Whitner had all the notice the Constitution requires.

2. Right to Privacy

Whitner argues that prosecuting her for using crack cocaine after her fetus attains viability unconstitutionally burdens her right of privacy, or, more specifically, her right to carry her pregnancy to term. We disagree.

. . .

First, the State's interest in protecting the life and health of the viable fetus is not merely legitimate. It is compelling. The United States Supreme Court in Casey recognized that the State possesses a profound interest in the potential life of the fetus, not only after the fetus is viable, but throughout the expectant mother's pregnancy.

Even more importantly, however, we do not think any fundamental right of Whitner's — or any right at all, for that matter — is Implicated under the present scenario. It strains belief for Whitner to argue that using crack cocaine during pregnancy is encompassed within the constitutionally recognized right of privacy. Use of crack cocaine is illegal, period. No one here argues that laws criminalizing the use of crack cocaine are themselves unconstitutional. If the State wishes to impose additional criminal penalties on pregnant women who engage in this already illegal conduct because of the effect the conduct has on the viable fetus, it may do so. We do not see how the fact of pregnancy elevates the use of crack cocaine to the lofty status of a fundamental right.

Moreover, as a practical matter, we do not see how our interpretation of section 20-7-50 imposes a burden on Whitner's right to carry her child to term. . . . [D]uring her pregnancy after the fetus attained viability, Whitner enjoyed the same freedom to use cocaine that she enjoyed earlier in and predating her pregnancy — none whatsoever. Simply put, South Carolina's child abuse and endangerment statute as applied to this case does not restrict Whitner's freedom in any way that it was not already restricted. The State's imposition of an additional penalty when a pregnant woman with a viable fetus engages in the already proscribed behavior does not burden a woman's right to carry her pregnancy to term; rather, the additional penalty simply recognizes that a third party (the viable fetus or newborn child) is harmed by the behavior.

Section 20-7-50 does not burden Whitner's right to carry her pregnancy to term or any other privacy right. Accordingly, we find no violation of the Due Process Clause of the Fourteenth Amendment.

Conclusion

For the foregoing reasons, the decision of the PCR Court is Reversed.

Justice Finney, dissenting.

I respectfully dissent, and would affirm the grant of postconviction relief to respondent Whitner.

The issue before the Court is whether a fetus is a "child" within the meaning of S.C. Code Ann. § 20-7-50, a statute which makes it a misdemeanor for a "person having legal custody of any child or helpless person" to unlawfully neglect that child or helpless person. Since this is a penal statute, it is strictly construed against the State and in favor of respondent. [Note 1 states that, after this case arose, the statute was amended to change the classification from misdemeanor to felony.]

The term child for purposes of § 20-7-50 is defined as a "person under the age of eighteen" unless a different meaning is required by the circumstances. We have already held that this same definition found in another part of the Children's Code means a child in being and not a fetus. It would be incongruous at best to hold the definition of "child" in the civil context of Doe is more restrictive than it is in the criminal context we consider today.

More importantly, it is apparent from a reading of the entire statute that the word child in § 20-7-50 means a child in being and not a fetus. A plain reading of the entire child neglect statute demonstrates the intent to criminalize only acts directed at children, and not those which may harm fetuses. First, § 20-7-50 does not impose criminal liability on every person who neglects a child, but only on a person having legal custody of that child. The statutory requirement of legal custody is evidence of intent to extend the statute's reach only to children, because the concept of legal custody is simply inapplicable to a fetus. Second, § 20-7-50 refers to S. C. Code Ann. § 20-7-490 for the definition of neglect. Section 20-7-490 defines a neglected child as one harmed or threatened with harm, and further defines harm. The vast majority of acts which constitute statutory harm under § 20-7-490 are acts which can only be directed against a child, and not towards a fetus. The reliance upon § 20-7-490 in § 20-7-50 is further evidence that the term child as used in the child neglect statute does not encompass a fetus. Read in context, and in light of the statutory purpose of protecting persons of tender years, it is clear that "child" as used in § 20-7-50 means a child in being.

At most, the majority only suggests that the term "child" as used in § 20-7-50 is ambiguous. This suggestion of ambiguity is created not by reference to our decisions under the Children's Code or by reference to the statutory language and applicable rules of statutory construction, but by reliance on decisions in two different fields of the law, civil wrongful death and common law feticide. Here, we deal with the

Children's Code, and the meaning of language used in a criminal statute under that Code. We have already indicated that a child within the meaning of § 20-7-90(A) (1985), which criminalizes non-support, must be one already born. Even if these wrongful death, common law, and Children's Code decisions are sufficient to render the term child in § 20-7-50 ambiguous, it is axiomatic that the ambiguity must be resolved in respondent's favor.

I would affirm.

Justice Moore, concurring with the dissent.

I concur with the dissent in this case but write separately to express my concerns with today's decision.

In my view, the repeated failure of the legislature to pass proposed bills addressing the problem of drug use during pregnancy is evidence the child abuse and neglect statute is not intended to apply in this instance. This Court should not invade what is clearly the sole province of the legislative branch. At the very least, the legislature's failed attempts to enact a statute regulating a pregnant woman's conduct indicate the complexity of this issue. While the majority opinion is perhaps an argument for what the law should be, it is for the General Assembly, and not this Court, to make that determination by means of a clearly drawn statute. With today's decision, the majority not only ignores legislative intent but embarks on a course of judicial activism rejected by every other court to address the issue.

As discussed in the Chief Justice's dissent, we are bound by the rules of statutory construction to strictly construe a criminal statute in favor of the defendant and resolve any ambiguity in her favor. I cannot accept the majority's assertion that the child abuse and neglect statute unambiguously includes a "viable fetus." If that is the case, then why is the majority compelled to go to such great lengths to ascertain that a "viable fetus" is a "child?"

Contrary to the majority's strained analysis in this case, one need look no further than the language of § 20-7-50 to clearly discern legislative intent that the statute apply only to children in being. "Legal custody" is not a qualification applicable to a viable fetus. I simply disagree the legislature intended a statute entitled "Unlawful neglect of child or helpless person by legal custodian" to render a pregnant woman criminally liable for any type of conduct potentially harmful to the unborn fetus.

In construing this statute to include conduct not contemplated by the legislature, the majority has rendered the statute vague and set for itself the task of determining what conduct is unlawful. Is a pregnant woman's failure to obtain prenatal care unlawful? Failure to quit smoking or drinking? Although the majority dismisses this issue as not before it, the impact of today's decision is to render a pregnant woman potentially criminally liable for myriad acts which the legislature has not seen fit to criminalize. To ignore this "down-the-road" consequence in a case of this import is unrealistic. The majority insists that parents may already be held liable for drinking after a child is born. This is untrue, however, without some further act on the part of the parent. A parent who drinks and then hits her child or fails to come home may be guilty of criminal neglect. The mere fact of drinking, however, does not constitute neglect of a child in being.

The majority attempts to support an overinclusive construction of the child abuse and neglect statute by citing other legal protections extended equally to a viable fetus and a child in being. The only law, however, that specifically regulates the conduct of a mother toward her unborn child is our abortion statute under which a viable fetus is in fact treated differently from a child in being. [Note 1 highlights that a woman may have a legal abortion of a viable fetus if necessary to preserve her health while, of course, she may not justify the death of a child in being on this ground.]

The majority argues for equal treatment of viable fetuses and children, yet its construction of the statute results in even greater inequities. If the statute applies only when a fetus is "viable," a pregnant woman can use cocaine for the first twenty-four weeks of her pregnancy, the most dangerous period for the fetus, and be immune from prosecution under the statute so long as she quits drug use before the fetus becomes viable. Further, a pregnant woman now faces up to ten years in prison for ingesting drugs during pregnancy but can have an illegal abortion and receive only a two-year sentence for killing her viable fetus.

Because I disagree with the conclusion § 20-7-50 includes a viable fetus, I would affirm the grant of post-conviction relief.

Notes and Queries

1. The case explores well the central arguments made by proponents of criminalization efforts. Opponents of efforts to criminalize perinatal drug use find such efforts problematic and suggest that they: discriminate against individuals based on their gender, race, and poverty status; reduce access to proper care; and violate women's rights to privacy. Persuasive?

2. What directions should the legal system take if we accept current social findings relating to perinatal drug abuse? Reviews of social science repeatedly find two points. First, the best evidence links alcohol abuse to birth defects, and no other drug has yet to be shown to have such powerful effects. Second, the negative effects of drug abuse arise less from the drug abuse itself than from the environment and circumstances in which the mother and child find themselves: domestic violence, poverty, and the high needs of babies that may result from parental abuse. See Steven J. Ondersma, Sharon M. Simpson, Elizabeth V. Brestan & Martin Ward (2000). Prenatal drug exposure and social policy: The search for an appropriate response. *Child Maltreatment*, 5, 93–108; Stephen Magura & Alexandre B. Laudet (1996). Parental substance abuse and child maltreatment: Review and implications for intervention. *Children and Youth Services Review*, 18, 193–220.

Research Comments

1. Compared to research examining the effects of illicit drugs, research examining the impact of mothers' use of alcohol seems quite impressive. Much of the research has focused on the fetal alcohol syndrome (FAS), which refers to a constellation of physical, behavioral, and cognitive abnormalities. In addition to the classic dysmorphic facial features, prenatal and postnatal growth abnormalities, and mental retardation that define the condition, approximately 80 percent of children with FAS have microcephaly and behavioral abnormalities. As many as 50 percent of affected children also exhibit poor coordination, hypotonia, attention-deficit hyperactivity disorder, decreased adipose tissue, and identifiable facial anomalies, such as maxillary hypoplasia, cleft palate, and micrognathia. Cardiac defects, hemangiomas, and eye or ear abnormalities are also common. Importantly, researchers also use the terms alcohol-related neurodevelopmental disorder (ARND) and alcohol-related birth defects (ARBD) to describe conditions in which there is a history of maternal alcohol exposure (defined as substantial regular intake or heavy episodic drinking) and an outcome validated by clinical or animal research to be associated with that exposure. This new terminology uses a pathophysiologic basis for the diagnostic categories to describe conditions resulting from prenatal alcohol exposure. Children with FAS, ARND, and ARBD may manifest cognitive, behavioral, and psychosocial problems that cause lifelong disabilities. Most notably, researchers note abnormal cognitive functioning that manifests itself in many domains, including specific mathematical deficiency, difficulty with abstraction, and problems with generalizing from one situation to another. The affected persons also demonstrate poor attention and concentration skills, memory deficits, and impaired judgment, comprehension, and abstract reasoning. Behavioral issues, such as hyperactivity and impulsivity, and conduct problems, such as lying, stealing, stubbornness, and oppositional behavior, are noted as common and as quantitatively and qualitatively different from those found in other forms of mental retardation. They also tend to evidence maladaptive social functioning, as revealed by failure to consider consequences for their actions, lack of response to appropriate social cues, lack of reciprocal friendships, social withdrawal, sullenness, mood lability, teasing and bullying behavior, and periods of high anxiety and excessive unhappiness. Secondary disabilities, such as mental health problems, chemical dependency, failure to develop appropriate sexual behavior, and consequent legal problems, also are common in adults diagnosed with FAS. See Committee on Substance Abuse and Committee on Children with Disabilities (2000). Fetal alcohol syndrome and alcohol-related neurodevelopmental disorders. *Pediatrics*, 106, 358–361.

2. FAS is estimated to occur at the rate of 5.2/10,000 live births in the United States. Higher rates are reported among selected subgroups (e.g., 30/10,000 among Native Americans). As expected, a number of factors determine the outcome of

a pregnancy during which the mother consumes alcohol. Current data do not support the concept of a "safe level" of alcohol consumption by pregnant women below which no damage to a fetus will occur. Current evidence suggests that while IQ scores less than 70 in this population increase the likelihood of negative outcomes, early diagnosis and intervention may reduce the occurrence of secondary disabilities. See Committee on Substance Abuse and Committee on Children with Disabilities (2000). Fetal alcohol syndrome and alcohol-related neurodevelopmental disorders. *Pediatrics*, 106, 358–361.

3. With respect to the overall negative impact of parental drinking, research has examined the impact of alcoholism on family violence. Although clinical reports often indicate a strong link between parental alcoholism and family violence, the empirical data provides a highly inconsistent picture. Studies focusing first on family violence and second on incidence of parental alcoholism (as well as those reflecting on the dynamics of alcoholic families and subsequent assessment of family violence) both have resulted in highly inconsistent rates of reported spousal and child abuse. One review reported extremely wide-ranging rates, from 2 percent to 62 percent, of alcoholism among parents who abuse their children; another study found that the reported rate of child abuse among alcoholic parents varied between 0 percent and 92 percent. See Jeannette L. Johnson & Michelle Leff (1999). Children of substance abusers: Overview of research findings. *Pediatrics*, 103, 1085–1099.

Palmore v. Sidoti

466 U.S. 429; 104 S. Ct. 1879 (1984)

Chief Justice Burger delivered the opinion of the Court.

We granted certiorari to review a judgment of a state court divesting a natural mother of the custody of her infant child because of her remarriage to a person of a different race.

I

When petitioner Linda Sidoti Palmore and respondent Anthony J. Sidoti, both Caucasians, were divorced in May 1980 in Florida, the mother was awarded custody of their 3-year-old daughter.

In September 1981 the father sought custody of the child by filing a petition to modify the prior judgment because of changed conditions. The change was that the child's mother was then cohabiting with a Negro, Clarence Palmore, Jr., whom she married two months later. Additionally, the father made several allegations of instances in which the mother had not properly cared for the child.

After hearing testimony from both parties and considering a court counselor's investigative report, the court noted that the father had made allegations about the child's care, but the court made no findings with respect to these allegations. On the contrary, the court made a finding that "there is no issue as to either party's devotion to the child, adequacy of housing facilities, or respectability of the new spouse of either parent."

The court then addressed the recommendations of the court counselor, who had made an earlier report "in [another] case coming out of this circuit also involving the social consequences of an interracial marriage." From this vague reference to that earlier case, the court turned to the present case and noted the counselor's recommendation for a change in custody because "[the] wife [petitioner] has chosen for herself and for her child, a life-style unacceptable to the father and to society.... The child ... is, or at school age will be, subject to environmental pressures not of choice."

The court then concluded that the best interests of the child would be served by awarding custody to the father. The court's rationale is contained in the following:

> The father's evident resentment of the mother's choice of a black partner is not sufficient to wrest custody from the mother. It is of some significance, however, that the mother did see fit to bring a man into her home and carry on a sexual relationship with him without being married to him. Such action tended to place gratification of her own desires ahead of her concern for the child's future welfare. This Court feels that despite the strides that have been made in bettering relations between the races in this country, it is inevitable that Melanie will, if allowed to remain in her present situation and attains school age and thus more vulnerable to peer pressures, suffer from the social stigmatization that is sure to come.

The Second District Court of Appeal affirmed without opinion, thus denying the Florida Supreme Court jurisdiction to review the case. We granted certiorari and we reverse.

II

The judgment of a state court determining or reviewing a child custody decision is not ordinarily a likely candidate for review by this Court. However, the court's opinion, after stating that the "father's evident resentment of the mother's choice of a black partner is not sufficient" to deprive her of custody, then turns to what it regarded as the damaging impact on the child from remaining in a racially mixed household. This raises important federal concerns arising from the Constitution's commitment to eradicating discrimination based on race.

The Florida court did not focus directly on the parental qualifications of the natural mother or her present husband, or indeed on the father's qualifications to have custody of the child. The court found that "there is no issue as to either party's devotion to the child, adequacy of housing facilities, or respectability of the new spouse of either parent." This, taken with the absence of any negative finding as to the quality of the care provided by the mother, constitutes a rejection of any claim of petitioner's unfitness to continue the custody of her child.

The court correctly stated that the child's welfare was the controlling factor. But that court was entirely candid and made no effort to place its holding on any ground other than race. Taking the court's findings and rationale at face value, it is clear that the outcome would have been different had petitioner married a Caucasian male of similar respectability.

A core purpose of the Fourteenth Amendment was to do away with all governmentally imposed discrimination based on race. Classifying persons according to their race is more likely to reflect racial prejudice than legitimate public concerns; the race, not the person, dictates the category. Such classifications are subject to the most exacting scrutiny; to pass constitutional muster, they must be justified by a compelling governmental interest and must be "necessary . . . to the accomplishment" of their legitimate purpose.

The State, of course, has a duty of the highest order to protect the interests of minor children, particularly those of tender years. In common with most states, Florida law mandates that custody determinations be made in the best interests of the children involved. The goal of granting custody based on the best interests of the child is indisputably a substantial governmental interest for purposes of the Equal Protection Clause.

It would ignore reality to suggest that racial and ethnic prejudices do not exist or that all manifestations of those prejudices have been eliminated. There is a risk that a child living with a stepparent of a different race may be subject to a variety of pressures and stresses not present if the child were living with parents of the same racial or ethnic origin.

The question, however, is whether the reality of private biases and the possible injury they might inflict are permissible considerations for removal of an infant child from the custody of its natural mother. We have little difficulty concluding that they are not. The Constitution cannot control such prejudices but neither can it tolerate them. Private biases may be outside the reach of the law, but the law cannot, directly or indirectly, give them effect. "Public officials sworn to uphold the Constitution may not avoid a constitutional duty by bowing to the hypothetical effects of private racial prejudice that they assume to be both widely and deeply held."

. . .

. . . The effects of racial prejudice, however real, cannot justify a racial classification removing an infant child from the custody of its natural mother found to be an appropriate person to have such custody. . . .

The judgment of the District Court of Appeal is reversed.

It is so ordered.

Notes and Queries

1. This case finds that private biases and social prejudices have no place in custody determinations, that they are not permissible considerations for removal of children from the custody of their natural parents. Given what you know so far about parental adequacy, does this seem true in reality?

2. Taking the Court's reasoning seriously and expansively would have a dramatic impact on laws regulating family relationships, especially parent–child relationships. Why is this case rarely used to challenge laws overtly imposing moral values on parent–child relationships? What do we still learn from *Palmore v. Sidoti*?

Bottoms v. Bottoms

249 Va. 410; 457 S.E.2d 102 (Va. Sup. Ct., 1995)

Justice Compton delivered the opinion of the court.

This is a child custody dispute between a child's mother and maternal grandmother. The sole issue is whether the Court of Appeals erred in deciding that the child's best interests would be served by awarding custody to the mother. We conclude that the Court of Appeals erred, and reverse.

. . .

In March 1993, appellant Pamela Kay Bottoms filed a petition against her daughter, appellee Sharon Lynne Bottoms, . . . seeking an award of custody of the daughter's son, born in July 1991. In the petition, the grandmother alleged that the "infant is currently living in an environment which is harmful to his mental and physical well being." Following a hearing, at which both parties were represented by counsel, the juvenile court awarded custody to the grandmother and granted the mother restricted visitation rights. The mother appealed. . . .

. . .

The mother appealed to the Court of Appeals. A three-judge panel unanimously reversed and vacated the trial court's order, remanding the case to the circuit court for entry of an order "effectuating the resumption of custody by the mother of her son." We awarded the grandmother this appeal from the Court of Appeals' June 1994 order.

"In all child custody cases, including those between a parent and a non-parent, 'the best interests of the child are paramount and form the lodestar for the guidance of the court in determining the dispute.'" In a custody dispute between a parent and non-parent, "the law presumes that the child's best interests will be served when in the custody of its parent."

. . .

In custody cases, the welfare of the child takes precedence over the rights of the parent. But, when the contest is between parent and non-parent, this rule is conditioned upon the principle that a parent's rights "are to be respected if at all consonant with the best interests of the child." . . .

. . .

This child's mother, born in February 1970, "dropped out" of school in the twelfth grade. Until she was 18 years of age, she resided at home with her mother, who is a divorcee, and her mother's boyfriend.

Upon leaving home, the child's mother was supported by and lived with a cousin, a friend, and a sister respectively. In December 1989, the child's mother married Dennis Doustou, whom she had been dating for several years. She left Doustou after eight months of marriage, and resumed living with the cousin for a while. The child was born during the separation in July 1991. The parties were divorced, and the mother was awarded custody of her child. The child's father has expressed little interest in his son and pays no child support.

The maternal grandmother, born in January 1951, resides in the Richmond area. Her boyfriend ceased living with her shortly before the juvenile court hearing, and has not returned. The grandmother did not complete her high school education, and has worked as a nurse's aide and manager of a shoe store. She currently is employed as a "nanny," taking care of two children.

During the two-year period before the trial court hearing, the child had spent 70 percent of the time with the grandmother and 30 percent with his mother. The grandmother has kept the child for "weeks at a time" and during "every weekend since he's been born." On at least three occasions during that period, the mother left the child with the grandmother without informing her of the mother's whereabouts or how she could be reached "in the event something happened to the child."

Following the mother's separation from Doustou, she continued a "relationship" with another man that had begun during her marriage. She contracted a venereal disease during this relationship that prevents her from having additional children. During the child's first year, the mother "slept with two or three different guys, maybe four, in the same room" with the child "where his crib was." At the time, the mother "lived two blocks away" from the grandmother, and the mother kept the child's "suitcase packed" for visits to the grandmother's home. The mother said that she has "had trouble" with her temper, and that when the child was about "a year" old, she "popped him on his leg too hard a couple of times," and left her fingerprints there. She has had "counseling" in an effort to control her temper.

At "some point subsequent to" the child's birth, the mother lived in a dwelling with yet another man who supported her for more than a year. After the mother "left" this man, she "lived with" a lesbian "couple."

Except for brief employment as a grocery store cashier, the mother had been unemployed during most of the three-year period prior to the trial court hearing. She was receiving "welfare money" which often was spent to "do her fingernails before the baby would get any food."

During May 1992, ten months before the juvenile court hearing, 16 months before the trial court hearing, and when her son was ten months old, the mother met April Wade, a lesbian. Wade, born in April 1966, had been discharged from the U.S. Army in 1986. Wade is a "recovering alcoholic."

The mother and Wade "moved in together" in September 1992. From that time, with the exception of a two-week period, the mother and Wade have lived in "a lesbian relationship." According to the mother, the relationship involves hugging and kissing, patting "on the bottom," sleeping in the same bed, "fondling," and "oral sex." The mother testified that she loves Wade and that they "have a lifetime commitment."

At the time of the juvenile court hearing, the mother, the child, and Wade were living in a two-bedroom apartment with "Evelyn," another lesbian. "At one time," the child's bed was in the room where the mother and Wade slept, having "sex in the same bed." At one point in her testimony, however, when asked "how many times did you do it when the child was sleeping in the same bedroom," the mother responded, "None." She said that she and Wade displayed other signs of affection "in front of" the child.

Wade, employed as a gift shop manager, supports the mother. The pair lives in an apartment complex in Western Henrico County. Wade has become "a parent figure" to the child, who calls Wade "Da Da."

Two months before the petition for custody was filed, the mother revealed her lesbian relationship to the grandmother. This disclosure alienated the two.

During the period after the juvenile court hearing, when regimented visitation with the mother began, the child demonstrated certain traits. For example, when the child returned to the grandmother from being with the mother, he would "stomp" his foot, tell himself to "go to the corner," and then would stand in the corner of a room, facing the wall. He curses, saying "shit" and "damn," language never used in the grandmother's home. On one occasion, when the mother and Wade "came to pick him up," the child "held his breath, turned purple He didn't want to go with her," according to the grandmother. During a period in mid-1993, each time the mother "would come pick him up," the child would scream and cry.

Wade has admitted she "hit" the child. Also, on one occasion, when an argument developed between the mother and Wade, on the one hand, and the grandmother, on the other, about the timing of the exchange of the child for visitation, Wade said during the quarrel, "I might end up killing somebody." According to the grandmother, the child is "always neglected." For example, when the child returns to the grandmother's home, she testified that he "can't even sit down in the bathtub. That's neglect from changing his diaper. He is so red."

At the conclusion of the hearing, the guardian ad litem made a closing statement to the trial judge. Saying that he "took this appointment very seriously," the guardian ad litem stated he had "done extensive reading in many areas," including "the effect homosexuality will have on the rearing of children." He stated that he had "talked with psychiatrists in the field," and met "at length" with the mother, the grandmother, Wade, and the child, and "interviewed all of these parties as best I could." He asked another attorney, a woman, to assist him in order to obtain "another perspective." The guardian ad litem said that he and his associate "literally" spent the entire month before the hearing on the case.

In evaluating the case, the guardian ad litem said he is "a pretty open-minded guy" without any biases, "especially involving a homosexual issue." He stated that the child's father "should be ashamed of himself" for having no interest in the child and for contributing "nothing towards financial support of the child."

He stated that Wade is "a very nice person," but "she has a lot of baggage that she brings along with her" causing him to question her "stability." He observed that Wade genuinely "loves the child," but in view of her "rather sketchy" employment history, he was "curious as to how she will support the child if custody goes with" Wade and the mother.

Commenting on the mother, the guardian ad litem said he has "no question that she loves [the child] very much," but he found her to be a "very . . . immature young lady." He noted that she has "never really completed anything," has "jumped from relationship to relationship, from one place to another," and has "never really put roots down." Observing that "she has no employment to speak of, no skills, no education" and that her "future in the job market . . . is rather bleak," nevertheless, the guardian ad litem said, she is the child's natural mother, and "the love between a natural mother and child is something that's almost sacred." He stated that he "firmly" believed that the mother's love for the child "is an honest love" and "that she comes to this court with clean hands in that regard."

Referring to the grandmother, he said he found "her to be an equally very nice person, a very sincere person." He said he regarded her "as a bit more than" a third-party stranger, and that she has had "more than a typical grandmother relationship with the child." He noted she "has taken care of this child the majority of the child's life," and "has provided for the child financially, fed the child, clothed the child," and "taken the child to the doctor."

. . .

The trial judge, announcing his decision from the bench at the conclusion of the hearing, said the dispute "presents the question . . . whether the child's best interest is served by a transfer of the custody of the child from [his] mother to [his] maternal grandmother." Stating that the mother's conduct is "illegal," and constitutes a felony under the Commonwealth's criminal laws, and that "her conduct is immoral," the court recognized the "presumption in the law in favor of the custody being with the natural parent."

Mentioning the evidence of lesbianism and specified "other evidence" in the case not involving homosexual conduct, the trial court concluded from "all the facts and circumstances . . . of the case," that "the custody will be with the grandmother."

The Court of Appeals concluded that "the evidence fails to prove" that the mother "abused or neglected her son, that her lesbian relationship with April Wade has or will have a deleterious effect on her son, or that she is an unfit parent." "To the contrary," said the Court of Appeals, the evidence showed that the mother "is and has been a fit and nurturing parent who has adequately provided and cared for her son. No evidence tended to prove that the child will be harmed by remaining with his mother." The court held "that the trial court abused its discretion by invoking the state's authority to take the child from the custody of his natural mother . . . and by transferring custody to a non-parent, . . . the child's maternal grandmother."

We disagree. The Court of Appeals failed to give proper deference upon appellate review to the trial court's factual findings, and misapplied the law to the facts viewed from a proper appellate perspective.

The evidence plainly is sufficient, when applying the clear and convincing standard and when viewing the facts from the correct appellate perspective, to support the trial court's findings that the parental presumption has been rebutted, that the mother is an unfit custodian at this time, and that the child's best interests would be promoted by awarding custody to the grandmother.

Among the factors to be weighed in determining unfitness are the parent's misconduct that affects the child, neglect of the child, and a demonstrated unwillingness and inability to promote the emotional and physical well-being of the child. Other important considerations include the nature of the home environment and moral climate in which the child is to be raised.

We have held, however, that a lesbian mother is not per se an unfit parent. Conduct inherent in lesbianism is punishable as a Class 6 felony in the Commonwealth; thus, that conduct is another important consideration in determining custody.

And, while the legal rights of a parent should be respected in a custody proceeding, those technical rights may be disregarded if demanded by the interests of the child.

In the present case, the record shows a mother who, although devoted to her son, refuses to subordinate her own desires and priorities to the child's welfare. . . .

. . .

And, we shall not overlook the mother's relationship with Wade, and the environment in which the child would be raised if custody is awarded the mother. We have previously said that living daily under conditions stemming from active lesbianism practiced in the home may impose a burden upon a child by reason of the "social condemnation" attached to such an arrangement, which will inevitably afflict the child's relationships with its "peers and with the community at large." We do not retreat from that statement; such a result is likely under these facts. Also, Wade has struck the child and, when there was a dispute over visitation, she has threatened violence when her views were not accepted.

. . .

Thus, the judgment of the Court of Appeals will be reversed and the case will be remanded . . . awarding custody of the child to Pamela Kay Bottoms.

Reversed and remanded.

Justice Keenan, dissenting

This Court has held, as the majority states, that a lesbian mother is not per se an unfit parent. Nevertheless, the majority ignores the trial court's refusal to follow this established law of the Commonwealth.

The record plainly shows that the trial court made a per se finding of unfitness based on the mother's homosexual conduct. The trial court stated:

> I will tell you first that the mother's conduct is illegal. It is a Class 6 felony in the Commonwealth of Virginia. I will tell you that it is the opinion of this Court that her conduct is immoral. And it is the opinion of this Court that the conduct of Sharon Bottoms renders her an unfit parent.

The trial court added to this statement only by citing two other factors to support its custody award. These factors were the "social condemnation" that would "inevitably" affect the child, and "other evidence of the child being affected or afflicted with the evidence [sic] which is unrebutted of the cursing, the evidence of the child standing in the corner."

As the Court of Appeals properly recognized, "adverse effects of a parent's homosexuality on a child cannot be assumed without specific proof." Although there is no evidence in this record showing that the mother's homosexual conduct is harmful to the child, the majority improperly presumes that its own perception of societal opinion and the mother's homosexual conduct are germane to the issue whether the mother is an unfit parent. Thus, the majority commits the same error as the trial court by attaching importance to factors not shown by the evidence to have an adverse effect on the child.

. . .

Notes and Queries

1. This case is somewhat peculiar in that it pits a custody dispute by a biological mother against a grandmother. What is peculiar is that the parental rights are essentially terminated even though the child welfare system has neither determined abuse (at least to the extent that the child was not removed from her mother) nor has child welfare offered services to unify the family.

2. The court rules that the mother's sexual orientation does not make her "*per se* an unfit parent" but that, since lesbianism is a crime, it is an important consideration in awarding custody. The dissent interprets the court's approach as adopting a *per se* rule finding of unfitness based on the mother's homosexual conduct. Do you agree?

Research Comments

1. Attempts to classify states' legislative and judicial approaches to gay and lesbian parenting note that approximately one-third of states adopt a *per se* rule. That approach divests the trial court of any discretion to grant custody to particular individuals. For example, all prospective parents falling into a particular category — such as being gay or lesbian, or cohabiting with a same-sex adult to whom they are not married — are necessarily considered unfit or undesirable. If the adopting individual falls into any of the undesirable categories, the trial court does not need to examine the case's other specific facts relating to that individual. As a result, any openly gay or lesbian individual will fall into a prohibited category and will automatically be disqualified as a potential parent. This rule assumes that gay and lesbian parenting never furthers the best interests of the child. On the other hand, approximately two-thirds of state jurisdictions adopt a nexus test that gives judges broad discretion in assessing the best interests of the child. Using the nexus test, the judge considers a parent's character fitness, parenting ability, and the significance of any other specific characteristics or conduct on an individual basis. When the court must address issues involving a homosexual parent, it generally examines whether the parent's sexuality or sexual conduct will adversely impact the child. If there are no signs of adverse impact, then sexuality is not pertinent to determining the best interests of the child and sexual preference is irrelevant. Thus, a nexus or causal connection must exist between an individual parent's homosexuality and harm to the particular child in question before the parent's homosexuality is considered relevant to the adoption or custody determination. See Theodore J. Stein (1996). Child custody and visitation: The rights of lesbian and gay parents. *Social Service Review*, 70, 436–450.

2. Which test do you find most fair? Many approve of the nexus test, given that (1) it is based on the general family law principle that most parental characteristics are relevant only if they can be shown to have a negative impact on the child, and (2) it requires an individualized determination of parental fitness for each case and does not dictate any particular result in any case. Persuasive?

3. Many approve of the nexus test because it leaves broad road discretion to trial courts. That discretion, however, leads to both its strength as well as to its weaknesses. It is protective of parental rights in that lesbian and gay parents will not be automatically disqualified from adopting. On the other hand, it is not that

protective, most notably because a court's judicial discretion may lead a court to consider alternative theories or approaches that still end up discriminating against adoptions by gays and lesbians. Courts have articulated a nexus test in cases that both protect and discriminate against these parents. As the leading case suggests, courts often make the following arguments to support denying custody to gay and lesbian parents: Lesbianism and sodomy are criminal acts, gay parents pose a special risk for molesting/harming their children, they also increase the likelihood that the children will suffer social condemnation and stigma, homosexuality is a transmittable disease, and homosexual parents will adversely affect the moral development of their children. Which of these arguments do you find most persuasive?

4. The American Psychological Association (APA) submitted a brief to the Supreme Court of Virginia arguing that: (1) Social science research indicates that (a) there are no significant differences between children raised by lesbian mothers or gay fathers and those raised by heterosexual parents, (b) the overall psychological health of children raised by lesbian mothers or gay fathers does not differ from that of children raised by heterosexual parents, (c) no differences have been reported between the social relationships of children raised by lesbian mothers or gay fathers and children raised by heterosexual parents, (d) a parent's sexual orientation does not influence the gender identity, gender role behavior, or sexual orientation of his or her child, (e) lesbian mothers and gay fathers are not likely to be unfit parents, and (f) lesbian mothers and gay fathers have parenting skills comparable to those of heterosexual parents; (2) professional social science organizations have rejected the view that lesbians and gay men as a group are dysfunctional; (3) a natural parent in an openly lesbian or gay relationship is entitled to the presumption of parental fitness; and (4) the fact that sodomy continues to be punishable as a felony under Virginia law is not grounds for depriving a lesbian or gay parent of custody. See *Bottoms v. Bottoms*, Supreme Court of Virginia, No. 94-1166, Brief of Amici Curiae, American Academy of Child and Adolescent Psychiatry, American Psychological Association, National Association of Social Workers, Inc., et al. http://www.psyclaw.org/bottomsbrief.html. Do you agree with the APA's position? Should the APA and other scientific associations submit briefs to courts and take positions?

5. The American Academy of Pediatrics recently released a Technical Report concluding that, although gay and lesbian parents may not be able to protect their children fully from the effects of stigmatization and discrimination, a parent's sexual orientation is not a variable that, in itself, predicts the ability to provide a home environment that supports children's development. Gay fathers reveal substantial evidence of nurturance and investment in their paternal role and are no different from heterosexual fathers in providing appropriate recreation, encouraging autonomy, or dealing with general problems of parenting. Compared with heterosexual fathers, gay fathers adhere to stricter disciplinary guidelines, place

greater emphasis on guidance and the development of cognitive skills, and are more involved in their children's development. Similarly, few differences exist between lesbian and heterosexual mothers' self-esteem, psychological adjustment, and attitudes toward child-rearing. Lesbian mothers fall within the range of normal psychological functioning on interviews and psychological assessments; they do not differ from heterosexual mothers on standardized measures of self-esteem, anxiety, depression, and parenting stress. Lesbian mothers strongly endorse child-centered attitudes and commitment to their maternal roles; they evidence more concern with providing male role models for their children than divorced heterosexual mothers. Lesbian and heterosexual mothers describe themselves similarly in marital and maternal interests, current lifestyles, and child-rearing practices. They report similar role conflicts, social support networks, and coping strategies. Several studies comparing children who have a lesbian mother with children who have a heterosexual mother do not report significant differences between such groups on personality measures, measures of peer group relationships, self-esteem, behavioral difficulties, academic success, or warmth and quality of family relationships. See Ellen C. Perrin & Committee on Psychosocial Aspects of Child and Family Health (2002). Technical report: Co-parent or second-parent adoption by same-sex parents. *Pediatrics*, 109, 341–344.

In the Interests of Tiffany

214 Wis. 2d 302; 571 N.W.2d 872 (Wisc. Ct. App., 1997)

Justice Schudson delivered the opinion of the court.

Tiffany was born on September 5, 1990, to Patty and Allen, who are biological siblings. Tiffany is the second of three children Patty and Allen have produced through their incestuous relationship. On March 31, 1994, Tiffany was removed from her parental home and placed in foster care because Patty and Allen had abandoned her at the home of a baby-sitter. Tiffany had become sick while in the sitter's care and needed to see a doctor; her parents could not be found. Consequently, after the sitter contacted the authorities, Tiffany was taken into the custody of the Milwaukee County Department of Human Services.

On March 8, 1995, the juvenile court found Tiffany to be a Child in Need of Protection or Services, pursuant to § 48.13(10). The court entered a dispositional order placing Tiffany outside her parents' home for one year and setting conditions for Tiffany's return to them. On April 1, 1996, the State filed a petition to terminate Patty's and Allen's parental rights to Tiffany on the ground of their incestuous parenthood.

A trial to the court was held on August 29, 1996. In the first phase, the fact-finding hearing under § 48.424, the State established that Patty and Allen are biological siblings and that Tiffany is their biological daughter. Neither Patty nor Allen contested the evidence of their incestuous parenthood of Tiffany and, consequently, the trial court found Patty and Allen unfit and proceeded to the dispositional phase under § 48.427(2).

During the dispositional phase, Dr. David Tick, a former professor of genetics at the Milwaukee County Medical College, testified about Tiffany's profound development delays, her psychosocial deprivation, and her stunted physical development. He testified based not only on his two examinations of Tiffany, but also on the medical reports prepared by Dr. June Dobbs, who had examined Tiffany on two previous occasions-shortly after her removal from the parental home, and three months later. Dr. Tick explained that when Dr. Dobbs first examined Tiffany, she was a non-verbal, three and one-half year old who behaved and physically appeared more like a two-year-old child. She was not toilet trained or able to feed herself and she displayed little or no emotion. Dr. Tick testified, however, that after time with her foster family, Tiffany made great progress. Thus, he concluded that Tiffany's delays resulted, in significant part, from parental neglect.

Dr. Tick also testified that he had diagnosed Tiffany with an autosomal recessive disorder. [genetic defects resulting from recessive genes present in both parents]....

...

Cynthia Barczak, a psychotherapist who worked with Tiffany and Patty, also testified at the dispositional hearing. She described Tiffany as a child with dramatic special needs who would require extensive therapy. Barczak testified that Patty had great difficulty recognizing Tiffany's problems and was unable to help Tiffany master basic skills such as identifying colors or counting. Barczak concluded that Patty and Tiffany had not bonded, that Allen and Tiffany had no substantial relationship, and that nothing positive would come from a continuing relationship between Tiffany and her biological parents.

Mary Dirk, a Milwaukee County Department of Human Services social worker, also testified. She told the court that Patty had two daughters prior to Tiffany, one of whom was also fathered by Allen. Parental rights to that child were involuntarily terminated in Texas in 1989. Dirk also testified that Allen had been very uncooperative with the clinicians and social workers who were evaluating him and trying to assist him in meeting the CHIPS conditions for Tiffany's return. She stated that Patty had been more cooperative than Allen, but was still unable to comply with the conditions. Lastly, Dirk apprised the court that Patty had recently given birth to a baby boy, whom she believed was also fathered by Allen.

The trial court found:

... there is a great likelihood of adoption of the child, in that an adoptive home had been identified by MCDHS as an appropriate adoptive resource. The court further finds that there is no relationship between the child and her respective parents or extended family members which would be harmed; to the contrary, given the tenacity of dysfunction between Tiffany's parents who persist in maintaining an incestuous relationship which continues to produce children, the court finds that severance of all legal, emotional and physical ties with the extended ... family is in the child's best interest. The court further finds that there are no obstacles to adoption regarding the child's age or health, and that adoption would provide the best chance for a stable and permanent home for the child.

II. Analysis

A. Due Process

Patty and Allen argue that § 48.415(7) is unconstitutional and, therefore, the termination of their parental rights based on their incestuous parenthood of Tiffany denied them due process of law. In essence, they assert that even though the State has a compelling interest in preserving and promoting the welfare of children, a statute specifying incestuous parenthood as a ground for termination is not narrowly tailored to serve the State's interest. We disagree.

...

While "the Due Process Clause requires a showing of justification when the government intrudes on choices concerning family living arrangements in a manner which is contrary to deeply rooted traditions," there is no question that the "State may legitimately say that no one can marry his or her sibling." This determination is consistent with, not contrary to, deeply rooted traditions. Thus, no fundamental principle of justice is offended when a state determines that siblings, whom it can legitimately bar from marriage, are unfit to provide parenting for the children they produce through their non-marital, incestuous relationship.

B. Equal Protection

Patty and Allen also argue that termination of their parental rights pursuant to § 48.415(7) violates their rights to equal protection of law. They contend that the State's only compelling interest is the prevention of genetic mutations, and that this interest lapses once the child is born. Additionally, they claim that their kinship has no effect on their ability to be good parents. We disagree.

...

Patty and Allen argue that § 48.415(7) does not further the State's interest in the continuing welfare of its children because whatever genetic defect might have been caused by parental consanguinity has already taken place. Genetic mutation, however, is but one consequence of incest, and only one of many reasons why Wisconsin and other states have long prohibited incestuous marriage and criminalized incest. "The crime [of incest] is also punished to promote and protect family harmony, to protect children from the abuse of parental authority, and because society cannot function in an orderly manner when age distinctions, generations, sentiments and roles in family are in conflict."

As the Attorney General argues, a child raised by incestuous parents is a child raised in a home that mocks even the most rudimentary conception of family. A statute that declares incestuous parents unfit acknowledges the fundamentally disordered circumstances in which the child of an incestuous relationship will be raised. Moreover, it recognizes the vulnerability of the child and the compelling interest in protecting children from the psychological confusion and emotional damage they likely will suffer as a result of being born to and living within an incestuous family.

Therefore, we reject Patty's and Allen's argument that once a child is born, the State's compelling interest lapses. Not only does the State's compelling interest in the protection of that child continue, but the State's equally compelling interest in deterring additional incestuous parenthood, by those parents and others, remains. As one court explained in a termination case, "the [incestuous] parent by his actions has demonstrated that the natural, moral constraint of blood relationship has failed to prevent deviant conduct and thus cannot be relied upon to constrain similar conduct in the future." Thus, § 48.415(7), Stats., further promotes the State's compelling interest in deterring incest by, in effect, warning those who might contemplate incest that if they produce a child, they will not necessarily be permitted to parent the child.

. . .

As already noted, under § 458.427(2), Stats., the trial court has discretion to dismiss any petition for termination of parental rights where incestuous parenthood does not warrant termination. Although incestuous parenthood results in a finding of unfitness, that finding does not necessarily result in termination. Termination is authorized only if: (1) incestuous parenthood is proven by clear and convincing evidence; (2) incestuous parenthood is shown to warrant termination; and (3) termination serves the child's best interests. As the supreme court explained, "the legislature has in effect put a 'spin' on the word 'unfit' by giving the court the discretion to dismiss a petition if the circuit court 'finds that the evidence does not warrant the termination of parental rights.'"

. . .

By the Court.-Order affirmed.

Justice Fine, concurring. [omitted]

Notes and Queries

1. The psychotherapist notes that "nothing positive would come from a continuing relationship between Tiffany and her biological parents." Would you feel comfortable arguing for termination of parental rights?

2. The trial court found that there is no relationship between the child and her parents that would be harmed. What evidence do you have to the contrary?

3. The court aptly notes the state's compelling interest in prohibiting incest: The crime is punished to promote and protect family harmony, to protect children from the abuse of parental authority, and because society cannot function in an orderly

manner when age distinctions, generations, sentiments, and roles in family are in conflict. Does terminating parental rights appropriately address the state's compelling interest? By the time this case was addressed by the court, Patty and Allen already had had another child who was not the subject of CPS investigations/allegations.

4. Note that the last paragraph of the opinion explicitly states that a finding of unfitness does not necessarily mean termination of parental rights. Are these parents unfairly subjected to termination of their parent–child relationship?

5. The court notes that adoption was likely. Should that matter?

Mississippi Band of Choctaw Indians v. Holyfield

490 U.S. 30; 109 S. Ct. 1597 (1989)

Justice Brennan delivered the opinion of the Court.

This appeal requires us to construe the provisions of the Indian Child Welfare Act that establish exclusive tribal jurisdiction over child custody proceedings involving Indian children domiciled on the tribe's reservation.

I

A

The Indian Child Welfare Act of 1978 (ICWA) was the product of rising concern in the mid-1970's over the consequences to Indian children, Indian families, and Indian tribes of abusive child welfare practices that resulted in the separation of large numbers of Indian children from their families and tribes through adoption or foster care placement, usually in non-Indian homes. Senate oversight hearings in 1974 yielded numerous examples, statistical data, and expert testimony documenting what one witness called "[t]he wholesale removal of Indian children from their homes, . . . the most tragic aspect of Indian life today." Studies undertaken by the Association on American Indian Affairs in 1969 and 1974, and presented in the Senate hearings, showed that 25 to 35% of all Indian children had been separated from their families and placed in adoptive families, foster care, or institutions. Adoptive placements counted significantly in this total: in the State of Minnesota, for example, one in eight Indian children under the age of 18 was in an adoptive home, and during the year 1971–1972 nearly one in every four infants under one year of age was placed for adoption. The adoption rate of Indian children was eight times that of non-Indian children. Approximately 90% of the Indian placements were in non-Indian homes. A number of witnesses also testified to the serious adjustment problems encountered by such children during adolescence, as well as the impact of the adoptions on Indian parents and the tribes themselves.

Further hearings, covering much the same ground, were held during 1977 and 1978 on the bill that became the ICWA. While much of the testimony again focused on the harm to Indian parents and their children who were involuntarily separated by decisions of local welfare authorities, there was also considerable emphasis on the impact on the tribes themselves of the massive removal of their children. For example, Mr. Calvin Isaac, Tribal Chief of the Mississippi Band of Choctaw Indians and representative of the National Tribal Chairmen's Association, testified as follows:

> Culturally, the chances of Indian survival are significantly reduced if our children, the only real means for the transmission of the tribal heritage, are to be raised in non-Indian homes and denied exposure to the ways of their People. Furthermore, these practices seriously undercut the tribes' ability to continue as self-governing communities. Probably in no area is it more important that tribal sovereignty be respected than in an area as socially and culturally determinative as family relationships.

Chief Isaac also summarized succinctly what numerous witnesses saw as the principal reason for the high rates of removal of Indian children:

> One of the most serious failings of the present system is that Indian children are removed from the custody of their natural parents by nontribal government authorities who have no basis for intelligently evaluating the cultural and social premises underlying Indian home life and childrearing. Many of the individuals who decide the fate of our children are at best ignorant of our cultural values, and at worst contemptful of the Indian way and convinced that removal, usually to a non-Indian household or institution, can only benefit an Indian child.

The congressional findings that were incorporated into the ICWA reflect these sentiments. . . .

. . .

The ICWA thus, in the words of the House Report accompanying it, "seeks to protect the rights of the Indian child as an Indian and the rights of the Indian community and tribe in retaining its children in its society." It does so by establishing "a Federal policy that, where possible, an Indian child should remain in the Indian community," and by making sure that Indian child welfare determinations are not based on "a white, middle-class standard which, in many cases, forecloses placement with [an] Indian family."

. . .

B

This case involves the status of twin babies, known for our purposes as B. B. and G. B., who were born out of wedlock on December 29, 1985. Their mother, J. B., and father, W. J., were both enrolled members of appellant Mississippi Band of Choctaw Indians (Tribe), and were residents and domiciliaries of the Choctaw Reservation in Neshoba County, Mississippi. J. B. gave birth to the twins in Gulfport, Harrison County, Mississippi, some 200 miles from the reservation. On January 10, 1986,

J. B. executed a consent-to-adoption form before the Chancery Court of Harrison County. W. J. signed a similar form. On January 16, appellees Orrey and Vivian Holyfield filed a petition for adoption in the same court and the chancellor issued a Final Decree of Adoption on January 28. Despite the court's apparent awareness of the ICWA, the adoption decree contained no reference to it, nor to the infants' Indian background.

Two months later the Tribe moved in the Chancery Court to vacate the adoption decree on the ground that under the ICWA exclusive jurisdiction was vested in the tribal court. On July 14, 1986, the court overruled the motion, holding that the Tribe "never obtained exclusive jurisdiction over the children involved herein. . . ." The court's one-page opinion relied on two facts in reaching that conclusion. The court noted first that the twins' mother "went to some efforts to see that they were born outside the confines of the Choctaw Indian Reservation" and that the parents had promptly arranged for the adoption by the Holyfields. Second, the court stated: "At no time from the birth of these children to the present date have either of them resided on or physically been on the Choctaw Indian Reservation."

The Supreme Court of Mississippi affirmed. It rejected the Tribe's arguments that the state court lacked jurisdiction and that it, in any event, had not applied the standards laid out in the ICWA. The court recognized that the jurisdictional question turned on whether the twins were domiciled on the Choctaw Reservation. It answered that question as follows:

> At no point in time can it be said the twins resided on or were domiciled within the territory set aside for the reservation. Appellant's argument that living within the womb of their mother qualifies the children's residency on the reservation may be lauded for its creativity; however, apparently it is unsupported by any law within this state, and will not be addressed at this time due to the far-reaching legal ramifications that would occur were we to follow such a complicated tangential course.

The court distinguished Mississippi cases that appeared to establish the principle that "the domicile of minor children follows that of the parents." It noted that "the Indian twins . . . were voluntarily surrendered and legally abandoned by the natural parents to the adoptive parents, and it is undisputed that the parents went to some efforts to prevent the children from being placed on the reservation as the mother arranged for their birth and adoption in Gulfport Memorial Hospital, Harrison County, Mississippi." Therefore, the court said, the twins' domicile was in Harrison County and the state court properly exercised jurisdiction over the adoption proceedings. Indeed, the court appears to have concluded that, for this reason, none of the provisions of the ICWA was applicable. In any case, it rejected the Tribe's contention that the requirements of the ICWA applicable in state courts had not been followed: "[T]he judge did conform and strictly adhere to the minimum federal standards governing adoption of Indian children with respect to parental consent, notice, service of process, etc."

Because of the centrality of the exclusive tribal jurisdiction provision to the overall scheme of the ICWA, as well as the conflict between this decision of the Mississippi Supreme Court and those of several other state courts, we granted plenary review. We now reverse.

II

Tribal jurisdiction over Indian child custody proceedings is not a novelty of the ICWA. Indeed, some of the ICWA's jurisdictional provisions have a strong basis in pre-ICWA case law in the federal and state courts....

The state-court proceeding at issue here was a "child custody proceeding." That term is defined to include any "'adoptive placement' which shall mean the permanent placement of an Indian child for adoption, including any action resulting in a final decree of adoption." Moreover, the twins were "Indian children." The sole issue in this case is, as the Supreme Court of Mississippi recognized, whether the twins were "domiciled" on the reservation.

A

The meaning of "domicile" in the ICWA is, of course, a matter of Congress' intent. The ICWA itself does not define it. The initial question we must confront is whether there is any reason to believe that Congress intended the ICWA definition of "domicile" to be a matter of state law. While the meaning of a federal statute is necessarily a federal question in the sense that its construction remains subject to this Court's supervision, Congress sometimes intends that a statutory term be given content by the application of state law....

First, and most fundamentally, the purpose of the ICWA gives no reason to believe that Congress intended to rely on state law for the definition of a critical term; quite the contrary....

Second, Congress could hardly have intended the lack of nationwide uniformity that would result from state-law definitions of domicile. An example will illustrate. In a case quite similar to this one, the New Mexico state courts found exclusive jurisdiction in the tribal court pursuant because the illegitimate child took the reservation domicile of its mother at birth — notwithstanding that the child was placed in the custody of adoptive parents 2 days after its off-reservation birth and the mother executed a consent to adoption 10 days later. Had that mother traveled to Mississippi to give birth, rather than to Albuquerque, a different result would have obtained if state-law definitions of domicile applied. The same, presumably, would be true if the child had been transported to Mississippi for adoption after her off-reservation birth in New Mexico. While the child's custody proceeding would have been subject to exclusive tribal jurisdiction in her home State, her mother, prospective adoptive parents, or an adoption intermediary could have obtained an adoption decree in state court merely by transporting her across state lines. Even if we could conceive of a federal statute under which the rules of domicile (and thus of jurisdiction) applied differently to different Indian children, a statute under which different rules apply from time to time to the same child, simply as a result of his or her transport from one State to another, cannot be what Congress had in mind.

We therefore think it beyond dispute that Congress intended a uniform federal law of domicile for the ICWA.

B

It remains to give content to the term "domicile" in the circumstances of the present case. The holding of the Supreme Court of Mississippi that the twin babies were not domiciled on the Choctaw Reservation appears to have rested on two findings of fact by the trial court: (1) that they had never been physically present there, and (2) that they were "voluntarily surrendered" by their parents. The question before us, therefore, is whether under the ICWA definition of "domicile" such facts suffice to render the twins nondomiciliaries of the reservation.

We have often stated that in the absence of a statutory definition we "start with the assumption that the legislative purpose is expressed by the ordinary meaning of the words used." We do so, of course, in the light of the "'object and policy'" of the statute. We therefore look both to the generally accepted meaning of the term "domicile" and to the purpose of the statute.

. . .

. . . "Domicile" is not necessarily synonymous with "residence," and one can reside in one place but be domiciled in another. For adults, domicile is established by physical presence in a place in connection with a certain state of mind concerning one's intent to remain there. One acquires a "domicile of origin" at birth, and that domicile continues until a new one (a "domicile of choice") is acquired. Since most minors are legally incapable of forming the requisite intent to establish a domicile, their domicile is determined by that of their parents. In the case of an illegitimate child, that has traditionally meant the domicile of its mother. Under these principles, it is entirely logical that "[o]n occasion, a child's domicile of origin will be in a place where the child has never been."

It is undisputed in this case that the domicile of the mother (as well as the father) has been, at all relevant times, on the Choctaw Reservation. Thus, it is clear that at their birth the twin babies were also domiciled on the reservation, even though they themselves had never been there. The statement of the Supreme Court of Mississippi that "[a]t no point in time can it be said the twins . . . were domiciled within the territory set aside for the reservation," may be a correct statement of that State's law of domicile, but it is inconsistent with generally accepted doctrine in this country and cannot be what Congress had in mind when it used the term in the ICWA.

Nor can the result be any different simply because the twins were "voluntarily surrendered" by their mother. Tribal jurisdiction under § 1911(a) was not meant to be defeated by the actions of individual members of the tribe, for Congress was concerned not solely about the interests of Indian children and families, but also about the impact on the tribes themselves of the large numbers of Indian children adopted by non-Indians. The numerous prerogatives accorded the tribes through the ICWA's substantive provisions must, accordingly, be seen as a means of protecting not only the interests of individual Indian children and families, but also of the tribes themselves.

In addition, it is clear that Congress' concern over the placement of Indian children in non-Indian homes was based in part on evidence of the detrimental impact on the children themselves of such placements outside their culture. Congress determined to subject such placements to the ICWA's jurisdictional and other provisions, even in cases where the parents consented to an adoption, because of concerns going beyond the wishes of individual parents. As the 1977 Final Report of the congressionally established American Indian Policy Review Commission stated, in summarizing these two concerns, "[r]emoval of Indian children from their cultural setting seriously impacts a long-term tribal survival and has damaging social and psychological impact on many individual Indian children."

These congressional objectives make clear that a rule of domicile that would permit individual Indian parents to defeat the ICWA's jurisdictional scheme is inconsistent with what Congress intended. The appellees in this case argue strenuously that the twins' mother went to great lengths to give birth off the reservation so that her children could be adopted by the Holyfields. But that was precisely part of Congress' concern. Permitting individual members of the tribe to avoid tribal exclusive jurisdiction by the simple expedient of giving birth off the reservation would, to a large extent, nullify the purpose the ICWA was intended to accomplish....

...

III

We are not unaware that over three years have passed since the twin babies were born and placed in the Holyfield home, and that a court deciding their fate today is not writing on a blank slate in the same way it would have in January 1986. Three years' development of family ties cannot be undone, and a separation at this point would doubtless cause considerable pain.

Whatever feelings we might have as to where the twins should live, however, it is not for us to decide that question. We have been asked to decide the legal question of who should make the custody determination concerning these children—not what the outcome of that determination should be. The law places that decision in the hands of the Choctaw tribal court. Had the mandate of the ICWA been followed in 1986, of course, much potential anguish might have been avoided, and in any case the law cannot be applied so as automatically to "reward those who obtain custody, whether lawfully or otherwise, and maintain it during any ensuing (and protracted) litigation." It is not ours to say whether the trauma that might result from removing these children from their adoptive family should outweigh the interest of the Tribe—and perhaps the children themselves—in having them raised as part of the Choctaw community. Rather, "we must defer to the experience, wisdom, and compassion of the [Choctaw] tribal courts to fashion an appropriate remedy."

The judgment of the Supreme Court of Mississippi is reversed, and the case is remanded for further proceedings not inconsistent with this opinion.

It is so ordered.

Justice Stevens, with whom The Chief Justice and Justice Kennedy join, dissenting.

The parents of these twin babies unquestionably expressed their intention to have the state court exercise jurisdiction over them. J. B. gave birth to the twins at a hospital 200 miles from the reservation, even though a closer hospital was available. Both parents gave their written advance consent to the adoption and, when the adoption was later challenged by the Tribe, they reaffirmed their desire that the Holyfields adopt the two children. As the Mississippi Supreme Court found, "the parents went to some efforts to prevent the children from being placed on the reservation as the mother arranged for their birth and adoption in Gulfport Memorial Hospital, Harrison County, Mississippi." Indeed, Appellee Vivian Holyfield appears before us today, urging that she be allowed to retain custody of B. B. and G. B.

Because J. B.'s domicile is on the reservation and the children are eligible for membership in the Tribe, the Court today closes the state courthouse door to her. I agree with the Court that Congress intended a uniform federal law of domicile for the Indian Child Welfare Act of 1978 (ICWA) and that domicile should be defined with reference to the objectives of the congressional scheme.... I cannot agree, however, with the cramped definition the Court gives that term. To preclude parents domiciled on a reservation from deliberately invoking the adoption procedures of state court, the Court gives "domicile" a meaning that Congress could not have intended and distorts the delicate balance between individual rights and group rights recognized by the ICWA.

The ICWA was passed in 1978 in response to congressional findings that "an alarmingly high percentage of Indian families are broken up by the removal, often unwarranted, of their children from them by nontribal public and private agencies," and that "the States, exercising their recognized jurisdiction over Indian child custody proceedings through administrative and judicial bodies, have often failed to recognize the essential tribal relations of Indian people and the cultural and social standards prevailing in Indian communities and families." The Act is thus primarily addressed to the unjustified removal of Indian children from their families through the application of standards that inadequately recognized the distinct Indian culture.

...

The Act gives Indian tribes certain rights, not to restrict the rights of parents of Indian children, but to complement and help effect them. The Indian tribe may petition to transfer an action in state court to the tribal court, but the Indian parent may veto the transfer. The Act provides for a tribal right of notice and intervention in involuntary proceedings but not in voluntary ones Finally, the tribe may petition the court to set aside a parental termination action upon a showing that the provisions of the ICWA that are designed to protect parents and Indian children have been violated.

. . .

When an Indian child is temporarily off the reservation, but has not been abandoned to a person off the reservation, the tribe has an interest in exclusive jurisdiction. The ICWA expresses the intent that exclusive tribal jurisdiction is not so frail that it should be defeated as soon as the Indian child steps off the reservation. Similarly, when the child is abandoned by one parent to a person off the reservation, the tribe and the other parent domiciled on the reservation may still have an interest in the exercise of exclusive jurisdiction. That interest is protected by the rule that a child abandoned by one parent takes on the domicile of the other. But when an Indian child is deliberately abandoned by both parents to a person off the reservation, no purpose of the ICWA is served by closing the state courthouse door to them. The interests of the parents, the Indian child, and the tribe in preventing the unwarranted removal of Indian children from their families and from the reservation are protected by the Act's substantive and procedural provisions. In addition, if both parents have intentionally invoked the jurisdiction of the state court in an action involving a non-Indian, no interest in tribal self-governance is implicated.

The interpretation of domicile adopted by the Court requires the custodian of an Indian child who is off the reservation to haul the child to a potentially distant tribal court unfamiliar with the child's present living conditions and best interests. Moreover, it renders any custody decision made by a state court forever suspect, susceptible to challenge at any time as void for having been entered in the absence of jurisdiction. Finally, it forces parents of Indian children who desire to invoke state-court jurisdiction to establish a domicile off the reservation. Only if the custodial parent has the wealth and ability to establish a domicile off the reservation will the parent be able to use the processes of state court. I fail to see how such a requirement serves the paramount congressional purpose of "promot[ing] the stability and security of Indian tribes and families."

The Court concludes its opinion with the observation that whatever anguish is suffered by the Indian children, their natural parents, and their adoptive parents because of its decision today is a result of their failure to initially follow the provisions of the ICWA. By holding that parents who are domiciled on the reservation cannot voluntarily avail themselves of the adoption procedures of state court and that all such proceedings will be void for lack of jurisdiction, however, the Court establishes a rule of law that is virtually certain to ensure that similar anguish will be suffered by other families in the future. Because that result is not mandated by the language of the ICWA and is contrary to its purposes, I respectfully dissent.

Notes and Queries

1. The ICWA provides, in part: "In any State court proceeding for the foster care placement of, or termination of parental rights to, an Indian child not domiciled or residing within the reservation of the Indian child's tribe, the court, in the absence of good cause to the contrary, shall transfer such proceeding to the jurisdiction of the tribe, absent objection by either parent, upon the petition of either parent or the Indian custodian or the Indian child's tribe: Provided, That such transfer shall be subject to declination by the tribal court of such tribe." Do you agree with the dissent's characterization of the Act? Does the Act place tribal rights over individual parents' rights as the majority opinion found?

2. The ICWA permits termination of parental rights solely upon "evidence beyond a reasonable doubt." Does this high standard indicate the highest respect given to parents' rights?

3. Are children's rights and interests served well by the ICWA?

4. Could the parents have avoided this litigation simply by severing their own links to the Choctaw tribe and culture?

5. In *Haaland v. Brackeen* (June 2023), the Supreme Court revisited the constitutionality of the ICWA. In that case, the state placed a 10-month-old Navajo boy in foster care. After the boy lived with his foster parents for over a year, they sought to adopt him. The prospective adoptive parents (the Brackeens) were a non-Native American couple; the boy's biological mother was Navaho and the father was Cherokee. The state court terminated the parental rights of both biological parents. All lived in Texas and the proceedings were in state court. The biological mother, father, and grandmother all supported the adoption. The Navajo and Cherokee Nations did not. Following the ICWA, the Navajo Nation sought to place the child with a Navajo family. The tribe was unsuccessful, which resulted in allowing the Brackeens to adopt the child. The Brackeens later sought to adopt the boy's sister. They did so in state court, to which the girl's extended family objected. The Brackeens then filed suit in federal court to overturn the ICWA on the grounds of racial discrimination. The appellate court ruled that Congress had the authority to enact the ICWA. The Supreme Court granted certiorari, along with three other cases. In a 7–2 decision, the Court affirmed and upheld the ICWA. Writing for the majority, Justice Amy Coney Barrett reaffirmed Congress's power while Justices Thomas and Alito viewed the law as inappropriately infringing on state sovereignty. Justice Kavanaugh concurred to underscore that the Court did not address the equal protection issue, as the plaintiffs did not have standing to argue the issue.

6. Kavanaugh's concurrence is of significance for children in foster care or adoption proceedings, and in the child welfare system more generally. It has yet to

be decided, for example, that a particular placement may be denied because of a child's race—even if the placement is otherwise determined to be in the child's best interests.

7. For a useful discussion that places transracial foster care and adoption into a broader perspective that highlights social and cultural factors and the reasons for controversy, see Fern L. Johnson, Stacie Mickelson & Mariana Lopez Davila (2013). Transracial foster care and adoption: Issues and realities. *New England Journal of Public Policy*, 25(1), 5. For useful overviews of transracial adoptee outcomes, see Jordan E. Montgomery & Nickolas A. Jordan (2018). Racial–ethnic socialization and transracial adoptee outcomes: A systematic research synthesis. *Child and Adolescent Social Work Journal*, 35, 439–458; Leslie Doty Hollingsworth (1997). Effect of transracial/transethnic adoption on children's racial and ethnic identity and self-esteem: A meta-analytic review. *Marriage & Family Review*, 25(1–2), 99–130.

Chapter 8

Seizing Children, Terminating Relationships, and Providing Alternative Care

Prior to the 1980s, "child welfare" was still essentially a relatively small, self-contained service system with few resources and minimal federal oversight and little public attention. That system made it difficult for most families to access services and equally difficult for children to leave out-of-home care. Service quality and coverage were uneven. Some agencies, primarily those in the voluntary sector, provided highly specialized, professional services to select children in long-term out-of-home care, unmarried mothers, healthy white infants, and adoptive parents. Other voluntary and public agencies struggled to provide a minimum level of care and protection to large numbers of dependent children. Brenda G. McGowan & Elaine M. Walsh (2000). Policy challenges for child welfare in the new century. *Child Welfare*, 79, 11–28.

The 1980s witnessed a major policy shift in the provision of services to children deemed maltreated or otherwise deemed in need of care. That shift resulted from a mix of factors, most notably the social action and civil rights initiatives of the 1960s, research and developmental theory regarding the negative consequences of "foster care drift" for children in care, political activity by groups of adoptive and foster parents, litigation by children's rights attorneys, and federal legislation. Together, they pointed to many deficiencies in the child welfare system, including: (1) Children entered care too easily, with little effort made to maintain them in their own homes; (2) foster care became permanent for many children even though it had been designed to be temporary; (3) agencies rarely developed written case plans for children; (4) services to help parents resolve the problems that necessitated placement of their children were rarely provided; and (5) parents were discouraged from visiting their children in foster care.

To address the above problems, Congress enacted the *Adoption Assistance and Child Welfare Act of 1980* (AACAW), Pub. L. No. 96-272, 94 Stat. 500 (1980), which was guided by three principles: (1) reasonable efforts to prevent placement, (2) permanency planning for children in out-of-home care, and (3) placement in the least detrimental alternative. AACWA focused on family preservation as it sought to prevent the removal of children from their own homes and, for those whose safety required removal, to facilitate family reunification. To avoid repetition of the problems that led to passage of AACWA, Congress conditioned the receipt of federal funds on states' making reasonable efforts to prevent the removal of children from their own homes, and for children removed, to reunite them with their parents. Judicial officers would conduct case-by-case determinations of state compliance with the reasonable efforts requirement. States also were mandated to provide each child with a written case plan describing, among other things, what the child's parents were to do to regain custody and what service providers were to do to assist parents. Finally, AACWA required that each child's case be reviewed no less than once every six months to determine the necessity of continued foster care and compliance with the case plan. Part of that requirement included a likely date by which the child could be returned home or placed for adoption or legal guardianship and a dispositional review no later than eighteen months after the child entered custody, with ongoing reviews thereafter.

The 1980s, however, also experienced major transformations in the need for child welfare services. The foster care system was beset by many internal and external challenges. Foster care became far from temporary for many children as the system frequently failed to provide children with stable, secure care. In addition, the system repeatedly failed to meet foster children's basic medical, psychological, and emotional needs. Although several reasons helped account for these failures, three were particularly determinative: (1) an upsurge in the number of children in need of care, (2) an overburdened system of agencies, and (3) an inadequate number of foster parents. Many of these issues resulted from the dramatic rise in child maltreatment complaints, which led to a sharp increase in out-of-home care entries. Although much controversy surrounds the validity of allegations of maltreatment, it seems difficult to dispute that the high number has been attributed to a complex mix of converging trends, including the growing number of placements related to drug and alcohol abuse, homelessness, and deteriorating family relationships. See Roger J. R. Levesque (1995). The failures of foster care reform: Challenging the most radical blueprint. *Maryland Journal of Contemporary Issues*, 6, 1–35.

In response to the above concerns, Congress, in 1997, enacted the *Adoption and Safe Families Act* (ASFA), Pub. L. No. 105-89, 111 Stat. 2115 (codified in scattered sections of 42 U.S.C.). ASFA reflects a shift in philosophy away from the family-preservation/family-reunification theme emphasized by the AACWA and toward a focus on achieving permanency through adoption. Like the AACWA, ASFA makes the safety of children a priority in all child welfare decision making. It also reaffirms the concept of permanency planning established under the AACWA and emphasizes the importance of "reasonable efforts" to preserve and reunify families. ASFA, however, does modify the reasonable efforts requirements of the AACWA by not making them required under four conditions: (1) if a judge determines that a parent has subjected a child to aggravated circumstances as defined in state law, which may include abandonment, torture, and extreme forms of physical or sexual abuse; (2) if a parent is criminally responsible for the death of another or her or his children; (3) if a parent's rights concerning a sibling have been involuntarily terminated; or (4) if a judicial determination finds that reasonable efforts are not required. These determinations rest on the need to preserve child safety, and many conditions are set forth as examples of assumed threat (e.g., cases in which parents have committed murder or voluntary manslaughter, have had their parental rights to a sibling of the child terminated, or have subjected the child to aggravated circumstances as defined by state law). In addition, ASFA mandates a permanency hearing after a child has been in care for twelve months and every twelve months thereafter, and expedites termination of parental rights by requiring states to file a termination petition in cases in which children have been in care for fifteen of the past twenty-two months, regardless of the child's age or special needs. The only exceptions are (1) when a child is in kinship care, (2) when the case plan documents a compelling reason termination would not be in the child's best interests, or (3) when the state has not made the required reasonable efforts to return the child home safely.

ASFA mandates that workers engage in concurrent planning, meaning that while they are providing family reunification services they also simultaneously must make plans for termination of parental rights and adoption in case of unsuccessful reunification efforts. When reasonable efforts are not required to return a child home because of potential danger to the child, ASFA mandates the making of reasonable efforts to complete whatever tasks are necessary to meet the child's alternative permanency plan. ASFA intends to put children on a fast track from foster care to permanent homes. States must actively recruit adoptive homes, document their child-specific recruitment efforts, and act expeditiously to approve adoptive homes and finalize adoptions. Exceptions to the mandate to pursue termination of parental rights apply to children who are in the care of a relative, for children for whom the state can justify in writing why it is not in the child's best interests to pursue adoption, and where the state has not made the required reasonable efforts to reunite the family. Although these are mandates, the reality is that they are supported by fiscal incentives. To receive federal funding, states need to move toward federal mandates, with a key one being an increase in the number of adoptions relative to prior years. States that do not comply with ASFA's provisions will be denied a portion of their Title IV-E and Title IV-B funds that finance foster care and other child welfare services.

The changing numbers of children in foster care are important for gaining perspective. Statistical findings from twenty years ago to recent reports indicate the Safe Families Act's success. In 1999, there were over 581,000 children in foster care. In 2021, there were 391,098 children in foster, which itself was a drop from 407,318 in 2020. Also importantly, in 1999, children stayed in care for an average of 32 months. In 2021, the averages stay in foster care was 21.7 months. These are dramatic drops. See U.S. Department of Health and Human Services (2001 and 2023). *The AFCARS Report*. Washington, DC: Author.

The dramatic drop in the number of children in care can result from many sources. As much as they may reveal success in moving along, they also can reveal greater hesitancy to remove children from their homes. The hesitancy itself may come from a variety of sources, which can mean increased services or actually the opposite in that systems may simply reduce interventions in the first place.

Putting aside the need for more research to understand the transformation of out of home care, the needs of children in foster care remain a fundamental challenge of our child protection systems. Children in care necessarily have been the victims of repeated abuse, prolonged neglect, or otherwise unstable environments. Given those realities and as we have seen, the need for intervention clearly exists. Such experiences are critical in the short- and long-term development and the ability to subsequently participate fully in society.

This chapter examines how we can most effectively ensure a transition in and out of care and protect children while in care. The fundamental issues to consider involve the extent to which we can protect children and make sound decisions in the placement of children in care and protect children released to their parents or placed for adoption. These issues are quite significant. As we will see, risk of violence and death actually may increase when returning children to their homes and removing children from homes is fraught with many judgment calls that can easily turn problematic. Providing care itself also necessarily remains complicated. Children in care do appear to have experienced disproportionately higher rates of physical, developmental, and mental health problems and have more unmet medical and mental health care needs; it seems mind-boggling to think that we expect volunteer families and parents to address those needs. The task is quite complex given the current and possible mix of rights, resources, needs, and the many decision points that require close attention and constant critical evaluation.

Lassiter v. Department of Social Services

452 U.S. 18; 101 S. Ct. 2153 (1981)

Justice Stewart delivered the opinion of the Court.

I

In the late spring of 1975, after hearing evidence that the petitioner, Abby Gail Lassiter, had not provided her infant son William with proper medical care, the District Court of Durham County, N. C., adjudicated him a neglected child and transferred him to the custody of the Durham County Department of Social Services, the respondent here. A year later, Ms. Lassiter was charged with first-degree murder, was convicted of second-degree murder, and began a sentence of 25 to 40 years of imprisonment. In 1978 the Department petitioned the court to terminate Ms. Lassiter's parental rights because, the Department alleged, she "has not had any contact with the child since December of 1975" and "has willfully left the child in foster care for more than two consecutive years without showing that substantial progress has been made in correcting the conditions which led to the removal of the child, or without showing a positive response to the diligent efforts of the Department of Social Services to strengthen her relationship to the child, or to make and follow through with constructive planning for the future of the child."

Ms. Lassiter was served with the petition and with notice that a hearing on it would be held. Although her mother had retained counsel for her in connection with an effort to invalidate the murder conviction, Ms. Lassiter never mentioned the forthcoming hearing to him (or, for that matter, to any other person except, she said, to "someone" in the prison). At the behest of the Department of Social Services' attorney, she was brought from prison to the hearing, which was held August 31, 1978. The hearing opened, apparently at the judge's instance, with a discussion of whether Ms. Lassiter should have more time in which to find legal assistance. Since the court concluded that she "has had ample opportunity to seek and obtain counsel prior to the hearing of this matter, and [that] her failure to do so is without just cause," the court did not postpone the proceedings. Ms. Lassiter did not aver that she was indigent, and the court did not appoint counsel for her.

A social worker from the respondent Department was the first witness. She testified that in 1975 the Department "received a complaint from Duke Pediatrics that William had not been followed in the pediatric clinic for medical problems and that they were having difficulty in locating Ms. Lassiter. . . ." She said that in May 1975 a social worker had taken William to the hospital, where doctors asked that he stay "because of breathing difficulties [and] malnutrition and [because] there was a great deal of scarring that indicated that he had a severe infection that had gone untreated." The witness further testified that, except for one "prearranged" visit and a chance meeting on the street, Ms. Lassiter had not seen William after he had come into the State's custody, and that neither Ms. Lassiter nor her mother had "made any contact with the Department of Social Services regarding that child." When asked whether William should be placed in his grandmother's custody, the social worker said he should not, since the grandmother "has indicated to me on a number of occasions that she was not able to take responsibility for the child" and since "I have checked with people in the community and from Ms. Lassiter's church who also feel that this additional responsibility would be more than she can handle." The social worker added that William "has not seen his grandmother since the chance meeting in July of '76 and that was the only time."

After the direct examination of the social worker, the judge said: "I notice we made extensive findings in June of '75 that you were served with papers and called the social services and told them you weren't coming; and the serious lack of medical treatment. And, as I have said in my findings of the 16th day of June '75, the Court finds that the grandmother, Ms. Lucille Lassiter, mother of Abby Gail Lassiter, filed a complaint on the 8th day of May, 1975, alleging that the daughter often left the children, Candina, Felicia and William L. with her for days without providing money or food while she was gone."

Ms. Lassiter conducted a cross-examination of the social worker, who firmly reiterated her earlier testimony. The judge explained several times, with varying degrees of clarity, that Ms. Lassiter should only ask questions at this stage; many of her questions were disallowed because they were not really questions, but arguments.

Ms. Lassiter herself then testified, under the judge's questioning, that she had properly cared for William. Under cross-examination, she said that she had seen William more than five or six times after he had been taken from her custody and that, if William could not be with her, she wanted him to be with her mother since, "He knows us. Children know they family.... They know they people, they know they family and that child knows us anywhere.... I got four more other children. Three girls and a boy and they know they little brother when they see him."

Ms. Lassiter's mother was then called as a witness. She denied, under the questioning of the judge, that she had filed the complaint against Ms. Lassiter, and on cross-examination she denied both having failed to visit William when he was in the State's custody and having said that she could not care for him.

The court found that Ms. Lassiter "has not contacted the Department of Social Services about her child since December, 1975, has not expressed any concern for his care and welfare, and has made no efforts to plan for his future." Because Ms. Lassiter thus had "wilfully failed to maintain concern or responsibility for the welfare of the minor," and because it was "in the best interests of the minor," the court terminated Ms. Lassiter's status as William's parent.

On appeal, Ms. Lassiter argued only that, because she was indigent, the Due Process Clause of the Fourteenth Amendment entitled her to the assistance of counsel, and that the trial court had therefore erred in not requiring the State to provide counsel for her. The North Carolina Court of Appeals decided that "[while] this State action does invade a protected area of individual privacy, the invasion is not so serious or unreasonable as to compel us to hold that appointment of counsel for indigent parents is constitutionally mandated." The Supreme Court of North Carolina summarily denied Ms. Lassiter's application for discretionary review and we granted certiorari to consider the petitioner's claim under the Due Process Clause of the Fourteenth Amendment.

...

A

The pre-eminent generalization that emerges from this Court's precedents on an indigent's right to appointed counsel is that such a right has been recognized to exist only where the litigant may lose his physical liberty if he loses the litigation....

... [I]t is the defendant's interest in personal freedom, and not simply the special Sixth and Fourteenth Amendments right to counsel in criminal cases, which triggers the right to appointed counsel....

Significantly, as a litigant's interest in personal liberty diminishes, so does his right to appointed counsel....

Finally, the Court has refused to extend the right to appointed counsel to include prosecutions which, though criminal, do not result in the defendant's loss of personal liberty. . . .

In sum, the Court's precedents speak with one voice about what "fundamental fairness" has meant when the Court has considered the right to appointed counsel, and we thus draw from them the presumption that an indigent litigant has a right to appointed counsel only when, if he loses, he may be deprived of his physical liberty. It is against this presumption that all the other elements in the due process decision must be measured.

B

The case of *Mathews v. Eldridge*, propounds three elements to be evaluated in deciding what due process requires, viz., the private interests at stake, the government's interest, and the risk that the procedures used will lead to erroneous decisions. We must balance these elements against each other, and then set their net weight in the scales against the presumption that there is a right to appointed counsel only where the indigent, if he is unsuccessful, may lose his personal freedom.

This Court's decisions have by now made plain beyond the need for multiple citation that a parent's desire for and right to "the companionship, care, custody, and management of his or her children" is an important interest that "undeniably warrants deference and, absent a powerful countervailing interest, protection." Here the State has sought not simply to infringe upon that interest, but to end it. If the State prevails, it will have worked a unique kind of deprivation. A parent's interest in the accuracy and justice of the decision to terminate his or her parental status is, therefore, a commanding one.

Since the State has an urgent interest in the welfare of the child, it shares the parent's interest in an accurate and just decision. For this reason, the State may share the indigent parent's interest in the availability of appointed counsel. If, as our adversary system presupposes, accurate and just results are most likely to be obtained through the equal contest of opposed interests, the State's interest in the child's welfare may perhaps best be served by a hearing in which both the parent and the State acting for the child are represented by counsel, without whom the contest of interests may become unwholesomely unequal. North Carolina itself acknowledges as much by providing that where a parent files a written answer to a termination petition, the State must supply a lawyer to represent the child.

The State's interests, however, clearly diverge from the parent's insofar as the State wishes the termination decision to be made as economically as possible and thus wants to avoid both the expense of appointed counsel and the cost of the lengthened proceedings his presence may cause. But though the State's pecuniary interest is legitimate, it is hardly significant enough to overcome private interests as important as those here, particularly in light of the concession in the respondent's brief that the "potential costs of appointed counsel in termination proceedings . . . is [sic] admittedly de minimis compared to the costs in all criminal actions."

Finally, consideration must be given to the risk that a parent will be erroneously deprived of his or her child because the parent is not represented by counsel. . . .

The respondent argues that the subject of a termination hearing—the parent's relationship with her child—far from being abstruse, technical, or unfamiliar, is one as to which the parent must be uniquely well informed and to which the parent must have given prolonged thought. The respondent also contends that a termination hearing is not likely to produce difficult points of evidentiary law, or even of substantive law, since the evidentiary problems peculiar to criminal trials are not present and since the standards for termination are not complicated. In fact, the respondent reports, the North Carolina Departments of Social Services are themselves sometimes represented at termination hearings by social workers instead of by lawyers.

Yet the ultimate issues with which a termination hearing deals are not always simple, however commonplace they may be. Expert medical and psychiatric testimony, which few parents are equipped to understand and fewer still to confute, is sometimes presented. The parents are likely to be people with little education, who have had uncommon difficulty in dealing with life, and who are, at the hearing, thrust into a distressing and disorienting situation. That these factors may combine to overwhelm an uncounseled parent is evident from the findings some courts have made. Thus, courts have generally held that the State must appoint counsel for indigent parents at termination proceedings. The respondent is able to point to no presently authoritative case, except for the North Carolina judgment now before us, holding that an indigent parent has no due process right to appointed counsel in termination proceedings.

C

The dispositive question, which must now be addressed, is whether the three *Eldridge* factors, when weighed against the presumption that there is no right to appointed counsel in the absence of at least a potential deprivation of physical liberty, suffice to rebut that presumption and thus to lead to the conclusion that the Due Process Clause requires the appointment of counsel when a State seeks to terminate an indigent's parental status. To summarize the above discussion of the *Eldridge* factors: the parent's interest is an extremely important one (and may be supplemented by the dangers of criminal liability inherent in some termination proceedings); the State shares with the parent an interest in a correct decision, has a relatively weak pecuniary interest, and, in some but not all cases, has a possibly stronger interest in informal procedures; and the complexity of the proceeding and the incapacity of the uncounseled parent could be, but would not always be, great enough to make the risk of an erroneous deprivation of the parent's rights insupportably high.

If, in a given case, the parent's interests were at their strongest, the State's interests were at their weakest, and the risks of error were at their peak, it could not be said that the *Eldridge* factors did not overcome the presumption against the right to appointed counsel, and that due process did not therefore require the appointment of counsel. But since the *Eldridge* factors will not always be so distributed, and since "due process is not so rigid as to require that the significant interests in informality, flexibility and economy must always be sacrificed," neither can we say that the Constitution requires that appointment of counsel in every parental termination proceeding. We therefore ... leave the decision whether due process calls for the appointment of counsel for indigent parents in termination proceedings to be answered in the first instance by the trial court, subject, of course, to appellate review.

III

... [B]ecause child-custody litigation must be concluded as rapidly as is consistent with fairness, we decide today whether the trial judge denied Ms. Lassiter due process of law when he did not appoint counsel for her.

The respondent represents that the petition to terminate Ms. Lassiter's parental rights contained no allegations of neglect or abuse upon which criminal charges could be based, and hence Ms. Lassiter could not well have argued that she required counsel for that reason. The Department of Social Services was represented at the hearing by counsel, but no expert witnesses testified, and the case presented no specially troublesome points of law, either procedural or substantive. While hearsay evidence was no doubt admitted, and while Ms. Lassiter no doubt left incomplete her defense that the Department had not adequately assisted her in rekindling her interest in her son, the weight of the evidence that she had few sparks of such an interest was sufficiently great that the presence of counsel for Ms. Lassiter could not have made a determinative difference. True, a lawyer might have done more with the argument that William should live with Ms. Lassiter's mother — but that argument was quite explicitly made by both Lassiters, and the evidence that the elder Ms. Lassiter had said she could not handle another child, that the social worker's investigation had led to a similar conclusion, and that the grandmother had displayed scant interest in the child once he had been removed from her daughter's custody was, though controverted, sufficiently substantial that the absence of counsel's guidance on this point did not render the proceedings fundamentally unfair. Finally, a court deciding whether due process requires the appointment of counsel need not ignore a parent's plain demonstration that she is not interested in attending a hearing. Here, the trial court had previously found that Ms. Lassiter had expressly declined to appear at the 1975 child custody hearing, Ms. Lassiter had not even bothered to speak to her retained lawyer after being notified of the termination hearing, and the court specifically found that Ms. Lassiter's failure to make an effort to contest the termination proceeding was without cause. In view of all these circumstances, we hold that the trial court did not err in failing to appoint counsel for Ms. Lassiter.

IV

In its Fourteenth Amendment, our Constitution imposes on the States the standards necessary to ensure that judicial proceedings are fundamentally fair. A wise public policy, however, may require that higher standards be adopted than those minimally tolerable under the Constitution. Informed opinion has clearly come to hold that an indigent parent is entitled to the assistance of appointed counsel not only in parental termination proceedings, but in dependency and neglect proceedings as well.... Most significantly, 33 States and the District of Columbia provide statutorily for the appointment of counsel in termination cases. The Court's opinion today in no way implies that the standards increasingly urged by informed public opinion and now widely followed by the States are other than enlightened and wise.

For the reasons stated in this opinion, the judgment is affirmed.

It is so ordered.

Chief Justice Burger, concurring.

I join the Court's opinion and add only a few words to emphasize a factor I believe is misconceived by the dissenters. The purpose of the termination proceeding at issue here was not "punitive." On the contrary, its purpose was protective of the child's best interests. Given the record in this case, which involves the parental rights of a mother under lengthy sentence for murder who showed little interest in her son, the writ might well have been a "candidate" for dismissal as improvidently granted. However, I am content to join the narrow holding of the Court, leaving the appointment of counsel in termination proceedings to be determined by the state courts on a case-by-case basis.

Justice Blackmun, with whom Justice Brennan and Justice Marshall join, dissenting.

The Court today denies an indigent mother the representation of counsel in a judicial proceeding initiated by the State of North Carolina to terminate her parental rights with respect to her youngest child. The Court most appropriately recognizes that the mother's interest is a "commanding one," and it finds no countervailing state interest of even remotely comparable significance. Nonetheless, the Court avoids what seems to me the obvious conclusion that due process requires the presence of counsel for a parent threatened with judicial termination of parental rights, and, instead, revives an ad hoc approach thoroughly discredited nearly 20 years ago.... Because I believe that the unique importance of a parent's interest in the care and custody of his or her child cannot constitutionally be extinguished through formal judicial proceedings without the benefit of counsel, I dissent.

I

...

It is not disputed that state intervention to terminate the relationship between petitioner and her child must be accomplished by procedures meeting the requisites of the Due Process Clause. Nor is there any doubt here about the kind of procedure North Carolina has prescribed. North Carolina law requires notice and a trial-type hearing before the State on its own initiative may sever the bonds of parenthood. The decisionmaker is a judge, the rules of evidence are in force, and the State is represented by counsel. The question, then, is whether proceedings in this mold, that relate to a subject so vital, can comport with fundamental fairness when the defendant parent remains unrepresented by counsel. As the Court today properly acknowledges, our consideration of the process due in this context, as in others, must rely on a balancing of the competing private and public interests, an approach succinctly described in *Mathews v. Eldridge*. As does the majority, I evaluate the "three distinct factors" specified in *Eldridge*: the private interest affected; the risk of error under the procedure employed by the State; and the countervailing governmental interest in support of the challenged procedure.

A

At stake here is "the interest of a parent in the companionship, care, custody, and management of his or her children." This interest occupies a unique place in our legal culture, given the centrality of family life as the focus for personal meaning and responsibility....

In this case, the State's aim is not simply to influence the parent–child relationship but to extinguish it. A termination of parental rights is both total and irrevocable. Unlike other custody proceedings, it leaves the parent with no right to visit or communicate with the child, to participate in, or even to know about, any important decision affecting the child's religious, educational, emotional, or physical development. It is hardly surprising that this forced dissolution of the parent–child relationship has been recognized as a punitive sanction by courts, Congress, and commentators. The Court candidly notes, as it must, that termination of parental rights by the State is a "unique kind of deprivation."

...

Rather than opting for the insensitive presumption that incarceration is the only loss of liberty sufficiently onerous to justify a right to appointed counsel, I would abide by the Court's enduring commitment to examine the relationships among the interests on both sides, and the appropriateness of counsel in the specific type of proceeding. The fundamental significance of the liberty interests at stake in a parental termination proceeding is undeniable, and I would find this first portion of the due process balance weighing heavily in favor of refined procedural protections. The second *Eldridge* factor, namely, the risk of error in the procedure provided by the State, must then be reviewed with some care.

B

The method chosen by North Carolina to extinguish parental rights resembles in many respects a criminal prosecution....

In addition, the proceeding has an obvious accusatory and punitive focus. In moving to terminate a parent's rights, the State has concluded that it no longer will try to preserve the family unit, but instead will marshal an array of public resources to establish that the parent–child separation must be made permanent. The State has legal representation through the county attorney. This lawyer has access to public records concerning the family and to professional social workers who are empowered to investigate the family situation and to testify against the parent. The State's legal representative may also call upon experts in family relations, psychology, and medicine to bolster the State's case. And, of course, the State's counsel himself is an expert in the legal standards and techniques employed at the termination proceeding, including the methods of cross-examination.

...

... When the parent is indigent, lacking in education, and easily intimidated by figures of authority, the imbalance may well become insuperable.

The risk of error thus is severalfold. The parent who actually has achieved the improvement or quality of parenting the State would require may be unable to establish this fact. The parent who has failed in these regards may be unable to demonstrate cause, absence of willfulness, or lack of agency diligence as justification. And errors of fact or law in the State's case may go unchallenged and uncorrected. Given the weight of the interests at stake, this risk of error assumes extraordinary proportions. By intimidation, inarticulateness, or confusion, a parent can lose forever all contact and involvement with his or her offspring.

C

The final factor to be considered, the interests claimed for the State, do not tip the scale against providing appointed counsel in this context....

The State may, and does, properly assert a legitimate interest in promoting the physical and emotional well-being of its minor children. But this interest is not served by terminating the rights of any concerned, responsible parent....

The State also has an interest in avoiding the cost and administrative inconvenience that might accompany a right to appointed counsel. But, as the Court acknowledges, the State's fiscal interest "is hardly significant enough to overcome private interests as important as those here." The State's financial concern indeed is a limited one, for the right to appointed counsel may well be restricted to those termination proceedings that are instituted by the State. Moreover, no difficult line-drawing problem would arise with respect to other types of civil proceedings. The instant due process analysis takes full account of the fundamental nature of the parental interest, the permanency of the threatened deprivation, the gross imbalance between the resources employed by the prosecuting State and those available to the indigent parent, and the relatively insubstantial cost of furnishing counsel. An absence of any one of these factors might yield a different result. But where, as here, the threatened loss of liberty is severe and absolute, the State's role is so clearly adversarial and punitive, and the cost involved is relatively slight, there is no sound basis for refusing to recognize the right to counsel as a requisite of due process in a proceeding initiated by the State to terminate parental rights.

II

. . .

B

The problem of inadequate representation is painfully apparent in the present case. . . .

At the termination hearing, the State's sole witness was the county worker who had met petitioner on the one occasion at the prison. This worker had been assigned to William's case in August 1977, yet much of her testimony concerned events prior to that date; she represented these events as contained in the agency record. Petitioner failed to uncover this weakness in the worker's testimony. That is hardly surprising, for there is no indication that an agency record was introduced into evidence or was present in court, or that petitioner or the grandmother ever had an opportunity to review any such record. The social worker also testified about her conversations with members of the community. In this hearsay testimony, the witness reported the opinion of others that the grandmother could not handle the additional responsibility of caring for the fifth child. There is no indication that these community members were unavailable to testify, and the County Attorney did not justify the admission of the hearsay. Petitioner made no objection to its admission.

The court gave petitioner an opportunity to cross-examine the social worker, but she apparently did not understand that cross-examination required questioning rather than declarative statements. At this point, the judge became noticeably impatient with petitioner. Petitioner then took the stand, and testified that she wanted William to live with his grandmother and his siblings. The judge questioned her for a brief period, and expressed open disbelief at one of her answers. The final witness was the grandmother. Both the judge and the County Attorney questioned her. She denied having expressed unwillingness to take William into her home, and vehemently contradicted the social worker's statement that she had complained to the Department about her daughter's neglect of the child. Petitioner was not told that she could question her mother, and did not do so. The County Attorney made a closing argument and the judge then asked petitioner if she had any final remarks. She responded: "Yes. I don't think its right."

It is perhaps understandable that the District Court Judge experienced difficulty and exasperation in conducting this hearing. But both the difficulty and the exasperation are attributable in large measure, if not entirely, to the lack of counsel. An experienced attorney might have translated petitioner's reaction and emotion into several substantive legal arguments. The State charged petitioner with failing to arrange a "constructive plan" for her child's future or to demonstrate a "positive response" to the Department's intervention. A defense would have been that petitioner had arranged for the child to be cared for properly by his grandmother, and evidence might have been adduced to demonstrate the adequacy of the grandmother's care of the other children. The Department's own "diligence" in promoting the family's integrity was never put in issue during the hearing, yet it is surely significant in light of petitioner's incarceration and lack of access to her child. Finally, the asserted willfulness of petitioner's lack of concern could obviously have been attacked since she was physically unable to regain custody or perhaps even to receive meaningful visits during 21 of the 24 months preceding the action.

III

Petitioner plainly has not led the life of the exemplary citizen or model parent. It may well be that if she were accorded competent legal representation, the ultimate result in this particular case would be the same. But the issue before the Court is not petitioner's character; it is whether she was given a meaningful opportunity to be heard when the State moved to terminate absolutely her parental rights. In light of the unpursued avenues of defense, and of the experience petitioner underwent at the hearing, I find virtually incredible the Court's conclusion today that her termination proceeding was fundamentally fair. To reach that conclusion, the Court simply ignores the defendant's obvious inability to speak effectively for herself, a factor the Court has found to be highly significant in past cases. I am unable to ignore that factor; instead, I believe that the record, and the norms of fairness acknowledged by the majority, compel a holding according counsel to petitioner and persons similarly situated.

Ours, supposedly, is "a maturing society," and our notion of due process is, "perhaps, the least frozen concept of our law." If the Court . . . was able to perceive as constitutionally necessary the access to judicial resources required to dissolve a marriage at the behest of private parties, surely it should perceive as similarly necessary the requested access to legal resources when the State itself seeks to dissolve the intimate and personal family bonds between parent and child. It will not open the "floodgates" that, I suspect, the Court fears. On the contrary, we cannot constitutionally afford the closure that the result in this sad case imposes upon us all.

I respectfully dissent.

Justice Stevens, dissenting.

A woman's misconduct may cause the State to take formal steps to deprive her of her liberty. The State may incarcerate her for a fixed term and also may permanently deprive her of her freedom to associate with her child. The former is a pure deprivation of liberty; the latter is a deprivation of both liberty and property, because statutory rights of inheritance as well as the natural relationship may be destroyed. Although both deprivations are serious, often the deprivation of parental rights will be the more grievous of the two. The plain language of the Fourteenth Amendment commands that both deprivations must be accompanied by due process of law.

Without so stating explicitly, the Court appears to treat this case as though it merely involved the deprivation of an interest in property that is less worthy of protection than a person's liberty. The analysis employed in *Mathews v. Eldridge*, in which the Court balanced the costs and benefits of different procedural mechanisms for allocating a finite quantity of material resources among competing claimants, is an appropriate method of determining what process is due in property cases. Meeting the Court on its own terms, Justice Blackmun demonstrates that the *Mathews v. Eldridge* analysis requires the appointment of counsel in this type of case. I agree with his conclusion, but I would take one further step.

In my opinion the reasons supporting the conclusion that the Due Process Clause of the Fourteenth Amendment entitles the defendant in a criminal case to representation by counsel apply with equal force to a case of this kind. The issue is one of fundamental fairness, not of weighing the pecuniary costs against the societal benefits. Accordingly, even if the costs to the State were not relatively insignificant but rather were just as great as the costs of providing prosecutors, judges, and defense counsel to ensure the fairness of criminal proceedings, I would reach the same result in this category of cases. For the value of protecting our liberty from deprivation by the State without due process of law is priceless.

Notes and Queries

1. What are the *Mathews v. Eldridge* factors?
2. The majority concludes that the rights of indigents to counsel in termination cases must be determined on a case-by-case basis by the trial judge and, failure to provide counsel remains subject to appellate review. Do you find their analysis persuasive? How would you justify focusing on appellate review protections when the issue is improper representation at trial? If the indigent cannot afford counsel at trial, why should it be assumed that they could appeal adverse decisions?
3. Do you think Ms. Lassiter would have benefitted from counsel? Justices Blackmun, Brennan, and Marshall offered the following excerpt from the trial court's hearing to argue that she in fact did need counsel. Persuasive? Do you find the evidence significant in light to their analysis of what competent counsel could have argued?

The Court: All right. Do you want to ask her any questions?

Petitioner: About what? About what she—

The Court: About this child.

Petitioner: Oh, yes.

The Court: All right. Go ahead.

Petitioner: The only thing I know is that when you say—

The Court: I don't want you to testify.

Petitioner: Okay.

The Court: I want to know whether you want to cross-examine her or ask any questions.

Petitioner: Yes, I want to. Well, you know, the only thing I know about is my part that I know about it. I know—

The Court: I am not talking about what you know. I want to know if you want to ask her any questions or not.

Petitioner: About that?

The Court: Yes. Do you understand the nature of this proceeding?

Petitioner: Yes.

The Court: And that is to terminate any rights you have to the child and place it for adoption, if necessary.

Petitioner: Yes, I know.

The Court: Are there any questions you want to ask her about what she has testified to?

Petitioner: Yes.

The Court: All right. Go ahead.

Petitioner: I want to know why you think you are going to turn my child over to a foster home? He knows my mother and he knows all of us. He knows her and he knows all of us.

The Court: Who is he?

Petitioner: My son, William.

Social Worker: Ms. Lassiter, your son has been in foster care since May of 1975 and since that time—

Petitioner: Yeah, yeah and I didn't know anything about it either.

The Court: Did you know that your mother filed a complaint on the 8th day of May, 1975 . . . ?

A: No, 'cause she said she didn't file no complaint.

The Court: That was some ghost who came up here and filed it I suppose.

The judge concluded his questioning by saying to the County Attorney: "All right, Mr. Odom, see what you can do."

This latter denial produced the following reaction from the court,

Q: [from respondent]: Did you tell Ms. Mangum on the 8th day of May, 1975, that when your daughter was in the hospital having William that she left the children in the cold house with no heat?

A: No, sir, no, sir, unh unh, no, sir.

Petitioner: That's a lie.

A: No, sir, no, sir. God knows, I'll raise my right hand to God and die saying that. Somebody else told that.

The Court: I wish you wouldn't talk like that it scares me to be in the same room with you.

The judge had initiated the examination of Mrs. Lassiter; subsequently he expressed exasperation with the rambling quality of her answers:

The Court: I tell you what, let's just stop all this. You question her, please. Just answer his questions. We'll be here all day at this rate. I mean, we are just wasting time, we're skipping from one subject to another—

4. Consider arguments for providing counsel in civil cases and whether *Lassiter* may provide a good case in point to support those arguments. First, civil litigants typically are unequipped for what is essential to a fair trial: knowledge of the law. Lay litigants do not have a mastery of the rules of evidence so that inadmissible evidence, such as hearsay or testimony pertaining to settlement negotiations, will not be admitted to their detriment. In addition, they may not be privy to the same resources and networking opportunities that are available to members of the Bar. What do you think of Mrs. Lassiter's lawyering skills? Second, failure to appoint counsel also compromises the neutrality and impartiality of the judiciary. When a litigant is without counsel, an undue and unethical responsibility may rest on judges to take the place of counsel. Does *Lassiter* illustrate the need for judges to remain impartial in our adversarial system? Third, the burden of proof in most civil cases, "a preponderance of the evidence," is a much lower standard that is much easier to reach than the "beyond a reasonable doubt" standard in criminal cases. This discrepency may become troublesome when unrepresented civil litigants face opposing parties with counsel, as the state of North Carolina did in *Lassiter*. Egregious? Lastly, the appearance of impropriety and lack of uniform application of the law may damage our system of justice. This particularly may be the case in light of the stratification of economic classes in the United States—often with disparate impact on minorities. Reasonable consideration? *Lassiter* may provide good support for these arguments, but what would be the countervailing factors?

Santosky v. Kramer

455 U.S. 745; 102 S. Ct. 1388 (1982)

Justice Blackmun delivered the opinion of the Court.

. . .

New York authorizes its officials to remove a child temporarily from his or her home if the child appears "neglected," within the meaning of Art. Once removed, a child under the age of 18 customarily is placed "in the care of an authorized agency," Soc. Serv. Law § 384-b.7.(a), usually a state institution or a foster home. At that point, "the state's first obligation is to help the family with services to . . . reunite it. . . ." § 384-b.1.(a)(iii). But if convinced that "positive, nurturing parent–child relationships no longer exist," § 384-b.1.(b), the State may initiate "permanent neglect" proceedings to free the child for adoption.

The State bifurcates its permanent neglect proceeding into "factfinding" and "dispositional" hearings. Fam. Ct. Act §§ 622, 623. At the factfinding stage, the State must prove that the child has been "permanently neglected," as defined by Fam. Ct. Act §§ 614.1.(a)–(d) and Soc. Serv. Law § 384-b.7.(a). The Family Court judge then determines at a subsequent dispositional hearing what placement would serve the child's best interests.

At the factfinding hearing, the State must establish, among other things, that for more than a year after the child entered state custody, the agency "made diligent efforts to encourage and strengthen the parental relationship." The State must further prove that during that same period, the child's natural parents failed "substantially and continuously or repeatedly to maintain contact with or plan for the future of the child although physically and financially able to do so." Should the State support its allegations by "a fair preponderance of the evidence," the child may be declared permanently neglected. That declaration empowers the Family Court judge to terminate permanently the natural parents' rights in the child. Termination denies the natural parents physical custody, as well as the rights ever to visit, communicate with, or regain custody of the child.

New York's permanent neglect statute provides natural parents with certain procedural protections. But New York permits its officials to establish "permanent neglect" with less proof than most States require. Thirty-five States, the District of Columbia, and the Virgin Islands currently specify a higher standard of proof, in parental rights termination proceedings, than a "fair preponderance of the evidence" The only analogous federal statute of which we are aware permits termination of parental rights solely upon "evidence beyond a reasonable doubt." [Indian Child Welfare Act of 1978] The question here is whether New York's "fair preponderance of the evidence" standard is constitutionally sufficient.

B

Petitioners John Santosky II and Annie Santosky are the natural parents of Tina and John III. In November 1973, after incidents reflecting parental neglect, respondent Kramer, Commissioner of the Ulster County Department of Social Services, initiated a neglect proceeding under Fam. Ct. Act § 1022 and removed Tina from her natural home. About 10 months later, he removed John III and placed him with foster parents. On the day John was taken, Annie Santosky gave birth to a third child, Jed. When Jed was only three days old, respondent transferred him to a foster home on the ground that immediate removal was necessary to avoid imminent danger to his life or health.

In October 1978, respondent petitioned the Ulster County Family Court to terminate petitioners' parental rights in the three children. Petitioners challenged the constitutionality of the "fair preponderance of the evidence" standard specified in Fam. Ct. Act § 622. The Family Court Judge rejected this constitutional challenge, and weighed the evidence under the statutory standard. While acknowledging that the Santoskys had maintained contact with their children, the judge found those visits "at best superficial and devoid of any real emotional content." After deciding that the agency had made "'diligent efforts' to encourage and strengthen the parental relationship," he concluded that the Santoskys were incapable, even with public assistance, of planning for the future of their children. The judge later held a dispositional hearing and ruled that the best interests of the three children required permanent termination of the Santoskys' custody.

Petitioners appealed, again contesting the constitutionality of § 622's standard of proof. The New York Supreme Court, Appellate Division, affirmed, holding application of the preponderance-of-the-evidence standard "proper and constitutional." That standard, the court reasoned, "recognizes and seeks to balance rights possessed by the child . . . with those of the natural parents. . . ."

The New York Court of Appeals then dismissed petitioners' appeal. . . . We granted certiorari to consider petitioners' constitutional claim.

II

. . .

The fundamental liberty interest of natural parents in the care, custody, and management of their child does not evaporate simply because they have not been model parents or have lost temporary custody of their child to the State. Even when blood relationships are strained, parents retain a vital interest in preventing the irretrievable destruction of their family life. If anything, persons faced with forced dissolution of their parental rights have a more critical need for procedural protections than do those resisting state intervention into ongoing family affairs. When the State moves to destroy weakened familial bonds, it must provide the parents with fundamentally fair procedures.

. . .

Thus, while private parties may be interested intensely in a civil dispute over money damages, application of a "fair preponderance of the evidence" standard indicates both society's "minimal concern with the outcome," and a conclusion that the litigants should "share the risk of error in roughly equal fashion." When the State brings a criminal action to deny a defendant liberty or life, however, "the interests of the defendant are of such magnitude that historically and without any explicit constitutional requirement they have been protected by standards of proof designed to exclude as nearly as possible the likelihood of an erroneous judgment." The stringency of the "beyond a reasonable doubt" standard bespeaks the "weight and gravity" of the private interest affected, society's interest in avoiding erroneous convictions, and a judgment that those interests together require that "society [impose] almost the entire risk of error upon itself."

. . .

This Court has mandated an intermediate standard of proof—"clear and convincing evidence"—when the individual interests at stake in a state proceeding are both "particularly important" and "more substantial than mere loss of money." Notwithstanding "the state's 'civil labels and good intentions,'" the Court has deemed this level of certainty necessary to preserve fundamental fairness in a variety of government-initiated proceedings that threaten the individual involved with "a significant deprivation of liberty" or "stigma."

. . .

III

In parental rights termination proceedings, the private interest affected is commanding; the risk of error from using a preponderance standard is substantial; and the countervailing governmental interest favoring that standard is comparatively slight. Evaluation of the three *Eldridge* factors compels the conclusion that use of a "fair preponderance of the evidence" standard in such proceedings is inconsistent with due process.

A

"The extent to which procedural due process must be afforded the recipient is influenced by the extent to which he may be 'condemned to suffer grievous loss.'" Whether the loss threatened by a particular type of proceeding is sufficiently grave to warrant more than average certainty on the part of the factfinder turns on both the nature of the private interest threatened and the permanency of the threatened loss.

Lassiter declared it "plain beyond the need for multiple citation" that a natural parent's "desire for and right to 'the companionship, care, custody, and management of his or her children'" is an interest far more precious than any property right. When the State initiates a parental rights termination proceeding, it seeks not merely to infringe that fundamental liberty interest, but to end it. "If the State prevails, it will have worked a unique kind of deprivation. . . . A parent's interest in the accuracy and justice of the decision to terminate his or her parental status is, therefore, a commanding one."

The factfinding does not purport — and is not intended — to balance the child's interest in a normal family home against the parents' interest in raising the child. Nor does it purport to determine whether the natural parents or the foster parents would provide the better home. Rather, the factfinding hearing pits the State directly against the parents. The State alleges that the natural parents are at fault. The questions disputed and decided are what the State did — "made diligent efforts," and what the natural parents did not do — "maintain contact with or plan for the future of the child." The State marshals an array of public resources to prove its case and disprove the parents' case. Victory by the State not only makes termination of parental rights possible; it entails a judicial determination that the parents are unfit to raise their own children.

At the factfinding, the State cannot presume that a child and his parents are adversaries. After the State has established parental unfitness at that initial proceeding, the court may assume at the dispositional stage that the interests of the child and the natural parents do diverge . . . (judge shall make his order "solely on the basis of the best interests of the child," and thus has no obligation to consider the natural parents' rights in selecting dispositional alternatives). But until the State proves parental unfitness, the child and his parents share a vital interest in preventing erroneous termination of their natural relationship. Thus, at the factfinding, the interests of the child and his natural parents coincide to favor use of error-reducing procedures.

B

Under *Mathews v. Eldridge*, we next must consider both the risk of erroneous deprivation of private interests resulting from use of a "fair preponderance" standard and the likelihood that a higher evidentiary standard would reduce that risk. Since the factfinding phase of a permanent neglect proceeding is an adversary contest between the State and the natural parents, the relevant question is whether a preponderance standard fairly allocates the risk of an erroneous factfinding between these two parties.

In New York, the factfinding stage of a state-initiated permanent neglect proceeding bears many of the indicia of a criminal trial. The Commissioner of Social Services charges the parents with permanent neglect. They are served by summons. The factfinding hearing is conducted pursuant to formal rules of evidence. The State, the parents, and the child are all represented by counsel. The State seeks to establish a series of historical facts about the intensity of its agency's efforts to reunite the family, the infrequency and insubstantiality of the parents' contacts with their child, and the parents' inability or unwillingness to formulate a plan for the child's future. The attorneys submit documentary evidence, and call witnesses who are subject to cross-examination. Based on all the evidence, the judge then determines whether the State has proved the statutory elements of permanent neglect by a fair preponderance of the evidence.

At such a proceeding, numerous factors combine to magnify the risk of erroneous factfinding. Permanent neglect proceedings employ imprecise substantive standards that leave determinations unusually open to the subjective values of the judge.

In appraising the nature and quality of a complex series of encounters among the agency, the parents, and the child, the court possesses unusual discretion to underweigh probative facts that might favor the parent. Because parents subject to termination proceedings are often poor, uneducated, or members of minority groups, such proceedings are often vulnerable to judgments based on cultural or class bias.

The State's ability to assemble its case almost inevitably dwarfs the parents' ability to mount a defense. No predetermined limits restrict the sums an agency may spend in prosecuting a given termination proceeding. The State's attorney usually will be expert on the issues contested and the procedures employed at the factfinding hearing, and enjoys full access to all public records concerning the family. The State may call on experts in family relations, psychology, and medicine to bolster its case. Furthermore, the primary witnesses at the hearing will be the agency's own professional caseworkers whom the State has empowered both to investigate the family situation and to testify against the parents. Indeed, because the child is already in agency custody, the State even has the power to shape the historical events that form the basis for termination.

The disparity between the adversaries' litigation resources is matched by a striking asymmetry in their litigation options. Unlike criminal defendants, natural parents have no "double jeopardy" defense against repeated state termination efforts. If the State initially fails to win termination, as New York did here, it always can try once again to cut off the parents' rights after gathering more or better evidence. Yet even when the parents have attained the level of fitness required by the State, they have no similar means by which they can forestall future termination efforts.

Coupled with a "fair preponderance of the evidence" standard, these factors create a significant prospect of erroneous termination. A standard of proof that by its very terms demands consideration of the quantity, rather than the quality, of the evidence may misdirect the factfinder in the marginal case. Given the weight of the private interests at stake, the social cost of even occasional error is sizable.

Raising the standard of proof would have both practical and symbolic consequences. The Court has long considered the heightened standard of proof used in criminal prosecutions to be "a prime instrument for reducing the risk of convictions resting on factual error." An elevated standard of proof in a parental rights termination proceeding would alleviate "the possible risk that a factfinder might decide to [deprive] an individual based solely on a few isolated instances of unusual conduct [or] . . . idiosyncratic behavior." "Increasing the burden of proof is one way to impress the factfinder with the importance of the decision and thereby perhaps to reduce the chances that inappropriate" terminations will be ordered.

The Appellate Division approved New York's preponderance standard on the ground that it properly "balanced rights possessed by the child . . . with those of the natural parents. . . ." By so saying, the court suggested that a preponderance standard properly allocates the risk of error between the parents and the child. That view is fundamentally mistaken.

The court's theory assumes that termination of the natural parents' rights invariably will benefit the child. Yet we have noted above that the parents and the child share an interest in avoiding erroneous termination. Even accepting the court's assumption, we cannot agree with its conclusion that a preponderance standard fairly distributes the risk of error between parent and child. Use of that standard reflects the judgment that society is nearly neutral between erroneous termination of parental rights and erroneous failure to terminate those rights. For the child, the likely consequence of an erroneous failure to terminate is preservation of an uneasy status quo. For the natural parents, however, the consequence of an erroneous termination is the unnecessary destruction of their natural family. A standard that allocates the risk of error nearly equally between those two outcomes does not reflect properly their relative severity.

C

Two state interests are at stake in parental rights termination proceedings—a parens patriae interest in preserving and promoting the welfare of the child and a fiscal and administrative interest in reducing the cost and burden of such proceedings. A standard of proof more strict than preponderance of the evidence is consistent with both interests.

"Since the State has an urgent interest in the welfare of the child, it shares the parent's interest in an accurate and just decision" at the factfinding proceeding. As parens patriae, the State's goal is to provide the child with a permanent home. Yet while there is still reason to believe that positive, nurturing parent–child relationships exist, the parens patriae interest favors preservation, not severance, of natural familial bonds. "[The] State registers no gain towards its declared goals when it separates children from the custody of fit parents."

The State's interest in finding the child an alternative permanent home arises only "when it is clear that the natural parent cannot or will not provide a normal family home for the child." At the factfinding, that goal is served by procedures that promote an accurate determination of whether the natural parents can and will provide a normal home.

Unlike a constitutional requirement of hearings, or court-appointed counsel, a stricter standard of proof would reduce factual error without imposing substantial fiscal burdens upon the State. As we have observed, 35 States already have adopted a higher standard by statute or court decision without apparent effect on the speed, form, or cost of their factfinding proceedings.

Nor would an elevated standard of proof create any real administrative burdens for the State's factfinders. . . . We cannot believe that it would burden the State unduly to require that its factfinders have the same factual certainty when terminating the parent–child relationship as they must have to suspend a driver's license.

IV

The logical conclusion of this balancing process is that the "fair preponderance of the evidence" standard prescribed by Fam. Ct. Act § 622 violates the Due Process

Clause of the Fourteenth Amendment. The Court noted in Addington: "The individual should not be asked to share equally with society the risk of error when the possible injury to the individual is significantly greater than any possible harm to the state." Thus, at a parental rights termination proceeding, a near-equal allocation of risk between the parents and the State is constitutionally intolerable. The next question, then, is whether a "beyond a reasonable doubt" or a "clear and convincing" standard is constitutionally mandated.

. . .

Like civil commitment hearings, termination proceedings often require the factfinder to evaluate medical and psychiatric testimony, and to decide issues difficult to prove to a level of absolute certainty, such as lack of parental motive, absence of affection between parent and child, and failure of parental foresight and progress. The substantive standards applied vary from State to State. Although Congress found a "beyond a reasonable doubt" standard proper in one type of parental rights termination case, another legislative body might well conclude that a reasonable-doubt standard would erect an unreasonable barrier to state efforts to free permanently neglected children for adoption.

A majority of the States have concluded that a "clear and convincing evidence" standard of proof strikes a fair balance between the rights of the natural parents and the State's legitimate concerns. We hold that such a standard adequately conveys to the factfinder the level of subjective certainty about his factual conclusions necessary to satisfy due process. We further hold that determination of the precise burden equal to or greater than that standard is a matter of state law properly left to state legislatures and state courts.

. . .

It is so ordered.

Justice Rehnquist, with whom The Chief Justice, Justice White, and Justice O'Connor join, dissenting.

I believe that few of us would care to live in a society where every aspect of life was regulated by a single source of law, whether that source be this Court or some other organ of our complex body politic. But today's decision certainly moves us in that direction. By parsing the New York scheme and holding one narrow provision unconstitutional, the majority invites further federal-court intrusion into every facet of state family law. If ever there were an area in which federal courts should heed the admonition of Justice Holmes that "a page of history is worth a volume of logic," it is in the area of domestic relations. This area has been left to the States from time immemorial, and not without good reason.

Equally as troubling is the majority's due process analysis. The Fourteenth Amendment guarantees that a State will treat individuals with "fundamental fairness" whenever its actions infringe their protected liberty or property interests. By adoption of the procedures relevant to this case, New York has created an exhaustive program to assist parents in regaining the custody of their children and to protect parents from the unfair deprivation of their parental rights. And yet the majority's myopic scrutiny of the standard of proof blinds it to the very considerations and procedures which make the New York scheme "fundamentally fair."

I

State intervention in domestic relations has always been an unhappy but necessary feature of life in our organized society. For all of our experience in this area, we have found no fully satisfactory solutions to the painful problem of child abuse and neglect. We have found, however, that leaving the States free to experiment with various remedies has produced novel approaches and promising progress.

. . .

The majority may believe that it is adopting a relatively unobtrusive means of ensuring that termination proceedings provide "due process of law." In fact, however, fixing the standard of proof as a matter of federal constitutional law will only lead to further federal-court intervention in state schemes. . . .

After fixing the standard of proof, therefore, the majority will be forced to evaluate other aspects of termination proceedings with reference to that point. . . . [T]he majority's approach will inevitably lead to the federalization of family law. Such a trend will only thwart state searches for better solutions in an area where this Court should encourage state experimentation. . . . It should not do so in the absence of a clear constitutional violation. As will be seen in the next part, no clear constitutional violation has occurred in this case.

. . .

As this account demonstrates, the State's extraordinary 4-year effort to reunite petitioners' family was not just unsuccessful, it was altogether rebuffed by parents unwilling to improve their circumstances sufficiently to permit a return of their children. At every step of this protracted process petitioners were accorded those procedures and protections which traditionally have been required by due process of law. Moreover, from the beginning to the end of this sad story all judicial determinations were made by one Family Court Judge. After four and one-half years of involvement with petitioners, more than seven complete hearings, and additional periodic supervision of the State's rehabilitative efforts, the judge no doubt was intimately familiar with this case and the prospects for petitioners' rehabilitation.

It is inconceivable to me that these procedures were "fundamentally unfair" to petitioners. Only by its obsessive focus on the standard of proof and its almost complete disregard of the facts of this case does the majority find otherwise. As the discussion above indicates, however, such a focus does not comport with the flexible standard of fundamental fairness embodied in the Due Process Clause of the Fourteenth Amendment.

B

In addition to the basic fairness of the process afforded petitioners, the standard of proof chosen by New York clearly reflects a constitutionally permissible balance of the interests at stake in this case. The standard of proof "represents an attempt to instruct the factfinder concerning the degree of confidence our society thinks he should have in the correctness of factual conclusions for a particular type of adjudication." In this respect, the standard of proof is a crucial component of legal process, the primary function of which is "to minimize the risk of erroneous decisions."

In determining the propriety of a particular standard of proof in a given case, however, it is not enough simply to say that we are trying to minimize the risk of error. Because errors in factfinding affect more than one interest, we try to minimize error as to those interests which we consider to be most important. . . .

. . .

On one side is the interest of parents in a continuation of the family unit and the raising of their own children. The importance of this interest cannot easily be overstated. Few consequences of judicial action are so grave as the severance of natural family ties. Even the convict committed to prison and thereby deprived of his physical liberty often retains the love and support of family members. "This Court's decisions have by now made plain beyond the need for multiple citation that a parent's desire for and right to 'the companionship, care, custody, and management of his or her children' is an important interest that 'undeniably warrants deference and, absent a powerful countervailing interest, protection.'" In creating the scheme at issue in this case, the New York Legislature was expressly aware of this right of parents "to bring up their own children."

. . .

When, in the context of a permanent neglect termination proceeding, the interests of the child and the State in a stable, nurturing homelife are balanced against the interests of the parents in the rearing of their child, it cannot be said that either set of interests is so clearly paramount as to require that the risk of error be allocated to one side or the other. Accordingly, a State constitutionally may conclude that the risk of error should be borne in roughly equal fashion by use of the preponderance-of-the-evidence standard of proof. This is precisely the balance which has been struck by the New York Legislature: "It is the intent of the legislature in enacting this section to provide procedures not only assuring that the rights of the natural parent are protected, but also, where positive, nurturing parent–child relationships no longer exist, furthering the best interests, needs, and rights of the child by terminating the parental rights and freeing the child for adoption."

III

For the reasons heretofore stated, I believe that the Court today errs in concluding that the New York standard of proof in parental-rights termination proceedings violates due process of law. The decision disregards New York's earnest efforts to aid parents in regaining the custody of their children and a host of procedural protections placed around parental rights and interests. The Court finds a constitutional violation only by a tunnel-vision application of due process principles that altogether loses sight of the unmistakable fairness of the New York procedure.

Even more worrisome, today's decision cavalierly rejects the considered judgment of the New York Legislature in an area traditionally entrusted to state care. The Court thereby begins, I fear, a trend of federal intervention in state family law matters which surely will stifle creative responses to vexing problems.

. . . Accordingly, I dissent.

Notes and Queries

1. What are the three standards of proof that may be used to sever parental rights? Which one would you argue most operates in the child's best interests?

2. The *Adoption Assistance Child Welfare Act* requires that intensive services be provided to try to keep children in their homes and provides that the state must make "reasonable efforts" to reunite the family. (New York state law requires "diligent efforts.") What outcome would you expect if the state did not fulfill its reasonable efforts obligations? Should the child–parent ties still be terminated? Should a state be required to prove that it in fact did pursue reasonable efforts to reunite the family? Should the state simply be required to show that the parent cannot provide a fit environment within a reasonable amount of time?

3. The majority emphasizes that the state "cannot presume that a child and his parents are adversaries." Since the state most likely intervened because the parents allegedly were failing in their responsibilities, is the assumption legitimate?

4. Termination proceedings typically occur after many other proceedings involving the removal of custody from parents. Should the clear and convincing standard, with appropriate exceptions, be applied at initial stages? Why?

5. Given *Lassiter*'s conclusion that the Fourteenth Amendment's Due Process Clause does not require the appointment of counsel for indigent parents in every parental status termination proceeding, would you have expected enunciation of a lower standard of proof?

6. Recall that *Lassiter* recognized but was not swayed enough by what it viewed as thirty-three states' good public policy of mandating counsel at termination proceedings. Yet, in this case, the Court at least found it persuasive that it was making the right decision as it referred to the majority of states' requirement that a mid-level standard of proof be required at termination hearings. Which approach properly addresses the role of states in establishing constitutional thresholds? In this regard, what do you make of Justice Rhenquist's dissent?

7. Much is made of the interests of the parent, child, and state. Do you agree with Justice Rhenquist's appraisal that, given that different situations differently result in making any of the interests more paramount than others, we should not fashion a standard of proof that assumes one would be more harmed? Assuming that he is correct, would that not argue for a higher standard of proof rather than the lower one?

Croft v. Westmoreland

103 F.3d 1123 (3rd Cir. Ct. App., 1997)

Circuit Judge Nygaard delivered the opinion of the court.

...

I.

On February 1, 1993, Gerald Sopko, Assistant Director of the Westmoreland County Children's Bureau received a call from Childline, informing him that Dr. Croft was sexually abusing his daughter, Chynna. Sopko was further told that the child slept with her parents and that she had recently been out of the house naked, walked to a neighbor's house, knocked on the door, and told the neighbors that she was "sleeping with mommy and daddy."

Barbara Jollie, Program Director for the Assessment Department of the Westmoreland County Children's Bureau, assigned the matter to Carla Danovsky for investigation. Danovsky, accompanied by State Police Trooper Griffin, went to the Croft home that night. Danovsky told Dr. Croft she was investigating him for possible sexual abuse of his daughter based on the Childline report. Dr. Croft consented to be interviewed.

Dr. Croft explained that Chynna had indeed, in April of 1992, left her bed without waking her parents, gone downstairs and outside, and locked herself out of the house. She then went to the house of her babysitter/nanny, a short distance from the Croft home, wearing her pajama top and holding her pajama bottoms with a soiled diaper inside. He further provided Danovsky with the telephone number of the nanny who could verify his version of events.

Dr. Croft agreed that his daughter had seen him naked and that, in fact, the family vacationed in the French West Indies where nude beaches are routine. Dr. Croft stated that his wife sunbathed nude around Chynna. He explained that Chynna suffered from seizures and, although she regularly slept in her parents' bed so they could be nearby if necessary, she slept naked only rarely. Henry and Carol Croft slept clothed. Dr. Croft told Danovsky that he had applied medicinal creams to her vaginal area when she had a rash. He denied sexually abusing Chynna.

Danovsky gave Dr. Croft an ultimatum: unless he left his home and separated himself from his daughter until the investigation was complete, she would take Chynna physically from the home that night and place her in foster care. Dr. Croft then left the room and Danovsky interviewed Carol Croft while Chynna sat in her lap. Carol Croft confirmed Dr. Croft's version of the April 1992 incident when Chynna locked herself out of the house. Finally, Danovsky questioned Chynna, who also confirmed Dr. Croft's version of the lock-out incident. Chynna provided no indication that she had ever been sexually abused. Danovsky then reiterated her ultimatum, that unless Dr. Croft immediately left his home and had no contact with his daughter, Danovsky would remove Chynna from the home that very night and place her in foster care. Faced with this dilemma, Dr. Croft complied with her ultimatum, and left his home, wife and daughter.

Danovsky testified to some inconsistencies between the statements of the Croft parents. She testified that Carol Croft said that Chynna never saw Henry Croft swimming naked, and that she sunbathed topless but not totally nude. One of the parents informed Danovsky that Chynna never slept naked in their bed, while the other said she was not clothed all the time. In sum, however, the differences were insignificant and reasonable under the circumstances. Danovsky also testified that, pursuant to County policy, a parent accused of sexual abuse must prove beyond any certainty that there was no sexual abuse before she would be permitted to leave a child with his or her parents. She further testified that if a County caseworker does not know whether or not the allegation is true, the child will be separated from the alleged perpetrator. Danovsky also testified that at the conclusion of her interview with the Crofts, she was uncertain whether any sexual abuse had occurred.

The Crofts filed a complaint in the federal district court against Westmoreland County Children and Youth Services (WCCYS), Carla Danovsky and Westmoreland County. They alleged that the defendants had impermissibly interfered with their Fourteenth Amendment liberty interest in the companionship of their daughter.

Defendants filed motions to dismiss the complaint, which, since discovery had been completed, were considered as motions for summary judgment. They argued that defendant Danovsky was entitled to qualified immunity for her actions and that the county and WCCYS enjoyed municipal immunity from the charges. The court entered summary judgment against the Crofts on all three counts, asserting that the Crofts would impermissibly have the court elevate their right to freedom of intimate association above Defendants' obligation to protect children. The Crofts timely appealed.

II.

We recognize the constitutionally protected liberty interests that parents have in the custody, care and management of their children. We also recognize that this interest is not absolute. Indeed, this liberty interest in familial integrity is limited by the compelling governmental interest in the protection of children particularly where the children need to be protected from their own parents. The right to familial integrity, in other words, does not include a right to remain free from child abuse investigations.

The Due Process Clause of the Fourteenth Amendment prohibits the government from interfering in familial relationships unless the government adheres to the requirements of procedural and substantive due process. In determining whether the Crofts' constitutionally protected interests were violated, we must balance the fundamental liberty interests of the family unit with the compelling interests of the state in protecting children from abuse. Whatever disruption or disintegration of family life the Croft's may have suffered as a result of the county's child abuse investigation does not, in and of itself, constitute a constitutional deprivation.

We realize there may be cases in which a child services bureau may be justified in removing either a child or parent from the home, even where later investigation proves no abuse occurred. However, a state has no interest in protecting children from their parents unless it has some reasonable and articulable evidence giving rise to a reasonable suspicion that a child has been abused or is in imminent danger of abuse.

Our focus here is whether the information available to the defendants at the time would have created an objectively reasonable suspicion of abuse justifying the degree of interference with the Crofts' rights as Chynna's parents. Absent such reasonable grounds, governmental intrusions of this type are arbitrary abuses of power.

Before the interviews, Danovsky possessed a six-fold hearsay report by an anonymous informant stating that the mother had told a friend that Dr. Croft had abused Chynna and that Chynna had recently been put out of the house naked, walked several miles, was found by a neighbor, and said she was sleeping with her parents.

Dr. Croft confirmed that an incident bearing only the barest resemblance to the anonymous tip had happened. Far from corroborating the anonymous tip, the Crofts' statements raised serious questions about the veracity of the informant. An anonymous tip may justify investigation but will not provide reasonable grounds for removal of a family member absent independent, articulable criteria of reliability; and certainly not when all evidence is to the contrary.

Danovsky was entitled to view the statements of an alleged perpetrator skeptically. She was not, however, entitled to rely on the unknown credibility of an anonymous informant unless she could corroborate the information through other sources which would have reduced the chance that the informant was recklessly relating incorrect information or had purposely distorted information.

Danovsky, in her deposition testimony, pointed to what she called "red flags"—statements given during the interviews which raised questions in her mind about whether the tip was true—as further justification for forcing Henry Croft from his home. The red flags cited by Defendants are incapable of providing the necessary reasonable grounds. For example, at one point during the interview, Dr. Croft told Danovsky that he had applied vaginal creams to Chynna when she had a rash, which Danovsky interpreted to mean that he regularly gave his daughter vaginal exams. Likewise, Danovsky's reliance on supposed inconsistencies between the statements of Carol and Dr. Croft is without foundation. None of the cited inconsistencies is evidence of child sexual abuse, nor did any of the statements in any way confirm the allegations of the anonymous tip. Even considered together, minor inconsistencies which provide no affirmative evidence of sexual abuse cannot alone establish the objectively reasonable grounds necessary to remove a family member from the family unit.

Most damaging to Defendants is Danovsky's deposition testimony that, after the interviews, she had no opinion one way or the other whether sexual abuse had occurred. Alternatively, Danovsky testified that she did not have enough information to make a determination and that further investigation was required. Under either statement, Danovsky did not have reasonable grounds, to any degree of certainty, that Chynna was sexually abused or was in imminent danger of abuse. She possessed no evidence of abuse beyond an anonymous tip. Danovsky had no physical evidence of sexual abuse with which to base an opinion. She was merely presented with an anonymous tip relating an incident which was reasonably explained by the accused parents. Record evidence establishes that Danovsky lacked any objective evidence of sexual abuse, and, indeed, that she had no belief that such abuse had occurred.

Considered in light of the circumstances surrounding the ultimatum, Danovsky's conduct was an arbitrary abuse of government power. Based on her lack of an opinion regarding whether sexual abuse had occurred, we hold that she lacked objectively reasonable grounds to believe the child had been sexually abused or was in imminent danger of sexual abuse. Combined with the total absence of objective evidence which would support a belief that sexual abuse had occurred, we hold that Danovsky's conduct will certainly not support the grant of summary judgment in the Defendants' favor. Because the Crofts did not cross-file for summary judgment, we, sitting as a court of review, must remand the cause to the district court for further proceedings.

III.

We will reverse the district court's entry of summary judgment.

. . .

Notes and Queries

1. In note one, the court highlights that defendants repeatedly characterize Dr. Croft's decision to leave as "voluntary." The court then proceeds to explicitly reject the contention by reasoning that the state's threat was blatantly coercive in that the state would take his four-year-old daughter and place her in foster care unless Dr. Croft left his home. Was the court reasonable?

2. The anonymous tip reported that "The mother told a friend . . ." of sexual abuse. Subsequently, the information went from the informant, to Childline, to Gerald Sopko, to Barbara Jollie, and then to Danovsky. The manner this report was filed is far from unusual, and such hearsay may often be the only available evidence

to alert child abuse investigators. Although such tips may not provide enough indicia of reliability to remove the child from the home, it does place the child protective agency in an awkward position since it must decide quickly whether to believe the parents, who may have at least some incentive not to tell the truth. Although the indicia of reliability may be insufficient to issue a warrant, do we want a high standard to determine the truth of allegations if the aim is to protect children? Should a social worker assume that parents are forthcoming? What harm is done by asking the father to leave for a few nights until an investigation puts the matter to rest or at least determines whether there is reasonable cause for intervention?

Review Problem

1. Acting voluntarily at the request of child welfare workers may have important practical implications. Consider these facts. A mother and her five children escape to a homeless shelter. Two of the children, a 7-day-old and a 1-year-old, are reported as having severe diaper and other rash and as not receiving medical treatment; one of the children has missed school since the family has been in the shelter. A social worker explains to the mother that, since there is no one else to care for the children, they may be better cared for in foster care, which she recommended as she explained DHS's two placement options: voluntary and involuntary. Although the mother was initially reluctant to place her children in foster care, she agreed that she had no other choice because she was unable to buy necessities for her children, such as milk and diapers. She further explained that she could not provide for her children because her boyfriend stole all her government assistance. On that same day the mother signed a voluntary placement agreement, placing her children in foster care. The voluntary placement agreement stated that plaintiff voluntarily and without coercion placed her children in foster care. Tragically, one of the children died in a fire set to the foster home by a foster child known to have set fires. The foster family had been properly approved and had passed all requirements. Does the mother have a claim? In this case, *Richardson v. City of Philadelphia, No. CIV.A.89-8901*, 1992 U.S. Dist. LEXIS 3345 (E.D. Pa. Mar. 6, 1992), the court found that if the child was placed voluntarily and without compelling the parent, the state was immune from civil damages; but if the state, through DHS and the Family Court system, affirmatively exercised its power to compel plaintiff to relinquish custody of the child because it believed that she was not capable of providing for his care, then it also assumed some duty to protect him from harm by private actors. The court also held that the municipality may be held liable under § 1983 for injuries resulting from a governmental policy or custom, if that policy or custom evidences a deliberate indifference to the rights of the person injured. In addition, it held that municipal defendants are immune from liability under state law. Would the mother have a § 1983 claim? (Recall that

a § 1983 civil action is one brought in federal courts that allows plaintiffs to seek relief for governmental violations of their rights, including constitutional, federal, and state rights.)

Research Comments

1. Voluntary separation often occurs in one of two ways: (1) the agency tells the parent suspected of abuse to leave the home; or (2) the agency tells the parents to place the child in the home of another family member for the duration of the investigation. This voluntary separation is attractive to agencies because it reduces the need for emergency shelter or foster care. It also is attractive to parents because it seems less threatening than the imagined horrors of bureaucratic care. Commentators note, however, that parents are often left with surprisingly serious and adverse consequences emerging from their initial separation decision. The emergency separation decision is accomplished informally, without a written document, and is treated by the state as a waiver or delay of the usual child welfare or dependency process, including a waiver or delay of the following: the parents' right to counsel, the parents' right to have prompt judicial review of the reasons for separation, and the parents' right to prompt planning for reunification of the child with the family. In addition, since the decision was made voluntarily, the caretaker was not a state agent, which makes the separation essentially not involve state protective custody or other reviewable state action. The voluntary agreement circumvents the traditional requirement of a prompt hearing and opportunity for the defendants to present their facts, an opportunity that is contemplated by most child welfare statutes and fundamental concepts of due process. Katherine C. Pearson (1998). Cooperate or we'll take your child: The parents' fictional voluntary separation decision and a proposal for change. *Tennessee Law Review*, 65, 835–873.

2. To counter problems with voluntary transfers, what do you think of the following proposal? In order to protect parents' fundamental rights, voluntary transfers would provide parents clear notice of the right to consult with counsel, provide counsel if indigent, give notice of the right to terminate the separation or placement with a simple request, mandate a clear statement of basic requirements, including duration of the transfer, require a written temporary separation agreement, and require indicia of informed, noncoerced consent. What would be the counter argument to these basic protections? Note that, where evidence of imminent threat or danger to the child clearly exists, government authorities are already armed with the potent tool of immediate, warrantless removal of the child followed by judicial review. Given that tool, why would the government pressure a parent for an amorphous voluntary separation agreement? Which approach best serves children's interests?

M. L. B. v. S. L. J.

519 U.S. 102; 117 S. Ct. 555 (1996)

Justice Ginsburg delivered the opinion of the Court.

By order of a Mississippi Chancery Court, petitioner M. L. B.'s parental rights to her two minor children were forever terminated. M. L. B. sought to appeal from the termination decree, but Mississippi required that she pay in advance record preparation fees estimated at $2,352.36. Because M. L. B. lacked funds to pay the fees, her appeal was dismissed.

Urging that the size of her pocketbook should not be dispositive when "an interest far more precious than any property right" is at stake, M. L. B. tenders this question, which we agreed to hear and decide: May a State, consistent with the Due Process and Equal Protection Clauses of the Fourteenth Amendment, condition appeals from trial court decrees terminating parental rights on the affected parent's ability to pay record preparation fees? We hold that, just as a State may not block an indigent petty offender's access to an appeal afforded others, so Mississippi may not deny M. L. B., because of her poverty, appellate review of the sufficiency of the evidence on which the trial court found her unfit to remain a parent.

I

Petitioner M. L. B. and respondent S. L. J. are, respectively, the biological mother and father of two children, a boy born in April 1985, and a girl born in February 1987. In June 1992, after a marriage that endured nearly eight years, M. L. B. and S. L. J. were divorced. The children remained in their father's custody, as M. L. B. and S. L. J. had agreed at the time of the divorce.

S. L. J. married respondent J. P. J. in September 1992. In November of the following year, S. L. J. and J. P. J. filed suit in Chancery Court in Mississippi, seeking to terminate the parental rights of M. L. B. and to gain court approval for adoption of the children by their stepmother, J. P. J. The complaint alleged that M. L. B. had not maintained reasonable visitation and was in arrears on child support payments. M. L. B. counterclaimed, seeking primary custody of both children and contending that S. L. J. had not permitted her reasonable visitation, despite a provision in the divorce decree that he do so.

After taking evidence on August 18, November 2, and December 12, 1994, the Chancellor, in a decree filed December 14, 1994, terminated all parental rights of the natural mother, approved the adoption, and ordered that J. P. J., the adopting parent, be shown as the mother of the children on their birth certificates. Twice reciting a segment of the governing Mississippi statute, the Chancellor declared that there had been a "substantial erosion of the relationship between the natural mother, [M. L. B.], and the minor children," which had been caused "at least in part by [M. L. B.'s] serious neglect, abuse, prolonged and unreasonable absence or unreasonable failure to visit or communicate with her minor children."

The Chancellor stated, without elaboration, that the natural father and his second wife had met their burden of proof by "clear and convincing evidence." Nothing in the Chancellor's order describes the evidence, however, or otherwise reveals precisely why M. L. B. was decreed, forevermore, a stranger to her children.

In January 1995, M. L. B. filed a timely appeal and paid the $100 filing fee. The Clerk of the Chancery Court, several days later, estimated the costs for preparing and transmitting the record: $1,900 for the transcript (950 pages at $2 per page); $438 for other documents in the record (219 pages at $2 per page); $4.36 for binders; and $10 for mailing.

Mississippi grants civil litigants a right to appeal, but conditions that right on prepayment of costs. Relevant portions of a transcript must be ordered, and its preparation costs advanced by the appellant, if the appellant "intends to urge on appeal," as M. L. B. did, "that a finding or conclusion is unsupported by the evidence or is contrary to the evidence."

Unable to pay $2,352.36, M. L. B. sought leave to appeal in forma pauperis. The Supreme Court of Mississippi denied her application in August 1995. Under its precedent, the court said, "the right to proceed in forma pauperis in civil cases exists only at the trial level."

. . .

Courts have confronted, in diverse settings, the "age-old problem" of "providing equal justice for poor and rich, weak and powerful alike." Concerning access to appeal in general, and transcripts needed to pursue appeals in particular, *Griffin* is the foundation case.

Griffin involved an Illinois rule that effectively conditioned thoroughgoing appeals from criminal convictions on the defendant's procurement of a transcript of trial proceedings. Indigent defendants, other than those sentenced to death, were not excepted from the rule, so in most cases, defendants without means to pay for a transcript had no access to appellate review at all. Although the Federal Constitution guarantees no right to appellate review, once a State affords that right, *Griffin* held, the State may not "bolt the door to equal justice,". . . .

The plurality in *Griffin* recognized "the importance of appellate review to a correct adjudication of guilt or innocence." "To deny adequate review to the poor," the plurality observed, "means that many of them may lose their life, liberty or property because of unjust convictions which appellate courts would set aside." Judging the Illinois rule inconsonant with the Fourteenth Amendment, the *Griffin* plurality drew support from the Due Process and Equal Protection Clauses.

. . . "This Court has never held that the States are required to establish avenues of appellate review, but it is now fundamental that, once established, these avenues must be kept free of unreasoned distinctions that can only impede open and equal access to the courts."

. . .

III

We have also recognized a narrow category of civil cases in which the State must provide access to its judicial processes without regard to a party's ability to pay court fees. In *Boddie v. Connecticut*, we held that the State could not deny a divorce to a married couple based on their inability to pay approximately $60 in court costs. Crucial to our decision in *Boddie* was the fundamental interest at stake. "Given the basic position of the marriage relationship in this society's hierarchy of values and the concomitant state monopolization of the means for legally dissolving this relationship," we said, due process "prohibits a State from denying, solely because of inability to pay, access to its courts to individuals who seek judicial dissolution of their marriages."

. . .

IV

Choices about marriage, family life, and the upbringing of children are among associational rights this Court has ranked as "of basic importance in our society," rights sheltered by the Fourteenth Amendment against the State's unwarranted usurpation, disregard, or disrespect. M. L. B.'s case, involving the State's authority to sever permanently a parent–child bond, demands the close consideration the Court has long required when a family association so undeniably important is at stake.

V

Guided by this Court's precedent on an indigent's access to judicial processes in criminal and civil cases, and on proceedings to terminate parental status, we turn to the classification question this case presents: Does the Fourteenth Amendment require Mississippi to accord M. L. B. access to an appeal-available but for her inability to advance required costs-before she is forever branded unfit for affiliation with her children? Respondents urge us to classify M. L. B.'s case with the generality of civil cases, in which indigent persons have no constitutional right to proceed in forma pauperis. M. L. B., on the other hand, maintains that the accusatory state action she is trying to fend off is barely distinguishable from criminal condemnation in view of the magnitude and permanence of the loss she faces. For the purpose at hand, M. L. B. asks us to treat her parental termination appeal as we have treated petty offense appeals; she urges us to . . . rule that Mississippi may not withhold the transcript M. L. B. needs to gain review of the order ending her parental status. Guided by *Lassiter* and *Santosky*, and other decisions acknowledging the primacy of the parent–child relationship, we agree. . . . We observe first that the Court's decisions concerning access to judicial processes . . . reflect both equal protection and due process concerns. . . .

. . .

. . . [T]he stakes for petitioner M. L. B. — forced dissolution of her parental rights — are large, "'more substantial than mere loss of money.'" In contrast to loss of custody, which does not sever the parent–child bond, parental status termination is "irretrievably destructive" of the most fundamental family relationship. And the risk of error, Mississippi's experience shows, is considerable.

VI

In numerous cases, respondents point out, the Court has held that government "need not provide funds so that people can exercise even fundamental rights." A decision for M. L. B., respondents contend, would dishonor our cases recognizing that the Constitution "generally confer[s] no affirmative right to governmental aid, even where such aid may be necessary to secure life, liberty, or property interests of which the government itself may not deprive the individual."

Complainants in the cases on which respondents rely sought state aid to subsidize their privately initiated action or to alleviate the consequences of differences in economic circumstances that existed apart from state action. M. L. B.'s complaint is of a different order. She is endeavoring to defend against the State's destruction of her family bonds, and to resist the brand associated with a parental unfitness adjudication. Like a defendant resisting criminal conviction, she seeks to be spared from the State's devastatingly adverse action. . . .

. . .

For the reasons stated, we hold that Mississippi may not withhold from M. L. B. "a 'record of sufficient completeness' to permit proper [appellate] consideration of [her] claims." Accordingly, we reverse the judgment of the Supreme Court of Mississippi and remand the case for further proceedings not inconsistent with this opinion.

It is so ordered.

Justice Kennedy, concurring in the judgment. [omitted]

Chief Justice Rehnquist, dissenting. [omitted]

Notes and Queries

1. How does the Court reason the need to provide the rights recognized in *M. L. B. v. S. L. J.* even though the Constitution emphasizes negative rights?
2. The Court obliquely suggests that dependency proceedings may not warrant the same level of protection since those proceedings deprive parents of custody only temporarily rather than permanently severing the parent–child bond. Would you agree that the difference in proceedings justifies different levels of protection? Do you agree with the Court's characterization of dependency hearings?

Deshaney v. Winnebago

489 U.S. 189; 109 S. Ct. 998 (1989)

Chief Justice Rehnquist delivered the opinion of the Court.

Petitioner is a boy who was beaten and permanently injured by his father, with whom he lived. Respondents are social workers and other local officials who received complaints that petitioner was being abused by his father and had reason to believe that this was the case, but nonetheless did not act to remove petitioner from his father's custody. Petitioner sued respondents claiming that their failure to act deprived him of his liberty in violation of the Due Process Clause of the Fourteenth Amendment to the United States Constitution. We hold that it did not.

I

The facts of this case are undeniably tragic. Petitioner Joshua DeShaney was born in 1979. In 1980, a Wyoming court granted his parents a divorce and awarded custody of Joshua to his father, Randy DeShaney. The father shortly thereafter moved to Neenah, a city located in Winnebago County, Wisconsin, taking the infant Joshua with him. There he entered into a second marriage, which also ended in divorce.

The Winnebago County authorities first learned that Joshua DeShaney might be a victim of child abuse in January 1982, when his father's second wife complained to the police, at the time of their divorce, that he had previously "hit the boy causing marks and [was] a prime case for child abuse." The Winnebago County Department of Social Services (DSS) interviewed the father, but he denied the accusations, and DSS did not pursue them further. In January 1983, Joshua was admitted to a local hospital with multiple bruises and abrasions. The examining physician suspected child abuse and notified DSS, which immediately obtained an order from a Wisconsin juvenile court placing Joshua in the temporary custody of the hospital. Three days later, the county convened an ad hoc "Child Protection Team"—consisting of a pediatrician, a psychologist, a police detective, the county's lawyer, several DSS caseworkers, and various hospital personnel—to consider Joshua's situation. At this meeting, the Team decided that there was insufficient evidence of child abuse to retain Joshua in the custody of the court. The Team did, however, decide to recommend several measures to protect Joshua, including enrolling him in a preschool program, providing his father with certain counselling services, and encouraging his father's girlfriend to move out of the home. Randy DeShaney entered into a voluntary agreement with DSS in which he promised to cooperate with them in accomplishing these goals.

Based on the recommendation of the Child Protection Team, the juvenile court dismissed the child protection case and returned Joshua to the custody of his father. A month later, emergency room personnel called the DSS caseworker handling Joshua's case to report that he had once again been treated for suspicious injuries. The caseworker concluded that there was no basis for action. For the next six months, the caseworker made monthly visits to the DeShaney home, during which she observed a number of suspicious injuries on Joshua's head; she also noticed that he had not been enrolled in school, and that the girlfriend had not moved out. The caseworker dutifully recorded these incidents in her files, along with her continuing suspicions that someone in the DeShaney household was physically abusing Joshua, but she did nothing more. In November 1983, the emergency room notified DSS that Joshua had been treated once again for injuries that they believed to be caused by child abuse. On the caseworker's next two visits to the DeShaney home, she was told that Joshua was too ill to see her. Still DSS took no action.

In March 1984, Randy DeShaney beat 4-year-old Joshua so severely that he fell into a life-threatening coma. Emergency brain surgery revealed a series of hemorrhages caused by traumatic injuries to the head inflicted over a long period of time. Joshua did not die, but he suffered brain damage so severe that he is expected to spend the rest of his life confined to an institution for the profoundly retarded. Randy DeShaney was subsequently tried and convicted of child abuse.

Joshua and his mother brought this action under 42 U. S. C. § 1983 in the United States District Court for the Eastern District of Wisconsin against respondents Winnebago County, DSS, and various individual employees of DSS. The complaint alleged that respondents had deprived Joshua of his liberty without due process of law, in violation of his rights under the Fourteenth Amendment, by failing to intervene to protect him against a risk of violence at his father's hands of which they knew or should have known. The District Court granted summary judgment for respondents.

The Court of Appeals for the Seventh Circuit affirmed, holding that petitioners had not made out an actionable § 1983 claim for two alternative reasons. First, the court held that the Due Process Clause of the Fourteenth Amendment does not require a state or local governmental entity to protect its citizens from "private violence, or other mishaps not attributable to the conduct of its employees." In so holding, the court specifically rejected the position endorsed by a divided panel of the Third Circuit . . . that once the State learns that a particular child is in danger of abuse from third parties and actually undertakes to protect him from that danger, a "special relationship" arises between it and the child which imposes an affirmative constitutional duty to provide adequate protection. Second, the court held, in reliance on our decision in *Martinez v. California*, that the causal connection between respondents' conduct and Joshua's injuries was too attenuated to establish a deprivation of constitutional rights actionable under § 1983. The court therefore found it unnecessary to reach the question whether respondents' conduct evinced the "state of mind" necessary to make out a due process claim. . . .

. . . [W]e granted certiorari. We now affirm.

II

The Due Process Clause of the Fourteenth Amendment provides that "[n]o State shall . . . deprive any person of life, liberty, or property, without due process of law." Petitioners contend that the State deprived Joshua of his liberty interest in "free[dom] from . . . unjustified intrusions on personal security," by failing to provide him with adequate protection against his father's violence. The claim is one invoking the substantive rather than the procedural component of the Due Process Clause; petitioners do not claim that the State denied Joshua protection without according him appropriate procedural safeguards, but that it was categorically obligated to protect him in these circumstances.

But nothing in the language of the Due Process Clause itself requires the State to protect the life, liberty, and property of its citizens against invasion by private actors. The Clause is phrased as a limitation on the State's power to act, not as a guarantee of certain minimal levels of safety and security. It forbids the State itself to deprive individuals of life, liberty, or property without "due process of law," but its language cannot fairly be extended to impose an affirmative obligation on the State to ensure that those interests do not come to harm through other means. Nor does history support such an expansive reading of the constitutional text. Like its counterpart in the Fifth Amendment, the Due Process Clause of the Fourteenth Amendment was intended to prevent government "from abusing [its] power, or employing it as an instrument of oppression." Its purpose was to protect the people from the State, not to ensure that the State protected them from each other. The Framers were content to leave the extent of governmental obligation in the latter area to the democratic political processes.

Consistent with these principles, our cases have recognized that the Due Process Clauses generally confer no affirmative right to governmental aid, even where such aid may be necessary to secure life, liberty, or property interests of which the government itself may not deprive the individual.... "Although the liberty protected by the Due Process Clause affords protection against unwarranted government interference... it does not confer an entitlement to such [governmental aid] as may be necessary to realize all the advantages of that freedom." If the Due Process Clause does not require the State to provide its citizens with particular protective services, it follows that the State cannot be held liable under the Clause for injuries that could have been averted had it chosen to provide them. As a general matter, then, we conclude that a State's failure to protect an individual against private violence simply does not constitute a violation of the Due Process Clause.

Petitioners contend, however, that even if the Due Process Clause imposes no affirmative obligation on the State to provide the general public with adequate protective services, such a duty may arise out of certain "special relationships" created or assumed by the State with respect to particular individuals. Petitioners argue that such a "special relationship" existed here because the State knew that Joshua faced a special danger of abuse at his father's hands, and specifically proclaimed, by word and by deed, its intention to protect him against that danger. Having actually undertaken to protect Joshua from this danger—which petitioners concede the State played no part in creating—the State acquired an affirmative "duty," enforceable through the Due Process Clause, to do so in a reasonably competent fashion. Its failure to discharge that duty, so the argument goes, was an abuse of governmental power that so "shocks the conscience," as to constitute a substantive due process violation.

We reject this argument. It is true that in certain limited circumstances the Constitution imposes upon the State affirmative duties of care and protection with respect to particular individuals. . . .

But these cases afford petitioners no help. Taken together, they stand only for the proposition that when the State takes a person into its custody and holds him there against his will, the Constitution imposes upon it a corresponding duty to assume some responsibility for his safety and general well-being. The rationale for this principle is simple enough: when the State by the affirmative exercise of its power so restrains an individual's liberty that it renders him unable to care for himself, and at the same time fails to provide for his basic human needs — e. g., food, clothing, shelter, medical care, and reasonable safety — it transgresses the substantive limits on state action set by the Eighth Amendment and the Due Process Clause. The affirmative duty to protect arises not from the State's knowledge of the individual's predicament or from its expressions of intent to help him, but from the limitation which it has imposed on his freedom to act on his own behalf. In the substantive due process analysis, it is the State's affirmative act of restraining the individual's freedom to act on his own behalf — through incarceration, institutionalization, or other similar restraint of personal liberty — which is the "deprivation of liberty" triggering the protections of the Due Process Clause, not its failure to act to protect his liberty interests against harms inflicted by other means.

Petitioners concede that the harms Joshua suffered occurred not while he was in the State's custody, but while he was in the custody of his natural father, who was in no sense a state actor. While the State may have been aware of the dangers that Joshua faced in the free world, it played no part in their creation, nor did it do anything to render him any more vulnerable to them. That the State once took temporary custody of Joshua does not alter the analysis, for when it returned him to his father's custody, it placed him in no worse position than that in which he would have been had it not acted at all; the State does not become the permanent guarantor of an individual's safety by having once offered him shelter. Under these circumstances, the State had no constitutional duty to protect Joshua.

It may well be that, by voluntarily undertaking to protect Joshua against a danger it concededly played no part in creating, the State acquired a duty under state tort law to provide him with adequate protection against that danger. But the claim here is based on the Due Process Clause of the Fourteenth Amendment, which, as we have said many times, does not transform every tort committed by a state actor into a constitutional violation. A State may, through its courts and legislatures, impose such affirmative duties of care and protection upon its agents as it wishes. But not "all common-law duties owed by government actors were . . . constitutionalized by the Fourteenth Amendment." Because, as explained above, the State had no constitutional duty to protect Joshua against his father's violence, its failure to do so — though calamitous in hindsight — simply does not constitute a violation of the Due Process Clause.

Judges and lawyers, like other humans, are moved by natural sympathy in a case like this to find a way for Joshua and his mother to receive adequate compensation for the grievous harm inflicted upon them. But before yielding to that impulse, it is well to remember once again that the harm was inflicted not by the State of Wisconsin, but by Joshua's father. The most that can be said of the state functionaries in this case is that they stood by and did nothing when suspicious circumstances dictated a more active role for them. In defense of them it must also be said that had they moved too soon to take custody of the son away from the father, they would likely have been met with charges of improperly intruding into the parent–child relationship, charges based on the same Due Process Clause that forms the basis for the present charge of failure to provide adequate protection.

The people of Wisconsin may well prefer a system of liability which would place upon the State and its officials the responsibility for failure to act in situations such as the present one. They may create such a system, if they do not have it already, by changing the tort law of the State in accordance with the regular lawmaking process. But they should not have it thrust upon them by this Court's expansion of the Due Process Clause of the Fourteenth Amendment.

Affirmed.

Justice Brennan, with whom Justice Marshall and Justice Blackmun join, dissenting.

"The most that can be said of the state functionaries in this case," the Court today concludes, "is that they stood by and did nothing when suspicious circumstances dictated a more active role for them." Because I believe that this description of respondents' conduct tells only part of the story and that, accordingly, the Constitution itself "dictated a more active role" for respondents in the circumstances presented here, I cannot agree that respondents had no constitutional duty to help Joshua DeShaney.

It may well be, as the Court decides, that the Due Process Clause as construed by our prior cases creates no general right to basic governmental services. That, however, is not the question presented here; indeed, that question was not raised in the complaint, urged on appeal, presented in the petition for certiorari, or addressed in the briefs on the merits. No one, in short, has asked the Court to proclaim that, as a general matter, the Constitution safeguards positive as well as negative liberties.

This is more than a quibble over dicta; it is a point about perspective, having substantive ramifications. In a constitutional setting that distinguishes sharply between action and inaction, one's characterization of the misconduct alleged under § 1983 may effectively decide the case. Thus, by leading off with a discussion (and rejection) of the idea that the Constitution imposes on the States an affirmative duty to take basic care of their citizens, the Court foreshadows — perhaps even preordains — its conclusion that no duty existed even on the specific facts before us. This initial discussion establishes the baseline from which the Court assesses the DeShaneys' claim that, when a State has — "by word and by deed" — announced an intention to protect a certain class of citizens and has before it facts that would trigger that protection under the applicable state law, the Constitution imposes upon the State an affirmative duty of protection.

The Court's baseline is the absence of positive rights in the Constitution and a concomitant suspicion of any claim that seems to depend on such rights. From this perspective, the DeShaneys' claim is first and foremost about inaction (the failure, here, of respondents to take steps to protect Joshua), and only tangentially about action (the establishment of a state program specifically designed to help children like Joshua). And from this perspective, holding these Wisconsin officials liable — where the only difference between this case and one involving a general claim to protective services is Wisconsin's establishment and operation of a program to protect children — would seem to punish an effort that we should seek to promote.

I would begin from the opposite direction. I would focus first on the action that Wisconsin has taken with respect to Joshua and children like him, rather than on the actions that the State failed to take.

. . .

Wisconsin has established a child-welfare system specifically designed to help children like Joshua. Wisconsin law places upon the local departments of social services such as respondent (DSS or Department) a duty to investigate reported instances of child abuse. While other governmental bodies and private persons are largely responsible for the reporting of possible cases of child abuse. Wisconsin law channels all such reports to the local departments of social services for evaluation and, if necessary, further action. Even when it is the sheriff's office or police department that receives a report of suspected child abuse, that report is referred to local social services departments for action; the only exception to this occurs when the reporter fears for the child's immediate safety. In this way, Wisconsin law invites — indeed, directs — citizens and other governmental entities to depend on local departments of social services such as respondent to protect children from abuse.

The specific facts before us bear out this view of Wisconsin's system of protecting children. Each time someone voiced a suspicion that Joshua was being abused, that information was relayed to the Department for investigation and possible action. When Randy DeShaney's second wife told the police that he had "'hit the boy causing marks and [was] a prime case for child abuse,'" the police referred her complaint to DSS. When, on three separate occasions, emergency room personnel noticed suspicious injuries on Joshua's body, they went to DSS with this information. When neighbors informed the police that they had seen or heard Joshua's father or his father's lover beating or otherwise abusing Joshua, the police brought these reports to the attention of DSS. And when respondent Kemmeter, through these reports and through her own observations in the course of nearly 20 visits to the DeShaney home, compiled growing evidence that Joshua was being abused, that information stayed within the Department — chronicled by the social worker in detail that seems almost eerie in light of her failure to act upon it. As to the extent of the social worker's involvement in, and knowledge of, Joshua's predicament, her reaction to the news of Joshua's last and most devastating injuries is illuminating: "'I just knew the phone would ring some day and Joshua would be dead.'"

Even more telling than these examples is the Department's control over the decision whether to take steps to protect a particular child from suspected abuse. While many different people contributed information and advice to this decision, it was up to the people at DSS to make the ultimate decision (subject to the approval of the local government's corporation counsel) whether to disturb the family's current arrangements. When Joshua first appeared at a local hospital with injuries signaling physical abuse, for example, it was DSS that made the decision to take him into temporary custody for the purpose of studying his situation — and it was DSS, acting in conjunction with the corporation counsel, that returned him to his father. Unfortunately for Joshua DeShaney, the buck effectively stopped with the Department.

In these circumstances, a private citizen, or even a person working in a government agency other than DSS, would doubtless feel that her job was done as soon as she had reported her suspicions of child abuse to DSS. Through its child-welfare program, in other words, the State of Wisconsin has relieved ordinary citizens and governmental bodies other than the Department of any sense of obligation to do anything more than report their suspicions of child abuse to DSS. If DSS ignores or dismisses these suspicions, no one will step in to fill the gap. Wisconsin's child-protection program thus effectively confined Joshua DeShaney within the walls of Randy DeShaney's violent home until such time as DSS took action to remove him. Conceivably, then, children like Joshua are made worse off by the existence of this program when the persons and entities charged with carrying it out fail to do their jobs.

It simply belies reality, therefore, to contend that the State "stood by and did nothing" with respect to Joshua. Through its child-protection program, the State actively intervened in Joshua's life and, by virtue of this intervention, acquired ever more certain knowledge that Joshua was in grave danger. . . .

It will be meager comfort to Joshua and his mother to know that, if the State had "selectively den[ied] its protective services" to them because they were "disfavored minorities," their § 1983 suit might have stood on sturdier ground. Because of the posture of this case, we do not know why respondents did not take steps to protect Joshua; the Court, however, tells us that their reason is irrelevant so long as their inaction was not the product of invidious discrimination. Presumably, then, if respondents decided not to help Joshua because his name began with a "J," or because he was born in the spring, or because they did not care enough about him even to formulate an intent to discriminate against him based on an arbitrary reason, respondents would not be liable to the DeShaneys because they were not the ones who dealt the blows that destroyed Joshua's life.

I do not suggest that such irrationality was at work in this case; I emphasize only that we do not know whether or not it was. I would allow Joshua and his mother the opportunity to show that respondents' failure to help him arose, not out of the sound exercise of professional judgment that we recognized . . . as sufficient to preclude liability, but from the kind of arbitrariness that we have in the past condemned.

As the Court today reminds us, "the Due Process Clause of the Fourteenth Amendment was intended to prevent government 'from abusing [its] power, or employing it as an instrument of oppression.'" My disagreement with the Court arises from its failure to see that inaction can be every bit as abusive of power as action, that oppression can result when a State undertakes a vital duty and then ignores it. Today's opinion construes the Due Process Clause to permit a State to displace private sources of protection and then, at the critical moment, to shrug its shoulders and turn away from the harm that it has promised to try to prevent. Because I cannot agree that our Constitution is indifferent to such indifference, I respectfully dissent.

Justice Blackmun, dissenting.

Today, the Court purports to be the dispassionate oracle of the law, unmoved by "natural sympathy." But, in this pretense, the Court itself retreats into a sterile formalism which prevents it from recognizing either the facts of the case before it or the legal norms that should apply to those facts. As Justice Brennan demonstrates, the facts here involve not mere passivity, but active state intervention in the life of Joshua DeShaney—intervention that triggered a fundamental duty to aid the boy once the State learned of the severe danger to which he was exposed.

The Court fails to recognize this duty because it attempts to draw a sharp and rigid line between action and inaction. But such formalistic reasoning has no place in the interpretation of the broad and stirring Clauses of the Fourteenth Amendment.

Like the antebellum judges who denied relief to fugitive slaves, the Court today claims that its decision, however harsh, is compelled by existing legal doctrine. On the contrary, the question presented by this case is an open one, and our Fourteenth Amendment precedents may be read more broadly or narrowly depending upon how one chooses to read them. Faced with the choice, I would adopt a "sympathetic" reading, one which comports with dictates of fundamental justice and recognizes that compassion need not be exiled from the province of judging.

Poor Joshua! Victim of repeated attacks by an irresponsible, bullying, cowardly, and intemperate father, and abandoned by respondents who placed him in a dangerous predicament and who knew or learned what was going on, and yet did essentially nothing except, as the Court revealingly observes, "dutifully recorded these incidents in [their] files." It is a sad commentary upon American life, and constitutional principles—so full of late of patriotic fervor and proud proclamations about "liberty and justice for all"—that this child, Joshua DeShaney, now is assigned to live out the remainder of his life profoundly retarded. Joshua and his mother, as petitioners here, deserve—but now are denied by this Court—the opportunity to have the facts of their case considered in the light of the constitutional protection that 42 U. S. C. § 1983 is meant to provide.

Notes and Queries

1. Why did the state not violate Joshua's constitutional rights?
2. What actions did the state take in response to Joshua's abuse?
3. Once returned to his father's custody after state removal, was Joshua really placed in no worse position than that in which he would have been had the state not acted at all?
4. The Court notes that "Had the State by the affirmative exercise of its power removed Joshua from free society and placed him in a foster home operated by its agents, we might have a situation sufficiently analogous to incarceration or institutionalization to give rise to an affirmative duty to protect. We express no view on the validity of this analogy, however, as it is not before us in the present case." Following the Court's reasoning in *DeShaney*, what do you suppose should be the outcome of the proffered situation?

Ernst v. Child and Youth Services

(3rd Cir. Ct. App., 1997)

Circuit Judge Stapleton delivered the decision of the court.

I. Facts

Sylvia Ernst ("Ernst") was the sole guardian of her minor granddaughter Susanne from infancy until the child was nine years old. [Note that the father had died and the mother had rare phone contact with her daughter.] At about that time, during the 1987–88 school year, a number of people in the Downingtown, Pennsylvania area where Ernst and Susanne lived became concerned about Susanne's well-being. A mover who had moved Ernst and Susanne into an apartment in Downingtown contacted police and expressed concern that there was something wrong in the relationship between Ernst and Susanne. He reported that Susanne looked unwell and appeared too young to be Ernst's daughter.

The Downingtown police conducted an investigation and learned that the Family Court of Nassau County, New York, had issued warrants for the arrest of Ernst and her daughter for child neglect and that a petition for custody of Susanne had been filed in 1981 but never served on Ernst. Nassau County officials informed the Downingtown police that the warrants had been vacated and the petition for custody of Susanne had been withdrawn. The police informed a CYS employee of its investigation and of the status of the warrants, but the CYS personnel responsible for the decision to seek custody of Susanne were apparently unaware at the time of their decision that the Nassau County warrants had been withdrawn.

School officials at several schools Susanne attended became concerned about Susanne's frequent tardiness, poor attendance, and inability to separate from Ernst at the start of the school day. The days would often begin with a scene outside Susanne's classroom during which Susanne would cry and scream and refuse to let go of her grandmother. On May 3, 1988, after another morning tantrum, officials at the East Ward School in Downingtown contacted CYS and requested immediate intervention. CYS believed Susanne's attachment to Ernst was sufficiently extreme to be unhealthy and filed a petition that same day seeking an adjudication of dependency and emergency custody of Susanne. After an immediate detention hearing, Judge Stively of the Chester County Court of Common Pleas found that a prima facie case of dependency had been presented, and ordered Susanne placed in a psychiatric institution for a complete evaluation.

At a subsequent hearing on May 18, 1988, the parties stipulated to an adjudication of dependency, which resulted in temporary legal custody remaining with CYS. The stipulation provided that CYS's goal was the reunification of the family and that Ernst could receive counseling and treatment at the institution at which Susanne was being treated.

CYS retained custody of Susanne for the next five years. During that time, Ernst and CYS waged an intense legal battle over Susanne's dependency status and custody. They also developed an extremely contentious relationship. CYS caseworkers found Ernst to be uncooperative, antagonizing, and unwilling to acknowledge her parenting problems. They also complained that she frequently made negative comments about CYS and Susanne's foster families during visits with Susanne. As CYS caseworkers became increasingly frustrated with Ernst, they sought and obtained restrictions on her visits with Susanne. Ultimately, with the approval of the Chester County Court of Common Pleas and the Superior Court of Pennsylvania, they changed CYS's goal for Susanne from family reunification to long-term foster placement. Meanwhile, Susanne occupied eight different placements at various foster homes and institutions. Ultimately, her emotional and intellectual development deteriorated significantly.

Finally, in April 1993, a new judge assigned to review Susanne's placement recognized that "the adversarial air of the proceeding [concerning Susanne's dependency] . . . at times . . . captured the focus of many of those involved in this case instead of focusing on Susanne." Concluding that "we have come to the point where state intervention in Susanne's life is now doing more harm than good," the court ordered that physical custody of Susanne be returned to Ernst, with legal custody remaining with CYS. Ernst was granted legal custody on November 17, 1993.

During the pendency of the state court proceedings, Ernst filed this action in federal court under 42 U.S.C. § 1983 against CYS, various CYS caseworkers who were involved in Susanne's case (the "CYS defendants"), three officials from the Downingtown Area School District, and Rita Borzillo, a private attorney who represented CYS throughout Susanne's dependency proceedings. Ernst's complaint alleged (1) violation of procedural and substantive due process by all defendants for their improper "seizure" of Susanne; (2) violation of substantive due process by CYS, the CYS defendants, and Borzillo for the imposition of restrictions on visitation and for the recommendation of long-term placement instead of reunification; (3) violations of procedural due process in the course and conduct of state court proceedings; and (4) violation of the First Amendment by the Pennsylvania statute that presumptively closes juvenile dependency proceedings to the public. The district court joined the Judiciary of the Commonwealth of Pennsylvania to defend the First Amendment claim.

A bench trial ensued on the claims that survived summary judgment. After the trial, the court granted judgment to CYS, the CYS defendants, and the Judiciary of Pennsylvania. Although the court criticized the CYS defendants for flawed social work practice and inability "to submerge their personal views in dealing with a difficult woman" and focus on Susanne's welfare, it ultimately concluded that the CYS defendants' actions "were not so devoid of professional judgment or so clearly outrageous as to impose liability for constitutional violations." The court held that CYS was not liable for any violations by the CYS defendants or Borzillo because Ernst had not shown that the actions were done by an official with policy-making authority or pursuant to a "policy" or "custom" of CYS. Finally, the district court held that Ernst lacked standing to bring her First Amendment challenge to Pennsylvania's juvenile court closure provision because she could not raise the right of the "third-party" public and press to access to the courts.

On the other hand, the court granted judgment in favor of Ernst against Borzillo. The court held that Borzillo, who was a state actor for purposes of § 1983 while she represented CYS, violated Ernst's substantive due process rights when she sought appellate review of an order granting Ernst an unsupervised visit with Susanne. The court found that Borzillo challenged the order primarily out of "animosity and anger at Ernst's small victory" in securing permission for an unsupervised visit. Nevertheless, the court found that the harm suffered by Ernst as a result of Borzillo's actions was de minimis, consisting only of the difference between the value of the unsupervised visit ordered and the supervised visit Ernst actually had with Susanne, and awarded only nominal damages and attorneys' fees.

...

III. Ernst's Appeal

A. CYS Defendants' Absolute Immunity

Ernst challenges the district court's grant of partial summary judgment to the CYS defendants based on absolute immunity "insofar as they acted in their prosecutorial capacity of filing petitions and making recommendations to the court." ...

Section 1983 provides that "every person who, under color of any statute, ordinance, regulation, custom, or usage, of any State ... subjects ... any citizen of the United States ... to the deprivation of any rights, privileges, or immunities secured by the Constitution and laws shall be liable to the party injured." Instead, courts must determine whether a particular governmental official is entitled to immunity according to the following analysis:

> [The] initial inquiry is whether [the] official claiming immunity under § 1983 can point to a common-law counterpart to the privilege he asserts. If "an official was accorded immunity from tort actions at common law when the Civil Rights Act was enacted in 1871, the Court next considers whether § 1983's history or purposes nonetheless counsel against recognizing the same immunity in § 1983 actions."

Courts "look to the common law and other history for guidance because [their] role is 'not to make a freewheeling policy choice,' but rather to discern Congress' likely intent in enacting § 1983."

The fact that a particular public official did not enjoy absolute immunity at common law is not, however, determinative of the absolute immunity issue. Where the official claiming immunity occupies a governmental position that did not exist at common law, he may still be entitled to immunity if he performs official functions that are analogous to functions performed by those who were immune at common law. It is therefore necessary for us to review the functions performed by officials to whom absolute immunity has been accorded in order to determine if child welfare workers perform analogous functions.

Under its historical and functional approach, the Supreme Court has held that certain officials "functioning as integral parts of the judicial process" are absolutely immune from civil suits under § 1983. For example, the Court has declared that judges, prosecutors, and witnesses, are entitled to absolute immunity when they perform judicial or quasi-judicial acts that are integral parts of the judicial process.

... The relevant public policy considerations were numerous. First, a prosecutor's exercise of his independent judgment would likely be compromised if he were threatened with suits for damages for his actions in initiating and prosecuting criminal cases in court. Such suits "could be expected with some frequency, for a defendant often will transform his resentment at being prosecuted into the ascription of improper and malicious actions to the State's advocate." Second, the prosecutor's energy would be diverted from his official duties if he were forced to defend himself against § 1983 actions. Third, defending against § 1983 actions likely would be particularly difficult for a prosecutor:

> The honest prosecutor would face greater difficulty in meeting the standards of qualified immunity than other executive or administrative officials. Frequently acting under serious constraints of time and even information, a prosecutor inevitably makes many decisions that could engender colorable claims of constitutional deprivation. Defending these decisions, often years after they were made, could impose unique and intolerable burdens upon a prosecutor responsible annually for hundreds of indictments and trials.

Fourth, failure to afford absolute immunity to prosecutors might undermine the functioning of the criminal justice system because it might lead prosecutors concerned about personal liability not to tender evidence that, while relevant, might conceivably turn out to be fabricated by the witness. Fifth, failure to afford absolute immunity might weaken the fairness of the criminal justice system by clouding postconviction review with "the subconscious knowledge that a post-trial decision in favor of the accused might result in the prosecutor's being called upon to respond in damages for his error or mistaken judgment." Finally, the court noted that absolute immunity for prosecutors would not leave the public without any means to punish or deter unconstitutional conduct because the availability of both judicial review and professional disciplinary procedures would protect the public and punish the errant prosecutor. Thus, the Court concluded that "in initiating a prosecution and in presenting the State's case, the prosecutor is immune from a civil suit for damages under § 1983."

Applying the principles set forth ... the instant case, we hold that the CYS defendants are entitled to absolute immunity for their actions on behalf of the state in preparing for, initiating, and prosecuting dependency proceedings. Their immunity is broad enough to include the formulation and presentation of recommendations to the court in the course of such proceedings. We reach this conclusion because (1) the functions performed by the CYS defendants in dependency proceedings are closely analogous to the functions performed by prosecutors in criminal proceedings; (2) the public policy considerations that countenance immunity for prosecutors are applicable to child welfare workers performing these functions; and (3) dependency proceedings incorporate important safeguards that protect citizens from unconstitutional actions by child welfare workers....

The functions performed by child welfare workers like the CYS defendants in dependency proceedings are closely analogous to those performed by prosecutors.

...

Moreover, we conclude that the public policy considerations supporting absolute immunity for prosecutors are equally applicable to child welfare workers acting in a quasi-prosecutorial capacity in dependency proceedings. Like a prosecutor, a child welfare worker must exercise independent judgment in deciding whether or not to bring a child dependency proceeding, and such judgment would likely be compromised if the worker faced the threat of personal liability for every mistake in judgment. Certainly, we want our child welfare workers to exercise care in deciding to interfere in parent–child relationships. But we do not want them to be so overly cautious, out of fear of personal liability, that they fail to intervene in situations in which children are in danger.

In the absence of absolute immunity, we would expect suits in retaliation for the initiation of dependency proceedings to occur with even greater frequency than suits against prosecutors. Parents involved in seemingly unjustified dependency proceedings are likely to be even more resentful of state interference in the usually sacrosanct parent–child relationship than are defendants of criminal prosecution. In turn, the likely frequency of such suits would result in a significant diversion of the energies of child welfare workers away from their official duties to the defense of § 1983 litigation. Further, defending against § 1983 actions would likely be as difficult for child welfare workers as it would be for prosecutors because child welfare workers, like prosecutors, must make quick decisions on the basis of limited information. "Defending these decisions, often years after they are made, could impose unique and intolerable burdens on [child welfare workers] responsible annually for hundreds of [dependency and child abuse cases]."

Finally, as with prosecutors, there are alternative mechanisms other than the threat of § 1983 liability that protect the public against unconstitutional conduct by child welfare workers. First, the judicial process itself provides significant protection. Child welfare workers must seek an adjudication of dependency from a neutral judge whose decisions are guided by the "best interests of the child" and subject to appellate review. Second, although child welfare workers are not subject to the comprehensive system of professional responsibility applicable to prosecutors, they are under the supervision of the agency that employs them. The agency has an incentive to ensure that its employees do not violate constitutional rights because it is not immune from suit for abuses committed by employees with policy-making authority or acting pursuant to agency policy or custom.

Reviewing Ernst's Third Amended Complaint, it is clear that all of the claims against the CYS defendants concern actions taken by the defendants in connection with the formulation and presentation of recommendations to the state court regarding Susanne's dependency status and disposition. Because all of these actions are analogous to a prosecutor's preparation for and initiation and presentation of a criminal prosecution, we hold that the CYS defendants are entitled to absolute immunity for the conduct that Ernst challenges here.

V.

The district court found it "disappointing that [the CYS] professionals were unable to submerge their personal views in dealing with a difficult woman or to give her sufficient credit for fighting placements out of genuine concern for [Susanne's] welfare." There is ample evidence in the record to support this view, as well as the view that their inability to do so had unfortunate consequences for Susanne and her grandmother. Nevertheless, we must acknowledge, as did the district court, the interest of the state in ensuring the independent and effective operation of the agency charged with protecting the state's children. That overriding interest precludes this court from affording Ernst compensation for whatever injuries she may have suffered at the hands of CYS. We will affirm the district court's grant of judgment in favor of CYS and the CYS defendants. We will reverse the grant of judgment in favor of Ernst against Borzillo and remand for entry of judgment in favor of Borzillo.

Notes and Queries

1. The court finds it "disappointing" that the CYS failed to respond more appropriately. The court further found that CYS's inabilities had "unfortunate consequences for Suzanne and her daughter." Why does the court then proceed to ignore the mother and daughters' plight?

2. The court seems concerned with protecting the rights of the "honest prosecutor." What do you make of that since it would seem that the concern should be placed on protecting individuals from overzealous state officials?

3. Do caseworkers have too much discretion in determining removal of children from their homes? Should a caseworker be held liable for wrongful removal?

4. What do the principles offered in this case tell us about whether *DeShaney* was rightly decided?

Research Comment

1. At the conclusion of their investigations, child protective service workers make critical decisions. They either can (1) close the case, (2) open it for protective service intervention or intensive in-home family preservation services, or (3) opt for out-of-home care. These are challenging decisions. Family relationships are dynamic and difficult to assess. To complicate matters, investigative staff and managers bring different values, educational backgrounds, and perspectives. Families themselves exhibit differences in values and practices. This mix of conditions increases the chances that the child welfare system engages in widespread disparity in its case decision making. If conclusions regarding risk in a particular case depend on who does the rating rather than the needs of families under scrutiny, then the child welfare system may leave some children in situations with a high potential for continued maltreatment while some could have stayed safely in their homes instead of being placed in out-of-home care. Mistakes can have enormous consequences, ranging from unnecessary expenditures, emotional upheaval and trauma, and serious injury to a child's death. Because risk assessment has important consequences, much effort is now being placed on the hope that it can be done more consistently and accurately.

   Risk assessment typically involves three procedures: (1) categorizing cases on the basis of severity of risk, (2) assessing the child and family's needs, and (3) determining the likelihood that a given person will harm a child in the future. See Michael S. Wald & Maria Woolverton (1990). Risk assessment: The emperor's new clothes? *Child Welfare*, 69, 483–511. To determine risk, agencies and researchers have developed five models: (1) matrix models, which use tables of risk factors rated in terms of their severity; (2) empirical predictor models, which use small sets of factors found to be predictive of substantiation or recurrence; (3) behaviorally anchored models that assess levels of child or parent functioning; (4) comprehensive ecologically structured models, which, for example, examine factors organized around five concerns (child, parent, family, maltreatment, and intervention); and (5) computerized "expert systems," which blend child protective services' expertise and artificial intelligence to derive computer-based decision rules. See Diana J. English & Peter J. Pecora (1994). Risk assessment as a practice method in child protective services. *Child Welfare*, 73, 451–473.

Despite important progress and recognition that the task of risk assessment is extremely challenging, the field of risk assessment has been repeatedly criticized. Criticisms charge that current risk assessments are inadequate and agencies use them in confused and inappropriate ways. These concerns are especially significant because most models have been developed through a process of consensus rather than through an empirically based process. Furthermore, virtually no basic research examines the correlates and predictive factors involved in the recurrence of any type of maltreatment; and even though there would be solid research, definitional and methodological problems plague assessment models, which makes it difficult to extrapolate conclusions with any degree of certainty. There also is no reason to assume that the same variables predict both occurrence and recurrence. In addition, developers of child abuse screening inventories have only recently considered the relevance of cultural factors in the definitions of maltreatment, family functioning, and abusive parenting. Lastly, although risk assessment models may have some degree of face validity and concurrent validity, the empirical evidence does not exist to support their predictive validity. These considerations support the conclusion that the accuracy of current risk assessment models and their use leave much to be desired.

The challenges in child protection risk assessment, however, are not peculiar to the child welfare system. Risk assessment research has long uncovered significant inadequacies in clinical judgment. Given those failures, some have argued a need to make greater use of actuarial models. Current evidence from actuarial studies of child maltreatment suggests a conclusion now endorsed in many other fields. Actuarial risk assessments derived from relatively simple, empirically validated instruments can efficiently estimate the risk of future maltreatment and substantially improve the clinical risk assessment performed by individual caseworkers. Actuarial models lead to more consistent estimates of risk. Likewise, inter-rater reliability for actuarial models is much higher than that of the other systems. As a result, it seems fair to conclude that the actuarial approach more accurately classifies cases to different risk levels. See Christopher Baird & Dennis Wagner (1999). Risk assessment in child protective services: Consensus and actuarial model reliability. *Child Welfare*, 78, 723–748.

Although it may seem that risk assessments would have improved over the years, it actually has not. A scoping review, which takes the broadest approach to finding studies, found only 25 studies that evaluated the risks assessment tools used by child protective services. The review found the research about validity and reliability (essentially, their scientific merit) to be dated, heterogenous in methodology, and varied in conceptualization of risk and its operationalization. In the end, they found a general dearth of evidence that supported the effective use of tools, especially across demographic subgroups. They even found a lack of agreement of how to assess tools, interpret findings, and determine their overall effectiveness. After decades of realizing the importance of risk assessment, evidence remains too limited to make confident recommendations about the validity and utility of existing tools. See Claire R. McNellan, Daniel J. Gibbs, Ann S. Knobel & Emily Putnam-Hornstein (2022). The evidence base for risk assessment tools used in US child protection investigations: A systematic scoping review. *Child Abuse & Neglect*, 134.

How do these findings influence your decision as to whether social workers should be held accountable and the standard of proof needed to show that they acted inappropriately? Given the limitations in the ability to assess risk, how justifiable is the power given to child protective services workers? Many now find that actuarial models are more reliable and consistent and that they have the greater potential to improve child welfare decision making and better protect at-risk children. Would you opt for actuarial approaches or opt for continuing to involve greater social worker discretion? Note that improving consistency in the way families are deemed at risk does not necessarily remove the problem that the risk assessment model itself can be wrong and contribute to inappropriate intervention.

Youngberg v. Romeo

457 U.S. 307; 112 S. Ct. 2425 (1982)

Justice Powell delivered the opinion of the Court.

The question presented is whether respondent, involuntarily committed to a state institution for the mentally retarded, has substantive rights under the Due Process Clause of the Fourteenth Amendment to (i) safe conditions of confinement; (ii) freedom from bodily restraints; and (iii) training or "habilitation." Respondent sued under 42 U. S. C. § 1983 three administrators of the institution, claiming damages for the alleged breach of his constitutional rights.

I

Respondent Nicholas Romeo is profoundly retarded. Although 33 years old, he has the mental capacity of an 18-month-old child, with an I. Q. between 8 and 10. He cannot talk and lacks the most basic self-care skills. Until he was 26, respondent lived with his parents in Philadelphia. But after the death of his father in May 1974, his mother was unable to care for him. Within two weeks of the father's death, respondent's mother sought his temporary admission to a nearby Pennsylvania hospital.

Shortly thereafter, she asked the Philadelphia County Court of Common Pleas to admit Romeo to a state facility on a permanent basis. Her petition to the court explained that she was unable to care for Romeo or control his violence. As part of the commitment process, Romeo was examined by a physician and a psychologist. They both certified that respondent was severely retarded and unable to care for himself. On June 11, 1974, the Court of Common Pleas committed respondent to the Pennhurst State School and Hospital, pursuant to the applicable involuntary commitment provision of the Pennsylvania Mental Health and Mental Retardation Act.

At Pennhurst, Romeo was injured on numerous occasions, both by his own violence and by the reactions of other residents to him. Respondent's mother became concerned about these injuries. After objecting to respondent's treatment several times, she filed this complaint on November 4, 1976, in the United States District Court for the Eastern District of Pennsylvania as his next friend. The complaint alleged that "[during] the period July, 1974 to the present, plaintiff has suffered injuries on at least sixty-three occasions." The complaint originally sought damages and injunctive relief from Pennhurst's director [Youngberg] and two supervisors; it alleged that these officials knew, or should have known, that Romeo was suffering injuries and that they failed to institute appropriate preventive procedures, thus violating his rights under the Eighth and Fourteenth Amendments.

Thereafter, in late 1976, Romeo was transferred from his ward to the hospital for treatment of a broken arm. While in the infirmary, and by order of a doctor, he was physically restrained during portions of each day. These restraints were ordered by Dr. Gabroy, not a defendant here, to protect Romeo and others in the hospital, some of whom were in traction or were being treated intravenously. Although respondent normally would have returned to his ward when his arm healed, the parties to this litigation agreed that he should remain in the hospital due to the pending lawsuit. Nevertheless, in December 1977, a second amended complaint was filed alleging that the defendants were restraining respondent for prolonged periods on a routine basis. The second amended complaint also added a claim for damages to compensate Romeo for the defendants' failure to provide him with appropriate "treatment or programs for his mental retardation." All claims for injunctive relief were dropped prior to trial because respondent is a member of the class seeking such relief in another action.

An 8-day jury trial was held in April 1978. Petitioners introduced evidence that respondent participated in several programs teaching basic self-care skills. A comprehensive behavior-modification program was designed by staff members to reduce Romeo's aggressive behavior, but that program was never implemented because of his mother's objections. Respondent introduced evidence of his injuries and of conditions in his unit.

At the close of the trial, the court instructed ... the jury was instructed that only if they found the defendants "[deliberately] [indifferent] to the serious medical [and psychological] needs" of Romeo could they find that his Eighth and Fourteenth Amendment rights had been violated. The jury returned a verdict for the defendants, on which judgment was entered.

The Court of Appeals for the Third Circuit, sitting en banc, reversed and remanded for a new trial. The court held that the Eighth Amendment, prohibiting cruel and unusual punishment of those convicted of crimes, was not an appropriate source for determining the rights of the involuntarily committed. Rather, the Fourteenth Amendment and the liberty interest protected by that Amendment provided the proper constitutional basis for these rights. In applying the Fourteenth Amendment, the court found that the involuntarily committed retain liberty interests in freedom of movement and in personal security. These were "fundamental liberties" that can be limited only by an "overriding, non-punitive" state interest. It further found that the involuntarily committed have a liberty interest in habilitation designed to "treat" their mental retardation.

The en banc court did not, however, agree on the relevant standard to be used in determining whether Romeo's rights had been violated. Because physical restraint "raises a presumption of a punitive sanction," the majority of the Court of Appeals concluded that it can be justified only by "compelling necessity." A somewhat different standard was appropriate for the failure to provide for a resident's safety. The majority considered that such a failure must be justified by a showing of "substantial necessity." Finally, the majority held that when treatment has been administered, those responsible are liable only if the treatment is not "acceptable in the light of present medical or other scientific knowledge."

Chief Judge Seitz, concurring in the judgment, considered the standards articulated by the majority as indistinguishable from those applicable to medical malpractice claims. In Chief Judge Seitz' view, the Constitution "only requires that the courts make certain that professional judgment in fact was exercised." He concluded that the appropriate standard was whether the defendants' conduct was "such a substantial departure from accepted professional judgment, practice, or standards in the care and treatment of this plaintiff as to demonstrate that the defendants did not base their conduct on a professional judgment."

We granted the petition for certiorari because of the importance of the question presented to the administration of state institutions for the mentally retarded.

II

We consider here for the first time the substantive rights of involuntarily committed mentally retarded persons under the Fourteenth Amendment to the Constitution. In this case, respondent has been committed under the laws of Pennsylvania, and he does not challenge the commitment. Rather, he argues that he has a constitutionally protected liberty interest in safety, freedom of movement, and training within the institution; and that petitioners infringed these rights by failing to provide constitutionally required conditions of confinement.

The mere fact that Romeo has been committed under proper procedures does not deprive him of all substantive liberty interests under the Fourteenth Amendment. Indeed, the State concedes that respondent has a right to adequate food, shelter, clothing, and medical care. We must decide whether liberty interests also exist in safety, freedom of movement, and training. If such interests do exist, we must further decide whether they have been infringed in this case.

A

Respondent's first two claims involve liberty interests recognized by prior decisions of this Court, interests that involuntary commitment proceedings do not extinguish. The first is a claim to safe conditions. In the past, this Court has noted that the right to personal security constitutes a "historic liberty interest" protected substantively by the Due Process Clause. And that right is not extinguished by lawful confinement, even for penal purposes. If it is cruel and unusual punishment to hold convicted criminals in unsafe conditions, it must be unconstitutional to confine the involuntarily committed — who may not be punished at all — in unsafe conditions.

Next, respondent claims a right to freedom from bodily restraint. In other contexts, the existence of such an interest is clear in the prior decisions of this Court. Indeed, "[liberty] from bodily restraint always has been recognized as the core of the liberty protected by the Due Process Clause from arbitrary governmental action." This interest survives criminal conviction and incarceration. Similarly, it must also survive involuntary commitment.

B

Respondent's remaining claim is more troubling. In his words, he asserts a "constitutional right to minimally adequate habilitation." This is a substantive due process claim that is said to be grounded in the liberty component of the Due Process Clause of the Fourteenth Amendment. The term "habilitation," used in psychiatry, is not defined precisely or consistently in the opinions below or in the briefs of the parties or the amici. . . . [T]he term refers to "training and development of needed skills." Respondent emphasizes that the right he asserts is for "minimal" training and he would leave the type and extent of training to be determined on a case-by-case basis "in light of present medical or other scientific knowledge."

In addressing the asserted right to training, we start from established principles. As a general matter, a State is under no constitutional duty to provide substantive services for those within its border. When a person is institutionalized — and wholly dependent on the State — it is conceded by petitioners that a duty to provide certain services and care does exist, although even then a State necessarily has considerable discretion in determining the nature and scope of its responsibilities. Nor must a State "choose between attacking every aspect of a problem or not attacking the problem at all."

Respondent, in light of the severe character of his retardation, concedes that no amount of training will make possible his release. And he does not argue that if he were still at home, the State would have an obligation to provide training at its expense. The record reveals that respondent's primary needs are bodily safety and a minimum of physical restraint, and respondent clearly claims training related to these needs. As we have recognized that there is a constitutionally protected liberty interest in safety and freedom from restraint, training may be necessary to avoid unconstitutional infringement of those rights. On the basis of the record before us, it is quite uncertain whether respondent seeks any "habilitation" or training unrelated to safety and freedom from bodily restraints. In his brief to this Court, Romeo indicates that even the self-care programs he seeks are needed to reduce his aggressive behavior. And in his offer of proof to the trial court, respondent repeatedly indicated that, if allowed to testify, his experts would show that additional training programs, including self-care programs, were needed to reduce his aggressive behavior. If, as seems the case, respondent seeks only training related to safety and freedom from restraints, this case does not present the difficult question whether a mentally retarded person, involuntarily committed to a state institution, has some general constitutional right to training per se, even when no type or amount of training would lead to freedom.

Chief Judge Seitz, in language apparently adopted by respondent, observed: "I believe that the plaintiff has a constitutional right to minimally adequate care and treatment. The existence of a constitutional right to care and treatment is no longer a novel legal proposition."

Chief Judge Seitz did not identify or otherwise define — beyond the right to reasonable safety and freedom from physical restraint — the "minimally adequate care and treatment" that appropriately may be required for this respondent. In the circumstances presented by this case, and on the basis of the record developed to date, we agree with his view and conclude that respondent's liberty interests require the State to provide minimally adequate or reasonable training to ensure safety and freedom from undue restraint. In view of the kinds of treatment sought by respondent and the evidence of record, we need go no further in this case.

III

A

We have established that Romeo retains liberty interests in safety and freedom from bodily restraint. Yet these interests are not absolute; indeed to some extent they are in conflict. In operating an institution such as Pennhurst, there are occasions in which it is necessary for the State to restrain the movement of residents — for example, to protect them as well as others from violence. Similar restraints may also be appropriate in a training program. And an institution cannot protect its residents from all danger of violence if it is to permit them to have any freedom of movement. The question then is not simply whether a liberty interest has been infringed but whether the extent or nature of the restraint or lack of absolute safety is such as to violate due process.

In determining whether a substantive right protected by the Due Process Clause has been violated, it is necessary to balance "the liberty of the individual" and "the demands of an organized society." In seeking this balance in other cases, the Court has weighed the individual's interest in liberty against the State's asserted reasons for restraining individual liberty. . . .

Accordingly, whether respondent's constitutional rights have been violated must be determined by balancing his liberty interests against the relevant state interests. If there is to be any uniformity in protecting these interests, this balancing cannot be left to the unguided discretion of a judge or jury. We therefore turn to consider the proper standard for determining whether a State adequately has protected the rights of the involuntarily committed mentally retarded.

B

We think the standard articulated by Chief Judge Seitz affords the necessary guidance and reflects the proper balance between the legitimate interests of the State and the rights of the involuntarily committed to reasonable conditions of safety and freedom from unreasonable restraints. He would have held that "the Constitution only requires that the courts make certain that professional judgment in fact was exercised. It is not appropriate for the courts to specify which of several professionally acceptable choices should have been made." Persons who have been involuntarily committed are entitled to more considerate treatment and conditions of confinement than criminals whose conditions of confinement are designed to punish. At the same time, this standard is lower than the "compelling" or "substantial" necessity tests the Court of Appeals would require a State to meet to justify use of restraints or conditions of less than absolute safety. We think this requirement would place an undue burden on the administration of institutions such as Pennhurst and also would restrict unnecessarily the exercise of professional judgment as to the needs of residents.

Moreover, we agree that respondent is entitled to minimally adequate training. In this case, the minimally adequate training required by the Constitution is such training as may be reasonable in light of respondent's liberty interests in safety and freedom from unreasonable restraints. In determining what is "reasonable" — in this and in any case presenting a claim for training by a State — we emphasize that courts must show deference to the judgment exercised by a qualified professional. By so limiting judicial review of challenges to conditions in state institutions, interference by the federal judiciary with the internal operations of these institutions should be minimized. Moreover, there certainly is no reason to think judges or juries are better qualified than appropriate professionals in making such decisions. For these reasons, the decision, if made by a professional, is presumptively valid; liability may be imposed only when the decision by the professional is such a substantial departure from accepted professional judgment, practice, or standards as to demonstrate that the person responsible actually did not base the decision on such a judgment. In an action for damages against a professional in his individual capacity, however, the professional will not be liable if he was unable to satisfy his normal professional standards because of budgetary constraints; in such a situation, good-faith immunity would bar liability.

IV

In deciding this case, we have weighed those postcommitment interests cognizable as liberty interests under the Due Process Clause of the Fourteenth Amendment against legitimate state interests and in light of the constraints under which most state institutions necessarily operate. We repeat that the State concedes a duty to provide adequate food, shelter, clothing, and medical care. These are the essentials of the care that the State must provide. The State also has the unquestioned duty to provide reasonable safety for all residents and personnel within the institution. And it may not restrain residents except when and to the extent professional judgment deems this necessary to assure such safety or to provide needed training. In this case, therefore, the State is under a duty to provide respondent with such training as an appropriate professional would consider reasonable to ensure his safety and to facilitate his ability to function free from bodily restraints. It may well be unreasonable not to provide training when training could significantly reduce the need for restraints or the likelihood of violence.

Respondent thus enjoys constitutionally protected interests in conditions of reasonable care and safety, reasonably nonrestrictive confinement conditions, and such training as may be required by these interests. Such conditions of confinement would comport fully with the purpose of respondent's commitment. In determining whether the State has met its obligations in these respects, decisions made by the appropriate professional are entitled to a presumption of correctness. Such a presumption is necessary to enable institutions of this type—often, unfortunately, overcrowded and understaffed—to continue to function. A single professional may have to make decisions with respect to a number of residents with widely varying needs and problems in the course of a normal day. The administrators, and particularly professional personnel, should not be required to make each decision in the shadow of an action for damages.

In this case, we conclude that the jury was erroneously instructed on the assumption that the proper standard of liability was that of the Eighth Amendment. We vacate the decision of the Court of Appeals and remand for further proceedings consistent with this decision.

So ordered.

Justice Blackmun, with whom Justice Brennan and Justice O'Connor join, concurring.

I join the Court's opinion. I write separately, however, to make clear why I believe that opinion properly leaves unresolved two difficult and important issues.

The first is whether the Commonwealth of Pennsylvania could accept respondent for "care and treatment," as it did under the Pennsylvania Mental Health and Mental Retardation Act of 1966 and then constitutionally refuse to provide him any "treatment," as that term is defined by state law. Were that question properly before us, in my view there would be a serious issue whether, as a matter of due process, the State could so refuse. I therefore do not find that issue to be a "frivolous" one, as the Chief Justice does.

In *Jackson v. Indiana*, this Court, by a unanimous vote of all participating Justices, suggested a constitutional standard for evaluating the conditions of a civilly committed person's confinement: "At the least, due process requires that the nature and duration of commitment bear some reasonable relation to the purpose for which the individual is committed." Under this standard, a State could accept a person for "safekeeping," then constitutionally refuse to provide him treatment. In such a case, commitment without treatment would bear a reasonable relation to the goal for which the person was confined.

If a state court orders a mentally retarded person committed for "care and treatment," however, I believe that due process might well bind the State to ensure that the conditions of his commitment bear some reasonable relation to each of those goals. In such a case, commitment without any "treatment" whatsoever would not bear a reasonable relation to the purposes of the person's confinement.

In respondent's case, the majority and principal concurring opinions in the Court of Appeals agreed that "[by] basing [respondent's] deprivation of liberty at least partially upon a promise of treatment, the state ineluctably has committed the community's resources to providing minimal treatment." Neither opinion clarified, however, whether respondent in fact had been totally denied "treatment," as that term is defined under Pennsylvania law. To the extent that the majority addressed the question, it found that "the evidence in the record, although somewhat contradictory, suggests not so much a total failure to treat as an inadequacy of treatment."

This Court's reading of the record supports that conclusion. Moreover, the Court today finds that respondent's entitlement to "treatment" under Pennsylvania law was not properly raised below. Given this uncertainty in the record, I am in accord with the Court's decision not to address the constitutionality of a State's total failure to provide "treatment" to an individual committed under state law for "care and treatment."

The second difficult question left open today is whether respondent has an independent constitutional claim, grounded in the Due Process Clause of the Fourteenth Amendment, to that "habilitation" or training necessary to preserve those basic self-care skills he possessed when he first entered Pennhurst—for example, the ability to dress himself and care for his personal hygiene. In my view, it would be consistent with the Court's reasoning today to include within the "minimally adequate training required by the Constitution," such training as is reasonably necessary to prevent a person's pre-existing self-care skills from deteriorating because of his commitment.

The Court makes clear that even after a person is committed to a state institution, he is entitled to such training as is necessary to prevent unreasonable losses of additional liberty as a result of his confinement—for example, unreasonable bodily restraints or unsafe institutional conditions. If a person could demonstrate that he entered a state institution with minimal self-care skills, but lost those skills after commitment because of the State's unreasonable refusal to provide him training, then, it seems to me, he has alleged a loss of liberty quite distinct from — and as serious as — the loss of safety and freedom from unreasonable restraints. For many mentally retarded people, the difference between the capacity to do things for themselves within an institution and total dependence on the institution for all of their needs is as much liberty as they ever will know.

Although respondent asserts a claim of this kind, I agree with the Court that "[on] the basis of the record before us, it is quite uncertain whether respondent [in fact] seeks any 'habilitation' or training unrelated to safety and freedom from bodily restraints." Since the Court finds respondent constitutionally entitled at least to "such training as may be reasonable in light of [his] liberty interests in safety and freedom from unreasonable restraints," I accept its decision not to address respondent's additional claim.

If respondent actually seeks habilitation in self-care skills not merely to reduce his aggressive tendencies, but also to maintain those basic self-care skills necessary to his personal autonomy within Pennhurst, I believe he is free on remand to assert that claim. Like the Court, I would be willing to defer to the judgment of professionals as to whether or not, and to what extent, institutional training would preserve respondent's pre-existing skills. As the Court properly notes, "[professionals] in the habilitation of the mentally retarded disagree strongly on the question whether effective training of all severely or profoundly retarded individuals is even possible."

If expert testimony reveals that respondent was so retarded when he entered the institution that he had no basic self-care skills to preserve, or that institutional training would not have preserved whatever skills he did have, then I would agree that he suffered no additional loss of liberty even if petitioners failed to provide him training. But if the testimony establishes that respondent possessed certain basic self-care skills when he entered the institution, and was sufficiently educable that he could have maintained those skills with a certain degree of training, then I would be prepared to listen seriously to an argument that petitioners were constitutionally required to provide that training, even if respondent's safety and mobility were not imminently threatened by their failure to do so.

The Court finds it premature to resolve this constitutional question on this less than fully developed record. Because I agree with that conclusion, I concur in the Court's opinion.

Chief Justice Burger, concurring in the judgment.

I agree with much of the Court's opinion. However, I would hold flatly that respondent has no constitutional right to training, or "habilitation," per se. The parties, and the Court, acknowledge that respondent cannot function outside the state institution, even with the assistance of relatives. Indeed, even now neither respondent nor his family seeks his discharge from state care. Under these circumstances, the State's provision of food, shelter, medical care, and living conditions as safe as the inherent nature of the institutional environment reasonably allows, serves to justify the

State's custody of respondent. The State did not seek custody of respondent; his family understandably sought the State's aid to meet a serious need.

I agree with the Court that some amount of self-care instruction may be necessary to avoid unreasonable infringement of a mentally retarded person's interests in safety and freedom from restraint; but it seems clear to me that the Constitution does not otherwise place an affirmative duty on the State to provide any particular kind of training or habilitation — even such as might be encompassed under the essentially standardless rubric "minimally adequate training," to which the Court refers. Since respondent asserts a right to "minimally adequate" habilitation "[quite] apart from its relationship to decent care," unlike the Court I see no way to avoid the issue.

I also point out that, under the Court's own standards, it is largely irrelevant whether respondent's experts were of the opinion that "additional training programs, including self-care programs, were needed to reduce [respondent's] aggressive behavior" — a prescription far easier for "spectators" to give than for an institution to implement. The training program devised for respondent by petitioners and other professionals at Pennhurst was, according to the Court's opinion, "presumptively valid"; and "liability may be imposed only when the decision by the professional is such a substantial departure from accepted professional judgment, practice, or standards as to demonstrate that the person responsible actually did not base the decision on such a judgment." Thus, even if respondent could demonstrate that the training programs at Pennhurst were inconsistent with generally accepted or prevailing professional practice — if indeed there be such — this would not avail him so long as his training regimen was actually prescribed by the institution's professional staff.

...

Notes and Queries

1. What are the implications of *DeShaney* and *Youngberg* for the voluntary and involuntary surrender of children to foster care? In *DeShaney*, the Court had refused to follow *Youngberg* because, in that case, the plaintiff was within the custody of the state and the Court emphasized that Joshua had not been in state custody. The Court explained that the plaintiff's reliance on *Youngberg* was misguided because of the difference in the type of custodial relationship; but the Court left open the possibility that had Joshua been in foster care, there might be a "situation sufficiently analogous ... to give rise to an affirmative duty to protect." *DeShaney*, at 201, n9.

2. What else does this case add to *DeShaney*? After determining that a custodial relationship exists, a court must then determine the standard of care that will be given to the person in custody. In *Youngberg*, the Court specifically held that "persons who have been involuntarily committed are entitled to more considerate treatment

and conditions of confinement than criminals whose conditions of confinement are designed to punish." This may be significant for children in care in that, for example, a child "confined" in the foster care system is "confined" for care, not for punishment. If that is the case, the "professional judgment" standard appears applicable. In *Youngberg*, the Court defined a qualified professional as someone who can make a decision concerning an issue because he or she is competent through training, education, or experience. Under this standard, long-term treatment decisions are made by professionals, qualified to work in the relevant area, who establish the standard by which care should be given.

3. The Court in *Youngberg* took an extremely controversial stance: Romeo had positive rights. The Constitution required the state not just to refrain from doing things to Romeo, but actively to do certain things for him. Above and beyond the uncontroversial assertion that the state must provide food, shelter, clothing, and medical care, the Court held that the duty to keep Romeo safe while in custody could necessitate the state's taking additional affirmative actions, such as, for example, providing such training as an appropriate professional would consider reasonable to ensure his safety and to facilitate his ability to function free from bodily restraints. It might well be unreasonable not to provide training when training could significantly reduce the need for restraints or the likelihood of violence. Arguably, these affirmative duties addressed incapacities springing not from the state's having deprived him of the liberty to fend for himself, but from the particular and personal consequences of mental retardation. The constitutional standard flowed from the condition of the person in custody. What are the particular and personal consequences of being a child in custody and do those consequences differ if the child has been maltreated?

Research Comments

1. The *DeShaney* court not only referenced *Youngberg* to describe the possible rights of children in custody; it also cited to *Estelle v. Gamble*, 429 U.S. 97 (1976), which involved the rights of an entirely different group. *Estelle* concerned a prisoner who alleged that prison doctors and guards violated his Eighth Amendment right to be free from "cruel and unusual punishment" when they failed to respond to his repeated complaints about a back injury and forced him to continue the labor that was part of his sentence. The record showed that although some of Gamble's (the prisoner's) ailments were addressed, there was evidence that his back injury could have been better diagnosed and treated if an X-ray had been taken. Despite denying Gamble's Eighth Amendment claim, Justice Marshall wrote for the Court that "deliberate indifference to serious medical needs of prisoners constitutes the 'unnecessary and wanton infliction of pain' ... proscribed by the Eighth Amendment." The Court illuminated the meaning of the phrase "deliberate indifference" in two ways. First, it contrasted situations that, while possibly actionable under

state tort law, were not actionable under 42 U.S.C. § 1983 because there was no showing of deliberate indifference to a prisoner's medical needs. While § 1983 would preclude, in such situations, "intentionally denying or delaying access to medical care" or "intentionally interfering with . . . treatment," it would not prohibit mere "negligence in diagnosing or treating a medical condition," or "an inadvertent failure to provide adequate medical care. . . ." Similarly, in the case of a prisoner forced to undergo a second attempt at electrocution when a mechanical malfunction interfered with the first attempt, Marshall observed that the Court had rejected a claim of cruel and unusual punishment because the need for the second attempt was "an unforeseeable accident" and an "innocent misadventure." But, the Court noted, had the second electrocution been part of a "single, cruelly willful attempt" or even just "a series of abortive attempts," it would have violated the Eighth Amendment. Second, the Court compared deliberate indifference to professional judgment and strongly implied that the professional judgment standard was to be construed more harshly against the state. The point was made in the Court's summary of a prisoner's rights case: a "doctor's choosing the 'easier and less efficacious treatment' of throwing away the prisoner's ear and stitching the stump may be attributable to 'deliberate indifference . . . rather than professional judgment." Following the decision to its logical conclusion, the Court set a requirement that plaintiffs show the state of mind (the mens rea) of the defendant as it attached significance to the subjective motivation of the defendant as a criterion for determining whether the action involves cruel and unusual punishment.

2. Do you conceive of children in foster homes more like prisoners or like patients in need of care? Some circuits, by adopting a "deliberate indifference" standard, have read the Constitution to provide a state with no legal duty to keep its foster homes safer than it keeps its prisons. See Brendan P. Kearse (1996). Abused again: Competing constitutional standards for the state's duty to protect foster children. *Columbia Journal of Law & Social Problems*, 29, 385–410.

Review Problems

1. Some view the picture that emerges from *Estelle* as one that develops the deliberate indifference standard as being extremely difficult for a plaintiff to satisfy. Do you agree that it is hard to imagine behavior by a state actor short of torture that would be found culpable under this standard of liability?

2. After *Youngberg* and *Estelle*, the Supreme Court revisited the standard on which to hold government actors liable under § 1983 claims. It notably did so in *Sacramento v. Lewis*, 523 U.S. 833 (1998), which involved a high-speed chase between Sacramento County sheriff's deputies and two men on a motorcycle, one of whom was a passenger named Lewis. The chase reached speeds up to 100 miles an hour as they wove in and out of moving traffic. The driver of the motorcycle eventually

lost control. As the bike tipped over, deputies could not stop quickly enough and hit Lewis, killing him. Lewis's parents brought a clam against the sheriff's department on the grounds that the officer violated Lewis's substantive due process by causing his death through reckless indifference to life in a high-speed chase aimed at apprehending a suspected offender. The circuit court concluded that a police officer's deliberate indifference to, or reckless disregard for, a person's right to life and security during a high-speed chase could establish liability under § 1983.

The Supreme Court unanimously disagreed. The Court noted that the conduct of the officer fell within the middle range of culpability, somewhere between negligence, which is "categorically beneath the threshold of constitutional due process," and "conduct intended to injure in some way unjustifiable by any government interest." The Court held that, with regard to high-speed police chases, deliberate indifference, rather than being the highest degree of misconduct required, is insufficient to establish liability. Given that the chase involved no intent to harm suspects, the Court concluded that the officer's actions did not give rise to liability under the Fourteenth Amendment, redressable by an action under § 1983.

In its reasoning, the Court emphasized that only the most egregious official conduct can be said to be "arbitrary in the constitutional sense." The Court also stated that it had repeatedly held that the Due Process Clause was intended to prevent government officials from abusing their power, or employing it as an instrument of oppression. The Court reiterated the cognizable level of executive abuse of power as that which shocks the conscience. Addressing what that meant for a high-speed chase, the Court concluded that only a purpose to cause harm unrelated to the legitimate object of arrest satisfies the element of arbitrary conduct shocking to the conscience, necessary for a due process violation.

In reaching its conclusion, the Court emphasized the need for an exact analysis of circumstances before any abuse of power is condemned as conscience shocking. The Court distinguished between imposing liability for deliberate indifference in a high-speed chase situation and imposing liability for deliberate indifference to inmate welfare. The primary distinction rests upon the fact that, in a high-speed chase, the officer must act decisively and show restraint at the same moment. Under such circumstances, little time exists for deliberation and, as use of the term deliberate indifference implies, the standard is sensibly employed only when actual deliberation is practical. In contrast to high-speed chases, situations that involve prison officials have time for reflection. In doing so, the Court held situations that allowed for the government to take thought and make reasonable provisions to a higher standard, as opportunities to do better are teamed with protracted failure even to care, indifference is truly shocking. In this case, the "deliberate indifference" accusation does not make sense, since in a high-speed chase there is no time for deliberation.

3. *Youngberg* and its progeny gain significance to the extent that parents voluntarily or involuntarily release their children to the state. Consider this case. Kathleen

was admitted to Hawthorn Children's Psychiatric Hospital, a state facility, as a voluntary inpatient at her parents' request. Immediately before Kathleen's admission to Hawthorn, she had been a psychiatric inpatient in a private hospital. Her parents' insurance coverage had been exhausted, necessitating the move. The Kennedys had been advised that, if they did not voluntarily admit Kathleen to a mental health facility, Kathleen would be involuntarily committed. The only affordable option open to them was a state-run facility where they would be charged in accordance with their ability to pay. Once admitted, Kathleen remained an inpatient at Hawthorn for several months. Due to her mental condition and her expressed desire to commit suicide, she was placed on the precaution "1:1 Constant Staff Supervision." Patients under this precaution must be within the eyesight of, and no more than three feet away from, staff members at all times. One month after being placed on 1:1, Kathleen was placed on "Protective Suicide Precautions." This precaution is for patients who are at a "moderate to low risk" for suicide, and requires nursing staff members to keep the patient "in constant eye-sight." Additionally, the nursing staff must directly interact with these patients every 15 to 20 minutes so that changes in their mental status or behavior may be detected. A few days after having been placed on Protective Suicide Precautions, the staff in Cottage D, where Kathleen was residing, told Hawthorn's nursing supervisor, Dunlap, that the number of nurses assigned to work the evening shift was inadequate to meet the patients' needs. Dunlap failed to find additional help, and, in fact, declined an offer by the day-shift supervisor to help locate additional nursing assistance. Compounding the problems, the nurse in Cottage D who was responsible for assigning a staff member to care for Kathleen failed to do so. This nurse was, at the time, on extended probation because of her past deficiencies in assigning work duties to the nursing staff. The evening shift began duty at 2:30 p.m. on April 8. Kathleen was not in the "constant eye-sight" of any nursing staff member. No one interacted with her every 15 to 20 minutes. When someone finally checked on her at 5:10 p.m., she was dead, hanging from a bed sheet in her room.

Kathleen's parents allege that these staffing problems were nothing new for Hawthorn. They assert that employees had complained about the chronic understaffing on several occasions. Moreover, they claim that Hawthorn officials falsified records, causing the staffing needs of the hospital to appear to be less than they actually were. These actions, they contend, establish a pattern of deliberate indifference to the health and safety of Hawthorn's patients. This deliberate indifference, in turn, deprived their daughter of her constitutionally protected liberty interest in a safe and humane environment. That deprivation, they assert, led to Kathleen's suicide.

Assuming that the parents' alleged facts are true, and based on *Estelle*, *Youngberg*, and *DeShaney*, do the parents win? Note that, legally, Kathleen had been institutionalized voluntarily, which raised the issue whether the manner in which a patient enters a state care facility is the dispositive question. If we look at the amount of control the state actors, here hospital employees, exerted over

Kathleen's life, a court could conclude that no apparent distinction should be made between involuntary and voluntary mental health care. After *DeShaney*, courts typically refused to grant due-process protection to those who voluntarily entered the state's custody. The issue that arose in this case led the court to remand the case for further findings concerning whether Kathleen's change in mental condition and course of treatment may have effectively converted her status from that of voluntary patient to involuntary patient. If so, then the court ruled that this situation is sufficiently similar to incarceration or institutionalization to give rise to § 1983 liability for a failure to protect, following *Youngberg*. Would you agree with the dissent in that case, which concluded that *DeShaney* requires a finding of no duty, which then leads to no *Youngberg* duty? The argument is that Kathleen was voluntarily admitted, not committed, and no evidence suggests that her status as a voluntary patient actually changed before her death. Her parents did not request her release, she was not restrained against her will or her parents' will, and there was no affirmative exercise of power by the state that was keeping Kathleen restrained of her liberty at the time of her death. See *Kennedy v. Schafer*, 71 F.3d 292 (7th Cir., 1995).

4. Consider *Weatherford v. Arizona*, 81 P.3d 320 (2003). The case involves social workers' liability for failing to protect a child placed in a foster care shelter. Below is the Supreme Court of Arizona's articulation of the standards relevant to § 1983 claims in the foster care context.

   The case arose out of the alleged sexual assault of twelve-year-old Michael L. by two minors held at a foster care facility. The assaults reportedly occurred over the course of four months in 1996 and 1997, after Claudette Washington, Michael's intake social worker, had arranged for Michael's placement at the shelter following his removal from his home because of unsanitary conditions. In mid-December 1996, Parthenia Gibson became Michael's social worker. Shirley Lewis supervised both Washington and Gibson throughout Michael's placement at the shelter.

   Cheryl Weatherford, acting as Michael's guardian ad litem, sued the State of Arizona, Washington, Gibson, and Lewis for negligence and for depriving Michael of his constitutional rights, in violation of § 1983. During summary judgment proceedings, Washington, Gibson, and Lewis did not dispute that, acting in their capacity as social workers, they failed to comply with various agency requirements, including failures to timely complete an initial case plan, to assess Michael's needs and his compatibility with other shelter residents, and to visit the shelter within twenty-four hours of Michael's placement. In addition, they did not dispute that they made only two of the sixteen required weekly supervised visits to the shelter between November 14, 1996, and the disclosure of the alleged sexual abuse on March 4, 1997.

   The superior court nonetheless granted summary judgment in favor of each of the defendants based upon qualified immunity, 42 U.S.C. § 1983, and protective services immunity, A.R.S. § 8-805.A (2001). The court of appeals reversed the order dismissing Weatherford's negligence and § 1983 claims. The court held that a foster child's right to reasonable safety while in foster care was clearly established in 1996 and that a social worker's failure to exercise professional judgment in the placement and monitoring of a child in state foster care may subject the social worker to individual liability under § 1983.

At oral argument, the social workers conceded that a foster child's substantive due process right to reasonable safety while in foster care was clearly established in 1996. As a result, the issue before the Arizona supreme court was whether the social workers' conduct, viewed in the light most favorable to Weatherford, could subject them to individual liability under § 1983.

The Arizona supreme court held that a foster child could establish § 1983 liability against a state official by showing that the official, without justification, acted with deliberate indifference by placing a child in foster care or by maintaining a placement when the official knew that the placement exposed the child to danger or would have known of the danger but for the official's deliberate indifference. The court reasoned that, if a state worker, with time to consider the placement for a foster child, acts with such deliberate indifference as to ignore information indicating that the placement will result in danger to the child or refuses to obtain information that, if considered, would reveal a danger to the child, the official's indifference is sufficiently egregious to justify imposing liability under § 1983.

The Arizona supreme court found that the standard reflected the United States Supreme Court's admonition that executive behavior violates § 1983 only if it involves an element of using the state's power in an oppressive manner. Following that finding, the Arizona supreme court reasoned that an official faces liability not for placing a child in foster care, but for placing the child in a dangerous foster care situation of which the official knew or would have known but for the official's deliberate indifference.

The Arizona supreme court further reasoned that the standard also incorporated the United States Supreme Court's admonition that anything less than deliberate indifference is not sufficient to establish § 1983 liability. It found, however, that the standard reflected the principle that the state, once it undertakes to make a person dependent upon its care, also undertakes an affirmative duty to assume responsibility for that person's safety and general well-being. Additionally, according to the court, the standard considers the difficult decisions imposed upon state workers in making and maintaining foster child placements. In deciding whether the worker made a particular decision "without justification," a court must consider the totality of the circumstances: A social worker cannot be held liable if safe placement cannot be found or if financial constraints prevent any choice other than that made. Whether an initial placement decision reaches a "constitutionally shocking" level may involve different factual considerations than whether a decision to continue a placement rises to this level.

The Arizona supreme court also noted that the articulated standard is like the standard of conduct required by other circuit courts of appeals, whether denominated a "deliberate indifference" or "professional judgment" standard, in the foster care context, and proceeded to provide two examples from the tenth and second circuits' cases that involved child welfare systems.

In *Yvonne L.*, for example, the plaintiffs asserted the right "not to be placed in a foster care environment involving a known or reasonably suspected risk of harm by a third party." The Tenth Circuit adopted a standard it labeled the "professional judgment" standard and held that this standard, "while it does not require actual knowledge the children will be harmed, [it] implies abdication of the duty to act professionally in making the placements." Similarly, in *Doe*, the Second Circuit, purporting to adopt the "deliberate indifference" standard, held that child placement agency officials may be held liable under § 1983 if they "exhibited deliberate indifference to a known injury, a known risk, or a specific duty, and their failure to perform the duty or act to ameliorate the risk or injury was a proximate cause of plaintiff's deprivation of rights under the Constitution."

The Arizona supreme court reasoned that *Doe* and *Yvonne L.* demonstrate, when applied to the unique facts of the foster care context, not much difference exists between the "deliberate indifference" and "professional judgment" standards. As a result, the court did not find it particularly helpful to label this standard of conduct "deliberate indifference" or "professional judgment."

Applying this standard to the facts of this case, the court reversed the trial court's grant of summary judgment. On remand, the court was tasked to consider whether, under the standard articulated, undisputed material facts permit the court to conclude, as a matter of law, that defendant social workers acted with deliberate indifference sufficient to impose responsibility either for the decision to place Michael in the shelter or for the decision to continue the placement.

What do you make of the liability standard that equates "deliberate indifference" to "professional judgment"? How reasonable is the use of "totality of the circumstances" standard to evaluate whether the actions meet the standard of liability? What about not holding case workers responsible unless they acted "without justification"? Are these appropriate standards for the foster care context? Thoughts on whether the case workers in this case would end up responsible? What do you make of the reason for the removal and the child's experience in foster care? Does the "without justification" standard work well in a case like this?

The case exemplifies how courts use rules developed in one context and apply it to another. In this case, the court enlists this from police liability cases: executive behavior violates § 1983 only if it involves an element of using the state's power in an "oppressive manner." Relevant to the foster care context? What does the "oppressive manner" consideration bring to the foster care context?

Suter v. Artist

503 U.S. 347; 112 S. Ct. 1360 (1992)

Chief Justice Rehnquist delivered the opinion of the Court.

This case raises the question whether private individuals have the right to enforce by suit a provision of the Adoption Assistance and Child Welfare Act of 1980. The Court of Appeals for the Seventh Circuit held that 42 U.S.C. § 671(a)(15) contained an implied right of action, and that respondents could enforce this section of the Act through an action brought under § 1983 as well. We hold that the Act does not create an enforceable right on behalf of respondents.

The Adoption Act establishes a federal reimbursement program for certain expenses incurred by the States in administering foster care and adoption services. The Act provides that States will be reimbursed for a percentage of foster care and adoption assistance payments when the State satisfies the requirements of the Act.

To participate in the program, States must submit a plan to the Secretary of Health and Human Services for approval by the Secretary.

... As relevant here, the Act provides:

> (a) Requisite features of State plan
>
> In order for a State to be eligible for payments under this part, it shall have a plan approved by the Secretary which—
>
> ...
>
> (3) provides that the plan shall be in effect in all political subdivisions of the State, and, if administered by them, be mandatory upon them;
>
> ...
>
> (15) effective October 1, 1983, provides that, in each case, reasonable efforts will be made (A) prior to the placement of a child in foster care, to prevent or eliminate the need for removal of the child from his home, and (B) to make it possible for the child to return to his home....

Petitioners in this action are Sue Suter and Gary T. Morgan, the Director and the Guardianship Administrator, respectively, of the Illinois Department of Children and Family Services (DCFS). DCFS is the state agency responsible for, among other things, investigating charges of child abuse and neglect and providing services to abused and neglected children and their families....

Respondents filed this class-action suit seeking declaratory and injunctive relief under the Adoption Act. They alleged that petitioners, ... failed to make reasonable efforts to prevent removal of children from their homes and to facilitate reunification of families where removal had occurred. This failure occurred, as alleged by respondents, because DCFS failed promptly to assign caseworkers to children placed in DCFS custody and promptly to reassign cases when caseworkers were on leave from DCFS. The District Court, without objection from petitioners, certified two separate classes seeking relief, including all children who are or will be wards of DCFS and are placed in foster care or remain in their homes under a judicial protective order. The District Court denied a motion to dismiss filed by petitioners, holding, as relevant here, that the Adoption Act contained an implied cause of action and that suit could also be brought to enforce the Act under 42 U.S.C. § 1983.

The Court of Appeals affirmed . . . [and] held that the "reasonable efforts" clause of the Adoption Act could be enforced through an action under § 1983 . . . [and] also found that the Adoption Act created an implied right of action such that private individuals could bring suit directly under the Act to enforce the provisions relied upon by respondents. We granted certiorari, and now reverse.

In *Maine v. Thiboutot*, we first established that § 1983 is available as a remedy for violations of federal statutes as well as for constitutional violations. We have subsequently recognized that § 1983 is not available to enforce a violation of a federal statute "where Congress has foreclosed such enforcement of the statute in the enactment itself and where the statute did not create enforceable rights, privileges, or immunities within the meaning of § 1983."

In *Pennhurst State School and Hospital v. Halderman*, we held that § 111 of the Developmentally Disabled Assistance and Bill of Rights Act of 1975, did not confer an implied cause of action. That statute, as well as the statute before us today, was enacted by Congress pursuant to its spending power. In *Pennhurst*, we noted that it was well established that Congress has the power to fix the terms under which it disburses federal money to the States. As stated in Pennhurst:

> The legitimacy of Congress' power to legislate under the spending power thus rests on whether the State voluntarily and knowingly accepts the terms of the 'contract.' There can, of course, be no knowing acceptance if a State is unaware of the conditions or is unable to ascertain what is expected of it. Accordingly, if Congress intends to impose a condition on the grant of federal moneys, it must do so unambiguously.

We concluded that the statutory section sought to be enforced by the *Pennhurst* respondents did not provide such unambiguous notice to the States because it spoke in terms "intended to be hortatory, not mandatory."

. . .

Did Congress, in enacting the Adoption Act, unambiguously confer upon the child beneficiaries of the Act a right to enforce the requirement that the State make "reasonable efforts" to prevent a child from being removed from his home, and once removed to reunify the child with his family? We turn now to that inquiry.

. . . to obtain federal reimbursement, a State have a plan which "provides that, in each case, reasonable efforts will be made . . . to prevent or eliminate the need for removal of the child from his home, and . . . to make it possible for the child to return to his home. . . ." As recognized by petitioners, respondents, and the courts below, the Act is mandatory in its terms. However, in the light shed by *Pennhurst*, we must examine exactly what is required of States by the Act. Here, the terms of § 671(a) are clear: "In order for a State to be eligible for payments under this part, it shall have a plan approved by the Secretary." Therefore the Act does place a requirement on the States, but that requirement only goes so far as to ensure that the State have a plan approved by the Secretary which contains the 16 listed features.

Respondents do not dispute that Illinois in fact has a plan approved by the Secretary which provides that reasonable efforts at prevention and reunification will be made. Respondents argue, however, that § 1983 allows them to sue in federal court to obtain enforcement of this particular provision of the state plan. This argument is based, at least in part, on the assertion that 42 U.S.C. § 671(a)(3) requires that the State have a plan which is "in effect." This section states that the state plan shall "provide that the plan shall be in effect in all political subdivisions of the State, and, if administered by them, be mandatory upon them." But we think that "in effect" is directed to the requirement that the plan apply to all political subdivisions of the State, and is not intended to otherwise modify the word "plan."

In the present case, however, the term "reasonable efforts" to maintain an abused or neglected child in his home, or return the child to his home from foster care, appears in quite a different context. No further statutory guidance is found as to how "reasonable efforts" are to be measured. This directive is not the only one which Congress has given to the States, and it is a directive whose meaning will obviously vary with the circumstances of each individual case. How the State was to comply with this directive, and with the other provisions of the Act, was, within broad limits, left up to the State.

Other sections of the Act provide enforcement mechanisms for the "reasonable efforts" clause of 42 U.S.C. § 671(a)(15). The Secretary has the authority to reduce or eliminate payments to a State on finding that the State's plan no longer complies with § 671(a) or that "there is a substantial failure" in the administration of a plan such that the State is not complying with its own plan. § 671(b). The Act also requires that in order to secure federal reimbursement for foster care payments made with respect to a child involuntarily removed from his home the removal must be "the result of a judicial determination to the effect that continuation [in the child's home] would be contrary to the welfare of such child and (effective October 1, 1983) that reasonable efforts of the type described in section 671(a)(15) of this title have been made." While these statutory provisions may not provide a comprehensive enforcement mechanism so as to manifest Congress' intent to foreclose remedies under § 1983, they do show that the absence of a remedy to private plaintiffs under § 1983 does not make the "reasonable efforts" clause a dead letter.

The regulations promulgated by the Secretary to enforce the Adoption Act do not evidence a view that § 671(a) places any requirement for state receipt of federal funds other than the requirement that the State submit a plan to be approved by the Secretary. The regulations provide that to meet the requirements of § 671(a)(15) the case plan for each child must "include a description of the services offered and the services provided to prevent removal of the child from the home and to reunify the family." Another regulation, entitled "requirements and submittal," provides that a state plan must specify "which preplacement preventive and reunification services are available to children and families in need." What is significant is that the regulations are not specific and do not provide notice to the States that failure to do anything other than submit a plan with the requisite features, to be approved by the Secretary, is a further condition on the receipt of funds from the Federal Government. Respondents contend that "neither [petitioners] nor amici supporting them present any legislative history to refute the evidence that Congress intended to be enforceable." To the extent such history may be relevant, our examination of it leads us to conclude that Congress was concerned that the required reasonable efforts be made by the States, but also indicated that the Act left a great deal of discretion to them.

Careful examination of the language relied upon by respondents, in the context of the entire Act, leads us to conclude that the "reasonable efforts" language does not unambiguously confer an enforceable right upon the Act's beneficiaries. The term "reasonable efforts" in this context is at least as plausibly read to impose only a rather generalized duty on the State, to be enforced not by private individuals, but by the Secretary in the manner previously discussed.

We conclude that 42 U.S.C. § 671(a)(15) neither confers an enforceable private right on its beneficiaries nor creates an implied cause of action on their behalf.

The judgment of the Court of Appeals is therefore

Reversed.

Justice Blackmun, with whom Justice Stevens joins, dissenting. [omitted]

Notes and Queries

1. As we have seen, the *Adoption and Safe Families Act of 1997* requires states to hold permanency planning hearings within twelve months of child placement and specifies situations in which "reasonable efforts" to reunify the family are not required. The act also requires termination proceedings to be filed (with some exceptions) when a child has been in placement for fifteen of the most recent twenty-two months. How would you argue that the reforms are enforceable under 42 U.S.C. § 1983? Would these limits mean that states no longer have a generalized duty? If so, what could be the utility of this line of reasoning?

Smith v. O.F.F.E.R.

431 U.S. 816; 97 S. Ct. 2094 (1977)

Mr. Justice Brennan delivered the opinion of the Court.

Appellees, individual foster parents and an organization of foster parents, brought this civil rights class action pursuant to 42 U.S.C. § 1983 in the United States District Court for the Southern District of New York, on their own behalf and on behalf of children for whom they have provided homes for a year or more. They sought declaratory and injunctive relief against New York State and New York City officials, alleging that the procedures governing the removal of foster children from foster homes . . . violated the Due Process and Equal Protection Clauses of the Fourteenth Amendment. The District Court appointed independent counsel for the foster children to forestall any possibility of conflict between their interests and the interests asserted by the foster parents. A group of natural mothers of children in foster care were granted leave to intervene on behalf of themselves and others similarly situated.

A divided three-judge District Court concluded that "the pre-removal procedures presently employed by the State are constitutionally defective," holding that "before a foster child can be peremptorily transferred from the foster home in which he has been living, be it to another foster home or to the natural parents who initially placed him in foster care, he is entitled to a hearing at which all concerned parties may present any relevant information to the administrative decisionmaker charged with determining the future placement of the child." . . . We reverse.

I

A detailed outline of the New York statutory system regulating foster care is a necessary preface to a discussion of the constitutional questions presented.

A

The expressed central policy of the New York system is that "it is generally desirable for the child to remain with or be returned to the natural parent because the child's need for a normal family life will usually best be met in the natural home, and . . . parents are entitled to bring up their own children unless the best interests of the child would be thereby endangered[.]" But the State has opted for foster care as one response to those situations where the natural parents are unable to provide the "positive, nurturing family relationships" and "normal family life in a permanent home" that offer "the best opportunity for children to develop and thrive."

Foster care has been defined as "[a] child welfare service which provides substitute family care for a planned period for a child when his own family cannot care for him for a temporary or extended period, and when adoption is neither desirable nor possible." Thus, the distinctive features of foster care are, first, "that it is care in a family, it is noninstitutional substitute care," and, second, "that it is for a planned period — either temporary or extended. This is unlike adoptive placement, which implies a permanent substitution of one home for another."

Under the New York scheme children may be placed in foster care either by voluntary placement or by court order. Most foster-care placements are voluntary. They occur when physical or mental illness, economic problems, or other family crises make it impossible for natural parents, particularly single parents, to provide a stable home life for their children for some limited period. Resort to such placements is almost compelled when it is not possible in such circumstance to place the child with a relative or friend, or to pay for the services of a homemaker or boarding school.

Voluntary placement requires the signing of a written agreement by the natural parent or guardian, transferring the care and custody of the child to an authorized child welfare agency. Although by statute the terms of such agreements are open to negotiation, it is contended that agencies require execution of standardized forms. The agreement may provide for return of the child to the natural parent at a specified date or upon occurrence of a particular event, and if it does not, the child must be returned by the agency, in the absence of a court order, within 20 days of notice from the parent.

The agency may maintain the child in an institutional setting, but more commonly acts under its authority to "place out and board out" children in foster homes. Foster parents, who are licensed by the State or an authorized foster-care agency, provide care under a contractual arrangement with the agency, and are compensated for their services. The typical contract expressly reserves the right of the agency to remove the child on request. Conversely, the foster parent may cancel the agreement at will.

The New York system divides parental functions among agency, foster parents, and natural parents, and the definitions of the respective roles are often complex and often unclear. The law transfers "care and custody" to the agency, but day-to-day supervision of the child and his activities, and most of the functions ordinarily associated with legal custody, are the responsibility of the foster parent. Nevertheless, agency supervision of the performance of the foster parents takes forms indicating that the foster parent does not have the full authority of a legal custodian. Moreover, the natural parent's placement of the child with the agency does not surrender legal guardianship; the parent retains authority to act with respect to the child in certain circumstances. The natural parent has not only the right but the obligation to visit the foster child and plan for his future; failure of a parent with capacity to fulfill the obligation for more than a year can result in a court order terminating the parent's rights on the ground of neglect.

Children may also enter foster care by court order. The Family Court may order that a child be placed in the custody of an authorized child-care agency after a full adversary judicial hearing under Art. 10 of the New York Family Court Act, if it is found that the child has been abused or neglected by his natural parents. In addition, a minor adjudicated a juvenile delinquent, or "person in need of supervision" may be placed by the court with an agency. The consequences of foster-care placement by court order do not differ substantially from those for children voluntarily placed, except that the parent is not entitled to return of the child on demand . . . termination of foster care must then be consented to by the court. [The court notes that: "the record shows that in 1973–1974 approximately 80% of the children removed from foster homes in New York State after living in the foster home for one year or more were transferred to another foster placement. Thirteen percent were returned to the biological parents, and 7 were adopted."]

B

The provisions of the scheme specifically at issue in this litigation come into play when the agency having legal custody determines to remove the foster child from the foster home, either because it has determined that it would be in the child's best interests to transfer him to some other foster home, or to return the child to his natural parents in accordance with the statute or placement agreement. Most children are removed in order to be transferred to another foster home. The procedures by which foster parents may challenge a removal made for that purpose differ somewhat from those where the removal is made to return the child to his natural parent.

[The statute], provides that the "authorized agency placing out or boarding [a foster] child ... may in its discretion remove such child from the home where placed or boarded." Administrative regulations implement this provision. The agency is required, except in emergencies, to notify the foster parents in writing 10 days in advance of any removal. The notice advises the foster parents that if they object to the child's removal they may request a "conference" with the Social Services Department. The department schedules requested conferences within 10 days of the receipt of the request. The foster parent may appear with counsel at the conference, where he will "be advised of the reasons [for the removal of the child] and be afforded an opportunity to submit reasons why the child should not be removed." The official must render a decision in writing within five days after the close of the conference, and send notice of his decision to the foster parents and the agency. The proposed removal is stayed pending the outcome of the conference.

If the child is removed after the conference, the foster parent may appeal to the Department of Social Services for a "fair hearing," that is, a full adversary administrative hearing ... however, the removal is not automatically stayed pending the hearing and judicial review.

This statutory and regulatory scheme applies statewide. In addition, regulations ... provide even greater procedural safeguards there.... [I]n place of or in addition to the conference provided by the state regulations, the foster parents may request a full trial-type hearing before the child is removed from their home. This procedure applies, however, only if the child is being transferred to another foster home, and not if the child is being returned to his natural parents.

One further preremoval procedural safeguard is available. The Family Court has jurisdiction to review, on petition of the foster parent or the agency, the status of any child who has been in foster care for 18 months or longer. The foster parents, the natural parents, and all interested agencies are made parties to the proceeding.

After hearing, the court may order that foster care be continued, or that the child be returned to his natural parents, or that the agency take steps to free the child for adoption. Moreover, § 392(8) authorizes the court to issue an "order of protection" which "may set forth reasonable conditions of behavior to be observed for a specified time by a person or agency who is before the court." Thus, the court may order not only that foster care be continued, but additionally, "in assistance or as a condition of" that order, that the agency leave the child with the present foster parent. In other words, § 392 provides a mechanism whereby a foster parent may obtain preremoval judicial review of an agency's decision to remove a child who has been in foster care for 18 months or more.

. . .

The relief sought in this case is entirely procedural. Our task is only to determine whether the District Court correctly held that the present procedures preceding the removal from a foster home of children resident there a year or more are constitutionally inadequate. To that task we now turn.

II

A

Our first inquiry is whether appellees have asserted interests within the Fourteenth Amendment's protection of "liberty" and "property."

. . .

The appellees' basic contention is that when a child has lived in a foster home for a year or more, a psychological tie is created between the child and the foster parents which constitutes the foster family the true "psychological family" of the child. That family, they argue, has a "liberty interest" in its survival as a family protected by the Fourteenth Amendment. Upon this premise they conclude that the foster child cannot be removed without a prior hearing satisfying due process. Appointed counsel for the children . . . however, disagrees, and has consistently argued that the foster parents have no such liberty interest independent of the interests of the foster children, and that the best interests of the children would not be served by procedural protections beyond those already provided by New York law. The intervening natural parents of children in foster care . . . also oppose the foster parents, arguing that recognition of the procedural right claimed would undercut both the substantive family law of New York, which favors the return of children to their natural parents as expeditiously as possible, and their constitutionally protected right of family privacy, by forcing them to submit to a hearing and defend their rights to their children before the children could be returned to them.

. . .

It is, of course, true that "freedom of personal choice in matters of . . . family life is one of the liberties protected by the Due Process Clause of the Fourteenth Amendment." There does exist a "private realm of family life which the state cannot enter," that has been afforded both substantive and procedural protection. But is the relation of foster parent to foster child sufficiently akin to the concept of "family" recognized in our precedents to merit similar protection? Although considerable difficulty has attended the task of defining "family" for purposes of the Due Process Clause, we are not without guides to some of the elements that define the concept of "family" and contribute to its place in our society.

First, the usual understanding of "family" implies biological relationships, and most decisions treating the relation between parent and child have stressed this element. . . .

Thus the importance of the familial relationship, to the individuals involved and to the society, stems from the emotional attachments that derive from the intimacy of daily association, and from the role it plays in "promot[ing] a way of life" through the instruction of children, as well as from the fact of blood relationship. No one would seriously dispute that a deeply loving and interdependent relationship between an adult and a child in his or her care may exist even in the absence of blood relationship. . . . For this reason, we cannot dismiss the foster family as a mere collection of unrelated individuals.

But there are also important distinctions between the foster family and the natural family. First, unlike the earlier cases recognizing a right to family privacy, the State here seeks to interfere, not with a relationship having its origins entirely apart from the power of the State, but rather with a foster family which has its source in state law and contractual arrangements. The individual's freedom to marry and reproduce is "older than the Bill of Rights." Accordingly, unlike the property interests that are also protected by the Fourteenth Amendment, the liberty interest in family privacy has its source, and its contours are ordinarily to be sought, not in state law, but in intrinsic human rights, as they have been understood in "this Nation's history and tradition." Here, however, whatever emotional ties may develop between foster parent and foster child have their origins in an arrangement in which the State has been a partner from the outset. While the Court has recognized that liberty interests may in some cases arise from positive-law sources, in such a case, and particularly where, as here, the claimed interest derives from a knowingly assumed contractual relation with the State, it is appropriate to ascertain from state law the expectations and entitlements of the parties. In this case, the limited recognition accorded to the foster family by the New York statutes and the contracts executed by the foster parents argue against any but the most limited constitutional "liberty" in the foster family.

A second consideration related to this is that ordinarily procedural protection may be afforded to a liberty interest of one person without derogating from the substantive liberty of another. Here, however, such a tension is virtually unavoidable. Under New York law, the natural parent of a foster child in voluntary placement has an absolute right to the return of his child in the absence of a court order obtainable only upon compliance with rigorous substantive and procedural standards, which reflect the constitutional protection accorded the natural family. Moreover, the natural parent initially gave up his child to the State only on the express understanding that the child would be returned in those circumstances. These rights are difficult to reconcile with the liberty interest in the foster family relationship claimed by appellees. It is one thing to say that individuals may acquire a liberty interest against arbitrary governmental interference in the family-like associations into which they have freely entered, even in the absence of biological connection or state-law recognition of the relationship. It is quite another to say that one may acquire such an interest in the face of another's constitutionally recognized liberty interest that derives from blood relationship, state-law sanction, and basic human right—an interest the foster parent has recognized by contract from the outset. Whatever liberty interest might otherwise exist in the foster family as an institution, that interest must be substantially attenuated where the proposed removal from the foster family is to return the child to his natural parents.

As this discussion suggests, appellees' claim to a constitutionally protected liberty interest raises complex and novel questions. It is unnecessary for us to resolve those questions definitively in this case, however, for, like the District Court, we conclude that "narrower grounds exist to support" our reversal. We are persuaded that, even on the assumption that appellees have a protected "liberty interest," the District Court erred in holding that the preremoval procedures presently employed by the State are constitutionally defective.

. . .

It is true that "[b]efore a person is deprived of a protected interest, he must be afforded opportunity for some kind of a hearing, 'except for extraordinary situations where some valid governmental interest is at stake that justifies postponing the hearing until after the event.'" But the hearing required is only one "appropriate to the nature of the case." "[D]ue process is flexible and calls for such procedural protections as the particular situation demands." Only last Term, the Court held that "identification of the specific dictates of due process generally requires consideration of three distinct factors: First, the private interest that will be affected by the official action; second, the risk of an erroneous deprivation of such interest through the procedures used, and the probable value, if any, of additional or substitute procedural safeguards; and finally, the Government's interest, including the function involved and the fiscal and administrative burdens that the additional or substitute procedural requirement would entail." Consideration of the procedures employed by the State and New York City in light of these three factors requires the conclusion that those procedures satisfy constitutional standards.

Turning first to the procedure applicable in New York City provides that before a child is removed from a foster home for transfer to another foster home, the foster parents may request an "independent review." The District Court's description of this review is set out in the margin. Such a procedure would appear to give a more elaborate trial-type hearing to foster families than this Court has found required in other contexts of administrative determinations. The District Court found the procedure inadequate on four grounds, none of which we find sufficient to justify the holding that the procedure violates due process.

First, the court held that the "independent review" administrative proceeding was insufficient because it was only available on the request of the foster parents. In the view of the District Court, the proceeding should be provided as a matter of course, because the interests of the foster parents and those of the child would not necessarily be coextensive, and it could not be assumed that the foster parents would invoke the hearing procedure in every case in which it was in the child's interest to have a hearing. Since the child is unable to request a hearing on his own, automatic review in every case is necessary. We disagree. As previously noted, the constitutional liberty, if any, sought to be protected by the New York procedures is a right of family privacy or autonomy, and the basis for recognition of any such interest in the foster family must be that close emotional ties analogous to those between parent and child are established when a child resides for a lengthy period with a foster family. If this is so, necessarily we should expect that the foster parents will seek to continue the relationship to preserve the stability of the family; if they do not request a hearing, it is difficult to see what right or interest of the foster child is protected by holding a hearing to determine whether removal would unduly impair his emotional attachments to a foster parent who does not care enough about the child to contest the removal. Thus, consideration of the interest to be protected and the likelihood of erroneous deprivations, the first two factors identified in *Mathews v. Eldridge*, as appropriate in determining the sufficiency of procedural protections, do not support the District Court's imposition of this additional requirement. Moreover, automatic provision of hearings as required by the District Court would impose a substantial additional administrative burden on the State. According to appellant city officials, during the approximately two years between the institution of SSC Procedure No. 5 in August 1974 and June 1976, there were approximately 2,800 transfers per year in the city, but only 26 foster parents requested hearings. It is not at all clear what would be gained by requiring full hearings in the more than 5,500 cases in which they were not requested.

Second, the District Court faulted the city procedure on the ground that participation is limited to the foster parents and the agency, and the natural parent and the child are not made parties to the hearing. This is not fatal in light of the nature of the alleged constitutional interests at stake. When the child's transfer from one foster home to another is pending, the interest arguably requiring protection is that of the foster family, not that of the natural parents. Moreover, the natural parent can generally add little to the accuracy of factfinding concerning the wisdom of such a transfer, since the foster parents and the agency, through its caseworkers, will usually be most knowledgeable about conditions in the foster home. Of course, in those cases where the natural parent does have a special interest in the proposed transfer or particular information that would assist the factfinder, nothing in the city's procedure prevents any party from securing his testimony.

Much the same can be said in response to the District Court's statement:

> [I]t may be advisable, under certain circumstances, for the agency to appoint an adult representative better to articulate the interests of the child.

> In making this determination, the agency should carefully consider the child's age, sophistication and ability effectively to communicate his own true feelings.

But nothing in the New York City procedure prevents consultation of the child's wishes, directly or through an adult intermediary. We assume, moreover, that some such consultation would be among the first steps that a rational factfinder, inquiring into the child's best interests, would pursue. Such consultation, however, does not require that the child or an appointed representative must be a party with full adversary powers in all preremoval hearings.

The other two defects in the city procedure found by the District Court must also be rejected. One is that the procedure does not extend to the removal of a child from foster care to be returned to his natural parent. But as we have already held, whatever liberty interest may be argued to exist in the foster family is significantly weaker in the case of removals preceding return to the natural parent, and the balance of due process interests must accordingly be different. . . .

. . . We do not think that the 18-month limitation on § 392 actions renders the New York scheme constitutionally inadequate. The assumed liberty interest to be protected in this case is one rooted in the emotional attachments that develop over time between a child and the adults who care for him. But there is no reason to assume that those attachments ripen at less than 18 months or indeed at any precise point. Indeed, testimony in the record as well as material in published psychological texts suggests that the amount of time necessary for the development of the sort of tie appellees seek to protect varies considerably depending on the age and previous attachments of the child. In a matter of such imprecision and delicacy, we see no justification for the District Court's substitution of its view of the appropriate cutoff date for that chosen by the New York Legislature, given that any line is likely to be somewhat arbitrary and fail to protect some families where relationships have developed quickly while protecting others where no such bonds have formed. If New York sees 18 months rather than 12 as the time at which temporary foster care begins to turn into a more permanent and family-like setting requiring procedural protection and/or judicial inquiry into the propriety of continuing foster care, it would take far more than this record provides to justify a finding of constitutional infirmity in New York's choice.

. . .

Finally, the § 392 hearing is available to foster parents, both in and outside New York City, even where the removal sought is for the purpose of returning the child to his natural parents. Since this remedy provides a sufficient constitutional preremoval hearing to protect whatever liberty interest might exist in the continued existence of the foster family when the State seeks to transfer the child to another foster home, a fortiori the procedure is adequate to protect the lesser interest of the foster family in remaining together at the expense of the disruption of the natural family.

... Since we hold that the procedures provided by New York State ... are adequate to protect whatever liberty interests appellees may have, the judgment of the District Court is

Reversed.

Mr. Justice Stewart, with whom The Chief Justice and Mr. Justice Rehnquist join, concurring in the judgment.

The foster parent–foster child relationship involved in this litigation is, of course, wholly a creation of the State. New York law defines the circumstances under which a child may be placed in foster care, prescribes the obligations of the foster parents, and provides for the removal of the child from the foster home "in [the] discretion" of the agency with custody of the child. The agency compensates the foster parents, and reserves in its contracts the authority to decide as it sees fit whether and when a child shall be returned to his natural family or placed elsewhere. Were it not for the system of foster care that the State maintains, the relationship for which constitutional protection is asserted would not even exist.

The New York Legislature and the New York courts have made it unmistakably clear that foster care is intended only as a temporary way station until a child can be returned to his natural parents or placed for adoption. ... "[U]nnecessary stays may deprive these children of positive, nurturing family relationships and have deleterious effects on their development into responsible, productive citizens." And, specifically repudiating the contention that New York law contemplates that a child will have a "secure, stable and continuous" relationship with a third-party custodian as the child's "psychological parent," the New York Court of Appeals has "[p]articularly rejected the notion, if that it be, that third-party custodians may acquire some sort of squatter's rights in another's child."

In these circumstances, I cannot understand why the Court thinks itself obliged to decide these cases on the assumption that either foster parents or foster children in New York have some sort of "liberty" interest in the continuation of their relationship. Rather than tiptoeing around this central issue, I would squarely hold that the interests asserted by the appellees are not of a kind that the Due Process Clause of the Fourteenth Amendment protects.

... Not every loss, however "grievous," invokes the protection of the Due Process Clause. Its protections extend only to a deprivation by a State of "life, liberty, or property." And when a state law does operate to deprive a person of his liberty or property, the Due Process Clause is applicable even though the deprivation may not be "grievous." "[T]o determine whether due process requirements apply in the first place, we look not to the 'weight' but to the nature of the interest at stake."

Clearly, New York has deprived nobody of his life in these cases. It seems to me just as clear that the State has deprived nobody of his liberty or property. Putting to one side the District Court's erroneous "grievous loss" analysis, the appellees are left with very little ground on which to stand. ...

. . .

What remains of the appellees' argument is the theory that the relation of the foster parent to the foster child may generate emotional attachments similar to those found in natural families. The Court surmises that foster families who share these attachments might enjoy the same constitutional interest in "family privacy" as natural families.

. . .

But under New York's foster-care laws, any case where the foster parents had assumed the emotional role of the child's natural parents would represent not a triumph of the system, to be constitutionally safeguarded from state intrusion, but a failure. The goal of foster care, at least in New York, is not to provide a permanent substitute for the natural or adoptive home, but to prepare the child for his return to his real parents or placement in a permanent adoptive home by giving him temporary shelter in a family setting. . . . Perhaps it is to be expected that children who spend unduly long stays in what should have been temporary foster care will develop strong emotional ties with their foster parents. But this does not mean, and I cannot believe, that such breakdowns of the New York system must be protected or forever frozen in their existence by the Due Process Clause of the Fourteenth Amendment.

One of the liberties protected by the Due Process Clause, the Court has held, is the freedom to "establish a home and bring up children." *Meyer v. Nebraska*, If a State were to attempt to force the breakup of a natural family, over the objections of the parents and their children, without some showing of unfitness and for the sole reason that to do so was thought to be in the children's best interest, I should have little doubt that the State would have intruded impermissibly on "the private realm of family life which the state cannot enter." But this constitutional concept is simply not in point when we deal with foster families as New York law has defined them. The family life upon which the State "intrudes" is simply a temporary status which the State itself has created. It is a "family life" defined and controlled by the law of New York, for which New York pays, and the goals of which New York is entitled to and does set for itself.

For these reasons I concur in the judgment of the Court.

Notes and Queries

1. What liberty interests do the foster parents assert? Suppose a child had stayed two years with a foster family. What rationales could be used to argue that the state must provide the child a hearing before the transfer?

2. The case presents many different images of the foster care system. The state, for example, premises its foster care system on the accepted principle that the placement of a child into foster care is solely a temporary, transitional action intended to lead to the future reunion of the child with his natural parent or parents, or if such a reunion is not possible, to legal adoption and the establishment of a new

permanent home for the child. On the other hand, the Court notes that others present a very different perspective. For example, from the standpoint of natural parents, foster care has been condemned as a class-based intrusion into the family life of the poor. Over 50 percent of all children in foster care in New York City are from female-headed families receiving Aid to Families with Dependent Children. Minority families are also more likely to turn to foster care; 52.3 percent of the children in foster care in New York City are Black and 25.5 percent are Puerto Rican. The poor have little choice but to submit to state-supervised childcare when family crises strike. The extent to which "voluntary" placements are in fact voluntary has been questioned on other grounds as well. For example, it has been said that many "voluntary" placements are in fact coerced by threat of neglect proceedings and are not in fact voluntary in the sense of the product of an informed consent. Foster parents also note that children often stay in "temporary" foster care for much longer than contemplated by the theory of the system. The District Court found as a fact that the median time spent in foster care in New York was over four years. Indeed, many children apparently remain in this "limbo" indefinitely. The District Court also found that the longer a child remains in foster care, the more likely it is that he will never leave: "[T]he probability of a foster child being returned to his biological parents declined markedly after the first year in foster care." It is not surprising, then, that many children often develop deep emotional ties with their foster parents, particularly those that enter foster care at a very early age and have little or no contact with their natural parents. Yet such ties do not seem to be regarded as obstacles to transfer of the child from one foster placement to another. The record in this case indicates that nearly 60 percent of the children in foster care in New York City have experienced more than one placement, and about 28 percent have experienced three or more. The intended stability of the foster home management is further damaged by the rapid turnover among social work professionals who supervise the foster care arrangements on behalf of the state. Moreover, even when it is clear that a foster child will not be returned to his natural parents, it is rare that he achieves a stable home life through final termination of parental ties and adoption into a new permanent family. Should these facts have swayed the Court in a different direction?

3. Can foster parents challenge the decisions of foster children's counsel when the counsel opposes the foster parents' wishes? The Court answered in the following manner:

> Appellants argue, with the dissenting judge below that in any event appellee foster parents have no standing to rely upon a supposed right of the foster children to avoid "grievous loss," because the foster children are independently represented by court-appointed counsel, who has consistently opposed the relief requested by appellees, and denied that the children have any such right. This argument misunderstands the peculiar circumstances of this lawsuit. Ordinarily, it is true, a party would not have

> standing to assert the rights of another, himself a party in the litigation; the third party himself can decide how best to protect his interests. But children usually lack the capacity to make that sort of decision, and thus their interest is ordinarily represented in litigation by parents or guardians. In this case, however, the State, the natural parents, and the foster parents, all of whom share some portion of the responsibility for guardianship of the child, are parties, and all contend that the position they advocate is most in accord with the rights and interests of the children. In this situation, the District Court properly appointed independent counsel to represent the children, so that the court could have the benefit of an independent advocate for the welfare of the children, unprejudiced by the possibly conflicting interests and desires of the other parties. It does not follow, however, that that independent counsel, who is not a guardian ad litem of the children, is solely authorized to determine the children's best interest.... We believe it would be most imprudent to leave entirely to court-appointed counsel the choices that neither the named foster children nor the class they represent are capable of making for themselves, especially in litigation in which all parties have sufficient attributes of guardianship that their views on the rights of the children should at least be heard.

Research Comments

1. Kinship care refers to a formal custody arrangement in which care for a child is legally transferred through a court order to the child welfare system, and in which the child's kin become his or her foster parents. Under this arrangement, the kin have physical custody and the state retains legal custody. Since the early part of the 1980s, kinship care has grown from a relatively rare form of child welfare placement to a very common one. Its use emerged out of necessity. As the number of children in need of placement increases and the number of foster families plummets, child welfare agencies increasingly turn to relatives as a vital placement resource. Their use was further encouraged by important legal developments. The Supreme Court, in a relatively ignored case, *Miller v. Youakim*, 440 U.S. 125 (1979), held that relatives were entitled to receive state payments for acting as foster parents. That decision eased the burden on relatives who otherwise could not afford to care for these children. Likewise, statutes now require agencies to attempt to place children in kinship care prior to placing them with strangers. See Roger J. R. Levesque (1995). The failures of foster care reform: Challenging the most radical blueprint. *Maryland Journal of Contemporary Issues*, 6, 1–35.

2. Kinship care has been known to bring obvious benefits to children. Most notably, siblings are more likely to stay together, children are less traumatized if they

remain with relatives, and they are less likely to be shuttled from foster home to foster home. See Laurel K. Leslie, John Landsverk, Mark B. Horton, William Ganger & Rae R. Newton (2000). The heterogeneity of children and their experiences in foster care. *Child Welfare*, 79, 315–334. Although praised and increasingly being used by child welfare agencies, kinship care still continues to be highly criticized. The view that relatives should take care of their own kin and not place additional burdens on the state often means that kinship foster parents may not receive the financial support and services that stranger foster families receive from the government. Several studies report that children in kinship foster care have significant physical, mental health, behavioral, and educational problems; but they and their foster families receive fewer services than children placed in nonrelative family foster care. This is of considerable significance given that service needs may be even greater for children in kinship care than for those in the care of nonrelatives, since kinship caregivers tend to be older, have fewer financial resources, and have more health problems than nonrelative foster parents. Family history also may indicate that a particular kinship foster parent is actually inappropriate due to previous abuse and neglect. It may be difficult to control whether or not an abusive or otherwise dangerous parent has unsupervised visits with the child when the child is placed with a relative. While kinship care has been touted as promoting stability for children, children in such placements are less likely to be reunited with their parents and are more likely to stay in out-of-home care for longer periods. Others question whether formal kinship care placements may be inappropriately replacing informal kinship care, which has traditionally taken place outside of the child welfare system. The concern is that families are being required to transfer their children's legal custody to the state and suffer greater intrusion into their lives instead of simply receiving enough support to raise their children themselves. See James P. Gleeson, John O'Donnell & Faith Johnson Bonecutter (1997). Understanding the complexity of practice in kinship foster care. *Child Welfare*, 76, 801–826; Mark E. Courtney (1998). The costs of child protection in the context of welfare reform. *The Future of Children*, 8, 88–103.

3. Research in this area remains limited, as revealed by two threads of important research. First, the most recent review of the literature indicates that, despite beliefs that children in kinship care fare better, no clear advantage exists for kinship vs. foster care on a wide variety of factors. The review also noted that no studies have examined the critical factors that would influence the relationship between the placement type and child well-being as well as overall placement outcomes. Alison Hassall, Elmie Janse van Rensburg, Sebastian Trew, David J. Hawes & Dave S. Pasalic (2021). Does kinship vs. foster care better promote connectedness? A systematic review and meta-analysis. *Clinical Child and Family Psychology Review*, 24(4), 813–832. Second, despite a lack of focus on kin carers vs. foster carers, the research that does exist (with much of it coming from Australia) supports expected findings given the reasons for using kinship care. Compared to foster carers, kin carers report (1) greater stress and mental health concerns, (2) accessing fewer services,

training, and support, and (3) less contact with service providers. Leith Harding, Kate Murray, Jane Shakespeare-Finch & Ron Frey. (2020). The wellbeing of foster and kin carers: A comparative study. *Children and Youth Services Review*, 108, 104566.

4. Would a relative foster parent have a liberty interest in her relationship to a foster child to which she is biologically related? Quite interestingly, the issue has been rarely litigated and the *O.F.F.E.R.* Court had left open the possibility that "long-term" foster parents may have certain protections due to the family ties and relationships that develop. One case that has examined the issue, *Rivera v. Marcus*, 696 F.2d 1016 (2d Cir. 1982), provides an important analysis. In *Rivera*, Betty Jean Ross and her two children moved in with Rivera in 1968. Rivera was a blood relation because she had the same biological father as the two children. During this time, they lived together as a family and she acted as a "surrogate mother" due to Ross's psychological problems. When Ross was committed to a mental institution, Rivera became the children's foster parent. The children were removed in 1974. During the time they were not in her care, Rivera was not able to talk to her half brother and sister or to learn their whereabouts. In determining Rivera's due process interest, the court found that the constitutional conception of "family" has evolved to include relationships among members of what has commonly become known as the "extended family." It further noted that the significance of biological connections in extending the constitutional protections for parent and child to other types of bonds. In its analysis, the *Rivera* court listed factors to use as a guide to determine the interests of a foster parent. These factors are (1) the biological relationship between the parties, (2) the expectation of the parties at the time the relationship was commenced, and (3) the age and previous living experience of the children prior to entering the foster care environment. Based on these considerations, the court found that the state had inappropriately infringed on Rivera's liberty interest in associating with her half brother and sister.

5. Why do you suppose that cases like *Rivera* seem to remain quite rare? Much speculation attempts to explain why these issues seem to not be litigated. It may well be that the problem is self-correcting in that where the facts are as strong as they were in *Rivera*, caseworkers are less likely to remove the children. It also may be because of lack of legal services, given that biological parents may have rights to an attorney while foster parents generally do not. Likewise, removals involving kin may be occurring in an acceptable manner to all parties or the foster parents simply may be unaware that they may request a hearing. See Gabrielle A. Paupeck (2001). When Grandma becomes Mom: The liberty interests of kinship foster parents. *Fordham Law Review*, 70, 527–561.

6. Given the significance of sibling bonds, it would seem that siblings have a right to associate, and because their relationship is more similar to a parent–child bond than to any third-party bond, that the state would need considerable evidence before separating siblings into different placements. Yet there is no single trend in

the statutory treatment of siblings' rights to associate. All states have at least one statute recognizing the importance of sibling bonds, but the recognition seems quite minimal given the potential significance of siblings. Most state statutes do not create a right to sibling visitation or right to be placed together. Instead, they find that the sibling bond may be one variable in a best interest test to determine where children should be placed once separated from their parents. Some states require "reasonable efforts" to place siblings together, while others create a presumption that sibling visitation is in the children's best interest. More recently, some states have revised their statutes to grant siblings standing to raise visitation issues including pre-adoptive sibling visitation and post-adoptive or permanency plan visitation. See William Wesley Patton (2001). The status of sibling's rights: A view into the new millennium. *Depaul Law Review*, 51, 1–38

Baltimore v. Bouknight

493 U.S. 549; 110 S. Ct. 900 (1990)

Justice O'Connor delivered the opinion of the Court.

In this action, we must decide whether a mother, the custodian of a child pursuant to a court order, may invoke the Fifth Amendment privilege against self-incrimination to resist an order of the juvenile court to produce the child. We hold that she may not.

I

Petitioner Maurice M. is an abused child. When he was three months old, he was hospitalized with a fractured left femur, and examination revealed several partially healed bone fractures and other indications of severe physical abuse. In the hospital, respondent Bouknight, Maurice's mother, was observed shaking Maurice, dropping him in his crib despite his spica cast, and otherwise handling him in a manner inconsistent with his recovery and continued health. Hospital personnel notified Baltimore City Department of Social Services (BCDSS) of suspected child abuse. In February 1987, BCDSS secured a court order removing Maurice from Bouknight's control and placing him in shelter care. Several months later, the shelter care order was inexplicably modified to return Maurice to Bouknight's custody temporarily. Following a hearing held shortly thereafter, the juvenile court declared Maurice to be a "child in need of assistance," thus asserting jurisdiction over Maurice and placing him under BCDSS' continuing oversight. BCDSS agreed that Bouknight could continue as custodian of the child, but only pursuant to extensive conditions set forth in a court-approved protective supervision order. The order required Bouknight to "cooperate with BCDSS," "continue in therapy," participate in parental aid and training programs, and "refrain from physically punishing [Maurice]." The order's terms were "all subject to the further Order of the Court." Bouknight's attorney signed the order, and Bouknight in a separate form set forth her agreement to each term.

Eight months later, fearing for Maurice's safety, BCDSS returned to juvenile court. BCDSS caseworkers related that Bouknight would not cooperate with them and had in nearly every respect violated the terms of the protective order. BCDSS stated that Maurice's father had recently died in a shooting incident and that Bouknight, in light of the results of a psychological examination and her history of drug use, could not provide adequate care for the child. On April 20, 1988, the court granted BCDSS' petition to remove Maurice from Bouknight's control for placement in foster care. BCDSS officials also petitioned for judicial relief from Bouknight's failure to produce Maurice or reveal where he could be found. The petition recounted that on two recent visits by BCDSS officials to Bouknight's home, she had refused to reveal the location of the child or had indicated that the child was with an aunt whom she would not identify. The petition further asserted that inquiries of Bouknight's known relatives had revealed that none of them had recently seen Maurice and that BCDSS had prompted the police to issue a missing persons report and referred the case for investigation by the police homicide division. Also on April 20, the juvenile court, upon a hearing on the petition, cited Bouknight for violating the protective custody order and for failing to appear at the hearing. Bouknight had indicated to her attorney that she would appear with the child, but also expressed fear that if she appeared the State would "'snatch the child.'" The court issued an order to show cause why Bouknight should not be held in civil contempt for failure to produce the child. Expressing concern that Maurice was endangered or perhaps dead, the court issued a bench warrant for Bouknight's appearance.

Maurice was not produced at subsequent hearings. At a hearing one week later, Bouknight claimed that Maurice was with a relative in Dallas. Investigation revealed that the relative had not seen Maurice. The next day, following another hearing at which Bouknight again declined to produce Maurice, the juvenile court found Bouknight in contempt for failure to produce the child as ordered. There was and has been no indication that she was unable to comply with the order. The court directed that Bouknight be imprisoned until she "purge[d] herself of contempt by either producing [Maurice] before the court or revealing to the court his exact whereabouts."

The juvenile court rejected Bouknight's subsequent claim that the contempt order violated the Fifth Amendment's guarantee against self-incrimination. The court stated that the production of Maurice would purge the contempt and that "the contempt is issued not because she refused to testify in any proceeding . . . [but] because she has failed to abide by the Order of this Court, mainly [for] the production of Maurice M." While that decision was being appealed, Bouknight was convicted of theft and sentenced to 18 months' imprisonment in separate proceedings. The Court of Appeals of Maryland vacated the juvenile court's judgment upholding the contempt order. The Court of Appeals found that the contempt order unconstitutionally compelled Bouknight to admit through the act of production "a measure of continuing control and dominion over Maurice's person" in circumstances in which "Bouknight has a reasonable apprehension that she will be prosecuted." Chief Justice Rehnquist granted BCDSS' application for a stay of the judgment and mandate of the Maryland Court of Appeals, pending disposition of the petition for a writ of certiorari. We granted certiorari and we now reverse.

II

The Fifth Amendment provides that "No person . . . shall be compelled in any criminal case to be a witness against himself." The Fifth Amendment's protection "applies only when the accused is compelled to make a testimonial communication that is incriminating." The juvenile court concluded that Bouknight could comply with the order through the unadorned act of producing the child, and we thus address that aspect of the order. When the government demands that an item be produced, "the only thing compelled is the act of producing the [item]." The Fifth Amendment's protection may nonetheless be implicated because the act of complying with the government's demand testifies to the existence, possession, or authenticity of the things produced. But a person may not claim the Amendment's protections based upon the incrimination that may result from the contents or nature of the thing demanded. Bouknight therefore cannot claim the privilege based upon anything that examination of Maurice might reveal, nor can she assert the privilege upon the theory that compliance would assert that the child produced is in fact Maurice (a fact the State could readily establish, rendering any testimony regarding existence or authenticity insufficiently incriminating). Rather, Bouknight claims the benefit of the privilege because the act of production would amount to testimony regarding her control over, and possession of, Maurice. Although the State could readily introduce evidence of Bouknight's continuing control over the child—e. g., the custody order, testimony of relatives, and Bouknight's own statements to Maryland officials before invoking the privilege—her implicit communication of control over Maurice at the moment of production might aid the State in prosecuting Bouknight.

The possibility that a production order will compel testimonial assertions that may prove incriminating does not, in all contexts, justify invoking the privilege to resist production. Even assuming that this limited testimonial assertion is sufficiently incriminating and "sufficiently testimonial for purposes of the privilege," Bouknight may not invoke the privilege to resist the production order because she has assumed custodial duties related to production and because production is required as part of a noncriminal regulatory regime.

The Court has on several occasions recognized that the Fifth Amendment privilege may not be invoked to resist compliance with a regulatory regime constructed to effect the State's public purposes unrelated to the enforcement of its criminal laws. . . .

These principles readily apply to this case. Once Maurice was adjudicated a child in need of assistance, his care and safety became the particular object of the State's regulatory interests. Maryland first placed Maurice in shelter care, authorized placement in foster care, and then entrusted responsibility for Maurice's care to Bouknight. By accepting care of Maurice subject to the custodial order's conditions (including requirements that she cooperate with BCDSS, follow a prescribed training regime, and be subject to further court orders), Bouknight submitted to the routine operation of the regulatory system and agreed to hold Maurice in a manner consonant with the State's regulatory interests and subject to inspection by BCDSS. In assuming the obligations attending custody, Bouknight "has accepted the incident obligation to permit inspection." The State imposes and enforces that obligation as part of a broadly directed, noncriminal regulatory regime governing children cared for pursuant to custodial orders.

Persons who care for children pursuant to a custody order, and who may be subject to a request for access to the child, are hardly a "'selective group inherently suspect of criminal activities.'" The juvenile court may place a child within its jurisdiction with social service officials or "under supervision in his own home or in the custody or under the guardianship of a relative or other fit person, upon terms the court deems appropriate." Children may be placed, for example, in foster care, in homes of relatives, or in the care of state officials. Even when the court allows a parent to retain control of a child within the court's jurisdiction, that parent is not one singled out for criminal conduct, but rather has been deemed to be, without the State's assistance, simply "unable or unwilling to give proper care and attention to the child and his problems." The provision that authorized the juvenile court's efforts to gain production of Maurice reflects this broad applicability. This provision "fairly may be said to be directed at . . . parents, guardians, and custodians who accept placement of juveniles in custody."

Similarly, BCDSS' efforts to gain access to children, as well as judicial efforts to the same effect, do not "focu[s] almost exclusively on conduct which was criminal." Many orders will arise in circumstances entirely devoid of criminal conduct. Even when criminal conduct may exist, the court may properly request production and return of the child, and enforce that request through exercise of the contempt power, for reasons related entirely to the child's well-being and through measures unrelated to criminal law enforcement or investigation. This case provides an illustration: concern for the child's safety underlay the efforts to gain access to and then compel production of Maurice. Finally, production in the vast majority of cases will embody no incriminating testimony, even if in particular cases the act of production may incriminate the custodian through an assertion of possession or the existence, or the identity, of the child. These orders to produce children cannot be characterized as efforts to gain some testimonial component of the act of production. The government demands production of the very public charge entrusted to a custodian, and makes the demand for compelling reasons unrelated to criminal law enforcement and as part of a broadly applied regulatory regime. In these circumstances, Bouknight cannot invoke the privilege to resist the order to produce Maurice.

We are not called upon to define the precise limitations that may exist upon the State's ability to use the testimonial aspects of Bouknight's act of production in subsequent criminal proceedings. But we note that imposition of such limitations is not foreclosed. The same custodial role that limited the ability to resist the production order may give rise to corresponding limitations upon the direct and indirect use of that testimony. The State's regulatory requirement in the usual case may neither compel incriminating testimony nor aid a criminal prosecution, but the Fifth Amendment protections are not thereby necessarily unavailable to the person who complies with the regulatory requirement after invoking the privilege and subsequently faces prosecution. In a broad range of contexts, the Fifth Amendment limits prosecutors' ability to use testimony that has been compelled.

III

The judgment of the Court of Appeals of Maryland is reversed, and the cases are remanded to that court for further proceedings not inconsistent with this opinion.

So ordered.

Justice Marshall, with whom Justice Brennan joins, dissenting.

. . .

I

The Court correctly assumes that Bouknight's production of her son to the Maryland court would be testimonial because it would amount to an admission of Bouknight's physical control over her son. The Court also assumes that Bouknight's act of production would be self-incriminating. I would not hesitate to hold explicitly that Bouknight's admission of possession or control presents a "'real and appreciable'" threat of self-incrimination. Bouknight's ability to produce the child would conclusively establish her actual and present physical control over him and thus might "prove a significant 'link in a chain' of evidence tending to establish [her] guilt."

Indeed, the stakes for Bouknight are much greater than the Court suggests. Not only could she face criminal abuse and neglect charges for her alleged mistreatment of Maurice, but she could also be charged with causing his death. The State acknowledges that it suspects that Maurice is dead, and the police are investigating his case as a possible homicide. In these circumstances, the potentially incriminating aspects to Bouknight's act of production are undoubtedly significant.

II

Notwithstanding the real threat of self-incrimination, the Court holds that "Bouknight may not invoke the privilege to resist the production order because she has assumed custodial duties related to production and because production is required as part of a noncriminal regulatory regime." In characterizing Bouknight as Maurice's "custodian," and in describing the relevant Maryland juvenile statutes as part of a noncriminal regulatory regime, the Court relies on two distinct lines of Fifth Amendment precedent, neither of which applies to this litigation.

A

The Court's first line of reasoning turns on its view that Bouknight has agreed to exercise on behalf of the State certain custodial obligations with respect to her son, obligations that the Court analogizes to those of a custodian of the records of a collective entity. This characterization is baffling, both because it is contrary to the facts of this case and because this Court has never relied on such a characterization to override the privilege against self-incrimination except in the context of a claim of privilege by an agent of a collective entity.

Jacqueline Bouknight is Maurice's mother; she is not, and in fact could not be, his "custodian" whose rights and duties are determined solely by the Maryland juvenile protection law. Although Bouknight surrendered physical custody of her child during the pendency of the proceedings to determine whether Maurice was a "child in need of assistance" (CINA) within the meaning of the Maryland Code, Maurice's placement in shelter care was only temporary and did not extinguish her legal right to custody of her son. When the CINA proceedings were settled, Bouknight regained physical custody of Maurice and entered into an agreement with the Baltimore City Department of Social Services (BCDSS). In that agreement, which was approved by the juvenile court, Bouknight promised, among other things, to "cooperate with BCDSS," but she retained legal custody of Maurice.

A finding that a child is in need of assistance does not by itself divest a parent of legal or physical custody, nor does it transform such custody to something conferred by the State. Thus, the parent of a CINA continues to exercise custody because she is the child's parent, not because the State has delegated that responsibility to her. Although the State has obligations "to provide for the care, protection, and wholesome mental and physical development of children" who are in need of assistance, these duties do not eliminate or override a parent's continuing legal obligations similarly to provide for her child.

In light of the statutory structure governing a parent's relationship to a CINA, Bouknight is not acting as a custodian in the traditional sense of that word because she is not acting on behalf of the State. In reality, she continues to exercise her parental duties, constrained by an agreement between her and the State. That agreement, which includes a stipulation that Maurice was a CINA, allows the State, in certain circumstances, to intercede in Bouknight's relationship with her child. It does not, however, confer custodial rights and obligations on Bouknight in the same way corporate law creates the custodial status of a corporate agent.

...

Jacqueline Bouknight is not the agent for an artificial entity that possesses no Fifth Amendment privilege. Her role as Maurice's parent is very different from the role of a corporate custodian who is merely the instrumentality through whom the corporation acts. I am unwilling to extend the collective entity doctrine into a context where it denies individuals, acting in their personal rather than representative capacities, their constitutional privilege against self-incrimination.

B

The Court's decision rests as well on cases holding that "the ability to invoke the privilege may be greatly diminished when invocation would interfere with the effective operation of a generally applicable, civil regulatory requirement." The cases the

Court cites have two common features: they concern civil regulatory systems not primarily intended to facilitate criminal investigations, and they target the general public. In contrast, regulatory regimes that are directed at a "'selective group inherently suspect of criminal activities,'" do not result in a similar diminution of the Fifth Amendment privilege.

1

Applying the first feature to this case, the Court describes Maryland's juvenile protection scheme as "a broadly directed, noncriminal regulatory regime governing children cared for pursuant to custodial orders." The Court concludes that Bouknight cannot resist an order necessary for the functioning of that system. The Court's characterization of Maryland's system is dubious and highlights the flaws inherent in the Court's formulation of the appropriate Fifth Amendment inquiry. Virtually any civil regulatory scheme could be characterized as essentially noncriminal by looking narrowly or, as in this case, solely to the avowed noncriminal purpose of the regulations. If one focuses instead on the practical effects, the same scheme could be seen as facilitating criminal investigations. The fact that the Court holds Maryland's juvenile statute to be essentially noncriminal, notwithstanding the overlapping purposes underlying that statute and Maryland's criminal child abuse statutes, proves that the Court's test will never be used to find a relationship between the civil scheme and law enforcement goals significant enough to implicate the Fifth Amendment.

The regulations embodied in the juvenile welfare statute are intimately related to the enforcement of state criminal statutes prohibiting child abuse. State criminal decisions suggest that information supporting criminal convictions is often obtained through civil proceedings and the subsequent protective oversight by BCDSS. . . .

. . . [T]he Court here disregards the practical implications of the civil scheme and holds that the juvenile protection system does not "'focu[s] almost exclusively on conduct which was criminal.'" I cannot agree with this approach. The State's goal of protecting children from abusive environments through its juvenile welfare system cannot be separated from criminal provisions that serve the same goal. When the conduct at which a civil statute aims — here, child abuse and neglect — is frequently the same conduct subject to criminal sanction, it strikes me as deeply problematic to dismiss the Fifth Amendment concerns by characterizing the civil scheme as "unrelated to criminal law enforcement or investigation." A civil scheme that inevitably intersects with criminal sanctions may not be used to coerce, on pain of contempt, a potential criminal defendant to furnish evidence crucial to the success of her own prosecution.

I would apply a different analysis, one that is more faithful to the concerns underlying the Fifth Amendment. This approach would target respondent's particular claim of privilege, the precise nature of the testimony sought, and the likelihood of self-incrimination caused by this respondent's compliance. "To sustain the privilege, it need only be evident from the implications of the question, in the setting in which it is asked, that a responsive answer to the question or an explanation of why it cannot be answered might be dangerous because injurious disclosure could result." This analysis unambiguously indicates that Bouknight's Fifth Amendment privilege must be respected to protect her from the serious risk of self-incrimination.

An individualized inquiry is preferable to the Court's analysis because it allows the privilege to turn on the concrete facts of a particular case, rather than on abstract characterizations concerning the nature of a regulatory scheme. Moreover, this particularized analysis would not undermine any appropriate goals of civil regulatory schemes that may intersect with criminal prohibitions. Instead, the ability of a State to provide immunity from criminal prosecution permits it to gather information necessary for civil regulation, while also preserving the integrity of the privilege against self-incrimination. The fact that the State throws a wide net in seeking information does not mean that it can demand from the few persons whose Fifth Amendment rights are implicated that they participate in their own criminal prosecutions. Rather, when the State demands testimony from its citizens, it should do so with an explicit grant of immunity.

2

The Court's approach includes a second element; it holds that a civil regulatory scheme cannot override Fifth Amendment protection unless it is targeted at the general public. Such an analysis would not be necessary under the particularized approach I advocate. Even under the Court's test, however, Bouknight's right against self-incrimination should not be diminished because Maryland's juvenile welfare scheme clearly is not generally applicable. A child is considered in need of assistance because "he is mentally handicapped or is not receiving ordinary and proper care and attention, and . . . his parents . . . are unable or unwilling to give proper care and attention to the child and his problems." The juvenile court has jurisdiction only over children who are alleged to be in need of assistance, not over all children in the State. It thus has power to compel testimony only from those parents whose children are alleged to be CINA's. In other words, the regulatory scheme that the Court describes as "broadly directed," is actually narrowly targeted at parents who through abuse or neglect deny their children the minimal reasonable level of care and attention. Not all such abuse or neglect rises to the level of criminal child abuse, but parents of children who have been so seriously neglected or abused as to warrant allegations that the children are in need of state assistance are clearly "a selective group inherently suspect of criminal activities."

III

In the end, neither line of precedents relied on by the Court justifies riding roughshod over Bouknight's constitutional privilege against self-incrimination. The Court cannot accurately characterize her as a "custodian" in the same sense as the Court has used that word in the past. Nor is she the State's "agent," whom the State may require to act on its behalf. Moreover, the regulatory scheme at issue here is closely intertwined with the criminal regime prohibiting child abuse and applies only to parents whose abuse or neglect is serious enough to warrant state intervention.

Although I am disturbed by the Court's willingness to apply inapposite precedent to deny Bouknight her constitutional right against self-incrimination, especially in light of the serious allegations of homicide that accompany this civil proceeding, I take some comfort in the Court's recognition that the State may be prohibited from using any testimony given by Bouknight in subsequent criminal proceedings. Because I am not content to deny Bouknight the constitutional protection required by the Fifth Amendment now in the hope that she will not be convicted later on the basis of her own testimony, I dissent.

Notes and Queries

1. Which opinion best reflects the nexus between civil child abuse investigations and the criminal justice system? A look at the actual laws that define maltreatment reveals that the criminal justice system can be used as well as the civil justice system. Prosecutions are left with much discretion, one which mirrors "wobblers" that allow for prosecuting the same actions as either felonies or misdemeanors. While they can be intertwined, the legal system has a long history of ignoring that intersection. Recall the *Walker* case in which parents were deemed exempt from responsibility under civil child neglect laws but not under criminal neglect for failing to obtain life-saving medical treatment for their child who died of meningitis. The court in that case accepted how religious exemptions for medical treatment in child welfare law were not available in the criminal justice system. *Walker v. Superior Court*, 47 Cal.3d 112, 763 P.2d 852 (1988).

2. Do you read the majority's opinion to find that Fifth Amendment protections are available against a prosecutor's use of evidence compelled through a regulatory regime? Should the Court explicitly decide that issue before compelling Bouknight to produce Maurice? If there is no firm rule, should a prosecutor offer Bouknight immunity in order to determine what happened to Maurice and determine whether Maurice is in need of assistance?

Chapter 9

Expertise and Testimony in the Courts

Unless opposing parties stipulate to the truth of evidence, whether evidence will be used to decide a dispute depends on a complex set of rules. These rules are necessary because testimony, documents, and records vary in their relevance, reliability, and potential for prejudicial affects. To ensure a fair, impartial, and just result, the court performs a gatekeeper role. Although the rules of evidence are complex, we can understand how they work by examining a few general rules that help courts determine whether to admit evidence at trials. The cases that follow address how the court determines the reliability of evidence, whether the evidence possesses enough indicia of reliability that it should be considered by factfinders. For our purposes, four areas of law raise the most important concerns.

What experts may testify to and the scope of their testimony is one of the most fundamental issues to understand when considering responses to child maltreatment. Generally, once a witness has been qualified as an expert, the expert may render an opinion. The admissibility of expert testimony depends on four factors: whether the subject matter of the testimony is outside the average judge's or jury's knowledge or experience, whether the state of the art of that field permits an expert opinion, whether the witness qualifies as an expert on that subject matter, and whether the basis of the expert's opinion is reasonably reliable. One of the major issues to address is the extent to which experts must rely on scientific evidence, an issue that becomes rather controversial when experts proffer evidence based on novel scientific principles. Once it has been determined that an expert may testify, the central issue then becomes determining the scope of the testimony. An expert witness may (depending on the state) be permitted to corroborate a claim of child maltreatment by testifying that the alleged victim presents psychological and behavioral patterns similar to those of other children known to have been maltreated. Again depending on the state, the court may allow expert testimony regarding syndromes. Such testimony involves the expert's description of a cluster of factors that have been identified with child maltreatment and have become known, collectively, as a syndrome. The witness (or another witness) will then explain consistencies between these factors and the child's condition.

Experts rarely are permitted to testify about two points. They must not testify whether they believe the child is telling the truth about the alleged abuse or render an opinion about witness credibility; those determinations are within the exclusive province of the jury or judge's power. Likewise, most states still prohibit expert testimony as to the ultimate issue (i.e., whether the child was, in fact, abused), since this too is considered within the role of the judge or jury alone. As we will see, however, these rules often become difficult to apply in practice. The opinion of experts can be highly persuasive and their findings on certain matters may run the risk of becoming tantamount to determining guilt or liability.

Special privileges defendants may hold raise another set of issues particularly important for child maltreatment law. Statements made to doctors, lawyers, and others in their professional capacity are generally considered privileged communications and cannot be disclosed in court. The major exception to that rule is if the patient or client consents to disclosure. The exception and the general rule make considerable sense in light of the rationale for privileges. This privilege rule aims to encourage those who seek professional assistance to communicate freely and openly with their service providers without fear of public exposure or legal repercussions. The scope of these privileges and the particular professional relationships to which they apply varies. In some states, privileges are abrogated by statute in child protection proceedings. In addition, all states have abuse reporting laws that mandate the reporting of suspected child abuse, often even when the reporter's suspicion originates from privileged communications. Conversations between husbands and wives are also privileged in most types of cases, which sometimes prevents one spouse from testifying against another. However, in a case alleging child maltreatment, this privilege is generally not applied. The major reason for abridging this privilege, in addition to showing concern for child safety, is that abuse or neglect already has destroyed the family harmony that the privilege was designed to protect. Importantly, attorneys generally are not mandated reporters, which highlights the great respect given to our adversarial system and its belief that attorneys do in fact stand for their clients when they represent them.

Character evidence provides a third important area to consider. Character witnesses generally are not permitted to testify in court. However, judges retain discretion to allow the alleged offender to present evidence concerning a pertinent trait of his/her own character or of the character of the victim. Character evidence regarding either the offender or the victim generally may only be used by the petitioner or prosecutor as rebuttal if the defendant already has raised the issue of character. A character witness may not testify to specific good or bad acts performed by the accused or the victim on direct examination unless character is an element of the case. Once that witness has testified, however, specific acts may be inquired about on cross-examination. Related to character evidence is evidence of prior misconduct. Courts routinely exclude evidence of misconduct by the defendant that occurred prior to the alleged abuse. However, past conduct may be so similar to the alleged maltreatment that it may be admitted to show that the offender had an overall plan, motive, or intent to abuse. The law has undergone a rapid transformation on this issue, with the trend toward a much more permissible use of prior conduct that would have been admitted even in the last decade.

The last set of issues to consider involves hearsay evidence. Briefly stated, hearsay is a statement made outside the courtroom that is presented in court proceedings by someone other than the original speaker to prove the truth of the original speaker's statement. The hearsay rule, however, is notable for its long list of exceptions that permit the use of hearsay. The underlying rationale for these exceptions is that some hearsay statements, when made under circumstances that suggest that they are trustworthy, are reliable enough to be used in court without being subject to the usual protections that adversarial processes provide to ensure the reliability and truthfulness of evidence. The first frequent exception involves an accused's admissions of wrongful conduct. When parties make out-of-court admissions, such admissions may be testified to by another under a hearsay rule exception. For example, a caseworker would be permitted to repeat the disclosure of an allegedly abusive parent in court even if the accused denied the wrongdoing at issue. The rationale for this exception is that an admission has presumably high reliability given that an alleged offender has nothing to gain from fabricating a damaging statement. The second exception involves statements spontaneously made under extreme emotional excitement. Excited utterances are deemed trustworthy because the excitement presumably does not allow speakers time to fabricate a story. The third major exception involves records, such as records held by agencies or other professionals who have interacted with children. Although records are hearsay because they contain second-hand information, their contents could be admissible if the records were kept regularly, systematically, and routinely. The regularity of the record-keeping process by persons with a duty to supply accurate data is thought to ensure trustworthiness and reliability. Importantly, this exception may seem like a broad rule, but the evidence is allowed only after it has been redacted of opinions and conclusions. The fourth exception relates to the third as it involves statements made to doctors and other medical personnel if they are made for the purpose of diagnosis or treatment. In some states, this exception could extend to a patient's description of past symptoms and even to the cause of the patient's injury and the perpetrator's identity. This rule assumes that, for the sake of seeking appropriate treatment, patients will be truthful. Lastly, a residual exception category provides courts with the discretion to allow the use of hearsay statements that do not fall under a traditional hearsay exception. This catch-all exception permits, in the interests of justice, the admission of hearsay that has circumstantial guarantees of trustworthiness.

Federal Rules of Evidence

Excerpts

Rule 401. Definition of "Relevant Evidence"

"Relevant evidence" means evidence having any tendency to make the existence of any fact that is of consequence to the determination of the action more probable or less probable than it would be without the evidence.

Rule 402. Relevant Evidence Generally Admissible; Irrelevant Evidence Inadmissible

All relevant evidence is admissible, except as otherwise provided by the Constitution of the United States, by Act of Congress, by these rules, or by other rules prescribed by the Supreme Court pursuant to statutory authority. Evidence which is not relevant is not admissible.

Rule 403. Exclusion of Relevant Evidence on Grounds of Prejudice, Confusion, or Waste of Time

Although relevant, evidence may be excluded if its probative value is substantially outweighed by the danger of unfair prejudice, confusion of the issues, or misleading the jury, or by considerations of undue delay, waste of time, or needless presentation of cumulative evidence.

Rule 701. Opinion Testimony by Lay Witnesses

If the witness is not testifying as an expert, the witness' testimony in the form of opinions or inferences is limited to those opinions or inferences which are (a) rationally based on the perception of the witness, and (b) helpful to a clear understanding of the witness' testimony or the determination of a fact in issue, and (c) not based on scientific, technical, or other specialized knowledge within the scope of Rule 702.

Rule 702. Testimony by Experts

If scientific, technical, or other specialized knowledge will assist the trier of fact to understand the evidence or to determine a fact in issue, a witness qualified as an expert by knowledge, skill, experience, training, or education, may testify thereto in the form of an opinion or otherwise, if (1) the testimony is based upon sufficient facts or data, (2) the testimony is the product of reliable principles and methods, and (3) the witness has applied the principles and methods reliably to the facts of the case.

Rule 703. Bases of Opinion Testimony by Experts

The facts or data in the particular case upon which an expert bases an opinion or inference may be those perceived by or made known to the expert at or before the hearing. If of a type reasonably relied upon by experts in the particular field in forming opinions or inferences upon the subject, the facts or data need not be admissible in evidence in order for the opinion or inference to be admitted. Facts or data that are otherwise inadmissible shall not be disclosed to the jury by the proponent of the opinion or inference unless the court determines that their probative value in assisting the jury to evaluate the expert's opinion substantially outweighs their prejudicial effect.

Rule 704. Opinion on Ultimate Issue

(a) Except as provided in subdivision (b), testimony in the form of an opinion or inference otherwise admissible is not objectionable because it embraces an ultimate issue to be decided by the trier of fact.

(b) No expert witness testifying with respect to the mental state or condition of a defendant in a criminal case may state an opinion or inference as to whether the defendant did or did not have the mental state or condition constituting an element of the crime charged or of a defense thereto. Such ultimate issues are matters for the trier of fact alone.

Daubert v. Merrell Dow

509 U.S. 579; 113 S. Ct. 2786 (1993)

Justice Blackman delivered the opinion of the Court.

In this case we are called upon to determine the standard for admitting expert scientific testimony in a federal trial.

I

Petitioners Jason Daubert and Eric Schuller are minor children born with serious birth defects. They and their parents sued respondent in California state court, alleging that the birth defects had been caused by the mothers' ingestion of Bendectin, a prescription antinausea drug marketed by respondent. Respondent removed the suits to federal court on diversity grounds.

After extensive discovery, respondent moved for summary judgment, contending that Bendectin does not cause birth defects in humans and that petitioners would be unable to come forward with any admissible evidence that it does. In support of its motion, respondent submitted an affidavit of Steven H. Lamm, physician and epidemiologist, who is a well-credentialed expert on the risks from exposure to various chemical substances. Doctor Lamm stated that he had reviewed all the literature on Bendectin and human birth defects — more than 30 published studies involving over 130,000 patients. No study had found Bendectin to be a human teratogen (i.e., a substance capable of causing malformations in fetuses). On the basis of this review, Doctor Lamm concluded that maternal use of Bendectin during the first trimester of pregnancy has not been shown to be a risk factor for human birth defects.

Petitioners did not (and do not) contest this characterization of the published record regarding Bendectin. Instead, they responded to respondent's motion with the testimony of eight experts of their own, each of whom also possessed impressive credentials. These experts had concluded that Bendectin can cause birth defects. Their conclusions were based upon "in vitro" (test tube) and "in vivo" (live) animal studies that found a link between Bendectin and malformations; pharmacological studies of the chemical structure of Bendectin that purported to show similarities between the structure of the drug and that of other substances known to cause birth defects; and the "reanalysis" of previously published epidemiological (human statistical) studies.

The District Court granted respondent's motion for summary judgment. The court stated that scientific evidence is admissible only if the principle upon which it is based is "'sufficiently established to have general acceptance in the field to which it belongs.'" The court concluded that petitioners' evidence did not meet this standard. Given the vast body of epidemiological data concerning Bendectin, the court held, expert opinion which is not based on epidemiological evidence is not admissible to establish causation. Thus, the animal-cell studies, live-animal studies, and chemical-structure analyses on which petitioners had relied could not raise by themselves a reasonably disputable jury issue regarding causation. Petitioners' epidemiological analyses, based as they were on recalculations of data in previously published studies that had found no causal link between the drug and birth defects, were ruled to be inadmissible because they had not been published or subjected to peer review.

The United States Court of Appeals for the Ninth Circuit affirmed. Citing *Frye v. United States* (1923), the court stated that expert opinion based on a scientific technique is inadmissible unless the technique is "generally accepted" as reliable in the relevant scientific community. The court declared that expert opinion based on a methodology that diverges "significantly from the procedures accepted by recognized authorities in the field . . . cannot be shown to be 'generally accepted as a reliable technique.'"

The court emphasized that other Courts of Appeals considering the risks of Bendectin had refused to admit reanalyses of epidemiological studies that had been neither published nor subjected to peer review. Those courts had found unpublished reanalyses "particularly problematic in light of the massive weight of the original published studies supporting [respondent's] position, all of which had undergone full scrutiny from the scientific community." Contending that reanalysis is generally accepted by the scientific community only when it is subjected to verification and scrutiny by others in the field, the Court of Appeals rejected petitioners' reanalyses as "unpublished, not subjected to the normal peer review process and generated solely for use in litigation." The court concluded that petitioners' evidence provided an insufficient foundation to allow admission of expert testimony that Bendectin caused their injuries and, accordingly, that petitioners could not satisfy their burden of proving causation at trial.

We granted certiorari in light of sharp divisions among the courts regarding the proper standard for the admission of expert testimony.

II

A

In the 70 years since its formulation in the *Frye* case, the "general acceptance" test has been the dominant standard for determining the admissibility of novel scientific evidence at trial. Although under increasing attack of late, the rule continues to be followed by a majority of courts, including the Ninth Circuit.

The *Frye* test has its origin in a short and citation-free 1923 decision concerning the admissibility of evidence derived from a systolic blood pressure deception test, a crude precursor to the polygraph machine. In what has become a famous (perhaps infamous) passage, the then Court of Appeals for the District of Columbia described the device and its operation and declared:

> Just when a scientific principle or discovery crosses the line between the experimental and demonstrable stages is difficult to define. Somewhere in this twilight zone the evidential force of the principle must be recognized, and while courts will go a long way in admitting expert testimony deduced from a well-recognized scientific principle or discovery, the thing from which the deduction is made must be sufficiently established to have gained general acceptance in the particular field in which it belongs.

Because the deception test had "not yet gained such standing and scientific recognition among physiological and psychological authorities as would justify the courts in admitting expert testimony deduced from the discovery, development, and experiments thus far made," evidence of its results was ruled inadmissible.

The merits of the *Frye* test have been much debated, and scholarship on its proper scope and application is legion. Petitioners' primary attack, however, is not on the content but on the continuing authority of the rule. They contend that the *Frye* test was superseded by the adoption of the Federal Rules of Evidence. We agree.

We interpret the legislatively enacted Federal Rules of Evidence as we would any statute. Rule 402 provides the baseline:

> All relevant evidence is admissible, except as otherwise provided by the Constitution of the United States, by Act of Congress, by these rules, or by other rules prescribed by the Supreme Court pursuant to statutory authority. Evidence which is not relevant is not admissible.

"Relevant evidence" is defined as that which has "any tendency to make the existence of any fact that is of consequence to the determination of the action more probable or less probable than it would be without the evidence." Rule 401. The Rules' basic standard of relevance thus is a liberal one.

Frye, of course, predated the Rules by half a century. In *United States v. Abel* we considered the pertinence of background common law in interpreting the Rules of Evidence. We noted that the Rules occupy the field, ... explained that the common law nevertheless could serve as an aid to their application:

> In principle, under the Federal Rules no common law of evidence remains. "All relevant evidence is admissible, except as otherwise provided...." In reality, of course, the body of common law knowledge continues to exist,

> though in the somewhat altered form of a source of guidance in the exercise of delegated powers.

We found the common-law precept at issue in the *Abel* case entirely consistent with Rule 402's general requirement of admissibility, and considered it unlikely that the drafters had intended to change the rule. In *Bourjaily v. United States*, (1987), on the other hand, the Court was unable to find a particular common-law doctrine in the Rules, and so held it superseded.

Here there is a specific Rule that speaks to the contested issue. Rule 702, governing expert testimony, provides:

> If scientific, technical, or other specialized knowledge will assist the trier of fact to understand the evidence or to determine a fact in issue, a witness qualified as an expert by knowledge, skill, experience, training, or education, may testify thereto in the form of an opinion or otherwise.

Nothing in the text of this Rule establishes "general acceptance" as an absolute prerequisite to admissibility. Nor does respondent present any clear indication that Rule 702 or the Rules as a whole were intended to incorporate a "general acceptance" standard. The drafting history makes no mention of *Frye*, and a rigid "general acceptance" requirement would be at odds with the "liberal thrust" of the Federal Rules and their "general approach of relaxing the traditional barriers to 'opinion' testimony." Given the Rules' permissive backdrop and their inclusion of a specific rule on expert testimony that does not mention "general acceptance," the assertion that the Rules somehow assimilated *Frye* is unconvincing. *Frye* made "general acceptance" the exclusive test for admitting expert scientific testimony. That austere standard, absent from, and incompatible with, the Federal Rules of Evidence, should not be applied in federal trials.

B

That the *Frye* test was displaced by the Rules of Evidence does not mean, however, that the Rules themselves place no limits on the admissibility of purportedly scientific evidence. Nor is the trial judge disabled from screening such evidence. To the contrary, under the Rules the trial judge must ensure that any and all scientific testimony or evidence admitted is not only relevant, but reliable.

The primary locus of this obligation is Rule 702, which clearly contemplates some degree of regulation of the subjects and theories about which an expert may testify. "If scientific, technical, or other specialized knowledge will assist the trier of fact to understand the evidence or to determine a fact in issue" an expert "may testify thereto." The subject of an expert's testimony must be "scientific . . . knowledge." The adjective "scientific" implies a grounding in the methods and procedures of science. Similarly, the word "knowledge" connotes more than subjective belief or unsupported speculation. The term "applies to any body of known facts or to any body of ideas inferred from such facts or accepted as truths on good grounds." Of course, it would be unreasonable to conclude that the subject of scientific testimony must be "known" to a certainty; arguably, there are no certainties in science. . . . But, in order to qualify as "scientific knowledge," an inference or assertion must be derived by the scientific method. Proposed testimony must be supported by appropriate validation—i.e., "good grounds," based on what is known. In short, the requirement that an expert's testimony pertain to "scientific knowledge" establishes a standard of evidentiary reliability.

Rule 702 further requires that the evidence or testimony "assist the trier of fact to understand the evidence or to determine a fact in issue." This condition goes primarily to relevance. "Expert testimony which does not relate to any issue in the case is not relevant and, ergo, non-helpful." The consideration has been aptly described by Judge Becker as one of "fit." "Fit" is not always obvious, and scientific validity for one purpose is not necessarily scientific validity for other, unrelated purposes. The study of the phases of the moon, for example, may provide valid scientific "knowledge" about whether a certain night was dark, and if darkness is a fact in issue, the knowledge will assist the trier of fact. However (absent creditable grounds supporting such a link), evidence that the moon was full on a certain night will not assist the trier of fact in determining whether an individual was unusually likely to have behaved irrationally on that night. Rule 702's "helpfulness" standard requires a valid scientific connection to the pertinent inquiry as a precondition to admissibility.

That these requirements are embodied in Rule 702 is not surprising. Unlike an ordinary witness, see Rule 701, an expert is permitted wide latitude to offer opinions, including those that are not based on knowledge or observation. Presumably, this relaxation of the usual requirement of firsthand knowledge—a rule which represents "a 'most pervasive manifestation' of the common law insistence upon 'the most reliable sources of information,'" is premised on an assumption that the expert's opinion will have a reliable basis in the knowledge and experience of his discipline.

C

Faced with a proffer of expert scientific testimony, then, the trial judge must determine at the outset, pursuant to Rule 104(a), whether the expert is proposing to testify to (1) scientific knowledge that (2) will assist the trier of fact to understand or determine a fact in issue. This entails a preliminary assessment of whether the reasoning or methodology underlying the testimony is scientifically valid and of whether that reasoning or methodology properly can be applied to the facts in issue. We are confident that federal judges possess the capacity to undertake this review. Many factors will bear on the inquiry, and we do not presume to set out a definitive checklist or test. But some general observations are appropriate.

Ordinarily, a key question to be answered in determining whether a theory or technique is scientific knowledge that will assist the trier of fact will be whether it can be (and has been) tested. "Scientific methodology today is based on generating hypotheses and testing them to see if they can be falsified; indeed, this methodology is what distinguishes science from other fields of human inquiry."

Another pertinent consideration is whether the theory or technique has been subjected to peer review and publication. Publication (which is but one element of peer review) is not a sine qua non of admissibility; it does not necessarily correlate with reliability and in some instances well-grounded but innovative theories will not have been published. Some propositions, moreover, are too particular, too new, or of too limited interest to be published. But submission to the scrutiny of the scientific community is a component of "good science," in part because it increases the likelihood that substantive flaws in methodology will be detected. The fact of publication (or lack thereof) in a peer reviewed journal thus will be a relevant, though not dispositive, consideration in assessing the scientific validity of a particular technique or methodology on which an opinion is premised.

Additionally, in the case of a particular scientific technique, the court ordinarily should consider the known or potential rate of error and the existence and maintenance of standards controlling the technique's operation.

Finally, "general acceptance" can yet have a bearing on the inquiry. A "reliability assessment does not require, although it does permit, explicit identification of arelevant scientific community and an express determination of a particular degree of acceptance within that community." Widespread acceptance can be an important factor in ruling particular evidence admissible, and "a known technique which has been able to attract only minimal support within the community" may properly be viewed with skepticism.

The inquiry envisioned by Rule 702 is, we emphasize, a flexible one. Its overarching subject is the scientific validity—and thus the evidentiary relevance and reliability—of the principles that underlie a proposed submission. The focus, of course, must be solely on principles and methodology, not on the conclusions that they generate.

Throughout, a judge assessing a proffer of expert scientific testimony under Rule 702 should also be mindful of other applicable rules. Rule 703 provides that expert opinions based on otherwise inadmissible hearsay are to be admitted only if the facts or data are "of a type reasonably relied upon by experts in the particular field in forming opinions or inferences upon the subject." Rule 706 allows the court at its discretion to procure the assistance of an expert of its own choosing. Finally, Rule 403 permits the exclusion of relevant evidence "if its probative value is substantially outweighed by the danger of unfair prejudice, confusion of the issues, or misleading the jury. . . ." Judge Weinstein has explained: "Expert evidence can be both powerful and quite misleading because of the difficulty in evaluating it. Because of this risk, the judge in weighing possible prejudice against probative force under Rule 403 of the present rules exercises more control over experts than over lay witnesses."

III

We conclude by briefly addressing what appear to be two underlying concerns of the parties and amici in this case. Respondent expresses apprehension that abandonment of "general acceptance" as the exclusive requirement for admission will result in a "free-for-all" in which befuddled juries are confounded by absurd and irrational pseudoscientific assertions. In this regard respondent seems to us to be overly pessimistic about the capabilities of the jury and of the adversary system generally. Vigorous cross-examination, presentation of contrary evidence, and careful instruction on the burden of proof are the traditional and appropriate means of attacking shaky but admissible evidence. Additionally, in the event the trial court concludes that the scintilla of evidence presented supporting a position is insufficient to allow a reasonable juror to conclude that the position more likely than not is true, the court remains free to direct a judgment and likewise to grant summary judgment. These conventional devices, rather than wholesale exclusion under an uncompromising "general acceptance" test, are the appropriate safeguards where the basis of scientific testimony meets the standards of Rule 702.

Petitioners and, to a greater extent, their amici exhibit a different concern. They suggest that recognition of a screening role for the judge that allows for the exclusion of "invalid" evidence will sanction a stifling and repressive scientific orthodoxy and will be inimical to the search for truth.It is true that open debate is an essential part of both legal and scientific analyses. Yet there are important differences between the quest for truth in the courtroom and the quest for truth in the laboratory. Scientific conclusions are subject to perpetual revision. Law, on the other hand, must resolve disputes finally and quickly. The scientific project is advanced by broad and wide-ranging consideration of a multitude of hypotheses, for those that are incorrect will eventually be shown to be so, and that in itself is an advance. Conjectures that are probably wrong are of little use, however, in the project of reaching a quick, final, and binding legal judgment — often of great consequence — about a particular set of events in the past. We recognize that, in practice, a gatekeeping role for the judge, no matter how flexible, inevitably on occasion will prevent the jury from learning of authentic insights and innovations. That, nevertheless, is the balance that is struck by Rules of Evidence designed not for the exhaustive search for cosmic understanding but for the particularized resolution of legal disputes.

V

To summarize: "General acceptance" is not a necessary precondition to the admissibility of scientific evidence under the Federal Rules of Evidence, but the Rules of Evidence — especially Rule 702 — do assign to the trial judge the task of ensuring that an expert's testimony both rests on a reliable foundation and is relevant to the task at hand. Pertinent evidence based on scientifically valid principles will satisfy those demands.

The inquiries of the District Court and the Court of Appeals focused almost exclusively on "general acceptance," as gauged by publication and the decisions of other courts. Accordingly, the judgment of the Court of Appeals is vacated, and the case is remanded for further proceedings consistent with this opinion.

It is so ordered.

Chief Justice Rehnquist, with whom Justice Stevens joins, concurring in part and dissenting in part.

The petition for certiorari in this case presents two questions: first, whether the rule of *Frye v. United States* (1923), remains good law after the enactment of the Federal Rules of Evidence; and second, if *Frye* remains valid, whether it requires expert scientific testimony to have been subjected to a peer review process in order to be admissible. The Court concludes, correctly in my view, that the *Frye* rule did not survive the enactment of the Federal Rules of Evidence, and I therefore join Parts I and II-A of its opinion. The second question presented in the petition for certiorari necessarily is mooted by this holding, but the Court nonetheless proceeds to construe Rules 702 and 703 very much in the abstract, and then offers some "general observations."

"General observations" by this Court customarily carry great weight with lower federal courts, but the ones offered here suffer from the flaw common to most such observations—they are not applied to deciding whether particular testimony was or was not admissible, and therefore they tend to be not only general, but vague and abstract. This is particularly unfortunate in a case such as this, where the ultimate legal question depends on an appreciation of one or more bodies of knowledge not judicially noticeable, and subject to different interpretations in the briefs of the parties and their amici. Twenty-two amicus briefs have been filed in the case, and indeed the Court's opinion contains no fewer than 37 citations to amicus briefs and other secondary sources.

The various briefs filed in this case are markedly different from typical briefs, in that large parts of them do not deal with decided cases or statutory language—the sort of material we customarily interpret. Instead, they deal with definitions of scientific knowledge, scientific method, scientific validity, and peer review—in short, matters far afield from the expertise of judges. This is not to say that such materials are not useful or even necessary in deciding how Rule 702 should be applied; but it is to say that the unusual subject matter should cause us to proceed with great caution in deciding more than we have to, because our reach can so easily exceed our grasp.

But even if it were desirable to make "general observations" not necessary to decide the questions presented, I cannot subscribe to some of the observations made by the Court. In Part II-B, the Court concludes that reliability and relevancy are the touchstones of the admissibility of expert testimony. Federal Rule of Evidence 402 provides, as the Court points out, that "evidence which is not relevant is not admissible." But there is no similar reference in the Rule to "reliability." The Court constructs its argument by parsing the language "if scientific, technical, or other specialized knowledge will assist the trier of fact to understand the evidence or to determine a fact in issue, ... an expert ... may testify thereto. ..." It stresses that the subject of the expert's testimony must be "scientific ... knowledge," and points out that "scientific" "implies a grounding in the methods and procedures of science" and that the word "knowledge" "connotes more than subjective belief or unsupported speculation."

From this it concludes that "scientific knowledge" must be "derived by the scientific method." Proposed testimony, we are told, must be supported by "appropriate validation." Indeed, the Court decides that "in a case involving scientific evidence, evidentiary reliability will be based upon scientific validity."

Questions arise simply from reading this part of the Court's opinion, and countless more questions will surely arise when hundreds of district judges try to apply its teaching to particular offers of expert testimony. Does all of this dicta apply to an expert seeking to testify on the basis of "technical or other specialized knowledge" — the other types of expert knowledge to which Rule 702 applies — or are the "general observations" limited only to "scientific knowledge"? What is the difference between scientific knowledge and technical knowledge; does Rule 702 actually contemplate that the phrase "scientific, technical, or other specialized knowledge" be broken down into numerous subspecies of expertise, or did its authors simply pick general descriptive language covering the sort of expert testimony which courts have customarily received? The Court speaks of its confidence that federal judges can make a "preliminary assessment of whether the reasoning or methodology underlying the testimony is scientifically valid and of whether that reasoning or methodology properly can be applied to the facts in issue." The Court then states that a "key question" to be answered in deciding whether something is "scientific knowledge" "will be whether it can be (and has been) tested." Following this sentence are three quotations from treatises, which not only speak of empirical testing, but one of which states that the "'criterion of the scientific status of a theory is its falsifiability, or refutability, or testability.'"

I defer to no one in my confidence in federal judges; but I am at a loss to know what is meant when it is said that the scientific status of a theory depends on its "falsifiability," and I suspect some of them will be, too.

I do not doubt that Rule 702 confides to the judge some gatekeeping responsibility in deciding questions of the admissibility of proffered expert testimony. But I do not think it imposes on them either the obligation or the authority to become amateur scientists in order to perform that role. I think the Court would be far better advised in this case to decide only the questions presented, and to leave the further development of this important area of the law to future cases.

Notes and Queries

1. Did the *Frye* rule survive the Federal Rules of Evidence?
2. Are we to interpret the Court's approach as a liberal rule (one which would admit more evidence)?
3. The dissent complains about the Court's focus on reliability. Do you prefer a focus on relevance to one on reliability? How does the Court guide reliability analyses?

4. Should we have greater faith in juries to parcel out junk science from good science? Was the rejected evidence here junk science?

G. E. v. Joiner

522 U.S. 136; 118 S. Ct. 512 (1997)

Chief Justice Rehnquist delivered the opinion of the Court.

We granted certiorari in this case to determine what standard an appellate court should apply in reviewing a trial court's decision to admit or exclude expert testimony under *Daubert v. Merrell Dow Pharmaceuticals, Inc.*, (1993). We hold that abuse of discretion is the appropriate standard. We apply this standard and conclude that the District Court in this case did not abuse its discretion when it excluded certain proffered expert testimony.

I

Respondent Robert Joiner began work as an electrician in the Water & Light Department of Thomasville, Georgia (City) in 1973. This job required him to work with and around the City's electrical transformers, which used a mineral-based dielectric fluid as a coolant. Joiner often had to stick his hands and arms into the fluid to make repairs. The fluid would sometimes splash onto him, occasionally getting into his eyes and mouth. In 1983 the City discovered that the fluid in some of the transformers was contaminated with polychlorinated biphenyls (PCBs). PCBs are widely considered to be hazardous to human health. Congress, with limited exceptions, banned the production and sale of PCBs in 1978.

Joiner was diagnosed with small cell lung cancer in 1991. He sued petitioners in Georgia state court the following year. Petitioner Monsanto manufactured PCBs from 1935 to 1977; petitioners General Electric and Westinghouse Electric manufactured transformers and dielectric fluid. In his complaint Joiner linked his development of cancer to his exposure to PCBs and their derivatives, polychlorinated dibenzofurans (furans) and polychlorinated dibenzodioxins (dioxins). Joiner had been a smoker for approximately eight years, his parents had both been smokers, and there was a history of lung cancer in his family. He was thus perhaps already at a heightened risk of developing lung cancer eventually. The suit alleged that his exposure to PCBs "promoted" his cancer; had it not been for his exposure to these substances, his cancer would not have developed for many years, if at all.

Petitioners removed the case to federal court. Once there, they moved for summary judgment. They contended that (1) there was no evidence that Joiner suffered significant exposure to PCBs, furans, or dioxins, and (2) there was no admissible scientific evidence that PCBs promoted Joiner's cancer. Joiner responded that there were numerous disputed factual issues that required resolution by a jury. He relied largely on the testimony of expert witnesses. In depositions, his experts had testified that PCBs alone can promote cancer and that furans and dioxins can also promote cancer. They opined that since Joiner had been exposed to PCBs, furans, and dioxins, such exposure was likely responsible for Joiner's cancer.

The District Court ruled that there was a genuine issue of material fact as to whether Joiner had been exposed to PCBs. But it nevertheless granted summary judgment for petitioners because (1) there was no genuine issue as to whether Joiner had been exposed to furans and dioxins, and (2) the testimony of Joiner's experts had failed to show that there was a link between exposure to PCBs and small cell lung cancer. The court believed that the testimony of respondent's experts to the contrary did not rise above "subjective belief or unsupported speculation." Their testimony was therefore inadmissible.

The Court of Appeals for the Eleventh Circuit reversed. It held that "because the Federal Rules of Evidence governing expert testimony display a preference for admissibility, we apply a particularly stringent standard of review to the trial judge's exclusion of expert testimony." Applying that standard, the Court of Appeals held that the District Court had erred in excluding the testimony of Joiner's expert witnesses. The District Court had made two fundamental errors. First, it excluded the experts' testimony because it "drew different conclusions from the research than did each of the experts." The Court of Appeals opined that a district court should limit its role to determining the "legal reliability of proffered expert testimony, leaving the jury to decide the correctness of competing expert opinions." Second, the District Court had held that there was no genuine issue of material fact as to whether Joiner had been exposed to furans and dioxins. This was also incorrect, said the Court of Appeals, because testimony in the record supported the proposition that there had been such exposure.

We granted petitioners' petition for a writ of certiorari and we now reverse.

II

Petitioners challenge the standard applied by the Court of Appeals in reviewing the District Court's decision to exclude respondent's experts' proffered testimony. They argue that that court should have applied traditional "abuse of discretion" review. Respondent agrees that abuse of discretion is the correct standard of review. He contends, however, that the Court of Appeals applied an abuse of discretion standard in this case. As he reads it, the phrase "particularly stringent" announced no new standard of review. It was simply an acknowledgment that an appellate court can and will devote more resources to analyzing district court decisions that are dispositive of the entire litigation. All evidentiary decisions are reviewed under an abuse of discretion standard. He argues, however, that it is perfectly reasonable for appellate courts to give particular attention to those decisions that are outcome-determinative.

We have held that abuse of discretion is the proper standard of review of a district court's evidentiary rulings.... The Court of Appeals suggested that *Daubert* somehow altered this general rule in the context of a district court's decision to exclude scientific evidence. But *Daubert* did not address the standard of appellate review for evidentiary rulings at all. It did hold that the "austere" *Frye* standard of "general acceptance" had not been carried over into the Federal Rules of Evidence. But the opinion also said:

> That the *Frye* test was displaced by the Rules of Evidence does not mean, however, that the Rules themselves place no limits on the admissibility of purportedly scientific evidence. Nor is the trial judge disabled from screening such evidence. To the contrary, under the Rules the trial judge must ensure that any and all scientific testimony or evidence admitted is not only relevant, but reliable.

Thus, while the Federal Rules of Evidence allow district courts to admit a somewhat broader range of scientific testimony than would have been admissible under *Frye*, they leave in place the "gatekeeper" role of the trial judge in screening such evidence. A court of appeals applying "abuse of discretion" review to such rulings may not categorically distinguish between rulings allowing expert testimony and rulings which disallow it.

. . .

We hold that the Court of Appeals erred in its review of the exclusion of Joiner's experts' testimony. In applying an overly "stringent" review to that ruling, it failed to give the trial court the deference that is the hallmark of abuse of discretion review.

III

We believe that a proper application of the correct standard of review here indicates that the District Court did not abuse its discretion. Joiner's theory of liability was that his exposure to PCBs and their derivatives "promoted" his development of small cell lung cancer. In support of that theory he proffered the deposition testimony of expert witnesses. Dr. Arnold Schecter testified that he believed it "more likely than not that Mr. Joiner's lung cancer was causally linked to cigarette smoking and PCB exposure." Dr. Daniel Teitelbaum testified that Joiner's "lung cancer was caused by or contributed to in a significant degree by the materials with which he worked."

Petitioners contended that the statements of Joiner's experts regarding causation were nothing more than speculation. Petitioners criticized the testimony of the experts in that it was "not supported by epidemiological studies . . . [and was] based exclusively on isolated studies of laboratory animals." Joiner responded by claiming that his experts had identified "relevant animal studies which support their opinions." He also directed the court's attention to four epidemiological studies on which his experts had relied.

The District Court agreed with petitioners that the animal studies on which respondent's experts relied did not support his contention that exposure to PCBs had contributed to his cancer. The studies involved infant mice that had developed cancer after being exposed to PCBs. The infant mice in the studies had had massive doses of PCBs injected directly into their peritoneums or stomachs. Joiner was an adult human being whose alleged exposure to PCBs was far less than the exposure in the animal studies. The PCBs were injected into the mice in a highly concentrated form. The fluid with which Joiner had come into contact generally had a much smaller PCB concentration of between 0–500 parts per million. The cancer that these mice developed was alveologenic adenomas; Joiner had developed small-cell carcinomas. No study demonstrated that adult mice developed cancer after being exposed to PCBs. One of the experts admitted that no study had demonstrated that PCBs lead to cancer in any other species.

Respondent failed to reply to this criticism. Rather than explaining how and why the experts could have extrapolated their opinions from these seemingly far-removed animal studies, respondent chose "to proceed as if the only issue [was] whether animal studies can ever be a proper foundation for an expert's opinion." Of course, whether animal studies can ever be a proper foundation for an expert's opinion was not the issue. The issue was whether these experts' opinions were sufficiently supported by the animal studies on which they purported to rely. The studies were so dissimilar to the facts presented in this litigation that it was not an abuse of discretion for the District Court to have rejected the experts' reliance on them.

The District Court also concluded that the four epidemiological studies on which respondent relied were not a sufficient basis for the experts' opinions. The first such study involved workers at an Italian capacitor plant who had been exposed to PCBs. The authors noted that lung cancer deaths among ex-employees at the plant were higher than might have been expected, but concluded that "there were apparently no grounds for associating lung cancer deaths (although increased above expectations) and exposure in the plant." Given that [the authors] were unwilling to say that PCB exposure had caused cancer among the workers they examined, their study did not support the experts' conclusion that Joiner's exposure to PCBs caused his cancer.

The second study followed employees who had worked at Monsanto's PCB production plant. The authors of this study found that the incidence of lung cancer deaths among these workers was somewhat higher than would ordinarily be expected. The increase, however, was not statistically significant and the authors of the study did not suggest a link between the increase in lung cancer deaths and the exposure to PCBs.

The third and fourth studies were likewise of no help. The third involved workers at a Norwegian cable manufacturing company who had been exposed to mineral oil. A statistically significant increase in lung cancer deaths had been observed in these workers. The study, however, (1) made no mention of PCBs and (2) was expressly limited to the type of mineral oil involved in that study, and thus did not support these experts' opinions. The fourth and final study involved a PCB-exposed group in Japan that had seen a statistically significant increase in lung cancer deaths. The subjects of this study, however, had been exposed to numerous potential carcinogens, including toxic rice oil that they had ingested.

Respondent points to *Daubert*'s language that the "focus, of course, must be solely on principles and methodology, not on the conclusions that they generate." He claims that because the District Court's disagreement was with the conclusion that the experts drew from the studies, the District Court committed legal error and was properly reversed by the Court of Appeals. But conclusions and methodology are not entirely distinct from one another. Trained experts commonly extrapolate from existing data. But nothing in either *Daubert* or the Federal Rules of Evidence requires a district court to admit opinion evidence which is connected to existing data only by the ipse dixit of the expert. A court may conclude that there is simply too great an analytical gap between the data and the opinion proffered. That is what the District Court did here, and we hold that it did not abuse its discretion in so doing.

We hold, therefore, that abuse of discretion is the proper standard by which to review a district court's decision to admit or exclude scientific evidence. We further hold that, because it was within the District Court's discretion to conclude that the studies upon which the experts relied were not sufficient, whether individually or in combination, to support their conclusions that Joiner's exposure to PCBs contributed to his cancer, the District Court did not abuse its discretion in excluding their testimony. These conclusions, however, do not dispose of this entire case.

Respondent's original contention was that his exposure to PCBs, furans, and dioxins contributed to his cancer. The District Court ruled that there was a genuine issue of material fact as to whether Joiner had been exposed to PCBs, but concluded that there was no genuine issue as to whether he had been exposed to furans and dioxins. The District Court accordingly never explicitly considered if there was admissible evidence on the question whether Joiner's alleged exposure to furans and dioxins contributed to his cancer. The Court of Appeals reversed the District Court's conclusion that there had been no exposure to furans and dioxins. Petitioners did not challenge this determination in their petition to this Court. Whether Joiner was exposed to furans and dioxins, and whether if there was such exposure, the opinions of Joiner's experts would then be admissible, remain open questions. We accordingly reverse the judgment of the Court of Appeals and remand this case for proceedings consistent with this opinion.

It is so ordered.

Justice Breyer, concurring.

The Court's opinion, which I join, emphasizes *Daubert*'s statement that a trial judge, acting as "gatekeeper," must "'ensure that any and all scientific testimony or evidence admitted is not only relevant, but reliable.'" This requirement will sometimes ask judges to make subtle and sophisticated determinations about scientific methodology and its relation to the conclusions an expert witness seeks to offer — particularly when a case arises in an area where the science itself is tentative or uncertain, or where testimony about general risk levels in human beings or animals is offered to prove individual causation. Yet, as amici have pointed out, judges are not scientists and do not have the scientific training that can facilitate the making of such decisions.

Of course, neither the difficulty of the task nor any comparative lack of expertise can excuse the judge from exercising the "gatekeeper" duties that the Federal Rules impose. . . . To the contrary, when law and science intersect, those duties often must be exercised with special care.

. . . It is, thus, essential in this science-related area that the courts administer the Federal Rules of Evidence in order to achieve the "ends" that the Rules themselves set forth, not only so that proceedings may be "justly determined," but also so "that the truth may be ascertained."

I therefore want specially to note that, as cases presenting significant science-related issues have increased in number, judges have increasingly found in the Rules of Evidence and Civil Procedure ways to help them overcome the inherent difficulty of making determinations about complicated scientific or otherwise technical evidence. Among these techniques are an increased use of Rule 16's pretrial conference authority to narrow the scientific issues in dispute, pretrial hearings where potential experts are subject to examination by the court, and the appointment of special masters and specially trained law clerks.

In the present case, the *New England Journal of Medicine* has filed an amici brief "in support of neither petitioners nor respondents" in which the *Journal* writes:

> [A] judge could better fulfill this gatekeeper function if he or she had help from scientists. Judges should be strongly encouraged to make greater use of their inherent authority . . . to appoint experts. . . . Reputable experts could be recommended to courts by established scientific organizations, such as the National Academy of Sciences or the American Association for the Advancement of Science.

Given this kind of offer of cooperative effort, from the scientific to the legal community, and given the various Rules-authorized methods for facilitating the courts' task, it seems to me that *Daubert*'s gatekeeping requirement will not prove inordinately difficult to implement; and that it will help secure the basic objectives of the Federal Rules of Evidence; which are, to repeat, the ascertainment of truth and the just determination of proceedings.

Justice Stevens, concurring in part and dissenting in part.

. . .

The Court of Appeals' discussion of admissibility is faithful to the dictum in *Daubert* that the reliability inquiry must focus on methodology, not conclusions. Thus, even though I fully agree with both the District Court's and this Court's explanation of why each of the studies on which the experts relied was by itself unpersuasive, a critical question remains unanswered: When qualified experts have reached relevant conclusions on the basis of an acceptable methodology, why are their opinions inadmissible?

Daubert quite clearly forbids trial judges from assessing the validity or strength of an expert's scientific conclusions, which is a matter for the jury. Because I am persuaded that the difference between methodology and conclusions is just as categorical as the distinction between means and ends, I do not think the statement that "conclusions and methodology are not entirely distinct from one another," is either accurate or helps us answer the difficult admissibility question presented by this record.

In any event, it bears emphasis that the Court has not held that it would have been an abuse of discretion to admit the expert testimony. The very point of today's holding is that the abuse of discretion standard of review applies whether the district judge has excluded or admitted evidence. And nothing in either *Daubert* or the Federal Rules of Evidence requires a district judge to reject an expert's conclusions and keep them from the jury when they fit the facts of the case and are based on reliable scientific methodology.

Accordingly, while I join Parts I and II of the Court's opinion, I do not concur in the judgment or in Part III of its opinion.

Notes and Queries

1. Justice Breyer emphasizes that a Court should not hesitate to go beyond the expertise proffered by the parties and utilize its powers to appoint independent experts, as Rule 706 of the Federal Rules of Evidence authorizes. Helpful suggestion?
2. If the experts would be qualified as experts, why is it that a court can reject their evidence derived from their expertise?
3. What is meant by "abuse of discretion"? How wrong must a judge be to abuse her discretion? Were animal studies good and relevant enough at least to be presented to a jury?

Kumho Tire v. Carmichael

526 U.S. 137; 119 S. Ct. 1167 (1999)

Justice Breyer delivered the opinion of the Court.

In *Daubert v. Merrell Dow Pharmaceuticals, Inc.* (1993), this Court focused upon the admissibility of scientific expert testimony. It pointed out that such testimony is admissible only if it is both relevant and reliable. And it held that the Federal Rules of Evidence "assign to the trial judge the task of ensuring that an expert's testimony both rests on a reliable foundation and is relevant to the task at hand." The Court also discussed certain more specific factors, such as testing, peer review, error rates, and "acceptability" in the relevant scientific community, some or all of which might prove helpful in determining the reliability of a particular scientific "theory or technique."

This case requires us to decide how *Daubert* applies to the testimony of engineers and other experts who are not scientists. We conclude that *Daubert*'s general holding—setting forth the trial judge's general "gatekeeping" obligation—applies not only to testimony based on "scientific" knowledge, but also to testimony based on "technical" and "other specialized" knowledge. We also conclude that a trial court may consider one or more of the more specific factors that *Daubert* mentioned when doing so will help determine that testimony's reliability. But, as the Court stated in *Daubert*, the test of reliability is "flexible," and *Daubert*'s list of specific factors neither necessarily nor exclusively applies to all experts or in every case. Rather, the law grants a district court the same broad latitude when it decides how to determine reliability as it enjoys in respect to its ultimate reliability determination. Applying these standards, we determine that the District Court's decision in this case—not to admit certain expert testimony—was within its discretion and therefore lawful.

I

On July 6, 1993, the right rear tire of a minivan driven by Patrick Carmichael blew out. In the accident that followed, one of the passengers died, and others were severely injured. In October 1993, the Carmichaels brought this diversity suit against the tire's maker and its distributor, whom we refer to collectively as Kumho Tire, claiming that the tire was defective. The plaintiffs rested their case in significant part upon deposition testimony provided by an expert in tire failure analysis, Dennis Carlson, Jr., who intended to testify in support of their conclusion.

Carlson's depositions relied upon certain features of tire technology that are not in dispute. A steel-belted radial tire like the Carmichaels' is made up of a "carcass" containing many layers of flexible cords, called "plies," along which (between the cords and the outer tread) are laid steel strips called "belts." Steel wire loops, called "beads," hold the cords together at the plies' bottom edges. An outer layer, called the "tread," encases the carcass, and the entire tire is bound together in rubber, through the application of heat and various chemicals. The bead of the tire sits upon a "bead seat," which is part of the wheel assembly. That assembly contains a "rim flange," which extends over the bead and rests against the side of the tire.

...

Carlson's testimony also accepted certain background facts about the tire in question. He assumed that before the blowout the tire had traveled far.... He conceded that the tire tread had at least two punctures which had been inadequately repaired.

Despite the tire's age and history, Carlson concluded that a defect in its manufacture or design caused the blow-out. He rested this conclusion in part upon three premises which for present purposes, we must assume are not in dispute: First, a tire's carcass should stay bound to the inner side of the tread for a significant period of time after its tread depth has worn away. Second, the tread of the tire at issue had separated from its inner steel-belted carcass prior to the accident. Third, this "separation" caused the blowout.

...

Carlson added that he had inspected the tire in question. He conceded that the tire to a limited degree showed greater wear on the shoulder than in the center, some signs of "bead groove," some discoloration, a few marks on the rim flange, and inadequately filled puncture holes (which can also cause heat that might lead to separation). But, in each instance, he testified that the symptoms were not significant, and he explained why he believed that they did not reveal overdeflection. For example, the extra shoulder wear, he said, appeared primarily on one shoulder, whereas an overdeflected tire would reveal equally abnormal wear on both shoulders. Carlson concluded that the tire did not bear at least two of the four overdeflection symptoms, nor was there any less obvious cause of separation; and since neither overdeflection nor the punctures caused the blowout, a defect must have done so.

Kumho Tire moved the District Court to exclude Carlson's testimony on the ground that his methodology failed Rule 702's reliability requirement. The court agreed with Kumho that it should act as a *Daubert*-type reliability "gatekeeper," even though one might consider Carlson's testimony as "technical," rather than "scientific." The court then examined Carlson's methodology in light of the reliability-related factors that *Daubert* mentioned, such as a theory's testability, whether it "has been a subject of peer review or publication," the "known or potential rate of error," and the "degree of acceptance . . . within the relevant scientific community." The District Court found that all those factors argued against the reliability of Carlson's methods, and it granted the motion to exclude the testimony (as well as the defendants' accompanying motion for summary judgment).

The plaintiffs, arguing that the court's application of the *Daubert* factors was too "inflexible," asked for reconsideration. And the Court granted that motion. After reconsidering the matter, the court agreed with the plaintiffs that *Daubert* should be applied flexibly, that its four factors were simply illustrative, and that other factors could argue in favor of admissibility. It conceded that there may be widespread acceptance of a "visual-inspection method" for some relevant purposes. But the court found insufficient indications of the reliability of

> the component of Carlson's tire failure analysis which most concerned the Court, namely, the methodology employed by the expert in analyzing the data obtained in the visual inspection, and the scientific basis, if any, for such an analysis.

It consequently affirmed its earlier order declaring Carlson's testimony inadmissable and granting the defendants' motion for summary judgment.

The Eleventh Circuit reversed. . . . It noted that "the Supreme Court in *Daubert* explicitly limited its holding to cover only the 'scientific context,'" adding that "a *Daubert* analysis" applies only where an expert relies "on the application of scientific principles," rather than "on skill- or experience-based observation." It concluded that Carlson's testimony, which it viewed as relying on experience, "falls outside the scope of *Daubert*," that "the district court erred as a matter of law by applying *Daubert* in this case," and that the case must be remanded for further (non-*Daubert*-type) consideration under Rule 702.

Kumho Tire petitioned for certiorari, asking us to determine whether a trial court "may" consider *Daubert*'s specific "factors" when determining the "admissibility of an engineering expert's testimony." We granted certiorari in light of uncertainty among the lower courts about whether, or how, *Daubert* applies to expert testimony that might be characterized as based not upon "scientific" knowledge, but rather upon "technical" or "other specialized" knowledge.

II

A

In *Daubert*, this Court held that Federal Rule of Evidence 702 imposes a special obligation upon a trial judge to "ensure that any and all scientific testimony . . . is not only relevant, but reliable." The initial question before us is whether this basic gatekeeping obligation applies only to "scientific" testimony or to all expert testimony. We, like the parties, believe that it applies to all expert testimony.

For one thing, Rule 702 itself says:

> If scientific, technical, or other specialized knowledge will assist the trier of fact to understand the evidence or to determine a fact in issue, a witness qualified as an expert by knowledge, skill, experience, training, or ducation, may testify thereto in the form of an opinion or otherwise.

This language makes no relevant distinction between "scientific" knowledge and "technical" or "other specialized" knowledge. It makes clear that any such knowledge might become the subject of expert testimony. In *Daubert*, the Court specified that it is the Rule's word "knowledge," not the words (like "scientific") that modify that word, that "establishes a standard of evidentiary reliability." Hence, as a matter of language, the Rule applies its reliability standard to all "scientific," "technical," or "other specialized" matters within its scope. We concede that the Court in *Daubert* referred only to "scientific" knowledge. But as the Court there said, it referred to "scientific" testimony "because that was the nature of the expertise" at issue.

Neither is the evidentiary rationale that underlay the Court's basic *Daubert* "gatekeeping" determination limited to "scientific" knowledge. . . . The Rules grant that latitude to all experts, not just to "scientific" ones.

Finally, it would prove difficult, if not impossible, for judges to administer evidentiary rules under which a gatekeeping obligation depended upon a distinction between "scientific" knowledge and "technical" or "other specialized" knowledge. There is no clear line that divides the one from the others. Disciplines such as engineering rest upon scientific knowledge. Pure scientific theory itself may depend for its development upon observation and properly engineered machinery. And conceptual efforts to distinguish the two are unlikely to produce clear legal lines capable of application in particular cases.

Neither is there a convincing need to make such distinctions. Experts of all kinds tie observations to conclusions. . . . And whether the specific expert testimony focuses upon specialized observations, the specialized translation of those observations into theory, a specialized theory itself, or the application of such a theory in a particular case, the expert's testimony often will rest "upon an experience confessedly foreign in kind to [the jury's] own." The trial judge's effort to assure that the specialized testimony is reliable and relevant can help the jury evaluate that foreign experience, whether the testimony reflects scientific, technical, or other specialized knowledge.

We conclude that *Daubert*'s general principles apply to the expert matters described in Rule 702. The Rule, in respect to all such matters, "establishes a standard of evidentiary reliability." It "requires a valid ... connection to the pertinent inquiry as a precondition to admissibility." And where such testimony's factual basis, data, principles, methods, or their application are called sufficiently into question, see Part III, infra, the trial judge must determine whether the testimony has "a reliable basis in the knowledge and experience of [the relevant] discipline."

B

The petitioners ask more specifically whether a trial judge determining the "admissibility of an engineering expert's testimony" may consider several more specific factors that *Daubert* said might "bear on" a judge's gate-keeping determination. These factors include:

- Whether a "theory or technique ... can be (and has been) tested";
- Whether it "has been subjected to peer review and publication";
- Whether, in respect to a particular technique, there is a high "known or potential rate of error" and whether there are "standards controlling the technique's operation"; and
- Whether the theory or technique enjoys "general acceptance" within a "relevant scientific community."

Emphasizing the word "may" in the question, we answer that question yes.

Engineering testimony rests upon scientific foundations, the reliability of which will be at issue in some cases. In other cases, the relevant reliability concerns may focus upon personal knowledge or experience.... Our emphasis on the word "may" thus reflects *Daubert*'s description of the Rule 702 inquiry as "a flexible one." *Daubert* makes clear that the factors it mentions do not constitute a "definitive checklist or test." And *Daubert* adds that the gatekeeping inquiry must be "'tied to the facts'" of a particular "case." ... Too much depends upon the particular circumstances of the particular case at issue.

...

We must therefore disagree with the Eleventh Circuit's holding that a trial judge may ask questions of the sort *Daubert* mentioned only where an expert "relies on the application of scientific principles," but not where an expert relies "on skill- or experience-based observation." We do not believe that Rule 702 creates a schematism that segregates expertise by type while mapping certain kinds of questions to certain kinds of experts. Life and the legal cases that it generates are too complex to warrant so definitive a match.

To say this is not to deny the importance of *Daubert*'s gatekeeping requirement. The objective of that requirement is to ensure the reliability and relevancy of expert testimony. It is to make certain that an expert, whether basing testimony upon professional studies or personal experience, employs in the courtroom the same level of intellectual rigor that characterizes the practice of an expert in the relevant field. Nor do we deny that, as stated in *Daubert*, the particular questions that it mentioned will often be appropriate for use in determining the reliability of challenged expert testimony. Rather, we conclude that the trial judge must have considerable leeway in deciding in a particular case how to go about determining whether particular expert testimony is reliable. That is to say, a trial court should consider the specific factors identified in *Daubert* where they are reasonable measures of the reliability of expert testimony.

C

The trial court must have the same kind of latitude in deciding how to test an expert's reliability, and to decide whether or when special briefing or other proceedings are needed to investigate reliability, as it enjoys when it decides whether that expert's relevant testimony is reliable. Our opinion in *Joiner* makes clear that a court of appeals is to apply an abuse-of-discretion standard when it "reviews a trial court's decision to admit or exclude expert testimony." . . . Thus, whether *Daubert*'s specific factors are, or are not, reasonable measures of reliability in a particular case is a matter that the law grants the trial judge broad latitude to determine. And the Eleventh Circuit erred insofar as it held to the contrary.

III

We further explain the way in which a trial judge "may" consider *Daubert*'s factors by applying these considerations to the case at hand. . . .

In sum, Rule 702 grants the district judge the discretionary authority, reviewable for its abuse, to determine reliability in light of the particular facts and circumstance of the particular case. The District Court did not abuse its discretionary authority in this case. Hence, the judgment of the Court of Appeals is

Reversed.

Justice Scalia, with whom Justice O'Connor and Justice Thomas join, concurring.

I join the opinion of the Court, which makes clear that the discretion it endorses—trial-court discretion in choosing the manner of testing expert reliability—is not discretion to abandon the gatekeeping function. I think it worth adding that it is not discretion to perform the function inadequately. Rather, it is discretion to choose among reasonable means of excluding expertise that is fausse and science that is junky. Though, as the Court makes clear today, the *Daubert* factors are not holy writ, in a particular case the failure to apply one or another of them may be unreasonable, and hence an abuse of discretion.

Justice Stevens, concurring in part and dissenting in part.

The only question that we granted certiorari to decide is whether a trial judge "may . . . consider the four factors set out by this Court in *Daubert v. Merrell Dow Pharmaceuticals, Inc.* (1993), in a Rule 702 analysis of admissibility of an engineering expert's testimony." That question is fully and correctly answered in Parts I and II of the Court's opinion, which I join.

Part III answers the quite different question whether the trial judge abused his discretion when he excluded the testimony of Dennis Carlson. Because a proper answer to that question requires a study of the record that can be performed more efficiently by the Court of Appeals than by the nine Members of this Court, I would remand the case to the Eleventh Circuit to perform that task. There are, of course, exceptions to most rules, but I firmly believe that it is neither fair to litigants nor good practice for this Court to reach out to decide questions not raised by the certiorari petition.

Accordingly, while I do not feel qualified to disagree with the well-reasoned factual analysis in Part III of the Court's opinion, I do not join that Part, and I respectfully dissent from the Court's disposition of the case.

Notes and Queries

1. Justice Stevens would not rule on the particular facts of the case, only the legal rule it raises. Fair?

2. All Justices agree that the Court's reliability factors may be used by lower courts to exclude expert testimony. Should trial judges perform that role?

Estelle v. McGuire

502 U.S. 62; 112 S. Ct. 475 (1991)

Chief Justice Rehnquist delivered the opinion of the Court.

Respondent Mark Owen McGuire was found guilty in a California state court of second-degree murder for the killing of his infant daughter. After unsuccessfully challenging his conviction on appeal in the state courts, McGuire sought federal habeas relief, and the United States Court of Appeals for the Ninth Circuit set aside his conviction. We hold that in so doing the Court of Appeals exceeded the limited scope of federal habeas review of state convictions.

McGuire and his wife brought their 6-month-old daughter, Tori, to a hospital in Hayward, California. The baby was bluish in color and was not breathing. The attending physician noticed a large and relatively recent bruise on Tori's chest with multiple bruises around it, as well as black and blue marks around her ears. Efforts to revive the child were unsuccessful; Tori died 45 minutes after being brought to the hospital. An autopsy revealed 17 contusions on the baby's chest, 29 contusions in her abdominal area, a split liver, a split pancreas, a lacerated large intestine, and damage to her heart and one of her lungs. The autopsy also uncovered evidence of rectal tearing, which was at least six weeks old, and evidence of partially healed rib fractures, which were approximately seven weeks old.

The police questioned McGuire and his wife. McGuire stated his belief that Tori's injuries must have resulted from a fall off the family couch. He told the police that when his wife went out to make a telephone call, he went upstairs, leaving Tori lying on the couch; when he heard the baby cry, he came back downstairs to find her lying on the floor. After a police officer expressed skepticism at this explanation, McGuire replied that "maybe some Mexicans came in" while he was upstairs. During separate questioning, McGuire's wife stated that she had not hit Tori, and that she was unsure whether her husband had done so.

McGuire was charged with second-degree murder. At trial, the prosecution introduced both the statements made by McGuire to police and the medical evidence, including the evidence of prior rectal tearing and fractured ribs. Two physicians testified that Tori was a battered child, relying in part on the prior rib and rectal injuries, as well as on the more recent injuries. McGuire's neighbor testified that she had seen McGuire carry Tori by one of her arms to the car and roughly pinch her cheeks together when she cried. The neighbor added that McGuire's wife had expressed fear in leaving Tori alone with McGuire, because he had been rough with the baby and "did bad things" to her.

In addition, the prosecution called a witness who had overheard a conversation between McGuire and his wife in the hospital emergency room the night of Tori's death. According to the witness, McGuire's wife several times insistently asked, "What really happened?" McGuire replied that he "didn't know," and that he "guessed" the baby fell off the couch. His wife continued to press for an answer, stating, "I am very patient. I can wait a long time. I want to know what really happened." Finally, she told McGuire that "the baby was alright when I left. You are responsible." McGuire's wife was called by the prosecution to testify at trial, after having been granted transactional immunity from future prosecution. In contrast to her prior statement to the police and her declarations at the hospital, she stated that she had beaten Tori on the day of her death before her husband arrived home. The jury convicted McGuire of second-degree murder.

The California Court of Appeal affirmed McGuire's conviction. The court observed that the evidence of prior rib and rectal injuries was introduced to prove "battered child syndrome." That syndrome exists when a child has sustained repeated and/or serious injuries by nonaccidental means. After reviewing California authority on the subject, the court concluded that "proof of Tori's 'prior injuries' tending to establish the 'battered child syndrome' was patently proper." The California Supreme Court denied review.

McGuire then filed a petition for habeas corpus relief in the United States District Court for the Northern District of California. That court denied relief. The Court of Appeals for the Ninth Circuit reversed and granted McGuire's habeas petition. The court ruled that the prior injury evidence was erroneously admitted to establish battered child syndrome, because no evidence linked McGuire to the prior injuries and no claim had been made at trial that the baby died accidentally. In addition, the court believed that the trial court's instruction on the use of prior act evidence allowed a finding of guilt based simply on a judgment that McGuire committed the prior bad acts. The court concluded that the admission of the evidence, in conjunction with the prejudicial instruction, "rendered [McGuire's] trial arbitrary and fundamentally unfair" in violation of due process. We hold that none of the alleged errors rise to the level of a due process violation, and so reverse.

[Note: The court instructed the jury:

> Evidence has been introduced for the purpose of showing that the Defendant committed acts similar to those constituting a crime other than that for which he is on trial. Such evidence, if believed, was not received, and may not be considered by you[,] to prove that he is a person of bad character or that he has a disposition to commit crimes. Such evidence was received and may be considered by you only for the limited purpose of determining if it tends to show three things:
>
>> 1. The impeachment of Daisy McGuire's testimony that she had no cause to be afraid of the Defendant; 2. To establish the battered child syndrome; and 3. Also a clear connection between the other two offense[s] and the one of which the Defendant is accused, so that it may be logically concluded that if the Defendant committed other offenses, he also committed the crime charged in this case. For the limited purpose for which you may consider such evidence, you must weigh it in the same manner as you do all other evidence in the case. You are not permitted to consider evidence for any other purpose.]

I

We first consider whether the admission of the prior injury evidence justified habeas relief. In ruling that McGuire's due process rights were violated by the admission of the evidence, the Court of Appeals relied in part on its conclusion that the evidence was "incorrectly admitted ... pursuant to California law." Such an inquiry, however, is no part of a federal court's habeas review of a state conviction. We have stated many times that "federal habeas corpus relief does not lie for errors of state law." ...

We thus turn to the question whether the admission of the evidence violated McGuire's federal constitutional rights. California law allows the prosecution to introduce expert testimony and evidence related to prior injuries in order to prove "battered child syndrome." The demonstration of battered child syndrome "simply indicates that a child found with [serious, repeated injuries] has not suffered those injuries by accidental means." Thus, evidence demonstrating battered child syndrome helps to prove that the child died at the hands of another and not by falling off a couch, for example; it also tends to establish that the "other," whoever it may be, inflicted the injuries intentionally. When offered to show that certain injuries are a product of child abuse, rather than accident, evidence of prior injuries is relevant even though it does not purport to prove the identity of the person who might have inflicted those injuries. Because the prosecution had charged McGuire with second-degree murder, it was required to prove that Tori's death was caused by the defendant's intentional act. Proof of Tori's battered child status helped to do just that; although not linked by any direct evidence to McGuire, the evidence demonstrated that Tori's death was the result of an intentional act by someone, and not an accident. The Court of Appeals, however, ignored the principle of battered child syndrome evidence in holding that this evidence was incorrectly admitted. For example, the court stated that "evidence cannot have probative value unless a party connects it to the defendant in some meaningful way." We conclude that the evidence of prior injuries presented at McGuire's trial, whether it was directly linked to McGuire or not, was probative on the question of the intent with which the person who caused the injuries acted.

In holding the prior injury evidence inadmissible, the Court of Appeals also relied on the theory that, because no claim was made at trial that Tori died accidentally, the battered child syndrome evidence was irrelevant and violative of due process. This ruling ignores the fact that the prosecution must prove all the elements of a criminal offense beyond a reasonable doubt. In this second-degree murder case, for example, the prosecution was required to demonstrate that the killing was intentional. By eliminating the possibility of accident, the evidence regarding battered child syndrome was clearly probative of that essential element, especially in light of the fact that McGuire had claimed prior to trial that Tori had injured herself by falling from the couch. The Court of Appeals, however, ruled that the evidence should have been excluded because McGuire did not raise the defense of accidental death at trial. But the prosecution's burden to prove every element of the crime is not relieved by a defendant's tactical decision not to contest an essential element of the offense. In the federal courts, "[a] simple plea of not guilty . . . puts the prosecution to its proof as to all elements of the crime charged." Neither the Court of Appeals nor the parties have given us any reason to think that the rule is different in California. The evidence of battered child syndrome was relevant to show intent, and nothing in the Due Process Clause of the Fourteenth Amendment requires the State to refrain from introducing relevant evidence simply because the defense chooses not to contest the point.

. . .

II

The Court of Appeals, however, did not rely solely on a finding that the admission of the evidence was unconstitutional. It based its decision in part on a belief that the instruction given by the trial court, allowed the jury to consider the prior injury evidence for more than simply proof of the battered child syndrome, and thereby violated McGuire's due process rights. McGuire focuses on the portion of the instruction explaining to the jury that the prior injury evidence

> was received and may be considered by you only for the limited purpose of determining if it tends to show . . . a clear connection between the other two offense[s] and the one of which the Defendant is accused, so that it may be logically concluded that if the Defendant committed other offenses, he also committed the crime charged in this case.

McGuire argues that, despite the absence of any direct evidence showing that he caused the rib and rectal injuries, the instruction told the jury to find that he had committed those prior offenses. Furthermore, he argues, the instruction left the jury with the mistaken impression that it could base its finding of guilt on the simple fact that he had previously harmed Tori. Under McGuire's reading, the instruction is transformed into a propensity instruction, allowing the jury to consider as evidence of his guilt the fact that his prior acts show a disposition to commit this type of crime. This, he contends, violates the Due Process Clause.

In arguing his point, McGuire makes much of the fact that, in giving its instruction, the trial court deviated in part from standard jury instruction. As we have stated above, however, the fact that the instruction was allegedly incorrect under state law is not a basis for habeas relief. . . .

McGuire first claims that the instruction directed the jury to find that he had caused the prior injuries, thereby effectively taking that question from the jury. One might argue that the "two offense[s]" referred to in the instruction were McGuire's pinching of the child's cheeks and the lifting of the child by her arm. When read in context, however, we conclude that the most likely interpretation is that the reference was to the rectal tearing and fractured ribs. McGuire argues that, despite the lack of any direct evidence linking him to those injuries, the instruction directed the jury to find that he had committed them. This claim is clearly foreclosed, however, by the language of the instruction. The challenged portion of the instruction included the words "if the Defendant committed other offenses." By including this phrase, the trial court unquestionably left it to the jury to determine whether McGuire committed the prior acts; only if the jury believed he was the perpetrator could it use the evidence in deciding whether McGuire was guilty of the crime charged. Therefore, if the jury did not believe McGuire caused the prior injuries, he was not harmed by the challenged portion of the instruction. To the extent that the jury may have believed McGuire committed the prior acts and used that as a factor in its deliberation, we observe that there was sufficient evidence to sustain such a jury finding by a preponderance of the evidence. The proof of battered child syndrome itself narrowed the group of possible perpetrators to McGuire and his wife, because they were the only two people regularly caring for Tori during her short life. A neighbor testified that she had seen McGuire treat Tori roughly on two occasions, and that McGuire's wife was scared to leave Tori alone with McGuire because he "did bad things" to her; the neighbor further testified that she had never seen McGuire's wife abuse the child in any way. Futhermore, when being questioned by the police after Tori died, McGuire's wife stated that she observed bruises on the baby's body when bathing her. When asked by the police for an explanation, she replied, "I don't really know, you know, I am not the only one who is taking care of her." The evidence described, along with other evidence in the record, convinces us that there was sufficient proof for the jury to conclude, if it so desired, that McGuire caused the prior rib and rectal injuries.

...

We therefore hold that neither the introduction of the challenged evidence, nor the jury instruction as to its use, "so infused the trial with unfairness as to deny due process of law." The judgment of the Court of Appeals is therefore

Reversed.

Justice O'Connor, with whom Justice Stevens joins, concurring in part and dissenting in part.

I agree with the Court that the evidence of battered child syndrome was relevant. The State had to prove that Mark McGuire intended to kill his daughter, and the evidence that Tori was a battered child was probative of causation and intent. I therefore join Part I of the Court's opinion.

I do not join Part II of the opinion because I think there is a reasonable likelihood that the jury misapplied the prior acts instruction. The trial court instructed the jury that evidence of Tori's prior injuries had been admitted to show that McGuire had committed offenses similar to that for which he was on trial, and that, if the jury found a "clear connection" between the prior offenses and the charged offense, "it may be logically concluded that if the Defendant committed other offenses, he also committed the crime charged in this case." In my view, the instruction encouraged the jury to assume that McGuire had inflicted the prior injuries and then directed the jury to conclude that the prior abuser was the murderer. Because the instruction may have relieved the State of its burden of proving the identity of Tori's murderer beyond a reasonable doubt, I would hold that the instruction was error and remand to the Court of Appeals for a determination of whether that error was harmless.

The fact that a 6-month-old child was repeatedly beaten in the course of her short life is so horrifying that a trial court should take special care to inform the jury as to the significance of that evidence. As the Court notes, the demonstration of battered child syndrome is relevant because it "'indicates that a child found with [serious, repeated injuries] has not suffered those injuries by accidental means.'" I therefore agree that proof of Tori's battered child status, although "not linked by any direct evidence to McGuire," was properly admitted because "the evidence demonstrated that Tori's death was the result of an intentional act by someone, and not an accident." Precisely because the relevance of battered child syndrome is not tied to the identity of the abuser, however, I believe that a jury instruction clarifying the limited probative value of that evidence was required.

Instead of an instruction limiting the use of evidence of Tori's prior injuries, the trial judge gave an instruction limiting the use of evidence of McGuire's prior bad acts. In so doing, the trial judge himself appears to have assumed that the prior injuries could be attributed to McGuire. The judge told the jury that "evidence has been introduced for the purpose of showing that the Defendant committed acts similar to those constituting a crime other than that for which he is on trial." The State concedes that this category of evidence encompasses both the acts for which McGuire was positively identified as the actor (carrying the child by one arm and roughly pinching her cheeks) and the far more brutal acts for which no actor was identified (the fractured ribs and the rectal tearing). The grouping of these two distinct classes of evidence created a reasonable likelihood that the jury would believe that McGuire had been identified—at least in the eyes of the trial judge—as the prior abuser.

The trial court's error in implying that McGuire had been identified as the prior abuser was compounded by its further instruction that, if the jury found a "clear connection" between the prior offenses and the charged offense, "it may be logically concluded that if the Defendant committed other offenses, he also committed the crime charged in this case." The Court finds it "likely" that the jury understood the instruction to mean that "if it found a 'clear connection' between the prior injuries and the instant injuries, and if it found that McGuire had committed the prior injuries, then it could use that fact in determining that McGuire committed the crime charged." In my view, there is a reasonable likelihood that the jury did not understand this single sentence to establish a two-step process.

The jury was instructed to "consider" the evidence that McGuire had "committed acts similar" to the crime charged and to "determine" whether there was a "clear connection" between these prior acts and the ones that resulted in Tori's death. The trial court did not instruct the jury that it must first "determine" whether McGuire had in fact inflicted the prior injuries. The part of the instruction relied upon by the Court—"it may be logically concluded that if the defendant committed other offenses, he also committed the crime charged in this case"—does not make clear that it is the jury's role to ascertain whether McGuire was the perpetrator of the prior abuse. Rather, coming as it does in the middle of what appears to be a conclusion of law, it is reasonably likely that the jury understood that such a determination had already been made and that its role was merely to determine if there was a "clear connection" between Tori's prior injuries and the injuries that killed her.

... [I]t is well established that the fundamental fairness guarantee of the Due Process Clause requires the prosecution to prove beyond a reasonable doubt every element of the offense. This constitutional principle "prohibits the State from using evidentiary presumptions in a jury charge that have the effect of relieving the State of its burden of persuasion beyond a reasonable doubt of every essential element of a crime." ...

In this case, the instruction perhaps was intended to posit a permissive inference that whoever had inflicted Tori's prior injuries was likely to have inflicted the injuries that caused her death. But the trial court did not make clear that the State first had to prove the predicate facts from which the inference was to be drawn. Furthermore, the wording of the instruction is such that the jury may well have assumed that it had no choice but to "logically conclude" that McGuire was the murderer once it found a "clear connection" between the prior injuries and the fatal ones. Because I cannot say with any confidence that the instruction allowed a mere permissive inference drawing from proven facts, I think the instruction should be treated as a mandatory presumption that may have relieved the State of its burden of proving the identity of Tori's killer beyond a reasonable doubt.

Had the instruction been clearly worded, I would agree with the Court that there is sufficient circumstantial evidence in the record to support a finding that McGuire was the perpetrator of the prior injuries. After all, as the Court points out, "the proof of battered child syndrome itself narrowed the group of possible perpetrators to McGuire and his wife, because they were the only two people regularly caring for Tori." In this case, however, it is important to remember that the other person regularly caring for Tori — Daisy McGuire — took the stand and testified, under a grant of immunity, that she was the one who inflicted the fatal injuries on the night of July 7, 1981.

McGuire's jury deliberated for three days before returning a verdict of guilty. Any evaluation of the jury instruction must be conducted against the background of Daisy McGuire's surprise testimony and the dilemma it so clearly posed for the jury. In my view, the jury instruction on similar acts was so "ambiguous," that there was a reasonable likelihood that the jury was encouraged to make assumptions and conclusions about the identity of Tori's murderer that relieved the State of having to prove that element of the offense beyond a reasonable doubt. In cases where the Court has found that jury instructions included mandatory presumptions inconsistent with the guarantees of the Due Process Clause, the Court has remanded to determine whether the erroneous instruction was harmless, which is the course that should be followed here.

Notes and Queries

1. Do the facts of this case leave you comfortable with the decision that the father was guilty of battering his child? What would you do with the mother's in-court testimony that she beat the child?

2. Does the evidence that Tori was a battered child seem strong?

3. Does it seems fair to find someone guilty of a crime because of actions that are not proven in court? Do you think that the testimony of acts constituting the battered child mean that the facts are proven?

4. Evidence of the battered child syndrome was admitted to help prove intent, a necessary element of the charges against the defendant. Should the state simply forgo charging such crimes?

5. Assuming that the case was tried in federal court, do the Federal Rules of Evidence require more from the expert witnesses? Would their evidence be excluded?

Research Comments

1. Generally, a person is tried for his specific acts, not for his bad character or his alleged propensity to commit bad acts. The Supreme Court identified the underlying concerns that motivated the character bar in *Michelson v. United States*, 335 U.S. 469 (1948). Explaining why common law had disallowed the admission of evidence of a defendant's evil character to demonstrate that he did the alleged act, Justice Jackson stated: "The inquiry is not rejected because character is irrelevant; on the contrary, it is said to weigh too much with the jury and to so overpersuade them as to prejudge one with a bad general record and deny him a fair opportunity to defend against a particular charge." Id. at 475–476.

2. The battered child syndrome explicitly concerns prior bad acts. The syndrome is defined as the collection of injuries sustained by a child as a result of repeated mistreatment or beating. Battered child syndrome is suspected if a child's injuries indicate intentional trauma or appear to be more severe than could reasonably be expected to result from an accident. Some of the most suspicious signs include: (1) appearance at an emergency room with an injured child and an improbable explanation; (2) delayed appearance at an emergency room with an injured child; (3) bruise marks shaped like hands, fingers, or objects (belt); (4) specific patterns of scalding seen when a conscious child is immersed in hot water; (5) burns from an electric stove, radiator, heater, or other hot objects on the child's hands or buttocks; (6) cigarette burns on exposed areas or the genitals; (7) black eyes in an infant; (8) human bite marks; (9) lash marks; (10) choke marks around neck; (11) circular marks around wrists or ankles (twisting); (12) sutures-separated; (13) bulging soft spot (fontanel) on the infants head; and (14) unexplained unconsciousness in infant. National attention to this syndrome emerged in 1962, with the publication of a now-famous article that conceptualized the "battered child syndrome," reframed society's concept of child physical abuse, and lead to the massive reforms in child protection laws. C. Henry Kempe, N. Freederick Silverman, Brandt F. Steele, William Droegemueller & Henry K. Silver (1962). The battered child syndrome. *Journal of the American Medical Association*, 181, 17–24.

3. Prior bad acts also have become an important and controversial issue in sexual maltreatment cases. Today, the majority of states govern the admission of prior sexual misconduct evidence either with the "lustful disposition" doctrine or the *Molineux* rule. The *Molineux* rule was set forth in the case of *People v. Molineux*, 61 N.E. 286 (N.Y. 1901), where the New York court stated that evidence of other offenses of misconduct by the defendant that are not part of the charged offense should not be received into evidence. However, the *Molineux* approach provided

a list of exceptions that allow for admitting prior acts for non-propensity purposes such as motive, intent, absence of mistake, common scheme or plan, and identity. Many states broadly interpret the enumerated *Molineux* exceptions for sex offense cases. In these states, evidence of past conduct is admitted as evidence of "intent" or "plan," even though under the normal understanding of those exceptions such evidence arguably would not be allowed. The majority of states adopt the "lustful disposition" exception for prior acts evidence in sex offense cases. Under this rule, evidence of past misconduct is admitted to show that the defendant has a propensity to engage in aberrant sexual behavior. Thomas J. Reed (1993). Reading gaol revisited: Admission of uncharged misconduct evidence in sex offender cases. *American Journal of Criminal Law*, 21, 127–180.

4. In September 1994, the United States Congress turned two centuries of evidentiary common law upside down. The Federal Rules generally follow the character bar, which is contained in Federal Rule 404(b). That Rule states, in part, that "Evidence of other crimes, wrongs, or acts is not admissible to prove the character of a person in order to show action in conformity therewith. It may, however, be admissible for other purposes, such as proof of motive, opportunity, intent, preparation, plan, knowledge, identity, or absence of mistake or accident. . . ." But how the rule applies to sex offenders was radically transformed by the *Violent Crime Control and Law Enforcement Act of 1994*, Pub. L. No. 103-322, 320935, 108 Stat. 1796, 2135–37 (1994) (codified as amended at 28 U.S.C. app. Fed. R. Evid. 413–415 (1994), which contained three new Federal Rules of Evidence (Rules 413, 414, and 415). These new rules, now being referred to as the "sexual character evidence rules," were designed to bolster prosecution of sexual assault and child molestation offenders, as well as to assist plaintiffs in civil cases predicated on sexual assault or child molestation. The rules allow the admission of evidence of charged or uncharged prior sexual misconduct to be used against a defendant in a sexual offense case and apparently changes the well-established rule against the use of propensity evidence to show that the defendant was acting in conformity with the defendant's character. Rules 413 through 415 address this admissibility in both criminal and civil cases. Rule 413 applies to criminal prosecutions for "sexual assault." The Rule states, "In a criminal case in which the defendant is accused of an offense of sexual assault, evidence of the defendant's commission of another offense or offenses of sexual assault is admissible, and may be considered for its bearing on any matter to which it is relevant." Rule 414 substitutes "child molestation" for "sexual assault." The Rule states, "In a criminal case in which the defendant is accused of an offense of child molestation, evidence of the defendant's commission of another offense or offenses of child molestation is admissible, and may be considered for its bearing on any matter to which it is relevant." Rule 415 is the civil analog to Rules 413 and 414. Rule 415 states: "In a civil case in which a claim for damages or other relief is predicated on a party's alleged commission of conduct constituting an offense of sexual assault or child molestation, evidence of that party's commission of another offense or offenses of sexual assault or child molestation is admissible and may

be considered as provided in Rule 413 and Rule 414. . . ." The new rules also set forth time frames for the disclosure to the other party that the other acts evidence is expected to be used. In criminal and civil cases, disclosure must occur at least fifteen days prior to trial, except for good cause, and disclosure must include any "statements of witnesses or a summary of the substance of any testimony that is expected to be offered." See Rules 413(b), 414(b), 415(b).

5. In deciding if prior acts evidence should be admitted under the new federal rules, the Tenth Circuit provided a useful four-prong test to use in determining if the evidence is substantially similar. In *United States v. Guardia*, 135 F.3d 1326, 1332 (10th Cir. 1998), the court reasoned that: (1) the case must be a trial for a sexual offense; (2) the prior bad acts evidence must be another sexual-type offense; (3) the evidence must be relevant, showing both that the defendant had a certain propensity and the propensity has bearing on the crime charged; and (4) the court must perform a Rule 403 balancing test to determine if the probative value of the evidence outweighs the prejudice to the defendant.

Review Problems

1. LeCompte was charged under 18 U.S.C. sections 2244(a)(1) and 2246(3) for the alleged sexual abuse of C. D., his wife's 11-year-old niece. On at least one occasion, LeCompte allegedly exposed himself to C. D. while they played games together at her aunt's trailer. On another occasion, LeCompte allegedly joined C. D. on the couch, forced her to touch his penis, and touched her breasts while C. D.'s siblings were sleeping on the floor next to her. Before trial, the government provided LeCompte with notice that it intended to offer evidence under Rule 414 of prior uncharged sex offenses against T. T., another of his nieces. The incidents involving T. T. allegedly had occurred eight to ten years prior to the current incidents on which he was being tried. According to the prosecutors, T. T. was prepared to testify at trial that LeCompte had played games with her at her aunt's house, had exposed himself to her, had forced her to touch his penis, and had touched her private parts. LeCompte moved to exclude the evidence. After applying the Rule 403 balancing test, the district court ruled that the evidence was inadmissible because the potential for unfair prejudice outweighed the limited probative value of the evidence. The district court found significant the eight-year period separating the incidents. The court also found that the testimony obviously would be highly prejudicial evidence against the defendant given that child sexual abuse carries a unique stigma in our society. Given that the evidence was highly prejudicial, the court reasoned that the evidence should carry a very high degree of probative value for it to be admitted. How should the circuit court reviewing this case rule? The Eighth Circuit rejected the district court's analysis. The court stated that although Rule 414 is subject to the requirements of Rule 403, it must be applied to allow Rule 414 its intended effect, namely to supersede the restrictive aspects of Rule 404(b).

The court ruled, "In light of the strong legislative judgment that evidence of prior sexual offenses should ordinarily be admissible, we think the District Court erred in its assessment that the probative value of T. T.'s testimony was substantially outweighed by the danger of unfair prejudice." *United States v. LeCompte*, 131 F.3d 767, 769 (8th Cir. 1997). The court found that the offenses committed against the two girls were substantially similar. The court also noted that even the district court acknowledged that the eight-year period between the offenses may not be as significant as it appears at first glance; in fact, the defendant was imprisoned for a portion of the time between the offenses, which deprived defendant of the opportunity to abuse any children. Arguably even more significantly, the court flatly rejected the district court's emphasis on the "unique stigma" of child sexual abuse — the danger that the jury might convict based on LeCompte's propensity to commit child sexual abuse, rather than on the facts directly supporting the offense against C. D. The court concluded that "it is for this reason that the evidence was previously excluded, and it is precisely such holdings that Congress intended to overrule." Id. at 770.

2. Fumiko Kimura lives in a fairly isolated Japanese immigrant enclave in Los Angeles. Upon learning of her husband's adulterous conduct, she attempts to drown herself and her two children in Santa Monica Bay. Both children die but she is rescued by good samaritans. Kimura contends that she was attempting a traditional Japanese ritual, *oyako-shinju*, parent–child suicide. According to this ancient custom, when women have been wronged by their husbands, they may choose to remove themselves from this world rather than bring shame to their families and communities. Taking their children with them into the afterlife is encouraged; leaving children behind with no one to attend to them would be a sign of poor motherhood. *Oyako-shinju*, although not officially condoned, is rarely prosecuted in Japan. How should a court go about determining whether to consider the appropriateness of expert evidence on *oyako-shinju*? See Roger J. R. Levesque (2000). Cultural evidence, child maltreatment, and the law. *Child Maltreatment*, 5, 146–160.

3. Kim Logerquist alleges that her pediatrician sexually abused her on several occasions between 1971 and 1973, when she was 8 to 10 years old. She further alleges that she had amnesia about those events until 1991, when her memory was triggered by watching a television commercial featuring a pediatrician. She sought to introduce evidence, through expert testimony, that severe childhood trauma, including sexual abuse, can cause a repression of memory, and that in later years this memory can be recalled with accuracy. The trial judge granted Defendant's motion that a *Frye* hearing be held to assess the admissibility of expert testimony regarding repressed memory. [Note that the jurisdiction in which she sought relief, Arizona, follows the *Frye* standard.] Two experts testified at the *Frye* hearing. Plaintiff called Dr. Bessell van der Kolk, a clinical psychiatrist who specializes in dissociative amnesia. He testified regarding the large number of patients who

alleged such phenomenon and about his diagnoses of dissociative amnesia or post-traumatic stress disorder in such patients. He would testify among other things, that his experience and observations over many years, together with the extensive literature on the subject, have led him to conclude the phenomenon exists in some patients. Defendant's expert, Dr. Richard Kihlstrom, a research psychologist, testified there were serious flaws in the many studies supporting repressed memory and cited other studies finding trauma usually enhances memory rather than causes amnesia. Doctor Kihlstrom did not, however, have any personal experience treating or dealing with people claiming to suffer from repressed memory; nor had he participated in any studies on trauma's effect on memory. After a lengthy hearing, the trial judge determined the theories advanced by Plaintiff's experts were not generally accepted in the relevant scientific community of trauma memory researchers. The judge therefore ordered excluding expert testimony of Plaintiff's alleged repressed memory and Plaintiff's theory that such evidence can be recalled with accuracy. How should the reviewing court rule? The reviewing court ruled *Frye* inapplicable. The court noted that it was apparent that they were not dealing with an alchemist attempting to change lead into gold or an astrologer predicting events from the movements of the stars but one of the leading researchers and authorities in behavioral science. The court found it strange that a witness so well qualified and experienced would not be permitted to testify on an issue beyond the experience of the average juror. The court then noted that *Frye* applies to the use of novel scientific theories or processes to produce results and that the issues at hand were not scientific. Neither parties had claimed that some scientific process, theory, or formula may be applied to test whether her memories of having been molested are true and accurate or whether the memories were imagined, suggested, implanted, or even invented. As a result, the court concluded that the truth of Plaintiff's testimony that she actually and accurately recalled or remembered the events, as distinguished from inventing them or having had them suggested or implanted, is for a jury to decide. The court also examined the issue, assuming *Frye* applied, of whether the trial judge abused his discretion by concluding the theory of repressed memory, post-traumatic stress disorder, or dissociative amnesia did not meet the general acceptance test. The court noted that court rulings have split on that question but that, from the record, one might conclude that in finding a lack of general acceptance, the judge gave undue weight to the views of research psychologists and too little to those of clinicians—psychiatrists and psychologists—who work in the field. *Logerquist v. McVey*, 1 P.3d 113 (Ariz. 2000) (en banc). Note that the psychiatric and psychological community remains divided over whether reliable scientific support exists to validate repressed memories. See Sheila Taub (Ed.) (1999). *Recovered Memories of Child Sexual Abuse: Psychological, Social, and Legal Perspectives on a Contemporary Mental Health Controversy.* Springfield, IL: Charles C. Thomas. These concerns would seem important to the legal decision to admit such testimony at trial as courts address whether to admit expert testimony on repressed memories. Courts differ, however, as to what evidentiary standard applies to such testimony. Some jurisdictions apply a heightened evidentiary standard by requiring the trial court to assess the reliability of the expert testimony; others merely require that the testimony pass on general relevance grounds, a rather low-level evidentiary standard. Which admissibility standard seems appropriate?

4. Consideration of evidence means much more than determining whether evidence could be admitted. When evidence is deemed admissible, the next concern involves determining what can be said about the evidence. Evidence and testimony involving post-traumatic stress disorder (PTSD) is illustrative. PTSD is quite relevant to child maltreatment because it is a common diagnosis for individuals who have been sexually maltreated. For PTSD to be diagnosed, the individual must have experienced events involving injury (including threats) and the response to those events involve intense fear, helplessness, or horror. In addition, the individual must re-experience the symptoms, avoid certain stimuli (e.g., avoid cars), experience increased arousal symptoms (e.g., unable to sleep), and have symptoms that reach clinical levels (e.g., really serious), and those symptoms must last at least one month. Several issues are raised by efforts to link PTSD with sexual maltreatment: (1) PTSD does not mean maltreatment occurred; (2) PTSD may be present with other disorders and comorbidity means that the other disorder may have caused the problem and that PTSD is not a distinct disorder; (3) individuals may be malingering to make a stronger case; and (4) from 80 to 90 percent of cases are correctly identified, which means that 20 percent are potentially inaccurate. In addition to issues involving PTSD diagnoses, several issues arise when it becomes sought as evidence in trials. The issues involve the breadth of the testimony. Typically, five forms of testimony may be offered and each varies in terms of its admissibility. Evidence may be proffered to understand typical victim's behavior during or after maltreatment, which generally is allowed. Testimony may also seek to provide a general education for jurors about PTSD, which generally is allowed. Testimony also may seek to apply PTSD testimony to the particular case by demonstrating consistency between the victim's behavior and PTSD, all offered without the expert's examination of the victim or commenting about the victim's credibility. That testimony is more controversial, even though research reveals that the testimony does tend to counteract myths and does not seem to prejudice defendants. Testimony stating that the victim does have PTSD is also quite controversial; and research is less clear about the impact of that evidence. Lastly, testimony may move beyond the diagnosis and state that the victim has been maltreated or that the victim is telling the truth, which tends to be viewed as inappropriate. What breadth of testimony do you see as appropriate? What rationales do you use to support your position: Is it because of the nature of the science, the role of the jury, the abilities of experts, or another factor? For an analysis dealing with these issues in the context of PTSD diagnosis for rape trauma testimony, see Laura E. Boeschen, Bruce D. Sales & Mary P. Koss (1998). Rape trauma experts in the courtroom. *Psychology, Public Policy, and the Law*, 4, 414–432.

5. Consider the following case. Velarde appeals his conviction by a jury on one count of aggravated sexual abuse of a child on grounds that expert testimony was unreliable and erroneously admitted. Dr. Ornelas began her testimony by recounting her usual procedures in examining a child where sexual abuse has been alleged and then testified that L. had a "normal" physical exam, which was, she opined, "consistent with what [L.] said happened." Dr. Ornelas testified that a normal exam is "the most common physical findings for a child who has been sexually abused." This is so, Dr. Ornelas opined, because "the type of contact that most commonly occurs between adults and children that's sexual is oral kinds of contact, touching, and what's called labial coitus." "Dr. Ornelas also testified that L.'s behavior of withdrawing from her family, staying inside of her room, not being communicative, not being her regular bubbly, running-around kind of self, and . . . waking up at night and touching her mother to make sure that her mother was there in bed with her . . . having sleep disturbances and some behavioral changes," was "consistent with child sexual abuse." Finally, she testified as follows: "Q. Doctor, if you had those symptoms or some of those symptoms and a report by a child of sexual abuse, are you comfortable forming a diagnosis of child sexual abuse in such a case? A. I would base that diagnosis on the child's statements about what had happened to them." When the defendant challenged the expert's reliability on the grounds that she exceeded her expertise in testifying about psychology, the trial judge refused a separate hearing, stating that he had "heard this testimony before in trials." The Tenth Circuit reversed because of a lack of any reliability determination by the court. The court also noted that the trial court improperly assumed that Dr. Ornelas's proffered testimony fell within the category of testimony in "ordinary" cases where courts may "avoid unnecessary 'reliability' proceedings . . . where the reliability of an expert's methods is properly taken for granted" and gave no indication why this case could be viewed as such an "ordinary" case, or why Dr. Ornelas's methods could be "properly taken for granted," except for the court's remark that "I've had this testimony before in trials, and it's not new and novel." The court further found the testimony problematic because she had testified that the victim had normal physical exams but exhibited behaviors consistent with sexual abuse; and she had testified that she believed sexual abuse had in fact occurred because the victim alleged that such abuse had occurred. *United States v. Velarde*, 214 F.3d 1204 (10th Cir. 2000).

6. What do you make of testimony offered in *United States v. Romero*, 189 F.3d 576 (7th Cir. 1999)? Thirty-six-year-old Romero "met" a 12-year-old Erich in a "chat room" on the Internet devoted to UFOs and extraterrestrials. After developing a relationship through e-mail, he enticed the boy to run away from home in Illinois. The two boarded a bus in Chicago bound for St. Petersburg. Some quick investigative work by the local police and the FBI foiled the trip, as Romero and Erich were intercepted at the Greyhound bus station in Louisville, Kentucky. Among other charges, Romero was eventually charged with kidnaping and transporting a minor with intent to engage in criminal sexual activity for inveigling

Erich to leave his home and travel to Kentucky; and charged with traveling in interstate commerce for the purpose of engaging in a sexual act with a juvenile. At closing argument in his second trial, the defense argued that Erich consented to travel with Romero, which negated, if believed, the kidnaping charge. Romero did not dispute his keen interest in child pornography or his sexual fantasies about Erich, but he argued that he did not intend to follow through on his fantasies. The second jury rejected these defenses and convicted Romero of the kidnaping and transportation charges. Judge Kocoras then sentenced him to 327 months in prison.

At issue on appeal was whether Judge Kocoras abused his discretion when he admitted the testimony of the prosecution's FBI expert on child molesters. Before trial, the government filed a notice of its intent to use the testimony of Agent Kenneth V. Lanning, who had spent many years studying the sexual exploitation of children and produced over twenty publications, to inform the jury about child molestation. The prosecution proposed to have Agent Lanning testify regarding (1) characteristics of "preferential" child molesters and the methods they used to attract and abuse children and (2) his opinion that Romero is a child molester with an interest in adolescent boys and that Romero had a sexual interest in Erich. Romero had filed a motion *in limine* to exclude Agent Lanning's testimony, arguing that the expert could not offer his opinion about Romero's intent with respect to Erich under Federal Rule of Evidence 704(b) because it would involve the ultimate issue the jury was impaneled to decide. Romero also had argued that Lanning's testimony would be unduly prejudicial under Rule 403 because it amounted to impermissible "profiling."

In response to the defense arguments, the government had offered that it would limit Lanning's testimony to the methods and techniques employed by preferential child molesters. The prosecution would not ask Lanning to give his opinion about Romero or to comment about his intent or culpability. Subject to these limitations, Judge Kocoras allowed Agent Lanning to testify, noting that the testimony would be highly probative:

> Here is a man who studied the field extensively, an acknowledged expert in the field. And I do not think there is any question whatever that his testimony meets all the criteria of the 700 series, and is particularly helpful to the jury because he has had an abundance of training and experience far beyond any lay person, certainly, and far beyond, I think, most experts in the field.

Judge Kocoras thus denied the motion to exclude Lanning's "testimony in general." Kocoras, however, agreed with the defense's concern that Lanning's testimony could possibly invade the province of the jury and usurp their function in determining whether Romero had the requisite criminal intent. For that reason, Judge Kocoras encouraged the defense to object to Lanning's testimony on a question-by-question basis if it seemed that he was going too far.

At trial Lanning testified that his observations arose from his expertise about child molesters in general, not from the specific facts of the case. He then explained his role:

> As I understand it, what I am going to do is provide or share the information that I have concerning the nature of certain types of offenders and provide this information to people who would not otherwise be aware and have this kind of knowledge because of their experiences and work.

Lanning then opined that child sex offenders fall on a spectrum from "situational sex offenders," whose activities are based on an accident of circumstance, to "preferential sex offenders," who have a definite preference for sexual contact with children and methodically pursue such contact. He identified four general traits usually exhibited by preferential sex offenders, all of which he had described in published materials long before the Romero case. He noted that the conduct of a preferential child molester occurs over a long period of time, is extremely persistent, and can involve enormous amounts of time on the Internet trying to meet children and develop seemingly innocent relationships with them; that preferential sex offenders have very specific interests and that they focus on certain kinds of children; that preferential sex offenders typically identify a need in a child and then move forward to temporarily fill that need in the child as part of this process; and that preferential offenders engage in fantasy and need-driven behavior. Not surprisingly, the hypotheticals described actions taken by Romero that had already been produced in evidence: Establishing a 9-month relationship with a young (age 12 at the time it started) boy on the Internet; traveling hundreds of miles to meet a 13-year-old; meeting a young boy in a hotel room; spending long hours communicating with multiple young boys; and discussing a sexual interest in children with another adult. Lanning testified that each of these actions would indicate that the offender in question would act upon his fantasies.

The appellate court rejected the defense's claim that Judge Kocoras erred in finding that Lanning's testimony generally would be reliable and helpful to the jury. The court viewed the testimony as critical in dispelling from the jurors' minds the widely held stereotype of a child molester and the court recognized the value of expert testimony in explaining a complicated criminal methodology that may look innocent on the surface but is not as innocent as it appears. Would you have admitted Lanning's testimony about the spectrum of sex offenders? Would it matter whether his research writings are peer-reviewed?

Research Comments

1. A syndrome is a group of signs and symptoms that are based on their frequent mutual occurrence that may suggest a common underlying course, pattern, or treatment selection, but do not necessarily imply a specific cause. In thinking of

syndromes, it is important to consider the extent to which they are diagnostic. The classic example of a diagnostic syndrome is the battered child syndrome because a group of findings convincingly indicate abuse. The battered child syndrome has a very high degree of diagnostic certainty; physicians look for injuries to the child that are inconsistent with the description of how the injuries came about and they also look for previous unreported injuries. Other syndromes fall outside the traditional meaning of syndrome as they do not point to a particular cause. The Child Sexual Abuse Accommodation Syndrome (CSAAS) is an excellent example of a non-diagnostic syndrome. The CSAAS was first identified by Dr. Roland Summit in a 1983 article in which he described five experiences typically occurring in sexually abused children: (1) secrecy about the sexual abuse, often ensured by threats of negative consequences of disclosure; (2) emotional helplessness to resist or complain; (3) entrapment and accommodation, where the child sees no way to escape ongoing abuse and thus learns to adapt; (4) delayed, conflicted, and unconvincing disclosure of the abuse; and (5) retraction of the child's allegations in an attempt to restore order to the family structure when the disclosure threatens to destroy it. Roland C. Summit (1983). The child sexual abuse accommodation syndrome. *Child Abuse & Neglect*, 7, 177–193. Rather than detecting abuse, the CSAAS makes the assumption that sex abuse already has occurred and it explains the possible reactions that an abused child may experience. Accommodation is not evidence of abuse. Moreover, a child need not show a cluster of accommodation symptoms in order to be accommodating abuse. For example, a child may delay reporting, yet never recant. The syndrome was developed not to prove that abuse occurred but to explain children's reactions to sexual abuse.

If a syndrome is not diagnostic, it would seem that it should not be admissible to establish the cause of a patient's symptom. This seems to make sense given that there is no single behavioral symptom, or syndrome that is characteristic or indicative of child sexual maltreatment. In an authoritative meta-analysis of the effects of sexual maltreatment, a review of forty-five studies found that no one symptom characterized a majority of the sexually abused children. Most importantly, they found that approximately one-third of the victims had no identifiable symptoms whatsoever. Kathleen A. Kendall-Tackett, Linda Meyer Williams & David Finkelhor (1993). Impact of sexual abuse on children: A review and synthesis of recent empirical studies. *Psychological Bulletin*, 113, 164–180. When a child exhibits one or more symptoms of child sexual abuse accommodation (e.g., delayed disclosure), this does not increase the likelihood that the child was abused. There is no reason to believe that true allegations are more likely than false allegations to be delayed. Therefore, it is inappropriate to use accommodation symptoms as "substantive evidence" of abuse. The purpose of accommodation symptoms, however, is to challenge the assumption that children who exhibit accommodation symptoms must not have been abused. From this perspective, it seems appropriate to tell the jury that accommodation frequently occurs among abused children in order to disabuse the jury of misconceptions regarding how abused children ought to behave. In legal terms, describing the symptoms of accommodation is an appropriate means by which one may "rebut" attacks on or "rehabilitate" a child's credibility. For example, if the defense argues that abuse did not occur since the child did not report abuse until long after exposure to the defendant, the prosecution could offer expert testimony that victims of abuse often delay reporting due to guilt and fear. The proper foundation for relevance of CSAAS testimony is the inference raised by the defense that an inconsistent pattern of disclosures by the child is indicative of deceit. It is generally believed that an abstract presentation of the CSAAS by an expert who has never seen the child and knows virtually nothing about the case would provide the jury with a demonstrably objective reflection. What do you make of this approach to using evidence that otherwise would not be admissible? Does admitting this type of testimony invade the province of the jury?

2. Base rates are one of the most critical points to understand when evaluating indicators, signs, symptoms, or syndromes of maltreatment. Witnesses may testify, for example, that, if a given child displays a number of signs, symptoms, or behaviors (such as "sexualized behavior" or "recantation" or "delayed recall"), then the child has most likely experienced sexual abuse. The problem with such statements is that some behaviors that have been put forth, including sexualized behavior, as indicators of sexual abuse are also found in non-abused children. To understand the reliability of a syndrome, we must know the prevalence of the syndrome in abused versus non-abused children. The current understanding of sexualized behavior is illustrative. Freud asserted that children are polymorphous perverse and are capable of generating sexual fantasies without sexual experience. As Freud was psychoanalyzing young women with hysteria, he found that they related childhood histories of sexual victimization. He concluded that the etiology of hysteria was a childhood experience of sexual abuse. He apparently was severely criticized by his colleagues and eventually altered his theory. He decided it was not actual incest but incestuous fantasies or wishes that were being reported by his female patients. See Jeffrey Moussaieff Masson (1998). *Assault on the Truth.* New York: Pocket Books. The controversy continues. An opinion that advanced sexual knowledge and explicit sexual behavior can be self-generated is not supported by research findings. Yet not all sexually abused children exhibit sexualized behavior nor manifest advanced sexual knowledge. In addition, children may learn about sex from sources other than sexual victimization. Nevertheless, sexualized behavior is the marker most often asserted as most likely to distinguish sexually abused from nonabused children. See William Friedrich (1993). Sexual victimization and sexual behavior in children: A review of recent literature. *Child Abuse & Neglect*, 17, 59–66.

Chapter 10

Representing and Protecting Children in Courts and Other State Interventions

The meteoric rise in child maltreatment cases during the 1980s has contributed to a record number of children involved in the court system, hastened efforts to accommodate children's needs in court proceedings, and even led to efforts to rethink the rights of children outside of courtrooms. Recognition of the need to address children's special needs has led to a massive amount of reforms. Most notably, the recognition that legal matters involving children and families need to be addressed differently than criminal matters or money disputes led many states to establish a specific family court with its own infrastructure and administration. Other states may continue to process family cases by a court structure that primarily addresses civil or criminal matters, but they too have undergone important changes. Even the criminal justice system has undergone changes to address the needs of children.

Typically, child protection cases arise under the jurisdiction of juvenile or family court and do so under the *parens patriae* role of the court, the state's interest in and responsibility for the well-being of all children in the state. In this arena, a child witness may be asked to provide factual information to the court that might result in a determination to take the child into state custody. Depending on the state, the child may or may not be a witness and rarely will be a party to the proceeding. The child's case is brought to court by the state child protective agency that files suit against the parents. The child may or may not be represented by an attorney or have an appointed guardian ad litem. Guardians ad litem may be attorneys, but most are lay guardians. It is their responsibility to assess the child's interest and needs and present them to the court on behalf of the minor child. The investigation of alleged child maltreatment leads to court action and also may have implications for how the court is able to proceed in making its judgment. Cases involving serious physical harm and allegations of child sexual maltreatment typically involve law enforcement investigations. As a result, children may not only become witnesses in family courts but also criminal courts.

Different courts raise different issues. One of the central issues involves whether child victims can make competent, reliable witnesses. The dilemma currently faced involves the criminal court and the extent to which children's evidence should be relied upon to reform traditional legal requirements and procedures in order to enable children to be heard in court, without infringing on the rights of the accused. In addition to issues involving children's basic competence, equally important are issues regarding the need to protect children from adverse affects of court proceedings. Again, the protection of children from traumatization as witnesses must be balanced with protection of defendants from false charges and breech of their constitutional rights. Likewise, when the legal system does not involve criminal matters, there has been an increasing tendency to consider representation of children in proceedings that tend to be framed in terms of the rights of parents to raise their children against the state's obligation to intervene in the name of child protection. As a result, the legal system has devised special rules to accommodate child witnesses and present their needs in court.

The most controversial legislative and jurisprudential developments involve criminal law, especially criminal law's important elaborations of hearsay exceptions. Several states have created, by statute, special exceptions to the hearsay rule especially for out-of-court statements made by a child victim of sexual and physical abuse. These innovations are deemed necessary when the child's hearsay statements do not fall within existing exceptions. Although the wording of these special exceptions varies, all statutes require that the child be found unavailable to testify in court and that his/her statements be particularly trustworthy. Importantly, a child's unavailability need not be literal; the child may be deemed unavailable to testify under these exceptions if it would be traumatized by testifying in court. Judges will generally require that evidence (often expert testimony) be presented to support claims that a child's in-court testimony would cause the child harm. All of these efforts reveal the immense challenges the law faces, in and outside of court, in representing and presenting children's concerns.

Wheeler v. United States

159 U.S. 523; 16 S. Ct. 93 (1895)

Mr. Justice Brewer delivered the opinion of the court.

On January 2, 1895, George L. Wheeler was by the Circuit Court of the United States for the Eastern District of Texas adjudged guilty of the crime of murder and sentenced to be hanged. Whereupon he sued out this writ of error....

The remaining objection is to the action of the court in permitting the son of the deceased to testify. The homicide took place on June 12, 1894, and this boy was five years old on the 5th of July following. The case was tried on December 21, at which time he was nearly five and a half years of age. The boy, in reply to questions put to him on his voir dire, said among other things that he knew the difference between the truth and a lie; that if he told a lie the bad man would get him, and that he was going to tell the truth. When further asked what they would do with him in court if he told a lie, he replied that they would put him in jail. He also said that his mother had told him that morning to "tell no lie," and in response to a question as to what the clerk said to him, when he held up his hand, he answered, "don't you tell no story."

Other questions were asked as to his residence, his relationship to the deceased, and as to whether he had ever been to school, to which latter inquiry he responded in the negative. As the testimony is not all preserved in the record we have before us no inquiry as to the sufficiency of the testimony to uphold the verdict, and are limited to the question of the competency of this witness.

That the boy was not by reason of his youth, as a matter of law, absolutely disqualified as a witness, is clear. While no one would think of calling as a witness an infant only two or three years old, there is no precise age which determines the question of competency. This depends on the capacity and intelligence of the child, his appreciation of the difference between truth and falsehood, as well as of his duty to tell the former. The decision of this question rests primarily with the trial judge, who sees the proposed witness, notices his manner, his apparent possession or lack of intelligence, any may resort to any examination which will tend to disclose his capacity and intelligence as well as his understanding of the obligations of an oath. As many of these matters cannot be photographed into the record the decision of the trial judge will not be disturbed on review unless from that which is preserved it is clear that it was erroneous. These rules have been settled by many decisions, and there seems to be no dissent among the recent authorities. . . .

These principles and authorities are decisive in this case. So far as can be judged from the not very extended examination which is found in the record, the boy was intelligent, understood the difference between truth and falsehood, and the consequences of telling the latter, and also what was required by the oath which he had taken. At any rate, the contrary does not appear. Of course, care must be taken by the trial judge, especially where, as in this case, the question is one of life or death. On the other hand, to exclude from the witness stand one who shows himself capable of understanding the difference between truth and falsehood, and who does not appear to have been simply taught to tell a story, would sometimes result in staying the hand of justice.

We think that under the circumstances of this case the disclosures on the voir dire were sufficient to authorize the decision that the witness was competent, and, therefore, there was no error in admitting his testimony. These being the only questions in the record, the judgment must be

Affirmed.

Notes and Queries

1. What standard must a child meet to be deemed competent? Is this more than what we require from adults?

2. Consider the following colloquy between the court and a 5-year-old child who was to testify about his sexual victimization by his father. His father appealed the guilty verdict by challenging his son's competency to testify:

The Court: Let me ask you this ***. Has anybody told you what you are supposed to say here today?

Witness: No.

The Court: No body has told you that you have to say anything?

Witness: Just what Ray done, right?

The Court: Is that what you plan to say?

Witness: My Mom told me everything he did to me?

The Court: Who told you that?

Witness: My mom.

The Court: Did you know it before your mother told you?

Witness: No. Except before my mother told me I remembered what he done.

The Court: Do you remember that?

Witness: I remember what Ray done.

The Court: Did you remember before she told you?

Witness: Uh huh.

The Court: Did anybody else talk to you and tell you what you were supposed to say?

Witness: No.

The Court: Nobody else talked to you about what to say?

Witness: No.

The Court: Let me ask you this ***, are you going to say what you remember Ray did or are you going to say what your mother said?

Witness: I just remember three times of it.

The Court: And you remember that without having been told by your mother?

Witness: Yes.

The Court: Your mother didn't tell you those three times did she?

Witness: Yeah, I think she did.

In this case, the appeals court ruled that the lower court had not abused its discretion in finding the child competent to testify. See *People v. McNichols*, 139 Ill. App. 3d 947; 487 N.E.2d 1252 (1986).

Kentucky v. Stincer

482 U.S. 730; 107 S. Ct. 2658 (1987)

Justice Blackmun delivered the opinion of the Court.

The question presented in this case is whether the exclusion of a defendant from a hearing held to determine the competency of two child witnesses to testify violates the defendant's rights under the Confrontation Clause of the Sixth Amendment or the Due Process Clause of the Fourteenth Amendment.

I

Respondent Sergio Stincer was indicted in the Circuit Court of Christian County, Ky., and charged with committing first-degree sodomy with T. G., an 8-year-old girl, N. G., a 7-year-old girl, and. . . . After a jury was sworn, but before the presentation of evidence, the court conducted an in-chambers hearing to determine if the two young girls were competent to testify. Over his objection, respondent, but not his counsel (a public defender), was excluded from this hearing.

The two children were examined separately and the judge, the prosecutor, and respondent's counsel asked questions of each girl to determine if she were capable of remembering basic facts and of distinguishing between telling the truth and telling a lie. T. G., the 8-year-old, was asked her age, her date of birth, the name of her school, the names of her teachers, and the name of her Sunday school. She was also asked whether she knew what it meant to tell the truth, and whether she could keep a promise to God to tell the truth. N. G., the 7-year-old girl, was asked similar questions. The two children were not asked about the substance of the testimony they were to give at trial. The court ruled that the girls were competent to testify. Respondent's counsel did not object to these rulings.

Before each of the girls began her substantive testimony in open court, the prosecutor repeated some of the basic questions regarding the girl's background that had been asked at the competency hearing. T. G. then testified, on direct examination, that respondent had placed a sock over her eyes, had given her chocolate pudding to eat, and then had "put his d-i-c-k" in her mouth. N. G., on direct examination, testified to a similar incident.

On cross-examination, respondent's counsel asked each girl questions designed to determine if she could remember past events and if she knew the difference between the truth and a lie. Some of these questions were similar to those that had been asked at the competency hearing. After the testimony of the girls was concluded, counsel did not request that the trial court reconsider its ruling that the girls were competent to testify. The jury convicted respondent of first-degree sodomy for engaging in deviate sexual intercourse and fixed his sentence at 20 years' imprisonment.

On appeal to the Supreme Court of Kentucky, respondent argued, among other things, that his exclusion from the competency hearing of the two girls denied him due process and violated his Sixth Amendment right to confront the witnesses against him. The Kentucky Supreme Court, by a divided vote, agreed that, under the Sixth Amendment of the Federal Constitution and under § 11 of the Bill of Rights of the Kentucky Constitution (the right "to meet the witnesses face to face"), respondent had an absolute right to be present at the competency hearing because the hearing "was a crucial phase of the trial." The court explained that respondent's trial "might not have taken place had the trial court determined that the children were not competent to testify." Two justices, however, dissented, concluding that respondent's right to confront the witnesses against him was not violated because respondent had the opportunity to assist counsel fully in cross-examining the two witnesses at trial.

We granted certiorari to determine whether respondent's constitutional rights were violated by his exclusion from the competency hearing.

II

A

The Sixth Amendment's Confrontation Clause provides: "In all criminal prosecutions, the accused shall enjoy the right . . . to be confronted with the witnesses against him." This right is secured for defendants in state as well as in federal criminal proceedings. . . . The opportunity for cross-examination, protected by the Confrontation Clause, is critical for ensuring the integrity of the factfinding process. Cross-examination is "the principal means by which the believability of a witness and the truth of his testimony are tested." Indeed, the Court has recognized that cross-examination is the "'greatest legal engine ever invented for the discovery of truth.'" The usefulness of cross-examination was emphasized by this Court in an early case explicating the Confrontation Clause:

> The primary object of the constitutional provision in question was to prevent depositions or ex parte affidavits . . . being used against the prisoner in lieu of a personal examination and cross-examination of the witness in which the accused has an opportunity, not only of testing the recollection and sifting the conscience of the witness, but of compelling him to stand face to face with the jury in order that they may look at him, and judge by his demeanor upon the stand and the manner in which he gives his testimony whether he is worthy of belief.

The right to cross-examination, protected by the Confrontation Clause, thus is essentially a "functional" right designed to promote reliability in the truth-finding functions of a criminal trial. The cases that have arisen under the Confrontation Clause reflect the application of this functional right. These cases fall into two broad, albeit not exclusive, categories: "cases involving the admission of out-of-court statements and cases involving restrictions imposed by law or by the trial court on the scope of cross-examination."

. . .

B

The Commonwealth argues that respondent's exclusion from the competency hearing of the two children did not violate the Confrontation Clause because a competency hearing is not "a stage of trial where evidence or witnesses are being presented to the trier of fact." Distinguishing between a "trial" and a "pretrial proceeding" is not particularly helpful here, however, because a competency hearing may well be a "stage of trial." In this case, for instance, the competency hearing was held after the jury was sworn, in the judge's chambers, and in the presence of opposing counsel who asked questions of the witnesses. Moreover, although questions regarding the guilt or innocence of the defendant usually are not asked at a competency hearing, the hearing retains a direct relationship with the trial because it determines whether a key witness will testify. Further, although the preliminary determination of a witness' competency to testify is made at this hearing, the determination of competency is an ongoing one for the judge to make based on the witness' actual testimony at trial.

Instead of attempting to characterize a competency hearing as a trial or pretrial proceeding, it is more useful to consider whether excluding the defendant from the hearing interferes with his opportunity for effective cross-examination. No such interference occurred when respondent was excluded from the competency hearing of the two young girls in this case. After the trial court determined that the two children were competent to testify, they appeared and testified in open court. At that point, the two witnesses were subject to full and complete cross-examination, and were so examined. Respondent was present throughout this cross-examination and was available to assist his counsel as necessary. There was no Kentucky rule of law, nor any ruling by the trial court, that restricted respondent's ability to cross-examine the witnesses at trial. Any questions asked during the competency hearing, which respondent's counsel attended and in which he participated, could have been repeated during direct examination and cross-examination of the witnesses in respondent's presence.

Moreover, the type of questions that were asked at the competency hearing in this case were easy to repeat on cross-examination at trial. . . . Thus, questions at a competency hearing usually are limited to matters that are unrelated to the basic issues of the trial. Children often are asked their names, where they go to school, how old they are, whether they know who the judge is, whether they know what a lie is, and whether they know what happens when one tells a lie.

In Kentucky, as in certain other States, it is the responsibility of the judge, not the jury, to decide whether a witness is competent to testify based on the witness' answers to such questions.

. . .

In this case both T. G. and N. G. were asked several background questions during the competency hearing, as well as several questions directed at what it meant to tell the truth. Some of the questions regarding the witnesses' backgrounds were repeated by the prosecutor on direct examination, while others—particularly those regarding the witnesses' ability to tell the difference between truth and falsehood—were repeated by respondent's counsel on cross-examination. At the close of the children's testimony, respondent's counsel, had he thought it appropriate, was in a position to move that the court reconsider its competency rulings on the ground that the direct and cross-examination had elicited evidence that the young girls lacked the basic requisites for serving as competent witnesses. Thus, the critical tool of cross-examination was available to counsel as a means of establishing that the witnesses were not competent to testify, as well as a means of undermining the credibility of their testimony.

Because respondent had the opportunity for full and effective cross-examination of the two witnesses during trial, and because of the nature of the competency hearing at issue in this case, we conclude that respondent's rights under the Confrontation Clause were not violated by his exclusion from the competency hearing of the two girls.

Respondent argues that his rights under the Due Process Clause of the Fourteenth Amendment were violated by his exclusion from the competency hearing. . . .

We conclude that respondent's due process rights were not violated by his exclusion from the competency hearing in this case. We emphasize, again, the particular nature of the competency hearing. No question regarding the substantive testimony that the two girls would have given during trial was asked at that hearing. All the questions, instead, were directed solely to each child's ability to recollect and narrate facts, to her ability to distinguish between truth and falsehood, and to her sense of moral obligation to tell the truth. Thus, although a competency hearing in which a witness is asked to discuss upcoming substantive testimony might bear a substantial relationship to a defendant's opportunity better to defend himself at trial that kind of inquiry is not before us in this case.

Respondent has given no indication that his presence at the competency hearing in this case would have been useful in ensuring a more reliable determination as to whether the witnesses were competent to testify. He has presented no evidence that his relationship with the children, or his knowledge of facts regarding their background, could have assisted either his counsel or the judge in asking questions that would have resulted in a more assured determination of competency. On the record of this case, therefore, we cannot say that respondent's rights under the Due Process Clause of the Fourteenth Amendment were violated by his exclusion from the competency hearing.

The judgment of the Supreme Court of Kentucky is reversed.

It is so ordered.

Justice Marshall, with whom Justice Brennan and Justice Stevens join, dissenting.

The Court today defines respondent's Sixth Amendment right to be confronted with the witnesses against him as guaranteeing nothing more than an opportunity to cross-examine these witnesses at some point during his trial. The Confrontation Clause protects much more. In this case, it secures at a minimum respondent's right of presence to assist his lawyer at the in-chambers hearing to determine the competency of the key prosecution witnesses. Respondent's claim under the Due Process Clause of the Fourteenth Amendment, though similar in this testimonial context to his claim under the Confrontation Clause, was not addressed by the court below and should not be decided here. Were this issue properly before the Court, however, I would again dissent. Due process requires that respondent be allowed to attend every critical stage of his trial.

I

The Sixth Amendment guarantees the criminal defendant "the right . . . to be confronted with the witnesses against him." The text plainly envisions that witnesses against the accused shall, as a rule, testify in his presence. I can only marvel at the manner in which the Court avoids this manifest import of the Confrontation Clause. Without explanation, the Court narrows its analysis to address exclusively what is accurately identified as simply a primary interest the Clause was intended to secure: the right of cross-examination. This use of analytical blinders is undoubtedly convenient. Since respondent ultimately did receive an opportunity for full cross-examination of the witnesses in his presence, the narrowly drawn standard enables the Court to conclude with relative ease that respondent's confrontation rights were not violated, even though the in-chambers competency hearing admittedly was, in this case, a "crucial" phase of respondent's trial from which he was physically excluded.

Although cross-examination may be a primary means for ensuring the reliability of testimony from adverse witnesses, we have never held that standing alone it will suffice in every case. . . . Not until today has this Court gone so far as to substitute a defendant's subsequent opportunity for cross-examination for his right to confront adverse witnesses in a prior testimonial proceeding. . . . Though "confrontation means more than being allowed to confront the witness physically," it must by implication encompass the right of physical presence at any testimonial proceeding. As this Court has previously recognized, "it is this literal right to 'confront' the witness at the time of trial that forms the core of the values furthered by the Confrontation Clause," guaranteeing the accused an opportunity to compel the witness to meet him "face to face" before the trier of fact.

Physical presence of the defendant enhances the reliability of the factfinding process. Under Kentucky law, in a witness competency proceeding the trial judge must assess the witness' ability to observe and recollect facts with accuracy and with committed truthfulness. This determination necessarily requires the judge to make independent factual findings against which can be measured the accuracy of the witness' testimony at the competency proceeding, whether addressing facts such as the witness' name, age, and relation to the defendant, or events concerning the alleged offense itself. These findings are critical to the trial judge's assessment of the witness' competency to testify, and they often concern matters about which the defendant, and not his counsel, possesses the knowledge needed to expose inaccuracies in the witness' answers. Having the defendant present ensures that these inaccuracies are called to the judge's attention immediately — before the witness takes the stand with the trial court's imprimatur of competency and testifies in front of the jury as to the defendant's commission of the alleged offense. It is both functionally inefficient and fundamentally unfair to attribute to the defendant's attorney complete knowledge of the facts which the trial judge, in the defendant's involuntary absence, deems relevant to the competency determination. That determination, which turns entirely on the trial court's evaluation of the witness' statements, cannot be made out of the physical presence of the defendant without violating the basic guarantee of the Confrontation Clause:

> [A] fact which can be primarily established only by witnesses cannot be proved against an accused . . . except by witnesses who confront him at the trial, upon whom he can look while being tried, whom he is entitled to cross-examine, and whose testimony he may impeach in every mode authorized by the established rules governing the trial or conduct of criminal cases. The presumption of innocence of an accused attends him throughout the trial and has relation to every fact that must be established in order to prove his guilt beyond reasonable doubt.

But more than the reliability of the competency determination is at stake in this case . . . the constitutional guarantee of the right of confrontation serves certain "symbolic goals" as well:

> The right to confront and cross-examine adverse witnesses contributes to the establishment of a system of criminal justice in which the perception as well as the reality of fairness prevails. To foster such a system, the Constitution provides certain safeguards to promote to the greatest possible degree society's interest in having the accused and accuser engage in open and even contest in a public trial. The Confrontation Clause advances these goals by ensuring that convictions will not be based on the charges of unseen and unknown — and hence unchallengeable — individuals.

This appearance of fairness is woefully lacking in the present case. The Commonwealth did not request that respondent be excluded from the competency hearing. The trial judge raised this issue sua sponte, and only the personal protestations of respondent, a recent Cuban immigrant whose fluency in the English language was limited, preserved the issue for appeal. Neither the prosecuting attorney nor the trial judge articulated any reason for excluding him. From this defendant's perspective, the specter of the judge, prosecutor, and court-appointed attorney conferring privately with the key prosecution witnesses was understandably upsetting. From a constitutional perspective, the unrequested and unjustified exclusion constitutes an intolerable subversion of the symbolic functions of the Confrontation Clause.

Had respondent invoked his Sixth Amendment right of self-representation and appeared pro se, there would be little doubt that he would have been entitled to attend the competency hearing and cross-examine the child witnesses.

. . .

. . . Given these well-founded constitutional pronouncements, today's decision may create for the criminal defendant a difficult dilemma: a choice between continuing to exercise his right to assistance of counsel, thereby being excluded from the competency hearing, and appearing pro se so that he may be in attendance at this critical stage of his trial. This Court has on occasion held that a forced choice between two fundamental constitutional guarantees is untenable. . . . Today's decision neglects the serious question whether this choice is constitutionally defensible.

II

Respondent's right to be present at the competency hearing does not flow exclusively from the Sixth Amendment. The confrontation right attaches in this context because the competency proceeding was testimonial in nature. As the Court acknowledges, however, respondent also claims a right independently grounded in the Fourteenth Amendment's Due Process Clause to attend any trial proceeding in which his presence "has a relation, reasonably substantial, to the fulness of his opportunity to defend against the charge." That the competency hearing in this case bore a reasonably substantial relation to respondent's defense can hardly be doubted. As the Court correctly acknowledges, "although questions regarding the guilt or innocence of the defendant usually are not asked at a competency hearing, the hearing retains a direct relationship with the trial because it determines whether a key witness will testify."

Reviewing the transcript of the competency hearing, the Court concludes that respondent's due process rights were not violated because no question regarding the substantive testimony of the witnesses was asked and respondent has given no indication that his presence would have assisted in achieving more reliable competency determinations. But the propriety of the decision to exclude respondent from this critical stage of his trial should not be evaluated in light of what transpired in his absence. To do so transforms the issue from whether a due process violation has occurred into whether the violation was harmless. Neither issue was addressed by the court below. More importantly, however, the Court, unfairly shifts the burden of proving harm from this constitutional deprivation to the excluded criminal defendant, who was in no way responsible for the error and is least able to demonstrate what would have occurred had he been allowed to attend. The Fourteenth Amendment does not permit this presumption that the involuntary exclusion of a defendant from a critical stage of his trial is harmless.

I respectfully dissent.

Notes and Queries

1. The Court pays particular attention to the facts of the case in deciding the constitutional rule, when in other cases we have seen the facts of the particular case do not have such a dominant place in the opinion. By focusing on the facts, did the Court do disservice to the Constitution?

2. The Court emphasizes that the respondent gave no indication that his presence at the competency hearing in this case would have been useful in ensuring a more reliable determination as to whether the witnesses were competent to testify. If that is an issue, then does it not argue for his presence? How can an accused provide such evidence without knowing that it could be an issue in the first instance? Does this matter? Does the Court's approach, as the dissent points out, impermissibly shift the burden to prove innocence to the defendant (rather than the burden by the state to prove guilt)?

3. According to the Court, what dual purpose does the Constitution's Confrontation Clause serve?

Coy v. Iowa

487 U.S. 1012; 108 S. Ct. 2798 (1988)

Justice Scalia delivered the opinion of the Court.

Appellant was convicted of two counts of lascivious acts with a child after a jury trial in which a screen placed between him and the two complaining witnesses blocked him from their sight. Appellant contends that this procedure, authorized by state statute, violated his Sixth Amendment right to confront the witnesses against him.

I

In August 1985, appellant was arrested and charged with sexually assaulting two 13-year-old girls earlier that month while they were camping out in the backyard of the house next door to him. According to the girls, the assailant entered their tent after they were asleep wearing a stocking over his head, shined a flashlight in their eyes, and warned them not to look at him; neither was able to describe his face. In November 1985, at the beginning of appellant's trial, the State made a motion pursuant to a recently enacted statute to allow the complaining witnesses to testify either via closed-circuit television or behind a screen. The trial court approved the use of a large screen to be placed between appellant and the witness stand during the girls' testimony. After certain lighting adjustments in the courtroom, the screen would enable appellant dimly to perceive the witnesses, but the witnesses to see him not at all.

Appellant objected strenuously to use of the screen, based first of all on his Sixth Amendment confrontation right. He argued that, although the device might succeed in its apparent aim of making the complaining witnesses feel less uneasy in giving their testimony, the Confrontation Clause directly addressed this issue by giving criminal defendants a right to face-to-face confrontation. He also argued that his right to due process was violated, since the procedure would make him appear guilty and thus erode the presumption of innocence. The trial court rejected both constitutional claims, though it instructed the jury to draw no inference of guilt from the screen.

...

II

The Sixth Amendment gives a criminal defendant the right "to be confronted with the witnesses against him." ...

Most of this Court's encounters with the Confrontation Clause have involved either the admissibility of out-of-court statements, or restrictions on the scope of cross-examination. The reason for that is not, as the State suggests, that these elements are the essence of the Clause's protection — but rather, quite to the contrary, that there is at least some room for doubt (and hence litigation) as to the extent to which the Clause includes those elements, whereas, as Justice Harlan put it, "[s]imply as a matter of English" it confers at least "a right to meet face to face all those who appear and give evidence at trial." Simply as a matter of Latin as well, since the word "confront" ultimately derives from the prefix "con-" (from "contra" meaning "against" or "opposed") and the noun "frons" (forehead). Shakespeare was thus describing the root meaning of confrontation when he had Richard the Second say: "Then call them to our presence — face to face, and frowning brow to brow, ourselves will hear the accuser and the accused freely speak. . . ."

We have never doubted, therefore, that the Confrontation Clause guarantees the defendant a face-to-face meeting with witnesses appearing before the trier of fact. . . .

The Sixth Amendment's guarantee of face-to-face encounter between witness and accused serves ends related both to appearances and to reality. This opinion is embellished with references to and quotations from antiquity in part to convey that there is something deep in human nature that regards face-to-face confrontation between accused and accuser as "essential to a fair trial in a criminal prosecution." What was true of old is no less true in modern times. President Eisenhower once described face-to-face confrontation as part of the code of his hometown of Abilene, Kansas. In Abilene, he said, it was necessary to "[m]eet anyone face to face with whom you disagree. You could not sneak up on him from behind, or do any damage to him, without suffering the penalty of an outraged citizenry. . . . In this country, if someone dislikes you, or accuses you, he must come up in front. He cannot hide behind the shadow." The phrase still persists, "Look me in the eye and say that." Given these human feelings of what is necessary for fairness, the right of confrontation "contributes to the establishment of a system of criminal justice in which the perception as well as the reality of fairness prevails."

The perception that confrontation is essential to fairness has persisted over the centuries because there is much truth to it. A witness "may feel quite differently when he has to repeat his story looking at the man whom he will harm greatly by distorting or mistaking the facts. He can now understand what sort of human being that man is." It is always more difficult to tell a lie about a person "to his face" than "behind his back." In the former context, even if the lie is told, it will often be told less convincingly. The Confrontation Clause does not, of course, compel the witness to fix his eyes upon the defendant; he may studiously look elsewhere, but the trier of fact will draw its own conclusions. Thus the right to face-to-face confrontation serves much the same purpose as a less explicit component of the Confrontation Clause that we have had more frequent occasion to discuss — the right to cross-examine the accuser; both "ensur[e] the integrity of the factfinding process." The State can hardly gainsay the profound effect upon a witness of standing in the presence of the person the witness accuses, since that is the very phenomenon it relies upon to establish the potential "trauma" that allegedly justified the extraordinary procedure in the present case. That face-to-face presence may, unfortunately, upset the truthful rape victim or abused child; but by the same token it may confound and undo the false accuser, or reveal the child coached by a malevolent adult. It is a truism that constitutional protections have costs.

III

The remaining question is whether the right to confrontation was in fact violated in this case. The screen at issue was specifically designed to enable the complaining witnesses to avoid viewing appellant as they gave their testimony, and the record indicates that it was successful in this objective. It is difficult to imagine a more obvious or damaging violation of the defendant's right to a face-to-face encounter.

The State suggests that the confrontation interest at stake here was outweighed by the necessity of protecting victims of sexual abuse. It is true that we have in the past indicated that rights conferred by the Confrontation Clause are not absolute, and may give way to other important interests. The rights referred to in those cases, however, were not the right narrowly and explicitly set forth in the Clause, but rather rights that are, or were asserted to be, reasonably implicit — namely, the right to cross-examine; the right to exclude out-of-court statements and the asserted right to face-to-face confrontation at some point in the proceedings other than the trial itself. To hold that our determination of what implications are reasonable must take into account other important interests is not the same as holding that we can identify exceptions, in light of other important interests, to the irreducible literal meaning of the Clause: "a right to meet face to face all those who appear and give evidence at trial." We leave for another day, however, the question whether any exceptions exist. Whatever they may be, they would surely be allowed only when necessary to further an important public policy. The State maintains that such necessity is established here by the statute, which creates a legislatively imposed presumption of trauma. Our cases suggest, however, that even as to exceptions from the normal implications of the Confrontation Clause, as opposed to its most literal application, something more than the type of generalized finding underlying such a statute is needed when the exception is not "firmly . . .

rooted in our jurisprudence." The exception created by the Iowa statute, which was passed in 1985, could hardly be viewed as firmly rooted. Since there have been no individualized findings that these particular witnesses needed special protection, the judgment here could not be sustained by any conceivable exception.

The State also briefly suggests that any Confrontation Clause error was harmless beyond a reasonable doubt. . . . We have recognized that other types of violations of the Confrontation Clause are subject to that harmless-error analysis and see no reason why denial of face-to-face confrontation should not be treated the same. An assessment of harmlessness cannot include consideration of whether the witness' testimony would have been unchanged, or the jury's assessment unaltered, had there been confrontation; such an inquiry would obviously involve pure speculation, and harmlessness must therefore be determined on the basis of the remaining evidence. The Iowa Supreme Court had no occasion to address the harmlessness issue, since it found no constitutional violation. In the circumstances of this case, rather than decide whether the error was harmless beyond a reasonable doubt, we leave the issue for the court below.

We find it unnecessary to reach appellant's due process claim. Since his constitutional right to face-to-face confrontation was violated, we reverse the judgment of the Iowa Supreme Court and remand the case for further proceedings not inconsistent with this opinion.

It is so ordered.

Justice O'Connor, with whom Justice White joins, concurring.

I agree with the Court that appellant's rights under the Confrontation Clause were violated in this case. I write separately only to note my view that those rights are not absolute but rather may give way in an appropriate case to other competing interests so as to permit the use of certain procedural devices designed to shield a child witness from the trauma of courtroom testimony.

Child abuse is a problem of disturbing proportions in today's society. Just last Term, we recognized that "[c]hild abuse is one of the most difficult problems to detect and prosecute, in large part because there often are no witnesses except the victim." Once an instance of abuse is identified and prosecution undertaken, new difficulties arise. Many States have determined that a child victim may suffer trauma from exposure to the harsh atmosphere of the typical courtroom and have undertaken to shield the child through a variety of ameliorative measures. We deal today with the constitutional ramifications of only one such measure, but we do so against a broader backdrop. Iowa appears to be the only State authorizing the type of screen used in this case. A full half of the States, however, have authorized the use of one- or two-way closed-circuit television. Statutes sanctioning one-way systems generally permit the child to testify in a separate room in which only the judge, counsel, technicians, and in some cases the defendant, are present. The child's testimony is broadcast into the courtroom for viewing by the jury. Two-way systems permit the child witness to see the courtroom and the defendant over a video monitor. In addition to such closed-circuit television procedures, 33 States (including 19 of the 25 authorizing closed-circuit television) permit the use of videotaped testimony, which typically is taken in the defendant's presence.

While I agree with the Court that the Confrontation Clause was violated in this case, I wish to make clear that nothing in today's decision necessarily dooms such efforts by state legislatures to protect child witnesses. Initially, many such procedures may raise no substantial Confrontation Clause problem since they involve testimony in the presence of the defendant. . . .

Thus, I would permit use of a particular trial procedure that called for something other than face-to-face confrontation if that procedure was necessary to further an important public policy. The protection of child witnesses is, in my view and in the view of a substantial majority of the States, just such a policy. The primary focus therefore likely will be on the necessity prong. I agree with the Court that more than the type of generalized legislative finding of necessity present here is required. But if a court makes a case-specific finding of necessity, our cases suggest that the strictures of the Confrontation Clause may give way to the compelling state interest of protecting child witnesses. Because nothing in the Court's opinion conflicts with this approach and this conclusion, I join it.

Justice Blackmun, with whom The Chief Justice joins, dissenting.

. . .

Two witnesses against appellant in this case were the 13-year-old girls he was accused of sexually assaulting. During their testimony, as permitted by a state statute, a one-way screening device was placed between the girls and appellant, blocking the man accused of sexually assaulting them from the girls' line of vision. This procedure did not interfere with what this Court previously has recognized as the "purposes of confrontation." Specifically, the girls' testimony was given under oath, was subject to unrestricted cross-examination, and "the jury that [was] to decide the defendant's fate [could] observe the demeanor of the witness[es] in making [their] statement[s], thus aiding the jury in assessing [their] credibility." In addition, the screen did not prevent appellant from seeing and hearing the girls and conferring with counsel during their testimony, did not prevent the girls from seeing and being seen by the judge and counsel, as well as by the jury, and did not prevent the jury from seeing the demeanor of the defendant while the girls testified. Finally, the girls were informed that appellant could see and hear them while they were on the stand. Thus, appellant's sole complaint is the very narrow objection that the girls could not see him while they testified about the sexual assault they endured.

. . . [T]he minimal extent of the infringement on appellant's Confrontation Clause interests is relevant in considering whether competing public policies justify the procedures employed in this case. . . . I fear that the Court's apparent fascination with the witness' ability to see the defendant will lead the States that are attempting to adopt innovations to facilitate the testimony of child victims of sex abuse to sacrifice other, more central, confrontation interests, such as the right to cross-examination or to have the trier of fact observe the testifying witness.

The weakness of the Court's support for its characterization of appellant's claim as involving "the irreducible literal meaning of the Clause" is reflected in its reliance on literature, anecdote, and dicta from opinions that a majority of this Court did not join. . . .

. . .

Indisputably, the state interests behind the Iowa statute are of considerable importance. . . .

Thus, the fear and trauma associated with a child's testimony in front of the defendant have two serious identifiable consequences: They may cause psychological injury to the child, and they may so overwhelm the child as to prevent the possibility of effective testimony, thereby undermining the truth-finding function of the trial itself. Because of these effects, I agree with the concurring opinion that a State properly may consider the protection of child witnesses to be an important public policy. In my view, this important public policy, embodied in the Iowa statute that authorized the use of the screening device, outweighs the narrow Confrontation Clause right at issue here — the "preference" for having the defendant within the witness' sight while the witness testifies.

Appellant argues, and the Court concludes that even if a societal interest can justify a restriction on a child witness' ability to see the defendant while the child testifies, the State must show in each case that such a procedure is essential to protect the child's welfare. I disagree. As the many rules allowing the admission of out-of-court statements demonstrate, legislative exceptions to the Confrontation Clause of general applicability are commonplace. . . .

For these reasons, I do not believe that the procedures used in this case violated appellant's rights under the Confrontation Clause.

II

Appellant also argues that the use of the screening device was "inherently prejudicial" and therefore violated his right to due process of law. . . .

. . .

During the girls' testimony, the screening device was placed in front of the defendant. In order for the device to function properly, it was necessary to dim the normal courtroom lights and focus a panel of bright lights directly on the screen, creating, in the trial judge's words, "sort of a dramatic emphasis" and a potentially "eerie" effect. Appellant argues that the use of the device was inherently prejudicial because it indicated to the jury that appellant was guilty. I am unpersuaded by this argument.

Unlike clothing the defendant in prison garb or having the defendant shackled and gagged, using the screening device did not "brand [appellant] . . . 'with an unmistakable mark of guilt.'" A screen is not the sort of trapping that generally is associated with those who have been convicted. It is therefore unlikely that the use of the screen had a subconscious effect on the jury's attitude toward appellant.

In addition, the trial court instructed the jury to draw no inference from the device:

. . .

Given this helpful instruction, I doubt that the jury—which we must assume to have been intelligent and capable of following instructions—drew an improper inference from the screen, and I do not see that its use was inherently prejudicial. After all, "every practice tending to single out the accused from everyone else in the courtroom [need not] be struck down."

I would affirm the judgment of conviction.

Notes and Queries

1. If you were a member of the jury, do you think a screen would prejudice you against the defendant?
2. Do you think that the "helpful instruction" to the jury cures potential prejudices?
3. Assuming that the statute in question did allow for more particularized findings that specific child witnesses needed protection, would the standard survive? What standard would you propose?

Maryland v. Craig

497 U.S. 836; 110 S. Ct. 3157 (1990)

Justice O'Connor delivered the opinion of the Court.

This case requires us to decide whether the Confrontation Clause of the Sixth Amendment categorically prohibits a child witness in a child abuse case from testifying against a defendant at trial, outside the defendant's physical presence, by one-way closed circuit television.

I

In October 1986, a Howard County grand jury charged respondent, Sandra Ann Craig, with child abuse, first and second degree sexual offenses, perverted sexual practice, assault, and battery. The named victim in each count was a 6-year-old girl who, from August 1984 to June 1986, had attended a kindergarten and prekindergarten center owned and operated by Craig.

In March 1987, before the case went to trial, the State sought to invoke a Maryland statutory procedure that permits a judge to receive, by one-way closed circuit television, the testimony of a child witness who is alleged to be a victim of child abuse. To invoke the procedure, the trial judge must first "determine that testimony by the child victim in the courtroom will result in the child suffering serious emotional distress such that the child cannot reasonably communicate." Once the procedure is invoked, the child witness, prosecutor, and defense counsel withdraw to a separate room; the judge, jury, and defendant remain in the courtroom. The child witness is then examined and cross-examined in the separate room, while a video monitor records and displays the witness' testimony to those in the courtroom. During this time the witness cannot see the defendant. The defendant remains in electronic communication with defense counsel, and objections may be made and ruled on as if the witness were testifying in the courtroom.

In support of its motion invoking the one-way closed circuit television procedure, the State presented expert testimony that the named victim, as well as a number of other children who were alleged to have been sexually abused by Craig, would suffer "serious emotional distress such that [they could not] reasonably communicate," §9-102(a)(1)(ii), if required to testify in the courtroom. The Maryland Court of Appeals characterized the evidence as follows:

> The expert testimony in each case suggested that each child would have some or considerable difficulty in testifying in Craig's presence. For example, as to one child, the expert said that what 'would cause him the most anxiety would be to testify in front of Mrs. Craig. . . .' The child 'wouldn't be able to communicate effectively.' As to another, an expert said she 'would probably stop talking and she would withdraw and curl up.' With respect to two others, the testimony was that one would 'become highly agitated, that he may refuse to talk or if he did talk, that he would choose his subject regardless of the questions' while the other would 'become extremely timid and unwilling to talk.'

Craig objected to the use of the procedure on Confrontation Clause grounds, but the trial court rejected that contention, concluding that although the statute "take[s] away the right of the defendant to be face to face with his or her accuser," the defendant retains the "essence of the right of confrontation," including the right to observe, cross-examine, and have the jury view the demeanor of the witness. The trial court further found that, "based upon the evidence presented . . . the testimony of each of these children in a courtroom will result in each child suffering serious emotional distress . . . such that each of these children cannot reasonably communicate." The trial court then found the named victim and three other children competent to testify and accordingly permitted them to testify against Craig via the one-way closed circuit television procedure. The jury convicted Craig on all counts, and the Maryland Court of Special Appeals affirmed the convictions.

The Court of Appeals of Maryland reversed and remanded for a new trial.

. . .

We granted certiorari to resolve the important Confrontation Clause issues raised by this case.

II

The Confrontation Clause of the Sixth Amendment, made applicable to the States through the Fourteenth Amendment, provides: "In all criminal prosecutions, the accused shall enjoy the right ... to be confronted with the witnesses against him."

...

We have never held, however, that the Confrontation Clause guarantees criminal defendants the absolute right to a face-to-face meeting with witnesses against them at trial. Indeed, in *Coy v. Iowa*, we expressly "left for another day ... the question whether any exceptions exist" to the "irreducible literal meaning of the Clause: 'a right to meet face to face all those who appear and give evidence at trial.'" ... Because the trial court in this case made individualized findings that each of the child witnesses needed special protection, this case requires us to decide the question reserved in *Coy*.

The central concern of the Confrontation Clause is to ensure the reliability of the evidence against a criminal defendant by subjecting it to rigorous testing in the context of an adversary proceeding before the trier of fact. The word "confront," after all, also means a clashing of forces or ideas, thus carrying with it the notion of adversariness.... [T]he right guaranteed by the Confrontation Clause includes not only a "personal examination," but also "(1) insures that the witness will give his statements under oath—thus impressing him with the seriousness of the matter and guarding against the lie by the possibility of a penalty for perjury; (2) forces the witness to submit to cross-examination, the 'greatest legal engine ever invented for the discovery of truth'; [and] (3) permits the jury that is to decide the defendant's fate to observe the demeanor of the witness in making his statement, thus aiding the jury in assessing his credibility."

The combined effect of these elements of confrontation—physical presence, oath, cross-examination, and observation of demeanor by the trier of fact—serves the purposes of the Confrontation Clause by ensuring that evidence admitted against an accused is reliable and subject to the rigorous adversarial testing that is the norm of Anglo-American criminal proceedings.

...

... we have never insisted on an actual face-to-face encounter at trial in every instance in which testimony is admitted against a defendant. Instead, we have repeatedly held that the Clause permits, where necessary, the admission of certain hearsay statements against a defendant despite the defendant's inability to confront the declarant at trial....

...

That the face-to-face confrontation requirement is not absolute does not, of course, mean that it may easily be dispensed with. As we suggested in *Coy*, our precedents confirm that a defendant's right to confront accusatory witnesses may be satisfied absent a physical, face-to-face confrontation at trial only where denial of such confrontation is necessary to further an important public policy and only where the reliability of the testimony is otherwise assured.

III

Maryland's statutory procedure, when invoked, prevents a child witness from seeing the defendant as he or she testifies against the defendant at trial. We find it significant, however, that Maryland's procedure preserves all of the other elements of the confrontation right: The child witness must be competent to testify and must testify under oath; the defendant retains full opportunity for contemporaneous cross-examination; and the judge, jury, and defendant are able to view (albeit by video monitor) the demeanor (and body) of the witness as he or she testifies. Although we are mindful of the many subtle effects face-to-face confrontation may have on an adversary criminal proceeding, the presence of these other elements of confrontation — oath, cross-examination, and observation of the witness' demeanor — adequately ensures that the testimony is both reliable and subject to rigorous adversarial testing in a manner functionally equivalent to that accorded live, in-person testimony. These safeguards of reliability and adversariness render the use of such a procedure a far cry from the undisputed prohibition of the Confrontation Clause: trial by ex parte affidavit or inquisition. Rather, we think these elements of effective confrontation not only permit a defendant to "confound and undo the false accuser, or reveal the child coached by a malevolent adult," but may well aid a defendant in eliciting favorable testimony from the child witness. Indeed, to the extent the child witness' testimony may be said to be technically given out of court (though we do not so hold), these assurances of reliability and adversariness are far greater than those required for admission of hearsay testimony under the Confrontation Clause. We are therefore confident that use of the one-way closed circuit television procedure, where necessary to further an important state interest, does not impinge upon the truth-seeking or symbolic purposes of the Confrontation Clause.

The critical inquiry in this case, therefore, is whether use of the procedure is necessary to further an important state interest. The State contends that it has a substantial interest in protecting children who are allegedly victims of child abuse from the trauma of testifying against the alleged perpetrator and that its statutory procedure for receiving testimony from such witnesses is necessary to further that interest.

We have of course recognized that a State's interest in "the protection of minor victims of sex crimes from further trauma and embarrassment" is a "compelling" one....

We likewise conclude today that a State's interest in the physical and psychological well-being of child abuse victims may be sufficiently important to outweigh, at least in some cases, a defendant's right to face his or her accusers in court....

The statute at issue in this case, for example, was specifically intended "to safeguard the physical and psychological well-being of child victims by avoiding, or at least minimizing, the emotional trauma produced by testifying." ...

Given the State's traditional and "'transcendent interest in protecting the welfare of children,'" and buttressed by the growing body of academic literature documenting the psychological trauma suffered by child abuse victims who must testify in court, we will not second-guess the considered judgment of the Maryland Legislature regarding the importance of its interest in protecting child abuse victims from the emotional trauma of testifying. Accordingly, we hold that, if the State makes an adequate showing of necessity, the state interest in protecting child witnesses from the trauma of testifying in a child abuse case is sufficiently important to justify the use of a special procedure that permits a child witness in such cases to testify at trial against a defendant in the absence of face-to-face confrontation with the defendant.

The requisite finding of necessity must of course be a case-specific one: The trial court must hear evidence and determine whether use of the one-way closed circuit television procedure is necessary to protect the welfare of the particular child witness who seeks to testify. The trial court must also find that the child witness would be traumatized, not by the courtroom generally, but by the presence of the defendant. Denial of face-to-face confrontation is not needed to further the state interest in protecting the child witness from trauma unless it is the presence of the defendant that causes the trauma. In other words, if the state interest were merely the interest in protecting child witnesses from courtroom trauma generally, denial of face-to-face confrontation would be unnecessary because the child could be permitted to testify in less intimidating surroundings, albeit with the defendant present. Finally, the trial court must find that the emotional distress suffered by the child witness in the presence of the defendant is more than de minimis, i.e., more than "mere nervousness or excitement or some reluctance to testify." We need not decide the minimum showing of emotional trauma required for use of the special procedure, however, because the Maryland statute, which requires a determination that the child witness will suffer "serious emotional distress such that the child cannot reasonably communicate" clearly suffices to meet constitutional standards.

. . .

In sum, we conclude that where necessary to protect a child witness from trauma that would be caused by testifying in the physical presence of the defendant, at least where such trauma would impair the child's ability to communicate, the Confrontation Clause does not prohibit use of a procedure that, despite the absence of face-to-face confrontation, ensures the reliability of the evidence by subjecting it to rigorous adversarial testing and thereby preserves the essence of effective confrontation. . . .

IV

The Maryland Court of Appeals held, as we do today, that although face-to-face confrontation is not an absolute constitutional requirement, it may be abridged only where there is a "'case-specific finding of necessity.'" Given this latter requirement, the Court of Appeals reasoned that "the question of whether a child is unavailable to testify . . . should not be asked in terms of inability to testify in the ordinary courtroom setting, but in the much narrower terms of the witness's inability to testify in the presence of the accused." "The determinative inquiry required to preclude face-to-face confrontation is the effect of the presence of the defendant on the witness or the witness's testimony." The Court of Appeals accordingly concluded that, as a prerequisite to use of the procedure, the Confrontation Clause requires the trial court to make a specific finding that testimony by the child in the courtroom in the presence of the defendant would result in the child suffering serious emotional distress such that the child could not reasonably communicate. This conclusion, of course, is consistent with our holding today.

In addition, however, the Court of Appeals interpreted our decision in *Coy* to impose two subsidiary requirements. First, the court held that "ordinarily cannot be invoked unless the child witness initially is questioned (either in or outside the courtroom) in the defendant's presence." Second, the court asserted that, before using the one-way television procedure, a trial judge must determine whether a child would suffer "severe emotional distress" if he or she were to testify by two-way closed circuit television.

Reviewing the evidence presented to the trial court in support of the finding required under § 9-102(a)(1)(ii), the Court of Appeals determined that "the finding of necessity required to limit the defendant's right of confrontation through invocation of § 9-102 . . . was not made here." The Court of Appeals noted that the trial judge "had the benefit only of expert testimony on the ability of the children to communicate; he did not question any of the children himself, nor did he observe any child's behavior on the witness stand before making his ruling. He did not explore any alternatives to the use of one-way closed-circuit television." The Court of Appeals also observed that "the testimony in this case was not sharply focused on the effect of the defendant's presence on the child witnesses."

. . .

The Court of Appeals appears to have rested its conclusion at least in part on the trial court's failure to observe the children's behavior in the defendant's presence and its failure to explore less restrictive alternatives to the use of the one-way closed circuit television procedure. Although we think such evidentiary requirements could strengthen the grounds for use of protective measures, we decline to establish, as a matter of federal constitutional law, any such categorical evidentiary prerequisites for the use of the one-way television procedure. The trial court in this case, for example, could well have found, on the basis of the expert testimony before it, that testimony by the child witnesses in the courtroom in the defendant's presence "will result in [each] child suffering serious emotional distress such that the child cannot reasonably communicate." So long as a trial court makes such a case-specific finding of necessity, the Confrontation Clause does not prohibit a State from using a one-way closed circuit television procedure for the receipt of testimony by a child witness in a child abuse case. Because the Court of Appeals held that the trial court had not made the requisite finding of necessity under its interpretation of "the high threshold required by [*Coy*] before § 9-102 may be invoked," we cannot be certain whether the Court of Appeals would reach the same conclusion in light of the legal standard we establish today. We therefore vacate the judgment of the Court of Appeals of Maryland and remand the case for further proceedings not inconsistent with this opinion.

It is so ordered.

Justice Scalia, with whom Justice Brennan, Justice Marshall, and Justice Stevens join, dissenting.

Seldom has this Court failed so conspicuously to sustain a categorical guarantee of the Constitution against the tide of prevailing current opinion. The Sixth Amendment provides, with unmistakable clarity, that "in all criminal prosecutions, the accused shall enjoy the right . . . to be confronted with the witnesses against him." The purpose of enshrining this protection in the Constitution was to assure that none of the many policy interests from time to time pursued by statutory law could overcome a defendant's right to face his or her accusers in court. . . .

Because of this subordination of explicit constitutional text to currently favored public policy, the following scene can be played out in an American courtroom for the first time in two centuries: A father whose young daughter has been given over to the exclusive custody of his estranged wife, or a mother whose young son has been taken into custody by the State's child welfare department, is sentenced to prison for sexual abuse on the basis of testimony by a child the parent has not seen or spoken to for many months; and the guilty verdict is rendered without giving the parent so much as the opportunity to sit in the presence of the child, and to ask, personally or through counsel, "it is really not true, is it, that I — your father (or mother) whom you see before you — did these terrible things?" Perhaps that is a procedure today's society desires; perhaps (though I doubt it) it is even a fair procedure; but it is assuredly not a procedure permitted by the Constitution.

Because the text of the Sixth Amendment is clear, and because the Constitution is meant to protect against, rather than conform to, current "widespread belief," I respectfully dissent.

I

According to the Court, "we cannot say that [face-to-face] confrontation [with witnesses appearing at trial] is an indispensable element of the Sixth Amendment's guarantee of the right to confront one's accusers." That is rather like saying "we cannot say that being tried before a jury is an indispensable element of the Sixth Amendment's guarantee of the right to jury trial." The Court makes the impossible plausible by recharacterizing the Confrontation Clause, so that confrontation (redesignated "face-to-face confrontation") becomes only one of many "elements of confrontation." The reasoning is as follows: The Confrontation Clause guarantees not only what it explicitly provides for — "face-to-face" confrontation — but also implied and collateral rights such as cross-examination, oath, and observation of demeanor (TRUE); the purpose of this entire cluster of rights is to ensure the reliability of evidence (TRUE);

the Maryland procedure preserves the implied and collateral rights (TRUE), which adequately ensure the reliability of evidence (perhaps TRUE); therefore the Confrontation Clause is not violated by denying what it explicitly provides for—"face-to-face" confrontation (unquestionably FALSE). This reasoning abstracts from the right to its purposes, and then eliminates the right. It is wrong because the Confrontation Clause does not guarantee reliable evidence; it guarantees specific trial procedures that were thought to assure reliable evidence, undeniably among which was "face-to-face" confrontation. Whatever else it may mean in addition, the defendant's constitutional right "to be confronted with the witnesses against him" means, always and everywhere, at least what it explicitly says: the "'right to meet face to face all those who appear and give evidence at trial.'"

The Court supports its antitextual conclusion by cobbling together scraps of dicta from various cases that have no bearing here....

... But we are not talking here about denying expansive scope to a Sixth Amendment provision whose scope for the purpose at issue is textually unclear; "to confront" plainly means to encounter face to face, whatever else it may mean in addition. And we are not talking about the manner of arranging that face-to-face encounter, but about whether it shall occur at all. The "necessities of trial and the adversary process" are irrelevant here, since they cannot alter the constitutional text.

II

...

The Court's test today requires unavailability only in the sense that the child is unable to testify in the presence of the defendant. That cannot possibly be the relevant sense. If unconfronted testimony is admissible hearsay when the witness is unable to confront the defendant, then presumably there are other categories of admissible hearsay consisting of unsworn testimony when the witness is unable to risk perjury, un-cross-examined testimony when the witness is unable to undergo hostile questioning, etc., *California v. Green* (1970), is not precedent for such a silly system. That case held that the Confrontation Clause does not bar admission of prior testimony when the declarant is sworn as a witness but refuses to answer. But in *Green*, as in most cases of refusal, we could not know why the declarant refused to testify. Here, by contrast, we know that it is precisely because the child is unwilling to testify in the presence of the defendant. That unwillingness cannot be a valid excuse under the Confrontation Clause, whose very object is to place the witness under the sometimes hostile glare of the defendant. "That face-to-face presence may, unfortunately, upset the truthful rape victim or abused child; but by the same token it may confound and undo the false accuser, or reveal the child coached by a malevolent adult." To say that a defendant loses his right to confront a witness when that would cause the witness not to testify is rather like saying that the defendant loses his right to counsel when counsel would save him, or his right to subpoena witnesses when they would exculpate him, or his right not to give testimony against himself when that would prove him guilty.

III

The Court characterizes the State's interest which "outweigh[s]" the explicit text of the Constitution as an "interest in the physical and psychological well-being of child abuse victims," an "interest in protecting" such victims "from the emotional trauma of testifying." That is not so. A child who meets the Maryland statute's requirement of suffering such "serious emotional distress" from confrontation that he "cannot reasonably communicate" would seem entirely safe. Why would a prosecutor want to call a witness who cannot reasonably communicate? And if he did, it would be the State's own fault. Protection of the child's interest—as far as the Confrontation Clause is concerned—is entirely within Maryland's control. The State's interest here is in fact no more and no less than what the State's interest always is when it seeks to get a class of evidence admitted in criminal proceedings: more convictions of guilty defendants. That is not an unworthy interest, but it should not be dressed up as a humanitarian one.

And the interest on the other side is also what it usually is when the State seeks to get a new class of evidence admitted: fewer convictions of innocent defendants—specifically, in the present context, innocent defendants accused of particularly heinous crimes. The "special" reasons that exist for suspending one of the usual guarantees of reliability in the case of children's testimony are perhaps matched by "special" reasons for being particularly insistent upon it in the case of children's testimony. Some studies show that children are substantially more vulnerable to suggestion than adults, and often unable to separate recollected fantasy (or suggestion) from reality. The injustice their erroneous testimony can produce is evidenced by the tragic Scott County investigations of 1983–1984, which disrupted the lives of many (as far as we know) innocent people in the small town of Jordan, Minnesota. At one stage those investigations were pursuing allegations by at least eight children of multiple murders, but the prosecutions actually initiated charged only sexual abuse. Specifically, 24 adults were charged with molesting 37 children. In the course of the investigations, 25 children were placed in foster homes. Of the 24 indicted defendants, one pleaded guilty, two were acquitted at trial, and the charges against the remaining 21 were voluntarily dismissed. There is no doubt that some sexual abuse took place in Jordan; but there is no reason to believe it was as widespread as charged.... The value of the confrontation right in guarding against a child's distorted or coerced recollections is dramatically evident with respect to one of the misguided investigative techniques the report cited: some children were told by their foster parents that reunion with their real parents would be hastened by "admission" of their parents' abuse. Is it difficult to imagine how unconvincing such a testimonial admission might be to a jury that witnessed the child's delight at seeing his parents in the courtroom? Or how devastating it might be if, pursuant to a psychiatric evaluation that "trauma would impair the child's ability to communicate" in front of his parents, the child were permitted to tell his story to the jury on closed-circuit television?

In the last analysis, however, this debate is not an appropriate one. I have no need to defend the value of confrontation, because the Court has no authority to question it. It is not within our charge to speculate that, "where face-to-face confrontation causes significant emotional distress in a child witness," confrontation might "in fact disserve the Confrontation Clause's truth-seeking goal." If so, that is a defect in the Constitution—which should be amended by the procedures provided for such an eventuality, but cannot be corrected by judicial pronouncement that it is archaic, contrary to "widespread belief," and thus null and void. For good or bad, the Sixth Amendment requires confrontation, and we are not at liberty to ignore it. To quote the document one last time (for it plainly says all that need be said): "In all criminal prosecutions, the accused shall enjoy the right . . . to be confronted with the witnesses against him."

The Court today has applied "interest-balancing" analysis where the text of the Constitution simply does not permit it. We are not free to conduct a cost-benefit analysis of clear and explicit constitutional guarantees, and then to adjust their meaning to comport with our findings. The Court has convincingly proved that the Maryland procedure serves a valid interest, and gives the defendant virtually everything the Confrontation Clause guarantees (everything, that is, except confrontation). I am persuaded, therefore, that the Maryland procedure is virtually constitutional. Since it is not, however, actually constitutional I would affirm the judgment of the Maryland Court of Appeals reversing the judgment of conviction.

Notes and Queries

1. The Court finds the child's testimony permissible given that it may be both reliable and subject to adversarial processes. Is that really true? What symbolic purposes of the Confrontation Clause protections are lost?
2. The Maryland statute requires that the child be questioned, either in or outside of the courtroom, in the defendant's presence before determining whether the closed-circuit television can be used. Why require that? Why not just wait and have the child testify before a jury?
3. The Supreme Court only requires that the trial judge make a case-specific finding of necessity. The trial judge may rely on an expert or conduct the inquiry herself. Would you encourage one approach over the other?
4. Does Justice Scalia have a more persuasive argument? Should a parent, with all the rights that they have over their children, have a right to sit in front of the child and ask her to tell the truth?
5. The dissent notes that the majority inappropriately places the interest of child protection ahead of a defendant's interests. Do you agree?

6. The American Psychological Association provided a brief noting that the presence of a defendant makes many children less communicative and less accurate witnesses. See Gail S. Goodman, Murray Levine, Gary B. Melton & David W. Ogden (1991). Child witnesses and the Confrontation Clause: The American Psychological Association brief in *Maryland v. Craig*. *Law & Human Behavior*, 15, 13–29. If that is so, are defendant's rights really infringed by means aimed to protect children from emotional distress in courts?

7. Do you find persuasive the argument that children need special accommodations because they would otherwise refuse to testify, or testify less completely, because they fear the defendant? What do you think about the underlying assumptions about the fears children may have? Would you find that the assumption that the fear is caused by the child's having been abused by the defendant inappropriately assumes guilt and violates the presumption of innocence? Fear may come from many sources. It could be argued that a child witness, in the interim between an accusation and testimony, may have been taught by adults to fear the accused. Fear also may have resulted from others repeatedly telling a child that the accused is bad and is to be feared. Are these possibilities enough to reject efforts to reduce the child's fears in court? For criticisms of the Court's assumptions, see Ralph Underwager & Hollida Wakefield (1992). Poor psychology produces poor law. *Law & Human Behavior*, 16, 233–243.

Research Comment

1. Although *Coy v. Iowa* and *Maryland v. Craig* allow us to shield child witnesses, whether we should do so remains complicated. Shielding appears not to affect the verdict in most mock trial studies. Likewise, shielded testimony may not be inherently less reliable, if we define it in terms of accuracy and honesty. Gail S. Goodman, Ann E. Tobey, Jennifer M. Batterman-Faunce, Holly Orcutt, Sherry Thomas, Cheryl Shapiro & Toby Sachsenmaier (1998). Face-to-face confrontation: Effects of closed-circuit technology on children's eyewitness testimony and jurors' decisions. *Law & Human Behavior*, 22, 165–203. But shielding a child witness from the rigors of confrontation may permit jurors to discount the child more easily or to take the child's story less seriously. See Ann E. Tobey, Gail S. Goodman, Jennifer M. Batterman-Faunce, Holly Orcutt & Toby Sachsenmaier (1995). Balancing the rights of children and defendants: Effects of closed-circuit television on children's accuracy and jurors' perceptions. In Maria S. Zaragoza, John R. Graham, Richard Hirschman & Yoseff S. Ben-Porath (Eds.). *Memory and Testimony in the Child Witness* (pp. 214–239). Thousand Oaks, CA: Sage. What do you make of this evidence?

Review Problem

1. James Danner was found guilty of raping and sodomizing his daughter, now 15 years old. The trial court conducted the following inquiry:

> Q. Why is it that him being there in the room would make you unable to tell your side?
>
> A. I don't know. I just can't. I just can't be near him.
>
> Q. We've already talked about that you're not afraid of him, are you?
>
> A. No.
>
> Q. I know it's difficult to exactly put a finger on what it is about; but why do you think that you could tell when he's not in the room but you couldn't tell it with him in the room?
>
> A. I don't know. I just can't be near him. I don't know why. I just can't.
>
> Q. Do you think that if you were to try and you know if we had to take breaks or something, you would be able to do it?
>
> A. I don't know.

The trial court found, and the Kentucky Supreme Court affirmed, the following reasoning:

> The court finds that due to factors which I cannot define but yet go much further than anxiety or nervousness, as referred to the various cases that have been cited, that compelling need exists for the use of the electronic equipment. And although I am not making this decision simply for the witnesses [sic] convenience, or to prevent her from being nervous or anxious, as that no doubt happens to all witnesses, the Court is convinced that due to the nature of [the] testimony and the age of the witness that face-to-face arrangement would inhibit the witness to a degree that the jury's search for the truth would be clouded.

Danner v. Kentucky, 525 U.S. 1010 (1998). *cert denied*, Scalia, with whom Thomas joined, dissenting. Do you agree with the trial court's ruling?

Globe Newspaper Co. v. Superior Court

457 U.S. 596; 102 S. Ct. 2613 (1982)

Justice Brennan delivered the opinion of the Court.

Section 16A of Chapter 278 of the Massachusetts General Laws, as construed by the Massachusetts Supreme Judicial Court, requires trial judges, at trials for specified sexual offenses involving a victim under the age of 18, to exclude the press and general public from the courtroom during the testimony of that victim. The question presented is whether the statute thus construed violates the First Amendment as applied to the States through the Fourteenth Amendment.

The case began when appellant, Globe Newspaper Co. (Globe), unsuccessfully attempted to gain access to a rape trial conducted in the Superior Court for the County of Norfolk, Commonwealth of Massachusetts. The criminal defendant in that trial had been charged with the forcible rape and forced unnatural rape of three girls who were minors at the time of trial—two 16 years of age and one 17. In April 1979, during hearings on several preliminary motions, the trial judge ordered the courtroom closed. Before the trial began, Globe moved that the court revoke this closure order, hold hearings on any future such orders, and permit appellant to intervene "for the limited purpose of asserting its rights to access to the trial and hearings on related preliminary motions." The trial court denied Globe's motions . . . and ordered the exclusion of the press and general public from the courtroom during the trial. The defendant immediately objected to that exclusion order, and the prosecution stated for purposes of the record that the order was issued on the court's "own motion and not at the request of the Commonwealth."

. . .

Before Globe appealed to the full court, the rape trial proceeded and the defendant was acquitted.

Nine months after the conclusion of the criminal trial, the Supreme Judicial Court issued its judgment, dismissing Globe's appeal.

. . .

For the reasons that follow, we reverse, and hold that the mandatory closure rule contained in § 16A violates the First Amendment.

II

In this Court, Globe challenges that portion of the trial court's order, approved by the Supreme Judicial Court of Massachusetts, that holds that § 16A requires, under all circumstances, the exclusion of the press and general public during the testimony of a minor victim in a sex-offense trial. . . .

III

A

The Court's recent decision in Richmond Newspapers firmly established for the first time that the press and general public have a constitutional right of access to criminal trials. Although there was no opinion of the Court in that case, seven Justices recognized that this right of access is embodied in the First Amendment, and applied to the States through the Fourteenth Amendment.

...

Two features of the criminal justice system, emphasized in the various opinions in Richmond Newspapers, together serve to explain why a right of access to criminal trials in particular is properly afforded protection by the First Amendment. First, the criminal trial historically has been open to the press and general public....

Second, the right of access to criminal trials plays a particularly significant role in the functioning of the judicial process and the government as a whole. Public scrutiny of a criminal trial enhances the quality and safeguards the integrity of the factfinding process, with benefits to both the defendant and to society as a whole. Moreover, public access to the criminal trial fosters an appearance of fairness, thereby heightening public respect for the judicial process. And in the broadest terms, public access to criminal trials permits the public to participate in and serve as a check upon the judicial process — an essential component in our structure of self-government. In sum, the institutional value of the open criminal trial is recognized in both logic and experience.

B

Although the right of access to criminal trials is of constitutional stature, it is not absolute. But the circumstances under which the press and public can be barred from a criminal trial are limited; the State's justification in denying access must be a weighty one....

IV

The state interests asserted to support § 16A, though articulated in various ways, are reducible to two: the protection of minor victims of sex crimes from further trauma and embarrassment; and the encouragement of such victims to come forward and testify in a truthful and credible manner. We consider these interests in turn.

We agree with appellee that the first interest — safeguarding the physical and psychological well-being of a minor — is a compelling one. But as compelling as that interest is, it does not justify a mandatory closure rule, for it is clear that the circumstances of the particular case may affect the significance of the interest. A trial court can determine on a case-by-case basis whether closure is necessary to protect the welfare of a minor victim. Among the factors to be weighed are the minor victim's age, psychological maturity and understanding, the nature of the crime, the desires of the victim, and the interests of parents and relatives. Section 16A, in contrast, requires closure even if the victim does not seek the exclusion of the press and general public, and would not suffer injury by their presence In the case before us, for example, the names of the minor victims were already in the public record, and the record indicates that the victims may have been willing to testify despite the presence of the press. If the trial court had been permitted to exercise its discretion, closure might well have been deemed unnecessary. In short, § 16A cannot be viewed as a narrowly tailored means of accommodating the State's asserted interest: That interest could be served just as well by requiring the trial court to determine on a case-by-case basis whether the State's legitimate concern for the well-being of the minor victim necessitates closure. Such an approach ensures that the constitutional right of the press and public to gain access to criminal trials will not be restricted except where necessary to protect the State's interest.

Nor can § 16A be justified on the basis of the Commonwealth's second asserted interest — the encouragement of minor victims of sex crimes to come forward and provide accurate testimony. The Commonwealth has offered no empirical support for the claim that the rule of automatic closure contained in § 16A will lead to an increase in the number of minor sex victims coming forward and cooperating with state authorities. Not only is the claim speculative in empirical terms, but it is also open to serious question as a matter of logic and common sense. . . .

V

For the foregoing reasons, we hold that § 16A . . . violates the First Amendment to the Constitution. Accordingly, the judgment of the Massachusetts Supreme Judicial Court is

Reversed.

Justice O'Connor, concurring in the judgment.

. . .

This case, however, does involve a criminal trial. Moreover, it involves a statute mandating automatic exclusion of the public from certain testimony. As the Court explains, Massachusetts has demonstrated no interest weighty enough to justify application of its automatic bar to all cases, even those in which the victim, defendant, and prosecutor have no objection to an open trial. Accordingly, I concur in the judgment.

Chief Justice Burger, with whom Justice Rehnquist joins, dissenting.

Historically our society has gone to great lengths to protect minors charged with crime, particularly by prohibiting the release of the names of offenders, barring the press and public from juvenile proceedings, and sealing the records of those proceedings. Yet today the Court holds unconstitutional a state statute designed to protect not the accused, but the minor victims of sex crimes. In doing so, it advances a disturbing paradox. Although states are permitted, for example, to mandate the closure of all proceedings in order to protect a 17-year-old charged with rape, they are not permitted to require the closing of part of criminal proceedings in order to protect an innocent child who has been raped or otherwise sexually abused.

The Court has tried to make its holding a narrow one by not disturbing the authority of state legislatures to enact more narrowly drawn statutes giving trial judges the discretion to exclude the public and the press from the courtroom during the minor victim's testimony. I also do not read the Court's opinion as foreclosing a state statute which mandates closure except in cases where the victim agrees to testify in open court. But the Court's decision is nevertheless a gross invasion of state authority and a state's duty to protect its citizens—in this case minor victims of crime. . . . Accordingly, I dissent.

. . .

Justice Stevens, dissenting. [omitted]

Notes and Queries

1. What must a court consider in evaluating whether to exclude the press? Which factors would best address a child's physical and psychological well-being?
2. What argument can be made against a state's right to require the exclusion of the public from all sex abuse cases?

Research Comments

1. The Supreme Court has not yet had occasion to address the issue of public access in the child protection context. Should the rule developed in *Globe Newspaper* be extended to child protection proceedings? Consider this case. Defendant's wife and infant child died in an automobile collision with a drunk driver. The defendant gained a degree of publicity through his subsequent efforts to combat drunk driving. The defendant suffers from manic-depressive disorder as well as post-traumatic stress syndrome, conditions for which he receives medical and psychological treatment. According to his doctor, defendant's occasional failure to take regular dosages of the prescription drug lithium sulphate invariably leads to debilitating episodes of mental illness. When so afflicted, defendant has been known to leave his surviving 3-year-old son in the care of neighbors or relatives. An anonymous report alerted the Division of Youth and Family Services (DYFS) to the possibility that defendant's mental illness was seriously affecting his parenting ability. As a result of the ensuing investigation, DYFS removed defendant's child from his custody without court order. DYFS served defendant with a notice of emergency removal and advised him that an order to show cause and a verified complaint would be presented at a preliminary hearing on the following day. When defendant appeared in court to answer the complaint, he was accompanied by four members of the press who asked for permission to view the proceedings. Should the press be allowed? DYFS opposed opening the proceedings. Defendant argued in favor of admitting the press. After extended argument from all parties, including the child's law guardian, the court ordered that the press would

have access to the preliminary hearing. In its ruling the trial court considered the question of press access based on the "best interests of the child" standard. The court discounted the defendant's desire to have the press report on the proceeding. The court maintained that no *per se* rule could govern, that determinations must be made on a case-by-case basis. The court then considered the possibility that the child might be harmed by press coverage of the hearing. The court considered the nature of the complaint made by DYFS and determined that the allegations did not involve any type of sexual abuse or direct insult upon the child. Rather, the complaint concerned the psychological and psychiatric well-being of the defendant and whether he is capable to carry on his duties as a parent to nurture and care for the child. The court specifically determined that nothing in the complaint would be an "embarrassment" to the child if it became public knowledge. The court therefore concluded that public disclosure of the content of the proceedings would be unlikely to have a detrimental effect on the child. *New Jersey Division of Youth & Family Services v. J.B.*, 576 A.2d 261 (N.J. 1990).

2. What should happen if all the parties oppose having the court open to the press? Consider this case. The Department of Public Social Services for the County of San Bernardino (DPSS) filed petitions to have the seven minor children of Joseph S. and Sandra S. declared dependents of the juvenile court. The primary basis for each of the petitions was allegations of neglect and abuse by the parents against their daughter, Rose. According to reports published in the *Sun Newspaper* (*Sun*), Rose had been kept locked in a closet by the parents for most of ten years. When she was found, Rose was lying in her own feces and in urine-stained clothes. The *Sun* ran numerous articles about the incident, and the case gained some national attention as well. The *Sun* filed a request for access to the juvenile court's files and records regarding the minors. DPSS, the minors, and the parents all opposed access. A hearing was held on the issue of whether the *Sun* would be permitted access to the court files and records and to the court proceedings. At the hearing the court took evidence regarding the effects further publicity would have on the minors and on reunification efforts by the family. The court then issued its order denying the *Sun* access to the court records and files. However, it granted the *Sun* permission to attend the court proceedings but prohibited the *Sun* from (1) publishing the names of any of the minors; (2) publishing any likeness, characters, cartoons, or photographs of the minors; (3) interviewing any of the minors unless their attorney is present; (4) interviewing the minors' caretakers in front of the minors; (5) interviewing any mental health professional to whom the minors had been referred; and (6) in the future, doing any act which might interfere with reunification or have a negative impact upon the providing of reunification services. The *Sun* appealed, contending that the court's order permitting access to the proceedings was proper but that the conditions imposed on that permission were unconstitutional. The appellate court found that the restrictions were egregious interferences with the freedom of the press, given that the *Sun* could get much of the materials outside of the hearing. The court, however, vacated the permission

of the *Sun* to attend proceedings. The trial court had allowed access based on the rationale that it could control the information the press would publish rather than on a reasoning that considered the children's interests. The appellate court remanded the case with the following instruction. The trial court's discretion must be directed at determining what is in the best interests of the minors. At the same time, the court should give proper consideration to the important social values that are fostered by allowing public or press access to the proceedings. In attempting to balance these competing interests, the court should attempt to apply these broad principles to the unique facts of this case and may properly consider such factors as the age of each child, the nature of the allegations, the extent of the present and/or expected publicity, and its effect, if any, on the children and on family reunification. After proper consideration of such factors and circumstances, the court should allow press access unless there is a reasonable likelihood that such access will be harmful to the child's or children's best interest in this case. *San Bernardino County v. Superior Court*, 232 Cal. App. 3d 188 (1991).

3. Typically, the following reasons are given for allowing the press's presence in dependency hearings: (1) discourage perjury, (2) encourage witnesses to come forward, (3) allow for more accurate fact finding, (4) check judicial abuse, (5) provide an outlet for community concern, and (6) educate the public on how the system works. *San Bernardino County v. Superior Court*, 232 Cal. App. 3d 188, 202–04 (1991). Persuasive enough?

Idaho v. Wright

497 U.S. 805; 110 S. Ct. 3139 (1990)

Justice O'Connor delivered the opinion of the Court.

This case requires us to decide whether the admission at trial of certain hearsay statements made by a child declarant to an examining pediatrician violates a defendant's rights under the Confrontation Clause of the Sixth Amendment.

I

Respondent Laura Lee Wright was jointly charged with Robert L. Giles of two counts of lewd conduct with a minor under 16.... The alleged victims were respondent's two daughters, one of whom was $5^{1/2}$ and the other $2^{1/2}$ years old at the time the crimes were charged.

Respondent and her ex-husband, Louis Wright, the father of the older daughter, had reached an informal agreement whereby each parent would have custody of the older daughter for six consecutive months. The allegations surfaced in November 1986 when the older daughter told Cynthia Goodman, Louis Wright's female companion, that Giles had had sexual intercourse with her while respondent held her down and covered her mouth and that she had seen respondent and Giles do the same thing to respondent's younger daughter. The younger daughter was living with her parents — respondent and Giles — at the time of the alleged offenses.

Goodman reported the older daughter's disclosures to the police the next day and took the older daughter to the hospital. A medical examination of the older daughter revealed evidence of sexual abuse. One of the examining physicians was Dr. John Jambura, a pediatrician with extensive experience in child abuse cases. Police and welfare officials took the younger daughter into custody that day for protection and investigation. Dr. Jambura examined her the following day and found conditions "strongly suggestive of sexual abuse with vaginal contact," occurring approximately two to three days prior to the examination.

At the joint trial of respondent and Giles, the trial court conducted a voir dire examination of the younger daughter, who was three years old at the time of trial, to determine whether she was capable of testifying. The court concluded, and the parties agreed, that the younger daughter was "not capable of communicating to the jury."

At issue in this case is the admission at trial of certain statements made by the younger daughter to Dr. Jambura in response to questions he asked regarding the alleged abuse. Over objection by respondent and Giles, the trial court permitted Dr. Jambura to testify before the jury as follows:

> Q. [By the prosecutor] Now, calling your attention then to your examination of [the younger daughter] on November 10th. What — would you describe any interview dialogue that you had with [her] at that time? Excuse me, before you get into that, would you lay a setting of where this took place and who else might have been present?
>
> A. This took place in my office, in my examining room, and, as I recall, I believe previous testimony I said that I recall a female attendant being present, I don't recall her identity.
>
> I started out with basically, 'Hi, how are you,' you know, 'What did you have for breakfast this morning?' Essentially a few minutes of just sort of chitchat.
>
> Q. Was there response from [the daughter] to that first — those first questions?
>
> A. There was. She started to carry on a very relaxed animated conversation. I then proceeded to just gently start asking questions about, 'Well, how are things at home,' you know, those sorts. Gently moving into the domestic situation and then moved into four questions in particular, as I reflected in my records, 'Do you play with daddy? Does daddy play with you? Does daddy touch you with his pee-pee? Do you touch his pee-pee?' And again we then established what was meant by pee-pee, it was a generic term for genital area.
>
> Q. Before you get into that, what was, as best you recollect, what was her response to the question 'Do you play with daddy?'

A. Yes, we play—I remember her making a comment about yes we play a lot and expanding on that and talking about spending time with daddy.

Q. And 'Does daddy play with you?' Was there any response?

A. She responded to that as well, that they played together in a variety of circumstances and, you know, seemed very unaffected by the question.

Q. And then what did you say and her response?

A. When I asked her 'Does daddy touch you with his pee-pee,' she did admit to that. When I asked, 'Do you touch his pee-pee,' she did not have any response.

Q. Excuse me. Did you notice any change in her affect or attitude in that line of questioning?

A. Yes.

Q. What did you observe?

A. She would not—oh, she did not talk any further about that. She would not elucidate what exactly—what kind of touching was taking place, or how it was happening. She did, however, say that daddy does do this with me, but he does it a lot more with my sister than with me.

Q. And how did she offer that last statement? Was that in response to a question or was that just a volunteered statement?

A. That was a volunteered statement as I sat and waited for her to respond, again after she sort of clammed-up, and that was the next statement that she made after just allowing some silence to occur.

On cross-examination, Dr. Jambura acknowledged that a picture that he drew during his questioning of the younger daughter had been discarded. Dr. Jambura also stated that although he had dictated notes to summarize the conversation, his notes were not detailed and did not record any changes in the child's affect or attitude.

The trial court admitted these statements under Idaho's residual hearsay exception....

Respondent and Giles were each convicted of two counts of lewd conduct with a minor under 16 and sentenced to 20 years' imprisonment. Each appealed only from the conviction involving the younger daughter. Giles contended that the trial court erred in admitting Dr. Jambura's testimony under Idaho's residual hearsay exception. The Idaho Supreme Court disagreed and affirmed his conviction. Respondent asserted that the admission of Dr. Jambura's testimony under the residual hearsay exception nevertheless violated her rights under the Confrontation Clause. The Idaho Supreme Court agreed and reversed respondent's conviction.

The Supreme Court of Idaho held that the admission of the inculpatory hearsay testimony violated respondent's federal constitutional right to confrontation because the testimony did not fall within a traditional hearsay exception and was based on an interview that lacked procedural safeguards. The court found Dr. Jambura's interview technique inadequate because "the questions and answers were not recorded on videotape for preservation and perusal by the defense at or before trial; and blatantly leading questions were used in the interrogation." The statements also lacked trustworthiness, according to the court, because "this interrogation was performed by someone with a preconceived idea of what the child should be disclosing." Noting that expert testimony and child psychology texts indicated that children are susceptible to suggestion and are therefore likely to be misled by leading questions, the court found that "the circumstances surrounding this interview demonstrate dangers of unreliability which, because the interview was not [audio or video] recorded, can never be fully assessed." The court concluded that the younger daughter's statements lacked the particularized guarantees of trustworthiness necessary to satisfy the requirements of the Confrontation Clause and that therefore the trial court erred in admitting them. Because the court was not convinced, beyond a reasonable doubt, that the jury would have reached the same result had the error not occurred, the court reversed respondent's conviction on the count involving the younger daughter and remanded for a new trial.

We granted certiorari and now affirm.

II

...

In *Ohio v. Roberts*, we set forth "a general approach" for determining when incriminating statements admissible under an exception to the hearsay rule also meet the requirements of the Confrontation Clause. We noted that the Confrontation Clause "operates in two separate ways to restrict the range of admissible hearsay." "First, in conformance with the Framers' preference for face-to-face accusation, the Sixth Amendment establishes a rule of necessity. In the usual case ... the prosecution must either produce, or demonstrate the unavailability of, the declarant whose statement it wishes to use against the defendant." Second, once a witness is shown to be unavailable, "his statement is admissible only if it bears adequate 'indicia of reliability.' Reliability can be inferred without more in a case where the evidence falls within a firmly rooted hearsay exception. In other cases, the evidence must be excluded, at least absent a showing of particularized guarantees of trustworthiness."

...

Applying the *Roberts* approach to this case, we first note that this case does not raise the question whether, before a child's out-of-court statements are admitted, the Confrontation Clause requires the prosecution to show that a child witness is unavailable at trial—and, if so, what that showing requires. The trial court in this case found that respondent's younger daughter was incapable of communicating with the jury, and defense counsel agreed. The court below neither questioned this finding nor discussed the general requirement of unavailability. For purposes of deciding this case, we assume without deciding that, to the extent the unavailability requirement applies in this case, the younger daughter was an unavailable witness within the meaning of the Confrontation Clause.

The crux of the question presented is therefore whether the State, as the proponent of evidence presumptively barred by the hearsay rule and the Confrontation Clause, has carried its burden of proving that the younger daughter's incriminating statements to Dr. Jambura bore sufficient indicia of reliability to withstand scrutiny under the Clause. The court below held that, although the trial court had properly admitted the statements under the State's residual hearsay exception, the statements were "fraught with the dangers of unreliability which the Confrontation Clause is designed to highlight and obviate." The State asserts that the court below erected too stringent a standard for admitting the statements and that the statements were, under the totality of the circumstances, sufficiently reliable for Confrontation Clause purposes.

In *Roberts*, we suggested that the "indicia of reliability" requirement could be met in either of two circumstances: where the hearsay statement "falls within a firmly rooted hearsay exception," or where it is supported by "a showing of particularized guarantees of trustworthiness."

We note at the outset that Idaho's residual hearsay exception, Idaho Rule Evid. 803(24), under which the challenged statements were admitted is not a firmly rooted hearsay exception for Confrontation Clause purposes. Admission under a firmly rooted hearsay exception satisfies the constitutional requirement of reliability because of the weight accorded longstanding judicial and legislative experience in assessing the trustworthiness of certain types of out-of-court statements. The residual hearsay exception, by contrast, accommodates ad hoc instances in which statements not otherwise falling within a recognized hearsay exception might nevertheless be sufficiently reliable to be admissible at trial. Hearsay statements admitted under the residual exception, almost by definition, therefore do not share the same tradition of reliability that supports the admissibility of statements under a firmly rooted hearsay exception. Moreover, were we to agree that the admission of hearsay statements under the residual exception automatically passed Confrontation Clause scrutiny, virtually every codified hearsay exception would assume constitutional stature, a step this Court has repeatedly declined to take.

The State in any event does not press the matter strongly and recognizes that, because the younger daughter's hearsay statements do not fall within a firmly rooted hearsay exception, they are "presumptively unreliable and inadmissible for Confrontation Clause purposes," and "must be excluded, at least absent a showing of particularized guarantees of trustworthiness." The court below concluded that the State had not made such a showing, inlarge measure because the statements resulted from an interview lacking certain procedural safeguards. The court below specifically noted that Dr. Jambura failed to record the interview on videotape, asked leading questions, and questioned the child with a preconceived idea of what she should be disclosing.

Although we agree with the court below that the Confrontation Clause bars the admission of the younger daughter's hearsay statements, we reject the apparently dispositive weight placed by that court on the lack of procedural safeguards at the interview. Out-of-court statements made by children regarding sexual abuse arise in a wide variety of circumstances, and we do not believe the Constitution imposes a fixed set of procedural prerequisites to the admission of such statements at trial. The procedural requirements identified by the court below, to the extent regarded as conditions precedent to the admission of child hearsay statements in child sexual abuse cases, may in many instances be inappropriate or unnecessary to a determination whether a given statement is sufficiently trustworthy for Confrontation Clause purposes. Although the procedural guidelines propounded by the court below may well enhance the reliability of out-of-court statements of children regarding sexual abuse, we decline to read into the Confrontation Clause a preconceived and artificial litmus test for the procedural propriety of professional interviews in which children make hearsay statements against a defendant.

The State responds that a finding of "particularized guarantees of trustworthiness" should instead be based on a consideration of the totality of the circumstances, including not only the circumstances surrounding the making of the statement, but also other evidence at trial that corroborates the truth of the statement. We agree that "particularized guarantees of trustworthiness" must be shown from the totality of the circumstances, but we think the relevant circumstances include only those that surround the making of the statement and that render the declarant particularly worthy of belief. This conclusion derives from the rationale for permitting exceptions to the general rule against hearsay:

> The theory of the hearsay rule . . . is that the many possible sources of inaccuracy and untrustworthiness which may lie underneath the bare untested assertion of a witness can best be brought to light and exposed, if they exist, by the test of cross-examination. But this test or security may in a given instance be superfluous; it may be sufficiently clear, in that instance, that the statement offered is free enough from the risk of inaccuracy and untrustworthiness, so that the test of cross-examination would be a work of supererogation.

In other words, if the declarant's truthfulness is so clear from the surrounding circumstances that the test of cross-examination would be of marginal utility, then the hearsay rule does not bar admission of the statement at trial. The basis for the "excited utterance" exception, for example, is that such statements are given under circumstances that eliminate the possibility of fabrication, coaching, or confabulation, and that therefore the circumstances surrounding the making of the statement provide sufficient assurance that the statement is trustworthy and that cross-examination would be superfluous.

We think the "particularized guarantees of trustworthiness" required for admission under the Confrontation Clause must likewise be drawn from the totality of circumstances that surround the making of the statement and that render the declarant particularly worthy of belief. Our precedents have recognized that statements admitted under a "firmly rooted" hearsay exception are so trustworthy that adversarial testing would add little to their reliability. Because evidence possessing "particularized guarantees of trustworthiness" must be at least as reliable as evidence admitted under a firmly rooted hearsay exception, we think that evidence admitted under the former requirement must similarly be so trustworthy that adversarial testing would add little to its reliability. Thus, unless an affirmative reason, arising from the circumstances in which the statement was made, provides a basis for rebutting the presumption that a hearsay statement is not worthy of reliance at trial, the Confrontation Clause requires exclusion of the out-of-court statement.

The state and federal courts have identified a number of factors that we think properly relate to whether hearsay statements made by a child witness in child sexual abuse cases are reliable. Although these cases (which we cite for the factors they discuss and not necessarily to approve the results that they reach) involve the application of various hearsay exceptions to statements of child declarants, we think the factors identified also apply to whether such statements bear "particularized guarantees of trustworthiness" under the Confrontation Clause. These factors are, of course, not exclusive, and courts have considerable leeway in their consideration of appropriate factors. We therefore decline to endorse a mechanical test for determining "particularized guarantees of trustworthiness" under the Clause. Rather, the unifying principle is that these factors relate to whether the child declarant was particularly likely to be telling the truth when the statement was made.

... [W]e are unpersuaded by the State's contention that evidence corroborating the truth of a hearsay statement may properly support a finding that the statement bears "particularized guarantees of trustworthiness." To be admissible under the Confrontation Clause, hearsay evidence used to convict a defendant must possess indicia of reliability by virtue of its inherent trustworthiness, not by reference to other evidence at trial....

In short, the use of corroborating evidence to support a hearsay statement's "particularized guarantees of trustworthiness" would permit admission of a presumptively unreliable statement by bootstrapping on the trustworthiness of other evidence at trial, a result we think at odds with the requirement that hearsay evidence admitted under the Confrontation Clause be so trustworthy that cross-examination of the declarant would be of marginal utility. Indeed, although a plurality of the Court in *Dutton v. Evans* looked to corroborating evidence as one of four factors in determining whether a particular hearsay statement possessed sufficient indicia of reliability, we think the presence of corroborating evidence more appropriately indicates that any error in admitting the statement might be harmless, rather than that any basis exists for presuming the declarant to be trustworthy.

... Corroboration of a child's allegations of sexual abuse by medical evidence of abuse, for example, sheds no light on the reliability of the child's allegations regarding the identity of the abuser. There is a very real danger that a jury will rely on partial corroboration to mistakenly infer the trustworthiness of the entire statement....

Finally, we reject respondent's contention that the younger daughter's out-of-court statements in this case are per se unreliable, or at least presumptively unreliable, on the ground that the trial court found the younger daughter incompetent to testify at trial. First, respondent's contention rests upon a questionable reading of the record in this case. The trial court found only that the younger daughter was "not capable of communicating to the jury." Although Idaho law provides that a child witness may not testify if he "appear[s] incapable of receiving just impressions of the facts respecting which they are examined, or of relating them truly," the trial court in this case made no such findings. Indeed, the more reasonable inference is that, by ruling that the statements were admissible under Idaho's residual hearsay exception, the trial court implicitly found that the younger daughter, at the time she made the statements, was capable of receiving just impressions of the facts and of relating them truly. In addition, we have in any event held that the Confrontation Clause does not erect a per se rule barring the admission of prior statements of a declarant who is unable to communicate to the jury at the time of trial. Although such inability might be relevant to whether the earlier hearsay statement possessed particularized guarantees of trustworthiness, a per se rule of exclusion would not only frustrate the truthseeking purpose of the Confrontation Clause, but would also hinder States in their own "enlightened development in the law of evidence."

III

The trial court in this case, in ruling that the Confrontation Clause did not prohibit admission of the younger daughter's hearsay statements, relied on the following factors:

> In this case, of course, there is physical evidence to corroborate that sexual abuse occurred. It also would seem to be the case that there is no motive to make up a story of this nature in a child of these years. We're not talking about a pubescent youth who may fantasize. The nature of the statements themselves as to sexual abuse are such that they fall outside the general believability that a child could make them up or would make them up. This is simply not the type of statement, I believe, that one would expect a child to fabricate.
>
> We come then to the identification itself. Are there any indicia of reliability as to identification? From the doctor's testimony it appears that the injuries testified to occurred at the time that the victim was in the custody of the Defendants. The [older daughter] has testified as to identification of [the] perpetrators. Those — the identification of the perpetrators in this case are persons well known to the [younger daughter]. This is not a case in which a child is called upon to identify a stranger or a person with whom they would have no knowledge of their identity or ability to recollect and recall. Those factors are sufficient indicia of reliability to permit the admission of the statements.

Of the factors the trial court found relevant, only two relate to circumstances surrounding the making of the statements: whether the child had a motive to "make up a story of this nature," and whether, given the child's age, the statements are of the type "that one would expect a child to fabricate." The other factors on which the trial court relied, however, such as the presence of physical evidence of abuse, the opportunity of respondent to commit the offense, and the older daughter's corroborating identification, relate instead to whether other evidence existed to corroborate the truth of the statement. These factors, as we have discussed, are irrelevant to a showing of the "particularized guarantees of trustworthiness" necessary for admission of hearsay statements under the Confrontation Clause.

We think the Supreme Court of Idaho properly focused on the presumptive unreliability of the out-of-court statements and on the suggestive manner in which Dr. Jambura conducted the interview. Viewing the totality of the circumstances surrounding the younger daughter's responses to Dr. Jambura's questions, we find no special reason for supposing that the incriminating statements were particularly trustworthy. The younger daughter's last statement regarding the abuse of the older daughter, however, presents a closer question. According to Dr. Jambura, the younger daughter "volunteered" that statement "after she sort of clammed-up." Although the spontaneity of the statement and the change in demeanor suggest that the younger daughter was telling the truth when she made the statement, we note that it is possible that "if there is evidence of prior interrogation, prompting, or manipulation by adults, spontaneity may be an inaccurate indicator of trustworthiness." Moreover, the statement was not made under circumstances of reliability comparable to those required, for example, for the admission of excited utterances or statements made for purposes of medical diagnosis or treatment. Given the presumption of inadmissibility accorded accusatory hearsay statements not admitted pursuant to a firmly rooted hearsay exception, we agree with the court below that the State has failed to show that the younger daughter's incriminating statements to the pediatrician possessed sufficient "particularized guarantees of trustworthiness" under the Confrontation Clause to overcome that presumption.

The State does not challenge the Idaho Supreme Court's conclusion that the Confrontation Clause error in this case was not harmless beyond a reasonable doubt, and we see no reason to revisit the issue. We therefore agree with that court that respondent's conviction involving the younger daughter must be reversed and the case remanded for further proceedings. Accordingly, the judgment of the Supreme Court of Idaho is affirmed.

It is so ordered.

Justice Kennedy, with whom The Chief Justice, Justice White, and Justice Blackmun join, dissenting.

The issue is whether the Sixth Amendment right of confrontation is violated when statements from a child who is unavailable to testify at trial are admitted under a hearsay exception against a defendant who stands accused of abusing her. The Court today holds that it is not, provided that the child's statements bear "particularized guarantees of trustworthiness." I agree. My disagreement is with the rule the Court invents to control this inquiry and with the Court's ultimate determination that the statements in question here must be inadmissible as violative of the Confrontation Clause.

... The majority errs, in my view, by adopting a rule that corroboration of the statement by other evidence is an impermissible part of the trustworthiness inquiry. The Court's apparent ruling is that corroborating evidence may not be considered in whole or in part for this purpose. This limitation, at least on a facial interpretation of the Court's analytic categories, is a new creation by the Court; it likely will prove unworkable and does not even square with the examples of reliability indicators the Court itself invokes; and it is contrary to our own precedents.

I see no constitutional justification for this decision to prescind corroborating evidence from consideration of the question whether a child's statements are reliable. It is a matter of common sense for most people that one of the best ways to determine whether what someone says is trustworthy is to see if it is corroborated by other evidence. In the context of child abuse, for example, if part of the child's hearsay statement is that the assailant tied her wrists or had a scar on his lower abdomen, and there is physical evidence or testimony to corroborate the child's statement, evidence which the child could not have fabricated, we are more likely to believe that what the child says is true. Conversely, one can imagine a situation in which a child makes a statement which is spontaneous or is otherwise made under circumstances indicating that it is reliable, but which also contains undisputed factual inaccuracies so great that the credibility of the child's statements is substantially undermined. Under the Court's analysis, the statement would satisfy the requirements of the Confrontation Clause despite substantial doubt about its reliability. Nothing in the law of evidence or the law of the Confrontation Clause countenances such a result; on the contrary, most federal courts have looked to the existence of corroborating evidence or the lack thereof to determine the reliability of hearsay statement not coming within one of the traditional hearsay exceptions. Specifically with reference to hearsay statements by children, a review of the cases has led a leading commentator on child witness law to conclude flatly: "If the content of an out-of-court statement is supported or corroborated by other evidence, the reliability of the hearsay is strengthened." ... States are of course free, as a matter of state law, to demand corroboration of an unavailable child declarant's statements as well as other indicia of reliability before allowing the statements to be admitted into evidence. Until today, however, no similar distinction could be found in our precedents interpreting the Confrontation Clause. If anything, the many state statutes requiring corroboration of a child declarant's statements emphasize the relevance, not the irrelevance, of corroborating evidence to the determination whether an unavailable child witness' statements bear particularized guarantees of trustworthiness, which is the ultimate inquiry under the Confrontation Clause. In sum, whatever doubt the Court has with the weight to be given the corroborating evidence found in this case is no justification for rejecting the considered wisdom of virtually the entire legal community that corroborating evidence is relevant to reliability and trustworthiness.

. . .

The short of the matter is that both the circumstances existing at the time the child makes the statements and the existence of corroborating evidence indicate, to a greater or lesser degree, whether the statements are reliable. If the Court means to suggest that the circumstances surrounding the making of a statement are the best indicators of reliability, I doubt this is so in every instance. And, if it were true in a particular case, that does not warrant ignoring other indicators of reliability such as corroborating evidence, absent some other reason for excluding it. If anything, I should think that corroborating evidence in the form of testimony or physical evidence, apart from the narrow circumstances in which the statement was made, would be a preferred means of determining a statement's reliability for purposes of the Confrontation Clause, for the simple reason that, unlike other indicators of trustworthiness, corroborating evidence can be addressed by the defendant and assessed by the trial court in an objective and critical way.

In this case, the younger daughter's statements are corroborated in at least four respects: (1) physical evidence that she was the victim of sexual abuse; (2) evidence that she had been in the custody of the suspect at the time the injuries occurred; (3) testimony of the older daughter that their father abused the younger daughter, thus corroborating the younger daughter's statement; and (4) the testimony of the older daughter that she herself was abused by their father, thus corroborating the younger daughter's statement that her sister had also been abused. These facts, coupled with the circumstances surrounding the making of the statements acknowledged by the Court as suggesting that the statements are reliable, give rise to a legitimate argument that admission of the statements did not violate the Confrontation Clause. Because the Idaho Supreme Court did not consider these factors, I would vacate its judgment reversing respondent's conviction and remand for it to consider in the first instance whether the child's statements bore "particularized guarantees of trustworthiness" under the analysis set forth in this separate opinion.

Notes and Queries

1. The Court makes the point that the hearsay statements at issue were not the kind "one would expect a child to fabricate." Do you agree?

2. What do you make of Dr. Jambura's interviewing skills? What do you make of his record-keeping skills? Does his testimony support the prosecution?

3. If hearsay statements bear "particularized guarantees of trustworthiness" they may be admitted when the child is unavailable to testify at trial. To determine trustworthiness, a court must examine the statement in the totality of circumstances

regarding the statement itself *not* including evidence that goes to the truth of the statement, such as corroborating evidence. Does this seem appropriate? Should a court have to determine the existence of indicators of truthfulness?

Research Comment

1. Hearsay evidence regarding children's out-of-court statements presents complex problems to the extent that allowing the evidence is based on the belief that it protects children from confrontational stress. Despite the theoretical possibility of receiving children's hearsay in lieu of children's live testimony, the reality is different. Children's hearsay is typically admitted in addition to, rather than in lieu of, their courtroom testimony. See John E. B. Myers, Allison D. Redlich, Gail S. Goodman, Lori P. Prizmich & Edward Imwinkelried (1999). Jurors' perceptions of hearsay in child sexual abuse cases. *Psychology, Public Policy, & Law*, 5, 388–419. What would you suggest policy makers do with these findings? Does it disturb the Court's rationales for creating special rules to accommodate child witnesses?

White v. Illinois

502 U.S. 346; 112 S. Ct. 736 (1992)

Chief Justice Rehnquist delivered the opinion of the Court.

In this case, we consider whether the Confrontation Clause of the Sixth Amendment requires that, before a trial court admits testimony under the "spontaneous declaration" and "medical examination" exceptions to the hearsay rule, the prosecution must either produce the declarant at trial or the trial court must find that the declarant is unavailable. The Illinois Appellate Court concluded that such procedures are not constitutionally required. We agree with that conclusion.

Petitioner was convicted by a jury of aggravated criminal sexual assault, residential burglary, and unlawful restraint. The events giving rise to the charges related to the sexual assault of S. G., then four years old. Testimony at the trial established that in the early morning hours of April 16, 1988, S. G.'s babysitter, Tony DeVore, was awakened by S. G.'s scream. DeVore went to S. G.'s bedroom and witnessed petitioner leaving the room, and petitioner then left the house. DeVore knew petitioner because petitioner was a friend of S. G.'s mother, Tammy Grigsby. DeVore asked S. G. what had happened. According to DeVore's trial testimony, S. G. stated that petitioner had put his hand over her mouth, choked her, threatened to whip her if she screamed and had "touched her in the wrong places." Asked by DeVore to point to where she had been touched, S. G. identified the vaginal area.

Tammy Grigsby, S. G.'s mother, returned home about 30 minutes later. Grigsby testified that her daughter appeared "scared" and a "little hyper." Grigsby proceeded to question her daughter about what had happened. At trial, Grigsby testified that S. G. repeated her claims that petitioner had choked and threatened her. Grigsby also testified that S. G. stated that petitioner had "put his mouth on her front part." Grigsby also noticed that S. G. had bruises and red marks on her neck that had not been there previously. Grigsby called the police.

Officer Terry Lewis arrived a few minutes later, roughly 45 minutes after S. G.'s scream had first awakened DeVore. Lewis questioned S. G. alone in the kitchen. At trial, Lewis' summary of S. G.'s statement indicated that she had offered essentially the same story as she had first reported to DeVore and to Grigsby, including a statement that petitioner had "used his tongue on her in her private parts."

After Lewis concluded his investigation, and approximately four hours after DeVore first heard S. G.'s scream, S. G. was taken to the hospital. She was examined first by Cheryl Reents, an emergency room nurse, and then by Dr. Michael Meinzen. Each testified at trial, and their testimony indicated that, in response to questioning, S. G. again provided an account of events that was essentially identical to the one she had given to DeVore, Grigsby, and Lewis.

S. G. never testified at petitioner's trial. The State attempted on two occasions to call her as a witness, but she apparently experienced emotional difficulty on being brought to the courtroom and in each instance left without testifying. The defense made no attempt to call S. G. as a witness, and the trial court neither made, nor was asked to make, a finding that S. G. was unavailable to testify.

Petitioner objected on hearsay grounds to DeVore, Grigsby, Lewis, Reents, and Meinzen being permitted to testify regarding S. G.'s statements describing the assault. The trial court overruled each objection. With respect to DeVore, Grigsby, and Lewis the trial court concluded that the testimony could be permitted pursuant to an Illinois hearsay exception for spontaneous declarations. Petitioner's objections to Reents' and Meinzen's testimony was similarly overruled, based on both the spontaneous declaration exception and an exception for statements made in the course of securing medical treatment. The trial court also denied petitioner's motion for a mistrial based on S. G.'s "presence [and] failure to testify."

Petitioner was found guilty by a jury, and the Illinois Appellate Court affirmed his conviction. It held that the trial court operated within the discretion accorded it under state law in ruling that the statements offered by DeVore, Grigsby, and Lewis qualified for the spontaneous declaration exception and in ruling that the statements offered by Reents and Meinzen qualified for the medical examination exception.... The Illinois Supreme Court denied discretionary review, and we granted certiorari limited to the constitutional question whether permitting the challenged testimony violated petitioner's Sixth Amendment Confrontation Clause right.

...

We therefore now turn to petitioner's principal contention that our prior decision in *Roberts* requires that his conviction be vacated. In *Roberts* we considered a

Confrontation Clause challenge to the introduction at trial of a transcript containing testimony from a probable-cause hearing, where the transcript included testimony from a witness not produced at trial but who had been subject to examination by defendant's counsel at the probable-cause hearing. In the course of rejecting the Confrontation Clause claim in that case, we used language that might suggest that the Confrontation Clause generally requires that a declarant either be produced at trial or be found unavailable before his out-of-court statement may be admitted into evidence. However, we think such an expansive reading of the Clause is negated by our subsequent decision in Inadi.

In *Inadi* we considered the admission of out-of-court statements made by a co-conspirator in the course of the conspiracy. As an initial matter, we rejected the proposition that *Roberts* established a rule that "no out-of-court statement would be admissible without a showing of unavailability." To the contrary, rather than establishing "a wholesale revision of the law of evidence" under the guise of the Confrontation Clause, we concluded that "*Roberts* must be read consistently with the question it answered, the authority it cited, and its own facts." So understood, *Roberts* stands for the proposition that unavailability analysis is a necessary part of the Confrontation Clause inquiry only when the challenged out-of-court statements were made in the course of a prior judicial proceeding.

Having clarified the scope of *Roberts*, the Court in *Inadi* then went on to reject the Confrontation Clause challenge presented there. In particular, we refused to extend the unavailability requirement established in *Roberts* to all out-of-court statements. Our decision rested on two factors. First, unlike former in-court testimony, co-conspirator statements "provide evidence of the conspiracy's context that cannot be replicated, even if the declarant testifies to the same matters in court." Also, given a declarant's likely change in status by the time the trial occurs, simply calling the declarant in the hope of having him repeat his prior out-of-court statements is a poor substitute for the full evidentiary significance that flows from statements made when the conspiracy is operating in full force.

Second, we observed that there is little benefit, if any, to be accomplished by imposing an "unavailability rule." Such a rule will not work to bar absolutely the introduction of the out-of-court statements; if the declarant either is unavailable, or is available and produced for trial, the statements can be introduced. Nor is an unavailability rule likely to produce much testimony that adds meaningfully to the trial's truth-determining process. Many declarants will be subpoenaed by the prosecution or defense, regardless of any Confrontation Clause requirement, while the Compulsory Process Clause and evidentiary rules permitting a defendant to treat witnesses as hostile will aid defendants in obtaining a declarant's live testimony. And while an unavailability rule would therefore do little to improve the accuracy of factfinding, it is likely to impose substantial additional burdens on the factfinding process. The prosecution would be required to repeatedly locate and keep continuously available each declarant, even when neither the prosecution nor the defense has any interest in calling the witness to the stand. An additional inquiry would be injected into the question of admissibility of evidence, to be litigated both at trial and on appeal.

These observations, although expressed in the context of evaluating co-conspirator statements, apply with full force to the case at hand. We note first that the evidentiary rationale for permitting hearsay testimony regarding spontaneous declarations and statements made in the course of receiving medical care is that such out-of-court declarations are made in contexts that provide substantial guarantees of their trustworthiness. But those same factors that contribute to the statements' reliability cannot be recaptured even by later in-court testimony. A statement that has been offered in a moment of excitement — without the opportunity to reflect on the consequences of one's exclamation — may justifiably carry more weight with a trier of fact than a similar statement offered in the relative calm of the courtroom. Similarly, a statement made in the course of procuring medical services, where the declarant knows that a false statement may cause misdiagnosis or mistreatment, carries special guarantees of credibility that a trier of fact may not think replicated by courtroom testimony. They are thus materially different from the statements at issue in *Roberts*, where the out-of-court statements sought to be introduced were themselves made in the course of a judicial proceeding, and where there was consequently no threat of lost evidentiary value if the out-of-court statements were replaced with live testimony.

The preference for live testimony in the case of statements like those offered in *Roberts* is because of the importance of cross-examination, "the greatest legal engine ever invented for the discovery of truth." Thus courts have adopted the general rule prohibiting the receipt of hearsay evidence. But where proffered hearsay has sufficient guarantees of reliability to come within a firmly rooted exception to the hearsay rule, the Confrontation Clause is satisfied.

We therefore think it clear that the out-of-court statements admitted in this case had substantial probative value, value that could not be duplicated simply by the declarant later testifying in court. To exclude such probative statements under the strictures of the Confrontation Clause would be the height of wrongheadedness, given that the Confrontation Clause has as a basic purpose the promotion of the "'integrity of the factfinding process.'" And as we have also noted, a statement that qualifies for admission under a "firmly rooted" hearsay exception is so trustworthy that adversarial testing can be expected to add little to its reliability. Given the evidentiary value of such statements, their reliability, and that establishing a generally applicable unavailability rule would have few practical benefits while imposing pointless litigation costs, we see no reason to treat the out-of-court statements in this case differently from those we found admissible in *Inadi*. A contrary rule would result in exactly the kind of "wholesale revision" of the laws of evidence that we expressly disavowed in *Inadi*. We therefore see no basis in *Roberts* or *Inadi* for excluding from trial, under the aegis of the Confrontation Clause, evidence embraced within such exceptions to the hearsay rule as those for spontaneous declarations and statements made for medical treatment.

. . .

For the foregoing reasons, the judgment of the Illinois Appellate Court is

Affirmed.

Justice Thomas, with whom Justice Scalia joins, concurring in part and concurring in the judgment.

. . .

The standards that the Court has developed to implement its assumption that the Confrontation Clause limits admission of hearsay evidence have no basis in the text of the Sixth Amendment. Ever since *Ohio v. Roberts*, the Court has interpreted the Clause to mean that hearsay may be admitted only under a "firmly rooted" exception or if it otherwise bears "particularized guarantees of trustworthiness." This analysis implies that the Confrontation Clause bars only unreliable hearsay. Although the historical concern with trial by affidavit and anonymous accusers does reflect concern with the reliability of the evidence against a defendant, the Clause makes no distinction based on the reliability of the evidence presented. Nor does it seem likely that the drafters of the Sixth Amendment intended to permit a defendant to be tried on the basis of ex parte affidavits found to be reliable. Reliability is more properly a due process concern. There is no reason to strain the text of the Confrontation Clause to provide criminal defendants with a protection that due process already provides them.

. . . I believe it is possible to interpret the Confrontation Clause along the lines suggested by the United States in a manner that is faithful to both the provision's text and history. One possible formulation is as follows: The federal constitutional right of confrontation extends to any witness who actually testifies at trial, but the Confrontation Clause is implicated by extrajudicial statements only insofar as they are contained in formalized testimonial materials, such as affidavits, depositions, prior testimony, or confessions. It was this discrete category of testimonial materials that was historically abused by prosecutors as a means of depriving criminal defendants of the benefit of the adversary process and under this approach, the Confrontation Clause would not be construed to extend beyond the historical evil to which it was directed.

Such an approach would be consistent with the vast majority of our cases, since virtually all of them decided before *Ohio v. Roberts* involved prior testimony or confessions, exactly the type of formalized testimonial evidence that lies at the core of the Confrontation Clause's concern. This narrower reading of the Confrontation Clause would greatly simplify the inquiry in the hearsay context. Furthermore, this interpretation would avoid the problem posed by the Court's current focus on hearsay exceptions that are "firmly rooted" in the common law. The Court has never explained the Confrontation Clause implications of a State's decision to adopt an exception not recognized at common law or one not recognized by a majority of the States. Our current jurisprudence suggests that, in order to satisfy the Sixth Amendment, the State would have to establish in each individual case that hearsay admitted pursuant to the newly created exception bears "particularized guarantees of trustworthiness," and would have to continue doing so until the exception became "firmly rooted" in the common law, if that is even possible under the Court's standard. This result is difficult to square with the Clause itself. Neither the language of the Clause nor the historical evidence appears to support the notion that the Confrontation Clause was intended to constitutionalize the hearsay rule and its exceptions. Although the Court repeatedly has disavowed any intent to cause that result I fear that our decisions have edged ever further in that direction.

For the foregoing reasons, I respectfully suggest that, in an appropriate case, we reconsider how the phrase "witness against" in the Confrontation Clause pertains to the admission of hearsay. I join the Court's opinion except for its discussion of the narrow reading of this phrase proposed by the United States.

Notes and Queries

1. *Inadi* involved a co-conspirator exception. Such statements clearly are made against one's own interest. How can disclosures of maltreatment be deemed comparable?
2. Are statements made during medical care made in a context that provides "substantial guarantees of trustworthiness"? Recall that the defendant's counsel in *Roberts* had examined the witnesses at a preliminary hearing. Does the medical context appear similarly trustworthy?

Crawford v. Washington

541 U.S. 36, 124 S. Ct. 1354 (2004)

Justice Scalia delivered the opinion of the Court.

Petitioner Michael Crawford stabbed a man who allegedly tried to rape his wife, Sylvia. At his trial, the State played for the jury Sylvia's tape-recorded statement to the police describing the stabbing, even though he had no opportunity for cross-examination. The Washington Supreme Court upheld petitioner's conviction after determining that Sylvia's statement was reliable. The question presented is whether this procedure complied with the Sixth Amendment's guarantee that, "[i]n all criminal prosecutions, the accused shall enjoy the right . . . to be confronted with the witnesses against him."

I

On August 5, 1999, Kenneth Lee was stabbed at his apartment. Police arrested petitioner later that night. After giving petitioner and his wife Miranda warnings, detectives interrogated each of them twice. Petitioner eventually confessed that he and Sylvia had gone in search of Lee because he was upset over an earlier incident in which Lee had tried to rape her. The two had found Lee at his apartment, and a fight ensued in which Lee was stabbed in the torso and petitioner's hand was cut.

Petitioner gave the following account of the fight:

> "Q. Okay. Did you ever see anything in [Lee's] hands?
>
> "A. I think so, but I'm not positive.
>
> "Q. Okay, when you think so, what do you mean by that?
>
> "A. I coulda swore I seen him goin' for somethin' before, right before everything happened. He was like reachin', fiddlin' around down here and stuff . . . and I just . . . I don't know, I think, this is just a possibility, but I think, I think that he pulled somethin' out and I grabbed for it and that's how I got cut . . . but I'm not positive. I, I, my mind goes blank when things like this happen. I mean, I just, I remember things wrong, I remember things that just doesn't, don't make sense to me later."

Sylvia generally corroborated petitioner's story about the events leading up to the fight, but her account of the fight itself was arguably different—particularly with respect to whether Lee had drawn a weapon before petitioner assaulted him. . . .

. . .

The State charged petitioner with assault and attempted murder. At trial, he claimed self-defense. Sylvia did not testify because of the state marital privilege, which generally bars a spouse from testifying without the other spouse's consent. In Washington, this privilege does not extend to a spouse's out-of-court statements admissible under a hearsay exception, so the State sought to introduce Sylvia's tape-recorded statements to the police as evidence that the stabbing was not in self-defense. Noting that Sylvia had admitted she led petitioner to Lee's apartment and thus had facilitated the assault, the State invoked the hearsay exception for statements against penal interest.

Petitioner countered that, state law notwithstanding, admitting the evidence would violate his federal constitutional right to be "confronted with the witnesses against him." According to our description of that right in *Ohio v. Roberts* (1980), it does not bar admission of an unavailable witness's statement against a criminal defendant if the statement bears "adequate 'indicia of reliability.'" To meet that test, evidence must either fall within a "firmly rooted hearsay exception" or bear "particularized guarantees of trustworthiness." The trial court here admitted the statement on the latter ground, offering several reasons why it was trustworthy: Sylvia was not shifting blame but rather corroborating her husband's story that he acted in self-defense or "justified reprisal"; she had direct knowledge as an eyewitness; she was describing recent events; and she was being questioned by a "neutral" law enforcement officer. The prosecution played the tape for the jury and relied on it in closing, arguing that it was "damning evidence" that "completely refutes [petitioner's] claim of self-defense." The jury convicted petitioner of assault.

The Washington Court of Appeals reversed. It applied a nine-factor test to determine whether Sylvia's statement bore particularized guarantees of trustworthiness, and noted several reasons why it did not: . . .

The Washington Supreme Court reinstated the conviction, unanimously concluding that, although Sylvia's statement did not fall under a firmly rooted hearsay exception, it bore guarantees of trustworthiness: . . .

. . .

We granted certiorari to determine whether the State's use of Sylvia's statement violated the Confrontation Clause.

II

The Sixth Amendment's Confrontation Clause provides that, "[i]n all criminal prosecutions, the accused shall enjoy the right . . . to be confronted with the witnesses against him." We have held that this bedrock procedural guarantee applies to both federal and state prosecutions. As noted above, *Roberts* says that an unavailable witness's out-of-court statement may be admitted so long as it has adequate indicia of reliability—i.e., falls within a "firmly rooted hearsay exception" or bears "particularized guarantees of trustworthiness." Petitioner argues that this test strays from the original meaning of the Confrontation Clause and urges us to reconsider it.

A

The Constitution's text does not alone resolve this case. One could plausibly read "witnesses against" a defendant to mean those who actually testify at trial, those whose statements are offered at trial, or something in-between. We must therefore turn to the historical background of the Clause to understand its meaning.

. . .

III

This history supports two inferences about the meaning of the Sixth Amendment.

A

First, the principal evil at which the Confrontation Clause was directed was the civil-law mode of criminal procedure, and particularly its use of ex parte examinations as evidence against the accused. It was these practices that the Crown deployed in notorious treason cases like Raleigh's; that the Marian statutes invited; that English law's assertion of a right to confrontation was meant to prohibit; and that the founding-era rhetoric decried. The Sixth Amendment must be interpreted with this focus in mind.

Accordingly, we once again reject the view that the Confrontation Clause applies of its own force only to in-court testimony, and that its application to out-of-court statements introduced at trial depends upon "the law of Evidence for the time being." Leaving the regulation of out-of-court statements to the law of evidence would render the Confrontation Clause powerless to prevent even the most flagrant inquisitorial practices. Raleigh was, after all, perfectly free to confront those who read Cobham's confession in court.

This focus also suggests that not all hearsay implicates the Sixth Amendment's core concerns. An off-hand, overheard remark might be unreliable evidence and thus a good candidate for exclusion under hearsay rules, but it bears little resemblance to the civil-law abuses the Confrontation Clause targeted. On the other hand, ex parte examinations might sometimes be admissible under modern hearsay rules, but the Framers certainly would not have condoned them.

The text of the Confrontation Clause reflects this focus. It applies to "witnesses" against the accused—in other words, those who "bear testimony." "Testimony," in turn, is typically "[a] solemn declaration or affirmation made for the purpose of establishing or proving some fact." An accuser who makes a formal statement to government officers bears testimony in a sense that a person who makes a casual remark to an acquaintance does not. The constitutional text, like the history underlying the common-law right of confrontation, thus reflects an especially acute concern with a specific type of out-of-court statement.

Various formulations of this core class of "testimonial" statements exist: "ex parte in-court testimony or its functional equivalent–that is, material such as affidavits, custodial examinations, prior testimony that the defendant was unable to cross-examine, or similar pretrial statements that declarants would reasonably expect to be used prosecutorially," "statements that were made under circumstances which would lead an objective witness reasonably to believe that the statement would be available for use at a later trial. These formulations all share a common nucleus and then define the Clause's coverage at various levels of abstraction around it. Regardless of the precise articulation, some statements qualify under any definition—for example, ex parte testimony at a preliminary hearing.

Statements taken by police officers in the course of interrogations are also testimonial under even a narrow standard. Police interrogations bear a striking resemblance to examinations by justices of the peace in England. The statements are not sworn testimony, but the absence of oath was not dispositive....

That interrogators are police officers rather than magistrates does not change the picture either.... The involvement of government officers in the production of testimonial evidence presents the same risk, whether the officers are police or justices of the peace.

In sum, even if the Sixth Amendment is not solely concerned with testimonial hearsay, that is its primary object, and interrogations by law enforcement officers fall squarely within that class.

B

The historical record also supports a second proposition: that the Framers would not have allowed admission of testimonial statements of a witness who did not appear at trial unless he was unavailable to testify, and the defendant had had a prior opportunity for cross-examination. The text of the Sixth Amendment does not suggest any open-ended exceptions from the confrontation requirement to be developed by the courts. . . .

[The historical sources] . . . suggest that this requirement was dispositive, and not merely one of several ways to establish reliability. This is not to deny, as The Chief Justice notes, that "[t]here were always exceptions to the general rule of exclusion" of hearsay evidence. . . . But there is scant evidence that exceptions were invoked to admit testimonial statements against the accused in a criminal case. Most of the hearsay exceptions covered statements that by their nature were not testimonial. . . .

IV

Our case law has been largely consistent with these two principles. Our leading early decision, for example, involved a deceased witness's prior trial testimony. *Mattox v. United States.* In allowing the statement to be admitted, we relied on the fact that the defendant had had, at the first trial, an adequate opportunity to confront the witness: . . .

Our later cases conform to *Mattox*'s holding that prior trial or preliminary hearing testimony is admissible only if the defendant had an adequate opportunity to cross-examine. . . .

Even our recent cases, in their outcomes, hew closely to the traditional line. . . .

. . .

Our cases have thus remained faithful to the Framers' understanding: Testimonial statements of witnesses absent from trial have been admitted only where the declarant is unavailable, and only where the defendant has had a prior opportunity to cross-examine.

V

Although the results of our decisions have generally been faithful to the original meaning of the Confrontation Clause, the same cannot be said of our rationales. *Roberts* conditions the admissibility of all hearsay evidence on whether it falls under a "firmly rooted hearsay exception" or bears "particularized guarantees of trustworthiness." This test departs from the historical principles identified above in two respects. First, it is too broad: It applies the same mode of analysis whether or not the hearsay consists of ex parte testimony. This often results in close constitutional scrutiny in cases that are far removed from the core concerns of the Clause. At the same time, however, the test is too narrow: It admits statements that do consist of ex parte testimony upon a mere finding of reliability. This malleable standard often fails to protect against paradigmatic confrontation violations.

Members of this Court and academics have suggested that we revise our doctrine to reflect more accurately the original understanding of the Clause. They offer two proposals: First, that we apply the Confrontation Clause only to testimonial statements, leaving the remainder to regulation by hearsay law—thus eliminating the overbreadth referred to above. Second, that we impose an absolute bar to statements that are testimonial, absent a prior opportunity to cross-examine—thus eliminating the excessive narrowness referred to above.

In *White*, we considered the first proposal and rejected it. Although our analysis in this case casts doubt on that holding, we need not definitively resolve whether it survives our decision today, because Sylvia Crawford's statement is testimonial under any definition. This case does, however, squarely implicate the second proposal.

A

Where testimonial statements are involved, we do not think the Framers meant to leave the Sixth Amendment's protection to the vagaries of the rules of evidence, much less to amorphous notions of "reliability." Certainly none of the authorities discussed above acknowledges any general reliability exception to the common-law rule. Admitting statements deemed reliable by a judge is fundamentally at odds with the right of confrontation. To be sure, the Clause's ultimate goal is to ensure reliability of evidence, but it is a procedural rather than a substantive guarantee. It commands, not that evidence be reliable, but that reliability be assessed in a particular manner: by testing in the crucible of cross-examination. The Clause thus reflects a judgment, not only about the desirability of reliable evidence (a point on which there could be little dissent), but about how reliability can best be determined.

The *Roberts* test allows a jury to hear evidence, untested by the adversary process, based on a mere judicial determination of reliability. It thus replaces the constitutionally prescribed method of assessing reliability with a wholly foreign one....

...

Dispensing with confrontation because testimony is obviously reliable is akin to dispensing with jury trial because a defendant is obviously guilty. This is not what the Sixth Amendment prescribes.

B

The legacy of *Roberts* in other courts vindicates the Framers' wisdom in rejecting a general reliability exception. The framework is so unpredictable that it fails to provide meaningful protection from even core confrontation violations.

Reliability is an amorphous, if not entirely subjective, concept. There are countless factors bearing on whether a statement is reliable....

The unpardonable vice of the *Roberts* test, however, is not its unpredictability, but its demonstrated capacity to admit core testimonial statements that the Confrontation Clause plainly meant to exclude....

...

C

Roberts' failings were on full display in the proceedings below. Sylvia Crawford made her statement while in police custody, herself a potential suspect in the case. Indeed, she had been told that whether she would be released "depend[ed] on how the investigation continues." In response to often leading questions from police detectives, she implicated her husband in Lee's stabbing and at least arguably undermined his self-defense claim. Despite all this, the trial court admitted her statement, listing several reasons why it was reliable. In its opinion reversing, the Court of Appeals listed several other reasons why the statement was not reliable. Finally, the State Supreme Court relied exclusively on the interlocking character of the statement and disregarded every other factor the lower courts had considered. The case is thus a self-contained demonstration of *Roberts'* unpredictable and inconsistent application.

Each of the courts also made assumptions that cross-examination might well have undermined. . . .

. . .

Where nontestimonial hearsay is at issue, it is wholly consistent with the Framers' design to afford the States flexibility in their development of hearsay law—as does *Roberts*, and as would an approach that exempted such statements from Confrontation Clause scrutiny altogether. Where testimonial evidence is at issue, however, the Sixth Amendment demands what the common law required: unavailability and a prior opportunity for cross-examination. We leave for another day any effort to spell out a comprehensive definition of "testimonial." Whatever else the term covers, it applies at a minimum to prior testimony at a preliminary hearing, before a grand jury, or at a former trial; and to police interrogations. These are the modern practices with closest kinship to the abuses at which the Confrontation Clause was directed.

In this case, the State admitted Sylvia's testimonial statement against petitioner, despite the fact that he had no opportunity to cross-examine her. That alone is sufficient to make out a violation of the Sixth Amendment. *Roberts* notwithstanding, we decline to mine the record in search of indicia of reliability. Where testimonial statements are at issue, the only indicium of reliability sufficient to satisfy constitutional demands is the one the Constitution actually prescribes: confrontation.

The judgment of the Washington Supreme Court is reversed, and the case is remanded for further proceedings not inconsistent with this opinion.

It is so ordered.

Chief Justice Rehnquist, with whom Justice O'Connor joins, concurring in the judgment.

I dissent from the Court's decision to overrule *Ohio v. Roberts* (1980). I believe that the Court's adoption of a new interpretation of the Confrontation Clause is not backed by sufficiently persuasive reasoning to overrule long-established precedent. Its decision casts a mantle of uncertainty over future criminal trials in both federal and state courts, and is by no means necessary to decide the present case.

. . .

. . . The Court grandly declares that "[w]e leave for another day any effort to spell out a comprehensive definition of 'testimonial.' " But the thousands of federal prosecutors and the tens of thousands of state prosecutors need answers as to what beyond the specific kinds of "testimony" the Court lists is covered by the new rule. They need them now, not months or years from now. Rules of criminal evidence are applied every day in courts throughout the country, and parties should not be left in the dark in this manner.

To its credit, the Court's analysis of "testimony" excludes at least some hearsay exceptions, such as business records and official records. To hold otherwise would require numerous additional witnesses without any apparent gain in the truth-seeking process. Likewise to the Court's credit is its implicit recognition that the mistaken application of its new rule by courts which guess wrong as to the scope of the rule is subject to harmless-error analysis.

But these are palliatives to what I believe is a mistaken change of course. It is a change of course not in the least necessary to reverse the judgment of the Supreme Court of Washington in this case. The result the Court reaches follows inexorably from *Roberts* and its progeny without any need for overruling that line of cases. In *Idaho v. Wright* (1990) we held that an out-of-court statement was not admissible simply because the truthfulness of that statement was corroborated by other evidence at trial. As the Court notes, the Supreme Court of Washington gave decisive weight to the "interlocking nature of the two statements." No re-weighing of the "reliability factors," which is hypothesized by the Court, is required to reverse the judgment here. A citation to *Idaho v. Wright* would suffice. For the reasons stated, I believe that this would be a far preferable course for the Court to take here.

Notes and Queries

1. *Crawford* is remarkable for being a 9–0 opinion and known for spurring a dramatic shift away from evidence-based prosecutions. Such prosecutions rely on hearsay exceptions rather than victims' in-court testimony. Given the challenges of children's testimony in child maltreatment cases, the case was seen as particularly problematic. That would seem particularly so given how Justice Scalia explicitly stated that "testimonial" out-of-court statements are inadmissible unless (1) the declarant is unavailable to testify in court and (2) the defendant has had a prior

opportunity to cross-examine them. The case certainly called into question the validity of *Maryland v. Craig*. The counterargument to concerns about *Crawford*'s impact on *Craig* is that the two-way system permits cross-examination at trial, and that those procedures, when used to further a pressing public policy interest, arguably appear legitimate.

2. It is fair to say that *Crawford* would apply to many types of efforts to introduce witnesses' statements from declarants that counsel does not expect to have appear as witnesses for cross-examinations at trial. For example, it could apply to non-testifying victims' statements made to first responders, family members, social workers, teachers, or doctors. Essentially, the child would need to appear in court to testify. Yet complications arise as to what is "testimonial," which has led to considerable commentary and litigation. For example, evidence may be offered for purposes other than truth against the defendant, which brings no Confrontation Clause problem. In this regard, much evidence may be admissible to impeach, be part of an expert's opinion, corroborate an opinion, or explain an investigation or someone's reactions.

3. The nature of cases involving child maltreatment is also important to consider. *Crawford* may not be relevant to the vast majority of child maltreatment cases given that they often avoid litigation altogether. For those that do end up litigated, *Crawford* does pose challenges. Yet those challenges may not be that problematic given what prosecutors typically need to prosecute through actual trials rather than guilty pleas. In a national survey of prosecutors, child testimony ranked as more frequent than any other type of evidence. Rather than rely on hearsay and other court testimony modifications, prosecutors' trial preparations rely on victim assistants and exposure to courtrooms (tours). See Theodore P. Cross & Debra Whitcomb (2017). The practice of prosecuting child maltreatment: Results of an online survey of prosecutors. *Child Abuse & Neglect*, 69, 20–28. Cases that are litigated, then, are those that rely on witnesses, which means that prosecutors limit their litigated cases to those with witnesses who could withstand cross-examination. That should not be surprising given that prosecutors go to trial with strong cases and confidence that witnesses will support their cases. This makes *Crawford* not so problematic given that so few cases actually do go to trial. Cases deemed problematic to prosecute are closed by either guilty pleas or dismissed. It is true, however, that *Crawford* may have altered the calculus litigants engage in when deciding plea bargains. However, studies have long shown that prosecutors pursue child maltreatment trials, such as those involving child sexual abuse, when, for example, children are older and have caregiver support. See Stephanie D. Block, Hannah M. Johnson, Linda M. Williams, Kristy L. Shockley, Eric Wang & Keith F. Widaman (2023). Predictors of prosecutorial decisions in reports of child sexual abuse. *Child Maltreatment*, 28(3), 488–499.

Parham v. J. R.

442 U.S. 584; 99 S. Ct. 2493 (1978)

Mr. Chief Justice Burger delivered the opinion of the Court.

The question presented in this appeal is what process is constitutionally due a minor child whose parents or guardian seek state administered institutional mental health care for the child and specifically whether an adversary proceeding is required prior to or after the commitment.

I

(a) Appellee J. R., a child being treated in a Georgia state mental hospital, was a plaintiff in this class action based on 42 U. S. C. § 1983, in the District Court for the Middle District of Georgia. Appellants are the State's Commissioner of the Department of Human Resources, the Director of the Mental Health Division of the Department of Human Resources, and the Chief Medical Officer at the hospital where appellee was being treated. Appellee sought a declaratory judgment that Georgia's voluntary commitment procedures for children under the age of 18, violated the Due Process Clause of the Fourteenth Amendment and requested an injunction against their future enforcement.

... After considering expert and lay testimony and extensive exhibits and after visiting two of the State's regional mental health hospitals, the District Court held that Georgia's statutory scheme was unconstitutional because it failed to protect adequately the appellees' due process rights.

To remedy this violation, the court enjoined future commitments based on the procedures in the Georgia statute. It also commanded Georgia to appropriate and expend whatever amount was "reasonably necessary" to provide nonhospital facilities deemed by the appellant state officials to be the most appropriate for the treatment of those members of plaintiffs' class, who could be treated in a less drastic, nonhospital environment.

Appellants challenged all aspects of the District Court's judgment.

...

(c) Appellee J. R. was declared a neglected child by the county and removed from his natural parents when he was 3 months old. He was placed in seven different foster homes in succession prior to his admission to Central State Hospital at the age of 7.

Immediately preceding his hospitalization, J. R. received outpatient treatment at a county mental health center for several months. He then began attending school where he was so disruptive and incorrigible that he could not conform to normal behavior patterns. Because of his abnormal behavior, J. R.'s seventh set of foster parents requested his removal from their home. The Department of Family and Children Services then sought his admission at Central State. The agency provided the hospital with a complete sociomedical history at the time of his admission. In addition, three separate interviews were conducted with J. R. by the admission team of the hospital.

It was determined that he was borderline retarded, and suffered an "unsocialized, aggressive reaction of childhood." It was recommended unanimously that he would "benefit from the structured environment" of the hospital and would "enjoy living and playing with boys of the same age."

J. R.'s progress was re-examined periodically. In addition, unsuccessful efforts were made by the Department of Family and Children Services during his stay at the hospital to place J. R. in various foster homes. On October 24, 1975, J. R. filed this suit requesting an order of the court placing him in a less drastic environment suitable to his needs.

(d) Georgia Code provides for the voluntary admission to a state regional hospital of children.... Under that provision, admission begins with an application for hospitalization signed by a "parent or guardian." Upon application, the superintendent of each hospital is given the power to admit temporarily any child for "observation and diagnosis." If, after observation, the superintendent finds "evidence of mental illness" and that the child is "suitable for treatment" in the hospital, then the child may be admitted "for such period and under such conditions as may be authorized by law."

Georgia's mental health statute also provides for the discharge of voluntary patients. Any child who has been hospitalized for more than five days may be discharged at the request of a parent or guardian. Even without a request for discharge, however, the superintendent of each regional hospital has an affirmative duty to release any child "who has recovered from his mental illness or who has sufficiently improved that the superintendent determines that hospitalization of the patient is no longer desirable."

Georgia's Mental Health Director has not published any statewide regulations defining what specific procedures each superintendent must employ when admitting a child under 18. Instead, each regional hospital's superintendent is responsible for the procedures in his or her facility. There is substantial variation among the institutions with regard to their admission procedures and their procedures for review of patients after they have been admitted....

...

The District Court nonetheless rejected the State's entire system of providing mental health care on both procedural and substantive grounds. The District Court found that 46 children could be "optimally cared for in another, less restrictive, non-hospital setting if it were available." These "optimal" settings included group homes, therapeutic camps, and home-care services. The Governor of Georgia and the chairmen of the two Appropriations Committees of its legislature, testifying in the District Court, expressed confidence in the Georgia program and informed the court that the State could not justify enlarging its budget during fiscal year 1977 to provide the specialized treatment settings urged by appellees in addition to those then available.

Having described the factual background of Georgia's mental health program and its treatment of the named plaintiffs, we turn now to examine the legal bases for the District Court's judgment.

II

In holding unconstitutional Georgia's statutory procedure for voluntary commitment of juveniles, the District Court first determined that commitment to any of the eight regional hospitals constitutes a severe deprivation of a child's liberty. The court defined this liberty interest in terms of both freedom from bodily restraint and freedom from the "emotional and psychic harm" caused by the institutionalization. Having determined that a liberty interest is implicated by a child's admission to a mental hospital, the court considered what process is required to protect that interest. It held that the process due "includes at least the right after notice to be heard before an impartial tribunal."

...

The parties agree that our prior holdings have set out a general approach for testing challenged state procedures under a due process claim. Assuming the existence of a protectible property or liberty interest, the Court has required a balancing of a number of factors:

> First, the private interest that will be affected by the official action; second, the risk of an erroneous deprivation of such interest through the procedures used, and the probable value, if any, of additional or substitute procedural safeguards; and finally, the Government's interest, including the function involved and the fiscal and administrative burdens that the additional or substitute procedural requirement would entail.

In applying these criteria, we must consider first the child's interest in not being committed. Normally, however, since this interest is inextricably linked with the parents' interest in and obligation for the welfare and health of the child, the private interest at stake is a combination of the child's and parents' concerns. Next, we must examine the State's interest in the procedures it has adopted for commitment and treatment of children. Finally, we must consider how well Georgia's procedures protect against arbitrariness in the decision to commit a child to a state mental hospital.

(a) It is not disputed that a child, in common with adults, has a substantial liberty interest in not being confined unnecessarily for medical treatment and that the state's involvement in the commitment decision constitutes state action under the Fourteenth Amendment. We also recognize that commitment sometimes produces adverse social consequences for the child because of the reaction of some to the discovery that the child has received psychiatric care. This reaction, however, need not be equated with the community response resulting from being labeled by the state as delinquent, criminal, or mentally ill and possibly dangerous. The state through its voluntary commitment procedures does not "label" the child; it provides a diagnosis and treatment that medical specialists conclude the child requires. In terms of public reaction, the child who exhibits abnormal behavior may be seriously injured by an erroneous decision not to commit. Appellees overlook a significant source of the public reaction to the mentally ill, for what is truly "stigmatizing" is the symptomatology of a mental or emotional illness. The pattern of untreated, abnormal behavior—even if nondangerous—arouses at least as much negative reaction as treatment that becomes public knowledge. A person needing, but not receiving, appropriate medical care may well face even greater social ostracism resulting from the observable symptoms of an untreated disorder.

However, we need not decide what effect these factors might have in a different case. For purposes of this decision, we assume that a child has a protectible interest not only in being free of unnecessary bodily restraints but also in not being labeled erroneously by some persons because of an improper decision by the state hospital superintendent.

(b) We next deal with the interests of the parents who have decided, on the basis of their observations and independent professional recommendations, that their child needs institutional care. Appellees argue that the constitutional rights of the child are of such magnitude and the likelihood of parental abuse is so great that the parents' traditional interests in and responsibility for the upbringing of their child must be subordinated at least to the extent of providing a formal adversary hearing prior to a voluntary commitment.

Our jurisprudence historically has reflected Western civilization concepts of the family as a unit with broad parental authority over minor children. Our cases have consistently followed that course; our constitutional system long ago rejected any notion that a child is "the mere creature of the State" and, on the contrary, asserted that parents generally "have the right, coupled with the high duty, to recognize and prepare [their children] for additional obligations." Surely, this includes a "high duty" to recognize symptoms of illness and to seek and follow medical advice. The law's concept of the family rests on a presumption that parents possess what a child lacks in maturity, experience, and capacity for judgment required for making life's difficult decisions. More important, historically it has recognized that natural bonds of affection lead parents to act in the best interests of their children.

As with so many other legal presumptions, experience and reality may rebut what the law accepts as a starting point; the incidence of child neglect and abuse cases attests to this. That some parents "may at times be acting against the interests of their children" . . . creates a basis for caution, but is hardly a reason to discard wholesale those pages of human experience that teach that parents generally do act in the child's best interests. The statist notion that governmental power should supersede parental authority in all cases because some parents abuse and neglect children is repugnant to American tradition.

Nonetheless, we have recognized that a state is not without constitutional control over parental discretion in dealing with children when their physical or mental health is jeopardized. Moreover, the Court recently declared unconstitutional a state statute that granted parents an absolute veto over a minor child's decision to have an abortion. Appellees urge that these precedents limiting the traditional rights of parents, if viewed in the context of the liberty interest of the child and the likelihood of parental abuse, require us to hold that the parents' decision to have a child admitted to a mental hospital must be subjected to an exacting constitutional scrutiny, including a formal, adversary, pre-admission hearing.

Appellees' argument, however, sweeps too broadly. Simply because the decision of a parent is not agreeable to a child or because it involves risks does not automatically transfer the power to make that decision from the parents to some agency or officer of the state. The same characterizations can be made for a tonsillectomy, appendectomy, or other medical procedure. Most children, even in adolescence, simply are not able to make sound judgments concerning many decisions, including their need for medical care or treatment. Parents can and must make those judgments. . . .

. . .

In defining the respective rights and prerogatives of the child and parent in the voluntary commitment setting, we conclude that our precedents permit the parents to retain a substantial, if not the dominant, role in the decision, absent a finding of neglect or abuse, and that the traditional presumption that the parents act in the best interests of their child should apply. We also conclude, however, that the child's rights and the nature of the commitment decision are such that parents cannot always have absolute and unreviewable discretion to decide whether to have a child institutionalized. They, of course, retain plenary authority to seek such care for their children, subject to a physician's independent examination and medical judgment.

(c) The State obviously has a significant interest in confining the use of its costly mental health facilities to cases of genuine need. The Georgia program seeks first to determine whether the patient seeking admission has an illness that calls for inpatient treatment. To accomplish this purpose, the State has charged the superintendents of each regional hospital with the responsibility for determining, before authorizing an admission, whether a prospective patient is mentally ill and whether the patient will likely benefit from hospital care. In addition, the State has imposed a continuing duty on hospital superintendents to release any patient who has recovered to the point where hospitalization is no longer needed.

The State in performing its voluntarily assumed mission also has a significant interest in not imposing unnecessary procedural obstacles that may discourage the mentally ill or their families from seeking needed psychiatric assistance. The parens patriae interest in helping parents care for the mental health of their children cannot be fulfilled if the parents are unwilling to take advantage of the opportunities because the admission process is too onerous, too embarrassing, or too contentious. It is surely not idle to speculate as to how many parents who believe they are acting in good faith would forgo state-provided hospital care if such care is contingent on participation in an adversary proceeding designed to probe their motives and other private family matters in seeking the voluntary admission.

The State also has a genuine interest in allocating priority to the diagnosis and treatment of patients as soon as they are admitted to a hospital rather than to time-consuming procedural minuets before the admission. One factor that must be considered is the utilization of the time of psychiatrists, psychologists, and other behavioral specialists in preparing for and participating in hearings rather than performing the task for which their special training has fitted them. Behavioral experts in courtrooms and hearings are of little help to patients.

The amici brief of the American Psychiatric Association et al. points out at page 20 that the average staff psychiatrist in a hospital presently is able to devote only 47% of his time to direct patient care. One consequence of increasing the procedures the state must provide prior to a child's voluntary admission will be that mental health professionals will be diverted even more from the treatment of patients in order to travel to and participate in—and wait for—what could be hundreds—or even thousands—of hearings each year. Obviously the cost of these procedures would come from the public moneys the legislature intended for mental health care.

(d) We now turn to consideration of what process protects adequately the child's constitutional rights by reducing risks of error without unduly trenching on traditional parental authority and without undercutting "efforts to further the legitimate interests of both the state and the patient that are served by" voluntary commitments. We conclude that the risk of error inherent in the parental decision to have a child institutionalized for mental health care is sufficiently great that some kind of inquiry should be made by a "neutral factfinder" to determine whether the statutory requirements for admission are satisfied. That inquiry must carefully probe the child's background using all available sources, including, but not limited to, parents, schools, and other social agencies. Of course, the review must also include an interview with the child. It is necessary that the decisionmaker have the authority to refuse to admit any child who does not satisfy the medical standards for admission. Finally, it is necessary that the child's continuing need for commitment be reviewed periodically by a similarly independent procedure.

We are satisfied that such procedures will protect the child from an erroneous admission decision in a way that neither unduly burdens the states nor inhibits parental decisions to seek state help.

Due process has never been thought to require that the neutral and detached trier of fact be law trained or a judicial or administrative officer. Surely, this is the case as to medical decisions, for "neither judges nor administrative hearing officers are better qualified than psychiatrists to render psychiatric judgments." Thus, a staff physician will suffice, so long as he or she is free to evaluate independently the child's mental and emotional condition and need for treatment.

It is not necessary that the deciding physician conduct a formal or quasi-formal hearing. A state is free to require such a hearing, but due process is not violated by use of informal, traditional medical investigative techniques. Since well-established medical procedures already exist, we do not undertake to outline with specificity precisely what this investigation must involve. The mode and procedure of medical diagnostic procedures is not the business of judges. What is best for a child is an individual medical decision that must be left to the judgment of physicians in each case. We do no more than emphasize that the decision should represent an independent judgment of what the child requires and that all sources of information that are traditionally relied on by physicians and behavioral specialists should be consulted.

Here, the questions are essentially medical in character: whether the child is mentally or emotionally ill and whether he can benefit from the treatment that is provided by the state. . . .

Although we acknowledge the fallibility of medical and psychiatric diagnosis, we do not accept the notion that the shortcomings of specialists can always be avoided by shifting the decision from a trained specialist using the traditional tools of medical science to an untrained judge or administrative hearing officer after a judicial-type hearing. Even after a hearing, the nonspecialist decisionmaker must make a medical-psychiatric decision. Common human experience and scholarly opinions suggest that the supposed protections of an adversary proceeding to determine the appropriateness of medical decisions for the commitment and treatment of mental and emotional illness may well be more illusory than real.

Another problem with requiring a formalized, factfinding hearing lies in the danger it poses for significant intrusion into the parent–child relationship. Pitting the parents and child as adversaries often will be at odds with the presumption that parents act in the best interests of their child. It is one thing to require a neutral physician to make a careful review of the parents' decision in order to make sure it is proper from a medical standpoint; it is a wholly different matter to employ an adversary contest to ascertain whether the parents' motivation is consistent with the child's interests.

Moreover, it is appropriate to inquire into how such a hearing would contribute to the successful long-range treatment of the patient. Surely, there is a risk that it would exacerbate whatever tensions already exist between the child and the parents. Since the parents can and usually do play a significant role in the treatment while the child is hospitalized and even more so after release, there is a serious risk that an adversary confrontation will adversely affect the ability of the parents to assist the child while in the hospital. Moreover, it will make his subsequent return home more difficult. These unfortunate results are especially critical with an emotionally disturbed child; they seem likely to occur in the context of an adversary hearing in which the parents testify. A confrontation over such intimate family relationships would distress the normal adult parents and the impact on a disturbed child almost certainly would be significantly greater.

It has been suggested that a hearing conducted by someone other than the admitting physician is necessary in order to detect instances where parents are "guilty of railroading their children into asylums" or are using "voluntary commitment procedures in order to sanction behavior of which they [disapprove]." Curiously, it seems to be taken for granted that parents who seek to "dump" their children on the state will inevitably be able to conceal their motives and thus deceive the admitting psychiatrists and the other mental health professionals who make and review the admission decision. It is elementary that one early diagnostic inquiry into the cause of an emotional disturbance of a child is an examination into the environment of the child. It is unlikely, if not inconceivable, that a decision to abandon an emotionally normal, healthy child and thrust him into an institution will be a discrete act leaving no trail of circumstances. Evidence of such conflicts will emerge either in the interviews or from secondary sources. It is unrealistic to believe that trained psychiatrists, skilled in eliciting responses, sorting medically relevant facts, and sensing motivational nuances will often be deceived about the family situation surrounding a child's emotional disturbance. Surely a lay, or even law-trained, factfinder would be no more skilled in this process than the professional.

By expressing some confidence in the medical decisionmaking process, we are by no means suggesting it is error free. On occasion, parents may initially mislead an admitting physician or a physician may erroneously diagnose the child as needing institutional care either because of negligence or an overabundance of caution. That there may be risks of error in the process affords no rational predicate for holding unconstitutional an entire statutory and administrative scheme that is generally followed in more than 30 states. "[Procedural] due process rules are shaped by the risk of error inherent in the truthfinding process as applied to the generality of cases, not the rare exceptions." In general, we are satisfied that an independent medical decisionmaking process, which includes the thorough psychiatric investigation described earlier, followed by additional periodic review of a child's condition, will protect children who should not be admitted; we do not believe the risks of error in that process would be significantly reduced by a more formal, judicial-type hearing. The issue remains whether the Georgia practices, as described in the record before us, comport with these minimum due process requirements.

. . .

We are satisfied that the voluminous record as a whole supports the conclusion that the admissions staffs of the hospitals have acted in a neutral and detached fashion in making medical judgments in the best interests of the children. The State, through its mental health programs, provides the authority for trained professionals to assist parents in examining, diagnosing, and treating emotionally disturbed children. Through its hiring practices, it provides well-staffed and well-equipped hospitals and—as the District Court found—conscientious public employees to implement the State's beneficent purposes.

. . .

(a) Our discussion in Part III was directed at the situation where a child's natural parents request his admission to a state mental hospital. Some members of appellees' class, including J. R., were wards of the State of Georgia at the time of their admission. Obviously their situation differs from those members of the class who have natural parents. While the determination of what process is due varies somewhat when the state, rather than a natural parent, makes the request for commitment, we conclude that the differences in the two situations do not justify requiring different procedures at the time of the child's initial admission to the hospital.

For a ward of the state, there may well be no adult who knows him thoroughly and who cares for him deeply. Unlike with natural parents where there is a presumed natural affection to guide their action, the presumption that the state will protect a child's general welfare stems from a specific state statute.

. . .

Since the state agency having custody and control of the child in loco parentis has a duty to consider the best interests of the child with respect to a decision on commitment to a mental hospital, the State may constitutionally allow that custodial agency to speak for the child, subject, of course, to the restrictions governing natural parents. On this record, we cannot declare unconstitutional Georgia's admission procedures for wards of the State.

(b) It is possible that the procedures required in reviewing a ward's need for continuing care should be different from those used to review the need of a child with natural parents. As we have suggested earlier, the issue of what process is due to justify continuing a voluntary commitment must be considered by the District Court on remand. In making that inquiry, the District Court might well consider whether wards of the State should be treated with respect to continuing therapy differently from children with natural parents.

The absence of an adult who cares deeply for a child has little effect on the reliability of the initial admission decision, but it may have some effect on how long a child will remain in the hospital. We noted . . . that "the concern of family and friends generally will provide continuous opportunities for an erroneous commitment to be corrected." For a child without natural parents, we must acknowledge the risk of being "lost in the shuffle." Moreover, there is at least some indication that J. R.'s commitment was prolonged because the Department of Family and Children Services had difficulty finding a foster home for him. . . .

V

It is important that we remember the purpose of Georgia's comprehensive mental health program. It seeks substantively and at great cost to provide care for those who cannot afford to obtain private treatment and procedurally to screen carefully all applicants to assure that institutional care is suited to the particular patient. The State resists the complex of procedures ordered by the District Court because in its view they are unnecessary to protect the child's rights, they divert public resources from the central objective of administering health care, they risk aggravating the tensions inherent in the family situation, and they erect barriers that may discourage parents from seeking medical aid for a disturbed child.

On this record, we are satisfied that Georgia's medical factfinding processes are reasonable and consistent with constitutional guarantees. Accordingly, it was error to hold unconstitutional the State's procedures for admitting a child for treatment to a state mental hospital. The judgment is therefore reversed, and the case is remanded to the District Court for further proceedings consistent with this opinion.

Reversed and remanded.

Mr. Justice Stewart, concurring in the judgment.

For centuries it has been a canon of the common law that parents speak for their minor children. So deeply imbedded in our traditions is this principle of law that the Constitution itself may compel a State to respect it. In ironic contrast, the District Court in this case has said that the Constitution requires the State of Georgia to disregard this established principle. I cannot agree.

. . .

I realize, of course, that a parent's decision to commit his child to a state mental institution results in a far greater loss of liberty than does his decision to have an appendectomy performed upon the child in a state hospital. But if, contrary to my belief, this factual difference rises to the level of a constitutional difference, then I believe that the objective checks upon the parents' commitment decision, embodied in Georgia law and thoroughly discussed, are more than constitutionally sufficient.

To be sure, the presumption that a parent is acting in the best interests of his child must be a rebuttable one, since certainly not all parents are actuated by the unselfish motive the law presumes. Some parents are simply unfit parents. But Georgia clearly provides that an unfit parent can be stripped of his parental authority under laws dealing with neglect and abuse of children.

Mr. Justice Brennan, with whom Mr. Justice Marshall and Mr. Justice Stevens join, concurring in part and dissenting in part.

I

Rights of Children Committed to Mental Institutions

Commitment to a mental institution necessarily entails a "massive curtailment of liberty." . . . Persons incarcerated in mental hospitals are not only deprived of their physical liberty, they are also deprived of friends, family, and community. Institutionalized mental patients must live in unnatural surroundings under the continuous and detailed control of strangers. They are subject to intrusive treatment which, especially if unwarranted, may violate their right to bodily integrity. Such treatment modalities may include forced administration of psychotropic medication, aversive conditioning, convulsive therapy, and even psychosurgery. Furthermore, as the Court recognizes, persons confined in mental institutions are stigmatized as sick and abnormal during confinement and, in some cases, even after release.

Because of these considerations, our cases have made clear that commitment to a mental hospital "is a deprivation of liberty which the State cannot accomplish without due process of law." In the absence of a voluntary, knowing, and intelligent waiver, adults facing commitment to mental institutions are entitled to full and fair adversary hearings in which the necessity for their commitment is established to the satisfaction of a neutral tribunal. At such hearings they must be accorded the right of "be present with counsel, have an opportunity to be heard, be confronted with witnesses against

[them], have the right to cross-examine, and to offer evidence of [their] own." These principles also govern the commitment of children. "Constitutional rights do not mature and come into being magically only when one attains the state-defined age of majority. Minors, as well as adults, are protected by the Constitution and possess constitutional rights."

Indeed, it may well be argued that children are entitled to more protection than are adults. The consequences of an erroneous commitment decision are more tragic where children are involved. Children, on the average, are confined for longer periods than are adults. Moreover, childhood is a particularly vulnerable time of life and children erroneously institutionalized during their formative years may bear the scars for the rest of their lives. Furthermore, the provision of satisfactory institutionalized mental care for children generally requires a substantial financial commitment that too often has not been forthcoming. Decisions of the lower courts have chronicled the inadequacies of existing mental health facilities for children.

In addition, the chances of an erroneous commitment decision are particularly great where children are involved. Even under the best of circumstances psychiatric diagnosis and therapy decisions are fraught with uncertainties. These uncertainties are aggravated when, as under the Georgia practice, the psychiatrist interviews the child during a period of abnormal stress in connection with the commitment, and without adequate time or opportunity to become acquainted with the patient. These uncertainties may be further aggravated when economic and social class separate doctor and child, thereby frustrating the accurate diagnosis of pathology.

These compounded uncertainties often lead to erroneous commitments since psychiatrists tend to err on the side of medical caution and therefore hospitalize patients for whom other dispositions would be more beneficial. The National Institute of Mental Health recently found that only 36% of patients below age 20 who were confined at St. Elizabeths Hospital actually required such hospitalization. Of particular relevance to this case, a Georgia study Commission on Mental Health Services for Children and Youth concluded that more than half of the State's institutionalized children were not in need of confinement if other forms of care were made available or used.

II

Rights of Children Committed by Their Parents

A

Notwithstanding all this, Georgia denies hearings to juveniles institutionalized at the behest of their parents. Georgia rationalizes this practice on the theory that parents act in their children's best interests and therefore may waive their children's due process rights. Children incarcerated because their parents wish them confined, Georgia contends, are really voluntary patients. I cannot accept this argument.

In our society, parental rights are limited by the legitimate rights and interests of their children. "Parents may be free to become martyrs themselves. But it does not follow they are free, in identical circumstances, to make martyrs of their children before they have reached the age of full and legal discretion when they can make that choice for themselves." This principle is reflected in the variety of statutes and cases that authorize state intervention on behalf of neglected or abused children and that, inter alia, curtail parental authority to alienate their children's property, to withhold necessary medical treatment, and to deny children exposure to ideas and experiences they may later need as independent and autonomous adults.

This principle is also reflected in constitutional jurisprudence. Notions of parental authority and family autonomy cannot stand as absolute and invariable barriers to the assertion of constitutional rights by children. States, for example, may not condition a minor's right to secure an abortion on attaining her parents' consent since the right to an abortion is an important personal right and since disputes between parents and children on this question would fracture family autonomy.

. . .

Additional considerations counsel against allowing parents unfettered power to institutionalize their children without cause or without any hearing to ascertain that cause. The presumption that parents act in their children's best interests, while applicable to most child-rearing decisions, is not applicable in the commitment context. Numerous studies reveal that parental decisions to institutionalize their children often are the results of dislocation in the family unrelated to the children's mental condition. Moreover, even well-meaning parents lack the expertise necessary to evaluate the relative advantages and disadvantages of inpatient as opposed to outpatient psychiatric treatment. Parental decisions to waive hearings in which such questions could be explored, therefore, cannot be conclusively deemed either informed or intelligent. In these circumstances, I respectfully suggest, it ignores reality to assume blindly that parents act in their children's best interests when making commitment decisions and when waiving their children's due process rights.

B

This does not mean States are obliged to treat children who are committed at the behest of their parents in precisely the same manner as other persons who are involuntarily committed. The demands of due process are flexible and the parental commitment decision carries with it practical implications that States may legitimately take into account. While as a general rule due process requires that commitment hearings precede involuntary hospitalization, when parents seek to hospitalize their children special considerations militate in favor of postponement of formal commitment proceedings and against mandatory adversary preconfinement commitment hearings.

First, the prospect of an adversary hearing prior to admission might deter parents from seeking needed medical attention for their children. Second, the hearings themselves might delay treatment of children whose home life has become impossible and who require some form of immediate state care. Furthermore, because adversary hearings at this juncture would necessarily involve direct challenges to parental authority, judgment, or veracity, preadmission hearings may well result in pitting the child and his advocate against the parents. This, in turn, might traumatize both parent and child and make the child's eventual return to his family more difficult.

Because of these special considerations, I believe that States may legitimately postpone formal commitment proceedings when parents seek inpatient psychiatric treatment for their children. Such children may be admitted, for a limited period, without prior hearing, so long as the admitting psychiatrist first interviews parent and child and concludes that short-term inpatient treatment would be appropriate.

. . .

I do not believe, however, that the present Georgia juvenile commitment scheme is constitutional in its entirety. Although Georgia may postpone formal commitment hearings, when parents seek to commit their children, the State cannot dispense with such hearings altogether. Our cases make clear that, when protected interests are at stake, the "fundamental requirement of due process is the opportunity to be heard 'at a meaningful time and in a meaningful manner.'" . . .

The informal postadmission procedures that Georgia now follows are simply not enough to qualify as hearings — let alone reasonably prompt hearings. . . .

The special considerations that militate against preadmission commitment hearings when parents seek to hospitalize their children do not militate against reasonably prompt postadmission commitment hearings. In the first place, postadmission hearings would not delay the commencement of needed treatment. Children could be cared for by the State pending the disposition decision.

Second, the interest in avoiding family discord would be less significant at this stage since the family autonomy already will have been fractured by the institutionalization of the child. In any event, postadmission hearings are unlikely to disrupt family relationships. At later hearings, the case for and against commitment would be based upon the observations of the hospital staff and the judgments of the staff psychiatrists, rather than upon parental observations and recommendations. The doctors urging commitment, and not the parents, would stand as the child's adversaries. As a consequence, postadmission commitment hearings are unlikely to involve direct challenges to parental authority, judgment, or veracity. To defend the child, the child's advocate need not dispute the parents' original decision to seek medical treatment for their child, or even, for that matter, their observations concerning the child's behavior. The advocate need only argue, for example, that the child had sufficiently improved during his hospital stay to warrant outpatient treatment or outright discharge. Conflict between doctor and advocate on this question is unlikely to lead to family discord.

As a consequence, the prospect of a postadmission hearing is unlikely to deter parents from seeking medical attention for their children and the hearing itself is unlikely so to traumatize parent and child as to make the child's eventual return to the family impracticable.

Nor would postadmission hearings defeat the primary purpose of the state juvenile mental health enterprise. Under the present juvenile commitment scheme, Georgia parents do not enjoy absolute discretion to commit their children to public mental hospitals. Superintendents of state facilities may not accept children for long-term treatment unless they first determine that the children are mentally ill and will likely benefit from long-term hospital care. If the superintendent determines either condition is unmet, the child must be released or refused admission, regardless of the parents' desires. No legitimate state interest would suffer if the superintendent's determinations were reached through fair proceedings with due consideration of fairly presented opposing viewpoints rather than through the present practice of secret, ex parte deliberations.

. . .

III

Rights of Children Committed by Their State Guardians

Georgia does not accord prior hearings to juvenile wards of the State of Georgia committed by state social workers acting in loco parentis. The Court dismisses a challenge to this practice on the grounds that state social workers are obliged by statute to act in the children's best interest. I find this reasoning particularly unpersuasive. With equal logic, it could be argued that criminal trials are unnecessary since prosecutors are not supposed to prosecute innocent persons.

To my mind, there is no justification for denying children committed by their social workers the prior hearings that the Constitution typically requires. In the first place, such children cannot be said to have waived their rights to a prior hearing simply because their social workers wished them to be confined. The rule that parents speak for their children, even if it were applicable in the commitment context, cannot be transmuted into a rule that state social workers speak for their minor clients. The rule in favor of deference to parental authority is designed to shield parental control of child rearing from state interference. The rule cannot be invoked in defense of unfettered state control of child rearing or to immunize from review the decisions of state social workers. The social worker-child relationship is not deserving of the special protection and deference accorded to the parent–child relationship, and state officials acting in loco parentis cannot be equated with parents.

Second, the special considerations that justify postponement of formal commitment proceedings whenever parents seek to hospitalize their children are absent when the children are wards of the State and are being committed upon the recommendations of their social workers. The prospect of preadmission hearings is not likely to deter state social workers from discharging their duties and securing psychiatric attention for their disturbed clients. Moreover, since the children will already be in some form of state custody as wards of the State, prehospitalization hearings will not prevent needy children from receiving state care during the pendency of the commitment proceedings. Finally, hearings in which the decisions of state social workers are reviewed by other state officials are not likely to traumatize the children or to hinder their eventual recovery.

For these reasons, I believe that, in the absence of exigent circumstances, juveniles committed upon the recommendation of their social workers are entitled to preadmission commitment hearings. As a consequence, I would hold Georgia's present practice of denying these juveniles prior hearings unconstitutional.

IV

Children incarcerated in public mental institutions are constitutionally entitled to a fair opportunity to contest the legitimacy of their confinement. They are entitled to some champion who can speak on their behalf and who stands ready to oppose a wrongful commitment. Georgia should not be permitted to deny that opportunity and that champion simply because the children's parents or guardians wish them to be confined without a hearing. The risk of erroneous commitment is simply too great unless there is some form of adversary review. And fairness demands that children abandoned by their supposed protectors to the rigors of institutional confinement be given the help of some separate voice.

Notes and Queries

1. Do you agree with the Court that "what is best for the child is an individual medical decision that must be left to the judgment of physicians in each case"?
2. How does the Court justify providing parents with so much control over their child's commitment?
3. Common law allowed mature minors to make their own decisions about medical treatment without their parents' consent. Should the right extend to civil commitment? Should hearings be provided for all children or simply those who are sufficiently mature to make autonomous decisions?
4. How does the Court justify not providing counsel for a child in order to avoid inappropriate commitment and to identify alternatives for treatment in a noninstitutional setting?
5. Many commentators suggest that commitment has been used to deal with troublesome children rather than children who suffer severe mental disorders. How can *Parham* be used to address the inappropriate commitment of children?
6. The Court places emphasis on the natural bonds of affection between parent and child that will lead the parents to act in their children's best interests. Do you find that argument persuasive? When considering wards of the state, the Court finds that the absence of an adult who cares deeply for a child has little effect on the reliability of the initial admission decision. The Court reasons that statutory

obligations require the state to act in the ward's best interest. Does that obligation persuade you that the state will in fact act in the child's best interests?

7. Do you agree with Justice Stewart who proposes that parents should be presumed to act in their children's best interests and that, if they do not, child maltreatment laws protect children from erroneous admissions to mental health institutions?

8. The Court reasons that providing less costly procedural protections to children is reasonable given that Georgia's comprehensive mental health program seeks substantively and at great cost to provide care for those who cannot afford to obtain private treatment. Should similar rationales support reduced protections for children's admission to private institutions? What admission procedures should private institutions implement?

9. What do you make of the Commission on Mental Health Services for Children and Youth's conclusion that more than half of Georgia's institutionalized children were not in need of confinement if other forms of care were made available or used?

Review Problem

1. A program of psychotherapy ("reparative" therapy) attempts to "cure" homosexuals by turning them into heterosexuals. The American Psychological Association has announced its opposition to these efforts and maintains that scientific evidence does not show that reparative or conversion therapy works. Further, the American Psychological Association does not view homosexuality as an illness. Suppose parents want their 15-year-old son committed for reparative therapy. Do parents retain that right? Suppose the son objects; are the parents being abusive? Suppose the son is sexually active in a state that has sodomy laws; should the parent be held responsible if the son engages in proscribed homosexual activity? Suppose the son is not homosexual but is sexually active. Could the parent commit the child to help stop his delinquent activities?

Research Comments

1. The *Child Abuse Prevention and Treatment Act* has moved toward establishing a statutory right to representation, although not necessarily by counsel, for all children who are the subjects of child protection proceedings. Specifically, as a condition for receiving federal funds, "in every case involving an abused or neglected child which results in a judicial proceeding," each state is required to "provide a guardian ad litem ... to represent the child." 42 U.S.C.A. § 5106a(b)(6) (West Supp. 2001). Congress specified that the guardian ad litem (GAL) may "be

an attorney or a court appointed special advocate (or both)" and that the purpose of such appointment shall be "(I) to obtain first-hand, a clear understanding of the situation and needs of the child; and (II) to make recommendations to the court concerning the best interests of the child." No further congressional guidance was or has been given as to the role of the GAL or the purpose of the representation.

2. What do you make of the use of Court Appointed Special Advocates (CASA)? CASA programs may follow one of four models: (1) the GAL model—the CASA is the child's GAL; (2) the "friend of the court" model—the CASA serves as an impartial observer, conducts investigations with key people, and makes recommendations to the court (children assigned a CASA under this model also have attorney GALs); (3) the "team" model—the CASA and attorney are appointed by the court to perform the functions of the GAL, and the CASA works "for" the attorney by providing the attorney with needed information to represent the child in judicial proceedings; and (4) the "monitor" model—the CASA monitors court orders for compliance and alerts the court about failures to comply, but has little, if any, contact with the children and families.

3. Which CASA model would be most effective in representing children? What factors would you consider in determining effectiveness: cost, re-entry into state care, time needed to achieve permanency, extent and nature of services received, case closure rates, moves by children from more restrictive (i.e., group homes and institutions) to less restrictive (i.e., parent, relative, family foster home) placements, the type of maltreatment, extent to which a child appears content with the proceedings, and/or other factors? Three major barriers hamper the effective representation of children: a lack of qualified personnel, insufficient funding, and time and compensation constraints. How would you address these issues in considering which models to follow?

4. Current trends in the representation of children seek to eliminate the use of attorneys, or at least not have attorneys act as attorneys when they represent children in maltreatment cases. Instead, they would have the attorney act as a GAL who would seek to operate in the child's best interest. Several rationales support the trend: Attorneys use too much of their discretion and biases; the use of attorneys minimizes the child's role; children do not have the same "autonomous rights" as adults, therefore they do not require attorney representation; and attorneys simply are not needed because the law focuses on parental rights and assumes that the state will be acting in the interests of children. Importantly, several rationales would support an opposite approach: Attorneys help ensure that parties will follow statutory requirements; the presiding judge must balance parental, state, and children's interests and thus cannot focus on the child's interest alone; children's interests may differ from those of their parents as well as those of the child welfare agency; and attorneys are needed to monitor the state's progress and failure. Many criticisms have been levied against not having legal counsel. If the GAL simply represents the child, then the child has no legal counsel. Lay GALs are unable to

provide "legal" counsel and cannot, for example, present evidence, examine witnesses, appeal adverse decisions, or advise the client of the ramifications of legal matters. Lay GALs attempting to serve in the role of legal counsel are engaging in the unauthorized practice of law. Additionally, lay representatives are less accountable than professionals for their actions because their conduct is not governed by ethical and legal standards.

5. Another model adopts a hybrid approach that has the attorney function as guardian ad litem. This model provides an attorney to represent the child and instructs the attorney to represent the child's "best interests." The attorney GAL advocates for a result that he/she believes (not necessarily what the child believes) is in the child's "best interests." Rather than taking direction from the client, as is the case in traditional attorney representation of adults, the attorney GAL is charged with forming the client's position by using his/her own judgment. Under this model, the attorney GAL's judgment as to the child's "best interests" takes precedence over the client's wishes. This model is favored in that it allows young children to be heard even though they cannot meaningfully participate in their litigation and it protects older children from the harm of their own bad choices. Critics view this approach as an "old fashioned," paternalistic model of representation that treats children as chattel rather than empowering them in the system. Critics further charge that this approach is ethically suspect because: (1) Attorneys should not disregard their clients' directives; (2) attorneys are not qualified to make "best interests" determinations; and (3) the legal system requires that attorneys be zealous advocates for a client's position, not agents of the court.

6. Regarding attorneys' roles, the American Bar Association has adopted the American Bar Association (1982). *Model Rules of Professional Conduct*. Chicago, IL: Author. Model Rule 1.14 was the first legal ethics rule that specifically addressed the representation of child clients. The Rule provides that:

   > (a) When a client's ability to make adequately considered decisions in connection with the representation is impaired, whether because of minority, mental disability or for some other reason, the lawyer shall, as far as reasonably possible, maintain a normal client–lawyer relationship with the client.
   >
   > (b) A lawyer may seek the appointment of a guardian, or take other protective action with respect to a client, only when the lawyer reasonably believes that the client cannot adequately act in the client's own interest.

This traditional attorney model seeks to allow attorneys to function as a client-directed advocate. Proponents of this approach understand its benefits as giving voice and autonomy to the client and as empowering children within the system. Another benefit is that it allows attorneys to function in a familiar setting and thus produces good outcomes for children because it encourages independent, zealous advocacy, and the attorney is not confused by the role or duties. Critics charge that the model does not work for young children who cannot meaningfully direct their litigation or for older children who may misdirect their litigation. The provisions do appear riddled with challenges. First, attorneys may not be able to adequately determine when clients have the ability to make "adequately considered decisions." For example, children's lawyers may assume that a child's ability to make decisions is somehow impaired simply because the client chooses a course of action not recommended by counsel. The Rule authorizes a lawyer's taking "protective action," but only when counsel believes the client is unable to "adequately act in the client's own interest." The rule runs the risk of excluding the participation of older children in their case if the attorney "reasonably believes" those clients unable to adequately act in their own interest. Second, the Rule assumes that lawyers can determine when child clients are unable to adequately act in their own interest. Third, the language of the Rule's second paragraph may be construed as a license to overrule a client's stated wishes. Because the Rule authorizes the attorney to determine client competence, the rule gives attorneys ethical license to disregard a child client's directions. Lastly, the Rule fails to address whether attorneys are required to serve as guardians or advocates. Without training, and even with training, attorneys may not be able to recognize that they need assistance.

7. To counter problems that arise when attorneys represent child clients, the American Bar Association has adopted new standards of practice that provide as follows:

> B-4. Client Preferences. The child's attorney should elicit the child's preferences in a developmentally appropriate manner, advise the child, and provide guidance. The child's attorney should represent the child's expressed preferences and follow the child's direction throughout the course of litigation.
>
> > (1) To the extent that a child cannot express a preference, the child's attorney shall make a good faith effort to determine the chil"s wishes and advocate accordingly or request appointment of a guardian ad litem.
> >
> > (2) To the extent that a child does not or will not express a preference about particular issues, the child's attorney should determine and advocate the child's legal interests.
> >
> > (3) If the child's attorney determines that he child's expressed preference would be seriously injurious to the child (as opposed to merely being contrary to the lawyer's opinion of what would be in the child's interests), the lawyer may request appointment of a separate guardian ad litem and continue to represent the child's expressed preference, unless the child's position is prohibited by law or without any factual foundation. The child's attorney shall not reveal the basis of the request for appointment of a guardian ad litem which would compromise the child's position.

> B-5. Child's Interests. The determination of the child's legal interests should be based on objective criteria as set forth in the law that are related to the purposes of the proceedings. The criteria should address the child's specific needs and preferences, the goal of expeditious resolution of the case so the child can remain or return home or be placed in a safe, nurturing, and permanent environment, and the use of the least restrictive or detrimental alternatives available.

See American Bar Association (1996). *ABA Standards of Practice for Lawyers Who Represent Children in Abuse & Neglect Cases*. Chicago, IL: Author. Available online at http://www.abanet.org/child/. Critics argue that the model still does not work well for young children and that the directive to resort to representation of the child's "legal interests" may not be a meaningful directive. Critics complain that focusing on "legal interests" is unsatisfactory because the legal interests of the child may be unclear or contradictory. The Standards also are criticized for including broad exceptions to the client-directed ideal and thus giving the lawyer unfettered and unreviewed discretion identifying the goals of the child.

8. The National Association of Counsel for Children (NACC) model modifies Standard B-4 of the ABA Standards. Some members of the NACC board believed the ABA Standards gave too much autonomy to the child client and was unrealistic where young children were concerned. The distinction between the ABA Standards and the NACC Revised ABA Standards is that where the ABA remained consistent with the client-directed attorney throughout, the NACC carved out a significant exception where the client cannot meaningfully participate in the formulation of his or her position. In such cases, the NACC's version calls for a GAL-type judgment using objective criteria. Additionally, the NACC's version requires the attorney to request the appointment of a separate GAL, after unsuccessful attempts at counseling the child or when the child's wishes are considered to be seriously injurious to the child. Proponents believe this is the best blending of the traditional attorney and attorney/GAL, providing the best of both options. Some suggest, however, that blending the attorney and GAL roles dilutes the strengths of both models. The NACC model is also criticized for giving the lawyer unfettered and unreviewed discretion identifying the goals of the child. National Association of Counsel for Children (2001). *ABA Standards of Practice for Lawyers Who Represent Children in Abuse & Neglect Cases, (NACC Revised Version)*. Denver, CO: Author. Available online at http://naccchildlaw.org/.

Chapter 11

Specific Prevention of Maltreatment

Prevention sciences have come of age, and policies have started to respond more deliberately to them. Although the study of prevention often uses different phrases for similar approaches, it most typically involves three possible prevention strategies: primary, secondary, and tertiary approaches. Tertiary prevention attempts to prevent long-term distress or dysfunction. It is preventative in that it consists of rehabilitative efforts that take place after the symptoms have become chronic. Secondary prevention includes interventions that take place soon after the appearance of the earliest symptoms, with the aim of preventing the disorder from becoming severe or chronic. Secondary prevention efforts seek to curtail the duration of the dysfunction, typically through early case finding and prompt intervention. These programs are preventative in that they reduce prevalence of dysfunction if the cases are treated successfully and the duration is shortened. Primary prevention involves interventions before exposure to risk factors and attempts to prevent symptoms and actually reduce the incidence of targeted dysfunctions. Gerald Caplan (1964). *Principles of Preventive Psychiatry*. New York: Basic Books.

Although the groupings were first developed in psychiatry, they have been used to envision and understand efforts to address social problems like child maltreatment. Tertiary prevention activities focus efforts on families where maltreatment has already occurred. These programs seek to prevent maltreatment from recurring and to reduce the negative consequences associated with maltreatment (e.g., social-emotional problems in children, lower academic achievement, and decreased family functioning). These prevention programs may include services such as intensive family preservation services with trained mental health counselors available to families twenty-four hours per day for a short period of time (e.g., six to eight weeks); parent mentor programs with stable, nonabusive families serving as "role models" and providing support to families in crisis; mental health services for children and families affected by maltreatment to improve family communication and functioning; and support groups for perpetrators, including sex offender programs in the criminal justice system and the civil commitment of offenders.

Secondary prevention activities focus efforts and resources on children and families known to be at higher risk for maltreatment. Several risk factors such as substance abuse, young maternal age, developmental disabilities, and domestic violence associate with child maltreatment. Secondary prevention programs may direct services to individuals, families, communities, or neighborhoods that have a high incidence of any or all of these risk factors. Examples of secondary prevention programs include home visitation programs for families deemed at risk, parent education programs for parents at risk, respite care for families in crisis, and parent support groups for parents at risk.

Primary prevention activities raise the awareness of the general public, service providers, and decision makers about the scope and problems associated with child maltreatment. Primary prevention efforts would include general public education about proper parenting such as to encourage parents to use nonviolent forms of discipline; public service announcements on the radio or television to inform, for example, citizens how and where to report suspected child abuse and neglect; and educational efforts to develop parenting skills during adolescence, such as efforts to teach adolescents age-appropriate expectations.

Given the wide variety of possible approaches to prevention, it is not surprising to find an equally wide variety of programs with varying degrees of documented success. It also is not surprising that, when implemented, programs end up addressing more than one mode of prevention. The ultimate adoption of prevention measures and the focus of those measures on different prevention objectives results from a complex balancing of our best social science understanding of the issues, prevailing popular beliefs, resources, and political limitations, and what the law permits and can foster. Understanding the forces in the balancing is quite significant, for the balancing sometimes means that responses are adopted even despite their documented ineffectiveness.

This chapter examines cases and materials that address a wide range of issues specifically aiming to prevent maltreatment: reporting abuse, stopping specific abusive behaviors, home visits, investigative visits and searches, registering child abusers and victims, notifying communities of specific offenders, and the civil commitment of offenders. These measures encompass both secondary and tertiary measures. Primary prevention efforts, the ones most distinguishable for their broad reach, are addressed in the next chapter.

Landeros v. Flood

17 Cal. 3d 399; 551 P.2d 389 (Ca. Sup. Ct., 1976)

Judge Mosk delivered the opinion of the court.

In this medical malpractice action plaintiff Gita Landeros, a minor, appeals from a judgment of dismissal....

The material factual allegations of the amended complaint are as follows. Plaintiff was born on May 14, 1970. On repeated occasions during the first year of her life she was severely beaten by her mother and the latter's common law husband, one Reyes. On April 26, 1971, when plaintiff was 11 months old, her mother took her to the San Jose Hospital for examination, diagnosis, and treatment. The attending physician was defendant Flood, acting on his own behalf and as agent of defendant San Jose Hospital. At the time plaintiff was suffering from a comminuted spiral fracture of the right tibia and fibula, which gave the appearance of having been caused by a twisting force. [Note 2 explains that a comminuted fracture is "a fracture in which the bone is splintered or crushed into numerous pieces."] Plaintiff's mother had no explanation for this injury. Plaintiff also had bruises over her entire back, together with superficial abrasions on other parts of her body. In addition, she had a nondepressed linear fracture of the skull, which was then in the process of healing. Plaintiff demonstrated fear and apprehension when approached. Inasmuch as all plaintiff's injuries gave the appearance of having been intentionally inflicted by other persons, she exhibited the medical condition known as the battered child syndrome.

It is alleged that proper diagnosis of plaintiff's condition would have included taking X-rays of her entire skeletal structure, and that such procedure would have revealed the fracture of her skull. Defendants negligently failed to take such X-rays, and thereby negligently failed to diagnose her true condition. It is further alleged that proper medical treatment of plaintiff's battered child syndrome would have included reporting her injuries to local law enforcement authorities or juvenile probation department. Such a report would have resulted in an investigation by the concerned agencies, followed by a placement of plaintiff in protective custody until her safety was assured. Defendants negligently failed to make such report.

The complaint avers that as a proximate result of the foregoing negligence plaintiff was released from the San Jose Hospital without proper diagnosis and treatment of her battered child syndrome, and was returned to the custody of her mother and Reyes who resumed physically abusing her until she sustained traumatic blows to her right eye and back, puncture wounds over her left lower leg and across her back, severe bites on her face, and second and third degree burns on her left hand.

On July 1, 1971, plaintiff was again brought in for medical care, but to a different doctor and hospital. Her battered child syndrome was immediately diagnosed and reported to local police and juvenile probation authorities, and she was taken into protective custody. Following hospitalization and surgery she was placed with foster parents, and the latter subsequently undertook proceedings to adopt her. Plaintiff's mother and Reyes fled the state, but were apprehended, returned for trial, and convicted of the crime of child abuse.

...

The standard of care in malpractice cases is also well known. With unimportant variations in phrasing, we have consistently held that a physician is required to possess and exercise, in both diagnosis and treatment, that reasonable degree of knowledge and skill which is ordinarily possessed and exercised by other members of his profession in similar circumstances.

The first question presented, accordingly, is whether the foregoing standard of care includes a requirement that the physician know how to diagnose and treat the battered child syndrome.

...

While helpful, the foregoing general history of the battered child syndrome is not conclusive on the precise question in the case at bar. The question is whether a reasonably prudent physician examining this plaintiff in 1971 would have been led to suspect she was a victim of the battered child syndrome from the particular injuries and circumstances presented to him, would have confirmed that diagnosis by ordering X-rays of her entire skeleton, and would have promptly reported his findings to appropriate authorities to prevent a recurrence of the injuries. There are numerous recommendations to follow each of these diagnostic and treatment procedures in the medical literature cited above.

Despite these published admonitions to the profession, however, neither this nor any other court possesses the specialized knowledge necessary to resolve the issue as a matter of law. We simply do not know whether the views espoused in the literature had been generally adopted in the medical profession by the year 1971, and whether the ordinarily prudent physician was conducting his practice in accordance therewith. The question remains one of fact, to be decided on the basis of expert testimony: "The standard of care against which the acts of a physician are to be measured is a matter peculiarly within the knowledge of experts; it presents the basic issue in a malpractice action and can only be proved by their testimony [citations], unless the conduct required by the particular circumstances is within the common knowledge of the layman."

Inasmuch as the "common knowledge" exception to the foregoing rule does not apply on the facts here alleged, the trial court could not properly conclude as a matter of law that defendants' standard of professional care did not include the diagnostic and treatment procedures outlined in the complaint. Plaintiff is therefore entitled to the opportunity to prove by way of expert testimony that in the circumstances of this case a reasonably prudent physician would have followed those procedures.

The second principal question in the case is proximate cause. Under the allegations of the complaint it is evident that the continued beating inflicted on plaintiff by her mother and Reyes after she was released from the San Jose Hospital and returned to their custody constituted an "intervening act" that was the immediate cause in fact of the injuries for which she seeks to recover. It is well settled in this state, however, that an intervening act does not amount to a "superseding cause" relieving the negligent defendant of liability if it was reasonably foreseeable: "[An] actor may be liable if his negligence is a substantial factor in causing an injury, and he is not relieved of liability because of the intervening act of a third person if such act was reasonably foreseeable at the time of his negligent conduct." Moreover . . . foreseeability may arise directly from the risk created by the original act of negligence: "If the likelihood that a third person may act in a particular manner is the hazard or one of the hazards which makes the actor negligent, such an act whether innocent, negligent, intentionally tortious, or criminal does not prevent the actor from being liable for harm caused thereby."

As we recently observed with respect to a determination of duty, however, "foreseeability is a question of fact for the jury." The same rule applies when the issue is whether the intervening act of a third person was foreseeable and therefore did not constitute a superseding cause: in such circumstances "The foreseeability of the risk generally frames a question for the trier of fact".

We cannot say categorically that an ordinarily prudent physician who had correctly diagnosed that plaintiff was a victim of the battered child syndrome would not have foreseen the likelihood of further serious injuries to her if she were returned directly to the custody of her caretakers. On the contrary, it appears from the professional literature that one of the distinguishing characteristics of the battered child syndrome is that the assault on the victim is not an isolated, atypical event but part of an environmental mosaic of repeated beatings and abuse that will not only continue but will become more severe unless there is appropriate medicolegal intervention. If the risk of a resumption of physical abuse is thus a principal reason why a doctor's failure to diagnose and treat the battered child syndrome constitutes negligence . . . the fact that the risk eventuates does not relieve him of responsibility.

Accordingly, the trial court in the case at bar could not properly rule as a matter of law that the defendants' negligence was not the proximate cause of plaintiff's injuries. Plaintiff is entitled to prove by expert testimony that defendants should reasonably have foreseen that her caretakers were likely to resume their physical abuse and inflict further injuries on her if she were returned directly to their custody.

. . .

The judgment is reversed.

Notes and Queries

1. *Landeros* is the leading pro-liability decision. Statutes have addressed this issue and typically instruct that "reasonable suspicion" or "reasonable cause to suspect or believe" triggers duties to report. Failure to report reasonable suspicion may

not lead to liability. Imposing liability may depend on the applicable statutory standard, such as willfully not reporting versus acting out of negligence.

2. How are we to define reasonableness? The leading case used "a reasonably prudent physician" standard. The California statute attempts to define the standard: "'reasonable suspicion' means that it is objectively reasonable for a person to entertain such suspicion, based upon facts that could cause a person in a like position, drawing when appropriate on his or her training and experience, to suspect child abuse." Cal. Penal Code § 11166 (West 1998). The standard of reasonableness depends on the reporter's training and experience. Is this preferred to taking no account of the reporter's profession or training?

3. Several jurisdictions explicitly reject the *Landeros* approach and refuse to impose civil liability for breach of reporting duties. For example, in *Borne v. Northwest Allen County School Corp.*, 532 N.E.2d 1196 (Ind. Ct. App., 1989), the Indiana Court of Appeals concluded that the legislative purpose in enacting Indiana's child abuse statutory scheme was not to create a private right of action against nonreporters of abuse. Since the legislature did not intend for a private right of action, statutory negligence, in turn, would not lie.

Review Problems

1. Should a health clinic be required to report, as child abuse, instances where minor patients under the age of 14 years are diagnosed as being pregnant, as having a sexually transmitted disease, or as suffering from complications of an abortion? What policies should be in place? Should clinics adopt the practice of telling patients that the law requires them to report possible statutory rape before they ask them about their sexual relationships? Why would a clinic do that?

2. Consider the following case. In November 1984, Vivian, age 13, began a voluntary sexual relationship with her 21-year-old boyfriend, Josh. On January 23, 1985, Dr. Law diagnosed Vivian as being pregnant. Dr. Law referred Vivian to a clinic for treatment. The clinic performed the requested medical care. The clinic did not report Vivian's pregnancy to any child protective agency. On February 21, 1985, Vivian's mother found out about the pregnancy. Her mother reported the pregnancy to the local sheriff and demanded that Vivian's boyfriend be "brought to justice." Following an investigation, the district attorney filed a civil complaint against the clinic alleging that its failure to report Vivian's pregnancy to a child protective agency violated child abuse reporting laws. The district attorney sought civil penalties and a permanent injunction enjoining the clinic from intentionally violating the law. The clinic contends that the law does not require the reporting of a minor's voluntary sexual conduct regardless of the age of the minor or the minor's partner. In effect, the clinic argues that they can determine whether the acts were abusive and, if they deem them abusive, then they must report the

case to proper authorities. In a nutshell, the reporting at issue is mandated by a provision that provides, in pertinent part, that "any . . . health practitioner . . . who has knowledge of or observes a child in his or her professional capacity . . . whom he or she knows or reasonably suspects has been the victim of child abuse shall report the known or suspected instance of child abuse to a child protective agency. . . ." Importantly, state statutes define child abuse as, among other things, sexual abuse of a child, which means sexual assault or sexual exploitation, lewd or lascivious acts upon a child under 14 years of age. The sexual relationship undoubtedly violates criminal law, but is there doubt that the clinic should report? Similar facts were litigated in *People v. Stockton Pregnancy Control Medical Clinic*, 203 Cal. App. 3d 225 (Cal. Ct. App., 1988). In that case, the court concluded that reasonable suspicions of voluntary sexual conduct between a minor under age 14 and a person of disparate age constituting a violation of the sexual abuse statute must be reported. The court also concluded that such reporting to a child protective agency serves a compelling state interest and therefore does not violate the state or federal constitutional privacy rights of affected minors. The court further concluded that the retention of substantiated reports of child abuse by the department of justice also serves a compelling state interest and therefore does not violate affected minors' rights to informational privacy under the state constitution. The court also emphasized that the provision does not currently require the reporting of all adolescents' sexual acts, which protects adolescents' rights. The law does not require reports of voluntary sexual conduct between minors under age 14 where both are of a similar age. The practical result is that the law exempts from reporting as "child abuse" the voluntary sexual conduct of sexually mature boyfriends and girlfriends and the conduct of younger children of similar ages who voluntarily play doctor or otherwise engage in sexual experimentation. Reasonable?

Reviews of Reporting Laws

1. State laws primarily govern who is required to report suspicions of child abuse and neglect. In addition, reporting laws include ways to increase the effectiveness of mandates. As a result, they state who qualifies as mandated reporters, which can focus on professionals and go as broad as including "anyone" who suspects maltreatment. They also address training requirements for mandated reporters, especially professionals who are in positions that potentially involve child maltreatment, such as physicians, teachers, therapists, and other service providers. Reporting laws also detail the responsibilities of institutions in making reports. They also typically involve the standards for making reports as well protections for privileged communications as well as confidentiality to protect reporters. They also detail the potential outcomes for failing to report. For a detailed review of state reporting laws, see Child Welfare Information Gateway (2023).

Mandatory reporting of child abuse and neglect. U.S. Department of Health and Human Services, Administration for Children and Families, Children's Bureau. https://www.childwelfare.gov/resources/mandatory-reporting-child-abuse-and-neglect/. See also Joel M. Geiderman & Catherine A. Marco (2020). Mandatory and permissive reporting laws: Obligations, challenges, moral dilemmas, and opportunities. *Journal of the American College of Emergency Physicians Open*, 1(1), 38–45.

2. Even though mandatory reporting laws may be useful to detect maltreatment, it is important to recognize their potential limitations. Limitations include false accusations, invasions of family privacy, disparities in reporting due to prejudice, harming children by the separation from families, parental reluctance to seek help, and overburdening child welfare systems with allegations that are unsubstantiated. See, e.g., Douglas J. Besharov (1994). Responding to child sexual abuse: The need for a balanced approach. *The future of children*, 135–155.

Gross v. Myers

229 Mont. 509; 748 P.2d 459 (Mont. Sup. Ct., 1987)

Justice Weber delivered the opinion of the court.

...

The plaintiff, Mrs. Gross, enrolled in the therapy group. Both parties agree that Mrs. Gross was adequately assured of strict confidentiality concerning matters raised during the group sessions. During one of these sessions, Mrs. Gross told the group about some incidents of sexual abuse which occurred between her husband and her daughters approximately 16 years earlier. When Mrs. Gross had originally learned of these incidents, she and her husband went for counseling to a mental health clinic, but state authorities were not notified.

After the third group session in 1986, Ms. Myers told Mrs. Gross that she was required by Montana law to report the incidents to state authorities. The parties agreed that Mrs. Gross was given an opportunity to make the report herself but chose not to do so. At the time of this conversation, all of the Gross' children were over nineteen years of age, and none of them were living with Mr. and Mrs. Gross.

Ms. Myers made the report by telephone to Mary Schulze of the Department of Human Services. Due to the remoteness of the incident, Mary Schulze made no further report or investigation of the matter.

Mrs. Gross brought this action in district court to recover damages allegedly caused by the report of child abuse made by Ms. Myers. Ms. Myers filed an answer, and during discovery, took Mrs. Gross' deposition. The parties also exchanged interrogatories. Ms. Myers then moved for summary judgment which was granted. From this order Mrs. Gross appeals.

I

Did the District Court err in concluding that the defendant, a clinical social worker running a therapy group, was subject to the reporting mandate of Section 41-3-201(1), MCA (1985), under the circumstances of this case?

Sections 41-3-201(1) and (2), MCA (1985), provide as follows:

> When the professionals and officials listed in Subsection (2) know or have reasonable cause to suspect that a child known to them in their professional or official capacity is an abused or neglected child, they shall report the matter promptly to the department of social and rehabilitation services or its local affiliate. . . .

. . .

Ms. Myers, as a licensed social worker and mental health professional, is included in the list of professionals . . . and is subject to the mandatory reporting requirements if she had reasonable cause to suspect that a child known to her in her professional capacity was abused or neglected. Section 41-3-102(2), MCA, contains the following definition of "abused or neglected child":

> An 'abused or neglected child' means a child whose normal physical or mental health or welfare is harmed or threatened with harm by the acts or omissions of his parent or other person responsible for his welfare.

Mrs. Gross argues that the statutory mandate to report exists only when the professional suspects current child abuse. In one sense she is correct. Section 41-3-102(6), MCA, defines threatened harm as "imminent risk of harm". Ms. Myers' cause for suspicion must be based upon a perceived present real harm or a perceived present imminent risk of harm. This perception need not always be based entirely upon current, culpable acts of those responsible for the child. The primary purpose of the statute is the protection of the child. If Ms. Myers, in her professional opinion had reasonable cause to suspect that a child presently is threatened with harm, she must report, whether her suspicion is based upon past acts, present acts, or both.

The question is whether Ms. Myers' suspicion was a reasonable one. In her affidavit in support of summary judgment she stated her concerns:

> My primary purpose in making the report was a concern for Joyce Gross's grandchildren. My training and experience leads me to the opinion that child sexual abuse is a chronic behavior which, without therapeutic intervention, is subject to repetition, even after long lapses of time.

Reasonable cause as anticipated by Section 41-3-201(1), MCA, clearly must be a subjective standard. While Section 41-3-201, MCA, contains the reporting requirement for a professional such as Ms. Myers, it is essential that such professionals also be aware of their potential liability under Section 41-3-207, MCA, in the event of a failure to report. Section 41-3-207, MCA, provides for both civil and criminal liability on the part of a professional who fails to report known or suspected child abuse. In the present case, Ms. Myers, as a professional, was required to exercise her own reasonable judgment within the circumstances presented. The purpose of the statutory requirement for the report of child abuse is to allow qualified persons in SRS, the county attorney, or peace officers to make the necessary investigation. The statutes do not require that the named professionals investigate to determine whether or not child abuse in fact has occurred. Ms. Myers submitted the affidavit of another therapist which supported her own professional opinion that sexual abuse toward children is chronic behavior which may reoccur even after a substantial lapse of time. Mrs. Gross submitted no evidence that Ms. Myers' suspicions were not reasonable. We conclude that the facts establish that the defendant had reasonable cause to suspect that a child may have been the subject of abuse or neglect. We hold the District Court did not commit error under these circumstances when it concluded that Ms. Myers was subject to the reporting mandate....

II

Did the District Court err in granting defendant's motion for summary judgment on the issue of her statutory immunity from civil liability?

The District Court granted summary judgment under Section 41-3-203, MCA, which provides immunity from liability. That statute reads:

> Anyone investigating or reporting any incident of child abuse or neglect ... is immune from any liability, civil or criminal, that might otherwise be incurred or imposed, unless the person acted in bad faith or with malicious purpose.

Unless Ms. Myers acted in bad faith or with malicious purpose, she is immune from civil liability and summary judgment would be proper. Mrs. Gross in her deposition admitted that Ms. Myers did not intend to harm or embarrass her. She concedes that the defendant had no malice toward her. As a result we need consider only the issue of bad faith.

...

Ms. Myers, as noted earlier, submitted an affidavit in support of her motion for summary judgment. In this affidavit she stated that her purposes for reporting were her concern for the grandchildren of Mrs. Gross and her desire to protect those children. She also said that she had no intent to harm or embarrass Mrs. Gross or the family.

Mrs. Gross filed no affidavit alleging facts which might support her allegation of bad faith....

...

... Mrs. Gross has failed to meet this burden and summary judgment was proper. As a result, Ms. Myers is immune from civil liability for reporting in this instance. We affirm.

Justice Sheehy, dissenting.

I dissent to the over-broad and unwarranted interpretation of the reporting mandate....

Where, under the statute, is the child that was known to Barbara Myers in this case to be an abused or neglected child which required her report? There is none. There is no abused child here under 18 years of age.

The "child" must be a person under 18 years of age....

The alleged abuser must be either the parent of any abused child under the statute, or he must be responsible for the child's welfare. This alleged abuser does not fit the statute.

Where is the "abused child" in this case? Barbara Myers had no knowledge that the alleged abuser was the parent of any child who was so harmed and threatened as described to constitute an abused child, and certainly knew of no child for whom the alleged abuser was responsible for the child's welfare.

Where is the harm or threatened harm to the child's health and welfare in this case? The statute states that it means the harm that occurs whenever the parent or other person responsible for the child's welfare "commits or allows to be committed a sexual assault against the child or expose the child or allows the child to be exploited for sexual purposes or commits or allows to be committed the act of sexually abusing the children."

In this case therefore, there is absolutely nothing within Section 41-3-201, MCA, which required a report by Barbara Myers so damaging to the husband of Joyce Gross. There was no "child known" to Barbara Myers; there was no "abused child"; there was no "harm to a child's health or welfare" threatened or present against a child based on sexual assault or one exploited for sexual purposes or otherwise sexually abused, and there was no child for whose welfare the alleged abuser was responsible. We have only a professional busybody.

The "threatened harm" required under the statute must be an "imminent risk of harm." Section 41-3-102(6). The majority opinion has transformed "imminent" into barely possible; perhaps; maybe; well, it could happen.

... [i]n my view, the immunity statute does not apply, because in this case Barbara Myers was not acting within Section 41-3-201(1), MCA, when she violated the confidence reposed in her by Joyce Gross.

Notes and Queries

1. *Gross* presents the general rule that a mandated reporter who reports child abuse in good faith is immune from civil and criminal liability regardless of whether the abuse is confirmed.

2. Does the dissent raise a persuasive argument, at least to the extent that, in this case, there actually is no child abuse and no harm? Does it seem legitimate to protect the reporting therapist who violates patient–client confidentiality to report a situation that does not constitute child abuse? Would you find the therapist negligent?

Research Comment

1. Research reveals important findings about the manner by which mental health professionals (e.g., psychiatrists, psychologists, and social workers) deal with the need to report cases of suspected child maltreatment concerning their clients. One study of surveys completed by 258 mental health professionals known to have reported a case of suspected child abuse and maltreatment to the New York State Central Register (NYSCR) revealed the following: (1) About 40 percent did not inform the client about the limits of confidentiality until reportable material came up; (2) many clinicians learned about abuse/maltreatment after approximately three months of therapy; (3) clinicians most typically informed the client about the report directly and before it was made, but did not call the NYSCR in the presence of the client; (4) most clinicians reported that informing clients about the limits of confidentiality did not deter them from entering treatment; (5) in over 72 percent of the cases, making the report did not disrupt the relationship, and in many instances it was helpful in the therapeutic process; and (6) about 27 percent were continuously resistant or terminated therapy shortly after the report was made. Barbara Weinstein, Murray Levine, Nathan Kogan, Jill Harkavy-Friedman & Joseph M. Miller (2000). Mental health professionals' experiences reporting suspected child abuse and maltreatment. *Child Abuse & Neglect*, 24, 1317–1328.

Zamstein v. Marvasti

692 A.2d 781 (Conn. Sup. Ct., 1997)

Justice Borden delivered the opinion of the court.

...

... In November, 1988, Sharon Zamstein brought an action in the Hartford Superior Court for dissolution of her marriage to the plaintiff. Sometime after initiating the dissolution proceeding, Sharon Zamstein accused the plaintiff of sexually abusing the couple's two children. In September, 1989, members of the Avon police department arrested the plaintiff on charges that he had sexually assaulted his two children, and the state's attorney for the Hartford judicial district commenced prosecution. Also in September, 1989, Sharon Zamstein retained the defendant, a psychiatrist licensed to practice in the state of Connecticut, to perform a sexual abuse evaluation of the children. The defendant met with the children on several occasions, videotaping each session. The plaintiff's complaint alleged further that in March, 1990, the defendant provided an edited version of the videotapes of his sessions with the children to the state's attorney's office and the plaintiff's criminal defense counsel. The plaintiff also alleged that the defendant had deleted exculpatory portions of the videotape before providing the tape to the state's attorney's office. On January 3, 1991, the marriage between the plaintiff and Sharon Zamstein was dissolved. The court awarded joint custody of the minor children to the plaintiff and Sharon Zamstein. The criminal trial of the plaintiff commenced in July, 1991. Following a three month trial, in which the defendant testified for the state, the plaintiff was acquitted of the criminal charges. The plaintiff alleged that the state's attorney's prosecution of the plaintiff would not have continued but for the defendant's provision of the edited videotapes.

. . .

The defendant moved to strike the plaintiff's amended complaint in its entirety. . . . In striking counts one through three, the plaintiff's negligence claims, the court ruled that, in the absence of an allegation of some special relationship between the plaintiff and the defendant, the defendant owed no duty of care to the plaintiff. . . .

II

We turn now to the principal issue in this appeal. The plaintiff . . . asks this court to extend existing law in Connecticut to recognize that psychiatrists, or other mental health professionals, who evaluate children for evidence of sexual abuse, owe a duty to exercise reasonable care in the performance of the evaluation, to the person suspected of committing the abuse. He contends that the need to protect individuals from false accusations of sexual abuse of children warrants the imposition of such a duty in the present case. . . . He argues that, because mental health professionals in Connecticut are already held to a standard of due care when they evaluate children for evidence of sexual abuse, extending the duty to encompass the parent or parents of the child who are alleged to have committed the abuse would not impose a greater burden on such mental health professionals, but rather would encourage them to perform their evaluations in accordance with the recognized standard of care. We disagree.

. . .

We conclude that imposing upon mental health professionals, who have been engaged to evaluate whether there has been sexual abuse, a duty of care running to the benefit of the alleged sexual abuser would be contrary to the public policy of this state. The legislature has expressed the strong public policy of encouraging medical professionals and other persons to report actual and suspected child abuse to the appropriate authorities and agencies. . . .

. . .

We conclude that imposing a duty on mental health professionals pursuant to the plaintiff's theory of liability in the present case would carry with it the impermissible risk of discouraging such professionals in the future from performing sexual abuse evaluations of children altogether, out of a fear of liability to the very persons whose conduct they may implicate. Such a result would necessarily run contrary to the state's policy of encouraging the reporting and investigation of suspected child abuse because effective evaluation and diagnosis of children is a necessary component of discovering the abuse in the first instance. In addition, imposing such a duty creates too high a risk that, in close cases, mental health professionals would conclude that no sexual abuse had occurred because they feared potential liability to the suspected abusers, rather than because of their professional judgment that, in all likelihood, no abuse had occurred. Because "rules of law have an impact on the manner in which society conducts its affairs"; we conclude that the sounder judicial ruling is to hold that no such duty exists.

...

... In our view, mental health professionals retained to evaluate children for evidence of child abuse should be allowed to focus their complete attention on the child whom they are to evaluate. The primary responsibility of such professionals is to determine whether the child has been sexually abused. They should not be distracted from their duty by the specter of potential liability to the suspected abuser in the event that their assessment of the child eventually turns out to be incorrect but honest.

We acknowledge that persons falsely charged with sexual abuse of children on the basis of incorrect evaluations may suffer great harm in both their social and personal relationships, and that such accusations have the potential of causing serious damage to a person's reputation. We are persuaded, however, that recognizing a cause of action under the circumstances pleaded in the plaintiff's complaint would have consequences detrimental to the community as a whole that outweigh any benefit that persons falsely charged with sexual abuse might derive if we were to permit such an action to proceed. Accordingly, we conclude that the trial court properly struck counts one through three of the plaintiff's amended complaint.

...

The judgment is affirmed.

Justice Berdon, dissenting.

The majority holds that, based upon what it presumes to be the public policy of this state, a psychiatrist or other mental health professional is absolutely immune from liability in an action brought by a parent as a result of the mental health professional's negligence in accusing the parent of sexually abusing his or her children. I disagree that the public policy of this state sanctions such immunity from civil liability.

The plaintiff, Jacob Zamstein, in his complaint seeking damages from the defendant, Jamshid Marvasti, a psychiatrist, alleges a tale of horror caused by the defendant's negligent conduct. On November 14, 1988, the plaintiff's wife, Sharon Zamstein, brought an action for dissolution of marriage against the plaintiff. The plaintiff and Sharon Zamstein, entered into a stipulation to have James C. Black, a psychiatrist, appointed to evaluate parental roles and to prepare a custody evaluation.

Thereafter, while the custody of the Zamsteins' minor children, J and R, was at issue, Sharon Zamstein accused the plaintiff of having sexually abused the two children. On September 14, 1989, an arrest warrant was executed and the plaintiff was taken into custody on charges of sexual assault. Later that month, Sharon Zamstein was referred to the defendant by her attorney in the dissolution proceeding in order to evaluate R and J for evidence of sexual abuse. At the request of Sharon Zamstein, the defendant undertook the evaluation. At the time that the defendant agreed to perform the evaluation, he knew that the children were the subject of a custody dispute between the plaintiff and Sharon Zamstein, and that, on the complaint of Sharon Zamstein, the plaintiff had been arrested on charges involving the alleged sexual abuse of his children. The defendant evaluated R during five sessions and J during three sessions, and the defendant videotaped all of these sessions. During these sessions, the defendant used several improper techniques to elicit incriminating responses from R and J, including the use of coercive interview techniques, asking leading or suggestive questions, and offering candy as a reward. At no time during his evaluation did the defendant ever meet or speak with the plaintiff.

On December 20, 1990, Black, having found no evidence of sexual abuse, recommended that the criminal charges against the plaintiff be dismissed and that unsupervised visitation between the plaintiff and the minor children commence immediately. Thereafter, on January 3, 1991, the family court issued a judgment dissolving the marriage between the plaintiff and Sharon Zamstein. The family court awarded joint custody of the minor children to the plaintiff and Sharon Zamstein.

Subsequently, the defendant presented to the state's attorney's office in Hartford and to the plaintiff's criminal defense counsel an edited version of the videotapes of the sessions with R and J, which he believed demonstrated that sexual abuse had occurred. In the edited version of the videotapes, the defendant had deleted the children's statements and actions exculpating the plaintiff from the allegations of sexual abuse.

Despite the findings of Black and the judgment of the family court, the state's attorney's office persisted with the prosecution of the plaintiff based on the defendant's presentation of the edited videotape. The criminal trial lasted more than three months and was the focus of numerous newspaper articles and televised news stories. At trial, the only expert testimony presented by the state was that of the defendant. Only after cross-examination of the defendant by the plaintiff's defense counsel at the criminal trial was it discovered that the defendant had edited the videotape to delete all of the exculpatory statements and actions by R and J. The plaintiff was subsequently acquitted of all criminal charges.

I agree with the majority that in determining whether a defendant owes a duty to another requires a two part inquiry: (1) whether it is foreseeable that harm of the general nature suffered by the plaintiff may result if care is not exercised; and (2) whether the imposition of such a duty is consistent with the public policy of this state. It is clear that the harm caused to the plaintiff in this case was foreseeable. The defendant was aware of the pending divorce proceeding and the criminal action during his evaluation of the minor children. Indeed, the defendant provided the edited videotape to the state's attorney's office for the purpose of assisting in the prosecution of the plaintiff for sexual abuse. Accordingly, the defendant knew or should have known that his actions would have a direct impact on the plaintiff's criminal prosecution and on the child custody proceedings, and could cause irreparable harm to the plaintiff and to his relationship with his children.

Nevertheless, the majority concludes that the defendant owed no duty to the plaintiff because the imposition of such a duty would be contrary to the public policy of this state. Although this court may assume what the public policy of this state is when the legislature is silent, once the legislature has spoken on a subject, it establishes the public policy of the state.

In my view, the legislature has recognized that it is not contrary to the public policy of this state to impose on psychiatrists and other mental health professionals a duty to persons they negligently accuse of abusing children. I agree with the majority that General Statutes demonstrates the state's strong public policy to report actual and suspected abuse. The majority, however, ignores the import of § 17a-101 (h), which provides in part that psychiatrists and others who "in good faith, [make] the report required by this section shall be immune from any liability, civil or criminal, which might otherwise be incurred or imposed. . . ." In other words, even in those situations in which mental health professionals are required to report child abuse, the granting of such immunity is predicated on the exercise of "good faith." Therefore, because the legislature in adopting § 17a-101 (h) refused to grant absolute immunity from civil liability to mental health professionals for reporting child abuse when required by law, it cannot possibly be the public policy of this state that mental health professionals owe no duty under any circumstances to persons they negligently accuse of child abuse. [Note 2 states that the majority of courts in other jurisdictions have concluded that, under the express language of child abuse reporting statutes similar to § 17a-101 (h), the immunity granted to mandatory reporters is limited to reports that were submitted in good faith.]

Under the allegations of the plaintiff"s complaint, it is inconceivable that such immunity would be available to the defendant. For example, the plaintiff alleges that the defendant had: (1) coercively obtained statements from the children that they were sexually abused by the plaintiff; (2) videotaped the interviews; and (3) furnished to the state's attorney's office a videotape edited to delete exculpatory portions. If, as a result of the edited videotape, the state continued with its prosecution of the plaintiff for sexual abuse, requiring him to endure a three month criminal trial during which it was discovered for the first time that the videotape was edited and at which he was found not guilty, the defendant would be hard pressed to convince a trier of fact that he acted in good faith.

. . .

The majority opinion has serious repercussions. It will allow mental health professionals to act negligently in their evaluation without any civil restraint, even when one parent's motivation for accusing the other parent of sexual abuse of his or her child is a dissolution proceeding involving a hotly contested custody issue. I, of course, agree with the majority that mental health professionals should not be discouraged from reporting child abuse. The concern that subjecting those professionals to civil liability for their negligent conduct could affect their professional judgment is allayed for several reasons. First, any parent who seeks to impose civil liability must prove that the mental health professional was negligent — that is, he or she failed to meet the appropriate standard of care. Indeed, if we were to apply the majority's reasoning, it would be contrary to the state's public policy to recognize that a physician has a duty to a patient not to commit malpractice because of concern that the physician would be reluctant to treat his patient aggressively when that treatment is in the patient's best interest. More importantly, when mental health professionals report child abuse cases to the state as required by § 17a-101, they are granted absolute immunity in civil, as well as criminal, cases if they acted in good faith. Finally, requiring psychiatrists and other health care professionals to answer for their negligence would have a salutary effect of causing the profession to regulate itself by establishing appropriate standards of care. The substantial harm that could result to a person when a professional like the defendant is not subject to civil sanctions is demonstrated in this case. That harm affects not only the parent, but also the children that the majority purports to protect, because such negligent conduct could destroy the relationship between a parent and his or her children.

. . .

Accordingly, I dissent.

Notes and Queries

1. An action for medical malpractice is essentially an action in tort brought against a physician or other health care provider for negligence. In order to maintain a medical malpractice action, the plaintiff must prove the elements of a negligence suit: (1) a duty owed by the physician to the plaintiff, (2) a breach of that duty by the physician, (3) a causal relationship between the breach of the duty by the physician and the plaintiff's injury, and (4) a resulting injury to the plaintiff. As the principal case illustrates, to sustain a medical malpractice action, a plaintiff typically must prove the existence of a physician–patient relationship.

2. Not all courts attach liability only in the presence of a physician–patient relationship as a result of a contract. In *Montoya v. Bebensee*, 761 P.2d 285 (Colo. Ct. App., 1988), the Colorado Court of Appeals abandoned the requirement of a physician–patient relationship in holding that a psychologist who was evaluating and treating a child for suspected child abuse owed a duty to the accused parent to exercise due care. The child's mother engaged the defendant psychologist during a dissolution proceeding for the purpose of rendering an opinion as to whether the father

had sexually abused the child. After the defendant examined the child, he filed a report of suspected abuse with the social services department and testified at a dissolution hearing that the father had sexually abused his child. The father sued the psychologist, alleging that he was negligent in his evaluation of the child. The court of appeals held that the defendant owed the father a duty of care. The court undertook a balancing test to determine whether to expand physician liability to accused child abusers, weighing the risk, the foreseeability, and the likelihood of the injury against the social utility of the actor's conduct, the magnitude of the burden of guarding against the injury or harm, and the consequences of imposing a duty on the actor. The court stressed the significant risk of severe injury to one who is falsely accused of child abuse. In addition, the court determined that the harm resulting from negligent false accusations was readily foreseeable. The court highlighted the public interest of having therapists report suspected child abuse and reasoned that the burden upon therapists to use due care is no greater than the duty of reasonable care required of all professionals. After considering all these factors, the court determined that "a mental health care provider owes a duty to any person, who is the subject of any public report or other adverse recommendation by that provider, to use due care in formulating any opinion upon which such a report or recommendation is based." Id. at 289.

Illinois v. Maness

191 Ill. 2d 478; 732 N.E.2d 545 (Ill. Sup. Ct., 2000)

Justice Bilandic delivered the opinion of the court:

This case involves the constitutionality of section 5.1 of the Wrongs to Children Act. We hold that section 5.1 is unconstitutionally vague.

Statute

Section 5.1 of the Wrongs to Children Act (Act) prohibits the offense of "permitting the sexual abuse of a child." For purposes of this case, section 5.1 provides:

> A. A parent or step-parent who knowingly allows or permits an act of criminal sexual abuse or criminal sexual assault as defined in Section 12-13, 12-14, 12-15 or 12-16 of the 'Criminal Code of 1961,' upon his or her child and fails to take reasonable steps to prevent its commission or future occurrences of such acts commits the offense of permitting the sexual abuse of a child. For purposes of this Section, 'child' means a minor under the age of 17 years.
>
> B. Any person convicted of permitting the sexual abuse of a child shall be guilty of a Class A misdemeanor.

Relevant to the facts of this case is the underlying provision of the criminal sexual abuse statute, section 12-15 of the Criminal Code of 1961, which provides that "the accused commits criminal sexual abuse if he or she commits an act of sexual penetration or sexual conduct with a victim who was at least 13 years of age but under 17 years of age and the accused was less than 5 years older than the victim." Criminal sexual abuse is a Class A misdemeanor.

. . .

Facts

On November 19, 1997, defendant, Kathy Maness, was charged in the circuit court of Randolph County with the offense of permitting the sexual abuse of a child. The charging instrument alleged that defendant, the mother of Lynlee Jo Otten, a minor under the age of 17 years, knowingly allowed or permitted Leonard A. Owens, Jr. to commit an act of criminal sexual abuse upon Lynlee, "in that Leonard A. Owens, Jr. committed an act of sexual penetration with Lynlee Jo Otten, who was at least 13 years of age, but under 17 years of age when the act was committed, in that Leonard A. Owens, Jr. placed his penis in the vagina of Lynlee Jo Otten, and Leonard A. Owens, Jr. was less than five years older than Lynlee Jo Otten, and the defendant did fail to take reasonable steps to prevent its commission." Defendant was alleged to have committed this offense in Randolph County, Illinois, where she and Lynlee lived, between the months of January and August of 1997.

. . . Between December 1996, and approximately April 1997, when the pair terminated their relationship, Lynlee and Leonard had sexual intercourse 15 to 20 times.

At some point after the sexual relationship began, Lynlee told defendant, her mother, that she and Leonard were having sexual intercourse. Defendant confronted both Lynlee and Leonard about the sexual relationship, expressed her disapproval, and discussed the implications of sexual intercourse.

Defendant obtained birth control pills for Lynlee and allowed Leonard on numerous occasions to spend the night at the family home. Defendant was aware that, on some of these occasions, Leonard slept in Lynlee's bedroom and had sexual intercourse with Lynlee. Defendant was also aware that, during the relevant time period, Leonard was 17 years old, and Lynlee was 13 years old. The record shows that Leonard pled guilty to criminal sexual abuse in connection with the facts of this case.

According to an investigative report from the Department of Children and Family Services (DCFS), defendant stated that she did not know what steps to take to prevent the sexual relationship between Lynlee and Leonard. Defendant further stated that Leonard "was a nice boy and was better than most of the younger boys Lynlee was hanging around with," and that "it was safer for Lynlee to be having sex with [Leonard] at home than [with] somebody else out of the home environment." The DCFS report discloses that defendant "feels she has some control of the daughter's sexual activities if it occurs in the home."

Defendant filed a motion to dismiss the charge, arguing that section 5.1 is unconstitutionally vague as to what constitutes "reasonable steps" to prevent the commission of future acts of sexual abuse. According to defendant, the statute exposes any parent to prosecution if a child "becomes pregnant, sires a child, asks for birth control devices, or seeks any counsel from the teenager's parents regarding sexual activity." Defendant also argued that section 5.1 of the Act, both on its face and as applied in this case, violates defendant's fundamental liberty right to raise her child free from undue state influence as guaranteed by the fourteenth amendment to the United States Constitution and article I, section 2, of the Illinois Constitution of 1970.

. . .

Analysis

We review de novo a circuit court's holding with respect to the constitutionality of a statute. Statutes carry a strong presumption of constitutionality, and the party challenging the constitutionality of a statute bears the burden of rebutting this presumption. Here, that party is defendant, who for the reasons set forth below has met this burden.

A cornerstone of our jurisprudence is that no person shall be deprived of life, liberty, or property without due process of law. Due process of law requires that the proscriptions of a criminal statute be clearly defined. To satisfy the vagueness doctrine, a criminal statute must meet two requirements. First, the statute must provide a person of ordinary intelligence a reasonable opportunity to distinguish between lawful and unlawful conduct so that he or she may act accordingly. "'No one may be required at peril of life, liberty or property to speculate as to the meaning of penal statutes. All are entitled to be informed as to what the State commands or forbids.'" Thus, a statute is unconstitutionally vague "if its terms are so indefinite that 'persons of common intelligence must necessarily guess at its meaning and differ as to its application.'"

Second, the statute must adequately define the offense in order to prevent arbitrary and discriminatory enforcement. The statute must provide explicit standards to regulate the discretion of governmental authorities who apply the law. If the legislature fails to provide minimal guidelines to govern law enforcement, a criminal law "may permit 'a standardless sweep [that] allows policemen, prosecutors, and juries to pursue their personal predilections.'"

Section 5.1 does not satisfy these requirements. To be charged under section 5.1, a parent must knowingly allow or permit an enumerated act of criminal sexual abuse or sexual assault to be committed upon his or her child, and fail to take "reasonable steps" to prevent its commission or future occurrences. It is unclear what the "reasonable steps" are that a parent must take in order to comply with the statute. The facts of this case demonstrate this uncertainty. As the record reveals, defendant's 13-year-old daughter confided in defendant that she was having sexual intercourse with her 17-year-old boyfriend. At this point, defendant, as a parent, took steps. She confronted her daughter and her daughter's boyfriend about the sexual relationship, expressed her disapproval, and discussed the implications of sexual intercourse. The statute does not set forth what more the statute commands.

We recognize that defendant obtained birth control pills for her daughter and allowed her daughter's boyfriend to spend the night at the family home. Defendant was aware that at times her daughter and her daughter's boyfriend slept together in her daughter's bedroom and had sexual intercourse with each other. Defendant, however, stated that she did not know what steps to take to prevent the sexual relationship between her daughter and her daughter's boyfriend, and that she felt she had more control over her daughter's sexual activities if they occurred in the home. We are in no position to determine whether defendant's actions constituted "reasonable steps" under the statute. We find that section 5.1 leaves a parent to speculate as to what the statute commands.

Furthermore, section 5.1 risks arbitrary and discriminatory enforcement. As we have discussed, the statute does not set forth standards to regulate what constitute "reasonable steps." There are no guidelines for authorities to follow in evaluating what "reasonable steps" are from case to case. This is certainly not a decision that should be left to the "personal predilections" of the governmental authorities who must apply section 5.1. Section 5.1 enumerates several underlying offenses. Regardless of the underlying offense, it is unclear what a parent must do to take "reasonable steps" under the statute, and authorities remain without standards to guide their enforcement of section 5.1.

... A person of ordinary intelligence is left to guess at its meaning and disagree as to its application. Due process of law requires that the proscriptions of a criminal statute be clearly defined. Section 5.1 fails to satisfy this requirement.

...

The dissent further contends that there "are numerous instances in which application of the statute would be proper," and then purports to give an example. The dissent's reasoning is flawed. The legal test for whether a statute withstands a vagueness challenge is well settled. To satisfy the vagueness doctrine, a criminal statute must provide both fair warning of the prohibited conduct and explicit guidelines for those who must apply the law Section 5.1 fails to meet this test. Section 5.1 requires a parent who knowingly allows an enumerated act to be committed upon his or her child to take "reasonable steps" to prevent the commission of the enumerated act. However, it is not clear what the "reasonable steps" are that a parent must take in order to comply with the statute and avoid criminal prosecution. The dissent's answer, that "a mother who gave express permission to one of her adult male friends to have sex with her 12-year-old daughter would clearly fall within the statute's prohibitions" begs the question of what a parent must in fact do in the first instance to comply with section 5.1's requirement of taking "reasonable steps" to prevent the enumerated act. The statute criminally punishes all parents who knowingly permit an enumerated act to occur and fail to take "reasonable steps" to prevent the act. Do "reasonable steps" mean that the parent must call the police, ban the offender from the home, send the child away, speak with the offender? The point is that, regardless of the underlying conduct, section 5.1 leaves a parent to speculate as to what the statute commands.

The dissent also concludes that defendant took "no steps" to prevent the abuse. The record reveals otherwise. Defendant confronted her daughter and her daughter's boyfriend about the sexual relationship, expressed her disapproval, and discussed the implications of sexual intercourse. What the dissent really appears to be saying is that defendant did not do enough. However, neither section 5.1, nor the dissent for that matter, specifies what more defendant must have done to avoid criminal prosecution.

Conclusion

We hold that section 5.1 is unconstitutionally vague. We therefore affirm the circuit court's order dismissing the charge against defendant. Consequently, we need not determine whether section 5.1 unconstitutionally infringes upon defendant's fundamental right to raise her child. We also note that, because the offense of permitting the sexual abuse of a child is no longer a Class 1 felony, we need not address defendant's argument raised in this court that applying section 5.1 to her conduct violates the constitutional prohibition against disproportionate penalties.

Affirmed.

Chief Justice Harrison, dissenting:

Section 5.1 of the Wrongs to Children Act imposes on parents a duty to take "reasonable steps" to prevent the commission or future occurrence of criminal sexual abuse of their children. Although my colleagues find this standard problematic, I do not believe that it renders the statute unconstitutionally vague. A penal statute comports with due process so long as the statute's prohibitions are sufficiently definite, when measured by common understanding and practices, to give a person of ordinary intelligence fair warning as to what conduct is prohibited, and the statute marks boundaries sufficiently distinct for judges and juries fairly to administer the law in accordance with the intent of the legislature.

Section 5.1 satisfies these requirements. While the statute does not specifically enumerate what constitute "reasonable steps" to prevent the commission or future occurrence of criminal sexual abuse, it is not alone in this regard. A similar standard has been employed successfully in many other areas of the law. For example, section 1(D)(m) of the Adoption Act provides that where a child has been removed from a parent by the State, the parent's failure to make "reasonable efforts" to correct the conditions that were the basis for removal of the child is grounds for finding the parent unfit. As a matter of common law, hospitals and physicians must take "reasonable steps" to avoid a foreseeable tragedy in their facility. Under the Domestic Violence Act of 1986 law enforcement officials have a duty to promptly undertake "all reasonable steps" to assist persons protected by the Act. Tort law dictates that if an accident is reasonably foreseeable, a party is charged with responsibility to take "reasonable steps" to avoid it.

Whether a party has acted reasonably will necessarily depend on the facts and circumstances of each particular case. What action is reasonable under the circumstances is not always easy to assess. Experience has shown, however, that when dealing with diverse and unpredictable situations, a "reasonableness" standard is the best measure for judging human conduct. Accordingly, the "reasonable man" standard has become a fundamental part of our jurisprudence. We constantly call upon citizens and law enforcement officials to follow and apply this standard. Again, examples are easy to summon. "Reasonableness" plays a pivotal role in assessing the legality of police stops. It is integral to the law of self-defense and the law governing trade secrets.

The majority has not cited any authority for the proposition that a "reasonableness" standard renders a criminal statute unconstitutionally vague, and I see no basis for reaching that conclusion with respect to section 5.1. Even if one could hypothesize circumstances in which application of the statute would be uncertain, that is not the test. A statute is unconstitutionally vague on its face only if it is incapable of any valid application, i.e., where "'no set of circumstances exists under which the [statute] would be valid.'"

Section 5.1 is not infirm under this standard. There are numerous instances in which application of the statute would be proper. For example, a mother who gave express permission to one of her adult male friends to have sex with her 12-year-old daughter would clearly fall within the statute's prohibitions.

Because there are valid applications for the statute and because the law does not involve first amendment rights, the determination as to whether the statute is constitutionally infirm must be made in the factual context of this particular case. Maness does not have standing to argue that the statute might be vague as applied to someone else. A defendant may be prosecuted under a statute without violating her due process rights if her conduct clearly falls within the statutory proscription even though the statute may be vague as to other conduct.

What Maness is alleged to have done in this case clearly falls within the prohibitions of section 5.1 of the Wrongs to Children Act. Maness knowingly permitted Leonard Owens, Jr., a 17-year-old boy, to repeatedly commit criminal sexual abuse of her 13-year-old daughter. Although Maness confronted the couple about their activities, counseled them and expressed her disapproval, the record also shows that she facilitated the criminal sexual abuse by allowing Owens to sleep with her daughter in her daughter's bedroom. When Owens had sex with Maness' daughter, it was usually in the bedroom and usually while Maness and her husband were at home. Maness was aware of this sexual activity and took no steps to stop it. Her view was that if her daughter was going to have sex with Owens, it was safer if she did so at home where Maness had some control.

Maness' contention that she was uncertain as to the law's application is unpersuasive. While persons of ordinary intelligence may sometimes be left to speculate as to what constitute "reasonable steps" to prevent the commission of criminal sexual abuse, this is not one of those situations. Maness is not being prosecuted because of how she counseled her daughter regarding her sexuality or because she obtained birth control medication and prophylactics for her daughter to use. Maness' problem is that the law in Illinois prohibits 17-year-olds from having sex with 13-year-olds, and Maness repeatedly and expressly allowed a 17-year-old to have sex with her daughter in her house. Any person of ordinary intelligence would understand that such conduct constitutes a failure to take "reasonable steps" to prevent criminal sexual abuse within the meaning of the law.

There is likewise no merit to Maness' contention that the statute is invalid because it unduly infringes on a parent's right to raise her child. Under the fourteenth amendment, parents have a "fundamental liberty interest *** in the care, custody, and management of their child[ren,]" with which the government may not interfere unduly. Parental autonomy, however, is not absolute. In matters concerning child abuse and neglect, a parent's rights yield to the state's interest in protecting its children.

The right to be a parent does not encompass the right to abuse one's child or to allow one's child to be abused. If Maness had knowingly allowed Owens to inject her daughter with heroin and provided the couple with a place in her home where the drugs could be injected, there would be no question that Maness could be prosecuted for child endangerment or worse, without offending the constitution. The result should not be different because the abuse involves illegal sex rather than illegal drugs.

For the foregoing reasons, the judgment of the circuit court should be reversed and the cause should be remanded for further proceedings. I therefore dissent.

Justices Miller and McMorrow join in this dissent.

Notes and Queries

1. How is the statute impermissibly vague? What is the standard for determining whether a statute is impermissibly vague?

2. The majority does not address whether the statute unconstitutionally impinges on parental rights. Was Maness acting reasonably? Should she have the right to act as she did given the fundamental right, and the high duty, she has in directing the upbringing of her child? As the court properly notes, if she was not acting reasonably, what should she have done? If there is no clear answer to that question, then the legal system, following the vagueness doctrine, must leave the actions and decisions to parental discretion or at least not hold the parent liable. If the law does so, is it abdicating its responsibility to protect children from harm? How does the legal system address harms in cases like Lynlee and Leonard's?

Campbell v. Wyoming

999 P.2d 649 (Wyo. Sup. Ct., 2000)

Justice Golden delivered the opinion of the court.

Appellant Casey Campbell appeals her conviction for felony child endangerment contending that constitutional and evidentiary errors require reversal.

We affirm the order of judgment and sentence.

...

Facts

In 1992, Casey Campbell's eight-month-old daughter, HC, suffered severe injuries at the hands of Campbell's live-in boyfriend, Floid Boyer. The Department of Family Services (DFS) removed HC from Campbell's custody and placed her in foster care. Campbell was convicted of misdemeanor child endangerment. HC was returned to her mother's care on September 16, 1994. Campbell still lived with Boyer and her two other children that he had fathered since HC was removed. On June 27, 1995, while left alone with Boyer, HC received second and third degree burns over eighteen percent of her body. The burns were on the left side of her body from below her shoulders, extending down her left side, thigh and leg.

Boyer admitted causing the burns but claimed the burns were inflicted when he tripped and spilled coffee on the child sometime during the day. Shortly after 7:00 p.m. that evening, Campbell arrived home from work with a friend and the friend's fourteen-year-old daughter who planned to babysit Campbell's children that evening. The three observed the burns and at least one large blister. The friend recommended that Campbell take HC to the doctor. Campbell and Boyer decided not to follow that advice and, without providing medications for the babysitter, left to play darts at a local bar. The babysitter observed that HC was in pain that evening and dressed her in a large t-shirt. The babysitter confirmed that photographs taken of HC's burns hours later at the hospital accurately reflected the appearance of the burns at 7:00 p.m. that evening. Campbell and Boyer returned home at midnight. By 2:00 a.m., HC's pain was severe, and Campbell decided the burns were serious and required that she take HC to the hospital. Campbell wrapped the child, placed her in a stroller, and walked the few blocks to the hospital.

The treating physician was the same doctor who had cared for HC in 1992. Although Campbell explained that the burns were caused by spilled coffee, the doctor believed the injuries were not consistent with hot liquid as the source. The police were contacted, and a criminal investigation began. Police went to the home and checked the carpet where Boyer alleged that he had spilled the coffee, finding no signs of a spill because the carpet was dry as was the padding underneath, and there was a layer of chalky dust underneath the pad. Boyer agreed to questioning at the police station, and DES was contacted to care for the two children still in the home. The conditions of the home were deemed deplorable, and DES decided that Campbell's other two children should be placed in protective custody. Eventually, these two children were placed with Boyer's parents.

Campbell was arrested on charges of child abuse and child endangerment, released on bond, and had a preliminary hearing....

On December 16, 1996, shortly before trial began, ... defense counsel requested a continuance so that it could explore a battered woman's syndrome defense. That continuance was denied, and Cambell went to trial. Before Campbell's trial, Boyer pled guilty to misdemeanor child endangerment.

At trial, the State alleged that Campbell had failed to protect HC from Boyer although she knew Boyer was abusive to the child and failed to get immediate medical care for HC after observing her injuries. The State contended that the unclean condition of Campbell's home required immediate attention because of the risk of infection to a burn victim. In support of its failure to protect claim, the State contended that Campbell knew Boyer was a danger to HC because he disliked HC because he was not her father and because HC was of a different race. In Campbell's defense, Boyer testified that he thought he was HC's father, and had spilled coffee on the child accidentally, causing the burns. He testified that Campbell wanted to take the child to the hospital at 7:00 p.m. that evening, but that he believed the burns were not serious enough to require them to forgo playing darts. He testified that he had been physically abusive to Campbell for years, and he believed that Campbell played darts that night to avoid angering him. Campbell testified that she had been abused by her brother since she was seven years old, by her stepfather since a teenager, and by Boyer since she was sixteen years old, and Boyer had violently assaulted her with knives and guns on past occasions. At the time of HC's injuries, she feared for herself and HC if she defied Boyer that night by refusing to play darts. By 2:00 a.m., she believed that HC's condition had changed because she now had blistered severely, and Boyer and Campbell both testified that they agreed that the child should be taken to the hospital for medical care.

At the jury instruction conference, the defense requested an instruction on the defense of duress and coercion. This instruction was denied by the district court. Campbell was convicted of felony child endangerment and sentenced to prison.

Discussion

...

In her second argument, Campbell attacks the child endangerment statute as facially vague and as applied to the facts of her case. She contends that it is facially vague because the statute specifies no standard of conduct at all.

Wyo. Stat. Ann. § 6-4-403 states:

> (a) No parent, guardian or custodian of a child shall: ...
>
> (ii) Knowingly or with criminal negligence cause, permit or contribute to the endangering of the child's life or health by violating a duty care, protection or support.

... The ultimate test under a vagueness challenge is whether a person of ordinary intelligence could read the statute and comprehend what conduct is prohibited.... "Laws must provide explicit standards for those who apply them. A vague law impermissibly delegates basic policy matters to policemen, judges, and juries for resolution on an ad hoc and subjective basis, with the attendant dangers of arbitrary and discriminatory application."

"[E]very law must be presumed to be constitutional, with all doubt resolved in its favor." In considering statutory language, the plain, ordinary and usual meaning of the words used controls in the absence of clear statutory provisions to the contrary....

Campbell contends that the child endangerment statute is standardless because the term "endangering of the child's life or health by violating a duty of care, protection or support" provides no guidance as to what behavior definitively falls within the prohibited conduct....

...

... The statute is not unconstitutionally vague because it does not enumerate the kinds of prohibited conduct; it is sufficiently definite to give notice concerning the criminal conduct prohibited by the statute and does not violate the due process right to know what criminal conduct is proscribed.

Campbell also contends that the statute is vague as applied to her.... We must determine whether Campbell could reasonably understand that delaying eight hours in seeking medical care or failing to protect HC from Boyer's abuse is prohibited criminal conduct.

The State contends that Campbell endangered HC's life or health by failing to immediately seek medical care after seeing the burns when the lack of cleanliness in her home necessitated medical care without delay. The babysitter and her mother both saw the burns at the same time that Campbell first saw them and testified they believed the child required medical care and had so advised Campbell. Campbell herself testified that she believed the child needed medical care but was too afraid of Boyer to insist upon it at the time. The treating physician testified that the burns required immediate medical attention because of the risk of infection. Campbell did not seek immediate medical care but instead delayed for an eight hour period. Her testimony establishes that she understood that HC probably required immediate medical care and that she as the parent had the duty to provide that care. On this theory of child endangerment, the statute is not unconstitutionally vague as applied.

The State's failure to protect theory is more difficult to resolve. The State contends that "the statute points squarely at any mother who would fail to take reasonable steps to protect her child from known abuse." The State contends that the "known abuse" is the past abuse that HC suffered at the hands of Boyer and that Campbell "fully realized that she had a 'duty to protect' [HC] and that if she made any admission that her 'significant abuser' had been posing a danger to her child prior to the incident in question she would be convicted." The State submitted evidence of Boyer's 1992 abuse of HC which led to DFS removing HC from the home in support of its contention that Campbell had failed to protect HC from known abuse. Our concern with the State's contentions is that, if accepted, we would in essence be finding that Campbell was guilty of child endangerment as soon as she accepted the return of custody of her child because she still lived with Boyer. The State, however, also knew that a potentially abusive situation remained at Campbell's home for HC because of Boyer's presence, and, despite that knowledge, DES agreed that physical custody should be returned to Campbell, and the district court granted legal custody to Campbell. Upon these particular facts, we do not think that Campbell would know that accepting the return of HC's custody would violate the child endangerment statute. Accepting custody of one's child from the State while living with the abuser of whom the State knows does not violate the child endangerment statute.

One's suspicion that the abuser would again harm the child and failure to act despite the suspicion, however, is child endangerment, and evidence at trial established that Campbell held this belief. Campbell testified that Boyer continued to abuse her and she suspected that Boyer was abusing HC as well. . . .

Despite these fears, Campbell did leave HC alone with Boyer on the day that Boyer burned the child, and then permitted Boyer's further abuse of HC by agreeing with him that she would not seek medical care. Inaction, complicity, or permitting child abuse constitutes child endangerment for failing to protect a child from a dangerous situation, and Campbell's testimony establishes she knew that her conduct was prohibited. Under this theory, the statute is not unconstitutionally vague as applied.

Coercion and Duress

In her next issue, Campbell requests that this Court recognize that her status as a battered woman alters the elements of a coercion or duress defense. The trial court denied the defense's requested instruction on the defense of coercion and duress, finding no evidence of imminent bodily harm. Campbell contends that her years of abuse established evidence of her belief of an imminent danger of death or great bodily harm if she refused Boyer's demand that she leave HC to play darts. The State contends that the district court properly determined that the element of present, imminent or impending harm for a coercion or duress defense had not been met by Campbell's belief.

Coercion or duress has been recognized as a defense to criminal charges, other than a charge of taking the life of an innocent person. Coercion or duress must be present, imminent or impending, and of such a nature so as to induce a well-grounded fear of death or serious bodily harm if the otherwise criminal act is not done. The burden of demonstrating the elements of such a defense is upon the defendant.

Campbell contends that she demonstrated that Boyer's past abuse of her reasonably put her in fear of imminent death or serious bodily harm if she did not agree to go play darts that night. Conceding that her subjective fear alone does not support a theory of coercion or duress, she argues that her apprehension was objectively reasonable because she acted "under threats or conditions that a person of ordinary firmness would have been unable to resist." She contends that her years of abuse reasonably caused her to decide that a coffee burn with little visible blistering did not justify provoking an argument with her abuser, and an abused woman of ordinary firmness would have feared for her life that night if she acted to care for HC. The State contends that the court properly refused the instruction because this evidence does not establish present, imminent or impending death or serious bodily harm by refusing Boyer's demand that she not care for the child and play darts.

In response to this argument, Campbell contends that she should be able to raise the affirmative defense of coercion and duress if the abuse she suffered caused her to believe that she was in imminent danger of death or serious bodily harm if she did not endanger her child's life or health by delaying medical care in similar fashion to that permitted under the statute allowing expert evidence of battered woman syndrome. That statute provides:

> (a) The "battered woman syndrome" is defined as a subset under the diagnosis of Post-Traumatic Stress Disorder established in the Diagnostic and Statistical Manual of Mental Disorders III-Revised of the American Psychiatric Association.
>
> (b) If a person is charged with a crime involving the use of force against another, and the person raises the affirmative defense of self-defense, the person may introduce expert testimony that the person suffered from the syndrome, to establish the necessary requisite belief of an imminent danger of death or great bodily harm as an element of the affirmative defense, to justify the person's use of force.

The statute's plain language expressly limits its reach to the affirmative defense of self-defense. Self-defense does not apply when charged with child endangerment.

We are therefore limited to the elements established under the common law defense, and the issue is whether she presented evidence that she faced present, imminent or impending death or serious bodily harm if she acted to care for the child on the night burned. A trial court commits reversible error if it fails to submit a requested instruction that properly articulates Wyoming law, is supported by competent evidence, and is not already presented by another instruction. The evidence established that others were present in the house at the time Campbell made her decision and did not witness Campbell's refusing to play darts or witness Boyer's threatening Campbell if she cared for her child. Campbell made no attempt to seek medical advice, take her daughter to the hospital, dress her in loose clothing, or give her medications either for pain or to prevent infection. Campbell testified that she recognized that the burns were extensive and serious and required medical care, and she decided not to seek medical care because her past abuse caused her to realize that she would provoke Boyer. We agree with the district court that this record does not establish that she faced present, imminent or impending death or serious bodily harm, and the district court did not err in refusing to give her defense instruction.

. . .

Fair Trial Issues

Improper Opinions of Guilt

Campbell alleges that the prosecutor committed per se reversible error by asking a police officer and the treating physician questions eliciting opinions that she was guilty of child endangerment. An investigating officer was asked:

> . . . would you consider the conditions of the house unsafe for raising children?
>
> A. Most definitely, yes.
>
> Q. Would you consider it to be extremely unsafe to the individual that you observed the burns on, [HC]?
>
> A. Yes.

The State argues that these statements followed testimony describing the lack of sanitation in Campbell's home, and were not opinions of guilt because, in context, the witness' testimony was relevant to elements of the crime that Campbell violated her duty of care as a parent. The State alleges that this testimony was relevant to connect the lack of sanitation in the home to the risk of infection posed to the burned child.

The prosecutor asked the treating physician the following:

> Q. Is there, when somebody has second and third degree burns such as you stated HC had, is there a risk of infection on those kinds of burns?
>
> A. Yes.
>
> Q. Is it contributing to the endangerment of the child the longer you do not take them to the hospital?
>
> A. Yes, there is a degree of problems with not managing a burn.
>
> Q. Is that one of the things you are concerned with in burns like this is to take care of the wound as soon as possible so no infection begins?
>
> A. Yes. Infection is a high risk. When we have a burn injury of this nature, we use sterile blankets.

Campbell argues that the doctor was asked for and gave his opinion that she was guilty of child endangerment for delaying in seeking medical treatment. The State argues that again this testimony was required to establish elements of the crime, and it remained for the jury to decide whether Campbell was guilty of child endangerment.

In this child endangerment prosecution, the State had to prove that Campbell acted with awareness of the probable consequences as opposed to making a mistake in judgment. Thus, it is relevant whether the conditions of the house were unsafe to a child with the type of injuries suffered by HC to prove that Campbell acted criminally when she delayed seeking medical care. The investigating officer's testimony was relevant to establish the conditions of the home, and the doctor's testimony was relevant to establish that infection was likely and dangerous for the burn victim. Together, the testimony established necessary evidence that allowed the State to argue that Campbell, as a reasonable parent, should have known that she was endangering her child's health or life by delaying medical care for HC given the conditions that existed inside her home. Neither testimony amounts to an opinion that Campbell was guilty of child endangerment, and we find no error.

. . .

The order of judgment and sentence is affirmed.

Concur: Justice Macy, specially concurring. [omitted]

Notes and Queries

1. Does it seem reasonable to hold that a battered mother can claim abuse of herself against her criminal actions against her abuser but she cannot use it as a defense against her inability to protect her children?
2. The state knew that Campbell remained in her abusive home and even had returned HC to her and the abusive environment. Should that suffice to demonstrate that she had no notice that she could be charged with failure to protect?
3. The state emphasized the lack of sanitation in the home and argued that the testimony was important to establish the home as creating a risk of infection to the burned child. Are you persuaded?

Review Problem

1. Assume that the mother is not being battered. Should she be held responsible? Consider the following case. The defendant mother left her 3-year-old daughter in the care of an acquaintance and his wife for several days. When the mother returned at 1:00 p.m., her daughter was listless and feverish and covered with bruises. The child's caretaker claimed that the daughter had become ill after a bumpy motorcycle ride. Throughout the day, the daughter's condition worsened and she complained of stomach cramps, vomited, and finally lapsed into unconsciousness. The mother still did not take her to the hospital. Sometime after 9:30 p.m., a friend of the mother took the child to the hospital where the child was pronounced dead as a result of internal injuries. Evidence at trial showed the daughter might have survived if she had received surgery up to one hour before her death.

The state contended that the mother's failure to seek medical attention for her daughter was, as contemplated by the state's criminal child abuse statute, "cruel and inhumane treatment," which caused her daughter to sustain further injuries that led to her death. The language of the child abuse statute defined "abuse" to encompass any "physical injury or injuries sustained by a child as a result of cruel or inhumane treatment or as a result of malicious act or acts." Proper finding? The court held that, because of the language used, the legislature intended the scope of the statute to reach failure-to-act conduct, including the defendant's failures in this case. *State v. Fabritz*, 348 A.2d 275 (Md. 1975), rev'g 332 A.2d 324 (1975), cert. denied, 425 U.S. 942 (1976), rev'd sub nom., *Fabritz v. Traurig*, 583 F.2d 697 (4th Cir. 1978), cert. denied sub nom., *Hopkins v. Fabritz*, 443 U.S. 915 (1979). Eventually, the conviction was overturned in a habeas corpus action for failure to show that the defendant was aware of either the seriousness of her child's injuries or the foreseeable consequences of a failure to seek timely medical assistance. If statutes allow mothers to be held responsible for failing to act, what specifically is it about domestic violence that justifies exceptions?

Research Comments

1. Every state has a statute imposing some form of criminal liability for passive child abuse, with classifications ranging from a misdemeanor, or a felony with a maximum sentence of up to five years, to the possibility, in child fatality cases, of a murder or manslaughter charge if the person has the requisite mens rea. For example, if committed intentionally, knowingly, recklessly, or with criminal negligence, a parent's omission may constitute a more serious crime. See, e.g., Ariz. Rev. Stat. Ann. 13-3623 (West 1999 & Supp. 2000). Liability for failure to protect usually requires that (1) the defendant had a legal duty to protect the child, (2) the defendant had actual or constructive notice of the foreseeability of abuse, (3) the child was exposed to such abuse, and (4) the defendant failed to prevent such abuse. For a thorough discussion of failure-to-protect laws, see generally Bryan A. Liang & Wendy L. Macfarlane (1999). Murder by omission: Child abuse and the passive parent. *Harvard Journal on Legislation*, 35, 397–450. A few states provide statutory affirmative defenses where the accused fears that any preventative action would cause physical harm to herself or increase the danger for the child. Elizabeth M. Schneider (1992). Particularity and generality: Challenges of feminist theory and practice in work on women-abuse. *New York University Law Review*, 64, 520–568.

2. Victims of battering face many challenges when they attempt to leave abusive relationships. Batterers are motivated by an attempt to control the victim. Among other tactics the perpetrator uses to gain control are: violence, isolation from friends and family, economic abuse, sexual abuse, using the children, coercion and threats, using male privilege, intimidation, emotional abuse, and minimizing, denying, and blaming. Due to the batterer's systematic, repetitive infliction

of abuse, a battered woman is usually instilled with shame, humiliation, and fear, eventually reducing her ability to act. Among other responses to the violence, battered women typically have lowered self-esteem, accept blame for their abuse, experience feelings of helplessness and passivity, and deny and minimize the abuse. Barriers to leaving the relationship are enormous: (1) shame; (2) fear; (3) lack of personal resources; (4) lack of emotional support; (5) lack of access to money, transportation, jobs, education, and services; and (6) discrimination and isolation. Importantly, the batterer is at his most dangerous when he feels that he is losing control over his victim, which makes attempts to leave violent and increases the likelihood of being killed. Karen J. Wilson (1997). *When Violence Begins at Home: A Comprehensive Guide to Understanding and Ending Domestic Abuse.* Alameda, CA: Hunter House Publishers. For a leading authority's view of battering adult relationships, see Leonore E. Walker (2000). *The Battered Woman Syndrome* (2nd Ed.). New York: Springer.

Pope v. State

284 Md. 309; 396 A.2d 1054 (Md. Ct. App., 1979)

Justice Orth delivered the opinion of the court.

The Evidence

The evidence adduced at the trial established that Demiko Lee Norris, three months old, died as a result of physical injuries inflicted by his mother, Melissa Vera Norris. The abuse by the mother occurred over a period of several hours on a Sunday morning at Pope's home and in Pope's presence. Pope's involvement in the events leading to the child's abuse and death began on the preceding Friday evening when she and Melissa, with the child, were driven home by Pope's sister, Angela Lancaster, from a service held at the Christian Tabernacle Church. When they arrived at Melissa's grandparents' home, where Melissa was living, Melissa refused to enter the house, claiming that it was on fire, although in fact it was not. During the evening, Melissa had sporadically indicated mental distress. "She would at times seem caught up in a religious frenzy with a wild look about her, trying to preach and declaring that she was God. She would as quickly resume her normal self without ever seeming to notice her personality transitions." Pope agreed to take Melissa and the child into her home for the night because she did not want to put them "out on the street," and Angela would not let them stay in her home.... Melissa slept in Pope's bedroom. Pope kept the baby with her in the living room, telling Melissa: "[Y]ou can go to sleep ... I'll be up, I'll just stay up, I'll watch the baby...." She explained in her testimony: "And I don't know why it was just, just a funny feeling that I had, you know, and ever since the baby was there I just kept it close to me for some reason." Pope fed the baby and fixed a bed for it in a dresser drawer. She stayed with the baby to care for him during the night because he was spitting up. She could not sleep while Melissa was there.

The next morning, awakened by the crying of the child, Pope fed him. Throughout the day Melissa "changed back and forth." When Melissa was "herself" she took care of her child. When Melissa thought she was God, Pope undertook the maternal duties. Pope watched the child "like it was my own," because "I felt maybe [Melissa] could [hurt the child] when she confessed she was God. . . . I felt close to the baby, maybe because, you know, I felt I haven't had a baby for so long, you know, I enjoyed taking care of the baby and watching it." . . .

During a lucid period, Melissa prepared to go to church. She got a tub of water to bathe the baby. What next occurred is graphically described in the opinion of the Court of Special Appeals:

> Then, from her suddenly changed voice and appearance, [Pope] knew Melissa had changed again to 'God.' Calling out that Satan had hidden in the body of her son, Melissa began to verbally exorcize that spirit and physically abuse the child by punching and poking him repeatedly about the stomach, chest and privates. After she undressed the child, that which ensued was hardly describable. In her religious frenzy of apparent exorcism, Melissa poked the child's vitals and beat the child about the head. She reached her fingers down its throat, wiping mucus and blood on diapers at hand, and even lifted the child by inserting her hands in its mouth, and shook him like a rag.

Continuing to talk and stomp, Melissa began to squeeze the baby. Then, holding the child by the neck with one hand, she took him into the bathroom, acting like she did not know that Pope was present. . . . She admitted that she knew at some point that Melissa was hurting the baby and was "fearful, amazed and shocked at the 'unbelievable' and 'horrible' thing that was happening."

Melissa's frenzy diminished. Angela came to the house to take them to church. . . .

Pope, Melissa and Angela left with the child to go to church. At Melissa's request they stopped by her grandfather's house, arriving about 2:00 p.m. Pope told him the child was dead, but he did not believe her because all three were acting so strangely. He refused to take or look at the baby. The three women with the child went to Bel Pre Health Center, picked up another member of the Christian Tabernacle congregation, telling her that "God has a job for you to do," and proceeded to the church. En route, they passed several hospitals, police stations and rescue squads. At the church, the child was given to, or taken by the Reverend Leon Hart, who handed him to Mother Dorothy King for her prayers. She discovered that the baby's body was cool and sent for ambulance assistance. Police and rescue personnel arrived and determined that the child was dead. There was expert medical testimony that the child had died sometime during the period of fifteen minutes to several hours after it was injured. The medical expert expressed no opinion as to whether the child could have been successfully treated if the injury had been reported sooner.

. . .

Pope, Melissa and Angela attended the evening service at the church. Melissa reverted to God during the service and Reverend Hart restrained her and attempted to convince her that she was not Jesus Christ. Melissa refused to go to her grandfather's home and returned home with Pope. The next morning Pope was again interviewed at the police station and wrote a full explanation of what had happened. She later made an oral statement which was recorded.

I

The Crime of Child Abuse

. . .

Responsibility for Abuse of a Child

. . .

> [a]ny parent, adoptive parent or other person who has the permanent or temporary care or custody or responsibility for the supervision of a minor child under the age of eighteen years who causes abuse to such minor child shall be guilty of a felony. . . .

Persons subject to the statute are designated in those terms also in subsection (b) 7 (A) defining abuse and in subsection (b) 8 defining sexual abuse.

. . .

The child abuse statute speaks in terms of a person who "has" responsibility for the supervision of a minor child. It does not prescribe how such responsibility attaches or what "responsibility" and "supervision" encompass. A doubt or ambiguity exists as to the exact reach of the statute's provision with respect to "has responsibility for the supervision of," justifying application of the principle that permits courts in such circumstances to ascertain and give effect to the real intention of the Legislature. . . . "[R]esponsibility for the supervision of" is not bound by certain of the strictures required for one to stand in place of or instead of the parent. A person in loco parentis is "charged, factitiously, with a parent's rights, duties, and responsibilities." "A person in loco parentis to a child is one who means to put himself in the situation of the lawful father [or mother] of the child with reference to the father's [or mother's] office and duty of making provision for the child. . . . [A] person in loco parentis is one, 'assuming the parental character and discharging parental duties.' There must be some indication, in some form, of an intention to establish it. It is a question of intention." . . .

. . . Absent a court order or award by some appropriate proceeding pursuant to statutory authority, we think it to be self-evident that responsibility for supervision of a minor child may be obtained only upon the mutual consent, expressed or implied, by the one legally charged with the care of the child and by the one assuming the responsibility. . . . [O]nce responsibility for the supervision of a minor child has been placed in a third person, it may be terminated unilaterally by a parent by resuming responsibility, expressly or by conduct. The consent of the third party in such circumstances is not required; he may not prevent return of responsibility to the parent. But, of course, the third person in whom responsibility has been placed is not free to relinquish that responsibility without the knowledge of the parent. For example, a sitter may not simply walk away in the absence of the parents and leave the children to their own devices.

Under the present state of our law, a person has no legal obligation to care for or look after the welfare of a stranger, adult or child.

> Generally one has no legal duty to aid another person in peril, even when that aid can be rendered without danger or inconvenience to himself.... A moral duty to take affirmative action is not enough to impose a legal duty to do so.

... Ordinarily, a person may stand by with impunity and watch another being murdered, raped, robbed, assaulted or otherwise unlawfully harmed. "He need not shout a warning to a blind man headed for a precipice or to an absentminded one walking into a gunpowder room with a lighted candle in hand. He need not pull a neighbor's baby out of a pool of water or rescue an unconscious person stretched across the railroad tracks, though the baby is drowning, or the whistle of an approaching train is heard in the distance." The General Assembly has enacted two "Good Samaritan" statutes which afford protection to one who assists another in certain circumstances. Those statutes, however, impose no requirement that assistance be rendered.

...

In the face of this status of the law we cannot reasonably conclude that the Legislature, in bringing a person responsible for the supervision of a child within the ambit of the child abuse law, intended that such responsibility attach without the consent criteria we have set out. Were it otherwise, the consequences would go far beyond the legislative intent. For example, a person taking a lost child into his home to attempt to find its parents could be said to be responsible for that child's supervision. Or a person who allows his neighbor's children to play in his yard, keeping a watchful eye on their activities to prevent them from falling into harm, could be held responsible for the children's supervision. Or a person performing functions of a maternal nature from concern for the welfare, comfort or health of a child, or protecting it from danger because of a sense of moral obligation, may come within the reach of the act. In none of these situations would there be an intent to grant or assume the responsibility contemplated by the child abuse statute, and it would be incongruous indeed to subject such persons to possible criminal prosecution.

...

The mental or emotional state of the mother, whereby at times she held herself out as God, does not change the result. We see no basis in the statute for an interpretation that a person "has" responsibility for the supervision of a child, if that person believes or may have reason to believe that a parent is not capable of caring for the child. There is no right to make such a subjective judgment in order to divest parents of their rights and obligations with respect to their minor children, and therefore, no obligation to do so.

. . .

Eldridge, J., concurring in part and dissenting in part:

. . .

The majority appears to be concerned about the "good Samaritans" who watch a lost child, or allow neighbors' children to play in their yards and exercise supervision, or perform "functions of a maternal nature from concern for the welfare, comfort or health of a child." However, such "good Samaritans" have nothing to fear from the child abuse statute. But, if one of these same individuals assumes responsibility for the child and batters it, sexually molests it, locks it for a long period of time in a dark closet, etc., that person should be held just as accountable under the child abuse statute as someone else having responsibility for the child.

My concern in this case is not so much with the decision that the evidence was insufficient to convict Pope of child abuse. The evidence may not have been sufficient. Instead, what is troublesome in this case is the damage which the majority has done to the child abuse statute.

Notes and Queries

1. The court notes that a person may be convicted of a felony upon proof establishing that he committed the offense as a perpetrating actor (principal in the first degree), or that, being actually or constructively present, he did not himself commit the offense but aided and abetted in the commission of it (principal in the second degree). Given that, the court finds insufficient evidence to find Pope guilty. The court reasoned as follows:

> The evidence certainly showed that Pope "witnessed a terrible event" and that she "stood by" while the mother killed the child. But the culpability for her conduct during the abuse of the child must be determined strictly within the law or else the basic tenets of our system of justice are prostituted. There is an understandable feeling of outrage at what occurred, intensified by the fact that the mother, who actually beat the child to death, was held to be not responsible for her criminal acts [for reason of insanity]. But it is the law, not indignation, which governs. The law requires that Pope's conviction of the felony of child abuse be set aside as clearly erroneous due to evidentiary insufficiency.

   Do you agree with the court's reasoning?

Review Problem

1. The court found no evidence that Ms. Pope had assumed responsibility for the child, and thus her conviction was overturned. Those assuming responsibility are not immune from prosecution. Consider the prosecution of Sharon Degren. When the victim, Jennifer, was 12 years old, Jennifer's mother made custodial arrangements with Sharon Degren and her husband, Nick Degren, for Jennifer to remain at their home on two separate occasions; once in June, for a period of one week, and again in August, for a period of two weeks. Jennifer knew Sharon and Nick Degren and did not object to the arrangements. During the first of her visits to the Degren home, Jennifer testified that one night she fell asleep on Sharon and Nick's bed, and she awoke to Nick having sexual intercourse with her. While this was occurring, Sharon was sitting on the corner of the bed "watching television and watching them." When Nick asked Sharon "if she felt right with him having sexual intercourse" with Jennifer, Sharon responded that "she really didn't care." Nick stopped when Jennifer told him to get off of her, and Jennifer then left the room. Sharon denied this event ever took place. During her visit in August, Jennifer testified that she had intercourse with Nick on two separate occasions, and that during both times Sharon was aware of the intercourse and did nothing to intervene. On the first such occasion, August 10, Sharon was in the room while Jennifer and Nick had intercourse. Although Sharon acknowledged that she was present at the time her husband and Jennifer were having sex, she claimed she did not intervene because her husband could be abusive at times and she "was afraid that he would hit [her]." On the second occasion, August 15, Sharon acknowledged that she left the room as Jennifer and Nick were having intercourse. Sharon was found guilty of four counts of child abuse for her involvement in the molestation of Jennifer. She was sentenced to four concurrent ten-year sentences, and "five years of each sentence were suspended in favor of five years of probation." She later filed a Petition for Writ of Certiorari in the Maryland Court of Appeals asserting that the lower courts erred in their holding that a caretaker of a minor child may be guilty of sexual child abuse under the child abuse statute for failure to prevent the sexual molestation or exploitation of the minor child by a third party. Under Maryland Code "[a] parent or other person who has permanent or temporary care or custody or responsibility for the supervision of a child . . . who causes abuse to the child is guilty of a felony and on conviction is subject to imprisonment in the penitentiary for not more than 15 years." Abuse includes both "the sustaining of physical injury by a child as a result of cruel or inhumane treatment or as a result of a malicious act . . . under circumstances that indicate that the child's health or welfare is harmed or threatened thereby," and sexual abuse. Sexual abuse is defined as "any act that involves sexual molestation or exploitation of a child." The statute also provides that "'sexual abuse' includes, but is not limited to: 1. Incest, rape, or sexual offense in any degree; 2. Sodomy; and 3. Unnatural or perverted sexual practices."

Dergen argued that she should not be held criminally liable for the sexual abuse of Jennifer because her omission or failure to prevent another person's act of sexual molestation or exploitation is not punishable under the language of the statute. In support of this argument, she argued that the plain meaning of the word "act" as used in the statute denotes a deed or something affirmative as opposed to an omission. Should she be held as having "caused" Jennifer's victimization? The court was unconvinced by Degren's arguments and ruled that not only does the definition of sexual abuse include an omission or failure to act when a child is being sexually abused, but the definition itself encompasses what she actually did: the affirmative acts of watching and failing to intervene in the rape. *Degren v. State*, 352 Md. 400, 722 A.2d 887 (1999).

Research Comments

1. Judicial decisions have steadily eroded the no duty to rescue rule in two ways: by recognizing exceptions in which the law imposes a duty to aid strangers and by expanding the class of special relationships that give rise to affirmative duties. The courts have used seven major avenues to impose *criminal* sanctions on failures to act: (1) a duty to act can be based upon the relationship of the parties (e.g., parents have a legal duty to aid their children); (2) a duty can be based on contract (e.g., a security guard must protect individuals from harm); (3) a duty can be based on a voluntary assumption of care (e.g., once one undertakes to help a person in need, he may have a duty to aid until the victim is safe); (4) a duty can arise from the fact that the person created the risk from which the need for protection arose (e.g., a person hurts another and does not render assistance); (5) a duty can arise when a person becomes responsible for another's criminal action (e.g., parents can be held responsible for their children's criminal acts); (6) property owners can be held liable for dangerous conditions on their property (e.g., club owners may be responsible for deaths on their property); and (7) a duty may arise from a statutory duty to act (e.g., requirements to report child abuse or requirements to warn potential victims). If any one of the exceptions to the no duty rule is met, the law recognizes a duty to exercise reasonable care.

2. In further contrast to the general rule, a minority of states have imposed a legislative duty to act in special situations. There are generally two forms of a duty. The first comes in the form of duties to report. Child abuse reporting laws provide the clearest example. However, some states provide much broader mandates; e.g., Wis. Stat. Ann. § 940.34 (2)(a) (West Supp. 1999) (requiring that "any person who knows that a crime is being committed and that a victim is exposed to bodily harm shall summon law enforcement officers or other assistance or shall provide assistance to the victim"); Wash. Rev. Code Ann. § 9.69.100(1)(b)–(c) (West 1998) (indicating that any "person who witnesses the actual commission of a sexual offense or assault against a child or . . . an assault . . . that appears reasonably likely

to cause substantial bodily harm to the child" has a duty to report the incident to "the prosecuting attorney . . . or other public official"). The second form involves the more controversial duty to aid; e.g., Vt. Stat. Ann. tit. 12, § 519(a) (1967 & Supp. 1999) (demanding that any "person who knows that another is exposed to grave physical harm shall, to the extent that the same can be rendered without danger or peril to himself . . . give reasonable assistance to the exposed person unless that assistance or care is being provided by others"); R.I. Gen. Laws Ann. § 11-56-1 (Michie 1994) (explaining that "any person at the scene of an emergency who knows that another person is exposed to, or has suffered, [sic] grave physical harm shall, to the extent that he or she can do so without danger or peril to himself . . . give reasonable assistance to the exposed person"); Minn. Stat. Ann. § 604A.01(1) (West 1998) (requiring any "person at the scene of an emergency who knows that another person is exposed to or has suffered grave physical harm shall, to the extent that the person can do so without danger or peril to self or others, give reasonable assistance to the exposed person").

3. Good Samaritan legislation typically aims to shield from liability those who act to assist when they have no legal obligations to do so. Good Samaritan laws that require broad duties to aid are not that unheard of; they actually mark a return to the common law concept of misprison of a felony. At common law, misprison was the concealment of a felony of which a man knows but never assented to. The common law elements of the crime were (1) knowledge of the felony, (2) a reasonable opportunity to disclose the felony without harm, and (3) failure to report the felony. See Daniel B. Yeager (1993). A radical community of aid: A rejoinder to opponents of affirmative duties to help strangers. *Washington University Law Quarterly*, 71, 1–58. In our principal case, the court, in an extended discussion deleted from the above text, explicitly rejected the argument that the defendant was guilty under that common law concept. In addition to finding that the law had lain dormant for over 200 years, the court found persuasive the failure of the Maryland legislature to enact legislation declarative of the common law crime of misprision of felony or which may be deemed to have created a comparable offense.

Review Problem

1. The current no duty to rescue rule in tort law is rooted in the early common law distinction between misfeasance (or action) and nonfeasance (or inaction). The law imposed a duty of care in misfeasance cases because the defendant affirmatively acted to injure the plaintiff. However, the law did not recognize a comparable duty in nonfeasance cases — those in which a defendant's failure to act resulted in the plaintiff's injury. In part, this distinction was based on the idea that a person should be held responsible for the consequences of his conduct but not for risks which he did not create and thus arguably could not control. Consider the following case. In May 1997, high school senior Jeremy Strohmeyer raped and strangled

seven-year-old Sherrice Iverson in a restroom at a casino in Nevada. Strohmeyer's best friend, David Cash, Jr., observed Strohmeyer's initial assault of the child, but did not attempt to intervene. Instead, he exited the restroom after two minutes and waited for his friend in the casino. Twenty-four minutes later, Strohmeyer emerged from the rest room. He told Cash that he had sexually assaulted and killed Sherrice. The two boys gambled for a while longer and drove home. Strohmeyer was arrested and sentenced to life in prison without parole after he pled guilty to kidnaping, sexual assault, and murder. Should Cash be held legally responsible too? Cash was never indicted, even though he did nothing to help the victim and failed to notify either the police or any casino employee of Strohmeyer's actions. The acts led to considerable public furor and renewed federal legislative attempts to pass Good Samaritan laws to help child victims. See Jessica R. Givelber (1999). Imposing duties on witnesses to child sexual abuse: A futile response to bystander indifference. *Fordham Law Review*, 67, 3169–3204.

Swartz v. Swartz

887 S.W.2d 644 (Mo. Ct. App., 1994)

Justice Breckenridge delivered the opinion of the court.

. . .

Judith Swartz was born on November 18, 1968, to Pamela Van Beek. James Swartz legally adopted Judith Swartz in September of 1976, prior to his marriage to Ms. Van Beek in November of 1979. The couple was divorced in April of 1983. On February 28, 1983, Mr. Swartz was convicted by a Clay County jury of sexually abusing Judith Swartz, for which he was later sentenced to a prison term of fifteen years. Judith Swartz testified at the trial that the acts of abuse began in November of 1979 and ended on September 27, 1982. On November 17, 1992, Judith Swartz filed this action for damages against Mr. Swartz and Ms. Van Beek. In her first amended petition, Judith Swartz alleged as Count I that her mother negligently and carelessly provided supervision and care for her, negligently failed to warn her of the "dangers and character of her husband," and negligently failed to procure adequate medical care for her after a jury convicted Mr. Swartz of child sexual abuse. In Count II of her petition, Judith Swartz claimed that Mr. Swartz negligently allowed himself to be in her presence, negligently failed to remove himself from her presence, negligently failed to seek help from others for the purpose of protecting Judith Swartz from his abuse, and negligently failed to procure medical treatment for Judith Swartz after he was convicted of child sexual abuse. In Count III, Judith Swartz maintained that Mr. Swartz negligently inflicted emotional distress on her when he attempted to remove her by force from her home on October 18, 1982.

. . . The trial court granted summary judgment in favor of Mr. Swartz and Ms. Van Beek on September 9, 1993. In its order, the trial court concluded that Mr. Swartz and

Ms. Van Beek had "parental immunity for alleged acts or omissions which allegedly injured plaintiff on or before December 16, 1991." Judith Swartz now appeals the grant of summary judgment.

...

Judith Swartz contends as her first point on appeal that the trial court erred in relying on the doctrine of parental immunity in granting the summary judgment motions of Mr. Swartz and Ms. Van Beek. Judith Swartz maintains that parental immunity should not apply because the policy behind the doctrine would not be advanced by its use in this case.

...

The parental immunity doctrine was adopted by the Missouri Supreme Court in *Baker v. Baker*. The Supreme Court held in *Baker* that in the interest of preserving family harmony, a fifteen-month-old child could not sue her father for mere negligence arising from an auto accident. This initial formulation of the rule applied only to unintentional torts committed within the scope of "parental authority or duty."

...

On December 17, 1991, the Supreme Court abrogated the parental immunity rule established by *Baker*.... The Court explained that the policy of preserving family harmony was "less significant than the interest in the right of an injured child to recover for injuries," since damage to family harmony and relationships occurred at the time the wrong was committed....

...

In analyzing the appropriateness of the application of the doctrine of parental immunity to the facts of this case, ... the record shows no dispute concerning the facts relevant to the disruption of family harmony resulting from Judith Swartz's suit against Mr. Swartz. Mr. Swartz was arrested, charged, and convicted by a jury of the class B felony of the rape of Judith Swartz. He was sentenced to fifteen years in prison. Judith Swartz testified as a witness against Mr. Swartz in the criminal trial. Ms. Van Beek dissolved her marriage to Mr. Swartz two months after his sentencing, and custody of Judith Swartz was awarded to Ms. Van Beek following the dissolution of marriage. Considering these circumstances, the domestic tranquility of the home has clearly been destroyed as a matter of law, and will not be disturbed by Judith Swartz's action against Mr. Swartz. Nor will the policy behind the doctrine of parental immunity be advanced by its application in this case. Summary judgment in favor of Judith Swartz on Mr. Swartz's affirmative defense of parental immunity is appropriate.

On the other hand, it is more difficult to determine whether the maintenance of an action by Judith Swartz against Ms. Van Beek would destroy the peace and harmony of the family unit. As Hurst indicates, it is certainly possible for the parental immunity exception to apply to a parent who has breached parental duties by failing to protect a child from sexual abuse. This court cannot determine, however, that the undisputed facts in the record are sufficient, as a matter of law, to justify an exception to the doctrine of parental immunity with regard to the cause of action against Ms. Van Beek. An evidentiary hearing is necessary to resolve the factual issues relevant to the determination of the impact Judith Swartz's action against Ms. Van Beek would have on the harmony of the family unit.

...

Judith Swartz's claims against Mr. Swartz are neither precluded by the doctrine of parental immunity nor barred by the applicable statutes of limitation. Likewise, Judith Swartz's claims against Ms. Van Beek are not barred by the applicable statute of limitations. An evidentiary hearing is required to determine whether an exception to the parental immunity doctrine applies to Judith Swartz's claims against Ms. Van Beek. Therefore, the trial court erred in granting summary judgment in favor of Mr. Swartz and Ms. Van Beek. The summary judgment is reversed and the cause remanded for further proceedings.

...

Notes and Queries

1. Why do you think the court requests an evidentiary hearing to resolve the factual issues relevant to the determination of the impact Judith Swartz's action against Ms. Van Beek would have on the harmony of the family unit? Should the fact that Judith is bringing the lawsuit suffice?
2. We already have seen that parents could be held liable in criminal law for failing to protect. Why not extend that to tort actions?

Review Problem

1. Stephanie Anne Kennedy alleges that Boyd Kelsey Chaney, a close personal friend of her family, sexually assaulted her while she was in his home over an eight-year period beginning in 1980 when she was ten years of age. Kennedy filed this action against her alleged assailant, and Nancy Chaney (hereinafter Chaney) was joined on the theory that she caused Kennedy to suffer damages by negligently supervising her while she was in the Chaney home. Kennedy alleges that Boyd Chaney (her alleged assailant) paid "excessive attention" to her and was "excessive" in his gift giving. Nancy Chaney's alleged negligence consisted of failing to recognize these "signs" as indicative of the possibility that her husband was sexually molesting Kennedy, which caused her to fail to investigate the situation. As a result, Nancy Chaney "unintentionally provided unchecked access to [Kennedy] for [her husband]," which caused Kennedy to suffer "serious and lasting injury." The court noted that public policy requires that where a child is sexually assaulted

in the defendant wife's home by her husband, the wife's duty of reasonable care to the injured child depends on whether the husband's behavior was reasonably foreseeable. Without knowledge of her husband's deviant propensities, a wife will not be able to foresee that he poses a danger and thus will not have a duty to take measures to prevent the assault. Although a wife's knowledge may be proven by circumstantial evidence, such inference must reflect the wife's actual knowledge and not merely constructive knowledge or notice. "[A]ctual knowledge can be inferred from the circumstances only if, in the light of the evidence, such inference is not based on speculation or conjecture. Only where the circumstances are such that the defendant 'must have known' and not 'should have known' will an inference of actual knowledge be permitted." In this case, the court found that the plaintiff did not allege facts showing that the abuse was foreseeable (i.e., facts from which it can be inferred that the defendant wife must have known that her husband was engaging in, or wished to engage in, acts of sexual misconduct with a minor). *Chaney v. Superior Court*, 46 Cal. Rptr. 2d 73 (Cal. Ct. App., 1995). What does this case add to your understanding of *Swartz v. Swartz* and how we can address claims against parents?

Wyman v. James

400 U.S. 309; 91 S. Ct. 381 (1971)

Justice Blackmun delivered the opinion of the Court.

This appeal presents the issue whether a beneficiary of the program for Aid to Families with Dependent Children (AFDC) may refuse a home visit by the caseworker without risking the termination of benefits.

. . .

Plaintiff Barbara James is the mother of a son, Maurice, who was born in May 1967. They reside in New York City. Mrs. James first applied for AFDC assistance shortly before Maurice's birth. A caseworker made a visit to her apartment at that time without objection. The assistance was authorized.

Two years later, on May 8, 1969, a caseworker wrote Mrs. James that she would visit her home on May 14. Upon receipt of this advice, Mrs. James telephoned the worker that, although she was willing to supply information "reasonable and relevant" to her need for public assistance, any discussion was not to take place at her home. The worker told Mrs. James that she was required by law to visit in her home and that refusal to permit the visit would result in the termination of assistance. Permission was still denied.

On May 13 the City Department of Social Services sent Mrs. James a notice of intent to discontinue assistance because of the visitation refusal. The notice advised the beneficiary of her right to a hearing before a review officer. The hearing was requested and was held on May 27. Mrs. James appeared with an attorney at that hearing. They continued to refuse permission for a worker to visit the James home, but again expressed willingness to cooperate and to permit visits elsewhere. The review officer ruled that the refusal was a proper ground for the termination of assistance. His written decision stated:

> The home visit which Mrs. James refuses to permit is for the purpose of determining if there are any changes in her situation that might affect her eligibility to continue to receive Public Assistance, or that might affect the amount of such assistance, and to see if there are any social services which the Department of Social Services can provide to the family.

A notice of termination issued on June 2.

Thereupon, without seeking a hearing at the state level, Mrs. James, individually and on behalf of Maurice, and purporting to act on behalf of all other persons similarly situated, instituted the present civil rights suit under 42 U. S. C. § 1983. . . .

II

The federal aspects of the AFDC program deserve mention. . . . Section 405, 42 U. S. C. § 605, provides that

> Whenever the State agency has reason to believe that any payments of aid . . . made with respect to a child are not being or may not be used in the best interests of the child, the State agency may provide for such counseling and guidance services with respect to the use of such payments and the management of other funds by the relative . . . in order to assure use of such payments in the best interests of such child, and may provide for advising such relative that continued failure to so use such payments will result in substitution therefor of protective payments . . . or in seeking the appointment of a guardian . . . or in the imposition of criminal or civil penalties. . . .

III

When a case involves a home and some type of official intrusion into that home, as this case appears to do, an immediate and natural reaction is one of concern about Fourth Amendment rights and the protection which that Amendment is intended to afford. Its emphasis indeed is upon one of the most precious aspects of personal security in the home: "The right of the people to be secure in their persons, houses, papers, and effects. . . ." This Court has characterized that right as "basic to a free society." And over the years the Court consistently has been most protective of the privacy of the dwelling. . . .

IV

This natural and quite proper protective attitude, however, is not a factor in this case, for the seemingly obvious and simple reason that we are not concerned here with any search by the New York social service agency in the Fourth Amendment meaning of that term. It is true that the governing statute and regulations appear to make mandatory the initial home visit and the subsequent periodic "contacts" (which may include home visits) for the inception and continuance of aid. It is also true that the caseworker's posture in the home visit is perhaps, in a sense, both rehabilitative and investigative. But this latter aspect, we think, is given too broad a character and far more emphasis than it deserves if it is equated with a search in the traditional criminal law context. We note, too, that the visitation in itself is not forced or compelled, and that the beneficiary's denial of permission is not a criminal act. If consent to the visitation is withheld, no visitation takes place. The aid then never begins or merely ceases, as the case may be. There is no entry of the home and there is no search.

V

If however, we were to assume that a caseworker's home visit, before or subsequent to the beneficiary's initial qualification for benefits, somehow (perhaps because the average beneficiary might feel she is in no position to refuse consent to the visit), and despite its interview nature, does possess some of the characteristics of a search in the traditional sense, we nevertheless conclude that the visit does not fall within the Fourth Amendment's proscription. This is because it does not descend to the level of unreasonableness. It is unreasonableness which is the Fourth Amendment's standard. . . .

There are a number of factors that compel us to conclude that the home visit proposed for Mrs. James is not unreasonable:

1. The public's interest in this particular segment of the area of assistance to the unfortunate is protection and aid for the dependent child whose family requires such aid for that child. The focus is on the child and, further, it is on the child who is dependent. There is no more worthy object of the public's concern. . . .

2. The agency, with tax funds provided from federal as well as from state sources, is fulfilling a public trust. The State, working through its qualified welfare agency, has appropriate and paramount interest and concern in seeing and assuring that the intended and proper objects of that tax-produced assistance are the ones who benefit from the aid it dispenses. . . .

3. One who dispenses purely private charity naturally has an interest in and expects to know how his charitable funds are utilized and put to work. The public, when it is the provider, rightly expects the same. . . .

4. The emphasis of the New York statutes and regulations is upon the home, upon "close contact" with the beneficiary, upon restoring the aid recipient "to a condition of self-support," and upon the relief of his distress. The federal emphasis is no different. It is upon "assistance and rehabilitation," upon maintaining and strengthening family life, and upon "maximum self-support and personal independence consistent with the maintenance of continuing parental care and protection. . . ." And it is concerned about any possible exploitation of the child.

5. The home visit, it is true, is not required by federal statute or regulation. But it has been noted that the visit is "the heart of welfare administration"; that it affords "a personal, rehabilitative orientation, unlike that of most federal programs" . . . .

6. The means employed by the New York agency are significant. Mrs. James received written notice several days in advance of the intended home visit. The date was specified.... Privacy is emphasized. The applicant-recipient is made the primary source of information as to eligibility. Outside informational sources, other than public records, are to be consulted only with the beneficiary's consent. Forcible entry or entry under false pretenses or visitation outside working hours or snooping in the home are forbidden. All this minimizes any "burden" upon the homeowner's right against unreasonable intrusion.

7. Mrs. James, in fact, on this record presents no specific complaint of any unreasonable intrusion of her home and nothing that supports an inference that the desired home visit had as its purpose the obtaining of information as to criminal activity.... Mrs. James appears to want from the agency that provides her and her infant son with the necessities for life is the right to receive those necessities upon her own informational terms, to utilize the Fourth Amendment as a wedge for imposing those terms, and to avoid questions of any kind.

...

The visit is not one by police or uniformed authority. It is made by a caseworker of some training whose primary objective is, or should be, the welfare, not the prosecution, of the aid recipient for whom the worker has profound responsibility. As has already been stressed, the program concerns dependent children and the needy families of those children. It does not deal with crime or with the actual or suspected perpetrators of crime. The caseworker is not a sleuth but rather, we trust, is a friend to one in need.

10. The home visit is not a criminal investigation, does not equate with a criminal investigation, and despite the announced fears of Mrs. James and those who would join her, is not in aid of any criminal proceeding. If the visitation serves to discourage misrepresentation or fraud, such a byproduct of that visit does not impress upon the visit itself a dominant criminal investigative aspect. And if the visit should, by chance, lead to the discovery of fraud and a criminal prosecution should follow, then, even assuming that the evidence discovered upon the home visitation is admissible, an issue upon which we express no opinion, that is a routine and expected fact of life and a consequence no greater than that which necessarily ensues upon any other discovery by a citizen of criminal conduct.

11....

It seems to us that the situation is akin to that where an Internal Revenue Service agent, in making a routine civil audit of a taxpayer's income tax return, asks that the taxpayer produce for the agent's review some proof of a deduction the taxpayer has asserted to his benefit in the computation of his tax. If the taxpayer refuses, there is, absent fraud, only a disallowance of the claimed deduction and a consequent additional tax. The taxpayer is fully within his "rights" in refusing to produce the proof, but in maintaining and asserting those rights a tax detriment results and it is a detriment of the taxpayer's own making. So here Mrs. James has the "right" to refuse the home visit, but a consequence in the form of cessation of aid, similar to the taxpayer's resultant additional tax, flows from that refusal. The choice is entirely hers, and nothing of constitutional magnitude is involved.

...

We therefore conclude that the home visitation as structured by the New York statutes and regulations is a reasonable administrative tool; that it serves a valid and proper administrative purpose for the dispensation of the AFDC program; that it is not an unwarranted invasion of personal privacy; and that it violates no right guaranteed by the Fourth Amendment.

Reversed and remanded with directions to enter a judgment of dismissal.

It is so ordered.

Mr. Justice Douglas, dissenting.

...

... Whatever the semantics, the central question is whether the government by force of its largesse has the power to "buy up" rights guaranteed by the Constitution. But for the assertion of her constitutional right, Barbara James in this case would have received the welfare benefit.

...

Is a search of her home without a warrant made "reasonable" merely because she is dependent on government largesse?

Judge Skelly Wright has stated the problem succinctly:

> Welfare has long been considered the equivalent of charity and its recipients have been subjected to all kinds of dehumanizing experiences in the government's effort to police its welfare payments. In fact, over half a billion dollars are expended annually for administration and policing in connection with the Aid to Families with Dependent Children program. Why such large sums are necessary for administration and policing has never been adequately explained. No such sums are spent policing the government subsidies granted to farmers, airlines, steamship companies, and junk mail dealers, to name but a few. The truth is that in this subsidy area society has simply adopted a double standard, one for aid to business and the farmer and a different one for welfare.

If the welfare recipient was not Barbara James but a prominent, affluent cotton or wheat farmer receiving benefit payments for not growing crops, would not the approach be different? ...

...

I would place the same restrictions on inspectors entering the homes of welfare beneficiaries as are on inspectors entering the homes of those on the payroll of government, or the homes of those who contract with the government, or the homes of those who work for those having government contracts. . . .

. . .

The bureaucracy of modern government is not only slow, lumbering, and oppressive; it is omnipresent. It touches everyone's life at numerous points. It pries more and more into private affairs, breaking down the barriers that individuals erect to give them some insulation from the intrigues and harassments of modern life. Isolation is not a constitutional guarantee; but the sanctity of the sanctuary of the home is such—as marked and defined by the Fourth Amendment. What we do today is to depreciate it.

. . .

Mr. Justice Marshall, whom Mr. Justice Brennan joins, dissenting.

. . .

Simply stated, the issue in this case is whether a state welfare agency can require all recipients of AFDC benefits to submit to warrantless "visitations" of their homes. In answering that question, the majority dodges between constitutional issues to reach a result clearly inconsistent with the decisions of this Court. We are told that there is no search involved in this case; that even if there were a search, it would not be unreasonable; and that even if this were an unreasonable search, a welfare recipient waives her right to object by accepting benefits. I emphatically disagree with all three conclusions. . . .

I

The Court's assertion that this case concerns no search "in the Fourth Amendment meaning of that term" is neither "obvious" nor "simple." I should have thought that the Fourth Amendment governs all intrusions by agents of the public upon personal security. . . .

Even if the Fourth Amendment does not apply to each and every governmental entry into the home, the welfare visit is not some sort of purely benevolent inspection. No one questions the motives of the dedicated welfare caseworker. Of course, caseworkers seek to be friends, but the point is that they are also required to be sleuths. The majority concedes that the "visitation" is partially investigative, but claims that this investigative aspect has been given too much emphasis. Emphasis has indeed been given. Time and again, in briefs and at oral argument, appellants emphasized the need to enter AFDC homes to guard against welfare fraud and child abuse, both of which are felonies. The New York statutes provide emphasis by requiring all caseworkers to report any evidence of fraud that a home visit uncovers. And appellants have strenuously emphasized the importance of the visit to provide evidence leading to civil forfeitures including elimination of benefits and loss of child custody.

. . .

Conceding for the sake of argument that someone might view the "visitation" as a search, the majority nonetheless concludes that such a search is not unreasonable. However, its mode of reaching that conclusion departs from the entire history of Fourth Amendment case law. Of course, the Fourth Amendment test is reasonableness, but in determining whether a search is reasonable, this Court is not free merely to balance, in a totally ad hoc fashion, any number of subjective factors. An unbroken line of cases holds that, subject to a few narrowly drawn exceptions, any search without a warrant is constitutionally unreasonable. In this case, no suggestion that evidence will disappear, that a criminal will escape, or that an officer will be injured, justifies the failure to obtain a warrant. Instead, the majority asserts what amounts to three state interests that allegedly render this search reasonable. None of these interests is sufficient to carve out a new exception to the warrant requirement.

First, it is argued that the home visit is justified to protect dependent children from "abuse" and "exploitation." These are heinous crimes, but they are not confined to indigent households. Would the majority sanction, in the absence of probable cause, compulsory visits to all American homes for the purpose of discovering child abuse? Or is this Court prepared to hold as a matter of constitutional law that a mother, merely because she is poor, is substantially more likely to injure or exploit her children? Such a categorical approach to an entire class of citizens would be dangerously at odds with the tenets of our democracy.

Second, the Court contends that caseworkers must enter the homes of AFDC beneficiaries to determine eligibility. . . . The majority's implication that a biannual home visit somehow assures the verification of actual residence or actual physical presence in the home strains credulity in the context of urban poverty. Despite the caseworker's responsibility for dependent children, he is not even required to see the children as a part of the home visit. Appellants offer scant explanation for their refusal even to attempt to utilize public records, expenditure receipts, documents such as leases, non-home interviews, personal financial records, sworn declarations, etc. — all sources that governmental agencies regularly accept as adequate to establish eligibility for other public benefits. In this setting, it ill behooves appellants to refuse to utilize informational sources less drastic than an invasion of the privacy of the home.

We are told that the plight of Mrs. James is no different from that of a taxpayer who is required to document his right to a tax deduction, but this analogy is seriously flawed. The record shows that Mrs. James has offered to be interviewed anywhere other than her home, to answer any questions, and to provide any documentation that the welfare agency desires. The agency curtly refused all these offers and insisted on its "right" to pry into appellee's home. Tax exemptions are also governmental "bounty." A true analogy would be an Internal Revenue Service requirement that in order to claim a dependency exemption, a taxpayer must allow a specially trained IRS agent to invade the home for the purpose of questioning the occupants and looking for evidence that the exemption is being properly utilized for the benefit of the dependent. If such a system were even proposed, the cries of constitutional outrage would be unanimous.

Appellants offer a third state interest that the Court seems to accept as partial justification for this search. We are told that the visit is designed to rehabilitate, to provide aid. This is strange doctrine indeed. A paternalistic notion that a complaining citizen's constitutional rights can be violated so long as the State is somehow helping him is alien to our Nation's philosophy....

...

In deciding that the homes of AFDC recipients are not entitled to protection from warrantless searches by welfare caseworkers, the Court declines to follow prior case law and employs a rationale that, if applied to the claims of all citizens, would threaten the vitality of the Fourth Amendment.... I find no little irony in the fact that the burden of today's departure from principled adjudication is placed upon the lowly poor. Perhaps the majority has explained why a commercial warehouse deserves more protection than does this poor woman's home. I am not convinced; and, therefore, I must respectfully dissent.

Notes and Queries

1. The Court proposes that a home visit by a welfare caseworker does not constitute a search within the meaning of the Fourth Amendment in part on the "rehabilitative" character of welfare home visits and the need to protect dependent children. Do these visits, then, mean that they are investigatory to prevent harm to children?
2. Do you take the decision to also mean that residence entries in the course of civil child abuse investigations are not "searches" governed by Fourth Amendment? Based on other cases we have read, it may seem reasonable to not require social workers to have probable cause that the child is being harmed. Should social workers at least be required to obtain a warrant, one that at least may be based on reasonable suspicion rather than probable cause?

Research Comments

1. Home visitations programs have become so common that few challenge their legitimacy. Part of the reason they have become so routine has been due to impressive research suggesting their effectiveness in addressing many issues that directly relate to public health, including child maltreatment. The American Academy of Pediatrics' Council on Child and Adolescent Health recently reviewed the now immense literature on the effectiveness of home visitation programs. In terms of prenatal effects, it concluded that home visiting (1) increases use of prenatal care; (2) increases birth weight; (3) decreases preterm labor and increases length of gestation; (4) increases use of health and other community resources (e.g., prenatal visits,

well-child visits, family planning, and immunizations); (5) improves nutrition during pregnancy; (6) reduces urinary tract infections during pregnancy; (7) increases attendance at childbirth classes; (8) decreases maternal smoking; (9) increases fathers' interest in the pregnancy; and (10) increases the number of mothers having companions in the labor room. In terms of postnatal effects, the Council found that home visiting (1) reduces subsequent pregnancies; (2) increases spacing between pregnancies; (3) increases length of maternal employment; (4) increases rate of return to, or retention in, school by mothers; (5) reduces emergency department visits; (6) reduces accidental injuries and poisonings resulting in a visit to the physician; (7) decreases the number of verified incidents of child abuse and neglect; (8) decreases physical punishment and restriction of infants, with an increase in use of appropriate discipline for older children; (9) improves maternal–child interaction and maternal satisfaction with parenting; (10) increases use of appropriate play materials at home; (11) improves growth in low-birth-weight infants; and (12) increases developmental quotients in infants. The Council also reported trends in research indicating the components of more successful programs: (1) a focus on families in greater need of services (as opposed to universal programs that may avoid stigmatizing families but might dilute scarce resources), including families with low-birth-weight and pre-term infants; children with chronic illness and disabilities; low-income, unmarried teenage mothers; parents with low IQs; and families with a history of substance abuse; (2) intervention beginning in pregnancy and continuing through the second to fifth year of life; (3) flexibility and family specificity, so that the duration and frequency of visits and the kinds of services provided can be adjusted to a family's need and risk level; (4) active promotion of positive health-related behaviors and specific qualities of infant caregiving instead of focusing solely on social support; (5) a broad multiproblem focus to address the full complement of family needs (as opposed to a focus on a single domain such as increasing birth weights or reducing child abuse); (6) measures to reduce family stress by improving its social and physical environments; and (7) use of nurses or well-trained paraprofessionals. American Academy of Pediatrics Council on Child and Adolescent Health (1998). The role of home-visitation programs in improving health outcomes for children and families. *Pediatrics*, 101, 486–490.

2. Despite impressive links between home visits and a host of positive outcomes for individuals, families, and society, it is important to note that other evaluations of several national home visitation models find important limitations and indicate enormous variability in outcome study findings. Results vary widely across program goals, program models, and program sites, and across families within the same site. See Deanna S. Gomby, Mary B. Larner, Carol S. Stevenson, Eugene M. Lewit & Richard E. Behrman (1999). Home visiting: Recent program evaluations — analysis and recommendations. *Future of Children*, 9, 4–26. The most studied and long-standing program, the Nurse Home Visitation Program (NHVP) from Elmira and Memphis, is the one that provided the most robust research suggesting that nurse home visitation services, begun during pregnancy and continuing through

the first two years of a child's life, prevents child maltreatment. Specifically, findings from Elmira indicated that children of nurse-visited mothers were less likely to be abused or neglected than a control group during the first two years of the children's lives, and their mothers were less likely to be identified as perpetrators of child maltreatment during the period between the children's fourth and fifteenth birthdays. Recently, however, reports circumscribe those findings: Child maltreatment was not prevented in families with frequent domestic violence. Almost half (48 percent) of the mothers in the Elmira study reported experiencing some form of partner-perpetrated violence (ranging from being pushed to being beaten or being injured or threatened with a weapon) during the 15 years since program enrollment. For the 21 percent who reported more than 28 incidents of domestic violence during the follow-up period, the visitation intervention had no effect on child maltreatment rates. John Eckenrode, Barbara Ganzel, Charles R. Henderson, Elliott Smith, David L. Olds, Jane Powers, Robert Cole, Harriett Kitzman & Kimberly Sidora (2000). Preventing child abuse and neglect with a program of nurse home visitation: The limiting effects of domestic violence. *The Journal of the American Medical Association*, 284, 1385–1391. These are important limitations. Nationally, physical violence is estimated to occur in four to six million intimate relationships annually, and three to ten million children each year are thought to be exposed to domestic violence, with exposure ranging from witnessing a violent altercation to observing its aftermath. It is unclear what percentage of families enrolled in home visitation programs nationally experience domestic violence. On a nationwide scale, that could translate to millions of children whose abuse would not be prevented. Deanna S. Gomby (2000). Promise and limitations of home visitation. *The Journal of the American Medical Association*, 284, 1430–1431.

Franz v. Lytle

997 F.2d 784 (10th Cir. Ct. App., 1993)

Justice Moore delivered the opinion of the court.

. . .

. . . On October 19, 1988, police dispatch contacted Officer Lytle to investigate a report of a child who was possibly in need of care. That report had been called in by Ms. Susan Brickley, who told police her neighbors two-year-old daughter, Ashley Franz, was unsupervised, wet, and unclean. [Note 1 notes that Ms. Brickley initially called Kansas Social and Rehabilitative Services (SRS), which told her to call the police because it did not have a caseworker available.] Late that afternoon, Officer Lytle went to Ms. Brickley's home where Ashley was playing. Ms. Brickley told Officer Lytle Ashley had a severe diaper rash and stank from constantly being urine-soaked. Without contacting Ashley's mother, Officer Lytle asked Ms. Brickley to remove Ashley's diaper. Ms. Brickley laid Ashley down on the living room floor and removed her diaper permitting Officer Lytle to observe the child's vaginal area and take five or six photographs of what he believed was a "very severe rash." Officer Lytle then visited the home of Katherine and Timothy Franz, Ashley's parents, telling Mrs. Franz he had just examined Ashley, and she would be contacted by Social and Rehabilitative Services (SRS).

Upon returning to headquarters, Officer Lytle contacted SRS, filled out a standard Kansas Bureau of Investigation (KBI) report, and consulted with Capt. Gary Johnson. According to Capt. Johnson's report, Officer Lytle told Capt. Johnson he was investigating "a possible molesting case," was concerned about "leaving the children at the home because of the risk factor that if there was a molestation case," and "was shown the bruising of the vaginal area by the female caller." Capt. Johnson advised Officer Lytle he might want to take the child for a medical examination so that a doctor could determine what caused the bruising and "alleviate the problem of protective custody." Capt. Johnson also suggested Officer Lytle have a female officer accompany him when he returned to the house.

Late the following afternoon, after telephoning a former neighbor of the Franzes, Officer Lytle, accompanied by Officer Jeanette Schlabach, returned to the Franz home and requested to see Ashley again. Both officers were in uniform and carrying side arms. Mrs. Franz permitted them to enter her home and complied with their request to examine Ashley, removing her pants, laying her down on the floor, and spreading her legs apart as ordered. Kneeling over Ashley, Officer Lytle then touched her vaginal area in several places "checking for any soreness or swelling," and Ashley's reaction to his touch, asking her if the places he pressed hurt. Officer Lytle believed he saw some discoloration in the area.

In response to Mrs. Franz's explanation she had been trying to "potty train" Ashley, Officer Lytle asked her to "voluntarily take her up to Wesley [Hospital] ER and let the Doctor look at her." To her protests about the cost and her lack of transportation, Officer Lytle answered he could place Ashley in protective custody and "take her up there ourselves." Upset, Mrs. Franz telephoned her husband at work. Officer Lytle took the phone and told Mr. Franz he had received a report from SRS, checked it out, and "Ashley does have some type of discoloration, bruises, whatever it is on her legs and around her vaginal area and we need to have it checked." Officer Lytle told Timothy Franz he could either take the child voluntarily, or they would take Ashley into protective custody.

Mr. Franz returned home, and he and Mrs. Franz, escorted by the officers, drove to Wesley Hospital where Ashley was examined by an emergency room physician. Mrs. Franz and the officers remained in the examining room while Dr. Davidson examined the child, concluding Ashley had "mild redness to labial folds, no tears, bruising, or edema." The officers apologized, and the Franzes returned home.

II.

Surviving in this appeal are plaintiffs' Fourth Amendment and pendent state law claims based on invasion of privacy, trespass, and deprivation of liberty on which the district court denied defendant's qualified immunity defense. To reach this result, the district court . . . framed its crucial inquiry as "whether, at the time defendants acted, it was clearly established law that a child abuse investigation conducted by police officers is subject to the probable cause or warrant requirements." Cognizant of a seeming split in the Circuits over this issue, the district court drew a bright line between law enforcement officers trained and "expected to know the subtleties of the probable cause and warrant requirements" and social workers who "have no such fluency of the legal standards." The court found at all times defendant was conducting a criminal investigation involving searches "aimed at uncovering incriminating evidence of sexual abuse by one or both of the parents." This conduct, the court held, was circumscribed by the Fourth Amendment which "clearly prohibited police officers from conducting warrantless searches of a home and a child's body for evidence of criminal sexual abuse absent consent or exigent circumstances or any of the recognized exceptions to the warrant requirement." . . . [T]he court further concluded no reasonable officer acting on the sole information provided, that Ashley was wet, unclean, and unsupervised, would "have believed that the searches were lawful." [The court also stated that even if these circumstances created a basis for probable cause, defendant indicated no exigency preventing them from securing a warrant, nor could defendants reasonably believe plaintiffs gave consent to the searches.]

III.

. . . [D]efendant advocates we accord police officers investigating a complaint a child is in need of care or abused the same latitude to search he claims is granted social workers. . . .

. . . [W]e must then decide to sustain a claim of the lawful exercise of authority based on qualified immunity if, upon examining the information defendant possessed, we can conclude a reasonable officer in the same position in 1988, schooled in the governing principles of the Fourth Amendment, believed he was acting in accord with those principles. If so, his conduct was lawful, and he is entitled to qualified immunity. . . .

IV.

The boundary for defendant's conduct establishing the "contours of the right" involved is the Fourth Amendment, which proscribes unreasonable searches. In 1988, the case law had unimpeachably established "'the cardinal principle that searches conducted outside the judicial process, without prior approval by judge or magistrate, are per se unreasonable under the Fourth Amendment—subject only to a few specifically established and well-delineated exceptions.'" . . . While the presence of probable cause permits the issuance of a search warrant by a neutral magistrate, its absence can only be overcome by the well-delineated exceptions of consent, exigent circumstances, and administrative searches.

Given these well-established principles, it became "hornbook law" to the district court that "police officers are required to conduct searches that comport with the Fourth Amendment." Throughout the course of events, the court observed, defendant proceeded as a law enforcement officer conducting a criminal investigation of possible child abuse or neglect for which he undertook the warrantless searches. Under these circumstances, the court believed, defendant's conduct was clearly circumscribed by the warrant or probable cause requirement. Implicit in this conclusion was the court's rejection of defendant's attempt to align his conduct with that of social workers under similar circumstances.

Nevertheless, defendant continues to argue the warrantless searches at issue fall more properly within the administrative search exception. In doing so, defendant casts this case as one of first impression requiring we decide, in effect, whether social workers are relieved of the probable cause or warrant requirement when investigating cases of child abuse or neglect in order to make him ultimately the beneficiary of that analysis.

. . .

. . . What the district court perceived, and what cannot be overlooked, is that defendant's focus was not so much on the child as it was on the potential criminal culpability of her parents. That focus is the hallmark of a criminal investigation. In contrast, a social worker's principal focus is the welfare of the child. While a criminal prosecution may emanate from the social worker's activity, that prospect is not a part of the social worker's cachet. This distinction of focus justifies a more liberal view of the amount of probable cause that would support an administrative search.

Moreover, defendant's conduct cannot otherwise be transformed into that of a social worker given the uncontroverted facts he was in uniform and carrying a gun at all times; he recorded his meeting with Mrs. Franz, following police policy; he filed standard KBI reports of his investigation; and he informed his superior officer he was investigating a possible child molestation. Each of these facts, as the district court properly found, provides the script for a criminal investigation carried out by a law enforcement officer.

. . . In the present case, defendant, armed only with information the child was urine-soaked and unsupervised, indeed told only by Ms. Brickley that Ashley had a diaper rash, and without any medical expertise, proceeded to visually inspect and touch portions of the child's body which are normally clothed. Additionally, defendant told plaintiffs if they did not comply with his order, the child would be taken into protective custody. The Kansas Code for Care of Children, relied on by defendant, specifically requires a law enforcement officer have a court order or believe a court order has been issued unless "the officer has probable cause to believe that the child is a child in need of care and that there are reasonable grounds to believe that the circumstances or condition of the child is such that continuing in the place or residence in which the child has been found or in the care and custody of the person who has care or custody of the child would be harmful to the child."

Since defendant's conduct does not comply even with the governing principles required of social workers in Kansas, we must circumscribe his actions by the governing principles of the discipline he represented. . . .

This analysis is also consistent with our case law which has looked to the function the official performs to examine qualified immunity claims. "'Under that approach, we examine the nature of the functions with which a particular official or class of officials has been lawfully entrusted, and we seek to evaluate the effect that exposure to particular forms of liability would likely have on the appropriate exercise of those functions.'"

However, as the district court stated, this conclusion "does not end the inquiry," but requires we move on to consider "whether a reasonable officer could have believed [defendant's] warrantless search to be lawful, in light of the clearly established law and the information the searching officer possessed." At no time, defendant stated in his deposition, was he investigating a sexual assault. The only information defendant possessed was that Ashley had a severe rash. Because defendant does not challenge the court's failure to find as a matter of law plaintiffs voluntarily consented to the searches under all of the circumstances of this case and does not allege any exigency, we agree with the district court in denying defendant qualified immunity that no reasonable officer would consider the searches lawful.

...

Therefore, on this record and under the particular circumstances of this case, we must eschew defendant's suggestion to decide as a matter of first impression, in the investigation of claims of child abuse and neglect, police officers are absolved of a warrant or probable cause requirement. At the time of defendant's actions, the law was clearly established that the information the officer possessed rendered the present warrantless searches objectively unreasonable barring his claim of qualified immunity so that plaintiffs' § 1983 and pendent state law action may proceed.

Affirmed.

Research Comments

1. Child protective services are generally required to initiate an investigation within twenty-four hours of receiving any report of abuse or neglect. If it appears that the child is in imminent danger or that the family may flee, however, investigations must commence immediately upon receipt of the report. Ideally, the investigation accomplishes several objectives, including (1) direct contact with the child; (2) an interview with the child's caretaker; (3) a determination of the nature, extent, and cause of the abuse; (4) the discovery of the condition of any other children in the household; and (5) an evaluation of the home environment and the risk of leaving the children in that environment. The results of the investigation must be reported, in writing, to the state or district attorney. Child abuse investigations share several characteristics with searches traditionally labeled criminal. For example, the purpose of the search is to determine whether a criminal activity is taking place. In many cases, the police department is the investigating agency; when it is not, many

states require social services investigators to refer substantiated reports of abuse to the local district attorney or the police for prosecution. Despite these similarities to criminal searches, child abuse investigations conducted pursuant to valid statutory and administrative provisions are generally deemed administrative; as long as the administrative function of the search is not a "mere pretext," the search will be judged on administrative terms. Nearly every state has expressly declared the policy underlying such investigations to be the protection and welfare of the child, not the apprehension and punishment of the alleged abuser. Thus, so long as a search serves a valid administrative function it may be conducted by police officers for the purpose of uncovering evidence of criminal wrongdoing and still be labeled administrative. This in turn yields the conclusion that child abuse investigations are administrative, since they further a valid administrative objective. State legislatures have enacted statutes that confer various forms of immunity upon social workers in child abuse investigations. These statutes illustrate the states' concern that the threat of potential liability will likely deter child protection workers from exercising their best professional judgment in child abuse investigations.

2. The home visit itself usually begins with the investigator's requesting consent to enter the home and to speak with or examine the child. Even if consent is denied, however, the investigator has legal authority to enter and may summon the police or obtain a court order to aid the investigation. If there is reason to believe that the child may be in danger, the police may use reasonable force to gain entry. The investigator is empowered to inspect and photograph both the child and "those areas of the residence 'reasonably related to the allegations of abuse or neglect.'" Should the investigator determine that the child's environment presents an immediate danger, he may remove the child from the home without prior judicial approval and order any physical, psychological, or psychiatric examinations he deems necessary. Traditionally, intrusions by state agents into the privacy of the home have been considered the most grievous sort and hence have been required to meet the Fourth Amendment's most stringent requirements. However, most state statutory and administrative schemes governing child abuse investigations include provisions that either mandate or permit investigatory home visits, and many of these expressly give investigators the authority to enter the home without obtaining a warrant or establishing reasonable cause. Courts have rebuffed challenges to these schemes, finding the warrant requirement inapplicable in that it would seriously impair, if not wholly frustrate, the state's efforts to protect the child.

Review Problem

1. In April 1981, the Department of Children and Family Services (DCFS) received an anonymous report that B. D., a 10-year-old boy, had been beaten by his father. After speaking with the principal at B. D.'s school, the caseworker required B. D. to remove his pants and examined his back and buttocks. In November 1980, A. O.'s

mother contacted the DCFS seeking family counseling. During the conversation, she revealed that A. O. had been kicked and shoved by his stepfather. Four months later, a caseworker interviewed A. O. at school and required him to remove his shirt and pants as part of an examination for evidence of abuse. The parents brought a Fourth Amendment challenge against the Illinois DCFS for allowing social workers to conduct nude searches of their children for evidence of child abuse where certain "hot-line" criteria were met. They argued that the DCFS investigatory procedures violate the Fourth Amendment's prohibition against unreasonable searches and the right to privacy protected by the Fourteenth Amendment. How should a court rule? The Seventh Circuit held that visual inspections conducted by state officials of unclothed children for evidence of child abuse implicated Fourth Amendment concerns. The court concluded, however, that the search was constitutional because the state's compelling interest in safeguarding children from injury and death outweighed the substantial intrusion into a child's right to privacy. *Darryl H. v. Coler*, 801 F.2d 893 (7th Cir. 1986). Note that, in *Darryl*, the hotline criteria that constituted a report requiring further investigation by a DCFS caseworker was information that: (1) a child less than 18 years old is involved; (2) the child was either harmed or in danger of harm; (3) a specific incident of abuse is identified; (4) a parent, caretaker, sibling, or babysitter is the alleged perpetrator of neglect; or (5) a parent, caretaker, adult family member, adult individual residing in the child's home, parent's paramour, sibling, or babysitter is the alleged perpetrator of abuse.

Valmonte v. Bane

18 F.3d 99 (2nd Cir. Ct. App., 1994)

Justice Altimari delivered the opinion of the court.

. . .

The major issue presented in this appeal is whether the state's maintenance of a Central Register that identifies individuals accused of child abuse or neglect, and its communication of the names of those on the list to potential employers in the child care field, implicates a protectible liberty interest under the Fourteenth Amendment. If so, we must also determine whether the state's statutory procedures established to protect the liberty interest are constitutionally adequate.

. . .

I. Statutory Scheme

Valmonte is challenging the state's system for collecting and storing information about allegedly abusive and neglectful individuals. . . . New York Social Services Law governs the recording and investigation of reports of suspected maltreatment of children, and the administrative review process by which substantiated reports may be reviewed. The Central Register maintains reports of child abuse as part of a larger system to ensure the safety of children in New York and is maintained by both the state and various county departments of social services.

A. Reporting and Initial Placement on Register

The Central Register procedures are triggered by reports to the Central Register of suspected child abuse. The state DSS maintains a telephone hotline with a toll-free telephone number that is staffed full-time in order to receive complaints. State law places an affirmative duty on designated individuals such as health care workers, social workers, law enforcement agents, judicial officers, and education employees to report to the Central Register whenever they have reasonable cause to suspect that a child is maltreated. Calls to the hotline can be made, however, by any individuals, not only those with affirmative duties of reporting.

Upon receiving a complaint of suspected child abuse, hotline operators must determine whether the allegations, if true, would be legally sufficient to constitute child abuse. If so, the operator records the complaint on paper and relays it to the appropriate county or local DSS. The local DSS is responsible for investigating all complaints of suspected child maltreatment, SSL § 423(1), and must investigate the truth of the charges and complete an investigation within 60 days.

At the conclusion of the investigation, the local department must determine whether the complaint is "unfounded" or "indicated." Unfounded reports are expunged from the Central Register and all records destroyed. If the local DSS finds that there is "some credible evidence" to support the complaint, the complaint is marked "indicated" and the individual who is the subject of the report is listed on the Central Register. The Central Register accepts the findings of the county department, without making an independent determination.

B. Confidentiality of Central Register Determinations

As noted earlier, the information in the Central Register is generally confidential. The names of individuals on the Central Register are not publicly available, although there are numerous exceptions for, among others, public agencies, law enforcement personnel, and judicial officers.

More significant, for purposes of this case, are the statutory provisions requiring certain employers in the child care field to make inquiries to the Central Register to determine whether potential employees are among those listed. The purpose of these provisions is to ensure that individuals on the Central Register do not become or stay employed or licensed in positions that allow substantial contact with children, unless the licensing or hiring agency or business is aware of the applicant's status. Numerous state agencies, private businesses, and licensing agencies related to child care, adoption, and foster care are required by law to inquire whether potential employees or applicants are on the Central Register. For purposes of simplicity, this group will be referred to as "employers," even though licensing agencies are included within that designation.

When such employers make an inquiry, the state DSS will inform the potential employer if the individual is the subject of an indicated report on the Central Register. The state DSS will not inform the employer of the nature of the indicated report, but only that the report exists. . . .

C. Procedures for Appealing Initial Listing

There are certain procedures established by the statutory scheme to allow individuals included on the Central Register to appeal their designation. When a local DSS finds that a report is "indicated," the subject of the report is notified and has 90 days to request that the report be expunged. If a request is made, the state DSS is required to gather the material pertinent to the indicated report and conduct a two-step review. First, the state DSS must determine whether there is "some credible evidence" that the subject committed the acts charged. In the second step of the review, the state DSS must also ascertain whether the acts alleged could be "relevant and reasonably related" to the subject's employment in any child care provider area.

If there is no credible evidence of child abuse or maltreatment, the state DSS must expunge the record and notify the subject. If there is some credible evidence, and the department finds that the allegations are reasonably related to child care, the department must deny the expungement request. Finally, if there is some credible evidence of the act, but a finding by the department that the allegations are not reasonably related to child care, the report will not be expunged, but it will also not be disclosed to potential child care employers and licensing agencies.

If the expungement request is denied, an administrative hearing before the state DSS commissioner's office is scheduled (the "non-deprivation hearing"). The burden of proof at this hearing is placed on the "child protective service or the state agency which investigated the report." The nature of the proof required at this hearing is functionally identical to that required for the initial expungement request: the local DSS must prove to the commissioner the allegations against the subject by some credible evidence and then must prove that the allegations are reasonably related to employment in the child care field.

The consequences of the hearing are substantially similar to those at the expungement hearing: if there is no credible evidence substantiating the allegation, the record is expunged; if there is credible evidence, but the acts alleged are not reasonably related to child care, the department is precluded from notifying potential employers in the child care field of the complaint; finally, if there is some credible evidence and a finding that the acts are related to child care, the record will be maintained and will be available to child care provider agencies and employers.

In this initial hearing, any state family court finding of abuse or neglect against the subject with regard to the allegations in the report creates "an irrebuttable presumption" that the allegations are supported by some credible evidence. The inverse, however, is not true: the fact that a case brought against the subject in state family court has been dismissed is not considered conclusive proof that there is no credible evidence of the allegations.

If the report is not expunged after the hearing, the subject of the report can commence a proceeding pursuant to Article 78 of the New York Civil Practice Law and Rules to challenge the decision. The court's determination of such a proceeding is made under the "arbitrary and capricious" standard usually applied to state agency determinations.

D. Post-Deprivation Hearing

As noted earlier, certain employers and licensing agencies are required to ascertain whether potential employees or applicants are listed on the Central Register, and can only hire or license such applicants if they maintain a written record of their reasons for doing so. If the agency decides not to hire or license the individual, it must provide the individual with "a written statement setting forth whether its denial, failure to hire or failure to use was based, in whole or in part, on such indicated report, and if so, its reasons for the denial or failure to hire or failure to use." Similarly, the termination of an employee who is the subject of an indicated report must be accompanied with a written statement setting forth whether the termination was based on the report.

If the reasons for the termination or refusal to hire include the fact that the applicant was the subject of an indicated report, that subject has the right to a post-deprivation hearing before the state DSS. At this hearing:

> the sole question before the department shall be whether the applicant ... who was denied access to the children cared for by a provider agency has been shown by a fair preponderance of the evidence to have committed the act or acts of child abuse or maltreatment giving rise to the indicated report.... The failure to sustain the burden of proof at a hearing held pursuant to this section shall not result in the expungement of an indicated report but shall be noted on the report maintained by the state central register and shall preclude the department from notifying a party which subsequently makes an inquiry to the department pursuant to this section that the person about whom the inquiry is made is the subject of an indicated report.

At this post-deprivation hearing, therefore, the DSS bears the burden of proving the allegations not by "some credible evidence"—the standard for the initial determination by the local DSS, the initial expungement request, and the non-deprivation hearing—but by a "fair preponderance of the evidence." The failure to reach that level of proof will not result in expungement, but will prevent potential employers or licensing agencies from knowing that the applicant is the subject of an indicated report.

Unless expunged earlier, an indicated report is finally expunged 10 years after the youngest child referred to in the report turns 18.

II. Valmonte's Case

Valmonte became entangled in this system on December 1, 1989, when she slapped her eleven year-old daughter Vanessa on the side of her face with an open hand. Valmonte states in her complaint that she slapped Vanessa because Vanessa had been caught stealing and other forms of discipline had not been successful. An unidentified employee at Vanessa's school made a complaint to the child abuse hotline that Valmonte had mistreated her daughter. Subsequently, child abuse investigators working for the Orange County DSS concluded that Valmonte had engaged in "excessive corporal punishment," marked the complaint against her as "indicated," and commenced child protective proceedings against her.

The New York state family court subsequently dismissed the child protective proceedings against Valmonte. This dismissal, however, had no impact on Valmonte's inclusion on the Central Register.

During this time, Valmonte requested expungement of her indicated report from the state DSS. This request was denied. Valmonte then exercised her right to an administrative hearing before an agent of the state DSS. The state DSS again denied expungement, finding some credible evidence to support the allegations.

Subsequently, Valmonte brought an action in the district court challenging the constitutionality of the Central Register statutory scheme under 42 U.S.C. § 1983. The complaint contained numerous procedural due process claims, substantive due process claims, and appended related state law claims. The defendant state and local departments of social services moved to dismiss Valmonte's action for failure to state a claim upon which relief could be granted, principally because Valmonte failed to adequately show that she had a protected liberty interest that was implicated by the procedures of the Central Register.

...

Valmonte now appeals, arguing principally that the state has deprived her of a legitimate liberty interest by disseminating to potential employers her placement on the Central Register list, and that the procedures established to allow her to challenge her designation are constitutionally inadequate.

Discussion

I. Does Disclosure Violate a Liberty Interest?

Valmonte primarily argues that the state government has stigmatized her as a child abuser while simultaneously depriving her of her ability to seek employment.... The present question is whether Valmonte has a cognizable claim under the facts alleged in her complaint.

To formulate a claim under the Due Process Clause of the Fourteenth Amendment, a plaintiff must demonstrate that he or she possesses a constitutionally protected interest in life, liberty, or property, and that state action has deprived him or her of that interest. The Supreme Court has established that "we examine procedural due process questions in two steps: the first asks whether there exists a liberty or property interest which has been interfered with by the State; the second examines whether the procedures attendant upon that deprivation were constitutionally sufficient."

...

The central issue in this case is whether Valmonte has sufficiently alleged the deprivation of a protected liberty interest. Valmonte's strongest argument on this issue is that the state's dissemination of information from the list to potential employers in the child care field not only stigmatizes those on the list but also denies them employment in their chosen field.

The question of whether one's good name and standing, and the interest in protecting that reputation, constitutes a protectible liberty interest has been considered in a string of Supreme Court and Second Circuit cases. The Supreme Court held in 1971 that a protectible liberty interest may be implicated "where a person's good name, reputation, honor, or integrity is at stake because of what the government is doing to him." A year later, the Court held that a government employee's liberty interest would be implicated if he were dismissed based on charges that imposed "on him a stigma or other disability that foreclosed his freedom to take advantage of other employment opportunities."

... [A] few years later ... the Court held that damage to one's reputation is not "by itself sufficient to invoke the procedural protection of the Due Process Clause." Rather, the Court held, loss of reputation must be coupled with some other tangible element in order to rise to the level of a protectible liberty interest. We have previously interpreted this holding to mean that "stigma plus" is required to establish a constitutional deprivation. Consequently, we will examine Valmonte's claim first to determine whether inclusion on the Central Register constitutes "stigma," and then to determine whether the "plus" requirement has been satisfied.

1. Stigma

Valmonte first must prove that her inclusion on the Central Register will result in stigma, that is, in "public opprobrium" and damage to her reputation. The district court found in both decisions that the disclosure of Valmonte's status on the list to prospective employers was enough publication to implicate her reputation.

There is no dispute that Valmonte's inclusion on the list potentially damages her reputation by branding her as a child abuser, which certainly calls into question her "good name, reputation, honor, or integrity." The state contends, however, that there is no "stigma" attached to her inclusion because there is no disclosure of information on the Central Register except to authorized state agencies or potential employers in the child care field.

Dissemination to potential employers, however, is the precise conduct that gives rise to stigmatization.... In the instant situation, although Valmonte's presence on the Central Register will not be disclosed to the public, it will be disclosed to any employer statutorily required to consult the Central Register. Since Valmonte states that she will be applying for child care positions, her status will automatically be disclosed to her potential employers....

2. "Plus"

Because Valmonte has sufficiently alleged the defamation prong of the "stigma plus" test, we must now determine whether the second part of that test is met. As we have noted in the past, "it is not entirely clear what the 'plus' is." . . .

. . .

We agree that our prior decisions indicate that defamation is simply not enough to support a cognizable liberty interest. It therefore follows that the deleterious effects which flow directly from a sullied reputation would normally also be insufficient. . . .

. . . Valmonte alleges much more than a loss of employment flowing from the effects of simple defamation. The Central Register does not simply defame Valmonte, it places a tangible burden on her employment prospects. Valmonte has alleged that because of her inclusion on the Central Register, and because all child care providers must consult that list, she will not be able to get a job in the child-care field. In other words, by operation of law, her potential employers will be informed specifically about her inclusion on the Central Register and will therefore choose not to hire her. Moreover, if they do wish to hire her, those employers are required by law to explain the reasons why in writing.

This is not just the intangible deleterious effect that flows from a bad reputation. Rather, it is a specific deprivation of her opportunity to seek employment caused by a statutory impediment established by the state. Valmonte is not going to be refused employment because of her reputation; she will be refused employment simply because her inclusion on the list results in an added burden on employers who will therefore be reluctant to hire her.

. . .

We hold that Valmonte has adequately stated a cause of action for deprivation of a liberty interest not merely because of the defamatory aspect of the Central Register, but because that defamation occurs in conjunction with a statutory impediment to employment. In this case, we find that the requirement that puts burdens on employers wishing to hire individuals on the list results in a change of that individual's status significant enough to satisfy the "plus" requirement of the "stigma plus" test.

II. Procedural Due Process

Even though the Central Register implicates Valmonte's liberty interest, Valmonte still must show that the procedural safeguards of her interest established by the state are insufficient to protect her rights. Valmonte argues that the existing procedures violate due process by prohibiting expungement of a subject's indicated record if there is "any credible evidence" to support the allegation and only holding the county DSS to a higher "preponderance of the evidence" standard after a subject loses an opportunity for employment.

. . .

The standards for evaluating the constitutionality of these procedures are clear. In *Mathews v. Eldridge*, the Supreme Court articulated a three-factor test for evaluating administrative procedures, requiring examination of: (1) the nature of the private interest affected by the official action; (2) the risk of error and the effect of additional procedural safeguards; and (3) the governmental interest. We must balance these factors to determine "when, under our constitutional system, judicial-type procedures must be imposed upon administrative action to assure fairness." The *Mathews v. Eldridge* factors relating to personal and government interest will be considered initially, followed by the more pertinent discussion of the risk of error caused by the procedures established by the state.

A. Private Interest

Valmonte's argument in support of her private interest at stake is basically her argument in support of her liberty interest; that is, her interest in securing future employment in the child care field free from the defamatory label placed upon her by the state. She also asserts that her interest in the raising of her children is an implicated liberty interest, even though nothing in the Central Register impacts directly on her role as a parent, rather than her potential role as a child care worker. Although we disagree that her interest in child-rearing is implicated, Valmonte does have a legitimate interest in pursuing her chosen occupation.

B. Countervailing State Interest

Valmonte does not seriously challenge that the state, as parens patriae, has a significant interest in protecting children from abuse and maltreatment. We need not discuss at length the unfortunate reality that children are often victimized, and that the state has a strong interest in protecting them from the infliction of physical harm by those charged with their care. We agree with the appellees that there is a significant interest on the part of the state in maintaining the existence of the Central Register.

C. Risk of Erroneous Deprivation

The deciding factor in this case, the one that clearly shows the inadequacy of the procedural protections established by the state, is the enormous risk of error that has been alleged by Valmonte and acknowledged by the appellees. As noted earlier, the state only requires that the local DSS meet the "some credible evidence" standard in order to initially include a subject on the Central Register or to keep the subject on the list at the non-deprivation administrative hearing. It is only later, at the post-deprivation hearing, when the subject has already been denied employment due to his or her inclusion on the Central Register, that the local DSS is required to prove the allegations against the subject by a "fair preponderance of the evidence."

The distinction between the two standards is significant. Valmonte points out that, according to her figures, nearly 75% of those who seek expungement of their names from the list are ultimately successful. Half of that number obtain expungement only after they have lost employment or prospective employment because of their inclusion on the Central Register. This means that roughly one-third of those initially placed on the Central Register are eventually removed once the local DSS is required to prove the charges against the subject by a fair preponderance of the evidence. The fact that only 25% of those on the list remain after all administrative proceedings have been concluded indicates that the initial determination made by the local DSS is at best imperfect.

Much of this unacceptably high risk of error must be attributable to the standard of proof required at the initial determination, and at the non-deprivation hearing. The "some credible evidence" standard does not require the factfinder to weigh conflicting evidence, merely requiring the local DSS to present the bare minimum of material credible evidence to support the allegations against the subject. In contrast, the "fair preponderance" standard allows for the balancing of evidence from both sides, and gives the subject the opportunity to contest the evidence and testimony presented by the local DSS. As the Supreme Court has noted, the preponderance of the evidence standard indicates that the litigants should share the risk of error rather than have one litigant bear the brunt of the risk. Under the instant statutory scheme, however, the individual, not the state, bears the risk.

The "some credible evidence" standard is especially dubious in the context of determining whether an individual has abused or neglected a child. Such determinations are inherently inflammatory, and "unusually open to the subjective values of" the factfinder. They are especially open to such subjectivity when the factfinder is not required to weigh evidence and judge competing versions of events, and where one side has the greater ability to assemble its case.

Considering the minimal standard of proof, and the subjective nature of the inquiry, it is not altogether surprising that there is such a high risk of error. Another fact adduced at oral argument and noted in the record is that there are roughly 2,000,000 individuals on the rolls of the Central Register. This staggering figure has been cited to us by Valmonte, but it was not contested at oral argument. We find it difficult to fathom how such a huge percentage of New Yorkers could be included on a list of those suspected of child abuse and neglect, unless there has been a high rate of error in determinations. In any event, we rely more on the 75% than on the two million figure, the authenticity of which we are inclined to doubt.

The appellees, remarkably, do not challenge these figures, but argue that there is no real deprivation in cases where individuals contest the initial inclusion on the Central Register. According to the appellees, the subjects are not deprived of anything if their names are taken off the list. Moreover, they assert that the fact that reports are eventually expunged demonstrates that the state's procedures are working to correct mistakes in the original determination.

This is an inherently contradictory argument by the state. To argue that the extraordinarily high percentage of reversals supports the fairness of the system, as a desirable feature of that system, is a curious defense of administrative procedures. One does not normally purchase a car from a dealer who stresses that his repair staff routinely services and repairs the model after frequent and habitual breakdowns. If 75% of those challenging their inclusion on the list are successful, we cannot help but be skeptical of the fairness of the original determination.

D. Balancing

We hold that the high risk of error produced by the procedural protections established by New York is unacceptable. While the two interests at stake are fairly evenly balanced, the risk of error tilts the balancing test heavily in Valmonte's favor. The crux of the problem with the procedures is that the "some credible evidence" standard results in many individuals being placed on the list who do not belong there. Those individuals must then be deprived of an employment opportunity solely because of their inclusion on the Central Register, and subject to the concurrent defamation by state officials, in order to have the opportunity to require the local DSS to do more than merely present some credible evidence to support the allegations.

. . .

Conclusion

For these reasons, we reverse the judgment of the district court and remand for further proceedings not inconsistent with this opinion. Although we recognize the grave seriousness of the problems of child abuse and neglect, and the need for the state to maintain a Central Register for ensuring that those with abusive backgrounds not be inadvertently given access to children, we find the current system unacceptable.

Notes and Queries

1. States typically maintain arrest and criminal records, even after the persons implicated therein have been acquitted or the charges upon which those records are predicated are dropped. While it is true that such records may be expunged, there is no automatic right to expunction once an individual's name has been cleared. Expunction in those instances is a discretionary function of the court, rarely utilized absent extreme circumstances, and mere acquittal of the subsequent charge is an insufficient reason to grant expunction. Given that, do you find maintenance of civil records that egregious? Are the situations comparable? Does a prosecutor's charges or a grand jury's indictment compare more favorably to a potentially unreliable and vindictive anonymous report?

Research Comment

1. Central registries and the systematic record-keeping of child maltreatment reports serve to assist in the identification and protection of maltreated children. In many states, the names of all suspected persons are forwarded for inclusion in the central registry when a decision is made by a social worker to "indicate," "substantiate," or classify an allegation as "founded"—all meaning that credible evidence supports a finding of maltreatment. Reports contained in central registries are typically used to aid social services agencies in the investigation, treatment, and prevention of child maltreatment cases, and to maintain statistical information for staffing and funding purposes. Note that CPS investigations may also find the report as "unfounded," which means that insufficient evidence supports the allegation, or "unsubstantiated," which indicates that suspicion remains that the child is at risk for maltreatment but insufficient evidence exists to substantiate the report. Which findings should be included? States vary considerably in their approach. Cal. Penal Code § 11170(a)(1) (West Supp. 2001) records all reports except those "determined to be unfounded." Alaska Stat. § 47.17.040(a) (Michie Supp. 2001) requires a registry of "all investigation reports but not of the reports of harm." Ga. Code Ann. § 49-5-181 (2001) provides that the central registry "shall receive all information regarding confirmed and unconfirmed cases of child abuse reported." Ind. Code Ann. § 31-33-17-1 (Michie 2001) provides only for "substantiated reports of child abuse and neglect." N.H. Rev. Stat. Ann. § 169-C:35 (Supp. 2001) maintains "a record of information on each case of alleged abuse or neglect reported."

Review Problems

1. Consider the following case. After an investigation of C. S., the County Department of Social Services (DSS) concluded that there was sufficient evidence to show that C. S. was a child abuser. DSS made a finding that the incident was "indicated" abuse, meaning that credible evidence indicated that abuse, neglect, or sexual abuse occurred. This finding also indicated that the evidence was unsatisfactorily refuted. C. S. was notified that his name would be added to a computerized central registry system used by the state to track abuse and neglect cases and child abusers. Upon being notified that his case was "indicated," C. S. requested an administrative hearing to appeal the finding. The department reviewed its records and decided that the finding should not be changed. Thereafter, the department's records were forwarded to the Office of Administrative Hearings, and an administrative law judge (ALJ) upheld the finding of "indicated" child abuse. C. S. filed a petition for judicial review and a motion to stay the ALJ's order. In a unanimous decision, the Court of Appeals of Maryland, in *C. S. v. Prince George's County Department of Social Services*, 343 Md. 14, 680 A.2d 470 (1996), held that alleged child abusers

have the right to an independent contested case hearing before their name is added to a central registry computer system and that the individual is entitled to a full trial-like hearing with judicial review of the investigating agency's decision. Is this a better approach than the one taken in *Valmonte*?

2. Following *Valmonte*, do you find the case of David and Marsha Hodge rightly decided? The Hodges took their three-month-old son Joseph to the Carroll County General Hospital for examination and treatment of the child's swollen right arm. The examining physician diagnosed a fractured ulna "'without adequate historical explanation'" and, pursuant to state law, reported the case to the Carroll County DSS. An investigation was initiated the next day by a child protective services caseworker and a Maryland State police officer. Their investigation ultimately yielded no evidence of abuse. The caseworker filed a report with DSS classifying the case as "unsubstantiated" (a case with insufficient evidence) and "ruled out" (a finding that no abuse occurred). Within a week of the incident, the Hodges took Joseph to two medical specialists for further examination. The specialists diagnosed the swelling as osteomyelitis, a bacterial bone infection, and performed the necessary corrective surgery. Five days after the caseworker closed his investigation, Marsha Hodge called DSS with news of the corrected diagnosis. On February 16, 1989, David Hodge wrote to DSS, again informing them of the misdiagnosis and requesting a copy of any DSS case file on the incident. In March 1989, Katz, Assistant Director of DSS, replied by letter that "the Department's report reflects that suspected child abuse was ruled out and unsubstantiated," and attached a redacted copy of the case file. Between February 1989 and May 1990, the Hodges engaged in a campaign of communications with Katz and other DSS officials and Maryland Department of Human Resources requesting, among other things, the full report and the destruction or expunction of any DSS file or document regarding the Hodge investigation. Each request was refused under Maryland's statutory bar against disclosure of confidential materials. Continued refusals to disclose and expunge the investigation report prompted legal action complaining that maintenance of a record of "unsubstantiated" and "ruled out" child abuse violated their liberty interest in familial privacy, and that failure to provide notice and a hearing before maintaining that record violated their procedural due process rights. Do you find these arguments persuasive? On appeal, the court ruled that the maxim of familial privacy is neither absolute nor unqualified, and may be outweighed by a legitimate governmental interest. It further noted that, although the records retained by DSS reference the Hodge family, the Hodges' complaint revealed no more than a conclusory allegation of reputational injury, which, absent a cognizable stigma and the ensuing loss of a tangible interest, failed to state a cause of action under § 1983. Moreover, given the extensive confidentiality provisions protecting the Hodge investigation report, the court saw no avenue by which a stigma or defamation labeling the Hodges as child abusers could attach. Finally, the court disagreed with the Hodges' contention that the state lacks a legitimate governmental interest once an abuse report has

been deemed "unsubstantiated" or "ruled out." It reasoned that the retention of these investigation reports continues to serve legitimate state interests in the welfare of children. For instance, a series of "unsubstantiated" or "ruled out" entries for a given child may arouse suspicion of a pattern or practice of emotional and physical harm to a child, warranting further inquiry by the state. Retained records could, in fact, protect the individual whose record is kept by preventing repeated investigations when more than one person makes the same accusation. Finally, such records allow the state to defend itself in the event of a suit alleging inadequate investigation of a reported instance of child abuse. *Hodge v. Jones*, 161. 31 F.3d 157 (4th Cir. 1994). Do you find the court's reasoning persuasive? Was there no harm done to the Hodges?

Seling v. Young

531 U.S. 250; 121 S. Ct. 727 (2001)

Justice O'Connor delivered the opinion of the Court.

...

Washington State's Community Protection Act of 1990 (Act) was a response to citizens' concerns about laws and procedures regarding sexually violent offenders. One of the Act's provisions authorizes civil commitment of such offenders. The Act defines a sexually violent predator as someone who has been convicted of, or charged with, a crime of sexual violence and who suffers from a mental abnormality or personality disorder that makes the person likely to engage in predatory acts of sexual violence if not confined in a secure facility. The statute reaches prisoners, juveniles, persons found incompetent to stand trial, persons found not guilty by reason of insanity, and persons at any time convicted of a sexually violent offense who have committed a recent overt act. Generally, when it appears that a person who has committed a sexually violent offense is about to be released from confinement, the prosecuting attorney files a petition alleging that that person is a sexually violent predator. That filing triggers a process for charging and trying the person as a sexually violent predator, during which he is afforded a panoply of protections including counsel and experts (paid for by the State in cases of indigency), a probable cause hearing, and trial by judge or jury at the individual's option. At trial, the State bears the burden to prove beyond a reasonable doubt that the person is a sexually violent predator.

Upon the finding that a person is a sexually violent predator, he is committed for control, care, and treatment to the custody of the department of social and health services. Once confined, the person has a right to adequate care and individualized treatment. The person is also entitled to an annual examination of his mental condition. If that examination indicates that the individual's condition is so changed that he is not likely to engage in predatory acts of sexual violence, state officials must authorize the person to petition the court for conditional release or discharge. The person is entitled to a hearing at which the State again bears the burden of proving beyond a reasonable doubt that he is not safe to be at large. The person may also independently petition the court for release. At a show cause hearing, if the court finds probable cause to believe that the person is no longer dangerous, a full hearing will be held at which the State again bears the burden of proof.

The Act also provides a procedure to petition for conditional release to a less restrictive alternative to confinement. Before ordering conditional release, the court must find that the person will be treated by a state certified sexual offender treatment provider, that there is a specific course of treatment, that housing exists that will be sufficiently secure to protect the community, and that the person is willing to comply with the treatment and supervision requirements. Conditional release is subject to annual review until the person is unconditionally released.

B

Respondent, Andre Brigham Young, was convicted of six rapes over three decades. Young was scheduled to be released from prison for his most recent conviction in October 1990. One day prior to his scheduled release, the State filed a petition to commit Young as a sexually violent predator.

At the commitment hearing, Young's mental health experts testified that there is no mental disorder that makes a person likely to reoffend and that there is no way to predict accurately who will reoffend. The State called an expert who testified, based upon a review of Young's records, that Young suffered from a severe personality disorder not otherwise specified with primarily paranoid and antisocial features, and a severe paraphilia, which would be classified as either paraphilia sexual sadism or paraphilia not otherwise specified (rape). In the state expert's opinion, severe paraphilia constituted a mental abnormality under the Act. The State's expert concluded that Young's condition, in combination with the personality disorder, the span of time during which Young committed his crimes, his recidivism, his persistent denial, and his lack of empathy or remorse, made it more likely than not that he would commit further sexually violent acts. The victims of Young's rapes also testified. The jury unanimously concluded that Young was a sexually violent predator.

Young and another individual appealed their commitments in state court, arguing that the Act violated the Double Jeopardy, Ex Post Facto, Due Process, and Equal Protection Clauses of the Federal Constitution....

The Washington court reasoned that the claimants' double jeopardy and ex post facto claims hinged on whether the Act is civil or criminal in nature. Following this Court's precedents, the court examined the language of the Act, the legislative history, and the purpose and effect of the statutory scheme. The court found that the legislature clearly intended to create a civil scheme both in the statutory language and legislative history. The court then turned to examine whether the actual impact of the Act is civil or criminal. The Act, the court concluded, is concerned with treating committed persons for a current mental abnormality, and protecting society from the sexually violent acts associated with that abnormality, rather than being concerned with criminal culpability. The court distinguished the goals of incapacitation and treatment from the goal of punishment. The court found that the Washington Act is designed to further legitimate goals of civil confinement and that the claimants had failed to provide proof to the contrary.

...

As the Washington Supreme Court held and the Ninth Circuit acknowledged, we proceed on the understanding that the Washington Act is civil in nature. The Washington Act is strikingly similar to a commitment scheme we reviewed four Terms ago in *Kansas v. Hendricks* (1997). In fact, Kansas patterned its Act after Washington's. In *Hendricks*, we explained that the question whether an Act is civil or punitive in nature is initially one of statutory construction. A court must ascertain whether the legislature intended the statute to establish civil proceedings. A court will reject the legislature's manifest intent only where a party challenging the Act provides the clearest proof that the statutory scheme is so punitive in either purpose or effect as to negate the State's intention. We concluded that the confined individual in that case had failed to satisfy his burden with respect to the Kansas Act. We noted several factors: The Act did not implicate retribution or deterrence; prior criminal convictions were used as evidence in the commitment proceedings, but were not a prerequisite to confinement; the Act required no finding of scienter to commit a person; the Act was not intended to function as a deterrent; and although the procedural safeguards were similar to those in the criminal context, they did not alter the character of the scheme.

We also examined the conditions of confinement provided by the Act. The Court was aware that sexually violent predators in Kansas were to be held in a segregated unit within the prison system. We explained that the Act called for confinement in a secure facility because the persons confined were dangerous to the community. We noted, however, that conditions within the unit were essentially the same as conditions for other involuntarily committed persons in mental hospitals. Moreover, confinement under the Act was not necessarily indefinite in duration. Finally, we observed that in addition to protecting the public, the Act also provided treatment for sexually violent predators. We acknowledged that not all mental conditions were treatable. For those individuals with untreatable conditions, however, we explained that there was no federal constitutional bar to their civil confinement, because the State had an interest in protecting the public from dangerous individuals with treatable as well as untreatable conditions. Our conclusion that the Kansas Act was "nonpunitive thus removed an essential prerequisite for both *Hendricks*' double jeopardy and ex post facto claims."

...

With this in mind, we turn to the Court of Appeals' determination that respondent could raise an "as-applied" challenge to the Act on double jeopardy and ex post facto grounds and seek release from confinement. Respondent essentially claims that the conditions of his confinement at the Center are too restrictive, that the conditions are incompatible with treatment, and that the system is designed to result in indefinite confinement. Respondent's claims are in many respects like the claims presented to the Court in *Hendricks*, where we concluded that the conditions of confinement were largely explained by the State's goal to incapacitate, not to punish. Nevertheless, we do not deny that some of respondent's allegations are serious. Nor do we express any view as to how his allegations would bear on a court determining in the first instance whether Washington's confinement scheme is civil. Here, we evaluate respondent's allegations as presented in a double jeopardy and ex post facto challenge under the assumption that the Act is civil.

We hold that respondent cannot obtain release through an "as-applied" challenge to the Washington Act on double jeopardy and ex post facto grounds. We agree with petitioner that an "as-applied" analysis would prove unworkable. Such an analysis would never conclusively resolve whether a particular scheme is punitive and would thereby prevent a final determination of the scheme's validity under the Double Jeopardy and Ex Post Facto Clauses. Unlike a fine, confinement is not a fixed event. As petitioner notes, it extends over time under conditions that are subject to change. The particular features of confinement may affect how a confinement scheme is evaluated to determine whether it is civil rather than punitive, but it remains no less true that the query must be answered definitively. The civil nature of a confinement scheme cannot be altered based merely on vagaries in the implementation of the authorizing statute.

...

Our decision today does not mean that respondent and others committed as sexually violent predators have no remedy for the alleged conditions and treatment regime at the Center. The text of the Washington Act states that those confined under its authority have the right to adequate care and individualized treatment. As petitioner acknowledges, if the Center fails to fulfill its statutory duty, those confined may have a state law cause of action. It is for the Washington courts to determine whether the Center is operating in accordance with state law and provide a remedy.

State courts, in addition to federal courts, remain competent to adjudicate and remedy challenges to civil confinement schemes arising under the Federal Constitution. As noted above, the Washington Supreme Court has already held that the Washington Act is civil in nature, designed to incapacitate and to treat. Accordingly, due process requires that the conditions and duration of confinement under the Act bear some reasonable relation to the purpose for which persons are committed.

...

Whether a confinement scheme is punitive has been the threshold question for some constitutional challenges. Whatever these cases may suggest about the relevance of conditions of confinement, they do not endorse the approach of the dissent, which would render the inquiry into the effects of the statute, completely open ended. In one case, the Court refused to consider alleged confinement conditions because the parties had entered into a consent decree to improve conditions. The Court presumed that conditions were in compliance with the requirements of the consent decree. In another case, the Court found that anecdotal case histories and a statistical study were insufficient to render a regulatory confinement scheme punitive. In such cases, we have decided whether a confinement scheme is punitive notwithstanding the inherent difficulty in ascertaining current conditions and predicting future events.

We have not squarely addressed the relevance of conditions of confinement to a first instance determination, and that question need not be resolved here. An Act, found to be civil, cannot be deemed punitive "as applied" to a single individual in violation of the Double Jeopardy and Ex Post Facto Clauses and provide cause for release.

The judgment of the United States Court of Appeals for the Ninth Circuit is therefore reversed, and the case is remanded for further proceedings consistent with this opinion.

It is so ordered.

Justice Scalia, with whom Justice Souter joins, concurring.

I agree with the Court's holding that a statute, "found to be civil in nature, cannot be deemed punitive" or criminal "as applied" for purposes of the Ex Post Facto and Double Jeopardy Clauses. The Court accurately observes that this holding gives us "no occasion to consider the extent to which a court may look to actual conditions of confinement and implementation of the statute to determine in the first instance whether a confinement scheme is civil in nature." I write separately to dissociate myself from any implication that this reserved point may be an open question. I do not regard it as such since, three years ago, we rejected a similar double jeopardy challenge (based upon the statute's implementation "as applied" to the petitioner), where the statute had not yet been determined to be civil in nature, and where we were making that determination "in the first instance." . . .

. . .

The short of the matter is that, for Double Jeopardy and Ex Post Facto Clause purposes, the question of criminal penalty *vel non* depends upon the intent of the legislature; and harsh executive implementation cannot "transform what was clearly intended as a civil remedy into a criminal penalty," any more than compassionate executive implementation can transform a criminal penalty into a civil remedy.

. . .

Justice Thomas, concurring in the judgment.

. . . I write separately to express my view, first, that a statute which is civil on its face cannot be divested of its civil nature simply because of the manner in which it is implemented. . . .

. . .

The Washington Act does not provide on its face for punitive conditions of confinement, and the actual conditions under which the Act is implemented are of no concern to our inquiry. I therefore concur in the judgment of the Court.

Justice Stevens, dissenting.

...

... If a detainee comes forward with "'the clearest proof' that 'the statutory scheme [is] so punitive either in purpose or effect as to negate [the State's] intention' that the proceeding be civil, it must be considered criminal." Accordingly, we have consistently looked to the conditions of confinement as evidence of both the legislative purpose behind the statute and its actual effect....

The majority in this case, however, incorrectly assumes that the Act at issue is necessarily civil. The issue the majority purports to resolve is whether an Act that is otherwise civil in nature can be deemed criminal in a specific instance based on evidence of its application to a particular prisoner. However, respondent Young's petition did not present that issue. Rather, consistent with our case law, Young sought to introduce evidence of the conditions of confinement as evidence of the punitive purpose and effect of the Washington statute. Properly read, Hudson acknowledges that resolving whether an Act is civil or criminal in nature can take into account whether the statutory scheme has a punitive effect....

To be sure, the question whether an Act is civil or punitive in nature "is initially one of statutory construction." However, under the majority's analysis, there is no inquiry beyond that of statutory construction. In essence, the majority argues that because the constitutional query must be answered definitively and because confinement is not a "fixed event," conditions of confinement should not be considered at all, except in the first challenge to a statute, when, as a practical matter, the evidence of such conditions is most likely not to constitute the requisite "clearest proof." This seems to me quite wrong. If conditions of confinement are such that a detainee has been punished twice in violation of the Double Jeopardy Clause, it is irrelevant that the scheme has been previously labeled as civil without full knowledge of the effects of the statute.

In this case, Young has made detailed allegations concerning both the absence of treatment for his alleged mental illness and the starkly punitive character of the conditions of his confinement. If proved, those allegations establish not just that those detained pursuant to the statute are treated like those imprisoned for violations of Washington's criminal laws, but that, in many respects, they receive significantly worse treatment. If those allegations are correct, the statute in question should be characterized as a criminal law for federal constitutional purposes. I therefore agree with the Court of Appeals' conclusion that respondent should be given the opportunity to come forward with the "clearest proof" that his allegations are true.

Accordingly, I respectfully dissent.

Notes and Queries

1. Do the alternative remedies sufficiently protect the interests of sex offenders and society?

2. Are we to read the Court's opinion as allowing a civil commitment that is in fact punitive? Why would such facts not matter? The Court notes that a § 1983 action against the Center is pending in the Western District of Washington. The Center operates under an injunction that requires it to adopt and implement a plan for training and hiring competent sex offender therapists, to improve relations between residents and treatment providers, to implement a treatment program for residents containing elements required by prevailing professional standards, to develop individual treatment programs, and to provide a psychologist or psychiatrist expert in the diagnosis and treatment of sex offenders to supervise the staff. A Special Master has assisted in bringing the Center into compliance with the injunction. Should the fact that the Center currently is not doing what it is supposed to do matter?

Research Comment

1. Involuntary civil commitment statutes exist in every state. They allow the state to commit a person against their will if there is proof of a mental disability that poses a substantial threat of serious harm to oneself or others. The threat of harm must be real and present, and the burden of proof to establish dangerousness (to self or others) must be clear and convincing. Proponents of involuntary commitment view this form of treatment as a last resort effort to help the mentally disabled who are imminently dangerous and in desperate need of mental health treatment. Critics of the practice focus on the fact that there is no assurance that such commitment accomplishes the goal of treatment and improvement of mental conditions. See Robert M. Levy & Leonard S. Rubenstein (1996). *The Rights of People with Mental Disabilities*. Carbondale, IL: Southern Illinois University Press.

Review Problems

1. In *Kansas v. Hendricks*, the Court's opinion pointed out that "States have in certain narrow circumstances provided for the forcible civil detainment of people who are unable to control their behavior and who thereby pose a danger to the public health and safety." The Court noted that the Kansas "Act unambiguously requires a finding of dangerousness either to one's self or to others," and then "links

that finding to the existence of a 'mental abnormality' or 'personality disorder' that makes it difficult, if not impossible, for the person to control his dangerous behavior." And the Court ultimately determined that the statute's "requirement of a 'mental abnormality' or 'personality disorder' is consistent with the requirements of . . . other statutes that we have upheld in that it narrows the class of persons eligible for confinement to those who are unable to control their dangerousness." The *Hendricks* case was made easier in that (1) Hendricks suffered from pedophilia, (2) the psychiatric profession itself classifies that condition "as a serious mental disorder," and (3) he conceded that he cannot "'control the urge'" to molest children. As a result, the Court concluded that this "admitted lack of volitional control, coupled with a prediction of future dangerousness, adequately distinguishes Hendricks from other dangerous persons who are perhaps more properly dealt with exclusively through criminal proceedings." The issue that emerged was whether the state needed always to prove that a dangerous individual is completely unable to control his behavior, which the Court addressed in *Kansas v. Crane*, No. 00-957, Supreme Court, Jan. 22, 2002

Crane was convicted of lewd and lascivious behavior and pleaded guilty to aggravated sexual battery for two incidents that took place on the same day in 1993. In the first, Crane exposed himself to a tanning salon attendant. In the second, 30 minutes later, Crane entered a video store, waited until he was the only customer present, and then exposed himself to the clerk. Before running out of the store, he grabbed the clerk by the neck, demanded she perform oral sex on him, and threatened to rape her. Following Crane's plea to aggravated sexual battery, the state filed a petition in State District Court to have him evaluated and adjudicated a sexual predator under the SVPA. Several psychologists examined him and determined that he suffered from exhibitionism and antisocial personality disorder. Though exhibitionism alone would not support classification as a sexual predator, a psychologist concluded that the two in combination did place Crane's condition within the range of disorders covered by the SVPA, "citing the increasing frequency of incidents involving [Crane], increasing intensity of the incidents, [respondent's] increasing disregard for the rights of others, and his increasing daring and aggressiveness." Another psychologist testified that respondent's behavior was marked by "impulsivity or failure to plan ahead," indicating his unlawfulness "was a combination of willful and uncontrollable behavior." The State's experts agreed, however, that "respondent's mental disorder does not impair his volitional control to the degree he cannot control his dangerous behavior."

Crane moved for summary judgment, arguing that for his detention to comport with substantive due process the State was required to prove not merely what the statute requires — that by reason of his mental disorder he is "likely to engage in repeat acts of sexual violence" — but also that he is unable to control his violent behavior. The Supreme Court agreed with Kansas insofar as it argued that *Hendricks* set forth no requirement of total or complete lack of control. *Hendricks* referred to the Kansas Act as requiring a "mental abnormality" or "personality disorder" that makes it "difficult, if not impossible, for the [dangerous] person to control his dangerous behavior." The Court agreed that an absolutist approach was unworkable in that most severely ill people—even those commonly termed "psychopaths"—retain some ability to control their behavior and insistence upon absolute lack of control would risk barring the civil commitment of highly dangerous persons suffering severe mental abnormalities. But the Court also held that the Constitution does not permit commitment of the type of dangerous sexual offender considered in *Hendricks* without any lack-of-control determination. The Court, however, did not announce a standard, but only noted that it is enough to say that there must be proof of serious difficulty in controlling behavior.

2. The American Psychiatric Association denies clinical capacity to predict harm and future dangerousness. Importantly, the Court has allowed clinical predictions of dangerousness, even if inaccurate, to justify involuntary confinement. *Barefoot v. Estelle*, 463 U.S. 880 (1983). The American Psychiatric Association argues that relevant disorders, such as pedophilia, are not mental illness. Yet the Court, in *Kansas v. Hendricks*, 117 S. Ct. 2072 (1997), concluded that such controversies allow the states to set the boundaries of civil commitment for disorders. What arguments are to be made against following the advice of those who will be relied upon to implement and enforce the law?

Doe v. Poritz

142 N.J. 1; 662 A.2d 367 (NJ Sup. Ct., 1995)

Chief Justice Wilentz delivered the opinion of the court.

. . .

The legislative choice was undoubtedly influenced by the fact that if the law did not apply to previously-convicted offenders, notification would provide practically no protection now, and relatively little in the near future. The Legislature reached the irresistible conclusion that if community safety was its objective, there was no justification for applying these laws only to those who offend or who are convicted in the future, and not applying them to previously-convicted offenders. Had the Legislature chosen to exempt previously-convicted offenders, the notification provision of the law would have provided absolutely no protection whatsoever on the day it became law, for it would have applied to no one. The Legislature concluded that there was no justification for protecting only children of the future from the risk of reoffense by future offenders, and not today's children from the risk of reoffense by previously-convicted offenders, when the nature of those risks were identical and presently arose almost exclusively from previously-convicted offenders, their numbers now and for a fair number of years obviously vastly exceeding the number of those who, after passage of these laws, will be convicted and released and only then, for the first time, potentially subject to community notification.

I

The Legislative Purpose: Addressing the Problem of Repetitive Sex Offenders

The challenged laws before us in this case have two basic provisions. First, they require registration with law enforcement authorities of certain convicted sex offenders and spell out the offenses that trigger the registration requirement, registration of those convicted prior to their passage limited to offenders found to have repetitive and compulsive characteristics. Second, they provide for notice of the presence of such offenders in the community, the scope of that notice measured by the likelihood that such offenders will commit another sex offense: where the risk of such reoffense is low, only law enforcement authorities are notified; where it is moderate, institutions and organizations having the responsibility to care for and supervise children and women are notified; and where the risk is high, those members of the public likely to encounter the offender are notified.

. . .

Based on statistical and other studies the Legislature could have found, and presumably did find, the following facts, essentially reflected in its statement of purpose, and its enactment of the laws:

> Studies describing recidivism by sex offenders indicate the severity of the problem the Legislature addressed in Megan's Law. Studies report that rapists recidivate at a rate of 7 to 35%; offenders who molest young girls, at a rate of 10 to 29%, and offenders who molest young boys, at a rate of 13 to 40%. Further, of those who recidivate, many commit their second crime after a long interval without offense. In cases of sex offenders, as compared to other criminals, the propensity to commit crimes does not decrease over time. . . . In one study, 48% of the recidivist sex offenders repeated during the first five years and 52% during the next 17 years. . . .

As Doe acknowledges, successful treatment of sex offenders appears to be rare. . . .

Further information gleaned from similar studies strongly reinforces the foregoing:

> Sexual crimes are notoriously underreported. Such data as are available, however, demonstrate that their impact is substantial and widespread. . . .
>
> Sexual assault takes a heavy toll on its victims, particularly on children. . . . Thus, apart from the substantial personal trauma caused to the victims of such crimes, sexual crimes against children exact heavy social costs as well.

On the critical issue of recidivism, the Legislature presumably adopted the view suggested in the following information, supportive of that stated in the studies relied on by the Attorney General:

> Sex offender recidivism compounds the problem. As a group, sex offenders are significantly more likely than other repeat offenders to reoffend with sex crimes or other violent crimes, and that tendency persists over time. . . .

> These figures comport with other data on sex offender recidivism. A major Justice Department study of state prisoners released in one year showed that 7.7% of released rapists were rearrested for rape within three years. Moreover, 27.5% of released rapists were rearrested during that period for some kind of violent offense (murder, rape, robbery, or assault).... A recent review of the most frequently cited studies of sex offender recidivism indicates that rapists repeat their offenses at [] rates up to 35%; offenders who molest young girls, at [] rates up to 29%; and offenders who molest young boys, at [] rates up to 40%....

Clearly, both the Legislature's and the public's increasing awareness of the dangers posed by sex ...

... The remedy selected by our Legislature goes beyond the ability of citizens to request the criminal record of their neighbors when they may have no reason to make such requests. The remedy goes directly to the question of what a community can do to protect itself against the potential of reoffense by a group the Legislature could find had a relatively high risk of recidivism involving those crimes most feared, and those crimes to which the most vulnerable and defenseless were exposed — the children of society. The spectacle of offenses committed by neighbors, known in the public records as significantly potential reoffenders, but not known to anyone else, and especially not known to those most likely to be affected, their neighbors, suggested the most obvious and practical degree of protection: a law that would tell neighbors and others who night be affected, of the presence of such offenders, no more and no less.

The concern for the potential unfairness of identification has some justification, but it is wrong to assume the people of this State and the media will not understand that potential. The Attorney General points to information, far from complete because of the injunction against the implementation of these laws, that suggests that harassment and vigilantism have been minimal. This Court has no right to assume that the public will be punitive when the Legislature was not, that the public, instead of protecting itself as the laws intended, will attempt to destroy the lives of those subject to the laws, and this Court has no right to assume that community leaders, public officials, law enforcement authorities, will not seek to educate the public concerning the Legislature's intent, including appropriate responses to notification information, responses that are not at all punitive, but seek merely to protect their children, their families, and others from reoffense....

...

... We do not perceive in this case a society clamoring for blood, demanding the names of previously-convicted sex offenders in order to further punish them, but rather families concerned about their children who want information only in order to protect them. Presumably, some citizens will harass, and presumably they will be prosecuted, but we believe that overwhelmingly our citizens are law-abiding citizens. We do not share the certainty of the dissent in the probability of community reaction that would gut the protective purpose of these laws and convert them into punishment. We decline to decide this case on that assumption.

II

The Laws and the Attorney General's Guidelines

Despite complexities of detail, the Registration Law is basically simple. It requires registration of sex offenders convicted after its effective date and all prior-convicted offenders whose conduct was found to be repetitive and compulsive. The sex offenses that trigger the laws for those previously convicted are aggravated sexual assault, sexual assault, aggravated criminal sexual contact, kidnapping pursuant to N.J.S.A. 2C:13-1(c)(2), and for those convicted after their effective date, added to the foregoing are various laws concerning endangering the welfare of a child, luring or enticing, criminal sexual contact if the victim is a minor, and kidnapping, criminal restraint, or false imprisonment if the victim is a minor and the offender not the parent; and in all cases an attempt to commit any of the foregoing.

Registration requires, in the case of those no longer in custody—generally those who committed the offense before adoption of the laws—appearance at a local police station for fingerprinting, photographing, and providing information for a registration form that will include a physical description, the offense involved, home address, employment or school address, vehicle used, and license plate number. For those in custody, the procedure is effected at that location. The forms, information, fingerprints, and photographs (or copies) are centrally collected by the State Police and prosecutors. The registration requirement applies to all convicts, all juveniles, no matter what their age, found delinquent because of the commission of those offenses, and to all found not guilty by reason of insanity. The requirements apply as well to sex offenders convicted elsewhere who relocate to this state. Registrants whose conduct was repetitive and compulsive must verify their addresses with the local law enforcement agency quarterly, other registrants must do so annually. Upon relocation to another municipality, re-registration is required there, and, apparently, any change of address requires notice to the local law enforcement agency.

All of these are lifetime requirements unless the registrant has been offense-free for fifteen years following conviction or release from a correctional facility (whichever is later) and, on application to terminate these obligations, can persuade the court that he or she is not likely to pose a threat to the safety of others. Registration records are open to any law enforcement agency in the state, or any other state, or any federal law enforcement agency. Failure to comply with the Registration Law is a fourth-degree crime.

The Community Notification Law requires the local chief of police to give notification of the registrant's presence in the community, such notification also required if the registrant changes address (presumably whether within or outside of the community although the statutory language refers only to the latter). The law provides for three levels of notification (referred to as Tiers One, Two and Three in the Guidelines) depending on the risk of reoffense.

> (1) If risk of reoffense is low, law enforcement agencies likely to encounter the person registered shall be notified;
>
> (2) If risk of reoffense is moderate, organizations in the community including schools, religious and youth organizations shall be notified in accordance with the Attorney General's Guidelines, in addition to the notice required by paragraph (1) of this subsection;
>
> (3) If risk of reoffense is high, the public shall be notified through means in accordance with the Attorney General's Guidelines designed to reach members of the public likely to encounter the person registered, in addition to the notice required by paragraphs (1) and (2) of this subsection.

No suggestion has been made that any registrant could be classified as posing no risk of reoffense: presumably then, all registrants will be subjected at the very least to Tier One Notification (called "Law Enforcement Alert" in the Guidelines). Although the statute provides that the risk of reoffense, and therefore the extent (the level, the Tier) of notification shall be assessed by the prosecutors of the county of conviction and the county of residence together with any law enforcement officials that either deems appropriate, the Guidelines appear to require the final assessment to be made by one prosecutor, apparently the prosecutor of the county of residence.

. . .

We are aware of the uncertainties that surround all aspects of the subject of sex offender recidivism and the effectiveness of preventive measures. Legislatures, despite uncertainty, must sometimes act to deal with public needs, basing such action on what they conclude, in a welter of conflicting opinions, to be the probable best course. Our Legislature could reasonably conclude that risk of reoffense can be fairly measured, and that knowledge of the presence of offenders provides increased defense against them. Given those conclusions, the system devised by the Legislature is propriately designed to achieve the laws' purpose of protecting the public.

. . .

IV

Interpretation of Statute: Revision of Attorney General's Guidelines; Judicial Review

. . .

. . . [D]espite its constitutionality, the statute sufficiently impinges on liberty interests to trigger both procedural due process and the fairness doctrine in our state, those subject to the statute are entitled to the protection of procedures designed to assure that the risk of reoffense and the extent of notification are fairly evaluated before Tier Two or Tier Three notification is implemented. Although the provisions of the statute and the implementing Guidelines are obviously designed to assure such evaluation, and although there is no reason to believe that the prosecutors and other law enforcement personnel charged with the decision-making power that controls both the level of notification and the specific steps that will determine the amount of notification will not discharge their duties competently and fairly, we have concluded that judicial review through a summary proceeding should be available prior to notification if sought by any person covered by the law. The Attorney General, therefore, as a condition to the enforcement of this law, shall formulate procedures designed to assure that notice is given in sufficient time prior to Tier Two or Tier Three notification to allow the offender to object. We realize that in some cases it may be impossible as a practical matter to give such notice, or to give it timely, and in those cases it may be dispensed with.

. . .

The only issue for the court on the Tier level of notification is the risk of reoffense. In that sense the factors of the Guidelines noting the characteristics of prior offenses or of the offender are relevant only to the risk of reoffense, i.e., the likelihood of its occurrence. That is the clear intent of the statute. All offenders required to register are, by statute, subject to at least Tier One notification, meaning that no matter how low the risk of reoffense, the Legislature has concluded Tier One notification is required.

We note further that quite obviously none of these standards or classes suggests the court must make a finding of likelihood of reoffense, for the Legislature did not impose either Tier Two or Tier Three notification only when it was probable that reoffense would occur, but rather only when the risk—however quantified—was sufficient to warrant such notification. The quality of the offense—a sex offense—undoubtedly led to this legislative conclusion that notification was warranted even when reoffense was not probable, and that legislative conclusion is unassailable in any proceedings before the court. Therefore the probability of reoffense on the part of moderate- or high-risk offenders is not the issue before the court, but rather the relatively greater risk of reoffense compared either to the low-risk offender class or the moderate-risk offender class.

. . .

As for the manner of notification, the limitations set forth in our opinion are mandatory. For Tier Two notification, only those community organizations that own or operate an establishment where children gather under their care, or where women are cared for, shall qualify, and only those that are "likely to encounter" the offender as discussed in connection with Tier Three. The notice that goes out to such organizations shall specifically direct them not to notify anyone else, that being the acknowledged intent of the statute as interpreted by the Attorney General, an interpretation with which we agree. Organizations concerned with the welfare of children and women, but not having them under their custody or care, do not qualify, and as we understand the Guidelines, the Attorney General does not take a different position. There shall be no automatic inclusion of an organization simply because it is "registered." Tier Two notification can easily amount to the same notification as required for Tier Three if these limitations are not observed.

That dangers exist beyond those organizations "likely to encounter" the offender is obvious, for the offender may travel many miles before he or she offends, suggesting the possibility that greater safety would be assured if every organization in the state were notified. That is not at all the intent of the Legislature, the law having struck the balance between the need for safety and individual rights through the "likely to encounter" standard. The word "likely" shall be taken in its usual sense: to mean not "possibly" but "likely," not in the sense of "probably" but rather in the sense of "having a fair chance to encounter."

As for the manner and extent of notification under Tier Three, "likely to encounter" clearly includes the immediate neighborhood of the offender's residence and not just the people next door. It presumably would include (since Tier Three includes Tier Two notification) all schools within the municipality, depending on its size, and we see no reason why it should not include schools and other institutions in adjacent municipalities depending upon their distance from the offender's residence, place of work, or school. . . .

We do not automatically exclude, however, notification to a group carefully selected to include only those "likely to encounter" the offender. . . .

. . .

We assume that the media will exercise responsibility in this matter in recognition of the critical societal interest involved. In particular, we assume that the media will not knowingly frustrate the explicit legislative goal of confining notification to those likely to encounter the offender. . . .

. . .

VI

Privacy

. . .

In assessing plaintiff's claim, we must determine whether, and to what extent, plaintiff has a reasonable expectation of privacy in the information disclosed under the Registration and Notification Laws. If there is a reasonable expectation of privacy in the information disclosed, we must decide whether the intrusion on the right of privacy is justified, balancing the governmental interest in disclosure against the private interest in confidentiality.

We first address plaintiff's expectation of privacy in the information disclosed under the Registration Law. Information that is readily available to the public, which an individual cannot expect to remain private, is not within the ambit of constitutional protection. . . . Requiring disclosure of plaintiff's prior arrest and conviction, therefore, does not implicate the right to privacy, as those records are publicly available. . . .

. . .

Likewise, requiring the disclosure of other information, such as plaintiff's age and legal residence or a description of his vehicle, does not infringe on any expectation of privacy. As the trial court noted, that information is readily available through public records.... Plaintiff therefore cannot have a reasonable expectation of privacy in the information contained therein.

Lastly, an individual cannot expect to have a constitutionally protected privacy interest in matters that are exposed to public view. Because a person's physical appearance is necessarily and constantly exposed to public view, no person can have a reasonable expectation of privacy in his appearance. Similarly, no person can have a reasonable expectation of privacy in her fingerprints. Requiring a description or photograph and fingerprints, therefore, does not implicate any privacy interest.

...

X
Conclusion

We sail on truly uncharted waters, for no other state has adopted such a far-reaching statute. All other notification statutes apparently make public notification discretionary on the part of officials; the statute before us, however, mandates it. Despite the unavoidable uncertainty of our conclusion, we remain convinced that the statute is constitutional. To rule otherwise is to find that society is unable to protect itself from sexual predators by adopting the simple remedy of informing the public of their presence. That the remedy has a potentially severe effect arises from no fault of government, or of society, but rather from the nature of the remedy and the problem; it is an unavoidable consequence of the compelling necessity to design a remedy.

There is no point in predicting the extent of potential ostracism, in avoiding the conclusion that some ostracism will result, or in calming concerns by observing that the offenders themselves are responsible for their plight for having committed their crimes in the first place, for that justification would apply to any excessive punishment by government. Here government has done all it can to confine that impact, allowing it only where clearly necessary to effect public safety, and if the Tier level selected and the methods of notification conform to the statute and its intent, as defined and limited herein, Tier Two and Tier Three public notification will be appropriately confined and applied only to those whose apparent future dangerousness requires it, and the statute will not only have survived constitutional attack, but in fact will operate as the Legislature intended. We must not prejudge society with the ogre of vigilantism or harassment, although its potential obviously calls for the vigorous steps suggested by the Attorney General, and we must not assume that those in responsible positions will violate the intent of this law by giving notification far beyond that which is authorized, and we must not assume that the press, for whatever reason, will disregard the notification confinement which this law requires.

...

Justice Stein, dissenting. [omitted]

Notes and Queries

1. Critics have assailed community notification and registration laws, with charges ranging from their ineffectiveness and their tendency to cause vigilantism, to their significant stigmatic and liberty-depriving effects and their inappropriate focus on crazed sex offenders who commit only a minority of sex crimes. How does *Doe v. Poritz* respond to these criticisms?

2. Community notification and registration laws are in a state of flux. Recent efforts engage in actuarial justice. This influence is most apparent in jurisdictions that eschew individual risk assessments in favor of legislative imposition of compulsory registration and notification for those offenders convicted of specified sex offenses. Do you find that trend more or less problematic than individualized assessments? Consider your answer in light of our previous discussion that experts are not necessarily adequate evaluators of risk. What other factors are relevant to your decision?

Research Comment

1. One of the arguments for using community notification laws is that offenders simply are not incarcerated long enough. Little research has examined this concern. Existing studies reveal that sentences generally tend to be lenient, ranging from five to nine years of prison with very wide deviations that range even farther than the average sentence. It also has found that the criminal justice system does seem to incarcerate and punish more severely (in terms of prison time) those society is most worried about—persistent predators who abuse several children. Interestingly, research also indicates that individual victims' experiences are generally less predictive of sentencing outcomes than perpetrators' characteristics and that intra-family and stranger abuse seem to be taken equally seriously. See Roger J. R. Levesque (2000). Sentencing sex crimes against children: An empirical and policy analysis. *Behavioral Sciences & the Law*, 18, 331–341.

Chapter 12

General Prevention of Maltreatment

Several decades ago, leading experts in responses to child maltreatment provided a blueprint to reshape child welfare systems in the United States. The U.S. Advisory Board on Child Abuse and Neglect concluded that only a universal system of early intervention, grounded in the creation of caring communities, could provide an effective foundation for confronting the child abuse crisis. United States Advisory Board on Child Abuse and Neglect (1993). *Neighbors Helping Neighbors: A New National Strategy for the Protection of Children.* Washington, DC: U.S. Department of Health and Human Services. Their conclusion and recommendations were not surprising. It is generally held that successful strategies for preventing child maltreatment require intervention at all levels of society. However, no consensus has formed regarding which programs or services should be offered to prevent child maltreatment. In part, lack of consensus continues because research on the prevention of child abuse is limited by the complexity of the problem, the difficulty in measuring and interpreting intervention outcomes, and the lack of attention to the interaction among variables in determining risk status for subsequent maltreatment.

Many characteristics are associated with general (or primary) prevention efforts. Among the most typically noted ideal considerations are programs that build on participants' strengths rather than focus on deficits; take a proactive stance rather than wait for maltreatment; use educational/teaching-oriented strategies; focus on the development of people by promoting personal and social competencies, including problem solving, self-awareness, communication, decision making, self-control, stress management, and the use of social support networks; offer participants a comprehensive range of services and options; allow for participants to voluntarily choose from the variety of services rather than being required to do so; are culturally responsive and designed to encourage sharing and partnerships between participants in the programs and the service providers; and use programs with broad admission criteria, aimed at large groups of the population and diverse participants.

Although a broad range of programs has been developed and implemented by public and private agencies at many levels, little evidence supports the effectiveness of programs specifically aiming to prevent maltreatment. A 1994 retrospective review of 1,526 studies on the primary prevention of child abuse found that only 30 studies were methodologically sound. Only two of the eleven studies dealing primarily with physical abuse and neglect showed a decrease in child abuse as measured by a reduction in hospital admissions, emergency department visits, or reports to child protective services. As of 2024, only one study had followed up to review primary studies' effects on child maltreatment. That review was published in 2007 and found 188 primary prevention interventions that addressed a broad range of risk factors. Despite that high number, few had been evaluated rigorously. In addition, only a handful of the studies demonstrated an impact on risk factors of child maltreatment or on child maltreatment itself. The study concluded that the field of public health, broadly defined, had yet to develop and systematically evaluate interventions that target identified risk factors, such as social norms tolerating violence against children, poverty, and partner violence. Harriet L. MacMillan, James H. MacMillan, David R. Offord, Lauren Griffith & Angus MacMillan (1994). Primary prevention of child physical abuse and neglect: A critical review. Part I. *Journal of Child Psychology and Psychiatry and Allied Disciplines*, 35, 835–856; Neil B. Guterman (1997). Early prevention of physical child abuse and neglect: Existing evidence and future directions. *Child Maltreatment*, 2, 12–34. Joanne Klevens & Daniel J. Whitaker. (2007). Primary prevention of child physical abuse and neglect: Gaps and promising directions. *Child Maltreatment*, 12(4), 364–377.

Existing reviews of the literature indicate several key points. Better designed research studies are needed to evaluate the effectiveness of prevention strategies that target the well-known risk and demographic factors presented in the first chapter of this book. Reviews are needed to evaluate the feasibility of interventions, as the lack of rigorous interventions and evaluations counsels a shift toward interventions that may be low cost or require minimal efforts from recipients and the public. What is known about child maltreatment simply does not appear to provide sufficient support for developing more effective responses when weighed against support for many other social interests and concerns. Despite that discouraging conclusion, it is important to recognize that broad and deep progress has been made (e.g., the creation and continued existence of child welfare systems exemplify a fundamental shift in society's commitment to protecting children). However, so much more remains to be done to reach expected effectiveness.

Despite lack of success in efforts to prove effectiveness, researchers tend to present the need for two forms of intervention that eventually will address child maltreatment. The first involves broad social interventions. Social strategies for preventing child abuse seem obvious, but they actually remain largely uninvestigated and unproven. Broad intervention efforts would typically include the need to increase the value society places on children; increase the economic self-sufficiency of families; enhance communities and their resources; discourage excessive use of corporal punishment and other forms of violence; make health care more accessible and affordable; expand and improve coordination of social services; improve treatment for alcohol and drug abuse; improve the identification and treatment of mental health problems; increase the availability of affordable child care; and prevent the births of unwanted children through sex education, family planning, abortion, and adoption.

The second approach involves supporting families and meeting basic needs. This approach focuses on different levels of responses starting with basic requirements for food, shelter, clothing, safety, and medical care. The next step involves addressing financial concerns and identifies and treats parents who abuse alcohol or drugs, or who suffer from spousal abuse. The next higher level of need includes education about time management and budgeting skills, stress management, coping and parenting skills such as appropriate discipline, knowledge of child development, nutrition and feeding problems, and safety issues. This approach gains considerable significance in that long-term home visitation (up to several years) has been found to be effective in reducing the incidence of child abuse as measured by hospital admissions, emergency department visits, and reports to child protective services. However, without an infrastructure of support services such as health care, social services, and child care, home visitors obviously are unable to deliver needed services.

This chapter examines how legal efforts could be used to address two sets of issues that frequently recur in social science analyses of general prevention. The first set of issues concerns how the legal system addresses issues of poverty and lack of adequate resources, factors which frequently link to child maltreatment and the failure of institutions to protect children. Given those links, we examine cases that preceded, foreshadowed, and influenced the enactment of the *Personal Responsibility and Work Opportunity Act of 1996*, Pub. L. No. 104-193, 110 Stat. 2105, codified in 42 U.S.C. 601 et seq. (1999). This act, known as the dramatic welfare overhaul measure that abolished welfare "as we knew it," may have a powerful impact on child welfare as it continues to shape anti-poverty programs. With the well-established association between child neglect and poverty, changes in child poverty may affect the number of children at risk for maltreatment.

The focus on access to basic resources may require a leap of faith given how policy changes have evolved without rigorous empirical support and how that support would be needed to develop effective strategies. But the need to address basic resources and changes in access to them quickly led commentators to identify several reasonable concerns about the potential impact of welfare reform laws on the child welfare system itself: (1) States may be expected—without additional resources—to care for additional children who are likely to enter care because their parents are unable to provide for them due to poverty; (2) due to the loss of Social Security Income (SSI) benefits, additional parents may have to place their children with special needs because they do not have the financial resources required to care for them at home; (3) the five-year time limit on receipt of income subsidies and work benefits may mean that many kinship foster parents will no longer be able to care for their relatives' children, thereby overtaxing an already overburdened system; (4) many families are likely to do without assistance given that voluntary agencies find themselves unable to fill the broadening gaps; (5) child welfare agencies are likely to experience significant difficulty implementing family reunification plans for children in out-of-home care if parents are expected to meet work requirements that limit their availability for child visiting and family counseling; (6) the prohibition against parents who are convicted of substance abuse felonies receiving public assistance will make it extremely difficult for preventive service or foster care workers to provide assistance to the increasing number of mothers with substance abuse problems whom they are seeing on their caseloads; and (7) Title IV-E makes proprietary organizations eligible to receive state out-of-home care payments, which may create problematic competition between nonprofit and for-profit facilities given that large managed mental health care providers are primarily responsible to their shareholders, not their clients. For a thorough examination of welfare reform's potential impact on family violence, see Ruth A. Brandwein (Ed.) (1999). *Battered Women, Children, and Welfare Reform: The Ties that Bind*. Thousand Oaks, CA: Sage Publications.

The second set of issues examines ways to address victimization during adolescence and the special needs adolescents have as future parents and responsible citizens. As with links between child poverty and child maltreatment, numerous reasons suggest that we must consider the special needs of adolescents. The victimization of adolescents present several important issues as we consider how adolescents, compared to children, occupy a different place in families and society. Most notably, adolescents spend more time in schools and with peers as they often develop intimate relationships that mirror the many problems adults face, such as relationship violence and rape. See Roger J. R. Levesque (2002). *Violent Adolescents, Model Adolescents: Shaping the Role and Promise of Education*. New York: Kluwer/Plenum. How we can address the victimization of adolescents in schools can help us understand the special place of adolescents. How schools respond to child maltreatment and can help in preventing maltreatment also is an important consideration. Much of that consideration revolves around the extent to which schools can offer programs aimed at both child maltreatment prevention and at building skills and knowledge necessary to become effective parents.

Research Comments

1. The effectiveness of programs in promoting family wellness and preventing child maltreatment has led to considerable controversy. A meta-analysis of fifty-nine programs attempted to identify factors that moderate program success. It found the following: The effectiveness of proactive intervention was much larger at follow-up than at post-assessment, while the effectiveness for reactive interventions were higher at post-assessment than follow-up. The least effective home visitation programs on child maltreatment were for programs with twelve or fewer visits and less than a six-month duration. Intensive family preservation programs with high levels of participant involvement, an empowerment/strengths-based approach, and a component of social support were more effective than programs without those elements. Both home visitation and intensive family preservation interventions were reported as more effective if they had a mix of participants from different socioeconomic status (SES) than only low SES participants. Jennifer MacLeod

& Geoffrey Nelson (2000). Programs for the promotion of family wellness and the prevention of child maltreatment: A meta-analytic review. *Child Abuse & Neglect*, 24, 1127–1149.

2. Efforts to enhance parents' skills, an obvious area for general intervention, have become popular but subject to numerous criticisms. Among the most notable criticisms are the burden that home programming imposes on parents, the nature of relationships between parents and professionals in parent education programs, the implicit blaming of parents, the role conflict for parents, and the potential cultural bias of parent education. Despite the frequency of these concerns in the early intervention literature, surprisingly few empirical studies examine the extent to which parents actually experience parent education as being culturally biased, resulting in an undesired burden, implying blame, or interfering with their primary role as parents. Little empirical information exists about the manner in which parent education is delivered, the relationship between parents and professionals as a context for parent education, or the value that parents perceive in the skills taught to them. See Gerald Mahoney & Ann Kaiser (1999). Parent education in early intervention: A call for a renewed focus. *Topics in Early Childhood Special Education*, 19, 131–141. Despite the pervasive lack of research directly addressing implementation concerns, parent education programs have multiplied rapidly and many directly seek to prevent child maltreatment. Parenting education has been fueled by bodies of research exploring two different theoretical perspectives: that numerous family and parental factors limit the ability of maltreating parents to provide their children with adequate parenting and that enhancing parental approaches to child-rearing plays a key role in shaping young maltreated children's social and emotional functioning. As a result, programs that provide parenting education seek to teach parents new skills that will improve parental resources, coping skills, and competencies in child-rearing. In addition, parenting education may provide a mechanism for parents to learn positive parenting techniques and attitudes from sources outside their own upbringing. Although programs continue to differ widely in their service delivery models, target populations, and curricula, important attempts have been made to systematize approaches to parent education and detail which efforts reach the most effectiveness. See N. Dickon Reppucci, Preston A. Britner & Jennifer L. Woolard (1997). *Preventing Child Abuse and Neglect Through Parent Education*. Baltimore, MD: Paul H. Brookes.

3. We do not lack calls for reform and reviews of what can be done to address child welfare systems' challenges. Yet comprehensive summaries of what those reform strategies would look like only appeared recently. One important scoping review, a review method that has the broadest reach, systematically examined the recommendations of 433 reviews of recommendation. The authors identified two general forms of recommendation, with some reviews recommending reform efforts at the macro level (e.g., addressing poverty) and others making recommendations for reform at the practice level (e.g., implementing evidence-based

parenting programs). The authors conclude with the need to evaluate how these can be transformed into policy solutions that work. Essentially, the authors call for thinking about programs that might work in light of what we know about laws and policies relating to families and child development. Jill R. McTavish, Christine McKee, Masako Tanaka, & Harriet L. MacMillan. (2022). Child welfare reform: A scoping review. *International Journal of Environmental Research and Public Health*, 19(21), 14071.

King v. Smith

392 U.S. 309; 88 S. Ct. 2128 (1968)

Justice Warren delivered the opinion of the Court.

Alabama, together with every other State, Puerto Rico, the Virgin Islands, the District of Columbia, and Guam, participates in the Federal Government's Aid to Families With Dependent Children (AFDC) program, which was established by the Social Security Act of 1935. This appeal presents the question whether a regulation of the Alabama Department of Pensions and Security, employed in that Department's administration of the State's federally funded AFDC program, is consistent with Subchapter IV of the Social Security Act and with the Equal Protection Clause of the Fourteenth Amendment. At issue is the validity of Alabama's so-called "substitute father" regulation which denies AFDC payments to the children of a mother who "cohabits" in or outside her home with any single or married able-bodied man. Appellees brought this class action against appellants, officers, and members of the Alabama Board of Pensions and Security, in the United States District Court for the Middle District of Alabama, under 42 U.S.C. § 1983, seeking declaratory and injunctive relief....

I.

The AFDC program is one of three major categorical public assistance programs established by the Social Security Act of 1935. The category singled out for welfare assistance by AFDC is the "dependent child," who is defined in § 406 of the Act as an age-qualified "needy child ... who has been deprived of parental support or care by reason of the death, continued absence from the home, or physical or mental incapacity of a parent, and who is living with" any one of several listed relatives. Under this provision, and, insofar as relevant here, aid can be granted only if "a parent" of the needy child is continually absent from the home. Alabama considers a man who qualifies as a "substitute father" under its regulation to be a nonabsent parent within the federal statute. The State therefore denies aid to an otherwise eligible needy child on the basis that his substitute parent is not absent from the home.

Under the Alabama regulation, an "able-bodied man, married or single, is considered a substitute father of all the children of the applicant ... mother" in three different situations: (1) if "he lives in the home with the child's natural or adoptive mother for the purpose of cohabitation"; or (2) if "he visits [the home] frequently for the purpose of cohabiting with the child's natural or adoptive mother"; or (3) if "he does not frequent the home but cohabits with the child's natural or adoptive mother elsewhere." Whether the substitute father is actually the father of the children is irrelevant. It is also irrelevant whether he is legally obligated to support the children, and whether he does in fact contribute to their support. What is determinative is simply whether he "cohabits" with the mother. [Note 9 states that, under the regulation, when "there appears to be a substitute father," the mother bears the burden of proving that she has discontinued her relationship with the man before her AFDC assistance will be resumed. The mother's claim of discontinuance must be "corroborated by at least two acceptable references in a position to know. Examples of acceptable references are: law-enforcement officials; ministers; neighbors; grocers." There is no hearing prior to the termination of aid, but an applicant denied aid may secure state administrative review.]

The testimony below by officials responsible for the administration of Alabama's AFDC program establishes that "cohabitation," as used in the regulation, means essentially that the man and woman have "frequent" or "continuing" sexual relations. With regard to how frequent or continual these relations must be, the testimony is conflicting. One state official testified that the regulation applied only if the parties had sex at least once a week; another thought once every three months would suffice; and still another believed once every six months sufficient. The regulation itself provides that pregnancy or a baby under six months of age is prima facie evidence of a substitute father.

Between June 1964, when Alabama's substitute father regulation became effective, and January 1967, the total number of AFDC recipients in the State declined by about 20,000 persons, and the number of children recipients by about 16,000, or 22%. As applied in this case, the regulation has caused the termination of all AFDC payments to the appellees, Mrs. Sylvester Smith and her four minor children.

Mrs. Smith and her four children, ages 14, 12, 11, and 9, reside in Dallas County, Alabama. For several years prior to October 1, 1966, they had received aid under the AFDC program. By notice dated October 11, 1966, they were removed from the list of persons eligible to receive such aid. This action was taken by the Dallas County welfare authorities pursuant to the substitute father regulation, on the ground that a Mr. Williams came to her home on weekends and had sexual relations with her.

Three of Mrs. Smith's children have not received parental support or care from a father since their natural father's death in 1955. The fourth child's father left home in 1963, and the child has not received the support or care of his father since then. All the children live in the home of their mother, and except for the substitute father regulation are eligible for aid. The family is not receiving any other type of public assistance, and has been living, since the termination of AFDC payments, on Mrs. Smith's salary of between $16 and $20 per week which she earns working from 3:30 a.m. to 12 noon as a cook and waitress.

Mr. Williams, the alleged "substitute father" of Mrs. Smith's children, has nine children of his own and lives with his wife and family, all of whom are dependent upon him for support. Mr. Williams is not the father of any of Mrs. Smith's children. He is not legally obligated, under Alabama law, to support any of Mrs. Smith's children. Further, he is not willing or able to support the Smith children, and does not in fact support them. His wife is required to work to help support the Williams household.

II.

The AFDC program is based on a scheme of cooperative federalism. It is financed largely by the Federal Government, on a matching fund basis, and is administered by the States. States are not required to participate in the program, but those which desire to take advantage of the substantial federal funds available for distribution to needy children are required to submit an AFDC plan for the approval of the Secretary of Health, Education, and Welfare (HEW). The plan must conform with several requirements of the Social Security Act and with rules and regulations promulgated by HEW.

One of the statutory requirements is that "aid to families with dependent children . . . shall be furnished with reasonable promptness to all eligible individuals. . . ." As noted above, § 406 (a) of the Act defines a "dependent child" as one who has been deprived of "parental" support or care by reason of the death, continued absence, or incapacity of a "parent." In combination, these two provisions of the Act clearly require participating States to furnish aid to families with children who have a parent absent from the home, if such families are in other respects eligible.

The State argues that its substitute father regulation simply defines who is a non-absent "parent" under 406 (a) of the Social Security Act. The State submits that the regulation is a legitimate way of allocating its limited resources available for AFDC assistance, in that it reduces the caseload of its social workers and provides increased benefits to those still eligible for assistance. Two state interests are asserted in support of the allocation of AFDC assistance achieved by the regulation: first, it discourages illicit sexual relationships and illegitimate births; second, it puts families in which there is an informal "marital" relationship on a par with those in which there is an ordinary marital relationship, because families of the latter sort are not eligible for AFDC assistance.

We think it well to note at the outset what is not involved in this case. There is no question that States have considerable latitude in allocating their AFDC resources, since each State is free to set its own standard of need and to determine the level of benefits by the amount of funds it devotes to the program. Further, there is no question that regular and actual contributions to a needy child, including contributions from the kind of person Alabama calls a substitute father, can be taken into account in determining whether the child is needy. In other words, if by reason of such a man's contribution, the child is not in financial need, the child would be ineligible for AFDC assistance without regard to the substitute father rule. The appellees here, however, meet Alabama's need requirements; their alleged substitute father makes no contribution to their support; and they have been denied assistance solely on the basis of the substitute father regulation. Further, the regulation itself is unrelated to need, because the actual financial situation of the family is irrelevant in determining the existence of a substitute father.

Also not involved in this case is the question of Alabama's general power to deal with conduct it regards as immoral and with the problem of illegitimacy. This appeal raises only the question whether the State may deal with these problems in the manner that it has here — by flatly denying AFDC assistance to otherwise eligible dependent children.

Alabama's argument based on its interests in discouraging immorality and illegitimacy would have been quite relevant at one time in the history of the AFDC program. However, subsequent developments clearly establish that these state interests are not presently legitimate justifications for AFDC disqualification. Insofar as this or any similar regulation is based on the State's asserted interest in discouraging illicit sexual behavior and illegitimacy, it plainly conflicts with federal law and policy. A significant characteristic of public welfare programs during the last half of the 19th century in this country was their preference for the "worthy" poor. Some poor persons were thought worthy of public assistance, and others were thought unworthy because of their supposed incapacity for "moral regeneration." This worthy-person concept characterized the mothers' pension welfare programs, which were the precursors of AFDC. Benefits under the mothers' pension programs, accordingly, were customarily restricted to widows who were considered morally fit.

In this social context it is not surprising that both the House and Senate Committee Reports on the Social Security Act of 1935 indicate that States participating in AFDC were free to impose eligibility requirements relating to the "moral character" of applicants. During the following years, many state AFDC plans included provisions making ineligible for assistance dependent children not living in "suitable homes." As applied, these suitable home provisions frequently disqualified children on the basis of the alleged immoral behavior of their mothers.

In the 1940's, suitable home provisions came under increasing attack. Critics argued, for example, that such disqualification provisions undermined a mother's confidence and authority, thereby promoting continued dependency; that they forced destitute mothers into increased immorality as a means of earning money; that they were habitually used to disguise systematic racial discrimination; and that they senselessly punished impoverished children on the basis of their mothers' behavior, while inconsistently permitting them to remain in the allegedly unsuitable homes. In 1945, the predecessor of HEW produced a state letter arguing against suitable home provisions and recommending their abolition. Although 15 States abolished their provisions during the following decade, numerous other States retained them.

In the 1950's, matters became further complicated by pressures in numerous States to disqualify illegitimate children from AFDC assistance. Attempts were made in at least 18 States to enact laws excluding children on the basis of their own or their siblings' birth status. All but three attempts failed to pass the state legislatures, and two of the three successful bills were vetoed by the governors of the States involved. In 1960, the federal agency strongly disapproved of illegitimacy disqualifications.

Nonetheless, in 1960, Louisiana enacted legislation requiring, as a condition precedent for AFDC eligibility, that the home of a dependent child be "suitable," and specifying that any home in which an illegitimate child had been born subsequent to the receipt of public assistance would be considered unsuitable. In the summer of 1960, approximately 23,000 children were dropped from Louisiana's AFDC rolls. In disapproving this legislation, then Secretary of Health, Education, and Welfare Flemming issued what is now known as the Flemming Ruling, stating that as of July 1, 1961,

> A State plan ... may not impose an eligibility condition that would deny assistance with respect to a needy child on the basis that the home conditions in which the child lives are unsuitable, while the child continues to reside in the home. Assistance will therefore be continued during the time efforts are being made either to improve the home conditions or to make arrangements for the child elsewhere.

Congress quickly approved the Flemming Ruling, while extending until September 1, 1962, the time for state compliance. At the same time, Congress acted to implement the ruling by providing, on a temporary basis, that dependent children could receive AFDC assistance if they were placed in foster homes after a court determination that their former homes were, as the Senate Report stated, "unsuitable because of the immoral or negligent behavior of the parent."

In 1962, Congress made permanent the provision for AFDC assistance to children placed in foster homes and extended such coverage to include children placed in child-care institutions. At the same time, Congress modified the Flemming Ruling by amending § 404 (b) of the Act. As amended, the statute permits States to disqualify from AFDC aid children who live in unsuitable homes, provided they are granted other "adequate care and assistance."

Thus, under the 1961 and 1962 amendments to the Social Security Act, the States are permitted to remove a child from a home that is judicially determined to be so unsuitable as to "be contrary to the welfare of such child." The States are also permitted to terminate AFDC assistance to a child living in an unsuitable home, if they provide other adequate care and assistance for the child under a general welfare program. The statutory approval of the Flemming Ruling, however, precludes the States from otherwise denying AFDC assistance to dependent children on the basis of their mothers' alleged immorality or to discourage illegitimate births.

The most recent congressional amendments to the Social Security Act further corroborate that federal public welfare policy now rests on a basis considerably more sophisticated and enlightened than the "worthy-person" concept of earlier times. State plans are now required to provide for a rehabilitative program of improving and correcting unsuitable homes; to provide voluntary family planning services for the purpose of reducing illegitimate births; and to provide a program for establishing the paternity of illegitimate children and securing support for them.

In sum, Congress has determined that immorality and illegitimacy should be dealt with through rehabilitative measures rather than measures that punish dependent children, and that protection of such children is the paramount goal of AFDC. In light of the Flemming Ruling and the 1961, 1962, and 1968 amendments to the Social Security Act, it is simply inconceivable, as HEW has recognized, that Alabama is free to discourage immorality and illegitimacy by the device of absolute disqualification of needy children. Alabama may deal with these problems by several different methods under the Social Security Act. But the method it has chosen plainly conflicts with the Act.

III.

Alabama's second justification for its substitute father regulation is that "there is a public interest in a State not undertaking the payment of these funds to families who because of their living arrangements would be in the same situation as if the parents were married, except for the marriage." In other words, the State argues that since in Alabama the needy children of married couples are not eligible for AFDC aid so long as their father is in the home, it is only fair that children of a mother who cohabits with a man not her husband and not their father be treated similarly. The difficulty with this argument is that it fails to take account of the circumstance that children of fathers living in the home are in a very different position from children of mothers who cohabit with men not their fathers: the child's father has a legal duty to support him, while the unrelated substitute father, at least in Alabama, does not. We believe Congress intended the term "parent" in § 406 (a) to include only those persons with a legal duty of support.

The Social Security Act of 1935 was part of a broad legislative program to counteract the depression. Congress was deeply concerned with the dire straits in which all needy children in the Nation then found themselves. In agreement with the President's Committee on Economic Security, the House Committee Report declared, "the core of any social plan must be the child." The AFDC program, however, was not designed to aid all needy children. The plight of most children was caused simply by the unemployment of their fathers. With respect to these children, Congress planned that "the work relief program and . . . the revival of private industry" would provide employment for their fathers. As the Senate Committee Report stated: "Many of the children included in relief families present no other problem than that of providing work for the breadwinner of the family." Implicit in this statement is the assumption that children would in fact be supported by the family "breadwinner."

The AFDC program was designed to meet a need unmet by programs providing employment for breadwinners. It was designed to protect what the House Report characterized as "one clearly distinguishable group of children." This group was composed of children in families without a "breadwinner," "wage earner," or "father," as the repeated use of these terms throughout the Report of the President's Committee,

Committee Hearings and Reports and the floor debates makes perfectly clear. To describe the sort of breadwinner that it had in mind, Congress employed the word "parent." A child would be eligible for assistance if his parent was deceased, incapacitated or continually absent.

The question for decision here is whether Congress could have intended that a man was to be regarded as a child's parent so as to deprive the child of AFDC eligibility despite the circumstances: (1) that the man did not in fact support the child; and (2) that he was not legally obligated to support the child. The State correctly observes that the fact that the man in question does not actually support the child cannot be determinative, because a natural father at home may fail actually to support his child but his presence will still render the child ineligible for assistance. On the question whether the man must be legally obligated to provide support before he can be regarded as the child's parent, the State has no such cogent answer. We think the answer is quite clear: Congress must have meant by the term "parent" an individual who owed to the child a state-imposed legal duty of support.

It is clear, as we have noted, that Congress expected "breadwinners" who secured employment would support their children. This congressional expectation is most reasonably explained on the basis that the kind of breadwinner Congress had in mind was one who was legally obligated to support his children. We think it beyond reason to believe that Congress would have considered that providing employment for the paramour of a deserted mother would benefit the mother's children whom he was not obligated to support.

By a parity of reasoning, we think that Congress must have intended that the children in such a situation remain eligible for AFDC assistance notwithstanding their mother's impropriety. AFDC was intended to provide economic security for children whom Congress could not reasonably expect would be provided for by simply securing employment for family breadwinners. We think it apparent that neither Congress nor any reasonable person would believe that providing employment for some man who is under no legal duty to support a child would in any way provide meaningful economic security for that child.

A contrary view would require us to assume that Congress, at the same time that it intended to provide programs for the economic security and protection of all children, also intended arbitrarily to leave one class of destitute children entirely without meaningful protection. Children who are told, as Alabama has told these appellees, to look for their food to a man who is not in the least obliged to support them are without meaningful protection. Such an interpretation of congressional intent would be most unreasonable, and we decline to adopt it.

...

... We think that these provisions corroborate the intent of Congress that the only kind of "parent," under § 406 (a), whose presence in the home would provide adequate economic protection for a dependent child is one who is legally obligated to support him. Consequently, if Alabama believes it necessary that it be able to disqualify a child on the basis of a man who is not under such a duty of support, its arguments should be addressed to Congress and not this Court.

IV.

Alabama's substitute father regulation, as written and as applied in this case, requires the disqualification of otherwise eligible dependent children if their mother "cohabits" with a man who is not obligated by Alabama law to support the children. The regulation is therefore invalid because it defines "parent" in a manner that is inconsistent with § 406 (a) of the Social Security Act. In denying AFDC assistance to appellees on the basis of this invalid regulation, Alabama has breached its federally imposed obligation to furnish "aid to families with dependent children . . . with reasonable promptness to all eligible individuals. . . ." Our conclusion makes unnecessary consideration of appellees' equal-protection claim, upon which we intimate no views.

We think it well, in concluding, to emphasize that no legitimate interest of the State of Alabama is defeated by the decision we announce today. The State's interest in discouraging illicit sexual behavior and illegitimacy may be protected by other means, subject to constitutional limitations, including state participation in AFDC rehabilitative programs. Its interest in economically allocating its limited AFDC resources may be protected by its undisputed power to set the level of benefits and the standard of need, and by its taking into account in determining whether a child is needy all actual and regular contributions to his support.

All responsible governmental agencies in the Nation today recognize the enormity and pervasiveness of social ills caused by poverty. The causes of and cures for poverty are currently the subject of much debate. We hold today only that Congress has made at least this one determination: that destitute children who are legally fatherless cannot be flatly denied federally funded assistance on the transparent fiction that they have a substitute father.

Affirmed.

Justice Douglas concurring.

The Court follows the statutory route in reaching the result that I reach on constitutional grounds. It is, of course, traditional that our disposition of cases should, if possible, be on statutory rather than constitutional grounds, unless problems of statutory construction are insurmountable.

We do have, however, in this case a long-standing administrative construction that approves state AFDC plans containing a man-in-the-house provision. Certainly that early administrative construction, which so far as I can ascertain has been a consistent one, is entitled to great weight.

The Department of Health, Education, and Welfare balked at the Alabama provision only because it reached all nonmarital sexual relations of the mother, not just nonmarital relations on a regular basis in the mother's house. Since I cannot distinguish between the two categories, I reach the constitutional question.

The Alabama regulation describes three situations in which needy children, otherwise eligible for relief, are to be denied financial assistance. In none of these is the child to blame. The disqualification of the family, and hence the needy child, turns upon the "sin" of the mother.

First, if a man not married to the mother and not the father of the children lives in her home for purposes of cohabiting with her, the children are cast into the outer darkness.

Second, if a man who is not married to the mother and is not the father of the children visits her home for the purpose of cohabiting with her, the needy children meet the same fate.

Third, if a man not married to the mother and not the father of the children cohabits with her outside the home, then the needy children are likewise denied relief. In each of these three situations the needy family is wholly cut off from AFDC assistance without considering whether the mother's paramour is in fact aiding the family, is financially able to do so, or is legally required to do so. Since there is "sin," the paramour's wealth or indigency is irrelevant.

In other words, the Alabama regulation is aimed at punishing mothers who have nonmarital sexual relations. The economic need of the children, their age, their other means of support, are all irrelevant. The standard is the so-called immorality of the mother.

The other day in a comparable situation we held that the Equal Protection Clause of the Fourteenth Amendment barred discrimination against illegitimate children. We held that they cannot be denied a cause of action because they were conceived in "sin," that the making of such a disqualification was an invidious discrimination. I would think precisely the same result should be reached here. I would say that the immorality of the mother has no rational connection with the need of her children under any welfare program.

. . .

Notes and Queries

1. The rather complicated formula for federal funding is contained in 42 U.S.C. § 603. The level of benefits is within the state's discretion, but the federal government's contribution is a varying percentage of the total AFDC expenditures within each state. The benefit levels vary greatly from state to state. For example, for May 1967, the average payment to a family under AFDC was about $224 in New Jersey, $221 in New York, $39 in Mississippi, $20 in Puerto Rico, and $53 in Alabama.

2. What do you make of the Flemming Ruling? Note 18 cites to a case record, for example, where a mother whose conduct with men displeased a social worker was required, as a condition of continued assistance, to sign an affidavit stating that,

"I . . . do hereby promise and agree that until such time as the following agreement is rescinded, I will not have any male callers coming to my home nor meeting me elsewhere under improper conditions." What are your thoughts of the relevance of this rule to child protection?

3. Alabama argued that it was merely interpreting federal law in its allocation of limited resources and that it chose to do so in a manner that discouraged immorality. The Supreme Court rejected that argument partly because the federal government's own rejection of punitive suitable home rules in favor of rehabilitative measures. Assuming that Congress had adopted the suitable home rule, what would have been the outcome of this case?

Review Problem

1. The program described in *King v. Smith* was originally known as "Aid to Dependent Children." In subsequent amendments to the Act, however, the name of the program was changed to "Aid to Families With Dependent Children," or AFDC. In 1996, the program was abolished as Congress replaced AFDC with the Temporary Assistance for Needy Families (TANF) block grant programs. 42 U.S.C. 601–17 (2000). TANF seeks to ensure biological fathers' responsibility for welfare mothers' children. Critics charge that these policies withhold from unmarried mothers who seek welfare the only basic sexual rights, consensual heterosexual sex between adults, shielded by privacy under reigning jurisprudence. Mandatory paternity establishment and child support provisions require a mother to identify her child's biological father in order to be eligible for welfare. Some find that these provisions single out nonmarital mothers for scrutiny and punishment, as paternity is automatically established at birth if a mother is married. See Gwendolyn Mink (1998). *Welfare's End.* Ithaca, NY: Cornell University Press. Would you agree? Are these simply a continuation of policies examined under *King v. Smith*? TANF continues AFDC efforts. Under AFDC, a mother who was not married, who did not know who her child's biological father was, or who did not want anything to do with him, nevertheless had to provide welfare officials with information about him. Critics of the manner AFDC treated women's rights asserted that paternity establishment rules compromised recipient's privacy. To obtain needed information, welfare officials and courts had required independent mothers to answer such questions as, "How many sexual partners have you had? . . . whom did you have sex with before you got pregnant? . . . how often did you have sex? . . . where did you have sex? . . . when did you have sex?" See Lisa Kelly (1995). If anybody asks who I am: An outsider's story of the duty to establish paternity. *The American University Journal of Gender & the Law*, 3, 247–256. Do you find these legitimate questions? Does your reading of *King v. Smith* lead you to conclude that such efforts are constitutionally suspect?

Research Comment

1. How generous are welfare programs to recipients? A look at national averages the year before TANF went into effect reveals that families on AFDC in 1995 averaged cash incomes equal to 41 percent of the poverty line. At the high end, in four states, AFDC families' average incomes reached 60 percent of poverty or above (Alaska, California, Connecticut, and Hawaii). At the low end, in fifteen states, average incomes for AFDC families were only 30 percent of the poverty threshold or below (Alabama, Arkansas, Florida, Indiana, Kentucky, Louisiana, Mississippi, North Carolina, Missouri, Oklahoma, South Carolina, Tennessee, Texas, Virginia, and West Virginia). The average monthly benefit was $381.00, ranging from $724.00 in Alaska down to $120 in Mississippi. The states cited in *King v. Smith* reveal that benefits, over about a thirty-year period, went up as follows: NJ: $224 to $357; NY: $221 to $555; MI: $39 to $120; AL: $53 to $150. Sheila Zedlewski & Linda Giannarelli (1997). Diversity among State Welfare Programs. Washington, DC: Urban Institute. Also available online at http://newfederalism.urban.org/html/anf_a1.htm#authors.

Dandridge v. Williams

397 U.S. 471; 90 S. Ct. 1153 (1970)

Justice Stewart delivered the opinion of the Court.

This case involves the validity of a method used by Maryland, in the administration of an aspect of its public welfare program, to reconcile the demands of its needy citizens with the finite resources available to meet those demands. Like every other State in the Union, Maryland participates in the Federal Aid to Families With Dependent Children (AFDC) program which originated with the Social Security Act of 1935. Under this jointly financed program, a State computes the so-called "standard of need" of each eligible family unit within its borders. Some States provide that every family shall receive grants sufficient to meet fully the determined standard of need. Other States provide that each family unit shall receive a percentage of the determined need. Still others provide grants to most families in full accord with the ascertained standard of need, but impose an upper limit on the total amount of money any one family unit may receive. Maryland, through administrative adoption of a "maximum grant regulation," has followed this last course. This suit was brought by several AFDC recipients to enjoin the application of the Maryland maximum grant regulation on the ground that it is in conflict with the Social Security Act of 1935 and with the Equal Protection Clause of the Fourteenth Amendment....

The operation of the Maryland welfare system is not complex. By statute the State participates in the AFDC program. It computes the standard of need for each eligible family based on the number of children in the family and the circumstances under which the family lives. In general, the standard of need increases with each additional person in the household, but the increments become proportionately smaller. The regulation here in issue imposes upon the grant that any single family may receive an upper limit of $250 per month in certain counties and Baltimore City, and of $240 per month elsewhere in the State. The appellees all have large families, so that their standards of need as computed by the State substantially exceed the maximum grants that they actually receive under the regulation. The appellees urged in the District Court that the maximum grant limitation operates to discriminate against them merely because of the size of their families, in violation of the Equal Protection Clause of the Fourteenth Amendment. They claimed further that the regulation is incompatible with the purpose of the Social Security Act of 1935, as well as in conflict with its explicit provisions.

...

I

The appellees contend that the maximum grant system is contrary to § 402 (a) (10) of the Social Security Act, as amended, which requires that a state plan shall "provide ... that all individuals wishing to make application for aid to families with dependent children shall have opportunity to do so, and that aid to families with dependent children shall be furnished with reasonable promptness to all eligible individuals." The argument is that the state regulation denies benefits to the younger children in a large family. Thus, the appellees say, the regulation is in patent violation of the Act, since those younger children are just as "dependent" as their older siblings under the definition of "dependent child" fixed by federal law. Moreover, it is argued that the regulation, in limiting the amount of money any single household may receive, contravenes a basic purpose of the federal law by encouraging the parents of large families to "farm out" their children to relatives whose grants are not yet subject to the maximum limitation.

It cannot be gainsaid that the effect of the Maryland maximum grant provision is to reduce the per capita benefits to the children in the largest families. Although the appellees argue that the younger and more recently arrived children in such families are totally deprived of aid, a more realistic view is that the lot of the entire family is diminished because of the presence of additional children without any increase in payments. It is no more accurate to say that the last child's grant is wholly taken away than to say that the grant of the first child is totally rescinded. In fact, it is the family grant that is affected. Whether this per capita diminution is compatible with the statute is the question here. For the reasons that follow, we have concluded that the Maryland regulation is permissible under the federal law.

...

Thus the starting point of the statutory analysis must be a recognition that the federal law gives each State great latitude in dispensing its available funds.

The very title of the program, the repeated references to families added in 1962, and the words of the preamble quoted above, show that Congress wished to help children through the family structure. The operation of the statute itself has this effect. From its inception the Act has defined "dependent child" in part by reference to the relatives with whom the child lives. When a "dependent child" is living with relatives, then "aid" also includes payments and medical care to those relatives, including the spouse of the child's parent. Thus, as the District Court noted, the amount of aid "is . . . computed by treating the relative, parent or spouse of parent, as the case may be, of the 'dependent child' as a part of the family unit." Congress has been so desirous of keeping dependent children within a family that in the Social Security Amendments of 1967 it provided that aid could go to children whose need arose merely from their parents' unemployment, under federally determined standards, although the parent was not incapacitated.

The States must respond to this federal statutory concern for preserving children in a family environment. Given Maryland's finite resources, its choice is either to support some families adequately and others less adequately, or not to give sufficient support to any family. We see nothing in the federal statute that forbids a State to balance the stresses that uniform insufficiency of payments would impose on all families against the greater ability of large families — because of the inherent economies of scale — to accommodate their needs to diminished per capita payments. The strong policy of the statute in favor of preserving family units does not prevent a State from sustaining as many families as it can, and providing the largest families somewhat less than their ascertained per capita standard of need. Nor does the maximum grant system necessitate the dissolution of family bonds. For even if a parent should be inclined to increase his per capita family income by sending a child away, the federal law requires that the child, to be eligible for AFDC payments, must live with one of several enumerated relatives. The kinship tie may be attenuated but it cannot be destroyed.

The appellees rely most heavily upon the statutory requirement that aid "shall be furnished with reasonable promptness to all eligible individuals." But since the statute leaves the level of benefits within the judgment of the State, this language cannot mean that the "aid" furnished must equal the total of each individual's standard of need in every family group. Indeed the appellees do not deny that a scheme of proportional reductions for all families could be used that would result in no individual's receiving aid equal to his standard of need. As we have noted, the practical effect of the Maryland regulation is that all children, even in very large families, do receive some aid. We find nothing in 42 U. S. C. § 602 (a)(10) that requires more than this. So long as some aid is provided to all eligible families and all eligible children, the statute itself is not violated.

This is the view that has been taken by the Secretary of Health, Education, and Welfare (HEW), who is charged with the administration of the Social Security Act and the approval of state welfare plans. The parties have stipulated that the Secretary has, on numerous occasions, approved the Maryland welfare scheme, including its provision of maximum payments to any one family, a provision that has been in force in various forms since 1947. Moreover, a majority of the States pay less than their determined standard of need, and 20 of these States impose maximums on family grants of the kind here in issue. The Secretary has not disapproved any state plan because of its maximum grant provision. On the contrary, the Secretary has explicitly recognized state maximum grant systems.

Finally, Congress itself has acknowledged a full awareness of state maximum grant limitations. In the Amendments of 1967 Congress added to § 402 (a) a subsection, 23: "[The State shall] provide that by July 1, 1969, the amounts used by the State to determine the needs of individuals will have been adjusted to reflect fully changes in living costs since such amounts were established, and any maximums that the State imposes on the amount of aid paid to families will have been proportionately adjusted." This specific congressional recognition of the state maximum grant provisions is not, of course, an approval of any specific maximum. The structure of specific maximums Congress left to the States, and the validity of any such structure must meet constitutional tests. However, the above amendment does make clear that Congress fully recognized that the Act permits maximum grant regulations.

For all of these reasons, we conclude that the Maryland regulation is not prohibited by the Social Security Act.

II

Although a State may adopt a maximum grant system in allocating its funds available for AFDC payments without violating the Act, it may not, of course, impose a regime of invidious discrimination in violation of the Equal Protection Clause of the Fourteenth Amendment. Maryland says that its maximum grant regulation is wholly free of any invidiously discriminatory purpose or effect, and that the regulation is rationally supportable on at least four entirely valid grounds. The regulation can be clearly justified, Maryland argues, in terms of legitimate state interests in encouraging gainful employment, in maintaining an equitable balance in economic status as between welfare families and those supported by a wage-earner, in providing incentives for family planning, and in allocating available public funds in such a way as fully to meet the needs of the largest possible number of families. . . .

. . .

In the area of economics and social welfare, a State does not violate the Equal Protection Clause merely because the classifications made by its laws are imperfect. If the classification has some "reasonable basis," it does not offend the Constitution simply because the classification "is not made with mathematical nicety or because in practice it results in some inequality." "The problems of government are practical ones and may justify, if they do not require, rough accommodations — illogical, it may be, and unscientific." "A statutory discrimination will not be set aside if any state of facts reasonably may be conceived to justify it."

To be sure, the cases cited, and many others enunciating this fundamental standard under the Equal Protection Clause, have in the main involved state regulation of business or industry. The administration of public welfare assistance, by contrast, involves the most basic economic needs of impoverished human beings. We recognize the dramatically real factual difference between the cited cases and this one, but we can find no basis for applying a different constitutional standard. It is a standard that has consistently been applied to state legislation restricting the availability of employment opportunities. And it is a standard that is true to the principle that the Fourteenth Amendment gives the federal courts no power to impose upon the States their views of what constitutes wise economic or social policy.

Under this long-established meaning of the Equal Protection Clause, it is clear that the Maryland maximum grant regulation is constitutionally valid. We need not explore all the reasons that the State advances in justification of the regulation. It is enough that a solid foundation for the regulation can be found in the State's legitimate interest in encouraging employment and in avoiding discrimination between welfare families and the families of the working poor. By combining a limit on the recipient's grant with permission to retain money earned, without reduction in the amount of the grant, Maryland provides an incentive to seek gainful employment. And by keying the maximum family AFDC grants to the minimum wage a steadily employed head of a household receives, the State maintains some semblance of an equitable balance between families on welfare and those supported by an employed breadwinner.

It is true that in some AFDC families there may be no person who is employable. It is also true that with respect to AFDC families whose determined standard of need is below the regulatory maximum, and who therefore receive grants equal to the determined standard, the employment incentive is absent. But the Equal Protection Clause does not require that a State must choose between attacking every aspect of a problem or not attacking the problem at all. It is enough that the State's action be rationally based and free from invidious discrimination. The regulation before us meets that test.

We do not decide today that the Maryland regulation is wise, that it best fulfills the relevant social and economic objectives that Maryland might ideally espouse, or that a more just and humane system could not be devised. Conflicting claims of morality and intelligence are raised by opponents and proponents of almost every measure, certainly including the one before us. But the intractable economic, social, and even philosophical problems presented by public welfare assistance programs are not the business of this Court. The Constitution may impose certain procedural safeguards upon systems of welfare administration. But the Constitution does not empower this Court to second-guess state officials charged with the difficult responsibility of allocating limited public welfare funds among the myriad of potential recipients.

The judgment is reversed.

. . .

Appendix to opinion of the Court. [omitted]

Justice Black, with whom Justice Harlan joins, concurring. [omitted]

Justice Douglas, with whom Justice Marshall joins, dissenting. [omitted]

Justice Marshall, with whom Mr. Justice Brennan joins, dissenting.

. . . I believe that the Court has erroneously concluded that Maryland's maximum grant regulation is consistent with the federal statute. In my view, that regulation is fundamentally in conflict with the basic structure and purposes of the Social Security Act.

More important in the long run than this misreading of a federal statute, however, is the Court's emasculation of the Equal Protection Clause as a constitutional principle applicable to the area of social welfare administration. The Court holds today that regardless of the arbitrariness of a classification it must be sustained if any state goal can be imagined that is arguably furthered by its effects. This is so even though the classification's underinclusiveness or overinclusiveness clearly demonstrates that its actual basis is something other than that asserted by the State, and even though the relationship between the classification and the state interests which it purports to serve is so tenuous that it could not seriously be maintained that the classification tends to accomplish the ascribed goals.

The Court recognizes, as it must, that this case involves "the most basic economic needs of impoverished human beings," and that there is therefore a "dramatically real factual difference" between the instant case and those decisions upon which the Court relies. The acknowledgment that these dramatic differences exist is a candid recognition that the Cour's decision today is wholly without precedent. I cannot subscribe to the Court's sweeping refusal to accord the Equal Protection Clause any role in this entire area of the law, and I therefore dissent from both parts of the Court's decision.

I

At the outset, it should be emphasized exactly what is involved in determining whether this maximum grant regulation is consistent with and valid under the federal law. In administering its AFDC program, Maryland has established its own standards of need, and they are not under challenge in this litigation. Indeed, the District Court specifically refused to require additional appropriations on the part of the State or to permit appellees to recover a monetary judgment against the State. At the same time, however, there is no contention, nor could there be any, that the maximum grant regulation is in any manner related to calculation of need. Rather, it arbitrarily cuts across state-defined standards of need to deny any additional assistance with respect to the fifth or any succeeding child in a family. In short, the regulation represents no less than the refusal of the State to give any aid whatsoever for the support of certain dependent children who meet the standards of need that the State itself has established.

Since its inception in the Social Security Act of 1935, the focus of the federal AFDC program has been to provide benefits for the support of dependent children of needy families with a view toward maintaining and strengthening family life within the family unit. As succinctly stated by the Senate Committee on Finance, "the objective of the aid to dependent children program is to provide cash assistance for needy children in their own homes." In meeting these objectives, moreover, Congress has provided the outlines that the AFDC plan is to follow if a State should choose to participate in the federal program. The maximum grant regulation, however, does not fall within these outlines or accord with the purposes of the Act. And the Court by approving it allows for a complete departure from the congressional intent.

The phrase "aid to families with dependent children," from which the AFDC program derives its name, appears in § 402 (a)(10) of the Act, 42 U. S. C. § 602 (a)(10), and is defined in 42 U. S. C. § 606 (b) as, inter alia, "money payments with respect to . . . dependent children." Moreover, the term "dependent child" is also extensively defined in the Act. Nowhere in the Act is there any sanction or authority for the State to alter those definitions — that is, to select arbitrarily from among the class of needy dependent children those whom it will aid. Yet the clear effect of the maximum grant regulation is to do just that, for the regulation creates in effect a class of otherwise eligible dependent children with respect to whom no assistance is granted.

It was to disapprove just such an arbitrary device to limit AFDC payments that Congress amended § 402 (a)(10) in 1950 to provide that aid "shall be furnished with reasonable promptness to all eligible individuals." Surely, as my Brother Douglas demonstrates, this statutory language means at least that the State must take into account the needs of, and provide aid with respect to, all needy dependent children. Indeed, that was our assessment of the congressional design embodied in the AFDC program in *King v. Smith*.

The opinion of the Court attempts to avoid this reading of the statutory mandate by the conclusion that parents will see that all the children in a large family share in whatever resources are available so that all children "do receive some aid." And "so long as some aid is provided to all eligible families and all eligible children, the statute itself is not violated." The Court also views sympathetically the State's contention that the "all eligible individuals" clause was designed solely to prevent discrimination against new applicants for AFDC benefits. I am unpersuaded, however, by the view that Congress simultaneously prohibited discrimination against one class of dependent children — those in families not presently receiving benefits — and at the same time sanctioned discrimination against another class — those children in large families. Furthermore, the Court's interpretation would permit a State to impose a drastically reduced maximum grant limitation — or, indeed, a uniform payment of, say, $25 per family per month — as long as all families were subject to the rule. Thus, merely by purporting to compute standards of need and granting some benefits to all eligible families, the State would comply with the federal law — in spite of the fact that the needs of no or very few dependent children would thereby be taken into account in the actual assistance granted. I cannot agree that Congress intended that a State should be entitled to participate in the federally funded AFDC program under such circumstances.

. . .

A second effect of the maximum family grant regulation further demonstrates its inconsistency with the federal program. As administered in Maryland, the regulation serves to provide a strong economic incentive to the disintegration of large families. This is so because a family subject to the maximum regulation can, merely by placing the ineligible children in the homes of other relatives, receive additional monthly payments for the support of these additional dependent children. When families are receiving support that is concededly far below their bare minimum subsistence needs, the economic incentive that the maximum grant regulation provides to divide up large families can hardly be viewed as speculative or negligible. The opinion of this Court does not even dispute this effect. The Court answers by saying that the family relationship "may be attenuated but it cannot be destroyed." Yet it was just this kind of attenuation that, as the legislative history conclusively demonstrates, Congress was concerned with eliminating in establishing the AFDC program. The Court's rationale takes a long step backwards toward the time when persons were dependent upon the charity of their relatives — the very situation meant to be remedied by AFDC.

Despite its denial of the principle that payments should be made with regard to all eligible individuals and its conflict with the basic purposes of the Act, the Maryland regulation is nevertheless found by the Court to be consistent with the federal law because the existence of such regulations has been recognized by Congress. To bolster this view, the Court argues that the same conclusion has been reached by the department charged with administering the Act. On neither score is the Court convincing.

...

II

Having decided that the injunction issued by the District Court was proper as a matter of statutory construction, I would affirm on that ground alone. However, the majority has of necessity passed on the constitutional issues. I believe that in overruling the decision of this and every other district court that has passed on the validity of the maximum grant device, the Court both reaches the wrong result and lays down an insupportable test for determining whether a State has denied its citizens the equal protection of the laws.

The Maryland AFDC program in its basic structure operates uniformly with regard to all needy children by taking into account the basic subsistence needs of all eligible individuals in the formulation of the standards of need for families of various sizes. However, superimposed upon this uniform system is the maximum grant regulation, the operative effect of which is to create two classes of needy children and two classes of eligible families: those small families and their members who receive payments to cover their subsistence needs and those large families who do not.

This classification process effected by the maximum grant regulation produces a basic denial of equal treatment. Persons who are concededly similarly situated (dependent children and their families), are not afforded equal, or even approximately equal, treatment under the maximum grant regulation. Subsistence benefits are paid with respect to some needy dependent children; nothing is paid with respect to others. Some needy families receive full subsistence assistance as calculated by the State; the assistance paid to other families is grossly below their similarly calculated needs.

Yet, as a general principle, individuals should not be afforded different treatment by the State unless there is a relevant distinction between them, and "a statutory discrimination must be based on differences that are reasonably related to the purposes of the Act in which it is found." Consequently, the State may not, in the provision of important services or the distribution of governmental payments, supply benefits to some individuals while denying them to others who are similarly situated.

In the instant case, the only distinction between those children with respect to whom assistance is granted and those children who are denied such assistance is the size of the family into which the child permits himself to be born. The class of individuals with respect to whom payments are actually made (the first four or five eligible dependent children in a family), is grossly underinclusive in terms of the class that the AFDC program was designed to assist, namely, all needy dependent children. Such underinclusiveness manifests "a prima facie violation of the equal protection requirement of reasonable classification," compelling the State to come forward with a persuasive justification for the classification.

The Court never undertakes to inquire for such a justification; rather it avoids the task by focusing upon the abstract dichotomy between two different approaches to equal protection problems that have been utilized by this Court.

Under the so-called "traditional test," a classification is said to be permissible under the Equal Protection Clause unless it is "without any reasonable basis." On the other hand, if the classification affects a "fundamental right," then the state interest in perpetuating the classification must be "compelling" in order to be sustained.

This case simply defies easy characterization in terms of one or the other of these "tests." The cases relied on by the Court, in which a "mere rationality" test was actually used, are most accurately described as involving the application of equal protection reasoning to the regulation of business interests. The extremes to which the Court has gone in dreaming up rational bases for state regulation in that area may in many instances be ascribed to a healthy revulsion from the Court's earlier excesses in using the Constitution to protect interests that have more than enough power to protect themselves in the legislative halls. This case, involving the literally vital interests of a powerless minority—poor families without breadwinners—is far removed from the area of business regulation, as the Court concedes. Why then is the standard used in those cases imposed here? We are told no more than that this case falls in "the area of economics and social welfare," with the implication that from there the answer is obvious.

In my view, equal protection analysis of this case is not appreciably advanced by the a priori definition of a "right," fundamental or otherwise. Rather, concentration must be placed upon the character of the classification in question, the relative importance to individuals in the class discriminated against of the governmental benefits that they do not receive, and the asserted state interests in support of the classification. As we said only recently, "In determining whether or not a state law violates the Equal Protection Clause, we must consider the facts and circumstances behind the law, the interests which the State claims to be protecting, and the interests of those who are disadvantaged by the classification."

It is the individual interests here at stake that, as the Court concedes, most clearly distinguish this case from the "business regulation" equal protection cases. AFDC support to needy dependent children provides the stuff that sustains those children's lives: food, clothing, shelter. And this Court has already recognized several times that when a benefit, even a "gratuitous" benefit, is necessary to sustain life, stricter constitutional standards, both procedural and substantive, are applied to the deprivation of that benefit.

Nor is the distinction upon which the deprivation is here based — the distinction between large and small families — one that readily commends itself as a basis for determining which children are to have support approximating subsistence and which are not. Indeed, governmental discrimination between children on the basis of a factor over which they have no control — the number of their brothers and sisters — bears some resemblance to the classification between legitimate and illegitimate children which we condemned as a violation of the Equal Protection Clause in *Levy v. Louisiana.*

The asserted state interests in the maintenance of the maximum grant regulation, on the other hand, are hardly clear. In the early stages of this litigation, the State attempted to rationalize the maximum grant regulation on the theory that it was merely a device to conserve state funds, in the language of the motion to dismiss, "a legitimate way of allocating the State's limited resources available for AFDC assistance." Indeed, the initial opinion of the District Court concluded that the sole reason for the regulation, as revealed by the record, was "to fit the total needs of the State's dependent children, as measured by the State's standards of their subsistence requirements, into an inadequate State appropriation." The District Court quite properly rejected this asserted justification, for "the saving of welfare costs cannot justify an otherwise invidious classification."

In post-trial proceedings in the District Court, and in briefs to this court, the State apparently abandoned reliance on the fiscal justification. In its place, there have now appeared several different rationales for the maximum grant regulation, prominent among them being those relied upon by the majority — the notions that imposition of the maximum serves as an incentive to welfare recipients to find and maintain employment and provides a semblance of equality with persons earning a minimum wage.

With regard to the latter, Maryland has urged that the maximum grant regulation serves to maintain a rough equality between wage earning families and AFDC families, thereby increasing the political support for — or perhaps reducing the opposition to — the AFDC program. It is questionable whether the Court really relies on this ground, especially when in many States the prescribed family maximum bears no such relation to the minimum wage. But the Court does not indicate that a different result might obtain in other cases. Indeed, whether elimination of the maximum would produce welfare incomes out of line with other incomes in Maryland is itself open to question on this record. It is true that government in the United States, unlike certain other countries, has not chosen to make public aid available to assist families generally in raising their children. Rather, in this case Maryland, with the encouragement and assistance of the Federal Government, has elected to provide assistance at a subsistence level for those in particular need — the aged, the blind, the infirm, and the unemployed and unemployable, and their children. The only question presented here is whether, having once undertaken such a program, the State may arbitrarily select from among the concededly eligible those to whom it will provide benefits. And it is too late to argue that political expediency will sustain discrimination not otherwise supportable.

Vital to the employment-incentive basis found by the Court to sustain the regulation is, of course, the supposition that an appreciable number of AFDC recipients are in fact employable. For it is perfectly obvious that limitations upon assistance cannot reasonably operate as a work incentive with regard to those who cannot work or who cannot be expected to work. In this connection, Maryland candidly notes that "only a very small percentage of the total universe of welfare recipients are employable." The State, however, urges us to ignore the "total universe" and to concentrate attention instead upon the heads of AFDC families. Yet the very purpose of the AFDC program since its inception has been to provide assistance for dependent children. The State's position is thus that the State may deprive certain needy children of assistance to which they would otherwise be entitled in order to provide an arguable work incentive for their parents. But the State may not wield its economic whip in this fashion when the effect is to cause a deprivation to needy dependent children in order to correct an arguable fault of their parents.

Even if the invitation of the State to focus upon the heads of AFDC families is accepted, the minimum rationality of the maximum grant regulation is hard to discern. The District Court found that of Maryland's more than 32,000 AFDC families, only about 116 could be classified as having employable members, and, of these, the number to which the maximum grant regulation was applicable is not disclosed by the record. The State objects that this figure includes only families in which the father is unemployed and fails to take account of families in which an employable mother is the head of the household. At the same time, however, the State itself has recognized that the vast proportion of these mothers are in fact unemployable because they are mentally or physically incapacitated, because they have no marketable skills, or, most prominently, because the best interests of the children dictate that the mother remain in the home. Thus, it is clear, although the record does not disclose precise figures, that the total number of "employable" mothers is but a fraction of the total number of AFDC mothers. Furthermore, the record is silent as to what proportion of large families subject to the maximum have "employable" mothers. Indeed, one must assume that the presence of the mother in the home can be less easily dispensed with in the case of large families, particularly where small children are involved and alternative provisions for their care are accordingly more difficult to arrange. In short, not only has the State failed to establish that there is a substantial or even a significant proportion of AFDC heads of households as to whom the maximum grant regulation arguably serves as a viable and logical work incentive, but it is also indisputable that the regulation at best is drastically overinclusive since it applies with equal vigor to a very substantial number of persons who like appellees are completely disabled from working.

Finally, it should be noted that, to the extent there is a legitimate state interest in encouraging heads of AFDC households to find employment, application of the maximum grant regulation is also grossly underinclusive because it singles out and affects only large families. No reason is suggested why this particular group should be carved out for the purpose of having unusually harsh "work incentives" imposed upon them. Not only has the State selected for special treatment a small group from among similarly situated families, but it has done so on a basis — family size — that bears no relation to the evil that the State claims the regulation was designed to correct. There is simply no indication whatever that heads of large families, as opposed to heads of small families, are particularly prone to refuse to seek or to maintain employment.

The State has presented other arguments to support the regulation. However, they are not dealt with specifically by the Court, and the reason is not difficult to discern. The Court has picked the strongest available; the others suffer from similar and greater defects. Moreover, it is relevant to note that both Congress and the State have adopted other measures that deal specifically with exactly those interests the State contends are advanced by the maximum grant regulation. Thus, for example, employable AFDC recipients are required to seek employment through the congressionally established Work Incentive Program which provides an elaborate system of counseling, training, and incentive payments for heads of AFDC families. The existence of these alternatives does not, of course, conclusively establish the invalidity of the maximum grant regulation. It is certainly relevant, however, in appraising the overall interest of the State in the maintenance of the regulation.

In the final analysis, Maryland has set up an AFDC program structured to calculate and pay the minimum standard of need to dependent children. Having set up that program, however, the State denies some of those needy children the minimum subsistence standard of living, and it does so on the wholly arbitrary basis that they happen to be members of large families. One need not speculate too far on the actual reason for the regulation, for in the early stages of this litigation the State virtually conceded that it set out to limit the total cost of the program along the path of least resistance. Now, however, we are told that other rationales can be manufactured to support the regulation and to sustain it against a fundamental constitutional challenge.

However, these asserted state interests, which are not insignificant in themselves, are advanced either not at all or by complete accident by the maximum grant regulation. Clearly they could be served by measures far less destructive of the individual interests at stake. Moreover, the device assertedly chosen to further them is at one and the same time both grossly underinclusive — because it does not apply at all to a much larger class in an equal position — and grossly overinclusive — because it applies so strongly against a substantial class as to which it can rationally serve no end. Were this a case of pure business regulation, these defects would place it beyond what has heretofore seemed a borderline case and I do not believe that the regulation can be sustained even under the Court's "reasonableness" test.

In any event, it cannot suffice merely to invoke the spectre of the past and to recite from *Lindsley v. Natural Carbonic Gas Co.* and *Williamson v. Lee Optical Co.* to decide the case. Appellees are not a gas company or an optical dispenser; they are needy dependent children and families who are discriminated against by the State. The basis of that discrimination — the classification of individuals into large and small families — is too arbitrary and too unconnected to the asserted rationale, the impact on those discriminated against — the denial of even a subsistence existence — too great, and the supposed interests served too contrived and attenuated to meet the requirements of the Constitution. In my view Maryland's maximum grant regulation is invalid under the Equal Protection Clause of the Fourteenth Amendment.

I would affirm the judgment of the District Court.

Notes and Queries

1. The Court notes that the "intractable economic, social, and even philosophical problems presented by public welfare assistance programs are not the business of this Court." It then recognizes that the Court may intervene only to the extent that the Constitution may require procedural safeguards. Fair?

Research Comments

1. In *Dandridge*, the Court refuses to recognize a substantive constitutional right to welfare, a rule that results from the Supreme Court's reading of the Constitution as providing negative rather than positive liberties. That same year, however, the Court decided the landmark case, *Goldberg v. Kelly*, 397 U.S. 254 (1970), which established that welfare benefits were a form of property and thus could not be terminated without the due process protections of prior notice and a hearing. Significantly, the *Goldberg* Court rejected the argument that welfare benefits were a "privilege," rather than a "right," and held that "such benefits are a matter of statutory entitlement for persons qualified to receive them." Id. at 262. In *Goldberg*, the Court noted that procedural due process applied to the termination of welfare benefits because such benefits are a matter of statutory entitlement for persons qualified to receive them and that their termination involves state action that adjudicates important rights. Thus, the Supreme Court implicitly found that welfare recipients had a constitutionally protected property interest in their benefits that guaranteed them a right to due process before their benefits could be terminated.

The Court further defined the concept of an entitlement in *Board of Regents v. Roth*, 408 U.S. 564 (1972). In *Roth*, the Court held that an assistant professor teaching under a one-year contact did not have a property interest in continued employment. That case is significant in that the Court explained that it is the nature, rather than the weight of the interest at stake, that determines whether due process protections apply. The Court stated, "to have a property interest in a benefit, a person clearly must have more than an abstract need or desire for it. He must have more than a unilateral expectation of it. He must, instead, have a legitimate claim of entitlement to it." Id. at 577. Legitimate claims of entitlement "are created and . . . defined by existing rules or understandings that stem from an independent source such as state law. . . ." Id.

What implications arise from these cases? Taken together, these cases mean that rules create reasonable expectations of entitlements, while discretionary systems cannot. Thus, where courts conclude that the decision maker has unfettered discretion in awarding the public benefit, they will not find an entitlement. As a result, the search for entitlement status requires a careful parsing of the statute creating the benefit in a search for substantive standards that constrain the discretion of the official decision maker. Important consequences follow from this approach. It allows applicants for benefits, as well as recipients, to claim a legitimate expectation of entitlement. Where the law sets forth objective criteria for the receipt of benefits, an applicant who meets the criteria has a "reasonable expectation" of their receipt. Do you find it suspect that the *Roth* test also creates the outcome that the more discretion a decision maker has in administering a government benefit, the less likely that benefit is to obtain entitlement status? Do you find that the approach gives the legislature too much control over whether an entitlement is created, which runs the risk of leaving the poor entirely at the mercy of the political process? What arguments would you make to support the claim that leaving these issues to the political process is the fairest way to address such intractable problems?

2. As we already have seen, TANF also regulates women's sexuality in the manner it requires states to punish noncooperating mothers with benefit cuts, because mothers must sign child support income over to the state as a condition of receiving welfare, and because the federal government offers states incentives and services to boost paternity establishment rates. The TANF regime also lets stand "family cap" policies, which are state-level policies withholding benefits from children born to mothers who are enrolled on welfare. A close look also reveals a host of other ways the new reforms directly regulate women's sexuality and parenting. Most notably, it views women who do not cooperate with service providers as at risk for maltreating their children. See Gwendolyn Mink (1998). *Welfare's End*. Ithaca, NY: Cornell University Press.

United States v. Moreno

413 U.S. 528; 93 S. Ct. 2821 (1973)

Justice Brennan delivered the opinion of the Court.

This case requires us to consider the constitutionality of § 3 (e) of the Food Stamp Act of 1964, 7 U. S. C. § 2012 (e), as amended in 1971, 84 Stat. 2048, which, with certain exceptions, excludes from participation in the food stamp program any household containing an individual who is unrelated to any other member of the household. In practical effect, § 3 (e) creates two classes of persons for food stamp purposes: one class is composed of those individuals who live in households all of whose members are related to one another, and the other class consists of those individuals who live in households containing one or more members who are unrelated to the rest. The latter class of persons is denied federal food assistance. A three-judge District Court for the District of Columbia held this classification invalid as violative of the Due Process Clause of the Fifth Amendment. We noted probable jurisdiction. We affirm.

I

The federal food stamp program was established in 1964 in an effort to alleviate hunger and malnutrition among the more needy segments of our society. Eligibility for participation in the program is determined on a household rather than an individual basis. An eligible household purchases sufficient food stamps to provide that household with a nutritionally adequate diet. The household pays for the stamps at a reduced rate based upon its size and cumulative income. The food stamps are then used to purchase food at retail stores, and the Government redeems the stamps at face value, thereby paying the difference between the actual cost of the food and the amount paid by the household for the stamps.

As initially enacted, § 3 (e) defined a "household" as "a group of related or non-related individuals, who are not residents of an institution or boarding house, but are living as one economic unit sharing common cooking facilities and for whom food is customarily purchased in common." In January 1971, however, Congress redefined the term "household" so as to include only groups of related individuals. Pursuant to this amendment, the Secretary of Agriculture promulgated regulations rendering ineligible for participation in the program any "household" whose members are not "all related to each other."

Appellees in this case consist of several groups of individuals who allege that, although they satisfy the income eligibility requirements for federal food assistance, they have nevertheless been excluded from the program solely because the persons in each group are not "all related to each other." Appellee Jacinta Moreno, for example, is a 56-year-old diabetic who lives with Ermina Sanchez and the latter's three children. They share common living expenses, and Mrs. Sanchez helps to care for appellee. Appellee's monthly income, derived from public assistance, is $75; Mrs. Sanchez receives $133 per month from public assistance. The household pays $135 per month for rent, gas, and electricity, of which appellee pays $50. Appellee spends $10 per month for transportation to a hospital for regular visits, and $5 per month for laundry. That leaves her $10 per month for food and other necessities. Despite her poverty, appellee has been denied federal food assistance solely because she is unrelated to the other members of her household. Moreover, although Mrs. Sanchez and her three children were permitted to purchase $108 worth of food stamps per month for $18, their participation in the program will be terminated if appellee Moreno continues to live with them.

Appellee Sheilah Hejny is married and has three children. Although the Hejnys are indigent, they took in a 20-year-old girl, who is unrelated to them, because "we felt she had emotional problems." The Hejnys receive $144 worth of food stamps each month for $14. If they allow the 20-year-old girl to continue to live with them, they will be denied food stamps by reason of § 3 (e).

Appellee Victoria Keppler has a daughter with an acute hearing deficiency. The daughter requires special instruction in a school for the deaf. The school is located in an area in which appellee could not ordinarily afford to live. Thus, in order to make the most of her limited resources, appellee agreed to share an apartment near the school with a woman who, like appellee, is on public assistance. Since appellee is not related to the woman, appellee's food stamps have been, and will continue to be, cut off if they continue to live together.

These and two other groups of appellees instituted a class action against the Department of Agriculture, its Secretary, and two other departmental officials, seeking declaratory and injunctive relief against the enforcement of the 1971 amendment of § 3 (e) and its implementing regulations. In essence, appellees contend, and the District Court held, that the "unrelated person" provision of § 3 (e) creates an irrational classification in violation of the equal protection component of the Due Process Clause of the Fifth Amendment. We agree.

II

Under traditional equal protection analysis, a legislative classification must be sustained if the classification itself is rationally related to a legitimate governmental interest. The purposes of the Food Stamp Act were expressly set forth in the congressional "declaration of policy":

> It is hereby declared to be the policy of Congress . . . to safeguard the health and well-being of the Nation's population and raise levels of nutrition among low-income households. The Congress hereby finds that the limited food purchasing power of low-income households contributes to hunger and malnutrition among members of such households. The Congress further finds that increased utilization of food in establishing and maintaining adequate national levels of nutrition will promote the distribution in a beneficial manner of our agricultural abundances and will strengthen our agricultural economy, as well as result in more orderly marketing and distribution of food. To alleviate such hunger and malnutrition, a food stamp

> program is herein authorized which will permit low-income households to purchase a nutritionally adequate diet through normal channels of trade.

The challenged statutory classification (households of related persons versus households containing one or more unrelated persons) is clearly irrelevant to the stated purposes of the Act. As the District Court recognized, "the relationships among persons constituting one economic unit and sharing cooking facilities have nothing to do with their abilities to stimulate the agricultural economy by purchasing farm surpluses, or with their personal nutritional requirements."

Thus, if it is to be sustained, the challenged classification must rationally further some legitimate governmental interest other than those specifically stated in the congressional "declaration of policy." Regrettably, there is little legislative history to illuminate the purposes of the 1971 amendment of § 3 (e). The legislative history that does exist, however, indicates that that amendment was intended to prevent so-called "hippies" and "hippie communes" from participating in the food stamp program. The challenged classification clearly cannot be sustained by reference to this congressional purpose. For if the constitutional conception of "equal protection of the laws" means anything, it must at the very least mean that a bare congressional desire to harm a politically unpopular group cannot constitute a legitimate governmental interest. As a result, "[a] purpose to discriminate against hippies cannot, in and of itself and without reference to [some independent] considerations in the public interest, justify the 1971 amendment."

Although apparently conceding this point, the Government maintains that the challenged classification should nevertheless be upheld as rationally related to the clearly legitimate governmental interest in minimizing fraud in the administration of the food stamp program. In essence, the Government contends that, in adopting the 1971 amendment, Congress might rationally have thought (1) that households with one or more unrelated members are more likely than "fully related" households to contain individuals who abuse the program by fraudulently failing to report sources of income or by voluntarily remaining poor; and (2) that such households are "relatively unstable," thereby increasing the difficulty of detecting such abuses. But even if we were to accept as rational the Government's wholly unsubstantiated assumptions concerning the differences between "related" and "unrelated" households, we still could not agree with the Government's conclusion that the denial of essential federal food assistance to all otherwise eligible households containing unrelated members constitutes a rational effort to deal with these concerns. [Note 7 highlights that the Government initially argued to the District Court that the challenged classification might be justified as a means to foster "morality." In rejecting that contention, the District Court noted that "interpreting the amendment as an attempt to regulate morality would raise serious constitutional questions." The District Court observed that it was doubtful, at best, whether Congress, "in the name of morality," could "infringe the rights to privacy and freedom of association in the home." The Government itself has now abandoned the "morality" argument.]

At the outset, it is important to note that the Food Stamp Act itself contains provisions, wholly independent of § 3 (e), aimed specifically at the problems of fraud and of the voluntarily poor. For example, with certain exceptions, § 5 (c)) of the Act, 7 U. S. C. § 2014 (c)), renders ineligible for assistance any household containing "an able-bodied adult person between the ages of eighteen and sixty-five" who fails to register for, and accept, offered employment. Similarly, §§ 14 (b) and (c)), 7 U. S. C. §§ 2023 (b) and (c)), specifically impose strict criminal penalties upon any individual who obtains or uses food stamps fraudulently. The existence of these provisions necessarily casts considerable doubt upon the proposition that the 1971 amendment could rationally have been intended to prevent those very same abuses.

Moreover, in practical effect, the challenged classification simply does not operate so as rationally to further the prevention of fraud. As previously noted, § 3 (e) defines an eligible "household" as "a group of related individuals . . . [1] living as one economic unit [2] sharing common cooking facilities [and 3] for whom food is customarily purchased in common." Thus, two unrelated persons living together and meeting all three of these conditions would constitute a single household ineligible for assistance. If financially feasible, however, these same two individuals can legally avoid the "unrelated person" exclusion simply by altering their living arrangements so as to eliminate any one of the three conditions. By so doing, they effectively create two separate "households," both of which are eligible for assistance. Indeed, as the California Director of Social Welfare has explained:

> The 'related household' limitations will eliminate many households from eligibility in the Food Stamp Program. It is my understanding that the Congressional intent of the new regulations are specifically aimed at the 'hippies' and 'hippie communes.' Most people in this category can and will alter their living arrangements in order to remain eligible for food stamps. However, the AFDC mothers who try to raise their standard of living by sharing housing will be affected. They will not be able to utilize the altered living patterns in order to continue to be eligible without giving up their advantage of shared housing costs.

Thus, in practical operation, the 1971 amendment excludes from participation in the food stamp program, not those persons who are "likely to abuse the program" but, rather, only those persons who are so desperately in need of aid that they cannot even afford to alter their living arrangements so as to retain their eligibility. Traditional equal protection analysis does not require that every classification be drawn with precise "'mathematical nicety.'" But the classification here in issue is not only "imprecise," it is wholly without any rational basis. The judgment of the District Court holding the "unrelated person" provision invalid under the Due Process Clause of the Fifth Amendment is therefore

Affirmed.

Justice Douglas, concurring.

. . .

These appellees instituted a class action to enjoin the enforcement of the "unrelated" person provision of the Act.

The "unrelated" person provision of the Act creates two classes of persons for food stamp purposes: one class is composed of people who are all related to each other and all in dire need; and the other class is composed of households that have one or more persons unrelated to the others but have the same degree of need as those in the first class. The first type of household qualifies for relief, the second cannot qualify, no matter the need. It is that application of the Act which is said to violate the conception of equal protection that is implicit in the Due Process Clause of the Fifth Amendment.

The test of equal protection is whether the legislative line that is drawn bears "some rational relationship to a legitimate" governmental purpose. The requirement of equal protection denies government "the power to legislate that different treatment be accorded to persons placed by a statute into different classes on the basis of criteria wholly unrelated to the objective" of the enactment.

This case involves desperately poor people with acute problems who, though unrelated, come together for mutual help and assistance. The choice of one's associates for social, political, race, or religious purposes is basic in our constitutional scheme. It extends to "the associational rights of the members" of a trade union.

I suppose no one would doubt that an association of people working in the poverty field would be entitled to the same constitutional protection as those working in the racial, banking, or agricultural field. I suppose poor people holding a meeting or convention would be under the same constitutional umbrella as others. The dimensions of the "unrelated" person problem under the Food Stamp Act are in that category. As the facts of this case show, the poor are congregating in households where they can better meet the adversities of poverty. This banding together is an expression of the right of freedom of association that is very deep in our traditions.

Other like rights have been recognized that are only peripheral First Amendment rights—the right to send one's child to a religious school, the right to study the German language in a private school, the protection of the entire spectrum of learning, teaching, and communicating ideas, the marital right of privacy.

As the examples indicate, these peripheral constitutional rights are exercised not necessarily in assemblies that congregate in halls or auditoriums but in discrete individual actions such as parents placing a child in the school of their choice. Taking a person into one's home because he is poor or needs help or brings happiness to the household is of the same dignity.

Congress might choose to deal only with members of a family of one or two or three generations, treating it all as a unit. Congress, however, has not done that here. Concededly an individual living alone is not disqualified from the receipt of food stamp aid, even though there are other members of the family with whom he might theoretically live. Nor are common-law couples disqualified: they, like individuals living alone, may qualify under the Act if they are poor—whether they have abandoned their wives and children and however antifamily their attitudes may be. In other words, the "unrelated" person provision was not aimed at the maintenance of normal family ties. It penalizes persons or families who have brought under their roof an "unrelated" needy person. It penalizes the poorest of the poor for doubling up against the adversities of poverty.

But for the constitutional aspects of the problem, the "unrelated" person provision of the Act might well be sustained as a means to prevent fraud. Fraud is a concern of the Act. Able-bodied persons must register and accept work or lose their food stamp rights. I could not say that this "unrelated" person provision has no "rational" relation to control of fraud. We deal here, however, with the right of association, protected by the First Amendment. People who are desperately poor but unrelated come together and join hands with the aim better to combat the crises of poverty. The need of those living together better to meet those crises is denied, while the need of households made up of relatives that is no more acute is serviced. Problems of the fisc are legitimate concerns of government. But government "may not accomplish such a purpose by invidious distinctions between classes of its citizens."

The legislative history of the Act indicates that the "unrelated" person provision of the Act was to prevent "essentially unrelated individuals who voluntarily chose to cohabit and live off food stamps"—so-called "hippies" or "hippy communes"—from participating in the food stamp program. As stated in the Conference Report, the definition of household was "designed to prohibit food stamp assistance to communal 'families' of unrelated individuals."

The right of association, the right to invite the stranger into one's home is too basic in our constitutional regime to deal with roughshod. If there are abuses inherent in that pattern of living against which the food stamp program should be protected, the Act must be "narrowly drawn" to meet the precise end. The method adopted and applied to these cases makes § 3 (e) of the Act unconstitutional by reason of the invidious discrimination between the two classes of needy persons.

. . .

The "unrelated" person provision of the present Act has an impact on the rights of people to associate for lawful purposes with whom they choose. When state action "may have the effect of curtailing the freedom to associate" it "is subject to the closest scrutiny." The "right of the people peaceably to assemble" guaranteed by the First Amendment covers a wide spectrum of human interests—including, "political, economic, religious, or cultural matters." Banding together to combat the common foe of hunger is in that category. The case therefore falls within the zone [of prior cases that held] . . . that a waiting period on welfare imposed by a State on the "immigration of indigents" penalizing the constitutional right to travel could not be sustained absent a "compelling governmental interest."

Justice Rehnquist, dissenting.

. . . I am unable to agree with the Court's disposition of this case. Here appellees challenged a provision in the Federal Food Stamp Act, 7 U. S. C. § 2011 et seq., which limited food stamps to related people living in one "household." The result of this provision is that unrelated persons who live under the same roof and pool their resources may not obtain food stamps even though otherwise eligible.

The Court's opinion would make a very persuasive congressional committee report arguing against the adoption of the limitation in question. Undoubtedly, Congress attacked the problem with a rather blunt instrument and, just as undoubtedly, persuasive arguments may be made that what we conceive to be its purpose will not be significantly advanced by the enactment of the limitation. But questions such as this are for Congress, rather than for this Court; our role is limited to the determination of whether there is any rational basis on which Congress could decide that public funds made available under the food stamp program should not go to a household containing an individual who is unrelated to any other member of the household.

I do not believe that asserted congressional concern with the fraudulent use of food stamps is, when interpreted in the light most favorable to sustaining the limitation, quite as irrational as the Court seems to believe. A basic unit which Congress has chosen for determination of availability for food stamps is the "household," a determination which is not criticized by the Court. By the limitation here challenged, it has singled out households which contain unrelated persons and made such households ineligible. I do not think it is unreasonable for Congress to conclude that the basic unit which it was willing to support with federal funding through food stamps is some variation on the family as we know it — a household consisting of related individuals. This unit provides a guarantee which is not provided by households containing unrelated individuals that the household exists for some purpose other than to collect federal food stamps.

Admittedly, as the Court points out, the limitation will make ineligible many households which have not been formed for the purpose of collecting federal food stamps, and will at the same time not wholly deny food stamps to those households which may have been formed in large part to take advantage of the program. But, as the Court concedes, "traditional equal protection analysis does not require that every classification be drawn with precise 'mathematical nicety.'" And earlier this Term, the constitutionality of a similarly "imprecise" rule promulgated pursuant to the Truth in Lending Act was challenged on grounds such as those urged by appellees here. In *Mourning v. Family Publications Service, Inc.*, the imposition of the rule on all members of a defined class was sustained because it served to discourage evasion by a substantial portion of that class of disclosure mechanisms chosen by Congress for consumer protection.

The limitation which Congress enacted could, in the judgment of reasonable men, conceivably deny food stamps to members of households which have been formed solely for the purpose of taking advantage of the food stamp program. Since the food stamp program is not intended to be a subsidy for every individual who desires low-cost food, this was a permissible congressional decision quite consistent with the underlying policy of the Act. The fact that the limitation will have unfortunate and perhaps unintended consequences beyond this does not make it unconstitutional.

Notes and Queries

1. The unrelated-person rule was apparently meant to deny food stamps to groups of "hippies." The Court determined that if equal protection of the laws means anything, it must at the very least mean that a bare congressional desire to harm a politically unpopular group cannot constitute a legitimate governmental interest. The significance of this case cannot be underestimated. What implications do you think the approach has for addressing child maltreatment?

Research Comment

1. The approach adopted in *Moreno* has lead to protecting several groups from invidious discrimination. Consider the following cases and the implications they may have for addressing the environments linked to child maltreatment.

   In *City of Cleburne v. Cleburne Living Center*, 473 U.S. 432 (1985), the Court held that Cleburne's requirement that group homes for mentally retarded people obtain special zoning permits, when other types of group residences did not require such a permit, violated the Equal Protection Clause. The Court determined that the Equal Protection Clause required only that the zoning ordinance be a rational means to serve a legitimate end. The special zoning requirement for group homes for the mentally retarded could not meet this standard because the requirement's relationship to the asserted goal was so attenuated as to render the distinction arbitrary or irrational. The Court also made clear that the desire to harm a politically unpopular group could not be a legitimate state goal.

   Plyler v. Doe, 457 U.S. 202 (1981), dealt with Texas's attempt to exclude children who were not legally admitted into the United States from its public schools. While determining that undocumented aliens were not a suspect classification and that education was not a fundamental right, the Court nonetheless found the exclusion from public schools a violation of the Equal Protection Clause. The Court concluded that it was difficult to conceive of a rational justification for penalizing these children for their presence within the United States.

   In *Romer v. Evans*, 517 U.S. 620 (1996), the Court addressed the question of what constitutes a legitimate state interest when a governmental classification is made based on sexual orientation. The Court struck down an amendment to Colorado's Constitution that prospectively prohibited the enactment of anti-discrimination laws based on sexual orientation. The Court explained that because the Colorado amendment neither burdens a fundamental right nor targets a suspect class, the amendment would be upheld if it bears a rational relation to some legitimate end. The touchstone in applying this standard is the purpose of the Equal Protection Clause, which the Court described as requiring government action that neither knows nor tolerates classes among citizens. The Court found that the amendment in *Romer* could not meet the requirements of the Equal Protection Clause because it imposed a broad and undifferentiated disability on a single named group and because the breadth of the amendment was so discontinuous with the reasons offered for it that the amendment seemed inexplicable by anything but animus toward the class it affects; it lacked a rational relationship to legitimate state interests. The amendment could not survive rational basis scrutiny because it did not further any identifiable legitimate purpose or discrete objective. The amendment sought to place a special burden on a group that could not be justified by the rationales offered by Colorado. The purpose of the amendment, the Court determined, was based not on a legitimate public purpose but on a desire to harm an unpopular group and to make them unequal to everyone else.

Bowen v. Gilliard

483 U.S. 587; 107 S. Ct. 3008 (1987)

Justice Stevens delivered the opinion of the Court.

As part of its major effort to reduce the federal deficit through the Deficit Reduction Act of 1984, 98 Stat. 494, Congress amended the statute authorizing Federal Aid to Families with Dependent Children (AFDC) to require that a family's eligibility for benefits must take into account, with certain specified exceptions, the income of all parents, brothers, and sisters living in the same home. The principal question presented in this litigation is whether that requirement violates the Fifth Amendment to the United States Constitution when it is applied to require a family wishing to receive AFDC benefits to include within its unit a child for whom child support payments are being made by a noncustodial parent.

I

This litigation began in 1970. At that time the federal statute did not require that all parents and siblings be included in an AFDC filing unit. Thus, for example, if a teenage child had significant income of her own, perhaps from wages or perhaps in support payments from an absent parent, the other members of her family could exclude her from the filing unit in order to avoid disqualifying the entire family from benefits or reducing its level of benefits.

Beaty Mae Gilliard, one of the named class members in the 1970 suit, began receiving public assistance from North Carolina under AFDC in 1962. In February 1970, after her seventh child was born, the State automatically included him in the filing unit, thereby increasing the family's monthly allotment from $217 to $227 to reflect the difference between the benefit for a family of seven and the benefit for a family of eight. Gilliard was, however, also receiving $43.33 each month in child support from the baby's father. When a formal parental support order was entered in April 1970, the State credited the support payments against her account and reduced her monthly benefit to $184. Gilliard sued, contending that she had a statutory right to exclude her seventh child from the unit and thus to continue to receive the $217 benefit for a family of seven and also to retain the $43.33 paid by her youngest child's father. A three-judge District Court agreed with her reading of the statute and entered an order requiring the State to reinstate her benefits at the $217 level and to reimburse her for the improper credits of $43 per month. The District Court also granted classwide relief. We affirmed that judgment. No constitutional question was decided at that time.

Congress amended the AFDC program in 1975 to require, as a condition of eligibility, that applicants for assistance must assign to the State any right to receive child support payments for any member of the family included in the filing unit. In response, North Carolina amended its laws to provide that the acceptance of public assistance on behalf of a dependent child would constitute an assignment of any right to support for that child. These amendments, however, did not harm recipients like Gilliard because they did not affect the right to define the family unit covered by an application and thereby to exclude children with independent income, such as a child for whom support payments were being made.

In 1983, the Secretary of Health and Human Services proposed certain amendments to the Social Security Act to "assure that limited Federal and State resources are spent as effectively as possible." ...

...

Because the 1984 amendment forced families to include in the filing unit children for whom support payments were being received, the practical effect was that many families' total income was reduced. The burden of the change was mitigated somewhat by a separate amendment providing that the first $50 of child support collected by the State must be remitted to the family and not counted as income for the purpose of determining its benefit level. Thus, the net effect of the 1984 amendments for a family comparable to Gilliard's would include three changes: (1) the addition of the child receiving support would enlarge the filing unit and entitle the family to a somewhat larger benefit; (2) child support would be treated as family income and would be assigned to the State, thereby reducing the AFDC benefits by that amount; and (3) the reduction would be offset by $50 if that amount was collected from an absent parent. In sum, if the assigned support exceeded $50 plus the difference in the benefit level caused by adding the child or children receiving support, the family would suffer; if less than $50 and the difference in the benefit level was collected as support, it would not.

After North Carolina adopted regulations to comply with the 1984 amendments, some members of the class that had earlier obtained relief filed a motion to reopen the 1971 decree and obtain further relief on behalf of the class. The State impleaded the Secretary of Health and Human Services, contending that if the State's compliance with the federal statute resulted in any liability to appellees, the Federal Government should share in any payment of additional AFDC benefits. The District Court found that North Carolina's and the Department of Health and Human Services' regulations were in conformance with the statute, but concluded that the statutory scheme violated both the Due Process Clause and the Takings Clause of the Fifth Amendment.

The court interpreted North Carolina law as imposing a duty on the custodial parent to use child support money exclusively for the benefit of the child for whom it had been obtained, and reasoned that a forced assignment of the support money to the State in exchange for AFDC benefits for the entire family was a taking of the child's private property. Additionally, the court reasoned that the use of the child's support money to reduce the Government's AFDC expenditures was tantamount to punishing the child for exercising the fundamental right to live with his or her family. Because of the serious impact on the autonomy of the family—including the child's potential relationship with his or her noncustodial parent—"special judicial scrutiny" was considered appropriate and the deprivation of property and liberty effected by the statutory scheme could not, in the court's view, survive such scrutiny. We noted probable jurisdiction.

The District Court was undoubtedly correct in its perception that a number of needy families have suffered, and will suffer, as a result of the implementation of the DEFRA amendments to the AFDC program. Such suffering is frequently the tragic byproduct of a decision to reduce or to modify benefits to a class of needy recipients. Under our structure of Government, however, it is the function of Congress—not the courts—to determine whether the savings realized, and presumably used for other critical governmental functions, are significant enough to justify the costs to the individuals affected by such reductions. The Fifth Amendment "gives the federal courts no power to impose upon [Congress] their views of what constitutes wise economic or social policy," by telling it how "to reconcile the demands of . . . needy citizens with the finite resources available to meet those demands." Unless the Legislative Branch's decisions run afoul of some constitutional edict, any inequities created by such decisions must be remedied by the democratic processes. The District Court believed that the amendment at issue did conflict with both the Due Process Clause and the Takings Clause of the Fifth Amendment. We consider these arguments in turn, and reject them.

III

The precepts that govern our review of appellee' due process and equal protection challenges to this program are similar to those we have applied in reviewing challenges to other parts of the Social Security Act:

> Our review is deferential. 'Governmental decisions to spend money to improve the general public welfare in one way and not another are "not

> confided to the courts. The discretion belongs to Congress unless the choice is clearly wrong, a display of arbitrary power, not an exercise of judgment.'

This standard of review is premised on Congress' "plenary power to define the scope and the duration of the entitlement to . . . benefits, and to increase, to decrease, or to terminate those benefits based on its appraisal of the relative importance of the recipients' needs and the resources available to fund the program."

The District Court had before it evidence that the DEFRA amendment was severely impacting some families. For example, some noncustodial parents stopped making their support payments because they believed that their payments were helping only the State, and not their children. It is clear, however, that in the administration of a fund that is large enough to have a significant impact on the Nation's deficit, general rules must be examined in light of the broad purposes they are intended to serve. The challenged amendment unquestionably serves Congress' goal of decreasing federal expenditures. The evidence that a few noncustodial parents were willing to violate the law by not making court-ordered support payments does not alter the fact that the entire program has resulted in saving huge sums of money.

The rationality of the amendment denying a family the right to exclude a supported child from the filing unit is also supported by the Government's separate interest in distributing benefits among competing needy families in a fair way. Given its perceived need to make cuts in the AFDC budget, Congress obviously sought to identify a group that would suffer less than others as a result of a reduction in benefits. When considering the plight of two five-person families, one of which receives no income at all while the other receives regular support payments for some of the minor children, it is surely reasonable for Congress to conclude that the former is in greater need than the latter. This conclusion is amply supported by Congress' assumption that child support payments received are generally beneficial to the entire family unit, see Senate Print, at 980, and by "the common sense proposition that individuals living with others usually have reduced per capita costs because many of their expenses are shared."

It was therefore rational for Congress to adjust the AFDC program to reflect the fact that support money generally provides significant benefits for entire family units. This conclusion is not undermined by the fact that there are no doubt many families in which some — or perhaps all — of the support money is spent in a way that does not benefit the rest of the family. In determining how best to allocate limited funds among the extremely large class of needy families eligible for AFDC benefits, Congress is entitled to rely on a classwide presumption that custodial parents have used, and may legitimately use, support funds in a way that is beneficial to entire family units. As we have repeatedly explained:

> If the classification has some 'reasonable basis,' it does not offend the Constitution simply because the classification 'is not made with mathematical nicety or because in practice it results in some inequality.' 'The problems

> of government are practical ones and may justify, if they do not require, rough accommodations — illogical, it may be, and unscientific.' 'A statutory discrimination will not be set aside if any state of facts reasonably may be conceived to justify it.'

We have no doubt that the DEFRA amendment satisfies this test.

Appellees argue (and the District Court ruled), however, that finding that Congress acted rationally is not enough to sustain this legislation. Rather, they claim that some form of "heightened scrutiny" is appropriate because the amendment interferes with a family's fundamental right to live in the type of family unit it chooses. We conclude that the District Court erred in subjecting the DEFRA amendment to any form of heightened scrutiny. That some families may decide to modify their living arrangements in order to avoid the effect of the amendment, does not transform the amendment into an act whose design and direct effect are to "intrud[e] on choices concerning family living arrangements." As was the case with the marriage-related provision upheld in *Califano v. Jobst*, "Congress adopted this rule in the course of constructing a complex social welfare system that necessarily deals with the intimacies of family life. This is not a case in which government seeks to foist orthodoxy on the unwilling."

Last Term we rejected a constitutional challenge to a provision in the Federal Food Stamp Program, which determines eligibility and benefit levels on a "household" rather than an individual basis. We held that the guarantee of equal treatment in the Due Process Clause of the Fifth Amendment was not violated by the statutory requirement that generally treated parents, children, and siblings who lived together as a single household, and explained:

> The disadvantaged class is that comprised by parents, children, and siblings. Close relatives are not a 'suspect' or 'quasi-suspect' class. As a historical matter, they have not been subjected to discrimination; they do not exhibit obvious, immutable, or distinguishing characteristics that define them as a discrete group; and they are not a minority or politically powerless. In fact, quite the contrary is true.
>
> Nor does the statutory classification 'directly and substantially' interfere with family living arrangements and thereby burden a fundamental right.

In light of this, we concluded in Lyng that the "District Court erred in judging the constitutionality of the statutory distinction under 'heightened scrutiny.'" In this case the District Court committed the same error.... [T]he standard of review here is whether "Congress had a rational basis" for its decision. And ... "the justification for the statutory classification is obvious." The provisions at issue do not violate the Due Process Clause.

IV

Aside from holding that the amendment violated the Due Process Clause of the Fifth Amendment and its equal protection component, the District Court invalidated the DEFRA amendments as a taking of private property without just compensation. The court based this holding on the premise that a child for whom support payments are made has a right to have the support money used exclusively in his or her "best interest." Yet, the court reasoned, the requirements (1) that a custodial parent who applies for AFDC must include a child's support money in computing family income, and (2) that the support must be assigned to the State, effectively converts the support funds that were once to be used exclusively for the child's best interests into an AFDC check which, under federal law, must be used for the benefit of all the children. Therefore, the District Court held that the State was "taking" that child's right to exclusive use of the support money. In addressing this issue, it is helpful to look first at whether the State "takes" the child's property when it considers the support payments as part of the family's income in computing AFDC eligibility. We will then consider whether the requirement that support payments be assigned to the State requires a finding that the amendments violate the taking prohibition.

Some perspective on the issue is helpful here. Had no AFDC program ever existed until 1984, and had Congress then instituted a program that took into account support payments that a family receives, it is hard to believe that we would seriously entertain an argument that the new benefit program constituted a taking. Yet, somehow, once benefits are in place and Congress sees a need to reduce them in order to save money and to distribute limited resources more fairly, the "takings" label seems to have a bit more plausibility. For legal purposes though, the two situations are identical. Congress is not, by virtue of having instituted a social welfare program, bound to continue it at all, much less at the same benefit level. Thus, notwithstanding the technical legal arguments that have been advanced, it is imperative to recognize that the amendments at issue merely incorporate a definitional element into an entitlement program. It would be quite strange indeed if, by virtue of an offer to provide benefits to needy families through the entirely voluntary AFDC program, Congress or the States were deemed to have taken some of those very family members' property.

The basic requirement that the AFDC filing unit must include all family members living in the home, and therefore that support payments made on behalf of a member of the family must be considered in determining that family's level of benefits, does not even arguably take anyone's property. The family members other than the child for whom the support is being paid certainly have no takings claim, since it is clear that they have no protected property rights to continued benefits at the same level. Nor does the simple inclusion of the support income in the benefit calculation have any legal effect on the child's right to have it used for his or her benefit. To the extent that a child has the right to have the support payments used in his or her "best interest," he or she fully retains that right. Of course, the effect of counting the support payments as part of the filing unit's income often reduces the family's resources, and hence increases the chances that sharing of the support money will be appropriate. But given the unquestioned premise that the Government has a right to reduce AFDC benefits generally, that result does not constitute a taking of private property without just compensation.

The only possible legal basis for appellees' takings claim, therefore, is the requirement that an applicant for AFDC benefits must assign the support payments to the State, which then will remit the amount collected to the custodial parent to be used for the benefit of the entire family. This legal transformation in the status of the funds, the argument goes, modifies the child's interest in the use of the money so dramatically that it constitutes a taking of the child's property. As a practical matter, this argument places form over substance, and labels over reality. Although it is true that money which was earmarked for a specific child's or children's "best interest" becomes a part of a larger fund available for all of the children, the difference between these concepts is, as we have discussed, more theoretical than practical. [Note 20 points out that, in analyzing the effect of the assignment it is again instructive to ask what would happen to the support payments if there were no AFDC program at all. In that case, it would appear that custodial parents would have to use a much greater portion of the support payments to sustain the family unit, since it could hardly be deemed in the child's best interest for his custodial parent and siblings to have no funds whatsoever. The overall practical effect of the AFDC program (even after the1984 amendment), therefore, is to enhance the probability that a child whose custodial parent is receiving support payments in the child's behalf will obtain direct economic benefit from those funds, in addition to the benefits that result from preserving the family unit. A reduction in that enhancement is no more a taking than any other reduction in a Social Security program.]

In evaluating whether governmental regulation of property constitutes a "taking" we have "eschewed the development of any set formula . . . and have relied instead on ad hoc, factual inquiries into the circumstances of each particular case." "To aid in this determination, however, we have identified three factors which have 'particular significance': (1) 'the economic impact of the regulation on the claimant'; (2) 'the extent to which the regulation has interfered with distinct investment-backed expectations'; and (3) 'the character of the governmental action.'" Here, each of these three factors refutes the conclusion that there has been a taking.

First, in evaluating the economic impact of the assignment, it is important to remember that it is the impact on the child, not on the entire family unit, that is relevant. Thus, the fact that the entire family's net income may be reduced does not necessarily mean that the amount of money spent for the benefit of a supported child will be any less than the amount of the noncustodial parent's support payments. The reality is that the money will usually continue to be used in the same manner that it was previously since the typical AFDC parent will have used the support money as part of the general family fund even without its being transferred through AFDC. Moreover, any diminution in the value of the support payments for the child is mitigated by the extra $50 that the family receives as a result of the assignment, by the extra AFDC benefits that are received by the inclusion of an additional family member in the unit, and by the fact that the State is using its own enforcement power to collect the support payments, and is bearing the risk of nonpayment in any given month. Whatever the diminution in value of the child's right to have support funds used for his or her "exclusive" benefit may be, it is not so substantial as to constitute a taking under our precedents.

Second, the child receiving support payments holds no vested protectable expectation that his or her parent will continue to receive identical support payments on the child's behalf, and that the child will enjoy the same rights with respect to them. The prospective right to support payments, and the child's expectations with respect to the use of such funds, are clearly subject to modification by law, be it through judicial decree, state legislation, or congressional enactment. For example, one of the chief criteria in assessing a child support obligation is the noncustodial parent's ability to make payments, and an adverse change in that parent's ability may, of course, require a modification of the decree. Any right to have the State force a noncustodial parent to make payments is, like so many other legal rights (including AFDC payments themselves), subject to modification by "the public acts of government." As the District Court explained, Congress, and the States, through their implementing statutes and regulations, have modified those rights through passage of (and the States' compliance with) the DEFRA amendments. This prospective change in the child's expectations concerning future use of support payments is far from anything we have ever deemed a taking.

Finally, the character of the governmental action here militates against a finding that the States or Federal Government unconstitutionally take property through the AFDC program. It is obviously necessary for the Government to make hard choices and to balance various incentives in deciding how to allocate benefits in this type of program. But a decision to include child support as part of the family income certainly does not implicate the type of concerns that the Takings Clause protects. This is by no means an enactment that forces "some people alone to bear public burdens which, in all fairness and justice, should be borne by the public as a whole."

The law does not require any custodial parent to apply for AFDC benefits. Surely it is reasonable to presume that a parent who does make such an application does so because she or he is convinced that the family as a whole—as well as each child committed to her or his custody—will be better off with the benefits than without. In making such a decision, the parent is not taking a child's property without just compensation; nor is the State doing so when it responds to that decision by supplementing the collections of support money with additional AFDC benefits.

V

Writing for a unanimous Court, Justice Stewart described the courts' role in cases such as this:

> We do not decide today that the . . . regulation is wise, that it best fulfills the relevant social and economic objectives that [Congress] might ideally espouse, or that a more just and humane system could not be devised. Conflicting claims of morality and intelligence are raised by opponents and proponents of almost every measure, certainly including the one before us.

> But the intractable economic, social, and even philosophical problems presented by public welfare assistance programs are not the business of this Court. The Constitution may impose certain procedural safeguards upon systems of welfare administration. But the Constitution does not empower this Court to second-guess . . . officials charged with the difficult responsibility of allocating limited public welfare funds among the myriad of potential recipients.

The judgment of the District Court is

Reversed.

Justice Brennan, dissenting.

Government in the modern age has assumed increasing responsibility for the welfare of its citizens. This expansion of responsibility has been accompanied by an increase in the scale and complexity of the activities that government conducts. Respect for the enormity of the administrative task that confronts the modern welfare state, as well as for the scarcity of government resources, counsels that public officials enjoy discretion in determining the most effective means of fulfilling their responsibilities.

The very pervasiveness of modern government, however, creates an unparalleled opportunity for intrusion on personal life. In a society in which most persons receive some form of government benefit, government has considerable leverage in shaping individual behavior. In most cases, we acknowledge that government may wield its power even when its actions likely influence choices involving personal behavior. On certain occasions, however, government intrusion into private life is so direct and substantial that we must deem it intolerable if we are to be true to our belief that there is a boundary between the public citizen and the private person.

This is such a case. The Government has told a child who lives with a mother receiving public assistance that it cannot both live with its mother and be supported by its father. The child must either leave the care and custody of the mother, or forgo the support of the father and become a Government client. The child is put to this choice not because it seeks Government benefits for itself, but because of a fact over which it has no control: the need of other household members for public assistance. A child who lives with one parent has, under the best of circumstances, a difficult time sustaining a relationship with both its parents. A crucial bond between a child and its parent outside the home, usually the father, is the father's commitment to care for the material needs of the child, and the expectation of the child that it may look to its father for such care. The Government has thus decreed that a condition of welfare eligibility for a mother is that her child surrender a vital connection with either the father or the mother.

The Court holds that the Government need only show a rational basis for such action. This standard of review has regularly been used in evaluating the claims of applicants for Government benefits, since "a noncontractual claim to receive funds from the public treasury enjoys no constitutionally protected status." Plaintiff child support recipients in this case, however, are children who wish not to receive public assistance, but to continue to be supported by their noncustodial parent. Their claim is not that the Government has unfairly denied them benefits, but that it has intruded deeply into their relationship with their parents. More than a mere rational basis is required to withstand this challenge, and, as the following analysis shows, the Government can offer no adequate justification for doing such damage to the parent-child relationship.

. . .

Justice Blackmun, dissenting. [omitted]

Notes and Queries

1. The decision follows the rule that the government may attach conditions to the receipt of its benefits. The argument is that the state need not provide the benefit and that the recipient need not have to apply for the benefit. The assumption is that recipients voluntarily apply for the benefit. What arguments support this approach?

Harris v. McRae

448 U.S. 297; 100 S. Ct. 2671 (1980)

Mr. Justice Stewart delivered the opinion of the Court.

This case presents statutory and constitutional questions concerning the public funding of abortions under Title XIX of the Social Security Act, commonly known as the "Medicaid" Act, and recent annual Appropriation Acts containing the so-called "Hyde Amendment." The statutory question is whether Title XIX requires a State that participates in the Medicaid program to fund the cost of medically necessary abortions for which federal reimbursement is unavailable under the Hyde Amendment. The constitutional question, which arises only if Title XIX imposes no such requirement, is whether the Hyde Amendment, by denying public funding for certain medically necessary abortions, contravenes the liberty or equal protection guarantees of the Due Process Clause of the Fifth Amendment, or either of the Religion Clauses of the First Amendment.

I

The Medicaid program was created in 1965, when Congress added Title XIX to the Social Security Act, for the purpose of providing federal financial assistance to States that choose to reimburse certain costs of medical treatment for needy persons. Although participation in the Medicaid program is entirely optional, once a State elects to participate, it must comply with the requirements of Title XIX.

One such requirement is that a participating State agree to provide financial assistance to the "categorically needy" with respect to five general areas of medical treatment: (1) inpatient hospital services, (2) outpatient hospital services, (3) other laboratory and X-ray services, (4) skilled nursing facilities services, periodic screening and diagnosis of children, and family planning services, and (5) services of physicians. Although a participating State need not "provide funding for all medical treatment falling within the five general categories, [Title XIX] does require that [a] state Medicaid [plan] establish 'reasonable standards . . . for determining . . . the extent of medical assistance under the plan which . . . are consistent with the objectives of [Title XIX].'"

Since September 1976, Congress has prohibited—either by an amendment to the annual appropriations bill for the Department of Health, Education, and Welfare or by a joint resolution—the use of any federal funds to reimburse the cost of abortions under the Medicaid program except under certain specified circumstances. This funding restriction is commonly known as the "Hyde Amendment," after its original congressional sponsor, Representative Hyde. The current version of the Hyde Amendment, applicable for fiscal year 1980, provides:

> [None] of the funds provided by this joint resolution shall be used to perform abortions except where the life of the mother would be endangered if the fetus were carried to term; or except for such medical procedures necessary for the victims of rape or incest when such rape or incest has been reported promptly to a law enforcement agency or public health service.

This version of the Hyde Amendment is broader than that applicable for fiscal year 1977, which did not include the "rape or incest" exception but narrower than that applicable for most of fiscal year 1978, and all of fiscal year 1979, which had an additional exception for "instances where severe and long-lasting physical health damage to the mother would result if the pregnancy were carried to term when so determined by two physicians."

On September 30, 1976, the day on which Congress enacted the initial version of the Hyde Amendment, these consolidated cases were filed in the District Court for the Eastern District of New York. The plaintiffs—Cora McRae, a New York Medicaid recipient then in the first trimester of a pregnancy that she wished to terminate, the New York City Health and Hospitals Corp., a public benefit corporation that operates 16 hospitals, 12 of which provide abortion services, and others—sought to enjoin the enforcement of the funding restriction on abortions. They alleged that the Hyde Amendment violated the First, Fourth, Fifth, and Ninth Amendments of the Constitution insofar as it limited the funding of abortions to those necessary to save the life of the mother, while permitting the funding of costs associated with childbirth. Although the sole named defendant was the Secretary of Health, Education, and Welfare, the District Court permitted Senators James L. Buckley and Jesse A. Helms and Representative Henry J. Hyde to intervene as defendants.

. . .

After a lengthy trial, which inquired into the medical reasons for abortions and the diverse religious views on the subject, the District Court filed an opinion and entered a judgment invalidating all versions of the Hyde Amendment on constitutional grounds. The District Court rejected the plaintiffs' statutory argument, concluding that even though Title XIX would otherwise have required a participating State to fund medically necessary abortions, the Hyde Amendment had substantively amended Title XIX to relieve a State of that funding obligation. Turning then to the constitutional issues, the District Court concluded that the Hyde Amendment, though valid under the Establishment Clause, violates the equal protection component of the Fifth Amendment's Due Process Clause and the Free Exercise Clause of the First Amendment. With regard to the Fifth Amendment, the District Court noted that when an abortion is "medically necessary to safeguard the pregnant woman's health, . . . the disentitlement to [Medicaid] assistance impinges directly on the woman's right to decide, in consultation with her physician and in reliance on his judgment, to terminate her pregnancy in order to preserve her health." The court concluded that the Hyde Amendment violates the equal protection guarantee because, in its view, the decision of Congress to fund medically necessary services generally but only certain medically necessary abortions serves no legitimate governmental interest. As to the Free Exercise Clause of the First Amendment, the court held that insofar as a woman's decision to seek a medically necessary abortion may be a product of her religious beliefs under certain Protestant and Jewish tenets, the funding restrictions of the Hyde Amendment violate that constitutional guarantee as well.

Accordingly, the District Court ordered the Secretary to "[cease] to give effect" to the various versions of the Hyde Amendment insofar as they forbid payments for medically necessary abortions. It further directed the Secretary to "[continue] to authorize the expenditure of federal matching funds [for such abortions]." In addition, the court recertified the McRae case as a nationwide class action on behalf of all pregnant and potentially pregnant women eligible for Medicaid who wish to have medically necessary abortions, and of all authorized providers of abortions for such women.

The Secretary then applied to this Court for a stay of the judgment pending direct appeal of the District Court's decision. We denied the stay, but noted probable jurisdiction of this appeal.

II

It is well settled that if a case may be decided on either statutory or constitutional grounds, this Court, for sound jurisprudential reasons, will inquire first into the statutory question. This practice reflects the deeply rooted doctrine "that we ought not to pass on questions of constitutionality . . . unless such adjudication is unavoidable." Accordingly, we turn first to the question whether Title XIX requires a State that participates in the Medicaid program to continue to fund those medically necessary abortions for which federal reimbursement is unavailable under the Hyde Amendment. If a participating State is under such an obligation, the constitutionality of the

Hyde Amendment need not be drawn into question in the present case, for the availability of medically necessary abortions under Medicaid would continue, with the participating State shouldering the total cost of funding such abortions.

The appellees assert that a participating State has an independent funding obligation under Title XIX because (1) the Hyde Amendment is, by its own terms, only a limitation on federal reimbursement for certain medically necessary abortions, and (2) Title XIX does not permit a participating State to exclude from its Medicaid plan any medically necessary service solely on the basis of diagnosis or condition, even if federal reimbursement is unavailable for that service. It is thus the appellees' view that the effect of the Hyde Amendment is to withhold federal reimbursement for certain medically necessary abortions, but not to relieve a participating State of its duty under Title XIX to provide for such abortions in its Medicaid plan.

The District Court rejected this argument. It concluded that, although Title XIX would otherwise have required a participating State to include medically necessary abortions in its Medicaid program, the Hyde Amendment substantively amended Title XIX so as to relieve a State of that obligation. This construction of the Hyde Amendment was said to find support in the decisions of two Courts of Appeals and to be consistent with the understanding of the effect of the Hyde Amendment by the Department of Health, Education, and Welfare in the administration of the Medicaid program.

We agree with the District Court, but for somewhat different reasons. The Medicaid program created by Title XIX is a cooperative endeavor in which the Federal Government provides financial assistance to participating States to aid them in furnishing health care to needy persons. Under this system of "cooperative federalism," if a State agrees to establish a Medicaid plan that satisfies the requirements of Title XIX, which include several mandatory categories of health services, the Federal Government agrees to pay a specified percentage of "the total amount expended . . . as medical assistance under the State plan. . . ." The cornerstone of Medicaid is financial contribution by both the Federal Government and the participating State. Nothing in Title XIX as originally enacted, or in its legislative history, suggests that Congress intended to require a participating State to assume the full costs of providing any health services in its Medicaid plan. Quite the contrary, the purpose of Congress in enacting Title XIX was to provide federal financial assistance for all legitimate state expenditures under an approved Medicaid plan.

Since the Congress that enacted Title XIX did not intend a participating State to assume a unilateral funding obligation for any health service in an approved Medicaid plan, it follows that Title XIX does not require a participating State to include in its plan any services for which a subsequent Congress has withheld federal funding. Title XIX was designed as a cooperative program of shared financial responsibility, not as a device for the Federal Government to compel a State to provide services that Congress itself is unwilling to fund. Thus, if Congress chooses to withdraw federal funding for a particular service, a State is not obliged to continue to pay for that service as a condition of continued federal financial support of other services. This is not to say that

Congress may not now depart from the original design of Title XIX under which the Federal Government shares the financial responsibility for expenses incurred under an approved Medicaid plan. It is only to say that, absent an indication of contrary legislative intent by a subsequent Congress, Title XIX does not obligate a participating State to pay for those medical services for which federal reimbursement is unavailable.

Thus, by the normal operation of Title XIX, even if a State were otherwise required to include medically necessary abortions in its Medicaid plan, the withdrawal of federal funding under the Hyde Amendment would operate to relieve the State of that obligation for those abortions for which federal reimbursement is unavailable. The legislative history of the Hyde Amendment contains no indication whatsoever that Congress intended to shift the entire cost of such services to the participating States. Rather, the legislative history suggests that Congress has always assumed that a participating State would not be required to fund medically necessary abortions once federal funding was withdrawn pursuant to the Hyde Amendment. Accordingly, we conclude that Title XIX does not require a participating State to pay for those medically necessary abortions for which federal reimbursement is unavailable under the Hyde Amendment.

III

Having determined that Title XIX does not obligate a participating State to pay for those medically necessary abortions for which Congress has withheld federal funding, we must consider the constitutional validity of the Hyde Amendment. The appellees assert that the funding restrictions of the Hyde Amendment violate several rights secured by the Constitution — (1) the right of a woman, implicit in the Due Process Clause of the Fifth Amendment, to decide whether to terminate a pregnancy, (2) the prohibition under the Establishment Clause of the First Amendment against any "law respecting an establishment of religion," and (3) the right to freedom of religion protected by the Free Exercise Clause of the First Amendment. The appellees also contend that, quite apart from substantive constitutional rights, the Hyde Amendment violates the equal protection component of the Fifth Amendment.

It is well settled that, quite apart from the guarantee of equal protection, if a law "impinges upon a fundamental right explicitly or implicitly secured by the Constitution [it] is presumptively unconstitutional." Accordingly, before turning to the equal protection issue in this case, we examine whether the Hyde Amendment violates any substantive rights secured by the Constitution.

A

We address first the appellees' argument that the Hyde Amendment, by restricting the availability of certain medically necessary abortions under Medicaid, impinges on the "liberty" protected by the Due Process Clause as recognized in *Roe v. Wade* and its progeny.

. . .

It is evident that a woman's interest in protecting her health was an important theme in *Wade*. In concluding that the freedom of a woman to decide whether to terminate her pregnancy falls within the personal liberty protected by the Due Process Clause, the Court in *Wade* emphasized the fact that the woman's decision carries with it significant personal health implications — both physical and psychological. In fact, although the Court in *Wade* recognized that the state interest in protecting potential life becomes sufficiently compelling in the period after fetal viability to justify an absolute criminal prohibition of nontherapeutic abortions, the Court held that even after fetal viability a State may not prohibit abortions "necessary to preserve the life or health of the mother." Because even the compelling interest of the State in protecting potential life after fetal viability was held to be insufficient to outweigh a woman's decision to protect her life or health, it could be argued that the freedom of a woman to decide whether to terminate her pregnancy for health reasons does in fact lie at the core of the constitutional liberty identified in *Wade*.

But, regardless of whether the freedom of a woman to choose to terminate her pregnancy for health reasons lies at the core or the periphery of the due process liberty recognized in *Wade*, it simply does not follow that a woman's freedom of choice carries with it a constitutional entitlement to the financial resources to avail herself of the full range of protected choices. The reason why was explained in *Maher*: although government may not place obstacles in the path of a woman's exercise of her freedom of choice, it need not remove those not of its own creation. Indigency falls in the latter category. The financial constraints that restrict an indigent woman's ability to enjoy the full range of constitutionally protected freedom of choice are the product not of governmental restrictions on access to abortions, but rather of her indigency. Although Congress has opted to subsidize medically necessary services generally, but not certain medically necessary abortions, the fact remains that the Hyde Amendment leaves an indigent woman with at least the same range of choice in deciding whether to obtain a medically necessary abortion as she would have had if Congress had chosen to subsidize no health care costs at all. We are thus not persuaded that the Hyde Amendment impinges on the constitutionally protected freedom of choice recognized in Wade.

Although the liberty protected by the Due Process Clause affords protection against unwarranted government interference with freedom of choice in the context of certain personal decisions, it does not confer an entitlement to such funds as may be necessary to realize all the advantages of that freedom. To hold otherwise would mark a drastic change in our understanding of the Constitution. It cannot be that because government may not prohibit the use of contraceptives or prevent parents from sending their child to a private school, government, therefore, has an affirmative constitutional obligation to ensure that all persons have the financial resources to obtain contraceptives or send their children to private schools. To translate the limitation on governmental power implicit in the Due Process Clause into an affirmative funding obligation would require Congress to subsidize the medically necessary abortion of an indigent woman even if Congress had not enacted a Medicaid program to subsidize other medically necessary services. Nothing in the Due Process Clause supports such an extraordinary result. Whether freedom of choice that is constitutionally protected warrants federal subsidization is a question for Congress to answer, not a matter of constitutional entitlement. Accordingly, we conclude that the Hyde Amendment does not impinge on the due process liberty recognized in *Wade*.

B

The appellees also argue that the Hyde Amendment contravenes rights secured by the Religion Clauses of the First Amendment. It is the appellees' view that the Hyde Amendment violates the Establishment Clause because it incorporates into law the doctrines of the Roman Catholic Church concerning the sinfulness of abortion and the time at which life commences. Moreover, insofar as a woman's decision to seek a medically necessary abortion may be a product of her religious beliefs under certain Protestant and Jewish tenets, the appellees assert that the funding limitations of the Hyde Amendment impinge on the freedom of religion guaranteed by the Free Exercise Clause.

1

It is well settled that "a legislative enactment does not contravene the Establishment Clause if it has a secular legislative purpose, if its principal or primary effect neither advances nor inhibits religion, and if it does not foster an excessive governmental entanglement with religion." Applying this standard, the District Court properly concluded that the Hyde Amendment does not run afoul of the Establishment Clause. Although neither a State nor the Federal Government can constitutionally "pass laws which aid one religion, aid all religions, or prefer one religion over another," it does not follow that a statute violates the Establishment Clause because it "happens to coincide or harmonize with the tenets of some or all religions." That the Judaeo-Christian religions oppose stealing does not mean that a State or the Federal Government may not, consistent with the Establishment Clause, enact laws prohibiting larceny. The Hyde Amendment, as the District Court noted, is as much a reflection of "traditionalist" values towards abortion, as it is an embodiment of the views of any particular religion. In sum, we are convinced that the fact that the funding restrictions in the Hyde Amendment may coincide with the religious tenets of the Roman Catholic Church does not, without more, contravene the Establishment Clause.

2

We need not address the merits of the appellees' arguments concerning the Free Exercise Clause, because the appellees lack standing to raise a free exercise challenge to the Hyde Amendment. The named appellees fall into three categories: (1) the indigent pregnant women who sued on behalf of other women similarly situated, (2) the two officers of the Women's Division, and (3) the Women's Division itself. The named appellees in the first category lack standing to challenge the Hyde Amendment on free exercise grounds because none alleged, much less proved, that she sought an abortion under compulsion of religious belief. Although the named appellees in the second category did provide a detailed description of their religious beliefs, they failed to allege either that they are or expect to be pregnant or that they are eligible to receive Medicaid. These named appellees, therefore, lack the personal stake in the controversy needed to confer standing to raise such a challenge to the Hyde Amendment.

Finally, although the Women's Division alleged that its membership includes "pregnant Medicaid eligible women who, as a matter of religious practice and in accordance with their conscientious beliefs, would choose but are precluded or discouraged from obtaining abortions reimbursed by Medicaid because of the Hyde Amendment," the Women's Division does not satisfy the standing requirements for an organization to assert the rights of its membership. One of those requirements is that "neither the claim asserted nor the relief requested requires the participation of individual members in the lawsuit." Since "it is necessary in a free exercise case for one to show the coercive effect of the enactment as it operates against him in the practice of his religion," the claim asserted here is one that ordinarily requires individual participation. In the present case, the Women's Division concedes that "the permissibility, advisability and/or necessity of abortion according to circumstance is a matter about which there is diversity of view within ... our membership, and is a determination which must be ultimately and absolutely entrusted to the conscience of the individual before God." It is thus clear that the participation of individual members of the Women's Division is essential to a proper understanding and resolution of their free exercise claims. Accordingly, we conclude that the Women's Division, along with the other named appellees, lack standing to challenge the Hyde Amendment under the Free Exercise Clause.

C

It remains to be determined whether the Hyde Amendment violates the equal protection component of the Fifth Amendment. This challenge is premised on the fact that, although federal reimbursement is available under Medicaid for medically necessary services generally, the Hyde Amendment does not permit federal reimbursement of all medically necessary abortions. The District Court held, and the appellees argue here, that this selective subsidization violates the constitutional guarantee of equal protection.

The guarantee of equal protection under the Fifth Amendment is not a source of substantive rights or liberties, but rather a right to be free from invidious discrimination in statutory classifications and other governmental activity. It is well settled that where a statutory classification does not itself impinge on a right or liberty protected by the Constitution, the validity of classification must be sustained unless "the classification rests on grounds wholly irrelevant to the achievement of [any legitimate governmental] objective." This presumption of constitutional validity, however, disappears if a statutory classification is predicated on criteria that are, in a constitutional sense, "suspect," the principal example of which is a classification based on race.

1

For the reasons stated above, we have already concluded that the Hyde Amendment violates no constitutionally protected substantive rights. We now conclude as well that it is not predicated on a constitutionally suspect classification. In reaching this conclusion, we again draw guidance from the Court's decision in *Maher v. Roe*. As to whether the Connecticut welfare regulation providing funds for childbirth but not for nontherapeutic abortions discriminated against a suspect class, the Court in *Maher* observed:

> An indigent woman desiring an abortion does not come within the limited category of disadvantaged classes so recognized by our cases. Nor does the fact that the impact of the regulation falls upon those who cannot pay lead to a different conclusion. In a sense, every denial of welfare to an indigent creates a wealth classification as compared to nonindigents who are able to pay for the desired goods or services. But this Court has never held that financial need alone identifies a suspect class for purposes of equal protection analysis.

Thus, the Court in *Maher* found no basis for concluding that the Connecticut regulation was predicated on a suspect classification.

It is our view that the present case is indistinguishable from *Maher* in this respect. Here, as in *Maher*, the principal impact of the Hyde Amendment falls on the indigent. But that fact does not itself render the funding restriction constitutionally invalid, for this Court has held repeatedly that poverty, standing alone, is not a suspect classification. That *Maher* involved the refusal to fund nontherapeutic abortions, whereas the present case involves the refusal to fund medically necessary abortions, has no bearing on the factors that render a classification "suspect" within the meaning of the constitutional guarantee of equal protection.

The remaining question then is whether the Hyde Amendment is rationally related to a legitimate governmental objective. It is the Government's position that the Hyde Amendment bears a rational relationship to its legitimate interest in protecting the potential life of the fetus. We agree.

In *Wade*, the Court recognized that the State has an "important and legitimate interest in protecting the potentiality of human life." That interest was found to exist throughout a pregnancy, "[growing] in substantiality as the woman approaches term." Moreover, in *Maher*, the Court held that Connecticut's decision to fund the costs associated with childbirth but not those associated with nontherapeutic abortions was a rational means of advancing the legitimate state interest in protecting potential life by encouraging childbirth.

It follows that the Hyde Amendment, by encouraging childbirth except in the most urgent circumstances, is rationally related to the legitimate governmental objective of protecting potential life. By subsidizing the medical expenses of indigent women who carry their pregnancies to term while not subsidizing the comparable expenses of women who undergo abortions (except those whose lives are threatened), Congress has established incentives that make childbirth a more attractive alternative than abortion for persons eligible for Medicaid. These incentives bear a direct relationship to the legitimate congressional interest in protecting potential life. Nor is it irrational that Congress has authorized federal reimbursement for medically necessary services generally, but not for certain medically necessary abortions. Abortion is inherently different from other medical procedures, because no other procedure involves the purposeful termination of a potential life.

After conducting an extensive evidentiary hearing into issues surrounding the public funding of abortions, the District Court concluded that "[the] interests of . . . the federal government . . . in the fetus and in preserving it are not sufficient, weighed in the balance with the woman's threatened health, to justify withdrawing medical assistance unless the woman consents . . . to carry the fetus to term." In making an independent appraisal of the competing interests involved here, the District Court went beyond the judicial function. Such decisions are entrusted under the Constitution to Congress, not the courts. It is the role of the courts only to ensure that congressional decisions comport with the Constitution.

Where, as here, the Congress has neither invaded a substantive constitutional right or freedom, nor enacted legislation that purposefully operates to the detriment of a suspect class, the only requirement of equal protection is that congressional action be rationally related to a legitimate governmental interest. The Hyde Amendment satisfies that standard. It is not the mission of this Court or any other to decide whether the balance of competing interests reflected in the Hyde Amendment is wise social policy. If that were our mission, not every Justice who has subscribed to the judgment of the Court today could have done so. But we cannot, in the name of the Constitution, overturn duly enacted statutes simply "because they may be unwise, improvident, or out of harmony with a particular school of thought." Rather, "when an issue involves policy choices as sensitive as those implicated [here] . . . , the appropriate forum for their resolution in a democracy is the legislature."

IV

For the reasons stated in this opinion, we hold that a State that participates in the Medicaid program is not obligated under Title XIX to continue to fund those medically necessary abortions for which federal reimbursement is unavailable under the Hyde Amendment. We further hold that the funding restrictions of the Hyde Amendment violate neither the Fifth Amendment nor the Establishment Clause of the First Amendment. It is also our view that the appellees lack standing to raise a challenge to the Hyde Amendment under the Free Exercise Clause of the First Amendment. Accordingly, the judgment of the District Court is reversed, and the case is remanded to that court for further proceedings consistent with this opinion.

It is so ordered.

Mr. Justice White, concurring. [omitted]

Mr. Justice Brennan, dissenting.

I agree entirely with my Brother Stevens that the State's interest in protecting the potential life of the fetus cannot justify the exclusion of financially and medically needy women from the benefits to which they would otherwise be entitled solely because the treatment that a doctor has concluded is medically necessary involves an abortion. I write separately to express my continuing disagreement with the Court's mischaracterization of the nature of the fundamental right recognized in *Roe v. Wade*, and its misconception of the manner in which that right is infringed by federal and state legislation withdrawing all funding for medically necessary abortions.

. . .

Mr. Justice Marshall, dissenting.

Three years ago, in *Maher v. Roe*, the Court upheld a state program that excluded nontherapeutic abortions from a welfare program that generally subsidized the medical expenses incidental to pregnancy and childbirth. At that time, I expressed my fear "that the Court's decisions will be an invitation to public officials, already under extraordinary pressure from well-financed and carefully orchestrated lobbying campaigns, to approve more such restrictions" on governmental funding for abortion.

That fear has proved justified. Under the Hyde Amendment, federal funding is denied for abortions that are medically necessary and that are necessary to avert severe and permanent damage to the health of the mother. The Court's opinion studiously avoids recognizing the undeniable fact that for women eligible for Medicaid—poor women—denial of a Medicaid-funded abortion is equivalent to denial of legal abortion altogether. By definition, these women do not have the money to pay for an abortion themselves. If abortion is medically necessary and a funded abortion is unavailable, they must resort to back-alley butchers, attempt to induce an abortion themselves by crude and dangerous methods, or suffer the serious medical consequences of attempting to carry the fetus to term. Because legal abortion is not a realistic option for such women, the predictable result of the Hyde Amendment will be a significant increase in the number of poor women who will die or suffer significant health damage because of an inability to procure necessary medical services.

The legislation before us is the product of an effort to deny to the poor the constitutional right recognized in *Roe v. Wade* even though the cost may be serious and long-lasting health damage. As my Brother Stevens has demonstrated, the premise underlying the Hyde Amendment was repudiated in *Roe v. Wade*, where the Court made clear that the state interest in protecting fetal life cannot justify jeopardizing the life or health of the mother. The denial of Medicaid benefits to individuals who meet all the statutory criteria for eligibility, solely because the treatment that is medically necessary involves the exercise of the fundamental right to chose abortion, is a form of discrimination repugnant to the equal protection of the laws guaranteed by the Constitution. The Court's decision today marks a retreat from *Roe v. Wade* and represents a cruel blow to the most powerless members of our society. I dissent.

. . .

Mr. Justice Blackmun, dissenting.

I join the dissent of Mr. Justice Brennan and agree wholeheartedly with his and Mr. Justice Stevens' respective observations and descriptions of what the Court is doing in this latest round of "abortion cases." ... There is "condescension" in the Court's holding that "she may go elsewhere for her abortion"; this is "disingenuous and alarming"; the Government "punitively impresses upon a needy minority its own concepts of the socially desirable, the publicly acceptable, and the morally sound"; the "financial argument, of course, is specious"; there truly is "another world 'out there,' the existence of which the Court, I suspect, either chooses to ignore or fears to recognize"; the "cancer of poverty will continue to grow"; and "the lot of the poorest among us," once again, and still, is not to be bettered.

Mr. Justice Stevens, dissenting.

"The federal sovereign, like the States, must govern impartially. The concept of equal justice under law is served by the Fifth Amendment's guarantee of due process, as well as by the Equal Protection Clause of the Fourteenth Amendment." When the sovereign provides a special benefit or a special protection for a class of persons, it must define the membership in the class by neutral criteria; it may not make special exceptions for reasons that are constitutionally insufficient.

These cases involve the pool of benefits that Congress created by enacting Title XIX of the Social Security Act in 1965. Individuals who satisfy two neutral statutory criteria — financial need and medical need — are entitled to equal access to that pool. The question is whether certain persons who satisfy those criteria may be denied access to benefits solely because they must exercise the constitutional right to have an abortion in order to obtain the medical care they need. Our prior cases plainly dictate the answer to that question.

A fundamentally different question was decided in *Maher v. Roe*. Unlike these plaintiffs, the plaintiffs in *Maher* did not satisfy the neutral criterion of medical need; they sought a subsidy for nontherapeutic abortions — medical procedures which by definition they did not need. In rejecting that claim, the Court held that their constitutional right to choose that procedure did not impose a duty on the State to subsidize the exercise of that right. Nor did the fact that the State had undertaken to pay for the necessary medical care associated with childbirth require the State also to pay for abortions that were not necessary; for only necessary medical procedures satisfied the neutral statutory criteria. Nontherapeutic abortions were simply outside the ambit of the medical benefits program. Thus, in *Maher*, the plaintiffs' desire to exercise a constitutional right gave rise to neither special access nor special exclusion from the pool of benefits created by Title XIX.

These cases involve a special exclusion of women who, by definition, are confronted with a choice between two serious harms: serious health damage to themselves on the one hand and abortion on the other. The competing interests are the interest in maternal health and the interest in protecting potential human life. It is now part of our law that the pregnant woman's decision as to which of these conflicting interests shall prevail is entitled to constitutional protection.

. . .

If a woman has a constitutional right to place a higher value on avoiding either serious harm to her own health or perhaps an abnormal childbirth than on protecting potential life, the exercise of that right cannot provide the basis for the denial of a benefit to which she would otherwise be entitled. The Court's sterile equal protection analysis evades this critical though simple point. The Court focuses exclusively on the "legitimate interest in protecting the potential life of the fetus." It concludes that since the Hyde Amendments further that interest, the exclusion they create is rational and therefore constitutional. But it is misleading to speak of the Government's legitimate interest in the fetus without reference to the context in which that interest was held to be legitimate. For *Roe v. Wade* squarely held that the States may not protect that interest when a conflict with the interest in a pregnant woman's health exists. It is thus perfectly clear that neither the Federal Government nor the States may exclude a woman from medical benefits to which she would otherwise be entitled solely to further an interest in potential life when a physician, "in appropriate medical judgment," certifies that an abortion is necessary "for the preservation of the life or health of the mother." The Court totally fails to explain why this reasoning is not dispositive here.

It cannot be denied that the harm inflicted upon women in the excluded class is grievous. As the Court's comparison of the differing forms of the Hyde Amendment that have been enacted since 1976 demonstrates, the Court expressly approves the exclusion of benefits in "instances where severe and long-lasting physical health damage to the mother" is the predictable consequence of carrying the pregnancy to term. Indeed, as the Solicitor General acknowledged with commendable candor, the logic of the Court's position would justify a holding that it would be constitutional to deny funding to a medically and financially needy person even if abortion were the only lifesaving medical procedure available. Because a denial of benefits for medically necessary abortions inevitably causes serious harm to the excluded women, it is tantamount to severe punishment. In my judgment, that denial cannot be justified unless government may, in effect, punish women who want abortions. But as the Court unequivocally held in *Roe v. Wade*, this the government may not do.

Nor can it be argued that the exclusion of this type of medically necessary treatment of the indigent can be justified on fiscal grounds. There are some especially costly forms of treatment that may reasonably be excluded from the program in order to preserve the assets in the pool and extend its benefits to the maximum number of needy persons. Fiscal considerations may compel certain difficult choices in order to improve the protection afforded to the entire benefited class. But, ironically, the exclusion of medically necessary abortions harms the entire class as well as its specific victims. For the records in both *McRae* and *Zbaraz* demonstrate that the cost of an abortion is only a small fraction of the costs associated with childbirth. Thus, the decision to tolerate harm to indigent persons who need an abortion in order to avoid "serious and long-lasting health damage" is one that is financed by draining money out of the pool that is used to fund all other necessary medical procedures. Unlike most invidious classifications, this discrimination harms not only its direct victims but also the remainder of the class of needy persons that the pool was designed to benefit.

In *Maher* the Court stated:

> The Constitution imposes no obligation on the States to pay the pregnancy-related medical expenses of indigent women, or indeed to pay any of the medical expenses of indigents. But when a State decides to alleviate some of the hardships of poverty by providing medical care, the manner in which it dispenses benefits is subject to constitutional limitations.

Having decided to alleviate some of the hardships of poverty by providing necessary medical care, the government must use neutral criteria in distributing benefits. It may not deny benefits to a financially and medically needy person simply because he is a Republican, a Catholic, or an Oriental—or because he has spoken against a program the government has a legitimate interest in furthering. In sum, it may not create exceptions for the sole purpose of furthering a governmental interest that is constitutionally subordinate to the individual interest that the entire program was designed to protect. The Hyde Amendments not only exclude financially and medically needy persons from the pool of benefits for a constitutionally insufficient reason; they also require the expenditure of millions and millions of dollars in order to thwart the exercise of a constitutional right, thereby effectively inflicting serious and long-lasting harm on impoverished women who want and need abortions for valid medical reasons. In my judgment, these Amendments constitute an unjustifiable, and indeed blatant, violation of the sovereign's duty to govern impartially.

I respectfully dissent.

Notes and Queries

1. Under *McRae*'s ruling, states do not violate a woman's reproductive rights when it favors childbirth over abortion to the extent that it can subsidize the former and not the latter. The Court essentially finds that the government has no duty to remove the obstacle of poverty it did not create. Do you agree that the government did not create obstacles to the extent that it did not take action? Does the state create obstacles through its inaction?

2. The Court refuses to apply heightened scrutiny of the class of poor women affected by the statute. On what basis does it support this claim?

3. Assume that, as an empirical matter, it could be shown that the Hyde Amendment resulted in the denial of abortions to poor women. What would you make of that finding? The legislators obviously sought to deter poor women from obtaining abortions, correct? If that is the case, then does the legislation seem suspect? Would you have expected a different outcome based on *U.S. v. Moreno* and its progeny? How do you distinguish these cases?

United States v. Morrison

529 U.S. 598; 120 S. Ct. 1740 (2000)

Chief Justice Rehnquist delivered the opinion of the Court.

...

Petitioner Christy Brzonkala enrolled at Virginia Polytechnic Institute (Virginia Tech) in the fall of 1994. In September of that year, Brzonkala met respondents Antonio Morrison and James Crawford, who were both students at Virginia Tech and members of its varsity football team. Brzonkala alleges that, within 30 minutes of meeting Morrison and Crawford, they assaulted and repeatedly raped her. After the attack, Morrison allegedly told Brzonkala, "You better not have any ... diseases." In the months following the rape, Morrison also allegedly announced in the dormitory's dining room that he "liked" to get girls drunk and. ..." The omitted portions, quoted verbatim in the briefs on file with this Court, consist of boasting, debased remarks about what Morrison would do to women, vulgar remarks that cannot fail to shock and offend.

Brzonkala alleges that this attack caused her to become severely emotionally disturbed and depressed. She sought assistance from a university psychiatrist, who prescribed antidepressant medication. Shortly after the rape Brzonkala stopped attending classes and withdrew from the university.

In early 1995, Brzonkala filed a complaint against respondents under Virginia Tech's Sexual Assault Policy. During the school-conducted hearing on her complaint, Morrison admitted having sexual contact with her despite the fact that she had twice told him "no." After the hearing, Virginia Tech's Judicial Committee found insufficient evidence to punish Crawford, but found Morrison guilty of sexual assault and sentenced him to immediate suspension for two semesters.

Virginia Tech's dean of students upheld the judicial committee's sentence. However, in July 1995, Virginia Tech informed Brzonkala that Morrison intended to initiate a court challenge to his conviction under the Sexual Assault Policy. University officials told her that a second hearing would be necessary to remedy the school's error in prosecuting her complaint under that policy, which had not been widely circulated to students. The university therefore conducted a second hearing under its Abusive Conduct Policy, which was in force prior to the dissemination of the Sexual Assault Policy. Following this second hearing the Judicial Committee again found Morrison guilty and sentenced him to an identical 2-semester suspension. This time, however, the description of Morrison's offense was, without explanation, changed from "sexual assault" to "using abusive language."

Morrison appealed his second conviction through the university's administrative system. On August 21, 1995, Virginia Tech's senior vice president and provost set aside Morrison's punishment. She concluded that it was "'excessive when compared with other cases where there has been a finding of violation of the Abusive Conduct Policy.'" Virginia Tech did not inform Brzonkala of this decision. After learning from a newspaper that Morrison would be returning to Virginia Tech for the fall 1995 semester, she dropped out of the university.

In December 1995, Brzonkala sued Morrison, Crawford, and Virginia Tech in the United States District Court for the Western District of Virginia. Her complaint alleged that Morrison's and Crawford's attack violated § 13981 and that Virginia Tech's handling of her complaint violated Title IX of the Education Amendments of 1972. Morrison and Crawford moved to dismiss this complaint on the grounds that it failed to state a claim and that § 13981's civil remedy is unconstitutional. The United States, petitioner in No. 99-5, intervened to defend § 13981's constitutionality.

The District Court dismissed Brzonkala's Title IX claims against Virginia Tech for failure to state a claim upon which relief can be granted. It then held that Brzonkala's complaint stated a claim against Morrison and Crawford under § 13981, but dismissed the complaint because it concluded that Congress lacked authority to enact the section under either the Commerce Clause or § 5 of the Fourteenth Amendment.

A divided panel of the Court of Appeals reversed the District Court, reinstating Brzonkala's § 13981 claim.... The full Court of Appeals vacated the panel's opinion and reheard the case en banc. The en banc court then issued an opinion affirming the District Court's conclusion that Brzonkala stated a claim under § 13981 because her complaint alleged a crime of violence and the allegations of Morrison's crude and derogatory statements regarding his treatment of women sufficiently indicated that his crime was motivated by gender animus. Nevertheless, the court by a divided vote affirmed the District Court's conclusion that Congress lacked constitutional authority to enact § 13981's civil remedy. Because the Court of Appeals invalidated a federal statute on constitutional grounds, we granted certiorari.

Section 13981 was part of the Violence Against Women Act of 1994. It states that "persons within the United States shall have the right to be free from crimes of violence motivated by gender." To enforce that right, subsection (c)) declares:

> A person (including a person who acts under color of any statute, ordinance, regulation, custom, or usage of any State) who commits a crime of violence motivated by gender and thus deprives another of the right declared in subsection (b) of this section shall be liable to the party injured, in an action for the recovery of compensatory and punitive damages, injunctive and declaratory relief, and such other relief as a court may deem appropriate.

Section 13981 defines a "crime" of violence motivated by "gender" as "a crime of violence committed because of gender or on the basis of gender, and due, at least in part, to an animus based on the victim's gender." It also provides that the term "crime of violence" includes any

> (A) . . . act or series of acts that would constitute a felony against the person or that would constitute a felony against property if the conduct presents a serious risk of physical injury to another, and that would come within the meaning of State or Federal offenses described in section 16 of Title 18, whether or not those acts have actually resulted in criminal charges, prosecution, or conviction and whether or not those acts were committed in the special maritime, territorial, or prison jurisdiction of the United States; and
>
> (B) includes an act or series of acts that would constitute a felony described in subparagraph (A) but for the relationship between the person who takes such action and the individual against whom such action is taken.

Further clarifying the broad scope of § 13981's civil remedy, subsection (e)(2) states that "[n]othing in this section requires a prior criminal complaint, prosecution, or conviction to establish the elements of a cause of action under subsection (c)) of this section." And subsection (e)(3) provides a § 13981 litigant with a choice of forums: Federal and state courts "shall have concurrent jurisdiction" over complaints brought under the section.

Although the foregoing language of § 13981 covers a wide swath of criminal conduct, Congress placed some limitations on the section's federal civil remedy. Subsection (e)(1) states that "[n]othing in this section entitles a person to a cause of action under subsection (c)) of this section for random acts of violence unrelated to gender or for acts that cannot be demonstrated, by a preponderance of the evidence, to be motivated by gender." Subsection (e)(4) further states that § 13981 shall not be construed "to confer on the courts of the United States jurisdiction over any State law claim seeking the establishment of a divorce, alimony, equitable distribution of marital property, or child custody decree."

Every law enacted by Congress must be based on one or more of its powers enumerated in the Constitution. . . . Congress explicitly identified the sources of federal authority on which it relied in enacting § 13981. It said that a "federal civil rights cause of action" is established "pursuant to the affirmative power of Congress . . . under section 5 of the Fourteenth Amendment to the Constitution, as well as under section 8 of Article I of the Constitution." We address Congress' authority to enact this remedy under each of these constitutional provisions in turn.

II

Due respect for the decisions of a coordinate branch of Government demands that we invalidate a congressional enactment only upon a plain showing that Congress has exceeded its constitutional bounds. With this presumption of constitutionality in mind, we turn to the question whether § 13981 falls within Congress' power under

Article I, § 8, of the Constitution. Brzonkala and the United States rely upon the third clause of the Article, which gives Congress power "to regulate Commerce with foreign Nations, and among the several States, and with the Indian Tribes."

As we discussed at length in *Lopez*, our interpretation of the Commerce Clause has changed as our Nation has developed....

As we observed in *Lopez*, modern Commerce Clause jurisprudence has "identified three broad categories of activity that Congress may regulate under its commerce power." "First, Congress may regulate the use of the channels of interstate commerce." "Second, Congress is empowered to regulate and protect the instrumentalities of interstate commerce, or persons or things in interstate commerce, even though the threat may come only from intrastate activities." "Finally, Congress' commerce authority includes the power to regulate those activities having a substantial relation to interstate commerce ... i.e., those activities that substantially affect interstate commerce."

Petitioners do not contend that these cases fall within either of the first two of these categories of Commerce Clause regulation. They seek to sustain § 13981 as a regulation of activity that substantially affects interstate commerce. Given § 13981's focus on gender-motivated violence wherever it occurs (rather than violence directed at the instrumentalities of interstate commerce, interstate markets, or things or persons in interstate commerce), we agree that this is the proper inquiry.

Since *Lopez* most recently canvassed and clarified our case law governing this third category of Commerce Clause regulation, it provides the proper framework for conducting the required analysis of § 13981. In *Lopez*, we held that the Gun-Free School Zones Act of 1990, which made it a federal crime to knowingly possess a firearm in a school zone, exceeded Congress' authority under the Commerce Clause. Several significant considerations contributed to our decision.

First, we observed that § 922(q) [of the statute] was "a criminal statute that by its terms has nothing to do with 'commerce' or any sort of economic enterprise, however broadly one might define those terms." ...

...

The second consideration that we found important in analyzing § 922(q) was that the statute contained "no express jurisdictional element which might limit its reach to a discrete set of firearm possessions that additionally have an explicit connection with or effect on interstate commerce." Such a jurisdictional element may establish that the enactment is in pursuance of Congress' regulation of interstate commerce.

Third, we noted that neither § 922(q) "'nor its legislative history contains express congressional findings regarding the effects upon interstate commerce of gun possession in a school zone.'" While "Congress normally is not required to make formal findings as to the substantial burdens that an activity has on interstate commerce," the existence of such findings may "enable us to evaluate the legislative judgment that the activity in question substantially affects interstate commerce, even though no such substantial effect [is] visible to the naked eye."

Finally, our decision in *Lopez* rested in part on the fact that the link between gun possession and a substantial effect on interstate commerce was attenuated. The United States argued that the possession of guns may lead to violent crime, and that violent crime "can be expected to affect the functioning of the national economy in two ways. First, the costs of violent crime are substantial, and, through the mechanism of insurance, those costs are spread throughout the population. Second, violent crime reduces the willingness of individuals to travel to areas within the country that are perceived to be unsafe." The Government also argued that the presence of guns at schools poses a threat to the educational process, which in turn threatens to produce a less efficient and productive workforce, which will negatively affect national productivity and thus interstate commerce. We rejected these "costs of crime" and "national productivity" arguments because they would permit Congress to "regulate not only all violent crime, but all activities that might lead to violent crime, regardless of how tenuously they relate to interstate commerce." . . .

With these principles underlying our Commerce Clause jurisprudence as reference points, the proper resolution of the present cases is clear. Gender-motivated crimes of violence are not, in any sense of the phrase, economic activity. While we need not adopt a categorical rule against aggregating the effects of any noneconomic activity in order to decide these cases, thus far in our Nation's history our cases have upheld Commerce Clause regulation of intrastate activity only where that activity is economic in nature.

. . .

In contrast with the lack of congressional findings that we faced in *Lopez*, § 13981 is supported by numerous findings regarding the serious impact that gender-motivated violence has on victims and their families. But the existence of congressional findings is not sufficient, by itself, to sustain the constitutionality of Commerce Clause legislation. As we stated in *Lopez*, "'Simply because Congress may conclude that a particular activity substantially affects interstate commerce does not necessarily make it so.'" Rather, "'whether particular operations affect interstate commerce sufficiently to come under the constitutional power of Congress to regulate them is ultimately a judicial rather than a legislative question, and can be settled finally only by this Court.'"

In these cases, Congress' findings are substantially weakened by the fact that they rely so heavily on a method of reasoning that we have already rejected as unworkable if we are to maintain the Constitution's enumeration of powers. Congress found that gender-motivated violence affects interstate commerce

> by deterring potential victims from traveling interstate, from engaging in employment in interstate business, and from transacting with business, and in places involved in interstate commerce; . . . by diminishing national

> productivity, increasing medical and other costs, and decreasing the supply of and the demand for interstate products.

Given these findings and petitioners' arguments, the concern that we expressed in *Lopez* that Congress might use the Commerce Clause to completely obliterate the Constitution's distinction between national and local authority seems well founded.... If accepted, petitioners' reasoning would allow Congress to regulate any crime as long as the nationwide, aggregated impact of that crime has substantial effects on employment, production, transit, or consumption. Indeed, if Congress may regulate gender-motivated violence, it would be able to regulate murder or any other type of violence since gender-motivated violence, as a subset of all violent crime, is certain to have lesser economic impacts than the larger class of which it is a part.

Petitioners' reasoning, moreover, will not limit Congress to regulating violence but may, as we suggested in *Lopez*, be applied equally as well to family law and other areas of traditional state regulation since the aggregate effect of marriage, divorce, and childrearing on the national economy is undoubtedly significant. Congress may have recognized this specter when it expressly precluded § 13981 from being used in the family law context. Under our written Constitution, however, the limitation of congressional authority is not solely a matter of legislative grace.

We accordingly reject the argument that Congress may regulate noneconomic, violent criminal conduct based solely on that conduct's aggregate effect on interstate commerce. The Constitution requires a distinction between what is truly national and what is truly local. In recognizing this fact we preserve one of the few principles that has been consistent since the Clause was adopted. The regulation and punishment of intrastate violence that is not directed at the instrumentalities, channels, or goods involved in interstate commerce has always been the province of the States. Indeed, we can think of no better example of the police power, which the Founders denied the National Government and reposed in the States, than the suppression of violent crime and vindication of its victims.

III

Because we conclude that the Commerce Clause does not provide Congress with authority to enact § 13981, we address petitioners' alternative argument that the section's civil remedy should be upheld as an exercise of Congress' remedial power under § 5 of the Fourteenth Amendment. As noted above, Congress expressly invoked the Fourteenth Amendment as a source of authority to enact § 13981.

The principles governing an analysis of congressional legislation under § 5 are well settled. Section 5 states that Congress may "'enforce,' by 'appropriate legislation' the constitutional guarantee that no State shall deprive any person of 'life, liberty or property, without due process of law,' nor deny any person 'equal protection of the laws.'" Section 5 is "a positive grant of legislative power" that includes authority to "prohibit conduct which is not itself unconstitutional and [to] intrude into 'legislative spheres of autonomy previously reserved to the States.'" However, "[a]s broad as the congressional enforcement power is, it is not unlimited." In fact, as we discuss in detail below, several limitations inherent in § 5's text and constitutional context have been recognized since the Fourteenth Amendment was adopted.

Petitioners' § 5 argument is founded on an assertion that there is pervasive bias in various state justice systems against victims of gender-motivated violence. This assertion is supported by a voluminous congressional record. Specifically, Congress received evidence that many participants in state justice systems are perpetuating an array of erroneous stereotypes and assumptions. Congress concluded that these discriminatory stereotypes often result in insufficient investigation and prosecution of gender-motivated crime, inappropriate focus on the behavior and credibility of the victims of that crime, and unacceptably lenient punishments for those who are actually convicted of gender-motivated violence. Petitioners contend that this bias denies victims of gender-motivated violence the equal protection of the laws and that Congress therefore acted appropriately in enacting a private civil remedy against the perpetrators of gender-motivated violence to both remedy the States' bias and deter future instances of discrimination in the state courts.

As our cases have established, state-sponsored gender discrimination violates equal protection unless it "'serves "important governmental objectives and . . . the discriminatory means employed" are "substantially related to the achievement of those objectives."'" "However, the language and purpose of the Fourteenth Amendment place certain limitations on the manner in which Congress may attack discriminatory conduct. These limitations are necessary to prevent the Fourteenth Amendment from obliterating the Framers' carefully crafted balance of power between the States and the National Government. Foremost among these limitations is the time-honored principle that the Fourteenth Amendment, by its very terms, prohibits only state action. The principle has become firmly embedded in our constitutional law that the action inhibited by the first section of the Fourteenth Amendment is only such action as may fairly be said to be that of the States. That Amendment erects no shield against merely private conduct, however discriminatory or wrongful."

Shortly after the Fourteenth Amendment was adopted, we decided two cases interpreting the Amendment's provisions. . . . We concluded that this law exceeded Congress' § 5 power because the law was "directed exclusively against the action of private persons, without reference to the laws of the State, or their administration by her officers." . . .

. . .

Section 13981 is not aimed at proscribing discrimination by officials which the Fourteenth Amendment might not itself proscribe; it is directed not at any State or state actor, but at individuals who have committed criminal acts motivated by gender bias.

. . .

Section 13981 is also different from these previously upheld remedies in that it applies uniformly throughout the Nation. Congress' findings indicate that the problem of discrimination against the victims of gender-motivated crimes does not exist in all States, or even most States. . . .

For these reasons, we conclude that Congress' power under § 5 does not extend to the enactment of § 13981.

IV

Petitioner Brzonkala's complaint alleges that she was the victim of a brutal assault. But Congress' effort in § 13981 to provide a federal civil remedy can be sustained neither under the Commerce Clause nor under § 5 of the Fourteenth Amendment. If the allegations here are true, no civilized system of justice could fail to provide her a remedy for the conduct of respondent Morrison. But under our federal system that remedy must be provided by the Commonwealth of Virginia, and not by the United States. The judgment of the Court of Appeals is

Affirmed.

Justice Thomas, concurring. [omitted]

Justice Souter, dissenting.

The Court says both that it leaves Commerce Clause precedent undisturbed and that the Civil Rights Remedy of the Violence Against Women Act of 1994, 42 U.S.C. § 13981, exceeds Congress's power under that Clause. I find the claims irreconcilable and respectfully dissent.

I

Our cases, which remain at least nominally undisturbed, stand for the following propositions. Congress has the power to legislate with regard to activity that, in the aggregate, has a substantial effect on interstate commerce. The fact of such a substantial effect is not an issue for the courts in the first instance, ibid., but for the Congress, whose institutional capacity for gathering evidence and taking testimony far exceeds ours. By passing legislation, Congress indicates its conclusion, whether explicitly or not, that facts support its exercise of the commerce power. The business of the courts is to review the congressional assessment, not for soundness but simply for the rationality of concluding that a jurisdictional basis exists in fact. Any explicit findings that Congress chooses to make, though not dispositive of the question of rationality, may advance judicial review by identifying factual authority on which Congress relied. Applying those propositions in these cases can lead to only one conclusion.

One obvious difference from *United States v. Lopez*, is the mountain of data assembled by Congress, here showing the effects of violence against women on interstate commerce. Passage of the Act in 1994 was preceded by four years of hearings, which included testimony from physicians and law professors; from survivors of rape and domestic violence; and from representatives of state law enforcement and private business. The record includes reports on gender bias from task forces in 21 States, and we have the benefit of specific factual findings in the eight separate Reports issued by Congress and its committees over the long course leading to enactment.

. . .

Based on the data thus partially summarized, Congress found that

> crimes of violence motivated by gender have a substantial adverse effect on interstate commerce, by deterring potential victims from traveling interstate, from engaging in employment in interstate business, and from transacting with business, and in places involved, in interstate commerce . . . [,] by diminishing national productivity, increasing medical and other costs, and decreasing the supply of and the demand for interstate products. . . .

Congress thereby explicitly stated the predicate for the exercise of its Commerce Clause power. Is its conclusion irrational in view of the data amassed? True, the methodology of particular studies may be challenged, and some of the figures arrived at may be disputed. But the sufficiency of the evidence before Congress to provide a rational basis for the finding cannot seriously be questioned.

. . .

The fact that the Act does not pass muster before the Court today is therefore proof, to a degree that *Lopez* was not, that the Court's nominal adherence to the substantial effects test is merely that. Although a new jurisprudence has not emerged with any distinctness, it is clear that some congressional conclusions about obviously substantial, cumulative effects on commerce are being assigned lesser values than the once-stable doctrine would assign them. These devaluations are accomplished not by any express repudiation of the substantial effects test or its application through the aggregation of individual conduct, but by supplanting rational basis scrutiny with a new criterion of review.

Thus the elusive heart of the majority's analysis in these cases is its statement that Congress's findings of fact are "weakened" by the presence of a disfavored "method of reasoning." This seems to suggest that the "substantial effects" analysis is not a factual enquiry, for Congress in the first instance with subsequent judicial review looking only to the rationality of the congressional conclusion, but one of a rather different sort, dependent upon a uniquely judicial competence.

This new characterization of substantial effects has no support in our cases (the self-fulfilling prophecies of *Lopez* aside), least of all those the majority cites. . . .

. . .

Obviously, it would not be inconsistent with the text of the Commerce Clause itself to declare "noncommercial" primary activity beyond or presumptively beyond the scope of the commerce power. That variant of categorical approach is not, however, the sole textually permissible way of defining the scope of the Commerce Clause, and any such neat limitation would at least be suspect in the light of the final sentence of Article I, § 8, authorizing Congress to make "all Laws . . . necessary and proper" to give effect to its enumerated powers such as commerce. Accordingly, for significant periods of our history, the Court has defined the commerce power as plenary, unsusceptible to categorical exclusions, and this was the view expressed throughout the latter part of the 20th century in the substantial effects test. . . .

. . .

. . . The legitimacy of the Court's current emphasis on the noncommercial nature of regulated activity, then, does not turn on any logic serving the text of the Commerce Clause or on the realism of the majority's view of the national economy. The essential issue is rather the strength of the majority's claim to have a constitutional warrant for its current conception of a federal relationship enforceable by this Court through limits on otherwise plenary commerce power. This conception is the subject of the majority's second categorical discount applied today to the facts bearing on the substantial effects test.

B

The Court finds it relevant that the statute addresses conduct traditionally subject to state prohibition under domestic criminal law, a fact said to have some heightened significance when the violent conduct in question is not itself aimed directly at interstate commerce or its instrumentalities. Again, history seems to be recycling, for the theory of traditional state concern as grounding a limiting principle has been rejected previously, and more than once. . . .

The objection to reviving traditional state spheres of action as a consideration in commerce analysis, however, not only rests on the portent of incoherence, but is compounded by a further defect just as fundamental. The defect, in essence, is the majority's rejection of the Founders' considered judgment that politics, not judicial review, should mediate between state and national interests as the strength and legislative jurisdiction of the National Government inevitably increased through the expected growth of the national economy. Whereas today's majority takes a leaf from the book of the old judicial economists in saying that the Court should somehow draw the line to keep the federal relationship in a proper balance, Madison, Wilson, and Marshall understood the Constitution very differently.

. . .

Amendments that alter the balance of power between the National and State Governments, like the Fourteenth, or that change the way the States are represented within the Federal Government, like the Seventeenth, are not rips in the fabric of the Framers' Constitution, inviting judicial repairs. The Seventeenth Amendment may indeed have lessened the enthusiasm of the Senate to represent the States as discrete sovereignties, but the Amendment did not convert the judiciary into an alternate shield against the commerce power.

C

The Court's choice to invoke considerations of traditional state regulation in these cases is especially odd. . . . Today's majority, however, finds no significance whatever in the state support for the Act based upon the States' acknowledged failure to deal adequately with gender-based violence in state courts, and the belief of their own law enforcement agencies that national action is essential.

The National Association of Attorneys General supported the Act unanimously and Attorneys General from 38 States urged Congress to enact the Civil Rights Remedy, representing that "the current system for dealing with violence against women is inadequate." It was against this record of failure at the state level that the Act was passed to provide the choice of a federal forum in place of the state-court systems found inadequate to stop gender-biased violence. The Act accordingly offers a federal civil rights remedy aimed exactly at violence against women, as an alternative to the generic state tort causes of action found to be poor tools of action by the state task forces. As the 1993 Senate Report put it, "The Violence Against Women Act is intended to respond both to the underlying attitude that this violence is somehow less serious than other crime and to the resulting failure of our criminal justice system to address such violence. Its goals are both symbolic and practical. . . ."

The collective opinion of state officials that the Act was needed continues virtually unchanged, and when the Civil Rights Remedy was challenged in court, the States came to its defense. Thirty-six of them and the Commonwealth of Puerto Rico have filed an amicus brief in support of petitioners in these cases, and only one State has taken respondents' side. It is, then, not the least irony of these cases that the States will be forced to enjoy the new federalism whether they want it or not. . . .

III

All of this convinces me that today's ebb of the commerce power rests on error, and at the same time leads me to doubt that the majority's view will prove to be enduring law. There is yet one more reason for doubt. . . . This one will end when the majority realizes that the conception of the commerce power for which it entertains hopes would inevitably fail the test expressed in Justice Holmes's statement that "the first call of a theory of law is that it should fit the facts." The facts that cannot be ignored today are the facts of integrated national commerce and a political relationship between States and Nation much affected by their respective treasuries and constitutional modifications adopted by the people. The federalism of some earlier time is no more adequate to account for those facts today than the theory of laissez-faire was able to govern the national economy 70 years ago.

Justice Bryer, dissenting.

No one denies the importance of the Constitution's federalist principles. Its state/federal division of authority protects liberty—both by restricting the burdens that government can impose from a distance and by facilitating citizen participation in government that is closer to home. The question is how the judiciary can best implement that original federalist understanding where the Commerce Clause is at issue.

I

The majority holds that the federal commerce power does not extend to such "noneconomic" activities as "noneconomic, violent criminal conduct" that significantly affects interstate commerce only if we "aggregate" the interstate "effects" of individual instances. Justice Souter explains why history, precedent, and legal logic militate against the majority's approach. I agree and join his opinion. I add that the majority's holding illustrates the difficulty of finding a workable judicial Commerce Clause touchstone—a set of comprehensible interpretive rules that courts might use to impose some meaningful limit, but not too great a limit, upon the scope of the legislative authority that the Commerce Clause delegates to Congress.

A

Consider the problems. The "economic/noneconomic" distinction is not easy to apply. Does the local street corner mugger engage in "economic" activity or "noneconomic" activity when he mugs for money? Would evidence that desire for economic domination underlies many brutal crimes against women save the present statute?

The line becomes yet harder to draw given the need for exceptions. The Court itself would permit Congress to aggregate, hence regulate, "noneconomic" activity taking place at economic establishments. And it would permit Congress to regulate where that regulation is "an essential part of a larger regulation of economic activity, in which the regulatory scheme could be undercut unless the intrastate activity were regulated." Given the former exception, can Congress simply rewrite the present law and limit its application to restaurants, hotels, perhaps universities, and other places of public accommodation? Given the latter exception, can Congress save the present law by including it, or much of it, in a broader "Safe Transport" or "Workplace Safety" act?

More important, why should we give critical constitutional importance to the economic, or noneconomic, nature of an interstate-commerce-affecting cause? If chemical emanations through indirect environmental change cause identical, severe commercial harm outside a State, why should it matter whether local factories or home fireplaces release them? The Constitution itself refers only to Congress' power to "regulate Commerce . . . among the several States," and to make laws "necessary and proper" to implement that power. The language says nothing about either the local nature, or the economic nature, of an interstate-commerce-affecting cause.

This Court has long held that only the interstate commercial effects, not the local nature of the cause, are constitutionally relevant. Nothing in the Constitution's language, or that of earlier cases prior to *Lopez*, explains why the Court should ignore one highly relevant characteristic of an interstate-commerce-affecting cause (how "local" it is), while placing critical constitutional weight upon a different, less obviously relevant, feature (how "economic" it is).

Most important, the Court's complex rules seem unlikely to help secure the very object that they seek, namely, the protection of "areas of traditional state regulation" from federal intrusion. The Court's rules, even if broadly interpreted, are underinclusive. The local pickpocket is no less a traditional subject of state regulation than is the local gender-motivated assault. Regardless, the Court reaffirms, as it should, Congress' well-established and frequently exercised power to enact laws that satisfy a commerce-related jurisdictional prerequisite — for example, that some item relevant to the federally regulated activity has at some time crossed a state line.

And in a world where most everyday products or their component parts cross interstate boundaries, Congress will frequently find it possible to redraft a statute using language that ties the regulation to the interstate movement of some relevant object, thereby regulating local criminal activity or, for that matter, family affairs. Although this possibility does not give the Federal Government the power to regulate everything, it means that any substantive limitation will apply randomly in terms of the interests the majority seeks to protect. How much would be gained, for example, were Congress to reenact the present law in the form of "An Act Forbidding Violence Against Women Perpetrated at Public Accommodations or by Those Who Have Moved in, or through the Use of Items that Have Moved in, Interstate Commerce"? Complex Commerce Clause rules creating fine distinctions that achieve only random results do little to further the important federalist interests that called them into being. That is why modern (pre-*Lopez*) case law rejected them.

The majority, aware of these difficulties, is nonetheless concerned with what it sees as an important contrary consideration. To determine the lawfulness of statutes simply by asking whether Congress could reasonably have found that aggregated local instances significantly affect interstate commerce will allow Congress to regulate almost anything. Virtually all local activity, when instances are aggregated, can have "substantial effects on employment, production, transit, or consumption." Hence Congress could "regulate any crime," and perhaps "marriage, divorce, and childrearing" as well, obliterating the "Constitution's distinction between national and local authority."

This consideration, however, while serious, does not reflect a jurisprudential defect, so much as it reflects a practical reality. We live in a Nation knit together by two centuries of scientific, technological, commercial, and environmental change. Those changes, taken together, mean that virtually every kind of activity, no matter how local, genuinely can affect commerce, or its conditions, outside the State — at least when considered in the aggregate. And that fact makes it close to impossible for courts to develop meaningful subject-matter categories that would exclude some kinds of local activities from ordinary Commerce Clause "aggregation" rules without, at the same time, depriving Congress of the power to regulate activities that have a genuine and important effect upon interstate commerce.

Since judges cannot change the world, the "defect" means that, within the bounds of the rational, Congress, not the courts, must remain primarily responsible for striking the appropriate state/federal balance. Congress is institutionally motivated to do so. Its Members represent state and local district interests. They consider the views of state and local officials when they legislate, and they have even developed formal procedures to ensure that such consideration takes place. Moreover, Congress often can better reflect state concerns for autonomy in the details of sophisticated statutory schemes than can the judiciary, which cannot easily gather the relevant facts and which must apply more general legal rules and categories. Not surprisingly, the bulk of American law is still state law, and overwhelmingly so.

B

I would also note that Congress, when it enacted the statute, followed procedures that help to protect the federalism values at stake. It provided adequate notice to the States of its intent to legislate in an "area of traditional state regulation." And in response, attorneys general in the overwhelming majority of States (38) supported congressional legislation, telling Congress that "our experience as Attorneys General strengthens our belief that the problem of violence against women is a national one, requiring federal attention, federal leadership, and federal funds."

Moreover, as Justice Souter has pointed out, Congress compiled a "mountain of data" explicitly documenting the interstate commercial effects of gender-motivated crimes of violence. After considering alternatives, it focused the federal law upon documented deficiencies in state legal systems. And it tailored the law to prevent its use in certain areas of traditional state concern, such as divorce, alimony, or child custody. Consequently, the law before us seems to represent an instance, not of state/federal conflict, but of state/federal efforts to cooperate in order to help solve a mutually acknowledged national problem.

I call attention to the legislative process leading up to enactment of this statute because, as the majority recognizes, it far surpasses that which led to the enactment of the statute we considered in *Lopez*. And even were I to accept *Lopez* as an accurate statement of the law, which I do not, that distinction provides a possible basis for upholding the law here. This Court on occasion has pointed to the importance of procedural limitations in keeping the power of Congress in check.

Commentators also have suggested that the thoroughness of legislative procedures — e.g., whether Congress took a "hard look" — might sometimes make a determinative difference in a Commerce Clause case, say when Congress legislates in an area of traditional state regulation. . . . I continue to agree with Justice Souter that the Court's traditional "rational basis" approach is sufficient. But I recognize that the law in this area is unstable and that time and experience may demonstrate both the unworkability of the majority's rules and the superiority of Congress' own procedural approach — in which case the law may evolve towards a rule that, in certain difficult Commerce Clause cases, takes account of the thoroughness with which Congress has considered the federalism issue.

For these reasons, as well as those set forth by Justice Souter, this statute falls well within Congress's Commerce Clause authority, and I dissent from the Court's contrary conclusion.

II

Given my conclusion on the Commerce Clause question, I need not consider Congress' authority under § 5 of the Fourteenth Amendment. Nonetheless, I doubt the Court's reasoning rejecting that source of authority. The Court points out that . . . § 5 does not authorize Congress to use the Fourteenth Amendment as a source of power to remedy the conduct of private persons. That is certainly so. The Federal Government's argument, however, is that Congress used § 5 to remedy the actions of state actors, namely, those States which, through discriminatory design or the discriminatory conduct of their officials, failed to provide adequate (or any) state remedies for women injured by gender-motivated violence — a failure that the States, and Congress, documented in depth.

. . .

The Court responds directly to the relevant "state actor" claim by finding that the present law lacks "'congruence and proportionality'" to the state discrimination that it purports to remedy. That is because the law, unlike federal laws prohibiting literacy tests for voting, imposing voting rights requirements, or punishing state officials who intentionally discriminated in jury selection is not "directed . . . at any State or state actor."

But why can Congress not provide a remedy against private actors? Those private actors, of course, did not themselves violate the Constitution. But this Court has held that Congress at least sometimes can enact remedial "legislation . . . [that] prohibits conduct which is not itself unconstitutional." The statutory remedy does not in any sense purport to "determine what constitutes a constitutional violation." It intrudes little upon either States or private parties. It may lead state actors to improve their own remedial systems, primarily through example. It restricts private actors only by imposing liability for private conduct that is, in the main, already forbidden by state law. Why is the remedy "disproportionate"? And given the relation between remedy and violation — the creation of a federal remedy to substitute for constitutionally inadequate state remedies — where is the lack of "congruence"?

The majority adds that Congress found that the problem of inadequacy of state remedies "does not exist in all States, or even most States." But Congress had before it the task force reports of at least 21 States documenting constitutional violations. And it made its own findings about pervasive gender-based stereotypes hampering many state legal systems, sometimes unconstitutionally so. The record nowhere reveals a congressional finding that the problem "does not exist" elsewhere. Why can Congress not take the evidence before it as evidence of a national problem? This Court has not previously held that Congress must document the existence of a problem in every State prior to proposing a national solution. And the deference this

Court gives to Congress' chosen remedy under § 5 suggests that any such requirement would be inappropriate.

Despite my doubts about the majority's § 5 reasoning, I need not, and do not, answer the § 5 question, which I would leave for more thorough analysis if necessary on another occasion. Rather, in my view, the Commerce Clause provides an adequate basis for the statute before us. And I would uphold its constitutionality as the "necessary and proper" exercise of legislative power granted to Congress by that Clause.

Notes and Queries

1. The *Morrison* decision may be seen as an example of a congressional enactment being subjected to a higher standard of review than rational basis. Congress had accumulated massive amounts of findings to support the civil rights remedy of the *Violence Against Women Act*. However, the holding in *Morrison* demonstrates that findings are not enough to demonstrate that a particular activity substantially affects interstate commerce. As a result, it may well be that, if Congress identifies a non-economic activity that substantially affects interstate commerce, it would be powerless to regulate the activity under the Commerce Clause, making any regulation of it subject to much stricter judicial review. What implications for addressing child maltreatment flow from this approach?

2. *Morrison* still lets Congress exercise the "power of the purse." An example of acceptable federal legislation might be a well-funded mandate for states to develop programs to prevent child abuse. What problems do you envision with this approach? How would you address the "recalcitrant state" problem, the concern that states may forgo government money in order to avoid having to implement an unpopular program?

Bowen v. Kendrick

487 U.S. 589; 108 S. Ct. 2562 (1988)

Chief Justice Rehnquist delivered the opinion of the Court.

[This] ... litigation involves a challenge to a federal grant program that provides funding for services relating to adolescent sexuality and pregnancy. Considering the federal statute both "on its face" and "as applied," the District Court ruled that the statute violated the Establishment Clause of the First Amendment insofar as it provided for the involvement of religious organizations in the federally funded programs. We conclude, however, that the statute is not unconstitutional on its face, and that a determination of whether any of the grants made pursuant to the statute violate the Establishment Clause requires further proceedings in the District Court.

I

The Adolescent Family Life Act (AFLA or Act) was passed by Congress in 1981 in response to the "severe adverse health, social, and economic consequences" that often follow pregnancy and childbirth among unmarried adolescents. Like its predecessor, the Adolescent Health Services and Pregnancy Prevention and Care Act of 1978, the AFLA is essentially a scheme for providing grants to public or nonprofit private organizations or agencies "for services and research in the area of premarital adolescent sexual relations and pregnancy." These grants are intended to serve several purposes, including the promotion of "self discipline and other prudent approaches to the problem of adolescent premarital sexual relations," the promotion of adoption as an alternative for adolescent parents, the establishment of new approaches to the delivery of care services for pregnant adolescents, and the support of research and demonstration projects "concerning the societal causes and consequences of adolescent premarital sexual relations, contraceptive use, pregnancy, and child rearing."

In pertinent part, grant recipients are to provide two types of services: "care services," for the provision of care to pregnant adolescents and adolescent parents, and "prevention services," for the prevention of adolescent sexual relations. While the AFLA leaves it up to the Secretary of Health and Human Services (the Secretary) to define exactly what types of services a grantee must provide, the statute contains a listing of "necessary services" that may be funded. These services include pregnancy testing and maternity counseling, adoption counseling and referral services, prenatal and postnatal health care, nutritional information, counseling, child care, mental health services, and perhaps most importantly for present purposes, "educational services relating to family life and problems associated with adolescent premarital sexual relations."

In drawing up the AFLA and determining what services to provide under the Act, Congress was well aware that "the problems of adolescent premarital sexual relations, pregnancy, and parenthood are multiple and complex." Indeed, Congress expressly recognized that legislative or governmental action alone would be insufficient:

> [S]uch problems are best approached through a variety of integrated and essential services provided to adolescents and their families by other family members, religious and charitable organizations, voluntary associations, and other groups in the private sector as well as services provided by publicly sponsored initiatives.

Accordingly, the AFLA expressly states that federally provided services in this area should promote the involvement of parents, and should "emphasize the provision of support by other family members, religious and charitable organizations, voluntary associations, and other groups." The AFLA implements this goal by providing that demonstration projects funded by the government

> shall use such methods as will strengthen the capacity of families to deal with the sexual behavior, pregnancy, or parenthood of adolescents and to

> make use of support systems such as other family members, friends, religious and charitable organizations, and voluntary associations.

In addition, AFLA requires grant applicants, among other things, to describe how they will, "as appropriate in the provision of services[,] involve families of adolescents[, and] involve religious and charitable organizations, voluntary associations, and other groups in the private sector as well as services provided by publicly sponsored initiatives." This broad-based involvement of groups outside of the government was intended by Congress to "establish better coordination, integration, and linkages" among existing programs in the community, to aid in the development of "strong family values and close family ties," and to "help adolescents and their families deal with complex issues of adolescent premarital sexual relations and the consequences of such relations."

In line with its purposes, the AFLA also imposes limitations on the use of funds by grantees. First, the AFLA expressly states that no funds provided for demonstration projects under the statute may be used for family planning services (other than counseling and referral services) unless appropriate family planning services are not otherwise available in the community. Second, the AFLA restricts the awarding of grants to "programs or projects which do not provide abortions or abortion counseling or referral," except that the program may provide referral for abortion counseling if the adolescent and her parents request such referral. Finally, the AFLA states that "grants may be made only to projects or programs which do not advocate, promote, or encourage abortion. . . ."

Since 1981, when the AFLA was adopted, the Secretary has received 1,088 grant applications and awarded 141 grants. Funding has gone to a wide variety of recipients, including state and local health agencies, private hospitals, community health associations, privately operated health care centers, and community and charitable organizations. It is undisputed that a number of grantees or subgrantees were organizations with institutional ties to religious denominations.

In 1983, this lawsuit against the Secretary was filed in the United States District Court for the District of Columbia by appellees, a group of federal taxpayers, clergymen, and the American Jewish Congress. Seeking both declaratory and injunctive relief, appellees challenged the constitutionality of the AFLA on the grounds that on its face and as applied the statute violates the Religion Clauses of the First Amendment. Following cross-motions for summary judgment, the District Court held for appellees and declared that the AFLA was invalid both on its face and as applied "insofar as religious organizations are involved in carrying out the programs and purposes of the Act."

. . .

II

. . .

Given this statutory framework, there are two ways in which the statute, considered "on its face," might be said to have the impermissible primary effect of advancing religion. First, it can be argued that the AFLA advances religion by expressly recognizing that "religious organizations have a role to play" in addressing the problems associated with teenage sexuality. In this view, even if no religious institution receives aid or funding pursuant to the AFLA, the statute is invalid under the Establishment Clause because, among other things, it expressly enlists the involvement of religiously affiliated organizations in the federally subsidized programs, it endorses religious solutions to the problems addressed by the Act, or it creates symbolic ties between church and state. Secondly, it can be argued that the AFLA is invalid on its face because it allows religiously affiliated organizations to participate as grantees or subgrantees in AFLA programs. From this standpoint, the Act is invalid because it authorizes direct federal funding of religious organizations which, given the AFLA's educational function and the fact that the AFLA's "viewpoint" may coincide with the grantee's "viewpoint" on sexual matters, will result unavoidably in the impermissible "inculcation" of religious beliefs in the context of a federally funded program.

We consider the former objection first. As noted previously, the AFLA expressly mentions the role of religious organizations in four places. . . .

Putting aside for the moment the possible role of religious organizations as grantees, these provisions of the statute reflect at most Congress' considered judgment that religious organizations can help solve the problems to which the AFLA is addressed. Nothing in our previous cases prevents Congress from making such a judgment or from recognizing the important part that religion or religious organizations may play in resolving certain secular problems. Particularly when, as Congress found, "prevention of adolescent sexual activity and adolescent pregnancy depends primarily upon developing strong family values and close family ties," it seems quite sensible for Congress to recognize that religious organizations can influence values and can have some influence on family life, including parents' relations with their adolescent children. To the extent that this congressional recognition has any effect of advancing religion, the effect is at most "incidental and remote." In addition, although the AFLA does require potential grantees to describe how they will involve religious organizations in the provision of services under the Act, it also requires grantees to describe the involvement of "charitable organizations, voluntary associations, and other groups in the private sector." In our view, this reflects the statute's successful maintenance of "a course of neutrality among religions, and between religion and nonreligion."

This brings us to the second ground for objecting to the AFLA: the fact that it allows religious institutions to participate as recipients of federal funds. The AFLA defines an "eligible grant recipient" as a "public or nonprofit private organization or agency" which demonstrates the capability of providing the requisite services. As this provision would indicate, a fairly wide spectrum of organizations is eligible to apply for and receive funding under the Act, and nothing on the face of the Act suggests it is anything but neutral with respect to the grantee's status as a sectarian or purely secular institution. . . .

We note in addition that this Court has never held that religious institutions are disabled by the First Amendment from participating in publicly sponsored social welfare programs. . . .

Of course, even when the challenged statute appears to be neutral on its face, we have always been careful to ensure that direct government aid to religiously affiliated institutions does not have the primary effect of advancing religion. One way in which direct government aid might have that effect is if the aid flows to institutions that are "pervasively sectarian."

The reason for this is that there is a risk that direct government funding, even if it is designated for specific secular purposes, may nonetheless advance the pervasively sectarian institution's "religious mission." Accordingly, a relevant factor in deciding whether a particular statute on its face can be said to have the improper effect of advancing religion is the determination of whether, and to what extent, the statute directs government aid to pervasively sectarian institutions. . . .

In this lawsuit, nothing on the face of the AFLA indicates that a significant proportion of the federal funds will be disbursed to "pervasively sectarian" institutions. Indeed, the contention that there is a substantial risk of such institutions receiving direct aid is undercut by the AFLA's facially neutral grant requirements, the wide spectrum of public and private organizations which are capable of meeting the AFLA's requirements, and the fact that, of the eligible religious institutions, many will not deserve the label of "pervasively sectarian." . . .

Nor do we agree with the District Court that the AFLA necessarily has the effect of advancing religion because the religiously affiliated AFLA grantees will be providing educational and counseling services to adolescents. . . . But nothing in our prior cases warrants the presumption adopted by the District Court that religiously affiliated AFLA grantees are not capable of carrying out their functions under the AFLA in a lawful, secular manner. Only in the context of aid to "pervasively sectarian" institutions have we invalidated an aid program on the grounds that there was a "substantial" risk that aid to these religious institutions would, knowingly or unknowingly, result in religious indoctrination. . . .

We also disagree with the District Court's conclusion that the AFLA is invalid because it authorizes "teaching" by religious grant recipients on "matters [that] are fundamental elements of religious doctrine," such as the harm of premarital sex and the reasons for choosing adoption over abortion. On an issue as sensitive and important as teenage sexuality, it is not surprising that the Government's secular concerns would either coincide or conflict with those of religious institutions. But the possibility or even the likelihood that some of the religious institutions who receive AFLA funding will agree with the message that Congress intended to deliver to adolescents through the AFLA is insufficient to warrant a finding that the statute on its face has the primary effect of advancing religion. Nor does the alignment of the statute and the religious views of the grantees run afoul of our proscription against "fund[ing] a specifically religious activity in an otherwise substantially secular setting." The facially neutral projects authorized by the AFLA—including pregnancy testing, adoption counseling and referral services, prenatal and postnatal care, educational services, residential care, child care, consumer education, etc.—are not themselves "specifically religious activities," and they are not converted into such activities by the fact that they are carried out by organizations with religious affiliations.

As yet another reason for invalidating parts of the AFLA, the District Court found that the involvement of religious organizations in the Act has the impermissible effect of creating a "crucial symbolic link" between government and religion. If we were to adopt the District Court's reasoning, it could be argued that any time a government aid program provides funding to religious organizations in an area in which the organization also has an interest, an impermissible "symbolic link" could be created, no matter whether the aid was to be used solely for secular purposes. This would jeopardize government aid to religiously affiliated hospitals, for example, on the ground that patients would perceive a "symbolic link" between the hospital—part of whose "religious mission" might be to save lives—and whatever government entity is subsidizing the purely secular medical services provided to the patient. We decline to adopt the District Court's reasoning and conclude that, in this litigation, whatever "symbolic link" might in fact be created by the AFLA's disbursement of funds to religious institutions is not sufficient to justify striking down the statute on its face.

A final argument that has been advanced for striking down the AFLA on "effects" grounds is the fact that the statute lacks an express provision preventing the use of federal funds for religious purposes. Clearly, if there were such a provision in this statute, it would be easier to conclude that the statute on its face could not be said to have the primary effect of advancing religion, but we have never stated that a statutory restriction is constitutionally required....

This, of course, brings us to ... the question whether the AFLA leads to "'an excessive government entanglement with religion.'" There is no doubt that the monitoring of AFLA grants is necessary if the Secretary is to ensure that public money is to be spent in the way that Congress intended and in a way that comports with the Establishment Clause. Accordingly, this litigation presents us with yet another "Catch-22" argument: the very supervision of the aid to assure that it does not further religion renders the statute invalid....

Here, by contrast, there is no reason to assume that the religious organizations which may receive grants are "pervasively sectarian" in the same sense as the Court has held parochial schools to be. There is accordingly no reason to fear that the less intensive monitoring involved here will cause the Government to intrude unduly in the day-to-day operation of the religiously affiliated AFLA grantees. Unquestionably, the Secretary will review the programs set up and run by the AFLA grantees, and undoubtedly this will involve a review of, for example, the educational materials that a grantee proposes to use. The Secretary may also wish to have Government employees visit the clinics or offices where AFLA programs are being carried out to see whether they are in fact being administered in accordance with statutory and constitutional requirements. But in our view, this type of grant monitoring does not amount to "excessive entanglement," at least in the context of a statute authorizing grants to religiously affiliated organizations that are not necessarily "pervasively sectarian."

In sum, in this somewhat lengthy discussion of the validity of the AFLA on its face, we have concluded that the statute has a valid secular purpose, does not have the primary effect of advancing religion, and does not create an excessive entanglement of church and state. We note, as is proper given the traditional presumption in favor of the constitutionality of statutes enacted by Congress, that our conclusion that the statute does not violate the Establishment Clause is consistent with the conclusion Congress reached in the course of its deliberations on the AFLA. As the Senate Committee Report states:

> In the committee's view, provisions for the involvement of religious organizations [in the AFLA] do not violate the constitutional separation between church and state. Recognizing the limitations of Government in dealing with a problem that has complex moral and social dimensions, the committee believes that promoting the involvement of religious organizations in the solution to these problems is neither inappropriate or illegal.

For the foregoing reasons we conclude that the AFLA does not violate the Establishment Clause "on its face."

III

We turn now to consider whether the District Court correctly ruled that the AFLA was unconstitutional as applied. . . .

On the merits of the "as applied" challenge, it seems to us that the District Court did not follow the proper approach in assessing appellees' claim that the Secretary is making grants under the Act that violate the Establishment Clause of the First Amendment. Although the District Court stated several times that AFLA aid had been given to religious organizations that were "pervasively sectarian," it did not identify which grantees it was referring to, nor did it discuss with any particularity the aspects of those organizations which in its view warranted classification as "pervasively sectarian." The District Court did identify certain instances in which it felt AFLA funds were used for constitutionally improper purposes, but in our view the court did not adequately design its remedy to address the specific problems it found in the Secretary's administration of the statute. Accordingly, although there is no dispute that the record contains evidence of specific incidents of impermissible behavior by AFLA grantees, we feel that this lawsuit should be remanded to the District Court for consideration of the evidence presented by appellees insofar as it sheds light on the manner in which the statute is presently being administered. It is the latter inquiry to which the court must direct itself on remand.

In particular, it will be open to appellees on remand to show that AFLA aid is flowing to grantees that can be considered "pervasively sectarian" religious institutions, such as we have held parochial schools to be.... [I]t is not enough to show that the recipient of a challenged grant is affiliated with a religious institution or that it is "religiously inspired."

The District Court should also consider on remand whether in particular cases AFLA aid has been used to fund "specifically religious activit[ies] in an otherwise substantially secular setting." ... [E]vidence that the views espoused on questions such as premarital sex, abortion, and the like happen to coincide with the religious views of the AFLA grantee would not be sufficient to show that the grant funds are being used in such a way as to have a primary effect of advancing religion.

...

IV

We conclude, first, that the District Court erred in holding that the AFLA is invalid on its face, and second, that the court should consider on remand whether particular AFLA grants have had the primary effect of advancing religion. Should the court conclude that the Secretary's current practice does allow such grants, it should devise a remedy to insure that grants awarded by the Secretary comply with the Constitution and the statute. The judgment of the District Court is accordingly

Reversed.

Justice O'Connor, concurring.

This litigation raises somewhat unusual questions involving a facially valid statute that appears to have been administered in a way that led to violations of the Establishment Clause. I agree with the Court's resolution of those questions, and I join its opinion. I write separately, however, to explain why I do not believe that the Court's approach reflects any tolerance for the kind of improper administration that seems to have occurred in the Government program at issue here.

The dissent says, and I fully agree, that "[p]ublic funds may not be used to endorse the religious message." As the Court notes, "there is no dispute that the record contains evidence of specific incidents of impermissible behavior by AFLA grantees." Because the District Court employed an analytical framework that did not require a detailed discussion of the voluminous record, the extent of this impermissible behavior and the degree to which it is attributable to poor administration by the Executive Branch is somewhat less clear. In this circumstance, two points deserve to be emphasized. First, any use of public funds to promote religious doctrines violates the Establishment Clause. Second, extensive violations—if they can be proved in this case—will be highly relevant in shaping an appropriate remedy that ends such abuses. For that reason, appellees may yet prevail on remand, and I do not believe that the Court's approach entails a relaxation of "the unwavering vigilance that the Constitution requires against any law 'respecting an establishment of religion.'"

...

Justice Kennedy, with whom Justice Scalia joins, concurring.

I join the Court's opinion, and write this separate concurrence to discuss one feature of the proceedings on remand. The Court states that "it will be open to appellees on remand to show that AFLA aid is flowing to grantees that can be considered 'pervasively sectarian' religious institutions, such as we have held parochial schools to be." In my view, such a showing will not alone be enough, in an as applied challenge, to make out a violation of the Establishment Clause.

Though I am not confident that the term "pervasively sectarian" is a well-founded juridical category, I recognize the thrust of our previous decisions that a statute which provides for exclusive or disproportionate funding to pervasively sectarian institutions may impermissibly advance religion and as such be invalid on its face. We hold today, however, that the neutrality of the grant requirements and the diversity of the organizations described in the statute before us foreclose the argument that it is disproportionately tied to pervasively sectarian groups. Having held that the statute is not facially invalid, the only purpose of further inquiring whether any particular grantee institution is pervasively sectarian is as a preliminary step to demonstrating that the funds are in fact being used to further religion. In sum, where, as in this litigation, a statute provides that the benefits of a program are to be distributed in a neutral fashion to religious and nonreligious applicants alike, and the program withstands a facial challenge, it is not unconstitutional as applied solely by reason of the religious character of a specific recipient. The question in an as-applied challenge is not whether the entity is of a religious character, but how it spends its grant.

Justice Blackmun, with whom Justice Brennan, Justice Marshall, and Justice Stevens join, dissenting.

In 1981, Congress enacted the Adolescent Family Life Act . . . in a broad-scale effort to alleviate some of the problems associated with teenage pregnancy. It is unclear whether Congress ever envisioned that public funds would pay for a program during a session of which parents and teenagers would be instructed:

> You want to know the church teachings on sexuality. . . . You are the church. You people sitting here are the body of Christ. The teachings of you and the things you value are, in fact, the values of the Catholic Church.

Or of curricula that taught:

> The Church has always taught that the marriage act, or intercourse, seals the union of husband and wife, (and is a representation of their union on all levels.) Christ commits Himself to us when we come to ask for the sacrament of marriage. We ask Him to be active in our life. God is love. We ask Him to share His love in ours, and God procreates with us, He enters into our physical union with Him, and we begin new life.

Or the teaching of a method of family planning described on the grant application as "not only a method of birth regulation but also a philosophy of procreation," and promoted as helping "spouses who are striving . . . to transform their married life into testimony[,] . . . to cultivate their matrimonial spirituality[, and] to make themselves better instruments in God's plan," and as "facilitat[ing] the evangelization of homes."

Whatever Congress had in mind, however, it enacted a statute that facilitated and, indeed, encouraged the use of public funds for such instruction, by giving religious groups a central pedagogical and counseling role without imposing any restraints on the sectarian quality of the participation. As the record developed thus far in this litigation makes all too clear, federal tax dollars appropriated for AFLA purposes have been used, with Government approval, to support religious teaching. Today the majority upholds the facial validity of this statute and remands the action to the District Court for further proceedings concerning appellees' challenge to the manner in which the statute has been applied. Because I am firmly convinced that our cases require invalidating this statutory scheme, I dissent.

. . .

As is evident from the parties' arguments, the record compiled below, and the decision of the District Court, this lawsuit has been litigated primarily as a broad challenge to the statutory scheme as a whole, not just to the awarding of grants to a few individual applicants. The thousands of pages of depositions, affidavits, and documentary evidence were not intended to demonstrate merely that particular grantees should not receive further funding. Indeed, because of the 5-year grant cycle, some of the original grantees are no longer AFLA participants. This record was designed to show that the AFLA had been interpreted and implemented by the Government in a manner that was clearly unconstitutional, and appellees sought declaratory and injunctive relief as to the entire statute.

. . .

It is true, of course, that the Court has recognized that the Constitution does not prohibit the government from supporting secular social-welfare services solely because they are provided by a religiously affiliated organization. But such recognition has been closely tied to the nature of the subsidized social service: "the State may send a cleric, indeed even a clerical order, to perform a wholly secular task." There is a very real and important difference between running a soup kitchen or a hospital, and counseling pregnant teenagers on how to make the difficult decisions facing them. The risk of advancing religion at public expense, and of creating an appearance that the government is endorsing the medium and the message, is much greater when the religious organization is directly engaged in pedagogy, with the express intent of shaping belief and changing behavior, than where it is neutrally dispensing medication, food, or shelter.

There is also, of course, a fundamental difference between government's employing religion because of its unique appeal to a higher authority and the transcendental nature of its message, and government's enlisting the aid of religiously committed individuals or organizations without regard to their sectarian motivation. In the latter circumstance, religion plays little or no role; it merely explains why the individual or organization has chosen to get involved in the publicly funded program. In the former, religion is at the core of the subsidized activity, and it affects the manner in which the "service" is dispensed. For some religious organizations, the answer to a teenager's question "Why shouldn't I have an abortion?" or "Why shouldn't I use barrier contraceptives?" will undoubtedly be different from an answer based solely on secular considerations. Public funds may not be used to endorse the religious message.

. . .

Notes and Queries

1. In a footnote, the ruling opinion specifies that the closest the lower court came to finding impermissible behavior by grantees was to identify "at least ten AFLA grantees or subgrantees [that] were themselves 'religious organizations,' in the sense that they have explicit corporate ties to a particular religious faith and by-laws or policies that prohibit any deviation from religious doctrine." The Court responds by noting that, while these factors are relevant to the determination of whether an institution is "pervasively sectarian," they are not conclusive, and did not find the court's conclusion that these institutions are "religious organizations" to be equivalent to a finding that their secular purposes and religious mission are "inextricably intertwined." What more evidence would have been needed? How can those grantees not be "pervasively sectarian"?

2. Do you agree that the statute does not encourage religious messages and does not support religious institutions? Why not simply declare the statute unconstitutional rather than look for instances in which religious institutions act impermissibly? Which approach would best protect the rights of adolescents? Are the examples provided by the dissent the type of material that would be deemed impermissible on remand to the lower court?

3. What implications do you think *Kendrick* holds for addressing child maltreatment? Schools are the most often used sites for teaching children about maltreatment and for providing child abuse prevention programs.

Research Comments

1. How policies address sexuality has important implications for addressing child maltreatment. One of the most obvious implications of the manner we allow schools and organizations to address materials that are sexually charged involves sexual abuse prevention programs. These programs are more controversial than we may expect. Their effectiveness often has been questioned. The first study to examine the long-term effectiveness of school-based child sexual abuse prevention

programs found that it associated with a reduced incidence of child sexual maltreatment. Out of 825 subjects, 8 percent of respondents who reported ever having had a prevention program also reported having been subsequently sexually abused, compared to 14 percent of respondents who did not ever have a prevention program. Laura E. Gibson & Harold Leittenberg (2000). Child sexual abuse prevention programs: Do they decrease the occurrence of child sexual abuse? *Child Abuse & Neglect*, 24, 1115–1125. A meta-analysis of sixteen evaluation studies of school programs aimed at the prevention of child sexual victimization found that victimization prevention programs are successful in teaching children sexual abuse concepts and self-protection skills. The analysis also found that intervention characteristics such as duration and content of the program, and child characteristics such as age and SES were important moderators of effectiveness (effect sizes). The authors conclcuded that their findings indicated a preference for programs that focus on training skills and that allow sufficient time for children to integrate self-protection skills into their cognitive repertoire. Jan Rispens, Andre Aleman & Paul P. Goudena (1997). Prevention of child sexual abuse victimization: A meta-analysis of school programs. *Child Abuse & Neglect*, 21, 975–988. Similar findings have been reported in other studies. Although much controversy attaches to the effectiveness of prevention programs, it is clear that more comprehensive and long-term programs have the strongest impact. See M. Katherine Davis & Christine A. Gidycz (2000). Child sexual abuse prevention programs: A meta-analysis. *Journal of Clinical Child Psychology*, 29, 257–265; David Finkelhor, Nancy Asdigian & Jennifer Dziuba-Leatherman (1995). Victimization prevention programs for children. *American Journal of Public Health*, 85, 1684–1689. These are important findings. The more comprehensive programs become, which research seems to indicate is necessary to reach effectiveness, the more likely they are to raise *Bownen v. Kendrick* issues.

2. Although programs may increase knowledge of maltreatment, whether programs actually prevent maltreatment remains controversial. One of the most comprehensive examinations of sexual abuse prevention programs, a national survey of 200 youth ages 10–16, found that children who had been exposed to more comprehensive school-based prevention programs scored better on a test of knowledge about sexual abuse. It was also found that programs aimed at preventing victimization of children may not be effective in actually preventing the occurrence of sexual abuse or other crimes, but may improve children's ability to deal with such victimizations. Children in recent prevention programs were more likely than those without programs to use recommended protection methods such as threatening to tell or telling the abuser to leave them alone. Children in prevention programs also were more likely to tell an adult about their victimization, to feel that they had dealt with the experience well, and to avoid blaming themselves. However, these programs did not appear to reduce the number of victimizations or the chance of injury. David Finkelhor, Nancy Asdigian & Jennifer Dziuba-Leatherman. (1995). Victimization prevention programs for children: A

follow-up. *The American Journal of Public Health*, 85, 1684–1690; David Finkelhor & Jennifer Dziuba-Leatherman (1995). Victimization prevention programs: A national survey of children's exposures and reactions. *Child Abuse & Neglect*, 19, 129–139. Follow-up reviews reveal similar positive findings, but they are important to consider in light of the limitation that they generally do not address actual victimizations and injuries. Jan Rispens, Andre Aleman & Paul P. Goudena (1997). Prevention of child sexual abuse victimization: A meta-analysis of school programs. *Child Abuse & Neglect*, 21(10), 975–987. Emma Brennan & Rosaleen McElvaney (2020). What helps children tell? A qualitative meta-analysis of child sexual abuse disclosure. *Child Abuse Review*, 29(2), 97–113. What implications may be drawn from these findings?

3. Even if studies could show program effectiveness, the extent to which they can be implemented outside of original contexts remains debatable. In this area of research, this issue is one of "implementation fidelity." One systematic review of fidelity in the implementation of sexual abuse prevention programs found cause for concern. The study used the National Institute of Health Behavioral Change Consortium (NIHBCC) Fidelity Checklist. As a result, they assessed fidelity quality across the domains of: intervention design, training providers, intervention delivery, intervention receipt, and enactment of skills. They found that no study achieved high fidelity. Jenny Lynas & Russell Hawkins (2017). Fidelity in school-based child sexual abuse prevention programs: A systematic review. *Child Abuse & Neglect*, 72, 10–21.

4. The extent to which schools help foster parenting skills also has been deemed important. The primary responsibility for the health and welfare of a child, and for themselves, has and will remain largely in the hands of the parents. In order to be prepared to provide for the health, safety, and well-being of their children, however, parents either must have extensive knowledge and skills in these areas, or be able to seek, obtain, evaluate, and use resources that may help them in the provision of such care. Despite the need for such skills and abilities within a rapidly changing society, no systematic and comprehensive effort has tried to provide education that would address these issues. Some sporadic efforts have emerged, but commentators are quick to note that programs have been woefully inadequate because their provision invariably has been in response to startling consequences of sociopolitical inaction (e.g., child maltreatment, domestic violence, dropping out of school, teen pregnancy, or youth violence). As a result and given expectations, commentators agree, parent education is short lived, minimalistic, fraught with untested methods, and ineffectual. The premise behind the lack in provision of more childcare education is the assumption that people will develop the requisite knowledge and skills and will adapt to changing circumstances over the child's development on their own and/or with available resources. The assumption has important consequences. The result is that parents with greater formal education and with adequate finances, social supports, and other resources are likely to be

able to seek, obtain, and properly use requisite childcare knowledge or services. These parents also are more likely already to have a substantial initial foundation of self- and child health care, safety, and well-being knowledge they can use to build upon and adapt to changing needs. Given these resources, these parents also are more likely to be able to adapt to economic downturns, political changes, or to personal or familial difficulties. In the absence of services, this group also is more able (and more likely) to mount effective lobbying efforts to address this absence or to have others do so on their behalf. See Edward Zigler, Sharon L. Kagan & Nancy W. Hall (Eds.) (1996). *Children, Families, and Government: Preparing for the Twenty-First Century*. New York: Cambridge University Press.

5. Pregnancy prevention programs also have been the subject of much inquiry that relates directly to issues raised in *Bowen v. Kendrick*. Although we tend to view these programs as school based, they actually have several other dimensions. The first dimension involves the locus of intervention, whether community based, school based, or school linked. The second dimension involves type of program administered, whether clinic or nonclinic. The third dimension is the type of intervention emphasized: abstinence only, sex education either with or without contraception, and contraceptive knowledge building with or without distribution. The final dimension is the micropractice focus of the intervention, whether skills building is a central goal of intervention. The practice dimension of skills building has become an especially important practice emphasis in the success of programs, and the importance of this intervention is discussed in more detail later. What do you make of research indicating that "best practices" (what we should do based on current knowledge) would include community-based and school-based clinics, programs offering contraceptive knowledge building along with comprehensive sex education and skills training, and sex education curricula based on social learning theory and skills training? See Cynthia Franklin & Jacqueline Corcoran (2000). Preventing adolescent pregnancy: A review of programs and practices. *Social Work*, 45, 40–53.

6. Sex education has emerged as a dominant approach to addressing pregnancies, spread of diseases, and relationship problems. Numerous studies over the past twenty-five years were conducted to examine effects of sexuality education programs. The vast majority of results from these studies have been inconsistent and controversial. Many studies continue to indicate that sexuality education programs tend to be ineffective, while others provide evidence of valuable and effective results. Although many results may not be politically popular, it does seem that at least one persistent finding tends to emerge and be championed as critical to successful sexuality education reform: More comprehensive, long-term programs generally reach greater effectiveness. How these findings can be addressed in light of *Bowen v. Kendrick* remains to be seen. See Roger J. R. Levesque (2000). Sexuality education: What adolescents' educational rights require. *Psychology, Public Policy, & Law*, 6, 953–988.

7. As with other prevention programs, effectiveness relies on fidelity. In the context of sexuality education, research may show that comprehensive programs may be more effective. But what actually constitutes "comprehensive" remains elusive and may challenge efforts to achieve effectiveness. The importance of this issue becomes even more important for efforts to evaluate effectiveness in light of recent reviews that reveal that reaching a consensus on what constitutes comprehensiveness may not only be impossible but also not desirable. Esther Miedema, Marielle LJ Le Mat & Frances Hague (2020). But is it comprehensive? Unpacking the 'comprehensive' in comprehensive sexuality education. *Health Education Journal*, 79(7), 747–762.

Davis v. Monroe County Board of Education

526 U.S. 629; 119 S. Ct. 1661 (1999)

Justice O'Connor delivered the opinion of the Court.

Petitioner brought suit against the Monroe County Board of Education and other defendants, alleging that her fifth-grade daughter had been the victim of sexual harassment by another student in her class. Among petitioner's claims was a claim for monetary and injunctive relief under Title IX of the Education Amendments of 1972 (Title IX). The District Court dismissed petitioner's Title IX claim on the ground that "student-on-student," or peer, harassment provides no ground for a private cause of action under the statute. The Court of Appeals for the Eleventh Circuit, sitting en banc, affirmed. We consider here whether a private damages action may lie against the school board in cases of student-on-student harassment. We conclude that it may, but only where the funding recipient acts with deliberate indifference to known acts of harassment in its programs or activities. Moreover, we conclude that such an action will lie only for harassment that is so severe, pervasive, and objectively offensive that it effectively bars the victim's access to an educational opportunity or benefit.

I

Petitioner's Title IX claim was dismissed under Federal Rule of Civil Procedure 12(b)(6) for failure to state a claim upon which relief could be granted. Accordingly, in reviewing the legal sufficiency of petitioner's cause of action, "we must assume the truth of the material facts as alleged in the complaint."

Petitioner's minor daughter, LaShonda, was allegedly the victim of a prolonged pattern of sexual harassment by one of her fifth-grade classmates at Hubbard Elementary School, a public school in Monroe County, Georgia. According to petitioner's complaint, the harassment began in December 1992, when the classmate, G. F., attempted to touch LaShonda's breasts and genital area and made vulgar statements such as "'I want to get in bed with you'" and "'I want to feel your boobs.'" Similar conduct allegedly occurred on or about January 4 and January 20, 1993. LaShonda reported each of these incidents to her mother and to her classroom teacher, Diane Fort. Petitioner, in turn, also contacted Fort, who allegedly assured petitioner that the school principal, Bill Querry, had been informed of the incidents. Petitioner contends that, notwithstanding these reports, no disciplinary action was taken against G. F.

G. F.'s conduct allegedly continued for many months. In early February, G. F. purportedly placed a door stop in his pants and proceeded to act in a sexually suggestive manner toward LaShonda during physical education class. LaShonda reported G. F.'s behavior to her physical education teacher, Whit Maples. Approximately one week later, G. F. again allegedly engaged in harassing behavior, this time while under the supervision of another classroom teacher, Joyce Pippin. . . . Again, LaShonda allegedly reported the incident to the teacher, and again petitioner contacted the teacher to follow up.

Petitioner alleges that G. F. once more directed sexually harassing conduct toward LaShonda in physical education class in early March, and that LaShonda reported the incident to both Maples and Pippen. In mid-April 1993, G. F. allegedly rubbed his body against LaShonda in the school hallway in what LaShonda considered a sexually suggestive manner, and LaShonda again reported the matter to Fort.

The string of incidents finally ended in mid-May, when G. F. was charged with, and pleaded guilty to, sexual battery for his misconduct. The complaint alleges that LaShonda had suffered during the months of harassment, however; specifically, her previously high grades allegedly dropped as she became unable to concentrate on her studies and, in April 1993, her father discovered that she had written a suicide note. The complaint further alleges that, at one point, LaShonda told petitioner that she "'didn't know how much longer she could keep [G. F.] off her.'"

Nor was LaShonda G. F.'s only victim; it is alleged that other girls in the class fell prey to G. F.'s conduct. At one point, in fact, a group composed of LaShonda and other female students tried to speak with Principal Querry about G. F.'s behavior. According to the complaint, however, a teacher denied the students' request with the statement, "'If [Querry] wants you, he'll call you.'"

Petitioner alleges that no disciplinary action was taken in response to G. F.'s behavior toward LaShonda. In addition to her conversations with Fort and Pippen, petitioner alleges that she spoke with Principal Querry in mid-May 1993. When petitioner inquired as to what action the school intended to take against G. F., Querry simply stated, "'I guess I'll have to threaten him a little bit harder.'" Yet, petitioner alleges, at no point during the many months of his reported misconduct was G. F. disciplined for harassment. Indeed, Querry allegedly asked petitioner why LaShonda "'was the only one complaining.'"

Nor, according to the complaint, was any effort made to separate G. F. and LaShonda. On the contrary, notwithstanding LaShonda's frequent complaints, only after more than three months of reported harassment was she even permitted to change her classroom seat so that she was no longer seated next to G. F. Moreover, petitioner alleges that, at the time of the events in question, the Monroe County Board of Education (Board) had not instructed its personnel on how to respond to peer sexual harassment and had not established a policy on the issue.

B

On May 4, 1994, petitioner filed suit in the United States District Court for the Middle District of Georgia against the Board, Charles Dumas, the school district's superintendent, and Principal Querry. The complaint alleged that the Board is a recipient of federal funding for purposes of Title IX, that "the persistent sexual advances and harassment by the student G. F. upon [LaShonda] interfered with her ability to attend school and perform her studies and activities," and that "the deliberate indifference by Defendants to the unwelcome sexual advances of a student upon LaShonda created an intimidating, hostile, offensive and abusive school environment in violation of Title IX." The complaint sought compensatory and punitive damages, attorney's fees, and injunctive relief.

The defendants (all respondents here) moved to dismiss petitioner's complaint under Federal Rule of Civil Procedure 12(b)(6) for failure to state a claim upon which relief could be granted, and the District Court granted respondents' motion. . . .

We granted certiorari in order to resolve a conflict in the Circuits over whether, and under what circumstances, a recipient of federal educational funds can be liable in a private damages action arising from student-on-student sexual harassment. We now reverse.

II

Title IX provides, with certain exceptions not at issue here, that

> no person in the United States shall, on the basis of sex, be excluded from participation in, be denied the benefits of, or be subjected to discrimination under any education program or activity receiving Federal financial assistance.

Congress authorized an administrative enforcement scheme for Title IX. Federal departments or agencies with the authority to provide financial assistance are entrusted to promulgate rules, regulations, and orders to enforce the objectives . . . and these departments or agencies may rely on "any . . . means authorized by law," including the termination of funding to give effect to the statute's restrictions.

There is no dispute here that the Board is a recipient of federal education funding for Title IX purposes. Nor do respondents support an argument that student-on-student harassment cannot rise to the level of "discrimination" for purposes of Title IX. Rather, at issue here is the question whether a recipient of federal education funding may be liable for damages under Title IX under any circumstances for discrimination in the form of student-on-student sexual harassment.

A

Petitioner urges that Title IX's plain language compels the conclusion that the statute is intended to bar recipients of federal funding from permitting this form of discrimination in their programs or activities. She emphasizes that the statute prohibits a student from being "subjected to discrimination under any education program or activity receiving Federal financial assistance." . . .

Here, however, we are asked to do more than define the scope of the behavior that Title IX proscribes. We must determine whether a district's failure to respond to student-on-student harassment in its schools can support a private suit for money damages. This Court has indeed recognized an implied private right of action under Title IX and we have held that money damages are available in such suits. . . .

. . . [R]espondents urge that Title IX provides no notice that recipients of federal educational funds could be liable in damages for harm arising from student-on-student harassment. Respondents contend, specifically, that the statute only proscribes misconduct by grant recipients, not third parties. Respondents argue, moreover, that it would be contrary to the very purpose of Spending Clause legislation to impose liability on a funding recipient for the misconduct of third parties, over whom recipients exercise little control.

We agree with respondents that a recipient of federal funds may be liable in damages under Title IX only for its own misconduct. . . .

We disagree with respondents' assertion, however, that petitioner seeks to hold the Board liable for G. F.'s actions instead of its own. Here, petitioner attempts to hold the Board liable for its own decision to remain idle in the face of known student-on-student harassment in its schools. . . .

. . . [*Gebser* ruled that] a recipient intentionally violates Title IX, and is subject to a private damages action, where the recipient is deliberately indifferent to known acts of teacher–student discrimination. Indeed, whether viewed as "discrimination" or "subjecting" students to discrimination, Title IX "unquestionably . . . placed on [the Board] the duty not" to permit teacher-student harassment in its schools and recipients violate Title IX's plain terms when they remain deliberately indifferent to this form of misconduct.

We consider here whether the misconduct identified in *Gebser* — deliberate indifference to known acts of harassment — amounts to an intentional violation of Title IX, capable of supporting a private damages action, when the harasser is a student rather than a teacher. We conclude that, in certain limited circumstances, it does.

. . .

The common law, too, has put schools on notice that they may be held responsible under state law for their failure to protect students from the tortious acts of third parties.

This is not to say that the identity of the harasser is irrelevant. On the contrary, both the "deliberate indifference" standard and the language of Title IX narrowly circumscribe the set of parties whose known acts of sexual harassment can trigger some duty to respond on the part of funding recipients. Deliberate indifference makes sense as a theory of direct liability under Title IX only where the funding recipient has some control over the alleged harassment. A recipient cannot be directly liable for its indifference where it lacks the authority to take remedial action.

The language of Title IX itself—particularly when viewed in conjunction with the requirement that the recipient have notice of Title IX's prohibitions to be liable for damages—also cabins the range of misconduct that the statute proscribes. The statute's plain language confines the scope of prohibited conduct based on the recipient's degree of control over the harasser and the environment in which the harassment occurs. If a funding recipient does not engage in harassment directly, it may not be liable for damages unless its deliberate indifference "subjects" its students to harassment. That is, the deliberate indifference must, at a minimum, "cause [students] to undergo" harassment or "make them liable or vulnerable" to it. Moreover, because the harassment must occur "under" "the operations of" a funding recipient.

These factors combine to limit a recipient's damages liability to circumstances wherein the recipient exercises substantial control over both the harasser and the context in which the known harassment occurs. Only then can the recipient be said to "expose" its students to harassment or "cause" them to undergo it "under" the recipient's programs. . . .

Where, as here, the misconduct occurs during school hours and on school grounds—the bulk of G. F.'s misconduct, in fact, took place in the classroom—the misconduct is taking place "under" an "operation" of the funding recipient. In these circumstances, the recipient retains substantial control over the context in which the harassment occurs. More importantly, however, in this setting the Board exercises significant control over the harasser. . . . We thus conclude that recipients of federal funding may be liable for "subjecting" their students to discrimination where the recipient is deliberately indifferent to known acts of student-on-student sexual harassment and the harasser is under the school's disciplinary authority.

. . .

We stress that our conclusion here—that recipients may be liable for their deliberate indifference to known acts of peer sexual harassment—does not mean that recipients can avoid liability only by purging their schools of actionable peer harassment or that administrators must engage in particular disciplinary action. We thus disagree with respondents' contention that, if Title IX provides a cause of action for student-on-student harassment, "nothing short of expulsion of every student accused of misconduct involving sexual overtones would protect school systems from liability or damages." Likewise, the dissent erroneously imagines that victims of peer harassment now have a Title IX right to make particular remedial demands. In fact, as we have previously noted, courts should refrain from second guessing the disciplinary decisions made by school administrators.

School administrators will continue to enjoy the flexibility they require so long as funding recipients are deemed "deliberately indifferent" to acts of student-on-student harassment only where the recipient's response to the harassment or lack thereof is clearly unreasonable in light of the known circumstances. The dissent consistently mischaracterizes this standard to require funding recipients to "remedy" peer harassment and to "ensure that . . . students conform their conduct to" certain rules. Title IX imposes no such requirements. On the contrary, the recipient must merely respond to known peer harassment in a manner that is not clearly unreasonable. This is not a mere "reasonableness" standard, as the dissent assumes. In an appropriate case, there is no reason why courts, on a motion to dismiss, for summary judgment, or for a directed verdict, could not identify a response as not "clearly unreasonable" as a matter of law.

Like the dissent, we acknowledge that school administrators shoulder substantial burdens as a result of legal constraints on their disciplinary authority. . . . We believe, however, that the standard set out here is sufficiently flexible to account both for the level of disciplinary authority available to the school and for the potential liability arising from certain forms of disciplinary action. A university might not, for example, be expected to exercise the same degree of control over its students that a grade school would enjoy and it would be entirely reasonable for a school to refrain from a form of disciplinary action that would expose it to constitutional or statutory claims.

. . .

B

The requirement that recipients receive adequate notice of Title IX's proscriptions also bears on the proper definition of "discrimination" in the context of a private damages action. We have elsewhere concluded that sexual harassment is a form of discrimination for Title IX purposes and that Title IX proscribes harassment with sufficient clarity to satisfy *Pennhurst*'s notice requirement and serve as a basis for a damages action. Having previously determined that "sexual harassment" is "discrimination" in the school context under Title IX, we are constrained to conclude that student-on-student sexual harassment, if sufficiently severe, can likewise rise to the level of discrimination actionable under the statute. . . . Students are not only protected from discrimination, but also specifically shielded from being "excluded from participation in" or "denied the benefits of" any "education program or activity receiving Federal financial assistance." The statute makes clear that, whatever else it prohibits, students must not be denied access to educational benefits and opportunities on the basis of gender. We thus conclude that funding recipients are properly held liable in damages only where they are deliberately indifferent to sexual harassment, of which they have actual knowledge, that is so severe, pervasive, and objectively offensive that it can be said to deprive the victims of access to the educational opportunities or benefits provided by the school.

The most obvious example of student-on-student sexual harassment capable of triggering a damages claim would thus involve the overt, physical deprivation of access to school resources. Consider, for example, a case in which male students physically threaten their female peers every day, successfully preventing the female students from using a particular school resource — an athletic field or a computer lab, for instance. District administrators are well aware of the daily ritual, yet they deliberately ignore requests for aid from the female students wishing to use the resource. The district's knowing refusal to take any action in response to such behavior would fly in the face of Title IX's core principles, and such deliberate indifference may appropriately be subject to claims for monetary damages. It is not necessary, however, to show physical exclusion to demonstrate that students have been deprived by the actions of another student or students of an educational opportunity on the basis of sex. Rather, a plaintiff must establish sexual harassment of students that is so severe, pervasive, and objectively offensive, and that so undermines and detracts from the victims' educational experience, that the victim-students are effectively denied equal access to an institution's resources and opportunities.

Whether gender-oriented conduct rises to the level of actionable "harassment" thus "depends on a constellation of surrounding circumstances, expectations, and relationships," including, but not limited to, the ages of the harasser and the victim and the number of individuals involved. Courts, moreover, must bear in mind that schools are unlike the adult workplace and that children may regularly interact in a manner that would be unacceptable among adults. Indeed, at least early on, students are still learning how to interact appropriately with their peers. It is thus understandable that, in the school setting, students often engage in insults, banter, teasing, shoving, pushing, and gender-specific conduct that is upsetting to the students subjected to it. Damages are not available for simple acts of teasing and name-calling among school children, however, even where these comments target differences in gender. Rather, in the context of student-on-student harassment, damages are available only where the behavior is so severe, pervasive, and objectively offensive that it denies its victims the equal access to education that Title IX is designed to protect.

... It is not enough to show, as the dissent would read this opinion to provide, that a student has been "teased," or "called ... offensive names." Comparisons to an "overweight child who skips gym class because the other children tease her about her size," the student "who refuses to wear glasses to avoid the taunts of 'four-eyes,'" and "the child who refuses to go to school because the school bully calls him a 'scaredy-cat' at recess," are inapposite and misleading. Nor do we contemplate, much less hold, that a mere "decline in grades is enough to survive" a motion to dismiss. The drop-off in LaShonda's grades provides necessary evidence of a potential link between her education and G.F.'s misconduct, but petitioner's ability to state a cognizable claim here depends equally on the alleged persistence and severity of G.F.'s actions, not to mention the Board's alleged knowledge and deliberate indifference. We trust that the dissent's characterization of our opinion will not mislead courts to impose more sweeping liability than we read Title IX to require.

Moreover, the provision that the discrimination occur "under any education program or activity" suggests that the behavior be serious enough to have the systemic effect of denying the victim equal access to an educational program or activity. Although, in theory, a single instance of sufficiently severe one-on-one peer harassment could be said to have such an effect, we think it unlikely that Congress would have thought such behavior sufficient to rise to this level in light of the inevitability of student misconduct and the amount of litigation that would be invited by entertaining claims of official indifference to a single instance of one-on-one peer harassment. By limiting private damages actions to cases having a systemic effect on educational programs or activities, we reconcile the general principle that Title IX prohibits official indifference to known peer sexual harassment with the practical realities of responding to student behavior, realities that Congress could not have meant to be ignored. Even the dissent suggests that Title IX liability may arise when a funding recipient remains indifferent to severe, gender-based mistreatment played out on a "widespread level" among students.

. . .

C

Applying this standard to the facts at issue here, we conclude that the Eleventh Circuit erred in dismissing petitioner's complaint. Petitioner alleges that her daughter was the victim of repeated acts of sexual harassment by G. F. over a 5-month period, and there are allegations in support of the conclusion that G. F.'s misconduct was severe, pervasive, and objectively offensive. The harassment was not only verbal; it included numerous acts of objectively offensive touching, and, indeed, G. F. ultimately pleaded guilty to criminal sexual misconduct. Moreover, the complaint alleges that there were multiple victims who were sufficiently disturbed by G. F.'s misconduct to seek an audience with the school principal. Further, petitioner contends that the harassment had a concrete, negative effect on her daughter's ability to receive an education. The complaint also suggests that petitioner may be able to show both actual knowledge and deliberate indifference on the part of the Board, which made no effort whatsoever either to investigate or to put an end to the harassment.

On this complaint, we cannot say "beyond doubt that [petitioner] can prove no set of facts in support of [her] claim which would entitle [her] to relief." Accordingly, the judgment of the United States Court of Appeals for the Eleventh Circuit is reversed, and the case is remanded for further proceedings consistent with this opinion.

It is so ordered.

Justice Kennedy, with whom The Chief Justice, Justice Scalia, and Justice Thomas join, dissenting.

. . . The only certainty flowing from the majority's decision is that scarce resources will be diverted from educating our children and that many school districts, desperate to avoid Title IX peer harassment suits, will adopt whatever federal code of student conduct and discipline the Department of Education sees fit to impose upon them. The Nation's schoolchildren will learn their first lessons about federalism in classrooms where the federal government is the ever-present regulator. The federal government will have insinuated itself not only into one of the most traditional areas of state concern but also into one of the most sensitive areas of human affairs. This federal control of the discipline of our Nation's schoolchildren is contrary to our traditions and inconsistent with the sensible administration of our schools. Because Title IX did not give States unambiguous notice that accepting federal funds meant ceding to the federal government power over the day-to-day disciplinary decisions of schools, I dissent.

I

. . . Schools cannot be held liable for peer sexual harassment because Title IX does not give them clear and unambiguous notice that they are liable in damages for failure to remedy discrimination by their students. . . .

A

In any event, a plaintiff cannot establish a Title IX violation merely by showing that she has been "subjected to discrimination." Rather, a violation of Title IX occurs only if she is "subjected to discrimination under any education program or activity," where "program or activity" is defined as "all of the operations of" a grant recipient. Under the most natural reading of this provision, discrimination violates Title IX only if it is authorized by, or in accordance with, the actions, activities, or policies of the grant recipient. This reading reflects the common legal usage of the term "under" to mean pursuant to, in accordance with, or as authorized or provided by.

It is not enough, then, that the alleged discrimination occur in a "context subject to the school district's control." The discrimination must actually be "controlled by"—that is, be authorized by, pursuant to, or in accordance with, school policy or actions.

This reading is also consistent with the fact that the discrimination must be "under" the "operations" of the grant recipient. The term "operations" connotes active and affirmative participation by the grant recipient, not merely inaction or failure to respond.

Teacher sexual harassment of students is "under" the school's program or activity in certain circumstances, but student harassment is not. . . .

. . .

I am aware of no basis in law or fact, however, for attributing the acts of a student to a school and, indeed, the majority does not argue that the school acts through its students. Discrimination by one student against another therefore cannot be "under" the school's program or activity as required by Title IX. The majority's imposition of liability for peer sexual harassment thus conflicts with the most natural interpretation of Title IX's "under a program or activity" limitation on school liability. At the very least, my reading undermines the majority's implicit claim that Title IX imposes an unambiguous duty on schools to remedy peer sexual harassment.

B

1

Quite aside from its disregard for the "under the program" limitation of Title IX, the majority's reading is flawed in other respects. The majority contends that a school's deliberate indifference to known student harassment "subjects" students to harassment — that is, "causes [students] to undergo" harassment. The majority recognizes, however, that there must be some limitation on the third-party conduct that the school can fairly be said to cause. In search of a principle, the majority asserts, without much elaboration, that one causes discrimination when one has some "degree of control" over the discrimination and fails to remedy it.

To state the majority's test is to understand that it is little more than an exercise in arbitrary line-drawing. The majority does not explain how we are to determine what degree of control is sufficient — or, more to the point, how the States were on clear notice that the Court would draw the line to encompass students.

. . .

2

The majority nonetheless appears to see no need to justify drawing the "enough control" line to encompass students. In truth, however, a school's control over its students is much more complicated and limited than the majority acknowledges. A public school does not control its students in the way it controls its teachers or those with whom it contracts. Most public schools do not screen or select students, and their power to discipline students is far from unfettered.

Public schools are generally obligated by law to educate all students who live within defined geographic boundaries. Indeed, the Constitution of almost every State in the country guarantees the State's students a free primary and secondary public education. . . . Schools that remove a harasser from the classroom and then attempt to fulfill their continuing-education obligation by placing the harasser in any kind of group setting, rather than by hiring expensive tutors for each student, will find themselves at continuing risk of Title IX suits brought by the other students in the alternative education program.

. . .

The practical obstacles schools encounter in ensuring that thousands of immature students conform their conduct to acceptable norms may be even more significant than the legal obstacles. School districts cannot exercise the same measure of control over thousands of students that they do over a few hundred adult employees. The limited resources of our schools must be conserved for basic educational services. Some schools lack the resources even to deal with serious problems of violence and are already overwhelmed with disciplinary problems of all kinds.

. . .

No one contests that much of this "dizzying array of immature or uncontrollable behaviors by students" is inappropriate, even "objectively offensive" at times and that parents and schools have a moral and ethical responsibility to help students learn to interact with their peers in an appropriate manner. It is doubtless the case, moreover, that much of this inappropriate behavior is directed toward members of the opposite sex, as children in the throes of adolescence struggle to express their emerging sexual identities.

It is a far different question, however, whether it is either proper or useful to label this immature, childish behavior gender discrimination. Nothing in Title IX suggests that Congress even contemplated this question, much less answered it in the affirmative in unambiguous terms. The majority, nevertheless, has no problem labeling the conduct of fifth graders "sexual harassment" and "gender discrimination." . . .

. . .

The difficulties schools will encounter in identifying peer sexual harassment are already evident in teachers' manuals designed to give guidance on the subject. For example, one teachers' manual on peer sexual harassment suggests that sexual harassment in kindergarten through third grade includes a boy being "put down" on the playground "because he wants to play house with the girls" or a girl being "put down because she shoots baskets better than the boys." Yet another manual suggests that one student saying to another, "You look nice" could be sexual harassment, depending on the "tone of voice," how the student looks at the other, and "who else is around." Blowing a kiss is also suspect. This confusion will likely be compounded once the sexual-harassment label is invested with the force of federal law, backed up by private damages suits.

The only guidance the majority gives schools in distinguishing between the "simple acts of teasing and name-calling among school children," said not to be a basis for suit even when they "target differences in gender," and actionable peer sexual harassment is, in reality, no guidance at all. . . .

The majority's reference to a "systemic effect" does nothing to clarify the content of its standard. The majority appears to intend that requirement to do no more than exclude the possibility that a single act of harassment perpetrated by one student on one other student can form the basis for an actionable claim. That is a small concession indeed.

The only real clue the majority gives schools about the dividing line between actionable harassment that denies a victim equal access to education and mere inappropriate teasing is a profoundly unsettling one: On the facts of this case, petitioner has stated a claim because she alleged, in the majority's words, "that the harassment had a concrete, negative effect on her daughter's ability to receive an education." In petitioner's words, the effects that might have been visible to the school were that her daughter's grades "dropped" and her "ability to concentrate on her school work [was] affected." Almost all adolescents experience these problems at one time or another as they mature.

III

The majority's inability to provide any workable definition of actionable peer harassment simply underscores the myriad ways in which an opinion that purports to be narrow is, in fact, so broad that it will support untold numbers of lawyers who will prove adept at presenting cases that will withstand the defendant school districts' pretrial motions. Each of the barriers to run-away litigation the majority offers us crumbles under the weight of even casual scrutiny.

... The majority seems oblivious to the fact that almost every child, at some point, has trouble in school because he or she is being teased by his or her peers. The girl who wants to skip recess because she is teased by the boys is no different from the overweight child who skips gym class because the other children tease her about her size in the locker room; or the child who risks flunking out because he refuses to wear glasses to avoid the taunts of "four-eyes"; or the child who refuses to go to school because the school bully calls him a "scarey-cat" at recess. Most children respond to teasing in ways that detract from their ability to learn. The majority's test for actionable harassment will, as a result, sweep in almost all of the more innocuous conduct it acknowledges as a ubiquitous part of school life.

The string of adjectives the majority attaches to the word "harassment"—"severe, pervasive, and objectively offensive"—likewise fails to narrow the class of conduct that can trigger liability, since the touchstone for determining whether there is Title IX liability is the effect on the child's ability to get an education. Indeed, the Court's reliance on the impact on the child's educational experience suggests that the "objective offensiveness" of a comment is to be judged by reference to a reasonable child at whom the comments were aimed. Not only is that standard likely to be quite expansive, it also gives schools—and juries—little guidance, requiring them to attempt to gauge the sensitivities of, for instance, the average seven year old.

...

Another professed limitation the majority relies upon is that the recipient will be liable only where the acts of student harassment are "known." The majority's enunciation of the standard begs the obvious question: known to whom? Yet the majority says not one word about the type of school employee who must know about the harassment before it is actionable.

...

The majority's limitations on peer sexual harassment suits cannot hope to contain the flood of liability the Court today begins.

...

There will be no shortage of plaintiffs to bring such complaints. Our schools are charged each day with educating millions of children. Of those millions of students, a large percentage will, at some point during their school careers, experience something they consider sexual harassment. A 1993 Study by the American Association of University Women Educational Foundation, for instance, found that "fully 4 out of 5 students (81%) report that they have been the target of some form of sexual harassment during their school lives." The number of potential lawsuits against our schools is staggering.

The cost of defending against peer sexual harassment suits alone could overwhelm many school districts, particularly since the majority's liability standards will allow almost any plaintiff to get to summary judgment, if not to a jury. In addition, there are no damages caps on the judicially implied private cause of action under Title IX. As a result, school liability in one peer sexual harassment suit could approach, or even exceed, the total federal funding of many school districts. Petitioner, for example, seeks damages of $500,000 in this case. Respondent school district received approximately $679,000 in federal aid in 1992–1993. The school district sued in *Gebser* received only $120,000 in federal funds a year. Indeed, the entire 1992–1993 budget of that district was only $1.6 million.

. . .

The prospect of unlimited Title IX liability will, in all likelihood, breed a climate of fear that encourages school administrators to label even the most innocuous of childish conduct sexual harassment. It would appear to be no coincidence that, not long after the DOE issued its proposed policy guidance warning. . . .

. . .

Even schools that resist overzealous enforcement may find that the most careful and reasoned response to a sexual harassment complaint nonetheless provokes litigation. . . .

. . .

Even more important, in most egregious cases the student will have state-law remedies available to her. The student will often have recourse against the offending student (or his parents) under state tort law. In some cases, like this one, the perpetrator may also be subject to criminal sanctions. And, as the majority notes, the student may, in some circumstances, have recourse against the school under state law.

Disregarding these state-law remedies for student misbehavior and the incentives that our schools already have to provide the best possible education to all of their students, the majority seeks, in effect, to put an end to student misbehavior by transforming Title IX into a Federal Student Civility Code. . . .

In the final analysis, this case is about federalism. Yet the majority's decision today says not one word about the federal balance. Preserving our federal system is a legitimate end in itself. It is, too, the means to other ends. It ensures that essential choices can be made by a government more proximate to the people than the vast apparatus of federal power. Defining the appropriate role of schools in teaching and supervising children who are beginning to explore their own sexuality and learning how to express it to others is one of the most complex and sensitive issues our schools face. Such decisions are best made by parents and by the teachers and school administrators who can counsel with them. The delicacy and immense significance of teaching children about sexuality should cause the Court to act with great restraint before it displaces state and local governments.

Heedless of these considerations, the Court rushes onward, finding that the cause of action it creates is necessary to effect the congressional design. It is not. Nothing in Title IX suggests that Congress intended or contemplated the result the Court reaches today, much less dictated it in unambiguous terms. Today's decision cannot be laid at the feet of Congress; it is the responsibility of the Court.

. . .

Perhaps the most grave, and surely the most lasting, disservice of today's decision is that it ensures the Court's own disregard for the federal balance soon will be imparted to our youngest citizens. The Court clears the way for the federal government to claim center stage in America's classrooms. Today's decision mandates to teachers instructing and supervising their students the dubious assistance of federal court plaintiffs and their lawyers and makes the federal courts the final arbiters of school policy and of almost every disagreement between students. Enforcement of the federal right recognized by the majority means that federal influence will permeate everything from curriculum decisions to day-to-day classroom logistics and interactions. After today, Johnny will find that the routine problems of adolescence are to be resolved by invoking a federal right to demand assignment to a desk two rows away.

. . . We can be assured that like suits will follow — suits, which in cost and number, will impose serious financial burdens on local school districts, the taxpayers who support them, and the children they serve. Federalism and our struggling school systems deserve better from this Court. I dissent.

Notes and Queries

1. Does the majority eviscerate Title IX as it finds peer-to-peer harassment actionable? What precisely is the standard the Court sets under which a school could be held liable?
2. The dissent concerns itself with the costs of litigating the rule set by the majority. Is that really a fair concern?

Research Comments

1. The American Association of University Women's study of the prevalence of sexual harassment in schools throughout the United States engendered a flood of legal debate regarding the sexual harassment of students. The study was the first major United States study of sexual harassment in schools and outlined the prevalence of student-on-student harassment in the American school system. The

study reported that four out of five students said they experienced unwanted and unwelcome sexual behavior at school or during a school-related activity. In addition, four out of five students reported an incident of sexual harassment by their classmates, while only 18 percent reported harassment by an adult in the school system. More than 65 percent of students reported that the harassment took place in school hallways, and 55 percent reported that the harassment took place in the classroom itself. In addition, the study outlined the effect of sexual harassment on victims. Sexually harassed students reported that they did not want to attend school, were less inclined to participate in class, found it hard to study, stayed home from school or cut class, had lower grades, or had second thoughts about whether they would graduate from high school. In all but one category, the number of girls who reported a negative impact on their education was twice the number of boys. In addition, significantly higher numbers of girls than boys reported feeling negative emotions, including embarrassment, self consciousness, loss of confidence, fear, and confusion. American Association of University Women (1993). *Hostile Hallways: The AAUW Survey on Sexual Harassment in America's Schools*. American Association of University Women Educational Foundation.

2. Rigorous programs that would focus on addressing sexual harassment in primary and secondary school levels remain rare. Still, some do show effectiveness. Gaby P. A. de Lijster, Hanneke Felten, Gerjo Kok & Paul L. Kocken (2016). Effects of an interactive school-based program for preventing adolescent sexual harassment: A cluster-randomized controlled evaluation study. *Journal of Youth and Adolescence*, 45, 874–886. Reviews of programs tend to be difficult to provide clear guidance as they tend to focus on other forms of violence, particularly dating and relationship violence. Noreen Orr, Annah Chollet, Andrew J. Rizzo, Naomi Shaw, Caroline Farmer, Honor Young, Emma Rigby, Vashti Berry, Chris Bonell & G. J. Melendez-Torres. (2022). School-based interventions for preventing dating and relationship violence and gender-based violence: A systematic review and synthesis of theories of change. *Review of Education*, 10(3), e3382. The bulk of research relating to preventing sexual harassment focuses on university levels or the workplace. For an important review that disentangles studies focusing on adult women from girls, see Leesa Hooker, Jessica Ison, Grant O'Sullivan, Christopher Fisher, Nicola Henry, Kirsty Forsdike, Felicity Young & Angela Taft. (2020). Primary prevention of sexual violence and harassment against women and girls: Combining evidence and practice knowledge. *Evidence Review and Data Synthesis*.

Review Problems

1. Consider the following. On October 11, 1993, Brian Seamons was assaulted by five of his upper-class football teammates in the locker room at Sky View High School. Brian was grabbed as he came out of the shower, forcibly restrained, and bound to a towel rack with adhesive tape. Brian's genital area was also taped. After

Brian was restrained, one of his teammates brought a girl that Brian had dated into the locker room to view him. All of this took place while other members of the team looked on. Brian reported this incident to school administrators and other authorities, including the football coach, Douglas Snow (the "coach"), and the school principal, Myron Benson (the "principal"). The coach brought Brian before the football team, accused Brian of betraying the team by bringing the incident to the attention of the administration and others, and told Brian to apologize to the team. When Brian refused to apologize, the coach dismissed Brian from the team. The five individuals who assaulted Brian were permitted to play in the next football game. The school district responded to the whole incident by canceling the final game of the season, a state playoff game. Brian alleges that he was subjected to a "hostile environment" because he was branded as the cause of the football team's demise, and that he was threatened and harassed. Eventually the principal suggested to Brian and his parents that Brian should leave the high school. Brian did so and enrolled in a distant county. Brian does not complain of the original assault against him. However, he does allege that the Defendants' response to that assault was sexually discriminatory and harassing. For example, Brian contends Defendants expected him to conform to a macho male stereotype, as evidenced by their suggestion to him that he "should have taken it like a man." In addition, the coach reportedly explained the incident by stating "boys will be boys," and characterizing the assault as "hazing," or consistent with "pranks" that are rites of passage on the football team. Following *Davis*, does Brian win his claim? The facts were ligated, in *Seamons v. Snow*, 84 F.3d 1226 (10th Cir. 1996), and the court rejected his claim. The court found that Brian had failed to allege facts sufficient to indicate that the conduct being challenged (which it must be remembered, postdates the locker room assault) was "sexual" in nature. It also found that Brian had failed to allege any facts that would suggest he was subjected to unwelcome sexual advances or requests for sexual favors, or that sex was used to contribute to a hostile environment for him. Following *Davis*, would the court rule differently?

2. In August 1999, the State College Area School District ("SCASD") adopted an Anti-Harassment Policy ("the Policy"). The Policy begins by setting forth its goal — "providing all students with a safe, secure, and nurturing school environment" — and noting that "disrespect among members of the school community is unacceptable behavior which threatens to disrupt the school environment and well being of the individual." The second paragraph contains what appears to be the Policy's operative definition of harassment: "Harassment means verbal or physical conduct based on one's actual or perceived race, religion, color, national origin, gender, sexual orientation, disability, or other personal characteristics, and which has the purpose or effect of substantially interfering with a student's educational performance or creating an intimidating, hostile or offensive environment." The Policy continues by providing several examples of harassment: "Harassment can include any unwelcome verbal, written or physical conduct which offends, denigrates or belittles an individual because of any of the characteristics described

above. Such conduct includes, but is not limited to, unsolicited derogatory remarks, jokes, demeaning comments or behaviors, slurs, mimicking, name calling, graffiti, innuendo, gestures, physical contact, stalking, threatening, bullying, extorting or the display or circulation of written material or pictures." These examples are followed by a lengthy section captioned "Definitions," which defines various types of prohibited harassment, including "Sexual harassment," "Racial and color harassment," "Harassment on the basis of religion," "Harassment based on national origin," "Disability harassment," and "Other harassment" on the basis of characteristics such as "clothing, physical appearance, social skills, peer group, intellect, educational program, hobbies or values, etc." The definitions state that harassment "can include unwelcome verbal, written or physical conduct directed at" the particular characteristic. Examples of specific types of harassment are also provided. For example, "Racial and color harassment" is said to include "nicknames emphasizing stereotypes, racial slurs, comments on manner of speaking, and negative references to racial customs." Religious harassment reaches "derogatory comments regarding surnames, religious tradition, or religious clothing, or religious slurs or graffiti." National origins harassment includes "negative comments regarding surnames, manner of speaking, customs, language, or ethnic slurs." Harassment on the basis of sexual orientation extends to "negative name calling and degrading behavior." Disability harassment encompasses "imitating manner of speech or movement." The Policy provides that "any harassment of a student by a member of the school community is a violation of this policy." It establishes procedures for the reporting, informal mediation, and formal resolution of complaints. In addition, the Policy sets a list of punishments for harassment, "including but not limited to warning, exclusion, suspension, expulsion, transfer, termination, discharge . . . , training, education, or counseling."

Plaintiff David Saxe is a member of the Pennsylvania State Board of Education and serves as an unpaid volunteer for SCASD. He is the legal guardian of both student-plaintiffs, who are enrolled in SCASD schools. After the Anti-Harassment Policy was adopted, Saxe filed suit in District Court, alleging that the Policy was facially unconstitutional under the First Amendment's free speech clause. In his Complaint, he alleged that all Plaintiffs openly and sincerely identify themselves as Christians. They believe, and their religion teaches, that homosexuality is a sin. They further believe that they have a right to speak out about the sinful nature and harmful effects of homosexuality and feel compelled by their religion to speak out on other topics, especially moral issues. They further alleged that they feared that they were likely to be punished under the Policy for speaking out about their religious beliefs, engaging in symbolic activities reflecting those beliefs, and distributing religious literature. They sought to have the policy declared unconstitutionally vague and overbroad and its operation permanently enjoined. What result? The court held that the school district's anti-harassment policy violated the free speech guarantees of the U.S. Constitution, particularly since the policy was not confined to such federally protected classes as gender, race, religion, and national origin, but encompassed sexual orientation, clothing, physical appearance, social skills, peer groups, income, intellect, educational program, hobbies, or values. The court found that not only did the school board extend the reach of its policy well beyond categories protected by statute, it also failed to demonstrate a pervasive discriminatory or disruptive effect from the proscribed harassment. The court was especially critical of the attempt to proscribe harassment on the basis of "values," such as the parent's religious beliefs, saying such a prohibition strikes at the heart of moral and political discourse. *Saxe v. State College Area School District*, 240 F.3d 200 (3d Cir., 2001).

Chapter 13

Legal Advocacy and Advancing Child Welfare Policy

Agencies that provide child welfare services confront significant challenges in their efforts to protect children and to address a wide variety of pressing needs. Most notably, and as we have repeatedly seen, the child protection system explicitly aims to protect children from harm. Yet it often finds itself criticized for failing to balance appropriately the rights of parents with the basic safety of children in their charge. The system is often accused of supplying insufficient safeguards and services to children, in some cases, while being too punitive and stigmatizing to families in others instances. These issues certainly reflect the real complexities and human limitations operating in the child welfare system

Commentators and practitioners have not been too quick to dismiss the possibility that the system itself may be at fault and that its many inadequacies could be ameliorated if the legal system and broader society took children more seriously and committed itself to structural reform. Although critics appropriately emphasize that it would be unwise to ignore how child welfare workers do provide many children with adequate care, they do highlight well the systematic challenges that run the risk of resulting in alarming failures, especially (1) inadequate service delivery and no services at all; (2) poorly organized or inadequate family needs/risk assessment and investigation; (3) lack of emphasis on the development of natural or informal "helping networks" such as friends, relatives, clergy, neighbors, and community groups; (4) failure to link CPS to substance abuse and domestic violence treatment services, despite the identification of substance abuse as the primary presenting problem in CPS case load; (5) lack of coordination with other systems affecting children, a problem exacerbated by the inadequacies and failure of those systems (such as income support systems as well as schools and juvenile justice systems); and (6) failure to achieve permanency for out-of-home placements in a timely manner and thereby limit the risks posed by multiple placements and disrupted attachment for the child. Given these deeply entrenched deficiencies, it is no surprise that even the federal government's agencies, commissions, and advisory boards routinely find a national emergency and crisis in the manner society protects children. United States Advisory Board on Child Abuse and Neglect (1993). *The Continuing Child Protection Emergency: A Challenge to the Nation*. Washington, DC: U.S. Department of Health and Human Services.

Given the potential for failure and the need for reform, it is sometimes surprising to realize that legal advocates seeking to engage in child welfare law and system reform actually do have numerous devices available to them. The modes used to seek reform vary from cause to cause and advocate to advocate. Approaches range from impact litigation, legislative advocacy, grassroots organizational efforts, public education, and media strategies to civil disobedience. Advocates often use many of these tools in response to the complexity of situations in which children find themselves. Despite wide diversity, the approach most often assumed as appropriate for broad policy reform and social change has been lawsuits, especially class actions that themselves evince important differences. These differences are revealed in the wide variety of appellations: from impact layering, cause lawyering, community lawyering, social change litigation, structural litigation, and political lawyering, to social justice lawyering. Despite potentially wide diversity, the general belief tends to be that this type of advocacy effectively highlights issues with deep cultural import, which thereby forces the government and broader society to examine them. Many now accept the reality, however, that litigation, in the traditional sense of seeking judicial relief, often fails to interest and engage the public in effective ways and that, although the courts can help produce social change, judicial decisions must be part of long-term multifaceted social movements. See Gerald N. Rosenberg (1991). *The Hollow Hope: Can Courts Bring About Social Change*? Chicago, IL: University of Chicago Press.

Given the significance of advocacy efforts, it is surprising to realize that tools for legal reform remain virtually ignored in the study of child welfare. Yet commentaries and research urging consideration of different arenas and modes of seeking reform have particular significance for efforts to address the way we think of children, families, and the law. Given that necessity, an appropriate framework for evaluating social change efforts through law necessarily must involve much more than a focus on federal and state judicial and legislative actions. Evaluating social change also would include the potential utility and effects of alternative regimes established by and on behalf of disenfranchised people to create services and programs denied to them by the formal legal system. Equally importantly, understanding the impact of reform would involve addressing its impact on a broad view of the term "law," which would include the norms about which individuals come to have consciousness, whether that consciousness derives from judicial decisions, statutes, or more general sources of rights to object to mistreatment. To make major changes in critical social relationships, one must change the way people think about issues. See Roger J. R. Levesque (2001). *Culture and Family Violence: Fostering Change through Human Rights Law.* Washington, DC: American Psychological Association.

Many espouse the view that litigation and lobbying to expand or improve child welfare programs will only reach effectiveness with the support of the general public and the enforcement of changed laws. The hope is that a new law that fundamentally affects a large number of people creates the potential for culture shifting. Unless a new law promotes public awareness and adherence to its mandates, as well as provides appropriate sanctions for their disregard, the hoped-for culture shifting cannot occur.

In the absence of an effort to also engage in broader reform, attempts at law reform may only succeed on a formal level and may not have any real impact on the larger cultural context. From this view, effective advocacy reconstructs values in the dominant culture, thus encouraging greater sensitivity to the injustices faced by the underrepresented and mobilizing greater resources for them.

Many salutary effects can emerge from efforts to foster broad reforms. One frequently touted result involves the mobilization and empowerment of those seeking legal assistance and strengthening the represented constituency or community organization seeking assistance for those in need. Much value attaches to this empowerment because all can then work toward larger, more fundamental change. This way, the community will view the law as a tool to accomplish change rather than see legal reform as the end goal in and of itself. Another salutary result involves the manner the advocacy engages with the profound moral issues underlying child welfare. Legal commentators have long documented the impact of judicial reasoning and legislators' discourse on the moral rhetoric surrounding controversial issues. Because of the potentially powerful nature of its surrounding rhetoric, successful litigation necessarily involves struggling with deep moral concerns. When significant changes occur and public awareness of those changes are widespread, the changes gain public legitimacy and contribute to a culture shift that allows for continuous, overall enforcement of changes. See Thomas B. Stoddard (1997). Bleeding heart: Reflections on using the law to make social change. *New York University Law Review*, 72, 967–991; Nan D. Hunter (1997). Lawyering for social justice. *New York University Law Review*, 72, 1009–1022; Chai R. Feldblum (1997). The moral rhetoric of legislation. *New York University Law Review*, 72, 992–1008.

Questions remain as to whether the use of these legal tools to effect social change is a legitimate form of legal practice. Scholars support both sides of the debate. Opponents of political lawyering raise two main contentions. One argument concerns the impact of political lawyering on the lawyer–client relationship. The primary concerns raised regarding the lawyer–client relationship focus on how attorneys can manipulate their clients and how they may elevate the interests of their broader cause over those of their individual clients. Typically, attorneys are asked to submerge themselves in their client's position and represent that position effectively and vigorously. The belief is that clients bear the consequences of their own decisions and are therefore best situated to understand both the legal and non-legal significance of their choices. Consequently, an attorney counsels clients most effectively by helping them explore all possible results of their actions so that they may make decisions that best serve their own needs. Another objection to lawyering for social change stems from the perception that it is a way of permitting the courts to supercede the democratic process. This type of litigation involves judges and lawyers in shaping broad, long-lasting injunctive relief and in making administrative and political decisions affecting the everyday policies and practices of public institutions and service systems. As a result, this type of lawyering may be perceived as inappropriately asking courts to legislate social policy and usurping the will of the people with their own. These are rather powerful charges that go to the foundation of our civil society: Attorneys are accused of commandeering the democratic process, thwarting legislative and executive decisions, and wielding unconstrained power to realize their own conceptions of the public good. See Robert H. Mnookin & Robert A. Burt (Eds.) (1996). *In the Interest of Children: Advocacy, Law Reform, and Public Policy.* Cambridge, MA: Program on Negotiation at Harvard Law School.

Proponents of lawyering for social change typically advance two positions. The first relates to the nature of the law as an articulation of social morality. This approach finds it legitimate to use lawyering to effect social change because the law reflects society's morals and standards. This view envisions lawyers as engaging the law to advance their own visions of an ideal society in furtherance of the notion that the law must reflect societal values. The second argument regards the structure of the legal system and the rights of all to gain access to justice. This view relies on the unique role that attorneys play in the legal system. Lawyers retain a monopoly on legal services, which obligates them to work for those in need not merely because of the demand for public services, but because of the implicit right to equal justice under law. This view also, then, goes to the foundation of our civil society; equal justice for all is one of the fundamental legitimizing principles of the American legal system. The argument is that advocacy for structural reform safeguards the basic civil rights of groups of people who are prevented by discrimination, poverty, disability, or other factors from participating fairly and equally in the political process. See David Luban (1988). *Lawyers and Justice: An Ethical Study.* Princeton, NJ: Princeton University Press.

Efforts to foster child welfare reform certainly involve ambitious and often controversial goals but they generally entail basic litigation (or threat of litigation) to initiate efforts to address systematic failures. The litigation of interest to us in this chapter, then, is the type that undertakes to effect changes in the rules and practices of public institutions or social service systems such as schools, juvenile justice facilities, mental hospitals, foster care systems, or welfare programs. As expected by the clients these institutions often serve, the sought-after changes are intended to improve protections for the civil liberties, safety, health, and well-being of the usually poor and minority children and families these systems affect. Although there may be diverse methods, all do tend to seek broad reform for specific clients, including those who will be treated by the system in the future, and often aim to transform society.

As we will see, even agreeing on the need to use structural reform litigation raises important issues. Even ardent defenders of structural reform litigation have been worried about losing sight of their clients, especially children. Young children often cannot state their own needs and desires. Older children may be able to articulate their desires, but their desires may not necessarily influence the actions of their counsel. Moreover, most structural reform cases on behalf of children involve poor and minority children, where parents and communities may also be unable to serve as a check on attorney power. At the same time, children usually cannot participate directly in the political process by voting, lobbying, organizing, or influencing the administrators of public agencies. With children who have been maltreated by their families, these issues present important challenges. The typical response to the concerns about the legitimacy of attorneys' representation of children is for the attorney to take direction from the child's parents or guardians. How we are to balance the rights and obligations of children, parents, families, communities, and governmental institutions yet again becomes our major concern.

Mallard v. United States District Court

490 U.S. 296; 109 S. Ct. 1814 (1989)

Justice Brennan delivered the opinion of the Court.

We are called upon to decide whether 28 U.S.C. § 1915(d) authorizes a federal court to require an unwilling attorney to represent an indigent litigant in a civil case. We hold that it does not.

I

Section 1915(d) provides: "The court may request an attorney to represent any [person claiming in forma pauperis status] unable to employ counsel and may dismiss the case if the allegation of poverty is untrue, or if satisfied that the action is frivolous or malicious." In *Nelson v. Redfield Lithograph Printing*, the Court of Appeals for the Eighth Circuit ordered "the chief judge of each district to seek the cooperation of the bar associations and the federal practice committees of the judge's district to obtain a sufficient list of attorneys practicing throughout the district so as to supply the court with competent attorneys who will serve in pro bono situations," such as in forma pauperis proceedings conducted under 28 U.S.C. § 1915. The District Court for the Southern District of Iowa heeded the Court of Appeals' command. Under the system in force since February 1986, once the District Court has determined that an indigent party qualifies for representation under § 1915(d), the Clerk of the Court forwards a copy of the court file to the Volunteer Lawyers Project (VLP), a joint venture of the Legal Services Corporation of Iowa and the Iowa State Bar Association. The VLP keeps a copy of a roster prepared by the District Court of all attorneys admitted to practice before the court and in good standing. After deleting the names of lawyers who have volunteered for VLP referrals of pro bono state-court cases, the VLP selects lawyers from the list nonalphabetically for § 1915(d) assignments. Lawyers who are chosen under the plan may apply to the District Court for reimbursement of out-of-pocket costs. They may also keep any fee award provided by statute, but are not guaranteed even minimal compensation for their own services. The VLP assists lawyers assigned to litigate in areas of the law with which they are unfamiliar by providing written materials, holding periodic seminars, and facilitating consultations with experienced attorneys.

Petitioner Mallard was admitted to practice before the District Court in January 1987, and entered his first appearance the following month. In June 1987 he was asked by the VLP to represent two current inmates and one former inmate who sued prison officials under 42 U.S.C. § 1983, alleging that prison guards and administrators had filed false disciplinary reports against them, mistreated them physically, and endangered their lives by exposing them as informants. After reviewing the case file, Mallard filed a motion to withdraw with the District Court. In his motion, petitioner stated that he had no familiarity with the legal issues presented in the case, that he lacked experience in deposing and cross-examining witnesses, and that he would willingly volunteer his services in an area in which he possessed some expertise, such as bankruptcy and securities law. The VLP opposed petitioner's motion, claiming that he was competent, that he had an ethical duty to do whatever was necessary to try the case, and that permitting an exception to the rule of assignment would create a dangerous precedent. A Magistrate denied petitioner's motion.

Mallard then appealed to the District Court. Although he reiterated his unfamiliarity with § 1983 actions, he contended that he should be permitted to withdraw not because of his inexperience in interpreting the statute and its case law, but because he was not a litigator by training or temperament. Forcing him to represent indigent inmates in a complex action requiring depositions and discovery, cross-examination of witnesses, and other trial skills, Mallard asserted, would compel him to violate his ethical obligation to take on only those cases he could handle competently and would exceed the court's authority under § 1915(d). In an accompanying affidavit, Mallard added: "I do not like the role of confronting other persons in a litigation setting, accusing them of misdeeds, or questioning their veracity. Because of my reluctance to become involved in these activities, I do not feel confident that I would be effective in litigating a case such as the instant case."

Unmoved, the District Court upheld the Magistrate's decision. Based on the quality of petitioner's brief in support of his motion to withdraw, the court pronounced him competent, notwithstanding his very slight acquaintance with trial litigation. The court also held that § 1915(d) empowers federal courts to make compulsory appointments in civil actions. In November 1987, Mallard sought a writ of mandamus from the Court of Appeals for the Eighth Circuit to compel the District Court to allow his withdrawal. The Court of Appeals denied the petition without opinion. We granted certiorari to resolve a conflict among the Courts of Appeals over whether § 1915(d) authorizes compulsory assignments of attorneys in civil cases. We now reverse.

II

Interpretation of a statute must begin with the statute's language. Section 1915(d)'s operative term is "request": "The court may request an attorney to represent" an indigent litigant. The import of the term seems plain. To request that somebody do something is to express a desire that he do it, even though he may not generally be disciplined or sanctioned if he declines. Of course, somebody who frequently refuses another person's requests might not win that person's favor. A soldier who regularly fails to fulfill his superior's requests might not rise in the ranks as rapidly as would someone who was more compliant. But somebody who refuses a request, as the word is ordinarily used, may not be penalized formally for doing so, as a soldier who disobeyed orders might be court-martialed. In everyday speech, the closest synonyms of the verb "request" are "ask," "petition," and "entreat." The verbs "require" and "demand" are not usually interchangeable with it.

There is little reason to think that Congress did not intend "request" to bear its most common meaning when it used the word in § 1915(d). Although "request" may double for "demand" or "command" when it is used as a noun, particularly when employed as a term of art in connection with wills, trusts, and probate proceedings, its ordinary and natural signification when used as a verb was precatory when Congress enacted the provision now appearing at 28 U.S.C. § 1915(d) in 1892.

. . .

An examination of state statutes governing in forma pauperis proceedings at the time § 1915(d) became law bolsters this conclusion. . . .

. . .

Comparing § 1915(d) with similar federal statutes strengthens our conclusion that Congress did not authorize mandatory appointments. The sole federal statute antedating § 1915(d) that provided for court-ordered representation allowed a capital defendant "to make his full defense by counsel learned in the law" and stated that "the court before whom such person shall be tried, or some judge thereof, shall . . . immediately, upon his request . . . assign to such person such counsel, not exceeding two, as such person shall desire. . . ." Thus, when Congress enacted § 1915(d), the verb "assign" was already part of the federal statutory lexicon; Congress' decision to depart from prior usage in fashioning a rule for civil cases involving indigent litigants might be taken to display a reluctance to require attorneys to serve, even though Congress apparently mandated service in the much more serious case of criminal defendants facing the death penalty.

This inference finds additional support in Congress' actions subsequent to § 1915(d)'s enactment. Every federal statute still in force that was passed after 1892 and that authorizes courts to provide counsel states that courts may "assign" or "appoint" attorneys, just as did the 1790 capital representation statute. . . .

Contrary to respondents' assertion, construing § 1915(d) to allow courts to ask but not compel lawyers to represent indigent litigants does not render § 1915(d) a nullity. Respondents contend that statutory authorization is unnecessary for a court simply to ask an attorney to represent someone; § 1915(d) would be superfluous if it did no more than that, and thus it must be read to confer coercive power upon the federal courts. Respondents' major premise, however, is too strong. Statutory provisions may simply codify existing rights or powers. Section 1915(d), for example, authorizes courts to dismiss a "frivolous or malicious" action, but there is little doubt they would have power to do so even in the absence of this statutory provision. Nor do respondents' premises compel their conclusion. Section 1915(d) plays a useful role in the statutory scheme if it informs lawyers that the court's requests to provide legal assistance are appropriate requests, hence not to be ignored or disregarded in the mistaken belief that they are improper, like a judge's request to cut short cross-examination so that he can go fishing. Section 1915(d) may meaningfully be read to legitimize a court's request to represent a poor litigant and therefore to confront a lawyer with an important ethical decision; one need not interpret it to authorize the imposition of sanctions should a lawyer decide not to serve in order to give purpose to the provision.

. . .

IV

We emphasize that our decision today is limited to interpreting § 1915(d). We do not mean to question, let alone denigrate, lawyers' ethical obligation to assist those who are too poor to afford counsel, or to suggest that requests made pursuant to § 1915(d) may be lightly declined because they give rise to no ethical claim. On the contrary, in a time when the need for legal services among the poor is growing and public funding for such services has not kept pace, lawyers' ethical obligation to volunteer their time and skills pro bono publico is manifest. Nor do we express an opinion on the question whether the federal courts possess inherent authority to require lawyers to serve. Although respondents and their amici urge us to affirm the Court of Appeals' judgment on the ground that the federal courts do have such authority, the District Court did not invoke its inherent power in its opinion below, and the Court of Appeals did not offer this ground for denying Mallard's application for a writ of mandamus. We therefore leave that issue for another day. We hold only that § 1915(d) does not authorize the federal courts to make coercive appointments of counsel. Accordingly, the judgment of the Court of Appeals is reversed, and the case is remanded for further proceedings consistent with this opinion.

So ordered.

Justice Kennedy, concurring.

Our decision today speaks to the interpretation of a statute, to the requirements of the law, and not to the professional responsibility of the lawyer. Lawyers, like all those who practice a profession, have obligations to their calling which exceed their obligations to the State. Lawyers also have obligations by virtue of their special status as officers of the court. Accepting a court's request to represent the indigent is one of those traditional obligations. Our judgment here does not suggest otherwise. To the contrary, it is precisely because our duties go beyond what the law demands that ours remains a noble profession.

I join in full the opinion of the Court.

Justice Stevens, with whom Justice Marshall, Justice Blackmun, and Justice O'Connor join, dissenting.

The relationship between a court and the members of its bar is not defined by statute alone. The duties of the practitioner are an amalgam of tradition, respect for the profession, the inherent power of the judiciary, and the commands that are set forth in canons of ethics, rules of court, and legislative enactments. This case involves much more than the parsing of the plain meaning of the word "request" as used in 28 U.S.C. § 1915(d). This case also does not concern the sufficiency of the lawyer's reasons for declining an appointment or the sanctions that may be imposed on an attorney who refuses to serve without compensation. There are, of course, many situations in which a lawyer may properly decline such representation. He or she may have a conflict of interest, may be engaged in another trial, may already have accepted more than a fair share of the uncompensated burdens that fall upon the profession, or may not have the qualifications for a particular assignment. As this case comes to us, however, the question is whether a lawyer may seek relief . . . simply because he would rather do something else with his time. For me, the answer is quite plain.

A few weeks ago we held that the Virgin Islands Bar could not exclude nonresidents from its membership. In that case, we expressly recognized the legitimacy of the bar's interest in requiring its entire membership to share in the burdens of providing representation to indigent defendants in criminal cases. That recognition reflects the fact that a court's power to require a lawyer to render assistance to the indigent is firmly rooted in the authority to define the terms and conditions upon which members are admitted to the bar and to exercise "those powers necessary to protect the functioning of its own processes." The lawyer's duty to provide professional assistance to the poor is part of the ancient traditions of the bar long recognized by this Court and the courts of the several States. As Justice Field, then sitting on the California Supreme Court, declared more than a century ago:

> [I]t is part of the general duty of counsel to render their professional services to persons accused of crime, who are destitute of means, upon the appointment of the Court, when not inconsistent with their obligations to others; and for compensation, they must trust to the possible future ability of the parties. Counsel are not considered at liberty to reject, under circumstances of this character, the cause of the defenseless, because no provision for their compensation is made by law.

Or, as Justice Sutherland declared for the Court more recently: "Attorneys are officers of the court, and are bound to render service when required by such an appointment."

Section 1915(d) embodies this authority to order counsel to represent indigent litigants even if it does not exhaust it. The statute was passed to give federal courts the same authority to allow in forma pauperis actions that the courts in the most progressive States exercised. In 1892, state courts had statutory authority to order lawyers to render assistance to indigent civil litigants in a dozen States and common-law power to appoint counsel in at least another 10 States. Congress intended to "open the United States courts" to impoverished litigants and "to keep pace" with the laws of these "[m]any humane and enlightened States." Congress also intended to ensure that the rights of litigants suing diverse parties in the most liberal of these States would not be defeated by the defendant's removal of the suit to federal court. To be faithful to the congressional design of ensuring the poor litigant equal justice whether the suit is prosecuted in federal or state court, the statute should be construed to require counsel to serve, absent good reason, when requested to do so by the court. The Court's niggardly construction to the contrary departs from the enlightened laws that Congress intended to track and defeats Congress' beneficent purpose.

I attach no particular significance to the difference, if any, between the ordinary meaning of the word "request" used in § 1915(d) and "assign" and "appoint" used in the various state statutes. The federal statute was introduced in the House and the Senate as an Act empowering courts to "assign" counsel for poor persons and uses the terms "assign" and "request" interchangeably. Significantly, it is entitled "An Act providing when plaintiff may sue as a poor person and when counsel shall be assigned by the court." Every contemporary decision uses the word "assign" to describe the judge's authority to secure counsel for parties under § 1915(d). It is evident that the drafters of this statute understood these terms to impose similar obligations and simply assumed that members of our profession would perform their assigned tasks when requested to do so by the court.

The notion that this petitioner had an absolute right to have his "motion to withdraw" granted by the District Court . . . is completely unacceptable to me. An attorney who has entered an appearance in a case may not withdraw without leave of court because the court's interest in making sure that a litigant is adequately represented and that the orderly prosecution of the lawsuit is not disrupted is paramount to a lawyer's personal interest in terminating a relationship with a client. In this unique case the petitioner apparently filed his motion to withdraw without first entering an appearance — thus, the motion might more appropriately have been captioned as a "petition to be excused from performing a nonexistent duty to enter an appearance in a pending case." Indeed, the very fact that the petitioner considered it appropriate to ask the Magistrate to allow him to "withdraw" is evidence of his recognition of some duty to accept the appointment unless there was a valid excuse for declining it.

The program adopted by the District Court for the Southern District of Iowa to provide representation for indigent litigants was in operation when petitioner became a member of that court's bar. In my opinion his admission to practice implicitly included an obligation to participate in that program. When a court has established a fair and detailed procedure for the assignment of counsel to indigent litigants, a formal request to a lawyer by the court pursuant to that procedure is tantamount to a command.

In context, I would therefore construe the word "request" in § 1915(d) as meaning "respectfully command." If that is not what Congress intended, the statute is virtually meaningless. There is no substance to the Court's speculation that Congress enacted this provision because of a concern that a court's requests to represent a poor litigant might otherwise be "disregarded in the mistaken belief that they are improper." There is no anecdotal or historical evidence to support this highly improbable speculation. In my opinion Congress gave its endorsement to these judicial "requests," assuming that it would be "unthinkable" for a lawyer to decline without an adequate reason.

I respectfully dissent.

Notes and Queries

1. Various courts, both state and federal, have interpreted certain statutes as authorizing them to appoint attorneys in civil *forma pauperis* cases. At the federal level, the courts of appeals were split on the interpretation of a particular statute, which stated that a federal court could "request" that an attorney serve an indigent civil litigant. In the principal case, the Supreme Court held that under this particular federal statute, federal courts could not mandate that an attorney accept a case involving an indigent civil litigant.

2. Assignment of attorneys in the common law tradition is generally limited to situations in which the due process rights of life and liberty apply, usually in criminal cases. Leading cases do demonstrate that the right to counsel exists in criminal cases; but the United States pro bono tradition does support coercive appointments in criminal cases to provide teeth to the due process guarantee. A clear line of cases does not exist supporting the right to counsel in non-criminal matters. The right to counsel generally only extends beyond the criminal case when a constitutionally guaranteed freedom is at stake.

3. We have seen in *Lassiter* that, despite the admittedly high interest a parent has in retaining parental rights for her children, and the arguably high possibility for error absent legal representation, the Court found that these factors did not rebut the presumption that right to counsel is not ordinarily provided in parental rights termination proceedings.

4. The case was decided on statutory grounds. What do you make of constitutional or policy grounds? The Fifth and Fourteenth amendments of the Constitution provide that private property shall not be taken for public use without just compensation. The parallel to the forced pro bono issue is clear. If an attorney's services (the attorney's private property) are used by the government without remuneration, then the government has engaged in an unconstitutional taking. In some circumstances, services may be deemed property. However, if the matter is one of public duty, the government is not taking private property and no compensation is owed. The Constitution's Thirteenth Amendment prohibits involuntary servitude within the United States, and grants Congress the power to enforce this provision. If law or force compels a person to work or perform, then the labor is considered involuntary. However, the constitutional provision against involuntary servitude has a public duty exception and the compelled service needs to benefit the public good. In the case of coercive appointments of attorneys, the government may argue that the public good (as in cases of military conscription) is served by compelling attorneys to render counsel to the indigent. Public policy arguments also may be made: Attorneys may not have adequate competence in an area and requiring them to accept certain cases may push them toward breaking professional rules of conduct. See Gail S. Guglietta (1991). *Mallard v.*

United States District Court: A case for volunteered pro bono representation. *New England Law Review*, 25, 923–957.

Research Comment

1. Poor people face a wide range of legal problems without legal representation. For example, right to counsel promoters recognize that low-income Americans face a wide range of legal problems, including those involving Social Security benefits, housing, consumer matters, insurance, welfare benefits, family crises, grinding financial problems, bankruptcies, repossessions, unemployment compensation, and many other crises involving legal disputes. Yet the American Bar Association reports that 40 percent of low-income households surveyed had civil legal problems in the last twelve months but could not obtain counsel. In the early nineties, two of five Americans surveyed could not afford legal help with everyday legal problems like contracts, housing, or domestic relations. See Patricia M. Wald (1992). Becoming a player: A credo for young lawyers in the 1990s. *Maryland Law Review*, 51, 422–433. Currently, the three highest contributors to legal services funding are direct pro bono services, federal funding through the Legal Services Corporation ("LSC"), and Income on Lawyer's Trust Accounts ("IOLTA") programs. See Joan Grace Ritchey (2001). Limits on justice: The United States' failure to recognize a right to counsel in civil litigation. *Washington University Law Quarterly*, 79, 317–341.

Legal Services Corporation v. Velazquez

531 U.S. 533; 121 S. Ct. 1043 (2001)

Justice Kennedy delivered the opinion of the Court.

In 1974, Congress enacted the Legal Services Corporation Act. The Act establishes the Legal Services Corporation (LSC) as a District of Columbia nonprofit corporation. LSC's mission is to distribute funds appropriated by Congress to eligible local grantee organizations "for the purpose of providing financial support for legal assistance in noncriminal proceedings or matters to persons financially unable to afford legal assistance."

LSC grantees consist of hundreds of local organizations governed, in the typical case, by local boards of directors. In many instances the grantees are funded by a combination of LSC funds and other public or private sources. The grantee organizations hire and supervise lawyers to provide free legal assistance to indigent clients. Each year LSC appropriates funds to grantees or recipients that hire and supervise lawyers for various professional activities, including representation of indigent clients seeking welfare benefits.

This suit requires us to decide whether one of the conditions imposed by Congress on the use of LSC funds violates the First Amendment rights of LSC grantees and their clients. For purposes of our decision, the restriction, to be quoted in further detail, prohibits legal representation funded by recipients of LSC moneys if the representation involves an effort to amend or otherwise challenge existing welfare law. As interpreted by the LSC and by the Government, the restriction prevents an attorney from arguing to a court that a state statute conflicts with a federal statute or that either a state or federal statute by its terms or in its application is violative of the United States Constitution.

Lawyers employed by New York City LSC grantees, together with private LSC contributors, LSC indigent clients, and various state and local public officials whose governments contribute to LSC grantees, brought suit in the United States District Court for the Southern District of New York to declare the restriction, among other provisions of the Act, invalid. The United States Court of Appeals for the Second Circuit approved an injunction against enforcement of the provision as an impermissible viewpoint-based discrimination in violation of the First Amendment. We granted certiorari, and the parties who commenced the suit in the District Court are here as respondents. The LSC as petitioner is joined by the Government of the United States, which had intervened in the District Court.

We agree that the restriction violates the First Amendment, and we affirm the judgment of the Court of Appeals.

I

From the inception of the LSC, Congress has placed restrictions on its use of funds. For instance, the LSC Act prohibits recipients from making available LSC funds, program personnel, or equipment to any political party, to any political campaign, or for use in "advocating or opposing any ballot measures." The Act further proscribes use of funds in most criminal proceedings and in litigation involving nontherapeutic abortions, secondary school desegregation, military desertion, or violations of the Selective Service statute. Fund recipients are barred from bringing class-action suits unless express approval is obtained from LSC.

The restrictions at issue were part of a compromise set of restrictions enacted in the Omnibus Consolidated Rescissions and Appropriations Act of 1996 and continued in each subsequent annual appropriations Act. The relevant portion of § 504(a)(16) prohibits funding of any organization

> that initiates legal representation or participates in any other way, in litigation, lobbying, or rulemaking, involving an effort to reform a Federal or State welfare system, except that this paragraph shall not be construed to preclude a recipient from representing an individual eligible client who is seeking specific relief from a welfare agency if such relief does not involve an effort to amend or otherwise challenge existing law in effect on the date of the initiation of the representation.

The prohibitions apply to all of the activities of an LSC grantee, including those paid for by non-LSC funds. We are concerned with the statutory provision which excludes LSC representation in cases which "involve an effort to amend or otherwise challenge existing law in effect on the date of the initiation of the representation."

In 1997, LSC adopted final regulations clarifying § 504(a)(16). LSC interpreted the statutory provision to allow indigent clients to challenge welfare agency determinations of benefit ineligibility under interpretations of existing law. For example, an LSC grantee could represent a welfare claimant who argued that an agency made an erroneous factual determination or that an agency misread or misapplied a term contained in an existing welfare statute. According to LSC, a grantee in that position could argue as well that an agency policy violated existing law. Under LSC's interpretation, however, grantees could not accept representations designed to change welfare laws, much less argue against the constitutionality or statutory validity of those laws. Even in cases where constitutional or statutory challenges became apparent after representation was well under way, LSC advised that its attorneys must withdraw.

After the instant suit was filed in the District Court alleging the restrictions on the use of LSC funds violated the First Amendment the court denied a preliminary injunction, finding no probability of success on the merits.

On appeal, the Court of Appeals for the Second Circuit ... upheld the restrictions on litigation, lobbying, and rulemaking "involving an effort to reform a Federal or State welfare system," ...

... The court invalidated, as impermissible viewpoint discrimination, the qualification that representation could "not involve an effort to amend or otherwise challenge existing law," because it "clearly seeks to discourage challenges to the status quo."

...

LSC filed a petition for certiorari challenging the Court of Appeals' conclusion that the § 504(a)(16) suits-for-benefits proviso was unconstitutional. We granted certiorari.

II

The United States and LSC rely on *Rust v. Sullivan* as support for the LSC program restrictions. In *Rust*, Congress established program clinics to provide subsidies for doctors to advise patients on a variety of family planning topics. Congress did not consider abortion to be within its family planning objectives, however, and it forbade doctors employed by the program from discussing abortion with their patients. ... The recipients argued that the regulations constituted impermissible viewpoint discrimination favoring an antiabortion position over a proabortion approach in the sphere of family planning. They asserted as well that Congress had imposed an unconstitutional condition on recipients of federal funds by requiring them to relinquish their right to engage in abortion advocacy and counseling in exchange for the subsidy.

We upheld the law, reasoning that Congress had not discriminated against viewpoints on abortion, but had "merely chosen to fund one activity to the exclusion of the other." The restrictions were considered necessary "to ensure that the limits of the federal program [were] observed." Title X did not single out a particular idea for suppression because it was dangerous or disfavored; rather, Congress prohibited Title X doctors from counseling that was outside the scope of the project.

The Court in *Rust* did not place explicit reliance on the rationale that the counseling activities of the doctors under Title X amounted to governmental speech; when interpreting the holding in later cases, however, we have explained *Rust* on this understanding. We have said that viewpoint-based funding decisions can be sustained in instances in which the government is itself the speaker or instances, like *Rust*, in which the government "used private speakers to transmit information pertaining to its own program." As we said in *Rosenberger*, "when the government disburses public funds to private entities to convey a governmental message, it may take legitimate and appropriate steps to ensure that its message is neither garbled nor distorted by the grantee." The latitude which may exist for restrictions on speech where the government's own message is being delivered flows in part from our observation that, "when the government speaks, for instance to promote its own policies or to advance a particular idea, it is, in the end, accountable to the electorate and the political process for its advocacy. If the citizenry objects, newly elected officials later could espouse some different or contrary position."

Neither the latitude for government speech nor its rationale applies to subsidies for private speech in every instance, however. As we have pointed out, "it does not follow ... that viewpoint-based restrictions are proper when the [government] does not itself speak or subsidize transmittal of a message it favors but instead expends funds to encourage a diversity of views from private speakers."

Although the LSC program differs from the program at issue in *Rosenberger* in that its purpose is not to "encourage a diversity of views," the salient point is that, like the program in *Rosenberger*, the LSC program was designed to facilitate private speech, not to promote a governmental message. Congress funded LSC grantees to provide attorneys to represent the interests of indigent clients. In the specific context of § 504(a)(16) suits for benefits, an LSC-funded attorney speaks on the behalf of the client in a claim against the government for welfare benefits. The lawyer is not the government's speaker. The attorney defending the decision to deny benefits will deliver the government's message in the litigation. The LSC lawyer, however, speaks on the behalf of his or her private, indigent client.

The Government has designed this program to use the legal profession and the established Judiciary of the States and the Federal Government to accomplish its end of assisting welfare claimants in determination or receipt of their benefits. The advice from the attorney to the client and the advocacy by the attorney to the courts cannot be classified as governmental speech even under a generous understanding of the concept. In this vital respect this suit is distinguishable from *Rust*.

...

By providing subsidies to LSC, the Government seeks to facilitate suits for benefits by using the State and Federal courts and the independent bar on which those courts depend for the proper performance of their duties and responsibilities. Restricting LSC attorneys in advising their clients and in presenting arguments and analyses to the courts distorts the legal system by altering the traditional role of the attorneys in much the same way broadcast systems or student publication networks were changed in the limited forum cases we have cited. Just as government in those cases could not elect to use a broadcasting network or a college publication structure in a regime which prohibits speech necessary to the proper functioning of those systems it may not design a subsidy to effect this serious and fundamental restriction on advocacy of attorneys and the functioning of the judiciary.

. . .

The restriction imposed by the statute here threatens severe impairment of the judicial function. Section 504(a)(16) sifts out cases presenting constitutional challenges in order to insulate the Government's laws from judicial inquiry. If the restriction on speech and legal advice were to stand, the result would be two tiers of cases. In cases where LSC counsel were attorneys of record, there would be lingering doubt whether the truncated representation had resulted in complete analysis of the case, full advice to the client, and proper presentation to the court. The courts and the public would come to question the adequacy and fairness of professional representations when the attorney, either consciously to comply with this statute or unconsciously to continue the representation despite the statute, avoided all reference to questions of statutory validity and constitutional authority. A scheme so inconsistent with accepted separation-of-powers principles is an insufficient basis to sustain or uphold the restriction on speech.

It is no answer to say the restriction on speech is harmless because, under LSC's interpretation of the Act, its attorneys can withdraw. This misses the point. The statute is an attempt to draw lines around the LSC program to exclude from litigation those arguments and theories Congress finds unacceptable but which by their nature are within the province of the courts to consider.

The restriction on speech is even more problematic because in cases where the attorney withdraws from a representation, the client is unlikely to find other counsel. The explicit premise for providing LSC attorneys is the necessity to make available representation "to persons financially unable to afford legal assistance." There often will be no alternative source for the client to receive vital information respecting constitutional and statutory rights bearing upon claimed benefits. Thus, with respect to the litigation services Congress has funded, there is no alternative channel for expression of the advocacy Congress seeks to restrict. This is in stark contrast to *Rust*. There, a patient could receive the approved Title X family planning counseling funded by the Government and later could consult an affiliate or independent organization to receive abortion counseling. Unlike indigent clients who seek LSC representation, the patient in *Rust* was not required to forfeit the Government-funded advice when she also received abortion counseling through alternative channels. Because LSC attorneys must withdraw whenever a question of a welfare statute's validity arises, an individual could not obtain joint representation so that the constitutional challenge would be presented by a non-LSC attorney, and other, permitted, arguments advanced by LSC counsel.

. . .

The effect of the restriction, however, is to prohibit advice or argumentation that existing welfare laws are unconstitutional or unlawful. Congress cannot recast a condition on funding as a mere definition of its program in every case, lest the First Amendment be reduced to a simple semantic exercise. Here, notwithstanding Congress' purpose to confine and limit its program, the restriction operates to insulate current welfare laws from constitutional scrutiny and certain other legal challenges, a condition implicating central First Amendment concerns. In no lawsuit funded by the Government can the LSC attorney, speaking on behalf of a private client, challenge existing welfare laws. As a result, arguments by indigent clients that a welfare statute is unlawful or unconstitutional cannot be expressed in this Government-funded program for petitioning the courts, even though the program was created for litigation involving welfare benefits, and even though the ordinary course of litigation involves the expression of theories and postulates on both, or multiple, sides of an issue.

It is fundamental that the First Amendment "was fashioned to assure unfettered interchange of ideas for the bringing about of political and social changes desired by the people." There can be little doubt that the LSC Act funds constitutionally protected expression; and in the context of this statute there is no programmatic message of the kind recognized in *Rust* and which sufficed there to allow the Government to specify the advice deemed necessary for its legitimate objectives. This serves to distinguish § 504(a)(16) from any of the Title X program restrictions upheld in *Rust*, and to place it beyond any congressional funding condition approved in the past by this Court.

Congress was not required to fund an LSC attorney to represent indigent clients; and when it did so, it was not required to fund the whole range of legal representations or relationships. The LSC and the United States, however, in effect ask us to permit Congress to define the scope of the litigation it funds to exclude certain vital theories and ideas. The attempted restriction is designed to insulate the Government's interpretation of the Constitution from judicial challenge. The Constitution does not permit the Government to confine litigants and their attorneys in this manner. We must be vigilant when Congress imposes rules and conditions which in effect insulate its own laws from legitimate judicial challenge. Where private speech is involved, even Congress' antecedent funding decision cannot be aimed at the suppression of ideas thought inimical to the Government's own interest.

For the reasons we have set forth, the funding condition is invalid. The Court of Appeals considered whether the language restricting LSC attorneys could be severed from the statute so that the remaining portions would remain operative. It reached the reasoned conclusion to invalidate the fragment of § 504(a)(16) found contrary to the First Amendment, leaving the balance of the statute operative and in place. That determination was not discussed in the briefs of either party or otherwise contested here, and in the exercise of our discretion and prudential judgment we decline to address it.

The judgment of the Court of Appeals is

Affirmed.

Justice Scalia, with whom The Chief Justice, Justice O'Connor, and Justice Thomas join, dissenting.

...

The Legal Services Corporation Act of 1974 (LSC Act) is a federal subsidy program, the stated purpose of which is to "provide financial support for legal assistance in noncriminal proceedings or matters to persons financially unable to afford legal assistance." Congress, recognizing that the program could not serve its purpose unless it was "kept free from the influence of or use by it of political pressures," has from the program's inception tightly regulated the use of its funds. No Legal Services Corporation (LSC) funds may be used, for example, for "encouraging . . . labor or antilabor activities," for "litigation relating to the desegregation of any elementary or secondary school or school system," or for "litigation which seeks to procure a nontherapeutic abortion." Congress discovered through experience, however, that these restrictions did not exhaust the politically controversial uses to which LSC funds could be put.

Accordingly, in 1996 Congress added new restrictions to the LSC Act and strengthened existing restrictions. Among the new restrictions is the one at issue here. Section 504(a)(16) of the Appropriations Act withholds LSC funds from every entity that "participates in any . . . way . . . in litigation, lobbying, or rulemaking . . . involving an effort to reform a Federal or State welfare system." It thus bans LSC-funded entities from participating on either side of litigation involving such statutes, from participating in rulemaking relating to the implementation of such legislation, and from lobbying Congress itself regarding any proposed changes to such legislation.

The restrictions relating to rulemaking and lobbying are superfluous; they duplicate general prohibitions on the use of LSC funds for those activities found elsewhere in the Appropriations Act. The restriction on litigation, however, is unique, and it contains a proviso specifying what the restriction does not cover. Funding recipients may "represent an individual eligible client who is seeking specific relief from a welfare agency if such relief does not involve an effort to amend or otherwise challenge existing law in effect on the date of the initiation of the representation." The LSC declares in its brief, and respondents do not deny, that under these provisions the LSC can sponsor neither challenges to nor defenses of existing welfare reform law. The litigation ban is symmetrical: Litigants challenging the covered statutes or regulations do not receive LSC funding, and neither do litigants defending those laws against challenge.

If a suit for benefits raises a claim outside the scope of the LSC program, the LSC-funded lawyer may not participate in the suit. As the Court explains, if LSC-funded lawyers anticipate that a forbidden claim will arise in a prospective client's suit, they "may not undertake [the] representation." Likewise, if a forbidden claim arises unexpectedly at trial, "LSC-funded attorneys must cease the representation at once." The lawyers may, however, and indeed must explain to the client why they cannot represent him. They are also free to express their views of the legality of the welfare law to the client, and they may refer the client to another attorney who can accept the representation.

II

The LSC Act is a federal subsidy program, not a federal regulatory program, and "there is a basic difference between [the two]." Regulations directly restrict speech; subsidies do not. Subsidies, it is true, may indirectly abridge speech, but only if the funding scheme is "'manipulated' to have a 'coercive effect'" on those who do not hold the subsidized position. Proving unconstitutional coercion is difficult enough when the spending program has universal coverage and excludes only certain speech—such as a tax exemption scheme excluding lobbying expenses. The Court has found such programs unconstitutional only when the exclusion was "aimed at the suppression of dangerous ideas." Proving the requisite coercion is harder still when a spending program is not universal but limited, providing benefits to a restricted number of recipients. The Court has found such selective spending unconstitutionally coercive only once, when the government created a public forum with the spending program but then discriminated in distributing funding within the forum on the basis of viewpoint. When the limited spending program does not create a public forum, proving coercion is virtually impossible, because simply denying a subsidy "does not 'coerce' belief" and because the criterion of unconstitutionality is whether denial of the subsidy threatens "to drive certain ideas or viewpoints from the marketplace." Absent such a threat, "the Government may allocate . . . funding according to criteria that would be impermissible were direct regulation of speech or a criminal penalty at stake."

In *Rust v. Sullivan*, the Court applied these principles to a statutory scheme that is in all relevant respects indistinguishable from § 504(a)(16). The statute in *Rust* authorized grants for the provision of family planning services, but provided that "none of the funds . . . shall be used in programs where abortion is a method of family planning." Valid regulations implementing the statute required funding recipients to refer pregnant clients "for appropriate prenatal . . . services by furnishing a list of available providers that promote the welfare of mother and unborn child," but forbade them to refer a pregnant woman specifically to an abortion provider, even upon request. We rejected a First Amendment free-speech challenge to the funding scheme, explaining that "the Government can, without violating the Constitution, selectively fund a program to encourage certain activities it believes to be in the public interest, without at the same time funding an alternative program which seeks to deal with the problem another way." This was not, we said, the type of "discrimination on the basis of viewpoint" that triggers strict scrutiny, ibid., because the "'decision not to subsidize the exercise of a fundamental right does not infringe the right.'"

The same is true here. The LSC Act, like the scheme in *Rust*, does not create a public forum. Far from encouraging a diversity of views, it has always, as the Court accurately states, "placed restrictions on its use of funds." Nor does § 504(a)(16) discriminate on the basis of viewpoint, since it funds neither challenges to nor defenses of existing welfare law. The provision simply declines to subsidize a certain class of litigation, and under Rust that decision "does not infringe the right" to bring such litigation. The Court's repeated claims that § 504(a)(16) "restricts" and "prohibits" speech and "insulates" laws from judicial review are simply baseless. No litigant who, in the absence of LSC funding, would bring a suit challenging existing welfare law is deterred from doing so by § 504(a)(16). *Rust* thus controls these cases and compels the conclusion that § 504(a)(16) is constitutional.

The Court contends that *Rust* is different because the program at issue subsidized government speech, while the LSC funds private speech. This is so unpersuasive it hardly needs response. If the private doctors' confidential advice to their patients at issue in *Rust* constituted "government speech," it is hard to imagine what subsidized speech would not be government speech. Moreover, the majority's contention that the subsidized speech in these cases is not government speech because the lawyers have a professional obligation to represent the interests of their clients founders on the reality that the doctors in *Rust* had a professional obligation to serve the interests of their patients,—which at the time of *Rust* we had held to be highly relevant to the permissible scope of federal regulation. Even respondents agree that "the true speaker in *Rust* was not the government, but a doctor."

The Court further asserts that these cases are different from *Rust* because the welfare funding restriction "seeks to use an existing medium of expression and to control it . . . in ways which distort its usual functioning." This is wrong on both the facts and the law. It is wrong on the law because there is utterly no precedent for the novel and facially implausible proposition that the First Amendment has anything to do with government funding that—though it does not actually abridge anyone's speech—"distorts an existing medium of expression." None of the three cases cited by the Court mentions such an odd principle. . . .

. . .

Finally, the Court is troubled "because in cases where the attorney withdraws from a representation, the client is unlikely to find other counsel." That is surely irrelevant, since it leaves the welfare recipient in no worse condition than he would have been in had the LSC program never been enacted. Respondents properly concede that even if welfare claimants cannot obtain a lawyer anywhere else, the Government is not required to provide one. It is hard to see how providing free legal services to some welfare claimants (those whose claims do not challenge the applicable statutes) while not providing it to others is beyond the range of legitimate legislative choice. . . .

The only conceivable argument that can be made for distinguishing *Rust* is that there even patients who wished to receive abortion counseling could receive the non-abortion services that the Government-funded clinic offered, whereas here some potential LSC clients who wish to receive representation on a benefits claim that does not challenge the statutes will be unable to do so because their cases raise a reform claim that an LSC lawyer may not present. This difference, of course, is required by the same ethical canons that the Court elsewhere does not wish to distort. Rather than sponsor "truncated representation," Congress chose to subsidize only those cases in which the attorneys it subsidized could work freely. And it is impossible to see how this difference from *Rust* has any bearing upon the First Amendment question, which, to repeat, is whether the funding scheme is "'manipulated' to have a 'coercive effect'" on those who do not hold the subsidized position. It could be claimed to have such an effect if the client in a case ineligible for LSC representation could eliminate the ineligibility by waiving the claim that the statute is invalid; but he cannot. No conceivable coercive effect exists.

This has been a very long discussion to make a point that is embarrassingly simple: The LSC subsidy neither prevents anyone from speaking nor coerces anyone to change speech, and is indistinguishable in all relevant respects from the subsidy upheld in *Rust v. Sullivan*. There is no legitimate basis for declaring § 504(a)(16) facially unconstitutional.

. . .

Today's decision is quite simply inexplicable on the basis of our prior law. The only difference between *Rust* and the present case is that the former involved "distortion" of (that is to say, refusal to subsidize) the normal work of doctors, and the latter involves "distortion" of (that is to say, refusal to subsidize) the normal work of lawyers. The Court's decision displays not only an improper special solicitude for our own profession; it also displays, I think, the very fondness for "reform through the courts"—the making of innumerable social judgments through judge-pronounced constitutional imperatives—that prompted Congress to restrict publicly funded litigation of this sort. The Court says today, through an unprecedented (and indeed previously rejected) interpretation of the First Amendment, that we will not allow this restriction—and then, to add insult to injury, permits to stand a judgment that awards the general litigation funding that the statute does not contain. I respectfully dissent.

Notes and Queries

1. The case addresses a clash in principles. One of the major purposes of the First Amendment is to protect the free discussion of governmental affairs. Since the freedom of speech serves to facilitate our representative democracy by advancing truth in the marketplace of ideas, debate on public issues are protected so that they can foster uninhibited, robust, and even sharp attacks on ideas championed by the

government and public officials. The Court views efforts to restrict viewpoints as the paradigmatic violation of the First Amendment, since such laws create one-sided public debates and disrupt the self-governing process. We have seen, however, that the government is constitutionally permitted to fund certain activities at the exclusion of others it deems in the public's interest. The argument is that, if the government is not constitutionally required to confer benefits, it may limit the conditions it places on such benefits. The clash occurs if Congress funds one viewpoint at the exclusion of another. Should the Court hold such funding laws presumptively invalid as viewpoint discriminating? Note here that the Second Circuit had concluded that the statute's prohibition on challenges to existing law was unconstitutional because it impermissibly discriminated on the basis of viewpoint, disfavoring those who opposed the status quo. Consequently, the Second Circuit had invalidated the portion of the statute that prohibited LSC-funded attorneys from contesting the validity of existing law. The Supreme Court affirmed, but it did so on different grounds. The Court distinguished the case from *Rust v. Sullivan*, which the LSC had urged was controlling. Whereas in *Rust* the government sought to promote its message through private speakers, the LSC program was "designed to facilitate private speech rather than to promote a governmental message." According to the majority, prior subsidized speech cases established that whether a restriction passes First Amendment scrutiny depends in part on the extent to which that subsidy condition distorts the "usual functioning" or "accepted usage" of the medium or vehicle for speech. Applying this test to section 504(a)(16), the majority concluded that the statute distorts the court system by "altering the traditional role of the attorneys" and by "prohibiting speech and expression upon which courts must depend for proper exercise of judicial power." The restriction violated the First Amendment because it unduly impaired the judiciary's ability to hear certain legal arguments. The Court has an interest in litigants' speech for it to perform its duties set forth in the Constitution. The difference between the cases is made obvious in Justice Scalia's dissent, which notes that the only difference between *Legal Services Corporation v. Velazquez* and the prior cases is that those cases did not involve attorneys. Are attorneys' roles important enough to justify an exception?

2. The LSCA states explicitly that the purpose of the LSC is to provide limited legal services to indigent clients. The LSCA restrictions show an intention to prevent grantees from using LSC funding to challenge or defend the status quo, partake in the political process of lawmaking, or express their own views over those of their clients. Why not make the same limitations apply to efforts for legal reform through the judiciary? *Velazquez* marks the first time that the Supreme Court has struck down a speech restriction on the ground that the restriction impaired a court's interest in receiving legal arguments. The case is significant for its novelty; is it also significant for it questionable theory based on the judiciary's institutional speech interest? What are we to make of the judiciary's interest in receiving legal arguments? Do you find that the majority exaggerates its fear about the extent

to which section 504(a)(16) would cause the judicial system to deviate from the Court's ideal? The system is already at odds with the majority's ideal model. Litigants do not always present all relevant arguments to courts. They may not do so for numerous reasons. Clients ultimately control litigation strategies and may not want attorneys to advance particular arguments; the court imposes page limits on briefs, forcing litigants to choose among arguments; tactical considerations require attorneys to choose among alternative arguments; and litigants simply may be incompetent. What would sway you against accepting those realities as dispositive? Recall that Article III of the Constitution protects the role of the independent judiciary within the constitutional scheme of tripartite government and assures impartial adjudication in federal courts. Do you view the case as an example of a congressional effort to infringe on the core function of an Article III court to say what the law is?

3. Does the majority's interpretation broaden the First Amendment's protections, leaving many congressional programs subsidizing speech vulnerable?

Baby Neal v. Casey

43 F.3d 48 (3rd Cir., 1994)

Justice Becker delivered the opinion of the court.

This appeal from orders of the district court for the Eastern District of Pennsylvania requires that we decide whether the court abused its discretion in denying class certification pursuant to FED. R. CIV. P. 23(b)(2) to a putative class of children in the legal care and custody of Philadelphia's Department of Human Services ("DHS"), who sought declaratory and injunctive relief against the officials responsible for operation of the child welfare system. Plaintiffs allege that systemic deficiencies prevent DHS from providing a variety of child welfare services legally mandated by the United States Constitution and by federal and state law. The district court held that the plaintiffs could not meet the commonality and typicality requirements of Rule 23, essentially because each of the plaintiffs' claims arose out of individual (and tragic) circumstances and hence they could not claim a single common injury and be appropriately entitled to class relief pursuant to Rule 23(b)(2). We reverse.

I. Facts and Procedural History

...

It is a matter of common knowledge (and it is not disputed here) that in recent years the system run by DHS and overseen by DPW has repeatedly failed to fulfill its mandates, and unfortunately has often jeopardized the welfare of the children in its care. Plagued by severe and widespread deficiencies in staff and revenues, the system has often demonstrated a lack of ability to provide abused and neglected children with the necessary welfare services.

The DHS acknowledged many of these deficiencies in its Three Year Plan 1991–1992. The Commonwealth defendants have also acknowledged these deficiencies: three times since April 1992, DPW denied a full operating license to the DHS. At those times, DPW announced that DHS had failed (1) to satisfy legal mandates for child protective services investigations; (2) to adhere to the caseload maximum of 30 cases per caseworker; (3) to assign to a substantial number of foster children a caseworker to monitor foster care placement and to ensure that the children received necessary and appropriate services; (4) to ensure that foster parents received the training necessary to permit them to care for foster children; and (5) to provide any child whose records were reviewed with an adequate case plan.

. . .

In factual terms, plaintiffs allege that the system has the following deficiencies: an insufficient number of trained caseworkers; an insufficient number of medical, psychiatric, psychological, and educational service providers; an insufficient number of trained foster parents; an insufficient number of placements for children who need environments that are more structured than foster homes; an insufficient number of potential adoptive parents; and a host of policies and procedures that are inefficient and deficient as measured against the standards of national organizations incorporated under federal law. The complaint portrays the impact of these deficiencies through accounts of the lives and conditions of the named plaintiffs. The stories are quite pathetic.

Doctrinally, these allegations comprise four separate claims for declaratory and injunctive relief. The first cause of action involves the alleged violations of rights conferred by the Adoption Assistance and Child Welfare Act of 1980, including the right to reasonable efforts to keep the children in their home or to enable them to return home; the right to timely written case plans; the right to placement in foster homes that meet nationally recommended standards; the right to appropriate services; the right to placement in the least restrictive, most family-like setting; the right to proper care while in custody; the right to a plan and to services that will assure permanent placement; the right to dispositional hearings within eighteen months of entering custody and periodically thereafter; and the right to receive services in a child welfare system with an adequate information system.

The second cause of action lies in alleged violations of the First, Ninth and Fourteenth Amendments to the United States Constitution. Specifically, plaintiffs claim that these amendments confer the right not to be deprived of a family relationship; the right not to be harmed while in state custody; the right to placement in the least restrictive, most appropriate placement; the right to medical and psychiatric treatment; the right to care consistent with competent professional judgment; and the right not to be deprived of liberty or property interests without due process of law.

The third cause of action alleges violations of rights conferred on the plaintiffs by the Child Abuse Prevention and Treatment Act, including the right to a prompt and appropriate investigation of reports of abuse or neglect; the right to protection from those who endanger their health and welfare; and the right to procedures, personnel, programs, and facilities that are necessary to deal effectively with child abuse and neglect. As with the first cause of action, defendants argue that this Act does not create any private rights of action.

The fourth cause of action provides an alternative basis in state law for some of the claims alleged under the three federal causes of action. These claims include the right to protection from abuse; the right to preventive rehabilitative services; the right to appropriate and timely case records and plans; the right to have every effort made to enable the children to remain in their homes or be returned to their homes; the right to appropriate services to assure proper permanent placement; and the right to adoption services.

Simultaneously with the filing of the complaint, the plaintiffs sought certification of a class consisting of "all children in Philadelphia who have been abused or neglected and are or should be known to the Philadelphia Department of Human Services." The Commonwealth defendants moved to dismiss the complaint on the grounds that the plaintiffs had no valid claim for relief under any of the relevant federal laws. The district court denied the defendants' motion, but it stayed the class certification motion during its consideration of this motion to dismiss. In response to defendants' asserted inability to complete the discovery necessary to oppose the certification, the district court stayed resolution of the class certification motion three additional times. During this period, the plaintiffs attempted to commence system-wide discovery. They now allege that the defendants never produced "much of the requested discovery."

The district court denied the class certification motion in an order dated January 6, 1992, based on the finding that the putative class had failed to satisfy the commonality and typicality requirements of Rule 23(a) and had also failed to satisfy Rule 23(b). The court based these determinations on its view that each of the plaintiffs had his or her own individual circumstances and needs, and that the class thus could not complain about a single, common injury. The plaintiffs moved for reconsideration or, in the alternative, for certification of subclasses. While this motion was pending, fourteen children intervened as plaintiffs, seeking relief for themselves and proffering a demonstration that children in DHS's custody and care continued to be harmed by DHS's failure to provide legally mandated child welfare services. The court subsequently denied the motion for reconsideration and for certification of subclasses.

The defendants then moved for summary judgment, repeating the argument made in the motion to dismiss that the plaintiffs had no private rights of action under the federal laws alleged, and arguing that the plaintiffs' claims had become moot. On August 24, 1992, the plaintiffs again moved for certification of subclasses. The district court stayed consideration of that motion pending the resolution of the summary judgment motion. In an order dated April 12, 1993, the court partially granted the defendants' motion for summary judgment, rejecting the plaintiffs' claims as to the existence of the private rights of action under the Child Abuse Prevention and Treatment Act and the Adoption Assistance and Child Welfare Act. The court denied the defendants' motion insofar as it asserted the mootness of all but twenty-three of the twenty-six plaintiffs' claims.

On May 10, 1993, the plaintiffs renewed their motion for subclass certification. On October 13, 1993, in an order denying certification the court held that the subclasses were not properly defined. The plaintiffs then moved for reconsideration, proposing new subclass definitions intended to address the court's concerns. The court denied this motion without comment, forbade plaintiffs from making any other class certification motions, and scheduled the case for trial.

By this time, nearly four years after the commencement of the litigation, almost all of the individual service needs of the plaintiff children had been met or otherwise resolved. The parties then settled the plaintiffs' remaining claims based on individual service needs and entered into a stipulation of entry of judgment, preserving the plaintiffs' right to appeal the denial of class certification and the grant of partial summary judgment as to the existence of private rights of action under the federal statutes. This appeal followed.

II. The Legal Requisites for Class Certification

A. Introduction

To obtain class action certification, plaintiffs must establish that all four requisites of Rule 23(a) and at least one part of Rule 23(b) are met. Rule 23(a) provides that

> one or more members of a class may sue or be sued as representative parties on behalf of all only if (1) the class is so numerous that joinder of all members is impracticable, (2) there are questions of law or fact common to the class, (3) the claims or defenses of the representative parties are typical of the claims or defenses of the class, and (4) the representative parties will fairly and adequately protect the interests of the class.

The requirements of Rule 23(a) are meant to assure both that class action treatment is necessary and efficient and that it is fair to the absentees under the particular circumstances. While numerosity addresses the first of these concerns, i.e., necessity, the last three requirements help determine whether the class action can be maintained in a fair and efficient manner. Class treatment makes no sense if there are no common issues; the trial court would gain nothing but logistical headaches from the combination of the cases for trial. Typicality asks whether the named plaintiffs' claims are typical, in common-sense terms, of the class, thus suggesting that the incentives of the plaintiffs are aligned with those of the class. Adequacy of representation assures that the named plaintiffs' claims are not antagonistic to the class and that the attorneys for the class representatives are experienced and qualified to prosecute the claims on behalf of the entire class.

In addition to satisfying the requirements of Rule 23(a), a putative class must also comply with one of the parts of subsection (b). In this case, plaintiffs seek certification pursuant to Rule 23(b)(2) which requires that "the party opposing the class has acted or refused to act on grounds generally applicable to the class, thereby making appropriate final injunctive relief or corresponding declaratory relief with respect to the class as a whole."

For the reasons explained below, we conclude that the plaintiffs satisfied all of the requirements of Rule 23, and that the district court abused its discretion in denying class certification on the grounds that plaintiffs failed to comply with subsections (a)(2) (commonality), (a)(3) (typicality), and (b)(2) (appropriateness of class relief) of Rule 23. There is, as we have noted, no dispute over numerosity ((a)(1)) or adequacy of representation ((a)(4)).

The concepts of commonality and typicality are broadly defined and tend to merge. Both criteria seek to assure that the action can be practically and efficiently maintained and that the interests of the absentees will be fairly and adequately represented. Despite their similarity, however, commonality and typicality are distinct requirements under Rule 23.

We turn to a more particularized discussion of these requisites. We underscore at the outset, however, that neither of these requirements mandates that all putative class members share identical claims and that factual differences among the claims of the putative class members do not defeat certification.

B. Commonality

The commonality requirement will be satisfied if the named plaintiffs share at least one question of fact or law with the grievances of the prospective class. Because the requirement may be satisfied by a single common issue, it is easily met, as at least one treatise has noted. Furthermore, class members can assert such a single common complaint even if they have not all suffered actual injury; demonstrating that all class members are subject to the same harm will suffice.

Challenges to a program's compliance with the mandates of its enabling legislation, even where plaintiff-beneficiaries are differently impacted by the violations, have satisfied the commonality requirement. Courts appear to consider "common" such challenges based on alleged violations of statutory standards. Moreover, because they do not also involve an individualized inquiry for the determination of damage awards, injunctive actions "by their very nature often present common questions satisfying Rule 23(a)(2)."

To the extent that the defendants assert that commonality requirements cannot be met in this case because of the individualized circumstances of the children, their argument has been squarely rejected by the Supreme Court. In *Califano v. Yamasaki*, plaintiffs challenged the adequacy of the procedures used to recoup overpayments under the Social Security Act. Rejecting an argument that the applicable statute only invited suits by individuals, the court explained that "class relief is consistent with the need for case-by-case adjudication," especially where "it is unlikely that differences in the factual background of each claim will affect the outcome of the legal issue." This is especially true where plaintiffs request declaratory and injunctive relief against a defendant engaging in a common course of conduct toward them, and there is therefore no need for individualized determinations of the propriety of injunctive relief. Indeed, (b)(2) classes have been certified in a legion of civil rights cases where commonality findings were based primarily on the fact that defendant's conduct is central to the claims of all class members irrespective of their individual circumstances and the disparate effects of the conduct.

. . .

Even where individual facts and circumstances do become important to the resolution, class treatment is not precluded. Classes can be certified for certain particularized issues, and, under well-established principles of modern case management, actions are frequently bifurcated. . . .

C. Typicality

The typicality inquiry is intended to assess whether the action can be efficiently maintained as a class and whether the named plaintiffs have incentives that align with those of absent class members so as to assure that the absentees' interests will be fairly represented. The typicality criterion is intended to preclude certification of those cases where the legal theories of the named plaintiffs potentially conflict with those of the absentees by requiring that the common claims are comparably central to the claims of the named plaintiffs as to the claims of the absentees. "Typicality entails an inquiry whether 'the named plaintiff's individual circumstances are markedly different or . . . the legal theory upon which the claims are based differs from that upon which the claims of other class members will perforce be based.'" Commentators have noted that cases challenging the same unlawful conduct which affects both the named plaintiffs and the putative class usually satisfy the typicality requirement irrespective of the varying fact patterns underlying the individual claims. Actions requesting declaratory and injunctive relief to remedy conduct directed at the class clearly fit this mold.

"Factual differences will not render a claim atypical if the claim arises from the same event or practice or course of conduct that gives rise to the claims of the class members, and if it is based on the same legal theory." . . .

Indeed, even relatively pronounced factual differences will generally not preclude a finding of typicality where there is a strong similarity of legal theories.

Where an action challenges a policy or practice, the named plaintiffs suffering one specific injury from the practice can represent a class suffering other injuries, so long as all the injuries are shown to result from the practice. In *Falcon*, the Supreme Court reversed certification of a class of Mexican Americans challenging hiring and promotion actions, which had been affirmed by the Fifth Circuit, on typicality grounds. Rather than standing for the proposition that a named plaintiff complaining of one specific injury (Falcon's not being promoted) cannot represent a class suffering perhaps a different injury (not being hired), *Falcon* merely requires that the class representative prove that there is a pervasive violation and that the various injuries alleged all stem from that common violation.

D. The Requisites of Rule 23(b)(2)

Besides meeting the requirements of Rule 23(a), plaintiffs must also satisfy one of the requirements of 23(b). The district court alternatively based its denial of certification on its conclusion that the plaintiffs failed this test. The plaintiffs maintain that their action satisfies Rule 23(b)(2), which is met if "the party opposing the class has acted or refused to act on grounds generally applicable to the class, thereby making appropriate final injunctive relief or corresponding declaratory relief with respect to the class as a whole."

In *Weiss v. York Hospital*, we explained that this requirement is almost automatically satisfied in actions primarily seeking injunctive relief. "When a suit seeks to define the relationship between the defendant(s) and the world at large, . . . (b)(2) certification is appropriate." Commentators have also noted that the language of (b)(2) does not even require that the defendant's conduct be directed or damaging to every member of the class. It is the (b)(2) class which serves most frequently as the vehicle for civil rights actions and other institutional reform cases that receive class action treatment. In fact, the injunctive class provision was "designed specifically for civil rights cases seeking broad declaratory or injunctive relief for a numerous and often unascertainable or amorphous class of persons."

What is important is that the relief sought by the named plaintiffs should benefit the entire class. The general applicability requirement of (b)(2) also aims to prevent prejudice to absentees by mandating that the putative class "demonstrate that the interests of the class members are so like those of the individual representatives that injustice will not result from their being bound by such judgment in the subsequent application of principles of res judicata." But injunctive actions, seeking to define the relationship between the defendant and the "world at large," will usually satisfy this requirement.

E. Precedents in Child Welfare Cases

A review of the jurisprudence in this area discloses that many very similar lawsuits challenging the provision of services to foster children have been certified despite the varieties of factual differences that characterize the plaintiffs in each case and despite the variety of legal claims any one class may make. Many of these cases also involve claims by classes that include differently situated plaintiffs, who were not, at the time of the litigation, suffering identical injuries from the defendants' conduct.

For example, in a class action brought in Vermont state court, the court certified a class of handicapped children challenging the provision of child welfare services over defendants' commonality and typicality objections based on factual differences of class members. The court explained:

> Certainly, the plaintiffs will have different stories to tell. However, it is apparent from the pleadings that plaintiffs legal claims are based on a common factual predicate: the defendants alleged failure to fulfill their duties in providing for a coordinated system that protects the welfare of class

> members. The individual treatment of handicapped youths, while important and crucial to plaintiffs' case, only serves to support a larger inquiry into the functioning of the state structure appropriated for administering programs that serve the handicapped.

Courts have also certified class actions alleging a variety of legal claims falling under the rubric of a systemic failure to provide certain child welfare services....

...

III. Did the District Court Abuse Its Discretion in Denying Class Certification?

Appellants contend that the district court abused its discretion when it denied certification. We agree. In our view, the district court applied an overly restrictive legal standard in evaluating the requirements of Rule 23 and in denying class certification. Although the court took cognizance of cases holding that common questions need only exist—not predominate—for (b)(2) actions, it nevertheless proceeded to demand higher demonstrations of commonality and typicality than the rule requires. It is axiomatic that errant conclusions of law constitute an abuse of discretion.

A. Commonality

As to commonality, the district court concluded that: "Not one of the common legal issues asserted by plaintiffs applies to every member of the proposed class.... The children's claims are based upon different legal theories depending on the individual circumstances of that child.... The services required to meet the needs of one child are vastly different from that of another child." These statements are at odds with the applicable standard. Plaintiffs are challenging common conditions and practices under a unitary regime. All the children in the class are subject to the risk that they will suffer from the same deprivations resulting from the DHS's alleged violations. Because the nature of foster placement is transitory and thus inherently variable, it is unreasonable to require that all plaintiffs suffer from the same injury simultaneously.

Defendants maintain that "proving systemwide failure does not establish that the law has been violated as to any child." However, the commonality standard requires only that a putative class share either the injury or the immediate threat of being subject to the injury. Here, systemwide deficiencies either violate class members' rights currently or subject them to the risk of such a violation.

Furthermore, all of the plaintiffs seek to force the DHS to comply with its statutory mandates, and all of their injuries alleged here would be cured if DHS remedied the systemic deficiencies. Insofar as the children challenge the scheme for the provision of child welfare services, their claims share a common legal basis.... Thus, we find the plaintiffs' attack on the DHS's systemic deficiencies in providing legally mandated child care services to be a sufficiently common legal basis to support class certification here.

The differing degree and nature of the plaintiffs' injuries also do not preclude a finding of commonality. Just as in *Yamasaki*, where the amounts of each class member's claim differed but where the class members nonetheless shared a common statutory claim, the putative class members in this case share the common legal claim that DHS's systemic deficiencies result in widespread violations of their statutory and constitutional rights, irrespective of their varying individual needs and complaints. As in *Yamasaki*, where the plaintiffs challenged the conduct of the defendant towards the class, the children here challenge DHS's conduct, which is generally applicable to them. Also, as in *Yamasaki*, where it did not matter that the amounts of the individuals' claims differed, it does not matter here that the children suffer in varying ways from the DHS's violation of its statutory mandates.

When it concluded that "not one factual issue pertains to the entire proposed class," the district court committed the error of overly fragmenting the plaintiffs' claims. A similar approach taken in another case has been characterized as "contrary to the clear language of the rule" and "irreconcilable with the majority of decisions on the common question issue." It is true that each plaintiff here has his or her own circumstances, but every plaintiff shares the essential circumstance of being in the custody or the care of DHS. Individual factual differences do not affect the central allegation that the DHS violates various statutory and constitutional rights in its provision of child care services to the class.

Because of the district court's capacity to bifurcate (or trifurcate) the proceedings, the individual circumstances of the children, even if they affect the issues presented by this case, would not preclude certification. And in this suit for declaratory relief, the court can substantially avoid examining those individualized circumstances, for the relief requested by the plaintiffs focuses entirely on the effort to reform defendants' conduct so that it complies with the various legal provisions raised here. Thus, while the children will undoubtedly be affected by the district court's rulings, the court need not consider the individual children's peculiar circumstances in fashioning its order.

The court's heavy emphasis on the factual differences of the 6,000 children also suggests that it did not take sufficient cognizance of the nature of the relief sought. Because the complaint does not seek damages, the factual differences are largely irrelevant. The complaint prays for declaratory and injunctive relief. Factual differences among the situations of the plaintiffs will thus not preclude the district court from determining whether the class claims are meritorious, or from ordering the appropriate relief in the event that they are.

. . .

In contrast to the cases we have distinguished, this case clearly presents common legal issues under the applicable standard. The children challenge DHS's pattern of conduct, which is subjecting them all to violations of their statutory and constitutional rights. Because of the dearth of trained caseworkers, for example, DHS (allegedly) fails to investigate reports of abuse and neglect promptly or adequately and fails to reliably provide the children in its care with written case plans, with appropriate placements, with proper care while in custody, and with periodical dispositional hearings. Similar violations of the rights of children in custody to be free from harm can (allegedly) be traced to the scarcity of properly trained foster parents or to DHS's lack of an adequate information system.

Moreover, trial will not require an individualized inquiry into a vast network of institutions. It is only the Philadelphia DHS's provision of the mandated services that is at issue, and the nature of the violations can be verified by reference to the applicable statutes; it is not necessary to examine each plaintiff's circumstances to evaluate the claims. The fact that all plaintiffs are subject to the risk of deprivation of services to which they are currently entitled (or which they may at some point in the future require) suffices to support their common claim against DHS.

B. Typicality

The district court also misconstrued the relevant standard of typicality. As with its analysis of the commonality issue, the court appeared to rely on the proposition that the plaintiffs were not challenging precisely the same conditions and practices because the services required by law differ depending on a child's individual situation. However . . . a claim framed as a violative practice can support a class action embracing a variety of injuries so long as those injuries can all be linked to the practice. Plaintiffs in this case attack a systemic failure by DHS to provide a broad range of legally mandated services. At any one time, the plaintiffs do not suffer from precisely the same deficiency, but they are all alleged victims of the systemic failures. Moreover, they each potentially face all of the system's deficiencies. A child not currently needing psychological services may well require such services sometime while in DHS custody. A child lucky enough to be receiving permanency planning, for example, faces the immediate threat of losing that service in a system characterized by the widespread absence of such services. Because being subject to the risk of an injury suffices under Hassine for both the commonality and the typicality inquiries, plaintiffs can allege these harms.

Furthermore, the fact that the common theme of attacking DHS's systemwide failure to comply with its legal mandates is equally central to the claims of the named plaintiffs as it is to the claims of the absentees reinforces the characterization of the plaintiffs' claims as typical. Indeed, this theme is central to each plaintiff. It bears remembering that the plaintiffs here seek only injunctive and declaratory relief; there are no other claims that could compromise the named plaintiffs' pursuit of the class claims.

Because there are no individual claims as such, the differences among the plaintiffs do not affect the central claim that DHS violates a variety of the children's (putative class members') constitutional and statutory rights by failing to provide mandated welfare services. We emphasize that the individual differences in the children's circumstances might indeed militate against certification if the action sought certification under 23(b)(3) because a court would need to evaluate those differences in the event that the plaintiffs prevailed and were entitled to monetary damages. In fashioning injunctive relief, however, a court would focus on the defendants rather than on the plaintiffs. Whether there are fifty or 6,000 plaintiffs, as in this case, the court's task is essentially the same. The court would not need to assure that every child received an "appropriate" case plan, for instance. Instead, the court would assure that the DHS had an adequate mechanism for generating and monitoring appropriate case plans. To the extent that some of the claims raised by the plaintiffs truly do require the court to engage in individualized determinations, the court retains the discretion to decertify or modify the class so that the class action encompasses only the issues that are truly common to the class.

Moreover, the prospect of class certification in this case does not present the sorts of dangers that the typicality requirement was intended to avoid. There is no danger here that the named plaintiffs have unique interests that might motivate them to litigate against or settle with the defendants in a way that prejudices the absentees. Many courts have noted that the "individual interest in pursuing litigation where the relief sought is primarily injunctive will be minimal." Indeed, because this suit seeks only declaratory and injunctive relief, the named plaintiffs are simply not asserting any claims that are not also applicable to the absentees. The common claims here are the only claims and must perforce occupy the same position of centrality for all class members. The putative class clearly satisfies the typicality requirement of Rule 23(a)(3); the district court abused its discretion in ruling that it did not.

C. The 23(b)(2) Showing

The district court also found that the plaintiffs failed to make the requisite showing under Rule 23(b)(2), concluding that the claims for relief were not generally applicable to the class. In so holding, the court failed to give effect to the proper role of (b)(2) class actions in remedying systemic violations of basic rights of large and often amorphous classes. While it is true that not all of the orders issued will immediately benefit every plaintiff, every plaintiff will benefit from relief designed to assure DHS compliance with the applicable standards.

Plaintiffs have alleged that systemic failure causes the DHS to violate various mandates under federal statutory and constitutional provisions. Because the children in the system are comparably subject to the injuries caused by this systemic failure, even if the extent of their individual injuries may be affected by their own individual circumstances, the challenge to the system constitutes a legal claim applicable to the class as a whole. An order forcing the DHS to comply with their statutory and constitutional mandates would constitute relief generally applicable to the entire putative class. Indeed, the violations alleged here are precisely the kinds targeted by Rule 23(b)(2). The writers of Rule 23 intended that subsection (b)(2) foster institutional reform by facilitating suits that challenge widespread rights violations of people who are individually unable to vindicate their own rights.

The fact that the plaintiffs in this case seek only injunctive and declaratory relief, not individual damages, further enhances the appropriateness of the class treatment. Clearly, this action aims to define the relationship of the defendants to the universe of children with whose care the defendants are charged. Plaintiffs simply ask the district court to declare the DHS's current provision of child welfare services to the plaintiffs to be violative of the cited statutory and constitutional provisions and to order DHS to implement a system that would enable it to comply with its legal mandates in the provision of these services. Furthermore, all of the class members will benefit from relief which forces the defendant to provide, in the manner required by law, the services to which class members either are currently or at some future point will become entitled.

While it is true that commonality, typicality, and the Rule 23(b)(2) general applicability requirements all manifest a concern about judicial efficiency and manageability, the district court's arguments on this score miss the mark. The district court clearly erred by finding that "it would be impossible to conceive of an Order this court could make granting class-wide injunctive relief which could address the specific case-by-case deficiencies in DHS's performance. . . ." But a court could, for example, order the DHS to develop training protocols for its prospective foster parents. Such an order would not, contrary to the district court's view, "create an enforcement problem of staggering proportions." The district court will thus not need to make individual, case-by-case determinations in order to assess liability or order relief. Rather, the court can fashion precise orders to address specific, system-wide deficiencies and then monitor compliance relative to those orders. Other courts have ordered the relief required by these types of cases without finding it to be either unworkable or unenforceable. . . . This is precisely the sort of order that is requested in this case. Because this suit challenges conduct generally applicable to the class and because the court can enter appropriate declaratory and injunctive relief, this action patently satisfies the (b)(2) standard.

IV. Conclusion

Because the claims alleged in the plaintiffs' complaint clearly meet the requirements of Rule 23, the district court's determination that they did not constitutes an abuse of discretion. We will therefore reverse the orders of the district court and remand for further proceedings consistent with this opinion. In so doing, we intimate no view on the merits, nor, should the plaintiffs succeed on merits, on the scope of the court's remedial power or on the appropriate remedy.

Notes and Queries

1. The court ruled that it had jurisdiction to consider the class certification issue, but not the summary judgment issues simply because it would be inappropriate for the court to reach the merits of this controversy in the present posture of the case because the facts had not been litigated.
2. As the opinion makes clear, denial of class certification is reviewed for abuse of discretion. What do you make of that standard?

Research Comments

1. A court's contempt power serves to enforce injunctions that seek to compel defendants to act or restrict them from acting in a specified way. Traditionally, courts recognized that injunctions would not be used as a remedy against personal rights because such rights were not grounded in property. That view came to an end with *Brown v. Board of Education*, 349 U.S. 294 (1955), the landmark case in which the Supreme Court issued an injunction that signified the beginning of the end for invidious school desegregation. As a result of that case, we saw the birth of civil rights injunctions that sought to reform entire institutions, such as mental health hospitals, correctional facilities, and public school systems. It did not take long for advocates to seek child welfare system reform through this mechanism. Do you see the rights of children in child welfare systems differently than those in other contexts? Arguments against the use of class actions and injunctions in child welfare cases typically claimed that injunctions were too difficult and expensive to manage and maintain and that they violated the separation of powers, compromised democratic principles, eroded federalism barriers, and required federal courts to proceed where they lacked expertise. Have these arguments become more or less potent today?

2. Bringing claims through class actions often pose major dilemmas for those attempting to address children's needs. Subgroups of children within class actions each have needs for resources that in a finite world will be met only through sacrifices by other subgroups. In addition, class actions challenge efforts to address significant interdependency issues, that is the extent to which individual children will have different needs. For example, making it more difficult to place a child in a juvenile detention center increases the chances that the juvenile either is relegated to an inadequate support network in the community or, depending on the age of the child and his or her alleged offense, is referred to criminal court and receives a disposition that involves either a prison sentence or admission to an adult psychiatric center. This is increasingly problematic in that child welfare class actions involve huge numbers of children and families in a vast spectrum of geographic and service settings. These "super class" actions acknowledge that many of the claims, which involve a variety of state and federal causes of action from substantive and procedural due process to the Medicaid statute and the Americans with Disabilities Act, do not apply to all of the children. See Peter Margulies (1999). The new class action jurisprudence and public interest law. *New York University Review of Law and Social Change*, 25, 487–538.

3. As much as class actions involving victims who suffer while under the failed care of child welfare systems raise compelling cases, commentators increasingly question their legitimacy. Many child welfare agencies have operated under court orders, and those that have, have tended to remain under those orders for many years, so

much so that their utility became questionable. As an example, commentators have shown how suits take so long that circumstances change, rendering the reason for the actions in the first place irrelevant. Critics view the approach as antidemocratic in the sense that plaintiff's attorneys and experts end up controlling agencies rather than individuals empowered by the electorate and those who work directly with children. The concern is not necessarily the usurpation of power by elites but more the loss of flexible solutions. The argument is that class actions result in management by paralysis rather than serve the interests of those they were meant to help, with those interests including their rights. For examples of these limitations, see Ross Sandler & David Schoenbrod (2003). *Democracy by Decree: What Happens When Courts Run Government*. New Haven, CT: Yale University Press. For counterarguments, see Mark V. Tushnet (2003). "Sir yes, sir!": The courts, Congress, and structural injunctions. *Constitutional Commentary*, 20(1), 189–204. For commentaries expressing concern about impact litigation in other contexts involving children, see Luis R. Fraga, Nick Rodriguez & Bari A. Erlichson (2005). Desegregation and school board politics: The limits of court-imposed policy change. In William G. Howell (Ed.). *Besieged: School Boards and the Future of Education Politics* (pp. 102–128). Washington, DC: Brookings Institution Press.

4. Analyses of class action litigation reveal recurring themes. A report summarizing key points of several important essays on class actions to reform child welfare systems reported the following:

> Improving child welfare system outcomes is a difficult multi-year endeavor; while pursuing that reform within the context of litigation has some advantages, it also presents additional challenges.
>
> . . .
>
> In spite of the fact that litigation is at its core an adversarial process, the jurisdictions that have made the most progress have done so by relying on approaches to reduce the distrust and conflict, to provide objective assessment and to build relationships and structures to foster cooperation and joint problem solving.
>
> . . .
>
> Getting to a candid understanding and assessment of a system's problems is a critical first step.
>
> . . .
>
> The structure of a court order whether entered through a Settlement Agreement or by the court after a contested hearing can either facilitate or cripple a reform effort.
>
> Begin with a clear understanding of the values and principles.
>
> Resist creating unrealistic expectations and overly ambitious timeframes.

> Pay attention to a system's leadership.
>
> Provide for phased implementation in any court-ordered reform plan.
>
> Ensure that the court order provides a mechanism for modification.
>
> A court order should include processes for problem solving outside of the courtroom.
>
> . . .
>
> A court order should include at the outset a plan for termination of court jurisdiction and exit.
>
> . . .
>
> The structures established and individuals selected for independent monitoring of progress under a court order should have qualities that ensure the confidence of the court, the defendants and the plaintiffs.
>
> . . .
>
> The most successful litigation-driven reform efforts have included the use of outside expertise at almost every stage of the process.

Center for the Study of Social Policy (2012). *For the Welfare of Children: Lessons Learned from Class Action Litigation*. Washington, DC: Author.

Appendix A
Key Federal Constitutional Provisions

Amendment I. Congress shall make no law respecting an establishment of religion, or prohibiting the free exercise thereof; or abridging the freedom of speech, or of the press; or the right of the people peaceably to assemble, and to petition the Government for a redress of grievances.

Amendment II. A well regulated militia, being necessary to the security of a free state, the right of the people to keep and bear arms, shall not be infringed.

Amendment III. Section 1. The judicial power of the United States, shall be vested in one Supreme Court, and in such inferior courts as the Congress may from time to time ordain and establish. . . . Section 2. The judicial power shall extend to all cases, in law and equity, arising under this Constitution, the laws of the United States, and treaties made, or which shall be made, under their authority; . . . to controversies to which the United States shall be a party; — to controversies between two or more states; — between a state and citizens of another state; — between citizens of different states; — between citizens of the same state claiming lands under grants of different states, and between a state, or the citizens thereof. . . .

Amendment IV. The right of the people to be secure in their persons, houses, papers, and effects, against unreasonable searches and seizures, shall not be violated, and no Warrants shall issue, but upon probable cause, supported by Oath or affirmation, and particularly describing the place to be searched, and the persons or things to be seized.

Amendment V. No person shall be held to answer for a capital, or otherwise infamous crime, unless on a presentment or indictment of a Grand Jury, except in cases arising in the land or naval forces, or in the Militia, when in actual service in time of War or public danger; nor shall any person be subject for the same offence to be twice put in jeopardy of life or limb; nor shall be compelled in any criminal case to be a witness against himself, nor be deprived of life, liberty, or property, without due process of law; nor shall private property be taken for public use, without just compensation.

Amendment VI. In all criminal prosecutions, the accused shall enjoy the right to a speedy and public trial, by an impartial jury of the State and district wherein the crime shall have been committed, which district shall have been previously ascertained by law, and to be informed of the nature and cause of the accusation; to be confronted with the witnesses against him; to have compulsory process for obtaining witnesses in his favor, and to have the Assistance of Counsel for his defense.

Amendment VIII. Excessive bail shall not be required, nor excessive fines imposed, nor cruel and unusual punishments inflicted.

Amendment IX. The enumeration in the Constitution, of certain rights, shall not be construed to deny or disparage others retained by the people.

Amendment X. The powers not delegated to the United States by the Constitution, nor prohibited by it to the States, are reserved to the States respectively, or to the people.

Amendment XIII. Section 1. Neither slavery nor involuntary servitude, except as a punishment for crime whereof the party shall have been duly convicted, shall exist within the United States, or any place subject to their jurisdiction. Section 2. Congress shall have power to enforce this article by appropriate legislation.

Amendment XIV. Section 1. All persons born or naturalized in the United States, and subject to the jurisdiction thereof, are citizens of the United States and of the state wherein they reside. No state shall make or enforce any law which shall abridge the privileges or immunities of citizens of the United States; nor shall any state deprive any person of life, liberty, or property, without due process of law; nor deny to any person within its jurisdiction the equal protection of the laws.

Amendment XV. Section 1. The right of citizens of the United States to vote shall not be denied or abridged by the United States or by any state on account of race, color, or previous condition of servitude. Section 2. The Congress shall have power to enforce this article by appropriate legislation.

Appendix B
Understanding Case Law

Nature of Cases: Formal cases typically begin in the trial court, where a trial judge (sometimes with the assistance of a jury) seeks to resolve a dispute. If one of the parties believes the decision makers erred in that phase, the party may appeal to a "higher" court, typically called a court of appeal. Courts of appeal review briefs. Briefs are the written arguments submitted by the appellant (the appealing party) and the appellee (the responding party). In addition to the briefs, the reviewing court may examine trial transcripts and documents introduced as evidence during the trial. To render decisions, courts often have attorneys appear to orally state their positions and to respond to questions from the justices. However, no trial takes place during the appellate phase; appellate courts take the facts as they were litigated and apply them to the law. Typically, one of the justices expresses the court's ruling in a written opinion.

Cite or Citation: This includes the parties and "citation" reference where the case can be located. The citation is the group of letters and numbers attached to the case, which tell you where the case was heard and when it was decided (e.g., U.S. or S.Ct. are U.S. Supreme Court case law reporters).

Facts: Material facts are the description of the events between the parties that led to the dispute. The facts indicate how the case came before the trial court and what was decided. If it is on appeal, it includes the alleged error.

Issues: Issues are the legal points or questions disputed by the parties. Typically, an issue combines the applicable rule of law with the material facts of the case.

Holdings: These are the court's rulings. Holdings are unlike dicta. Dicta are the arguments the court makes, but they are only binding on future courts if they relate to the question actually before it. The dicta, however, are important to consider in analyzing the court's thinking and possibilities.

Reasoning: This is the analysis the court used to support its decisions.

Opinions: The opinion of the court is the written decision. When more than one judge has heard the case, one of the judges typically writes the decision for the court, and that judge's name appears at the beginning of the opinion. Cases often have separate opinions, which may be concurring or dissenting. Concurring opinions agree with the principal holding but differ in its reasoning. Dissenting opinions dissent on the holding and the reasoning. If the court's opinion is joined in by a majority, it is called the majority opinion, which binds future cases. The common ground on which a majority agree becomes the law. Concurring opinions do not affect whether the reasoning will bind subsequent cases. However, when the opinion of the court is a plurality opinion, when a majority has concurred in the result only but not in the reasoning, then the plurality's reasoning does not bind future cases.

Policy Considerations: The social policies or goals that the decision maker seeks to further.

Appendix C
Understanding Legal Reasoning

This text seeks to help readers predict, argue, and decide legal outcomes through examining where the law is not self-explanatory and where different opinions offer different views of appropriate responses to issues. Examining these cases and views allows readers to better understand what decision makers use to create arguments to explain the law and negotiate its meaning with others. To those uninitiated to legal reasoning, it may make sense to delineate the principal methods of legal reasoning, the different source of law some decision makers deem appropriate, and the different sets of legal information used in determining the meaning of a legal rule or of a text's language. Although how legal decision makers decide the meaning of law has become an entire field of law in its own right, we see in the cases presented in this text that legal analyses tend to adopt a mixture of at least five types of legal reasoning.

Textual Analysis: This approach examines the language used in the legal document under review. Although there are different textual methods of interpretation, two appear particularly common: plain meaning and intratextual arguments. The "plain meaning" approach examines a text's language and, if it is clear on its face, finds no need for interpretation. Under this approach, if the text is clearly dispositive, the analysis ends (unless the language is absurd or clearly inappropriate). This approach places very stringent limitations on the evidence decision makers use to decipher meaning; they confine evidence of the law to the text itself. See William N. Eskridge, Jr. (1999). Norms, empiricism, and canons in statutory interpretation. *University of Chicago Law Review*, 66, 671–684. If the text is less than obvious, then a decision maker may simply use "intratextual arguments." This approach makes use of different parts of legal documents to give meaning to other parts. These arguments typically follow one of two formats: They either compare the words used in one part of the text with the words used in another part, or they deduce the meaning of portions of the text from their position within the organization of the text. Since intratextual arguments look to other parts of the document or the document as a whole, the approach makes more liberal use of evidence than does the plain meaning approach. See Akhil Reed Amar (1999). Intratextualism. *Harvard Law Review*, 112, 747–827.

Intent: The intent of the people who wrote, drafted, or participated in the text's construction also can serve to determine what the law means. Most notably, for example and in constitutional law, this method of interpretation is known as "original intent" or "the intent of the Framers." Evidence of intent may include previous versions of the text, its legislative history, contemporary commentary, and official comments. See Robert H. Bork (1971). Neutral principles and some First Amendment problems. *Indiana Law Journal*, 47, 1–35. Justice Stephen Breyer, for example, has described the value of examining legislative history. Breyer, when Chief Judge of the Court of Appeals for the First Circuit, outlined what he considered to be the five essential uses of legislative history. According to Breyer, legislative history must be used in order for the Court to: (1) avoid an absurd result, (2) illuminate and correct drafting errors, (3) ascertain specialized meanings, (4) identify a reasonable purpose, and (5) choose among reasonable interpretations of a politically controversial statute. Stephen Breyer (1992). On the uses of legislative history in interpreting statutes. *Southern California Law Review*, 65, 845–874.

Precedent: Precedent refers to the rules of law developed by courts or administrative agencies. This approach gives great weight to prior pronouncements on the meaning of the law. The permissible evidence to consider in determining the law's meaning is limited to statements in formal legal opinions or interpretations. Our legal system's reliance on legal precedent tends to be well-known and understood as based on the principle of *stare decisis*. At least in terms of constitutional law, the scope of *stare decisis* has been delineated well in *Planned Parenthood v. Casey*, 505 U.S. 833 (1992). In that case, the plurality offered four factors considered legitimate in following or rejecting precedent: the workability of the existing rule, society's reliance on the existing rule, whether the rule has been undermined by subsequent decisions, and whether the premises of fact underlying the decision have changed.

Tradition: Traditions provide another powerful source of legal authority used to interpret the meaning of law. For example, the Supreme Court often identifies "tradition" as the touchstone for determining our fundamental rights and the Court often describes constitutional rights as those so rooted in the traditions and conscience of our people as to be ranked as fundamental. Compared to the above three sources and methods of legal interpretation, proof of tradition has the potential to be much more expansive and tradition may involve considering many factors. For example, tradition may mean traditional ways of allocating governmental power or social traditions. Likewise, conflicting traditions may exist, such as the tradition of protecting the rights of parents and the tradition of protecting the rights of unitary families and the presumption that spouses are the parents of children born to their marriage. See *Michael H. v. Gerald D.*, 491 U.S. 110 (1989). As with the principle of *stare decisis*, reliance on tradition tends to limit the evidence used and encourages decision makers to reject interpretations of law that have no root in our past.

Policy Analysis: Policy analyses tend to predict the consequences that will flow from giving the law one interpretation or another and then decide which set of consequences is more consistent with the underlying values of the law. Unlike other sources of law, the decision maker need not attempt to ascertain the value choices made by others; rather, this approach balances the relevant values and interests affected by the decision to pursue a particular policy. As a result, the scope of what may be considered appropriate evidence tends to be extremely broad. For example, under the Federal Rules of Evidence Rule 201, a court may take judicial notice of "adjudicative facts" (those facts relating to issues to be decided by the trier of fact) if they are "generally known" or "capable of accurate and ready determination by resort to sources whose accuracy cannot reasonably be questioned." Courts also may take judicial notice of any "legislative facts" (those facts relating to questions of policy to be decided in interpreting the law) regardless of whether these facts are indisputable. As the federal rules advisory committee's notes reveal, judicial notice of "legislative facts" is not subject to the limitations of Rule 201 or any other rule of evidence. Unlike other approaches, this approach does not necessarily deal with the original sources of law. See Oliver Wendell Holmes (1897). The path of law. *Harvard Law Review*, 10, 457–478.

Appendix D

Understanding the Place of Social Science in Law

One of the heated issues that plays in the background of our analyses of child maltreatment law is the extent to which the courts incorporate social science into the law. When social science is used, positions that theorize the interaction between social science and the law fall into two general categories. Some predict that scientific findings will eventually assume a prominent role in legal decision making and policy making. The notion is that social science percolates into culture, indirectly affecting legal disputes and decisions. Some assert, for example, that modern Western culture as a whole has elevated science to a prominent, often commanding position. Judges incorporate social science into their opinions simply because they are products of their culture. This view also suggests that courts that are not now using social science can do so because we can overcome obstacles to its use. See, e.g., Richard Lempert (1988). "Between cup and lip": Social science influences on law and policy. *Law & Policy*, 10, 167–200. Other theories posit that social science will not have much of an impact on the law in the foreseeable future for a variety of reasons. This approach suggests that science will be used instrumentally to bolster decisions reached on other grounds and to conceal the true political and ideological bases for those decisions. Justices, the argument goes, will use social science findings only when it serves to reinforce their already decided positions. See Michael J. Saks & Charles H. Baron (1980). *The Use/Nonuse/Misuse of Applied Social Research in the Courts*. Cambridge, MA: Abt Books.

The issue on which no consensus has been reached is why courts often are reluctant to rely on empirical research. There are many reasons that the law may avoid social sciences. It may well be that no empirical research has been conducted on the issues being litigated and in some instances the Court may point to the absence of empirical data as one reason not to take a particular approach. For example, in *Addington v. Texas*, 441 U.S. 418 (1979), the Court was asked to determine the appropriate burden of proof in civil commitment trials. The Court lamented that there were no directly relevant empirical studies on how jurors interpret the phrases "preponderance of the evidence," "clear and convincing," and "beyond a reasonable doubt." Yet at least one such study did exist. Rita James Simon & Linda Mahan (1971). Quantifying burdens of proof: A view from the bench, the jury, and the classroom. *Law & Society Review*, 5, 319–330. In other instances, the research may be only tentative or inconclusive. For example, in *Kentucky v. Stincer*, 479 U.S. 1303 (1987), the Court was asked to rule on the constitutionality of a rule protecting child sex abuse victims from having to confront defendants. The American Psychological Association filed an amicus curiae brief stating that psychologists did not yet know whether face-to-face confrontation between the victim and the accused would cause particular trauma to the child. They cited the few studies that had been done, indicating that the results were inconclusive.

Another reason courts may appear reluctant to make full use of social science evidence is that the social sciences often rival law. This approach poses a series of contrasting characteristics that distinguish the social sciences from law: (1) Social science is innovative, while law resists innovation; (2) social science is based on data and observation, while law is based on precedent and hierarchy; (3) social science seeks an objective answer to problems, while law seeks an adversarial victory; (4) social science is descriptive, while law is prescriptive; (5) social science is nomothetic, while law is idiographic; (6) social science conclusions are probabilistic and tentative, while legal conclusions are irrevocable and must appear certain; (7) social science is proactive, while law is reactive; and (8) social science is abstract, while law deals with concrete issues. See Craig Haney (1980). Psychology and legal change: On the limits of a factual jurisprudence. *Law & Human Behavior*, 4, 147–199

Yet another approach to understanding why the legal system often fails to move toward directions suggested by social sciences suggests that the courts and social sciences are essentially incompatible. This approach suggests that the Supreme Court will perceive a branch of social science to be relevant to the formation of legal policy only if the science reflects the values advanced by the law. The more the two value systems converge, the more completely the Court's jurisprudence will incorporate social scientific information. The converse is also true. This approach suggests that we examine which areas of law share values with fields of social science and which do not. It also predicts that the less compatible the two systems are, the less likely it is that legal decision makers will incorporate social science information into their decisions. See Alexander J. Tanford (1990). The limits of a scientific jurisprudence: The Supreme Court and psychology. *Indiana Law Journal*, 66, 137–173.

Appendix E
Glossary of Legal Terms

Abandonment: A parent's or custodian's act of leaving a child without adequate care, supervision, support, or parental contact for an excessive period of time.

Ab initio: "From the beginning."

Action: A lawsuit or legal proceeding.

Acquit: To find not guilty or free from accusation.

Acquittal: Setting the person free from a charge of guilty by a finding of not guilty.

Adjudication: Pronouncing a judgment.

Adversary system: A judicial system involving opposing parties before an independent decision maker.

Affidavit: A written statement made under oath.

Affirm: To agree or uphold.

Allegation: Assertion or statement that a party expects to prove.

Amend: To change or modify.

Amicus curiae: "Friend of the court." A party that provides information, typically a brief, to a court even though the party is not directly involved in the case at hand.

Answer: Defendant's written response in a civil case.

Appeal: A request to overturn the legal ruling of a lower court.

Appeals court: See "appellate court" in this glossary.

Appellant: The party appealing a decision or judgment to a higher court. Opposite of appellee.

Appellate court: A court having jurisdiction to review.

Appellee: The party against whom the appellant appeals a legal decision.

Arraignment: Initial appearance before a judge in a criminal case.

Assault: Crime of attempting to kill or cause serious physical injury.

Aver: To allege; to assert formally.

Bad faith: Dishonesty or fraud.

Battery: Use of force or violence to inflict an injury.

Bench trial: A trial held before a judge and without a jury.

Beyond a reasonable doubt: The highest level of proof required to win a legal action.

Brief: Written document that outlines a party's legal arguments in a case.

Burden of proof: The duty of a party in a lawsuit to persuade the judge or the jury that enough facts exist to prove the allegations of the case.

Case law: The law created by judges when deciding individual disputes or cases; also known as common law.

Caveat emptor: "Buyer beware."

Certiorari: "To be informed of." The order a court issues to review the decision and proceedings in a lower court. (pronounced ser-shi-o-ra' ri)

Child abuse: Defined by state statutes. Usually occurs when a parent purposefully harms a child.

Child neglect: Defined by state statutes. Usually arises from a parent's passive indifference to a child's well-being, such as failing to feed a child or leaving a child alone for an extended time.

Citation: (1) Order to appear in court at a certain place at a specified time. Issuing a citation is not an arrest, and failure to accept it or to comply with it is not a crime. (2) Reference to legal authorities and precedents (such as constitutions, statutes, and reported cases) to substantiate a legal proposition.

Civil law: (1) The system of legal principles forming the basis of the law of most European countries and descended from common law as distinguished from the "common law" tradition of Anglo-American jurisdictions. (2) Body of law governing private or "civil" relationships, as distinguished from criminal law.

Circumstantial evidence: Indirect evidence that implies something occurred but doesn't directly prove it.

Claimant: Party asserting a right, demand or claim.

Clear and convincing evidence: Level of proof sometimes required in a civil case for the plaintiff to prevail. Is more than a preponderance of the evidence but less than beyond a reasonable doubt.

Code: A collection, compendium, or revision of laws, rules, and regulations enacted by legislative authority.

Common law: The law created by judges when deciding individual disputes or cases. Also known as case law.

Compensatory damages: Money awarded to reimburse actual costs, such as medical bills or pain and suffering.

Competency: Legally fit and qualified, such as to give testimony, waive rights, etc.

Complainant: Plaintiff, party that files the suit, same as plaintiff.

Complaint: The document that initiates a legal action.

Concur: To agree or act together.

Custodian: The party appointed to act on the child's behalf.

Damnum absque injuria: "A wrong without injury." The doctrine that the courts will not hear a case in which the wrongful act or omission of the potential defendant did not cause any harm to person, property, or rights. (pronounced dam'num abs'kwe in-joo'ri-a)

Decision: Judgment rendered by a court after a consideration of the facts and legal issues before it.

Declaratory judgment: Declares the rights of the parties or expresses the opinion of the courts on a question of law, without ordering anything to be done.

Decree: Decision or order of the court.

Defendant: In criminal cases, the person accused of the crime. In civil matters, the person or organization that is being sued.

Deposition: Part of the pre-trial discovery (fact-finding) process in which a witness testifies under oath. A deposition is held out of court with no judge present, but the answers often can be used as evidence in the trial.

De minimis: An abbreviation of "de minimis non curat lex," which literally means the law is not concerned with trivial matters. The phrase is generally used as a way of categorizing that which is not worth litigating over.

De novo: Anew.

Dependent child: A child who is homeless or without proper care through no fault of the parent, guardian, or custodian.

Deposition: The sworn testimony of a witness taken outside of court and transcribed by a reporter.

Dictum: That part of the opinion of a court which is not necessary for the decision of the issue before it and does not act as a binding precedent in later cases.

Direct evidence: Evidence that stands on its own to prove an alleged fact, such as testimony of a witness who says she saw a defendant pointing a gun at a victim during a robbery.

Direct examination: The initial questioning of a witness by the party that called the witness.

Directed verdict: A judge's order to a jury to return a specified verdict, usually because one of the parties failed to prove its case.

Discovery: Part of the pre-trial litigation process during which each party requests relevant information and documents from the other side in an attempt to "discover" pertinent facts.

Dismissal with prejudice: Case dismissed for good reason, which bars plaintiff from bringing an action on the same claim.

Dismissal without prejudice: Case dismissed, but plaintiff may bring a new suit on the same claim.

Disposition: Order of a juvenile court determining what is to be done with a minor. In criminal cases, the settlement of a case.

Dissent: Denotes the disagreement of one or more judges of a court with the decision of the majority.

Double jeopardy: Being tried twice for the same offense.

Due process: The notion that laws and legal proceedings must be fair. The Constitution guarantees that the government cannot take away a person's basic rights to "life, liberty or property, without due process of law." Courts have issued numerous rulings about what this means in particular cases.

Duty to warn: The legal obligation to warn people of a danger. Typically, manufacturers of hazardous products have a duty to warn customers of a product's potential dangers and to advise users of any precautions they should take.

Emancipation: Achieving independence from his or her parents, often by getting married before reaching age 18 or by becoming fully self-supporting.

En banc: "By the full court." When all the members of an appellate court hear an argument, they are sitting *en banc*.

Equal Protection Clause: Part of the Fourteenth Amendment to the U.S. Constitution that prohibits discrimination by state government institutions.

Equity: The spirit and habit of fairness and just dealing between people.

Error: An incorrect application of the law to some material aspect of a case, furnishing grounds for the review of the proceedings and reversal of judgment by an appellate court.

Establishment Clause: Part of the First Amendment to the U.S. Constitution that prohibits government from "establishing" a religion.

Et al.: An abbreviation of *et alia*, meaning "and others."

Et seq.: An abbreviation for *et sequentes*, or *et sequentia*, meaning "and the following."

Evidence: Matters presented in court to prove an alleged fact.

Exigent circumstances: Emergency conditions.

Ex parte: "By or for one party." Situation in which only one party (and not the adversary) appears before a judge.

Expert witness: A witness with a specialized knowledge of a subject.

Felony: Crime punishable by incarceration for a year or more.

Findings: A conclusion reached upon some matter by a judge or jury in a legal proceedings (e.g., a "finding of fact").

Foreseeability: A key issue in determining a person's liability. If a defendant could not reasonably have foreseen that someone might be hurt by his or her actions, then there may be no liability.

Garnishment: A court-ordered method of debt collection in which a portion of a person's salary is paid to a creditor.

Good faith: Honestly and without deception.

Grand jury: A group of citizens convened in a criminal case to consider the prosecutor's evidence and determine whether probable cause exists to prosecute a suspect for a felony.

Gross negligence: Failure to use even the slightest amount of care in a way that shows recklessness or willful disregard for the safety of others.

Guardian: Person assigned by the court to take care of minor children or incompetent adults.

Guardian ad litem: "Guardian at law." The person appointed by the court to look out for the best interests of the child during the course of legal proceedings.

Habeas corpus: "You have the body." It is a judicial mandate to a prison official ordering them to bring an inmate to the court so it can determine the lawfulness of the imprisonment.

Harmless error: An error committed by a lower court during a trial which is not prejudicial to the rights of the party and for which the appellate court will not reverse the judgment.

Health care proxy: Someone designated to make a broad range of decisions for a person who is not able to give informed consent.

Hearsay: Secondhand information that a witness only heard about from someone else and did not see or hear himself.

Holding: Part of a judicial opinion related to the material facts of a case, which binds later cases presenting similar issues.

Hung jury: A jury that is unable to reach a final verdict.

Immunity: Exemption from a legal duty, penalty, or prosecution.

Impeachment of witness: An attack on the credibility of a witness by the testimony of other witnesses or by the inconsistent testimony or statements of the witness made at an earlier time.

In camera: "In chambers." Refers to a hearing or inspection of documents that takes places in private, often in a judge's chambers.

Incapacity: The lack of power or the legal ability to act.

Incompetent: A person lacking the capacity, legal qualification, or fitness to manage affairs or to discharge a required duty.

Indictment: A formal accusation of a felony, issued by a grand jury after considering evidence presented by a prosecutor.

Indigent: Lacking in funds.

Information: A formal accusation of a crime, issued by a prosecutor. An alternative to an indictment.

Infractions: Minor offenses, often traffic tickets, which are punishable only by a fine.

In loco parentis: "In the place of the parent." Refers to actions of a custodian, guardian, or other person acting in the parent's place.

Intent, criminal: The exercise of intelligent will, where the mind is fully aware of the nature and consequences of an act done with such knowledge and with full liberty of action.

Inter alia: Among other things.

Joint custody: When both parents share custody of a child after a divorce.

Judgment: A court's official decision on the matters before it.

Judgment non obstante veredicto: A judgment notwithstanding the verdict. A decision by a trial judge to rule in favor of a losing party even though the jury's verdict was in favor of the other side.

Judicial notice: Acceptance by the court, without formal proof shown, of facts of common knowledge.

Jurisdiction: The power of a court to hear and determine cases or controversies brought before the court for resolution.

Jury charge: The judge's instructions to the jurors on the law that applies in a case and definitions of the relevant legal concepts.

Knowingly: With knowledge, willfully or intentionally with respect to a material element of an offense.

Legal custody: In a divorce, a type of child custody in which a parent who has legal custody has the right to be involved in all the decision making.

Lesser included offenses: Charges that contain elements of the most serious charge against a defendant.

Liability: Legal responsibility, duty, or obligation.

Malpractice: Failure of a professional to follow the accepted standards of practice of his or her profession.

Mandamus: A writ by which a court commands the performance of a particular act.

Mandatory sentence: A criminal sentence set by a legislature that establishes the minimum length of prison time for specified crimes.

Mens rea: "Guilty mind." Certain crimes require that a person intended to carry out the crime, and thus the prosecution would have to prove that there was *mens rea* at the time the offense was committed.

Minor: A person who does not have the legal rights of an adult.

Misdemeanor: Crime that is punishable by less than one year in jail.

Mitigating factors: Information about a defendant or the circumstances of a crime that might tend to lessen the sentence of the crime with which the person is charged.

Moral turpitude: Conduct contrary to honesty, modesty, or good morals.

Motion: A formal request asking a judge to issue a ruling or order on a legal matter.

Motion for directed verdict: In civil cases, a request asserting that the plaintiff has raised no genuine issue to be tried and asks the judge to rule in favor of the defense. Typically made after the plaintiff is done presenting his or her case.

Motion for summary judgment: In civil cases, a request asserting that the plaintiff has raised no genuine issue to be tried and asks the judge to rule in favor of the defense. Typically made before the trial.

Motion in limine: A written motion for a protective order against prejudicial questions and statements.

Motion to dismiss: In a civil case, a defendant's request asserting that even if all the allegations are true, the plaintiff is not entitled to any legal relief and thus the case should be dismissed.

Motion to suppress evidence: A request to keep out evidence at a trial or hearing.

Named plaintiffs: The originators of a class action suit.

Negligence: Failure to use the degree of care that a reasonable person would use under the same circumstances.

Nisi prius: Courts for the initial trial of issues of fact, as distinguished from appellate courts.

Oath: A solemn and formal declaration by a person that what they are about to say or write is the truth.

Parens patriae: "Parent of his country." Used when the government acts on behalf of a child or incompetent individuals.

Parties: Plaintiffs and defendants (petitioners and respondents) to lawsuits, also known as appellants and appellees in appeals, and their lawyers.

Pendente lite: Temporary arrangements for custody, child support, child visitation, alimony, use and possession of the family home, etc., until a final hearing.

Perjury: A crime in which a person knowingly makes a false statement while under oath in court.

Petition: A written application to the court asking for specific action to be taken.

Petty offenses: Minor crimes, such as traffic violations, which are generally punishable by a fine or short jail term.

Physical custody: In a divorce, the parent who has physical custody lives most of the time with the child.

Plaintiff: The person who initiates a lawsuit.

Pleadings: In a civil case, the allegations by each party of their claims and defenses.

Precedent: Previously decided case considered binding in the court where it was issued and in all lower courts in the same jurisdiction.

Preliminary hearing: Legal proceeding used in some states in which a prosecutor presents evidence to a judge in an attempt to show that there is probable cause that a person committed a crime.

Preponderance of the evidence: The level of proof required to prevail in most civil cases. The judge or jury must be persuaded that the facts more probably support one view (the plaintiff's) than another (the defendant's).

Prima facie: "At first view." Refers to the minimum amount of evidence a plaintiff must have to avoid having a case dismissed. It is said that the plaintiff must make a *prima facie* case.

Privileged communication: Conversation that takes place within the context of a protected relationship, such as that between an attorney and client, a husband and wife, a priest and penitent, and a doctor and patient.

Probable cause: A reasonable belief that a person has committed a crime.

Pro se: "For himself." A person who represents himself, sometimes with the assistance of a lawyer. (pronounced pro say)

Prosecutor: The government lawyer who investigates and tries criminal cases. Generally known as a district attorney, state's attorney, county attorney, or United States attorney.

Protective order: In litigation, an order that prevents the disclosure of sensitive information except to certain individuals under certain conditions. In a domestic dispute, an order that prevents one party from approaching another, often within a specified distance.

Proximate cause: In tort law, the negligent act which causes a plaintiff's injury or, when combined with other acts or omissions, most directly causes the plaintiff's injury or loss.

Public defender: A lawyer who works for a state or local agency representing clients accused of a crime who cannot afford to pay.

Punitive damages: Money awarded to a victim that is intended to punish a defendant and stop the person or business from repeating the type of conduct that caused an injury.

Quaere: A question.

Quash: To nullify, void.

Quid pro quo: Something for something. Exchanging something of value.

Reasonable care: The level of care a typical person would use if faced with the same circumstances.

Reasonable doubt: The level of certainty a juror must have to find a defendant guilty of a crime.

Remand: An appellate court's decision to send a case back to a lower court for further proceedings.

Res ipsa loquitur: "The thing speaks for itself." Refers to situations when it's assumed that a person's injury was caused by the negligent action of another party because the accident was the sort that would not occur unless someone was negligent.

Res judicata: A rule of civil law that once a matter has been litigated and final judgment has been rendered by a court, the matter cannot be relitigated by the parties.

Respondent: The party against whom an appeal is taken. See "appellee" in this glossary.

Right against self-incrimination: The Fifth Amendment right that allows a person to refuse to answer questions that would subject him or her to accusation of a criminal act.

Settlement: The resolution or compromise by the parties in a civil lawsuit.

Standard of care: The standard to which a defendant is held.

Standing: The legal right to initiate a lawsuit. Typically, a person must be sufficiently affected by the matter at hand, and there must be a case or controversy that can be resolved by legal action.

Stare decisis: "To stand by that which is decided." Refers to the principle of adhering to precedent when deciding a case.

Statute: The law as enacted by the legislative body, as opposed to case law developed by the courts.

Statutes of limitations: Laws setting deadlines for filing lawsuits within a certain time after events occur that are the source of a claim.

Strict liability: Liability even when there is no proof of negligence.

Subpoena: An order compelling a person to appear to testify or produce documents.

Substantive law: That part of the law dealing with rights, duties, and liabilities, as distinguished from procedural law, which is the law regulating procedure.

Summary judgment: Judgment entered when there is no genuine issue of material fact and party is entitled to prevail as a matter of law.

Summation: The closing argument in a trial.

Summons: A legal document that notifies a party that a lawsuit has been initiated and that states when and where the party must appear to answer the charges.

Tort: A civil wrong that results in an injury to a person or property.

Valid claim: A grievance that can be resolved by legal action.

Verdict: The formal decision issued by a jury on the issues of fact presented at trial.

Vicarious liability: When one person is liable for the negligent actions of another person, even though the first person was not directly responsible for the injury.

Visitation right: The right granted to a parent or other relative to visit a child on a specified basis. Usually occurs during a divorce proceeding.

Wanton: An act that is useless for any rightful purpose, is without any adequate legal provocation, and manifests a reckless indifference to the rights and interests of others.

Warrant: An official order authorizing a specific act, such as an arrest or the search of someone's home.

Willfully: Intentionally.

Without prejudice: A dismissal "without prejudice" allows a new suit to be brought on the same cause of action.

Writ: A judicial order.

Writ of Certiorari: A Supreme Court's order directing a lower court to transmit records for a case for which it will hear on appeal.

About the Author

Roger J. R. Levesque received his JD from Columbia University School of Law and his PhD in cultural psychology from the University of Chicago. Prior to his current appointment as professor of criminology and criminal justice as well as affiliate professor of law at Indiana University, he was professor of psychology and law at the University of Arizona and a fellow in the Law & Psychology Program at the University of Nebraska. He has published several dozen research and scholarly articles and book chapters that deal with family life and the law. His books include *Child Sexual Abuse: A Human Rights Perspective* (1999); *Adolescents, Sex, and the Law: Preparing Adolescents for Responsible Citizenship* (2000); *Culture and Family Violence: Fostering Change through Human Rights Law* (2001); *Dangerous Adolescents, Model Adolescents: Shaping the Role and Promise of Education* (2002); *Not by Faith Alone: Religion, Law and Adolescence* (2002); *Sexuality Education: What Adolescents' Rights Require* (2003); *Adolescence, Media and the Law* (2007); *Rethinking Child Maltreatment Law: Returning to First Principles* (2008); *Adolescence, Discrimination, and the Law: Addressing Dramatic Shifts in Equality Jurisprudence* (2015); *Adolescence, Privacy and the Law: A Developmental Science Perspective* (2016); *The Science and Law of School Segregation and Diversity* (2017); *Adolescents and Constitutional Law: Regulating Social Contexts of Development* (2019).

He serves as editor-in-chief of the *Journal of Youth and Adolescence*. In addition to being the first journal devoted to the study of adolescence (founded over fifty years ago), it is the most cited to journal of its kind as well as the most widely found in libraries worldwide; it also currently has the highest Impact Factor and Eigenfactors of journals devoted to the social science understanding of adolescence. He also is editor-in-chief of *Adolescent Research Review*, which publishes articles critically reviewing important contributions to the understanding of adolescence. Currently, the *Review* ranks among the top journals focusing on adolescent development.

He also edits *Advancing Responsible Adolescent Development*, a book series examining social and individual factors that contribute to adolescents' responsibility (including irresponsibility) in multiple contexts and settings. The book series is the largest devoted to the adolescent period; it includes twenty-five books and several forthcoming.

He is editor of the *Encyclopedia of Adolescence*, the most multidisciplinary, comprehensive research compendium focused on the period of adolescence.

Professor Levesque is the recipient of numerous awards, including for research and teaching, and has earned many distinctions. The Association for Psychological Science (APS) (previously the American Psychological Society) has elected him fellow in recognition of his outstanding contributions to developmental science. In addition, the American Psychological Association (APA) has elected him fellow in recognition of his contributions to the field of psychology and law as well as his contribution to psychology's place in the study of social issues; he is fellow in the American Psychology /Law Society as well as the Society for the Psychological Study of Social Issues. He also has gained fellow status for his contributions to youth policy development, in the Society for Child and Family Policy and Practice, as well as for his contributions to developmental science, in APA's Division 7: Developmental Psychology.

Table of Cases